$19.00

VALLEY

OF THE

UPPER MAUMEE RIVER

WITH HISTORICAL ACCOUNT OF ALLEN COUNTY AND THE CITY OF
FORT WAYNE, INDIANA. THE STORY OF ITS PROGRESS
FROM SAVAGERY TO CIVILIZATION.

VOLUME I.

ILLUSTRATED.

MADISON, WIS.:
BRANT & FULLER,
1889.

The reproduction of this book has been made possible through the sponsorship of The Allen County-Fort Wayne Historical Society of Fort Wayne, Indiana.

A Reproduction by UNIGRAPHIC, INC.
1401 North Fares Avenue
Evansville, Indiana 47711
Nineteen Hundred Seventy Four

INDEX TO VOLUME I.

GENERAL HISTORY.

	Page.
Aboit township	285
Academie	210
Adams township	205
Allen, Col. John	133
Annals of the township	205
Arcola	292
Besancon	401
Big Leg, murder of	186
Bondie, Antoine	134
Border warfare	74
Bouquet, Gen	54, 65
British expedition against Fort Wayne	146
British occupation	54
Canal, land office	201
Cedar Creek township	331
Cedarville	333
Centerville	422
Churches in the township	456
Church, Lutheran, in Allen county	465
Emanuel's, The	471
Gar Creek	472
Marion	472
Martin's	471
New Haven	472
St. John's (Fort Wayne)	472
St. John's (Hoagland)	472
St. Paul's	471
St. Peter's	471
Trinity	471
Zion's	471
Clark, Gen. George R	69
Cold and drought	196
Commanders at Ft. Wayne	106, 164
Concordia college	472
Coureurs de Bois	42
Drainage	285
Early explorations	42
Edwardsburg	388
Eel River township	300
Expeditions from Fort Wayne	142, 154
Fallen Timber, battle of	103
Farm settlement	201
Fort Dearborn massacre	130
Fort Defiance	101
Fort Meigs, siege of	151, 159
Fort Miami (old)	52, 108
Fort, the French	52, 108
Fort Miami, capture of	60
Fort Recovery	100
Fort Stephenson, siege of	160
Fort Wayne	106, 141, 143
Fur trade	111, 164, 179
Game, early	202
Gamelin, journal of	77
Geology and physical geography	171
Girty, Simon	89
Glacial action	171
Godefroi, Francis	62, 212
Hardin, Col. John	76, 83, 98

	Page.
Harlan	351
Harmar's campaign	81
Harmar's Ford, battle	35, 85
Harrison, Gov. W. H.	110, 113, 116, 120, 122, 126, 139, 143, 153, 158, 163.
Heller's Corners, battle near	84
Hesse Cassel	432
Hoagland	422
Huntertown	314
Indiana, territory of	110
Indians, distribution of	23
Intrigues of British	89, 100
Introduction	19
Jackson township	396
Jefferson township	400
Johnston, Stephen, killing of	135
Kekionga	67
LaBalme, expedition of	70
Lake township	291
Land cession disputes	73, 99, 122
Land office	198
La Salle, journeys of	45
at Kekionga	47
Leo	333
Logan, Capt	137, 139, 147
Lutheran church in Allen Co.	465
McCulloch, Hugh, reminiscenses of	188
Madison township	421
Mails, early	183, 185
Maples	401
Marion township	431
Massillon	422
Maumee, first map of	44
Maumee township	387
Maumee Valley Monumental Association	vi
Maysville	351
Metea	134
ambuscade of	141
Miami, fort, on Maumee	106
massacre at	153
Miamis, description of	24–30
principal chiefs	30
early history	37
treaties with	197
Middletown	433
Milan township	390
Mills, early	204
Mississinewa, expedition against	148
Monroe township	405
Monroeville	406
Morris, Capt., at Kekionga	62
New Haven	207
Northwest Territory	71, 109
Old Fort, residents at	180
rebuilding of	183
village at the	179, 196
Oliver, Wm., adventures of	137
Peace of Ghent	163
Peltier, Louis, reminiscenses of	191–195

	Page.
Perry township	312
Pleasant township	447
Pontiac, conspiracy of	56
death of	68
Portage to Wabash	47, 49, 53, 55, 108
Prehistoric remains	21
Prophet, The	112, 115, 126
Regimental Buttons	165
Relief of Fort Wayne	140
Residents, early, at Fort Wayne	186
Richardville, Chief	165
Riley, Capt. James	184
River Raisin, battle of	149
Royal Americans, The	54
Schools in Allen county	480
monroeville	491
private and church	481
public	483
township	491
Scipio township	382
Settlement and development	179
Settlers, customs of	202
Shane, Anthony	156
Shawnee run	185
Siege of Fort Wayne	132
Springfield township	350
St. Clair's campaign	87
St. Joseph township	211
Strata, geologic	178
Sheldon	448
Tecumseh	104
confederacy of	109
at Fort Wayne	126
in war of 1812	129, 153, 159
Tippecanoe, battle of	126
Townships, formation of	205
Traders, early	134, 183
Treaties, early	73
of Greenville	107, 163
at Fort Wayne	110, 119
at Vincennes	122
with Miamis	197
Urbana	333
Wabash-Erie trough	171
Wallen	210
Wars—	
Miamis and Iroquois	38, 51, 53
Indians and English	56
Revolutionary	68
Federal and Indian	81
of 1812	127
Washington, observations of	72
interest in the west	95
Washington township	209
Wayne, Gen. Anthony	167
campaign of	95
Wayne township	205
Wells, Captain	102, 129, 131
White Pigeon, expedition to	156
Williamsport	433
Woodburn	387

INDEX TO VOLUME I.

PERSONAL HISTORY.

Name	Page	Name	Page	Name	Page
Allen, Thomas	384	Doty, Solomon	395	Hauk, Samuel	429
Alligear, John D	415	Douglass, Albert	337	Hayes, H. F.	410
Amstutz, John	348	Douglass, John	336	Hayes, John	410
Anderson, A. H	414	Downing, J. B	220	Hellwarth, Michael	248
Andrews, Rapin, and sons	320	Driesbach, Isaac	363	Henderson, G. W.	334
Antrup, Henry E	270	Driesbach, Levi	364	Henry, Henry	377
Archer, John	252	Driver, Adam	365	Henderson, James A	366
Argo, M. E	427	Driver, David D	423	Herin, D. E. O.	340
Ashley, George L	261	Dryer, Charles R	494	Herrick, D. G. N	361
Ashton, Ambrose	388	Duly, Solomon	328	Herrick, Horace	365
Bacon, Henry	343	Dunten, H. F	315	Hettenger, Emanuel	379
Bair, Simon	338	Dunten, Thomas	314	Hilbert, Isaac	381
Baldwin, Timothy	398	Dupeyron, John B	405	Hillegass, Jacob	324
Bates, Alfred H	288	Edsall, William S.	187	Hoffman, George W., sr.	378
Bauman, William	380	Ehle, William	394	Hoffman, G. W.	379
Bauserman, W. H	426	Eloph, Henry	291	Holder, Chichester	415
Beams, Henry W	344	Esterline, W. J	290	Hollopeter, Cyrus	354
Beckman, Edward	253	Evard, Clement	400	Hollopeter, John W	339
Beckman, Fred	439	Evard, James	274	Hollopeter, Matthias	339
Beckman, N. F	440	Fairfield, Charles W	213	Hollopeter, William C	341
Beninghoff, William	385	Finan, Edward	414	Holmes, John W	312
Benward, John S	308	Fitch Nathaniel, and sons	316	Holman, Joseph	200
Berning, Charles W	435	Fleming, T. H	257	Holmes, Joshua	216
Betz, Samuel	373	Fletter, James M	273	Holmes, Roland	217
Bez, Rev. C. G	479	Fox, August	350	Hood, J. W	378
Bird, Oehmig	287	Franke, F. W	424	Houk, Hiram	373
Black, John T	28	Freeman, Robert L	304	Houser, John H	256
Bleke, Frederick	268	Freese, Franklin	409	Houser, Charles	430
Bleke, William	255	Friedt, Jacob	372	Howey, William C	346
Blume, Martin	278	Fry, John W	372	Howe, Estes	355
Bœuf, Octave	297	Foote, H. B	384	Hull, Adam	301
Bohde, Henry	279	Fulkerson, David L	340	Hunt, Col. John E.	180
Boston, Alexander	365	Furguson, Matthew	258	Hurson, John W	329
Boulton, Henry	362	Gable, F. L	428	Hyndman, Nelson	305
Brandeberry, Abraham	417	Gavin, James	497	Irwin, John S.	492
Brandeberry, G. W	418	Gearin, Cornelius	293	Jackson, Phanuel W	323
Breman, Charles J	414	Gibson, David	411	Jamison, O. E	442
Brooks, W. B	394	Gillett, Charles M	337	Jeffries, Adam	266
Brower, George, sr	428	Gillieron, Louis	280	Jones, Benjamin	295
Brudi, Carl L	240	Geiseking, F. W	255	Jones, Jasper W	396
Brudi, Gottleib	240	Gloyd, George B. and son	317	Jones, Thomas	419
Brudi, Joseph	240	Godfrey, George L	212	Johnson, Amariah	381
Bruick, John H	261	Godfroy, Francis	212	Johnson, F. A	385
Brueck, Philip	261	Goeglein, George	275	Johnston, John R	302
Bullard, George	286	Goeglein, Jacob	274	Johnston, Joseph	303
Bullerman, Fred	269	Goeglein, John	275	Juengel, Rev. Henry	474
Butts, B. S	296	Goheen, Wm	293	Juergens, Louis	271
Butts, W. W	296	Gotsch, Rev. Geo. Theo	476	Kammeyer, Frederick	255
Cartwright, Samuel	286	Grayless, Geo. W	295	Kampe, Rev. Gustav	478
Challenger, F. C	283	Greenawalt, Jesse	376	Kariger, Samuel	254
Challenger, E. D	283	Greenwell, C. L	310	Keim, Daniel	299
Chapman, Jonathan	250	Gresley, John	443	Kell, Geo. V	311
Chapman, Sol. C	328	Grier, Joseph H	217	Kell, Jacob	325
Chase, Levi	307	Griffin, A. C	330	Kell, Solomon	325
Chausse, Aime	279	Griffith, John	419	Keller, Sebastian	299
Clem, Noah	416	Grodrian, Frederick, and sons	426, 427	Kern, Caspar	245
Cline, John	398	Gronauer, Joseph	402	Kiser, Peter	195
Colter, Jacob	299	Grosjean, John	294	Klein, Rev. F. A	478
Comparet, Charles W	195	Grosjean, Edward	253	Klopfenstein, Michael	345
Comparet, Francis	195	Grosjean, John B	253	Knapp, John R	386
Corbaley, John A	412	Gross, Rev. Charles	474	Knisely, Daniel	364
Corey, John N	289	Gruber, Christian	353	Kochlinger, John H	242
Covington, Thomas	290	Grubb, Ira I	359	Koester, Christian, sr	270
Crall, Milton	379	Gump, George	327	Kohlmeier, A. F	268
Crozier, S. H	424	Haifley, George	370	Kramer, Charles	275
Cummins, Henry	366	Haifley, John B	371	Kronmuller, George	296
Cummins, Joseph D	367	Hake, John, and sons	435	Kucher, Rev. John J	475
Curtice, John F	201	Hall, Alvin	392	Lacroix, Louis	277
Dailey, Samuel	341	Hall, Nelson B	352	La Fontaine, Francis	36
Dannenfelser, Conrad	282	Hamilton, William A	285	Lahmeyer, John P	271
Darroch, A. M	289	Hamm, Adam	347	Lake, Curtis C	392
Daugharty, Alfred	256	Harper, John	287	Lake, George P	353
Delagrange, Constant	326	Harper, Edward	402	Landin, John	278
Dever, John	346	Harrod family	436	Landin, Michael	278
Diederich, Rev. H. W	477	Harter, William H	376	Lane, Chester T	493
Dorsey, George	383	Hathaway, Stephen	306	Lapp, Valentine	282
Dorsey, Robert	383			Larimore, Thomas	298

INDEX TO VOLUME I.

Name	Page	Name	Page	Name	Page
Lasselle, Gen. Hyacinth	179	Pfeiffer, John C	254	Stellhorn, J. H	218
Lawrence, Oliver	220	Poinsett, John S	252	Stephenson, John D	416
Lemon, John S	380	Price, Moses B	388	Stevick, Jacob	349
Leonard, Nelson	257	Price, Richard	360	Stickney, Maj. B. F	182
Lewis, Maj. Samuel	201	Rapp, George	219	Stirlen, Alexander	329
Little, H. A	390	Rapp, John	298	Stirling, W. R	297
Little Turtle	30	Redelsheimer, D. S	408	Stock, Rev. S. F. C. F	475
Lochner, John	347	Reemer. W. H	289	Strass, Morris	412
Lomas, Charles	283	Reichelderfer, Charles	359	Surfus, John	319
Loveland, H. W	247	Reichelderfer, Jacob	357	Suttenfield, William	182
McCarty, John	309	Reichelderfer, John D	356	Swaidner, John	375
McCombs, James	329	Reichelderfer, Louis	358	Swift, Dr. C. F	375
McConnel, John	399	Reichelderfer, William A	358	Taylor, Alfred M	262
McCoy, G. W	245	Repp, Peter	378	Taylor, John	400
McCrory, James	345	Reulle, Adolphe	404	Tecumseh	111
McDermut, Wilson E	497	Reuille, James	418	Tielker, Conrad	219
McKay, David	258	Reuille, Jules H	410	Tillman, John	403
McKee, Thomas L	307	Richards, Smith	374	Tipton, Gen. John	198
McLain, Nelson	432	Richardville, Jean Baptiste	33	Todd, Eli	425
McMaken, Henry C	214	Ridenour, E. B	418	Tracy, William	294
McNabb, William J	349	Ringwalt, William H	354	Treace, Henry A	330
Madden, W. W	297	Robinson, J. L	423	Trease, George W	343
Markle, Ephraim	362	Robinson, Warren	448	Trease, W. W	342
Martin, David	411	Rockhill, Edward	293	Tryon, John M	420
Masson, John B	326	Rockhill, William	293	Turner, H. K	445
Matthews, Samuel	310	Rodenbeck, Diederich	244	Tustison, Oliver	246
Mercer, Jacob	441	Rodenbeck, Henry	244	Valentine, Jackson	303
Merkel, Charles	348	Rogers, John	221	Vandolah, James, and sons	319
Metcalf, M. V	327	Rogers, Lamort M	221	VanZile, David	350
Meyer, Fred. A	266	Rogers, Orrin D	222	Viberg, C. H	348
Meyer, Frederick, sr	265	Rose, Christian F	264	Vollmer, Friedrich	272
Meyer, H. C. W	272	Rose, Christian H	264	Vonderau, H. G	280
Meyer, J. H. F. B	267	Roussey, Francis	404	Vonderau, Jacob	280
Miller, H. F. C	446	Roy, Florentin	326	Voirol, Florant	397
Miller, Michael	311	Sapp, Absalom	371	Wagner, Peter	215
Mills, Samuel	374	Sarazin, August	276	Waltke, William	271
Moellering, Charles F	218	Sauder, Jacob	342	Warner, George W	386
Mooney, Julius C	308	Sauer, Rev. H. G	473	Warner, Samuel	323
Moore, Latham	380	Schafer, Gottlieb	393	Waters, John	259
Moore, William A	359	Schaick, Christian	269	Waters, Martin	385
More, Lucas	254	Schepelmann, Henry	389	Wayne, Gen. Anthony	167
Moritz, John M	492	Schoene, John R	290	Wells, Delphine B	496
Moudy, John W	341	Sharp, Carrie B	495	Welsheimer, Luderick	298
Moudy, Martin L	342	Sheehan, John	416	West, F. C	331
Muller, W. M	335	Shirley, Robert B	389	Wetzel, William	283
Myers, John	265	Shoaff, D. M	322	Wheeler, Schuyler	320
Neff, P. J	423	Shoaff, W. S	306	Whitaker, Col. J. W	222
Nettelhorst, Louis	335	Shoaff, W. W	305	Whiteleather, James F	496
Notestine, Daniel	333	Shordon, George	263	Whitney, Mrs. Elmira	403
Notestine, Jacob	333	Shordon, William	263	Whittern, Charles	420
Notestine, Peter	333	Siemon, Rev. Otto	477	Wiegmann, Henry	276
Notestine, Uriah	260	Simmers, D. W	291	Wiese, Christian	241
Nusbaum, George W	366	Simon, Solomon	318	Wilkinson, John	216
Nuttle, A. D	391	Small, Joseph, and family	438	Willbur, George W	393
Oberholtzer, W. O	368	Smith, Jarvis	300	Wood, Albert	315
Omo, Frederick	360	Smitley, Jacob, and family	444	Worden, Ezra	356
Paff, Aaron	338	Snider, Philip	440	Wyckoff, Mrs. Nancy	399
Parker, Christian	259	Snyder, Anthony	370	Young, Henry	267
Parker, James D	265	Snyder, George R	364	Young, Julius	267
Parker, John R	413	Snyder, Nicholas	249	Zeimmer, John	362
Parnin, Eugene	328	Somers, Joseph	429	Zeimmer, Martin	363
Parnin, Francis	398	Spencer, Col. John	200	Zeis, Christopher	371
Peltier, James	181	Spindler, William A	394	Zeis, Lewis	377
Peltier, Louis	181	Spindler, W. S	395	Zimmerman, Samuel	344
Pepe, August	405	Sprankel, John	287	Zollinger, Henry C	243
Pernot, Constant	397	Squires, L. D	382	Zurbuch, F. J	248
Peters, John	369	Starr, Gilbert, and sons	368		

ILLUSTRATIONS.

Name	Page	Name	Page	Name	Page
Bell, R. C	144	Hettler, C. F	368	Randall, F. P	80
Boltz, Ferd. F	384	Jones, Jasper W	400	Robertson, R. S	48
Dawson, R. J	160	McClellan, C. A. O	112	Robinson, J. M	480
Dougall, Allen H	464	McDonald, R. T	304	Rogers, L. M	208
Foster, D. N	272	Niezer, J. B	416	Shirley, Robert B	336
Godfroy, G. L	176	O'Connor, Bernard	432	Wayne, Anthony	Frontispiece
Harper, Edward	240	Peltier, J. C	448		

THE MAUMEE VALLEY MONUMENTAL ASSOCIATION.

This patriotic association had its origin through the action of the "Pioneer association of the Maumee valley," at its annual meeting held in 1885, on the battlefield of "Fallen Timber."

A committee was then and there appointed to take into consideration and devise ways and means to secure the possession and control, and to protect and commemorate the most important historical points, such as battlefields and forts, in the Maumee valley.

The result of the deliberations of the committee, was the incorporation, under the laws of Ohio, of the Maumee valley monumental association.

The incorporators were all residents of Ohio, and were: D. W. H. Howard, of Fulton county; Asher Cook, of Wood county; William Baker, R. B. Mitchell, Samuel M. Young, R. C. Lemmon, Mavor Brigham, Henry Bennett, Richard Mott, John C. Lee, Foster R. Warren and John R. Osborn, of Lucas county.

The articles of incorporation were filed in the office of the secretary of state of Ohio, on the 28th day of July, 1885. Prior to this formal organization, however, the incorporators had perfected an organization by the election of a board of directors, and through an executive committee consisting of D. W. H. Howard, Asher Cook, and J. C. Lee, presented a memorial to congress, which resulted in an appropriation for a survey of the various historical localities, which survey has been under the charge of Gen. O. M. Poe, of the engineer corps, U. S. army, who has rendered to congress an exhaustive report of the survey of all the historic grounds of the valley, as well as Put-in-Bay, and recommends their purchase, improvement, and marking by substantial monuments, at an estimated cost of $65,000.

Originally the membership was restricted to residents of the valley, but that rule has been abrogated, and any person interested may become a member on the payment of $1.

Much of the success of the association thus far is due to the patriotism, zeal and energy of Gen. John C. Lee, of Toledo, its able, earnest and efficient secretary.

The first annual meeting of the association was held on the battlefield of Fallen Timber, Lucas county, Ohio, August 20, 1885. The board of directors there elected were Hon. Richard Mott, Samuel M. Young, of Toledo, Ohio; Hon. Asher Cook, of Perrysburgh, Ohio; Chief Justice M. R. Waite, Hon. Thomas Dunlap, of Toledo, Ohio; Mr. Joel Foot, of Wood county, Ohio; Hon. Reuben C. Lemmon, Foster R. Warren, esq., Col. D. W. H. Howard, of Fulton county, Ohio; Reuben B. Mitchell and Daniel F. Cook, of Lucas county; Peter Mangus of Defiance county; John C. Lee, of Toledo; J. Austin Scott, of Ann Arbor, Mich., and Hon. S. H. Cately, of Fulton county.

At a meeting of the board of directors on the 28th of August, 1885, Chief Justice M. R. Waite was elected president; Col. D. W. H. Howard, first vice president; Hon Richard Mott, second vice president; Hon. Asher Cook, third vice president; Foster R. Warren, treasurer; John C. Lee, secretary. Executive committee: Col. D. W. H. Howard, Hon. Asher Cook and John C. Lee.

The same persons constituted the board of directors and officers during the two succeeding years. In 1888, Hon. Richard Mott having deceased as well as Chief Justice Waite, five members of the board were elected at the annual meeting in Fort Wayne, the terms of regularly expiring members being filled by the re-election of the same members, and the vacancies from death, by the election of Lieut. Gov. Robert S. Robertson and Hon. Franklin P. Randall of Fort Wayne.

At the meeting of the board of directors on the 28th of August, the directorship to which Peter Mangus had been elected was declared vacant by reason of his having failed to appear and accept the office, and President R. B. Hayes was elected to fill that vacancy. At the same time officers for the ensuing year were elected as follows: President, R. B. Hayes; first vice president, Robert S. Robertson; second vice president, Samuel H. Cateley; third vice president, D. W. H. Howard; secretary, J. C. Lee; treasurer, Reuben B. Mitchell; executive committee, D. W. H. Howard, Asher Cook and J. C. Lee.

At the annual meeting held August 8th, 1889, on Old Fort Defiance, the three out-going members of the board of directors were re-elected, and since that time there has been no meeting of the board of directors for the election of officers for the ensuing year. This meeting will be held at no distant day.

The prominent points sought to be protected, and marked by monuments, are:

1. Fort Miami, seven miles from Toledo on the north bank of the Maumee (Miami of the Lakes), established in 1680 as a military and trading post by an expedition sent out by Frontenac, then French governor of Canada, but abandoned after a few years of occupation. Reoccupied in 1785 by Glencoe, British governor of Canada, as a military post, it fell into the hands of Gen. Wayne, August 20, 1794. In pursuance of the treaty between Great Britain and the United States, it was abandoned in 1795, and was again occupied by the British in 1813, and became memorable for the massacre of Col. Dudley's soldiers when made prisoners by the forces of Proctor and Tecumseh.

2. Fort Defiance, erected by Gen. Wayne in August, 1794, at the confluence of the Auglaize and the Maumee.

3. "Fallen Timber," the site of the famous battle of Wayne with the Indians under "Turkey Foot," August 16, 1794.

4. Fort Industry, built by Wayne at the mouth of Swan creek, now the site of the city of Toledo, after the battle of "Fallen Timber."

5. Fort Wayne, at the head of the Maumee, built by Wayne in 1794.

6. Fort Meigs, built by Gen. Harrison in February, 1813, on the southwest bank of the Maumee ten miles above Toledo, and besieged by Proctor and Tecumseh for several days in May, and again in July, of that year.

7. Put-in-Bay, where the dead of Perry's memorable naval battle are buried.

It is hoped that ere long, through the instrumentality of this society, all these historic spots will be owned by the United States, and marked with appropriate monuments, to perpetuate the memory of the heroic deeds of the pioneer soldiers of America on the western frontier, and to preserve them as sacred spots which may not only serve as memorials of valor, but be forever object lessons in patriotism for the generations to come.

TO THE READER.

In the preparation of this work the biographical sketches are usually arranged in connection with those parts of the general history to which they seem most appropriately to belong. This does not in any instance imply that these sketches were written by the person whose name may appear at the head of such chapter. In fact they were not written by the writers of the various portions of the work who have composed the chapters on the general history. The biographical sketches were compiled almost exclusively by a corps of men trained for that particular work. The large number of these which the book contains, needs no apology when the most enlightened sense of our civilization has approved the growing custom of publishing biographies of living persons, and thereby rendering the facts of history secure while the witnesses are yet able to judge of their accuracy.

THE PUBLISHERS.

THE VALLEY

OF

THE UPPER MAUMEE RIVER.

———

By COL. ROBERT S. ROBERTSON.

INTRODUCTION.

In preparing a history of the Valley of the Upper Maumee, it is no part of the plan to give a full account of the early discoveries upon the vast territory which was opened to the inspection of the world by Columbus, or of the travels and explorations of those hardy adventurers, who, led either by curiosity, or the search for wealth and honors, became the pioneers of civilization in the new world, but rather to be restricted to those explorations and events which connect themselves with the opening and settlement of this region of our country.

It is said that history repeats itself, and that this is true, is illustrated in many ways, and in none more vividly than in the explorations in Africa now passing under the observation of the living. We read of the adventures of a Livingstone and a Stanley, giving no thought to the fact that they are repeating the adventures of La Salle and others, and opening to civilization and settlement that hitherto unknown continent, just as La Salle and his compeers opened a path through the unknown wilds of America.

Then, as now, men were induced to undergo the fatigues and perils which are the lot of explorers, by motives of widely various character. Love of adventure may have been the impulse with some, but with most of them, it was search for wealth, for power, and for fame; wealth by obtaining new possessions, or trading in the products of the newly discovered countries; power, by becoming the leaders and governors in the new states or empires to be formed; and fame for themselves and posterity, by reason of the rank or honors they hoped to attain in the conquest and government of the new world they aided in opening, settling and placing among the nations of the world. Such were the powerful inducements which led men then as now, to abandon home, the advantages of civilization, and everything dear to civilized man, to become the companions of, savages, to traverse an unbroken country through forest and marsh, enduring fatigue and the terrors of disease, as well as dangers to them before unknown and not even to be imagined.

The first explorers of America were men cast in heroic mold, whether he were the traveler for adventure and discovery, the trader in search of peltries and furs, the seeker for gold, the seeker for the fountain of youth, or the priest and devotee who hoped to save souls for the kingdom of heaven.

We see the noble-born cavalier leaving the ball-rooms and salons of London and Paris, to become the explorer of America, the inmate of

Indian huts, in order to survey a new state which he may claim for his sovereign, and perchance become its governor.

We see the speculative trader, sent, perhaps, to represent some powerful trading company, enduring the same privations, in order to amass new wealth. We see the adventurer, seeking the El Dorado whose sands are golden, and whose dew drops congeal and become diamonds, incur all the dangers of savage life, that he may suddenly acquire great treasure; and in their train, we see the cowled and hooded priest, willing to die or endure the tortures of the fagot and the stake, that he may claim for his sovereign the souls of the heathen he encounters, and for himself a heavenly crown.

The example of each and all of these hardy adventurers and brave explorers is instructive, and has left an impress upon the centuries which will not soon be effaced. The grandeur and nobility of soul they exhibited when confronted by the most appalling dangers, and in the presence of a living terrible death, are well worthy of study and emulation, but their story has no place in a work like this, except as it connects itself with the record of the Maumee Valley, and that is what it is aimed to collate in this effort at local history.

The prehistoric remains of the region will be briefly mentioned, followed by a notice of the Indian tribes known to have possessed this part of the country. The next section will illustrate the period of discovery, and this will be followed by the history of the settlement, and devotion to the purposes of civilization. In preparing this historical sketch, many original sources have been searched, and credit should be given to such pioneers in Western history as have marked the way before us.

That part which embodies the military movements on the Maumee is largely taken from such works as Brice's History of Fort Wayne, Western Annals, and Dillon's History of Indiana. The works consulted are: Life of the Cavalier de La Salle, French; Margry's Exploration and Discoveries, French; Hennepin's Nouvelles Decouvertes, French; Du Pratz' Louisiane, French; Parkman's Discovery of the Great West, Parkman's Conspiracy of Pontiac, Parkman's Jesuits in North America, Parkman's Frontenac and New France, Dillon's History of Indiana, Dillon's Historical Notes, American Antiquarian, Magazine of American History, Western Annals, Colden's History of the Five Nations, McClung's Western Adventures, Washington's Journal, Pennsylvania Historical Society Publications, American State Papers, United States Statutes — Indian Treaties, Imlay's North America, Colonial History of New York, Documentary History of New York, Hopkins' Mission to Fort Wayne, 1804; Brice's History of Fort Wayne, Helm's Allen County History, McCoy's History of Baptist Indian Missions, Bancroft's United States, Lossing's Revolution, Lossing's War of 1812, McAfee's War of 1812, Dawson's Sketches in Fort Wayne Times, Williams' History First Presbyterian Church, Drake's Life of Tecumseh, Burnet's Notes on the North West Territory.

VALLEY OF THE UPPER MAUMEE RIVER.

PREHISTORIC REMAINS.

LONG before the era of Columbus, the valley of the Mississippi had been occupied by a comparatively dense population, and research tends to prove that it was inhabited, long before the advent of the red man known to the explorer, by a people whose history is lost forever, but which appears to have been fixed and permanent in habits, at least in a degree surpassing the races which followed it. This race, to which the indefinite name of the Moundbuilders has been given, had made some advances toward civilization, judged by the aboriginal standard, but did not rise much above the condition of barbarism, and perhaps was less civilized than the Aztecs. The origin and the fate of this race are shrouded in mystery. We know it was always the custom of the red savage to incorporate in his tribe the women and children and sometimes the men of conquered enemies, and it is probable that the remnants of the Moundbuilders were thus amalgamated with the conquering race, which would also acquire some of the habits of the conquered, and in some degree the language. In this way the difference in language and habits of the various tribes inhabiting the country may be partly explained. The remains of the early race appear to be closely related to the monuments of the races of the extreme south, and there is reason to believe that those tribes which inhabited the lake regions were driven south, and there the industry and peaceful habits which characterized them made a stronger impress upon the peoples which inhabited those regions at the era of discovery. Northern Indiana has many proofs of the presence of this race, and they have left some of their monuments in the valley of the Upper Maumee, but not so extensive as are found in other regions.

While some of the race were making settlements along the Ohio, others had passed up the Mississippi, discovered the Great Lakes, and mined copper to some extent on the shores of Lake Superior. Colonies had occupied Michigan, and as far south as the Kankakee in Indiana, and it is from them, perhaps, that Allen county received the marks of occupation. All along the valley of Cedar creek, in Dekalb county, their mounds and earthworks appear in considerable number, but are less numerous southward. Few, if any, are found along the Maumee, and the only traces of their settlement are along Cedar creek, or in the neighborhood of its junction with the St. Joseph.

On Cedar creek, near Stoner's station, was erected a group of four mounds. Two of them were on a line north and south, and about forty feet apart, and about fifteen rods east were two others, about the same distance apart, and on a line east and west. Excavations of two re vealed a large number of human bones, arrow heads and some copper ornaments. Another mound was excavated by the author, but there were found only lumps of charcoal and a layer of hard-baked earth at the base. Four miles south of these, on the Coldwater road, is a large oblong mound which was only partially explored, but in which were found a perforated piece of ribboned slate, much charcoal and a stratum of baked earth. At Cedarville were three mounds about a hundred feet apart, lying on a line nearly parallel with the river. These were found to contain charcoal in considerable quantities, as far as explored. Descending the St. Joseph, to the homestead of Peter Notestine, an old settler, there was found by early relic hunters a circular mound, called a "fort," which was finally conquered by the plow. Numerous fragments of pottery, flint and stone implements, and a large and rude pipe of pottery were found at this place. On the west side of the river, opposite the site of the Antrap's mill, is a semi-circular mound with its ends on the river bank. It is about 600 feet in arc. Very large trees had grown upon this work and gone to decay since its erection, and the falling of trees unearthed many fragments of pottery and flints. At the mouth of Cedar creek was the most southern mound in the county, possessing the usual characteristics.

The mound burial was a distinction of importance between these older peoples and the red men, for the Indians rarely erected mounds over the remains of their dead. The three most prominent Indian burying grounds were on the series of sand hills in the west end of Fort Wayne; on the St. Joseph, just north of the city, near the site of the Miami town; and at Cedarville, on the banks of the St. Joseph. The latter place appears to have been a site of considerable importance in a period of which not the slightest historical trace remains.

Stone implements have been found in the county in considerable quantity, but they belonged in large part to the red men, though some of these relics are of a beauty of finish that seems foreign to the character of the aborigines with whom the early settlers had to do. Flint arrow-heads and spear-heads, of every degree of finish and size, some neatly beveled, flint knives and scrapers, and stone ornaments and totems of various kinds, have been collected and adorn various cabinets.

THE MIAMIS AT KEKIONGA.

The region about the the head of the Maumee presented many attractions to the aboriginal inhabitants of the country. The Maumee is formed by the intersection of the St. Joseph and St. Mary's rivers, and itself flows in a northeasterly direction into Lake Erie. Almost interlocking with the headwaters of the St. Joseph are the sources of Eel river flowing in a southwesterly direction to find the Wabash, while the headwaters of the St. Mary's in like manner almost interlace with the more southerly sources of the same river.

But a short distance from the head of the Maumee, the Aboit and Little rivers have their rise in and near the prairie, and their waters go to swell the volume of the Wabash as well. The two water systems thus lie in a valley having the same general trend southwestwardly from the head of Lake Erie to the embouchure of the Wabash into the Ohio, but forming a remarkable watershed near the head of the Maumee, the waters from one side of the prairie, and the almost imperceptible divide, flowing northeasterly to the lake, and through the St. Lawrence system into the Atlantic, while the waters from the other side of the same prairie, by a route as long, seek and find a discharge into the gulf of Mexico. Heavily wooded, with openings here and there, which formed the beautiful prairies, or upon the alluvial bottoms bordering the rivers, it was a paradise for the fishermen and hunters who made it their home. Nature easily supplied the simple wants of the forest dwellers who preceded the white men, and there are many evidences that a spot thus favored by nature was a favorite dwelling place for the aboriginal tribes who claimed it as their own. Besides these advantages it was the gateway for the migrations of the various tribes that were wont from an early period to communicate at great distances with each other. Commencing at any point between Buffalo and the gulf, the voyager could float from one point to the other except for a short portage from the Maumee to the Little river, over which he would be obliged to carry his light canoe. Here, for a long period, dwelt the Miamis, and, with their kindred tribes, the Pottawatomies, the Shawnees, and the Delawares, all a part of the Algonquin sept, which, in its various divisions occupied a very large portion of what is now the United States east of the Mississippi, had their principal town, the capital of an incomplete and loosely bound confederacy. The Miamis were the head of this family, and next in rank were the Delawares, after whom came the Shawnees. Of kin to these were the Peorias, Kaskaskias, Weas, and Piankeshaws, collectively known as the Illinois Indians. Allied to them and belonging to the same Algonquin family were the Ottawas or Tawas, the Chippewas, the Nipissings, Ojibwas, the Kickapoos, and the Sacs and Foxes. Near them, on the east, were the Huron Iroquois, or the Wyandots, whose principal town was near Sandusky.*

It is no part of this history to trace the origin, migrations, wars, and downfall of the various Indian tribes, except in so far as they relate to the history of this region. Others have so well written the history of

---

*The spelling of tribal names adopted here is mainly that of Schoolcraft and Drake. The various forms of each, if pronounced as their originators intended, would be very similar in sound, though the orthography is diverse. Thus Maumee differs from Miami, originally pronounced Me-ah-me, only in the slurring of the first unaccented vowel. The two words are really identical, but while the explorer wrote of the Miami of the Ohio and the Miami of the Lake, the rivers are now distinguished by a partial change to English pronunciation, and known as the Maumee and the Miami. The "Me-ah-mees" were also sometimes called Omees. The name of the Shawnees has been written Shawanoe, Santanas, Shawanon, Chouanon, etc. The name survives in such various geographical forms as Shawano, Santee, and Suwanee.

this fast vanishing race, that it is unnecessary, and would be out of place here, to more than attempt to give an outline of those principal tribes which have dominated the valley we are describing. The great Algonquin sept was the most extended, and had the greatest number of dialects. They roamed at will from the Atlantic to the Mississippi, from the Arctic belt to the gulf. They met the early settlers at Plymouth and on the Potomac and Roanoke, and whenever the tide of civilization flowed towards the father of waters, it was met by parts of the same great family of the aboriginal tribes. The Indian knew no personal ownership of soil, and no other right of ownership than occupation by his tribe. He shunned the white man, and many a remnant of eastern tribes sought new hunting grounds towards the west, after trying to overcome inexorable fate by defying the incoming wave, and again met and fought their white enemies, whom they considered invaders of their new homes.

Among the western tribes which held the great basin east of the Mississippi none were greater in rank than the Miamis. Known from early times as "Linnewas," or "Minnewas," which means men, and later by the various names of "Omees," "Aumees," "Omamees," "Twightwees" or "Twa-twas," they were met everywhere, a century ago, in that vast territory from Detroit to the Ohio by way of the Great Miami, down the Ohio into the Mississippi, up that river to the region of the lakes. They proudly called themselves "men," and were considered the most stable, heroic and resolute of the western tribes. The several bands of this great tribe were located nearly as follows: The Miamis on the head waters of the Miami of the lake (the Maumee), on the St. Joseph of the lake near South Bend, and at Chicago. The Weas and the Piankeshaws were on the Wabash and southward. The Peorias were on the Illinois. The Mascoutins were between the Illinois and the Wabash. The Cahokias, the Kaskaskias, and the Tamawis were toward the Mississippi in what is now the state of Illinois, and the Michigammies were located at Des Moines. They all spoke one language, with but slightly varying dialects, and all were known as kin to, and part of, the Miamis proper. This confederacy was at an early period at war with the Sioux and Sacs and Foxes, and after many years of war, but few were left except the Miamis and the Weas, on the Maumee and Wabash, the remnants of the others being few and scattered.

The Miamis, with whom we have most to do, were feared by their enemies and were much sought as allies by those tribes needing assistance. By their position, they were destined to play an important part in molding the destinies of the New World, and they have left a deep impress upon the early history of the country. Their customs and habits were such as were common to all the savage tribes. In summer they hunted and fished, or made war upon other tribes with whom they came in contact. Before they came in contact with the whites, their arms were a spear or javelin, a bow and quiver of arrows, all pointed with barbs of stone, and the "casse tete," or "head-breaker," which was either the well-formed stone axe or hatchet fastened to a handle by withes, or the stone enclosed in a rawhide, the handle being twisted and hardened strips of the same material. In winter they gathered in their villages, and passed the time in games and play. The women were the workers; the men were veritable lords and masters. They raised corn, and some small fruits and vegetables near the permanent villages, but were generally improvident, feasting to-day, and fasting to-morrow. Their clothing was made of the skins of deer and other animals, the women being well clad with attempts at ornament, while the men were more than half naked and tattoed the exposed portions of the skin. They had one custom peculiar to themselves. They were monogamists, and if the wife were unfaithful, the husband could cut off her nose and send her away. They were hospitable to their friends but very cruel to their enemies. When a captive was taken in war he was certain to be put to death with the most cruel tortures by slow fire, the ceremony of living cremation often taking the whole of a day before the hapless victim was permitted to end his sufferings in death. No sex or condition was spared these cruel torments, unless some who had lost a member of their family chose to adopt the prisoner to take the place of the deceased.

They had one custom of peculiar atrocity. They seemed at an early period to have practiced cannibalism quite generally, but later, it was confined to eating prisoners of war, and finally the horrible practice seems to have become the prerogative of certain families — an honorary distinction, as it were. As a means of terror to their enemies, they early formed here what was commonly known as a "man-eating society," which, to make it the more fearful to their opponents, was firmly established on a hereditary basis, confined to one family alone, whose descendants continued to exercise, by right of descent, the savage rites and duties of the man-eating family. For these enormities, the Sacs and Foxes, when they took any of the Miamis prisoners, gave them up to their women to be buffeted to death. They speak also of the Mascoutins with abhorrence, on account of their cruelties. In proof of the foregoing, relative to the society of man-eaters among the Indians at this point, General Lewis Cass, in a speech delivered at the canal celebration of July 4th, 1843, in "Swinney's Grove," near the site of the present Catholic cemetery, said: "For many years during the frontier history of this place and region, the line of your canal was a bloody war-path, which has seen many a deed of horror. And this peaceful town has had its Moloch, and the records of human depravity furnish no more terrible examples of cruelty than were offered at his shrine. The Miami Indians, our predecessors in the occupation of this district, had a terrible institution whose origin and object have been lost in the darkness of aboriginal history, but which was continued to a late period, and whose orgies were held upon the very spot where we now are. It was called the man-eating society, and it was the duty of its associates to eat such prisoners as were preserved and delivered to them for that purpose. The members of this society belonged to a particular family, and the dreadful inheritance descended to all the children, male and female. The duties it imposed could not be avoided, and the sanctions of religion were added to the obligations of immemorial usage. The feast was a solemn ceremony, at which the whole tribe was collected as actors or spectators. The miserable victim was bound to a stake, and burned at a slow fire, with all the refinements of cruelty which savage ingenuity could invent. There was a traditionary ritual, which regulated with revolting precision the whole course of procedure at these ceremonies. Latterly the authority and obligations of the institution had declined, and I presume it has now wholly disappeared. But I have seen and conversed with the head of the family, the chief of the society, whose name was White Skin — with what feeling of disgust, I need not attempt to describe. I well knew an intelligent Canadian, who was present at one of the last sacrifices made at this horrible institution. The victim was a young American captured in Kentucky, toward the close of our revolutionary war. Here where we are now assembled, in peace and security, celebrating the triumph of art and industry, within the memory of the present generation, our countrymen have been thus tortured, and murdered, and devoured. But, thank God, that council-fire is extinguished. The impious feast is over; the war-dance is ended; the war-song is sung; the war-drum is silent, and the Indian has departed to find, I hope, in the distant west, a comfortable residence, and I hope also to find, under the protection, and, if need be, under the power of the United States, a radical change in the institutions and general improvement in his morals and condition. A feeble remnant of the once powerful tribe which formerly won their way to the dominion of this region by blood, and by blood maintained it, have to-day appeared among us like passing shadows, flitting round the places that know them no more. Their resurrection, if I may so speak, is not the least impressive spectacle which marks the progress of this imposing ceremony. They are the broken columns which connect us with the past. The edifice is in ruins, and the giant vegetation, which covered and protected it, lies as low as the once mighty structure which was sheltered in its recesses. They have come to witness the first great act of peace in our frontier history, as their presence here is the last in their own. The ceremonies upon which you heretofore gazed with interest, will never again be seen by the white man, in this seat of their former power. But thanks to our ascendency, these representations are but a pageant; but a theatrical exhibition which, with barbarous motions and sounds and contortions, shows how their ancestors conquered their enemies, and how they glutted their revenge in blood. To-day, this last of the race is here — to-morrow they will commence their journey towards the setting sun, where their fathers, agreeable to their rude faith, have preceded them, and where the red man will find rest and safety."

Many instances of the treatment of the prisoners whose misfortune it was to fall into the hands of these merciless demons of the forest, and whose sufferings by torture and at the stake are a part of the history of this now beautiful region where men now enjoy undisturbed the blessings of peace, and whose bodies served as torches to light the pathway of the new civilization which was destined to overspread and develop the virgin west, could be given, but the description of one would serve for all. In 1789, John May, of Virginia, was appointed government surveyor of lands for Kentucky, and started down the Ohio, with Charles Johnston, a youth of twenty, as clerk, on the boat of Jacob Skyles, a merchant who was taking a stock of goods into the wilderness. Another young man named Flinn, and two sisters named Fleming, were passengers. It was in the spring of 1790 that they started, and on reaching the mouth of the Scioto, they were decoyed to land by the piteous appeals of two white men, whom the Indians had captured, and now compelled to act as decoys to lure their compatriots into the hands of the savages. Landing to save these men they were themselves attacked. Flinn was captured as he leaped to the shore. One of the girls was killed and Skyles wounded. The hapless prisoners were distributed to the different bands and taken north to the Miami villages. Flinn was tortured and burned at the stake. The first news of his fate was received from a Delaware, who returned from the Miami villages with the intelligence that Flinn had been burned at the stake a few days before. He declared that he was present and assisted in torturing him, and had afterward eaten a portion of his flesh, which he declared "was sweeter than bear's meat."

A Canadian trader who was also present, described the scene. Flinn had at first entertained strong hopes of being adopted, but a wild council was held in which the most terrible sentiments regarding the whites were uttered, and the resolution proclaimed that henceforth no quarter should be given to any age, sex or condition. Flinn was seized and fastened to the stake. He appealed to the trader to save him, and he ran to the village and brought out several kegs of rum which he offered as a ransom. The Indians in a rage, broke in the heads of the kegs and spilled the rum upon the ground. The trader then brought out 600 silver brooches, but the Indians scornfully rejected them, and threatened the trader with the same fate if he again interfered. He communicated his ill success to Flinn, who heard him with composure, and only said, "Then all I have to say is, God have mercy upon my soul." The scene of torture then commenced with whoops and yells, which struck terror to the heart of the trader, but which Flinn bore with heroic fortitude. Not a groan escaped him. He walked calmly around the stake for several hours, until his flesh was roasted, and the fire had burned down. An old squaw approached to rekindle it, but Flinn, watching his opportunity, gave her so furious a kick in the breast, that she fell back insensible, and for some time was unable to take further part in the torture. The warriors then bored his ankles, and passing thongs through the sinews, confined them closely to the stake, so that he was unable to offer further resistance. His sufferings continued for many hours, until at last terminated by the tomahawk.

Skyles was also conducted to one of the towns on the Maumee, near the scene of Flinn's terrible execution, and was, according to custom, compelled to run the gauntlet. The Indian boys were his principal tormenters, one of the urchins displaying particular dexterity in the infernal art. He procured a stout thorn switch upon which the largest thorn was left, and this, as Skyles passed him, he drove up to the head into his naked back. It was left there, and carried by Skyles sticking in his flesh, to the end of his painful career. He was then turned over to his master, and made himself so useful and agreeable to his squaw, that one night she confided to him that his death had been resolved upon, to take place the following day. He could not at first believe it, but listening while they thought him sleeping, talking with her daughter, a girl of fifteen, all hope was dispelled. The old squaw thought he was a good man and ought to be saved, but the young girl exulted over the prospect of witnessing his torture. When they at last fell asleep, Skyles took the Indian's rifle, shot bag and corn pouch and started for the river. He plunged in and swam across, but ruined the gun in so doing, and threw it away. He started southward through the woods, but became bewildered, and after a hard tramp of six hours, found himself at the river where he had crossed. He wandered about for several days almost starved, and almost in despair entered a village from which the warriors were fortunately absent, and went into a trader's booth where he found a white man trading with some squaws. As he had blackened himself, he was not recognized, but made himself known to the trader, who assured him he would aid him, but that he was being sought for and was in great danger, and must leave at once. He told him of a boat, under charge of an English captain, which had gone down the Maumee laden with furs, and which he might overtake, and took him to the river where was a skiff, which he immediately took and started down the river. He was fortunate enough to overtake the Englishman, was aided by him and taken to Detroit, whence he finally reached the United States.

Johnston had been ransomed from the Indians by a Mr. Duchouquet, a French trader, at Sandusky, and while yet with him, the Cherokees, to whom Miss Fleming had fallen as a prisoner, and had also been taken to the Miami villages, returned after wasting their booty with their usual improvidence, bringing her with them. Her dress was tattered, her cheeks sunken, her eyes discolored with weeping, and she appeared wholly wretched. Johnston applied to the traders to aid in delivering her and they promptly complied. A white man, who had been taken from Pittsburgh when a boy and had been adopted among the Indians, and had known her there, where her father kept a small tavern, went with them; as soon as she saw him, she burst into tears, and implored him to save her from her cruel fate. He zealously engaged in the work, and solicited the intercession of an old chief known as "Old King

Crane," telling him the pardonable lie that the woman was his sister. The old man went to the Cherokee camp to try his eloquence upon them, but was refused with insults. This exasperated him, and he returned to his village in a passion, announcing that he would collect his young men and rescue the white squaw by force. This Whittaker applauded, and urged haste, lest the Cherokees, in dread of losing their prisoner, might put her to death. Before daylight King Crane assembled his young men, and advanced on the Cherokee camp. He found all but the miserable prisoner in a sound sleep. She had been stripped naked, her body painted black, and in this condition had been bound to a stake, around which hickory poles had been collected, and every arrangement completed for burning her alive at daylight. She was moaning in a low tone, and was so exhausted as not to be aware of the approach of her deliverers until King Crane cut her cords with his knife. He then ordered his young men to assist her in putting on her clothes, which they did with the utmost indifference. He then awakened the Cherokees and informed them that the squaw was his, and if they submitted quietly, well; but if not, he and his young men were ready for them. They were indignant, but in the presence of superior armed numbers, finally expressed a willingness to give her up, but hoped he would not be such a "beast" as to refuse to pay her ransom. He replied, that as he had her in his own hands, he would serve them right not to give them a single brooch, but that as he disdained receiving anything from them without an equivalent he would pay them 600 brooches. He then returned with her to Lower Sandusky, and placing her in charge of two trusty Indians, sent her to Pittsburgh. The Cherokees loudly protested and paraded the town that evening in war paint, declaring that they would not leave the town until they had shed the blood of a white man in revenge for the loss of their prisoner.

Such was the fate of many a noble character among those who sought new homes in this region, and such were the scenes which frequently were witnessed where now stands the populous and peaceful city of Fort Wayne. The principal burning place at this point, was on the north bank of the Maumee, at the point where the St. Joseph and St. Mary's unite to form that river, though it is known that some captives were burned at the stake, up the St. Mary's, near the site of the Godfroy place, on what is known as the Richardville reserve.

The Miamis had some considerable knowledge of agriculture, and had permanent lodges at their village sites, as well as the portable ones they used when scattered for the hunting season.

Their burial customs were probably not unlike those of other tribes. Cremation was not customary for the dead — only for living captives. They were not, at least in modern times, mound builders. Near their village sites are always found cemeteries, in which the deceased was laid in a recumbent position, in a shallow grave. With the dead was generally placed his weapons, his ornaments, and a dish or jar containing food, and thus we often discover in these graves stone hatchets, flint spear and arrow heads, beads and trinkets, and remains of pottery. Another form of burial was known to be practiced among them, but this was probably resorted to when death came to them while away on hunting or war parties. No grave was prepared, but the body was placed in a hollow log, the ends of which were closed, or a log would be split and its halves hollowed to receive the corpse, when it would either be tied with green withes, or confined to the earth by crossed stakes driven into the ground, surmounted by a rider. Again, the body would be placed upon the earth and a pen of logs erected over it, each course being drawn in, until they met at the top in a single log, heavy enough to keep the pen thus formed from being overturned by the beasts of the forest.

Principal Chiefs of the Miamis.—Aque-noch-qua was chief, and signed the first treaty between the British and Miamis, July 23, 1748. He lived in Turtle village, a few miles northwest of Fort Wayne, and here in 1751,* his son, the famous Little Turtle, was born.

Upon his death, Little Turtle (Me-che-can-noch-qua) became chief of the tribe. His mother was a Mohican, and was a woman of superior qualities, some of which she transmitted to her child. His courage, sagacity, and extraordinary talents, were developed at an early age, and when but a boy, his influence with his own tribe as well as with others of the confederation, was almost unbounded; his skill in the management of an army was not surpassed by those trained and schooled in the profession of arms. He was victorious in many a hotly contested battle, and it was not until he met "the man who never sleeps," as he called Gen. Wayne while addressing a council of war, did he meet his equal. Of a very inquiring turn of mind, he never lost an opportunity to gain some valuable information upon almost every subject or object that attracted his attention; and sought by every means in his power, during the latter days of his life, to relieve his people from every debasing habit—encouraging them only in the more peaceful, sober, and industrious ways of life. In 1797, accompanied by Capt. Wells, he visited Philadelphia, where he enjoyed the society of the distinguished Count Volney, and the Polish patriot, Kosciusko, and others. While in Philadelphia, he had his portrait painted, by order of the president. Stopping at the same house with Turtle, in Philadelphia, was an Irish gentleman, somewhat remarkable as a wit, who made it a point to "poke fun" at the chief whenever an occasion offered. He and Turtle happening to meet one morning in the studio of Stewart, the artist engaged in painting each of their portraits, the Irishman observed Turtle in a rather thoughtful mood, began to rally him upon his sober demeanor, and suggested, through Capt. Wells, that it was because of his inability to cope with him in the jocular contest. At this Turtle brightened up. "He mistakes," said he, to Capt. Wells, in reply; "I was just thinking of proposing to the man to paint us both on one board, and here I would stand, face to face with him, and confound him to all eternity."

---

* Some histories say Turtle was born in 1747, but in 1804 he stated to the Quakers who then visited Ft. Wayne, that he had seen fifty-three winters.

In the latter part of 1801, he again with other chiefs visited the east, and at a council held at Baltimore on the 26th of December, with a committee of the yearly meeting of Friends, he made a speech in which he spoke of the tools and two plows given him by the Philadelphia Friends, and said he had used them until they were worn out and useless to him. He added: "It is the real wish of your brothers, the Indians, to engage in the cultivation of our lands, and although the game is not yet so scarce but that we can get enough to eat, we know it is becoming scarce, and that we must begin to take hold of such tools as we see in the hands of the white people." He attributed most of the evils existing among the Indians to the liquor they had learned to drink from the whites, and said that it caused the young men to say: "We had better be at war with the white people," adding, "this liquor that they introduce into our country is more to be feared than the gun or the tomahawk. There are more of us dead since the treaty of Greenville, than we lost by the years of war before, and it is all owing to the introduction of this liquor among us," and after a touching description of the woes thus caused he declared that he wished what he had said might be made public.

In 1803, Little Turtle for the Miamis, and Five Medals for the Pottawatomies, joined in a letter to the "Friends" at Baltimore, in which they express their pleasure that the president had prevented the traders from selling liquor to their people, and their fears that he might be persuaded to permit the traffic, adding "if he does, your red brethren are lost forever," but at the same time expressing the hope that "the Great Spirit will change the minds of our people, and tell them it will be better for them to cultivate the earth than to drink whiskey." The following year, 1804, a delegation from the Baltimore yearly meeting was sent to Fort Wayne on a mission of amelioration to the Indians, and there met both these chiefs. Little Turtle was then "but half well," as he said. His complaint was the gout, and on the interpreter telling him his complaint was one that belonged to great folks and gentlemen, he said: "I always thought I was a gentleman."

At the general council of the Indians called to meet this delegation, which assembled at Fort Wayne, April 10, 1804, the subject of teaching agriculture to the Indians was the principal theme of discussion. Little Turtle expressed regret that his people had not accepted the idea of cultivating their lands, much as he had tried to convince them of its necessity, and his hope that the words of the Friends might turn their minds. A Friend named Philip Dennis had agreed to remain, intending to live among them to teach them practical farming. Little Turtle explained that the other chiefs and himself had agreed that he should be at neither of their villages, "lest our younger brothers should be jealous of our taking him to ourselves. We have determined to place him on the Wabash, where some of our families will follow him, where our young men, I hope, will follow him, and where he will be able to instruct them as he wishes." The point thus selected for the first "agricultural college" established in the west, was a little below Huntington, at a place then called "the boatyard," from the fact that Gen. Wilkinson had built some flat-boats there, to transport baggage and material down the river. The experiment was not a success, and Dennis found by experience that Little Turtle's misgivings in regard to the industry of the young men were fully verified. After he had enclosed his farm, only one, or at most two, of the red men evinced any disposition to labor. They would take a seat on a fence, or in the trees near his work, and watch with apparent interest his plowing and hoeing, but without offering to lend a helping hand. He left in the fall, discouraged, and so ended the first attempt to teach the savage the arts of peace.

In 1807, Little Turtle again visited Baltimore and Washington, accompanied by Richardville and other chiefs. He desired to have a flour mill erected at Fort Wayne, and appeared earnestly desirous of promoting the interests of his people. He is described as having a countenance placid beyond description and possessed of a very cordial disposition. On this visit he was entertained with other chiefs at the house of a former friend. He was the first to enter the parlor, bowed gracefully as he was introduced to the family, and in a short address, gracefully acknowledged his pleasure at meeting the wife and children of his friend. He exceeded all the other chiefs in dignity of appearance — a dignity which resulted from the character of his mind. He was of medium stature, with a complexion of the palest copper shade, and did not wear paint. His hair was worn full and had no admixture of gray. He was then dressed in a coat of blue cloth with gilt buttons, pantaloons of the same color, and buff waistcoat. He, together with the others, wore leggins and moccasins, and had gold rings in his ears. This dress was completed by a long, red, military sash around his waist, and a cocked hat surmounted by a red feather. On entering a house, he immediately removed the hat, and carried it under his arm. Altogether he was graceful and agreeable to an uncommon degree, and was admired by all who made his acquaintance.

On the 14th day of July, 1812, Little Turtle died in his lodge at the old orchard, a short distance north of the confluence of the St. Mary's and St. Joseph, in the yard fronting the house of his brother-in-law, Capt. William Wells. Turtle had suffered for many months previous with the gout, and came here from Little Turtle village, to be treated by the surgeon at the fort. It was a solemn and interesting occasion. After the treaty of Greenville, Turtle had remained the true and faithful friend of the Americans and the United States government. Tecumseh strove hard to gain his confidence and aid, but without effect, for nothing could move him from his purpose of peace and good-will towards the Americans. In the language of one who was present at his burial: "His body was borne to the grave with the highest honors, by his great enemy, the white man. The muffled drum, the solemn march, the funeral salute, announced that a great soldier had fallen, and even enemies paid tribute to his memory." His remains were interred about the center of the old orchard, with all his adornments, implements of war, a sword presented to him by Gen. Washington, together with a medal, with the likeness of Washington thereon — all laid by the side of the body, and hidden beneath the sod in one common grave. The exact spot of his grave is now unknown. Such was Me-che-can-noch-qua — the bravest among the brave, and wisest among the wise of the Indians of the northwest — leading an army of braves to sure victory one hour — cutting and slashing, as with the ferocity of a tiger, at one moment — and as passive and gentle as a child the next. Ever may his gentler and better deeds be perpetuated by the American people.

He was succeeded by Pe-chon, who was present at, and was one of the signers of, the treaty of July, 1814, at Greenville, and who died soon after at the residence of Richardville, who succeeded him as chief of the Miamis.

John Baptiste Richardville,* whose Indian name was "Pe-che-wa," or "The Wild Cat," was the son of Joseph Drouet de Richardville, who was of noble lineage, and was probably engaged as an officer in the French service in Canada, before being lured into the western wilds, by the prospect of amassing wealth in the fur trade. He was for a long time a trader among the Indians here, and took for a wife, as was customary at that date, Tah-cum-wah, a daughter of Aque-noch-qua, and sister of Little Turtle. Their son was born about 1761, in a hut under the boughs of the historic apple tree, which stood near the confluence of the St. Joseph and St. Mary's, but has long since disappeared.

Among the many thrilling and interesting incidents and narrations, as frequently recited by the chief to the late Allen Hamilton, he gave, some years ago, an account of his ascent to the chieftainship of his tribe. The occasion was not only thrilling and heroic, but, on the part of his famous mother and himself, will ever stand in history as one of the noblest and most humane acts known to any people, and would serve as a theme, both grand and eloquent, for the most gifted poet or dramatist of any land. It was in a wild and barbarous age. Kekionga still occasionally echoed with the shrieks and groans of captive men; and the young warriors of the region still rejoiced in the barbaric custom of burning prisoners at the stake. A white man had been captured and brought in by the warriors. A council had been convened, in which the question of his fate arose in debate and was soon settled. He was to be burned at the stake, and the braves and villagers generally were soon gathered about the scene of torture, making the air resound with their triumphant shouts of pleasure at the prospect of soon enjoying another hour of fiendish merriment at the expense of a miserable victim of torture. Already the man was lashed to the stake, and the

---

*According to Tanquay's "Dictionnaire Genealogique des Familles Canadiennes," there married at Champlain March 18, 1687, Claude Drouet, Sieur de Richardville, officer, born in 1657, son of Claude, Attorney, and Appolline Soisson, of Chartres. He had eight children, and it is reasonable to believe that from one of his sons descended that Drouet who was father of Jean Baptiste Druet de Richardville, whose name is written in numerous treaties and carved on the monument which marks his grave as John B. Richardville.

torch that was to ignite the cumbustible material placed about the same was in the hands of the brave appointed. But rescue was at hand. The man was destined to be saved from the terrible fate that surrounded him! Young Richardville had for some time been singled out as the future chief of the tribe, and his heroic mother saw in this a propitious and glorious moment for the assertion of his chieftainship, by an act of great daring and bravery — the rescue of the prisoner at the stake. Young Richardville and his mother were at some distance, but sufficiently near to see the movements of the actors in the tragedy about to be enacted, and could plainly hear the coarse ejaculations and shouts of triumph of the crowd. At that moment, just as the torch was about to be applied to the bark, as if touched by some angelic impulse of love and pity for the poor captive, the mother of young Richardville placed a knife in her son's hand, and bade him assert his chieftainship by the rescue of the prisoner. The magnetic force of the mother seemed instantly to have inspired the young warrior, and he quickly bounded to the scene, broke through the wild crowd, cut the cords that bound the man, and bid him be free. All was astonishment and surprise; and though by no means pleased at the loss of their prize, yet the young man, their favorite, for his daring conduct, was at once esteemed as a god by the crowd, and then became a chief of the first distinction and honor in the tribe. The mother of Richardville now took the man in charge, and soon quietly placing him in a canoe and covering him with hides, in charge of some friendly Indians he was soon gliding down the placid current of the Maumee, beyond the reach of the turbulent warriors of Kekionga.

At a later period in the life of the chief, being on his way to Washington, he came to a town in Ohio, where, stopping for a little while, a man came up to him, and suddenly recognizing in the stranger the countenance of his benefactor and deliverer of years before, threw his arms about the chief's neck, and embraced him with all the warmth of filial affection. He was indeed the rescued prisoner; and the meeting between the two was one of mingled pleasure and surprise. In stature, Richardville was about five feet ten inches, with broad shoulders, and weighed about one hundred and eighty pounds. His personal appearance was attractive; graceful in carriage and manner. Exempt from any expression of levity — he is said to have "preserved his dignity under all circumstances." His nose was Roman, his eyes were of a lightish blue, and slightly protruding, "his upper lip firmly pressed upon his teeth, and the under one slightly projecting." That he was an Indian half-breed, there can be no doubt. His own statements, and unvarying traditions conclusively prove that he inherited his position through his mother, by the laws of Indian descent, and contradict the theory that he was a Frenchman who obtained the chieftainship by trickery or purchase. In appearance he was remarkable in this — he was neither red nor white, but combined both colors in his skin, which was mottled or spotted red and white. His mother was a most remarkable woman.

Chief Richardville was an only son, and much beloved by her. Her reign continued for a period of some thirty years, prior to the war of 1812, during which time, according to the traditions of the Indians, "she ruled the tribe with a sway, power, and success as woman never ruled before." After her reign, " she retired and passed the mace of power to her son." Richardville was taciturn and was dignified in manner, a habit often almost assuming the form of extreme indifference; yet such was far from his nature, for he ever exercised the warmest and most attentive regard for all of his people and mankind in general; and "the needy never called in vain; his kind and charitable hand was never withheld from the distressed of his own people or from the stranger." So wisely did he manage the affairs of his tribe, with such wisdom and moderation did he adjust and settle all matters relating to his people, that he was not only held in the highest estimation by the Indians generally, throughout the northwest, but honored and trusted as their law-giver with the most unsuspecting confidence and implicit obedience, always adjusting affairs between his own people, as well as all inter-tribal relations, without resort to bloodshed. A patient and attentive listener, prudent and deliberate in his action, when once his conclusions were formed he rarely had occasion to change them. Averse to bloodshed, except against armed resistance, he was ever the strong and consistent friend of peace and good-will.

Many were the vivid recollections he recited years ago to early settlers. At the time of Harmar's movements and defeat, he was a boy of some ten or twelve years of age. But his narration of the way the Indians stole along the bank of the river, near the point, long since known as "Harmar's ford," was most thrilling. Not a man among the Indians, said he, was to fire a gun until the white warriors under Harmar had gained the stream, and were about to cross. Then the red men in the bushes, with the rifles leveled and ready for action, just as the detachment of Harmar began to near the center of the Maumee, opened a sudden and deadly fire upon them; and horses and riders fell in the stream, one upon the other, until the river was literally strewn from bank to bank with the slain, both horses and men; and the water ran dark with blood.

There seemed, in the settling of this section of the country, a rivalry between the settlers and the Indians, as to who should tender the chief the highest respect, for all admired who knew him.

At the treaty of St. Mary's, in 1818, a reserve of nine sections of land was made to him, including a tract some four or five miles from Fort Wayne, up the St. Mary's river, which, since his death, has been in the hands and keeping of his descendants, and is now owned by Archange (daughter of La Blonde, the first daughter of the chief), wife of James R. Godfroy, whose interesting family, with some three or four other persons, relatives of the same, living near, now constitute the only remnants of the once powerful Miami tribe in this part of their old stronghold. They have all long since assumed the garb of civilization, and successfully till one of the finest bodies of land in the northwest.

Richardville was at the treaties of Greenville in 1795, Fort Wayne in 1803, and Vincennes in 1805. He participated also, as civil chief of the tribe, in the treaty of St. Mary's, October 6, 1805, and went to Washington with Little Turtle in 1807.

About 1827, he built a house on the reservation on the St. Mary's. He had three daughters, La Blonde, Susan and Catharine. The daughter of La Blonde married James Godfroy, who has long lived at the old residence of the chief. Richardville was many years a trader at Fort Wayne, but in 1836 moved his goods to the forks of the Wabash, and continued business there a long time, although he retained his family residence near Fort Wayne, having for his housekeeper at the forks of the Wabash, Margaret La Folia, a French woman of prepossessing appearance. He was held in high esteem, and was the lawgiver of his people, trusted by them with the utmost confidence, and obeyed implicitly. He died at his family residence on the 13th of August, 1841; and to-day, in the Catholic cemetery, on the confines of his birth-place, is to be seen an enduring marble shaft, erected by his daughters, commemorating the beloved and famous chief of the Miamis.

Francis La Fontaine, whose Indian name was To-pe-ah, perhaps a contraction of the Pottawatomie name, To-pe-na-bin, was the immediate successor of Pe-che-wa (Richardville), as the principal chief of the Miamis. He was the lineal descendant of La Fontaine, who, during the latter part of the eighteenth century, was sent out by the French government in connection with the provincial management of Canada. His father was of French extraction, and at one time a resident of Detroit; his mother was a Miami woman, whose name does not appear very frequently in the history of the tribe, but who was, nevertheless, a woman of considerable force of character, as manifested in the qualities of her son. He was born near Fort Wayne, in 1810, and spent a great portion of his life in its immediate vicinity. When about the age of twenty-one years, he was married to Catharine (Po-con-go-qua), a daughter of Richardville. In his younger days, he was noted for great strength and activity, and was reputed to be the most fleet of foot in the tribe. His residence was on the south side of the prairie, between Huntington and Fort Wayne, on lands granted by the treaties of October 23, 1834, and November 6, 1838. Manifesting great interest in the welfare of his tribe, he became very popular, and, after the death of Chief Richardville, in 1841, he was elected principal chief of the Miamis. Subsequently, he moved to the forks of the Wabash, and resided in the frame building near the road, a few rods west of the fair grounds — the place belonging to his wife, who inherited it from her father.

When, under the provisions of their final treaty with the United States, his tribe, in the fall of 1846, moved to the reservation set apart to them, west of the Mississippi, he went with them and remained during the winter. The following spring he started homeward. At that time, the route of travel was from the Kansas Landing (now Kansas City), down the Missouri and Mississippi, to the mouth of the Ohio; up the Ohio to the mouth of the Wabash, and thence up the latter stream to La Fayette — all the way by steamboats. At St. Louis, he was taken sick, and his disease had made such progress that, upon his arrival at La Fayette, he was unable to proceed further, and died there, on the 13th of April, 1847, at the age of thirty-seven years. He was embalmed at La Fayette, and his remains were brought to Huntington, where he was buried in the grounds now occupied by the Catholic church. His body was subsequently removed to the new cemetery. At the time of the removal of his body, so perfect had been the embalming, little evidence of decay was manifested.

He was a tall, robust man, weighing about 350 pounds, and generally dressed in Indian costume. There are two portraits of him remaining, one painted by Freeman, and one by R. B. Croft. About twenty months after his death, his widow married F. D. Lasselle, of Fort Wayne, but lived only a short time. Of her seven children by La Fontaine, but two are now living — Mrs. Archange Engleman, in Huntington, and Mrs. Esther Washington, who removed to Kansas.

Early History of the Miamis.— At what period in their history the Miamis made Kekionga their "Central City," can not be definitely stated, but it was probably nearly contemporaneous with the early white settlements on the Atlantic coast. This statement is at variance, no doubt, with the opinions entertained by others, who believe that from time immemorial, "when the memory of man runneth not to the contrary," this typical band of the Algonquin family had inhabited and possessed this, to them, classic ground. The statement made by Little Turtle, in his address to Gen. Wayne, at the treaty of Greenville, in August, 1795, which is confirmed by the narratives of the early French voyageurs, is wholly inconsistent with such an assumption. That intelligent Miami chief said: "I hope you will pay attention to what I now say to you. I wish to inform you where your younger brothers, the Miamis, live, and also the Pottawatomies of St. Joseph, together with the Wabash Indians. You have pointed out to us the boundary line between the Indians and the United States; but I now take the liberty to inform you that the line cuts off from the Indians a large portion of country which has been enjoyed by my forefathers from time immemorial, without molestation or dispute. The prints of my ancestors' houses are everywhere to be seen in this portion. I was a little astonished at hearing you and my brothers who are now present, telling each other what business you had transacted together heretofore, at Muskingum, concerning this country. It is well known to all my brothers who are now present, that my forefather kindled the first fires at Detroit; thence he extended his lines to the west waters of the Sciota; thence to its mouth; from there down the Ohio to the mouth of the Wabash; and thence to Chicago, on Lake Michigan. At this place I first saw my elder brothers, the Shawnees. I have now informed you of the boundaries of the

Miami nation, where the Great Spirit placed my forefather long ago, and charged him not to sell or part with his lands, but preserve them for his posterity. This charge has been handed down to me." When they left the parent stock in the east, by what route they migrated westward, will probably never be known, and their own traditions in regard to it were vague and uncertain.

The first historical account of the tribe since it became known under the distinct name of Miamis, was in the year 1669, when they were found in the vicinity of Green Bay, by the French missionary, Father Allouez, and later by Father Dablon. In 1680, both of these renowned and devoted priests visited a town of the Miamis and Mascoutins, on the Fox river, above Lake Winnebago. St. Lusson, a French officer in the Canadian forces, found them at Green Bay during the same year. They received him with marked distinction, giving a sham battle for his entertainment, as well as the game of la crosse. On his return he gave a marvelous account of the dignity and state of the Miami chief who was his host and entertainer. From there they passed to the southward of Lake Michigan, in the vicinity of Chicago, subsequently locating on the St. Joseph of Lake Michigan, establishing there a village, another on the river Miami (Maumee) of Lake Erie, and a third on the Wabash, called Ouiatenon.

Some part of the tribe seems to have remained after the migration mentioned, for in 1673 Marquette visited the town of the Miamis formerly visited by Allouez and Dablon. On reaching the village he found a cross planted in its center. The Indians had decorated it with dressed deer skins, red girdles, bows and arrows, and other ornaments, in honor of the great Manitou of the French. He describes the Miamis as wearing long locks of hair over each ear, and says of the Mascoutins and Kickapoos, that they were mere boors as compared with their Miami townsmen. It may be, however, that prior to their location at Green Bay, they first assumed the character of a distinct tribe at Detroit, as stated by Little Turtle, and, in various wanderings, spread thence over the valley of the Scioto to the Ohio, and thence to the Wabash and northward, inhabiting from time to time, every portion of the territory they claimed, and of which their proprietorship was recognized by the surrounding tribes.

In 1680, the Iroquois decreed in their councils a war against the Illinois, then a numerous and powerful tribe. The chief town of the Miamis was on the way, and although the Miamis were kinsmen to the Illinois, the wily Iroquois visited them and induced them to join in the invasion as their allies. This was more easily accomplished, because there had been a jealousy of long standing between the two tribes, and the Miamis were unaware that they were already marked out by their treacherous allies, the Iroquois, as their next victims, and that one purpose of the alliance was doubtless to reduce the fighting number of the Miamis by means of this war with the Illinois. About the middle of September, the allies approached the Vermilion river, where the Illinois, warned of the invasion, had hastened to meet them, and were posted in the open prairie near the margin of the river. The Iroquois and their allies were numerous, and were armed in great measure with guns, pistols, and swords, obtained from the whites, while most of the Illinois were armed only with the primitive weapons of the savage, only about a hundred of them being armed with modern weapons. They exhibited every evidence of bravery and eagerness to meet the invaders, yelling, dancing and brandishing their weapons in the presence of their foes, who responded with similar manifestations of eagerness for the fray. Notwithstanding this apparent eagerness no battle was fought, and yielding to the mediation of La Salle, who had espoused their cause, the Illinois finally withdrew.

Subsequently, the Iroquois crossed to the Illinois side of the river, took possession, and erected a rude fort for immediate protection. Under the guise of making a treaty of peace, they prepared for a merciless slaughter of their victims. The French being withdrawn, the Illinois unfortunately for themselves, separated into different bands and scattered. The Iroquois, foiled in finding a living foe, wreaked their vengeance upon the dead, tearing down the burial scaffolds, and violating the graves, giving the bodies to the dogs or burning them, and fixing the skulls on stakes. They then pursued the fleeing Illinois to the Mississippi, scattering the remnants of the once powerful tribe in every direction. Few of the men were killed, but many women and children were captured, and for some time the Iroquois revelled in the tortures they inflicted upon these unhappy victims. At length, sated with their atrocities, the conquerers withdrew, taking with them a host of captives whose lives had been spared, not from any instinct of mercy, but because they could make them useful as slaves by incorporating them in their tribe. The total number of their prisoners has been stated as more than seven hundred.

In 1686 the Miamis were located on the Bay des Puans (Green Bay, Wisconsin). There they were attacked by their former allies the Iroquois, and suffered greatly at their hands, these fierce warriors desiring by the destruction of the Miamis to make themselves masters of Michillimackinac and of the bay, including in their objects the destruction of the Christian missionaries, and the extinction of the trade by way of the lakes, or the control of it for themselves. During the same year, Denonville writes that the Five Nations are making a large war party, supposed to be against the Oumiamis and other savages of the Bay des Puans, who were attacked this year, one of their villages having been destroyed by the Iroquois, on receiving notice whereof the hunters of those tribes pursued the Iroquois, whom they overtook and fought with considerable vigor, having recovered several prisoners and killed many of the Iroquois. During the years 1686–7 there were frequent difficulties between the Iroquois and Miamis, which occasioned much uneasiness among the English colonial officials, and the English governor called a council of his Iroquois allies to ascertain the true condition of affairs.

It was held at Albany on the 5th of August, 1687, when he proposed to them to send messages to the Ottawas, Twightwees and the further Indians, and some of the prisoners from those tribes were sent to make a covenant chain with them.

On the following day, one of the Maquase (Mohawk) sachems, named Sindachsegie, made a speech to the governor, explaining the cause of the disturbance between them and those nations in alliance with the French. He said: "Wee are resolved to speake the truth, and all the evill we have done them is that about six yeares agoe, some of the Sinnekes and some of the Onnondages went aboard of a French Barke att Onnyagaro, that was come to trade there, and took out of the said Barke a Caske of Brandy and cutt the Cable." It occurred, also, that in September, of the preceding year, the Senecas had visited the country of the Omianies (Miamis), and in a warlike expedition had taken of them 500 prisoners and lost twenty-nine killed, two of them in foray, and twenty-seven when the Touloucks (Outaouacs) and Illinois caught them.

Ten years later, Peter Schuyler and others, on behalf of the Senecas, in a communication to the English governor, Fletcher, dated September 28, 1697, made this statement: "Wee are sorry to have it to tell you the loss of our brethren, the Sinnekes, suffered in an engagement with ye Twichtwichts Indians; our young men killed several of the enemy, but, upon their retreat, some of their chiefe capts. were cut off. You know our custome is to condole ye dead, therefore, we desire you give us some for these Beavours; soe laid down ten Beavr. skins. The Wampum was immediately given them for said skins, and the day following appointed for a conference upon the first proposition made by them for powder & lead, &c." Further statement is made concerning the war between the Five Nations and the Miamis, in Robert Livingston's report to the secretary of Indian affairs, in April, 1700, from which it would seem that the war had been pending between these parties for many years, taken in connection with the preceding statement. He recommends "That all endeavors be used to obtain a peace between the 5 Nations and the Dowaganhaas, Twichtwicks & other far Nations of Indians whom the Governor of Canada stirs up to destroy them, not only the 5 Nations have been mortall enemies to the French & true to the English, but because they hinder his trade with the said far Nations, trucking with them themselves and bringing the beavers hither."

In a subsequent communication by the same writer, on the 29th of August of the same year, a better reason is given, perhaps, for the desire to induce a cessation of hostilities between those belligerent nations. "Brethren: You must needs be sensible that the Dowaganhaes, Twichtwicks, Ottawa & Diononades, and other remote Indians, are vastly more numerous than you 5 Nations, and that, by their continued warring upon you, they will, in a few years, totally destroy you."

In 1736, there was an enumeration of the Indian tribes with the number of their warriors and the armorial bearings of each nation, supposed to have been prepared by M. de Joncaire, a Frenchman who had been adopted into the Seneca tribe.

He mentions first the Pottawatomies, who call themselves the governor's eldest sons. They were located at the village of St. Joseph, on the river of that name (the St. Joseph of Lake Michigan) and numbered about one hundred warriors. He mentions that they had with them ten Miamis, who bear in their arms a crane.

He classes the Miamis under the head of "Lake Erie and its dependencies on the south side," and says of them: "The Miamis have for their device the hind and the crane. These [the Miamis and Pottawatomies] are the two principal tribes. There is likewise the device of the bear, and they numbered 200 men bearing arms. The Ouyattanons, Peauguichias, Petikokias are the same nation, though in different villages. They can place under arms 350 men. The devices of these savages are the serpent, the deer, and the small acorn."

In November, 1763, Sir William Johnson gave an account of the present state of the Indians, and mentions as a part of the Ottawa confederacy, the Miamis or Twightwees, located near the fort on the Miami river, numbering over 250 men. He says: "The Twightwees were originally a very powerful people, who, having been subdued by the Six Nations, were permitted to enjoy their possessions. There are many tribes and villages of them, but these are all that are certainly known."

In 1765, the Miami confederacy was composed of the following branches, situated and having warriors in number, viz.: Twightwees, at the head of the Maumee river, with 250 available warriors; the Ouiatenons, in the vicinity of Post Ouiatenon, on the Wabash, with 300 warriors; the Piankeshaws, on the Vermillion river, with 300 warriors, and the Shockeys, on territory lying on the Wabash, between Vincennes and Post Ouiatenon, with 200 warriors. At an earlier period, probably, the Miamis, with their confederates, were able to muster a much more formidable force, as the citation from the representatives of the Five Nations would seem to show.

In 1748, the English merchants and traders secured a limited trade with the Miamis, much, it is said, in consequence of the failure of the French traders, who had, during the preceding century, held the supremacy, to supply the increasing wants of the Miamis, especially those on the borders of the Ohio and its tributaries. Thus a favorable influence was exerted on the part of the Miamis toward the English, which resulted in a treaty of alliance and friendship between the English and the Twightwees (Miamis) on the 23d of July of the same year, whereby the latter became and were recognized as "Good Friends and Allies of the English Nation, subjects of the King of Great Britain, entitled to the privilege and protection of the English Laws." This treaty was signed by the representatives, "Deputies from the Twightwees (or Miamis) on or about the river Ouabache, a branch of the river Mississippi," three in number, the first and principal of whom was Aque-noch-qua, head chief of the Miamis, and the father of Me-che-can-noch-qua (LittleTurtle), at that time and for many years previous a resident of the Turtle village in this vicinity.

By their several treaties with the United States, the Miamis have ceded an aggregate of 6,853,020 acres of land. Aggregate of land given in exchange, 44,640 acres, the aggregate value of which was $55,800. The aggregate consideration paid for these lands, in money and goods, $1,205,907; total consideration paid, $1,261,707, as shown by the records of the department at Washington.

EARLY EXPLORATIONS.

The period when the white man first wended his way through the wilderness, and set his foot upon the spot where was the seat of authority among the Miamis, and where now rise the spires of the busy city of Fort Wayne, cannot with any certainty be determined. The first intrepid explorer was doubtless one of that class, who either from love of a life of wild adventure, or from desire to avoid the punishment due for misdemeanors committed, either in France, or the settlements on the St. Lawrence, joined the horde of adventurers known as " coureurs de bois," or wood rangers, and paddled his canoe along the borders of Lake Erie, thence up the Maumee to the portage, and perhaps still further down the Wabash in search of peltries, which he conveyed back to the settlements, or, if he feared to return, sold them to intermediate traders.

"The Coureur de Bois" was an unique figure in American history. Careless and rollicking in disposition, he fearlessly plunged into the wilds of the interior, freely mingling with the tribes he happened to come in contact with, making himself at home and welcomed in their villages, becoming one of them by adopting their habits and dress, allowing himself to be painted and sometimes adopted into their tribes, making love to, and contracting a temporary marriage with, the dusky girl who was willing to become the mistress of the wigwam of the pale-face; broke these bonds and ties to form others whenever his fortunes or his fancy took him to another village; returned by long voyages for occasional visits to the old settlements, where he spent his time in wild carousals until he had lost the wealth his peltries had brought him, when he would again plunge into the forest to seek some one of his deserted wives, and spend another period in amassing the necessary supplies for another visit and another debauch. Sometimes he left the scenes of civilized life behind him forever, and remained among his savage companions, becoming one of them, in so far as one born in civilization can become in truth a savage. Wild and reckless as he was, savage as he might become, he was the precursor of the advance of civilization, and blazed the path through hitherto trackless wilds for the entrance of the explorer and the priest, who led the advance, and became the pioneers of the western world. Let us treat his follies and his crimes with lenient judgment, for he, unwittingly perhaps, but nevertheless certainly, performed an inestimable service to the world, and to us who now enjoy the blessings of a civilization he seemed to flee from and shun.

That the route by way of the head of the Maumee and its portage to the Wabash was known and traversed at an early date may be said to be known with certainty, although any records of such travels may be wanting. The reader should remember that for many years after the discovery of America, the learned of the world believed it to be a part of the Indies, and they long sought a passage over our continent, to reach the South sea and the treasures of Cathay. It was not till long after La Salle discovered the Mississippi, that it dawned upon their minds that a new continent had been discovered, an unknown half of the world opened for future empire. In the mean time, the explorer and priest had followed fast upon the footsteps of the wood ranger and fur trader, and it is the record of their adventurous footsteps, as they opened and took possession of the valley of the Mississippi, and more particularly of the valley of the Maumee, with which we have to deal.

As early as 1504, and perhaps at an earlier date, the fisheries of Newfoundland were known and visited by the hardy and venturesome fishermen of France, and a map of the St. Lawrence was made in 1506, by Denys, a citizen of Honfleur. In 1508, Thomas Aubert of Dieppe sailed up the St. Lawrence, and from that time commenced an inter-communication and trade between the French and the Indians of the interior, which gradually extended to distant points. When Capt. John Smith discovered the Chesapeake, he discovered among the Indians of that region, articles of civilized manufacture, which must have come from the French settlements on the St. Lawrence through the Iroquois. Quebec was founded in 1608, and became the center from which wood ranger, trader, explorer, and priest, radiated in every direction, sowing seeds which were to fructify, and produce a marvelous harvest, far in the future.

The great profits realized from the fur trade were inducements for adventure, and numerous traders and other adventure-loving spirits found their way to the extensive domain of New France. Among these, of course, members of the society of Jesus were found, and, in 1611, a mission had been established among the Indians of that region. From that time forward, vigorous efforts were made for the furtherance of trade in connection with the establishment of missions for the conversion of the Indians. By means of the assiduous perseverance of the French traders and priests, these efforts were generally attended with success. As a result, it is stated that up to 1621, 500 convents of the Recollets had been established in New France. In 1635, a Jesuit college was founded at Quebec. During that year, Champlain, the first governor of New France, died, and with him much of the zeal incident to prosperous settlements.

The immediate successor of Champlain as governor, was Chasteaufort, who was superceded by De Montmagny, in 1636. With this latter appointment, a change in the affairs of the government was noticeable, the fur trade becoming the principal object of attention. A consequence of this policy was the exploration of other new territory, to enlarge the arena of trade. Rude forts were erected as a means of defense to the trading-houses and a protection to the 'trade. Not far remote — a never-failing auxiliary — was the chapel of the Jesuit, surmounted by a cross. Gradually, these explorations extended westward and southward along the margin of the lakes and their tributaries.

Champlain had in 1611-12, ascended as far as Lake Huron, which he called "the Fresh Sea," passing by the Maumee on his way. In 1640, Fathers Charles Raymbault and Claude Pijart were chosen and sent as missionaries to the Algonquins of the north and west. Where they labored is not known, but it is probable that they went little further than here at that early date. In August, 1604, two young and adventurous fur traders joined a band of Algonquins, and made a voyage of 500 leagues, coming in contact with many tribes, and even with the Sioux beyond Lake Superior.

The importance of maps, in tracing doubtful questions in history, is frequently overlooked. It may be said, without fear of dispute, that when we find a map upon which the site of habitations and the rivers and other topographical features are delineated even with a reasonable degree of exactness, that region has been visited by some one who carefully noted his discoveries, and was skilled in the work he sought to accomplish; and it is from such a map, that we know that the site of Fort Wayne was known at an earlier date than any recorded history has given.

In 1657, Sanson, who was the royal geographer of the French king, prepared a map of "Le Canada, ou Nouvelle France," on which Lake Erie is displayed, with a river flowing into it from the southwest, for a distance, and from a direction, clearly representing the Maumee in its course from the site of Fort Wayne to the lake. The St. Mary's and the St. Joseph are not represented, indicating that their courses had not yet been explored. In this map we have indubitable evidence that the Maumee had been traversed by intrepid French explorers prior to 1657.

On the 8th of August, 1660, Father Claude Allouez set out on a mission to the far west, and for many years thereafter was the spiritual adviser and saintly father of the Miamis, beloved by them, and devoting his life to their temporal and spiritual welfare. He found them between Green Bay and the head of Lake Superior. Two years later, he returned to Quebec, and urged the establishment of permanent missions among the western tribes, and succeeded so well that on his return in 1668 he was accompanied by Fathers Claude Dablon and James Marquette, then recently from France.

In 1669, Monsieur Talon, the intendant of justice, etc., for the province of New France, having visited France, and received instructions from the king to push the discoveries into the interior, appointed Robert Cavelier, Sieur de La Salle, a man of wonderful energy, sagacity, bravery and discretion, with instructions " to penetrate further than has ever been done, * * * to the southwest and south"; to keep a journal of his adventures in all instances, and on his return to reply to the written instructions embraced in his commission. These instructions required, also, that he take possession of all the new territory discovered, in the king's name, displaying the arms of France and issuing *proces verbaux* to settlers to serve as titles. Reporting this appointment to the king, he remarked: " His Majesty will probably have no news of him before two years from this, and when I shall return to France." At the same time, with like instructions, Sieur de St. Lusson was appointed to penetrate to the west and northwest.

Subsequently, in February, 1671, M. Colbert, the king's secretary, in a communication addressed to the intendant, says: "The resolution you have taken to send Sieur de La Salle toward the south, and Sieur de St. Lusson to the north, to discover the South sea passage, is very good; but the principal thing to which you ought to apply yourself in discoveries of this nature, is to look for the copper mine."

As a part of the annual report to the king, in November of the same year, he makes this announcement: " Sieur de La Salle has not yet returned from his journey to the southward of this country. But Sieur de Lusson is returned, after having advanced as far as 500 leagues from here (Quebec), and planted the cross and set up the king's arms in presence of seventeen Indian nations, assembled on this occasion, from all parts, all of whom voluntarily submitted themselves to the dominion of His Majesty, whom alone they regard as their sovereign protector." This meeting was held at the Falls of St. Mary, north of Lake Michigan. He reports, also, that " according to the calculations made from the reports of the Indians and from maps, there seems to remain not more than 1,500 leagues of navigation to Tartary, China and Japan. Such discoveries must be the work either of time or of the king." The route pursued by La Salle in his adventure is, to some extent, a matter of conjecture, since no record made by himself is now known to be extant, except so much as relates to his starting out on such an expedition with Messrs. Dollier and Gallinee; and becoming dissatisfied with the proposed plans of these two gentlemen, to his pursuing a route more in accord with his own judgment. Having thus separated from them, after a short period of silence, we hear of him a few leagues to the southward of Lake Erie, approaching the head-waters of the principal tributary of the Ohio, the Alleghany, no doubt, which he descends until met by a great fall in the river, understood to be the Falls of the Ohio, at Louisville. Here the direct narrative ends, and we are left to a consideration of pertinent circumstances for tracings of him during the succeeding two or three years. This was in the fall of 1669.

The correspondence of the government officials, from time to time, during the period of his absence, show that he had not yet returned.

Indeed, it was stated in the beginning that his return was not expected until the expiration of two years, at least; and later that he returned accordingly — all these facts tending to show that his movements were fully known by the authorities aforesaid, and were in compliance with instructions. Such being the conditions, let us examine, from the context, whether he retraced his steps, as some have affirmed, or took a different route to reach the point contemplated. This objective purpose was to find the outlet of the great river supposed to run to the southwest or south and fall into the Vermilion Sea (Gulf of California), on the western border of the continent. Animated with a desire to accomplish his mind's ideal of a more direct route to China and Japan, such as seemed to control his actions about the time of his separation from his companions in the vicinity of Lake Erie, is not presumable even, that he was so easily discouraged as to turn back after having reached the Falls of the Ohio, almost in direct line with his contemplated route. The less objectionable probability is that he either continued thence down the Ohio river to the Mississippi, the great "Father of Waters," or started overland toward the line of northern lakes, which might discharge an outlet to the westward. Or, again, he may have so far retraced his steps as to enable him to ascend one of those larger tributaries of the Ohio, the Scioto or Miami, toward the western extremity of Lake Erie, whence, proceeding northward, he may have traversed the strait to Lake Huron, and along the eastern boundary of the peninsula of Michigan to the strait of Michillimackinac; thence, passing to the westward around Green Bay and down the west side of Lake Michigan to its southern border. Leaving this point, his route seemed to lie in the direction of the Illinois, crossing which, he is said to have traced its course to the Mississippi, and, perchance, descended its muddy channel. This route is in part conjectural, but not wholly so, since the nearest approach to an account of his travels yet produced, incidentally refers to that portion of his travels after leaving Lake Erie, at a period subsequent to his passage down the Ohio.

Taking into consideration all the facts pertinent to the issue, thus far developed, the more probable route, after leaving the Falls of the Ohio, at Louisville, was down that river to the mouth of the Wabash, since, on a manuscript map, drawn in 1673, and still extant, exhibiting the area of discovery at that date, the Mississippi river is not shown, but the Ohio is traced a short distance below the Falls, and a part of eastern and northern Illinois delineated thereon. From this, the inference is naturally and reasonably drawn that, with the information manifestly in the possession of the compiler of that map, who must have been, at the same time, cognizant of the movements of M. de La Salle, if not a companion, it is highly probable that if the Mississippi had been then discovered, or La Salle had descended the Ohio below the mouth of the Wabash, these additional areas of discovery would have been represented also. "And this," says Mr. Parkman (who is the possessor of this map), in his account of M. de La Salle's proceedings at that time, "is very significant, as indicating the extent of La Salle's exploration of the following year, 1670."

Accepting this probability as true — and there seems to be little reason to doubt it — that he ascended the Wabash, where did he leave that stream? The obvious answer is, that if he subsequently embarked on the western extremity of Lake Erie, and ascended the strait to Lake St. Clair and beyond, as we have seen, he must have traversed it to "the carrying-place" on "La Riviere du Portage," or Little river, and thence, by the portage, to the river "de la Roche" (Maumee), at Kekionga, and down that river until it debouches into Lake Erie. This is the more probable, too, in view of the further fact that, being a trader as well as a discoverer, the greater inducement was in favor of the central or chief village of the Miamis, not only the principal arena of trade, but the great converging point of all the sources of information, as stated by Little Turtle in his address to Gen. Wayne at the treaty of Greenville; and his statement was not mere speculation, but founded on the traditions of his fathers from time immemorial. Hence, the route was practical, since it offered the means of acquiring more complete and accurate information than was obtainable from any other source, concerning what he most desired to know.

That this theory is correct, is strongly supported by his own claim, as we shall see hereafter, that he discovered the route by way of the Maumee to the Wabash, and by the account he gave of his later movements in 1676, when he built a fort at Crevecœur, "for the protection of the trade in those countries," as he had already done for several years, in the rivers Oyo, Ouabache and others in the surrounding neighborhood, which flow into the Mississippi, * * * adding, "the countries and rivers of the Oyo and Ouabache were inhabited by our Indians, the Chouanons, Miamis, and Illinois." If he had traversed the Wabash, and traded along it several years prior to 1676, at what time is it probable these voyages were made and the trading done? At what other time than in the fall of 1669, and during the years 1670 and 1671? If not within that period, when? for we have no account of his having done so between the years 1672 and 1676, the date at which the above account commences. Furthermore, if he was trading at that time on the Wabash, then his articles of traffic passed up La Riviere du Portage, were transported over "the carrying-place" to the St. Mary's, reshipped and taken down the Maumee to Lake Erie. What more probable route? What more natural point for the location of a fort, palisaded according to the necessities for protection and defense, than that at the head of the portage, on the St. Mary's? Without 'direct proof to the contrary, the propositions will be accepted as true, that he traded along the upper Wabash in 1669-71, visited Kekionga and perhaps established there one of his fortified trading posts, and used it as a base for his operations in that region.

The mission at Sault Ste. Marie was permanently established in 1668, and, the year following, Father Marquette having succeeded Allouez at

La Pointe, the latter then established himself at Green Bay, whence that earnest Father began to enlarge his field of labor, visiting the countries to the southward and westward of Lake Michigan. Although we have no direct account of the exact period when the mission was established among the Miamis, yet in view of the direction pursued by Allouez about this time, it is fair to presume that Kekionga was visited by one or more of these priests as early as 1669 or 1670, for, in May, 1671, a grand council of all the adjacent tribes, including the Miamis, previously visited or communicated with, was held at Sault Ste. Marie, in whose presence and with whose consent the governor general of New France took " possession, in the name of His Majesty, of all the lands lying between the east and west, and from Montreal to the south, so far as it could be done."

Meanwhile, Allouez had been pursuing his labors among the Miamis, and extending the beneficent influence of his holy faith; but it appears to have been reserved to Marquette to establish a mission among them, and erect there the standard of the cross, in the year 1673. On the 18th of May, 1675, Marquette died near the river that has since taken his name, near the margin of the lake, in western Michigan. Allouez died also, soon after, in the midst of his labors among the Miamis.

As early as 1672, so considerable a trade had grown up about the head-waters of the Maumee that the attention of the provincial government was drawn to the necessity of establishing and maintaining a military post for its protection. That such a post was established seems proven by the fact that in the account of transactions during 1696–7, it appears that Frontenac ordered the Sieur de Vincennes to the command of this post, and in a like report for 1704, it appears that he was again sent to command the same post by reason of his formerly having been stationed there, as appears from the statement as follows:

" Dispatched Father Valliant and Sieur de Joncaire to Seneca, and I sent Sieur de Vinsiene to the Miamis with my annexed order and message to be communicated to them.

" Sieur de Vinsiene, my lord, has been formerly commandant at the Miamis (1697), by whom he was much beloved; this led me to select him in preference to any other to prove to that nation how wrong they were to attack the Iroquois — our allies and theirs — without any cause; and we — M. de Beaucharnois and I — after consultation, permitted said Sieur de Vinsiene to carry some goods and to take with him six men and two canoes."

Again, in a communication from Vandrueil to Pontchartrain, dated October 19, 1705, the following further statement occurs: " I did myself the honor to inform you last year that I regarded the continuance of the peace with the Iroquois as the principal affair of this country, and as I have always labored on that principle, it is that also which obliged me to send Sieur de Joncaire to the Senecas and Sieur de Vinsiene to the Miamis."

In 1680, the route to the Mississippi by way of the Maumee and the

Yours truly
R. S. Robertson

Wabash is clearly alluded to by Pere Allouez, who says: "There is at the end of Lake Erie, ten leagues below the strait, a river by which we can traverse much of the road to the Illinois, being navigable to canoes about two leagues nearer than that by which they usually go there," i. e., by way of the St. Joseph of the Lake, and the Kankakee.

That the great, lion-hearted, but unfortunate La Salle, the grandest character among the early American explorers, knew of, and had himself discovered this route, can hardly be doubted in the light of some fragments of his writings, though the records which he always carefully kept of his explorations of this particular region were probably lost when his transports were wrecked, and their contents engulfed in the St. Lawrence, as he was returning to Quebec. In 1681, as he was about to start on his second expedition to the Mississippi, he drew up a will, in which he made the following devise: "I do give, cede and transfer, to the said Sieur Pleet, in case of my death, * * * all my rights over the country of the Miamis, Illinois, and others to the southward, with the settlements among the Miamis." In a report made by him to Frontenac in 1682, he mentions the route by the Maumee and Wabash to the Mississippi as the most direct. Notwithstanding this fact, the early explorers and traders long continued to go around by the route through the lakes to the site of Chicago, and thence to the Father of Waters, sometimes by the way of Green Bay, and the Illinois and Fox rivers, or by the head of Lake Michigan up the St. Joseph of the Lake, to the site of the present city of South Bend, thence by portage to the Kankakee, and down that river. Why they should so long travel by these tedious and difficult routes, when a shorter and easier one was well known, was long a mystery to the historian, until a hitherto unpublished letter of La Salle threw a flood of light upon the subject, and cleared away the mystery.

It is well known that about the time of the advent of the white man, the great Iroquois confederacy was waging a war of extermination against the Algonquin tribes, of which the Miamis and the Illinois were a part, and that their savage forays left a bloody trail through all this section of the country to the banks of the Mississippi. It was by reason of these murderous sallies, and the fact that the lower and shorter route was infested by roving bands of these savage warriors, enemies of the French, as well as of the Algonquins, that the longer route was followed. La Salle himself says, in a letter dated October, 1682, "Because I can no longer go to the Illinois but by the Lakes Huron and Illinois (Michigan), the other ways *which I have discovered by the head of Lake Erie*, and by the western coast of the same, becoming too dangerous by frequent encounters with the Iroquois." This letter is important, because it not only proves that he had traversed this route prior to that date, but also that he actually discovered it, and that his feet have trod the ground upon which a populous city now stands, when there was nothing to meet his view but a small cluster of Indian wigwams, and the unbroken forest surrounding it. We may consider this disputed question as proven, for La Salle was noted for stating none but exact facts, and when he says "I have discovered the route," it may be accepted as the truth.

When did he discover it? is the question which yet remains unsolved.

Hennepin says: "From this lake [Erie] to the Mississippi they have three different routes. The shortest by water is up the river Miamis or Ouamis, on the southwest of Lake Erie, on which river they sail about one hundred and fifty leagues without interruption, when they find themselves stopped by another landing of about three leagues, which they call a carrying-place, because they are generally obliged to carry their canoes overland in those places to the next river, and that where they next embark is a very shallow one, called La Riviere du Portage; hence they row about forty leagues to the river Ouabach, and from thence about one hundred and twenty leagues to the river Ohio, into which the Ouabach falls, as the river Ohio does about eighty leagues lower into the Mississippi, which continues its course for about three hundred and fifty leagues directly to the Bay of Mexico."

It is not only of interest, but importance, to trace briefly the movements of the great La Salle, for they were of weightier bearing upon the future of this region than those of any other explorer. During the period of the explorations of La Salle, he seemed to have been surrounded not only by the ordinary dangers which beset him on his journeys among savage tribes, but by greater dangers arising from the machinations of envious persons or rivals for fame among his own nationality. The tongue of malice and the hand of treachery always followed him wherever he went, and finally brought him to an untimely death, at the hands of a traitorous assassin. Much of this he attributed to the machinations of a rival order of the church, and there is doubtless much to prove that his worst enemies were the priests who belonged to an order different from that of which he was a devout and conscientious member, and these envious rivals had much to do in making his great work of discovery more dangerous, and in hindering his efforts to Christianize and civilize the Indian tribes of this region. In December, 1679, he left the fort of the Miamis of St. Joseph and went up that river to the Miami town where South Bend now stands. Five miles from there was one of the heads of the Kankakee by which he was to proceed to the Illinois. When he arrived at their village near Peoria, and was endeavoring to win their favor, he was met by intrigue. A Mascoutin chief named Monso, attended by several Miamis, reached the village and denounced him as a spy of the Iroquois. This La Salle attributed to Father Allouez, and in a letter to Frontenac, written in 1680, he states his conviction that Allouez, who was then stationed with the Miamis, had induced them to send Monso and his companions on their sinister errand. There had long been a jealousy between the Miamis and the Illinois, although they were kindred and neighbors, and the Iroquois, with deep cunning, strove to foment the Miamis to make war upon the Illinois, at a time when it is believed that they intended to make the Miamis their next victims, and Membre states that the enemies of La Salle intrigued successfully among the Miamis for the same end.

In 1681, La Salle, in order to defeat the purposes of conquest of the Iroquois, tried to gather about him at Fort Miamis, the Shawnees, the Illinois and the Miamis, and to reconcile the latter, and teach the Miamis the folly of their league with the Iroquois. In this effort he had little success, until a band of Iroquois, returning from the massacre of the Tamaroes, a sept of the Illinois, on the Mississippi, met and slaughtered a band of Miamis near the Ohio, and not only refused satisfaction, but remained and established themselves in three forts in the heart of the Miami country. La Salle went among the Illinois and succeeded in gaining their good will and returned to Fort Miami, and thence to the village at the portage between the Kankakee and the Saint Joseph. Here he found some emissaries from the Iroquois, whom he boldly rebuked and threatened in such manner that they secretly left. This convinced the Miamis of the deceit that had been practiced upon them by the Iroquois, and gave La Salle great standing and influence among them. He met here several bands of Indians lately come from the east, from Rhode Island, New York and Virginia, whence they had migrated on account of the encroachments of the whites. These he called to a council, and promised them protection and new homes in the west. They, in return, promised their aid in reconciling the Miamis with the Illinois. The next day the Miamis met in grand council, and were won over by the grace and eloquence of La Salle, and a bond of amity and defense was entered into.

In 1682, the Iroquois were preparing to renew their warfare upon the western tribes, particularly upon their late allies, the Miamis. La Salle determined to assist the latter, and gathered them and their allies into one great camp at Fort St. Louis on the Illinois river. There were the Illinois, numbering 1,200, the Miamis, from the St. Joseph and Kankakee, numbering 1,300, the Shawnees, Weas, Piankeshaws, and others, to the number in all, of 3,800 warriors. The Iroquois hesitated, and that summer passed in peace, but in March, 1683, they besieged the place for six days, when, finding their enemies well prepared, and under the command and direction of so able a leader as La Salle, they at length withdrew. In 1712, the Miamis were found again on the Maumee and the Wabash, and the Illinois were located on the river of that name. Both were much reduced by their long warfare with the Iroquois, and had dwindled so much that Father Marest, who then visited them, found but three villages, though Father Rasles, who visited them in 1723, found eleven. This difference in the number of villages found, may have arisen by reasons of the visits being made at different seasons, as they scattered in summer for hunting and fishing, and gathered in villages in winter for feasting and merrymaking.

During the period between La Salle's attempt to gather them into a confederacy, and this period, little mention is found in history of the use of the route from the mouth of the Maumee to the Wabash, doubtless because of its being shunned on account of the murderous forays of the Iroquois, but the author of Western Annals' states that in 1716 a route was established to the Mississippi, up the Maumee to the site of Fort Wayne, thence by a portage to the Wabash, and thence by way of the Wabash and Ohio, to the Mississippi.

Colden's History of the Five Nations, published in 1745, contains a map showing the portage from the St. Mary's to the "Ouabache," one from the St. Joseph of the Maumee to Huakiki" (Kankakee), and one from the Kankakee to the St. Joseph of Lake Michigan. Parkman says: "at the middle of the 18th century * * two posts on the Wabash, and one on the Maumee made France the mistress of the great trading highway from Lake Erie to the Ohio." History and tradition inform us that a French fort was destroyed here in 1747. If this be true, it must soon have been re-established, for in 1749, Captain Bienville de Celeron, a chevalier of the order of St. Louis, was sent by the Marquis de Gallissoniere, then governor of Canada, with orders to descend the Ohio and take possession of the country in the name of the French king. He descended the Ohio to the mouth of the great Miami, burying inscribed leaden plates at various points on his route, thence up the Miami to about Fort Loramie, thence across the portage and down the St. Mary's to the head of the Maumee. His party completed the portage on the 25th of September, and arrived at Kiskakon, then the Indian name for the site of Fort Wayne. It was then a French post, under the command of M. de Raymond. It was called Kiskakon from a branch of the Ottawas that removed here from Michillimackinac, where they had resided as late as 1682. Here de Celeron provided pirogues and provisions for the descent of the Maumee to Lake Erie. The Miami chief, "Pied Froid," or Cold Foot, resided in the village. He appears not to have been very constant in his allegiance either to the French or the English. Leaving Kiskakon on the 27th of September, part of the expedition proceeded overland to Detroit, and the remainder descended the river by canoe.

A map of the route traversed by de Celeron, prepared by Father Bonnecamp, who accompanied the expedition, shows with considerable exactness the course of the St. Mary's and Maumee, and the fort is located in the bend of the St. Mary's, south and east of the river. According to this map this fort stood not far from the late residence of Hon. Hugh McCulloch, which agrees with existing traditions. Vandreuil mentions the Fort Miamis on the Maumee in 1751. This must have been our Fort Miami, for, although there were four forts of that name in the west, the other Fort Miami of the Maumee was not erected until early in 1794, and then by the British.

It is interesting to note that Gen. George Washington, who was sent to Fort Duquesne on a mission to the French commandant by Gov. Dinwiddie, accompanied his report of his expedition with a map of the western country which indicates that if he could not himself tell an untruth, he could prepare maps which did. On his map a mountain range is located as trending from the northeast to the southwest within the peninsula of Michigan. On the east side of the mountain range, the "Miamis river," a very short stream, has its source, and flows directly east to Lake Erie, while the "Obaysh," or "River St. Jerome," rises on the same side of the range apparently near where the city of Jackson now stands, and flows only a little west of south to the Ohio.

In 1758 this route was described by Du Pratz in his " Histoire de Louisiane." He says: " From the Missouri to the Oubache [the Ohio], is a hundred leagues. It is by this river one goes to Canada, from New Orleans to Quebec. The voyage is made by going up the river to the Oubache [Ohio], then they go up this river to the river of the Miamis [the Wabash], continue this route to the portage and when they reach this place, seek natives of this nation, who make the portage in the space of two leagues. This road completed, they find a small river which flows into Lake Erie."

The French were then in possession of all west of the Alleghanies, but their domination was destined soon to come to an end. Historians have laid little stress upon one fact which perhaps more than any other gave direction to and changed the destiny of the new world. But for the savage war so long and relentlessly waged by the Iroquois against the western Indians, which rendered this route dangerous to traverse, and still more so for permanent occupation, there can be little doubt that the French would, long before this period, have established a strong, well manned and well equipped cordon of forts extending from the Saint Lawrence through the lakes, up the Maumee and down the Wabash to the Mississippi, and thence to the gulf, assuring the perpetuity of their power and firmly establishing a Gallic empire in America. As it was, the weak garrisons of the scattered palisaded forts of the west fell quickly before the arms of Great Britain, and most of them were surrendered and formally transferred to that power in the fall of 1760.

We have thus traced the history of the early explorations which opened this region, and established conclusively that the white man visited it long before the era of its settlement, and if anything were wanting to place far back in time the period of this partial occupation, it is a significant fact that the Indian names of the two rivers whose confluence form the Maumee, have been lost, or at least, are disputed, they having "from time immemorial" been known only by the names of St. Joseph and St. Mary's, names doubtless conferred upon them by that devoted pioneer priest, who so early assumed the spiritual charge of the Miamis, and who was probably the first to erect, at the junction of the rivers he so christened, the symbol of Christianity, the cross of the Christ whose devoted servant he was. He, and his companion soldiers of the cross, deserve long to be remembered as the forerunners of a civilization they dreamed not of.

THE BRITISH OCCUPATION.

It was on the 29th of November, 1760, that Detroit fell into the hands of the British, and soon after, an officer was sent southward to take possession of Fort Miami at the head of the Maumee, and of Fort Ouiatenon on the Wabash, both of which were intended to, and did, guard the communication between Lake Erie and the Ohio. This officer was Ensign Holmes, in command of a detachment of the Sixtieth Rifles, or "Royal Americans." A force not greater than 800 men from this historic regiment, garrisoned all the posts of the west, and stood for years between the savage hordes and the advancing settlements, which were the vanguard of our present civilization.

A history of this gallant regiment would form a large portion of the history of the French and Indian wars, from the Hudson and Lake Champlain to the Mississippi, and the subsequent wars down to the revolutionary period, but unfortunately that history is lacking, except as it can be gleaned from scattered documents and scanty traditions. "The Royal Americans" was organized in 1755 under the direction of the Duke of Cumberland, expressly for service in America. It was intended to consist of four battalions of 1,000 men each, to be raised from the German and Swiss emigrants, and £81,178 was voted by parliament to raise and equip it. German and Swiss officers were to be provided, and an act of parliament authorized them to be commissioned. Henry Bouquet was a Swiss of the canton of Berne, and was a soldier from boyhood, serving under the king of Sardinia, and subsequently under the king of Holland. He accepted a lieutenant-colonel's commission in the regiment in 1755, and was colonel of the first battalion at this period. He was made a brigadier general in 1765, and has left a heroic record, written on many bloody fields of Indian warfare.

Some of the battalions were filled from the Scotch emigrants who had left the highlands of Scotland on account of their participation in the rebellion of 1745, and these brave, hardy and experienced troops won distinction in the north and west, at Lake George, Bushy Run, and on other fields of danger and valor; stretching the thin lines of their little battalions almost half across the continent, and making possible the extension of the new Anglo-Saxon empire in the wilds of the interior of the continent. They were the guide posts, and the living wall which lined the great highway from the east to the west, upon which marched, with slow but steady tread, the advance guard of the mighty hosts of civilization which were beginning to press forward with eager footsteps and a grand impulse toward the setting sun. The regiment was honored with the post of danger in all the Indian wars along its very extended front. One of its battalions was pitted against Montcalm, and defended Fort George on the lake of that name. The story of its massacre and narrow escape from annihilation has been made immortal in the pages of history and romance. Another battalion guarded the

Pennsylvania frontier, and the rest were scattered among all the forts of the western country, exposed to all the horrors and dangers of savage warfare. They were the first soldiery of an English speaking race whose martial tread was heard upon the banks of the upper Maumee, and whose guns held the Indians in subjection here until overpowered by the last great uprising of an embittered, despairing race, in its futile and expiring attempt to stay the tide which was about to overwhelm it.

At the close of the French struggle, so great had been the havoc among the various tribes of the northwest, that, from the estimates of Sir William Johnson, it is presumed there were not more than 10,000 fighting men to be found in the whole territory lying " between the Mississippi on the west, and the ocean on the east; between the Ohio on the south, and Lake Superior on the north"; which, according to a further estimate by Sir William, in 1763, placed the Iroquois at 1,950; the Delawares at about 600; the Shawnees at about 300; the Wyandots at about 450; the Miamis, with their neighbors, the Kickapoos, at about 800; while the Ottawas, Ojibwas, and a few wandering tribes, northward, were left without any enumeration at all. At that period, so thin and scattered was the population, that, even in those parts which were thought well populated, one might sometimes journey for days together through the twilight forest, and meet no human form. Broad tracts were left in solitude. All Kentucky was a vacant waste, a mere skirmishing ground for hostile war parties of the north and south. A great part of upper Canada, of Michigan, and of Illinois, besides other portions of the west, were tenanted by wild beasts alone. At this period, says Parkman, "the Shawanoes had fixed their abode upon the Scioto and its branches. Farther toward the west, on the waters of the Wabash and the Maumee, dwelt the Miamis, who, less exposed, from their position, to the poison of the whiskey keg, and the example of debauched traders, retained their ancient character and custom in greater purity than their eastern neighbors." " From Vincennes," says the same writer, " one might paddle his canoe northward up the Wabash, until he reached the little wooden fort of Ouiatenon. Thence a path through the woods led to the banks of the Maumee. Two or three Canadians, or half-breeds, of whom there were numbers about the fort, would carry the canoe on their shoulders, or, for a bottle of whisky, a few Miami Indians might be bribed to undertake the task. On the Maumee, at the end of the path, stood Fort Miami, near the spot where Fort Wayne was afterward built. From this point one might descend the Maumee to Lake Erie, and visit the neighboring Fort of Sandusky; or, if he chose, steer through the strait of Detroit, and explore the watery wastes of the northern lakes, finding occasional harborage at the little military posts which commanded their important points. Most of these western posts were transferred to the English during the autumn of 1760; but the settlements of the Illinois (Kaskaskia, Cahokia, etc.) remained several years longer under French control."

The Indians of the northwest had lost their French father, and with him, for a time, their trinkets, and much besides in the form of powder, balls, etc., that they had long annually been accustomed to receive from that quarter. They could hardly realize, notwithstanding the many whisperings to that effect, that their French father was forever divested of his power in America, and that his rule this side of the great waters had ceased. They believed the oft repeated stories that their French father "had of late years fallen asleep," and that his numerous vessels and soldiers would soon be moving up the Mississippi and St. Lawrence, to drive the English from their dominions, leaving them again in quiet possession of their former hunting grounds. Every means was now resorted to by the French, scattered about the wilderness, to arouse the savages, and their efforts were not in vain. The rancor of the Indians was greatly increased from time to time, until at length, after a lapse of two years, a great scheme was developed for the overthrow and destruction of the English and the various posts so recently occupied by them. As had been frequent at other periods among the aborigines in the wilds of the new world, a great prophet suddenly began to exert a powerful influence among the tribes of the northwest. He held his mission under the Great Spirit, and earnestly enjoined upon the tribes to return again to their primitive habits — to throw away the weapons, apparel, etc., obtained from the pale-faces. Here, said he, is the starting point of success. The force of the new prophet's teachings was truly great, and the tribes came from long distances to hear him. For the most part his suggestions were much regarded by the tribes; but the weapons of the white man could not be dispensed with. These they retained. The prophet was a Delaware, and the great leader of the movement was an Ottawa chieftain, whose Indian name was Pontiac.

For over two years, Forts Miami and Ouiatenon remained in comparative security. The 10th of February, 1763, at length arriving, a treaty of peace was concluded at Paris, between France and England — the former surrendering to the latter all claims to the vast region lying east of the Mississippi, making the Father of Waters the boundary line of the British possessions in America. A few months later, on the 7th of October, the English government, " proportioning out her new acquisitions into separate governments," set apart " the valley of the Ohio and adjacent regions as an Indian domain," and, by proclamation, strictly forbade " the intrusion of settlers " thereon. But the seeds of future trouble had long since been sown, and the little forts in the wilderness, here (Fort Miami) and at Ouiatenon, were destined ere long to hear the murmurs of war. The great plot of Pontiac, and the efforts of the Delaware prophet for the destruction of the English and the capture of the posts so recently lost by the French, were rapidly though silently maturing. Intimations and surmises were all that could be gained, so still and cautious were the movements of the savages; and the first really positive assurance of the efforts and designs of the Ottawa chieftain and his followers, was disclosed at Fort Miami, opposite the present site of Fort Wayne.

With the utmost vigilance, and the greatest possible activity, Pontiac was pushing forward his scheme of destruction. War belts were dispatched to various tribes at a distance, inviting them to join in the overthrow of the invaders and capture of the forts; and soon the entire Algonquin race with the Senecas, the Wyandots, and many tribes from the valley of the lower Mississippi, were induced to join in the great scheme. The ensign of the Sixtieth Rifles was still in command, with a small body of men, at Fort Miami; and it was through Holmes that the first positive information of the plot of the Indians was received.

One day, early in the month of March, 1763, Holmes was startled by a friendly admonition. A neighboring Indian, through some acts of kindness, perhaps, on the part of Holmes, had formed a strong friendship for the ensign. The Indian told him that the warriors of one of the villages near by had recently received a *bloody belt*, with a "speech," pressing them to kill him (Holmes) and demolish the fort here, and which, whispered the friendly Indian, the warriors were then making preparation to do. The peril was imminent, and Holmes began at once to look about him. Summoning the neighboring Indians to a council, he boldly charged them with the design, which they finally acknowledged, with seeming contriteness and regret, charging the whole affair upon a tribe at another locality in the region. Holmes obtained the belt, and, from a speech of one of the chiefs of the Miamis, was at least partially induced to entertain the belief that all would now be tranquil.

A few days later, and the following letter, from Ensign Holmes, at this point, was on its way to Major Gladwyn, commanding at Detroit:

"FORT MIAMIS, MARCH 30TH, 1763.

"Since my Last Letter to You, wherein I Acquainted You of the Bloody Belt being in this village, I have made all the search I could about it, and have found it out to be True; Whereon I Assembled all the Chiefs of this Nation (the Miamis), and after a long and troublesome Spell with them, I Obtained the Belt, with a Speech, as you will Receive Enclosed; This Affair is very timely Stopt, and I hope the News of a Peace will put a Stop to any further Troubles with these Indians, who are the Principle Ones of Setting Mischief on Foot. I send You the Belt with this Packet, which I hope You will Forward to the General."

Signs of coming trouble with the Indians at length became more apparent. They had now begun to hang about the forts, with impenetrable faces, asking for tobacco, gunpowder and whisky. Now and then some slight intimation of danger would startle the garrison, and an English trader, coming in from the Indian villages, would report that, from their manners and behavior, he suspected them of mischievous designs. Occasionally, some half-breed would be heard boasting in his cups, that before the next summer he would have English hair to fringe his hunting-frock.

By the 27th of April, 1763, Pontiac having nearly matured his plans, great numbers of the villages and camps of the western tribes, including all grades and ages, women and children, assembled to celebrate the savage rites of war; magicians consulted their oracles, and prepared charms to insure success; many warriors, as was the Indian custom before great events in war, withdrew to the deep recesses of the forest, or hid in caves to fast and pray, that the Great Spirit might give them victory. A grand council was convened at the river Ecorces, where Pontiac delivered to the vast throng a speech both eloquent and artful.

On the morning of the great council, several old men, heralds of the camp, had passed to and fro among the lodges, calling the warriors to attend the meeting. They came from their cabins — the tall, naked figures of the wild Ojibwas, with quivers slung at their backs, and light war-clubs resting in the hollow of their arms; Ottawas, wrapped close in their gaudy blankets; Wyandots, fluttering in painted shirts, their heads adorned with feathers, and their leggins garnished with bells. All were soon seated in a wide circle upon the grass, row within row — a grave and silent assembly. Each savage countenance seemed carved in wood, and none could have detected the passions hidden beneath that unmovable exterior. Pipes, with ornamented stems, were lighted and passed from hand to hand.

Placing himself in the center of the silent multitude, with long, black hair flowing about his shoulders, stern, resolute, with an imperious, peremptory bearing, like that of a man accustomed to sweep away all opposition by force of his impetuous will, Pontiac began at once to arouse his auditors by a recital of the injustice of the English, and by drawing a contrast between the conduct of the French and the British toward the tribes assembled; presenting to them the terrible consequences of English supremacy — persisting that it was the aim of the British to destroy and drive them from the land of their fathers. They have driven away the French, he recounted, and now they seek an opportunity to remove us also. He told them that their French father had long been asleep, but that now he was awake again, and would soon return in his many canoes to regain his old possessions in Canada.

Every sentence was rounded with a fierce ejaculation; and as the impetuous orator proceeded, his audience grew restless to spring at once into the bloody arena of battle and bury the scalping knife and tomahawk in the bodies of the enemy. Turning to the opposite side of savage nature, appealing to their sense of the mysterious, in a somewhat mellowed tone, though still as earnest in demeanor, he said:

" A Delaware Indian conceived an eager desire to learn wisdom from the Master of Life; but being ignorant where to find him, he had recourse to fasting, dreaming, and magical incantations. By these means it was revealed to him, that, by moving forward in a straight, undeviating course, he would reach the abode of the Great Spirit. He told his purpose to no one, and having provided the equipments of a hunter — gun, powder-horn, ammunition, and a kettle for preparing his food — he setforth on his errand. For some time he journeyed on in high hope and confidence. On the evening of the eighth day, he stopped by the side of a brook, at the edge of a small prairie, where he began to make ready his evening meal, when looking up, he saw three large openings in the woods, on the opposite side of the meadow, and three well-beaten paths which enter them. He was much surprised, but his wonder increased, when, after it had grown dark, the three paths were more clearly visible than ever. Remembering the important object of his journey, he could neither rest nor sleep; and leaving his fire, he crossed the meadow, and entered the largest of the three openings. He had advanced but a short distance into the forest, when a bright flame sprang out of the ground before him, and arrested his steps. In great amazement, he turned back, and entered the second path, where the same wonderful phenomenon again encountered him; and now, in terror and bewilderment, yet still resolved to persevere, he pursued the last of the three paths. On this he journeyed a whole day without interruption, when, at length, emerging from the forest, he saw before him a vast mountain of dazzling whiteness. So precipitous was the ascent, that the Indian thought it hopeless to go farther, and looked around him in despair; at that moment, he saw, seated at some distance above, the figure of a beautiful woman arrayed in white, who arose as he looked upon her, and thus accosted him: 'How can you hope, encumbered as you are, to succeed in your design? Go down to to the foot of the mountain, throw away your gun, your ammunition, your provisions and your clothing; wash yourself in the stream which flows there, and then you will be prepared to stand before the Master of Life!' The Indian obeyed, and then began to ascend among the rocks, while the woman, seeing him still discouraged, laughed at his faintness of heart, and told him that, if he wished for success, he must climb by the aid of one hand and one foot only. After great toil and suffering, he at length found himself at the summit. The woman had disappeared and he was left alone. A rich and beautiful plain lay before him, and at a little distance he saw three great villages, far superior to the squalid dwellings of the Delawares. As he approached the largest, and stood hesitating whether he should enter, a man gorgeously attired stepped forth, and taking him by the hand, welcomed him to the celestial abode. He then conducted him into the presence of the Great Spirit, where the Indian stood confounded at the unspeakable splendor which surrounded him. The Great Spirit bade him be seated, and thus addressed him: 'I am the maker of heaven and earth, the trees, lakes, rivers, and all things else. I am the maker of mankind; and because I love you, you must do my will. The land on which you live I made for you and not for others. Why do you suffer the white man to dwell among you? My children, you have forgotten the customs and traditions of your fathers. Why do you not clothe yourselves in skins as they did, and use the bows and arrows and stone-pointed lances, which they used? You have bought guns, knives, kettles and blankets of the white man, until you can no longer do without them; and what is worse, you have drunk the poison fire-water, which turns you into fools. Fling all these away;

live as your wise fore-fathers lived before you. And, as for these English — these dogs dressed in red, who have come to rob you of your hunting-grounds, and drive away the game — you must lift the hatchet against them, wipe them from the face of the earth, and then you will win my favor back again, and once more be happy and prosperous. The children of your great father, the King of France, are not like the English. Never forget that they are your brethren. They are very dear to me, for they love the red men, and understand the true mode of worshiping me!' With some further admonition from the Great Spirit, of a moral and religious nature, the Indian took leave of the Master of Life, and returned again to terra firma, where, among his people, he told all he had seen and heard in the wonderful land of the Great Spirit."

After this address all was ripe for action. Pontiac's words had spread a fire among the great throng of listeners that nothing short of a desperate defeat would smother. The first blow was destined to fall upon Detroit.

The story of the attempt, and of its frustration by the prompt action of Maj. Gladwyn, who had been warned of the plot by his Ojibwa mistress, has been too often told to need repetition here. Nine posts, held by the English, had been included in the great conspiracy and sought to be captured, viz.: Detroit, Presque-Isle, Michillimackinac, Miami, Ouiatenon, Le Bœuf, Venango, Fort Pitt, and Fort Sandusky. The plan of capture seems to have embodied the cunning and resolution of Pontiac at every point; and preparations similar to those at first manifested at Detroit, were apparent at every post essayed to be taken; which one after another, excepting Detroit alone, fell into the hands of the Indians. Many were the bloody scenes enacted.

On the 16th of May, Sandusky fell; on the 1st of June, Ouiatenon was captured, Michillimackinac on the 12th, and Presque-Isle, on the 15th of June. After Presque-Isle was taken, the little posts of Le Bœuf and Venango shared its fate; farther south, at the forks of the Ohio, a host of Delaware and Shawnee warriors were gathering around Fort Pitt, and havoc reigned along the whole frontier.

Father Jonois, a Jesuit missionary, had reached Detroit and conveyed to the garrison a letter from Capt. Etherington, at Michillimackinac, giving an account of the capture of that post. Soon after, a letter from Lieut. Jenkins, at Ouiatenon, telling of the capture of that post, was received by Maj. Gladwyn. Close upon these tidings, came the news that Fort Miami was taken.

Holmes had been carefully watching the Miamis, although his fears had been somewhat quieted by the conference concerning the bloody belt. But unknown to him, savage ingenuity and deception were at work, and the ensign was destined to fall a victim to the perfidy of the conspirators.

The 27th of May had come. All nature was radiant with the beauties of spring. The expanding foliage of the forest waved gracefully over and partly shut out from the blaze of the sunlight the sweet-scented wild flowers that grew profusely beneath the majestic oaks, maples and sycamores, that lined the margins of our beautiful rivers. An Indian girl,* with whom Holmes had for some time been intimate, and in whom he placed much confidence, was compelled by the conspirators to come to the fort and tell Holmes that there was a sick squaw lying in a wigwam not far from the fort, and express a desire that he should go and see her. Unsuspecting, and kindly desiring to relieve the supposed sick squaw, he was soon without the enclosure, and advancing with cautious steps in the direction of the hut indicated. Nearing a cluster of huts, which are said to have been situated at the edge of an open space, hidden from view by an intervening spur of the woodland, the girl directed him to the hut wherein lay the supposed invalid. Another instant he fell bleeding to the ground, and the sudden crack of two rifles echoed over the little garrison. Startled, the sergeant thoughtlessly passed without the fort to ascertain the cause of the shots, when, with triumphant shouts, he was seized by the savages. This, in turn, brought the soldiers within, about nine in all, to the palisades of the garrison, when a Canadian, of the name of Godfroy, accompanied by two other white men, stepped forth and demanded a surrender of the fort, with the assurance to the soldiers that if they at once complied their lives would be spared; but, refusing, they should all be killed without mercy. The garrison gate soon swung back upon its hinges, and English rule at this point for a time ceased to be.

Encouraged by the fall of this weak and almost ungarrisoned post, Pontiac renewed his efforts to unite the tribes and destroy the remaining western forts, particularly aiming at the capture of Detroit. But the campaign he had already made had led to a vigorous movement on the part of the English government for the chastisement of the Indians. The plan of this campaign contemplated two armies — one to be led by Colonel Bouquet, and the other by Colonel Bradstreet, the former to move towards Fort Pitt, and to the country of the hostile Shawnees and Delawares, along the Scioto and Muskingum rivers; while Bradstreet was to push forward to Detroit. The one led by Bradstreet reached Detroit on the 26th of August, and relieved that long suffering and almost disheartened garrison, and the Indians gave up the hope of its capture.

Pontiac and his followers, sullen and intractable, left Detroit, and he again took up his abode, for the time, on the Maumee, a few miles below the site of Fort Wayne, whence he is said to have sent a haughty defiance to the English commander at Detroit. Many of the Indians about Detroit went with Pontiac, leaving there but a few remnant tribes, who, for the most part, exhibiting a desire for peace, were soon given

---

* Mrs. Suttenfield, lately deceased, stated that she became acquainted with this woman in 1815, when she had a son, a man of some years, who, the squaw said, was Saginash (English); and from the age of the man, the inference is drawn that he was a son of Holmes. After leaving here, the woman took up her residence at Raccoon Village. She lived to a great age, and was known to many of the early settlers of Fort Wayne.

a council at that point, on the 7th of September. Upon the condition— which they are said to have not understood at all, and which, not understanding, they accepted — that they become subjects of the king of England, a treaty of peace was concluded with them. At this council were present portions of the Miamis, Pottawatomies, Ottawas, Ojibwas, Sacs, and Wyandots. Said Wasson, an Ojibwa chief, to the English commander, on this occasion: "My Brother, last year God forsook us. God has now opened our eyes, and we desire to be heard. It was God's will you had such fine weather to come to us. It is God's will also that there should be peace and tranquility over the face of the earth and of the waters"— openly acknowledging that the tribes he represented were justly chargeable with the war, and deeply regretted their participation.

Before quitting Sandusky, Bradstreet had sent Captain Morris, accompanied by a number of Canadians and friendly Indians, toward the country of the Illinois, to treat with the Indians of that portion of the west. Ascending the Maumee in a canoe, he approached the camp of Pontiac, and was met by about 200 Indians, who treated him with great violence, while they offered a friendly welcome to the Iroquois and Canadian attendants. Accompanied by this clamorous escort they moved toward the camp. At its outskirts stood Pontiac himself. He met the ambassador with a scowling brow, and refused to offer his hand. "The English are liars," was his first fierce salutation. He then displayed a letter, addressed to himself, purporting to have been written by the king of France, containing as Morris declared, "the grossest calumnies which the most ingenious malice could devise, to incense the Indians against the English." The old story had not been forgotten. "Your French father," said the writer, "is neither dead nor asleep; he is already on his way, with sixty great ships, to revenge himself on the English, and drive them out of America." It is evident that the letter had emanated from either a French officer, or more probably a French fur trader, who, for his own aggrandizement, sought to arouse the antipathy of the natives to the further encroachment of the English.

"The Indians led me," says Morris, "up to a person who stood advanced before two slaves (prisoners of the Panis nation, taken in war and kept in slavery), who had arms, himself holding a fusee with the butt on the ground. By his dress and the air he assumed, he appeared to be a French officer: I afterwards found he was a native of old France, had been long in the regular troops as a drummer, and that his war name was St. Vincent. This fine-dressed, half-French, half-Indian figure desired me to dismount; a bear-skin was spread on the ground, and St. Vincent and I sat upon it, the whole Indian army, circle within circle, standing around us. Godefroi sat at a little distance from us; and presently came Pontiac, and squatted himself, after his fashion, opposite to me. This Indian has a more extensive power than ever was known among that people; for every chief used to command his own tribe, but eighteen nations, by French intrigue, had been brought to unite, and choose this man for their commander, after the English had conquered Canada; having been taught to believe, that, aided by France, they might make a vigorous push and drive us out of North America. * * * * Pondiac said to my chief: 'If you have made peace with the English, we have no business to make war on them. The war-belt came from you.' He afterward said to Godefroi: 'I will lead the nations to war no more; let 'em be at peace if they chuse it; but I myself will never be a friend to the English. I shall now become a wanderer in the woods; and if they come to seek me there, while I have an arrow left I will shoot at them.' He made a speech to the chiefs," continues Morris, "who wanted to put me to death, which does him honor; and shows that he was acquainted with the law of nations; 'We must not,' said he, 'kill ambassadors; do we not send them to the Flat-Heads, our greatest enemies, and they to us? Yet these are always treated with hospitality.'"

After relieving the party of all but their canoe, clothing and arms, they were permitted to resume their course without further molestation. Quitting the inhospitable camp of Pontiac, with poles and paddles, against a strong current, they continued their course up the beautiful Maumee, and in seven days from leaving Sandusky, in the morning they arrived within sight of Fort Miami, which, from the time of its capture, the previous year, had been without a garrison, its only occupants being a few Canadians who had erected some huts within the enclosure, and a small number of Indians. The open ground in the vicinity of the fort, at that time, was occupied by the wigwams of the Kickapoos, a large body of whom had lately arrived. On the opposite side, hidden by an intervening strip of forest, stood the Miami villages.

Having brought the canoe to a place of landing, a short distance below the fort, the attendants strode off through the strip of woods toward the village; and it is stated as most fortunate that Morris remained behind, for, scarcely had his attendants traversed the woods, than they were met by a band of savages, armed with spears, hatchets, and bows and arrows, seeking to destroy the Englishman. Morris' chiefs endeavored to dissuade them from their purpose, and succeeded in so far as sparing his life. But coming up, in a few moments, to where Morris stood, they began to threaten him and treat him very roughly, and took him to the fort, where he was commanded to remain, and the Canadians forbidden to admit him to their huts. A deputation of Shawnee and Delaware chiefs had recently come to the Miami village, with fourteen war-belts, with a view of arousing the Miamis again to arms against the English; and it was to these that was mainly ascribed Morris' treatment. From this point they had proceeded westward, arousing to war all the tribes from the Mississippi to the Ohio, avowing that they would never make friends with the English — that they would fight them as long as the sun shone.

Morris had not long remained at the fort, when two Miami warriors came to him, and with raised tomahawks grasped him by the arms, forced him without the garrison, and led him to the river. Walking forward into the water with him, Morris' first thought was that the Indians sought to drown him, and then take his scalp; but instead they led him across the stream, then quite low, and moved toward the center of the Miami village, on the west side of the St. Joseph. Nearing the wigwams, the Indians stopped and sought to undress him; but finding the task rather difficult, they became quite angry and Morris himself, in rage and despair, tore off his uniform. Then tying his arms behind him with his sash, the Indians drove him forward into the village. Speedily issuing from the wigwams to receive the prisoner, the Indians gathered about him like a swarm of angry bees, giving vent to terrific yells — "sounds compared to which, the nocturnal howlings of starved wolves are gentle and melodious." The largest portion of the villagers were for killing him; but a division arising between them, as to what was best to do with him, then was developed a vociferous debate. Finally the Canadians, Godfroy and St. Vincent, who had followed him to the village, came forward and interceded with the chiefs in behalf of their prisoner. A nephew of Pontiac was among the chiefs, a young man, possessing much of the bold spirit of his uncle, who heroically spoke against the propriety of killing the prisoner; and Godfroy insisted "that he would not see one of the Englishmen put to death, when so many of the Indians were in the hands of the army at Detroit." A Miami chief, called the Swan, is also represented as having protected the prisoner, and cut the sash binding his arms. Morris, beginning now to speak in his own defense, was seized by a chief called the White Cat, and bound to a post by the neck; at which another chief, called the Pacanne, rode up on horseback, cut the band with his hatchet, giving Morris his freedom again, exclaiming "I give this Englishman his life. If you want English meat, go to Detroit or to the lake, and you will find enough of it. What business have you with this man, who has come to speak with us?" The determined words of Pacanne had the desired effect. A change of feeling began to show itself; and the prisoner, without further words, was driven out of the village, whither he made his way to the fort. On his way, it is stated, an Indian met him, and, with a stick, beat his exposed body.

His position was yet most critical; for while the Canadians in the fort were disposed to protect him, they were yet loath to lay themselves liable to distrust, and the same warriors who had taken him to the village were now lurking about, ready to embrace the first opportunity to kill him; while the Kickapoos, near by, had sent him word that if the Miamis did not kill him, they would whenever he passed their camp. On considering whether he should proceed on his journey to the Illinois, his Canadian and Indian attendants strongly urged him to go no farther; and on the evening of this day they held a council with the Miami chiefs, wherein it became more evident that his situation was most perilous. Messages were continually reaching him, threatening an end to his life, should he attempt to fulfill his mission, and a report was also conveyed to him that several of the Shawnee deputies were returning to the garrison expressly to kill him. Under these circumstances, he speedily pushed his bark toward Detroit, where he arrived on the 17th of September.

The expedition under Bouquet penetrated to the center of the Delaware towns, and into the most extensive settlements of the Shawnees, about 150 miles from Fort Pitt. With a large body of regular and provincial troops, he soon humbled these tribes, and compelled them to deliver all the prisoners in their possession. During the frontier struggles, for some years prior to Bouquet's campaign, hundreds of families along the borders had been massacred and many carried away to the forest by the Indians; and when Bouquet started on his expedition to the interior, he was eagerly joined by many who, years before, had lost their friends. Among the many prisoners brought into the camp (over 200 in all), husbands found their wives, and parents their children, from whom they had been separated for years. Women, frantic between hope and fear, were running hither and thither, looking piercingly into the face of every child. Some of the little captives shrank from their forgotten mothers, and hid in terror in the blankets of the squaws that had adopted them. Some that had been taken away young, had grown up and married Indian husbands or Indian wives, now stood utterly bewildered with conflicting emotions. A young Virginian had found his wife; but his little boy, not two years old when captured, had been torn from her, and had been carried off, no one knew where. One day, a warrior came in leading a child. At first, no one seemed to own it. But soon the mother knew her offspring, and screaming with joy, folded her son to her bosom. An old woman had lost her grand-daughter in the French war, nine years before. All her other relatives had died under the knife. Searching with trembling eagerness, in each face, she at last recognized the altered features of her child. But the girl had forgotten her native tongue, and returned no answer, and made no sign. The old woman groaned, and complained bitterly, that the daughter she had so often sung to sleep on her knee, had forgotten her in her old age. Soldiers and officers were alike overcome. "Sing," said Bouquet to the old lady, "sing the song you used to sing." As the low, trembling tones began to ascend, the wild girl seemed startled, then listening for a moment longer, she burst into a flood of tears. She was indeed the lost child, but all else had been effaced from her memory, save the recollection of that sweet cradle song. The tender sensibilities were foreign, as a general rule, to the Indian heart; indeed, they held such emotions in contempt; but when the song of the old lady was seen by them to touch the captive's heart and bring her again to a mother's arms, they were overcome with sympathy. Many captive women who returned to the settlements with their friends soon afterward made their escape, and wandered back to their Indian husbands, so great was the change that had taken place in their natures.

The British having subdued the tribes of the northwest, and completed definite treaties with them at Niagara, contemplated a further move to the west and north, with the purpose of securing the country and posts along the Illinois and Mississippi. Of this Pontiac soon became aware, and leaving his place of seclusion on the Maumee, with four hundred of his chiefs, about the close of autumn he passed up to Fort Miami and after a short stay to the Wabash, and on to the Mississippi, arousing the tribes at every point to prepare to meet and destroy the English. Having gained the French settlements and other places where the French traders and *habitans* were to be met, and where the flag of France was still displayed, he received encouragement from the French fur traders and *engagés*, who dreaded the rivalry of the English in the fur trade. They insisted that the king of France was again awake, and his great armies were coming; "that the bayonets of the white-coated warriors would soon glitter amid the forests of the Mississippi." But Pontiac seemed doomed to disappointment and failure; and after repeated efforts, having visited New Orleans to gain the aid of the French governor of Louisiana, he returned to the west.

Determining to try the virtue of peace proposals in advance of the army, Sir William Johnson sent forward two messengers, Lieut. Fraser and George Croghan, to treat with the Indians on the Mississippi and Illinois. After many hardships, and the loss of their stores, through the severity of the winter, they reached Fort Pitt, whence, after some delay, Fraser, with a few attendants, made his way down the Ohio for a thousand miles; then coming to a halt, he met with very rough treatment from the Indians. A short time afterward, in the month of May, 1765, Croghan, with some Shawnee and Delaware attendants, moved down the Ohio as far as the mouth of the Wabash, where the party was fired upon by the Kickapoos and several of the attendants killed. Croghan and the remainder were taken prisoners, but finally proceeded to Vincennes, where, finding many friendly Indians, they were well received, and the Kickapoos strongly censured. From that point they went to Ouiatenon, arriving there on the 23d, where also Croghan found many friendly Indians. Here he made preparations for a council, and was met by a large number of Indians, who smoked the pipe of peace with him. Soon receiving an invitation from St. Ange to visit Fort Chartres, further down, Croghan, accompanied by a large number of Indians, left Ouiatenon for that point, and had not journeyed far when he met Pontiac and a large body of chiefs and warriors. Pontiac shook the hand of Croghan, who at once returned with the party to Ouiatenon, where a great concourse of chiefs and warriors were gathered.

Pontiac complained that the French had deceived him, and offered the calumet and peace-belt, professing concurrence with the Ouiatenon chiefs in their expressions of friendship for the English. At the conclusion of this meeting, collecting the tribes here he had desired to meet, he soon took up his line of march, followed by Pontiac and a large number of chiefs, and set out toward Detroit, crossing over to Fort Miami and the village adjacent. Having kept a regular journal of his mission, from which the foregoing is principally drawn, he wrote at this point:

"August 1st (1765). The Twigtwee village is situated on both sides of a river called St. Joseph. This river where it falls into the Miami [Maumee] river, about a quarter of a mile from this place, is 100 yards wide, on the east side of which stands a stockade fort somewhat ruinous.* The Indian village consists of about forty or fifty cabins, besides nine or ten French houses, a runaway colony from Detroit during the late Indian war; they were concerned in it, and being afraid of punishment, came to this point, where ever since they have spirited up the Indians against the English. * * * * * The country is pleasant, the soil is rich and well watered. After several conferences with these Indians, and their delivering me up all the English prisoners they had, on the 6th of August we set out for Detroit, down the Miamis river in a canoe."

Arriving on the 17th of August, he found many of the Ottawas, Pottawatomies and Ojibwas, and in the same council hall in which Pontiac had poured out his impassioned oratory to seduce the Indians into his great conspiracy, Croghan convened the relenting tribes, and addressing them in their own style, succeeded in extracting terms of peace in September, and a promise from Pontiac that he would visit Oswego in the spring to conclude the final terms of a treaty with the commandant, Sir William Johnson. Croghan then returned to Niagara.

About the period of the first snow, the Forty-second regiment of Highlanders, a hundred strong, having moved down the Ohio from Fort Pitt, commanded by Capt. Sterling, arrived at Fort Chartres. The *fleur de lis* of France was soon lowered, and, in its stead, the English planted their standard. When spring came, Pontiac, true to his word, left his old home on the Maumee, for Oswego, where he soon arrived, to make a great speech, and "seal his submission to the English" forever.

With his canoe laden with presents he had received at the great council of Oswego, he proceeded toward the Maumee, where he is said to have spent the following winter, living in the forest with his wives and children, and hunting like an ordinary warrior. In the spring of 1767, considerable discontent was manifested among the tribes "from the lakes to the Potomac." The Indians had been disturbed in the possession of their lands, and began the commission of atrocities along the frontier. Pontiac had strangely kept out of the way. That he had been party to the agitation along the border, was not known, but many had their suspicions. For two years subsequently, few, if any, but his immediate friends, knew of his whereabouts. In the month of April, 1769, however, he again visited the Illinois, and though his object was unknown, the English were excited by his movements. He soon afterward went to the French settlement at St. Louis, where he was

---

* It is worthy of notice that an English guinea dated 1765, the year of Croghan's visit, was found on the site of this old fort, and is now in possession of the writer. It is probably a specimen of the first British gold used to purchase *Americans.*

murdered. The account of his death is, that he was killed by an Illinois Indian, of the Kaskaskia tribe; that having feasted with some of the Creoles of Cahokia, opposite the site of St. Louis, he became drunk, and while he was entering an adjacent forest, the murderer stole upon him and dispatched him with a tomahawk. It was said that the assassin had been instigated to the act by an Englishman of the name of Williamson, who had agreed to give him a barrel of whisky, with a promise of something besides, if he would kill the Ottawa chieftain. Says Gouin's account: "From Miami, Pontiac went to Fort Chartres, on the Illinois. In a few years, the English, who had possession of the fort, procured an Indian of the Peoria nation to kill him. The news spread like lightning through the country. The Indians assembled in great numbers and attacked and destroyed all the Peorias, except about thirty families, which were received into the fort." Thus, the death of Pontiac was revenged. His spirit could rest in peace.

EPOCH OF SAVAGE TRIUMPHS.

Revolutionary period.— The British flag had no sooner waved in supremacy over the western frontier, than its lustre began to wane, and the power it represented began to lose its prestige on the American continent.

The principles from which grew the American revolution were already asserting themselves, and the thunders of a new war which was destined to change the policy of nations, began to be heard. During all the long years of the struggle for independence, the western frontier was again the scene of savage warfare, and, instigated by the British, and by their own revengeful instinct, the tomahawk and scalping knife were again seized by willing and ruthless hands, in the west, and long were held suspended, like the sword of Damocles, over the heads of the hardy settlers of the western frontier. These settlers were born in the midst of danger, and were warriors almost from the cradle. Even the women were of heroic mold, often themselves defending their homes and loved ones from danger, and always encouraging their husbands and brothers, and teaching their children, to bravely sustain their manhood in all the trials and dangers which surrounded them. So, when the war for independence came; when it was found that Great Britain, not content to meet her unruly sons in the open battle field, was secretly inciting the Indians to a murderous war along the frontier, there was little difficulty in raising hardy bands of brave men, skilled in the warfare of the woods, burning to avenge the slaughter of near relatives by their savage foes. With an iron will and endurance, these brave men responded to the call of country, and sprang to the defense of their hearthstones, no matter how humble the roof which covered them, and went forth to conquer gloriously, or perchance die a fearful death by torture.

The first campaign of importance was that of Gen. George Rogers

Clark, sent by Gov. Patrick Henry of Virginia, with a volunteer force to attack the British outpost at Kaskaskia, in 1778. The history of this campaign under its great-souled commander reads in some particulars like a chapter from the romances of the days of chivalry. The expedition resulted in the capture of all the far western British posts, Kaskaskia, Cahokia and Vincennes, in the face of largely superior forces and almost insuperable difficulties. The forts were manned by Americans, and the prowess of Clark's gallant forces soon made his name a terror among the Indians. Virginia extended her jurisdiction over these parts by creating the county of Illinois, and even the French settlers at Vincennes became friendly and peace seemed assured.

But when the news of Clark's success reached Detroit, by way of the Maumee, Hamilton, the British governor, determined to recapture the posts. With eighty regulars, a large number of Canadian militia, and 600 Indians, he ascended the Maumee, crossed over to the Wabash, and made a rapid movement upon Vincennes, thinking to take the fort by storm, and destroy all within the garrison. When the enemy approached, Capt. Helm, who was in command, was not to be dismayed. With an air as confident as if the fort were full of soldiers, he leaped upon the bastion near a cannon, and swinging his lighted match, shouted with great force as the enemy advanced, "Halt! or I will blow you to atoms!" At this the Indians precipitately took to the woods, and the Canadians fell back out of range. Fearing that the fort was well manned, and that a desperate encounter would ensue, Hamilton offered a parley. Capt. Helm declared that he would fight as long as a man was left to bear arms, unless permitted to march out with the full honors of war, which was after some parley agreed upon, and the garrison consisting of Helm and five men all told, marched out, to the astonishment of the British commander. But Helm was afterward detained in the fort as a prisoner.

The season now being late and unfavorable, Hamilton took no further steps toward the capture of the other posts till spring. In the meantime Clark, toward the last of January, 1779, received information of the recapture, and on the 7th of February, with 130 men, he took up his line of march through the forest for Vincennes, a distance of 150 miles, ordering Captain Rogers, with forty men, on board a large keelboat, with two four-pounders and four swivels, to ascend the Wabash to within a few miles of the mouth of White river, there to await further orders. The march through the wilderness was one of peril and hardship. The river bottoms were inundated, and, as they moved through these lowlands, the soldiers were often, while having to feel for the trail with their feet, compelled to hold their guns and ammunition above their heads. Their food on the march was parched corn and jerked beef. At length, on the evening of the 23d of February, arriving within sight of the fort, Clark ordered his men to parade about the summit of a hill overlooking the fort, keeping them marching for some time. By this stratagem the British commander was led to believe a large force was approaching — at least 1,000 men, he thought, with colors plainly visible. During the night a ditch was dug to within rifle-shot of the fort, and before day-break, a number of men were stationed there to pick off the garrison, and every gunner showing his head was shot by the unerring hunters. On the 25th the fort was surrendered, and Hamilton, Major Hay and a few others, as instigators of Indian murders on the frontier, were sent to Virginia to answer for the crimes charged upon them. They were put in irons and held for a time in close confinement in retaliation for the massacres that had occurred, but were finally released at the suggestion of General Washington. This achievement on the part of Clark and his brave comrades left them in possession of all the lower portion of the west until the close of the revolution, when, at the treaty of peace with the British in 1783, on the basis of its having been conquered and held by Col. Clark, Great Britain conceded all of this region to the United States.

At the period of the revolution Kekionga had become a place of much importance, in trading and military points of view, and as such, ranked next to Detroit and Vincennes. It was, accordingly, occupied by the British as a post or seat of an official for Indian affairs. Col. Clark, on the capture of Vincennes, had meditated an expedition against this place, as well as against Detroit; and though he seems never to have abandoned the idea, yet he could not succeed in his arrangements. But while the subject was still fresh in the minds of Clark and the inhabitants of the lower Wabash, another individual made his appearance to undertake what even the daring Clark with greater resources, did not deem prudent to venture upon. This was La Balme, a native of France, who had come to this country as an officer, with the French troops under La Fayette, in 1779. It is not known whether he came to the west on his own responsibility, or whether he was directed by some authority; but he is found in the summer of 1780, in Kaskaskia, raising volunteers for an expedition against the post of Kekionga, with the design in case of success, of extending his operations against Detroit. At Kaskaskia, he succeeded in obtaining only twenty to thirty men. With these he proceeded to Vincennes, where he sought recruits. But his expedition was looked upon as a forlorn hope, and it met with the encouragement, generally, of only the less considerate.

It is quite certain, that though a generous and gallant man, he was too reckless and inconsiderate to lead such an expedition. Sometime in the fall of 1780, with as is supposed, fifty to sixty men, he proceeded up the Wabash on his adventure. He conducted his march with such caution and celerity, that he appeared at the village of Kekionga before the watchful inhabitants had warning of his approach. The sudden appearance of a foe, unknown as to character, numbers and designs, threw them into the greatest alarm, and they fled on all sides. La Balme took possession of the place without resistance. It was probably his intention, in imitation of Clark's capture of Kaskaskia, to take the village and its inhabitants by surprise, and then by professions of kindness and friendship, to win them over to the American cause; but the inhabitants, including some six or eight French traders, eluded his grasp. His occupation of the village was not of long duration. After making plunder of the goods of some of the French traders and Indians he retired and encamped near the Aboit creek, not far from the place where that stream was crossed by the Wabash and Erie canal. The Indians having soon ascertained the number and character of La Balme's men, and learning that they were Frenchmen, were not disposed at first to avenge the attack. But two of the traders, Beaubien and La Fontaine, indignant at the invasion and plunder of the place, were not disposed to let the invaders off without a blow, and incited the Indians to follow and attack them. The warriors of the village and vicinity rallied under the lead of their war chief, Little Turtle, and falling on La Balme's camp in the night time, massacred the entire party. La Balme's expedition may not have been impelled by the most patriotic motives, nor guided by wise counsels, nor attended with results beneficial to the country; yet it is an interesting event connected with the early history of the upper Maumee valley.

Northwest Territory.— The need of some form of government for the growing settlements in the west, together with the fact that large numbers of the soldiers of the disbanded armies of the revolution were ready and willing to emigrate and found new homes, if guaranteed the necessary protection of the laws, led congress to listen to their demands, and in 1787, the ordinance was passed which created the "North West Territory," and provided a government therefor. This territory consisted of all of the lands lying northwest of the Ohio and east of the Mississippi, and comprised all of what are now the states of Ohio, Indiana, Michigan, Illinois and Wisconsin. Virginia ceded all her rights in the territory to the United States, and her example was followed by all the other states which claimed title under their original charters, which generally granted them the lands to the westward indefinitely.

In July, 1788, the seat of government was located at Marietta, Ohio, in the place called "Campus Martius." General Arthur St. Clair, a distinguished officer in the revolutionary war, was appointed governor, Winthrop Sargent, secretary, and three judges formed the executive council. The governor and judges were authorized to adopt for the new territory, laws from the other states not inconsistent with the ordinance, and under the laws so enacted the territory thrived for many years.

For the most part, the settlers of the northwest territory were men who were valiant soldiers and had spent much of their fortunes in the revolutionary war. Such was the character of a party of emigrants, under the leadership of General Rufus Putnam, which left New England in 1787-8, and descending the Ohio, began the settlement of Adelphia, later named Marietta, bringing with them, and re-establishing there, many of the primitive habits and customs of their ancestors. First erecting substantial buildings for their families, they set about the organization of a church and a school, toward which all contributed "with a right good will"; and these were the first institutions of the kind established in the northwestern territory.

A year later, in 1789, the first settlement was formed at or near the present site of Cincinnati, Ohio, which was first called Losantiville. Fort Washington was established there, and it was from that point that the first movement under Gen. Harmar was made against the Indians at the present site of Fort Wayne, under the administration of General Washington, in October, 1790. It was also from that region, which, at an early period was known as "the settlements," that came most of the earlier settlers of Fort Wayne, then still known as the Miami village or Omi.* The subsequent expeditions of Gens. St. Clair and Wayne also started from Fort Washington.

During 1780, 1781, to 1785–6, difficulties had arisen between the colonial government and the Spanish on the lower Mississippi, as to the navigation of that river, and the possession of a large part of the western territory, and there was much trouble with the Indians of the west, more especially along the Ohio, which continued to embarrass the settlements for some time. In addition to these troubles people in the southwest, early in that period, began and continued for several years, to manifest considerable dissatisfaction. The government had permitted the Spaniards of the south to control the navigation of the Mississippi; many privations had come upon the people of the west in consequence, and distrust of the government had gradually given rise to a desire for dissolution, especially in Kentucky, which, at that period was yet a part of Virginia. Washington had recognized this, and soon presented important suggestions, as he had done before the revolution, relative to the organization of commercial and navigation companies, as the best means of protecting and cementing the interests of the east and west. In a letter to Gov. Benjamin Harrison in the year 1784 he strenuously urged the importance of binding together all parts of the Union, and especially the west and east, with the indissoluble bonds of interest, with a view to prevent the formation of commercial and consequent political connections with either the Spaniards on the south, or the English on the north. He recommended the speedy survey of the Potomac and James rivers; of the portage to the waters of the Ohio; of the Muskingum, and the portage from that river to the Cuyahoga; for the purpose of opening a water communication for the commerce of the Ohio and the lakes, to the seaboard, which he denominated as an object of great political and commercial importance. To Richard Henry Lee, in the same year, Washington wrote: "Would it not be worthy of the wisdom and attention of congress to have the western waters well explored, the navigation of them fully ascertained and accurately laid down, and a complete and perfect map made of the country, at least as far westerly as the Miamis running into the Ohio and Lake Erie, and to see how the

---

* "A corrupt orthography and abridgment of the French term Aux Miamis; as Au Cas is a corruption of Aux Kaskaskias."

waters of these communicate with the river St. Joseph, which empties into Lake Michigan, and with the Wabash? for I cannot forbear observing that the Miami village points to a very important post for the Union."

It was not a custom with the French, at any of their settlements in the west, to make large purchases of lands from the Indians; small tracts about their settlements invariably served to supply their wants. At the treaty of Paris in 1763, these small grants about the forts of Detroit, Vincennes, Kaskaskia, Cahokia, etc., were all that they ceded to the British, and at the close of the revolution, in 1783, when Great Britain transferred her western claims to the United States, she might be said to have had no right to convey anything but what she had previously received from France, excepting the guarantee of the Six Nations and the southern tribes to a part of the land south of the Ohio; and it could be asserted that none of the territory claimed by the Miamis, western Delawares, Shawnees, Wyandots or Hurons, and some other tribes still to the west and north could be ceded to the United States by this treaty. But a different view of the matter was taken by congress. Concluding that the treaty guaranteed to the United States the full right to all territory then transferred, and at the same time considering the right of the Indians to the territory as forfeited by acts of warfare against the colonial government during the struggle for independence, the government made no movement toward a purchase of the lands from the Indians, but began to form treaties of peace with them, and to suggest its own boundary lines.

The stipulations of the treaty of October, 1783, had contemplated one great council of all the tribes; but in March, 1784, this plan was changed to that of holding councils with each separate tribe or nation; and the commissioners appointed by the government to superintend these affairs, refusing to pay further attention to the subject of a general council with the northern tribes, in October, 1784, against the wishes of Red Jacket, Brant, and other chiefs of the Iroquois, terminated the treaty of Fort Stanwix.

It was in this way that the United States obtained the right possessed by the Iroquois to the western territory, north and south of the Ohio. Though publicly and honorably concluded, the legality was questioned by many of the Iroquois, who claimed that the treaty was with only a part of the Indian tribes; and that it was the desire of the tribes that the United States government should treat with them as a body, including all the Indians bordering upon the lakes of the north. In January of the following year (1785), a treaty was concluded with the Wyandots, Delawares, Chippewas and Ottawas; but the legality of the former treaty seems not then to have been questioned, by the Wyandots and Delawares, at least; and yet it was asserted at a general council of some sixteen tribes of northwest Indians, in 1793, that the treaties of Forts Stanwix, McIntosh, and Finney (the latter at the mouth of the Miami), were the result of intimidation, and held only with single tribes, at which, they asserted, the Indians had been invited to form treaties of peace, but instead forced to make cession of land. In January, 1786, a third treaty was held by the United States, at Fort Finney, with the Shawnees; and the Wabash tribe being invited to be present, would not go. In 1789, confirmatory of preceding treaties, the fourth and fifth treaties were held at Fort Harmar, one with the Six Nations; the other with the Wyandots, Delawares, Ottawas, Chippewas, Pottawatomies, and Sacs; and it seems, from speeches made at a subsequent council of the confederated tribes, more particularly of the lake (1793), that they would not accept these treaties as at all binding upon them. Said one of the chiefs at this latter council:

"Brothers: We are in possession of the speeches and letters which passed on that occasion [council convened by Gov. Arthur St. Clair, in 1788], between those deputied by the confederate Indians, and Gov. St. Clair, the commissioner of the United States. These papers prove that your said commissioner in the beginning of the year 1789, after having been informed by the general council of the preceding fall that no bargain or sale of any part of these lands would be considered as valid or binding, unless agreed to by a general council, nevertheless persisted in collecting together a few chiefs of two or three nations only, and with them held a treaty for the cession of an immense country, in which they were no more interested than as a branch of the general confederacy, and who were in no manner authorized to make any grant or cession whatever.

"Brothers: How then was it possible for you to expect to enjoy peace, and quietly to hold these lands, when your commissioner was informed, long before he held the treaty of Fort Harmar, that the consent of a general council was absolutely necessary for the sale of any part of these lands to the United States."

From these facts it will be seen why the expeditions of 1790–91 and 1793–94, with the efforts of 1811–12 and '13, met with such stubborn and relentless resistance from the Miamis and other tribes, as detailed in subsequent pages. The impression that they would without remuneration or mercy, be despoiled of their lands and at length driven away, seems to have gained possession of the tribes of the northwest before and during the early campaigns of Harmar, St. Clair and Wayne; and the Miamis — though, as it would seem from Gamelin's journal, a strong spirit of unity did not prevail among the different tribes before and during 1780 — led the way under Little Turtle, with formidable effect.

An Indian War Cloud.— With a feeling of bitterness toward the United States, small bands of Indians had begun in the spring of 1789 to attack the settlements along the western borders of Virginia and Kentucky. The secretary of war, General Knox, in a report to the president, June 15, 1789, presented this subject as follows:

" By information from Brigadier-General Harmar, the commanding officer of the troops on the frontier, it appears that several murders have been lately committed on the inhabitants, by small parties of Indians, probably from the Wabash country. Some of the said murders having been perpetrated on the south side of the Ohio, the inhabitants on the waters of that river are exceedingly alarmed, for the extent of six or seven hundred miles along the same. It is to be observed that the United States have not formed any treaties with the Wabash Indians; on the contrary, since the conclusion of the war with Great Britain, hostilities have almost constantly existed between the people of Kentucky and the said Indians. The injuries and murders have been so reciprocal that it would be a point of critical investigation to know on which side they have been the greatest. Some of the inhabitants of Kentucky during the past year, roused by recent injuries, made an incursion into the Wabash country, and possessing an equal aversion to all bearing the name of Indians, they destroyed a number of peaceable Piankeshaws who prided themselves in their attachment to the United States. Things being thus circumstanced, it is greatly to be apprehended that hostilities may be so far extended as to involve the Indian tribes with whom the United States have recently made treaties. It is well known how strong the passion for war exists in the mind of a young savage, and how easily it may be inflamed, so as to disregard every precept of the older and wiser part of the tribes who may have a more just opinion of the force of a treaty. Hence, it results that unless some decisive measures are immediately adopted to terminate those mutual hostilities, they will probably become general among all the Indians northwest of the Ohio.

"In examining the question how the disturbances on the frontiers are to be quieted, two modes present themselves by which the object might perhaps be effected — the first of which is by raising an army and extirpating the refractory tribes entirely; or secondly, by forming treaties of peace with them in which their rights and limits should be explicitly defined, and the treaties observed on the part of the United States with the most rigid justice, by punishing the whites who should violate the same.

"In considering the first mode, an inquiry would arise, whether, under the existing circumstances of affairs, the United States have a clear right, consistently with the principles of justice and the laws of nature, to proceed to the destruction or expulsion of the savages on the Wabash, supposing the force for that object easily attainable. It is presumable that a nation solicitous of establishing its character on the broad basis of justice, would not only hesitate at but reject every proposition to benefit itself by the injury of any neighboring community, however contemptible and weak it may be, either with respect to its manners or power. When it shall be considered that the Indians derive their subsistence chiefly by hunting, and that, according to fixed principles, their population is in proportion to the facility with which they procure their food, it would most probably be found that the expulsion or destruction of the Indian tribes have nearly the same effect; for if they are removed from their usual hunting-grounds, they must necessarily encroach on the hunting-grounds of another tribe, who will not suffer the encroachment with impunity — hence they destroy each other. The Indians, being the prior occupants, possess the right of the soil. It can not be taken from them unless by their free consent, or by the right of conquest in case of a just war. To dispossess them on any other principle, would be a gross violation of the fundamental laws of nature, and of that distributive justice which is the glory of a nation. But if it should be decided, on an abstract view of the question, to be just to remove by force, the Wabash Indians from the territory they occupy, the finances of the United States would not at present admit of the operation.

"By the best and latest information, it appears that on the Wabash and its communications, there are from 1,500 to 2,000 warriors. An expedition against them, with a view of extirpating them, or destroying their towns, could not be undertaken with a probability of success with less than an army of 2,500 men. The regular troops of the United States on the frontiers are less than 600; of that number not more than 400 could be collected from the posts for the purpose of the expedition. To raise, pay, feed, arm, and equip 1,900 additional men, with the necessary officers for six months, and to provide every thing in the hospital and quartermaster's line, would require the sum of $200,000, a sum far exceeding the ability of the United States to advance, consistently with a due regard to other indispensable objects."

On the 26th of August, 1789, about 200 mounted volunteers, under the command of Colonel John Hardin, marched from the Falls of the Ohio to attack some of the Indian towns on the Wabash. This expedition returned to the Falls on the 28th of September, without the loss of a man — having killed six Indians, plundered and burnt one deserted village, and destroyed a considerable quantity of corn.

In a letter addressed to President Washington, bearing date September 14, 1789, Governor St. Clair pointed out with great care the embarrassments which would surround an expedition against the Indians on the Wabash, and the danger of precipitating a frontier Indian war, and considerable correspondence on the subject passed between President Washington and Governor St. Clair, and it was determined to make an effort for the government and safety of the western settlements.

About the 1st of January, 1790, Governor St. Clair, with the judges of the supreme court, descended the Ohio, from Marietta to Fort Washington, and on the 8th of January, 1790, the governor and Winthrop Sargent, secretary of the territory, arrived at Clarksville, whence they proceeded to the Illinois country, to organize the government in that quarter. Before the governor left Clarksville, he sent to Major Hamtramck, the commanding officer of Post Vincennes, dispatches containing speeches which were addressed to the Indian tribes on the Wabash. The latter officer, on the 15th of April, dispatched Antoine Gamelin with these speeches of St. Clair, which Gamelin delivered at all the villages bordering this stream, and came as far east as Kekionga. The following is the journal of Gamelin, which will give the reader a fair notion of the spirit of the Miamis at that period:

"The first village I arrived to, is called Kikapouguoi. The name of the chief of this village is called Les Jambes Croches. Him and his tribe have a good heart, and accepted the speech. The second village is at the river du Vermilion, called Piankeshaws. The first chief and all his warriors, were well pleased with the speeches concerning the peace: but they said they could not give presently a proper answer, before they consult the Miami nation, their eldest brethren. They desired me to proceed to the Miami town (Ke-ki-ong-gay), and, by coming back to let them know what reception I got from them. The said head chief told me that he thought the nations of the lake had a bad heart, and were ill disposed for the Americans: that the speeches would not be received, particularly by the Shawnees at Miamitown. * * The 11th of April, I reached a tribe of Kickapoos. The head chief and all the warriors being assembled, I gave them two branches of white wampum, with the speeches of his excellency Arthur St. Clair, and those of Major Hamtramck. It must be observed that the speeches have been in another hand before me. The messenger could not proceed further than the Vermilion, on account of some private wrangling between the the interpreter and some chief men of the tribe. Moreover, something in the speech displeased them very much, which is included in the third article, which says, '*I do now make you the offer of peace: accept it, or reject it as you please.*' These words appeared to displease all the tribes to whom the first messenger was sent. They told me they were menacing; and finding that it might have a bad effect, I took upon myself to exclude them; and, after making some apology, they answered that he and his tribe were pleased with my speech, and that I could go up without danger, but they could not presently give me an answer, having some warriors absent, and without consulting the Ouiatenons, being the owners of their lands. They desired me to stop at Quitepiconnoe [Tippecanoe], that they would have the chiefs and warriors of Ouiatenons and those of their nation assembled there, and would receive a proper answer. They said that they expected by me a draught of milk from the great chief, and the commanding officer of the post, for to put the old people in good humor; also some powder and ball for the young men for hunting, and to get some good broth for their women and children: that I should know a bearer of speeches should never be with empty hands. They promised me to keep their young men from stealing and to send speeches to their nations in the prairies for to do the same.

"The 14th April, the Ouiatenons and the Kickapoos were assembled. After my speech, one of the head chiefs got up and told me, 'You, Gamelin, my friend and son-in-law, we are pleased to see in our village, and to hear by your mouth, the good words of the great chief. We thought to receive a few words from the French people; but I see the contrary. None but the Big Knife is sending speeches to us. You know that we can terminate nothing without the consent of our brethren the Miamis. I invite you to proceed to their village and to speak to them. There is one thing in your speech I do not like; I will not tell of it; even was I drunk, I would perceive it; but our elder brethren will certainly take notice of it in your speech. You invite us to stop our young men. It is impossible to do it, being constantly encouraged by the British.' Another chief got up and said — 'The Americans are very flattering in their speeches; many times our nation went to their rendezvous. I was once myself. Some of our chiefs died on the route; and we always came back all naked; and you, Gamelin, you come with speech, with empty hands.' Another chief got up and said to his young men, 'If we are poor, and dressed in deer skins, it is our own fault. Our French traders are leaving us and our villages, because you plunder them every day; and it is time for us to have another conduct.' Another chief got up and said — 'Know ye that the village of Ouiatenon is the sepulchre of all our ancestors. The chief of America invites us to go to him if we are for peace. He has not his leg broke, having been able to go as far as the Illinois. He might come here himself; we should be glad to see him at our village. We confess that we accepted the ax, but it is by the reproach we continually receive from the English, and other nations, which received the ax first, calling us women; at the present time they invite our young men to war. As to the old people, they are wishing for peace.' They could not give me an answer before they received advice from the Miamis, their elder brethren.

"The 18th April I arrived at the river a l'Anguille [Eel river]. The chief of the village [which was on the north side of Eel river, six miles above the confluence of that stream with the Wabash], and those of war were not present. I explained the speeches to some of the tribe. They said they were well pleased; but they could not give me an answer, their chief men being absent. They desired me to stop at their village coming back; and they sent with me one of their men for to hear the answer of their eldest brethren.

"The 23d April I arrived at the Miami town. The next day I got the Miami nation, the Shawnees and Delawares all assembled. I gave to each nation two branches of wampum, and began the speeches, before the French and English traders, being invited by the chiefs to be present, having told them myself I would be glad to have them present, having nothing to say against any body. After the speech I showed them the treaty concluded at Muskingum [Fort Harmar], between his excellency, Governor St. Clair, and sundry nations, which displeased them. I told them that the purpose of this present time was not to submit them to any condition, but to offer them the peace, which made disappear their displeasure. The great chief told me that he was pleased with the speech; that he would soon give me an answer. In a private discourse with the great chief, he told me not to mind what the Shawnees would tell me, having a bad heart, and being the perturbators of all the nations. He said the Miamis had a bad name, on account of the mischief done on the river Ohio; but he told me, it was not occasioned by his young men, but by the Shawnees; his young men going out only for to hunt.

"The 25th of April, Blue Jacket, chief warrior of the Shawnees, invited me to go to his house, and told me — 'My friend, by the name and consent of the Shawnees and Delawares, I will speak to you. We are all sensible of your speech, and pleased with it; but, after consultation, we can not give an answer without hearing from our father at Detroit; and we are determined to give you back the two branches of wampum, and to send you to Detroit to see and hear the chief, or to stay here twenty nights for to receive his answer. From all quarters we receive speeches from the Americans, and not one is alike. We suppose that they intend to deceive us. Then take back your branches of wampum.'

"The 26th, five Pottawatomies arrived here with two negro men, which they sold to English traders. The next day I went to the great chief of the Miamis, called Le Gris. His chief warrior was present. I told him how I had been served by the Shawnees. He answered me that he had heard of it; that the said nations behaved contrary to his intentions. He desired me not to mind those strangers, and that he would soon give me a positive answer.

"The 28th of April, the great chief desired me to call at the French trader's and receive his answer. 'Don't take bad,' said he, 'of what I am to tell you. You may go back when you please. We can not give you a positive answer. We must send your speeches to all our neighbors, and to the lake nations. We can not give a definite answer without consulting the commandant at Detroit.' And he desired me to render him the two branches of wampum refused by the Shawnees; also a copy of speeches in writing. He promised me that, in thirty nights, he would send an answer to Post Vincennes by a young man of each nation. He was well pleased with the speeches, and said to be worthy of attention, and should be communicated to all their confederates, having resolved among them not to do anything without a unanimous consent. I agreed to his requisitions, and rendered him the two branches of wampum and a copy of the speech. Afterward he told me that the Five Nations, so called, or Iroquois, were training something; that five of them, and three Wyandots, were in this village with branches of wampum. He could not tell me presently their purpose, but he said I would know of it very soon.

"The same day Blue Jacket, chief of the Shawnees, invited me to his house for supper; and, before the other chiefs, told me that after another deliberation, they thought necessary that I should go myself to Detroit for to see the commandant, who would get all his children assembled to hear my speech. I told them I would not answer them in the night; that I was not ashamed to speak before the sun.

"The 29th of April I got them all assembled. I told them that I was not to go to Detroit; that the speeches were directed to the nations' of the river Wabash and the Miami; and that, for to prove the sincerity of the speech, and the heart of Gov. St. Clair, I have willingly given a copy of the speeches to be shown to the commandant at Detroit; and according to a letter wrote by the commandant of Detroit to the Miamis, Shawnees and Delawares, mentioning to you to be peaceable with the Americans, I would go to him very willingly, if it was in my directions, being sensible of his sentiments. I told them I had nothing to say to the commandant; neither him to me. You must immediately resolve if you intend to take me to Detroit, or else I am to go back as soon as possible. Blue Jacket got up and told me, 'My friend, we are well pleased with what you say. Our intention is not to force you to go to Detroit. It is only a proposal, thinking it for the best. Our answer is the same as the Miamis. We will send in thirty nights, a full and positive answer by a young man of each nation by writing to Post Vincennes.' In the evening, Blue Jacket, chief of the Shawnees, having taken me to supper with him, told me in a private manner, that the Shawnee nation was in doubt of the sincerity of the Big Knives, so called, having been already deceived by them. That they had first destroyed their lands, put out their fire, and sent away their young men, being a hunting, without a mouthful of meat; also had taken away their women—wherefore many of them would, with a great deal of pain, forget these affronts. Moreover, that some other nations were apprehending that offers of peace would, may be, tend to take away by degrees, their lands, and would serve them as they did before: a certain proof that they intend to encroach on our lands, is their new settlement on the Ohio. If they don't keep this side [of the Ohio] clear, it will never be a proper reconcilement with the nations Shawnees, Iroquois, Wyandots and perhaps many others. Le Gris, chief of the Miamis, asked me in a private discourse, what chiefs had made a treaty with the Americans at Muskingdum [Fort Harmar]? I answered him that their names were mentioned in the treaty. He told me he had heard of it some time ago; but they are not chiefs, neither delegates who made that treaty—they are only young men who, without authority and instructions from their chiefs have concluded that treaty, which will not be approved. They went to the treaty clandestinely, and they intend to make mention of it in the next council to be held.

"The 2d of May I came back to the river a l'Anguille. One of the chief men of the tribe being witness of the council at Miami town, repeated the whole to them; and whereas, the first chief was absent, they said they could not for the present time give answer, but they were willing to join their speech to those of their eldest brethren. 'To give you proof of an open heart, we let you know that one of our chiefs is gone to war on the Americans; but it was before we heard of you, for certain they would not have been gone thither.' They also told me that a few days after I passed their village, seventy warriors, Chippewas and Ottawas, from Michillimackinac, arrived there. Some of them were Pottawatomies, who meeting in their route the Chippewas and Ottawas,

Truly yours
F. P. Randall

joined them. 'We told them what we heard by you; that your speech is fair and true. We could not stop them from going to war. The Pottawatomies told us that, as the Chippewas and Ottawas were more numerous than them, they were forced to follow them.'

"The 3d of May I got to the Weas. They told me that they were waiting for an answer from their eldest brethren. 'We approve very much our brethren for not to give a definite answer, without informing of it all the lake nations; that Detroit was the place where the fire was lighted; then it ought first to be put out there; that the English commandant is their father, since he threw down our French father. They could do nothing without his approbation.' The 4th of May I arrived at the village of the Kickapoos. The chief, presenting me two branches of wampum, black and white, said: 'My son, we can not stop our young men from going to war. Every day some set off clandestinely for that purpose. After such behaviour from our young men, we are ashamed to say to the great chief at the Illinois and of the Post Vincennes, that we are busy about some good affairs for the reconcilement; but be persuaded that we will speak to them continually concerning the peace; and that, when our eldest brethren will have sent their answer, we will join ours to it.' The 5th of May I arrived at Vermilion. I found nobody but two chiefs; all the rest were gone a-hunting. They told me they had nothing else to say but what I was told going up."

Gov. St. Clair being at Kaskaskia, early in June of this year, received from Major Hamtramck the following, bearing date Post Vincennes, May 22d, 1790: "I now inclose the proceedings of Mr. Gamelin, by which your excellency can have no great hopes of bringing the Indians to a peace with the United States. The 8th of May, Gamelin arrived, and on the 11th some merchants arrived and informed me that, as soon as Gamelin had passed their villages on his return, all the Indians had gone to war; that a large party of Indians from Michillimackinac, and some Pottawatomies, had gone to Kentucky; and that three days after Gamelin had left the Miami village, an American was brought there and burnt."

Harmar's Campaign.— Being induced to believe from the dispatches received from Hamtramck, that there was no possibility of forming a treaty of peace with the Miamis and other tribes banded with them, St. Clair quit Kaskaskia and reached Fort Washington on the 13th of July. Having consulted with General Harmar, and concluding to send a formidable force against the Indians about the head-waters of the Wabash, by authority of President Washington, on the 15th of July, he addressed circular letters to a number of lieutenants of the western counties of Virginia [Kentucky] and Pennsylvania, for the purpose of raising 1,000 militia in the former, and 500 in the latter. The regular troops then in service in the west General Harmar estimated at about 400 efficient men, with whom the militia were to operate as follows: Of the Virginia militia, 300 were to rendezvous at Fort Steuben, and, with a garrison at that post, to proceed to Vincennes, to join Major Hamtramck, who had orders to call to his aid the militia of that place, and move up the Wabash, attacking such Indian villages along that river as his force might seem adequate to. The 1,200 militia remaining were to join the regular troops, under General Harmar, at Fort Washington. That the British commandant at Detroit might know the true cause of the movement, on the 19th of September Gov. St. Clair addressed a letter to him, assuring the said commandant that the purposes of the United States were pacific in so far as their relations to Great Britain were concerned; that the expedition was to quell the vindictive and intolerable spirit of the Indians toward the settlements against which they had so long, so inhumanly and destructively carried on their savage warfare. That the English, toward Lake Erie, notwithstanding this spirit of candor and courtesy on the part of St. Clair, gave aid to the Indians in their efforts against the United States during 1790-91, the evidence is clear enough; but to what extent they did so, was not fully known. The following paragraphs from a certificate of one Thomas Rhea, taken in the early part of 1790, will give some indication of the encouragement given the Indians by the British.

"At this place, the Miami," said Rhea, in his account, "were Colonels Brant and McKee, with his son Thomas; and Captains Bunbury and Silvie, of the British troops. These officers, &c., were all encamped on the south side of the Miami or Ottawa river, at the rapids above Lake Erie, about eighteen miles; they had clever houses, built chiefly by the Pottawatomies and other Indians; in these they had stores of goods, with arms, ammunition and provision, which they issued to the Indians in great abundance, viz.: corn, pork, peas, &c. The Indians came to this place in parties of one, two, three, four and five hundred at a time, from different quarters, and received from Mr. McKee and the Indian officers, clothing, arms, ammunition, provisions, &c., and set out immediately for the upper Miami towns, where they understood the forces of the United States were bending their course, and in order to supply the Indians from other quarters collected there, pirogues loaded with the above-mentioned articles were sent up the Miami [Maumee] river, wrought by French Canadians."

About the middle of September, the Virginia militia began to gather about the mouth of Licking river, opposite Cincinnati, for the most part badly armed and equipped; they were organized by General Harmar, and formed into three battalions, under Majors Hall, McMullen and Ray, with Trotter as lieutenant-colonel. About the 24th of September, came the militia of Pennsylvania, also badly prepared, and many of them substitutes—"old, infirm men, and young boys." These were formed into one battalion, under Lieut.-Colonel Truby and Major Paul; while four battalions of militia, subject to General Harmar's command, were commanded by Col. John Hardin. Majors John Plasgrave Wylles and John Doughty commanded the regular troops, in two small battalions. The artillery corps, with but three pieces of ordnance, was under the command of Captain William Ferguson; while under James Fontaine was placed a small battalion of light troops or mounted militia. The whole army contained about 1,453 regular and raw militia troops. The militia under Col. Hardin, on the 26th of September, advanced from Fort Washington into the country, for the double purpose of opening a road for the artillery and obtaining feed for their cattle. On the 30th of September, the regular troops marched, commanded by General Harmar, and on the 3d day of October joined the militia. A journal of the daily movements of the army was regularly kept by Captain John Armstrong, of the regulars, up to its arrival at the Miami village.

After an uninterrupted march of sixteen days, on the afternoon of the 15th of October, Colonel Hardin, with an advanced detachment, stole upon Kekionga, only to find it deserted by men, women and children. A few cows, some vegetables, about 20,000 bushels of corn in the ear, and empty wigwams, were all that greeted them; and the militia, in much disorder, soon began to scatter in search of plunder. On the 17th, about one o'clock, the main body of the army came up and crossed the Maumee to the village. Major McMullen, having discovered the tracks of women and children leading to the northwest, so reported to General Harmar, and the latter on the morning of the 18th, detailed Col: Trotter and Majors Hall, Ray and McMullen, with 300 men, among whom were thirty regulars, forty light-horse, and 230 active riflemen. Furnished with three days' provision, they were ordered to reconnoiter the country around the village. About one mile from the encampment, an Indian on horseback was discovered, pursued and killed by a part of the detachment, under Trotter; and before returning to the main body another Indian was seen, "when the four field officers left their commands and pursued him, leaving the troops for the space of about half an hour without any direction whatever." Being intercepted by the light-horsemen, one of whom he had wounded, the Indian was at length despatched. Changing the route of his detachment, and moving in different directions, till night, Col. Trotter, contrary to instructions, returned to the Miami village.

In consequence of the disorderly course of the militia on their arrival, General Harmar ordered cannon to be fired for the purpose of calling them to ranks, and also harangued the officers on the bad results liable to follow such indifference. On the 18th he issued the following general order:

"CAMP AT THE MIAMI VILLAGE, Oct. 18, 1790.

"The general is much mortified at the unsoldierlike behavior of many of the men in the army, who make it a practice to straggle from the camp in search of plunder. He, in the most positive terms, forbids this practice in future, and the guards will be answerable to prevent it. No party is allowed to go beyond the line of sentinels without a commissioned officer, who, if of the militia, will apply to Col. Hardin for his orders. The regular troops will apply to the general. All the plunder that may be hereafter collected, will be equally distributed among the army. The kettles, and every other article already taken, are to be collected by the commanding officers of battalions, and to be delivered to-morrow morning to Mr. Belli, the quartermaster, that a fair distribution may take place. The rolls are to be called at troop and retreat beating, and every man absent is to be reported. The general expects that these orders will be pointedly attended to; they are to be read to the troops this evening. The army is to march to-morrow morning early for their new encampment at Chillicothe, about two miles from hence. "JOSIAH HARMAR, *Brigadier-General*."

Col. Hardin having asked for the command of the troops returned to camp under Trotter, for the remaining two days, Gen. Harmar put that officer in command, and he on the next day led the detachment along an Indian trail to the northwest, in the direction of the Kickapoo villages. Coming to a point, near a morass, some five miles distant from the confluence of the St. Mary's and St. Joseph rivers, where on the preceding day there had been an Indian encampment, the detachment came to a halt, and was stationed in readiness for an attack should the enemy still be near. A half hour passed with no alarm. The order now being given to the front to advance, all marched forward except the company under Faulkner, which not having received the order, was left behind. Having advanced some three miles, two Indians afoot, with packs, were discovered; but they dropped their burdens at the sight of the troops and were soon lost sight of. The absence of Faulkner at this time becoming apparent, Major Fontaine, with a portion of the cavalry, was sent in pursuit of him, on the theory that he was lost.

The report of a gun to the front soon fell upon the attentive ear of Captain Armstrong in command of the regulars—an alarm gun, perhaps, suggested he. He had discovered the "tracks of a horse that had come down the road and returned." Captain Armstrong also observed the fires of the Indians in the distance. Hardin thought the Indians would not fight, and moved forward in the direction of the fires, neither giving orders or preparing for an attack. The band of 300 was now several miles from camp and marching through the forest, unaware that the enemy was in ambush, and Little Turtle was the leader. Behind the fires lay the red men with guns leveled. No sooner had the troops approached the fires than a destructive volley burst upon them from the ambush. The militia were panic stricken, and all but nine began a precipitate flight for the camp of Gen. Harmar. Hardin had retreated with them, and in vain strove to rally them. The regulars bravely faced the enemy, and returned the fire. The nine remaining militia were pierced by the balls of the enemy, and twenty-two of the regulars fell, Captain Armstrong, Ensign Hartshorn, and some five or six privates, alone making their escape. This bloody engagement was near the place now known as "Heller's Corners."

Having, after the departure of Hardin in the morning, destroyed the Miami village, Harmar moved about two miles down the Maumee to the Shawnee village, known as Chillicothe. On the 20th he issued the following order:

"CAMP AT CHILLICOTHE, *one of the Shawnese towns, on the Omee river*, Oct. 20th, 1790.

"The party under command of Captain Strong is ordered to burn and destroy every house and wigwam in this village, together with all the corn, etc., which he can collect. A party of 100 men (militia), properly officered, under the command of Col. Hardin, is to burn and destroy effectually, this afternoon, the Pickaway town, with all the corn, etc., which he can find in it and its vicinity.

"The cause of the detachment being worsted yesterday, was entirely owing to the shameful, cowardly conduct of the militia, who ran away, and threw down their arms, without firing scarcely a single gun. In returning to Fort Washington, if any officer or men presume to quit the ranks, or not to march in the form that they are ordered, the general will most assuredly order the artillery to fire on them. He hopes the check they received yesterday will make them in future obedient to orders.   JOSIAH HARMAR, *Brigadier-General.*"

From the scene of the smoking remains of the Indian village of Chillicothe, at ten o'clock on the morning of the 21st, the army under Harmar began march toward Fort Washington, and proceeded about seven miles, when a halt was made and the troops encamped for the night.

The evening was clear and beautiful — ushering in a glorious October night. There was no sign of the enemy and the hoarse calls of the night owl, mingled with the voices of the soldiery, were all the sounds that fell upon the attentive ears of the sentinels.

Reassured by this peaceful outlook, a desire for revenge came to the mind of Colonel Hardin. His desire for the chastisement of the Indian was by no means appeased by burning villages. The Miamis had perhaps returned to the village immediately after the departure of the army, thought he, and a most propitious opportunity was presented to return and surprise them. He urged upon General Harmar "that, as he had been unfortunate the other day, he wished to have it in his power to pick the militia and try it again." He sought to explain the cause of the militia not meeting the Indians on the 19th; and insisted that he wished to vindicate their valor. The earnest demeanor of Hardin prevailed, and Harmar gave his consent, as he was anxious that the Indians should be as well subdued as possible, that they might not give the army trouble on its March to Fort Washington. That night Hardin set out, intending to strike the Miami village before daylight. Under his command a body of 340 militia, and sixty regulars under Major Wyllys, took up its line of march, in three columns, the regulars in the center and the militia to the right and left. Captain Joseph Ashton moved at the head of the regulars, while Major Wyllys and Colonel Hardin were in his front. Contrary to Hardin's hopes, some delay having been caused by the halting of the militia, the banks of the Maumee were not gained till after sunrise. Indians were soon discovered by the spies, and Major Wyllys called the regulars to a halt, and ordered the militia on to a point in front, and presented his plan of attack to the commanding officers of the detachment. Major Hall was directed, with his battalion, to move round the bend of the Maumee, cross the St. Mary's and take a position in the rear of the Indians, until an attack should be made by Major McMullen's battalion, Major Fontaine's cavalry, and the regular troops under Major Wyllys, who were all ordered to cross the Maumee at or near the ford. Hardin and Wyllys had aimed to surround the Indians in their encampment; but Maj. Hall, having reached his flanking position unobserved, disregarded the orders given by firing upon an Indian that appeared in sight before the general attack was made. This startled the Indians, and small squads of them being seen hurrying away in many directions, they were rapidly pursued, contrary to orders, by the militia under McMullen and the cavalry under Fontaine, leaving Wyllys, at the head of the regulars, without support. In crossing the Maumee they were attacked by a superior body of Indians, under the lead of Little Turtle, and at length, after the fall of Wyllys and the larger part of the regular troops, were forced to retreat. Major Fontaine, at the head of the mounted militia, in a charge upon a small body of Indians, was killed, and a considerable number of his men fell, and the remainder sought safety in retreat. While the regulars were being slaughtered by Little Turtle, the militia under Hall and McMullen, at the confluence of the St. Mary's and St. Joseph, were briskly engaged with small parties of Indians, but when they learned of the misfortune of the regulars they scurried away toward the camp of Harmar. A single horseman having reached the camp of the main army with the news of the defeat about 11 o'clock a. m., Harmar at once ordered Major Ray, with his battalion, to advance to the aid of the retreating forces. But the effect of the panic on the militia was too great — but thirty men could be prevailed on to advance to the rescue under Major Ray, and those had gone but a short distance when they were met by Hardin and the retreating forces. Gaining the encampment, Colonel Hardin, flushed with excitement, and still entertaining a strong desire to fight the Indians, urged Harmar to set out at once with the entire force for the Miami village. But Harmar would not venture a return. Said he: "You see the situation of the army; we are now scarcely able to move our baggage; it will take up three days to go and return to this place; we have no more forage for our horses; the Indians have got a very good scourging; and I will keep the army in perfect readiness to receive them, should they think proper to follow."

The remains of Major Wyllys and Fontaine and eight other officers and men who fell in the engagement with Little Turtle, were buried in trenches near the river, some twenty rods below the site of the residence of J. J. Comparet, which was built just above the fatal ford. Before the destructive fire of the red men the soldiers fell in such numbers that the water, then of no great volume, became bloody. One of the soldiers wounded here, John Smith, managed to conceal himself on the bank, and after witnessing the triumph of the savages, escaped down the Maumee and reached Fort Washington. Returning with Gen. Wayne, he became a resident of the village about the fort

The militia had now become little better than wooden men in the eyes of Gen. Harmar. He had lost all faith in them, and on the morning of the 23d of October, after a loss of 183 killed and thirty-one wounded, the army again took up its march for Fort Washington, where it arrived on the 4th of November. Among the killed in this campaign were Maj. Wyllys and Lieut. Ebenezer Frothingham, of the regulars; Major Fontaine, Captains Thorpe, McMurtrey and Scott, Lieutenants Clark and Rogers, and Ensigns Bridges, Sweet, Higgins and Thielkeld, of the militia. The loss on the part of the Indians was thought to be about equal to that of the forces under Harmar.

Major Hamtramck, who had moved from Vincennes up the Wabash, had proceeded with his command to the mouth of the Vermilion river, and after laying waste several deserted villages, returned again to Vincennes. The campaign of 1790 against the Indians of the northwest was now closed, and the chilling blasts of another long, dreary winter, with its anxieties, its hardships, and its perils, had begun to set in about the lonely settlements.

St. Clair's Campaign.— The defeat of Harmar gave great encouragement to the Indians, as well it might, and brought corresponding depression to the settlements. So elated were the savages, that they renewed their attacks upon the frontier settlements with greater vigor and ferocity, if possible, than ever before, rendering it necessary for the settlers to combine and take prompt measures for their safety. Meetings were held all along the frontier. The government was freely criticised and in many instances severely denounced for the inefficient management of the campaigns of the past. Particularly, they denounced as unwise, the appointment of regular army officers, unused to Indian warfare, to command the militia, which was composed of men accustomed to study the Indian and his cunning from boyhood, and they earnestly implored the president to employ only the militia, under officers of its own choosing, for frontier defense, offering at once to raise a force sufficient not only for frontier defense, but to carry an aggressive war forthwith into the Indian country. This was not granted, but the president readily favored the increase of the regular army on the frontier, and appointed Gen. St. Clair to the command.

On the third of March, 1791, congress passed the "act for raising and adding another regiment to the militia establishment of the United States, and for making further provision for the protection of the frontier." It was proposed to place an army of some 3,000 men under the command of St. Clair. On the 21st of March, instructions were addressed, by the secretary of war, Gen. Henry Knox, to that general, which show what importance was attached to the possession of Kekionga. Said the secretary: "While you are making use of such desultory operations as in your judgment the occasion may require, you

will proceed vigorously in every preparation in your power, for the purpose of the main expedition; and having assembled your force, and all things being in readiness, if no decisive indications of peace should have been produced, either by the messengers or by the desultory operations, you will commence your march for the Miami village, in order to establish a strong and permanent military post at that place. In your advance you will establish such posts of communication with Fort Washington, on the Ohio, as you may judge proper. The post at Miami village is intended for awing and curbing the Indians in that quarter, and as the only preventive of future hostilities. It ought, therefore, to be rendered secure against all attempts and insults of the Indians. The garrison which should be stationed there ought not only to be sufficient for the defense of the place, but always to afford a detachment of five or six hundred men, either to chastise any of the Wabash or other hostile Indians, or to secure any convoy of provisions. The establishment of said post is considered as an important object of the campaign, and is to take place in all events. In case of a previous treaty, the Indians are to be conciliated upon this point if possible; and it is presumed good arguments may be offered to induce their acquiescence. * * *
Having commenced your march upon the main expedition, and the Indians continuing hostile, you will use every possible exertion to make them feel the effects of your superiority; and, after having arrived at the Miami village, and put your works in a defensible state, you will seek the enemy with the whole of your remaining force, and endeavor by all means possible to strike them with great severity. * * *
In order to avoid future wars, it might be proper to make the Wabash, and thence over to the Maumee, and down the same to its mouth at Lake Erie, the boundary [between the people of the United States and the Indians], excepting so far as the same should relate to the Wyandots and Delawares, on the supposition of their continuing faithful to the treaties. But if they should join in the war against the United States, and your army be victorious, the said tribes ought to be removed without the boundary mentioned."

Following this Brig.-Gen. Scott, of Kentucky, marched with about 800 mounted men toward Ouiatenon, and destroyed the villages and cornfields, and in a fight with the Indians killed thirty and took fifty-one prisoners. On the 5th of July, Gen. James Wilkinson was sent in command of another expedition against the Wabash and Red river Indians, and destroyed a number of towns and cornfields. These campaigns were undertaken principally with the object of weakening the strength, and destroying the resources of the Indians on the Wabash, and thus giving material aid to Gen. St. Clair in the campaign he was preparing to enter upon against the Miamis at Kekionga, but they accomplished little in that direction and served to increase the hatred of the Miamis, who, filled with desire for revenge, instead of slackening their efforts, or ceasing to make war upon the Americans, began to call to their aid numerous warriors from the surrounding tribes of the Pottawatomies,

Kickapoos, Delawares, Ottawas, Wyandots, and other tribes of the northwest. While Gen. St. Clair was making preparations to establish a military post at the Miami village, Little Turtle, the Shawnee chief Blue Jacket, and the Delaware chief, Buck-ong-a-helas, were actively engaged in an effort to organize a confederacy of tribes sufficiently powerful to drive the white settlers from the territory — receiving aid and counsel from Simon Girty, Alexander McKee, Matthew Elliott (the latter two sub-agents in the British Indian department), and from a number of British, French and American traders who generally resided among the Indians, and supplied them with arms and ammunition in exchange for peltries.

This Girty was a noted character in all the frontier Indian wars. A renegade white man who allied himself with the Wyandots, and for many years was their leader in battle, as well as the planner of their campaigns, he exhibited a savageness of disposition, and a heartlessness in witnessing (if he did not direct), the torture by his savage allies of their white prisoners, which display almost unparalleled depravity, but by means of it, he no doubt obtained and held a supremacy of control over their minds. He was often at the Miami villages of the Maumee, and is said to have resided for some time at the town of Chillicothe, two miles east of Fort Wayne, at the bend of that river.

It was unfortunate for the success of the movements against the Indian tribes, that although in the treaty of 1783 with Great Britain it was declared in the seventh article of that document that the king would, " with all convenient speed, and without causing any destruction, or carrying away any negroes or property of the American inhabitants, withdraw all his forces, garrisons and fleets from the United States, and from every post, place and harbor within the same, yet, at the time of Harmar's, St. Clair's and Wayne's campaigns, he still held and garrisoned the posts of Niagara, Detroit and Michillimackinac. From these points, under the plea that that part of the treaty of 1783, relating to the collection and payment of all debts theretofore contracted with and due to the king's subjects, had not been faithfully complied with by the Americans, the English government continued, from time to time, to give aid and comfort to the Indians and others in open warfare upon the United States forces and the settlements along the Ohio, and at other points in the west. Accordingly, while Gen. St. Clair was preparing to march upon the Miami village, the British at Niagara, Detroit and Michillimackinac, were using what means they could to defeat the purposes of the United States; and an insight into their movements, at that time in league with the Indians, would doubtless have discouraged St. Clair in his effort to capture the Miami village, or to establish a military post at this point. But the effort was destined to be made; and after much delay and many impeding and perplexing circumstances, in the early part of September, 1791, the main body of the army, under General Butler, marched from the vicinity of Fort Washington, and, moving northward some twenty-five miles, on the eastern bank of the river Miami erected a post, which they called Fort Hamilton. On the 4th of October the army continued its march, and having advanced forty-two miles from Fort Hamilton, they erected Fort Jefferson, six miles south of Greenville, Ohio. The season was now far advanced, and the 24th of October had arrived before the army again moved for the Miami village.

Some of the militia deserted, heavy rains fell, provisions became short, a reconnoitering party was fired upon, two were killed and one supposed to have been taken prisoner, and St. Clair was sick, during the nine days' march which followed. On the 3d of November the main army reached the site of Fort Recovery, and encamped at the headwaters of the Wabash, in view of several small creeks, about fifty miles from the Miami village. The chill of winter now begun to be felt — snow had already fallen. Some Indians were seen but they fled as soon as observed.

The famous Shawnee chief Tecumseh had been placed in charge of a party of spies and scouts, with which he had hung upon the route of the army of St. Clair as it advanced toward Greenville, and reported the movements and strength of his forces to the head chiefs of the Indians. The advance and general movement of St. Clair thus became well known to the confederated tribes and their allies, and this information inspired them with the determination to draw the army into their power by wiles and stratagems, and, if possible, destroy it. Under the lead of the famous Little Turtle, and Buckongahelas, and Blue Jacket, the renegade Simon Girty and several other white men, they prepared to meet St. Clair with a force of 1,400 warriors.

This force was assembled for review on an extensive plain about five miles southwest of the village on the banks of the St. Mary's [part of the Richardville reserve]. A considerable altercation arose among the Indians on the review ground relative to a commander-in-chief. Some were in favor of Buckongahelas, while others favored Little Turtle. At length Buckongahelas settled the controversy by yielding the command to Little Turtle, saying that he was the younger and more active man and that he preferred him to himself. This reconciled the opposing factions and Little Turtle took command.

He divided his warriors into bands or messes, to each mess twenty men. It was the duty of four of this number alternately to hunt for provisions. At noon of each day the hunters were to return to the main army with what they had killed, and by this regulation his commissariat was well supplied during the seven days they were advancing to the field of battle.

Meanwhile, at the camp of St. Clair, a site afterward known as Fort Recovery, the commander desiring a place of safety for the knapsacks of the soldiers, had, on the evening of the arrival of the army, concluded "to throw up a slight work," and then after the arrival of the regiment still on the way, to move on and attack the enemy. But before the sun had risen on November 4, following that hour which is accounted the darkest just before day, the Indian whoop startled the army of St. Clair, just getting under arms. A furious attack burst from the darkness, upon the militia, which soon gave way, and came rushing into the camp, through Major Butler's battalion, creating the wildest disorder on every side, and closely pursued by the Indians. The fire of the front line checked the red men, but almost instantly a very heavy attack began upon that line; and in a few minutes it was extended to the second likewise. The greatest pressure was directed against the center of each, where was placed the artillery, from which the men were repeatedly driven with great slaughter. Perceiving but little effect from the fire of the artillery, a bayonet charge was ordered, led by Lieut.-Col. Darke, which drove the Indians back some distance, but they soon returned to the attack and the troops of Darke were, in turn, compelled to give way; while, at the same time, the enemy had pushed their way into camp by the left flank, and the troops there also were in disorder. Repeated charges were now made by Butler's and Clark's battalions, but with great loss; many officers fell, leaving the raw troops without direction — Major Butler himself being dangerously wounded. In the Second regiment every officer had fallen, except three, and one of these had been shot through the body.

The artillery being now silenced, half the army fallen and all the officers killed, except Captain Ford, who was very badly wounded, it became necessary to regain the trail from which the troops were now cut off, and to make a retreat if possible. For this purpose the remnant of the army was formed, as well as circumstances would admit, toward the right of the encampment, from which, by the way of the second line, another charge was made upon the enemy, as if with the design to turn the right flank, but in fact to gain the route. This was effected, and as soon as it was open, the militia took the lead, followed by the troops, Major Clarke with his battalion covering the rear. Everything was now in confusion. The panic had produced a complete rout. The camp and artillery were all abandoned — not a horse was left alive to remove the cannon; and the soldiers threw away their arms and accoutrements as they ran, strewing the path for miles with them. The retreat began about half-past nine o'clock and continued a distance of twenty-nine miles, to Fort Jefferson, where the survivors arrived soon after sunset, St. Clair having lost thirty-nine officers killed, and 593 men killed and missing; twenty-two officers and 242 men wounded. The loss in stores and other valuable property was estimated at $32,810.75.

The officers who fell in this memorable occasion were: Major General Richard Butler; Lieutenant Colonel Oldham, of the Kentucky militia; Majors Ferguson, Clarke, and Hart; Captains Bradford, Phelon, Kirkwood, Price, Van Swearingen, Tipton, Smith, Purdy, Piatt, Guthrie, Cribbs, and Newman; Lieutenants Spear, Warren, Boyd, McMath, Bead, Burgess, Kelso, Little, Hopper and Lickens; Ensigns Balch, Cobb, Chase, Turner, Wilson, Brooks, Beatty, and Purdy; Quartermasters Reynolds and Ward; Adjutant Anderson, and Dr. Grasson.

The officers wounded were: Lieutenant Colonels Gibson, Darke, and Sargent (adjutant general); Major Butler; Captains Doyle, Trueman, Ford, Buchanan, Darke and Hough; Lieutenants Greaton, Davidson, De Butts, Price, Morgan, McCroa, Lysle, and Thompson; Ensign Bines; Adjutants Whisler and Crawford, and the Viscount Malartie, volunteer aid-de-camp to the commander-in-chief.

In this engagement, Little Turtle displayed feelings of humanity toward his retreating foes, of which few examples have been recorded in the history of Indian warfare, and which reflect honor on his character. On beholding the soldiers fleeing before the exasperated Indians, and falling every moment under the merciless blows of the tomahawks, his heart revolted, and ascending an eminence he gave a peculiar cry, which commanded his forces to cease from further pursuit and return to their camps. He also sent out messengers to inform them, wherever they might be, that they must be satisfied with the carnage, having killed enough. But this humane effort was of little effect.

Many women had followed the army of St. Clair in its march toward the Miami village, preferring to be with their husbands rather than remain behind. Most of them were destroyed or captured, and after the flight of the remnant of the army, the Indians began to avenge their own real and imaginary wrongs by perpetrating the most horrible acts of cruelty and brutality upon the bodies of the living and dead Americans who fell into their hands. Believing the whites made war merely to acquire land, the Indians crammed clay and sand into the eyes and down the throats of the dying and the dead. The unfortunate women who fell behind in the panic-stricken retreat, were subjected to the most indecent cruelty which the ingenuity of their lustful and merciless captors could devise, and the bodies of some of them were found with stakes as large as a man's arm driven through them.

B. Van Cleve, who was in the quartermaster-general's department, of the army of St. Clair, gave the following narrative of the affair: "On the fourth [of November] at daybreak, I began to prepare for returning [to Fort Washington], and had got about half my luggage on my horse, when the firing commenced. We were encamped just within the lines, on the right. The attack was made on the Kentucky militia. Almost instantaneously, the small remnant of them that escaped broke through the line near us, and this line gave away. Followed by a tremendous fire from the enemy, they passed me. I threw my bridle over a stump, from which a tent pole had been cut, and followed a short distance, when finding the troops had halted, I returned and brought my horse a little further. I was now between the fires, and finding the troops giving away again, was obliged to leave him a second time. As I quitted him he was shot down, and I felt rather glad of it, as I concluded that now I should be at liberty to share in the engagement. My inexperience prompted me to calculate on our forces being far superior to any that the savages could assemble, and that we should soon have the pleasure of driving them. Not more than five minutes had yet elapsed, when a soldier near me had his arm swinging with a wound. I requested his arms and accoutrements, as he was unable to use them, promising to return them to him, and commenced firing. The smoke was settled down to within about three feet of the ground, but I generally put one knee to the ground and with a rest from behind a tree, waited the appearance of an Indian's head from behind his cover, or for one to run and change his position. Before I was convinced of my mistaken calculation, the battle was half over and I had become familiarized to the scene. Hearing the firing at one time unusually brisk near the rear of the left wing, I crossed the encampment. Two levy officers were just ordering a charge. I had fired away my ammunition and some of the bands of my musket had flown off. I picked up another, and a cartridge box nearly full, and pushed forward with about thirty others. The Indians ran to the right, where there was a small ravine filled with logs. I bent my course after them, and on looking round, found I was with only seven or eight men, the others having kept straight forward and halted about thirty yards off. We halted also, and being so near to where the savages lay concealed, the second fire from them left me standing alone. My cover was a small sugar tree or beech, scarcely large enough to hide me. I fired away all my ammunition; I am uncertain whether with any effect or not. I then looked for the party near me, and saw them retreating and half way back to the lines. I followed them, running my best, and was soon in. By this time our artillery had been taken, I do not know whether the first or second time, and our troops had just retaken it, and were charging the enemy across the creek in front; and some person told me to look at an Indian running with one of our kegs of powder, but I did not see him. There were about thirty of our men and officers lying scalped around the pieces of artillery. It appeared that the Indians had not been in a hurry, for their hair was all skinned off.

"Daniel Bonham, a young man raised by my uncle and brought up with me, and whom I regarded as a brother, had by this time received a shot through his hips and was unable to walk. I procured a horse and got him on. My uncle had received a ball near his wrist that lodged near his elbow. The ground was literally covered with dead and dying men. Happening to see my uncle, he told me a retreat was ordered, and that I must do the best I could and take care of myself. Bonham insisted that he had a better chance of escaping than I had, and urged me to look to my own safety alone. I found the troops pressing like a drove of bullocks to the right. I saw an officer whom I took to be Lieut. Morgan, an aid to Gen. Butler, with six or eight men, start on a run a little to the left of where I was. I immediately ran and fell in with them. In a short distance we were so suddenly among the Indians, who were not apprised of our object, that they opened to us and ran to the right and left without firing. I think about 200 of our men passed through them before they fired, except a chance shot. When we had proceeded about two miles most of those mounted had passed me. A boy had been thrown or fell off a horse and begged my assistance. I ran, pulling him along about two miles further, until I had become nearly exhausted. Of the last two horses in the rear, one carried two men and the other three. I made an exertion and threw him on behind the two men. The Indians followed us but about half a mile further. The boy was thrown off some time afterwards, but escaped and got in safely. My friend Bonham I did not see on the retreat, but understood he was thrown off about this place, and lay on the left of the trace, where he was found in the winter and was buried. I took the cramp violently in my thighs and could scarcely walk, until I got within a hundred yards of the rear, where the Indians were tomahawking the old and wounded men; and I stopped here to tie my pocket handkerchief around a man's wounded knee. I saw the Indians close in pursuit at this time, and for a moment my spirits sunk and I felt in despair for my safety. I considered whether I should leave the road, or whether I was capable of any further exertion. If I left the road the Indians were in plain sight and could easily overtake me. I threw the shoes off my feet and the coolness of the ground seemed to revive me. I again began a trot, and recollect that, when a bend in the road offered, and I got before half a dozen persons, I thought it would occupy some time for the enemy to massacre them before my turn would come. By the time I had got to Stillwater, about eleven miles, I had gained the center of the flying troops, and, like them, came to a walk. I fell in with Lieut. Shaumburg, who, I think, was the only officer of artillery that got away unhurt, with Corp. Mott, and a woman who was called red-headed Nance. The latter two were both crying. Mott was lamenting the loss of his wife, and Nance that of an infant child. Shaumburg was nearly exhausted, and hung on Mott's arm. I carried his fusee and accoutrements and led Nance; and in this sociable way we arrived at Fort Jefferson a little after sunset.

"The commander-in-chief had ordered Col. Darke to press forward to the convoys of provisions, and hurry them on to the army. Major Truman, Captain Sedan and my uncle were setting forward with him. A number of soldiers, and packhorsemen on foot, and myself among them, joined them. We came on a few miles, when all, overcome with fatigue, agreed to a halt. Darius Curtus Orcutt, a packhorse master, had stolen at Jefferson, one pocket full of flour and the other full of beef. One of the men had a kettle, and one Jacob Fowler and myself groped about in the dark until we found some water where a tree had been blown out of root. We made a kettle of soup, of which I got a small portion among the many. It was then concluded, as there was a bend in the road a few miles further on, that the Indians might undertake to intercept us there, and we decamped and traveled about four or five miles further. I had got a rifle and ammunition at Jefferson from a wounded militiaman, an old acquaintance, to bring in. A sentinel was set, and we laid down and slept until the governor came up a few hours afterward. I think I never slept so profoundly. I could hardly get awake after I was on my feet. On the day before the defeat, the ground was covered with snow. The flats were now filled with water frozen over, the ice as thick as a knife-blade. I was worn out with fatigue, with my feet knocked to pieces against the roots in the night, and splashing through the ice without shoes. In the morning we got to a camp of packhorsemen, and amongst them I got a doughboy or water-dumpling, and proceeded. We got within seven miles of Hamilton on this day, and arrived there soon on the morning of the sixth."

On the 26th of December following, notwithstanding the ill-fortune which seemed to follow all movements against the Miamis, Gen. Knox, secretary of war, again urged the establishment of a strong military post at the head of the Maumee. In 1792, Rev. Samuel Kirkland was sent on a mission to the western Indians, one point of his journey to be the Miami village, to urge the Indians to make peace, and to learn what number was engaged against St. Clair, but he accomplished little by his mission. The 12th of May of the same year, Capt. Truman was sent from the Ohio river to the Maumee, on a similar errand, but was killed by an Indian on his way.

CAMPAIGN OF ANTHONY WAYNE.

George Washington, as early as 1750, had become as deeply interested in the great west as any enthusiast of the past few decades. His brothers were officers of the Ohio company, organized in 1749, and Washington, surveying in the Shenandoah valley, and dreaming of the future, obtained such broadened views of the destiny of the colonies, that the grand idea of a vast nation which should bind together all these regions, possessed his mind. He held fast to the conception of western development, even during the darkest hours of the revolution, and when some one coming to him with a rumor that Russia had made an alliance with England to crush the colonies, asked the heroic leader if that were true, what was to be done, Washington replied: "We will retire to the valley of the Ohio, and there be free." After the war he made a trip over the Alleghanies, and returned with a stronger national inspiration than ever, so that he wrote to La Fayette: "The honor, power and true interests of this country must be measured on a continental scale." Subsequently he made another western trip of seven hundred miles on horseback through the Indian country, and it was after that excursion that he wrote the letter to Benjamin Harrison, governor of Virginia, and great-grandfather of the president of the United States, which has been mentioned on a previous page.

Washington wished to encourage settlements in the Ohio region and beyond, and had a strong antipathy for the land-jobbers, speculators and monopolizers, a "parcel of banditti" he called them, who might "skim the cream of the country at the expense of the suffering officers and soldiers who fought and bled to obtain it." Throughout all the efforts to subdue and colonize the west, the majestic will of Washington was the ruling force. Strange as it may appear to a citizen of the commonwealth of Indiana, in the closing decade of the nineteenth century, his policy of opening the western lands was one of the pretexts for abuse and invective which has not been surpassed in the politics of later days. A strong party which opposed him would have preferred the military force of the government, if any were used, to be directed southward to open the Mississippi. The nation, in the year 1889, knows Washington better than he was ever known, even by his contemporaries. But among all that has been said and written of the father of his country, nothing causes a more inspiring realization of his profound wisdom and marvelous political insight than the words he addressed to those who advocated the policy of southern aggression. "The problem of the Mississippi will settle itself," he said, "if we simply let it alone and think only of multiplying communications between the west and the Atlantic." Less than a century later, the west, to which Washington threw his influence, was strong enough to again settle "the problem of the Mississippi," and establish the foundation principles of the northwest territory from the lakes to the gulf.

As has been indicated, the issue of the campaign of St. Clair had political bearings as well as military. If it failed the enemies of Washington could declaim with greater reason against the "waste" of money upon the "wild west." Furthermore, it was emphatically a campaign by Washington, in all but personal leadership. He had thrown himself heart and soul into the preparation for the campaign, and planned the movement to Kekionga with a knowledge of details made possible by his experience as an Indian fighter.

The courier reached the president's house at Philadelphia, on a December day, and Washington was called from the side of his wife at a reception to receive the news of a tragedy rivalling that of the defeat of Braddock at Fort DuQuesne. He read the dispatch, and quietly returned to the reception and calmly and courteously met every guest until all at a late hour had departed. Then in grim silence he walked up and down the room, his secretary alone being with him. Suddenly he broke the silence with a thunderous outburst: "It's all over; St. Clair defeated, routed, the officers nearly all killed, the men by wholesale; the rout complete; shocking to think of, and a surprise into the bargain. Here at the very spot I took leave of him, I wished him success and honor. You have your instructions, I said to him, from the secretary of war. I had a strict eye to them, and will add but one word: beware of a surprise. I repeat it, beware of a surprise. You know how the Indian fights us. He went off with that as my last solemn warning thrown into his ears. And yet, to suffer that army to be cut to pieces, hacked, butchered, tomahawked, by a surprise, the very thing I guarded him against. O God! O God! he is worse than a murderer. How can he answer to his country? The blood of the slain is upon him, the curse of widows and orphans, the curse of heaven." He walked long in silence, and then said, "This must not go beyond this room." Then again, "Gen. St. Clair shall have justice. I will hear him without prejudice. He shall have full justice."

Mankind knows Washington better, and loves him more, because the revelation alike of his passionate, warmly human nature, and the supreme self-control that inspired the closing declaration, did get " beyond that room." St. Clair received just and considerate treatment, and the president at once set about the formation of an army to renew the advance toward Kekionga. The army of the republic was re-organized on the basis of five thousand soldiers, and was styled the Legion of the United States. As major-general commanding this army, Washington considered Gen. Lee; but there were objections, and he selected Gen. Anthony Wayne, although there were grumblings thereat in Virginia. Wayne had won the admiration of the people by his daring and desperate valor and uniform success in the revolution. Whenever recklessness led him into danger, genius enabled him to alight on his feet where others would have been irretrievably ruined. He was selected because a rapid campaign was contemplated, but even the energy of both he and his chief could not hasten the march of events. Wayne was given two brigadiers, James Wilkinson and Thomas Posey, who had served honorably in the war of the revolution. Pittsburg was appointed as the rendezvous of the forces, and here Gen. Wayne arrived in June, 1792, to find a perplexing task before him. Many of the officers experienced in Indian warfare had fallen in the disastrous campaigns of Harmar and St. Clair, others had resigned, and nearly all the forces were without any knowledge of tactics and innocent of the meaning and importance of discipline. He began a daily drill of these raw levies to prepare for the impending campaign.

But some time was destined to elapse before his movement was effectively under way against the stronghold on the Maumee. The opposition to western development compelled the government to exhaust every peaceful resource before waging another costly war, while a strong party was opposed to any efforts tending toward conciliation, especially with the British who had been for five years inspiring the northwestern Indians to bloodshed, as well as committing depredations themselves at sea. The embassies that were sent out to treat with the Indians protested against any movements on the part of Gen. Wayne, on the ground that they tended to embarrass their diplomatic efforts, while Gen. Wayne no doubt felt the settlement of the trouble lay altogether in his hands. Furthermore, before he was ready to advance in force, the effect of European complications was felt, and it happened that the war which the republic of France waged against combined Europe delayed the establishment of Fort Wayne for many months. The government at Washington was embarrassed by the extraordinary conduct of Genet, minister of France, who, among other schemes, sent four agents to Kentucky to raise an army to invade Louisiana, then under Spanish dominion; and even the brave and discreet Gen. George Rogers Clark accepted a commission from the agents of Genet as "major-general of the armies of France." The enlistment of the army for the gigantic fillibustering scheme of clearing the Mississippi of Spanish forts was actively under way in Kentucky. Not only there, but throughout the union, a large and active party, in fact nearly all "popular sentiment," was in favor of an open alliance with the French, and an attack on Louisiana. This would have involved another immediate war with Great Britain on the part of a young, experimental government, with a bankrupt treasury; and all the actions of the English appeared to indicate that such a conflict was courted. Against this seemingly popular movement, though he was incensed at the British, and none more desired to chastise them, Washington stood firm as a rock, unmoved by a storm of abuse and misrepresentation and caricature. Throughout this most critical period his wonderful self-control was often nigh to exhaustion, but he finally triumphed. He maintained the national idea, that America must not allow her destinies to be associated with those of any other land, nor go to war as a subordinate of a foreign power, but should hold herself aloof as the equal of any nation, looking first of all to her own interests and self-development.

The negotiations for peace with the Indians made subsequently to St. Clair's defeat should be briefly noticed, as they throw much light upon the reason why Wayne was compelled to advance to the place which now bears his name. While Gen. Wayne was making his army ready, the government from early in 1792 until August, 1793, was constantly employing messengers with speeches, commissioners to make treaties, and spies with secret instructions. The Indians were assured that the United States made no claim to any land not already ceded by treaties. Major Hamtramck, stationed at Vincennes, concluded treaties of peace with some of the Weas and Eel river Indians, and subsequently Gen. Rufus Putnam at the same place made a treaty with some of the Wabash and Illinois tribes, on the basis that the land they occupied was theirs, and that the United States should not attempt to take it without purchase. But these were exceptions, and the proud Miamis and their allies still stood aloof. To them, Gen. Wilkinson sent two messengers, Freeman and Gerrard, April 7, 1792. They were captured by a party of Indians, who, on learning that they were embassadors, started with them for the Maumee. But the messengers were too inquisitive about the country and the strength of the savages, and their escort, concluding that the pale-faces were spies, killed them when within one day's march of the Indian camp. Undeterred by their fate, Maj. Alexander Truman, of the First regiment, and Col. John Hardin, of Kentucky, started on the same mission of peace from Fort Washington in May. They carried an eloquent letter, inviting the Indians to send a deputation to Philadelphia to talk with the president, and assuring them that they would not be despoiled of their lands. The embassadors were never seen again; but William May — who was with Freeman's party, and had deserted it according to orders, so that he might safely work his way back to the army with news, was captured afterward and sold to traders at the rapids — saw and recognized the scalps of the unfortunate peacemakers.

The last effort for peace was made by Benjamin Lincoln, Beverly Randolph and Timothy Pickering, who were appointed commissioners, and given private instructions which bound them to insist that the United States would give up none of the territory between Lake Erie and the Ohio, which had been ceded at the treaty of Fort Harmar, in 1789, but that if it clearly appeared that the Miamis and other tribes had a right to any of that land, and had not taken part in the treaty, they should be reimbursed for their interest in the territory. They were met at Niagara by Capt. Brant and other Indians representing, they said, the Five Nations, Wyandots, Shawnees, Delawares, Muncies, Miamis, Chippewas, Ottawas, Pottawatomies, Mingoes, Cherokees and Nantokokis, assembled on the Maumee. The commissioners were cheered by the talk of these diplomates and sent back a petition to Secretary Knox, to restrain the activity of Gen. Wayne until they could have an opportunity to again meet the red embassadors with their white belts and wampum. They proceeded to the Detroit river, where they were met by Buckongahelas and others who, adopting the plan of letter writing, had a paper ready, in which the United States was offered this ultimatum — the Ohio must be the boundary line, and all the whites must be removed beyond it. The commissioners objected that large numbers of whites had settled in this territory and the United States had given them lands which they could not now be dispossessed of without injustice. To this, the Indians, after returning to the council, where were the British agents, ingeniously rejoined that the large amount of money proposed to be paid them for their land had better be divided among these settlers, to extinguish their claims. They emphatically declared that the English had no right to convey any of the northwest to the United States, and that they refused to recognize the exclusive right of America to purchase their lands. The position of the Indians was in fact that they had a right to dispose of their lands to the English or any other nation they chose. This issue was an important one, in the then critical condition of the government, menaced by French intrigue, and with the British holding posts in the territory and thereby practically supporting the Indian policy. The commissioners could not settle it, and retired. It remained for Anthony Wayne to decide by his famous campaign against Kekionga, the question of the ownership of the northwest territory, now the seat of magnificent commonwealths which, as the most energetic members of an indissoluble Union, exert a dominant influence over the affairs of the western hemisphere.

During the period of negotiation the savages had continued to skirmish along the frontier, committing many atrocities, while the little forts which were established a short distance from Cincinnati, toward Kekionga, were held by a few patient soldiers, shirtless, shoeless and with several months' pay overdue. Major-General Wayne was near Fort Washington in October, 1793, and on the 7th marched for 'Fort

Jefferson with 2,600 regulars and about 400 auxiliaries. With unerring sagacity he wrote to Washington that the great tranquility just then prevailing proved to him that the Indians were massing for a battle, and in his plans he indicated a policy of taking advantage of the inability of the Indians to remain long massed without exhausting their provisions. Advancing to a point between Fort Jefferson and the field of St. Clair's battle, Gen. Wayne built a fort which he named Greenville for his friend Gen. Greene, and halted for the winter, sending home the militia. Two days before Christmas he sent Major Henry Burbeck with eight companies of infantry and a detachment of artillery, to take possession of the fatal field of 1791, and there on the site of St. Clair's rout, was erected Fort Recovery, aptly named. This midwinter approach appears to have startled the Indians for the time, and they sent a message expressing a desire to make peace, which was evidently intended to secure delay. But the activity of the French party gave the Indians enough time to collect their bands.

During this winter and the early spring the great intrigue reached a climax, and Wayne was required in April to send a detachment to make a fortification below the mouth of the Tennessee river, to overawe the proposed Louisiana army. It was just a little earlier that Lord Dorchester, governor general of Canada, told a number of Indian chiefs that "he would not be surprised if Great Britain and the United States would be at war in the course of a year." As if in earnest of this declaration, Lieutenant-Governor Simcoe was ordered to establish a British post at the foot of the Maumee rapids, within the territory ceded by England to the United States. Not only the British, but the Spanish, were preparing to take advantage of a war alliance between the United States and France; the governor of Louisiana invaded the American territory, and during this critical spring of 1794, a messenger from the Spaniards came up to the Maumee to assure the Indians of the co-operation of the occupants of the great river. It was not remarkable that under these circumstances, in the midst of these endless and mysterious intrigues which involved the fate of nations on both sides of the Atlantic, that the Indians boldly demanded that the northwest territory should be abandoned, or that the advance of Gen. Wayne was marked by extreme caution. Another defeat like that of St. Clair would have been "inexpressibly ruinous," as Washington himself declared, and would have involved the welfare of the young republic.

Wayne still remaining quiet, on the 30th of June, 1794, the Indians took the offensive at Fort Recovery. In the morning of that day, under the walls of the fort, Major McMahon, with an escort of ninety riflemen and fifty dragoons, was fiercely assailed by a body of some 1,500 Indians. Assisted by a number of British agents and a few French Canadian volunteers, the Indians, during a period of about twenty-four hours, made several sallies upon the fort, but finding their efforts unavailable, retired. The loss to the garrison, however, was by no means trifling — twenty-two men being killed and thirty wounded, and three were missing; 221

horses were killed, wounded and missing. The Indians carried away their dead during the night, by the light of torches, so that only eight or ten of their warriors were found dead near the fort. Major McMahon, Capt. Hartshorne, Lieut. Craig and Cornet Torry, fell on this occasion.

Major-Gen. Scott with some 1,600 mounted volunteers arrived at Fort Greenville on the 26th of July, and now it was time to move. Wayne had waited patiently. Now he struck with rapidity considering that his way lay through unbroken primeval forests. On the 28th the army began its march upon the Indian villages along the Maumee. Some twenty-four miles to the north of Fort Recovery, Wayne built and garrisoned a small post which he called Fort Adams. From this, on the 4th of August, the army moved toward the confluence of the Auglaize and Maumee rivers, where it arrived on the 8th of August. Here a strong stockade fort, with four blockhouses for bastions, was erected and called Fort Defiance. On the 14th of August, Gen. Wayne wrote to the secretary of war: "I have the honor to inform you that the army under my command took possession of this very important post on the morning of the 8th inst.; the enemy on the preceding evening having abandoned all their settlements, towns and villages, with such apparent marks of surprise and precipitation, as to amount to a positive proof that our approach was not discerned by them until the arrival of a Mr. Newman, of the quartermaster-general's department, who deserted from the army near the St. Mary's. * * * I had made such demonstrations, for a length of time previously to taking up our line of march, as to induce the savages to expect our advance by the route of the Miami villages, to the left, or toward Roche de Boeuf by the right, which feints appear to have produced the desired effect, by drawing the attention of the enemy to those points, and gave an opening for the army to approach undiscovered by a devious, i. e., in a central direction. Thus, sir, we have gained possession of the grand emporium of the hostile Indians of the west, without loss of blood. * * * Everything is now prepared for a forward move to-morrow morning toward Roche de Boeuf, or foot of the rapids. * * * Yet I have thought proper to offer the enemy a last overture of peace; and as they have everything that is dear and interesting now at stake, I have reason to expect that they will listen to the proposition mentioned in the enclosed copy of an address dispatched yesterday by a special flag [Christopher Miller], who I sent under circumstances that will insure his safe return, and which may eventually spare the effusion of much human blood. But should war be their choice, that blood be upon their own heads. America shall no longer be insulted with impunity. To an all-powerful and just God I therefore commit myself and gallant army."

In his address to the Indians, as dispatched by Miller "to the Delawares, Shawnees, Miamis, and Wyandots, and to each and every of them: and to all other nations of Indians northwest of the Ohio, whom it may concern," General Wayne said: "Brothers — Be no longer deceived or led astray by the false promises and language of the bad white men at the foot of the rapids; they have neither the power nor inclination to protect you. No longer shut your eyes to your true interest and happiness, nor your ears to this last overture of peace. But, in pity to your innocent women and children, come and prevent the further effusion of your blood. Let them experience the kindness and friendship of the United States of America, and the invaluable blessings of peace and tranquility." He urged them also — " each and every hostile tribe of Indians to appoint deputies" to assemble without delay " in order to settle the preliminaries of a lasting peace." The answer brought by Miller upon his return, on the 16th, was, " that if he (Gen. Wayne) waited where he was ten days, and then sent Miller to them, they would treat with him; but that if he advanced, they would give him battle."

Many of the Indians felt no little distrust as to their ability to defeat the great chief of the Americans who was making so masterful an advance with sleepless vigilance. A man afterward known as Captain Wells, who, at the age of twelve years, had been captured in Kentucky and adopted by the Miamis, and who had lived to manhood and raised a family among them, began to feel a strange conflict in his mind. He had fought by the side of Little Turtle against both Harmar and St. Clair; and it was said of him, that afterward, in times of calm reflection, with dim memories still of his childhood home, of brothers and playmates, he seemed to have been harrowed by the thought that amongst the slain by his own hand, may have been his kindred. He had resolved to break his attachment to the tribe, even to his wife and children. In this state of mind, with much of the Indian characteristics, he invited Little Turtle to accompany him to the " Big Elm," about two miles east of Fort Wayne. Wells there told the chief his purpose. " I now leave your nation," said he, " for my own people. We have long been friends. We are friends yet until the sun reaches that height," indicating an hour. " From that time we are enemies. Then if you wish to kill me, you may. If I want to kill you I may." At the time indicated Wells crossed the river, and was lost to the view of his old friend and chieftain, Little Turtle. Moving in an easterly course to strike the trail of Wayne's forces, he was successful in obtaining an interview with the general, and thereafter proved the fast friend of the Americans. This movement of Wells was a severe blow to the Miamis. To Turtle's mind it seemed to be an unmistakable foreboding of speedy defeat to the confederated tribes of the northwest.

On the 15th of August, Gen. Wayne moved toward the foot of the rapids, and came to a halt a few miles above that point, on the 18th, and the next day began the erection of a temporary post for the reception of stores and baggage, and began to reconnoiter the enemy's encampment, which lay "behind a thick, bushy wood and the British fort." This was Fort Miami, situated at the foot of the rapids on the northwestern bank of the Maumee, near the site of Maumee City.

The post established by Wayne was named Fort Deposit. The Miamis were now undecided as to policy notwithstanding the fact that they had succeeded in defeating the former expeditions of Harmar and St. Clair. At a general council of the confederated tribes, held on the 19th of August, Little Turtle was most earnest in his endeavors to persuade the Indians to make peace with Gen. Wayne. Said he, "We have beaten the enemy twice under different commanders. We cannot expect the same good fortune to attend us always. The Americans are now led by a chief who never sleeps. The nights and the days are alike to him, and during all the time that he has been marching on our villages, notwithstanding the watchfulness of our young men, we have never been able to surprise him. Think well of it. There is something whispers me, it would be prudent to listen to his offers of peace." But his words were little regarded. One of the chiefs of the council even went so far as to charge him with cowardice, which he readily enough spurned, for there were none braver or more ready to act where victory was to be won or a defense required, than Little Turtle. The council broke up, and Little Turtle, at the head of his braves, took his stand to give battle to the advancing army. The best account of the engagement is that given by Wayne in his report to Secretary Knox:

"At eight o'clock on the morning of the 20th the army again advanced in columns agreeably to the standing order of march; the legion on the right, its flank covered by the Maumee: one brigade of mounted volunteers on the left, under Brigadier-General Todd, and the other in the rear, under Brigadier-General Barbee. A select battalion of mounted volunteers moved in front of the legion, commanded by Major Price, who was directed to keep sufficiently advanced so as to give timely notice for the troops to form in case of action, it being yet undetermined whether the Indians would decide for peace or war.

"After advancing about five miles, Major Price's corps received so severe a fire from the enemy, who were secreted in the woods and high grass, as to compel them to retreat. The legion was immediately formed in two lines, principally in a close, thick wood, which extended for miles on our left and for a very considerable distance in front, the ground being covered with old fallen timber, probably occasioned by a tornado, which rendered it impracticable for the cavalry to act with effect, and afforded the enemy the most favorable covert for their savage mode of warfare. They were formed in three lines, within supporting distance of each other, and extending for near two miles, at right angles with the river. I soon discovered, from the weight of the fire and extent of their lines, that the enemy were in full force in front, in possession of their favorite ground, and endeavoring to turn our left flank. I therefore gave orders for the second line to advance and support the first; and directed Major-General Scott to gain and turn the right flank of the savages, with the whole of the mounted volunteers, by a circuitous route; at the same time I ordered the front line to advance and charge with trailed arms, and rouse the Indians from their coverts at the point of the bayonet, and when up, to deliver a close and well-directed fire on their backs, followed by a brisk charge, so as not to give them time to load again.

"I also ordered Capt. Mis Campbell, who commanded the legionary cavalry, to turn the left flank of the enemy next the river, and which afforded a favorable field for that corps to act in. All these orders were obeyed with spirit and promptitude; but such was the impetuosity of the charge by the first line of infantry, that the Indians and Canadian militia and volunteers were driven from all their coverts in so short a time that, although every possible exertion was used by the officers of the second line of the legion, and by Generals Scott, Todd, and Barbee, of the mounted volunteers, to gain their proper positions, but part of each could get up in season to participate in the action; the enemy being driven, in the course of one hour, more than two miles through the thick woods already mentioned by less than one-half their numbers. From every account, the enemy amounted to 2,000 combatants.* The troops actually engaged against them were short of 900. This horde of savages, with their allies, abandoned themselves to flight, and dispersed with terror and dismay, leaving our victorious army in full and quiet possession of the field of battle, which terminated under the influence of the guns of the British garrison."

Both the foresight and the valor of Little Turtle were now no longer to be questioned. At the council, on the night before the attack, he saw the end of all their efforts against the army of Wayne; and the Indians soon began to realize that their stronghold was lost.

Though it is not positively known whether Tecumseh was at the council or not, yet it is recorded in the narrative by Anthony Shane, that he led a party of Shawnees in the attack upon the army of Gen. Wayne. It was in this engagement that he first encountered the "white chief," William Henry Harrison, with whom, a few years later, he had so much to do. Says the account of Shane: "He occupied an advanced position in the battle, and while attempting to load his rifle, he put in a bullet before the powder, and was thus unable to use his gun. Being at this moment pressed in front by some infantry, he fell back with his party, till they met another detachment of Indians. Tecumseh urged them to stand fast and fight, saying if any one would lend him a gun, he would show them how to use it. A fowling-piece was handed to him, with which he fought for some time, till the Indians were again compelled to give ground. While falling back, he met another party of Shawnees; and, although the whites were pressing on them, he rallied the Indians, and induced them to make a stand in the thicket. When the infantry pressed close upon them, and had discharged their muskets into the bushes, Tecumseh and his party returned the fire, and then retreated

---

* There were about 450 Delawares, 175 Miamis, 275 Shawnees, 225 Ottawas, 275 Wyandots, and a small number of Senecas, Pottawatomies, and Chippewas. The number of white men who fought in defense of the Indians in this engagement, was about seventy, including a corps of volunteers from Detroit, under the command of Captain Caldwell.

till they had joined the main body of the Indians below the rapids of the Maumee."

To quote Wayne's report, "the bravery and conduct of every officer belonging to the army, from the generals down to the ensign, merit my highest approbation. There were, however, some whose rank and situation placed their conduct in a very conspicuous point of view, and which I observed with pleasure and the most lively gratitude. Among whom I must beg leave to mention Brig.-Gen. Wilkinson and Col. Hamtramck, the commandants of the right and left wings of the legion, whose brave example inspired the troops. To those I must add the names of my faithful and gallant aids-de-camp, Captains De Butt and T. Lewis, and Lieut. Harrison, who, with the adjutant-general, Major Mills, rendered the most essential service by communicating my orders in every direction, and by their conduct and bravery exciting the troops to press for victory.. Lieut. Covington, upon whom the command of the cavalry now devolved, cut down two savages with his own hand, and Lieut. Webb one, in turning the enemy's left flank. The wounds received by Captains Slough and Prior, and Lieutenants Campbell, Smith [an extra aid-de-camp to Gen. Wilkinson], of the legionary infantry, and Capt. Van Rensselear of the dragoons, Capt. Rawlins, Lieut. McKenny and Ensign Duncan of the mounted volunteers, bear honorable testimony of their bravery and conduct.

"Captains H. Lewis and Brock, with their companies of light infantry, had to sustain an unequal fire for some time, which they supported with fortitude. In fact, every officer and soldier who had an opportunity to come into action displayed that true bravery which will always ensure success. And here permit me to declare, that I never discovered more true spirit and anxiety for action, than appeared to pervade the whole of the mounted volunteers; and I am well persuaded that, had the enemy maintained their favorite ground for one-half hour longer, they would have most severely felt the prowess of that corps. But, while I pay this tribute to the living, I must not neglect the gallant dead, among whom we have to lament the early death of those worthy and brave officers, Capt. Mis Campbell, of the dragoons, and Lieut. Towles, of the light infantry of the legion, who fell in the first charge."

Of the killed and wounded in this engagement, according to the report of Gen. Wayne, the regular troops lost twenty-six killed, and eighty-seven wounded. Of the Kentucky volunteers, seven were killed and thirteen were wounded; and nine regulars and two volunteers died of their wounds before the 28th of the month. "The loss of the enemy was more than double that of the Federal army," and "the woods were strewn for a considerable distance with the dead bodies of Indians."

The army remained three days and nights on the banks of the Maumee, on the field of battle, during which time all the houses and cornfields were consumed and destroyed for a considerable distance both above and below Fort Miami, as well as within pistol shot of the garrison, who were compelled to remain quiet spectators of this general devastation and conflagration, which was Wayne's method of teaching the Indians that the British were powerless. Among the property destroyed were the houses and stores of Col. McKee, the British Indian agent, and principal stimulator of the war.

On the 27th, the army started upon its return march for Fort Defiance, laying waste, as it moved, villages and cornfields for a distance of some fifty miles along the Maumee. While the American forces occupied position within range of the British fort at the rapids, from the afternoon of the 20th to the forenoon of the 23d, five letters passed between Gen. Wayne and Major Campbell, who commanded Fort Miami with 460 men and 12 cannon; the first coming from the British commander, enquiring the cause of the army of the United States approaching so near his majesty's fort, asserting that he knew "of no war existing between Great Britain and America." To this Gen. Wayne replied: "Without questioning the authority or the propriety, sir, of your interrogatory, I think I may, without breach of decorum, observe to you, that, were you entitled to an answer, the most full and satisfactory one was announced to you from the muzzles of my small arms, yesterday morning, in the action against the horde of savages in the vicinity of your post, which terminated gloriously to the American arms; but, had it continued until the Indians, etc., were driven under the influence of the post and guns you mention, they would not have much impeded the progress of the victorious army under my command, as no such post was established at the commencement of the present war between the Indians and the United States." To which in turn, the British commander rejoined that the insults that had been offered the British, would, if repeated, compel him to have recourse to measures which the nations might regret. Wayne in reply reminded Campbell that he was committing a hostile act in occupying a fort within the limits of the United States, and ordered him to retire peacefully within the limits of the British lines. To which the British commandant replied that he certainly would not abandon the post at the summons of any power whatever, until he received orders to that effect from those he had the honor to serve under, or the fortunes of war should oblige him so to act, and again warned Wayne to beware of the cannon.

Reaching Fort Defiance again, the army soon began improving the works, and here remained till the morning of the 14th of September, 1794, when the legion began its march for Kekionga, whither it arrived at 5 o'clock p. m., September 17, and on the following day the troops fortified their camps, while "the commander-in-chief reconnoitered the ground and determined on the spot to build a garrison." Work began on the fort September 24th and on the 17th of October Wayne forwarded a description of the works to the war department.

On the morning of the 22d of October, 1794, the fort was in readiness, and Lieut.-Col. Hamtramck assumed command of the post, with the following sub-legions: Capt. Kingsbury's 1st; Capt. Greaton's 2d; Captains Spark's and Reed's 3d; Capt. Preston's 4th; and Capt. Porter's of artillery; and after firing fifteen rounds of cannon, Col. Hamtramck christened the post — Fort Wayne. Not less important than the shot that "echoed round the world" was the glad outburst of cannon, saluting the stars and stripes as it floated over this stockade fort in the heart of a boundless and lonely forest region. It signalled the birth of the imperial great west.

On the 28th of October, Gen. Wayne, with the main body of the regulars, took up his line of march for Fort Greenville, arriving there on the 2d of November. As the tidings of the victory of Wayne flew from town to town in the east, from settlement to settlement in the west, they awakened a thrill of inexpressible joy, that told how much more had been accomplished than the most sanguine had dared to expect. Congress, by resolution, complimented Wayne and his army. The heart of Washington was cheered as it had not been since he assumed the presidency. His administration was lifted beyond reproach; the continental policy he had so patiently fought for was forever established, the voice of faction which had embittered his life was hushed. The young republic suddenly acquired a strength and vigor of policy which Washington and Hamilton had striven almost in vain to impart. The Indians of the south at once hushed their warlike demonstrations. Ninety days after the battle of the Maumee, Minister Jay was able to conclude a satisfactory treaty with Lord Grenville. This was effected on the 19th of November; and one of its main stipulations was that of a withdrawal, "on or before the first day of June, 1796, of all troops and garrisons, from all posts and places within the boundary lines assigned to the United States by the treaty of peace of 1783."

After the battle of the Maumee, Wayne had continued to invite the Indians to a friendly meeting, but they for some time seemed to be depending upon support from the British. While Wayne was inviting them to meet him at Greenville to conclude a treaty, Lieut.-Gen. Simcoe, Col. McKee, and other officers of the British Indian department, persuaded Little Turtle, Blue Jacket, Buckongahelas and other distinguished chiefs, to agree to hold an Indian council at the mouth of Detroit river.

But when the news of Jay's treaty reached the Indians, they felt their last hope of aid from the English fading away, and began seriously to think of peace. During the months of December and January, 1794–5, small parties of Miamis, Ottawas, Chippewas, Pottawatomies, Sacs, Delawares and Shawnees visited Gen. Wayne at his headquarters at Greenville, signing preliminary articles of peace, and agreeing to meet Wayne at Greenville on or about the 15th of June, 1795, with all the sachems and war-chiefs of their nations, to arrange a final treaty of peace and amity.

During the period that elapsed between the departure of Wayne for Fort Greenville until the 17th of May, 1796, Col. Hamtramck remained in command at Fort Wayne; and nothing of a very important nature occurred during that time, the garrison being principally occupied in receiving parties from the various tribes, issuing rations to them, and otherwise endeavoring to bring about friendly relations with the disheartened savages, who had grown weary of a losing cause.

True to their promise, in the early part of June, 1795, deputations from the different tribes began to arrive at Greenville. The treaty, which was one of much interest throughout, lasted from the 16th of June to the 10th of August, many of the principal chiefs making strong speeches, and each nation openly and separately assenting to the articles and stipulations of the treaty. At the conclusion of his speech to the deputies on the 10th of August, at the termination of the treaty, Gen. Wayne addressed the assemblage as follows: "I now fervently pray to the Great Spirit, that the peace now established may be permanent, and that it may hold us together in the bonds of friendship, until time shall be no more. I also pray that the Great Spirit above may enlighten your minds, and open your eyes to your true happiness, that your children may learn to cultivate the earth, and enjoy the fruits of peace and industry. As it is probable, my children, that we shall not soon meet again in public council, I take this opportunity of bidding you all an affectionate farewell and wishing you a safe and happy return to your respective homes and families."

Little Turtle took a leading part in this treaty as he had in war, and he was the one selected to make a final protest against part of the boundary line proposed by Wayne. Speaking for the Pottawatomies, Weas and Shawnees, he asked that the boundary be put east of the present limits of Indiana at the south; and in regard to the lands to be taken in the Indian region, he said: "We wish you to take the six miles square on the side of the river where your fort [Wayne] now stands, as your younger brothers wish to inhabit that beloved spot again. The next place you pointed out was the Little river, and said you wanted two miles square at that place. This is a request that our fathers the French and British, never made us; it was always ours. The carrying place has heretofore proved, in a great degree, the subsistence of your younger brothers. That place has brought us, in the course of one day, the amount of one hundred dollars. Let us both own this place and enjoy in common the advantages it affords." Wayne replied: "I have traced the lines of two forts at Fort Wayne; one stood near the junction of the St. Joseph's with the St. Mary's and the other not far removed on the St. Mary's, and it is ever an established rule among Europeans to reserve as much ground around their forts as their cannon can command." As to the portage at Little river, as a source of wealth, "It may be true, but the traders laid the expense on their goods, and the Indians on the Wabash paid it." By this venerable argument, the Indians were persuaded to surrender the control of their commerce.

At this treaty the Indians ceded the land east of this line: from the mouth of the Cuyahoga river down to the portage to the Muskingum, west to the portage between the Miami and St. Mary's; thence to Fort Recovery; thence to about the mouth of the Kentucky river.

Within the present limits of Indiana, the following isolated tracts were ceded, besides the southeastern strip east of the boundary: One tract of land, six miles square, at the confluence of the St. Mary and St. Joseph rivers; one tract of land, two miles square, on the Wabash river, at the end of the portage from the head of the river Maumee, and about eight miles westward from Fort Wayne; one tract of land, six miles square, at Ouiatenon, the old Wea town on the river Wabash; one tract of 150,000 acres, near the falls of the Ohio, which tract was called the "Illinois Grant," or "Clark's Grant;" the town of Vincennes, on the river Wabash, and the adjacent lands to which the Indian title had been extinguished; and all similar lands, at other places, in possession of the French people, or other white settlers among them.

The happy conclusion of this treaty alone was needed to complete the victory of the Maumee. A feeling of rejoicing pervaded the country. The hopes of Washington were at last realized, in the tide of emigration that set in from the eastern states. Many immigrants selected sites along the Ohio, the Scioto, and Muskingum rivers; while others began settlements in the fertile regions lying between the Miami and Maumee. Log cabins arose here and there in the vast domain, the children raised in which were to colonize Indiana.

TECUMSEH'S CONFEDERACY.

Indiana Territory.— For nearly fifteen years after the events which terminated with the treaty of Greenville, peace reigned, and the settlements gradually increased toward the west. In the summer of 1796 Gen. Wayne returned to the northwest to supervise the evacuation of the British posts, and by his orders, about the 17th of May of this year, Col. Hamtramck left Fort Wayne, passing down the Maumee to Fort Deposit, and on the 11th of July the British fort, Miami, at the foot of the rapids, was evacuated, Capt. Moses Porter taking possession with federal troops. On the 13th of July, Col. Hamtramck took possession of the post at Detroit. Col. Thomas Hunt, with the first regiment, remained at Fort Wayne. In December, upon the death of Gen. Wayne, Gen. James Wilkinson was put in command of the western army of the United States.

On the 23d of April, 1798, a legislative session was convened at Cincinnati, which closed on the 7th of May, participated in by Winthrop Sargent, acting governor, and John Cleves Symmes, Joseph Gilman and Return Jonathan Meigs, Jr., territorial judges. On the 29th of October Gov. St. Clair issued a proclamation, directing the qualified voters of the northwestern territory to hold elections in their respective counties on the third Monday of December, to elect representatives to a general assembly, to convene at Cincinnati on January 22, 1799. The representatives having met at the appointed place, in compliance with the ordinance of 1787 for the establishment of a legislative council, nominated ten persons whose names were forwarded to the president of the United States, who, on the 2nd of March, 1799, selected Jacob Burnett,

James Findlay, Henry Vanderburgh, Robert Oliver and David Vance, as suitable persons to form the legislative council of the territory, which selection was, on the following day, confirmed by the senate. The legislature met again at Cincinnati on September 16, 1799, and was fully organized on the the 24th, Henry Vanderburgh being elected president, and William C. Schenk secretary of the council. In the house of representatives were nineteen members, representing the counties of Hamilton, Ross, Wayne, Adams, Knox, Jefferson and Washington. On the 3d of October, of this year, the names of two candidates, William H. Harrison and Arthur St. Clair, Jr., to represent the northwest territory in congress, being presented to that body, Harrison was chosen — he receiving eleven votes and the other ten.

In 1800, a division of the territory was made, and on the 13th of May William Henry Harrison was appointed governor of Indiana territory. The seat of government was established at Vincennes, the only other military post in Indiana, more convenient than Fort Wayne, on account of its accessibility from the Ohio by the Wabash. There the governor met with the judges on Monday the 12th of January, 1801, to promulgate "such laws as the exigencies of the times" might call for, and for the "performance of other acts conformable to the ordinances and laws of congress for the government of the territory."

From the time of the formation of the new territory until 1810, the principal subjects of attention were land speculations, the adjustment of land titles, the question of negro slavery, the purchase of Indian lands by treaties, the organization of territorial legislatures, the extension of the right of suffrage, the division of the Indiana territory, the movements of Aaron Burr, and the hostile views and proceedings of the Shawnee chief, Tecumseh, and his brother, the prophet.

With hope for good-will between the United States and the Indians of the northwest, Governor Harrison, at an early period of his administration, made efforts to induce the different tribes to engage in agricultural and other pursuits of a civilized nature, to the end that they might be more agreeably situated and live more in harmony with the settlers. Being also invested with power to negotiate treaties between the government and the different tribes in the Indian Territory, and to extinguish by such treaties, the Indian title to lands, the governor was most actively employed from 1802 to 1805.

On the 17th day of September, 1802, at a conference held at Vincennes, chiefs and head men of the Pottawatomie, Eel river, Piankeshaw, Wea, Kaskaskia, and Kickapoo tribes appointed the Miami chiefs, Little Turtle and Richardville, and the Pottawatomie chiefs, Winnemac and Topinepik to adjust by treaty the extinguishment of certain Indian claims to lands on the Wabash, near Vincennes. On the 7th of June, 1803, Governor Harrison held a treaty at Fort Wayne, with the Delaware, Shawnee, Pottawatomie, Eel river, Kickapoo, Piankeshaw, and Kaskaskia tribes, whereby was ceded to the United States about 1,600,000 acres of land.

During this period, abandoning schemes for war, the Indians seemed mainly to have betaken themselves to the forest and prairies in pursuit of game; and the result was that a considerable traffic was steadily carried on with them by fur-traders of Fort Wayne and Vincennes, and at small trading posts which were established on the Wabash river and its tributaries. The furs which were obtained from the Indians were generally transported to Detroit. The skins were dried, compressed, and secured in packs. Each pack weighed about 100 pounds. A pirogue, or boat, that was sufficiently large to carry forty packs, required the labor of four men to manage it on its voyage. In favorable stages of the Wabash river, such a vessel, under the management of skillful boatmen, was propelled by poles fifteen or twenty miles a day, against the current. After ascending the river Wabash and the Little River to the portage near Fort Wayne, the traders carried their packs over the portage, to the St. Mary's where they were again placed in pirogues, or in keelboats, to be transported to Detroit. At that place the furs and skins were exchanged for blankets, guns, knives, powder, bullets, intoxicating liquors, etc., with which the traders returned to their posts.

But already the mutterings of another Indian war began to be heard. The restless savages, chafing under the restraints of their surroundings, and always discontented and revengeful, began to grow uneasy, and to listen to the voice of the ever-present instigator of revolt.

Tecumseh and the Prophet.—The period approached during which the Shawnee nation was to present its highest types, Tecumseh, whom an author has called the Philip of the west, but who was in ability far above the need of such an historical association, and Capt. Logan, one of the bravest of Indians.

Tecumseh was born on the Mad river, six miles below Springfield, Ohio, about 1768. His father, Puckeshinwa, a chief, died in battle, leaving six sons and a daughter. The fourth child was Tecumseh, or Shooting-Star; the sixth and seventh, Lawlewasikaw and Kumskawkaw, who were twins. According to Anthony Shane, Tecumseh was also brought forth at the same birth. Tecumseh, in his boyhood, frolicked in sham battles, and became expert with the bow and arrow. His first engagement was against the Col. Logan who brought up the Indian Logan, and in his second skirmish with the whites, he was so revolted at the burning of a prisoner that he resolved never to witness or permit another outrage of the kind, a resolve he religiously observed. He sought adventures and speedily became famous, not only as a daring fighter, but the best hunter among the Shawnees. His skirmishes with the Kentuckians spread a terror of the young leader among the Americans. While Harmar was leading his expedition against Kekionga, Tecumseh was making an excursion through Ohio, in all essentials the same as those of the errant knights of an earlier age. He returned to assist in the attack on Fort Recovery, and watch Wayne's advance, and at the battle of the Maumee was first opposed to William Henry Harrison. Subsequently he attended various conferences with the settlers, and addressed without embarrassment large assemblages, which were awed by his magnificent presence and wonderful eloquence.

He was humane in the treatment of prisoners; his political schemes were sound in conception, and he was patient and masterly in their execution. We may take as a just estimate of his character these words by Gen. Harrison, written soon before the battle of Tippecanoe: "The implicit obedience and respect which the followers of Tecumseh pay to him, is really astonishing, and more than any other circumstance bespeaks him one of those uncommon geniuses which spring up occasionally to produce revolutions and overturn the established order of things. If it were not for the vicinity of the United States, he would, perhaps, be the founder of an empire that would rival in glory Mexico and Peru. No difficulties deter him. For four years he has been in constant motion. You see him to-day on the Wabash, and in a short time hear of him on the shores of Lake Erie or Michigan, or on the banks of the Mississippi; and wherever he goes he makes an impression favorable to his purposes."

In 1798, the Delawares residing on the White river invited Tecumseh and his followers to encamp with them, and he remained there several years. In 1805, some of the Shawnees on the headwaters of the Auglaize sent word to Tecumseh to come to the Tah-wah towns and endeavor to unite the nation, and the Shawnees on the Mississinewa being invited at the same time it happened that the two parties met at Greenville, where Lawlewasikaw persuaded them to stop. This brother of Tecumseh was an audacious, assertive man, given to boasting, and lacking in firmness and talent for command. About this time an old Shawnee prophet died, and Lawlewasikaw was prompted by his ambition for influence to grasp the dead man's place, a comfortable and important office. He changed his name to Tenskwatawah, The-Open-Door, in significance of his teachings of a new way of life. In November, 1805, he assembled the Shawnees, Wyandots, Ottawas and Senecas in considerable numbers at Wapakoneta, and made his first appearance in the character which he had assumed, and in which he was to exert a great influence as far as the upper lakes and beyond the Mississippi. It appears that nothing was then said about the confederacy, but he endeavored to win the reverence of the tribes by a claim of having been admitted to the glories of the "happy hunting grounds" of the future existence. He had, he asserted, fallen into a trance, during which his companions thought him dead, and had begun preparations for his burial when he returned to earth from the clouds. He was inspired, he said, to warn the Indians to give up drunkenness, to which he himself had been addicted, and he told them that he had seen all the drunkards who had died, in the dwelling of the devil, with flames continually burning from their mouths; which vivid picture led many to renounce the use of "firewater." He denounced the practice of intermarriage with the whites, and called on the red men to abandon all weapons and garments they

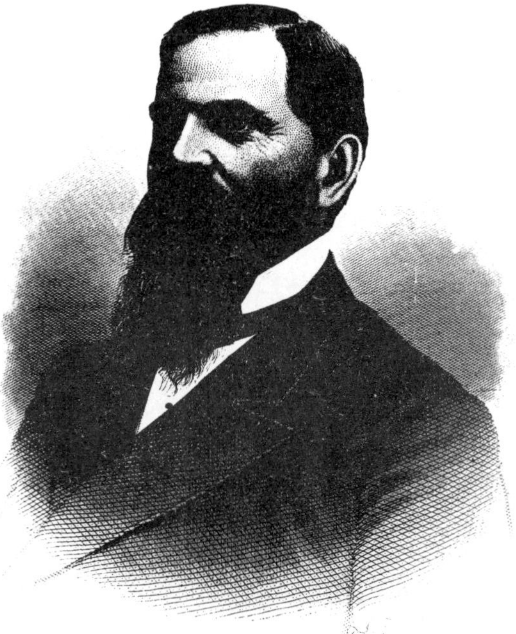

Western Engr. Pub. Co.

C. A. O. McClellan

had learned to use since the white occupation. The old and infirm they should tenderly care for, and all property should be held in common. Especially did he inveigh against witchcraft, which many believed in. In some way he learned the date of an approaching eclipse of the sun, and foretelling it, caused the Indians to believe he had supernatural power. Contrary to the sentiments of his brother, he began denouncing various Indians for witchcraft, and ordering them to be burned at the stake. Several Delawares were the first victims, and an old woman was toasted over the fire for four days. The old chief Teteboxti was burned on a pile he had himself helped to build, seeing that his death was inevitable. Finally, on the preparation for the destruction of another woman, her brother suddenly awakening to good sense took her from the prophet, and boldly rebuked him, considerably checking his influence.

On hearing of these cruelties, which, however, are not without parallel, Governor Harrison sent them a speech opening with these words:

"MY CHILDREN:—My heart is filled with grief, and my eyes are dissolved in tears at the news which has reached me. You have been celebrated for your wisdom above all the tribes of red people who inhabit this great island. Your fame as warriors has extended to the remotest nations, and the wisdom of your chiefs has gained for you the appellation of *grandfathers*, from all the neighboring tribes. From what cause, then, does it proceed, that you have departed from the wise counsel of your fathers, and covered yourselves with guilt?" He adjured them to drive the "imposter from them, and cease such abominable wickedness," and closed: "I charge you to stop your bloody career; and, if you value the friendship of your great father, the President—if you wish to preserve the good opinion of the Seventeen Fires, let me hear by the return of the bearer, that you have determined to follow my advice."

The Prophet's influence was greatest with the Kickapoos, next with the Delawares; most of the chiefs of his own nation were opposed to him, and complained of him at Fort Wayne. In the spring of 1807, he and Tecumseh assembled several hundred Indians at Greenville, and though little could be found out concerning the object of the meeting, great apprehension was felt at the settlements south of there. Capt. William Wells, who had been appointed Indian agent at Fort Wayne, received a letter from the president addressed to the leaders, requesting them to remove without the limits of the government's purchase, and Anthony Shane, a half-blood Shawnee, was sent to invite Tecumseh and his brother to come to Fort Wayne and hear the letter. Tecumseh replied that his fire was kindled on the spot appointed by the Great Spirit, and if Capt. Wells had any communication to make he must come there, and in six days. Shane was sent again at the day fixed, and read a copy of the letter to the Indians. Tecumseh was offended that Wells should presume to employ an ambassador in treating with him, and made a speech to the Indians of remarkable power. "These lands are

8

ours," he cried, "as to boundaries the Great Spirit knows none, nor will his red people acknowledge any." Then turning to Shane, he remarked with stately indifference, "If my great father, the president of the Seventeen Fires, has anything more to say to me, he must send a man of note as his messenger. I will hold no further intercourse with Capt. Wells."

Instead of dispersing, the Indians continued to flock to Greenville. Fully 1,500 had passed and repassed Fort Wayne, in their visits to the prophet, before the summer of 1807 had fairly set in. Messengers and runners passed from tribe to tribe, and were greatly aided by British agents in their mysterious operations.

At the close of summer, reliable persons bore testimony that nearly a thousand Indians, in possession of new rifles, were at Fort Wayne and Greenville, all under the control of the prophet.

The alarm had now become so general, that the governor of Ohio, in September, sent a deputation to Greenville to ascertain the meaning of the gathering. The commissioners were well received by the Indians — a council was called, and the governor's message read; at the close of which, one of the commissioners addressed them in explanation of their relationship to the United States government, urging them to desist from all aggressions and remain neutral, should a war with England ensue. Having heard the commissioner attentively, according to Indian usage they asked to be permitted to meditate upon the matter until the next day. Blue Jacket, who commanded in the battle with Gen. Wayne, was appointed to deliver the sentiments of the council; and at its re-assembling, that chief, through the interpreter, said:

"BRETHREN:— We are seated who heard you yesterday. You will get a true relation, so far as our connections can give it, who are as follows: Shawnees, Wyandots, Pottawatomies, Tawas, Chippewas, Winnepas, Menominees, Malockese, Lecawgoes, and one more from the north of the Chippewas. Brethren, you see all these men sitting before you, who now speak to you.

"About eleven days ago we had a council, at which the tribe of Wyandots, the elder brother of the red people, spoke and said God had kindled a fire, and all sat around it. In this council we talked over the treaties with the French and the Americans. The Wyandot said the French formerly marked a line along the Alleghany mountains, southerly, to Charleston [S. C.]. No man was to pass it from either side. When the Americans came to settle over the line, the English told the Indians to unite and drive off the French, until the war came on between the British and the Americans, when it was told them that King George, by his officers, directed them to unite and drive the Americans back.

"After the treaty of peace between the English and the Americans, the summer before Wayne's army came out, the English held a council with the Indians and told them if they would turn out and unite as one man, they might surround the Americans like deer in a ring of fire, and destroy them all. The Wyandot spoke further in the council. We see, said he, there is like to be war between the English and our white brethren, the Americans. Let us unite and consider the sufferings we have undergone, from interfering in the wars of the English. They have often promised to help us, and at last, when we could not withstand the army that came against us and went to the English fort for refuge, the English told us, 'I cannot let you in; you are painted too much, my children.' It was then we saw the British deal treacherously with us. We now see them going to war again. We do not know what they are going to fight for. Let us, my brethren, not interfere, was the speech of the Wyandot.

"Further, the Wyandot said, I speak to you, my little brother, the Shawnees at Greenville, and to you our little brothers all around. You appear to be at Greenville to serve the Supreme Ruler of the universe. Now send forth your speeches to all our brethren far around us, and let us unite to seek for that which shall be for our eternal welfare, and unite ourselves in a band of perpetual brotherhood. These, brethren, are the sentiments of all the men who sit around you; they all adhere to what the elder brother, the Wyandot, has said, and these are their sentiments. It is not that they are afraid of their white brothers, but that they desire peace and harmony, and not that their white brethren could put them to great necessity, for their former arms were bows and arrows, by which they get their living."

The Prophet, who improved every occasion to advance his own importance, informed the whites why his people had settled upon Greenville.

"About nine years since," said he, "I became convinced of the errors of my ways, and that I would be destroyed from the face of the earth if I did not amend them. Soon after I was told what I must do to be right. From that time I have continually preached to my red brethren; telling them the miserable situation they are in by nature, and striving to convince them that they must change their lives, live honestly and be just in all their dealings, kind to one other and also to their white brethren; affectionate in their families, put away lying and slandering, and serve the Great Spirit in the way I have pointed out; they must never think of war again; the tomahawk was not given them to go at war with one another. The Shawnees at Tawa town would not listen to me, but persecuted me. This made a division in the nation; those who adhered to me removed to this place, where I have constantly preached to them. They did not select this place because it looked fine or was valuable, for it was neither; but because it was revealed to me that this is the proper place where I must establish my doctrines. I mean to adhere to them while I live, for they are not mine but those of the Great Ruler of the world, and my future life shall prove to the whites the sincerity of my professions. In conclusion, my brethren, our six chiefs shall go with you to Chillicothe."

Tecumseh, Roundhead, Blue Jacket and Panther, returned with the commissioners to Chillicothe, where a council was called, in which they gave the governor positive assurances that they entertained none but peaceful intentions toward the whites. A speech which Tecumseh delivered at the time occupied between three and four hours in its delivery. It was eloquent and masterly, and showed that he possessed a thorough knowledge of all the treaties which had been made for years. While he expressed his pacific intentions if fairly treated, he told the governor to his face that every aggression or settlement upon their lands would be resisted, and that no pretended treaties would insure the squatters safety. Stephen Ruddell acted as interpreter upon the occasion. The governor, convinced that no instant danger was threatened Fort Wayne, disbanded the militia he had called into service. The chiefs returned to their people, and for a short time the settlers were free from apprehension.

Not long afterward the settlements were thrown into excitement by the murder of a man named Myers by the Indians, near where is now the town of Urbana, Ohio; and many of the settlers returned to their old homes in Kentucky. Being ordered to deliver up the murderers, Tecumseh and his brother disclaimed any knowledge of them—said they were not of their people. A council was finally held at Springfield with two parties of Indians, one from the north, the other from Fort Wayne, under Tecumseh. Being embittered against each other, each party was quite anxious that the other should receive the blame for the murder. Says Drake, the party from the north, at the request of the commissioners, left their arms a few miles behind them, but Tecumseh would not consent to attend unless his followers were allowed to keep theirs about them, adding that his tomahawk was his pipe, and he might wish to use it. At this a tall, lank-sided Pennsylvanian, who was standing among the spectators, and had no love for the glittering tomahawk of the self-willed chief, cautiously stepped up, and handed him a greasy, long-stemmed clay pipe, respectfully intimating that if he would only deliver up his dreadful tomahawk, he might use that article. The chief took it between his thumb and finger, held it up, looked at it a few seconds, then at the owner, who all the time was gradually backing away from him, and instantly threw it, with a contemptuous sneer, over his head into the bushes. The commissioners being compelled to waive this point, the council proceeded; and the verdict was, that the murder was an individual affair, sanctioned by neither party—which brought the council to a close, with a reconciliation of both parties, and the satisfaction of the settlers.

But the protestations of Tecumseh and the Prophet could not allay the uneasiness of the settlements; and before the end of the fall Governor Harrison sent the following speech, by an Indian agent, to the Shawnees:

"My Children:—Listen to me; I speak in the name of your father, the great chief of the Seventeen Fires.

"My children, it is now twelve years since the tomahawk, which you had seized by the advice of your father, the king of Great Britain, was buried at Greenville, in the presence of that great warrior, Gen. Wayne.

"My children, you then promised, and the Great Spirit heard it, that you would in future live in peace and friendship with your brothers, the Americans. You made a treaty with your father, and one that contained a number of good things, equally beneficial to all the tribes of the red people, who were parties to it.

"My children, you promised in that treaty to acknowledge no other father than the chief of the Seventeen Fires; and never to listen to the proposition of any foreign nation. You promised never to lift up the tomahawk against any of your father's children, and to give him notice of any other tribe that intended it; your father also promised to do something for you, particularly to deliver to you every year a certain quantity of goods; to prevent any white man from settling on your lands without your consent, or to do you any personal injury. He promised to run a line between your land and his, so that you might know your own; and you were to be permitted to live and hunt upon your father's land, as long as you behaved yourselves well. My children, which of these articles has your father broken? You know that he has observed them all with the utmost good faith. But, my children, have you done so? Have you not always had your ears open to receive bad advice from the white people beyond the lakes?

"My children, let us look back to times that are passed. It has been a long time since you called the king of Great Britain father. You know that it is the duty of a father to watch over his children, to give them good advice, and to do every thing in his power to make them happy. What has this father of yours done for you, during the long time that you have looked up to him for protection and advice? Are you wiser and happier than you were before you knew him, or is your nation stronger or more respectable? No, my children, he took you by the hand when you were a powerful tribe; you held him fast, supposing he was your friend, and he conducted you through paths filled with thorns and briers, which tore your flesh and shed your blood. Your strength was exhausted, and you could no longer follow him. Did he stay by you in your distress, and assist and comfort you? No, he led you into danger and then abandoned you. He saw your blood flowing and he would give you no bandage to tie up your wounds. This was the conduct of the man who called himself your father. The Great Spirit opened your eyes; you heard the voice of the chief of the Seventeen Fires speaking the words of peace. He called you to follow him; you came to him, and he once more put you on the right way, on the broad, smooth road that would have led to happiness. But the voice of your deceiver is again heard; and, forgetful of your former sufferings, you are again listening to him. My children, shut your ears and mind him not, or he will lead you to ruin and misery.

"My children, I have heard bad news. The sacred spot where the great council fire was kindled, around which the Seventeen Fires and ten tribes of their children smoked the pipe of peace — that very spot where the Great Spirit saw his red and white children encircle themselves with the chain of friendship — that place has been selected for dark and bloody councils. My children, this business must be stopped. You have called in a number of men from the most distant tribes, to listen to a fool, who spake not the words of the Great Spirit, but those of the devil, and of the British agents. My children, your conduct has much alarmed the white settlers near you. They desire that you will send away those people, and if they wish to have the impostor with them, they can carry him. Let him go to the lakes; he can hear the British more distinctly."

The Prophet's reply was, that evil birds had sung in the governor's ears; and he denied any correspondence with the British, protesting that he had no intentions whatever of disturbing the settlements. Tecumseh continued to urge a confederacy and the Prophet's influence extended. Even the Ojibways, far up the lakes, and their neighbors, came down in great numbers, and exhausting their provisions, were fed at Fort Wayne by order of Gov. Harrison.

The Pottawatomies and Kickapoos having granted them a tract of land, Tecumseh and the Prophet, in the spring of 1808, removed to Tippecanoe, where he collected some Shawnees and about 100 from the northern tribes. The Miamis and Delawares, being friendly to the whites, were greatly opposed to their coming, and even sent a delegation to stop them. But Tecumseh boldly told the party they were not to be thwarted in their purposes to ameliorate the condition of their brethren.

In August, the Prophet, accompanied by several of his followers, visited Governor Harrison, at Vincennes, protesting, as formerly, that his purposes were peaceable. In the course of his speech he made these remarkably wise and just observations:

"The Great Spirit told me to tell the Indians that he had made them, and made the world — that he had placed them on it to do good and not evil. I told all the red-skins, that the way they were in was not good, and that they ought to abandon it. That we ought to consider ourselves as one man: but we ought to live agreeably to our several customs, the red people after their mode and the white people after theirs; particularly, that they should not drink whisky; that it was not made for them, but the white people, who alone knew how to use it; and that it is the cause of all the mischiefs which the Indians suffer; and that they must always follow the directions of the Great Spirit, and we must listen to him, as it was He that made us; determine to listen to nothing that is bad; do not take up the tomahawk, should it be offered by the British or by the Long-Knives; do not meddle with anything that does not belong to you, but mind your own business, and cultivate the ground, that your women and your children may have enough to live on.

"I now inform you that it is our intention to live in peace with our father and his people forever, and I call the Great Spirit to witness the truth of my declaration. The religion which I have established for the last three years, has been attended to by the different tribes of Indians in this part of the world. These Indians were once different people;

they are now but one; they are all determined to practice what I have communicated to them, that has come immediately from the Great Spirit through me.

"I have listened to what you have said to us. You have promised to assist us. I now request you, in behalf of all the red people, to use your exertions to prevent the sale of liquor to us. We are all well pleased to hear you say that you will endeavor to promote our happiness. We give you every assurance that we will follow the dictates of the Great Spirit."

To test the influence of the Prophet over his followers, Gov. Harrison held conversations with and offered them spirits, but they always refused, and he became almost convinced that the Indian was sincere in his professions, and had no other ambition than to ameliorate the condition of his race.

During the following year Tecumseh and the Prophet sought quietly to add strength to their movement. Both were engaged in a deep game; and while the Prophet seemed the leading spirit, Tecumseh was yet the prime mover. The Prophet attempted but little without first getting the advice of his brother, though it is evident he was most headstrong in much that he undertook.

In the spring of 1809, Capt. Wells sent word to Gov. Harrison that many of the Indians were leaving the Prophet because of his requiring them to become parties to a scheme for the massacre of the inhabitants of Vincennes. The governor began the organization of two companies of militia, to garrison a post two miles from that town. But the Prophet's followers dispersed before the close of the summer.

On the 30th of September, 1809, Gov. Harrison concluded another treaty at Fort Wayne, in which the Delaware, Pottawatomie, Miami and Eel river tribes participated. According to this treaty, the Indians ceded about 2,900,000 acres of land, principally situated on the southeastern side of the river Wabash, and below the mouth of Raccoon creek, a little stream which empties into the Wabash, near what is now the boundary of Parke county. The chiefs of the Wea tribe, in the following month, having met Gov. Harrison at Vincennes, acknowledged the legality of this treaty; and by a treaty held at Vincennes on the 9th of December following, the Kickapoo tribe also confirmed the treaty. Up to this time, the land ceded to the United States by treaty stipulations between Governor Harrison and the different tribes of Indiana territory, amounted to 29,719,530 acres.

Having received, through a reliable source, information regarding an effort of Tecumseh and the Prophet to incite the Indians against the settlements, and that those who had left the ranks of the Prophet had again returned to his support; and further, that the British had their agents quietly at work among the tribes thus banded, and that the Indians were boasting to American traders that they were getting their ammunition without cost, Gov. Harrison, through instructions from the secretary of war, in July, 1810, began to prepare for the protection of the frontier.

As the summer of 1810 advanced, it became more and more evident to Governor Harrison that the true purpose of Tecumseh and the Prophet was to make war upon the whites. Early in June, Leatherlips, subsequently known as the "Doomed Warrior," a chief of the Wyandots, who held the "great belt," was accused of witchcraft and sentenced to death, and the sentence was carried out by breaking his skull with a tomahawk. From the best information Governor Harrison could obtain, this charge of witchcraft was made by the Prophet, and its penalty inflicted only against and upon those friendly to the United States. A few weeks after the death of the Wyandot chief, he learned that a plot was nearly matured for the surprise and massacre of the garrisons at Fort Wayne, Detroit, Chicago, Vincennes and St. Louis. Tecumseh and the Prophet were moving secretly but surely to that end.

There was still much opposition to the proposed union and war, and such chiefs as Winnemac, and various civil chiefs, remained friendly to Gen. Harrison. From one of the Iowas Harrison learned that a British agent had recently visited the Prophet, and encouraged the latter to continue in his efforts to unite the tribes, but to await a signal from the British before carrying out their designs against the Americans.

Finding that the most constant watchfulness was necessary, Gov. Harrison dispatched two agents to Tecumseh and his brother to ascertain, if possible, their real designs. Receiving the agents very courteously, in reply to the inquiries made, the Prophet told the agents that the assembling of the Indians upon that spot was by the explicit command of the Great Spirit.

The agent told him that his movements had excited so much alarm that the troops of Kentucky and Indiana were being called out, and preparations were being made for trouble.

In answer to the questions of the agents as to the cause of his complaints against the United States, the Prophet replied that his people had been cheated of their lands. Though told that his complaints would readily be listened to by Gov. Harrison, at Vincennes, the Prophet refused to go, saying that while there upon a former occasion he was badly treated.

Receiving this information, the governor at once wrote to the secretary, stating the cause, and telling him that all this caviling was merely a pretext on the part of Tecumseh and the Prophet; that he had been as liberal in the conclusion of treaties as his understanding of the views and opinions of the government would permit, and that none of the tribes had just cause for complaint.

Having heard, in July, that the Sacs and Foxes had formed an alliance with the Prophet, and were ready and willing to strike the Americans at any time, Governor Harrison sent the following address to the Prophet by a confidential interpreter:

"Notwithstanding the improper language which you have used toward me, I will endeavor to open your eyes to your true interests. Notwithstanding what bad white men have told you, I am not your personal enemy. You ought to know this from the manner in which I received and treated you on your visit to this place.

"Although I must say that you are an enemy to the Seventeen Fires, and that you have used the greatest exertions with other tribes to lead them astray. In this, you have been in some measure successful; as I am told they are ready to raise the tomahawk against their father; yet their father, notwithstanding his anger at their folly, is full of goodness, and is always ready to receive into his arms those of his children who are willing to repent, acknowledge their fault, and ask for his forgiveness.

"There is yet but little harm done, which may easily be repaired. The chain of friendship which united the whites with the Indians may be renewed, and be as strong as ever. A great deal of that work depends upon you — the destiny of those who are under you, depends upon the choice you may make of the two roads which are before you. The one is large, open and pleasant, and leads to peace, security and happiness; the other, on the contrary, is narrow and crooked, and leads to misery and ruin. Don't deceive yourselves; do not believe that all the nations of Indians united are able to resist the force of the Seventeen Fires. I know your warriors are brave, but ours are not less so; but what can a few brave warriors do against the innumerable warriors of the Seventeen Fires? Our blue-coats are more numerous than you can count; our hunters are like the leaves of the forest, or the grains of sand on the Wabash.

"Do not think that the red-coats can protect you; they are not able to protect themselves. They do not think of going to war with us. If they did, you would, in a few months, see our flag wave over all the forts of Canada.

"What reason have you to complain of the Seventeen Fires? Have they taken any thing from you? Have they ever violated the treaties made with the red-men? You say that they have purchased lands from them who had no right to sell them; show that this is true, and the land will be instantly restored. Show us the rightful owners of those lands which have been purchased — let them present themselves. The ears of your father will be open to your complaints, and if the lands have been purchased of those who did not own them, they will be restored to their rightful owners. I have full power to arrange this business; but if you would rather carry your complaints before your great father, the president, you shall be indulged. I will immediately take means to send you, with those chiefs which you may choose, to the city where your father lives. Every thing necessary shall be prepared for your journey, and means taken for your safe return."

After hearing this speech, the Prophet told the interpreter that, as his brother intended to pay Governor Harrison a visit in a few weeks, he would let him carry the reply to the governor's message. Receiving this information, Governor Harrison sent a message to Tecumseh, requesting him to bring but a small body of his followers, as it was inconvenient for him to receive many. To this Tecumseh paid no regard, and on the 12th of August, 1810, with four hundred warriors, all armed with tomahawks, war-clubs, and "painted in the most terrific manner," he began to descend the Wabash. Arriving near Vincennes, on the morning of the 15th, attended by about fifteen or twenty of his warriors, Tecumseh approached the house of the governor, who, in company with the judges of the supreme court, several army officers, a sergeant and a dozen men, besides a large number of citizens, waited upon the portico of his house to receive the chief.

During the milder season of the year, to hold a council other than in a grove, with logs or turf to sit upon, was distasteful to the Indians, and to the invitation to come forward and take seats upon the portico, he objected, signifying that it was not a fit place to hold a council, and at his request the governor and his attendants took seats beneath a grove of trees before the house.

With a firm and elastic step and with a proud and somewhat defiant look, Tecumseh advanced to the place where the governor and those who had been invited to attend the conference were sitting. This place had been fenced in to prevent the crowd from encroaching upon the council. As he stepped forward he seemed to scan the preparations which had been made for his reception, particularly the military part of it, with an eye of suspicion — by no means, however, with fear. As he came in front of the dias, an elevated portion of the place upon which the governor and the officers of the territory were seated, the governor invited him, through the interpreter, to take a seat with him and his counselors, premising the invitation by saying that it was the wish of their "great father," the president of the United States, that he should do so. Pausing for a moment, at the utterance of these words by the interpreter, and extending his tall figure to its greatest height, he looked upon the troops and then upon the crowd about him. Thus, for a moment, with keen, piercing eyes fixed upon Gov. Harrison, and then upward to the sky, he raised his sinewy arm toward the heavens, with a tone and gesture expressive of supreme contempt for the paternity assigned him, and in a clear, loud, full voice, exclaimed:

"My Father? — The sun is my father — the earth is my mother — and on her bosom I will recline." Having finished, he stretched himself with his warriors on the green sward. The effect is said to have been electrical — for some moments there was a perfect silence throughout the assembly.

Gov. Harrison said to Tecumseh through the interpreter, that he had understood he had complaints to make, and redress to ask for certain wrongs which he, Tecumseh, supposed had been done his tribe, as well as the others; that he felt disposed to listen to the one, and make satisfaction for the other, if it was proper he should do so. That in all his intercourse and negotiations with the Indians, he had endeavored to act justly and honorably with them, and believed he had done so, and had heard of no complaint of his conduct until he learned that Tecumseh was endeavoring to create dissatisfaction toward the government, not only among the Shawnees, but among the other tribes dwelling on the Wabash and Illinois; and had, in so doing, produced a great deal of mischief and trouble between them and the whites, by averring that the tribes, whose land the government had lately purchased, had no right to so sell, nor their chiefs any authority to convey. That the governor had invited him to attend the council with a view of learning from his own lips whether there was any truth in the reports, and to learn from him whether he, or his tribe, had any cause of complaint against the whites; and if so, as a man and a warrior, openly and boldly to avow it. That, as between himself and as great a warrior as Tecumseh, there should be no concealment—all should be done by them under a clear sky, and in an open path, and with these feelings on his own part, he was glad to meet him in council.

In appearance, Tecumseh was accounted one of the most splendid specimens of his tribe—who claimed that they were the first created and most perfect of men. Tall, athletic and manly, dignified and graceful, he was the *beau ideal* of an Indian chieftain. In a voice, at first low, but distinct, Tecumseh replied, stating at length his objections to the treaty at Fort Wayne, made by Gov. Harrison in the previous year; and in the course of his speech, boldly avowed the principle of his party to be that of resistance to every cession of land, unless made by all the tribes, which he contended, formed but one nation. He admitted that he threatened to kill the chiefs who signed the treaty of Fort Wayne; and that it was his fixed determination not to permit the village chiefs, in future, to manage their affairs, but to place the power with which they had been heretofore invested, in the hands of the war chiefs. The Americans, he said, had driven the Indians from the sea-coast, and would soon push them into the lakes; and while he disclaimed all intention of making war upon the United States, he declared it to be his unalterable resolution to make a stand, and resolutely oppose the further intrusion of the whites upon the Indian lands. He concluded with a brief but impassioned recital of the various wrongs and aggressions upon the Indians from the commencement of the revolutionary war.

The governor rose in reply, and in examining the right of Tecumseh and his party to make objections to the treaty of Fort Wayne, took occasion to say, that the Indians were not one nation, having a common property in the lands. The Miamis, he contended, were the real owners of the tract on the Wabash, ceded by the late treaty, and the Shawnees had no right to interfere in the case; that upon the arrival of the whites on this continent, they had found the Miamis in possession of this land, the Shawnees being then residents of Georgia, from which they had been driven by the Creeks, and that it was ridiculous to assert that the red men constituted but one nation; for, if such had been the intention of the Great Spirit, he would not have put different tongues in their heads, but have taught them all to speak the same language.

The governor having taken his seat, the interpreter commenced explaining the speech to Tecumseh, who, after listening to a portion of it, sprang to his feet, and began to speak with great vehemence of manner. The governor was surprised at his violent gestures, but as he did not understand him, he thought he was making some explanation, and suffered his attention to be drawn toward Winnemac, a friendly Indian lying on the grass before him, who was renewing the priming of his pistol, which he had kept concealed from the other Indians, but in full view of the governor. His attention, however, was again attracted toward Tecumseh, by hearing Gen. Gibson, who was intimately acquainted with the Shawnee language, say to Lieut. Jennings, " Those fellows intend mischief; you had better bring up the guard." At that moment, the followers of Tecumseh seized their tomahawks and war-clubs, and sprang upon their feet, their eyes turned upon the governor. As soon as he could disengage himself from the arm-chair in which he sat, he rose, drew a small sword which he had by his side, and stood on the defensive, Capt. G. R. Floyd who stood near him, drew a dirk, and the chief Winnemac cocked his pistol. The citizens present were more numerous than the Indians, but were unarmed; some of them procured clubs and brick-bats, and also stood on the defensive. The Rev. Mr. Winans, of the Methodist church, ran to the governor's house, got a gun, and posted himself at the door to defend the family. During this singular scene, no one spoke, until the guard came running up, and appeared to be in the act of firing, when the governor ordered then not to do so. He then demanded of the interpreter an explanation of what had happened, who replied that Tecumseh had interrupted him, declaring that all the governor had said was *false;* and that he and the Seventeen Fires had cheated and imposed on the Indians.

The governor then told Tecumseh that he was a bad man, and that he would hold no further communication with him; that as he had come to Vincennes under the protection of a council-fire, he might return in safety, but he must immediately leave the village. Here the council terminated. During the night, two companies of militia were brought in from the country, and that belonging to the town was also called out. Next morning Tecumseh requested the governor to afford him an opportunity of explaining his conduct on the previous day — declaring that he did not intend to attack the governor, and that he had acted under the advice of some of the white people. The governor consented to another interview, it being understood that each party should have the same armed force as on the previous day. On this occasion the deportment of Tecumseh was respectful and dignified. He again denied having any intention to make an attack upon the governor, and declared that he had been stimulated to the course he had taken, by two white men, who assured him that one-half the citizens were opposed to the governor, and willing to restore the land in question; that the governor would soon be put out of office, and a good man sent to fill his place, who would give up the land to the Indians. When asked by the governor whether he intended to resist the survey of these lands, Tecumseh replied that he and his followers were resolutely determined to insist upon the old boundary. When he had taken his seat, chiefs from the Wyandots, Kickapoos, Pottawatomies, Ottawas and Winnebagoes, spoke in succession, and distinctly avowed that they had entered into the Shawnee confederacy, and were determined to support the principles laid down by their leader. The governor, in conclusion, stated that he would make known to the president the claims of Tecumseh and his party, to the land in question; but that he was satisfied the government would never admit that the lands on the Wabash were the property of any other tribes than those who occupied them when the white people first arrived in America; and, as the title to these lands had been derived by purchase from those tribes, he might rest assured that the right of the United States would be sustained by the sword. Here the council adjourned.

On the following day, Gov. Harrison visited Tecumseh in his camp, attended only by the interpreter, and was politely received. A long conversation ensued, in which Tecumseh again declared that his intentions were really such as he had avowed them to be in the council; that the policy which the United States pursued, of purchasing land from the Indians, he viewed as mighty water, ready to overflow his people; and that the confederacy which he was forming among the tribes to prevent any individual tribe from selling without the consent of the others, was the dam he was erecting to resist this mighty water. He stated further, that he should be reluctantly drawn into war with the United States; and that if he, the governor, would induce the president to give up the lands lately purchased, and agreed never to make another treaty without the consent of all the tribes, he would be their faithful ally, and assist them in the war, which he knew was about to take place with England; that he preferred being the ally of the Seventeen Fires, but if they did not comply with his request, he would be compelled to unite with the British. The governor replied, that he would make known his views to the president, but that there was no probability of its being agreed to. "Well," said Tecumseh, " as the great chief is to determine the matter, I hope the Great Spirit will put sense enough into his head to induce him to give up this land; it is true, he is so far off, he will not be injured by the war; he may sit still in his town and drink his wine, while you and I will have to fight it out." This prophecy, it will be seen, was literally fulfilled; and the great chieftain who uttered it, attested that fulfillment with his blood. The governor, in conclusion, proposed to Tecumseh that in the event of hostilities between the Indians and the United States, he should use his influence to put an end to the cruel mode of warfare which the Indians were accustomed to wage upon women and children, and upon prisoners. To this he cheerfully assented; and it is due to the memory of Tecumseh to add, that he faithfully kept his promise.

Campaign of Tippecanoe.—Not long after this council, a Winnebago chief, who had been employed to watch the proceedings of Tecumseh, brought word to Gov. Harrison that the former was sending to each of the tribes a large wampum belt, with a view of uniting them in one great confederation; and that, upon a return of the belt, he saw a British agent fairly dance with joy—adding, with tears in his eyes, that he and all the village chiefs had been deprived of their power, and that the control of everything was in the hands of the warriors, who were greatly opposed to the United States. The governor of Missouri sent word that the Sac Indians had allied themselves to the confederacy; that Tecumseh himself was then doing all in his power to induce the tribes west of the Mississippi to join him; to which were added the reports of different Indian agents, who were generally of opinion that the period for a war with the Indians would soon arrive.

Early in 1811, as a part of the annuity to the Indians, Gov. Harrison sent a boat load of salt up the Wabash, a portion of which was to be given to the Prophet for the Shawnees and Kickapoos; but, upon the arrival of the boat at the point where the Prophet had his lodges, he made bold to seize the entire cargo, alleging as a reason for so doing that he had 2,000 men to feed, who had been without salt for two years. Upon being informed of this, Gov. Harrison felt justified in demanding aid from the government; and made application to the secretary of war to have Col. Boyd's regiment, then at Pittsburg, sent immediately to him, requesting, at the same time, to receive authority to act on the offensive as soon as it was known that the Indians were in actual hostility against the United States. The governor's apprehensions were well founded, and it soon became an acknowledged fact that Vincennes was to be the first point of attack.

A council was held in which Tecumseh participated, but was defiant, and closed an impassioned speech with the prophetic declaration: "I will stamp my foot at Tippecanoe, and the very earth shall shake." This was on the 30th day of July, 1811, and in the early morning of the 6th of November, was fought the battle of Tippecanoe, where, in the defeat of the Prophet, the gallant Harrison and his small but heroic army won lasting fame. Here the Prophet lost his influence, for he had made war against the orders of Tecumseh, then absent in the south. The latter on his return was deeply dejected. He sent word to Gov. Harrison that he wished to visit the president, but upon Gov. Harrison declining to allow him an escort, he refused to visit Washington.

Tecumseh at Fort Wayne.— One of the strange inconsistencies of the dealings of the general government, which has been apparent to the present day, is exhibited by what followed. Only a few days after the battle of Tippecanoe, on the 22d of November, 1810, the period for the annual meeting of the Indians to receive their annuities, having arrived, they began to assemble at Fort Wayne in great numbers. John Johnson was then Indian agent here. Many of the chiefs in attendance were fresh from Tippecanoe, claiming their portions of the annuity equally with the most peaceful of the tribes — representing that the Prophet's followers had him in confinement, and purposed taking his life; that he was chargeable with all their troubles; together with many other stories of a similar character, all more or less, in the main untrue, especially as regarded the Prophet's confinement. But the stories presented to Col. Johnson had the desired effect and he was induced thereby to inform the government that the Indians were all favorable to peace, and that no further hostilities should be committed against them; and yet, says M'Afee, in most of the nations here assembled, a British faction was boiling to the brim, and ready to flow on our devoted frontiers, wherever the British agents might think proper to increase the fire of their hostility. The old council-house was located near the spot lately occupied by Michael Hedekin. It was a two-story log building, about sixty feet long, by about twenty wide; and stood but a short distance to the southwest of the fort. It was in this building the agent lived.

The assemblage of the Indians to receive their annuity at the hands of Col. Johnson, after the battle of Tippecanoe, consisted principally of chiefs and head men of the Miamis, Delawares, the Pottawatomies, and Shawnees. Col. Johnson, on this occasion, made them a speech, presenting the importance of an adherence to peaceable relations on the part of the tribes and the United States, telling them that the president was desirous of living in peace and friendship with them; and that pardon would be granted to any of the hostile tribes who would put away their arms and be peaceable. To this Black-Hoof, a Shawnee chief, responded in behalf of all the tribes present, assuring him that they all had the strongest desire to lay hold of the chain of peace and friendship with the United States. It was believed that this expression was sincere on the part of the Shawnees and a large number of the Delawares; but that the Miamis and Pottawatomies had little or no intention of being peaceable after receiving their annuities. Little Turtle, now in the decline of life and influence, was the strenuous advocate of peace, but a majority of his people followed the counsels of Tecumseh. The Indians generally made great pretensions to a desire for peace.

Tecumseh made his appearance at Fort Wayne some time during the month of December. The result of his brother's recklessness had affected him deeply. His scheme was broken, but he was still for war — for freedom — for the expulsion of the white race that occupied the ancient hunting ground of his fathers. His air was haughty, and he was still obstinate in the opinions he had embraced. He made bitter reproaches against Harrison, and at the same time had the presumption to demand ammunition from the commander at Fort Wayne, which was refused him. He then said he would go to his British father, who would not deny him. He appeared thoughtful a while, then gave the war-whoop, and went away to join the British at Malden.

War with Great Britain.— Such was the spirit in which Tecumseh left Fort Wayne on this memorable occasion; and early in the spring of 1812, he and his party began to put their threats into execution. Small parties began to commit depredations on the frontier settlements of Indiana and Illinois territories, and part of Ohio. Twenty scalps were taken in Indiana territory alone before the first of June; and the people were compelled to protect themselves by going into forts. Volunteer companies of militia were organized, and the Indians were frequently pursued, but generally without success, as they fled at once after committing their depredations. Governor Harrison asked permission of the war department to raise a mounted force to penetrate to their towns, with a view of chastising them. But this was refused, the government hesitating to disturb them in that way at that time, fearing they would take a more active part with the British. The government was imbued with a "peace on any terms" policy, and the Indians accepted all that was given them, and laughed at the credulity of the giver. In June, 1812, war was declared with Great Britain, and congress passed acts authorizing the recruiting of the army, and the employment of 100,000 militia.

During this month the president made a requisition on the state of Ohio for 1200 militia, and the famous Fourth regiment, under command of Col. Miller, which had sometime before been ordered to the relief of Vincennes, was now ordered to Cincinnati, to join the militia, which was ordered by Governor Meigs to rendezvous on the 29th of April, at Dayton. As directed by the secretary of war, on the 25th of May following, Governor Meigs surrendered the command of the army to General Hull, for some time previous governor of Michigan territory, but who had been appointed a brigadier-general in the United States army. From Dayton the army under Hull marched for Staunton on the 1st of June. From Staunton it marched to Urbana. Here Governor Meigs and General Hull held a council with twelve chiefs of the Shawnee, Mingo and Wyandot nations, to obtain leave from them to march the army through their territory, and to erect such forts as might be deemed necessary. This was promptly granted, and every assistance which they could give the army in the wilderness was promised. Governor Meigs had held a council with these Indians on the 6th, in which it was agreed to adhere to the treaty of Greenville. On the 10th of June, the Fourth regiment, under Col. Miller, made its appearance at Urbana, and was escorted into camp through a triumphal arch, adorned with an eagle, and inscribed with the words, "Tippecanoe—Glory."

From Urbana the army, on the 16th, moved as far as King's Creek, and from this point opened a road as far as the Scioto, where they built two block-houses, which they called Fort M'Arthur, in honor of the officer whose regiment had opened the road. To this fort the whole army came on the 19th, and on the 21st Col. Findley was ordered to open the road as far as Blanchard's fork, on the Auglaize, whither the army, excepting a guard left at Fort M'Arthur, marched on the 22d. Here, amid rain and mud, another block-house was erected, which was called Fort Necessity. From Fort Necessity the army moved to Blanchard's fork, where Col. Findley had built a block-house, named in honor of that officer. A road was shortly after, under direction of Col. Cass, cut to the rapids, and the main army soon encamped on the banks of the Maumee, opposite the old battle ground of Gen. Wayne. From this point, after a day or two's rest, the army moved down just below the old British fort Miami. For a considerable period, the movements of the army under Hull were directed toward Detroit and the region of the lakes, and there, a great disaster was destined soon to come, which not only caused great perturbation among the settlers and frontier posts, but which really threatened them with destruction.

From the time of his abrupt departure from Fort Wayne up to the breaking out of the war of 1812, Tecumseh had plotted against the Americans, and from the first hostile movements of the British, had allied himself to their cause, and begun to take a most active part with the enemy, in whose army he was made a brigadier-general in the service of the king. Early in August, at the head of a party of Shawnees, accompanied by a number of British soldiers, he made an attack upon a company of Ohio militia sent to escort some volunteers engaged in bringing supplies for the army. This occurred at Brownstown, and was the first action after the declaration of war. Tecumseh and his party succeeded in drawing the company into an ambush, in which it suffered considerable loss, and it was then followed by Tecumseh in its retreat toward the river Ecorce. The movements of the army under Hull were directed toward Detroit, which became the headquarters of that force. Hull prepared orders to be sent to the forts giving warning of the necessity of preparing for defense, but there was remarkable delay in transmission.

The garrison at Mackinaw not having received the order of Gen. Hull, written about the 5th of July, relating to the declaration of war, that post was surrendered on the 17th of that month, which caused Gen. Hull to declare that the whole northern hordes of Indians would be let loose upon him. Fort Dearborn, at Chicago, was in a position as hazardous as that of Mackinaw. Toward the last of July, Gen. Hull began to think seriously of the situation at Chicago, and of the relief of the garrison under Capt. Heald, which was being surrounded by a party of Indians in communication with Tecumseh, which, though not yet attempting any acts of violence was only awaiting the necessary encouragement from the enemy. Hull took action by sending an express to Major B. F. Stickney, then Indian agent at Fort Wayne, requesting him to at once extend to Capt. Heald all the information, assistance and advice within his power, who was ordered to accept of such aid, and to conform to such instructions as he might receive from the Indian agent at Fort Wayne. Instructions were accordingly prepared by Major Stickney to accompany the order of Gen. Hull, and an agent dispatched to Chicago. In this letter Capt. Heald was promised military aid as soon as it was possible to render it.

Capt. William Wells was at that time Indian sub-agent here. He was a great favorite with the Miamis, and accounted a perfect master of everything pertaining to Indian life, both in peace and war, and withal a stranger to personal fear; and, says Major Stickney, "if Gen. Wayne desired a prisoner to obtain information, Capt. Wells could always furnish one." This capable man was selected to lead a party to the aid of

9

Capt. Heald, and Major Stickney suggested the raising of a band of thirty warriors. These he selected from the Miamis. The Pottawatomies were known to be in the vicinity of Chicago, and the fact of Wells being a favorite with the Miamis made the former tribe unfriendly toward him, there having arisen an enmity between the two tribes. So that Wells' position was at best, should trouble arise upon their arrival at Fort Dearborn, a most precarious one, a fact that he was by no means unacquainted with. But his nature was fearless. On the 3d of August, with his braves well equipped by the agent, he set out full of hope and courage, for the relief of the garrison at Chicago, whither they arrived on the 12th.

Wells and his party had not been long at the fort before he discovered unmistakable evidences of coming trouble. A large number of Pottawatomies and Winnebagoes, professing friendship, were encamped about the fort; and for some time Tecumseh and the British, through their runners, had kept up a regular correspondence with the Indians. On the night of the 14th, a runner having arrived among the Indians with the news from Tecumseh that Major Vanhorn had been defeated at Brownstown; that the army under Hull had returned from Canada to Detroit; and that there was prospect of success, the Indians at once decided to remain no longer inactive.

Wells was warmly attached to Capt. Heald. The latter had married his niece, and she was with her husband to share the dangers that surrounded them.

On the arrival of Wells with his warriors at the fort, Capt. Heald informed him that he had received the dispatch from the agent at Fort Wayne, with the order of Gen. Hull, and had then called together all the Indian warriors in his neighborhood, and had entered into a treaty with them. The leading terms were, that he was to deliver up to the Indians the fort with all its contents, except arms, ammunition and provisions necessary for their march to Fort Wayne. The Indians on their part were to permit him to pass unmolested. Wells at once protested against the terms of the treaty. There was a large quantity of ammunition and whisky in the fort. These, he declared, they should not have. He urged that if the Indians had the whisky they would get drunk, and pay no regard to the treaty; and he was for throwing the ammunition and whisky into the lake. The Indians learned what was going on, and determined to attack Heald and his party, at the first convenient point, after they should leave the fort. Wells understood Indian character so perfectly that he was aware of their intentions at a glance.

As soon as it was daybreak, Wells saw that the tomahawk was sharpening for them, and told Heald they must be off as quick as possible, hoping to move before the Indians were ready for them. No time was to be lost. Topeeneebee, a chief of the St. Joseph band, had, early in the morning, informed Mr. Kinzie of the mischief what was intended by the Pottawatomies, who had engaged to escort the detachment; and urged him to relinquish his design of accompanying the troops by land, promising him that the boat containing himself and family should be permitted to pass in safety to the St. Joseph. This offer was declined by Mr. Kinzie, on the ground that his presence might operate as a restraint upon the fury of the savages, so warmly were the greater part of them attached to himself and family.

As the garrison marched out on the morning of the 15th, the band struck up the Dead March, as if some invisible force had impressed upon them the fate many of them were soon to meet; and on they moved, solemn and thoughtful, in military array, Capt. Wells taking the lead, at the head of his little band of Miami warriors, his face blackened. Taking their route along the lake shore, as they gained a range of sand hills lying between the prairie and the beach, the escort of Pottawatomies, some 500 in number, instead of continuing along the beach with the Americans and Miamis, kept the level of the prairie. They had marched about a mile and a half, when Capt. Wells, who had ridden a little in advance with the Miamis, suddenly came galloping back, exclaiming: "They are about to attack us; form instantly, and charge upon them," telling his niece not to be alarmed, that "they would not hurt her, but that he would be killed." No sooner had he ceased to speak, than a volley was fired from among the sand hills. The little company being hastily brought into line, charged rapidly up the bank. A veteran, some seventy years, was the first to fall. Capt. Wells fell, pierced with many balls, and in the words of Mrs. Kinzie, "Pee-so-tum held dangling in his hand a scalp, which, by the black ribbon around the queue, I recognized as that of Capt. Wells." Their leader being killed, the Miamis fled; one of their chiefs, however, before leaving the scene of the disaster, rode up to the Pottawatomies, exclaimed to them: "You have deceived the Americans and us. You have done a bad action, and brandishing his tomahawk, I will be the first to head a party of Americans to return and punish your treachery;" and then galloped away over the prairie in pursuit of his companions, who were rapidly starting for Fort Wayne. "The troops," wrote Mrs. Kinzie, "behaved most gallantly. They were but a handful; but they seemed resolved to sell their lives as dearly as possible. Our horses pranced and bounded, and could hardly be restrained, as the balls whistled among them."

The Indians made desperate attempts to rush upon and tomahawk the soldiers, but every such effort was bravely repulsed. Several women and children were killed; and the ranks at length became so reduced as not to exceed twenty effective men; yet they were undaunted and resolute, and remained united while able to fire. Withdrawing a distance, the Indians sent a French boy to demand a surrender. The boy was Capt. Heald's interpreter, who had deserted to the side of the Indians in the early part of the engagement. Advancing very cautiously toward the Americans, a Mr. Griffith advanced to meet him, intending to kill him for his conduct in deserting; but the boy declaring that it was the only way he could save himself, and at the same time appearing quite sorry for having been obliged to act as he did, he was permitted to approach. He said the Indians proposed to spare the lives of the Americans, if they would surrender. But the surviving soldiers all refused. The boy soon returned, saying the Indians were very numerous, and strongly urged Mr. Griffith to use his endeavors to bring about a surrender, which was at length consented to. The men having laid down their arms, the Indians came forward to receive them; when, in the face of their promise, they tomahawked three or four of the men; and one Indian, it is stated, with the fury of a demon, approached Mrs. Heald, with his tomahawk raised to strike her. Much accustomed to danger, and being well acquainted with Indian character, with remarkable presence of mind she looked him earnestly in the face, and smiling said: "Surely you will not kill a squaw." The Indian's arm fell, and the brave lady was protected by the barbarous hand that was about to rob her of life. She was the daughter of Gen. Samuel Wells, of Kentucky, who fought most valiantly at the battle of Tippecanoe. The rage of the Indians was lavished upon the body of Capt. Wells. After this massacre, his head was cut off, and as his character was unequaled for bravery, the Indians took his heart from his body, cooked it, and divided it among themselves in very small pieces. They religiously believed that each one who ate of it, would thereby become as brave as he from whom it was taken.

In accordance with their ancient custom, the Indians now divided the prisoners. Captain Heald and wife and Mr. Griffith being selected by the Ottawas, were taken by this band to the lake shore, beyond the mouth of the river St. Joseph. Having been severely wounded, they considered their fate as inevitably sealed; but Griffith's eye fell upon a canoe, at a convenient point, sufficiently large to hold them, and one night soon afterward they succeeded in making their escape, traversing the lake in this frail bark some 200 miles to Mackinaw, where the British commander enabled them to reach the United States in safety.

On the next day after this disaster Gen. Hull filled the cup of misfortune in the west by surrendering Detroit without firing a gun, to an inferior British force, consisting of some 700 troops and about 600 Indians, under command of Gen. Brock. This placed the whole territory in the hands of the British. Said Gen. Brock, in writing to his superior officer: "When I detail my good fortune, you will be astonished." The nation shared his astonishment and added thereto disgust.

THE SIEGE OF FORT WAYNE.

The success of the Indians at Chicago gave them courage for still greater efforts for the overthrow of the whites, and the old dream was revived of driving them beyond the Ohio. With few exceptions, the tribes were now determined in their course, and devoted to the British interests. The few tribes continuing friendly to the United States were threatened with extermination by Tecumseh, who imagined he was fast bringing his great scheme to an issue by the aid of the English. Possessing an excellent memory, and being well acquainted with every important position in the northwest, he was able to point out to the British many important advantages. Before crossing at Detroit, at the time of Hull's surrender, General Brock took occasion to inquire of Tecumseh what sort of a country he should have to pass over, should he conclude to go beyond. Taking a roll of elm bark, and extending it on the ground by means of four stones, Tecumseh drew his scalping-knife, and began to etch upon the bark the position of the country, embracing its hills, roads, rivers, morasses, and woods, which being a demonstration of talent quite unexpected in Tecumseh, greatly delighted the Briton. His position and influence—strengthened by the British, and joined by a numerous army of his own blood—were now formidable, and he was determined to render them as potent as his strength and advantages would permit.

His great plan was now the siege and massacre of Fort Wayne and Fort Harrison (near Terre Haute). The Pottawatomies and Ottawas, aided by the British under Major Muir, were to lead in the movement upon Fort Wayne, while the Winnebagoes, and a portion of the Miamis who had been persuaded to join the Tecumseh party, were to surprise and capture Fort Harrison. The first of September was appointed as the earliest period of attack.

The government, in the meantime, had begun most active measures for the renewal and prosecution of the war. Talk of invasion of Canada, by Niagara, was soon upon the breeze and the British commander, Gen. Brock, early heard the rumor. Ohio and Kentucky, upon receipt of the news from Detroit, were aroused to patriotic determination. The governor of Ohio ordered the remaining portion of the detached militia of his state, numbering some 1,200 men, to be formed and marched to Urbana, under command of Brig.-Gen. Tupper; while the secretary of war had previously called on Gov. Scott, of Kentucky, for a body of 1,500 men, embracing the regulars enlisted in that state. In the early part of May, the governor of Kentucky had organized ten regiments, some 5,500 men, as the quota of that state. Among the many patriots of Kentucky who so eagerly enlisted under the standard of their country, was Col. John Allen, who took command of the rifle regiment. He was a lawyer of much distinction and a man in great favor with his fellow-citizens. From him Allen county derived its name.

After the massacre at Chicago, those Pottawatomies engaged in it spent several weeks about Fort Dearborn, and divided the spoils which had been given them. They then retired to their villages on the St. Joseph of Lake Michigan, where they were assembled in council by British emissaries, who instigated them to lay siege to Forts Wayne and Harrison. The British agents promised that in case the Indians would besiege those forts, and prevent their evacuation by the garrisons, they should be joined in one moon by a large British force from Malden and

Detroit, with artillery, who would be able to demolish the stockades, and would give up to the savages the garrisons for massacre and spoils. The siege was to be commenced in twenty days after the council adjourned.

At this time there was a trader residing near Fort Wayne, of French extraction, Antoine Bondie. He was about fifty years of age, and had lived among the Indians from the time he was twelve years old. He was an extraordinary character. At one time he would appear to be brave and generous, at another meanly selfish. He was recognized by the Miamis as one of their tribe — married one of their squaws, and conformed to their habits and mode of life. The hostile Pottawatomies, desirous of saving him from the destruction which they contemplated for the garrison, sent Metea, chief of their tribe, and a famous orator, to inform him of their intentions and his danger. Metea went to his cabin in the night, and under an injunction of great secrecy, informed him of all that was contemplated. He offered to come for Bondie and his family before the siege was commenced, with a sufficient number of pack horses to remove them and their moveable property to a place of safety. Bondie did not decline the offer.

The morning after Metea had made this revelation, Bondie, accompanied by Charles Peltier, a French interpreter, went to the agent very early, and with many injunctions of secrecy, informed him of it all. The agent was thankful for the information, but was doubtful whether to credit or reject it, as a mistake in a matter of so much importance, either way, would prove ruinous to his character and cause his disgraceful ejection from the important office which he held. He had been but three months in office or in the country and was acquainted with but few persons. The character of Bondie was not known to him, and the nature of his communication was such as to require great secrecy, and if true, immediate preparation for the defense of the fort. Stickney sent a note to Capt. Rhea, the commanding officer of the garrison, desiring a meeting with him in the open esplanade of the fort, where there could be no one to overhear what might be said. This officer having been long in the country had every opportunity of knowing Bondie. He met the agent, heard his communication and dismissed it by observing that Bondie was a trifling fellow and no reliance could be placed upon what he said. This increased the perplexity of the agent. He sent for Bondie and his interpreter, to have a cross-examination. This being completed, it remained for the agent either to pass the matter without notice and incur the chances of the siege by the Indians of the two posts, to be followed by a regular force of British troops with artillery, without any preparation for defense or relief from abroad, or to report the information, without attaching to it his official belief in its correctness, in which case it would have no effect. In weighing and comparing chances and consequences, he determined that it was better that he should be ruined in his reputation, and the government suffer all sacrifices consequent upon the falsity of the report, than that they should both suffer if it proved true. He, therefore, sent a second time to Capt.

Rhea, and declared his intention to make the report and give it his sanction. He informed him that he had just received a dispatch from Gov. Harrison, from Vincennes, saying that he was going to Cincinnati, where he must be addressed, if necessary, and that he should send an express to him, directed to that city, and another to Captain Taylor, at Fort Harrison. When nearly ready to dispatch his messenger, Capt. Rhea sent a note to him requesting that he would delay his express to Cincinnati, until he could write a letter to the governor of Ohio, informing him of the report. Stickney complied with this request, and the express was sent with letters to Gov. Harrison and Gov. Meigs. Active preparations were now begun by the little garrison of 100 for defense. Such men as could be spared with teams were employed to send off ladies who were there, with children, to the frontier; and it was subsequently ascertained that within a few hours after the messengers had started, the Indians drew their lines around the fort.

On the 5th of August, Major Stickney was prostrated by severe illness, from which he did not become convalescent for twelve days. He was then conveyed from the agency house to the fort for safety. It was now very plain that the statement of Bondie was no fiction. He, with his Indian family, moved into the fort. The Indian warriors, to the number of some 500, as then supposed, assembled in the neighborhood of the fort; and it was evident that they had hopes of getting possession of it by stratagem. They would lie in wait near the fort, day after day, a few near, but the majority of them as much out of sight as possible. Those near were watching an opportunity to force the sentries, but these were so faithful to their duty, that no chance was presented. Stephen Johnston, who was a clerk in the United States factory store, feeling very solicitous about the safety of his wife (who had been sent to the frontier in a delicate situation), accompanied by Peter Oliver and a discharged militiaman, attempted to elude the vigilance of the Indians, and visit the place of her abode. They left at 10 o'clock at night. When a short distance south of what is now known as the Hanna homestead, Johnson was fired upon by six Indians and killed instantly. Before the Indians could reload their pieces, the remaining two men made good their retreat to the fort; and for a reward of $20, an Indian was induced to bring in the body of Mr. Johnston. The Indians disclosed their purposes by other violent acts. One one occasion two soldiers were sent out on horseback, three or four miles, to drive in some cattle. One of them was taken prisoner, the other made his escape. The Indians obtained possession of both horses. They killed cattle and hogs near the fort, stole horses, and committed many other minor depredations.

Both parties wished to delay the final conflict — Major Stickney, to give time for Gen. Harrison to send the fort the necessary relief; and the Indians, from daily expectation of the arrival of the British force which had been promised them. The Indians, however, did not cease to employ many devices and stratagems, to accomplish their object before the arrival of the British. An Indian would occasionally come near the fort, and hold conversation with an interpreter, who would be sent out for that purpose. The interpreter would be informed that the depredations had been committed by the young men, contrary to the wishes of the chiefs — that the chiefs wished for peace. At length the Indians expressed a desire to be admitted to see the commandant of the post, that they might agree upon some terms for a cessation of hostilities; and asked for a signal by which they might approach the fort and be permitted to talk with their white father. A white cloth was accordingly sent to them to be used as a flag of truce. For several days they delayed making use of the flag, and continued their depredations. The agent finally sent a message to them, by an Indian, that they had dirtied his flag, and he could not suffer them to retain it any longer; that they must return it immediately. The next day, the whole body of Indians moved up to the fort, bearing the white flag in front, evidently hoping to obtain the admission of a large number of their warriors. But the agent was too well acquainted with Indian character to be deceived. Having with difficulty, being yet ill, walked to the gate, he designated by name the chiefs to be admitted, who, upon their entrance one by one, were disarmed by the guard, and examined very closely. Thirteen only were admitted, who followed the agent to his sleeping apartment. The officers in the garrison remained in their quarters. The agent now addressed a note to Capt. Rhea, desiring that the guard should be paraded and kept under arms during the continuance of the council. In accordance with the customs of such occasions, tobacco was presented to the chiefs that they might smoke.

When the pipes began to go out, Winnemac, the Pottawatomie, rose and addressed the agent, declaring that the Pottawatomies had no hand in killing Johnston, and that the chiefs could not control their young men. The soldiers and horses had been taken without the knowledge or consent of the chiefs, in opposition to whose wishes the young men had committed all their depredations. "But," continued Winnemac, "if my father wishes for war, I am a man." At this expression the chief struck his hand upon his knife, which he had concealed under his blanket. Bondie, who was present, and understood fully what was said, jumped quickly to his feet, and striking his knife sharply, shouted in Pottawatomie, "I am a man too." The interpreter turned pale, and the faces of the chiefs present bore a look of disappointment, as they saw the guard parading under arms. The conference was closed, and, although Major Stickney was convinced of the treachery, as the chiefs had been admitted under a flag of truce, they were permitted to go out unmolested. The plan of the Indians on this occasion was subsequently divulged. They were to obtain an entrance into the fort, for as many as possible. Winnemac was to be the speaker. When he should come to the expression "I am a man," he was to dispatch the agent. Other chiefs were to rush to each of the officers' quarters, to massacre them, and others were to open the gates of the fort, to the force without. The work was then to be finished, by butchering every soul in the fort.

The commandant, Captain Rhea, who was unfortunately addicted to his cups, invited Winnemac to his quarters and held a long consultation with him there. The agent learned from the interpreter that the captain had made great professions of friendship to the chief, and had invited him to breakfast with him in the morning. Going to attempt to dissuade from so rash a proceeding, he found the captain in such a state of intoxication that it was useless to attempt to reason with him, so he sought the two lieutenants, Ostrander and Curtis, and informed them of what had taken place, and giving it as his opinion that an attack would be made the next morning, urged upon them the necessity of all possible preparation. The next morning, aroused by the firing of rifles, the agent stepped out upon a gallery that projected from the second story of his quarters, and saw two soldiers fall, mortally wounded, about fifty yards from the fort. He then ascertained that no preparations had been made in anticipation of an attack. All was confusion in the garrison. The two men were taken into the fort, and died about one o'clock that day.

About the 3d of September, a most interesting occurrence took place. A white man and three Indians arrived at the fort, on horseback, "in full yell." It was the Indian yell of triumph. The white man proved to be William Oliver. He was accompanied by Capt. Logan and his two Shawnee companions. The garrison had long been in weary suspense, not knowing whether the express to Gov. Harrison had got through or not, and every day in expectation that the British force would arrive. All were on tiptoe to hear the news — William Oliver had arrived in defiance of 500 Indians — had broken through their lines and reached the fort in safety. He reported that about 2,000 volunteers had assembled in Kentucky, and had marched to Cincinnati. Harrison having received the dispatch from the agent at Fort Wayne, had determined to march to its relief. Ohio was raising volunteers. Eight hundred were then assembled at St. Mary's, sixty miles south of Fort Wayne. They intended to march to the relief of the fort in three or four days.

William Oliver, about twenty-three years of age, was a sutler with the garrison at Fort Wayne, but had made a visit to Cincinnati, and did not until he had returned as far as Piqua, learn of the siege. He immediately joined a rifle company, expecting to advance at once to the relief; but becoming impatient determined to go to Cincinnati and induce Col. Wells to advance with the Seventeenth regiment, or else try to reach the fort alone and encourage his friends to hold out. He found Harrison at Cincinnati, who assured him the troops would march at once. Oliver declared his intention of going through the Indian lines to carry the news to the fort, but the general warned him of the danger, and as he shook hands with him, observed "that he should not see him again." In four days he overtook the militia at the St. Mary's and learned that scouts reported the Indians in great force on the route to the fort. But he had taken his life in his hand and would not abandon the enterprise. On the next day, Gen. Thomas Worthington, then an Indian commissioner, joined him, and they secured an escort of sixty-eight militia and Logan and fifteen other Shawnees. On the second day, thirty-six of the party became frightened and returned; the remainder in the evening camped twenty-four miles from Fort Wayne. Here Worthington and the rest were persuaded to remain, while Oliver, Logan, Captain John and Bright-Horn pushed on.

Well armed and mounted, they started at daybreak of September 3d, and cautiously advanced. When within five miles of the fort, Logan discovered that the Indians had dug holes on either side of the trace, alternately, at such distances as to protect themselves from their own fire, and were ready to meet all attempts at communication. The party consequently struck across the country to the Maumee, which they reached a mile and a half below the fort. Tying their horses in a thicket, they crept forward until they discovered that the garrison was still in possession. They then returned to their horses, remounted, and riding at the greatest speed reached the gate of the esplanade. Finding this locked they rode down the river bank, and ascended to the northern gate. Fortune had favored them, for just at this time, the Indian hostiles were engaged in concocting another plan to capture the fort by stratagem, and at the gate the apparition of Oliver and his men surprised Winnemac and Five Medals, who were about to ask admittance with treacherous designs. Said one of the lieutenants of the fort: "The safe arrival of Oliver at this particular juncture may be considered miraculous. One hour sooner or one hour later, would no doubt have been inevitable destruction both to himself and his escort. It is generally believed by those acquainted with the circumstances, that not one hour, for eight days and nights preceding or following the hour which Mr. Oliver arrived, would have afforded an opportunity of any safety."

Oliver prepared a hasty letter to Washington, and Logan and his companions, supplied with new rifles, were cautiously let out of the gate, whence they started at the utmost speed of their horses. The hostiles made a desperate effort to intercept them, but the anxious garrison soon heard the couriers' yells of triumph far beyond the besiegers' lines.

From the 5th the siege was active. An incessant firing was kept up day and night; several times the buildings were set on fire by burning arrows which were shot within the stockade, but the vigilance of the garrison prevented a conflagration. A few days after Oliver's arrival, the Indians, in the evening, gained possession of a trading house near the fort, and from this point demanded a surrender. Protection was promised in that case, but extermination if the fort was carried by storm. To emphasize their demand, they claimed to have received large reinforcements, some pieces of British cannon, and artillerists; the demand was refused, and then with hideous yells, the savages swarmed in upon the fort, opening a heavy fire, in which two cannon joined. Every man in the garrison capable of duty stood at his post with several stands of loaded rifles at hand. Curtis, the acting lieutenant, gave orders not to fire until the enemy had approached within twenty-five paces. This order was executed and such a destructive fire opened that in twenty minutes the Indians retreated with a loss of eighteen men. It was afterward discovered that the cannon used were made of logs by some British traders. Only three loads were fired from them before they burst.

Gov. Harrison was so popular, that the governor of Kentucky disregarded the state law, and made him brigadier-general of the Kentucky militia, whom he led as rapidly as possible to the relief of Fort Wayne. The faithful Shawnees met the advancing army at Piqua, Ohio, where the message of Oliver was delivered to Gen. Harrison, who drew his men together, and made them a speech. Said he: "If there is a man under my command who lacks the patriotism to rush to the rescue, he, by paying back the money received from the government, shall receive a discharge, as I do not wish to command such." But one man responded to the proposition. His name was Miller, of the Kentucky militia; and having obtained his discharge, on the morning of the 6th, his comrades, not willing to let him return without some special manifestation of appreciation, put him on a rail, carried him around the lines to the music of the Rogue's March, and down to the Miami, where they took him off the rail, let him into the water and baptized him in the name of "King George, Aaron Burr, and the Devil." As he emerged, the men stood on the bank and threw handsful of mud at him, then, forming into two lines in an adjacent lane, made him run the gauntlet, each one contributing a handful of dirt. Harrison learned at this time that Gen. Winchester was to command, but that officer being yet in the rear, the hero of Tippecanoe resolved to push on and save Fort Wayne.

On the morning of the 6th the army began its march for Fort Wayne, encamping that evening in the woods some twelve miles from Piqua. Early on the morning of the 7th [Monday], the army resumed its march, made fifteen miles, and encamped on a branch three and a half miles from the St. Mary's. September 8th, they marched to St. Mary's where they lay till next day. There they were joined by 200 mounted volunteers under Col. Richard M. Johnson, who had volunteered for thirty days, on hearing that Fort Wayne was besieged. Wednesday, September 9th, they marched eighteen miles to Shane's Crossing, where they overtook a regiment of 800 men from Ohio, under Colonels Adams and Hawkins, who had started on to the relief of Fort Wayne. From this point Logan and four Shawnee companions acted as scouts for the army. Cols. Adams and Hawkins joined the army and all marched together, numbering about 3,500 men. They marched ten miles and encamped. A strong detachment of spies under Capt. James Sugget of Scott county, marched considerably ahead of the army, and Sugget came upon the trail of a large party which he immediately pursued. After following the trail some distance he was fired on by an Indian, who had secreted himself in a clump of bushes so near to Sugget that the powder burnt his clothes, but the ball missed him. The Indian jumped from his covert and attempted to escape, but Andrew Johnson, of Scott's, shot him. At the crack of the gun, the Indian's gun and blanket fell. Supposing that he had killed him, and being eager in pursuit of the trail, they made no halt; but before they could overtake the Indians they had to give up the pursuit on account of the lateness of the hour and the distance they were ahead of the army. On returning to where the Indian was shot they found the gun and blanket, but he had escaped. They followed the blood for some distance and found pieces of his handkerchief, which he had cut into plugs to stop the blood, but he had bled so profusely that it had forced them out of the wound. On returning to camp Logan held up the bloody blanket and exhibited it as he rode along the line. Orders were immediately issued for the troops to turn out and make a breastwork around the encampment, and before dark the same was fortified by a breastwork made by cutting down trees and piling them on each other. A strong picket guard was detailed and posted at a considerable distance from the line. Orders were given that in case two shots were heard in quick succession, the men were quickly to repair to the breastwork, and several alarms brought them to their post, but they proved to be false, arising from the fears of the militia, unused to war, although it was ascertained afterward that the Indians were prepared to attack had they not found the pickets so watchful.

On Saturday, September 10, after an early and scant breakfast, the army resumed its march toward Fort Wayne. From St. Mary's it moved in two lines, one on the right, and the other on the left of the trace, at a distance of about 100 yards therefrom, while the wagons kept the trace. Sugget's spies went ahead, and on coming to where they had left the trail of the wounded Indian, they again took it, and after following it a short distance, found his dead body. When he found he could not survive, he broke bushes and covered himself with them in order to hide his body.

The Indians prepared to draw Harrison into an ambush and give battle at a swamp five miles southeast of the fort, but finding him too wary and his force too strong, they kindled extensive fires to create an impression with the garrison that a battle had occurred, and then retreated past the fort in apparently great confusion, hoping to draw out the garrison. But this final ruse failed, and the Indians withdrew, ending a weary watch of about twenty days' duration. When Harrison perceived the stand of the enemy at the swamp, a halt was made, and the army disposed for battle. Col. Hawkins, of the Ohio mounted volunteers, left the lines and went some distance from the road. Being partly concealed by a clump of bushes, one of his men took him for an Indian and shot him through. The ball entered between the shoulders and came out at the breast, but fortunately did not prove mortal.

At the first grey of the morning of the 12th of September, the distant halloos of the disappointed savages revealed to the anxious inmates of the fort the approach of the army. Great clouds of dust could be seen from the fort, rolling up in the distance, as the soldiery under Gen. Harrison moved forward to the rescue; and in the evening, the army stood before the fort, while the woods resounded with the glad shouts of welcome to Harrison and the brave boys of Ohio and Kentucky.

The ambuscade at the five-mile swamp was directed by Metea, the most noted chief of the Pottawatomies, who at this time was in the zenith of his power. His villages were on the St. Joseph river, one at the table-land where Cedarville now stands, the other seven miles from Fort Wayne, on the section afterward known as the Bourie reserve. While preparing his ambuscade at the marsh, he was attacked by Major Mann and a few skirmishers, and shot by the Major. The chief's arm was broken, but he made his escape, although hotly pursued by the officer. Metea lived in the vicinity of Fort Wayne until May, 1827, when he died from poison, administered it is supposed by some Indians who were incensed at him for his adherence to the treaty of 1826. He was buried on the sand-hill near the site of Fort Wayne college.

The garrison during the siege had been well supplied with provisions, and there was a good well of water within the inclosure. Among the means of defense were four small field pieces. If it could be protected from fire, the post was able to withstand a considerable Indian siege. Capt. McAfee, a source of much of the information concerning this period, gave this military estimate of the fort: "It is delightfully situated, on an eminence on the south bank of the Miami of the lakes, immediately below the formation of that river by the junction of the St. Mary's from the southwest with the St. Joseph's from the north. It is well constructed of block houses and picketing, but could not resist a British force, as there are several eminences on the south side, from which it could be commanded by a six or nine pounder." The garrison had lost but three men. From subsequent information, it was believed that the Indian loss was about twenty-five. Eight were seen to fall. One Indian was killed at a distance of 300 yards, while standing in the St. Mary's river. A soldier named King, with a long, heavy rifle, fired, and the ball took effect in the back of the savage between his shoulders, and he fell into the water. This feat was witnessed by the whole garrison.

Previous to the beginning of the siege, there were several dwellings near the fort, forming a little village, but these were now in ruins, having been burned, as well as the government factory, by the hostiles. The handsome farm in the fork of the rivers, belonging to Captain Wells, and still known as the Wells reserve, was overrun and his buildings destroyed. The corn which had been cultivated by the villagers was nearly all gone, and the remnants served as forage for Harrison's cavalry.

Capt. Rhea had been so utterly incompetent that immediately after the arrival of Gen. Harrison, Lieuts. Ostrander and Curtis preferred charges against him, and called upon Major Stickney, the agent, as a witness. The general assembled his principal officers as a board of inquiry, and it was shown that Rhea was drunk six days during the siege. Gen. Harrison, out of consideration for the advanced age of the captain granted him leave to resign by the 1st of January.

THE LAST YEAR OF WAR.

On the second day after the arrival of the army, Gen. Harrison formed two detachments, with orders to destroy the Indian villages in northeastern Indiana, the first division being composed of the regiments under Cols. Lewis and Allen, and Captain Garrard's troop of horse, under Gen. Payne, accompanied by Gen. Harrison; the second division, under Col. Wells, accompanied by a battalion of his own regiment, under Major Davenport (Scott's regiment), the mounted battalion under Johnson, and the mounted Ohio men under Adams.

In order that the Indians' means of subsistence might also be cut off, it was determined while destroying the villages to cut up and destroy the corn and other products. After a march of a few miles, the troops under Payne came to the Miami villages, at the forks of the Wabash, where, finding the villages abandoned, the troops were ordered to cut up the corn and destroy the vegetables in the field adjacent. At this point was observed the tomb of a chief, built of logs, and bedaubed with clay. This chief was laid on his blanket, with his gun and his pipe by his side, a small tin pan on his breast, containing a wooden spoon, and a number of earrings and brooches — all deemed necessary, no doubt, on his journey to the other world.

On the 16th of September the body under Col. Wells had advanced to the Pottawatomie village, known as Five Medals, on the Elkhart river, near the site of Goshen. Having crossed the river, about three miles above the village, and formed in order of battle, in a plain thinly timbered, the division advanced to the right and left of the village, and then surrounded it; but, to the regret of all, the place was found deserted, the Indians having abandoned it two days before, leaving behind considerable quantities of corn, gathered and laid on scaffolds to dry, with abundance of beans, potatoes and other vegetables, which furnished an ample store of provisions for the men and forage for the horses. This village was called Five Medals, from a chief of that name, who made it his residence. On a pole, before the door of that chief, a red flag was hung, with a broom tied above it; and on another pole at the tomb of an old woman, a white flag was flying. The body of the old woman was entire, sitting upright, with her face toward the east; and a basket beside her, containing trinkets, such as owl and hawk bills and claws, a variety of bones, and bunches of roots tied together; all of which indicated that she had been revered as a sorceress. In one of the huts was found a morning report of one of Hull's captains, also a Liberty Hall newspaper, printed at Cincinnati, containing an account of Gen. Harrison's army. Several coarse bags, which appeared to have contained shot, and pieces of boxes with London and Malden printed on them, were also picked up in the cabin; which proved that these Indians were intimately connected with the British, and had been furnished with information by some one, perhaps, in our own country. This village, with some seventy acres of corn, was destroyed, and after a most fatiguing march, from the effects of which one man died soon after the return of the division, the force arrived again at the fort on the 18th, a few hours after the body under Payne had returned.

On the day before the return of these divisions, Col. Simrall, with a regiment of dragoons, armed with muskets, and numbering some 320 men, also a company of mounted riflemen, under Col. Farrow, from Montgomery county, Ky., had arrived at the fort; and on the evening of the return of Payne and Wells, Gen. Harrison sent them to destroy the village called Turtle, some twenty miles northwest of the fort, with orders not to molest the buildings formerly erected by the United States for the benefit of Little Turtle, whose friendship for the Americans had ever been firm after the treaty of Greenville.

In addition to these movements, Gen. Harrison took the precaution to remove all the undergrowth in the locality surrounding the fort, extending toward the confluence of the St. Joseph and St. Mary's, to where now stands Rudisill's mill, and westward to the point now occupied by the Fort Wayne college, thence southeast to about the site of the residence of the late Allen Hamilton, and to the east down the Maumee a short distance. So well cleared was the ground, including a large part of the present area of the city of Fort Wayne, that it was said that a sentinel " on the bastions of the fort, looking westward, could see a rabbit running across the grounds as far as so small an object was discernible by the naked eye." By this " extensive clearing" the Indians were left without any shelter for ambush. Some thirty or forty acres, of what is yet known as the Cole farm, extending to the junction of the rivers, and just opposite the Maumee, was then known as the Public Meadow, and had long been a considerable open space.

Gen. Harrison made an official report of his transactions to the war department, and about the 19th of September Brig.-Gen. James Winchester arrived at the fort to take command of the first division of Kentucky troops. Gen. Winchester had seen service in the revolutionary struggle, and at this period was somewhat advanced in years. He was a man of some wealth, and resided in Tennessee, where he is said to have lived many years in a degree of elegant luxury and ease, which was not calculated to season him for a northern campaign in the forest.

Gen. Harrison was ever a favorite with his soldiers, and commanded in a remarkable degree the love and confidence of both the rank and file. When Gen. Winchester arrived to take command of the forces there was great dissatisfaction among the troops. Indeed, so great was the aversion to the change, that many of the militia were disposed not to be under his command, and it was with much difficulty that Gen. Harrison and the field officers succeeded in reconciling them to the change of officers. During no other war of the United States was the value of a true leader so thoroughly demonstrated as in the campaign against the Miamis. The men were persuaded to march under Gen. Winchester, with the confident belief that Gen. Harrison would sooner or later again assume command of them. He did become commander-in-chief on the 24th; and while the unfortunate Winchester's career ended at the river Raisin, he won lasting fame at the river Thames.

On the 19th the command of the troops at the fort was transferred to Gen. Winchester, and any part of the infantry which he might deem necessary to the extension of his plans was placed at his disposal.

The same evening Gen. Harrison started toward Piqua, to take command of the forces collecting in the rear; and to arrange for a mounted expedition against Detroit — intending to surprise that point by marching on a route but little known, from Fort Wayne up the St. Joseph, and thence to the headwaters of the river Raisin. His troops consisted of three regiments from Kentucky, under Barbee, Payne and Jennings; three companies of mounted riflemen from the same state, under Capts. Roper, Bacon and Clarke; also a corps of mounted Ohioans who had rendezvoused at Dayton on the 15th, in obedience to a call by Govs. Meigs and Harrison, commanded by Col. Findley, who had re-entered the service since the surrender of Gen. Hull.

On the 20th Gen. Harrison met the mounted men and the regiment of Jennings at St. Mary's (Girty Town), the remainder of the infantry being still further in the rear. The general having left orders at Fort Wayne for Johnson's battalion and Col. Simrall's dragoons, which were not included in Gen. Winchester's command, to return to St. Mary's as early as possible, Major Johnson, on the morning of the 20th, began his line of march, but after an advance of some twenty miles, was met by orders from Gen. Harrison, to return to Fort Wayne again, and there await further orders. The force returned, excepting Ensign Wm. Holton, with about twenty-five men of Capt. Ward's company, who refusing to obey orders, started for Kentucky.

General Winchester had now removed his camp to the forks of the Maumee; and early on the 22d of September, he moved down the north side of that stream, over very nearly the same route as that by which Gen. Wayne's army had reached the Miami villages in 1794, intending to go as far as Fort Defiance, at the mouth of the Auglaize, with a view of forming a junction there with the infantry in the rear, who were to come from the St. Mary's, by way of the Auglaize.

Before leaving the forks of the Maumee, Winchester issued the following order:

"The front guard in three lines, two deep in the road, and in Indian files on the flanks at distances of fifty and one hundred yards, as the ground will admit. A fatigue party to consist of one captain, one

R C Bell

ensign, two sergeants, and two corporals, with fifty men, will follow the front guard for the purpose of opening the road. The remainder of the infantry to march on the flanks in the following order: Colonels Wells and Allen's regiments on the right, and Lewis' and Scott's on the left. The general and brigade baggage, commissaries and quartermaster's stores, immediately in the rear of the fatigue party. The cavalry in the following order: Capt. Garrard and twenty of his men to precede the guard in front, and equally divided at the head of each line; a lieutenant and eighteen men in the rear of the whole army and baggage; the balance of the cavalry equally divided on the flanks or the flank lines. The regimental baggage wagons will fall in according to the respective ranks of their commanding officers. The officers commanding corps previous to their marching will examine carefully the arms and ammunition of their respective corps, and see that they are in good order. They will also be particularly careful that the men do not waste their cartridges. No loaded muskets are to be put in the wagons. One-half of the fatigue party is to work at a time, and the others will carry their arms. The wagon master will attend to loading the wagons, and see that the various articles are put in, in good order, and that each wagon and team carry a reasonable load. The hour of march will be 9 o'clock this morning. The officer of the day is charged with this order. The line of battle will be the same as that of General Harrison in his last march to Fort Wayne."

The march down the Maumee was made with great precaution, at the rate of five or six miles each day, and the camp strongly fortified every night. Not many miles had been gained before a party of Indians were discovered, and the signs were strong that there were many more in the region. A volunteer company of scouts having been organized under Capt. Ballard, Lieut. Harrison Munday, of the rifle regiment, and Ensign Liggett, of the 17th U. S. infantry, they were kept in advance to reconnoiter the country. On the 25th, Ensign Liggett having obtained permission to proceed as far as Fort Defiance, he was accompanied by four men of McCracken's company from Woodford, Ky. Late that evening, while preparing some food, they were discovered by a Frenchman and eight Indians, who surprised them with a demand to surrender. On being assured that they would not be hurt, and would be permitted to wear their arms till they entered the British camp, they surrendered; but the Indians and Frenchman as they walked on, concocted and executed the following plan for their destruction: five of the Indians, each having marked his victim, walked behind and one side of the men, and, at a given signal fired upon them. Four of them fell dead; Liggett escaped the first fire and sprung to a tree, but was shot while raising his gun. Next day Capt. Ballard, with a part of his company, being in advance, discovered the dead bodies and a party of Indians watching near them. He formed his men for action with the Maumee on his right, but not liking his position, and perceiving that the Indians were too strong for him, he fell back 200 yards and formed in a stronger position. The enemy supposing he had fled, filed off from their right flank intending to surround him on his left, and cut off his retreat. He heard them pass by on his left without discovering him, and then filed off by the left in their rear, and by a circuitous route arrived safely at the camp.

Lieut. Munday, with another body of the scouts, presently happened at the same place, and discovering some Indians, who still remained there, formed his men and charged upon them, at the same time saluting them with their own yell. They fled precipitately, and Munday, on discovering their superior numbers, took advantage of their panic to withdraw. Next morning, the 27th, Capt. Ballard, with his spies and Capt. Garrard's troop of horse, accompanied by Major Woolford, aid to the general, and some other volunteers, went forward to bury the dead. The Indians were still in ambush; but Capt. Ballard expecting it, approached them in a different direction, so as to disconcert their plans. He attacked them with a brisk fire, and Capt. Garrard immediately ordered a charge, on which they fled in every direction, leaving trails of blood from their killed and wounded.

These Indians were the advance of an army organized to attack Fort Wayne, consisting of 200 regulars under Major Muir, of the British army, with four pieces of artillery, and about 1,000 Indians, commanded by Elliott. They had brought their baggage and artillery by water to old Fort Defiance, at the mouth of the Auglaize, where they had left their boats and were advancing up the south side of the Maumee toward Fort Wayne. Upon the approach of Winchester, they threw their cannon into the river, together with their fixed amunition, and retreated in great haste. Gen. Winchester did not pursue them.

Fort Harrison (near Terre Haute), had been besieged also, but here Zachary Taylor, then a young captain, first drew to himself the admiration of the nation by a gallant and successful defense.

Thus the plan of the British to take the posts of Forts Wayne and Harrison, then to give them up to massacre, and to turn about 1,500 Indians loose upon the frontier to kill and lay waste, had come to defeat.

The only other important military event for several weeks was a successful though perilous movement upon a party of British and Indians at the Rapids, by a small body of troops under Gen. Tupper, wherein the former were put to flight, but after the retreat a few of Tupper's men were killed by the Indians. The British and Indians now fell back upon the river Raisin, and Gen. Harrison prepared to establish at the Rapids a grand base of supplies for a campaign against Detroit and Canada.

Soon after this movement, Capt. James Logan, the faithful Shawnee chief, had proceeded with a small number of his tribe to make observations in the direction of the Rapids. Having met and been closely pursued by a superior force, he and his men were obliged to disperse and retreat, and Logan, with but two of his comrades, Captain John and Bright-Horn, succeeded in reaching the camp of Gen. Winchester.

The second officer in command of the Kentucky troops, without the slightest ground, accused Logan of infidelity and giving intelligence to the enemy. Indignant, and burning under the insult, Logan called in his friend Oliver, and told him he would start out next morning and either leave his body bleaching in the woods or return with such trophies as would vindicate his loyalty. Accordingly, on the 22d of November, accompanied by Captain John and Bright-Horn, he started down the Maumee about noon. Having stopped to rest, they were surprised by a party of seven of the enemy, mounted, among them young Elliott, the half-breed British officer, and the celebrated Winnemac. With great presence of mind Logan extended his hand to the chief and pretended that he had left the Americans and wished to join the British. Winnemac shrewdly proceeded to disarm the Shawnees, and his party surrounding them, they moved toward the British camp. But Logan persisted so strongly in his story that finally the arms were returned to him and his men. Overhearing Winnemac and Elliott talking of shooting them down if they made a move to escape, Logan determined to take the offensive, and managed to give the word to his companions. Captain John put some extra bullets in his mouth, with the expression "Me chaw heap tobac." It was soon determined to encamp for night, and as the British party scattered somewhat, Logan and his men opened fire upon them. By the first fire both Winnemac and Elliott fell; by the second a young Ottawa chief lost his life, and two more of the enemy were mortally wounded about the conclusion of the combat. But at this time Logan himself, as he was stooping down, received a ball just below the breast-bone which ranged downward and lodged under the skin of his back. Bright-Horn was also wounded by a ball which passed through his thigh. As soon as Logan was shot, he ordered a retreat; he and Bright-Horn, wounded as they were, jumped on the horses of the enemy and rode to Winchester's camp, a distance of twenty miles, in five hours. Captain John, after taking the scalp of Winnemac, also retreated in safety and arrived at the camp next morning.

Logan had wiped out the imputation against him, but he died after two or three days of extreme agony. He endured the pain with great fortitude and died satisfied. "More firmness and consummate bravery has seldom appeared on the military theatre," said Winchester, in his letter to the commanding general. "He was buried with all the honors due to his rank, and with sorrow as sincerely and generally displayed, as I ever witnessed," said Major Hardin, in a letter to Gov. Shelby.

Spemika-lawba, the High Horn, one of the Machachac tribe of Shawnees, obtained the name of Logan from Col. Logan, of Kentucky, who captured him when a boy, and made him for several years a member of his family. He finally returned to his tribe and became a civil chief. It has been stated, manifestly without reason, that he was related to Tecumseh. He married an Indian maiden, who, when young, had been taken prisoner by Col. Hardin, in 1789. In the army he had formed an attachment for Major Hardin, son of the colonel, and son-in-law of Gen. Logan, and on his death bed, requested him to see that the money due for his services was faithfully paid to his family. He also requested, that his family might be removed immediately to Kentucky, and his children educated and brought up in the manner of the white people. Logan was widely known as a friend of the whites. He was one of the guides for Gen. Hull, and prior to the siege of Fort Wayne, he was intrusted by John Johnston, of Piqua, with the delicate and dangerous duty of bringing the women and children from the threatened post. He conducted twenty-five women and children 100 miles in safety, and did not sleep from the time he left Fort Wayne until he arrived at Piqua.

About the time of Tupper's expedition to the Rapids, Gen. Harrison determined to send an expedition of horsemen against the Miamis, assembled in the towns on the Mississinewa river, a branch of the Wabash. A deputation of chiefs from those Indians met Gen. Harrison at St. Mary's, early in October, and sued for peace, agreeing to abide by the decision of the president, and in the meantime to send in five chiefs to be held as hostages. The president replied to the communication of the general on this subject, that, as the disposition of the several tribes would be known best by himself, he must treat them as their conduct and the public interest might, in his judgment, require. The hostages were never sent in, and further information of their intended hostility was obtained. At the time of their peace mission, they were alarmed by the successful movements which had been made against other tribes from Fort Wayne, and by a formidable expedition which was penetrating their country under Gen. Hopkins. But the failure of that expedition was soon afterward known to them, and they determined to continue hostile. A white man by the name of William Connor, who had resided many years with the Delawares, and had a wife among them, but who was firmly attached to the American cause in this war, was sent to the towns to watch the movements of the Miamis. He visited the villages on the Mississinewa river, and was present at several of their councils. The question of war with the United States and union with the British was warmly debated, and there was much division among the chiefs, but the war party at last prevailed. The presence of Tecumseh, and afterward the retreat of Gen. Hopkins, rendered them nearly unanimous for war.

To avert the evils of their hostility, was the object of the expedition against Mississinewa. Said Harrison: "The situation of this town, as it regards one line of operations, even if the hostility of the inhabitants was less equivocal, would render a measure of this kind highly proper; but from the circumstance of Gen. Hopkins' failure it becomes indispensable. Relieved from the fears excited by the invasion of their country, the Indians from the upper part of the Illinois river, and to the south of Lake Michigan, will direct all their efforts against Fort Wayne and the convoys which are to follow the left wing of the army. Mississinewa will be their rendezvous, where they will receive provisions and every assistance they may require for any hostile enterprise. From that place they can, by their runners, ascertain the period at which every convoy may set out from St. Mary's and with certainty intercept it on its way to the Maumee Rapids. But that place being broken up, and the provisions destroyed, there will be nothing to subsist any body of Indians, nearer than the Pottawatomie towns on the St. Joseph of the lake."

This expedition numbered about 600 mounted riflemen, under Lieut.-Col. Campbell. It left Franklinton on the 25th of November, by way of Dayton and Greenville; and reached the Indian towns on the Mississinewa toward the middle of December, suffering much from the cold. In a rapid charge upon the first village, eight warriors were killed, and forty-two taken prisoners, including men, women and children. About half an hour before day, the morning following this charge, the detachment was attacked by the Indians, and after a sharp but short encounter, in which Campbell lost eight killed, and forty-eight wounded, the enemy fled precipitately with a heavy loss.

Learning from a prisoner that Tecumseh was within eighteen miles of them, with a body of 600 warriors, with the number of wounded then to be cared for, it was deemed advisable to return, and the detachment, having previously destroyed the towns they had approached, started upon their return march, and reached Dayton during the early part of January. The good effect of the expedition was soon felt, as it disclosed who were friends and who were enemies among the Indians.

The winter being severe, and unfavorable to transportation, the army of Harrison suffered many privations for the want of sufficient provisions and clothing; yet though it was midwinter in the wild and trackless forests, the government and people were impatient, and anxiety was manifest for a forward march against the British.

At the River Raisin.—On January 10th, 1813, Gen. Winchester having received orders to advance toward the British lines, reached the Rapids, preceded by a detachment of 670 men, under Gen. Payne, who had been ordered to attack a party of Indians gathered in an old fortification at Swan creek. A large stone house was built within the encampment, at the Rapids, to secure the provisions and baggage. A considerable quantity of corn was also gathered in the fields, and apparatus for pounding and sifting it being made, it supplied the troops with very wholesome bread.

It soon became apparent that an attack was meditated by the British upon the forces under Winchester, they having heard through some Indians of the advance of the army. Consequently, on the morning of the 17th, Gen. Winchester detached Col. Lewis, with 550 men, for the river Raisin; and a few hours later, Lewis' detachment was followed by 110 more under Col. Allen. On the morning of this day Gen. Winchester sent a message to Gen. Harrison, acquainting him with the movements made, and desiring a reinforcement, in case of opposition in an effort to possess and hold Frenchtown. With this express was also sent word that 400 Indians were at the river Raisin, and that Elliott was expected from Malden, with an expedition to attack the camp at the Rapids.

Early on the morning of the 19th, the messenger reached Gen. Harrison, who ordered another detachment to proceed at once to the Rapids, which reached there on the morning of the 20th, accompanied by the commander-in-chief. In the meantime, on the 18th, the troops under Lewis and Allen, who had proceeded toward the river Raisin, to occupy Frenchtown, had been attacked by the enemy, who were driven back with considerable loss, leaving the town in the possession of the federal forces. On receipt of news of this action, Gen. Winchester set out with 250 men for the relief of the forces at Frenchtown, and arrived at the river Raisin on the 20th. The British and Indian advance, under Col. Proctor, was preparing to renew the attack of the 18th, and on the night of the 21st advanced unobserved very near the American lines. Early on the morning of the 22d, the enemy, from a position within about 300 yards of the American lines, opened a heavy fire with cannon and musketry, and soon succeeded in nearly surrounding the camp.

The Americans fought bravely, but were overpowered, and an indiscriminate slaughter followed. In their confusion and dismay, the Americans attempted to pass down a long narrow lane, through which the road ran from the village. The Indians were on both sides, and shot them down in great numbers. A large party, which had gained the wood, on the right, were surrounded and massacred, nearly 100 men being tomahawked within the distance of 100 yards. The most horrible destruction overwhelmed the fugitives in every direction.

Captain Simpson was shot and tomahawked at the edge of the woods, near the mouth of the lane. Col. Allen, who has been before mentioned, though wounded in his thigh, attempted to rally his men several times, entreating them to halt and sell their lives as dearly as possible. He had escaped about two miles, when, at length, wearied and exhausted, and disdaining perhaps to survive the defeat, he sat down on a log, determined to meet his fate. An Indian chief, observing him to be an officer of distinction, was anxious to take him prisoner. As soon as he came near the Colonel, he threw his gun across his lap, and told him in the Indian language to surrender and he should be safe. Another savage having, at the same time, advanced with a hostile appearance, Col. Allen, by one stroke of his sword, laid him dead at his feet. A third Indian, near by, had then the honor of shooting one of the first and greatest citizens of Kentucky. Capt. Mead, of the regular army, who had fought by the side of Col. Daviess, when he fell in the battle of Tippecanoe, was killed where the action was commenced. Finding that the situation of the corps was rendered desperate by the approach of the enemy, he gave orders to his men — " My brave fellows, charge upon them;" and a moment afterward he was no more.

A party with Lieut. Garrett, consisting of fifteen or twenty men, after retreating about a mile and a half, was compelled to surrender, and and all massacred, but the lieutenant. Another party of about thirty men had escaped nearly three miles, when they were overtaken by the savages, and having surrendered, about one-half of them were shot and tomahawked. In short, the greater part of those who were in the retreat, fell a sacrifice to the fury of the Indians. The snow was so deep, and the cold so intense, that they were soon exhausted, and unable to elude their pursuers. Gen. Winchester and Col. Lewis, with a few more, were captured at a bridge, about three-quarters of a mile from the village. Their coats being taken from them, they were carried back to the British lines.

A party, under Majors Graves and Madison, having placed themselves behind some picketing, maintained their position and fought bravely, until an order, reported as coming from Gen. Winchester, was brought by Proctor, who was accompanied by one of his aids, desiring them to surrender. Major Madison remarked "that it had been customary for the Indians to massacre the wounded and prisoners after a surrender, and that he would not agree to any capitulation, which Gen. Winchester might direct, unless the safety and protection of his men were stipulated." To which Proctor replied: "Sir, do you mean to dictate to me?" "No," said Madison; "I mean to dictate for myself, and we prefer selling our lives as dearly as possible, rather than be massacred in cold blood."

Terms embodying positive protection to all having at length been agreed upon, Madison surrendered and his party reached Malden in safety. But the Indians soon returned to the scene of disaster, and began an unmerciful slaughter of the wounded, stripping them, and even setting fire to the houses in which many of them were sheltered, burning them with the buildings. In this terrible affair about 400 Americans were killed and 520 made prisoners.

When Gen. Harrison received news of the opening of the engagement, he ordered Perkin's brigade to proceed to his relief, and soon after mounted his horse and overtook some reinforcements under Payne. But they had not proceeded far when they were met by some men from the scene of defeat, who told the sad story of the fate that had befallen their comrades. Its effect was to nerve Gen. Harrison to push on with greater speed. However, another party was met, and, after a council as to the wisdom of proceeding, it was deemed proper to venture no nearer the scene of disaster, as no succor could be rendered the victims of the furious red men and merciless British opponents, and a further advance would only tend to furnish more material for massacre and defeat. Subsequent to the battle, the British sent Gen. Winchester, Col. Lewis and Major Madison to Quebec, where and at Beaufort they were confined till the spring of 1814.

Siege of Fort Meigs.— After these events little of importance occurred until the latter part of April. On the 16th of February, the governor of Kentucky, in compliance with a law that had been recently passed in that state, had ordered a draft of 3,000 men, to be organized into four regiments, under Colonels Dudley, Boswell, Cox and Caldwell, under the command of Gen. Green Clay. As the season advanced, it became evident that the British would soon make an attack on the American lines at Fort Meigs, Harrison's base on the Maumee; and this was made the more certain from the fact that the enemy had recently learned the situation of affairs in the American army from a prisoner they had taken. This condition of affairs was communicated to the war department, and the propriety of calling out the remainder of the Kentucky draft, to be placed at Fort Wayne to keep the Indians in check, was pressed upon the attention of the government.

Both the American and British armies became active in their movements; and the British commander made bold to assert that he would march the northwestern army under Gen. Harrison, to Montreal by the first of June. During the latter part of April, the British had often been seen, in small bodies, near Fort Meigs, by scouts sent out by the commanding-general; and on the 26th of April, the enemy's advance was observed at the mouth of the bay. On the 28th, as Captain Hamilton was descending the Maumee, with a small reconnoitering party, he beheld the whole force of the British and Indians coming up the river within a few miles of the fort. The British, with a force of 3,000, took possession of old Fort Miami, just below the scene of Wayne's engagement with the Indians in 1794, opposite and two miles below Fort Meigs. Three batteries were erected opposite Fort Meigs, and the Indians, occupying the south side of the river, invested the garrison.

About the 1st of May, the British, having completed their batteries, commenced a heavy cannonade against Fort Meigs, which was continued for five days, with but little effect. The American batteries returned the fire, but with little energy, not wishing to waste ammunition.

Tecumseh and the Prophet, with a body of some 600 Indians, since the fatal affair at the Raisin river (Tecumseh not having been present at that engagement), had joined the British, and were directing the Indian operations against the Americans.

About the time of the opening of the British batteries, Gen. Harrison had expected a reinforcement under Gen. Green Clay; and when the movements of the British became fully apparent, Capt. Oliver, accompanied by a white man and an Indian, was sent as a messenger to Gen. Clay, with letters also for the governors of Ohio and Kentucky.

Fears had been entertained that the enemy would at length make an effort to gain a nearer approach to the fort, and erect a battery on the same side of the river. This was done on the 3d, and three field pieces and a howitzer were opened upon the American camp from a clump of bushes on the left, but were soon hushed by a few shots from the eighteen pounders of the American batteries. Changing their position, the batteries were again opened, but with little effect. Said Col. Wood, of the American forces: "With a plenty of ammunition, we should have been able to blow John Bull almost from the Miami. * * * It was extremely diverting to see with what pleasure and delight the Indians would yell, whenever in their opinion considerable damage was done in camp by the bursting of a shell. Their hanging about the camp, and occasionally coming pretty near, kept our lines almost constantly in a blaze of fire; for nothing can please a Kentuckian better than to get a shot at an Indian — and he must be indulged."

With a reinforcement of some 1,200 Kentuckians, Gen. Clay soon drew near. Capt. Oliver had met him at Fort Winchester. Gen. Harrison immediately sent an order to Gen. Clay, which was delivered by Capt. Hamilton, requesting him to detach " about 800 men from his brigade, and to land them at a point he would direct, about a mile or a mile and a half above Camp Meigs. I will then conduct the detachment," continued Gen. Harrison, " to the British batteries on the left [north] bank of the river. The batteries must be taken, the cannon spiked, and carriages cut down; and the troops must then return to their boats and cross over to the fort. The balance of your men," said he, " must land on the fort side of the river, opposite the first landing, and fight their way into the fort through the Indians."

As soon as Capt. Hamilton had delivered the orders, Gen. Clay, who was then in the thirteenth boat from the front directed him to go to Col. Dudley, with orders to take the twelve front boats and execute the plans of Gen. Harrison on the left bank, and to post the subaltern with the canoe on the right bank, as a beacon for his landing.

Col. Dudley gained the British batteries, and the British flag was cut down, amid the cheers of the American garrison. Gen. Harrison, who had been watching with great concern, through his field glass, from a battery next to the river, the movements of Dudley across the river, discovered that Dudley pursued the British, after spiking the guns, and was in imminent danger, if he did not at once obey the previous orders to retire as soon as that object was accomplished.

Tecumseh was on the south side, where a sortie from the fort was made to engage him, but seeing the movements opposite, he crossed the river and fell upon the rear of Dudley, whose right and center had moved two miles from the fort in pursuit of the enemy. The general sent Lieut. Campbell to warn Dudley of his danger, but he could not reach him in time. The left column still holding the batteries, was attacked by the British, largely reinforced, who overpowered the Americans, capturing some at the batteries, while others fled to the boats. The right and center being surrounded, surrendered. Col. Dudley had received a wound, and was finally tomahawked by the savages. The number that escaped and regained the fort was less than 200. The prisoners were taken down to headquarters, put into Fort Miami, and the Indians permitted to occupy the surrounding rampart, and amuse themselves by loading and firing at the crowd, or at any particular individual. Those who preferred to inflict a still more cruel and savage death, selected their victims, led them to the gateway, and there under the eye of General Proctor, and in the presence of the whole British army, tomahawked and scalped them.

For about two hours these acts of unmitigated ferocity and barbarity to the prisoners of war continued; during which time, upward of twenty prisoners were massacred in the presence of the magnanimous Britons, to whom they had surrendered. The chiefs, at the same time, were holding a council on the fate of the prisoners, in which the Pottawatomies, who were painted black, were for killing the whole, and by their warriors the murders were perpetrated. The Miamis and Wyandots were on the side of humanity, and opposed the wishes of the others. The dispute between them had become serious, when Tecumseh came down from the batteries, riding at great speed. With fury, he struck down two Indians about to murder a prisoner, and drawing his tomahawk, dared the horde to attempt to kill another American He demanded to be told where Proctor was, and seeing him, sternly inquired why he permitted the massacre. "Sir," said Proctor, "your Indians cannot be commanded." "Begone," retorted Tecumseh, "you are unfit to command; go and put on petticoats." Still later he said to the noble Briton, for whom he had contempt: "I conquer to save, you to murder."

The prisoners were retained at Fort Miami till night, many of the wounded for hours experiencing excruciating torments, and then were placed in the British boats and carried down the river to the brig Hunter and a schooner, where several hundred of them were stowed away in the hold of the brig, and kept there for two days and nights. Being finally liberated on parole, however, these prisoners were landed at the mouth of Huron river, below the Sandusky bay.

The division which landed on the Fort Meigs side of the river gained the works with little loss, and took part in a general sortie in which the British were severely punished and many taken prisoners. The disaster to Col. Dudley was only a lamentable incident in a day that, in spite of it, terminated to the glory of the American arms. The siege was soon abandoned, and Fort Miami evacuated. The Indians, who had been promised great things, including the person of Gen. Harrison for torture, were very much discouraged by the weakness of the great father across the sea.

Expeditions from Fort Wayne.—During much of the time after the transfer of the scene of warfare to the lower Maumee, but little of marked interest had occurred at Fort Wayne. The garrison had been watchful; the Indians had been active in the region, but their attention had mainly been called to the Rapids.

The principal object of the expeditions against the Indians, from Fort Wayne and other points, as the reader will remember, was to destroy their provisions and means of subsistence, thereby disabling them from aiding the British in the spring of 1813. Richard M. Johnson, who had witnessed the effect of these movements and the efficiency of the mounted riflemen, had, on his return to congress, laid before the war department a plan for a mounted expedition against the tribes during the winter of 1812–13.

The good effects of the expeditions were stated by him to be: "Security to the northwestern frontiers from Fort Wayne to the Mississippi—to the convoys of provisions for the northwestern army, when its force was diminished in the spring, and the neutrality of the savages in future, from the powerful impression that would be made on their fears; that the winter season would be most favorable for the movement—enabling the horsemen, while snow was on the ground, and the leaves off the bushes, to hunt out and destroy the Indians prowling about."

With this view, two regiments, consisting of about 1,280 men, were proposed to be employed, which were considered sufficient to traverse the entire Indian country, from Fort Wayne to the lower end of, and beyond, Lake Michigan, thence by way of the Illinois river, back to the river Ohio, near Louisville; and to disperse and destroy all the tribes of Indians and their resources to be found within that compass. Col. Johnson also presented this project to the governor of Kentucky, and it was finally submitted by the secretary of war to Gen. Harrison on the 26th of December, 1812. Said the secretary in this communication: "The president has it in contemplation to set on foot an expedition from Kentucky of about 1,000 mounted men, to pass by Fort Wayne, the lower end of Lake Michigan, and around by the Illinois back to the Ohio near Louisville, for the purpose of scouring that country, destroying the provisions collected in the Indian villages, scourging the Indians themselves, and disabling them from interfering with your operations. It is expected that this expedition will commence in February [1813]; and it will terminate in a few weeks. I give you the information, that you may take it into consideration in the estimate of those arrangements you may find it necessary to make, for carrying into effect the objects of the government. I send you a copy of the proposed plan, on which I wish to hear from you without delay. You will particularly state, whether you can effect these objects in the manner which is suggested by adequate portions of the force now in the field; and in that case, whether it will be better to suspend the movement of this force until the spring."

The general plans of Harrison were adopted, and Col. Johnson's regiment was accepted and ordered to proceed at once to Fort Wayne, where Johnson was to take command of that post, and the posts on the Auglaize; also to make incursions into the country of the Indians; to scour the northwestern frontiers; and, if possible, to cut off small parties who might infest the forest, or be marching from the Illinois and Wabash toward Malden and Detroit — never to remain at one place more than three days. An officer from each regiment was sent back to raise another body of men. The regiment under Johnson was officered as follows: R. M. Johnson, colonel; James Johnson, lieutenant-colonel. First battalion — Duval Payne, major; Robert B. McAfee, Richard Matison, Jacob Elliston, Benjamin Warfield, John Payne (cavalry), Elijah Craig, captains. Second battalion — David Thompson, major; Jacob Stucker, James Davidson, S. R. Combs, W. M. Price, James Coleman, captains. Staff — Jeremiah Kertly, adjutant; B. S. Chambers, quartermaster; Samuel Theobalds, judge-advocate; L. Dickinson, sergeant-major. James Sugget, chaplain and major of the spies; L. Sandford, quartermaster-sergeant; subsequently added, Dr. Ewing, surgeon, and Drs. Coburn and Richardson, surgeon's mates.

The regiment arrived at Fort Meigs on the 1st of June, 1813. From this point Col. Johnson proceeded alone to the Indian village of Wapakoneta, on the Auglaize, to procure some Shawnee Indians to act as guides and spies; and after a few days returned with thirteen Indians, among whom was Anthony Shane, whose father was a Frenchman, in whom great confidence was placed by the northwestern army. Shane had been an active opponent of Wayne, in 1794, but after the treaty of Greenville had been a most faithful friend of the United States.

On the 5th of June, Johnson broke camp, and when the troops reached Shane's crossing of the St. Mary's, about forty miles from Fort Wayne, they were halted and drilled for some time, and there remained over night. Heavy rains having but recently fallen, the St. Mary's was found impassable; and on the following morning a rude bridge was formed over this stream by felling trees across it, upon which the army crossed with their baggage and guns, while their horses were got over by swimming them by the side of the fallen timber. The remainder of the route to Fort Wayne proved very difficult; all the flats and marshes being covered with water, and the roads very miry. Reaching the fort on the evening of the 7th of June, it was found that the boats had all gained the common landing place, at the base of the hill, just below the garrison, in safety, but one which had stranded on a sand-bar a short distance above, in sight of the fort; and while attempting to get the boat off, the boatmen were fired upon by some Indians lurking near, and two of the men killed, while the third in attempting to swim to the shore was drowned. Arriving a little in advance of the regiment, Col. Johnson and staff, as soon as it was possible to get ready, mounted their horses and crossed to the boat. The Indians at once fired upon their advance and then retreated.

The scouts suggested that the Indians were considerably stronger than the party under Col. Johnson, and a pursuit was deferred until the arrival of the regiment, when a chase was continued for some ten miles; but rain beginning to fall heavily, the party was compelled to return to the fort again, without having gained sight of the Indians.

On the next day, after a council of officers, the expedition was formed to proceed in the direction of the southeast end of Lake Michigan. The regiment, toward evening, deposited their heavy baggage in the fort; supplied themselves with ten days' provisions, and crossed the St. Mary's, to encamp for the night in the forks opposite the garrison, where the river had now just begun to rise, though on the evening of the 5th, it had been at the top of its banks at Shane's crossing, but forty miles from its mouth by land.

Early on the following day, the regiment took the Indian trail leading toward the Pottawatomie village of Five Medals, which had been destroyed the previous year, but which it was thought had been rebuilt. The regiment marched forty miles this day. Stopping now to rest and permit their horses to graze, with a view to an attack upon the Indian village at daylight the next morning, a heavy rain came up, preventing the execution of the plan; but after encountering many obstacles in crossing high waters and marshes, they arrived at the Elkhart river before it had risen so as to be impassable, and in half an hour afterward the village of Five Medals was gained and surrounded, but found unoccupied.

Determining now to visit a village on the other side of the St. Joseph of the lake, known as Paravash, on the morning of the 11th the regiment began its march, but upon arriving at the St. Joseph, and finding it impassable, further movement upon this village was abandoned. A rapid advance was now made eastward upon the White Pigeon town, arriving there in the afternoon of that day, meeting a few Indians on the way, who made their escape in a canoe across a stream on the route, which was also found impassable. The village of White Pigeon had long been the most extensive Indian town in that region; and the main trace of the Indians, from Chicago and the Illinois country to Detroit, passed directly through this town, but appeared to have been but little traversed that spring. Near this village the regiment encamped till the following day, when, having fulfilled his instructions to visit this trace with a view to intercepting any movements of the enemy that might be making by this route, and finding also that the provisions of the troops had been considerably damaged by the rains encountered, Col. Johnson determined to return to Fort Wayne; and as there was an Indian trail leading directly from White Pigeon to Fort Wayne, the regiment took this path for the fort, where it arrived on the 14th after a march, with heavy rains every day, of some 200 miles.

Though not encountering the Indians in his route, or finding them at either of the villages visited, yet the movements of the expedition under Col. Johnson greatly increased his knowledge of the country; and it was ascertained that all the Indians in the British service who had been engaged in the siege of Fort Meigs, were still mainly held and maintained in the vicinity of Malden.

After a few days' stay at Fort Wayne, the regiment under Johnson proceeded down the Maumee, with an escort of provisions, to Fort Winchester. The provisions were placed in boats, with a number of men to man them, while the troops moved along the road opened by Gen. Winchester, on the north side of the Maumee, encamping every night with the boats. Arriving at Fort Winchester, Col. Johnson received a dispatch from Gen. Harrison, recommending him to make an attack on the enemy at Raisin and Brownstown. This advice, though by no means explicit, Col. Johnson sought to carry out, feeling that any suggestion emanating from Harrison should be executed, if possible. But, owing to his horses being much exhausted by the expedition from Fort Wayne, as well as for lack of a sufficient number of men, a detachment of his regiment having been engaged in escorting provisions from St. Mary's, he was unable to carry out immediately the plan proposed by Gen. Harrison. Its execution was considered most hazardous indeed; to have attempted a march of a hundred miles, through swamps and marshes, and over difficult rivers, with guides not very well acquainted with the country, and with horses greatly worn down, to attack a body of Indians who could, in a few hours, raise more than double the force of the regiment of 700 men then under Johnson, required some consideration as well as time and preparation.

Fortunately for the regiment, on the next day an express arrived from Gen. Clay, commanding at Fort Meigs, with information that the British and Indians threatened to invest that place again, and requesting that Col. Johnson would march his regiment there immediately for its relief. Such was the zeal and promptitude of both officers and men, that in half an hour they were all ready to march, and commenced crossing the Maumee, opposite the fort. The heads of the column were then drawn up in close order, and the colonel, in a short and impressive address, instructed them in their duties. If an enemy were discovered, the order of march was to be in two lines, one parallel to the river, and the other in front, stretching across from the head of the former to the river on the right. He concluded with saying: "We must fight our way through any opposing force, let what will be the consequences, as no retreat could be justifiable. It is no time to flinch — we must reach the fort or die in the attempt." Every countenance, responsive to the sentiments of the speaker, indicated the same desperate determination. The ground on which the enemy had gained their barbarous triumph over Dudley was again to be traversed; and his allies would doubtless hope to realize another 5th of May, in another contest with Kentucky militia. The regiment arrived at ten o'clock in the night, opposite Fort Meigs, without molestation, and encamped on the open plain between the river and the hill on which the British batteries had been erected. Information, gained from a Frenchman and an American prisoner, who arrived at Fort Meigs on the 20th of June, was to the effect that the British were determined to renew the attack on the fort, and were to start for that purpose about that period. At this time, Gen. Harrison was at Franklinton, where he was made acquainted with the determination of the British.

Before quitting Franklinton he held an important council with some chiefs of the friendly Indians of the Delaware, Shawnee, Wyandot and Seneca tribes, informing them that a crisis had arrived, which required all the tribes who remained neutral, and who were willing to engage in the war, to take a decided stand either for the Americans or against them — that the president wanted no false friends — that the proposal of Gen. Proctor to exchange the Kentucky militia for the tribes in our friendship indicated that he had received some hint of their willingness to take up the tomahawk against the Americans — and that to give the United States a proof of their disposition, they must either remove with their families into the interior, or the warriors must accompany him in the ensuing campaign and fight for the United States. To the latter condition, the chiefs and warriors unanimously agreed; and said they had long been anxious for an invitation to fight for the Americans. Tahe, the oldest Indian in the western country, who represented all the tribes, professed, in their name, the most indissoluble friendship for the United States. Gen. Harrison then told them he would let them know when they would be wanted in the service; "but," said he, "you must conform to our mode of warfare. You must not kill defenseless prisoners, old men, women or children." By their conduct, he also added, he would be able to tell whether the British could restrain their Indians from such horrible cruelty. For if the Indians fighting with him would forbear such conduct, it would prove that the British could also restrain theirs if they wished to so — humorously telling them he had been informed that Gen. Proctor had promised to deliver him into the hands of Tecumseh, if he succeeded against Fort Meigs, to be treated as that warrior might think proper. "Now," continued he, "if I can succeed in taking Proctor, you shall have him for your prisoner, provided you will agree to treat him *as a squaw*, and only put petticoats upon him; for he must be a coward who would kill a defenseless prisoner."

The government, with considerable reluctance, employed Indians against the Indians in the service of the British, as a measure of self-defense; but it was demonstrated that the North-American savage is not such a cruel and ferocious being that he cannot be restrained by civilized man within the bounds of civilized warfare. In several instances, strong corps of Indians fought under the American standard, and were uniformly distinguished for their orderly and humane conduct.

British Discomfiture.—On the 1st of July, General Harrison set out from Fort Meigs for Lower Sandusky, accompanied by seventy mounted men, under command of Capt. McAfee. Soon after his departure, the Indians began again to invest the vicinity of Fort Meigs; and late on the evening of the 20th of July, the vessels of the British army were to be seen in the Maumee, some distance below the fort. Early on the following morning, a picket-guard, of some eleven men, having been sent to a point about 300 yards below the fort, were surprised by the Indians, and seven of them killed. At this time a large body of British and Indians were seen encamped below old Fort Miami, on the north side of the river; and the woods in the rear of the fort were soon after possessed by the Indians, who occasionally fired into the fort, and captured some horses and oxen.

On the 23d, with a body of some 800 Indians, Tecumseh was seen moving up the river, with a view, as was supposed, of attacking Fort Winchester. On the 25th, the enemy removed his camp to the south side of the river, which induced the belief that an attempt would be made by the British to take the fort by storm. Gen. Harrison was kept advised of the movements of the British; but his force was not sufficient to enable him to reach the garrison as he had wished, though he continued to assure Gen. Clay that all needed aid would reach him from Ohio and other points in good season. On the evening of the 26th, some hours after the arrival at the fort of the express from Gen. Harrison, heavy firing was commenced on the Sandusky road, about the distance of a mile from Fort Meigs. The discharge of rifles and musketry, accompanied by the Indian yell, could be clearly distinguished; and by degrees the apparent contest approached toward the fort, though sometimes it appeared to recede. It lasted about an hour, and came in the end near the edge of the woods. The general pronounced it a sham battle, intended to draw out the garrison to relieve a supposed reinforcement. A few discharges of cannon at the fort, and a heavy shower of rain, at length put an end to the scheme, no doubt to the great mortification of its projectors. The express from Gen. Harrison had providentially arrived in time to preserve the garrison from the possibility of being deluded by this artifice of the enemy. On the next day the British moved over to their old encampment, and on the 28th embarked in their vessels and abandoned the siege. The force which Proctor and Tecumseh brought against the fort in this instance was about 5,000 strong. A greater number of Indians were collected by them for this expedition than ever were assembled in one body on any other occasion during the war.

Having raised the siege of Fort Meigs, the British sailed round into Sandusky bay, while a competent number of their Indian allies moved across through the swamps of Portage river, to co-operate in a combined attack on Lower Sandusky, expecting, no doubt, that Gen. Harrison's attention would be chiefly directed to Forts Winchester and Meigs. The general, however, had calculated on their taking this course, and had been careful to keep patrols down the bay, opposite the mouth of Portage river, where he supposed their forces would debark. Gen. Clay now took care to acquaint Gen. Harrison with the movements of the British, and on the 29th of July, the messenger from Fort Meigs having reached him, he called a council of war, consisting of McArthur, Cass, Ball, Paul, Wood, Hukill, Holmes and Graham.

By the 31st of July, the enemy had approached so near Fort Stephenson, which was held by Major Croghan, as to be able to throw their shells about; and a flag was soon seen approaching the garrison, which was met by Ensign Shipp. The bearer of the flag had been instructed by Gen. Proctor, who accompanied the fleet, to demand a surrender of the fort, which was positively refused, Shipp replying that it was the determination of the commander of the garrison to defend it to the last extremity, and to disappear amid the conflagration that should destroy it. The Indians, as on former occasions, "were not to be restrained," and the bearer of the flag expressed his "great pity that so fine a young man should fall into the hands of the savages." An Indian at this moment came out of an adjoining ravine, and advancing to the ensign, took hold of his sword and attempted to wrest it from him. The Englishman interfered, and having restrained the Indian, affected great anxiety to get Shipp safe into the fort. The enemy now opened a fire from their six-pounders in the gunboats and the howitzer on shore, which they continued through the night with but little intermission, and with very little effect. The forces of the enemy consisted of 500 regulars, and about 800 Indians, commanded by Dickson, the whole being commanded by General Proctor in person. Tecumseh was stationed on the road to Fort Meigs with a body of 2,000 Indians, expecting to intercept a reinforcement on that route.

REUBEN J. DAWSON.

The enemy had directed their fire against the northwestern angle of the fort, which induced the commander to believe that an attempt to storm his works would be made at that point. In the night Capt. Hunter was directed to remove the six-pounder to a block-house from which it would rake that angle. By great exertion Hunter accomplished this in secrecy. The embrasure was masked, and the piece loaded with a half charge of powder, and double charge of slugs and grape shot.

Early on the morning of the 2d, the enemy opened fire with their howitzer and three six-pounders, which they landed in the night and planted in a point of woods about 250 yards from the fort. About 4 o'clock p. m., they concentrated the fire of all their guns on the northwest angle, which convinced Major Croghan that they would endeavor to make a breach and storm the works at that point. Late in the evening, when the smoke of the firing had completely enveloped the fort, the enemy made the assault. Two feints were made toward the southern angle, where Capt. Hunter's lines were formed; and at the same time a column of 350 men were discovered advancing through the smoke within twenty paces of the northwestern angle. A heavy fire of musketry was opened upon them from the fort, which threw them into some confusion. Col. Short, who headed the principal column, soon rallied his men, and led them with great bravery up to the brink of the ditch. After a momentary pause, he leaped into the ditch, calling to his men to follow him, and in a few minutes it was full. The masked port-hole was now opened, and the six-pounder, at the distance of thirty feet, poured such destruction among them, that but few who had entered the ditch were fortunate enough to escape. A precipitate and confused retreat was the immediate result, although some of the officers attempted to rally their men. The other column, which was led by Col. Warburton and Major Chambers, was also routed in confusion by a destructive fire from the line commanded by Capt. Hunter. The whole of them fled into the adjoining wood, beyond the reach of the small arms of the fort. During the assault, which lasted half an hour, the enemy had kept up an incessant fire from their cannon. They left Col. Short, a lieutenant, and twenty-five privates dead in the ditch; and the total number of prisoners taken was twenty-six, most of them badly wounded. Major Muir was knocked down in the ditch, and lay among the dead till darkness of the night enabled him to escape in safety. The loss of the garrison was one killed and one slightly wounded. The total loss of the enemy was calculated at about 150 killed and wounded.

When night came on, which was soon after the assault, the wounded in the ditch were found to be in a desperate situation. Complete relief could not be brought to them by either side with any degree of safety. Major Croghan, however, relieved them as much as possible — conveying them water over the picketing in buckets, and a ditch was also opened under the picketing, by means of which those who were able and willing, were encouraged to crawl into the fort.

About 3 o'clock, on the morning of the 3d, the British and Indian force commenced a disorderly retreat. So great was their precipitation that they left a sail boat behind, containing some clothing and a considerable quantity of military stores; and on the next day seventy stands of arms and some braces of pistols were picked up around the fort. Their hurry and confusion was caused by the apprehension of an attack from Gen. Harrison, of whose position and force they had probably received an exaggerated account.

At the council held with McArthur, Cass and others, about the 1st of August, it had been determined that Major Croghan should abandon Fort Stephenson as "untenable against heavy artillery;" and as this fort was considered of little value as a military post, it was also concluded to destroy it at the moment of evacuation. Gen. Harrison immediately dispatched an order to that effect to Major Croghan, which, the messenger and his Indian guides having lost their way, failed to reach him in time. Then deeming it unsafe, in view of the near approach of the enemy, to attempt an evacuation and retreat, after a council with his officers, the most of whom readily coincided with him, Major Croghan at once started the messenger on his return to Gen. Harrison with the following note:

"Sir, I have just received yours of yesterday, 10 o'clock p. m., ordering me to destroy this place, and make good my retreat, which was received too late to be carried into execution. We have determined to maintain this place, and by heavens we can."

His main reason for writing thus positively was, that he feared that the messenger might be captured, and the note fall into the hands of the British. But Gen. Harrison, without knowing fully the motive of Croghan in thus replying to his order, presumed it to indicate disobedience of orders, and on the following morning, Colonel Wells, with an escort, was sent to relieve him, and Croghan was ordered to report at headquarters. His explanation of his course and the meaning of his note, received the ready approval of Harrison, and Croghan was at once ordered to return to his post and resume its command, with written orders similar to those he had received before.

In an official report of this siege, Gen. Harrison said: "It will not be among the least of Gen. Proctor's mortifications, to find that he has been baffled by a youth, who has just passed his twenty-first year. He is, however, a hero worthy of his gallant uncle, George R. Clark." "Never was there," said General Harrison, "a set of finer young fellows, viz: Lieutenants Johnson and Baylor of the Seventeenth, Anthony of the Twenty-fourth, Meeks of the Seventh, and Ensigns Shipp and Duncan of the Seventeenth." Lieutenant Anderson of the Twenty-fourth was also commended for marked good conduct; and soon after the siege of Fort Stephenson, Major Croghan was brevetted a lieutenant-colonel by President Madison; while the ladies of Chillicothe, Ohio, presented him with a splendid sword, accompanied by an appropriate address.

A little party of Wyandot Indians, after the retreat of the British from Fort Stephenson, were sent down the bay, with other scouts, for the purpose of intercepting the retreat of the enemy. Succeeding in capturing a few British soldiers, who had been left in the general retreat, the Indians brought them to the camp, without doing them any injury; and, conscious that they had done their duty, they were frequently seen telling the story to their brother warriors, and laughing at the terror which had been manifested by the soldiers, who, no doubt, expected to be massacred or carried off and destroyed by torture.

THE DAWN OF PEACE.

Soon after the events just described, occurred Perry's victory on Lake Erie, which caused the British army, so lately filled with elation over the hope it entertained of an easy victory over the frontier militia, the untrained men of the west, to put an end to all further attempts in that direction, and the theater of war was now transferred to Canada. At the great victory at the Thames, the powerful Tecumseh was killed, and the Indians who had followed him in the belief, as he had taught them, that he was invulnerable, became totally disheartened, and lacking leaders with as warlike instincts as he, they were ready, and more than willing, to sue for peace. Indeed, before Gen. Harrison marched his army in pursuit of the British, the Ottawas and Chippewas had asked for peace, which he had promised them on condition that they would bring in their families, and raise the tomahawk against the British. To these terms they readily acceded, and before his return the Miamis and Pottawatomies had solicited a cessation of hostilities from Gen. McArthur on the same conditions. Even the ferocious Mai-pock, of the Pottawatomies, now tendered his submission, and an armistice was concluded with seven of the hostile tribes, which was to continue till the pleasure of the president was known. They agreed to deliver up all their prisoners at Fort Wayne, and to leave hostages in security for their good behavior. Separated from their allies and deprived of their leader, they were now glad to accept the American friendship on any terms, that would save them from extermination by famine and the sword.

Gen. Harrison, feeling that the secretary of war entertained a dislike for him, resigned his position as commander-in-chief of the western forces on the 11th of May, 1814. Prior to his resignation, however, he had arranged for a treaty at Greenville, where, on the 22d of July, with Gen. Cass, on behalf of the United States, they had met the friendly Wyandots, Delawares, Shawnees, Senecas, and concluded a peace with the Miamis, Weas and Eel river Indians, and certain of the Pottawatomies, Ottawas and Kickapoos; all of whom had engaged to join the Americans, should the war continue; but all need of their services was ended by the treaty of Ghent, December 24, 1814.

The conference of July, 1814, at Greenville, was one of the largest that had ever been held with the tribes, and Pecon, as the representative of the Miamis, with 113 others, were signers of the treaty.

Twenty years had now elapsed since the fort was built at the head of the Maumee by Gen. Wayne, and it had withstood the ravages of time and the efforts of the Indians to destroy it remarkably well. From the period of Col. Hamtramck's occupation, after the departure of Gen. Wayne, it was in charge of various officers. After the resignation of Capt. Rhea, in 1812, Capt. Hugh Moore assumed command, who in 1813 was superseded by Joseph Jenkinson. In the spring of 1814, Major Whistler became its commander, who was succeeded in 1815, by Major Josiah H. Vose, who continued in command until its abandonment, April 19, 1819. Soon after the arrival of Major Whistler to assume command here, it was feared that the Indians might again make an effort to capture the post, and it being much out of repair, and most uncomfortable for the garrison in many respects, Major Whistler applied to the war department for permission to rebuild it, which was granted by Gen. Armstrong, and the main structure was replaced by new pickets and the officers' and other quarters within the enclosure were rebuilt. Though many Indians continued, for several years after the war of 1812, to congregate here for purposes of trade, to receive their annuity; and also from a feeling of sympathy and attraction for the scene of their old home and gathering-place, aside from some petty quarrels among themselves, in which killings often occurred, nothing war-like was ever again manifest in the relations of the Indians and the whites.

Still remote from the "settlements," Fort Wayne continued as in former years, to exist as an object of special interest to the nation as a frontier post, it not being known what conflicts might sooner or later call it into action again, in defense of the northwest.

Attached to the fort, running west to about where the "Old Fort House" was located, near Lafayette street, embracing about one acre of ground, was an excellent and well cultivated garden belonging to the commanding officer, always filled in season with the choicest vegetation. Still to the west of this was the company's garden, extending to about where the Hedekin House now stands, which was also well tilled. The road then mainly used, extended westward from the fort along what is now the canal, to the corner of Barr and Columbia streets.

Just to the south of the fort, in what is now called "Taber's Addition," was located the burial ground of the garrison, where also were interred others not immediately connected with the fort. Lieut. Ostrander, who had thoughtlessly fired upon a flock of birds passing over the fort, had been reprimanded by Capt. Rhea, and because of his refusal to be tried by a court-martial, was confined in a small room in the garrison, where he subsequently died, was among the number buried in this place.

Fort Wayne was then on the route for the transmission of immense quantities of furs, consisting principally of beaver, bear, otter, deer and coon, which were collected on the Wabash and Illinois rivers, and nearly all of which passed over the portage. They were the principal staple of the country, and among the traders the only currency, so that when debts were contracted, or payments to be made, notes were usually drawn payable in furs.

By means of this currency dry goods, boots, shoes, hardware, etc., were sold at very high prices to the Indians and others, by which means, and the early purchase of lands, at a very low figure, many in after years became very wealthy. Richardville, civil chief of the Miamis, who was licensed as a trader with the Indians as early as 1815, became the wealthiest Indian in America by this trade and the sale of lands. Schoolcraft estimated his wealth some years prior to his death at about $200,000 in specie; much of which had been so long buried in the earth that the boxes in which the money was enclosed had mainly decayed, and the silver itself become greatly blackened.

Soon after the war of 1812 broke out, with many other members of the tribe, including his family, this chief had made his way to the British lines for protection, intending, doubtless, to render some aid to the enemy, for but few among the tribes of the northwest remained neutral or failed to give aid in some way to the British cause. At the close of the war in 1814, he returned and passed on up the St. Mary's, about three miles from Fort Wayne, where he encamped. Major Whistler, desiring to see him, sent an interpreter, Crozier, requesting the chief to come immediately to the fort, which he did. The treaty of Greenville was then about to take place, and the major desired that the chief should be present, and so requested him; but Richardville was very indifferent about the matter, hesitated, and returned to his camp. A few days later, however, he came back to the fort, where he was now held as a hostage for some ten days, when he at length consented to attend the treaty, and was soon after accompanied thither by Robert Forsyth, a paymaster, who was on his way with a chief, Chondonnai, who had been implicated in the massacre at Chicago, and William Suttenfield joined the party.

In 1818 several French traders came to Fort Wayne, but not meeting with such inducements as they had desired, passed on after a few days, to the more remote regions of the west, where furs were supposed to be more abundant. In this year there were also a number of treaties held with the Indians at St. Mary's, Ohio, under the direction of Gov. Jennings and Benjamin Parke, of Indiana, and Gen. Lewis Cass, of Michigan.

The departure of the troops, in the following year, is said to have left the little band of citizens extremely lonesome, but henceforth peace instead of war was to reign about the historic confluence of the St. Joseph and St. Mary's.

No history has recorded what regiments were represented in the various garrisons which occupied Fort Wayne, but a collection of military buttons found in and about the site of the fort, and now in the posession of the writer, will doubtless furnish an approximate knowledge of who were its defenders.

These buttons were worn by soldiers of the First, Second, Third, Fifth, Sixth, Seventh, Eighth, Ninth, Tenth, Twelfth, Thirteenth and Fifteenth regiments of infantry, the First light artillery, and a rifle regiment.

Besides these numbered buttons, are several, representing no regiment, many of which were doubtless worn prior to the date of designating commands by numbers upon the buttons.

The oldest and most archaic in appearance is a flat pewter button with a rude eagle impressed. The next is slightly convex with the eagle and stars as upon the early United States coins. Then follows a convex button with an eagle standing on a shield, with the legend "United States Infantry," in the outer circle. A convex button with the eagle bearing a shield upon which is the letter I, in script. A flat button with a large letter I, in script, and a single star below. A flat button with the eagle over an oval, inscribed 1 Rt. A flat brass button with a bugle enclosing the figure 1, all surrounded by fifteen stars. A flat brass button with eagle, but no number or stars. A flat brass button with eagle perched on a cannon, below which is inscribed 1 Regt. A flat brass button with script monogram L. A., below which is an oval of stars enclosing the figure 1. A flat brass button with similar monogram, below which is a wreath enclosing an arrow. A flat silver-plated button with initials L. D.

Other buttons are without device of any kind to indicate the command to which the wearer belonged. And those who wore them have long since departed, leaving no other record of the pioneer heroes who opened, and held open, the "glorious gate" to the west, until the army of civilization could enter and take possession, and reap the fruits of their heroic daring. Let us not forget, but ever hold in grateful remembrance the brave men whose valor and privations secured to us this rich and favored region of our great country.

As has appeared in these pages, the importance of the head of the Maumee as a strategic point had not escaped the attention of the statesmen and military leaders of the new republic, and most of the campaigns in the west, if not all of them, were directed toward securing a post here, as the key to the western and southwestern country. Now at the opening of the era of peace, with which the writer will close this account of the early history of the Valley of the Upper Maumee, the attention of the generals of commerce was as strongly directed to this as a strategic point for industrial development.

McAfee, in his "History of the Late War," said in referring to the Wabash and St. Mary's: "A canal at some future day will unite these rivers, and thus render a town at Fort Wayne, as formerly, the most considerable place in that country;" and in 1819, Capt. James Riley, a surveyor, suggested the connection of the Maumee with the Wabash by means of a canal, a feat which was long afterward accomplished. This pioneer, making the ways straight for the coming civilization, with the voice of a true and sagacious prophet, hailed Fort Wayne as the "future Emporium of Indiana."

ANTHONY WAYNE.

THE HERO OF BRANDYWINE, STONY POINT, MONMOUTH, JAMESTOWN, AND THE MAUMEE.

A patriotic Pennsylvanian author, of half a century ago, defending the gallantry of his people, wrote: "They ask for our illustrious dead!" "At the sound, from his laureled grave in old Chester, springs to life again the hero of Pennsylvania's olden time, the undaunted general, the man of Paoli and of Stony Point, whose charge was like the march of the hurricane, whose night assault stunned the British as though a thunderbolt had fallen in their midst. We need not repeat his name. The aged matron, sitting at the farm-house door of old Chester, in the calm of summer twilight, speaks that name to the listening group of grandchildren, and the old revolutioner, trembling on the verge of the grave, his intellect faded, his mind broken, and his memory almost gone, will start and tremble with new life at the sound, and as he brushes a tear from the quivering eyelid of age, will exclaim with a feeling of pride that a weight of years cannot destroy, ' I — I, too, was a soldier with Mad Anthony Wayne!' "

* * *

In the month of September, 1777, rumors of war startled the homes in the valley of the Brandywine. Gen. Howe, with some 17,000 well-armed soldiers, had landed above the Susquehanna, and was to sweep like a tornado over the plains between him and the city of Philadelphia. To oppose him came Washington, with his ill-clad Continentals, from the direction of Wilmington. On the morning of the 11th there stood under a great chestnut tree, not half a mile from Chadd's ford, gathered around the one who towered above them all, majestic and graceful in form, a group of officers among whom could be seen the sagacious Greene, the rugged brow of Pulaski, the bluff good-humored visage of Knox, the frank, manly face of DeKalb; a boy whose blue eyes sparkled and whose sandy hair fell back gracefully from a noble forehead — Lafayette; and there also, with his eyes abrim with reckless daring, was the young hero of the north, who should be the theme of a thousand legends — Anthony Wayne. In the afternoon, Wayne, with his men, held a hill commanding Chadd's ford, fighting in the fields he had traversed in his boyhood wanderings. In stature the general was not more than an inch above the medium. His form was hardy and vigorous. Beneath the plume of red and white that surmounted his chapeau was the face of a warrior, broad forehead, aquiline nose, clear hazel eyes. Five thousand men, under Gen. Knyphausen, were moving to the attack. Over their heads floated the banners of Hesse and Anspach. Not of their own will, but by their rulers, they were hired to fight for the imbecile king, who occupied himself catching flies in his palace, while men who had not learned what freedom was, were ravaging the homes of heroes who were brave enough to swear that they and their land should be subject to no potentate nor regal power. The battle waged fiercely and attack after attack was repulsed until finally Knyphausen, glittering in black and gold, charged at the head of his guard, 400 ruthless dragoons, with whom war was a trade and slaughter a pastime. To meet these, Wayne shouted one command, "Come on," to his 200 troopers, and then under a blue flag on which gleamed the thirteen stars, he crashed against the overpowering force of the foreigners. His gallant band of Continentals charged in a wedge that drove the enemy apart in confusion. The Hessians were hurled back at the saber's edge, into the river and across it, and the left wing of the army was triumphant. Just at this moment, the remainder of the army of Washington began a retreat before superior numbers, but Wayne had saved the day from disaster, and he was the last to leave the field.

* * *

A few days later Wayne and his men were watching the movements of the British near Paoli, when the enemy suddenly appeared in force to give him battle. On account of the nature of his operations he was ready to move, and immediately ordered a retreat under the command of an inferior officer, while he remained on the field to protect the rear. Three orders were necessary to bring the subordinate to understand that he must move rapidly, and in consequence the British under Lord Grey were able to cut off a body of the Continentals. "It was "charge for England and St. George"; then a cry for quarter, and the brutal response, "Cut them down. No quarter." One hundred and fifty Continentals were butchered by the soldiers of England. After this the watchword was, "Remember Paoli."

* * *

Nearly two years later Wayne avenged Paoli in a way eternally to the glory of Americans. The British had seized Stony Point, a precipitous hill commanding King's Ferry on the Hudson, then the ordinary path of communication between the middle and eastern states. On two sides the hill was washed by the river, and the other approaches were covered by water except at low tide. The enemy encircled the position with a double row of abatis, and on the summit placed a fortification bristling with artillery. It was confidently believed to be impregnable. There was but one to entrust with the attempt to capture this fort, Anthony Wayne. The army and country were overwhelmed with gloom. He must strike for the honor of Washington and the welfare of the nation, as he was again called on to do in 1792. He accepted the task without hesitation, and at midnight after the 15th of July, 1779, his command was at the morass ready to advance. There were two columns to close in from opposite sides. First in each line was a forlorn hope of twenty men, with axes to cut away the abatis, then a small advance party followed by the main command. At the head of one regiment Wayne placed himself, and gave the order: "The first man that fires his piece shall be cut down. Trust to the bayonet. March on." As the troops were wading the morass, the sentinels at the fort perceived them and the rattle of drums came down the night air. Hardly had the axe begun its work on the abatis, than a torrent of grape-shot and musketry poured down upon the assailants. The forlorn hopes were swept away, but their places were taken, and in the face of a whirlwind of fire and roaring of cannon that shook the hill, the Continentals marched steadily upward, teeth clenched, bayonets fixed, without a word or the click of a hammer. A ball struck Wayne on the forehead and he fell, but rising again cried out, "March on, carry me into the fort, and if I must die, I will die at the head of the column." With such a leader the patriots were invincible. In a moment their steel flashed in the lurid light on the fortifications; both columns met in the enclosure, and the British begged for quarter as the patriots did at Paoli. Not a man was injured after the surrender, and every cry for quarter was sacredly heeded. So Anthony Wayne avenged Paoli.

* * *

This was the most brilliant affair of the war for independence. For many days nothing was talked of in Philadelphia but the glory of Gen. Wayne. Washington complimented him, and congress passed eulogistic resolutions. Lafayette sent word across the sea that he was "particularly delighted in hearing that this glorious affair had been conducted by my good friend Gen. Wayne." Wayne's wound was slight, and in an hour after the victory he was able to write a message to Washington, which has become historic:

"DEAR GENERAL:—The fort and garrison, with Col. Johnston, are ours. Our officers and men behaved like men who are determined to be free."

* * *

These glimpses of the revolution illustrate the hero's gallant service. But much more could be told: of how, at the battle of Germantown, Wayne led one division, and in the retreat saved the army by his undaunted courage; of how during the weary winter which Washington spent at Valley Forge, Wayne skirmished through New Jersey, repeatedly fighting the enemy; of the famous battle at Monmouth, where Wayne with 700 men, attacked and engaged the greater part of the British army, and being deserted by the retreat of Lee, managed to retire without loss, until he met Washington, under whom he then returned to win the day; or of that memorable occasion, when Lafayette having mistaken the force of the enemy about to retreat across the James toward Yorktown, sent Wayne with 700 to attack the rear. No incident of the war is more characteristic of the impetuous valor and cool discretion of Wayne than that event. He found he had struck the entire British army, the wings of which immediately advanced to enclose his regiment. Without the slightest hesitation he ordered a charge, and his little force drove the enemy back from their front at the point of the bayonet. Thinking that this movement could only be inspired by confidence in an army near at hand, the enemy drew back its advance, and Wayne was able to retreat in safety before the true situation was realized.

Anthony Wayne, though not distinctively a cavalry officer, was in the essential qualities of soldiership and personal influence the Sheridan of the revolution. A braver man never lived. There was nothing he feared to attempt; and he dared do, not only what others could, but deeds from which they shrank. The terrible power which he infused into a column of attack, was not equaled until the days of Winchester and Five Forks. His name became a synonym for unapproachable daring and invincible valor, and among all Washington's lieutenants, none can be more justly coupled with him in admiration. His history in detail can here be but briefly mentioned. He was born in Chester county, Penn., January 1, 1745, a grandson of an Anthony Wayne who was a captain under William of Orange. As a boy he drilled his schoolmates and he neglected his books for stories of battle, but on being shown the necessity of study, was as rapid and successful in that domain as in all his enterprises. Dr. Franklin selected him to survey lands in Nova Scotia, and subsequently he married, and became a member of the Pennsylvania legislature. As early as 1764 he read the signs of the times and began organizing military companies and drilling them. He was called to the front as a colonel in January, 1776, joined the expedition to Canada, was there wounded and became noted for valor, and subsequently was made a brigadier-general, a rank he held at Brandywine. After the surrender at Yorktown he went to Georgia at the head of 400 regulars and drove the British from that state in little more than a month, surprised and defeated the Creeks at Ogechee, and within a few days rendered the tribe inoffensive. When the British evacuated Charleston he and his men marched in at their heels amid huzzas and blare of trumpets. He became a legislator again, and served until he was appointed commander-in-chief of the United States army in 1792. Returning to Philadelphia after the Maumee campaign, February 6, 1796, he was met four miles from the city by a military escort, and as he entered the city, there was a salute of cannon, the church bells joined in the chorus, and all business was suspended to honor the hero. It was expected that he would be appointed secretary of war, but intrigue was revived in the west, and Wayne was again sent to the Lake Erie region with almost autocratic powers. With consummate wisdom he quelled all disturbances. Then sailing for Presque-Isle, the last post he was to visit before returning to the east, he was seized with the gout, which, attacking the stomach, caused his death December 15, 1796. Separated in early manhood from a family he loved, to fight for his country from the St. Lawrence to the Carolinas, he sacrificed all the comforts and joys of life to America, and after winning the great west, died in the line of duty, hundreds of miles from home and civilization. Long may the fair city which has arisen where he trod the forests, honor and keep green the memory of Major-General Anthony Wayne.

GEOLOGY AND PHYSICAL GEOGRAPHY.

By CHARLES R. DRYER, M. D.

ALLEN COUNTY is crossed by the parallel of 41 north latitude, the meridian of 85° west longitude and the annual isothermal of 51° F. Its average elevation is not far from 800 feet above sea level. Physically it forms a part of the Wabash–Erie region, a shallow trough which extends from Lake Erie southwestward nearly to the borders of Illinois. This trough is about 200 miles long, 100 miles wide and 200 feet deep. Allen county lies exactly midway of its length, and from a point just west of Fort Wayne, the bottom of the trough slopes gently toward either end. Along the axis of the trough extends one uninterrupted river channel, occupied at present, however, by different streams; from Lake Erie to Fort Wayne by the Maumee, at Fort Wayne for two miles by the St. Mary's, thence for twenty miles by the Little river prairie, thence by the Little Wabash river to its junction with the main stream, and thence by the Wabash river.

The Wabash-Erie trough is crossed transversely by a series of crescentic or arrowhead shaped ridges which are parallel with the southwest shore of Lake Erie, and have their convex sides or angles directed toward the southwest. These determine the position of the drainage lines, so that the principal streams which flow down the sides of the trough to the axial channel, the Mississinewa, the Salamonie, the Wabash above Huntington, the St. Mary's and the Auglaize on the south, and the Aboit, the St. Joseph and the Tiffin on the north, follow closely the western faces of the ridges. The general course of these streams indicates that they were once tributaries of the Wabash, but at present the eastern four join the Maumee and turn back upon themselves, so that in a course of ten miles the waters of the St. Joseph suffer a change in direction of 160°. Geologists are now prepared to explain the cause of this anomalous behavior.

The face of the earth in northern Indiana is covered by a vast sheet of clay, sand, gravel and boulders, the thickness of which in Allen county ranges from 40 to 280 feet. The pebbles and boulders are found to be composed of a variety of materials, of which quartz, granite, sienite, greenstone and silicious slate are most common. These are very hard minerals and entirely different from the limestone rock which underlies the region. The most casual observer would notice that some of the citizens of Allen county are foreigners and came from Germany, France or Ireland. In the same way geologists recognize these boulders as being emigrants, and as having come from the region north of the great lakes. Our soil is largely made up of foreign materials, and to the whole mass has been given the name of drift. The drift is distributed over the United States north of the Ohio and Missouri rivers, and has been deposited from continental glaciers, or vast sheets of ice which repeatedly descended southward from the Canadian highlands. During the last glacial occupation the southern edge of the ice was divided into tongues or lobes, each of which pushed southward as far as the slope of the country and the temperature permitted. One of these ice-tongues, after passing through the basin of Lake Erie, emerged from its southwest end and traversed the Wabash-Erie trough. The weight of an ice-sheet from 1,000 to 5,000 feet thick causes it to grind, plane and scratch the rock surface over which it passes, to scoop out and reduce to powder the soft rocks and to wear away, round and groove the harder ones. The materials thus prepared are pushed and carried forward by the glacier, and finally deposited by the melting of the ice. The extreme edge of the ice may remain in the same position for hundreds of years, while the whole mass is moving slowly toward that limit where the ice melts as fast as it comes. Along such a line a great accumulation of material occurs, forming a ridge of drift called a terminal moraine. In the case of the Erie lobe, owing to some comparatively sudden changes of climate, the melting was not uniform, but periods of rapid melting and retreat alternated with periods during which its edge was stationary. Each of these halting places is marked by a moraine or ridge of drift like a breastwork thrown up to cover the retreat of an army; and the parallel, crescentic ridges which cross the Wabash-Erie trough are terminal moraines of the Erie ice-lobe. During the melting of the ice immense volumes of water flowed away through various channels, the main drainage line being the St. Joseph-Wabash, then connected through the Little river prairie. As soon as the ice-fort was withdrawn to a line east of Fort Wayne, the trough sloped toward the ice, and the water being dammed back by the moraines to the westward formed the Maumee lake which, at a point four miles east of Fort Wayne, discharged its surplus by a short river flowing westward into the St. Joseph-Wabash.

Allen county is naturally divided into six regions: (1) the Maumee lake region, (2) the St. Mary's and St. Joseph moraine, (3) the St. Mary's basin, (4) the St. Joseph valley, (5) the Wabash-Aboit moraine, (6) the Aboit and Eel river region. The Maumee lake region comprises the township of Maumee and portions of Scipio, Jackson, Milan, Jefferson, Adams, St. Joseph and Springfield. Its surface is very nearly level and contains large tracts of swamp which are difficult of drainage. The soil is chiefly a black alluvium with large areas of clay and streaks and ridges of sand and gravel. All its peculiarities are such as would result from an occupation of the region for many years by a shallow lake. It is bounded on the southwest and northeast by a well marked beach line known as the Van Wert and Hicksville ridges. The Van Wert ridge upon the eastern border of Indiana is broken up into four which enter Allen county in sections 14, 15, 10, 11, 2 and 3, Monroe township. The principal and last formed ridge passes across sections 2, 3 and 4, Monroe, into section 32, Jackson. Then there is a gap of two miles, to pass through which the branches of Flat Rock creek gather from the west, south and southeast. The ridge begins again in section 36, Jefferson, and traverses sections 25, 23, 22, 21 and 16. Here it is double for about half a mile and thence westward lies upon the edge of the St. Mary's moraine, so that in sections 17 and 18, Jefferson, and 12 and 11, Adams, its northern face is high and bold. Near New Haven, it ends in a bluff about forty feet high, which is curved back southwards, the cemetery being located upon its apex. The Van Wert road follows the ridge pretty closely. "Irish ridge," in sections 9, 10 and 14, Jefferson, seems to be an off-shore sand-bar, but may have been temporarily the shore line. The Van Wert ridge is a superficial pile of sand and gravel from 10 to 30 feet high and from 5 to 20 rods wide, and presents all the characteristics of a lake beach.

The Hicksville ridge begins in section 4, St. Joseph township, and pursues a very direct course to the northeast corner of the county, being well indicated upon the map by the Hicksville road. It is for the most part more bold and continuous than the Van Wert ridge, chiefly because it coincides with the margin of the St. Joseph moraine. These ridges are prolonged westward to Fort Wayne, upon the sides of the channel through which the Maumee lake emptied into the St. Joseph-Wabash. In sections 14 and 15, Adams, there is a gap a mile and a half wide through which the St. Mary's river once emptied into the lake. It brought down a great quantity of sand which was deposited as a delta at its mouth. The New Haven delta extends from the center of section 5, Jefferson, westward five miles, and has an average width of one mile. Its northern boundary is marked by a conspicuous bluff, which once formed the south shore of the outlet of the lake. The Maumee river traverses the lake region in a very tortuous course, with a sluggish current which flows at the bottom of a channel twenty to forty feet deep. East of New Haven no stream of any size enters it from the south, the drainage being eastward parallel with the Maumee to the Auglaize. Near the northern border of the Maumee lake region "fountain" or artesian wells are numerous. Flowing water is struck at depths of from thirty-five to forty-five feet, a copious stream of which rises to the surface, being fed by reservoirs in the gravel beds of the St. Joseph moraine. The water-bearing gravel often contains rounded fragments of coal never larger than a cherry.

The St. Mary's and St. Joseph moraine is the most extensive and important ridge in the Wabash-Erie region. It extends along the right bank of the St. Mary's river and the left bank of the St. Joseph from Lima, Ohio, to Hudson, Michigan. It has been compared to a dead' wave on the surface of the ocean, hardly perceptible to the eye on account of its smoothness, but revealed by its effect on everything that encounters it. The crest of the ridge can be easily traced upon the map, since it forms the watershed between the St. Mary's and the Auglaize, and between the St. Joseph and the Maumee, being about four miles distant from the rivers on the west and sometimes thirty miles from those on the east. In Allen county, south of the Maumee, the Wayne trace follows the crest very closely. It is a slightly rolling strip of country four or five miles wide, elevated from fifty to eighty feet above the general level, and occupying the greater portion of the townships of Madison, Marion and Adams, part of Wayne, and the whole space between the Hicksville ridge and the St. Joseph river. A former channel of the St. Mary's cuts through the moraine from the great bend of that river in section 6, Marion township, along the course of Merriam's creek, the Trier ditch and Six-mile creek, to New Haven. It has a nearly uniform width of one-quarter of a mile, and its bottom is from forty to sixty feet below the summit of the moraine.

The St. Mary's basin lies almost entirely on the left bank of that river and consists in Indiana of a flat strip of country ten or twelve miles wide, occupying in Allen county, Pleasant township and portions of Marion, Lafayette and Wayne. The St. Mary's river is a sluggish, muddy stream, almost without bluffs or flood plain, the highest water seldom being more than sufficient to fill its channel. Its minimum flow has been estimated to be from 1,500 to 2,000 cubic feet per minute. In its lower course it has been tossed about from one channel to another repeatedly. The Six-mile creek channel, probably the oldest, has been described. A second channel leaves the present river at the southeast corner of section 22, Wayne township, and extends southwestward to section 35, about where it joins the Wabash-Erie channel. The Bluffton road crosses it at Chief Godfrey's. It now forms an arm of the prairie six miles long and one-half mile wide. A third and later channel leaves the river one mile below the second, near M. Strack's, and extends westward two and one-half miles to the Wabash-Erie channel.

The broad Wabash-Erie channel, above mentioned and previously referred to, deserves careful description. From the western apex of the Maumee lake in section 3, Adams township, to Fort Wayne, it originally gave passage to the waters of that lake westward. It is bounded on the north by a continuation of the Hicksville ridge, which, as it approaches the St. Joseph, curves sharply northward, parallel with that river, to a point two miles above its mouth. The new asylum for the feeble minded is built upon the edge of this bluff. The Wabash-Erie channel passes through the northern half of the city of Fort Wayne. Lines down from the Allen county jail to St. Vincent's orphan asylum, and from the Fort Wayne college to Lindenwood cemetery cross the channel at right angles. From Fort Wayne it extends southward twenty-seven miles, with a breadth varying from one, to one and a half miles. It is bounded on the north by a bluff forty to sixty feet high, and on the south by a system of ridges and bluffs hereafter described. This portion of the channel was originally occupied by a stream which carried the united waters of the Maumee lake, the St. Joseph and the St. Mary's, into the Wabash river below Huntington. This stream, which I have called the Wabash-Erie river, was thirty miles long, one mile wide, and may have had a depth of from 60 to 100 feet. For more than twenty miles, the channel is now occupied by a marsh called the Little river prairie, through which meanders an insignificant stream, the successor and heir of a river once comparable with the Detroit or the Niagara.

In the triangular space bounded by the Six-mile creek channel, the second St. Mary's channel and the Wabash-Erie channel are grouped a series of sand and gravel ridges, variously called by geologists kames and osars. They are portions of, or appendages to, the St. Mary's moraine. On the east the system is almost continuous with the Van Wert ridge, being separated from it by the Six-mile creek gap. Kame No. 1 forms the western border of that gap in section 15, Adams, on the farm of D. Rodenbeck. It is a file of gravel twenty rods wide, twenty feet high and half a mile long. Kame No. 2 lies on the eastern border of the city of Fort Wayne and extends from a point east of the Vordermark homestead westward about one mile to Holton avenue. It has been partially removed for the new freight yards of the P., Ft. W. & C. railway. West of these yards it rises in a conical hill, the summit of which is the highest point of the St. Mary's moraine in Allen county. Kame No. 3, very symmetrical and one-fourth of a mile long, extends parallel with No. 2 about forty rods north of its eastern end. Kame No. 4 begins near the Main street bridge over the St. Mary's, and extends southward one mile to Shawnee run. In the neighborhood of Fort Wayne college it has been graded down thirty or forty feet. The Swinney gravel pit has been extensively excavated out of it. The old Catholic cemetery and Riedmiller's grove are situated upon it. A low spur crosses Broadway near the McCulloch park. Kame No. 5 extends along Walnut street from Fairfield avenue to Shawnee run. Kame No. 6 begins south of the corner of Creighton avenue and Broadway, passes westward through the grounds of Byron Thompson, curves southward along Thompson avenue and ends at " the high banks " of the St. Mary's. Kame No. 7 begins north of the Allen county poor farm and extends southward one mile to the third St. Mary's channel. In front of the infirmary it forms the left bank of the St. Mary's river and is about forty feet high. Kame No. 8 lies west of No. 7 in the north halves of sections 21 and 20, Wayne township. It is very irregular, built along three parallel axes but not complete on either. Two branches extend northward from St. John's cemetery into section 16. West of the cemetery it is broken by gaps into a series of conical hills. Its western end at G. Rapp's is broad and slopes gently toward the prairie. It forms the north bank of the third St. Mary's channel. Kame No. 9 begins in a broad, high mass which occupies nearly the whole of the southwest quarter of section 22 on the east of the Bluffton road between Chief

Godfrey's and M. Strack's. It has been extensively excavated for moulding sand. Thence two branches extend westward, the southern along the south line of section 21 to its west line, the northern through the middle of sections 21 and 20. Kame No. 10 is also double and occupies the north half of section 29. Kame No. 11 lies a few rods south of the west end of No. 10. Nos. 9, 10 and 11 are parallel, *en echelon*, and form the divide between the second and third channels of the St. Mary's.

To this system belong several small islands in the Wabash-Erie channel, now the prairie. The Wabash railway crosses one on the west line of section 20 and another on the line between sections 19 and 30. The latter is known as Midway island. The most interesting and characteristic kame of the series forms Fox island in section 25, Aboit township. It is plainly visibly a few rods to the south of the Wabash railway, but should be visited to be appreciated. A road recently opened across the prairie gives easy access to its western end. Here one beautifully symmetrical ridge, lithe and graceful as a serpent, sweeps in a gentle curve like the Italic letter (S), three fourths of a mile long, 20–25 feet high and as steep as sand can be piled. Several wings and branches upon either side enclose coves and land-locked bays; and covered (as it still is) with luxuriant forests and embraced in mid-channel by the waters of the great river, it must have been one of the most charming and unique parks in the world.

The question of the origin and formation of kames is still an unsettled one. The present state of opinion among geologists inclines to the theory that they were in some way produced by sub-glacial streams or in dry cracks and tunnels under the ice; the materials may have fallen in from the top of the ice sheet, or they may have been squeezed and scraped up from below by the enormous pressure and unequal motion of its mass.

The St. Joseph valley lies between the St. Joseph moraine on the east and the Aboit moraine on the west. It has a nearly uniform width of a little more than half a mile, and is bounded by well marked bluffs often broken into several terraces. Between these the present river winds from side to side with a strong and clear stream, its minimum flow being estimated at 4,000 cubic feet per minute. As in the case of the St. Mary's, the basin of the St. Joseph lies almost wholly upon its western side, being fed from numerous lakes and streams in Steuben and Noble counties. Careful examination shows it to have been once a much larger stream than at present, to have flowed at a level about thirty-five feet higher and to have discharged its waters through the Wabash-Erie channel into the Wabash.

The Wabash-Aboit moraine is similar in character to the St. Mary's and St. Joseph moraine and parallel with it. It extends along the right bank of the upper Wabash river to the village of Murray, Wells county, thence into the southwest corner of Allen county, where it turns to the northeast and fills the space between the St. Joseph valley on the

George L. Godfrey

east, and the valleys of the Aboit river and Cedar creek on the west. It occupies the greater part of the townships of Lafayette, Aboit, Washington, Perry and Cedar Creek. The moraine has a breadth varying from four to eight miles and an elevation of from 80 to 120 feet above the St. Joseph river. It is a broad, rolling table land, the chief material of which is a gravelly clay, with frequent mounds, ridges and patches of sand and gravel. Along the line between Lafayette and Aboit townships, it is cut in two by the Wabash-Erie channel, on either side of which bluffs rise to a height of from 60 to 125 feet, the hill at Bowman's, section 8, La Fayette, being 873 feet above tide. In the northern part of the county it is cut across again by the gorge of Cedar creek, 50 to 100 feet deep and 800 feet wide. At the bend of Cedar creek, in sections 3, 10 and 11, Perry township, the moraine rises to an extraordinary height, where "Dutch Ridge" attains an elevation on the farm of H. Hensinger, of more than 100 feet above the creek and 925 feet above tide, being the highest point in Allen county. This region abounds in precipitous bluffs and deep ravines and deserves the name of the Alps of Allen. Its picturesque beauty is heightened by the presence of a few small lakes, Viberg's and Hollopeter's in section 7, Cedar Creek, being gems of their kind, and typical specimens of morainic lakes.

The Aboit and Eel River region comprises the townships of Lake and Eel River, and portions of Aboit and Perry. The Aboit and Eel rivers have their sources in a marshy prairie which lies in wide, tortuous channels, with various tongues, peninsulas and islands of dry land between. West of Huntertown the prairie is two or three miles wide, and from a bold bluff on the north shore the view across the marsh, diversified with wooded points and islands, is worthy of an artist's pencil. Living and extinct lakes are not rare, the largest being Mud lake, in section 8, Lake township, and White lake, section 3, Eel River. The northwest half of Eel River township lies upon the borders of the moraine formed between the Saginaw and the Erie ice-lobes, and is quite hilly. The peculiar morainic topography of mound and hollow, although upon a miniature scale, gives sufficient variety and irregularity to render this the most picturesque portion of the county.

Concerning the rocks which underlie the drift in Allen county nothing is known except in the isolated spots where deep well borings have been made. These are quite numerous in the vicinity of Fort Wayne. They all pass through the same strata and show that the variations of thickness and level are very slight. The following table embodies all the important geological results:

12

	Court House Square, Fort Wayne.	Bass Foundry.	Abbott Well.	Section 4, Perry Township.
Surface above tide	772	788	796	844
Drift	88	110	100	281
Limestone	802	} 1,040	868	749
Shale (Hudson)	260		176	430
Shale (Utica)	260	287	257	240
Limestone (Trenton)	1,590	21	493	52
Total depth	3,000	1,458	1,900	1,752

The bed rock in the southern half of Allen county is undoubtedly upper Silurian of the Niagara or waterlime group; in the northern part probably Devonian of the corniferous group, but the line of parting can hardly be conjectured. The chapter upon outcrops in Allen county resembles the famous one upon snakes in Ireland. Rumors are afloat of the existence of stone quarries at various localities, but all have proved to be mythical. There are strong indications that rock lies very near the surface in the bed of the Maumee at Bull Rapids; in the bed of the St. Mary's, on the farm of J. J. Essig, section 29, Marion township, and on the farm of J. Akey, section 35, Adams township. Mr. Frank Randall, jr., late of the county surveyor's office, reports a ledge of limestone upon the bank of the Aboit river, in section 20, Aboit township.

The surface of Allen county, together with that of the greater part of Indiana, remains to-day substantially as the mighty stamp of the glacier moulded it. To it we owe our landscape, our soil, our wealth and prosperity. Agriculture and brick manufacture are the only occupations in the county which depend upon the geological structure. Agriculturally the land may be divided into three classes: (1) Lacustrine land: lake bottom without muck; soil chiefly fine, tough clay with occasional streaks of sand and gravel; drainage difficult. (2) Bottom or muck land: the largest tracts are inter-moraine in old drainage channels, and basins of extinct lakes; soil black and mucky. (3) Moraine land: high and rolling; soil gravelly clay with mounds and ridges of sand and gravel; drainage easy. Perhaps in no other county of the state has drainage been more important or undertaken upon a larger scale. The Eel river ditch, completed in 1887, is eleven miles long and drains 3,000 acres of marsh. The Little river ditch, completed in 1889, with all its branches has a total length of forty miles, and furnishes an outlet for the water which falls upon 200,000 acres of land. At an expense of $170,000, 35,000 acres of marsh have been converted into rich farming lands, and a fertile source of miasma has been removed, greatly to the improvement of the sanitary condition of 50,000 people. This may be said to be the closing chapter in the history of the Wabash-Erie river. Its channel can never be obliterated, but nothing less than some great convulsion of nature can now divert it from the dominion and use of man.

SETTLEMENT AND DEVELOPMENT.

COMPILED WITH ASSISTANCE OF HON. F. P. RANDALL.

ROUND about the old fort, after peace came finally with the end of the struggles of 1812-14, the scene was one of rare beauty. The extensive clearing made by order of Gen. Wayne in 1794, and again by Gen. Harrison in 1812, was covered with waving grass, and circling this stood the primeval forest, like a wall of emerald, pierced by three gates through which flowed the gleaming rivers. The days of Indian warfare had come to an end, the day of white settlement was yet in anticipation. Nature smiled restfully, and the few who held this frontier fort spent their days in quiet, perhaps undisturbed by dreams of the whirl and excitement of the city that would rise in this lovely park, with block after block of lofty edifices; for no one then could picture to himself the reality of the flood of immigration that would people these vast solitudes and crowd the busy cities of northern Indiana.

The first business of the vicinity consisted in the portage of goods and furs by way of a well-worn trail seven miles long, from the bend of St. Mary's, one mile west of the fort, to Little river, from the Maumee to the Wabash, and this had previous to about the year 1800, been mainly controlled by the mother of Richardville, who engaged a large number of Frenchmen with ponies, and did a business, according to the representations made at the treaty of Greenville, that amounted to as much sometimes as $100 a day. Then Louis Bourie, of Detroit, established a branch trading house at the fort and carried on the transfer from 1803 to 1809, and his clerk here was an important intermediary in the shipment of goods for the traders from Detroit or Canada up the Maumee to Fort Wayne, and then by packhorses to the Wabash headwaters. This way the transportation would move in the summer and fall, and in the spring great collections of fur of beaver, otter, deer, coon and bear would pass in the other direction coming up from the wilds of Indiana and Illinois.

One notable among the early traders was Hyacinth Lasselle, who was the first white person born at the site of Fort Wayne, and it is believed, the first in northern Indiana. His father, Col. James Lasselle, removed from Montreal to the Indian village, Kekionga, opposite the site of the city, in the fall of 1776, having been appointed agent among the Indians for the British government. On February 25, 1777, Hyacinth Lasselle was born. The family remained at Kekionga until La-Balm's invasion in 1780, when they fled with most of the villagers down the Maumee. In this precipitate movement, the only daughter of the family fell from their boat and was drowned. Returning to Montreal, Hyacinth was put in school. At the age of sixteen he became a clerk with his brothers, James and Francis, traders at Detroit, which he reached after a voyage of two months in batteaux. When peace followed the establishment of Fort Wayne, Hyacinth was sent by his brothers to trade at that post, and he was in that business here for about eighteen months subsequent to May, 1795. He then descended the Wabash, but was a frequent visitor at the fort until 1804, when he made his home permanently at Vincennes. He served during the war of 1812, acting four years as an officer in the Rangers, and became major-general of militia. He died at Logansport, January 23, 1843. He was a great favorite with the Miamis, who called him Kekiah, or Little Miami, and his remarkable athletic powers made him famous among the Indians. The Miamis, at one time, challenged all the tribes to meet their Kekiah in a foot-race. The Winnebagoes, of Lake Michigan, sent their champion, with a delegation, and as the race neared the close with Lasselle in the lead, the Winnebagoes were so excited that they let fly their arrows at the victor, one of which pierced his thigh just as the race was won. As Lasselle was not seriously hurt, he prevailed on the Miamis to overlook the outrage, but it is not recorded that he was engaged in any more international contests. Another noted trader was Antoine Bondie, whose important services before and during the siege have already been described.

Another early birth at Fort Wayne was that of John Elliott Hunt. He was the son of Col. Thomas Hunt, of the First United States infantry, who fought at Lexington, Bunker Hill and Stony Point, and was in command at Fort Wayne from 1796 to 1798, having his wife, Eunice, with him. Within the fort, John E. Hunt was born, April 11, 1798. His early life was spent with his brother Henry at Detroit. He became known as Gen. Hunt, and in 1816 formed a partnership with Robert A. Forsyth, doing business at Maumee City. He was very energetic in promoting railroad and canal construction, and should be remembered as one of the benefactors of the Maumee valley. He was treasurer of Lucas county and postmaster at Toledo. Col. Hunt, the old commandant, died near St. Louis in 1806.

In May, 1814, when Major Whistler took command of the fort, among the residents are remembered the major's two daughters, William Suttenfield and his wife Laura, Lieut. Curtiss, Baptiste Maloch and wife, and James Peltier and wife. Within the stockade lived a French blacksmith, Louisaneau, who came about the time of the war of 1812, under government appointment. The remains of his shop were discovered in making an excavation for the residence of Judge Carson on Berry street, now owned by heirs of Samuel Hanna. Dr. Daniel Smith arrived in 1814, from Lancaster, Ohio. Dr. Turner came in 1815 and Dr. Trevitt in 1816. During the war of 1812, John P. Hedges was a clerk of John H. Piatt, commissary-general of the northwestern army, and visited Fort Wayne to report on the rations at the fort. At the treaty of Greenville, his father, Samuel P., and he, issued rations to the Indians, and subsequently, in 1814, John P. Hedges became one of the residents of the village at Fort Wayne. At this date George and John E. Hunt resided near the fort with a store of goods; Peter Oliver and Perry Kercheval, a clerk of Major Stickney's. A more extended notice of some of these pioneers and their descendants can here be appropriately given.

The son of a union between the Maloch and Peltier families, is Louis Peltier, the oldest living resident of Fort Wayne. The history of his parents is romantic and interesting. James Peltier, his father, was one of the early French traders, and a favorite with the Indians. After he had been carrying on this business here six or seven years, Baptiste Maloch, also a trader, and his wife, came to the post in 1807, bringing with them their sprightly grand-daughter, Emeline Chapeteau, who in 1814 became the wife of James Peltier. Miss Chapeteau was a great friend of the savage inhabitants of the region. On landing she was named by the Indians, "Golden Hair." Some time prior to the famous siege of 1812, she accompanied a pleasure party to the home of a French family a short distance down the Maumee. The party was menaced by a crowd of unfriendly Indians as soon as it was out of sight of the fort. Mlle. Chapeteau was at once appealed to by the white party for protection, and she managed to persuade the Indians to allow them to proceed without further molestation. At another time, when she happened to be alone in a cabin without the fort, a party of Indians made a sally upon the latter, and retiring baffled, some of them came to her lonely abode, and entered, but finding her, they made no hostile demonstrations, contented themselves with obtaining food and using the floor as a sleeping place. After they left in the morning, an officer ventured out, and finding Mlle. Chapeteau, to his surprise alive, insisted that she should remain within the fort, and she there resided with her uncle, David Bourie, during the subsequent siege. She was a native of Detroit, born in 1792, so that her life was spent, up to a good age, among the stirring scenes of frontier posts. After the death of James Peltier, at about eighty years of age, she married Mr. Griswold, and in February, 1876, she passed away. Three of her children are living. Louis Peltier, the second, was born at the old fort, March 14, 1814. When a boy, he learned the Miami tongue, and traded with that tribe until 1832. He then began the cabinet-maker's trade with James Wilcox, and four years later succeeded to the business, adding to it undertaking in 1840. This business he continued for many years, being engaged twenty-four years at his stand, opposite where is now Root & Co.'s store. This venerable citizen is a man of strict honesty and integrity, has been affectionate in his family, and has the good will and reverence of the community.

Throughout his long career he did a successful business, being known as one of the leading undertakers in northern Indiana, but so fair and equitable and lenient were his transactions, that in all his life he sued but one man. Politically he was a whig, but since Gen. Scott's campaign has been a democrat. He was married in 1833 to Laura Cushing, who died in 1850, and in 1856 he was united to Mary Nettlehorst, a native of Germany. He has three children, James C. and Ellen, by the first marriage, and Angeline by the second wife. James C., who carries on the undertaking business, was born in Fort Wayne September 21, 1843. He attended the Catholic schools of the city, and studied two years at Notre Dame, his college work being interrupted by the war. In 1862 he enlisted in Company K, Twelfth Indiana, and the following August was wounded at Richmond, Ky. He was honorably discharged in the winter of 1862 on account of physical disability. He then went into business with his father, and since 1882 has conducted the establishment in his own name. He is widely known as one of the leading undertakers of Indiana; is a Catholic in faith; and politically is a democrat. A prominent member of the Sion S. Bass post, G. A. R., he is the only one who has served two terms as commander, which position he filled in 1887–8. He was married December 25, 1866, to Selena F. Wadge, a native of England, and they have two children, William H. and Laura A. Mrs. Peltier is a member of the Episcopal church.

The river St. Mary's was a favorite route for the coming of visitors and settlers from "the settlements" in southwestern Ohio, and for a long period many flat-boats and pirogues would come down that river and tie up at the landing just above the fort. Among those who came by that route, as early as 1814, were William Suttenfield and his wife, and a party of friends, who made their home in the fort. Mr. Suttenfield was for a considerable period a non-commissioned officer at the fort, and for many months after his arrival, was employed with a squad of three or four men in bringing provisions and goods to the garrison from Piqua and other points. He was short and slender and very active and frequently declared that the Indians could not catch him. He subsequently arose to the rank, or title at least, of colonel. The first house in what is now called the old plat was erected by Mr. Suttenfield, at the northwest corner of Barr and Columbia streets, and he and his wife resided there many years in the comfortable log house. Mrs. Laura Suttenfield was born in Boston, Mass., in 1795, and survived her husband many years. She numbered among her friends in the early days, the agent, Major B. F. Stickney, a manly soldier, to whom so much credit belongs for the saving of Fort Wayne from capture in 1812, Gen. John Tipton and Col. John Johnson, two important leaders in their era.

Major Benjamin F. Stickney, appointed an Indian agent by President Jefferson, was one of the most famous pioneers of the Maumee valley. After leaving Fort Wayne, about 1820, he settled at Swan Creek, and he and Samuel Allen founded Vistula, which became part of Toledo. There was a question of boundary between Ohio and Michigan, and Stickney was the leader in the " secession " of the Toledo settlement from Ohio to Michigan, and afterward, during times of canal speculation, back to Ohio. The last move resulted in the Toledo war of 1835, worthy of the pen of " Diedrich Knickerbocker." Of this, Stickney was the hero. He was a man of considerable attainments, and had an estimable wife, Mary, daughter of the celebrated Gen. Stark. His eccentricities furnished much amusement, especially his selection of names for his children, the boys being dubbed One, Two, etc., and the girls named after the states.

In 1815 the fort was rebuilt, logs being hauled by the soldiers from the forest, covering the site of the residence of Samuel Hanna, deceased, and that vicinity. About the buildings a stockade was made of pickets, twelve and a half feet long, put in in sets of six, with a cross piece, two feet from the top, let in and spiked. They were firmly planted in a trench three and a half feet deep. Aside from the rivers there were no available routes in any direction, although there was the Wayne trace which could be followed by horsemen to Fort Recovery, one toward the site of Chicago, along which the carrier of the military mail found no hut or trace of white men until he reached Fort Dearborn; shorter traces that led down the Maumee on each side, and one to the reservation of the unfortunate Capt. Wells on Spy run. The fording places were Harmar's, 100 rods below the old Maumee bridge, now obliterated, and one above it. At the former ford the first observation of independence day that is recorded, occurred in 1810, by Capt. Rhea and other officers, who took dinner under an old elm, afterward known as the " post office," because on that very day the courier arrived with mail from Detroit and government dispatches. By this route, the mail was carried to Chicago and Green Bay for several years. In 1817, Major Whistler was removed to Missouri, being succeeded by Major Josiah H. Vose, of the Fifth regiment, who held command until April, 1819, when, much to the regret of the few settlers and traders, the fort was abandoned forever, and only the campfires of the numerous Indians and their noisy pow-wows, remained to furnish a variety to the life of the pioneers at the site of the future city. Among the residents then, were John B. Bourie, one of the earliest traders, and Samuel Hanna and James Barnett. Mr. Hanna built a hewn log house on the corner of Columbia and Barr, and he and Barnett opened a wholesale house to supply traders, in the following year, 1820. Their goods came from Boston by ship to New York, by way of Albany to Buffalo, by lake to Swan Creek (Toledo), and thence up the Maumee on pirogues. In 1820, Francis Comparet engaged in the Indian trade, and became with Alexis Coquillard, who afterward did business at South Bend, and Benjamin B. Kercheval, who became Indian agent, who came at the same time, the agents of the American Fur Company, which was established here in 1820. George W. and William G. Ewing began trading in 1822 and in 1825 Peter Kiser established himself as a butcher and issued rations to the Indians at the forks of the Wabash and on Eel river while treaties were being made with them. Allen Hamilton made his home here in 1823, as deputy register, and soon became the confidential adviser of Richardville.

The status of the settlement at about this time may be inferred from the letters of Capt. James Riley, who came from his survey in Ohio, to visit the place in 1819, and was impressed by the remarkable possibilities of the location as a "depot of immense trade." He said: "The fort is now only a small stockade. No troops are stationed here, and less than thirty dwelling houses, occupied by the French and American families, form the settlement. But as soon as the land shall be surveyed and offered for sale, inhabitants will pour in from all quarters to this future thoroughfare between the east and the Mississippi river. I was induced to visit this place for curiosity, to see the Indians receiving their annuities and to view the country. While here at that time, leveled the portage-ground from the St. Mary's to Little river, and made some practical observations, as aftertime has shown them to be." He wrote that the St. Mary's had been almost covered with boats at every freshet for several years. He describes this as a "central point combining more natural advantages to build up and support a town of importance, as a place of deposit and trade and a thoroughfare, than any point he had seen in the western country." He said at this time there were assembled about 1,000 whites from Ohio, Michigan, Indiana and New York, to trade with the Indians during payment, and that they brought whisky in abundance, which they dealt out to the Indians and kept them continually drunk and unfit for business. Horse-racing, drinking, gambling, debauchery, extravagance and waste were the order of the day and night, and the Indians were the least savage and more christianized, and the example of those whites was too indelicate to mention." This Capt. Riley had a world-wide notoriety on account of his shipwreck and captivity on the coast of Africa.

He advised the speedy survey of the lands which soon followed, and every inducement to rapid settlement, and encouragement by the government of this "future emporium of Indiana." As an earnest of his faith he purchased a number of tracts at Willshire, moved his family there, laid off a town, built a grist-mill, and surveyed, in 1822, all the country on both sides of the St. Mary's, embracing Fort Wayne, and also about twenty townships, of six miles square, between the St. Mary's and the Maumee. It will not detract from the value of his historical statements to recall that Capt. Riley was famous for snake stories, and that his most famous one related that snakes were so numerous in a certain field he was running a line across, that ever and anon an angry serpent would fasten its fangs in his leathern breeches. Slashing their heads off with his knife, he calmly proceeded, and after completing his work, found thirty-eight snake heads fastened to him. One of the houses outside the fort, but within range, was the council house, the headquarters of the Indian agent. The first was destroyed in the siege of 1812, but a new one was built in 1816, on lots 32 and 33, the county addition, and was first occupied by Major B. F. Stickney. This building was subsequently replaced by the residence of Mr. Hedekin, and the old council house well is still in use. The year following the erection of this house, Major Stickney, in a letter to the superintendent of Indian affairs, gives some interesting observations concerning the aborigines. He spoke despondingly of the prospect of civilizing the Indians, the insurmountable obstacles being the insatiable thirst for intoxicating liquors on their part, and the thirst for gain on the part of the white people. Not only were they averse to the civilization of the whites, but viewed the character of the latter in an unfavorable light on philosophical grounds, believing them to be always actuated by motives of trade and speculation. Said he: "All the Miamis and Eel River Miamis, are under my charge, about 1,400 in number; and there are something more than 2,000 Pottowatomies who come within my agency." The Indians gathered here in great numbers during 1815, to receive rations according to the treaty of Greenville, and they remained in the country, harmless in their relations to the whites, until about 1846, when all those not installed upon reservations were transferred to the plains beyond the Mississippi, a change which they endured with patient sorrow, for the power of the Miamis ended forever with the days of Little Turtle, their famous chieftain.

In 1822 the little village had a postoffice, of whom Samuel Hanna was the functionary; the Maumee mail came once a week by horseback, Mr. Suttenfield being the contractor. For one trip the Fort Dearborn mail was carried on foot by Samuel Bird, a Pleasant township settler, an old soldier who rebuilt the fort. He carried mail several years. In 1824 hotels were added to the conveniences by William Suttenfield and Alexander Ewing, who each paid a license of $12.50, and each occupied corners at the intersection of Columbia and Barr streets. "Washington Hall," as Ewing's tavern was known, was managed by him until 1829, when Robert Hood and Abner Gerard became the proprietors, and they in turn were succeeded by Samuel Sauer. To give an idea of the population at this time it may be stated that in 1823, when Indiana was divided into two congressional districts, and John Test was elected to congress from the first district, there were only about fifty votes cast in the whole of northern Indiana. In 1822 two famous men, Gen. Lewis Cass, and the historian, H. R. Schoolcraft, landed from a canoe by which they had come up the Maumee, en route to the Mississippi. A notable feature of the town site at that time was a pond, covering about one lot, lying about half a square east of the court-house and between Berry and Columbia streets. A little brook meandered from the southwest down the west side of what is now Harrison street past the Berry Street Methodist Episcopal church, into the St. Mary's. Near the site of the church was a "fishing hole," much frequented. Among the hazel bushes along this creek the Indians were accustomed to idle, and on its banks one day a Shawnee Indian, being asked to drink out of the stream by a Miami, received as he was stooping a deadly knife-thrust from his companion. The Shawnees who were encamped to the southeast were enraged, and two days later a band of that tribe painted and armed for the fray, came up and halted upon an elevation at what is now the corner of Clinton and Washington streets. Diplomacy was at once brought into action, and it was managed to appease the outraged tribe by the gift of several horses, and many trinkets and other goods. Thus, the story goes, the creek came to be known as Shawnee run.

Another famous Indian murder was the killing of a half-breed Indian-negro woman, by Newelingua, or Big-Leg, a Miami. The woman, whom he claimed as a slave, frequently stole meat from his cabin, he asserted, and he finally threatened to kill her if she did not desist. Her kleptomania was unconquerable, however, and she fled to Fort Wayne and took service in a white family to escape her fate. Big-Leg kept his promise, however. Finding her doing a washing, he stealthily crept up, and plunged a knife through her body. Looking at her corpse, he exclaimed, "Wasn't that nice!" The settlers took a different view of it, and although the not infrequent murders among the Indians were unpunished, except by their own vendetta, the villagers decided to draw the line at invasion of their homes for such outrages. Big-Leg was consequently imprisoned in the old county jail. Being told that he would be hung he was concerned about what the nature of that ceremony was, and finally concluded that it was something like the weighing of venison by the traders. He communicated this to his friends, who soon brought a dog near the jail, where Big-Leg could have a glimpse of them, and proceeded to "weigh" the canine with a rope about his neck upon an improvised scaffold. The violent contortions of the victim of this experiment gave the Indian a great aversion to "weighing," and he pleaded that he might be shot instead. His friends desired his release, and sought to exchange another Indian of less importance for him. He was prosecuted by James Perry, before Judge Charles H. Test, William N. Hood, associate judge, at the May, 1830, term of circuit court, and convicted, but recommended to mercy. The governor pardoned him, and he moved to Kansas, with other Miamis in 1848.

Among the well-known residents of Fort Wayne between 1812 and 1838, besides those already mentioned, were F. D. Lasselle, who became a merchant on the south side of Columbia street, and subsequently sold out to the Miami Indians, the store being then managed by Chapine (Richard Chute); William S. Edsall, a trader, associated with the Ewings; James Aveline (or St. Jule, as he was then called, father of Francis Aveline) who came from Vincennes previous to 1824; the father of Zenas Henderson, who kept a trading house at the site of the Dewald store, and was succeeded by his son (Zenas Henderson & Co. were licensed in 1831 to keep a ferry across the St. Mary's at the old ford, where the county road crosses leading to Pigeon Prairie, Mich.); Peter Gibeau, who manufactured candy, and his father, said to have lived to the age of one hundred and five years; Ribedeau, Francis Minie and

John B. Bequette, who manufactured trinkets for the traders all over the west; Benjamin Smith, a grocer; Anthony L. Davis, the first county clerk; Stephen Coles; Joseph L. and Thomas W. Swinney, respectively sheriff and treasurer; Thomas Johnson, a prominent lawyer; James Lillie, Samuel Lillie, who opened a hotel in 1835; Anthony Lintz, a shoemaker; Dr. Lewis G. Thompson, O. W. Jefferds, still living, proprietor of the woolen mill; Henry Cooper, the first school teacher and a famous lawyer; Robert Hood and Benjamin Cushman, who were the associate judges in 1837; Hon. I. D. G. Nelson and David H. Colerick, both distinguished in law; John Cochrane, builder of many of the old mansions; Samuel Sauer, a hotel keeper; Merchant W. Huxford; James B. Dubois, a jolly French tailor; Jesse L. Williams, Henry Rudisill, Royal W. Taylor, Philo Taylor, Samuel Freeman, merchants; F. P. Randall, Henry and John Steer, Thomas Hamilton, a merchant, brother of Allen; William Rockhill, one of the first county commissioners and justices, afterward congressman; Hugh Hanna, in 1826-7, and John Majors, 1836, pioneer carpenters; John Spencer, receiver public moneys; John E. Hill; Thomas Tigar, founder of the *Sentinel;* George W. Wood, of the same paper; John M. Wilt, L. P. Ferry, a prominent lawyer; Philo Rumsey, now living at Omaha; Major Samuel Edsall, who became state senator; Robert E. Fleming, clerk of the circuit court for sixteen years; William H. Coombs, a distinguished lawyer; Michael Hedekin, who became a contractor on the canal; Hon. Hugh McCulloch; Marshall S. Wines, a contractor on the canal, miller and legislator; John Trentman and Oliver Morgan, who each founded famous business houses; William N. Hood, an associate judge; Joseph Holman; David Pickering, elected sheriff in 1830; Dr. James Ormiston; Capt. Robert Brackenridge, register of the land office; Philip C. Cook, 1828, blacksmith; Isaac Marquis, and Absalom Holcomb, who built the first tannery in 1828.

Among the first farmers near by was Capt. Hackley, son-in-law of Capt. Wells, who cultivated in a primitive way a few acres now in the northern part of the city.

While the treaty of Greenville (1814) was going on, Peter Edsall and wife, from New York, kept a boarding house in a shanty, and saved enough to move to St. Mary's, where a similar gathering enabled them to clear enough to buy a farm on Shane's prairie. The father died and the mother and nine children moved to Fort Wayne in 1824. Before this the eldest boys, Samuel, John and Simon, made frequent trips to Fort Wayne, and cut hay on the prairie west of the fort where the water stood so high that the grass had to be carried to high ground to dry. Then Capt. Riley resided at Willshire, but there was only one house between Shane's prairie and Fort Wayne, that of George Ayres, on Twenty-four mile creek. The widow Edsall occupied a cabin on the St. Mary's, near the usual route of the Indians to the rival trading establishments of the Ewings, Barnett & Hanna, and Comparet & Coquillard. William S. Edsall was an attache of the corps of United States topographical engineers, under Col. Shriver, which was detailed in

1826 to survey a route for the Wabash & Erie canal. An idea of the fatality that accompanied that work may be obtained from the fact that after beginning work at Fort Wayne in the spring of that year, but very little was done before the entire party was prostrated by sickness, and soon afterward Col. Shriver died at the old fort. Col. Asa Moore succeeded him, and the survey was continued to the mouth of the Tippecanoe, and continued down the Maumee in 1827-8, until Col. Moore also fell a victim to the malaria. Young Edsall established a ferry and soon became acquainted with W. G. Ewing, and eventually became a clerk with the Ewings. He subsequently took charge of a branch house at Huntington, where he became county clerk and recorder. In 1836 he returned to Fort Wayne, and formed a partnership with his brother Samuel. In 1839 he became a partner in the great firm of Ewing, Edsall & Co. In that spring he took a horse-back ride through the west, as far as Madison, Wis. He became register of the land office in 1843, and in 1846, became a partner of his brother in merchandise and milling. The Edsalls originated the plank road from Fort Wayne to Bluffton about this time, a very important enterprise. In 1853, they made a contract for making the road-bed of the Wabash railroad from the state line forty-seven miles, and carried the job through, although they received little pay until they had completed the work, and meanwhile wages had risen, and the cholera had swept off workmen by hundreds. These are only instances of the large and beneficent enterprises in which the Edsalls were engaged. The second railroad they also did much to secure. Major Samuel Edsall died in February, 1865. In 1868, at the close of three years' business life in Chicago, William S. was elected clerk of the circuit court by the unanimous vote of the county.

Hon. Hugh McCulloch visited Fort Wayne in 1833, on the invitation of Dr. Lewis G. Thompson, whom he met at South Bend. He was making a trip of inspection, starting from Boston, and, says the distinguished writer, in his "Men and Measures of Half a Century," "Fort Wayne was about as uninviting in every respect except its site as any of the towns through which I had passed." "In 1833, the stockade of the fort, enclosing two or three acres, and a number of hewn log houses, was still standing." "Uninviting as Fort Wayne was in many respects it was fortunate in the character of its settlers — intelligent, far-seeing, wide-awake men, among the most prominent of whom was Samuel Hanna, one of that class to which the west has been indebted for its public improvements. Commencing business in a small way with his brother-in-law, James Barnett, he became the leader in all enterprises which were undertaken for Fort Wayne, and the country around it; the most important of which were the Ohio & Indiana, and the Fort Wayne & Chicago railroads. The construction of these roads was uphill work from the start. Again and again the companies were on the verge of bankruptcy, and nothing saved them but the faith, energy and unyielding tenacity of Mr. Hanna.

"Allen Hamilton was a protestant Irishman of a respectable but impoverished family. He joined a small party of his countrymen who were about to emigrate to Canada. In due time he reached Montreal, and after spending a few days in that city in fruitless efforts to find employment, he proceeded on foot to New York, and being equally unsuccessful there, he pushed on in the same way to Philadelphia. Here he was after a weary search kindly given a place by an old Quaker, and this was the turning point in his life. From that day his career was one of uninterrupted success. In a conversation with him in the spring of 1834, I said that a friend of mine, a ship-master, tired of the sea, was coming to Fort Wayne, with $15,000 in cash. 'That is a large sum,' said he, 'if I had that amount of clear cash, I should consider myself rich.' He died about twenty-five years from that time, leaving an estate worth a million or more. Nor was his good fortune confined to the acquisition of wealth. He was equally fortunate in his family relations. Especially fortunate was he in having sons who (unlike the sons of most rich men in the United States), are adding to the estate which their father left them, and at the same time maintaining his good reputation.

"William G. Ewing and his brother George W., formed the firm of 'W. G. & G. W. Ewing.' They had come from Ohio, and with Mr. Hanna, Mr. Hamilton and others whom I shall mention, were among the first settlers of northern Indiana. As there were at that time no surplus agricultural productions in that section, the only business opening for them was trade with the Indians and white hunters and trappers in furs and skins. Commencing in a small way at Fort Wayne, they rapidly extended their field of operations, and in a few years from that time at which they bought the first coonskin, the firm became one of the most widely known and successful in the northwest. But large and profitable as was their trade, the bulk of their large fortune was the result of investments in real estate, the most fortunate of which were in Chicago and St. Louis. Enterprising, laborious, adventurous men they were, but so devoted to business, so persistent in the pursuit of gain, that they had no time to enjoy the fruits of their labors. Charles W. Ewing, their brother, was a lawyer, and one of the most graceful and fascinating speakers, one of the most accomplished and agreeable men socially, that I ever became acquainted with. He had a splendid physique and a classic face. He was an excellent singer and story-teller. He had made a study of Shakespeare, and could quote the finest passages from the works of the great master in a manner that could hardly be surpassed by distinguished actors. So thoroughly equipped was he for success in the higher walks of life that the most distinguished positions would have been within his reach, if his convivial habits had not led him into dissipation which terminated prematurely a career, the opening of which was full of promise.

"Samuel Lewis, who had charge of the Wabash & Erie canal office, was a man of the purest character and of superior business capacity.

His wife, a lady of rare intelligence, was the aunt of Gen. Lew Wallace, who is adding to his high reputation as a soldier, enviable distinction as a writer. The house in which Mr. Lewis lived was a double log cabin, the latch-string of which was always out, a cabin which was rendered interesting in summer by the beauty and odors of the honeysuckles and climbing roses which covered its walls, and in winter by the cheerful blaze in its ample fireplaces, and which was always made doubly charming by the open-handed hospitality of its host.

"Jesse L. Williams, the chief engineer of the Wabash & Erie canal, was living at Fort Wayne in 1833. When the state engaged in an extensive system of public water works he was appointed chief engineer of the state, and went to Indianapolis, where he remained until the entire system collapsed in the general financial crash of 1837, and all hopes of its revival had been abandoned, when he returned to Fort Wayne, where he recently died, the last survivor of those whom I first met there. Few of our civil engineers have surpassed Mr. Williams in engineering skill, and I have never known his equal in industry and endurance. His labors as chief engineer of the Wabash & Erie canal, and other public works in Indiana, were prodigious, but he never failed to be equal to them. Week after week, and month after month, every day except Sunday, on which he always rested, he could be found upon the line of the public works, usually in the saddle, and in the evening, and until midnight, at his desk. Mr. Williams acquired a large property, and he was very fortunate in his family connections. His wife (the daughter of Judge Creighton, of Chillicothe, Ohio), who is still living, is a lady of superior culture, who has always been distinguished alike for her social qualities and active beneficence. His sons, while they do not come up to their father's standard in energy, will not discredit the name which they bear. The men whom I have thus mentioned, with Robert Breckenridge, register of the land office, a man who possessed the best qualities of the distinguished Breckenridge family of Kentucky, of which he was a distant connection; Marshall S. Wines, a man of extraordinary enterprise and force; John Spencer, receiver of the land office; Francis Comparet, and John B. Bourie, Canadian Frenchmen, who were just commencing what soon became a large trade in furs with the Indians, made up, with their families and a few stragglers, the population of Fort Wayne in the early summer of 1833. Since then I have been thrown among people of all grades; I have been brought into social relations with men standing high in public esteem; but the men of whom I have spoken, after the lapse of more than half a century, stand out before me in bold relief as remarkably intelligent, enterprising, far-seeing, and withal kind-hearted, generous men. Nor ought I to conclude what I have thought it proper for me to say about my early acquaintances in the west, without saying a few more words about a prominent and remarkable man, John B. Richardville, who succeeded Little Turtle as [civil] chief of the Miamis. He was a man of great natural shrewdness and sagacity, of whom no one ever got the better in a trade. Nor did he find an equal in diplomatic skill among the government commissioners when treaties were to be made with his nation. 'He is', said Senator Tipton, who often met him in councils, 'the ablest diplomat of whom I have any knowledge. If he had been born and educated in France, he would have been the equal of Talleyrand.' Although he dressed like a white man, and lived in a brick house, he had a commanding influence over the tribe. He was watchful of the interests of his people, but by no means unmindful of his own. In all treaties, large reservations of the choicest lands were secured to him and not a few boxes of silver were set apart for his special use." Mr. McCulloch reached Fort Wayne on the 26th of June and remained to deliver the Fourth of July oration, and before he had decided to make his home here was attacked by the malarious diseases which every new-comer at that time had to undergo. He was desperately ill, but his courage and pluck carried him through. Then, reduced almost to a skeleton, he took possession of a little office Dr. Thompson had built for him and began the practice of law, which, however, he abandoned in October, 1835, to begin as cashier of the branch of the State Bank that career in finance which has made his name a famous one.

Louis Peltier, before mentioned as the oldest native citizen of Fort Wayne, kindly furnishes for this work the following additional facts regarding the city in its infancy: Mrs. James Peltier came to Fort Wayne in 1807, with her uncle, Baptiste Maloch and wife, and lived where now stands Baker's saw-mill, east of which was situated a trading post owned by George Hunt. The first mission was at a shanty where the Methodist college now stands.

Baptiste Maloch and wife built a house on about the third lot from Clinton, on Columbia street, and there started the first bakery with Mr. Felix as baker. On the corner of Columbia and Clinton was situated a hewn log house (two-story) in which W. G. and G. W. Ewing conducted a dry goods store. East of Maloch's bakery Messrs. Anthony Davis and Walker had a dry goods store. Two lots from that Mr. Bourie kept a dry goods store. On the corner of Barr and Columbia streets Alexander Ewing kept a hotel. On the corner of Columbia and Barr streets (south side), was situated a two-story house where Dr. Cushman, of Vermont, the first physician in Fort Wayne, lived. On the north side of Columbia street where Monning's mill is now, was a log house in 1824 — Suttenfield's hotel. There was a blacksmith shop adjoining the hotel kept by Madore Katchee. Between that and the fort, Francis Aveline, grandfather of the present Avelines, made buckskin slippers, principally for the ladies. Mr. Peltier remembers when the fort was in good condition and Col. Tipton was acting as agent for the Indians, previous to his removal to Logansport. There was a porch extending around the fort under which a number of leathern buckets were kept, painted blue, and this constituted the fire department.

The original road of which so much has been said in connection with the proposed Maumee river bridge, ran about 200 yards from the present Main street bridge, west to the gas factory. On the northwest corner of Barr and Columbia, Samuel Hanna and James Barnett kept a general store, and Mr. Hanna's residence adjoined this. Squire Dubois and Samuel Stophlet had a tailor shop adjoining in a frame building. Capt. Bourie and mother lived on the adjoining lot. Capt. Brackenridge was next, in a hewn log building, where he conducted the land office. Tom Forsythe built a hewn log house next, which was afterward occupied by Brackenridge as a residence. Adjoining was a log house occupied by a shoe-maker named Halkins. Next was a frame house built by Mrs. Turner; next to that another frame house in which lived Mrs. William Ewing, which was occupied later by Bellamy, a shoe-maker. Adjoining that, where Schwieter's bakery now stands, James Barnett built a residence which was among the first brick houses in Fort Wayne. He also erected a building (frame) on the northeast corner for business purposes. On the northwest corner Allen Hamilton erected a frame building; adjoining which Tom Daniels put up a frame, in which he had a saloon. Next Chief Richardville kept a dry goods store, with John Forsythe as his clerk, and also Mr. Bruno. Benjamin Archer built a two-story brick next for a residence. William Henderson had a tailor shop in the adjoining building, which was frame; Henry Sharp had a hat store next; Zenas Henderson had a two-story brick building in which he had a hotel, bakery and saloon combined. As it had an ornamental front, Tom Swinney, the fancy painter of those days, spread a representation of two large eagles on the gable end of the house. On the northwest corner of Calhoun and Columbia streets was situated a story and a half brick house, with a log house adjoining, which was occupied by Robert Hood, justice of the peace. On the next lot was Hugh Hanna's carpenter shop, a frame building, with residence adjoining. Mr. Douglas, teamster, lived next. Conrad Nill had a shoe-maker shop next to that. Then came the Free Mason hall, where the canal basin was. Opposite to this was the first tannery, a log structure. A brick hotel building stood next, built by Joseph Holman, who conducted the tavern. Oliver Morgan, sr., was next with a hardware store, and near there was Squire Comparet's frame two-story residence; then came Alexander Chapman, a carpenter, in a frame building; then the frame house of Aveline, the tailor, who was a bachelor uncle of Frank Aveline, who built the Aveline House.

At the southwest corner of Calhoun and Columbia was a one-story frame building, built by Mr. Ewing, and on the southeast was the dwelling of Mr. Bruno. East of that was Lillie's hotel, a two-story brick; then came the residence of Dr. Thompson, a one-story brick; the residence of Comparet, one-story and a half brick; Squire Comparet's residence adjoined his father's residence, adjoining which was Comparet's store. The first house on the west side of Clinton street was a frame, occupied by Baptiste Becquette, silver-smith, adjoining which was his residence, a rude log house. On Clinton street at the corner of Main,

Allen Hamilton occupied a two-story frame house built by Hugh Hanna; at the corner of Berry, Abner Gerard lived in a two-story hewn log house; at the corner of Wayne, a one-story frame was occupied by Mr. Comey; at the corner of Lewis, a one-story frame was occupied fifty years ago by Father Miller; at the corner of Berry, northeast, Messrs. Rue & Crane kept a bakery shop sixty years ago; and on the southeast Madore Katchee had a dwelling house fifty-five years ago. Mrs. Turner's one-story frame house stood on the corner of Clinton and Wayne streets; on the north side of Wayne street, between Calhoun and Clinton streets, a brewery was kept by Henry Engle, fifty-four years ago. East of this lived a teamster named Strong.

At the northeast corner of Clinton and Wayne, where the Masonic Temple now stands, lived Zenas Henderson, who built a brick house; next to that was a frame house occupied by Mr. Whiteside, and at the northeast corner of Wayne and Clay streets lived Mr. Damen. On the second lot from Clay street on the south side, was a one-story frame house occupied by Taylor Frank fifty-four years ago, and at the corner of Barr and Wayne, was then a one-story frame owned by Mr. Weller. On the second lot south on Barr street, stood a one-story frame house occupied by Martin Noll.

The first hat shop was on Spy Run avenue, on Wells' reserve. It was owned by the Scotts, and was a one-story log structure, standing on the west side of the road, their residence being on the east side. North of Scott's was the residence of Mrs. Wells, a double log house, in which also lived Squire William Rockhill. From this place Mr. Rockhill moved to near what now is the McCulloch homestead, about fifty-five years ago; his house still stands on Greeley street. Colonel Wines, contractor, when he first came to Fort Wayne, also lived on the Wells' homestead. Adjoining the Wells' farm was that of Capt. Hackley, who married a Miss Wells. North of that some distance, Rudisill built the mill and also his residence.

Where the Foster block now stands was a two-story frame occupied by Col. Spencer, who had his land office on Main street in the public square.

On Court street, adjoining Spencer's residence, was a blacksmith shop, owned by Mr. Holloway. On the corner of Court and Berry streets was a log house which was bought by Grandma Anderson. On the corner of Berry and Calhoun stood a one-story frame house, owned by Mrs. Francis Minie, and aunt of Louis Peltier; the lot was 50x60 feet, and was bought by her for $500. Adjoining her lot on Berry street was a frame house in which the first gunsmith shop in Fort Wayne was established by Mosean, who also was a bell-maker. Next to that was the one-story frame residence of John Majors, a millwright by occupation. East from the government building was a one-story frame house built by Stophlet, and sold to Mrs. Peltier for $600, the lot being 60x150 feet. Next to that was a one-story frame where Madame Hinton resided. The corner of Barr and Berry streets was owned by Daniel Kiser.

Opposite Hon. F. P. Randall's residence of the present day, was in 1835, a frame house owned by Patrick Ryan, who was a shoemaker. East of Ryan lived Dr. Thompson in a brick house. On Main street at the corner of Clay, was Cyrus Fairfield's blacksmith shop, and at the corner of Barr was a two-story frame house occupied by Hugh McCulloch, in which place the first Mrs. McCulloch died. A two-story log house, on the corner of Calhoun and Berry streets, was owned by John P. Hedges. On the next two lots were two one-story houses, in one of which Squire Barnett and wife lived and died. Forty-five years ago Mr. Tinkham lived in a one-story frame house on Washington street, near Ewing. In 1842, an orphan asylum was built by Bernard Rekers, on the site where now stands August Trentman's residence, northwest corner of Wayne and Webster streets. Where now stands the Brunswick hotel was a sand bluff, and here the first garden stuff was raised and peddled by Grandma Morell, as she was then called. She also owned three lots where Jack Read's livery stable and Charles A. Munson's residence now are.

Forty-three years ago, the Hedekin house was built, and in 1842, Calvin Anderson, still living, became the first landlord. Betset Godfrey, of Detroit, had a bakery where the gas factory now stands. East of the bakery, Mrs. Charles Peltier lived over fifty-five years ago. On Superior street, at the corner of Barr, fifty-two years ago, stood a one story frame building, occupied by George Fallow, as a brewery; opposite, northwest corner, in 1834, was a blacksmith shop owned by Phillip Cook, and most of this was the fur packing establishment of Mr. Schovat about 1829; at the corner of Calhoun was a two-story log house in which Samuel Edsall's mother resided; and on the southwest corner, was a two-story frame house, built by Hugh Hanna and occupied by Capt. Bourie, in which Bourie and his wife both died; to the west of the latter was a cooper shop, owned by Gus Buerett, who made whisky kegs over fifty years ago. On Wells street, near the bridge, was a trading post kept by a man named Douglas. The first farm in Bloomingdale, in 1837, was owned by Hinton, who was Thomas Tigar's father-in-law. Another farm, opposite Swinney's, was owned by a man named Beeson. Joseph Holman, a Methodist preacher, lived on a farm north of the river, near Lindenwood cemetery. Near John Orff's homestead was a one-story building, which was the first distillery; it was owned by Squire Rockhill and brother. The first batch of liquor made by them attracted the Indians, forty or fifty in number, who began drinking with tin cups while it was still hot and finally got so hilarious that the proprietors had to send to town for Col. Tipton and James Peltier, who worked a night and day before they could leave the riotous crew. Where Eckarts' packing house now stands, Squire Rockhill built the first saw-mill, fifty-four or fifty-five years ago. The next saw-mill was built by Anthony Davis, Abel Beeson, Mr. Douglass and Peter Duprez. Duprez and his wife were both buried in the little orchard where Beaver's mill was afterward established. Before the saw-mill was completed, the owners became discouraged and were going to abandon the idea of corn-cracking, etc., when old Chief Richardville made them a present of $500, which encouraged them. He thought it might at some future date, keep his people from starving. On the opposite side of the river lived a Mr. Compton, who once became drunk and forced his son to go into a pen to unfasten a dog which he knew to be mad. The dog bit the boy, who afterward died of hydrophobia, which so enraged the Indians that they sought to shoot Compton, but were driven away.

Francis Comparet, mentioned above as one of the well-known early settlers of the city, was born at Monroe, Mich., October 12, 1798. That was then an Indian trading post, and his parents were engaged in that business. He was raised as a trader, and learned the Indian languages. In 1819 he was married to Eleanor Gwoin, a native of that post, and in March, 1820, they came to Fort Wayne, where he at once began to establish himself as a trader, and traveled extensively through the Indian territory. His trading house stood east of the alley on the south side of Columbia street between Clinton and Calhoun. He was agent for a number of years of the North American Fur Company, and had Henry Colerick as a partner in 1832-33, and subsequently Peter Kiser. The latter firm built a distillery on the south bank of the canal, east of Comparet's residence, and Mr. Comparet built a flouring mill which was very important at that day. He was active and energetic in business, and rendered efficient service in advancing the interests of the city. From 1824 to 1829 he served as county commissioner, forming with William Rockhill and James Wyman the first board. He took part in the building of several saw- and flouring-mills, and constructed the dam which forms the reservoir at Rome City, now famous as a summer resort. He had six children, all born in this city: Joseph, born in 1825, now resident of Washington territory; David, born in 1831; Alexander, born in 1833, now of Hicksville, Ohio; Theodore, born in 1835, now of Washington, D. C.; John M., born in 1837, now living at Blanco, Texas, and Louis, born in 1840, a resident of Des Moines, Iowa. In 1845 the successful career of Francis Comparet was cut short by death. David, the only one of his sons now residing here, was married at Fort Wayne in 1846, to Sarah Columbia, who was born in New York, in 1837. He was for many years identified with many of the leading interests of Fort Wayne. His son, Charles M. Comparet, was born in this city in 1851, and was educated in the city schools. He first engaged in the grain business with his father, and was bailiff of the criminal court six years under Judge Borden. In 1882 he engaged in the manufacture of shirts at 47 Hanna street, at which he is still engaged, doing a prosperous business, and giving employment to twenty-seven people. He was married in 1882 to Emma Shell, who was born in Clark county, Ind., and they have one child, Charles W. He is a member of the I. O. O. F., the K. of P., and the Patriarchal circle, and is in politics a democrat.

Hon. Peter Kiser, one of the most notable old settlers of Indiana, is a son of Richard Kiser, who was born in Rockingham county, Va. Rebecca Mossland, his mother, was from Cape May, N. J. They emigrated to Montgomery county, Ohio, where they were married in the year 1800. Peter was born in that county in August, 1805, or in 1810, as stated by some of the relatives, the family record having been destroyed by fire at an early day. Richard was a soldier in the war of 1812, and was at Detroit at the surrender of Gen. Hull, at that place, in August of that year. In 1822 the family removed to Shane's prairie, in Mercer county, Ohio, then a frontier settlement. Having no schools to attend, the youthful Peter engaged as a hand on the flat-boats, which at that time conveyed the products of the northwest to New Orleans. As early as 1825, Mr. Kiser was employed by Gen. Tipton, then Indian agent at Fort Wayne, to furnish the meat rations for the Indians during treaties and other councils with them, which employment was continued by other agents, until 1846. In the early years of the emigrants' Indian mission at Niles, in the territory of Michigan, Mr. Kiser assisted in conveying provisions to that station. For several years subsequent to 1838, he was associated with Francis Comparet, and then, having worked in the pork and provision business, he erected the first market-house at Fort Wayne, in 1835, and was the only butcher in the town. Mr. Kiser was married in January, 1842, to Rebecca Snyder, of Wells county, Ind., and they had eight children, all boys. In 1844, he commenced the mercantile business on Calhoun street. In 1828 he joined Wayne lodge of Masons, and has been a worthy member to this day. He has twice represented Allen county in the state legislature. He is still able, though feeble with the weight of years, to tread the streets of the city that has replaced the village at the fort, and he is esteemed as one whose business life has been characterized by honesty and integrity, whose relations toward his fellow men have been distinguished by unfailing kindness and benevolence, from whom the poor and needy have never gone empty-handed, as long as he had to give.

Cold and Drought.—There were two periods in the early days when the settlement experienced remarkable extremes of climate. The winter of 1831 was a most remarkable one. As early as the latter part of November, snow began to fall, and continued to lie upon the ground until the middle of March following; and the settlers, during this long season of snow, had a surfeit of sledding with their roughly-constructed pole " jumpers," and by frolics upon the ice of the rivers sought to enjoy the " long and dreary winter." So intense, much of the time, was the cold and great the depth of the snow during this long winter, that—though the settlers suffered but little from lack of food—the animals of the forest were unable to find any prey, and the wolves, of which there were still vast numbers throughout the northwest, were brought to such a state of hunger, that their fierce howlings were nightly heard at Fort Wayne, and it was unsafe for the settlers to venture far beyond the limits of the town. But even in this condition, the wolves would never make an attack upon a man unless their numbers were sufficient to insure success. The Indians' stores gave out during the winter and they suffered much from hunger. Some of them, it is said, were reduced to such a state that they devoured carrion. Several of them were killed and eaten by the wolves.

The summer and autumn of 1838 were signalized by a drought of longer duration and greater geographical extent than had been experienced since the first settlement of the country. On the estuary of the Maumee no rain fell from the 3rd of July to the 15th of October, and at Fort Wayne there was no rain-fall of any consequence from July to Christmas. The St. Mary's was so low that no provisions could be brought down from Ohio, and the supply of provisions in town was finally reduced to two barrels of flour. It was not until the next March that three flat-boats came down, laden with flour and bacon and whisky, and the arrival of these necessities was duly celebrated. During this drought all the smaller streams throughout the region were exhausted and their beds became dusty. The wild animals of every kind found in the forests collected on the banks of the rivers, and even approached the town. The wet prairies became dry, the wells failed and even the bogs of the Black Swamp below, dried and showed great cracks in the muck. The excavation of the canal was then going on in the lower valley and the mortality among the laborers was frightful.

Treaties with the Miamis.— The first land in the valley of the upper Maumee ceded to the United States by the Indians was a "piece six miles square, at or near the confluence of the rivers St. Joseph and St. Mary's," and a piece two miles square at the portage to the Little river. To these tracts the Indians relinquished their rights at the treaty they made with Gen. Anthony Wayne, at Greenville, Ohio, August 3, 1795.

On October 16, 1818, a treaty was concluded at St. Mary's, Ohio, by which the Miamis ceded the region thus bounded: Beginning at the Wabash river, near the mouth of Raccoon creek, thence up the Wabash to the reserve at its head near Fort Wayne; thence to the reserve at Fort Wayne; thence with the lines thereof to the St. Mary's river; thence up the St. Mary's to the reservation at the portage; thence with the line of the Wyandot session on 1817, to the reservation at Loramie's store, thence to Fort Recovery; thence to the place of beginning. There were reservations to Richardville of nine sections, with the right to convey; to Francois and Louis Godfrey twelve sections, and so on, in all forty-eight sections. For this cession the government agreed to pay a perpetual annuity of $15,000, build a grist-mill and saw-mill, and furnish a gunsmith and blacksmith for the Indians, and give them annually 160 bushels of salt. On October 23, 1826, a treaty was concluded at Mississinewa, by which the Miamis ceded all their claim to land in Indiana north and west of the Wabash, and of the cession just mentioned, and they were to receive for the latter $31,040.53 in goods, and cash $26,259.47, and annuities of $35,000 in 1827, $30,000 in 1828, and a permanent annuity, to include the former one agreed upon, of $25,000, as long as the tribe existed. There were various other smaller considerations and annuities. At the forks of the Wabash, October 23, 1834, another treaty was made conveying much of the reservations, and at the same place, November 6, 1838, the Miamis ceded nearly all that was left of the reservations for $335,680, and the government stipulated to possess the Miamis of, and guarantee to them forever, a country west of the Missouri river, to remove to, and settle on, whenever said tribe may be disposed to emigrate, and " this guarantee is hereby pledged. Said country to be sufficient in extent and suited to their wants and condition." The treaty sets out that whereas John B. Richardville is very old and infirm, his annuity shall be paid him without his removal. The latter received title again to several reservations and $6,800 in money. At the same place, November 28, 1840, the residue of the " big reserve," on the south side of the Wabash, was ceded, for $550,000 and other consideration, and there was an agreement to pay Richardville $25,000, and Francois Godfroy $15,000 for claims they had against the tribe. By the treaty of 1854, we learn that the Miamis ceded 500,000 acres set off to them by act of congress, February 25, 1841, west of Missouri (Kansas), on condition that they were to each take 200 acres, and near their reserves to have 70,000 acres in a body in common and a section for school purposes. There is a lengthy settlement of previous transactions; the $25,000 annuity is to cease in 1855, and an annuity of $7,500 is to be paid for twenty years, and $50,000 invested for the tribe. Finally, in 1868, the unfortunate Miamis, in spite of all the " forevers " and " pledges" theretofore made, are required to make a treaty by which they are removed to the Indian territory, and confederated with the Peorias, Kaskaskias, Weas, Piankeshaws, and from this last refuge, if any of them remain, no one can say how soon they will be called on to depart.

In the spring of 1828, the Indian agency at Fort Wayne was removed from Fort Wayne to Logansport, at the suggestion of Gen. John Tipton. This distinguished man had up to that time served as agent at Fort Wayne, with the Miami and Pottawatomie Indians, from March, 1823, and in the fall of 1826, he secured valuable concessions from the Indians. John Tipton was born in Sevier county, Tenn., August 14, 1786. When seven years old, he was orphaned by the murder of his father by the Cherokees. In 1807, he moved with his mother to the Indiana side of the Ohio. He served under Harrison before and during the battle of Tippecanoe, became a captain and advanced to the rank of brigadier-general. He served as sheriff, legislator, was one of the commissioners whe selected Indianapolis as the capital, was one to adjust the Indiana and Illinois boundary, and served as United States senator from 1832 to April 5, 1839, when he died at Logansport.

Opening of Land to Settlement.—After the treaty of St. Mary's congress passed an act, approved May 8, 1822, which provided that this new domain "lying east of the range line separating the first and second ranges east of the second principal meridian extended north to the present Indian boundary, and north of a line to be run, separating the tiers of townships numbered twenty and twenty-one, commencing on the old Indian boundary, in range thirteen east of the said principal meridian, in Randolph county, and the said district be bounded on the east by the line dividing the states of Ohio and Indiana, shall form a district, for which a land office shall be established at Fort Wayne." One of the provisions of that act was, that until the lands embraced in the specified limits had been surveyed, or a sufficient quantity thereof " in the opinion of the president, to authorize a public sale of lands within the same," a register of the land office and a receiver of public moneys should not be appointed. Consequently those offices were not filled until the year following, when President Monroe appointed Joseph Holman, of Wayne county, receiver of public moneys, and Samuel C. Vance, of Dearborn county, register. The necessary proclamation having been issued the land office was opened for the sale of lands to the highest bidder, on the 22d of October, 1823, the office being located in the old fort. At this first sale, John T. Barr, of Baltimore, Md., and John McCorkle, Piqua, Ohio, were the most extensive purchasers, the principal tract being described as "the north fraction of the southeast quarter of section 2, township 30 north, of range 12 east," upon which they subsequently laid out the original town of Fort Wayne, embracing 118 lots. The "Old Fort" grounds were not then subject to sale, having been reserved for the use of the Indian agency, including some forty acres.

Alexander Ewing was also a principal purchaser at this first sale, entering the east half of the southwest quarter of section 2, which lies immediately west of the Barr and McCorkle tract, and upon which Ewing's and Rockhill's additions were afterward laid out. The tract known as the "Wells' pre-emption," lying in the forks of the St. Joseph's and St. Mary's rivers, having been by act of congress, May 18, 1808, set apart to Capt. Wells, who was authorized to enter it, when adjacent lands should be subject to sale, at $1.25 per acre — was purchased by his heirs. The offices were continued here during a period of twenty-one years.

On the inauguration of President Jackson, in 1829, Capt. Robert Brackenridge succeeded Capt. Vance, and Gen. Jonathan McCarty, of Fayette county, became receiver. On the election of the latter to congress, he was succeeded by Col. John Spencer, who served until 1837. The officers after that date were: Receivers — 1837, Daniel Reid, of Wayne; 1841, Samuel Lewis, of Allen; 1841, I. D. G. Nelson, of Allen. Registers — 1837, James W. Borden, of Wayne county; 1841, William Polke, La Porte county; 1843, William S. Edsall, of Allen county.

At the time of Col. Spencer's taking the office, there were but 222 entries of sales of land on the books, and the receipts amounted to only about $100,000. The country around for a great distance, was then still an almost unbroken wilderness. Under the impulse given to speculation and emigration in the years 1835 and 1837, the sales increased to an enormous extent, so much so, that in the short period of eight months they reached the sum of $1,620,637, and in a single year to over $2,000,000. Col. John Spencer, who held the receivership at Fort Wayne for a longer period than any other man, incurred, on account of the large amounts of money he had to handle and the dangers of communication with other towns, extraordinary expenses in the administration of his office, and in the auditing of his accounts a deficit was found against him. His property was taken to meet this, and he was subjected to expensive and tedious litigation. He persistently contested the matter, and finally an accounting made under a special act of congress of 1847 showed that instead of a deficit, there was a balance due him of over $500. His property was returned to him. In a pamphlet he published to enforce his subsequent claim for damages, he gives the following facts regarding his history: He was born in Kentucky, and emigrated to Dearborn county, Ind., in 1797. At the age of twenty he became an ensign in the Indiana militia and was soon afterward captain. At the age of twenty-five he was elected sheriff of Dearborn county, served two terms, and after an interval of one term by another, he was elected again and re-elected. In 1822, he was made adjutant of the Fifteenth militia, and two years later, major. In 1825 he organized the Fifty-fifth regiment and served as its colonel six years.

Joseph Holman, first receiver of the land office, representative and treasurer of Allen county, was a prominent figure in the early days. He was born near Versailles, Ky., and was married November 22, 1810, and went to housekeeping two days afterward in a house built by himself of logs. He came to Wayne county, Ind., in 1805, one of the very first settlers there. In the war of 1812 he was a soldier, and built a block-house on his farm for the protection of the neighbors. He was a member of the convention which framed the constitution of the state of Indiana in 1816. His father, George Holman, when a young man was captured by the Indians and ran the gauntlet at Wapakoneta, and was sentenced to death at the stake; but after witnessing the burning of a companion, was saved by a Shawnee who had taken a fancy to him. Joseph Holman first became conspicuous in 1807 when he was selected by an anti-slavery "log-convention" to confer with the settlers at Clark's grant, concerning the nomination of a delegate to congress in opposition to the choice of the southern towns. He was instrumental in securing the election of Jonathan Jennings to that office. His brother William was a pioneer Methodist preacher.

In 1827, congress by an act approved March 2, granted to the state of Indiana, "for the purpose of constructing a canal from the head of navigation on the Wabash to the foot of the Maumee rapids," every alternate section of land equal to five miles in width on both sides of the line to be fixed for the canal. Consequently, the line not being yet known, the sale and entry of land was stopped for the time, and settlement considerably retarded within the supposed limits of the canal grant, and it was not until 1830 that an office for the sale of canal lands was opened at Logansport, and not until October, 1832, that the Fort Wayne office did business. The minimum price of these lands was $2.50 per acre, but so long credit was given the purchasers that the proceeds availed little for the prosecution of the work.

In the winter of 1830-31, Major Samuel Lewis was appointed commissioner of the Wabash and Erie canal and the canal land office, just referred to, a position he held for ten years. Major Lewis was one of the pioneers of Allen county, and a very prominent man in the early history of northeastern Indiana. He was a native of Mason county, Va., son of Col. Lewis, who was an officer in the war of the revolution. Major Lewis removed to Cincinnati in 1811, where he remained some time, and then at the age of twenty-one, went to Brookville, Ind., and engaged in business. He was elected to represent his county in the general assembly, and subsequently was appointed by President J. Q. Adams, Indian sub-agent, to fill which position he removed to Fort Wayne in 1827. By President William H. Harrison he was appointed receiver at this place, an office he held until the official revolution following the president's death. His various official functions, and natural ability, made him one of the foremost men of the embryo city. While at Brookville, he was married to Katherine Wallace, the sister of ex-governor David Wallace, of Indiana, and aunt of the distinguished soldier and author, Gen. Lew Wallace. Their daughter, Frances, born at this city, was in 1875, married to John F. Curtice, of Fort Wayne. He is a native of Indiana, born at Dublin, Wayne county, February 28, 1850, and is the elder of two living children of Dr. Solon Curtice, who was born in Clark county, Ohio, in 1820, and his wife, Mary Hazzard, born on the eastern shore of Maryland in 1820. He received his collegiate education at the Ohio Wesleyan university at Delaware, Ohio, which he entered in 1866, and was graduated in 1868. In 1869, he came to Fort Wayne, and after reading law in the office of Coombs & Miller, was admitted to the Allen county bar in 1871, but never practiced, the profession of the law not being to his taste. For several years he has been largely engaged in the real estate and loan business, and has been highly successful.

About 1823, the farm settlement in the valley of the upper Maumee began, though "squatters" had previously made them homes at various remote places. In 1819, four years previous, the nearest habitation of a white man on the Wayne trace was that of George Ayres, near Willshire, Ohio; on the St. Joseph trace, toward Lake Michigan, the nearest house was that of Col. Jackson, on Elkhart prairie; about the time of the opening of land for settlement, the house of Joel Bristol was erected near Wolf lake, in what is now Noble county; to the south and southwest the nearest habitations of white men were the house of one Robinson, distant thirty miles on the Wabash, and the mission station of a few Quakers, at the forks of the Wabash, where they gave the Indians instruction in agriculture. John Stratton, coming up from Richmond in 1824-5, mainly by the Robinson trace, found not more than six or eight houses between Richmond and Fort Wayne, the best one a hewn log house, used as a tavern. With the opening of the lands immigration began at once to set in, mostly from the state of Ohio, where the pioneers already began to feel crowded, and where the price of land had advanced considerably. Many from the southeast came down the St. Mary's with their goods in pirogues, which was the name for the hollowed sycamore logs, sometimes from trees of large size and made forty feet in length, capable of carrying five or six tons. The propelling power consisted of a man in each end who stood and with long poles pushed the boat against the current. It was customary to charge $3.00 per ton for freight from Toledo on these crafts. Some pioneers journeyed by wagon, finding, when they entered the Maumee valley, that it was a hard road to travel, up and down the sides of steep ravines, and guided by traces that were appropriately so called, for they were not roads. They found the land heavily wooded, in places covered with luxuriant vines, which in some instances the pioneer did not attempt at first to eradicate, but pushed aside as he planted the corn to find its way up from beneath them. The forest tangles were difficult to penetrate, and when the chosen spot was found then harder work followed with the axe, before a habitation could be made ready and the life of the settler be said really to begin. There was abundant supply of food ready for those who were ready with the rifle, and hardly any were not. Deer abounded. An old settler, Mr. Castleman, counted forty-five at one time in one drove on Little prairie, and for several years it was great sport to hunt deer on the Maumee. The hunter floating down silently in his pirogue, would find the animals in considerable numbers in the water to escape the mosquitoes, with only their heads protruding above the surface to furnish a mark for his unerring rifle. There was a profusion of smaller game, and the hunting of bears was a common thing. Daniel Notestine, an early settler in the Cedar creek district, tomahawked two in the forests, besides killing three with his rifle. The Indians were yet numerous and remained many years on their reservations, but in the days of settlement they were peaceable and kind to their pale-faced neighbors. With meat in abundance, and corn, potatoes and wheat from the little "deadenings," the settler had few wants to be supplied by the use of money, and it was well that it was so, for money was very scarce. The only things that would at all times command money were the pelts of the deer, mink and coon, and they almost attained the dignity of currency. Every spring, the settler's cabin would be well covered with coonskins, the reward of vigorous hunting, and each representing about $1.00. At weddings, corn bread served instead of cake, and venison took the place of the daintier modern dishes, but the marriage vows were not more lightly heeded.

Early Enterprises.— The early settlers suffered their main inconvenience on account of their distance from grist-mills. They must either make a wearisome journey into Ohio for a small grist, or by the use of a wooden mortar and pestle, crack corn into a coarse sort of meal, from which "johnny-cake" could be made, for the manufacture of which a "johnny-cake" board hung in every cabin. Or corn and pork could be boiled together, forming the favorite dish known as "hog and hominy." A primitive grist-mill, called the "corn-cracker," was a great convenience to a wide region about it, although the grinding was of a very imperfect sort. Such a mill was put in operation in 1828 on Six-mile creek in Adams township, by Joseph Townsend, who also used the water power to propel a saw-mill. Famous grist-mills in those days were that built by James Barnett and Samuel Hanna at the site of the later Esmond mills; Wines' mill, which was built on the south bank of the Maumee by one Coles, and sold in 1838 to Marshall Wines; and the mill built by Henry Rudisill and Henry Johns on the west bank of the St. Joseph, the water power being gained by a dam about 300 feet above the mill. When this mill was built in 1830, it was hailed with gratitude by the settlers to the north of Fort Wayne, who had been traveling many miles to mill, and they all joined heartily in the work of constructing the dam. The demand for lumber on the part of the early settler was very limited. He busied himself at first in felling the trees to make an opening, and to obtain logs for his cabin, and while this was being done, he, and ofttimes his wife and children also, slept in "God's first temples," the forests, under the shelter of a tree, or under a temporary hut of bark, raised on poles. The logs being cut into lengths, with the help of the other members of the little colony or the "neighbors" gathered from a wide territory, some logs without trimming or hewing other than the necessary notches at the ends, were laid as the foundation, and on these by means of skid-poles and forked sticks in the hands of the men, other similar rough logs were laid. The roof was made of rude clapboards, about three feet long, and six inches wide, called "shakes," laid somewhat as shingles are, and weighted with poles. The huge slab doors were pinned together with wooden pins, hung on wooden hinges, and from the wooden latch passed a buckskin "latch-string" to the outside. The light came through the door and down the chimney of mud and sticks or through a hole in the side covered by a greased cloth or paper. The stove or fire place was a sort of crib addition, with back walls and jams of clay. The floor was made of rough slabs or "puncheons," over which many a pioneer baby learned to walk, with many a bump. All that was needed for these buildings, or for the furniture, was made by the settler himself, with maul and wedge and axe, and clapboards and puncheons were the only lumber known at first.

But the settlers who came in after the opening of the lands in regular form, soon demanded better accommodation, and hewn log houses began to appear, which were a great advance over the previous rough structures, often not even chinked with mud. It was not long until the saw-mill began to supply lumber for the settlers' wants, for none of these primitive structures were adopted with any other motive than to provide temporarily for the necessities of life. Those who loved the unhewn log house went further west to keep on the edge of civilization.

In 1835 the first steam saw-mill in northern Indiana was built by Benjamin Archer and his sons, on the land of David Archer, on the St. Joseph river, two and a half miles north of the present city limits. David Archer and his son John went to Dayton, Ohio, for the boiler and other machinery, and it was hauled through the woods to the site of the mill from that distant point, the boiler being drawn by six yoke of oxen, and the rest of the machinery by horses. The magnitude of this operation, and its extreme tediousness, can hardly be imagined by one in this day of "fast freights." When the machine caravan reached Shane's prairie, bad roads were encountered, and young Archer was compelled to return home for another team of oxen before the journey could be completed. Unfortunately this mill was soon afterward destroyed by fire, and enterprise in this direction received a decided check in the upper Maumee valley. The mill was operated for three years by Benjamin Sunderland. The next steam saw-mill was that of Henry Rudisill, on the St. Joseph river, erected in 1841. He added an upper story and in that operated a carding mill also. In the same year that the Archers built their steam mill, Klinger & Comparet built a saw-mill on Beckett's run, which was operated by water power.

Clearings were not made by the early settlers until a considerable period after the opening of the land, except by cutting away the undergrowth of briers, grapes, haws, spice, gooseberries, pawpaws and the like. The bushes were cut down or grubbed out; the smaller trees were chopped down, and their bodies cut into lengths of twelve to fifteen feet, and the brush piled in heaps. The large trees were left standing, but "deadened" by girdling. In a dry time the brush heaps were burned over; a large area was scorched by the burning of the leaves, and the soil underneath would then be especially fertile. Sometimes the brush would be piled about the larger trees, which were easily killed in the same operation that removed the undergrowth. To get the logs out of the way, there would be a "log-rolling," to which the neighbors were invited, who came with wooden hand-spikes, and put all the logs in heaps, to be burned. The trees that did not fall were gradually cut down, and so the clearing proceeded hand in hand with tillage of the fields.

The best plow at first was the bar-share, the iron part of which was a bar of iron about two feet long, with a broad share of iron welded to it. At the extreme point was a coulter that passed through a beam six or seven feet long, to which were attached handles of corresponding length. The mold-board was of wood, split out of winding timber, or hewed into a winding shape. Some used on new ground only a shovel plow. Sown seed was brushed in with a sapling with a bushy top, dragged butt forward. The harrow or drag was of primitive construction, and was sometimes made of a crotched tree. The grain was harvested with the sickle until the trees were out of the road, and the threshing was done with the flail, two sticks of unequal length fastened together with a thong, with which the inexperienced were in more danger than the wheat piled on the floor.

ANNALS OF THE TOWNSHIPS.

In an account of the settlement of those portions of the valley of the upper Maumee without the limits of the city of Fort Wayne, reference will of necessity be frequently made to the townships as they are now limited, all being with slight exceptions bounded by the township and range lines of the government survey. In the days when the settlements were made however, these township divisions were mainly unknown. At the first session of the county board, May 31, 1824, Wayne township was defined as embracing the whole of Allen county. So it remained until January, 1826, when all that portion east of the line between ranges 12 and 13, or broadly, that part east of the juncture of the rivers, was formed into Adams township. In 1828, the northern halves of these townships were set apart as St. Joseph township, and this was four years later divided into Washington and St. Joseph.

The first division of Adams township was in September, 1834, when Root township was set off, including Marion and part of Adams county. Marion was given its present limits in August, 1835. Jackson was set off May, 1837; Jefferson and Madison, March, 1840; Monroe in March, 1841. From the original Washington township, Perry was set off in September, 1835, then embracing all township 32, range 12, the east half of range 11, and the territory north. Then Eel River was set apart, and Lake in May, 1837. Out of the former comprehensive St. Joseph township, Maumee was set off in March, 1836; Cedar Creek and Springfield in September, 1837; the latter at first included Scipio, which was established in 1843. Milan township was created in March, 1838, with irregular boundaries, and was given its present limits in September, 1840. From old Wayne township, Aboit was partitioned in May, 1836; Pleasant in June, 1842, and Lafayette in 1846. The boundary lines of these three townships were afterward adjusted somewhat to the courses of Little river and one of its tributaries.

WAYNE, ADAMS, WASHINGTON AND ST. JOSEPH.

These four townships which are now limited to the district twelve miles square, near the center of which the city lies, were the only townships known to the earliest settlers. Within their present limits, however, the first rural homes of Allen county were made. The history of the early settlement of Wayne township is so intimately connected with that of the city of Fort Wayne, that no attempt will be made to treat upon it further. No villages have been established in it except that of Lewisburg, which was platted by Lewis Mason, on section 30, January 2, 1837.

Adams Township.—The earliest considerable settlement was in Adams township, in 1823, when Jesse Adams, William Caswell, Eliphalet Edmunds, Charles Weeks, sr., Charles Weeks, jr., Martin Weeks, Israel Taylor, Philip Fall and Capt. Hurst, began to make them homes, at first "deadening," and in later years clearing away and ruthlessly destroying the heavy timber which encumbered the land, and was then of little value. Mr. Adams, who came from Rochester, N. Y., and settled near New Haven, was a man of much ability, and gave the township subsequently formed his name, not in his own honor, he declared, but in memory of John Quincy Adams. The closing years of his life were spent in Jefferson township. A daughter of this pioneer died in 1825, and was buried upon his farm, where a second interment, the body of Mrs. James Thatcher, was made in 1828. The spot became the cemetery for a large district, but the established cemetery afterward was upon land donated by D. W. Miller, in 1830, which is now included in the beautiful cemetery maintained by the Odd Fellows since 1875. In 1830 Caswell and the senior Weeks removed and became the first settlers of Perry township. Henry Cooper and Judge Wolcott settled in Adams township in 1824, and in December of the following year John and Jabez Rogers took possession of land in the woods. They were all of true pioneer stock, hardy, industrious and good citizens. Henry Cooper here laid the foundation of his fame as a lawyer by studying by the light of the log heaps. John Rogers came from Ohio, with a large family, and the survivors and their children are now among the best people of the county. In that year, 1825, a son was born to Mr. Rogers and wife, named John S., who was the first white child born within Adams township. He died at Fort Wayne at the age of twenty years. The first hewn-log house was erected this year by Mr. Rogers, and it was an architectural triumph for the locality in those days. This prominent old settler lived in the township twenty-five years, and then moved to the city, where he died in 1877. In 1826, Samuel Brown, from Ohio, settled, and in the following year John McIntosh, who entered land in 1823, was married to Ruth, a daughter of his neighbor Brown, the ceremony being performed by Squire Jesse Adams, who had been elected at the first election, held on the second Monday of March of the previous year, at the home of Eliphalet Edmunds. Two years elapsed before the next marriage, of David Miller to Rachel Townsend. In 1827 Henry Cooper sowed the first wheat, at a rather late season, November 15, but it turned out well, according to the tradition. In this year a number of good men were added to the population: John Blakely, John K. Senseny, Joseph Townsend, David W. and Abraham Miller, Thomas Daniels, John Troutner and Judge Nathan Coleman. The year 1827 is also memorable as the date of the survey of the first road, from Fort Wayne to a point just east of the site of New Haven. It was afterward extended as a stage line to Defiance, Ohio, and "the river road" became a popular thoroughfare. Henry Tilbury came in 1826 and Jeremiah Bateman in 1828, and in 1829 the Smith brothers, William, John, Thomas and Joseph, began clearing their farms. In this year immigration began to increase so rapidly as to make an accurate record almost impossible. Neighbors, before so scattered, began to touch elbow in the march of civilization, and the smoke from many stick chimneys told of happy families at home in rude cabins which were for all their rudeness the shrines of peace, religion and industry. The tide of immigrants led John Rogers, in 1832, to establish an inn on his farm, convenient to the river road and the Maumee, and many an immigrant's wagon stopped there, or pirogue hauled up to the bank to enjoy the hospitality of the "Hoosier Nest," as it was called. About the same time Rufus McDonald opened the "New York" inn on his farm, and in 1837 the postoffice was established there, and was kept by Mr. McDonald until 1842. During that period the mail was carried between Defiance and Fort Wayne, on horseback, by John Omans.

New Haven.— The land embraced in the original plat of New Haven was entered by one Gundy, who deadened the timber after the usual manner of the first settlers, and it was known as "Gundy's Deadening." The land passed from him to Samuel Hanna, then to Eben Burgess, who with his son, Henry, made the town plat March 16, 1839. Henry Burgess opened up the first store, and Elias Shafer kept a hotel near by. The expectations of prosperity from the canal traffic were not justified, but the building of the Wabash railway and the "Nickle-plate" through the town have made it an excellent railway point. In June, 1866, a petition was presented to the county commissioners by John Begue and others asking the incorporation of the town, and an election was ordered, which took place on June 7th, and resulted favorably to incorporation. In December, of the following year, upon the petition of A. H. Dougall and others, the corporation was made a voting precinct. Additions to the original plat were made by J. K. Edgerton in 1854, by Reuben Powers in May, 1853, and Nicholas Shookman in 1863. During the war, and for ten years later, there was extensive manufacture of staves, hoops, etc. Money was plentiful, and the town flourished as it has not since. But it is handsomely situated, and has many beautiful and well-kept residences. The population as taken by Trustee O. D. Rogers, in 1885, was 1,211. A pioneer industry of the town was the the New Haven flouring mill, which was erected in 1856 by Amasa Volney and John A. Powers, in the hands of one or more of whom it remained in whole or in part for many years. An interest was owned at one time by Allen H. Dougall. While owned by Volney Powers, it was destroyed by fire, January 7, 1884. L. M. Rogers, in partnership with John Begue and Levi Hartzell, founded the Maumee Valley flouring mill in 1864, an extensive establishment. Amása Rogers owned an interest subsequently, and for several years, up to 1871, it was managed by Louis and Charles Lepper. In the latter year a terrific explosion was caused by lack of water in the boiler, the proprietors and engineer were instantly killed, and the miller and two boys dangerously injured, and the building ruined. In 1875, the property was purchased by Joseph Brudi & Co., who are still operating it with full roller process. In 1854, John Begue started a cooper shop, to which stave manufacture was added in 1862, the Beugnot brothers becoming partners. Subsequent to 1870, under the management of Schnelker, Beugnot & Co., this became a great establishment.

In 1863 the planing mill was erected by Gustav Gothe and Carl and Joseph Brudi at the east end of town, which is now operated by Gothe & Co. A stave factory of considerable importance was founded in 1864 by B. Schnelker and J. E. McKendry, which in May, 1876, went into the hands of H. Schnelker & Co., they then employing ninety-five hands, and consuming in their manufacture, 12,000 cords of wood annually. It is now owned by H. F. Schnelker & Co., and is an extensive manufactory. In 1881, F. H. Bueter and A. R. Schnitker founded a handle factory, which is operated at present by Schnitker & Fischer. A large wood working factory is now in erection by M. S. Flowers. The more prominent business men at this time are: L. M. and W. S. Rogers, dry goods and groceries; Frank H. Bueter, general store and postmaster; G. Adolph Foellinger, druggist; Bartholomew Dowling, hardware; Henry Hager and Salvador Peltier, groceries; Rogers & Tustison, agricultural implements; O. D. Rogers, notary; Edward Harper, furniture; Mack & Gabet, brewers; Amos Miller, watchmaker; Henry Blaising, Hudson & Butler, meat markets; Chas. W. Cook, New Haven hotel; W. Zeddis, harness; George C. Hathaway & Co., lumber; Jacob Scheeler, tile manufacturer. The first physicians were distinguished more for natural talent than for college diplomas. Jesse Adams practiced for some time, administering relief to those who were sick, and Dr. Barnwell, a botanical doctor, and Opp, a physician of more skill, followed him in this work. Dr. Philip H. Clark came in 1840, but after six years, removed to Ashland county, Ohio, where he is still living. Dr. W. W. Martin, who became a surgeon of the Forty-fourth Indiana, and afterward committed suicide, practiced some time in New Haven, and was followed by Drs. Ross, Mitten and Diggens. The physicians at present are Drs. John W. Bilderbach, August G. Brudi, Charles J. Gilbert, Lycurgus S. Null. The societies of the town are Newman lodge, No. 376, F. & A. M., instituted February 3, 1868; New Haven lodge, No. 253, I. O. O. F., instituted March 6, 1866, which is distinguished for its work in establishing the famous cemetery; Jesse Adams post, G. A. R., No. 493, organized March 12, 1887.

In 1858, the trustees of Adams township erected a school building with two rooms, in which a district school was held. After the incorporation, the town added two rooms to this structure, and in December, 1866, Dr. James Anderson was employed as principal and authorized to grade the school by the school board of the town, L. M. Rogers, C. E. Bryant and John Begue. In 1885 this building was torn away, and a handsome brick building was erected, through the efforts of Trustee O. D. Rogers. The building contains four rooms besides an office, and is two stories high. The school board now consists of H. F. Schnelker, C. A. Miller and Joseph Brudi. The town officers are: Trustees, Dr. L. S. Null, D. H. F. Barbrick, J. J. Lee; marshal, Charles Bell; treas-

Lamot M. Rogers

urer, B. Dowling; clerk, H. H. Schnelker. The newspaper of the town, the *New Haven Palladium*, was founded October 25, 1872, by Thomas J. Foster, who continued to publish it until June 5, 1879, when it was rented by Orrin D. Rogers, who conducted it one year when the paper was suspended. Subsequently H. L. Williamson established the *Echo*, which had a short existence.

Washington Township.—The next township after Wayne and Adams in order of settlement was Washington. Immediately following the beginning of the sale of lands, Reinhard Cripe, a Pennsylvania-German, settled on Spy run, with his family. He was one of those who enjoyed the sport of hunting, and his good nature made him popular, but he left little to show for his residence when he removed a few years later, to Elkhart county. The first real beginning at the settlement and improvement of the township was made by the Archer family, which consisted of Benjamin Archer and wife, then past middle life, their three sons, David, John S., Benjamin, a daughter Susan and her husband Alexander Ballard, their daughter Elizabeth, who was the wife of Thomas Hatfield, also one of the party, and the daughter Sarah, with her husband, Edward Campbell, a French-Canadian. Andrew J. Moore was also a member of the party, and Adam Petit, who in 1828 married the daughter of David Archer. Thomas Hatfield had visited the township in the spring, and entered land, and in November, 1825, accompanied by the Archers, who had removed from Philadelphia to Dayton, they set out, and traveled thither by the Wayne trail, through the boundless forests, camping out by the way during the nights, which were made musical by the howling of wolves and screeching of wildcats. Benjamin Archer was well-to-do for those days, and his sons being grown men, were given tracts which he purchased, to improve. David settled on the St. Joseph, two and a half miles from the fort; John S. was given a quarter section near the site of the Catholic orphan asylum; and Benjamin went three miles to the northwest, upon land recently owned by Alexander McKinley. Mrs. Ballard was given a tract just east of the Wells reserve, but she and her husband, who worked as a brickmaker in the village, did not go upon it until 1830. The heirs of Thomas Hatfield, who was for many years a justice of the peace, and a minister of the gospel, still retain the lands the parents settled upon at that time. Near the same locality lay the lands allotted to the Campbells. All of the family were stalwart and healthful, and they have subdued hundreds of acres of forests and changed the somber hue of green to the golden gleam of ripening grain on many a landscape. In the year of his settlement Benjamin Archer established a brick kiln on section 35, where his sons, principally John S., engaged in making brick, supplying the demand in the town until 1830. In this family occurred the first birth, of David, son of David and Anna Archer, born January 1, 1827, and the first marriage, of Franklin Sunderland to Rebecca Archer, in 1828. In 1826 Isaac Klinger entered a tract near the site of Bloomingdale, and took possession in the following year, when Jonathan Cook arrived with his family and settled on section 34. His brother, Philip Cook, came with him, but in 1828 married Isabel Archer and removed to town. His latter years were spent upon the farm he took in 1827.

Late in the year 1827, two Virginians, Lovell Yates and Richard Shaw, settled, but their land transactions were confined to renting and tilling a small field. Their main occupation was hunting, and when the settlers became more numerous they went further west. James Sanders settled in the same year. He had been a minister of the Methodist church, and conducted meetings occasionally at the neighbors'. A Mr. Hudson and family settled in 1828, and Joseph Goins in 1830. In that year Col. John Spencer located roads through the township, one of which became the highway to Goshen, the other to Lima, Ind., the latter subsequently made a plank road (1839-40). Next year the same engineer located the Leesburg and Yellow river roads, so that the early settlers in Washington township were especially favored with primitive highways. The Lima road becoming a favorite thoroughfare, Mr. Poirson opened the first hotel upon it in a log building. About the year 1828, Jonathan Chapman, or "Daddy Appleseed," established a nursery and sold fruit trees. In 1829, David Archer brought a number of apple trees from Ohio, and these were set out in the pioneer orchards. In 1832, Joseph Gill came in from Pickaway county, Ohio, and soon after his settlement on section 15 his wife Mary died and was buried in the pioneer graveyard, which, one acre in extent, was donated by Thomas Hatfield, in 1830. It is still in use. Among the subsequent early settlers were Joshua and George Butler, Gavin Peyton and Babel Wainwright in 1832, Elias Walters, John B. Grosjean and Charles Schwab, the blacksmith, in 1834; Benjamin Sunderland in 1836. Early in the thirties Thomas Hinton, an Englishman, settled in the southeast, and he afterward kept an inn at the place where the Goshen road crosses the feeder canal, called the "Bullshead Tavern." His son, Samuel Hinton, is now an aged resident of Fort Wayne. In 1840 the population began to increase rapidly. The first election in the township was held in April, 1832, and John S. Archer was elected justice. In 1856, a tannery was established by Mr. Gray near the site of Centlivre's brewery, which became for a time a prosperous establishment, with stores in Fort Wayne, St. Louis, and elsewhere, but it finally failed.

The village of Wallen was founded in 1870, upon lands owned by J. K. Edgerton, adjoining the Grand Rapids & Indiana railroad, and the name was bestowed in honor of the then superintendent of the road. Additions were subsequently made by James P. Ross, who was the first postmaster, appointed in 1871. Important interests here are the sawmill of Grosjean Bros., established in 1872, and their tile manufactory established in 1882. This, and the branch at Arcola, manufacture about 3,000 tile annually, to the amount of $8,000, and give steady employment to about twenty-five men.

The village of Academie, so named because of the Catholic institution two miles east, was platted by S. Cary Evans in 1874, but has not developed.

St. Joseph Township, when first created, embraced all the territory in northeastern Indiana north of the township line north of Fort Wayne, and west to the western extremity of the jurisdiction of Allen county. Within its present limits, to which it was reduced in 1840, the first settler was Jeremiah Hudson, of Delaware, who established himself in the fall of 1828, and cleared a farm on the land afterward known as the " Ogle half-section." Charles H. De Rome, a native of Canada, who had married a half-breed Miami maiden at Vincennes, came to the township in 1829, and lived on the reserve which was granted his wife, Marie Christine. He was well educated, knew the English, French and Indian languages, and held positions in business houses in Fort Wayne. Jesse Klinger, a native of Pennsylvania, who settled on the Richardville reserve in 1829, and became a great favorite, and conspicuous for those kindly acts of neighborly kindness peculiar to the early days, was fairly embarked in making his farm, when he died in 1835, and was one of the first of those to be buried in the cemetery he had donated. His son, Samuel, born in 1830, was the first white native of the township. Thomas Griffis was another 1829 settler, and was unfortunate in losing the land he purchased of De Rome, on account of the president not giving his consent to the transfer. Another who lost his labor in the same way was John Klinger, a settler of 1829, who afterward improved a farm on the west side of the river. Other comers in this year were William Sturms, a famous hunter, but also an industrious farmer; Moses Sivotts, a good Pennsylvanian, who remained but a few years; and Martin Weeks, who settled on the ridge road. The latter was devoted to the chase, and was also a turbulent citizen, so amply endowed by nature that his neighbors were no match for him, and he was consequently avoided. Later, however, he underwent a remarkable change and became a popular minister of the Baptist church. In 1830, Abraham Dingman and William Butt came in from Ohio, and settled down to clearing and farming with such industry and obliviousness to everything else, that they became famous as workers in a community of forest-fellers. John Tilbury, another man of great energy, began work in 1832, on a farm on the ridge road three miles east of Fort Wayne, still owned by his descendants. The list of new people in 1833 includes James A. Royce, an industrious and popular man, who was one of the earliest school teachers; James Porter, who subsequently removed to Washington township; and Christian Parker, grandson of a revolutionary hero, who cleared a farm of 160 acres, and subsequently became the first justice, then county commissioner, and member of the state assembly for four successive terms.

In 1836, Job Lee, a quiet and pious man who had been in the war of 1812, came here. Others this year were True Pattee, who held religious meetings as a minister of the Methodist church; James Mayhew, John Harver, Silas, Charles and John La Vanway, and the Goodale brothers. In the list of pioneers should also be included Uriah J. Rock, Jeremiah Whitesides, Jedediah Halliday, William Matthews, Benjamin Coleman and Peter Parker. "Jerry" Whitesides was a conspicuous figure of those days. He was tall and slim, and had lost his right arm, it having been amputated half way above the elbow, leaving just enough to serve as a rest for a rifle, which was his inseparable companion. Throughout the valley of the upper Maumee he was known as Jerry Whitesides, the one-armed hunter. The first marriage in the township was performed by Justice Parker in 1835, Isaac Bush to Sarah Madden; and the first death was that of William Matthews, who died in 1834 and was buried at the Maumee settlement. In 1834, at the instance of Christian Parker, the road which was subsequently extended as the St. Joseph state road, was established from town to Jacob Notestine's farm, and in 1836 the Ridge road was surveyed. On this highway, in 1838-9, Mr. Rossington opened a small tavern, which became well known. Previously, the private hospitality of Christian Parker, for which he would accept no recompense, such was the courtesy of the good pioneer, was the main resource of travelers on that road.

On a beautiful and historic tract of land, four and a half miles from Fort Wayne, on the St. Mary's river, now reside the descendants of distinguished men whose names are frequently met in the annals of the upper Maumee valley, Richardville and Godefroi.

Francis Godfroy, or Godefroi, which is the old French form of the name, was a war chief of the Miamis of great power and influence, succeeding Little Turtle in 1812. His father was a Frenchman who took to wife a Miami maiden. Francis married Soc-a-jag-wa, a Miami girl, and they made their home on the Wabash, near Peru, about four miles east of the site of which town their son, James R. Godfrey, who is still living, was born in July, 1810. The latter came to Allen county about 1844 and was married to Montosoqua, daughter of La Blonde, the daughter of the famous civil chief of the Miamis, John Baptiste Richardville. She was born near Fort Wayne, in 1835, and died in March, 1885. They had twelve children, James, now deceased; Mary, now deceased; Louisa, wife of George Neid, residing on the reserve; John, who lives with four children on the reserve; Annie, wife of William Stuck; George L., and six who died in childhood. James, the oldest son, was born on the reserve in 1846. At the outbreak of war in 1861, he enlisted in the Eleventh Indiana battery, but contracting disease, was discharged on account of disability at Corinth, June 5, 1862. On the same day that he reached home his life ended.

George Lewis Godfrey, the youngest son of James R. Godfrey, was born at the family residence on the reservation, October 2, 1850. There he was reared and was given a good practical education in the public schools. He has followed farming as an avocation, residing on the reservation all his life. He is one of the very few Indians in Indiana or the country who are members of secret societies, and is the highest in Masonry of any Indian in Indiana and the world. He became a

Mason several years ago, joining Home lodge, No. 342. Since then he has become a member of the Fort Wayne chapter, No. 19; Fort Wayne council, No. 4, R. S. & M.; Fort Wayne commandery, No. 4, K. T.; Fort Wayne grand lodge of perfection, 14th degree; Urias council, 16th degree, and consistory S. P. R. S. of Indianapolis. He is also a member of the Phoenix lodge, No. 101, K. of P., and division No. 12, uniform rank, and was at one time a member of the United Order of Foresters, passing through all the chairs of the same, and was also a member of the Patriarchal Circle. He is a member of Wayne Street Methodist Episcopal church. There are now seventy-two residents of the reserve, embracing James R. Godfrey, his children and grandchildren.

Charles W. Fairfield, a prominent farmer of Wayne township, was born June 6, 1842, in a frame house which was built in the country, but now stands on Broadway street, Fort Wayne, south of the Wabash railroad tracks. His father, Charles Fairfield, one of the pioneers of Allen county, was born in Kennebunk Port, Maine, February 14, 1809, son of Capt. William Fairfield, a sea captain of Kennebunk Port, who was one of Gen. Washington's aides-de-camp during the revolutionary war. All the sons followed in the footsteps of their father and became sailors, two of them, Oliver and Asa, rising to the position of captains. They participated in the war of 1812, and were both captured on the sea by English men-of-war, and confined in English prisons, the former at Halifax, N. S., for sixteen months, and the latter at Dartmouth, England, for six months. When Charles Fairfield was fifteen years of age he went to sea, and continued for thirteen years, during the latter part of that time being in command of a vessel. In 1835, the three brothers, Oliver, Asa and Charles, came to Indiana. The brothers located first in Fort Wayne, Oliver engaging in the bakery business, while Asa and Charles began farming. Asa died October 4, 1868; Oliver, March 24, 1883, leaving Charles the oldest representative of the family in the west. About 1843, Mr. Fairfield removed to a farm on the St. Joseph road in St. Joseph township, and from there removed to Wayne township where he purchased over 400 acres of land on the Bluffton road. In 1862, he traded with the county commissioners for a farm of 290 acres, where his son now resides, three and one-half miles southwest from Fort Wayne. In May, 1889, he removed to his present home two miles from the city. He has been a worthy citizen throughout his residence in Allen county, but though he has accepted with reluctance various public trusts, he has always lived a quiet life. Being a careful business man he has been successful financially, owning 515 acres of improved farm land and city property. Known all over Allen county, he is everywhere esteemed. He was married December 4, 1837, to Sarah A. Browning, who was born near Marietta, Ohio, January 18, 1815, and is the daughter of Bazalia Browning, a native of New Jersey, who was an early settler of Ohio, a soldier of 1812, and a pioneer of Allen county, coming here as early as 1832. In 1887, Mr. and Mrs. Fairfield celebrated their golden wedding. To their union four sons and three daughters were born: George N., enlisted in 1861, while attending Lawrence university at Appleton, Wis., in the Fourth Wisconsin regiment; was transferred in 1863 to Company E, Sixteenth Indiana, of which he became captain, and died at Stony Point, near Vicksburg, Miss., in the fall of 1863; Olive A., now the wife of W. R. H. Edwards, an old citizen of Fort Wayne, now of Deer Lodge county, Mont.; Charles W.; Mary F., now the wife of Harry Davis of Washington territory; Edward B., of Montana; Frances, deceased wife of Cornelius Miller; Willard A., of Wayne township. Charles W. Fairfield was reared in Wayne township, and was educated in the log school-houses of that day. On April 19, 1861, he enlisted in Company E, Ninth Indiana infantry, for ninety days, and participated in the campaigns in West Virginia, in Gen. Morris' brigade, Eleventh corps, Army of the Potomac. Returning to Allen county, he engaged in saw-milling for two years. During the gold excitement in Idaho in 1864, he joined a party of thirty-five who made the entire trip there by ox teams in six months. This party was among the very first in the gold regions of southern Idaho, and they opened up the first road from North Platte Bridge, Neb., 400 miles to Virginia City, through the center of the Sioux country. The trip was a most perilous one. They were piloted by Bozeman, a scout, who founded Bozeman City, Mont. Two years later Mr. Fairfield returned to Allen county for a year, then going back to the mining regions, at that time only fourteen miles from the Union Pacific railroad. He located at Laramie City, Wy., where he was engaged on a contract on the Union Pacific railroad. While residing in Beaver Head county, Idaho, he served as sheriff for about one year. In the fall of 1868 he returned to Allen county, and began farming, his present occupation. He manages one of his father's farms and owns a good farm of 100 acres in the same township. He was married in Montana, November 22, 1864, to Emma Toothill, born in Pennsylvania, March 26, 1842, the daughter of Joseph Toothill, an Englishman, who died when she was in her fourth year. His wife was Hannah Smith, born in New York state, and died in Chicago, April 20, 1886, in her eighty-sixth year. Mr. and Mrs. Fairfield have had nine children, five of whom survive: Hattie M., wife of George M. Trick, of Pleasant township; George M., of the Indiana Machine Works, Fort Wayne; Charles E., Oliver Perry, and Ida. Mr. Fairfield is a member of Sion S. Bass post, G. A. R., and of Harmony lodge, I. O. O. F.

Henry C. McMaken, a well-known farmer of Wayne township, was born near New Haven, Adams township, June 15, 1844. His father, Joseph G. McMaken, who was born near Hamilton, Ohio, February 8, 1814, came to Allen county in the spring of 1832, with his father, Joseph H. McMaken, who settled at Fort Wayne, and kept for many years one of the first taverns, the Washington hotel, which stood on the corner of Calhoun and Columbia streets, the mammoth dry goods house of De Wald & Co. now occupying the site. In 1838, he removed to a farm in Adams township, and in 1847, purchased a farm on the Maysville pike, about three and one-half miles from the city. He was one of the best known citizens during his life, and after farming for years, died December 13, 1864. His widow, Dorothy Ruch, was born in Alsace-Loraine, France, about 1818, and came at about eleven years of age to America with her parents, who located in Pittsburg, then removed to Starke county, Ohio, and in 1837, came to Fort Wayne. In 1889, she removed to Fort Wayne. There were twelve children born, ten of whom are living: Henry C.; William B., farmer in Wayne township; Joseph H., on the homestead farm in Adams township; Sarah J., wife of S. S. Coleman, of Wayne township; Anna M.; Adelia C.; J. C. F., farmer of Lake township; Franklin A., residing in Fort Wayne; Elizabeth, and Lottie M., wife of Elmer Banks, of St. Joe township. Henry C. finished his education at the Methodist Episcopal college in Fort Wayne in 1857, and then worked on the farm until June, 1862, when he enlisted in Company E, Fifty-fifth Indiana regiment, and served three months. He was captured at Richmond, Ky., August 30, 1862, and four days later paroled. He was discharged at Indianapolis, September 9, 1862. Returning to the home farm, he worked until 1868, and then rented a farm. In 1874, he purchased sixty-two acres in Wayne township, his present farm. In 1874, he erected a two-story frame residence, and in 1885, a large and substantial barn. April 9, 1868, he was married to Frances J., daughter of Adam Link, born at Newark, Ohio, December 8, 1840. They have had seven children: Lottie May (deceased), Lucie L., Dora G., William H., Helen J., Adam J. (deceased), Elizabeth. Mr. McMaken is a member of Sion S. Bass post, No. 40, G. A. R.

Peter Wagner, a venerable farmer of Wayne township, residing one mile and a quarter south of the city limits, was born near the river Rhine, Germany, February 17, 1814. He left his home at Zweibrucken, April 6, 1833, with his parents, Peter and Anna Maria (Gross) Wagner, and arriving at New York in June, 1833, they reached Albany, N. Y., July 4th. Going to Buffalo on a canal boat, the family remained there about three months, and Peter crossed over to Canada, where he worked on a farm for John Forsythe, a wealthy citizen. Returning to Buffalo, he joined the family and they reached Detroit, after a voyage of two weeks. They came to the Maumee river by wagon, being two weeks on the way, having to cut their way through the woods, and on reaching the Maumee, they completed the journey to Ft. Wayne in pirogues. In the spring of 1834, the father entered eighty acres of canal land, where he farmed until his death, about 1854, his wife dying six weeks later. They were members of the Catholic church, and were well known and highly esteemed, liked by all who knew them. Of their ten children, three survived. Their son Peter Wagner, was married in 1839, to Mary Magdalene Baker, a sister of Jacob, Killian and John Baker, of Fort Wayne. Her death occurred December 31, 1887. They had ten children: John, Catherine, Magdalene (deceased), Mary, Jacob, George (deceased), Elizabeth, Henry, Agnes and Julian. When Mr. Wagner was married, he began farming on eighty acres of land in section 24, and he next purchased forty acres adjoining, in Adams township, then eighty acres more, making a farm of 200 acres, one of the finest in Wayne township. In 1867, he erected a two-story brick residence at a cost of $3,000. He also has fine houses and out buildings. Mr. Wagner has held various township offices, and was supervisor for seven years. He is a member of the Cathedral Catholic church. He has lived an upright life and is generally respected.

John Wilkinson, superintendent of the Allen county asylum and poor farm, was born in Washington township, February 26, 1844. His father, William Wilkinson, was born in County Cork, Ireland, about 1802. He married in Ireland Johanna Quinlan, who was born about 1804, and they immigrated in 1833 and located at Troy, N. Y., where the father was employed in Burden's iron works. In 1835 they located on a farm in Washington township, where the father farmed until his death in 1849. He was one of the worthy pioneers of Allen county. His widow died in 1876. They had seven children, five sons and two daughters, of whom one son is deceased. John Wilkinson attended the common schools and finished his education in the schools of Plymouth, Ind. He remained on the farm until 1871, and then lived at Alexandria, Va., about one year. Returning to Allen county, and locating at Fort Wayne in 1876, he was elected a member of the city council from the ninth ward, and was re-elected in 1878, and again in 1880, when he resigned. In 1879, while a member of the council, he was also appointed deputy clerk of the circuit court, holding that position until 1880, when he was appointed by the county commissioners superintendent of the Allen county asylum and poor farm, which position he has held for nine years with ability and to the general satisfaction. Mr. Wilkinson was married August 12, 1863, to Annie Maloney, who was born in Whitley county, Ind., the daughter of Patrick Maloney, a native of Ireland. They have three sons and four daughters. Mr. Wilkinson and wife are members of the Catholic cathedral. In politics he is a democrat. Capt. Francis Wilkinson, chief of police of Fort Wayne, is a brother to our subject.

Joshua Holmes, assistant assessor of Wayne township, one of the pioneers of Allen county, was born in Licking county, Ohio, October 13, 1813. His parents Joseph and Sarah (Haver) Holmes, natives of Pennsylvania, went to Ohio in early life and were there married; the father being of English and Scotch, and the mother of German and Welsh, descent. The father, a farmer, and soldier in the war of 1812, lived to be sixty-three years old. His father was a soldier in the revolution. The mother was fifty-one years of age when she died. Of their ten children only four survive, of whom the second born was Joshua. He was reared in Fairfield county, Ohio. In 1835, he visited Allen county, and came with his wife in 1836, arriving here September 7. In 1834 his father came to Allen county and entered 120 acres of land in his son's name, and 118 for himself. The land is situated on the Illinois road, four miles west of the city. Erecting a tent, he and wife lived in it until he could build a log cabin. In 1870, he removed to Fort Wayne, where he has since resided. In May, 1885, he sold the old homestead, retaining 80 acres he had purchased. Mr. Holmes was married March 8, 1836, to Mary M. Fountain, who was born in New Jersey, and reared in Guernsey county, Ohio. Her death occurred March 8, 1881. They had twelve children, six of whom survive: Sarah A., now Mrs. Thomas Donally, of Pittsburg; Bayliss, now of Mississippi; George, of Huntington county, Ind.; Clara, now Mrs. Tam, of Mississippi; John W., of Eel River township, and Roland. Mr. Holmes has served as assessor of Wayne township for a number of years, and for the past four years has been assistant under John Slater. He is a member of the Second Presbyterian church.

Roland Holmes, son of the above, was born on the old homestead, February 2, 1857. He was educated in the city and district schools, and for the last ten years has been following farming. He was married on August 18, 1875, to Ida Donley, who was born in Ohio, and they have two children: Nora and Willie.

Joseph H. Grier, a worthy and substantial citizen of Fort Wayne, residing at the corner of Pontiac and Oliver streets, was born in Williamsport, Penn., March 16, 1838. His father, Samuel Grier, was a native of Williamsport. The grandfather immigrated from Ireland to Philadelphia when a young man, and later became a pioneer of Lycoming county, Penn. He was a surveyor and laid out the plat of Williamsport, and also did most of the surveys for the county during the early days. Later in life he engaged in mercantile pursuits, and was the first postmaster of Williamsport. About 1837 Samuel Grier settled in Allen county, purchasing 200 acres of land in Marion township, on the Piqua road. He resided there until about 1852, when he removed to Michigan and purchased a farm in St. Joseph county. Later in life he retired from farming, and resided at Constantine, Mich., until his death, in 1883, in his seventy-fourth year. His wife, Elizabeth Hetner, was born in Lycoming county, Penn., the daughter of an early settler. She resides at Constantine, in her sixty-ninth year. Their only child, Joseph H., was reared in Allen county until his fifteenth year, and then finished his education in the schools of Florence, Mich. At twenty-four years of age he was married to Ellen B., daughter of B. F. Rice, a well-known citizen of South Wayne. She was born near Decatur, Ind. Mr. Grier began farming in St. Joseph county, Mich. In 1884 he removed to Constantine, and in March, 1886, to Fort Wayne. Mr. Grier owns a fine farm of 145 acres within sight of White Pigeon, Mich., also over 100 acres in the southeastern suburbs of Fort Wayne, and six lots within the city limits. In 1887 he erected his residence just across the city limits, a large two-story brick structure, built in modern style, surrounded by a beautiful lawn, decidedly the handsomest residence in southeast Fort Wayne. Mr. and Mrs. Grier are members of the Methodist church. They have two daughters, Viola and Edna. While residing in Michigan, Mr. Grier was supervisor of the township of Constantine, including the village, from 1878 to 1882. He was four years a director of the St. Joseph County Agricultural society, and for four years was a director in the Village insurance company. He was for several years a director of the St. Joseph County Horse-Thief association, a "regulator" society, and has acted as assignee in several important cases.

Charles F. Moellering, manager of the extensive brick-yards of William Moellering, in Wayne township, was born in Fort Wayne, December 5, 1858, son of Charles and Mary (Ehleid) Moellering, both natives of Germany. Charles, the father, came to America at an early day, and to Fort Wayne during the '40's. He was a brick-mason by trade, and contractor, doing an extensive business for twenty-six years. He was for some time a partner of his brother, William Moellering. Later in life he removed to a farm in Wayne township, where he died in March, 1885, at the age of sixty-two years. His wife, Mary Ehleid, died in 1870, at the age of forty years. By an earlier marriage, Mr. Moellering had children, one of whom, Elizabeth Bradtmiller, survives. To the second marriage seven children were born. All of the children survive. The oldest, Charles F. Moellering, was reared in Fort Wayne and educated in the Lutheran schools. He was on the farm until 1882, when he took charge of William Moellering's business at the brick yard. He owns the old homestead of eighty acres, on the Bluffton road, but makes his home at the yards. He was married to Annie, daughter of William Schafer, who was born in Wayne township in 1863. To this union one son, Frederick W., was born. Mr. and Mrs. Moellering are members of Emanuel Lutheran church.

J. H. Stellhorn, of Wayne township, a leading farmer and lumberman, was born in Fort Wayne, June 19, 1851. His father, Frederick Stellhorn, one of Allen county's pioneers, was born in Hanover, Germany, in 1818, and emigrated about 1844, coming directly to Fort Wayne. He resided there until the spring of 1861, when he purchased 100 acres in Wayne township. While in Fort Wayne he was engaged in the stone and lime business, but upon removing to the country, he began farming and running the water-power saw-mill on the place. He is a prominent citizen, and for a number of years held the position of supervisor, and was frequently solicited to make the race for county commissioner, but always declined. His wife was Fredericka Moellering, who was born in Prussia in 1824, and is the sister of William Moellering, of Fort Wayne. To these parents ten children were born, six of whom survive. The third born, J. H. Stellhorn, when fifteen years of age began work in his father's saw-mill, and continued until about his twenty-fourth year, when he purchased a steam saw-mill which he has since operated. His mill on the St. Mary's river, three and one-half miles south of the city limits, has a capacity of about 4,000 feet per day. In 1885, Mr. Stellhorn added grist-mill machinery, which he operates during the winter months, and averages about 5,000 bushels of feed and cornmeal per year. He has been quite prominent in his township. He has been supervisor of his district, and in 1883, was elected superintendent of all the township roads, and served ten months until the repeal of the law. Since 1885, he has been superintendent of Simons' No. 5 pike, an extension of Fairfield avenue. He was married in 1874, to Eliza Kline, of Adams county, who died eighteen months later, leaving one child, who survived six weeks. He was again married in 1877, to Sophia Poehler, of Wayne township. Mr. Stellhorn and wife are members of Lutheran Trinity church.

Conrad Tielker, a well-known farmer of Wayne township, was born in Westphalia, Prussia, November 24, 1824. His father, Christian Tielker, was a native of Prussia, and a soldier in the Napoleonic wars. He and his wife died in Prussia. Conrad, in 1846, after a voyage of seventy-two days, landed at New York, and soon afterward arriving at Fort Wayne, went to work in a brick-yard at $12 per month. Three months later he began to work on the canal, hauling stone to the city. He worked in the stone quarries at Huntington during the winter, and in May, 1847, went to Toledo, and thence to Chicago, and worked on a farm two years at Yankee settlement, southwest of Chicago. He returned to Fort Wayne, and worked in a warehouse, and then bought a fourth share in a canal boat, and for three years was engaged in boating, and then sold to his brother Henry. In 1852 he purchased school land in section sixteen, at $6 per acre. In 1853 he removed to the farm, and built a log house, 16x14, in which he lived eighteen years. In 1871, he erected a handsome dwelling, and in 1876, a large bank barn. In 1886, the latter was destroyed by fire, together with 800 bushels of grain and thirty-five tons of hay. His farm comprises eighty-six acres of first-class land. Mr. Tielker was married March 13, 1853, to Wilhelmina Baade, who was born in Westphalia, Prussia, May 19, 1834, and came to this country when ten years of age. They have had eight children, five of whom survive: Wilhelmina, Lizzie (dead), Christ. (killed by being kicked by a horse), Mary, wife of Elias Aumann, of St. Joseph township; Frederick, living in Bloomingdale; Sophia, William and Conrad (twins), William (dead). Mr. and Mrs. Tielker and family are members of the Lutheran church. Mr. Tielker is a democrat. After the defeat of his party in 1860, Mr. Tielker resolved that he would not cut his hair until a democrat was elected president, and he kept his word for twenty-four years. Upon the election of Cleveland his hair was cut, which was the occasion of a grand frolic by a number of his old friends at his residence. In 1865, Mr. Tielker made a visit of seven weeks in Europe, with his parents.

George Rapp, of Wayne township, was born in Germany, May 6, 1825. His parents, Nicholas and Margaret (Hotz) Rapp, were natives of Germany, the father being a farmer by occupation. The father died in 1839, in his forty-second year, and the mother in 1833, aged thirty-five. Their only child, George, learned the blacksmith trade, and when twenty-one years of age he emigrated, landing at New York, September 16. Going to Lancaster county, Penn., he worked at his trade one and a half years, and then, in 1848, located at Fort Wayne. He opened a shop on Main street, and six months later removed to Huntertown, where he kept a shop until 1861. He then removed to a farm in Wayne township. His farm embraces eighty-six acres of good land, three miles west from Fort Wayne, through which passes the Wabash railroad. Mr. Rapp has always been regarded as one of the leading citizens of his township. In 1886 he was appointed supervisor of road district No. 3, and in 1887 was elected for two years. He is a member of St. John's Lutheran church of Fort Wayne. January 4, 1848, Mr. Rapp was married to Elizabeth Saur, who was born in Germany, March 19, 1828, and immigrated in 1842 with her parents, who settled in Pennsylvania. Mrs. Rapp died January 29, 1882, leaving six children: Philip, born in 1850; Henry, 1856; George, 1858, died 1874; Mary, 1861; Lizzie, 1864; Charley, 1868; John, 1871. Mr. Rapp is a member of St. John's Lutheran church of Fort Wayne, as are all his children.

Oliver Lawrence, a well-known young farmer of Wayne township, living three miles west from the city, was born in Wayne county, Ohio, March 25, 1857. His father, George B. Lawrence, was a native of Ohio, born in 1834. He removed to Indiana in 1864, with his parents, and is at present a well-to-do farmer of Lafayette township, and a member of the county board of equalization. His wife, Elizabeth Geitgey, was born in Wayne county, Ohio, in 1836. Of their children, three sons and two daughters, the oldest is Oliver Lawrence. He was reared in Lafayette township, and was educated in the district schools; also attending the Fort Wayne college two years. He was married November 10, 1881, to Parynthia Pierce, who was born in Aboit township, the daughter of Ossa W. Pierce, now living in Washington territory. Mr. Lawrence removed to Wayne township April 2, 1882, and located on a farm of 102 acres, where he has a fine brick residence. He has one son, George Winslow, born May 19, 1885. Mr. Lawrence and wife are members of the Methodist Episcopal church in Wayne township.

J. B. Downing, of Wayne township, residing two miles south of the city, was born in New York state, May 31, 1835. His parents, David and Emily (Hotchkiss) Downing, natives of Connecticut, removed from that state to New York, and thence to Ohio, about 1845, and settled in Oxford township, Erie county, near Sandusky city, where the father farmed until his death, about 1857. The mother died about 1882. Of their ten children, six survive. J. B. Downing, in 1865, came to Allen county and purchased his present farm of 120 acres. He was married March 4, 1858, to Cynthia L. Sexton, who was born in Erie county, Ohio, daughter of Myron Sexton, a native of Connecticut, who settled in Erie county in 1826. He is now at eighty-seven years of age, a retired farmer of Seneca county, Ohio. Mr. and Mrs. Downing have one son, Myron Sexton, born October 2, 1859. He is a resident of Fort Wayne, and a traveling salesman for the wholesale confectionery house of Louis Fox. He was married in October, 1883, to Gracie, daughter of Henry Mensch. Mr. and Mrs. Downing are members of the Third

Presbyterian church of Fort Wayne. Mr. Downing is a member of Wayne lodge, No. 25, F. & A. M., of the thirty-second degree.

The early settler of Adams township whose impress upon its history seems most permanent, was John Rogers, who came from Preble county, Ohio, in 1825. He was born in 1785, in Somerset county, N. J., son of Simeon Rogers, who was born in that state, of Irish lineage. John Rogers was married at Springfield, Ohio, about 1815, to Tryphena J. Shipman, daughter of Jabez Shipman, whose ancestors came from Scotland. She was a native of Morris county, N. J., and was the second wife of Mr. Rogers. Two years later the family moved to Vernon, Ind., where they lived three years, afterward settling on a farm two miles north of Paris, Preble Co., Ohio. In 1825, they settled four miles east of Fort Wayne, on the south bank of the Maumee. This, Mr. Rogers cleared, and raised a large family of children, who honor their worthy parents. In 1850, he removed to a home they provided for him at New Haven, and here and at Fort Wayne he lived until September 15, 1877. Five of his children survive: Dorcas, wife of John Brown, of Fort Wayne, Lamort M., Alanson A., Orrin D. and Helen M., widow of Amasa Bowers, of Andrews.

Lamort M. Rogers, an honored pioneer citizen and a prominent merchant at New Haven, was born at Springfield, Ohio, January 17, 1817. Sixty-four years Mr. Rogers has resided in Adams township, continuously. His boyhood, youth and the first years of his manhood were spent on the homestead farm. The school privileges of those times were very poor, consequently his early schooling was quite limited, but his fund of general knowledge is now wide and varied. January 24, 1844, before leaving the homestead, he was married to Harriet N. Corlew, who was born near Plattsburgh, N. Y., October 7, 1822, the daughter of Lucy (Thornton) Corlew and her husband, the latter of whom was born in Canada, and the former near Springfield, Vt. Soon after their marriage, Mr. and Mrs. Rogers located on another farm, about two miles south of his father's. There his attention was given to agriculture until March, 1856, when he removed to New Haven, where he has lived ever since. During nearly his entire residence in New Haven, now thirty-three years, he has been engaged in merchandise, and as a business man he has become widely and favorably known throughout the eastern half of Allen county. His place of business, which has been headquarters for the people of the surrounding country, has an honorable reputation. During his residence in New Haven, Mr. Rogers has also dealt in grain, and for three years he was one of the proprietors of the Maumee Valley Mills, which he and two other gentlemen erected in 1864. He has also managed a farm which he owns in the vicinity of New Haven, and has dealt to some extent in real estate. Mr. Rogers has five children: Adelaide L., Willie S., Emma L., Frank and Jessie P., of whom only Willie S. and Jessie P. are living. The former is now the business partner of of his father. Mr. Rogers is a member of the Masonic and Odd Fellows lodges, of the chapter and council degrees in the former, and the encampment in the latter. He has the honor of being the first noble grand of New Haven lodge, No. 253, I. O. O. F. In politics, he cast his first presidential vote for William Henry Harrison, and since 1856 he has ardently supported the republican party. He has been honored with various township and municipal offices, and for a period of eleven years he was postmaster at New Haven.

Orrin D. Rogers, the fifth son of John Rogers, was born in Preble county, Ohio, April 2, 1824. He was but seventeen months old when his parents settled in Adams township. The school-house in which he received his first lessons was the old-fashioned cabin with greased paper for window lights, and slab floor. In early manhood he attended a select school in Fort Wayne nine months, and there received the greater part of his education. At the age of twenty-three he taught a term of school in Adams township, and subsequently taught two terms in Whitley county, and one in Jefferson township. April 22, 1851, he was married to Clarinda Rowe, who was born at Portage, N. Y., March 16, 1833, daughter of Sebastian H. and Louisa (Cary) Rowe. After his marriage Mr. Rogers learned the carpenter trade, which he has followed at times ever since. Gaining considerable acquaintance with law, he has acted as collecting agent, justice of the peace and notary public. He has served as justice of the peace about fourteen years. In politics he is a republican. Mr. Rogers served as first lieutenant of Company G, One Hundred and Fifty-second volunteer infantry, six months, beginning February 22, 1865. The date of his commission as first lieutenant was March 13, 1865. He was mustered out at Charleston, W. Va., on the 30th day of August following. He and wife have had five children: Eva A., Ella L., Clara D., Fitz Glen and a daughter that died unnamed. Ella L. is also dead. Mr. Rogers is a member of the G. A. R., being a post commander of Jesse Adams post, No. 493.

Col. Joseph W. Whitaker was born in Dearborn county, Ind., January 10, 1821. His parents, Daniel and Catharine (Shuman) Whitaker, were respectively natives of Pennsylvania and Virginia, the former chiefly of Scotch-Irish, and the latter of German, descent. The father was born about 1790, and served in the war of 1812, soon after the close of which he was married to Catharine Shuman, who was about two years his junior. For a short time afterward they resided in Hamilton county, Ohio, but in about 1817 they removed to Dearborn county, Ind. In 1835 the father came to Allen county and entered a tract of unimproved land in Marion township, about ten miles southeast of Fort Wayne, on the old Wayne trace. Col. Whitaker came to this land in 1836, and during about ten months was employed in improving it. In the fall he returned to Dearborn county, and in September, 1837, the entire family came and settled upon the homestead mentioned above, where the father and mother spent the rest of their lives, the former dying January 12, 1849, and the latter in April, 1874. In December, 1837, Col. Whitaker went to Fort Wayne and began an apprenticeship at the blacksmith trade, of four years with John Fairfield, by which time he had the trade well learned. For two or three years following this he worked in different places as a journeyman. March 5, 1846, he was married near Decatur, Ind., to Miss Susan De Vese, who was born in Milton township, Wayne co., Ohio, November 9, 1827, the daughter of Joseph and Elizabeth (Shafer) De Vese, both natives of Bucks county, Penn. They were married in their native county, and about two years later removed to Wayne county, Ohio. In November, 1836, they located in Adams county, where the mother died in March, 1863, and the father in August, 1866. In March, 1849, Mr. Whitaker left home for California, whither he arrived about 100 days later, having gone across the plains. He was engaged at mining until the fall of 1853, when he returned home by way of Panama and New York, arriving in Fort Wayne in December. He followed his trade at Fort Wayne until 1859, when he removed to New Haven. In September, 1861, he entered the service of the Union as captain of Company D, Thirtieth Indiana regiment. He served in that capacity three years, and was mustered out at Indianapolis, September 29, 1864. He commanded his company at Shiloh, Stone River, Chickamauga, Mission Ridge, the Atlanta campaign and battle of Jonesboro. In February, 1865, he re-entered the service as a recruiting officer and was mustered as lieutenant-colonel of the One Hundred and Fifty-second Indiana volunteer regiment at Indianapolis in the following month. He served in that capacity in the army of the Potomac until August 30, 1865, when he received his discharge at Charleston, W. Va. He was afterward mustered out at Indianapolis. Returning to his home in New Haven, he engaged in mercantile pursuits. In 1875 he was appointed postmaster and served as such ten years. Since 1885 he has been enjoying a comfortable and happy retired life. Col. Whitaker has had two children: Eugene Becklerd, born August 28, 1848, now a resident of New Haven, holding a responsible position with the New York, Chicago & St. Louis railway, and Joseph Spafford, born April 23, 1849, died March 15, 1852. Joseph was born after his father left for California and died before he returned. Mr. Whitaker is a Mason and Odd Fellow and a comrade of the Grand Army of the Republic. In politics he was formerly a whig, but since 1856, has been an ardent republican. Col. Whitaker is a man of more than ordinary ability and intelligence, and in military and civil life he has proven to be true and capable. He and wife have resided in the Maumee valley for more than half a century, and they are very highly esteemed.

The Brudi brothers, prominent in the annals of Adams township, are sons of John George and Anna Barbara (Handi) Brudi, who were married in Germany, their native land. Several years after their marriage, their union having been blessed meanwhile with six sons and two daughters, the parents decided to emigrate to America. The father came over in 1845, and bought a farm in Jefferson township, two miles southeast of New Haven. In the following year his wife and children came to their new home, all but the youngest child, who died on the ocean. The mother passed away in 1855, and a year or so later the father returned to Germany. He made a visit here afterward, and died in Germany, August 13, 1868. Their sons, Carl L., Gottlieb and Joseph are mentioned below.

Carl L. Brudi was born in Wurtemberg, Germany, February 5, 1831. For a few years after coming to this country, he remained at the home of his parents, working on the farm. In 1855 he was married to Mrs. Barbara Frauenfalder, and with her he settled on a farm in section 13, Adams township, where her death occurred about six months after the marriage. She was a native of Switzerland, where she was first married, her husband dying before she came to America. April 11, 1858, Mr. Brudi was married to Miss Mary M. Redenbaugh, who was born in Williams county, Ohio, February 21, 1839, daughter of Philip and Mary (Fischer) Redenbaugh, natives of Germany. In 1863, Mr. Brudi removed from his farm to New Haven, where for a year and a half he was engaged in a lumber and shingle business. He then returned to the farm which he has since occupied, giving his whole attention to agriculture. His farm of 190 acres, of first-class land, is well improved. Mr. Brudi and his present wife have had ten children: Sophia A., William F., John George, Emma T., Henry E., Carl Louis, August C., Gottlieb A., Mary A. and Philip C., all of whom are living except Sophia and Philip. William F. formerly worked for Henry W. Bond, of Fort Wayne, and afterward purchased a flour trade from Mr. Bond, and is now doing a successful business. George is in Mr. Bond's employ as foreman. Henry is a baker at Markle, Huntington county. Parents and children are members of the German Lutheran church. In politics Mr. Brudi is a democrat. He is progressive, prosperous and influential.

Gottlieb Brudi was born in Wurtemberg, Germany, June 14, 1833 He was married October 8, 1854, to Sophia Nester, a native of New Albany, Ind., born August 22, 1839, daughter of Christian and Sarah (Webber) Nester, natives of Germany. Immediately after his marriage Mr. Brudi located on a farm one mile west of New Haven, which he has owned ever since, and has occupied with the exception of four years from the fall of 1866, to January, 1871, when he resided at Fort Wayne, engaged in the grocery business. Aside from this his undivided attention has been given to farming, at which he has been successful. His farm, which is very desirably located, contains eighty acres of first-class land. He has recently provided it with a fish pond well stocked with German carp. He also owns a livery barn, business property and residence in Fort Wayne. He and wife have had nine children: Lizzie, Gottlieb (deceased), Sophia, Anna, Carrie, Amelia, Louis, Bertha and Martha. Mr. and Mrs. Brudi and family are members of the St. John's German Lutheran church, at Fort Wayne. In politics, Mr. Brudi is a democrat. He is a wide-awake and successful farmer, honorable and upright.

Joseph Brudi, a prominent miller and lumber dealer of New Haven, was born in Wurtemberg, Germany, February 11, 1837. He was married in Jefferson township to Mary M. Wagner, in October, 1862. She was born in Germany and came with her parents to America in the same year in which the Brudi family came. In 1863 Mr. and Mrs. Brudi removed from Jefferson township to New Haven. In the fall of 1864 he enlisted in Company F, One Hundred and Forty-second Indiana volunteer infantry, with which he served until the close of the war. His service consisted chiefly of guard duty in the vicinity of Nashville, Tenn. He was mustered out at Nashville in the latter part of July, 1865, and was honorably discharged at Indianapolis soon afterward. Mr. Brudi returned to New Haven and resumed the shingle and lumber business in which he had become engaged on locating there in 1863. He has dealt in lumber ever since, and kept up the manufacture of shingles until about 1885. Since 1877 he has also been one of the proprietors of the Maumee Valley flouring mills. In the milling and lumbering business he is the partner of Gustav Gothe, the former business being conducted under the name of J. Brudi & Co., and the latter under the name of G. Gothe & Co. They have been partners in business for twenty-six years. The marriage of Mr. Brudi resulted in the birth of eleven children: Anna, Johanna, Clara (deceased), Ottilie, Joseph (deceased), Frederick, Carl (deceased), Martha, Josephine, Albert and Joseph. The wife of Mr. Brudi died December 23, 1879. Mr. Brudi is a member of the German Lutheran church. In politics he is a democrat. He has served two terms as a member of the town board and is at present a member of the school board.

Gustav Gothe, the well-known manufacturer of New Haven, was born in Fuerstenthum Schwarzburg, Sondershausen, Germany, March 7, 1819. He is the son of Frederick Gothe, who died when Gustav was nineteen years of age. His mother died about a year later. At twenty-one years of age he took a situation in a hotel in Rodolstadt, Germany, and held it seven years. For four years after this he was employed in a hotel in Weimar, Germany. May 7, 1854, he embarked at Liverpool, and landed at New York on the 9th of June following. He immediately left for Tiffin, Ohio, where he remained two years, working upon a farm in that vicinity a short time, but mainly engaged as a contractor, in grading two miles of the Tiffin railroad, now a part of the Nickleplate line. Subsequently, he came to New Haven, arriving October 18, 1856. Here he took a contract of grading two miles of the Tiffin road, through New Haven, but after one-half mile of it was finished the company collapsed and the enterprise was abandoned. In 1858 he started a shingle factory in New Haven, and in 1859 took as a partner his brother-in-law, Carl Brudi, and in addition to the manufacture of shingles, the firm, which had taken the name of G. Gothe & Co., engaged in the lumber business. Carl Brudi was superseded by his brother Joseph Brudi, about two years later, and the firm composed of G. Gothe and Joseph Brudi, has existed ever since under the name of G. Gothe & Co. Mr. Gothe and Mr. Brudi bought the Maumee Valley Flouring Mills, at New Haven, in 1875. The property, which had been severely wrecked by an explosion about four years before, was rebuilt by them, and they have ever since owned and operated it under the name of J. Brudi & Co. Mr. Gothe was married December 21, 1858, to Miss Mary Brudi, sister of his business partner, who is also a native of Germany. Mr. and Mrs. Gothe are members of the German Lutheran church. In politics, Mr. Gothe is a staunch democrat. He has served seven years as a member of the town board, and five years as treasurer. Mr. Gothe gives his entire attention to the superintendence of the Maumee Valley Mills, which under his supervision, has gained an enviable reputation. It was provided with the new roller process about four years ago. Mr. Gothe is much devoted to church work, and for as much as fifteen years he has served in a official capacity. He is one of New Haven's worthiest citizens.

Herman Schnelker, who resides near New Haven, was born in Germany, August 13, 1831, the son of Herman H. and Catharine (Tobben) Schnelker. He was reared to the age of nineteen in his native country, attending school between the ages of six and fifteen; at the latter age he was apprenticed as a shoemaker and served four years. In 1850 he accompanied his father, mother, one brother and one sister to America, to join two brothers who had come to this country the year before. One of them, however, was dead when his parents arrived, having died September 8, 1849, nine weeks after his arrival at Fort Wayne. The family landed at New Orleans on November 24, 1850, after having been about eight weeks on the sea. They embarked on a Mississippi river steamer, and set out up the river. When about three days out from New Orleans the mother sickened with the cholera and two days later, when the vessel neared Vicksburg, she died. The remainder of the family continued their journey to Fort Wayne, arriving on December 21. Herman remained in Fort Wayne three years, working at the shoemaker's trade. In 1853 he removed to New Haven, near where, with the exception of two years, he has resided since. During the first year and a half of his residence there he conducted a boot and shoe shop. In 1855 he returned to Fort Wayne, and for two years, was engaged in the manufacture of soap and candles. In 1857, he became the partner of his brother, Bernard Schnelker, and his brother-in-law, Nicholas Schuckman, in mercantile pursuits at New Haven. The firm conducted a general store until 1867, and did a successful business. In 1867, Mr. Schnelker associated himself with Col. C. E. Briant, of Huntington, and George W. Hall, now deceased, in the manufacture of stoves, with factories at New Haven, and Delphos, Ohio. The firm, under the name of Schnelker, Hall & Co., did a profitable business three years. In 1870 Mr. Schnelker purchased the interests of Briant and Hall in the factory at New Haven, and sold to the latter his interest at Delphos. Soon afterward Mr. Schnelker entered into partnership with Bernard Schnelker, John Begue, John Beugnot and Anthony Beugnot in the manufacture of stoves, and the firm, under the name of Schnelker, Beugnot & Co., operated three factories at New Haven and one at Fort Wayne until 1874. In the meantime his brother, Bernard Schnelker, died in 1871. In 1874, one of the factories at New Haven was sold to John Begue. From 1874 to 1878, Mr. Schnelker and the Messrs. Beugnot, together with Bernard Schnelker's heirs, operated the two remaining factories at New Haven and the one at Fort Wayne. In 1878 Mr. Schnelker and the heirs purchased the interest of the Beugnots at New Haven, and sold to the Beugnots their interest at Fort Wayne. Herman Schnelker continued the business under the name of H. Schnelker & Co., until 1880, when he sold to his brother Bernard Schnelker's widow and her son, H. F. Schnelker, by whom it is now conducted under the name of H. F. Schnelker & Co. In 1880, Herman Schnelker removed to a farm, where his attention has since been given to agriculture. His farm contains 167 acres and occupies an eminence a quarter of a mile south of New Haven, with which it is connected by a gravel walk. It is splendidly improved with brick residence and good barn, and is altogether a beautiful country home. Mr. Schnelker was married in 1854, and has living eight children: Louise, Bernard H., Mary E., Edward, William, Agnes, Herman and Albin. Mr. and Mrs. Schnelker are members of the Roman Catholic church. He is a member of the St John's Benevolent and St Joseph's School societies, and in politics he is a staunch democrat. He served as trustee of Adams township two terms and made a good officer. He is *one of the county's best men.

Henry F. Schnelker, a prominent stave manufacturer of New Haven, was born at that place July 7, 1854. His parents, Bernard and Mary G. (Lupken) Schnelker, natives of Germany, came to America before marriage, with their families, the Schnelker family coming in 1844 and the Lupken family in 1847. Bernard first located in Cincinnati where he worked at his trade, that of a blacksmith. About a year later he removed to Fort Wayne, where he was married to Miss Lupken, in about 1852. Soon afterward they removed to New Haven, where the father's death occurred January 29, 1871, and where the mother now resides. Henry F. was reared to manhood in New Haven, where he received his earliest education. He afterward attended the Christian Brothers' school, at Fort Wayne, about two years, and still later Notre Dame university, near South Bend, Ind., three years. Returning home he took charge of the interest of his father, then deceased, in the Indiana Stave company, at New Haven and Fort Wayne. Upon the dissolution of the company in 1876, Henry F., with his mother and uncle, Herman Schnelker, purchased the factory at New Haven, and it was conducted under the name of H. Schnelker & Co. two years. In 1878 he and his mother purchased the interest of his uncle, and they still own and operate the factory under the name of H. F. Schnelker & Co. In connection with the stave business, for two years, from 1876 to 1878, Mr. Schnelker was also engaged in merchandise, as the partner in a general store, of F. H. Bueter. In 1879 Mr. Schnelker's stave factory was destroyed by fire. In the following year he rebuilt at New Haven, and erected another factory at Payne, Ohio, which he still owns and operates. For the past ten years he has also attended to the management of farms in the vicinity of New Haven, owning three farms, two of 160 acres each and one of 240 acres. His mother is his partner in both the factory and farming properties. Mr. Schnelker was married June 25, 1878, to Allie J. Allen, a native of Ohio, daughter of John G. and Mary C. Allen, the former of whom was killed in the battle of Shiloh. They have three children: Bernadette C., Irene H. and Norbet B. Mr. and Mrs. Schnelker are members of the Roman Catholic church. He is a member of the Catholic Knights and the Knights of St. Charles. He is a democrat in politics. For the past nine years he has been a member of the board of school trustees in New Haven.

John B. Beugnot, of New Haven, was born in Haute-Saône, France, April 19, 1833. He is the son of Francis and Collet (Perregot) Beugnot, with whom he came to America in March, 1843. The family came to Massillon, Ohio, in the latter part of April, and resided in Stark county, Ohio, five years, after which they located on a farm in Jefferson township, where the father died in 1858. The mother's death occurred at New Haven in March, 1870. While in Jefferson township, Mr. Beugnot learned the cooper's trade, beginning it at the age of nineteen, and serving his apprenticeship with John Begue, his brother-in-law. In 1854, he removed with the family of Mr. Begue to New Haven, and was employed for forty-eight days at grading the Wabash railway. After this, for eight years, he acted as foreman in Mr. Begue's cooper shop. In 1862, he entered into partnership with Mr. Begue in both cooperage and stave manufacture, Mr. Begue having established the latter in 1859. Anthony, a brother of Mr. Beugnot, also took an interest in 1862, and from that year until 1870 it was conducted by them under the name of J. Begue & Co. In 1870, they took in as partners, Bernard and Herman Schnelker, and the firm, under the name of Schnelker, Beugnot & Co., did an extensive business until 1878, operating three stave factories and two cooper shops in New Haven, and one cooper shop and one stave factory in Fort Wayne. In 1878, the firm dissolved, the two Messrs. Schnelker retaining the interests at New Haven and the two Messrs. Beugnot retaining those in Fort Wayne. In 1878, the latter removed the stave factory from Fort Wayne to Cecil, Ohio, where the firm has done an extensive stave and heading business ever since. The firm name until 1881 was J. B. Beugnot & Bro. Since then it has been J. B. Beugnot, Brother & Co., Mr. J. A. Schaab having had an interest since that year. For the past six years the firm has also operated in saw-milling in the vicinity of Cecil, and also owns a very large farm near that place, 200 acres of which are in cultivation. Mr. Beugnot was married November 27, 1856, to Miss Pelagie Girardot, a native of France, born September 25, 1835 to Joseph and Rene (Jacoutot) Girardot, with whom she came to America when she was eighteen years of age. Her father and mother were the parents of eleven children. They settled in Jefferson township, and moved to New Haven in

1866. The father died there May 19, 1884; the mother is still living, aged eighty-two, and makes her home with Mrs. Beugnot. Mr. and Mrs. Beugnot are members of the Roman Catholic church. Mr. Beugnot is a member of the St. John's Benevolent society, and in politics he is a democrat. He has served three years on the town board in New Haven, and two years as treasurer of the town. He has a beautiful home in New Haven, which is provided with all that is needed to make life pleasant. Mr. Beugnot ranks among the county's leading citizens, and as far as he is known, his reputation for honesty and uprightness is spotless.

Hon. Lycurgus S. Null, a scholarly physician of New Haven, and ex-state senator and representative, was born in Columbiana county, Ohio, August 24, 1839. His parents, Jesse and Lydia (Sampsel) Null, were respectively natives of Pennsylvania and Ohio. The paternal and maternal ancestors of Dr. Null came from Holland, the former settling near Gettysburg, Penn., and the latter in Maryland. When the doctor was but four years old his father died. He was reared to early manhood on a farm in his native county, and received a good knowledge of the ordinary branches of learning; later in youth he taught two terms of school. At the age of twenty he began the study of medicine with an uncle, Dr. Isaac Sampsell, in Morrow county, Ohio, and continued with him a year and a half. In 1862, at the Eclectic Medical Institute of Cincinnati, he attended one course of lectures. Early in 1863, he began the practice of his profession in Noble county, Ind., and in October he came to New Haven where he has since resided, and has been, except a few brief interruptions, in active practice. In October, 1864, he enlisted in Company F, One Hundred and Forty-second Indiana volunteer infantry. May 2, 1865, he was commissioned a second lieutenant, and was mustered out as such July 14, 1865, at Nashville, Tenn. Returning home he resumed his practice, and during the winter of 1865-6 he took another course of lectures in the Eclectic Medical Institute of Cincinnati, graduating in the latter year. He has since also taken two courses of lectures in the Miami Medical College of Cincinnati. Dr. Null was married April 11, 1876, to Susan, daughter of Levi and Mary Hartzell, and they have six children: Claude A. and Maude A. (twins), Winona, Ralph W., Jesse L. and Mary Edna, of whom Claude A. and Jesse L. are deceased. Dr. Null is an Odd Fellow, a thirty-second degree Mason and a Knight Templar. He takes an active part in politics as a democrat, and in the fall of 1880 he was elected a member of the lower branch of the state legislature, and served one term. In the fall of 1882 he was elected state senator for four years. He made a diligent and faithful officer, and discharged his duties in a creditable manner. Dr. Null is one of the able and successful physicians of the county, and as a citizen ranks among the best.

August R. Schnitker, a prominent manufacturer of New Haven, was born in Prussia, March 8, 1847. With his parents, Christian and Charlotte (Diederich) Schnitker, he came to America, in the eighth year of his age, 1854. The family came directly to Allen county, and settled on a farm in Jefferson township, where the mother died about two years later. Soon afterward the father with three children, August, Charles and Caroline, removed to New Haven, where, in 1858, he was married to Wilhelmina Reiling, who is still living. The father died in 1862. Charles and Caroline have since died, so that Mr. Schnitker's nearest relative, aside from his children, is a half-brother, Christian Schnitker of Fort Wayne. During his early manhood Mr. Schnitker was employed for several years in a stave factory in New Haven. In 1864 he began the trade of a harness maker, and served as an apprentice three years, the last two in Fort Wayne. In 1866 he started a harness shop in New Haven and has conducted a shop there ever since. In October, 1881, he became one of the founders of the New Haven handle factory in partnership with F. H. Bueter. They afterward took as a partner Mr. Jobst Fischer, and about two years later Mr. Schnitker and Mr. Fischer purchased the interest of Mr. Bueter and formed the firm of Schnitker & Fischer. Mr. Schnitker was married January 1, 1871, to Hannah W. Linnemann, a native of Prussia, born November 27, 1847. She is the daughter of Frederick and Louise Linnemann, with whom she came to America when a little girl. They first located in New York, but soon afterward removed to New Haven. Mr. and Mrs. Schnitker have had eight children: William F., Charles F., Emma W., Amelia, Henry (deceased), Frederick and two others who died in infancy. Mr. Schnitker and wife are members of the German Lutheran church. In politics he is a democrat. He has served as treasurer of the town of New Haven two years, being elected in 1880, and re-elected in 1881. Mr. Schnitker began business for himself with no means of his own whatever, and his present good circumstances speak very creditably of his energy and good management.

Jobst Fischer, the well known handle manufacturer of New Haven, was born in Bavaria, July 19, 1840, son of John E. and Catharine B. (Merkel) Fischer, with whom he came to America when he was between seven and eight years old. The family located in Onondago county, N. Y., where in early life he labored some on a farm, and during six to eight years at railroading. Before leaving Onondago county, N. Y., he also worked two or three years at coopering. In 1862 he accompanied his parents to Allen county, settled in Jefferson township; worked two years on the farm, and then came to the town of New Haven, which has been his home with the exception of nine months, ever since. For ten years after locating there he conducted a butcher shop. In 1875 he helped to re-build the Maumee Valley Flouring Mills, at New Haven, as the partner of Joseph Brudi and Gustav Gothe. He retained an interest in that property about two years after which Mr. Fischer formed a partnership with Franklin Hargrave, in the tile business, and he devoted his attention to it about two years. He then resumed butchering. Two or three years later he purchased a one-third interest in the New Haven handle factory, the other two-thirds being owned by A. R. Schnitker and F. H. Bueter. Subsequently, the interest of Mr. Bueter was purchased by the other two, who have since operated under the name of Schnelker & Fischer. Mr. Fischer was married December 18, 1866, to Margaret Wagner, a native of Fort Wayne, daughter of George and Anna Brigitte Wagner, and they have three children: John A. G., Ernst C. J., and Anna C. B. The parents are members of the German Lutheran church. Mr. Fischer is a democrat in politics. He has served three years as a member of the town board of New Haven. Mrs. Fischer's parents, George and Anna Brigitte (Wolf) Wagner, natives of Germany, were married there, and in 1844 immigrated and settled at Fort Wayne. There the father died in 1850. The mother now resides at New Haven, a venerable lady, aged seventy-one.

Gustav Adolph Foellinger, a prominent young druggist of New Haven, was born at Fort Wayne, August 23, 1855. He is the son of Jacob Foellinger, one of the pioneers of the Maumee valley, a history of whom appears elsewhere in this work. His boyhood was spent in Fort Wayne, where he attended the German Lutheran parochial schools until he was thirteen years of age, then he entered Eyser institute, a college at St. Louis, Mo., where he pursued his studies three years, obtaining in addition to Latin, French, botany and mathematics, a good knowledge of pharmacy. Returning home he soon afterward obtained a situation as clerk in a drug store at Kendallville, Ind., and held it six months. In April, 1872, he accepted a clerkship with Meyer Bros., of Fort Wayne, and continued with them three and one-half years. From 1875 to 1878, owing to ill health, he remained at the home of his father, assisting him at times in the boot and shoe business. In 1878, for the benefit of his health he went to Santa Fe, New Mexico, where for three years he held a position with the drug firm of Fischer & Co., Mr. Fischer being his brother-in-law. At the end of the second year in Santa Fe, he returned to Fort Wayne, and on July 22, 1880, was united in marriage to Sophia, daughter of Henry Roeniermann. Mrs. Foellinger was born at Fort Wayne, October 8, 1857. She accompanied her husband to Santa Fe, and in 1881, both returned to Fort Wayne, where in November, he engaged in the drug business. He conducted a store six months, and then for two years and a half held a position with Meyer Bros. In the spring of 1885 he opened business at New Haven, where he has since been engaged. His marriage has resulted in the birth of three children: Adelaide, Emma and Cornelia. Mr. Foellinger and wife are members of the German Lutheran church. He has served as treasurer of New Haven, one term.

Allen M. Hartzell, a leading young citizen of New Haven, son of the late Levi Hartzell, was born on the old Hartzell homestead, about one mile southwest of New Haven, August 25, 1856. He received his early education in the public schools of New Haven, and at the age of fourteen secured a teacher's license, and during the winter of 1870–71 taught a term of school in Adams township. In 1871 he attended the Fort Wayne Methodist college. In 1872–3 he attended college at

Oberlin, Ohio, and during the winter of 1873-4 completed a commercial course in the A. D. Wilt Commercial college of Dayton. In 1876 he entered upon the study of law at Fort Wayne, with Robert Stratton, now of Minneapolis. He was admitted to the bar about a year later, and for four years thereafter he was engaged at both the study and practice of law with Mr. Stratton. His legal efforts were rewarded with unusual success; however, though very much devoted to the profession, owing to ill-health he abandoned the practice. In September, 1881, he engaged in milling at New Haven, he and his brother Elias having purchased the New Haven flouring mills. The property was destroyed by fire January 6, 1882, and it has not since been rebuilt. In 1882 Mr. Hartzell turned his attention to farming and at the same time, he, in partnership with his younger brother, Warren, established a dairy on the old homestead and they did a very successful business for five years, marketing the products in Fort Wayne. They discontinued this in the spring of 1887, and, in connection with a large agricultural business, they have since given attention to the breeding of fine horses. Mr. Hartzell was married December 28, 1881, to Emma, daughter of Nathaniel and Sarah E. (De Long) Fitch. Her father formerly resided in Huntertown, where he died January 1, 1877. Her mother still lives at that place. Mrs. Hartzell was born in Huntertown February 1, 1861. Mr. Hartzell is a member of the I. O. O. F., and in politics he is an ardent republican. In the fall of 1886 he received the nomination of his party for the state legislature. He made a number of speeches throughout the county, acquitting himself with much credit, and by a strong canvass succeeded in reducing the democratic majority from 2,500 to 900. Mr. Hartzell is a young man of high moral worth and social standing.

Henry Tilbury (deceased), one of the earliest settlers of Adams township, was born October 2, 1801, son of Jacob and Barbara Tilbury. He was married in Lancaster county, Penn., about 1821, to Hannah Miller, who was born in that county February 22, 1804, the daughter of Daniel Miller. In 1826 they emigrated to Allen county and settled on a tract of land one mile east of Fort Wayne, which city then contained but three buildings besides the old fort. In 1827 Mr. Tilbury removed to another tract he had bought in the Bourie reserve, three miles east of Fort Wayne, where he farmed until his death, August 15, 1854; there his widow still resides, now a venerable lady, aged eighty-five years. She has lived on the same farm sixty-two years. She became the mother of fifteen children, as follows: George, born October 25, 1823, died August 15, 1838; Samuel, born February 25, 1825; Mary, born May 27, 1826, died aged about thirty-five; Amanda, born March 25, 1829, died in August, 1853; Allen, born September 9, 1832, died December 8, 1837; Nahum, born June 22, 1834, served in the Thirtieth Indiana regiment, was discharged on account of injuries received at Stone River, and later served as first lieutenant of Company B, One Hundred and Twenty-ninth Indiana until close of war; Jarius, born July 30, 1836, who served in Company D, Thirtieth Indiana regiment three years, was in several battles and was once taken prisoner but was soon paroled, now lives on the old homestead in Adams township; Anthony Wayne, born April 27, 1838, is a locomotive engineer on the G. R. & I. railroad, and resides at Kalamazoo, Mich.; Nathan, born February 2, 1840, farmer, lives in St. Joseph township; Marquis, born July 22, 1841, also served in Company D, Thirtieth Indiana regiment with his brother, is a farmer, and resides in Milan township; Harriet, born April 7, 1843, died May 30, 1870; Jasper, born July 22, 1845, served in Company B, One Hundred and Twenty-ninth Indiana regiment, under Capt. James Harper, from November 13, 1863, to the close of the war. His regiment joined Sherman's army at Blue Springs, Tenn., and participated with it in the Atlanta campaign, battles of Franklin and Nashville, after which the regiment was ordered to Washington, D. C., then to Wilmington, Fort Fisher and Newbern, N. C.; was at Raleigh when the rebel general, Joseph Johnston, surrendered to Gen. Sherman. The regiment was afterward stationed at Charlotte, N. C., where he was discharged August 29, 1865. He is a farmer, and resides on the old homestead. Melinda, born February 9, 1846, died February 9, 1846; Henry, born April 10, 1849, died August 26, 1851; Major General Winfield Scott, born January 26, 1852, is a cabinet-maker and resides in Fort Wayne. Henry Tilbury, in early days, also acted as mail carrier to some extent, and as guard when the Indians were paid. He was a member of the Universalist church, to which his widow also adheres.

Henry Linker, a successful farmer of Adams township, was born on the farm he now occupies, April 9, 1840. His parents, Englehardt and Anna Elizabeth (Weisheit) Linker, were born, reared and married in Hesse-Darmstadt, Germany, and emigrated to America in 1833. After stopping in Detroit a few months, they came by wagon, to Allen county, and for about three weeks lived in the old fort. After that they located on an eighty-acre tract of land in section 17, Adams township, which the husband had entered from the government. Here he and wife spent the rest of their lives, he dying on the 27th of June, 1845, and she on July 24th, 1874. She, however, was married after her first husband's death, to Frederick Weirs, who died June 11, 1858. Henry Linker has spent his life on the old homestead, giving his whole attention to farming. He now owns the homestead, and as a farmer is successful. He was married December 21, 1865, to Caroline Gurgens, who was born in Hanover, Germany, August 4, 1842, daughter of Henry F. and Wilhelmina (Bohde) Gurgens, with whom she came to Allen county in June, 1848. The parents located in St. Joseph township, where they still reside. Mr. and Mrs. Linker have had ten children: Anna Elizabeth, Henry Englehardt, Caroline Dora Elizabeth, Louis John August, Frederick William Ernst, Dora Louisa Christina, Louisa Mary Catharine, Mary Sophia Anna, Wilhelmina Augusta Mary and Frederick William Christian, all living except the fifth, a twin brother to Dora Louisa Christina, who died aged six weeks. Parents and children are members of the German Lutheran church. In politics Mr. Linker is a democrat.

Henry Weisheit, of Adams township, was born November 1, 1843. His parents, Peter and Anna Catharine (Trier) Weisheit, were born, reared and married in Hesse-Darmstadt, Germany. They emigrated to America in 1832, and on reaching this country came to Detroit and there lived one year; then coming to Allen county and locating on a 160-acre tract of wood-land in section 17, Adams township, which the father of Henry had purchased as canal land. There the father and mother resided until their decease, the former dying April 8, 1877, and the latter November 13, 1887. On his farm of 120 acres, Henry Weisheit was born, and there has resided ever since, busily occupied as a farmer. Mr. Weisheit was married November 12, 1868, to Mary Schleinbacker, a native of Adams township, born November 10, 1851. Her parents, George and Mary Schleinbacker, were natives of Germany and were married in America. The mother of Mrs. Weisheit was her father's second wife, and after her death he was again married. Mr. Weisheit and wife have had nine children: Margaret, Henry, Hannah, Christian, Mary, Martha, Frederick, Louisa and Herman, all living except Margaret, who died in infancy. Mr. and Mrs. Weisheit are members of the German Lutheran church; in politics, he is a republican. He is an industrious farmer and an honorable man.

Hon. Conrad Trier, an honored pioneer of Adams township, was born in Germany, August 6, 1811, the son of Henry Trier. He was reared in his native country, and in 1832 came to America, landing at Philadelphia, July 5. His father came over the same year. The first work Conrad did in this country was in Allegheny City, Penn., where he was employed in a hotel and livery barn eighteen months. In 1834, he came to Allen county and settled on land in Adams township, which he entered from the government. He has lived on the same farm a period of fifty-five years. His first house was a little log-cabin, the logs for which he carried on his back. For three years after he settled on his land he was also employed during a part of the time on the canal. He was married January 1, 1837, to Catharine Trier, also a native of Germany, but in no way related to him. She came to America with her parents in 1836. This marriage resulted in the birth of twelve children: Henry, John, Elizabeth, Sophia, Christian, William, Catharine, Peter, Paul, Herman, Martin and Martha, of whom Christian, William and Catharine are dead. Mrs. Trier died in February, 1879. She was a member of the German Lutheran church, and her surviving husband and children are members of the same church. Mr. Trier has served one term as a member of the Indiana legislature and two terms as trustee of Adams township. The Maumee valley has no more worthy citizen. When Mr. Trier came to America, he not only possessed nothing, but was in debt $99, cost of passage of himself, his father and his three brothers, which was paid by his uncle. He worked hard, prospered and became one of the wealthy farmers of Allen county, owning at one time 640 acres of land, which, however, he has since given to his children.

Herman Trier, son of the above, was born on the old homestead, October 10, 1851, upon which he has always lived, and has been occupied in farming. He was married November 7, 1878, to Anna Elizabeth, daughter of Valentine and Anna Lapp, born in St. Joseph township, August 22, 1859. They have the following children: Conrad V., Henry J., Theodore, Herman H. J. and Frieda, of whom Theodore and Frieda survive.

Elisha W. Green, a worthy and revered pioneer of Adams township, who resides one-half mile southeast of New Haven, was born in Clarendon township, Rutland co., Vt., July 29, 1815. He is the son of Walter and Lovina (Colvin) Green, respectively natives of Vermont and Rhode Island. His father was a soldier in the war of 1812, and was the son of Peleg Green, a native of Rhode Island, who was a soldier in the war of the revolution. Peleg Green was a cooper, and it is related of him that when a lad attending school, it was a part of his daily work to whittle out a quart of wooden pegs, to be used to plug the worm holes in the barrel staves. He removed from Rhode Island to Vermont, where he lived to the age of more than ninety years. For forty years prior to his death he was totally blind. The mother of Mr. Green was the daughter of Philip Colvin, also a native of Rhode Island. He and his wife spent their last years in Luzerne county, Penn., both living beyond ninety years of age. Both the paternal and maternal ancestors of Mr. Green were noted for longevity. Elisha W. was reared to manhood on the old homestead in Rutland county, Vt. He worked upon the farm in summer and attended an old-fashioned district school during three months of each winter, until he reached the age of eighteen. May 16, 1836, he set out for Allen county, a married sister being at that time a resident of Adams township, and reached this county June 20, and remained until the following fall, making his home with his sister and laboring at ten dollars per month. Before leaving he took the money thus earned and entered 120 acres of land in Adams township, it being the last entry made in the township. In September, 1836, he went to Chautauqua county, N. Y., where he remained eighteen months. In March, 1838, he set out upon a lumber raft, in Conewango creek, and drifted down into the Alleghany river, thence into the Ohio, and down that stream to Cincinnati, being in the employ, while on the trip, of Pope & Cowan, Chautauqua county lumbermen. From Cincinnati he walked across the country to Fort Wayne, 150 miles in three days. Soon afterward he sold the tract of land which he had entered, and bought another just east of the site of New Haven, a town which at that time was not in existence. This land is still in his possession; his home farm which lies just south of it has been occupied by him since 1843. He has devoted himself to farming and has been very successful; he owns 150 acres, his wife has eighty acres, and they jointly own 200 more, all first-class land. Mr. and Mrs. Green have given liberally to worthy enterprises, and have provided comfortably for their children. Mr. Green formerly gave considerable attention to lumbering, and for sixteen years he was the owner of a threshing outfit. His first marriage was in the fall of 1841, to Lucy Ludington, who died about a year later, leaving one child, Lucy B., now the wife of Dr. R. S. Knode, formerly a prominent physician of Fort Wayne, but now of Omaha, Neb. December 13, 1844, Mr. Green was married to Julia A. Doyle, who was born near Crestline, Ohio, May 6, 1822. Her parents, John and Jane (Maxwell) Doyle, both natives of Pennsylvania, were married in Jefferson county, of that state, and in an early day located in Richland county, Ohio. Mr. Green and his present wife have had seven children: Willis, born March 13, 1846, served as a volunteer soldier in Company B, One Hundred and Twenty-ninth Indiana regiment, and was killed December 16, 1864, in the battle of Nashville; Silas, born May 6, 1848, married to Lucretia Johnson, by whom he has two children, Charles and Minnie; is a farmer in Adams township; Lavina J., born June 6, 1850, married to Edgar S. McDonald by whom she had three children: Iva, who resides with her father, at Sioux Falls, Dakota, Willie Hayes, and an infant son who died in infancy — Mrs. McDonald died June 23, 1883; Annetta, born February 25, 1853, died March 11, 1853; Julia Catharine, born March 17, 1854, married to Franklin Grover, a farmer of Jefferson township; William J., born July 31, 1857, died January 10, 1860; and Foster M., born April 25, 1861, died December 30, 1873. Mr. Green is a member of Masonic and Odd Fellows lodges, and in politics is a staunch republican and a strong temperance man. He served as trustee of Adams township one term and discharged the duties of the office honorably. For a great many years he and wife have been devoted members of the Methodist Protestant church.

Levi Hartzell, deceased, formerly one of the most substantial men of Adams township, was born in Miami county, Ohio, March 3, 1813. He was the son of Philip and Elizabeth (Miller) Hartzell, the former a native of Kentucky, and the latter of Miami county, Ohio. In early manhood he learned the miller's trade. He was married in Miami county, February 25, 1842, to Mary Souders, who was born December 31, 1820, the daughter of John and Sarah (Grubb) Souders, both natives of Lancaster county, Penn. Her father accompanied his parents to Miami county in a very early day, and her mother moved to that county with her mother and brother at the same time. They had a family of six daughters and four sons, of whom Mrs. Hartzell was the oldest. A short time after their marriage Mr. and Mrs. Hartzell came to Adams township and located in section 14, on land Mr. Hartzell had purchased five or six years before. He had been a resident of Adams township from the time he bought the land until his marriage. When he and his wife settled on the farm it contained but eighty acres, only three of which were cleared. Mr. Hartzell set about improving his land, and his labors were rewarded with prosperity, and adjoining lands were purchased until finally he owned a fine farm of 390 acres, supplied with a large barn, handsome brick residence and other substantial improvements. He also owned two other farms in Adams township, containing 140 acres each, and at one time he was one of the proprietors of the Maumee Valley Mills at New Haven, which property he helped to erect. Mr. and Mrs. Hartzell had nine children: Joshua, Elias, Susan, Sarah J., John R., Philip, Allen M., Warren S. and Lucy, all of whom are living except Philip and Lucy. Joshua and Elias served in the war of the rebellion nearly three years, under Capt. James Harper. In politics Mr. Hartzell was a republican, taking a very active part, and was an influential worker. He served as assessor of Adams township six years, and as trustee one term. Mr. Hartzell died January 30, 1871. He was an honorable, upright man, and he led a life of industry and honor. Mrs. Hartzell still occupies the old homestead from which she has given a good part to her children. She is an estimable lady and is highly respected.

Lyman Noble, of Adams township, is a native of Dutchess county, N. Y., born September 4, 1833, the son of Nathaniel and Elizabeth Noble. His mother died when he was but eleven days old. Four years later, his father and step-mother removed to Allen county, and settled in Adams township in 1837. With the exception of two years in Wayne township, Mr. Noble has been a successful farmer of Adams township ever since. He was married December 17, 1857, to Hannah Ann Lillie, who was born within the present limits of Fort Wayne, September 13, 1835, the daughter of Samuel and Emily (Philley) Lillie. Mr. and Mrs. Noble have had seven children: Charles N., Edward D., Lillie C., Emily H., Flora M., John M. and one other that died unnamed. The parents are devoted members of the Methodist Episcopal church, and both are very active temperance workers. Mrs. Noble is vice-president of the Woman's Christian Temperance Union, of Fort Wayne. Her parents at one time occupied the old fort as their home, and one of her sisters was born there, and very appropriately, she was named Indiana. Mrs. Noble is the only living member of the Lillie family, her father, mother, sisters and brothers all having died. She takes a very active part in church work and gives encouragement to all things which have for their object the public good. In politics Mr. Noble is a republican. The father of Mr. Noble was a soldier in the war of 1812, and his grandfather was a soldier in the revolution, messing during the war with Gen. Washington. Mr. Noble is distantly related to ex-Gov. Noah Noble.

Meinrad Seiler (deceased), formerly a well-known farmer of Adams township, was born in Germany, October 4, 1810. His father was Joseph Seiler, and his mother's maiden name was Helen Wirtner. In 1836 he came to America, and after spending one year in New York, came to Fort Wayne. He was a carpenter by trade, and as such he worked both in New York and Fort Wayne—at the latter until 1843. In that year he settled upon a farm in Adams township, and there followed farming until his death. He was married July 13, 1844, to Barbara Allgeier, also a native of Germany, born May 8, 1827, to Lorenz and Salome (Brown) Allgeier, with whom she came to America in 1844. The family located near Fort Wayne, where the father and mother spent the rest of their lives. Mr. and Mrs. Seiler had ten children: Joseph, John, Mary, Joseph, Peter, Joseph, Helen, Henry, Frank and Charles, of whom the first Joseph, the second Joseph, Henry and Charles are dead. Mr. Seiler died April 27, 1875; he was a member of the Roman Catholic church, and his wife and children are also members. Mrs. Seiler still occupies the old homestead of 196 acres of good land, which belongs to her and her children. John Seiler, son of the above, was born in Adams township, October 1, 1846. He spent his boyhood and youth on a farm, and at twenty-one years of age began to learn the carpenter's trade. This for ten years he worked at in Adams, Jefferson, Madison, Marion and Wayne townships, constructing dwelling houses, barns, bridges, etc. February 3, 1880, he was married to Maggie, daughter of Matthias and Anna (Welling) Ros. She was born in Allen county, in June 1858. Immediately after their marriage they settled on a farm in section 3, Adams township, which Mr. Seiler had purchased in 1879. There they lived happily until May 13, 1887, when their union was broken by Mrs. Seiler's death. Since then Mr. Seiler has remained on the farm, which contains 143 acres of fine land and has two good houses and barns, one of the latter having been built by Mr. Seiler at a cost of $1,000 besides his labor. His farm is very desirably situated in the bend of the Maumee river. The marriage of Mr. Seiler resulted in the birth of two children, John and Mary. Mr. Seiler is a member of the Roman Catholic church, and in politics is a democrat. He owns two good business houses in Fort Wayne.

Friederich W. Hitzemann, an old and respected farmer of Adams township, was born in Prussia, July 3, 1823. He is the son of Friederich W. and Mary Louisa (Meyers) Hitzemann, the latter of whom died in 1825. He was reared on a farm, and at the age of seventeen, accompanied his father to America and settled in Fort Wayne, which was his home until 1855. He helped to construct the Wabash & Erie canal, and afterward gave his attention to boating on the canal for thirteen years, owning a boat during eight years of the time. In early manhood he was at different times in the employ of Allen Hamilton, J. W. Townley and William Ewing, working for each a few months. He was married December 29, 1853, to Mary Angeline Lindemann, who was born in Hanover, Germany, February 10, 1830, the daughter of Lewis and Mary (Drebert) Lindemann, with whom she came to America in 1842. In 1855, Mr. and Mrs. Hitzemann settled on a farm in section 15, Adams township, where they have resided ever since. Mr. Hitzemann continued boating, however, until 1860. Since then he has given his whole attention to agriculture. He owns a fine farm of 120 acres, which is splendidly improved with brick residence and good barn. Mr. and Mrs. Hitzemann have two children: Louisa Charlotte, wife of Henry Rennekamp, of Adams township, and Frederick L., who is at home. The parents and children are members of the German Lutheran church. Mr. Hitzemann is a worthy and upright man, sociable and agreeable.

Stephen Allgeier (deceased), formerly a worthy citizen of Adams township, was born in Baden, Germany, December 26, 1818, the son of Lorenz and Salome Allgeier. He came to America in 1836, and after spending a few years in New York came to Adams township and located on a tract of wood-land in section 16, becoming one of the early settlers of that locality. While in New York state he had learned and followed the cooper's trade, and after locating in Adams township, in addition to the improvement and cultivation of his land, he, for several years, occasionally worked at his trade. He was married at the age of twenty-six to Augusta Houser, who died July 22, 1854, leaving four children: Charles, Catharine, Frank J. and Matilda, all of whom are living. July 2, 1855, Mr. Allgeier was married to Mary, daughter of John and Barbara (Ostheimer) Baschab, natives of Germany. They came to America in about 1834 and located in Northampton county, Penn., where Mrs. Allgeier was born March 25, 1836. In 1839 they removed to Starke county, Ohio, and thence to Marion township in 1854. There her father died, December 22 of the same year. His wife survived him until October 5, 1876. By his second marriage Mr. Allgeier had six children: Mary (deceased), Henry, Daniel, Peter (deceased), August and Mary F. Mr. Allgeier died May 26, 1879. He was a member of the Roman Catholic church. Mrs. Allgeier still occupies the home place, which is now owned and cultivated by Daniel Allgeier, the second son.

Hermann Tibbet, a worthy resident of Adams township, was born in Hanover, Germany, September 12, 1815, son of Bernard Tibbet. He grew to manhood in his native country, attended school until he was past fourteen, and then worked on a farm. In 1841 he embarked at Bremen on June 10th and landed at New York on July 23. He arrived at Fort Wayne on August 12. An older brother, George, who had come to America about three years before, resided in Adams township, and with him Hermann made his home five months. His first work in this country was upon a stage boat in the canal, being thus employed twenty-two days. In 1842 he was employed four months on the construction of the reservoir in Paulding county, Ohio. For one year following this he was engaged in the manufacture of brick in Wayne township. He then began farming in Adams township. During the first six years he resided on a farm two miles from Fort Wayne, owned by Michael Hedekin. In 1851 he bought a farm in section 11, upon which he has resided thirty-eight years. His farm contains eighty acres of good land, and it is in a splendid state of improvement and cultivation. He also owns a farm of ninety acres in section 1. Mr. Tibbet was married November 25, 1841, to Adaline Holtal, a native of Hanover, born near Mr. Tibbet's birth-place, February 2, 1812. She came to America on the same vessel that brought her husband, the marriage following soon after their arrival at Fort Wayne. They have had five children: Bernard, Katharine, Mary, Rosa and Theodore, of whom only Bernard and Mary are living. Mr. Tibbet and wife are members of the Roman Catholic church. He is one of his township's best citizens, and he and wife are highly esteemed. Bernard Tibbet, the oldest child, was born on a farm two miles south of New Haven, in Adams township, September 28, 1842. By occupation he is a farmer. He was married June 22, 1871, to Josephine Pripsing, by whom he had one child, Catharine, who died in childhood. His wife died February 19, 1888. He is a member of the Roman Catholic church and of the Catholic Knights of America and of St. John's Benevolent society. He has filled out an unexpired term as trustee of Adams township. He owns twenty acres of land which adjoins the old home, and a brick business block in New Haven.

Martin P. Habecker, trustee of Adams township, and one of its prosperous farmers, was born in Lancaster county, Penn., September 19, 1837. His parents, Daniel and Elizabeth (Daugherty) Habecker, were also natives of Lancaster county. The Habecker family originally came from Germany, and the Daugherty family from Ireland. When Martin was between seven and eight years old his parents came to Adams township, in which they spent their lives, the mother dying March 5, 1859, and the father, September 28, 1864. Here Martin P. has lived forty-four years. The family first located on a farm in section 20. Mr. Habecker was married March 2, 1865, to Margaret, daughter of Charles and Louisa (Coleman) Doctor, the former of whom was born in Hesse-Darmstadt, Germany, and came to America with his parents when he was sixteen years old. The latter was a native of Ohio. They were married in Marion township, where Mrs. Habecker was born, January 17, 1844. From 1865 to 1868, Mr. and Mrs. Habecker resided on the old Habecker homestead in section 20. In 1868 they located on the farm they now occupy in section 17, where they have lived with the exception of four years, from May 13, 1873, to April 19, 1877, when they resided in section 33. Mr. Habecker and wife have had five children: Alice Mella, Mary Violetta (deceased), Minnie Adeline, Frances Marion (deceased), and Martin Franklin. Mr. and Mrs. Habecker are members of the English Lutheran church of Fort Wayne. Mr. Habecker is an honorable, upright official.

Gerard Henry Christopher Rebber (deceased), an early resident of Adams township, was born at Bohmte in Amte Wittlage, Hanover, January 29, 1822. He came with his parents, Gerard Henry and Dorothea Rebber and two brothers and two sisters, to America, when he was twenty years old. The family came directly to Allen county and after a few months in Wayne township, removed to Adams township, where Mr. Rebber and his parents spent the rest of their lives, his mother dying in 1851 and his father in 1870. Mr. Rebber was married in St. Paul's German Lutheran church, of Fort Wayne, August 16, 1849, by pastor Dr. Sihler, to Catherine Clara Rahen, who was born in Essen, Wittlage, Hanover, May 9, 1826, the daughter of Henry and Henrietta (Dressing) Rahen. She came to America in 1847, and after spending a year in Syracuse, N. Y., came to Fort Wayne, where she remained

Edward Harper

until her marriage. Her father and mother came to America in 1850, and located in that part of Fort Wayne north of St. Mary's river. They were the first settlers, and it was a brother of Mrs. Rebber that gave it the name of Bloomingdale. There her father died in 1857. His wife about ten years later, died at the home of Mrs. Rebber, in Adams township. As soon as they were married, Mr. and Mrs. Rebber located on a farm in section 16, Adams township. In April, 1859, they removed to another farm in the same section, where the family has resided ever since, the father dying there May 5, 1889. Mr. Rebber was a member of the German Lutheran church. Mr. and Mrs. Rebber had ten children: Gerard Henry, born August 7, 1850; Marie Henrietta, born September 29, 1851; Lewis Frederick, born October 29, 1854, died April 24, 1855; Henrietta Dorothea, born October 1, 1855; Frank Frederick Christian, born September 12, 1857; Henry Frederick Christopher, born May 19, 1859; Henry Frederick Christian, born October 7, 1861; John Henry, born November 30, 1863, died January 9, 1887; Sophia Elizabeth Clara, born September 28, 1865; and Henry Frederick Lewis, born December 5, 1867. Mr. Rebber left two good farms of eighty acres each, one being the home farm in section 16, which is provided with a handsome brick residence, good barn and other substantial improvements. The other farm lies in section 22, Adams township. Mrs. Rebber occupies the old homestead. She and the children are members of the German Lutheran church. Gerard Henry Rebber, the oldest child, has been in the employment of the Pittsburgh, Fort Wayne & Chicago railway since January 13, 1872. He began as a section hand, but June 27, 1876, he was promoted to section foreman, and he has since filled that position on section 26. In 1888, his section was awarded first premium. He owns eighty acres of land in Adams township.

Christian Wiese, a respected citizen of Adams township, was born in Prussia, March 9, 1829. He was but six years old when his father died. At the age of fifteen he accompanied his widowed mother to America. An older brother of his had come to this country four years before and located in Adams township, and to his home the remainder of the family came. Christian spent one year working at the tailor's trade in Fort Wayne, but this proved very distasteful, and he gave it up, and for nine years was employed on the Wabash and Erie canal, during the boating season, making his home with his brother in Adams township. He started as driver at $5 per month, and continued, with increasing wages, three years, when he and three others purchased a boat and he was engaged as one of its owners and steersman during the remaining six years. On retiring from the canal he took his earnings, which amounted to $700, and bought eighty acres of land in section 15, Adams township. As the price of the land was $1,200, he started $500 in debt, and he owed as much more for improvements, etc. In 1854 he set about clearing, and in the course of a few years he had developed a good farm. It is now as nice a farm, for its size, as any in the township, being splendidly improved and desirably situated. Mr. Weise has accumulated enough to buy two other farms, one of thirty acres in section 28, and another of 120 acres in Fayette county, Ill. The latter, however, he has given to one of his sons. His present wife owns a good residence property in Fort Wayne. In 1854 Mr. Wiese was married to Ann Elizabeth, daughter of Peter and Anna Katharine Weisheit. She was an infant child when her mother died, soon after which the family removed to America. She bore to Mr. Wiese eleven children: Sophia, Elizabeth, Christian, Charles, Martha, Louisa, Katharine, Henry, Marie, Sophia and one that died unnamed. Sophia, Elizabeth and Christian are dead. The first wife of Mr. Wiese died in 1880, and on October 16, 1881, he was married to Mrs. Lenore Böester, a native of Schaumburg-Lippe, Germany, born October 16, 1830, the daughter of Christian and Marie Mueller. She came to America in 1856, and was married two years later to Henry Böester, who died October 8, 1877. By him she had five children, all deceased. Mr. and Mrs. Wiese are members of the German Lutheran church. He has led an industrious life, and he is permitted to spend his declining years in comfortable circumstances.

John Henry Koehlinger, of Adams township, was born near Wetzler, Prussia, August 24, 1838. With his parents, Henry and Christina (Weber) Koehlinger, he came to America in the eleventh year of his age. The family landed at New York early in July, 1849, and arrived at Fort Wayne about eight days later. They settled on a tract of woodland in section 35, Adams township, where he remained helping to clear and cultivate the farm until he was twenty-one. There his father died in the latter part of July, 1868, and there his mother still resides in the eighty-fourth year of her age. At the age of twenty-one, Mr. Koehlinger began to learn the cooper's trade in New Haven. He followed this until he enlisted in Company G, Twelfth Indiana volunteer infantry, April 28, 1861, and served until May 19, 1862, when, owing to expiration of term of service, he was honorably discharged at Washington City. He was neither wounded nor taken prisoner, but while marching from Williamsport, Md., to Martinsburg, Va., on the night of March 1, 1862, he stepped on a stone which rolled in such a way as to throw his foot into a rut and his left ankle was thrown out of joint. It resulted in a permanent injury. He returned home and followed the cooper's trade in New Haven until 1864, when he purchased an interest in a shingle and lumber business, and for one year he was a member of the firm of G. Gothe & Co. He then resumed his trade until 1869. In the fall of that year he bought eighty acres of land in section 13, and located upon it in the following spring. Since then his attention has been given to farming, at which he has been successful. He has since bought an additional twenty, so that he now owns a handsome farm of 100 acres. Mr. Koehlinger was married October 21, 1862, to Johanna Brudi, a native of Wurtemberg, Germany, born January 21, 1842, the daughter of John George and Anna Barbara (Handi) Brudi. Mr. and Mrs.

Koehlinger have seven sons and three daughters: Gustav A., Frederick Edward, Emma K., Henry G., Carl William, Christian F. G., Philip A., Clara E., Louise S. and Gottlieb Arthur. Parents and children are members of Emanuel's church in New Haven, in which Mr. Koehlinger is active and influential. He is a progressive farmer and a worthy, upright man.

Henry C. Zollinger, a prominent citizen of Adams township, was born in Wiesbaden, Germany, April 18, 1841. He is the son of Christian and Elizabeth (Kühn) Zollinger, with whom he came to America when he was seven years old. The family arrived at Sandusky City, Ohio, early in May, 1848. In the summer of 1850, they came to Allen county and settled on a farm in Marion township, where the father and mother resided for about thirty years. The father was a turner by trade, and with him Henry learned the trade, beginning at the age of thirteen and following it at home until he was twenty-one. On August 12, 1862, he enlisted in the Eleventh Indiana battery, with which he served until late in 1864, and was in the entire campaign from Chattanooga to Atlanta. He was taken prisoner near Chattanooga, October 2, 1863, but was paroled about two weeks later. He accompanied Sherman over a portion of the march to the sea, then returned with his battery to Chattanooga and to Nashville, where he was transferred to the Eighteenth Indiana battery, with which he served until the close of the war. He was discharged at Indianapolis early in July, 1865. He received three wounds, but none of them proved serious. Returning home he soon afterward settled on a tract of land which he had bought in section 36, Adams township, where for a year he worked at the turner's trade. He was married April 9, 1866, to Miss Mary A. Gretzinger, who was born in Tuscarawas county, Ohio, December 5, 1846, the daughter of George and Christina Gretzinger, natives of Wurtemberg, Germany. Shortly after his marriage, Mr. Zollinger removed to Fort Wayne, where for about three years he was one of the proprietors of a chair factory. April 21, 1869, he returned to Adams township and located on a forty-acre farm which he had leased. In 1872 he bought an eighty-acre tract adjoining, and to this, in 1874, he added the forty which he had leased. His farm is in a splendid state of improvement, being provided with a nice residence and good barn. Mr. Zollinger has done but little farming himself, his farm during the greater part of the time being rented out. In 1870 he purchased a saw-mill which was located on the land he had leased, and he has owned and operated it ever since, doing a very large business. Since 1880, in connection with saw-milling, he has also been largely engaged in the manufacture of drain tile. Mr. Zollinger and wife have had eight children: Anna E., John L., Charles H., Henry A., George W. and Christian F. (twins), Julia L. and Maria K., all of whom are living except John L. and Charles H. He and wife are members of St. John's Reformed church, of Fort Wayne. He is a member of the Masonic and Odd Fellows lodges, and of the G. A. R., being a past commander in the last. In 1874 he was elected trustee of Adams township; he was re-elected in 1876, and again elected in 1878, serving three terms to the entire satisfaction of the public. He takes an active part in politics, and is an influential worker in the republican party. From 1876 to 1881 he served as postmaster at Adams station, resigning the position in the latter year.

Diederich Rodenbeck, of Adams township, was born in Prussia, January 1, 1832, the son of Frederick and Marie (Beck) Rodenbeck. He attended school between the ages of seven and fourteen, and spent his youth on a farm. In 1854 he emigrated to America and came directly to Fort Wayne. The first work he did in this country was upon Adam Brick's farm, in Adams township, where he was employed two months. In the hope of finding better employment, in August, 1854, he went to Indianapolis, but failing to secure work there then returned to Fort Wayne and during the twenty months which followed he worked on a farm in Wayne township at four dollars per month. In the fall of 1856 his father, mother, two brothers and four sisters came to America and were met by him in Fort Wayne. For a month the family remained at the place where he had been employed in Wayne township. They then located on a tract of land which the father had purchased in section 15, Adams township. There the father and mother resided until death, the former dying in August, 1865, and the latter July 8, 1869. She was born October 4, 1802. Until July, 1857, Diederich remained on the farm with his parents, and then became employed on the Wabash & Erie canal and followed the life of a boatman for over five years. March 4, 1862, he was married to Christina Zelter, a native of Prussia, born February 20, 1838. She is the daughter of Henry and Charlotte (Schmidt) Zelter. The mother died in Germany when Mrs. Rodenbeck was but ten years old. She came to America in February, 1861. Her father followed in March, 1868, and has since made his home with her. He is now in his ninety-first year, having been born February 4, 1799. Soon after their marriage Mr. and Mrs. Rodenbeck located on the farm they now occupy in section 15. He owns forty acres besides his home farm, which contains eighty acres of fine land, and is provided with a good barn and a handsome brick residence. Mr. Rodenbeck and wife have had ten children: Diederich (deceased), Sophia (deceased), the third died unnamed, Diederich, Wilhelmina, Sophia, Louisa, Henry, Frederick and Christina. Parents and children are members of the German Lutheran church. He is a progressive farmer and a first-class citizen.

Henry Rodenbeck (deceased), of Adams township, was born in Prussia, February 23, 1829, the son of Frederick and Mary (Baade) Rodenbeck. He grew to manhood in his native country working upon a farm. In August, 1854, he accompanied his parents to America, and located with them on a farm in section 15, where his father and mother spent the rest of their lives, the former dying in October, 1865, and the latter July 8, 1869. Here he also lived until his death. He was married September 11, 1856, to Wilhelmina Hitzemann, a native of Prussia, born January 3, 1832, the daughter of Conrad and Sophia (Wiebke) Hitzemann. Mrs. Rodenbeck came to America with a brother in 1853, and her parents came in the following year and settled in Wayne township, but afterward removed to Washington township, where the mother died June 20, 1871. Her father is living in his eighty-sixth year. Mr. and Mrs. Rodenbeck have had eight children: Mary, Louisa (deceased), Sophia (deceased), Louisa, Wilhelmina (deceased), Henry, Wilhelmina and Frederick. Mr. Rodenbeck died April 8, 1886. He was a member of the German Lutheran church, and was an honest, upright man and worthy citizen. His wife, who survives him, occupies the old homestead where she is spending the decline of life in comfort. She and children are members of the German Lutheran church.

Caspar Kern (deceased), formerly a well-known citizen of Adams township, was born September 24, 1821. His parents, John Michael and Anna Margaret Kern, came with him to America in 1837, and settled in Union county, Ohio. October 19, 1848, he was married in Franklin county, Ohio, to Elizabeth Spindler, a native of Lancaster county, Penn., born May 20, 1826, daughter of Matthias and Elizabeth Spindler, who also were natives of Pennsylvania. After their marriage, Mr. and Mrs. Kern resided in Union county, Ohio, until 1858. In that year they came to Allen county, and first settled in St. Joseph township. In 1861, they removed to Adams township, where the family has since occupied the same farm. Mr. Kern died April 4, 1884. His marriage resulted in the birth of nine children: Anna Margaret, John Jacob, David F., John F., Mary C., Edward F., Christian W., Lizzie M. and Anna M., of whom Anna Margaret (the oldest) and David F., are dead. Mrs. Kern still occupies the old homestead, which contains 192 acres of good land. She and children are, as was her husband, members of the German Lutheran church.

George W. McCoy, a prominent citizen of Adams township, was born near Greensburg, Ind., at a place now called McCoy's Station, January 30, 1827. His parents, Angus C. and Elizabeth (Smith) McCoy, were born, the former in Washington county, Penn., March 13, 1789, and the latter in Loudon county, Va., May 9, 1799. They were married in Bourbon county, Ky., February 16, 1815, and in 1825 they removed to Decatur county, Ind., where both spent their remaining years, the mother dying September 23, 1844, and the father in 1865. The paternal grandparents of George W., were Alexander and Nancy McCoy, natives of Scotland. His maternal grandparents were Zadok and Nancy Smith, natives of Virginia. George W. McCoy was reared to manhood on a farm in his native county. At the age of twenty he entered Wabash college, at Crawfordsville, in which he completed a full classical course, graduating in 1853. During his college life he also taught about four terms of school. During the winters of 1853-4 and 1854-5 he also taught school. In the fall of 1856 he entered Lane seminary, a theological institution at Cincinnati, which he attended three months, intending to prepare himself for the ministry. But circumstances compelled him to give up his theological studies and return home. In the spring of 1857, he taught another term of school in Decatur county. He then engaged in the warehouse business in Greensburg, and for two years dealt in wheat and agricultural implements. In 1859 he removed to Fort Wayne, and for fourteen months was engaged in the hardware business. In 1860 he located on a farm which he had purchased two miles northeast of Fort Wayne on the Maumee gravel road. This contained 144 acres, 109 of which lay in Adams township and thirty-five in St. Joseph. He first located on the part in St. Joseph, and in 1866 he sold it and removed to the part in Adams township, which he has occupied ever since. He has since made several purchases and sales of land, owning at one time 370 acres. His present farms contains 220 acres. Mr. McCoy was married January 12, 1859, to Martha J., daughter of B. W. Oakley, formerly of Fort Wayne. She died September 9, 1869. March 2, 1885, he was married to Catharine C. Ginther, his present wife. His first marriage resulted in the birth of five children: Elizabeth S., Charles O., George, Hattie A. and Jennie M., of whom only Charles and Jennie are living. He has one child, Angus C., by his present wife. The latter was born in Union county, Ohio, December 14, 1849, daughter of Joseph and Fidilla (Bowersmith) Ginther, respectively natives of Tuscarawas and Union counties, Ohio. Her father was the son of John and Lydia (Demuth) Ginther, natives of Pennsylvania. Her mother was the daughter of Jacob and Matilda (Jenkins) Bowersmith. Mrs. McCoy's father was born August 3, 1826, and her mother September 16, 1824. Mr. McCoy is a member of the Presbyterian church, and in politics has been a republican since the party was organized. Mr. McCoy is a highly intelligent man, and possesses a superior education. He is in comfortable circumstances, and his friends are numerous.

Oliver Tustison, a well-known citizen of Adams township, was born in Crawford county, Ohio, April 7, 1840, son of Nelson and Eusebia (Cox) Tustison. The father was born in Philadelphia, October 7, 1811, and the mother in Coshocton county, Ohio, September 5, 1816. The father was the son of Nelson and Jane (Brown) Tustison, the former a native of Denmark, and the latter of Philadelphia. His mother was the daughter of John and Rebecca (Hull) Cox, the former a native of Germany and the latter of Coshocton county, Ohio. When Oliver Tustison was four years old his parents removed to Williams, now Defiance county, Ohio, where he spent his youth on a farm, two miles west of Hicksville, Ohio. In the spring of 1861 the family settled on the farm which Mr. Tustison now occupies in Adams township. Here the mother died February 15, 1873, and the father, February 24, of the same year. Their daughter, Alvira, also died in the same month, February 9, 1873. Mr. Tustison remained on the farm until 1864, when he went to Montana territory; thence to Nevada a month later. There he remained three years engaged at farming. In 1867 he returned home by way of San Francisco, Panama and New York, and resumed farming at the old home place. October 20, 1868, he was married to Jennie M. Loveall, a native of Adams township, daughter of Samuel and Nancy Loveall. In 1869, Mr. and Mrs. Tustison removed to Marion county, Ill., where they resided three years. They returned to Adams township in 1872, where Mr. Tustison has resided ever since, excepting from October, 1886, to April, 1889, when he resided in New Haven. During 1875 and 1876, he was engaged in the pump business, and for the past three years has also dealt in agricultural implements. Aside from this his attention has been given to farming. His first wife died March 6, 1874. A child, Ina A., who was born to their marriage, had died April 25, 1872, aged three months. Mr. Tustison's brother, Matthias M. Tustison, died on the 8th of April, 1872, making six deaths in the family inside of two years. January 11, 1877, Mr. Tustison was married to Clara Dell, daughter of Orrin D. Rogers. She is a native of New Haven, and at the time of her marriage was a teacher by profession. This marriage has resulted in the birth of three children: Olive M., Nelson R. and Glenn C. Mr. and Mrs. Tustison are members of the Universalist church. He is a member of the I. O. O. F. lodge and encampment. In politics he is a democrat. He is now holding the office of justice of the peace, having been elected in 1888.

Hezekiah W. Loveland, one of the substantial farmers of Adams township, was born in Glastonbury township, Hartford co., Conn., about eight miles from the city of Hartford, March 17, 1827. His parents, Luther and Lucy (Wickam) Loveland, were natives of the same township. His father was born March 18, 1793, the son of Pelatia and Mollie (Sparks) Loveland, also natives of Glastonbury township, married December 17, 1774. His mother was also born in 1793. Both his paternal and maternal ancestors had resided in Glastonbury township for several generations. As far back as 1653, Thomas Loveland emigrated from Glastonbury, Eng., and became one of the earliest settlers of the new township, bearing the same name. It is thought that all persons bearing the name of Loveland in America, sprang from this same Thomas Loveland. The parents of Hezekiah were married May 15, 1814. When he was a little child but one year old, his parents removed from Connecticut to Erie county, Ohio, where he was reared on a farm. In March, 1850, he went to California, where, for three years, he was engaged at mining. He then returned by way of Panama and New York. On November 9, 1854, he was married in Defiance county, Ohio, to Delilah Tustison, who was born in Crawford county, Ohio, November 11, 1835, the daughter of Nelson and Eusebia (Cox) Tustison, the former of whom was born at Philadelphia. Immediately after his marriage, Mr. Loveland located on a farm in Scipio township, Allen county, which he had bought in 1849. In 1859, he removed to the old Loveland homestead in Erie county, Ohio, having purchased it from his father. In February, 1863, he located where he now resides, in Adams township. With the exception of the three years he was in California, he has been farming, at which pursuit he has been successful. Mr. Loveland has had seven children: Harriet, Maria, Mary, Lucius Nelson, Eusebia J., Emmet O. and Ernest A., all living except Ernest A., who died in childhood. Mrs. Loveland died April 8, 1877. Mr. Lovejoy is a member of the Masonic lodge, and in politics is a democrat. He owns a farm of 140 acres, which adjoins the town of New Haven on the west, and has a handsome brick residence, erected in 1885.

Francis J. Zurbuch (deceased), formerly a leading farmer of Adams township, was born in France, March 17, 1822, the son of Francis J. Zurbuch. He came to America with his father and mother when he was nine years old, and the family first located near Columbus, Ohio, but later settled in Mercer county, Ohio, where the father died. His widow afterward accompanied a son to Tennessee, where she died in 1877. Francis J. spent his youth chiefly in Mercer county, Ohio. He worked at farmwork and in early manhood learned the cooper's trade, and also the trade of a stone mason. He was married in Dayton, Ohio, January 29, 1849, to Rachel Miller, who was born in Baden, Germany, May 16, 1829. She was the daughter of John and Barbara Miller, with whom she came to America, when she was thirteen years of age. They settled near Dayton, Ohio, where both the father and mother spent the rest of their lives. Mr. and Mrs. Zurbuch began their married life in Dayton, where they resided about fourteen years, Mr. Zurbuch working at the cooper's trade. In 1863 they came to Adams township and settled about a mile northeast of New Haven, where Mr. Zurbuch was engaged at farming until the time of his death, on the 10th day of September, 1877. Mr. and Mrs. Zurbuch had seven children: John, Francis J., Mary, George, Anna F., Elizabeth and John, of whom the first named John and Mary, are dead. Mr. Zurbuch was an honorable man and commanded universal respect. He was a member of the Roman Catholic church, as are his family. His wife with two of her sons occupy the old homestead, which contains 147 acres of land and is well improved.

Michael Hellwarth, a substantial farmer of Adams township, was born in Mercer county, Ohio, about five miles from Celina, March 5, 1840. His father, George M. Hellwarth, was born January 24, 1803, in Wittemberg, Germany, son of Ulrich Hellwarth. He served ten years in the German army and then accompanied his father to America, about 1831, when he was twenty-eight years of age. His mother had died in Germany when he was but four years old. Caroline, who became his wife, lived only a few miles distant in the old country. They became engaged there, she came to America on the same vessel with him and their marriage followed soon after arrival. They located in Little York, Penn., but four years later moved to Springfield, Ohio. After residing there three years they removed to Mercer county and occupied the farm upon which their son Michael was born. They were among the early settlers of that county and lived there until death, the mother dying in 1837. The father was afterward married to Margaret Wappes, who still resides on the old homestead. He became the father of sixteen children, of whom the first five were born to his first wife. Nine of his children are still living. He died January 25, 1866. Michael was reared to manhood on the home farm, and was married to Miss Mary Furthmiller February 11, 1866. They soon afterward located on a farm adjoining his old home. October 18, 1868, he removed to Allen county; lived first on a farm in Jefferson township, and in the spring of 1869 purchased his present farm in Adams township. With the exception of one year he has given his whole attention to agriculture. He has a fine farm of 120 acres, with a good residence and barn. During the one year mentioned he was engaged at the butcher's trade in New Haven. The first wife of Mr. Hellwarth died November 6, 1876, and on November 20, 1877, he was married to Lucinda Mosimann, a native of Vera Cruz, Ind., daughter of Frederick and Elizabeth Mosimann. The first marriage of Mr. Hellwarth resulted in the birth of five children: Nelson W., Clara Agnes (died aged sixteen), Cora E., John A. and Herman E., and by the second marriage he had one child, Dellie, who died, aged three months. Mr. and Mrs. Hellwarth are members of the Evangelical church. In politics he is a republican. He is an intelligent and enterprising man and an industrious and successful farmer.

Nicholas Snyder, a prosperous farmer of Adams township, was born in Onondaga county, N. Y., October 19, 1839. His parents, Joseph and Catharine (Hullar) Snyder, were natives of Lorraine, France. His father was born in 1812, and came with his parents, Joseph and Margaret (Semley) Snyder, to America when he was nineteen years of age. They located in Onondaga county, N. Y., where both the grandparents spent the rest of their lives. The mother of Mr. Snyder came to America with her parents, who also settled in Onondaga county, N. Y., but about six years later her father and mother returned to France. Sixteen years later they again came to America and ended their days in Onondaga county, N. Y. Their names were Casper and Christina (Shepp) Hullar. Nicholas Snyder was reared in his native county, working at farm work. He was married there April 14, 1863, to Margaret Palz, born in Lorraine, April 22, 1840, the daughter of Conrad and Catharine (Zengiler) Palz, with whom she came to America when she was nine years old and settled in Onondaga county, N. Y., where her father died three years later. Her mother, for the past twenty-five years, has made her home with Mr. and Mrs. Snyder. She is now in the eightieth year of her age. From the month of March preceding his marriage to the spring of 1872, Mr. Snyder was in the employ of the New York Central & Hudson River railway. He began as a section hand, but at the end of one year he was promoted to section foreman and continued in that capacity eight years, during the last two of which he resided in Utica, N. Y., where he was foreman of the yards and work train. March 13, 1872, he resigned, and soon after removed to Allen county, and located in section 13, Adams township, on a farm which he had purchased in February, 1872. His attention since then has been given to agriculture. His farm contains sixty acres of fine land, and it is provided with a good residence and barn, and other substantial improvements. Mr. and Mrs. Snyder have had ten children: Helen, Magdalena, Joseph, George, Louis N., Frederick A., William H., John P., Emma M., and Leo A., all living except Joseph and George. Mr. and Mrs. Snyder are members of the Roman Catholic church. He is a member of St. John's Benevolent society. The maternal grandmother of Mrs. Snyder lived to be one hundred and four years old. Her husband died at the age of eighty-eight. The mother of Mr. Snyder died in Onondago county, N. Y., November 21, 1864. In the following February his father was married to Mrs. Hower, whose maiden name was Catharine Zion. In 1865 they came to Adams township. In the spring of 1882, they removed to Minnesota, where the father died July 25, 1883. His widow resides at Northfield, Minn.

A notable character in early times was Jonathan Chapman, better known as "Johnny Appleseed." "If ever there lived a man who deserved to have a monument erected to his memory by any people," said a great nurseryman at Rochester, N. Y., "that man was Jonathan Chapman." The people of western Pennsylvania, and especially those of Ohio and Indiana, might have appropriately raised such a monument years ago. Not less than 100,000 square miles of country between the Ohio river and the northern lakes, a famous fruit growing region, owe the origin of their fruitfulness largely to the peculiar labor and novel method of the person named. His bones lie in a neglected and forgotten grave, where they were placed about forty years ago; but there are some still living who remember well how his nurseries in the wilderness along the Ohio, Muskingum, Wabash and other streams, planted while he tramped through the woods from 1801 until 1840, supplied trees to the early settlers. He first appeared in western Pennsylvania, with early settlers, and beyond the fact that he was born in Boston, in 1775, nothing was known of his antecedents, or of his family, except that he had a sister, Persis Broom. He came among the settlers carrying a bag of appleseeds, which he planted through the Alleghany valley, and when that region became too thickly settled for his carrying out his novel idea, he entered the wilderness of Ohio with a horse loaded with leathern bags containing appleseeds collected at the Pennsylvania cider presses, where the first fruits from his pioneer orchards were used. He planted seeds along Licking creek, and there are a number of trees standing in Licking county, which are the original growth from his seeds. Chapman soon became known as Johnny Appleseed and his right name was unknown to many of the later generations. He selected the most fertile spots in the many valleys tributary to the Ohio river, sowing, it is said, as much as sixteen bushels of seed to the acre. When he had planted a nursery he enclosed it with a stout brush fence. He then left it and tramped to some other rich and loamy vales where he sowed and fenced as before. After planting along the Ohio tributaries in 1806, he planted all along the second route ever opened through the Ohio wilderness, which was from Fort Duquesne or Pittsburg via Sandusky to Detroit. When one stock of seeds was exhausted, this persistent enthusiast returned with his leathern bags to the cider presses and obtained more. When the trees in these strange nurseries were large enough to be sold, and there were farmers in the neighborhood to buy them, the planter would visit them or appoint an agent to look out for the sale of them. If the farmer had money Johnny Appleseed would take his price in cash, but he would accept old clothes, corn-meal, or any other article, even notes made payable when he called again and demanded the amount, but he was never known to ask payment of a note or to even keep one in his possession. What he did with these obligations is a mystery. If he received money he always gave it to needy settlers or purchased articles for them which they lacked. Johnny Appleseed carried with him on his long tramps through the forest, tracts and books on the doctrines of Swedenborg, of whom he was an ardent follower, and he never entered the cabin of a settler without reading something from one of these books, as a preliminary to anything else. At one cabin he would tear out a few leaves or a chapter and leave it there for the perusal of the settler and and his family, at another he would leave another section of the book, and so on until he had scattered a small library in tattered parts over a large extent of country. On subsequent rounds he would gather them up and leave other portions in their places. Thus he managed to furnish his reading matter to several families at the same time, the only objection being that as the subsequent distributions were made with no particular rotation of parts, the books had to be read by many of Johnny Appleseed's parishioners backward, and from the middle of the work to either end. This singular character lived the rudest and simplest of lives, and for forty years slept in the woods wherever night overtook him, and subsisted on fruits and vegetables alone. He believed it a sin to kill any living thing for food, and believed it wrong to even prune or graft a tree to increase or improve the fruit. He said that there should be eaten only the natural products of the seed as God had ordered. He was the constant and faithful friend of all dumb brutes, reptiles and insects. He made the care and protection of aged and infirm horses his special duty on his rounds. If he saw a settler working a horse that was lame or blind or afflicted in any way, as settlers were frequently compelled to do, he would purchase it at the owner's price and then give it to some one who could afford to treat it gently or turn it loose to end its days in peaceful pasture. Hundreds of reminiscences of his strange and beneficent doings are related by farmers from the Ohio to Lake Michigan. He always dressed in the cast-off clothing he received in exchange for apple trees, and made his journey usually barefooted and bareheaded. Once he went through the Muskingum valley arrayed in an old coffee sack, through a hole in the bottom of which his head was thrust, while from a hole cut in each side his hands and arms protruded. In the winter time he wore as a hat a large tin dipper, which he carried to cook his corn-meal mush in. The Indians regarded him as a great medicine man, and many stories are told of how his influence with the savages saved many a border family from tomahawk and firebrand. He came to Allen county as soon as there were settlements, and established nurseries at various places. He was a short, "chunky" man, restless, with bright, black eyes. In expounding his religion or describing his apples, he was remarkably eloquent, and used excellent language. He died at the home of Richard Worth, on the St. Joseph, in 1845.

Among those particularly prominent in the settlement of Washington township, was one still a resident, John Archer, who came here with his father in 1825. He was born in Montgomery county, Ohio, September 25, 1822, son of David and Anna (Crisenbury) Archer. David Archer was born near Philadelphia, in 1807, and died in Washington township in 1861. He was elected county commissioner in 1834 and served for four years. He was a man of indomitable energy. He was a Mason and a member of the Methodist Episcopal church. The mother of Mr. Archer was born in Boone county, Ky., and died in Washington township at about seventy years of age. John Archer is the eldest of three living children in a family of eleven. In the fall of 1844 he settled on his present farm of 240 acres. He attended school only three months with a teacher named Hague, but learned well his life occupation, farming. For nearly six years he was one of the board of trustees of Washington township, and for sixteen years was trustee under the present law, his last term expiring in 1886; he also served four years as assessor. He was formerly an old-line whig, and is now a republican. October 4, 1849, he was married to Mary Poinsett, born in Montgomery county, Ohio, July 6, 1825, and they have five children living: Anna E., Mary J., Oliver A., Winfield S. and Andrew J. Mr. Archer is the third oldest resident of the county living, and is one of its most honorable and worthy men.

John S. Poinsett, a son of a worthy pioneer, and himself a resident of Washington township since childhood, has become widely known as one of the leading farmers. He was born in Hanover township, Montgomery county, Ohio, November 23, 1818. His father, Peter Poinsett, was born in New Jersey, and died in the county of Allen at fifty-two years of age. He married Mary Rockhill, born in the same state, who died in Allen county at about the same age. Mr. Poinsett, the eldest of three living children, was raised on the farm. As early as 1828, he came with his father to Allen county and remained one season and then returned to Ohio. About 1834 the family made a permanent settlement. Mr. Poinsett has been occupied during life as a farmer and stock dealer. About 1855 he settled where he now lives, and owns 220 acres of well improved land. He was married in 1843 to Ellen Rockhill, born in Montgomery county, Ohio, and they have six children: William, John, Harriet, Joseph, Mary and Edward. In politics he is a republican, and cast his first presidential vote for William H. Harrison. He is one of the prosperous men of this county, but all has been won by his own exertions.

John B. Grosjean, a prominent pioneer of Washington township, is a native of France, born May 3, 1819, being one of the two survivors of five children of Claude and Frances Grosjean, natives of France. The family immigrated, reaching New York City, May 3, 1834, and on the 4th of June, arrived at Fort Wayne, taking a whole month to make the trip over land. The parents died in this county, many years ago. John B. Grosjean was raised on the farm, and in 1846, began farming for himself on the land he now owns, 137 acres of well improved land. He was married in 1848, to Miss Mary Porson, who was born in France, April 6, 1824, daughter of Bernard and Cecilia, natives of France, who died in Washington township, her father in 1858 and her mother in 1870. They built and kept the first tavern in Washington township. Mr. and Mrs. Grosjean have nine living children. He and wife are members of the Catholic church.

Edward Grosjean, son of the above, was born in Washington township, July 7, 1860, the fourth child of his worthy parents. He was raised on the farm, and received his education at the public schools and at Fort Wayne Methodist college. After leaving school he worked on the farm one year, and then in 1881, embarked in the saw-mill business on the Lima road. The next year he removed to Wallen, and has there been engaged in that business ever since. For six years he has also been manufacturing tile extensively. In 1884, he became associated with two brothers in the firm of Grosjean Brothers, manufacturers and dealers in hardwood lumber and drain tile, and they have done a prosperous business, now employing sixteen men. Their reputation as enterprising business men is widespread. Mr. Grosjean was married in 1881, to Martha Hudson, who was born in Allen county in 1860, and they have one child, Ray, born in September, 1884. Mrs. Grosjean is a member of the Methodist church, and he of the Catholic church. In politics he is a republican. He is a popular young man, and already occupies a leading position.

Edward Beckman, who has been for forty-five years a resident of Washington township, is the son of prominent pioneer parents. His father, Henry Beckman, and his mother, whose maiden name was Sophia Tegtmeyer, were both born in Germany in 1804, were married about fifty-two years ago, and came to Allen county in 1836. These venerable and esteemed people yet reside in the township where they made their home in the forests. The older of their two living children, Edward, was born in this county April 11, 1841. He was raised on the Washington township farm where he still lives, and obtained a good education in the Lutheran schools. November 12, 1862, he was married to Eliza Gerding, who was born in Washington township in 1844. They have nine children: Edward H., Lo\`is P., Louise, Sophia, Justa, Eliza, Frederick C., Harmon E. and Julia. Mr. Beckman has always occupied a high position in the esteem of the people of the county as a capable and straightforward man, and in 1880 the members of his party (democratic) testified their confidence in him by tendering him the nomination for township trustee. Unfortunate dissensions in the party alone prevented his election. He is a notable land owner and farmer, having 380 acres of fertile land, and his home is one of the most pleasant. He and family are members of the St. Paul's Lutheran church at Fort Wayne.

Samuel Kariger, who lives upon his fine farm of 160 acres in Washington township, four and a half miles northwest of the city, is one of a family of worthy pioneers. His parents, Frederick and Elizabeth (Lindsay) Kariger, natives of Pennsylvania, removed in the spring of 1836 from Ohio to Allen county, and settled on the land above mentioned. Here the father died January 21, 1846, in the fifty-ninth year of his age, and the mother died in 1871, in her eighty-second year. Frederick Kariger was the son of John Kariger, a native of Pennsylvania, who died in Knox county, Ohio, in 1845. He had a brother who lost his life in the revolution. Elizabeth Lindsay was the daughter of William Lindsay, who was born near Lancaster, Penn., and died at her husband's Ohio home in 1836. Samuel Kariger was born in Knox county, Ohio, March 22, 1821, the youngest of six children. March 3, 1847, he was married to Mary Ann Benz, who was born in Germany in 1830, and came to Allen county in 1836. Mrs. Kariger died June 24, 1873, leaving four children: Catherine, Mary E., Elsie A., and John. Mr. Kariger, being the oldest settler in his part of the township, and an honorable citizen, is highly esteemed. In politics he is a democrat, and for twenty-six years he has been a member of the Presbyterian church at Fort Wayne.

Among the industrious men who began their labors here prior to 1840, should be mentioned Lucas More. This early settler of Allen county was born in Lehigh county, Penn., September 11, 1816. His father, Henry More, was born in Pennsylvania in 1787, was a soldier of the war of 1812, and died in Whitley county in the eighty-ninth year of his age. His wife, Mary Smith, died in her seventy-sixth year, in 1878. They had eleven children, of whom the oldest, and one of the three living, is Lucas More. He came to Allen county in 1837, and lived in Fort Wayne until 1843, when he settled upon the farm in Washington township which he now owns. In 1843 he was married, September 5th, to Magdelena Gunder, who was born in France, September 12, 1821. They have four children: Melinda, William, Lavinia J. and Stephen. Mr. More cast his first presidential vote for W. H. Harrison, and has been an earnest republican. His occupation is farming, and he is quite successful. He is one of the worthiest of the pioneers who have done so much to develop the county, and having made his own way in life, has the esteem and good-will of all.

John C. Pfeiffer, one of the leading and most wealthy farmers of Allen county, was born July 27, 1821, to Christopher and Catherine Pfeiffer, natives of Germany, who emigrated to the United States in 1832, and settled at Buffalo, N. Y. Eight years later they came to Fort Wayne, and the remainder of their lives was spent here. Mr. Pfeiffer came to Allen county at nineteen years of age, and remained at home until twenty-seven, when he settled where he now lives, three miles from the city, about 1855. Here he has a fertile farm of 240 acres well improved and of great value, which is the reward of his industrious career. He was married in 1849, to Margaret Bosler, a native of Germany, and they have five children: Charles, Carrie, Sophia, Edward and Abbie. He is a republican in politics, and he and wife are members of the English Lutheran church.

Frederick W. Gieseking, a well-to-do farmer of Washington township, was born in Lake township, November 9, 1845, the second of three children of Diedrich William Gieseking. His father, a native of Prussia, born August 13, 1817, after two years' service in the Prussian army emigrated, reaching New York July 10, 1841. He came on to Allen county and found employment with Charles Zigens, of Eel River township, and was married April 5, 1843, to Mary Jokey, a native of Germany, who died November 10, 1876. By untiring industry he became the owner of an estate of 940 acres in this county. Subsequently he became the owner of a farm of 252 acres in Washington township. Frederick W. was educated in the public schools and the commercial college. He began farming for himself in 1881 on the same place which his father purchased in 1868, and has a well-improved farm of 160 acres, three and a half miles northwest of Fort Wayne. He was married in 1881 to Louisa Rose, who was born in Washington township, March 15, 1861, and they have two children: Mary L., born January 10, 1884, and Clarence F., born December 20, 1887. Mr. Gieseking is a member of the English Lutheran church, and in politics is a democrat.

Frederick Kammeyer, a leading farmer of Washington township, residing on section 30, was born in Germany, September 19, 1840, son of Frederick and Wilhelmina (Brenning) Kammeyer. The family came to Allen county in 1845, and here the father died two weeks after their arrival. The mother died in 1880. Mr. Kammeyer, the youngest of his father's children, was educated at the Lutheran schools of Fort Wayne. He settled where he now lives in 1868, and here owns 100 acres of well improved land, with improvements valued at $6,000. He was married in 1868 to Miss Caroline Bode, who was born in Germany in 1845, and came to Allen county about 1856. They have five children: Sophia, Henrietta, Minnie, Lizzie and Matilda. A son, Frederick, died at two years of age. Politically Mr. Kammeyer was formerly a republican, and cast his first presidential vote for Abraham Lincoln, but for many years he has been a democrat, and manifests much interest in the political affairs of the day. By trade he is a machinist, and for five years, from 1863 to 1868, was in the employ of the Pennsylvania railway company, in the Fort Wayne shops. He and family are members of the Lutheran church.

William Bleke, a prominent farmer of Washington township, was born in Prussia, October 23, 1842. His parents, Charles and Mary

(Gieseking) Bleke, were natives of Germany, and died in Allen county. William, the eldest of their two children living, came with them to Allen county in 1846. He was educated at the German Lutheran schools. In 1866 he settled where he now lives, three and a half miles from the city, upon a fine farm of over 200 acres. He is a successful farmer, enterprising and business-like, and is a stockholder and director of the Leo gravel road. He is a member of St. Paul's Lutheran church, and in politics democratic. In 1866 Mr. Bleke was married to Sarah Rupp, a native of Ohio, and they have five children, Charles, born in 1867; Frederick, born in 1870; William, born in 1876; John, born in 1878, and Augusta, born in 1875.

John A. Houser, a successful and prominent farmer of Washington township, residing just north of the city limits of Fort Wayne, was born in Bavaria, Germany. He accompanied his parents, George and Christina Houser, to America in 1844, when he was about seven years old. The family first resided at New York city, where the father died a few years later. In 1852 Mr. Houser with his widowed mother and two brothers came to Allen county, and settled in Washington township. October 23, 1861, he enlisted in Company D, Nineteenth United States infantry, and served three years; after the battle of Stone River he was transferred to Company A of the same regiment. He was in the battles of Shiloh, Corinth, Crab Orchard, Jackson, Stone River and Hoover's Gap. He was married October 24, 1865, to Miss Catharine, daughter of George Snider. She died June 9, 1883, leaving six children: George A., Mary C., Katie, Clara, Christina R. and John A. On May 9, 1888, he was married to Catharine E. Prentiss. Mr. and Mrs. Houser are members of the Roman Catholic church. He is a member of the Catholic Knights of America, has served as captain of St. Bernard's branch, No. 103, four years, and is now captain of St. John's branch. He is also a member of St. Joseph's society and the G. A. R.

Alfred Daugharty, an honored veteran of the war of the rebellion, and now the efficient trustee of Washington township, was born in Stark county, Ohio, May 9, 1840, son of James and Rebecca (Keck) Daugharty, natives of Pennsylvania. His father died in Ohio in 1841, where the mother is now living. In his youth he worked four years at the trade of blacksmith, but in 1861 came to Allen county, and in August of that year enlisted in Company D, of that gallant and famous Indiana regiment, the Forty-fourth. In its conspicuous service he did a noble part. He was in the battle of Fort Donelson, and in the famous engagement at Pittsburg Landing, where his regiment stood like an iron wall against the advancing and triumphant rebel forces on the first day, he was one of the many who fell seriously wounded. His wound was so grave that it was necessary to amputate a leg. His sacrifice to the cause of the nation is one that commends him to the grateful esteem of his fellow citizens. He was honorably discharged from the service June, 1864, and has ever since been a resident of the city. He has been variously engaged, always winning in every position the confidence and esteem of those with whom he was associated. For six years he was in the employ of the Fort Wayne, Jackson & Saginaw, now Lake Shore, railway. Subsequently, he was connected with the Fort Wayne post-office for nine years. In politics he is a republican, and though living in a democratic township, he was elected township trustee in 1886 by sixteen majority, and in 1888 was re-elected by a majority of fifty-five, although the same township gave sixty-two majority for the national ticket of the opposition. This is a notable testimonial to his worth and the esteem in which he is held by his neighbors. He is a comrade of the G. A. R., and in January, 1889, was installed as commander of Sion S. Bass post, No. 40. Mr. Daugharty was married July 3, 1864, to Martha E. Johnston, who was born in Greene county, Ind., in 1844. They have three children: Ulysses E., Nellie May, and Walter W. He and wife are members of the Methodist Episcopal church.

Thomas H. Fleming, of Washington township, was born in County Longford, Ireland, May 12, 1843. He is the son of James Fleming, born May 4, 1804, and his wife, Elizabeth Hysop, born in 1806, both of whom reside in Ireland. Of their ten children, four are living, of whom Mr. Fleming is the next to oldest. He was educated in Ireland, and in 1864 emigrated to Canada, but after two years in Ontario, came to Fort Wayne and was for fourteen years in the employ of Hoffman Brothers, five years with N. G. Olds & Sons, and two years with the New York, Chicago and St. Louis railroad company. In 1885, he removed to his well-improved farm, four miles north of the city. He has made his own way in life and has been quite successful and is esteemed as an honorable and upright man. He is a Mason of Summit City lodge, No. 170. In 1888, he was elected justice of the peace. Mr. Fleming was married June 14, 1868, to Frances Gibson, born in Ohio, August 14, 1845, and they have two children, Elizabeth Alice, born in 1869, and Josie Maud, born in 1878. He and wife are members of the Episcopal church.

Nelson Leonard, a prominent citizen of Washington township, comes from one of the earliest pioneer families of Indiana. His father, Thomas Leonard, was born in Pennsylvania in 1784, and emigrated to Indiana in 1803, becoming one of the pioneer school-teachers. His father served under Washington, and was a descendant of one of seven brothers who emigrated from England to the Carolinas about the middle of the last century. Thomas married Anna Rathburn, born in New York in 1786. He died in Delaware county in 1843, and she died two years later in Henry county. Of their five children living Nelson Leonard, born in Henry county, May 12, 1825, is the fourth. He was raised on a farm and obtained his education at the subscription schools. In 1845 he began work for himself, and in 1847 engaged in brickmaking at Muncie, whither he removed his family in 1854. In 1864 he engaged in farming, and in 1873 came to Allen county, and made his home in Washington township, where he has since been engaged in brickmaking. He has a pleasant home two miles from the court-house, and still owns his Delaware county farm. He is an enterprising man, one of the projectors, stockholders and directors of the Leo gravel road; is a republican in politics, a member of the Methodist church, and of the Odd Fellows since 1851. March 18, 1847, he was married to Drusilla Llewellyn, a native of West Virginia, and they have five children, Hannah J., Mary A., Mattie, Wilmer and Elma.

David McKay, of Washington township, is secretary and manager of the Brookside Farm company, of Fort Wayne, and one of the most prominent horsemen of the state. He was born at Hurkledale, Annan, Scotland, October 9, 1849. His father, David McKay, a Scotch farmer, was the fourth in line of the name of David, and the son of the subject is the sixth of that name, making six generations of the same name. All the ancestors were noted horse breeders, the McKay family being horsemen as far back as 1745. Mr. McKay was reared on the farm in Scotland and given a collegiate education. For several years he bred horses on the home farm in Scotland, which comprises 345 acres, of which he owns a portion, and in 1878 he came to America and settled near Rockford, Ill. A few months later he went to Chicago, where he was engaged two years in importing stock from Scotland. Removing to Arlington Heights, twenty-two miles from Chicago, he conducted a stock farm and imported for two years. In 1884 he came to Fort Wayne, and in company with J. H. Bass organized the Brookside Farm company, which has one of the largest and finest stock farms in the northwest. The company makes a specialty of importing and breeding Galoway cattle and Clydesdale horses, and their claim to the finest herd of Galoway cattle in America has never been disputed. Mr. McKay was married on October 7, 1884, to Ellen Sharp Roddick, a native of Scotland, and to their union three children have been born.

Matthew Furguson, a leading farmer of Washington township, was born at Greensburg, Penn., December 17, 1827. His father, John Furguson, was born in Pennsylvania in 1801, and died at St. Mary's, Ohio, in 1859, having moved to Ohio from Pennsylvania in 1833. His mother, whose maiden name was Henrietta Perkins, died at Delphos, Ohio, in 1873. Mr. Furguson is the only one living of six children born. In 1833, he removed with his parents, to Bellefontaine, Ohio, and in 1839, removed to St. Mary's. He was raised on the farm partly and obtained a common school education. In early life he worked at the carpenter's trade for some two years. In 1862, he enlisted in Company G, Eighty-first regiment, at Lima, Ohio, and served for one year, being mustered out at the close of the Vicksburg campaign, in 1863, as second lieutenant. He was engaged for some time in the saw-mill business. In 1870, he removed to Delphos, Ohio, and for many years, he was connected with the Delphos Wheel company, and for twelve years, was the purchasing agent, and a stockholder from the organization of the company, in 1871, until 1887. In 1883, he bought what is known as the Shultz farm of 180 acres, three miles north of the court-house, and in March, 1885, removed to it. He was married in 1857, to Susan L. Nopson, who was born near Syracuse, N. Y. They have nine children:

Henrietta, Mary J., Walter, John, Lucy, Grace, Matthew A., Anna and Augusta. He is a member of Hope lodge, F. & A. M., at Delphos, Ohio.

John Waters, an early settler in Washington township, was born in Pennsylvania, September 23, 1818. His parents, Elias and Mary (Clapper) Waters, were natives of Pennsylvania. They removed to Allen county and settled in Washington township in 1834, coming here from Ohio, where the family had resided for several years, having emigrated there from Pennsylvania in 1820. In 1833, the year before the coming of the family, the father came here and secured a home. He died in Allen county, and the mother also. John Waters is the oldest of four children living of these parents. Beginning with the coming of his parents, Mr. Waters has been a resident of Washington township ever since, and his many years here, and his numerous estimable traits of character, have made him a host of friends. He has prospered in financial matters, and now has a beautiful farm, substantially improved, and altogether owns 505 acres of valuable land. He cast his first presidential vote for William Henry Harrison, and since the organization of the republican party has affiliated with it. Mr. Waters was married in 1845, to Sarah Ann Ervin, a native of Pennsylvania. She died April 20, 1886. Five children were born to this union: Mary L., Elias A., John S., Sarah A. and James W. By the marriages of these children Mr. Waters has twenty-four grand-children.

Among the early settlers of St. Joseph township a conspicuous figure was Christian Parker, who was elected justice in 1834, county commissioner in 1839, and in 1844 as the whig candidate, representative in the state legislature, to which he was sent for four successive terms. He was born in Preble county, Ohio, September 11, 1807, of English ancestors. His grandfather, Amariah Parker, fled from Cornwall to escape impressment into the British army, and settled near Boston in 1761. He and his three brothers assisted in the revolutionary struggle, one of them falling at Bunker Hill, as a lieutenant-colonel. After the war, Amariah removed to New Jersey and married Tamar Munson, and lost all his fortune by the depreciation of continental money. His son, Jacob Parker, was left an orphan at thirteen, without home, and he was bound out to a blacksmith at New York. Escaping from harsh treatment he reached Fort Washington, Ohio, and enlisted under Gen. Wayne, and fought at the battle of the Maumee, August 20, 1794, receiving a wound there. After his discharge he settled near Middleton, Ohio, married Mary Loy, and settled in 1801 in Preble county. Christian Parker was the son of this soldier under Wayne. He cut his way from Fort Wayne into the St. Joseph township forests in October, 1833, and before the following February had a cabin built on section 20. He brought with him his wife, Rachel, daughter of Henry Cassell, of Preble county, born August 1, 1807, in Virginia. They were married June 18, 1829, and had the following children: Samuel C., born April 24, 1830; Francis A. C., December 21, 1831; Harriet (deceased),

August 22, 1833; Julia A. (died May 8, 1868), August 7, 1835; Jacob H. (deceased), July 17, 1837; Allen H. (deceased), April 9, 1839; Caroline, May 10, 1841; Henry C. (deceased April 20, 1875), February 4, 1844; Maria (deceased), January 14, 1846; Oliver P., October 13, 1848; Mary E. (deceased), January 21, 1851; Winfield S. (deceased), July 19, 1853. Mrs. Parker died February 4, 1879, and Christian Parker passed away August 24, 1888. Their son, Oliver P., was born on the St. Joseph township homestead, and there raised, receiving the common school education of those days. He now owns 160 acres of the old farm, a beautiful and productive tract of land. In 1868 Mr. Parker was married to Fanny Fike, born in 1844, by whom he had three children, two of whom are living, Ulysses Grant and Estella H. On December 24, 1876, Mr. Parker was married to Kitty Lischy, a native of Kosciusko county, born April 18, 1857, and they have two children, Mabel F. R. and Pansy D.

Uriah Notestine, well-known as a pioneer of Allen county, is one of a family who have done good service in clearing away the forests and bringing about the splendid agricultural development of the region. He was born in Fairfield county, Ohio, January 6, 1815, one of fifteen children of Jacob and Barbara A. (Gunder) Notestine. The family is of German origin, each of Mr. Notestine's grandparents having been born in Germany. In 1830 the family came to Fort Wayne, reaching there July 14. There they remained until the spring of 1834, when they moved and settled on the banks of the St. Joseph in Cedar Creek township. Here the parents died, and were buried in a spot of the ground purchased of the government by William Gunder, brother-in-law of Jacob Notestine, who bought the land of the former. Uriah Notestine began work in this state as a day laborer, with his father, who took the contract for digging the race for the old Rudisill mill. He also worked on the dam, and he and his brother scored the timber for that pioneer mill. Mr. Notestine's advantages for education were slight, but he attended school a few terms in Ohio and one term in the old log school-house that stood on the site of the Allen county jail. In the spring of 1834 Mr. Notestine made a trip from Fort Wayne to Darke county, Ohio, 120 miles through the woods on horseback, to obtain a deed to the first land he bought. In 1835 he carried the mail for the first time from Fort Wayne to White Pigeon, a distance of sixty miles, and four days were occupied by the trip. In all the adventures of the early days he was a conspicuous figure, but he prospered also as a farmer, and came to own a good farm of 100 acres. Among the relics of olden times in his possession is a food-adze made in Virginia in 1785, which belonged to his mother's father. February 12, 1838, he was married to Melinda Bowen, who died in March, 1839, in the twentieth year of her age. November 12, 1841, he was married to Maria L. Royce, born May 22, 1823, and they had six children, of whom James A., Aaron S., Eliza Ann, and Matilda E. are living. Mr. Notestine and wife are members of the United Presbyterian church. Politically he was a democrat, having voted for Jackson for president, but in 1884 became identified with the prohibition party. He served as constable of St. Joseph about four years, under Justices Sivitts, Cook, Royce and Eby.

One of the earliest German settlers of Adams township was Philip Brueck, who emigrated to America and settled there in the woods in 1833, buying eighty acres of land, upon which he and his family made them a home. Two years later, however, they removed to St. Joseph township, where his son, Moritz Brueck, became a prominent farmer. The latter was born in Franckenau, Germany, December 11, 1824, and passed his youth among the frontier scenes of Allen county. Deprived of the advantages of schools he taught himself to read and write and became an intelligent and wide-awake citizen. He and an elder brother cleared the homestead in St. Joseph township, and made a fine farm out of the wild land. At the time of his death he owned 360 acres of valuble land, mostly in cultivation, and good buildings. He was one of the leading citizens, and was noted for his honesty and industry. He was married October 21, 1847, to Martha Elizabeth Trier, daughter of John H. and Christina Trier, well-known pioneers of Adams township, who emigrated in 1835, and settled on eighty acres, and though poor at first, prospered, and left a good farm of 120 acres. Mr. and Mrs. Brueck had the following children: Anna C., born February 24, 1850; John H., born March 1, 1853; Adam, born March 5, 1855; Catharine E., born October 7, 1857; Christian M., born November 9, 1860; Heinrich V., born November 4, 1863; Paul W., born March 19, 1867; Jacob P., born April 5, 1872. Mrs. Brueck was born in Germany, November 16, 1829. She is a member of the Lutheran church, as was her husband, with all the members of the family, and is highly esteemed by all.

John H. Bruick, one of the progressive and enterprising farmers of the township of St. Joseph, is a native of the county. He was born March 1, 1853, the son of Moritz and Martha E. (Trier) Bruick. He was raised upon the farm of his estimable parents and received a common school education. He is one of the leaders among the younger citizens of the township, and has a fine farm of 140 acres of fertile land, well under cultivation, and supplied with a comfortable residence and good barns. He was married in 1877 to Louisa Donnenfelser, and their union was blessed by the birth of five children, of whom three are living: Clara, Otto and Paul. Mrs. Bruick was born in 1858. She and her husband are members of the German Lutheran church, and are highly esteemed.

Of the third generation of his family in Allen county, George L. Ashley, of St. Joseph township, is entitled to be called one of the pioneer boys of the county. His father, George Hale Ashley, a native of Greene county, N. Y., born June 14, 1814, married Esther Linzey, who was born in New York city, January 18, 1815. The father was an intelligent, well educated man. . In 1836 he emigrated to the west, looking for a new home, and came to Indiana with his father, John

Ashley, and his mother, and bought a half section of the wild land in Washington township. This they settled upon, built them a cabin, and there worked at clearing and improving for seven years. In 1844 George H. Ashley went to Maumee township, with the intention of building a grist-mill on the Maumee river. He erected the frame work of the building, when he discovered that the damming of the stream would not be allowed, and he then abandoned the project. He settled there, however, and bought more wild land, and made of it a farm, adding it to his original purchase until he owned 256 acres. In 1864 he bought 160 acres in St. Joseph township, which he improved with good buildings, and made this his home until his death, August 7, 1868. He was a leading citizen wherever he lived, and while in Maumee township served a number of years as justice and as trustee. He and wife were devoted members of the Methodist Episcopal church, of which he was a local preacher. His wife, who shared the hardships of his pioneer life, died February 18, 1879. Their son, George L. Ashley, was born in Maumee township, February 2, 1853, and received his education at the district school and at the Methodist college at Fort Wayne. Adopting farming as his vocation, he has followed that successfully. In 1875 he was married to Josephine, daughter of Silas Darling, born March 8, 1857. She died January 17, 1879, leaving one child, Charles, born March 11, 1877. February 17, 1881, he was married to Adessa, daughter of Jeremiah and Margaret (Stoner) Miller, born June 6, 1861. They have four children: Oliver, born March 29, 1882; Oscar J., March 5, 1885; George S., February 7, 1887; Josie M., February 14, 1889. Mr. Ashley and wife are members of the Methodist Episcopal church. He has a fine farm of 74½ acres.

Alfred M. Taylor, of St. Joseph township, has passed through an eventful and busy life, and is now widely known as one of the worthy and deserving old citizens of Allen county. He was born May 25, 1817, in Orleans county, Vt. His parents, Gideon M. and Phœbe (Walbridge) Taylor, removed with their family to Genesee county, N. Y., twelve years later, where Alfred grew to manhood, and received the education which the common schools of those days afforded. At the age of twenty-one he started out for himself, and first made a trip to New Orleans. He remained in the south four years, following boating and tending wood-yard, and overseeing a cotton plantation, and then went to Wisconsin, going into the mining district and driving team and farming for one year. Returning to New York he resumed farming there, and his father dying soon afterward, he was left in charge of the farm and family. He and his brother bought the farm, and subsequently he obtained entire control of the homestead of 250 acres. February 18, 1846, he was married to Mary V. Pond, who was born in New Hampshire, July 11, 1822, a well-read and intelligent lady. They remained on the homestead for ten years, and then removed to Illinois, where they lived four years. January 5, 1860, he settled on the farm where he now lives and which he had traded for without inspection in

1856. It was then all woods, and he and family moved into a little log cabin and began clearing it. As the result of his untiring industry he now has a fine farm of 160 acres. Mr. Taylor and wife are members of the Baptist church at Fort Wayne. He is a veteran Odd Fellow and has been a charter member of the following lodges: Oakfield lodge, No. 188, of Prospect Hill, N. Y.; New Haven lodge, No. 256, and Harlan lodge, No. 331. He is also a member of Summit City encampment. He was formerly a Mason. Mr. Taylor and wife are highly esteemed by their neighbors, indeed, by all who know them, which was evidenced by the fact that when the post-office was established under the administration of President Grant, all were in favor of putting it into the hands of Mr. and Mrs. Taylor. Appointed in 1869, they held the office sixteen years. On the election of Cleveland they resigned, but on the urgent request of the community they consented to hold it longer, and Mrs. Taylor was appointed, the office being moved and the name changed to Thurman. Mr. Taylor cast his first vote for W. H. Harrison, and since the organization of the republican party has voted for all of its presidential candidates.

George Shordon, a well-known farmer of St. Joseph township, was born in Springfield township, this county, October 12, 1839. Beginning with the pioneer days, he has grown with the development of the county, and has been an eye-witness of its marvelous development. He was reared to manhood at the home of his parents, Stephen and Catherine (Kieffer) Shordon, and received the education given in the pioneer school-houses. Appreciating its short-comings, he has bestowed upon all his children as good an education as he could obtain for them, and three are now teachers in the public schools. In July, 1862, he was married to Martha Bowers, by whom he had three children: Lilly D., Howard and Ethel. In the same year of his marriage he left the comforts of home to enlist in Company D, Eighty-eighth Indiana infantry, and served faithfully until peace came. He was with his regiment in all its engagements except Chickamauga, being then sick; he was with Sherman in the march to the sea, and received an honorable discharge at Indianapolis in 1865. On his return home, his father deeded him eighty acres of wild land, upon which he built a cabin and began the work of clearing. By industrious perseverance, he now has a handsome, well cultivated farm of 120 acres, with good and substantial buildings.

William Shordon, a son of the above named Stephen and Catherine Shordon, was born in Springfield township, July 3, 1848. Coming with the family to St. Joseph township, he settled where he now lives at the age of four or five years. Here he grew to manhood and received the education obtainable in those days, and remained with his parents until they removed to Fort Wayne. Adopting farming as his vocation, he followed it successfully, and now has a fine farm of ninety acres, upon which he lives, in St. Joseph township, as finely improved as any in the township, and 120 acres in Milan township. In addition to agriculture, he takes much interest in stock-raising, and gives particular attention to the breeding of Norman horses and Shropshire sheep. He is generally recognized as a valuable and prominent citizen, and has been for ten years the treasurer of the Maumee avenue turnpike. Mr. Shordon was married in 1869 to Senora Black, born June, 1851, daughter of John T. Black, elsewhere mentioned. She is a member of the Catholic church, to which Mr. Shordon also belongs.

A familiar name in Washington and St. Joseph townships, is that of Christian F. Rose, one of the early settlers and esteemed old people. He was born in Germany, May 28, 1812, the son of Frederick and Christina Rose. His father dying, he had after twelve years of age to care for the family, and his early years were toilsome. April 28, 1838, he left his native land, borrowing the money to pay his passage, and after arriving at Cincinnati worked there at $15 per month for the money to pay back the cost of his passage. After about two years in Cincinnati he came on foot to Indiana and found employment at Fort Wayne in digging on the canal. After one summer of this he found employment with Mr. Hubble for two years, and for one year with Hugh McCulloch. By economy he saved enough from his earnings by 1843, to buy eighty acres of timber land in Washington township. In 1844, he was married to Mary Schumaker, and they settled on the land in a log cabin, and began the tedious and toilsome work of clearing. The woods were so dense that he and his bride in going to their cabin from Fort Wayne, driving an ox-team, lost their way. They prospered, but in 1853, the wife died at the age of forty-one years, leaving two children: one, a son, died at the age of twenty-six, and the daughter married Frederick Blake. In 1854 Mr. Rose married Christina Brinckman, born in 1829, by whom he had eight children: Christian H., Frederick, Henry, Theodore, Louisa, Mina, one who died in infancy, and William who died in 1888. In 1871 Mr. Rose and family removed to St. Joseph township, settling where he now lives. He has a fine farm of 153 acres, with a two-story brick dwelling, and a large bank barn. He and wife are members of the German Lutheran church, and are highly thought of.

Christian H. Rose, eldest son of the above, now occupies the honored position of trustee of St. Joseph township. He was born in Washington township, November 10, 1856. His childhood was spent in that township, his residence in St. Joseph township beginning with the removal of the family there. May 11, 1882, he was married to Anna, daughter of Charles and Anna Moellering, and they have three sons: Theodore, born April 16, 1883; Henry, January 25, 1886; Frederick, January 1, 1888. Mrs. Rose was born in October, 1864. Mr. Rose being the eldest son in the family of his parents, much of the work of pioneer days fell upon him, and he is to be credited with much of the good results. In the spring of 1888, he was nominated by the democratic party for trustee of St. Joseph township, and elected by thirty-eight majority, the highest ever received by a candidate for that office. His administration has already added one brick school-house of the best model to the school facilities, and he is a competent and faithful officer.

In the fall of 1840, Peter and Elizabeth (Black) Parker, the husband a native of Ohio and the wife of Virginia, came to St. Joseph township from Ohio, and settled in the woods on an eighty-acre tract of land. They brought with them their son, James D. Parker, born March 30, of the same year, who is now one of the leading citizens of the township. The family settled in a little log cabin and entered heartily upon the work of clearing away the forest and tilling the soil. Industrious and intelligent, the father prospered in his affairs, and came to own a fine farm of 200 acres. He and wife were devoted members of the Lutheran church, and politically he was a staunch democrat. Being widely known as a worthy citizen he was twice chosen to serve as county commissioner, and his integrity and faithfulness in this position were never questioned. James D. Parker was reared in the pioneer home, and was busily occupied in youth with the labors of farm life. In 1860 he was married to Sophronia, daughter of Daniel Eby, born in 1840. They had three children: Anna E., Charles and Nina. Subsequent to the death of his first wife, Mr. Parker was married to Lovina, daughter of William and Sarah Wackard, by whom he has two children: William E. and Joseph R. Mrs. Parker, who was born February 15, 1858, is a member of the Grace Reformed church. Mr. Parker is a member of the Methodist Episcopal church. In 1863 Mr. Parker enlisted in Company E, One Hundred and Forty-second Indiana infantry, and served faithfully until the close of the war. He now owns forty-eight acres of the old homestead and is a worthy citizen.

During the year 1840 Frederick Meyer, sr., emigrated from Germany to America, and coming directly to Fort Wayne, found employment on the Wabash & Erie canal. He was born November 21, 1813, the son of Christian and Christina Meyer, both natives of Germany. By economy Mr. Meyer was soon able to send to Germany for his wife, Christina Dinkes, to whom he had been married in 1839, and buy a little farm of forty acres in the woods. There they made their home in a round-pole cabin, and began a life of patient endeavor, which resulted in their owning a good farm of 120 acres, in St. Joseph township, well improved. In 1887 the wife died at the age of seventy-six, leaving six children living, out of seven born: Frederick, Henry, John, Mary, Charles and William. Mr. Meyer, sr., is a member of the Lutheran church, as was his wife. He is generally known and highly esteemed throughout the country. John Myers, son of the above, was born in St. Joseph township, March 26, 1847. Though only a boy at the time, he enlisted in 1864, in Company F, One Hundred and Forty-second Indiana infantry, under Capt. Robert Swan, and served faithfully until the war was over. He was honorably discharged at Indianapolis, in 1865. After the war he traveled extensively through the west for about eight years, going twice to California. Finally, in 1877, he settled down, and was married to Sophia, daughter of Frederick Bullerman, and born in 1853. They have had five children, of whom two are living: Anna A. and Louisa. He and wife are members of the Lutheran church. He is a highly respected citizen, and has been successful financially, having a good farm of 100 acres.

Fred A. Meyer, a son of the above named Fred and Christina Meyer, was born in Prussia, April 14, 1840. His introduction to this country was at the age of three years, and being raised by his parents at their pioneer home he experienced all the trials and privations of a frontier life. At twenty years of age, he started out for himself, hiring as a farm hand, and continued to be engaged in this way until 1863, when he had accumulated enough to buy the eighty acres of land where he now has his home. It was then covered with dense forest, but by steady labor, every day, and many a night, he made of this a pleasant and fertile farm. This necessary toil, however, from the days of childhood, deprived him of those educational advantages that are now common. In 1869 Mr. Meyer was married to Caroline Mengensen, and they had six children, of whom four survive: Charles, Christina, Sophia and Caroline. Mrs. Meyer was born in 1846. She and her husband are faithful members of the Lutheran church. Mr. Meyer now has a good farm of 100 acres, in St. Joseph township, improved with substantial buildings.

Among the early settlers of the county, of English origin, one of the most prominent is Adam Jeffries, who was born in England, July 12, 1822, the son of Daniel and Susannah Jeffries. In his native land he received a good schooling until thirteen years of age, when he entered the law office of John W. Wall, of Devizes, Wilts, England, as copying and engrossing clerk. There he was engaged until past twenty years of age, and such proficiency did he attain in penmanship that when a congratulatory address was to be prepared for the queen upon the occasion of her escape from assassination at the hands of Edwin Oxford, young Jeffries was selected to do the work. In 1843, he emigrated to America, and his twenty-first birthday occurred while he was at sea. His voyage occupied eight weeks, and he remained one week in New York city and another week on the Hudson river, before he came to Allen county. He made his home first in Eel River township, where his parents had previously settled on a tract of forty acres. Here young Jeffries worked on the farm in summer and taught school in winter. After he had taught five terms, his father was badly crippled by the falling of a tree upon him, and Adam had to take charge of the farm. He followed agriculture up to 1874, when he retired from participation in the farm work. His life has been one of struggle and successful persistence. When he came to this country he had saved only $50 from his wages as clerk, having received only $3 a week as his highest wages. He accumulated property, and came to own 307 acres of land. He remained on this farm until 1874, when he sold out and removed to Texas. Thirteen months later they returned to Indiana, and until 1882, lived at Fort Wayne, moving then to St. Joseph township, where they now live. Mr. Jeffries was married April 13, 1848, to Rebecca, daughter of John and Elizabeth

(Johnson) Ashley, early settlers from Connecticut. Mrs. Jeffries was born June 24, 1817, and was at the time of her marriage the widow of Aaron Bixby. She and husband and children are members of the Methodist Episcopal church. Mr. and Mrs. Jeffries had five children, one of whom died at the age of four years and another in 1884, leaving three living: Mary, Ethel and Sarah R.

Julius Young, who came to Allen county in 1843, is one of the industrious settlers coming from Germany, who have done so much to develop the county. He was born in that land December 25, 1829, the son of Frederick and Dorothea Young, and came to America with an uncle, when only fourteen years of age. Coming into a strange land, unable to speak a word of English, his trials were many and he had to live at first on wages that amounted to only $4 per month. About 1858 he purchased on time forty acres of wild land, in St. Joseph township, and built a little log hut, to which in 1860, he took a wife, Sarah Bretteny, who shared his toil and pleasures. In 1862, Mr. Young enlisted in the Eleventh Indiana battery, and served with it until it was discharged, when he enlisted in the Eighteenth battery and served until the close of the war. His service was gallant and faithful, during which he incurred disabilities for which he receives the small pension of $6 a month. He was honorably discharged at Indianapolis in 1865, and returned to his home. His perseverance as a farmer has been rewarded by a handsome farm of 120 fertile acres, well improved, and he enjoys the respect and good-will of all who know of his early struggles and his deserved success. Mr. Young and wife are members of the United Brethren church, of which he is a trustee. He has four children: Sarah, William, Julius and Frederick.

John H. F. B. Meyer, a prosperous young farmer of St. Joseph township, is a son of one of the early German settlers, John Meyer, who came to this county with his parents in 1844, at the age of twelve years, and located in this township, where the family settled on eighty acres of woodland. John Meyer married Sophia Luhman, and by this union had six children, of whom five are living: Henry, Frederica, Mary, Dora, J. H. F. B. and Fred. The father was a true pioneer, who toiled long and faithfully to carve a home out of the wild-wood for his family. When he settled he first worked five years upon rented land, and then bought eighty acres, which he cleared and occupied until his death. He came to own 247 acres of farming land. He and wife were members of the Lutheran church, and were highly respected by all. John, their son, was raised on the homestead, and received a good education in the public and parochial schools. May 2, 1886, he was married to Katie Goegline, and they have a pleasant home on the farm of eighty acres which Mr. Meyer owns and cultivates.

When three years old, Henry Young, now a leading farmer of St. Joseph township, was brought here by his parents, Henry and Louisa (Blume) Young, and introduced to the scenes of pioneer life. He was born November 11, 1842, in Ohio. His father being a cripple, Henry found it necessary as soon as he was old enough, to stay at home and attend to the farm, thereby losing all opportunities for attendance on school, but he is by no means lacking in practical acquirements, and has a good education obtained by his own efforts. In 1863 he purchased eighty acres of land in the woods, which he has made into a good farm, and added to until he now owns 295 acres of fertile and valuable land, handsomely kept and provided with a commodious two-story brick dwelling and good barn. In 1864 he was married to Louisa Sheffer, who was born April 26, 1842, and they have had ten children, of whom eight are living: John H., Mary, William, Christina, Lizzie, Christian, Anna and Clara. About two years after his marriage he embarked in saw-milling in connection with agriculture, and followed the milling business about eleven years. He and wife are members of the Lutheran church, in which he has held an official position for eighteen or twenty years.

Anton F. Kohlmeier was born in Prussia, December 23, 1831, the son of Christian F. and Sophia L. Kohlmeier. With his family he came to America when about fourteen years of age, and first made his home at Fort Wayne, where he remained four years. His father then purchased seventy-two acres of the canal lands in Washington township, a tract then entirely wooded, upon which they cleared a little spot to erect a cabin upon, and there began the career of persevering industry, which was rewarded at last by the possession of a beautiful and rich farm. Being engaged in this labor nearly all the time, Mr. Kohlmeier had no leisure for school, but the education he has obtained is the result of his own natural aptness and home study. When he was sixteen years old he took a position with B. W. Oakley as a general chore boy, at Fort Wayne, and a year later became a clerk, a position he held for seven years, and received a salary of $4 per month. After the close of this service he returned to the farm of his father and remained there until 1858. In the latter year he was married to Sophia, widow of Anton Sleinkemper. He and wife are members of the Lutheran church, and he has been a warden of his church for twenty-two years. He has prospered in life and now has 160 acres of land in cultivation, with good buildings, in St. Joseph township, and a house and lot in Fort Wayne.

Frederick Bleke, one of the progressive farmers in the valley of the St. Joseph, is a son of the worthy old settlers, Charles Bleke and his wife, Mary Gieseking, who came to Allen county in 1846, and bought 260 acres of land, mostly unimproved, upon which they lived until their death. These parents had four children, of whom only two representatives are living. They, like their parents, are prominent in the affairs of their townships, and highly esteemed by all. Frederick Bleke was born in Germany, March 21, 1845, and was raised from the age of one year on the homestead in this county. He remained with his parents until twenty-eight years old, when he started out for himself, and was given by his father as a reward for his faithful help, the old homestead. This farm of 260 acres, now in his possession, is one of the handsomest and best improved in St. Joseph township, and is supplied with good and comfortable buildings. In the Lutheran church to which he and family belong he is prominent, and among the people of the township he is highly regarded. He holds the honorable position of president of the Fort Wayne and Leo gravel road. Mr. Bleke was married May 23, 1873, to Mary, daughter of C. F. Rose, and six children have been born to them, of whom three survive: Amelia, Louisa and Amanda. Mrs. Bleke was born in Allen county, May 31, 1849.

Frederick Bullerman, now a substantial citizen of St Joseph township, came from Germany at the age of twenty-two years, and found his first employment in New York state, where he worked upon a farm for two years. He then came to Allen county and settled in Adams township, where he leased ninety-two acres of land densely wooded, which he began to clear. Mr. Bullerman was born in Germany, September 7, 1822, son of Frederick and Sophia Bullerman, who followed him to this country two years after his arrival. In his native land he was educated in German, but his education in the English language was obtained by his own exertions. After Mr. Bullerman had toiled six years on the farm he leased, he managed to save enough from his hard earnings to make a payment on the farm he now occupies, which he purchased at that time. Here he renewed the toil of clearing, now cheered and encouraged by his wife, Maria Schrader, to whom he was married August 4, 1849. Mr. Bullerman began as a poor man, but he now has a fine farm of 120 acres, substantially improved, and enjoys the merited respect of his neighbors. He and wife are members of the Lutheran church. They have had ten children, of whom seven are living: Henry, now commissioner of Allen county, Fred, William, George, Christian, Sophia, Mary, Maria, Mina and Anna. Mrs. Bullerman was born April 8, 1825.

Among the leading settlers in 1846 were Martin and Anna Maria (Koester) Schaick, who settled upon forty acres of unimproved land. With them came their son, Christian Schaick, now a well-known citizen of the township, who was born at Wittenberg, Germany, July 29, 1839. About one year after the arrival of the family, the father died, and the oldest son having left home, the care of the family speedily fell upon Christian, who faithfully performed the duty which was thus imposed upon him. On this account his early life was toilsome and he was deprived of educational advantages. August 29, 1862, he enlisted in Company D, Forty-eighth Indiana, and served at the front, gallantly and faithfully, with the exception of six months on furlough on account of illness, until he was discharged at Washington, May 30, 1865. Returning to this county he began clearing forty acres he had purchased while in the service, and renewed the experiences of pioneer life. March 30, 1867, he was married to Elizabeth Griffith, born January 3, 1845, daughter of James and Margaret (Comfort) Griffith, natives of Pennsylvania. They were early settlers at Pickaway, near Columbus, Ohio, where the father worked as a carpenter until 1855, when they removed to Adams county, Ind., settling upon forty acres which they cleared. Four or five years later they came to Allen county and settled at Williamsport where he was postmaster during the war. Subsequently, he removed to Fort Wayne and remained there until his wife died, when he returned to Williamsport, where he now lives. Mrs. and Mrs. Schaick have had nine children, of whom eight are living: Margaret, George, Anna, Jacob, Mary, John, William and Louisa. He and wife are members of the English Lutheran church, and he was formerly a member of Sion S. Bass post, G. A. R., at Ft. Wayne. Mr. Schaick now has a good farm of eighty acres, well improved, in St. Joseph township.

Prominent among the respected old German residents of the county is Christian Koester, sr., who was born in Germany, November 11, 1813, son of Kordt and Mary (Stoppenhagen) Koester. He grew to manhood in his native state, and in 1846 emigrated to America. He came to Fort Wayne in the same year, and worked on the canal a year and a half. He continued to be engaged in employment of that nature for several years, and in 1853 embarked in the lime and stone business at Fort Wayne. In this he continued for sixteen years, and did well at his business. In 1879 he bought the farm on which he now lives, and moved upon it, retiring from business life. This handsome place of 151½ acres with two-story brick dwelling and good barn he deeded to his son Christian. He was married in 1853 to Minnie Stellhorn, and they have had six children, of whom Christian is the only survivor. He and wife are devoted members of the German Lutheran church. Christian Koester, jr., was born at Fort Wayne, December 30, 1857. He received a good common school education and attended Concordia college four years. He remained in Fort Wayne until 1880, when he was married April 29, to Mary, daughter of John F. and Mary Gerke, when he removed to the farm above mentioned. Mrs. Koester was born December 5, 1861. They have three children, Minnie, Emma and Frederick. He and wife are members of the German Lutheran church, and are highly regarded by all who know them. He is a thorough-going young farmer, and besides his home, owns a good frame dwelling and barn.

In 1847, there came to Fort Wayne, Henry E. Antrup, son of Herman and Catherine Antrup, who has done his share in the development of the county. The parents came to America in 1838, and settled in New York. Henry E. Antrup, now a respected citizen of St. Joseph township, was born in Prussia, March 27, 1827. His parents being poor, he was compelled by circumstances, to earn his own support from the age of thirteen. On coming to Fort Wayne, he was first employed as a boatman on the canal, and this was his occupation for four years. During this time he acquired some town property, which soon appreciated in value so that when he sold it he was able with the proceeds, to buy 160 acres of land, upon which he now lives. It was nearly all in woods at the time, and the task of clearing it and preparing it for tillage busily occupied him for a considerable period. He has prospered in life, and the ninety-one acres he still holds is well kept and provided with buildings. In 1849, he was married to Harriet Ashley, daughter of John and Diana (Potter) Ashley, and born in 1833. To them seven children were born, of whom two are living: Charles E. and Henrietta. Mr. Antrup has been a prominent citizen, was supervisor of the roads in an early day, and is an important member of the republican party. He has of late years been raising fruit for the market, with success, and making a specialty of breeding Shropshire sheep. He and wife are faithful members of the Presbyterian church, of which he has been elder for fourteen years.

Louis Juergens, a respected farmer of St. Joseph township, was born at Fort Wayne, July 26, 1848. His parents, Henry and Wilhelmina (Bode) Juergens, were natives of Germany, who came to America in 1848, and made their home for two years in Fort Wayne. At the end of that period, they removed to a farm of forty acres, partly cleared, and ten years later moved to the farm which was their subsequent residence. Louis was reared on the farm and as his parents were then poor, had little school advantages. In 1874, he was married to Louisa Busche, who was born in 1852, and to this union were born eight children, all now living: Wilhelmina, Ernst, Henry, August, Louis, Arthur and Adolph. Mr. Juergens has served one year as constable, then resigning the office, and has held the office of road supervisor one year. During the rebellion, he patriotically tendered his services to the government, but was rejected by the recruiting officers on account of his youth and size. He and his father and brother began in this county poor, but their energy and industry have made them prosperous, and none are more highly esteemed. He has a valuable farm of 125 acres, well improved, with a good residence and large and commodious barn.

John P. Lahmeyer, a native of Allen county, and a prominent citizen of St. Joseph township, was born in Adams township, December 22, 1848. His parents, Frederick and Dora Lahmeyer, were early settlers there. He was raised to manhood in Adams township, receiving a good common school education. He served an apprenticeship as a carpenter, and thus became able to construct his own buildings. In 1875 he was married to Martha Trier, who was born September, 1853, and this union was blessed with three children, John, Katie and Mary. Previous to his marriage, his father, with whom he had remained and worked on the farm until he was twenty-six years old, rewarded his assistance by giving him the farm on which he now lives, 100 acres of fine land, well kept and provided with substantial buildings, worthy of the progressive region in which he lives. Mr. and Mrs. Lahmeyer are members of the Lutheran church, of which he has served as a trustee about five years.

William Waltke, one of the industrious natives of Prussia who have prospered in this county in spite of discouraging circumstances, was born July 2, 1826. At the age of one year he was left an orphan by the death of his father, and grew up almost without a home. In

Prussia he received some education in German, and after coming to this country he acquired some knowledge of the English language. In 1849 he immigrated and landed at New York on the 7th of August. As he put his foot on the soil of the new land where he intended some way to buy him a little farm and be independent, he had but $5 in his pocket and this was not enough to pay his passage to Fort Wayne, his destination. He worked for about six weeks to obtain enough to pay his fare, and then came to Fort Wayne, where he obtained employment as a tanner. This he was engaged in for seven years, and he then found employment at marble cutting, which busied him sixteen years. Out of his wages he saved enough besides supporting his family to buy fifty-one acres in St. Joseph township where he now lives, and has a handsome home. In 1851 he was married to Hannah Gerke, who was born in 1832, and twelve children were born to them, of whom seven are living: George, Christian, Dora, William, John, Lizzie, and Sophia. He and wife are members of the Lutheran church.

In 1849 Friedrich Vollmer, now a prominent farmer of St. Joseph township, arrived in Fort Wayne from Germany, in search of a new home in the strange land. He had with him on his arrival but 50 cents, which he in deference to the patriotism of his adopted country, spent in celebrating the fourth of July. Mr. Vollmer was born in Germany, January 15, 1824, son of Henry and Sophia Vollmer. He received a good education in his native language, and after coming to America speedily acquired a general knowledge of English. He remained in Fort Wayne but a short time and then went to Crawfordsville, Ind., where he found work in railroad construction about three months at 75 cents per day. All his savings were lost through sickness, and then he went to Indianapolis, where he worked on a railroad three or four years, and managed to save $108, with which he made a payment upon the land he now owns in St. Joseph township. In 1853, he was married to Sophia Zuba, who died in the same year, and he then married Sophia Meyer, who was born December 31, 1829. Their union was blessed with nine children, six of whom survive: Frederick, William, Louis, Sophia, Mina and Lisetta. The next year after his marriage he went upon his farm and began the work of clearing. His years of toil are now rewarded by the possession of a good farm of eighty acres, and two houses and lots in Fort Wayne.

Henry C. W. Meyer, a prosperous farmer of Allen county, was born in Hanover, Germany, August 12, 1828, son of Henry and Elizabeth Meyer. The father dying when Henry was ten years of age, the latter was compelled by these adverse circumstances at the age of fourteen to seek his own fortune. By hard work and perseverance he accumulated the little sum of $25, and to this there was added $40 from the estate of his brother. With this capital he came to America, starting April 15, 1849. On reaching Fort Wayne he was in debt $2.25 for his passage, an amount he borrowed to secure his clothes from the transportation agents. He found employment as a boatman on the canal until

D. N. Foster

1854, meanwhile having bought seventy-six acres, which he paid for out of his wages. In 1854 he was married to Engel Gerke, and he and wife went upon their little farm, then mainly woods, which they have increased by wise foresight and patient industry to landed possessions of 246 acres, adorned with handsome and substantial buildings. Mrs. Meyer was born in December, 1831. She and her husband are members of the German Lutheran church. To their union three children have been born: Frederick G., Louis W. and Mary E.

James M. Fletter, a venerable and highly esteemed citizen of St. Joseph township, was born in Franklin county, Penn., January 10, 1813. His grandfather, a native of Germany, came to this country with a Hessian regiment during the revolutionary war. His company was taken prisoners by the continental army, and after this ancestor of the Fletter family had learned the ways of the country, and understood the struggle for independence, he became a citizen of America and determined to cast his lot with the colonies. His son Jacob was born in Pennsylvania, and became a soldier of the United States in the war of 1812, serving as a captain during the expedition into Canada. He was married to Lydia Crunkleson, and early in the twenties, with his family removed to Ohio and became a pioneer, clearing land and there raising his family. He was a potter by trade, at which he was also occupied. His emigration to Ohio was caused by losing all his property in Pennsylvania on account of becoming surety for others, a favor which his kindly nature could not refuse. Previously he served as sheriff of Franklin county, and was a prominent and influential citizen. He lived in Ohio until the death of his wife. Their son, James M. Fletter, came to Fort Wayne on a prospecting tour in 1831, and worked there a short time as a tailor, but the country being then very new, he returned to Ohio and there worked at his trade. May 26, 1836, he was married to Jane, daughter of Zephaniah Bell, a devoted member of the Methodist church and a good and true wife. She died March 6, 1846, and one of her three children survives, Caroline, widow of William Andrews, living in California. September 10, 1846, Mr. Fletter was married to Ann, daughter of Abraham Grose. She was born August 4, 1822, and died June 26, 1860. Six children were born to this marriage, of whom four survive, Sarah, John, Eliza and William. In 1849 Mr. Fletter removed with his family to St. Joseph township, upon the eighty acres which is now his home farm, and began life anew in a little log cabin. This was his first introduction to farming, but he was successful, and subsequently erected a good dwelling, which he had the misfortune to lose by fire in 1883. November 18, 1860, he was married to Charity, daughter of Moses Embre, and widow of Roscoe Bennett. Mr. Fletter, about 1864, sold his property and rented his farm and moved to Fort Wayne and remained two years, and in 1883 he embarked in general merchandise in Milan township, and then in Perry township, but less than three years later he returned to his farm, which has been his residence with these exceptions. Mrs. Fletter was born January 7, 1814, and is a member of the

United Brethren church, to which Mr. Fletter also belongs, although he was formerly a Methodist.

In 1850, among the settlers in Milan township, from beyond the sea, were the family of David and Mary A. (Devaux) Evard, natives of Switzerland. James Evard, one of the children of these worthy parents, was born in Switzerland, September 6, 1838. He received a good education, both in the old country and in Allen county. He was a blacksmith by trade, and by industry and economy earned enough at the anvil to purchase his fertile farm of eighty acres in St. Joseph township, which is his present abode. In 1861 he was one of the earliest to enlist for the preservation of the union, and enlisted in Company A, Thirtieth Indiana regiment, and served with his company until the battle of Shiloh, where he was wounded in the left foot so as to totally disable him for active service. He is now the recipient of a pension from the government in recognition of his sacrifices for his adopted country. In 1864 Mr. Evard was married to Corilla Bowers, who was born in 1840, and they have had five children, of whom four are living: Nellie, Jennie, Hortense and Lillie. The one who died was at the time of decease a teacher in the public schools. Her death was caused by fire, which caught in her clothing. Mr. Evard served one term as constable, and is a member of the Grand Army post at New Haven. He and wife are members of the Grace Reformed church at Fort Wayne.

The Goeglein family of St. Joseph township, prominent in the history of Allen county, are descendants of Daniel and Magdalena (Reuter) Goeglein, of German birth, who emigrated from Bavaria in 1838, and came to Meigs county, Ohio, where they remained until 1865, when they removed to St. Joseph township and resided there until their death. Daniel Goeglein was a worthy, pious and honorable man. While in the old country he was a soldier for a time in the Napoleonic war, and was wounded, and before he was able to return to the service, Napoleon had met his Waterloo. He came to this country a poor man, but by industry accumulated enough to make easy his declining years. He and wife are both members of the Lutheran church, and were the organizers of the church at Pomeroy, Ohio. He died at the age of seventy-six years.

Jacob Goeglein, son of the above, was born in Germany, January 25, 1827. Coming with his parents to America, he helped in their labors in clearing their eighty-acre farm in Ohio. He received a good common school education, and is one of the intelligent and progressive people of the county. Widely known throughout the county as an enterprising and valuable citizen, he was chosen to serve two terms in the responsible position of county commissioner. Though beginning life with no advantages he has prospered through the exercise of his own talents, and now has a good farm of 220 acres, with commodious buildings. Politically he is, with the other members of the family, a firm supporter of the democratic party. Mr. Goeglein was married in Ohio, to Otilia Mess, who was born in November, 1827, and they have had thirteen children, of whom eleven are living: John, Jacob, Mary,

Henry, Abraham, Sophia, Elizabeth, William, Christian, Valentine and Daniel. Mrs. Goeglein and her husband are members of the Lutheran church.

George Goeglein, another son of Daniel and Magdalena, was born in Meigs county, Ohio, June 21, 1840. He was reared in his native state to the age of twenty-five, and then came to St. Joseph township, where his abode has since been. In 1867 he began a general merchandise business which he has continued to the present with considerable success in connection with farming. In 1872, he purchased the farm upon which he now resides, which includes sixty-seven acres and is handsomely improved. He has been chosen by the people of his township to serve as trustee four years, a well appreciated mark of confidence and esteem. During President Arthur's administration he was appointed postmaster at the office which was created and named Goeglein, and since that time has served in this position to the entire satisfaction of the public. Mr. Goeglein was married in 1861 to Catherine Sauvage, and this union has been blessed with twelve children, of whom there are nine living: John H., George A., Valentine J., Katie M., Sophia, William, Gottlieb, Frederick and Theodore. Mrs. Goeglein was born in 1839. She and her husband are members of the German Lutheran church.

John Goeglein, son of the above mentioned Jacob Goeglein, was born in Meigs county, Ohio, June 1, 1848. Coming to Indiana with his parents, his residence in St. Joseph township began at the age of fifteen years. He was the eldest child, and much of the labor of the early days in this county fell upon him, so that he was deprived of extended educational advantages. At the age of twenty-one years he started out for himself as the manager of a threshing machine, a business he followed for about six years, in connection with farming. He now occupies his pleasant farm of eighty acres and has a comfortable home. May 4, 1871, he was married to Anna Bruick, who was born in 1850, and they have had eight children, of whom seven are living: Christian, Martin, Louis, Herman, Edward, Elizabeth and Anna. Immediately after his marriage he rented the farm of J. H. Bass in St. Joseph township, which he occupied five years, then going upon the farm he now lives upon. He and wife are members of the Lutheran church.

Charles Kramer, an enterprising and highly respected citizen of St. Joseph township, was born in Lucas county, Ohio, May 28, 1846. While a small child, he was brought by his parents, Frederick and Minnie Kramer, to Washington township, where he experienced much of the hard work and privations incident to the early days when all who were old enough to assist in any way found it necessary to take part in the arduous duties of clearing and brush burning. His early schooling was necessarily limited, but he is nevertheless an intelligent and wide-awake citizen. At the age of twenty-one he started out for himself, and worked four years as a farm hand. At about twenty-five years' of age he found employment in railroading, and was so employed for ten years, doing well in this business, and reaching the position of engineer. During seven years as engineer he did not have an accident, a record of which he is well proud. His savings while railroading enabled to make payment on a farm of 130 acres, which he sold seven years later and purchased a farm of 247 acres, which he now occupies. Upon this he has a fine house and barn, and all in all has one of the best farms in the township. Mr. Kramer was married June 6, 1872, to Sophia Rose, who was born December 22, 1845, and they have had nine children, of whom seven are living: Charles, Emma, Eliza, Adolph, Henry, Amanda and Arthur. He and his wife are members of the German Lutheran church.

Prominent among the German pioneers of the county is Henry Wiegmann, who was born in Germany, October 31, 1834. Left an orphan at the age of two years, his progress in the world was attended with much privation and hardship. Receiving a fair German education in the old country, he left there in 1851, and came to America. He remained one year in New York state, and then came to Fort Wayne. Here he was first employed by Judge Hanna, at $6, and worked for a year and a half at that wages. He then began to work upon the railroad, and was employed for two years carrying water and whisky to the men, both beverages being then considered indispensable. After that he hired out to Hon. F. P. Randall to make rails and clear land, upon the farm which he now occupies. Being economical and frugal he saved enough from his small earnings to start a small store in Fort Wayne, being the third German to open a grocery in the city. Two years later he went to Missouri and worked one year, and then after another short stay in Allen county, went to the gold fields of California, and remained four years and four months. Returning with some of the California gold, he re-established himself in the grocery business at Fort Wayne, and by fair dealing built up a good trade which remained with him while he was in business. He was a successful and prosperous business man. In 1877 he retired from business and removed to his farm of 110 acres one mile northeast of the city on the Maumee avenue turnpike. This is a beautiful and well improved place, and besides it he owns a business building and dwelling in the city. Mr. Wiegmann was married in 1863, to Sophia Waltermarth, and their union was blessed with nine children: Henry, Lizza, Sophia, Friedrich, Karl, Wilhelm, Caroline, Friedrich and Ludwig. He and wife are members of the German Lutheran church.

An industrious farmer of St. Joseph township, and prominent among the French settlers, is August Sarazin, who was born in France May 2, 1838, the son of Silas and Sophia Sarazin. Until fourteen years of age he remained in his native land, and being poor had there no chance to obtain an education. Since coming to America he has by his own efforts learned somewhat of English, and is an intelligent and capable citizen. His life has been devoted to industry, and he has prospered as a farmer, and though starting in this country without any advantages, now has a good farm of eighty-three acres, advantageously situated, fertile and well-cultivated, and he has his home in a comfortable two-story brick dwelling house. Mr. Sarazin was married in 1866 to Josephine Bobay, who was born in 1842, and this union has been blessed with eleven children, of whom ten are living: Julius, John, Pauline, August, Mary, Frederick, Louisa, Charles, Sophia and Sylvester. Mr. Sarazin and wife are members of the Catholic church.

Louis Lacroix, one of the leading French settlers of St. Joseph township, was born in France, August 17, 1832, son of Xavier and Frances Lacroix. When about thirteen years of age he came to the United States and first settled in New York state, where he began work as a laborer at $3 per month, and remained with the same employer five years, his wages being gradually raised to $13 per month. After a residence of seven years in New York, at the age of twenty years he returned to France for the family of his father, the latter having come to this country with him. His mother was then dead, but he brought over his four sisters, which cost him $400 of his hard-earned money. They remained in New York one summer and then came to Perry township, Allen county, where he first leased land, and then bought forty acres of woodland which he cleared. He then leased another forty and cleared that, and then bought eighty acres in St. Joseph township. After clearing this he bought sixty acres, of which he cleared thirteen, and then cleared forty acres for Mr. Griffith. In 1852 he began working on the Wabash railroad, and the following year worked for T. P. Anderson in getting out ties, and in general work. He then was employed on a canal boat two years to obtain money to pay for the land he and his father had bought. During the early years of his toilsome career he gained his education; in France he was in school five winters, in this country he obtained two months schooling by paying six cents per week, and after he was twenty he worked for his board while attending school two months. He now has a valuable farm of 140 acres, with good buildings, and is a leading citizen. In 1861 he was married to Mary Martin, who was born December, 1843, and of their eleven children eight are living: Francis, Clara, Julia, Joseph, Louis, Sophia, Charles and Henry. He and wife are members of the Catholic church. Mrs. Lacroix is a daughter of Charles J. and Frances J. Martin, natives of France, who came to this country in 1842, and two years later settled in Perry township. Her father was accidentally drowned in the St. Joseph river at the bridge just north of Fort Wayne, February 19, 1861. He was driving home from the city, the other occupants of his wagon being his wife, another lady and a priest. As they drove from the approach the wheels struck the edge of the bridge, which was higher than the approach, and the sudden shock broke one of the tugs. The horses were then unable to hold the wagon on the steep and narrow approach and it ran off into the river. All escaped except Mr. Martin, whose body was not found until five weeks afterward.

Michael Landin, a venerable and respected citizen of St. Joseph township, was born in Germany, June 8, 1808, son of Michael and Magdalena Landin. He was a weaver by trade, but most of his life in this country has been spent in farming. In 1836 he emigrated to America and settled at Buffalo, N. Y., where he remained seventeen years. He then moved to Toledo, Ohio, but six months later he came to this county. After living on rented land ten years he bought 160 acres of new land, which he cleared. He was married in 1832 to Mary M. Fisher, who was born August 7, 1810, and eight children were born to them, of whom six are living: Barbara, Catherine, Jacob, Michael, John and Mary M. He and his wife are prominent members of the Catholic church. He served as trustee of his church several years in Buffalo, and has helped to build four churches. Mr. Landin began in this country with nothing, but he succeeded well and was able to divide 160 acres of valuable farming land between his sons, John and Michael, who are to pay the shares of the other heirs. He is now eighty-one years of age, and his venerable wife, who has shared his toil, is aged seventy-nine.

Michael Landin, jr., son of the above, was born in New York, January 23, 1845. He assisted his father in the work of clearing and farming, and shared the toils of the early days. In 1877 he was married to Mary Ley, who was born in 1855, and to their union has been born five children, of whom four are living: Anna M., William H., Katie, Mary and Edward. He and wife are members of the Catholic church. They are now comfortably situated on a pleasant farm of eighty acres, handsomely improved with good house and barn, and are highly esteemed by all.

John Landin, another son of Michael and Mary M., was born in New York state, February 17, 1847. He also worked with his parents and is now rewarded by possession of a handsome eighty-acre farm. He was married in October, 1876, to Maggie Blinckner, who was born in Ohio, in 1856, and died July 15, 1887. She was a member of the Catholic church. April 10, 1887, he was married to Fannie Raw, who was born April 24, 1864. Mr. Landin and wife are members of the Catholic church and are popular and respected citizens.

Martin Blume, prominent among the young farmers of St. Joseph township, is a son of Martin and Margaret Blume, of this township. The latter Martin Blume, was born in Germany, August 10, 1825, son of Martin and Elizabeth Blume, who emigrated with their family to America about 1835, and settled in Pennsylvania. Four years later they moved to Perry county, Ohio, and ten years later to Hocking county, where they lived until death. The family have done a great work in the clearing of land, Martin Blume, sr., having brought under cultivation a farm of 300 acres, which he purchased in 1860. Martin Blume, jr., the subject of this mention, was born in Hocking county, Ohio, June 2, 1853, and came to Indiana when a small boy and had a share in the pioneer work in which his father engaged. In 1876 he was married to Cecilia Evard, who was born in 1853, and to this union have been born seven children, of whom six are living: Nora, Catherine C., Albert, Charles, Bessie and Eugene. Two years later he bought 157 acres of land of his father for $3,500, $2,000 of which his father gave him, and the remainder he paid. Of this farm he has cleared a considerable portion, and has built upon it a good two-story brick dwelling. He and wife are members of the United Brethren church.

Henry Bohde, an industrious and successful farmer of St. Joseph township, was born in Germany, January 17, 1818, the son of Frederick and Dora Bohde. He was reared in Hanover, and there received his education and learned the trade of a baker, which was his occupation about ten years. He was married in 1848 to Sophia Bohnon, who was born about 1824, and in 1854 he and family came to America. They settled in St. Joseph township, where he rented land for six years. He then bought forty acres of wild land, and was about to clear it when his wife died, in 1860, leaving three children: Henry, jr., Doris and Irma. She was a devoted member of the Lutheran church, and estimable wife, and was sincerely mourned. Mr. Bohde afterward boarded with his brother and began clearing his farm, then untouched by the hand of man, and in October, 1863, he was married to Doris Karnal, and moved into his little log cabin on his farm. Then began a life of sturdy endeavor, which has been rewarded by a handsome and productive farm, increased now to eighty acres, and provided with a comfortable house and roomy barn. Though now seventy years old, Mr. Bohde is still active and in the enjoyment of life. He and his good wife, who was born May 2, 1827, are members of the Lutheran church, and are respected by all. Henry Bohde, jr., who has always made his home with his father, was born in Germany, January 27, 1852. Coming to America at two years of age, he was early thrown into the activities of pioneer life, and his early years were busily occupied with the duties of the farm. He was married in 1881 to Mary, daughter of John and Sophia Meyer, elsewhere mentioned. She was born March 9, 1860. To this union were born four children, three of whom survive: Hannah, Emma and Clara. Mr. Bohde and wife are members of the Lutheran church. He owns forty acres adjoining the old homestead.

Aime Chausse, who has been an industrious and valuable citizen of the county since 1854, was born in Switzerland, December 4, 1828, son of Abraham and Emily (Marchand) Chausse. In his native country he received a good education, and since coming to America has taken time to teach himself the English language in his few leisure moments. He emigrated to America in March, 1849, and first settled in Wayne county, Ohio. Being familiar with both the trades of carpenter and cooper, he followed one or the other, when not farming, and remained in Ohio until 1854, when he came to Milan township, and settled on ninety-eight acres of wild land, which he purchased of F. P. Randall. In the same year he was married to Elise Bueche, who was born in August, 1838. They made their home on this uncultivated tract, where Mr. Chausse cut down the first tree, and worked hard to pay for the land, which he had bought on time. They succeeded well by patient industry, and in a few years had a productive farm adorned with good buildings. In 1869 he sold his farm and bought forty-three acres in St. Joseph township, all of which but five acres, it was necessary for him to clear. He now owns a valuable place of sixty-three acres, well-improved, with a pleasant residence and good barn. He is highly esteemed by his neighbors, and in 1878 he elected justice of the peace, and since then has been continuously elected without opposition. During the years of the Grange organization he was a prominent member and treasurer. He and wife and their family, consisting of four children, John, Edward, Helena and Bertha, are highly esteemed.

Jacob Vonderau, one of the prosperous farmers of St. Joseph township, was born December 8, 1819, the son of Jacob and Barbara Vonderau. In Germany, his native land, he received a good education, and after marriage in this country, through the kindness of his wife, he has become familiar with the English. He emigrated to America in 1842, arriving at New York, July 4th. He first settled in Pennsylvania, and a year later, moved further west to Union county, Ohio, which was his home for thirteen years. At the close of that period he came to this county and settled in Milan township, where he remained twenty years. Afterward he removed to the farm upon which he now lives. He was a tailor by trade in the old country, but he has been quite successful as a farmer. Beginning by renting land for twenty-five years, he then bought eighty acres of unimproved land, to which he subsequently added another eighty, and as he improved in circumstances he bought 120 more, and 168 in Maumee township. He highly deserves, as he generally receives, the appreciative esteem of the people who know him and his industrious career. In 1845 Mr. Vonderau was married to Margaret Kern, and to this union were born eleven children, all of whom are living. Parents and family are members of the Lutheran church.

Herman G. Vonderau, son of the above, was born in Union county, Ohio, February 11, 1855. He came with his parents to Allen county at the age of two years, so that nearly all his life has been spent in this county, where he is highly esteemed, and ranked among the deserving and worthy citizens. In this county he received a good common school education. He was married November 24, 1878, to Catherine Griebel, who was born March 13, 1856, and to this union have been born three children: George, Mary and John. He and wife are members of the Lutheran church. Beginning his career as a farmer, without any assistance from his father, he has succeeded well, and now has a good farm of eighty acres in St. Joseph township.

Louis Gillieron, prominent among the St. Joseph township farmers of Swiss origin, was born in the Alpine republic October 17, 1819. He was raised to manhood in his native land, and there acquired a good education in the French language. In 1859 he was married to Mrs. Mary A. Shaftef, who was also born in Switzerland, in March, 1822

To this union has been born one child, Louis. Mr. Gillieron served in the army of Switzerland thirteen years before coming to America, and afterward served four months in the Union army during the war of the rebellion. Taken sick at the end of that period he was honorably discharged. Though a poor man when he came to this country, he has prospered, through his industrious and economical habits, and now has a good farm of 120 acres, and a comfortable home. He and wife are members of the Lutheran church. His son, Louis, is married to Julia Guke, and they have two children, Louis and Joseph. Both are members of the Lutheran church.

John T. Black, of St. Joseph township, is one of the leading farmers of the county. Though coming to Allen county at a later day than many others, he had already experienced at his former home all the hard work and privations of pioneer life, and his prominent position among the prosperous people of the county is one honestly and laboriously earned. Blessed with such a vigorous constitution that he has never been confined to bed a day by sickness, his life has been busily occupied. His grandfather came from Germany, and his grandmother was of an English family that came to Delaware about 160 years ago. He was born February 22, 1824, in Maryland. On December 20, ten years later, his parents, John and Matilda (Lowe) Black, reached Erie county, Ohio, having traveled to the west with their family and goods in two one-horse emigrant wagons, occupying twenty-six days in the trip. The father brought with him $1,000 in silver, and bought 150 acres of new land bordering on Lake Erie. Here they built a cabin of rough hickory logs for their home, and father and son began the work of clearing. Money being scarce they had to earn what they got by boating wood to Huron. By working continuously almost day and night, the family soon became prosperous, and the father's lands increased in extent and value until they were worth $100,000. This land was divided among the children. The mother, a true and devoted member of the Methodist church, died in May, 1886, at the age of eighty-five years. The father, who in addition to his severe farm work, served as a soldier in the war of 1812, for which he now receives a pension, still retains much of his eyesight and is able to walk without a cane at the age of ninety-eight years. John T. Black obtained his education in subscription schools in Maryland, and in district schools in Ohio. May 23, 1850, he was married to Rachel M., daughter of Wilson and Keturah (Elson) Driver, of Maryland, and soon afterward settled upon the Ohio homestead which fell to him upon the division of his father's lands. Here he remained until 1864, when he removed to St. Joseph township and bought 160 acres, of which he has made a beautiful farm. He also owns eighty acres in Milan township, and a house and lot in Fort Wayne. By his first marriage he had eight children, of whom five are living, Senora, Calvin, William, Marion, May. The mother died in July, 1876. Mr. Black served as trustee in his township in Ohio six years. He has been a member of the Masonic order since 1860.

Among the citizens of St. Joseph township, of German birth, who are comfortably situated and well-to-do, should be mentioned Valentine Lapp. He was born in Germany, December 5, 1827, son of Henry and Eliza Lapp. Growing to manhood in his native land he was there well educated, but since coming to America has not given much attention to the study of English. He came to America in 1858, without money, but coming to Allen county, he worked out a short time and then bought the farm where he now lives, and he has been able to pay for it, and add many more acres. First buying forty acres, he built there his log cabin, which has now given way to a commodious two-story dwelling. He soon bought another forty and cleared that also, and now has in all 100 acres in St. Joseph township and eighty in Milan. His sturdy and estimable traits of character have won for the respect of all his neighbors. October 9, 1858, he was married to Elizabeth Amren, who was born December 26, 1832, and they have five children: Elizabeth, Henry, Martin, John and Valentine. Parents and children are members of the Lutheran church, of which Mr. Lapp has been one of the trustees for about three years.

Conrad Dannenfelser, a worthy and prosperous citizen of St. Joseph township, now deceased, was born in Germany, October 9, 1819, son of Henry D. Dannenfelser. He emigrated to America in 1849, and first made his home at Cleveland, Ohio, where he remained nine years. He then came to Allen county, and in 1867, moved upon the farm which was his home until his death. Mr. Dannenfelser came to this country a poor man, but was very successful in his enterprises, industrious and economical, and left an estate of 243 acres of well cultivated land. He died June 11, 1889, sincerely mourned by a great number of friends and acquaintances. He was one of the leading citizens of the township. On December 2, 1842, he was married to Dorothea Rhienfahrt, by whom he had five children, one of whom, Mary, survives, and after the death of this wife, he was married in 1855, to Catherine Mack, who was born December 5, 1826. She survives him with four of their five children, Louisa, Ernst, Alfred and George. Mrs. Dannenfelser, as was her husband, is a member of the Lutheran church.

In the southwest corner of St. Joseph township is the homestead of Joseph W. Challenger, now deceased, who was one of the worthiest citizens of the township. Joseph W. Challenger was born in Twerton, near Bath, England, January 17, 1823, and came to America with his parents when a mere child, and settled in Massachusetts. Leaving home at the age of ten years on account of ill-treatment at the hands of his father he was thrown upon the world, practically an orphan, and deprived of all educational advantages. By his own efforts, however, he became well educated in practical matters. Becoming a machinist he was presently a master of his trade and for a considerable time served as a locomotive engineer. He invested his savings in thirty acres of land one and a half miles from the court-house on the Maumee avenue road, and cleared this and built upon it a good house and barn, making it a productive and pleasant place. He was married January 8, 1856, to Margaret A. Willower, and to this union two children were born: Frank C. and Edward D. Appreciating the value of the advantages of which he was deprived, he gave his sons a good education, both attending the Fort Wayne commercial college. This worthy gentleman passed away April 16, 1888. The eldest son, Frank C. Challenger, was born December 3, 1856, at Lima, Ohio. He was raised in Fort Wayne, where he received a good education. June 15, 1880, he was married to Adelia Tilbury, daughter of Jarius and Eliza Tilbury. She was born in Fort Wayne, January 22, 1859. She and her husband are members of the Methodist Episcopal church. Their home is at the old farm, and they own besides that place three houses and lots and one vacant lot in the city. Edward D. Challenger, the second son of Joseph W., was born at Zanesville, Ohio, October 14, 1860. Coming to Indiana when a mere child, he grew up at Fort Wayne and there received a good education, including two years at the commercial college. February 18, 1882, he accepted a position as bookkeeper in the boiler shops of the Pennsylvania railroad company, which he has retained until the present, giving satisfaction to the company, and faithfully remaining at his post during all this period, except four days during the last illness of his father. He was married July 10, 1883, to Edith Hutson, daughter of James and Sarah Hutson, and they have one child, Maude, born June 6, 1885. He is an energetic young man, and highly esteemed.

William Wetzel, who was one of the prosperous farmers of St. Joseph township during his lifetime, was born in Germany, in 1817, and died in April, 1888. He remained in his native land until 1848, and in 1846 was married there to Mary Pflaumer, who was born in Germany in 1825. When they emigrated to America, they were without means, except to pay their passage, and after they had spent one night in the strange land, they were absolutely without money, and with two children to support. He borrowed $30 from a friend, and that carried him to Starke county, Ohio, where he began work as a day laborer in a brick yard. The next year he came to DeKalb county, and bought thirty acres of new land. This he cleared, meanwhile working for his living at day's labor. Subsequently he sold this land and bought another forty in DeKalb, which he sold and purchased eighty acres, which he cleared and improved. After remaining there some time, he came to Allen county and purchased 103 acres in St. Joseph township. To his marriage were born four children: William, Elizabeth, John and Henry. Mr. Wetzel was a faithful member of the German Reformed church, and was highly thought of by all who knew him.

Charles Lomas, now deceased, an industrious and popular citizen during his lifetime, was born June 29, 1835, at Manchester, England. He was the son of James and Ann (Ashton) Lomas. He grew to manhood in his native land, and there received a good education, and learned the trade of a moulder, which was his occupation for many years. In 1853, he was married in England, to Elizabeth, daughter of Edward and

Mary (Hopwood) Simpson. She was born May 17, 1835. In the same year they emigrated, and settled first at Brooklyn, N. Y., where they remained eighteen months, then going to Ohio, where they spent one year. Subsequently they remained four months in Kentucky, and then lived in Ohio again for two years. They then came to Fort Wayne, where the father found employment in the J. H. Bass foundry and machine shops, and retained his position for thirteen years. He then bought the farm in St. Joseph township, where his widow now resides; but his life was not long spared for the enjoyment of this new home. Two years after moving there he died November 30, 1878. He was a member of the I. O. O. F., and intelligent and enterprising. Since his death, his widow has made many improvements on the farm and now has a comfortable two-story dwelling and a good barn. To the marriage of Mr. and Mrs. Lomas were born ten children, of whom eight are living: William, Charles, Edward, James, Byron, Martha J., Sarah A., and Mary E.

ABOIT TOWNSHIP.

Near where the canal crossed the Aboit river La Balme and his little force from Kaskaskia and Vincennes encamped in the latter part of 1780, and were surprised and slaughtered by the Indians under Little Turtle. It has been stated that the word "Aboit" is a corruption of the French "Abattoir," or slaughter-house, given on account of that bloody event. But in an early treaty the river is called "*à Bouette*," which is a form of "*à Boitte*," and as a name for the stream signifies "Minnow river." This is undoubtedly the true derivation and meaning of the name. Unlike "à l'Anguille," the early name of Eel river, it was not translated, but was gradually transformed, and is yet often spelled Aboite. In the wilderness here the "Maryland settlement" was established in 1833. The colony, about thirty souls in all, was composed of the families of Enoch Turner, Richard Andrew, William E. Gouty and Richard Clark, all natives of Maryland. These were industrious and enterprising pioneers. The first religious services were held at the house of Mr. Andrew in 1834, by Rev. James Holman, a Methodist minister, and it was the regular place of meeting for a number of years. The same minister married Martin Kelley to Mary, daughter of Mr. Andrew, in 1834, that being the first ceremony of the kind in the township. At the same home the first township election was held in 1836, and Mr. Andrew and Samuel Dunlap were elected justices. There were just about enough voters to form the board and furnish candidates. Enoch Turner donated the ground for a cemetery in 1834, and afterward gave land for a log church which was built in 1842, and used for that purpose and also for a school-house for many years. In the year of this settlement, 1833, Jesse Vermilyea came. He was a prominent man, and when Aboit postoffice was established in 1839 he became the first postmaster, and served a considerable time. During the latter named year he manufactured brick and built the first brick house in the township. He kept a small stock of goods and traded with the Indians, though he did not open a store. The next comers were Lot S. Bayless and Benjamin Rogers, who came early in 1834. In 1848 Bayless built a saw-mill on Aboit river. In 1833, William Hamilton purchased a tract of land, and in after years he amassed a considerable fortune. In 1853 he erected a saw-mill on Aboit river. George Bullard, a prominent citizen, came in November, 1835, and purchased 240 acres on section 13, which he cleared almost without assistance. His energy is revealed in the record by the fact that he built the first hewn log house in 1836, and next year set out the first orchard. In the same year, through his generosity, the first school was taught on his land. Another among the early settlers was Raburn Beeson, who came from Ohio.

Along the Little river, in portions of the townships of Wayne, Aboit and Lafayette, a sunken basin extends for twelve miles, with an average width of three miles, which had been a miasmatic swamp from the earliest settlement until a recent date. Attempts were made to drain it, but the enterprise was too gigantic for any other than specially organized effort. Finally under the drainage law of 1883, a petition was filed to begin proceedings for a thorough drainage system. The drainage commissioners, Surveyor D. M. Allen, W. W. Shoaff and Edward Ely reported on this petition that there were 18,000 acres covered with water so as to be absolutely worthless, 17,000 only available in the dryest seasons, and that other land to the extent of 50,000 acres would be benefited by the drainage proposed. It was proposed to construct forty miles of ditches. The great expense of the work caused many to fear that the cost would exceed the benefit and there was a vigorous contest. The burden which fell upon some land owners was indeed almost crushing. But finally the work was ordered, and Mr. Ely appointed superintendent. The contract was let July 7, 1886, to the Little River Ditching company, consisting of H. C. Paul, C. S. Bash, Joseph Derheimer, F. C. Boltz and S. B. Bond. W. H. Goshorn was the engineer in chief. In June, 1889, the work was practically completed by blasting the ditch through the limestone ledge which was the main barrier to drainage. This immense tract, which was formerly in wet seasons so flooded with water that the track of the Wabash railway was submerged, is now rapidly becoming a beautiful, cultivated prairie, the soil of which is wonderfully fertile.

A son of one of the early settlers just named, William A. Hamilton, was born in Aboit township, December 1, 1835. His father, William Hamilton, first came to Allen county in 1833, from Albany, N. Y. After selecting his land, he returned for his family at Cleveland, Ohio, and brought them to the farm where A. M. Darroch now resides. His wife's maiden name was Joanna Van Huzen. She died May 21, 1875, and his death followed eight days later. They were the parents of four children, three of whom are now living: William A., Mary and Jane A. William A. Hamilton was educated in the common schools, and worked on the farm with his father until twenty-two years of age, when he engaged in agriculture on his own account. He was married April 15, 1858, to Barbara, daughter of John Scott, one of the early settlers of Allen county. They have ten children: Annie, John A., Alice A., George S., Francis W., Wilson A., Lillie B., Henry, Hugh and James.

George Bullard, one of the noted pioneers of the county, was born in St. Lawrence county, N. Y., December 23, 1802. His father, John Bullard, had been a dealer in cattle on a large scale, and a lumberman on the St. Lawrence, and was a man of great business capacity. He was in Ogdensburg when that place was taken by the British in 1814, and lost all his property. He died in December, 1825, and his wife, whose maiden name was Annie Hall, died November 10, 1841. George Bullard, when a boy, was employed for five years by his brothers in their store, and afterward he rented a farm of a brother, and lived upon it until 1823. Then he engaged in the grocery business at Belleville, N. Y., and after three years of that, purchased a salt block in Onondaga county, of a capacity of eighty barrels a week. This he attended to for two years, and was subsequently engaged in the grocery business at Henderson until 1834. In the fall of the latter year he came to Indiana, and purchased 1,100 acres of land in Aboit township, paying $1.25 for government and $2.50 for canal land. November 1, 1835, he arrived with his family, and took possession of the rude shanty he had built. The nearest neighbor west was two miles distant, roads were miserable, without bridges, and the market, Fort Wayne, contained only about 700 inhabitants, with very poor buildings. Mr. Bullard took rank then as one of the leaders, and he has ever since been recognized as a prominent citizen, public-spirited, sociable and generous. He has served the people several times as trustee, and for thirty years officiated as justice of the peace, receiving his first commission from Gov. Wright. He has resided at his present home for fifty-four years, with the exception of eighteen months spent in Fort Wayne, where he purchased property at one time. The faithful partner of his life was Rosamond Dawson, to whom he was married January 12, 1827. She was the daughter of James Dawson, of Henderson, N. Y., and was born October 9, 1802. She lived to the age of eighty-three years, but never used glasses, being able to read a paper by candle-light and thread a needle to the last. She died January 14, 1886. Of the eleven children of Mr. and Mrs. Bullard, four are living. Mr. Bullard is a member of the F. & A. M. lodge, and Fort Wayne chapter, Royal Arch Masons.

Notable among the pioneers of Aboit township are Samuel Cartwright and wife. Samuel Cartwright was born in Rockbridge county, Va., May 10, 1815, son of Charles and Elizabeth (Paxton) Cartwright, natives of Virginia. The father was a farmer by occupation and died in 1832. Mr. Cartwright received a limited education in the common schools of Virginia, and at his father's death managed the farm with the assistance of his brother until twenty-one years of age. He was then engaged as contractor on the Miami canal for about four years, and subsequently came to Indiana and was variously employed until 1845, when he purchased the land on which he now lives, settling in the woods. The farm now consists of 280 acres of land. He was married January 16, 1842, to Miss Lavina Pierce, daughter of Asa Pierce of Aboit township. They are the parents of three children, two of whom are living: Louis A., a resident of Aboit township, and James V., a physician at Paine, Ohio. Mrs. Cartwright is a member of the Methodist Episcopal church, and attended the dedication of the first church of that denomination in Fort Wayne. She taught the first school in Aboit township.

Oehmig Bird, of Aboit township, was born in Fort Wayne, September 11, 1849. His parents, James S. and Matilda (Eick) Bird, were natives of Pennsylvania, who came to Allen county in 1848. The father ran on the first railroad train in the United States. After coming to Indiana, farming was his principal occupation. He died December 3, 1855, and was followed by his widow, April 11, 1868, Mr. Bird worked on the farm until seventeen years of age, when he began to learn the carpenter's and joiner's trade which he followed for about thirteen years. Subsequently he resumed farming and stock-raising, his principal occupation, together with running a threshing machine. He is a worthy and enterprising man, and at present is superintendent of the Holmes gravel road in Aboit township. He was married November 25, 1879, to Elmira, daughter of S. B. Stouder. She was born June 24, 1859. They have had four children, all deceased. Mr. Bird is a member of Sol. D. Bayless lodge, No. 359, F. & A. M., of Fort Wayne, and politically he is a democrat.

John Harper, a prominent citizen of Aboit township, was born in Franklin county, Penn., near Chambersburg, November 16, 1817. He is the son of William and Rachel (Duley) Harper, natives of Pennsylvania. The father, whose occupation was farming and shoemaking, died February 7, 1848. Mr. Harper was educated in the common schools and worked with his father until twenty-one years of age. Then buying a small tract of land he engaged in farming, and seven years later, in 1848, moved to Allen county, Ind. He purchased 200 acres where he now lives, and settled in the woods to develop his present fine farm. He was married April 28, 1842, to Liza Byall, daughter of James Byall, a native of Maryland, who served in the war of 1812, and died in Ohio in 1855. Mr. and Mrs. Harper have had eight children, five of whom are living: Isaiah W., James B., Benjamin F., Eliza and Victoria. Isaiah W. is a farmer and resides near the old homestead. James B., lately deceased, was a prominent attorney, and Benjamin F. is in the same profession at Fort Wayne. Eliza is a clerk in the pension office at Washington, D. C. Politically Mr. Harper is a republican. He cast his first vote for William Henry Harrison in 1840.

John Sprankel, of Aboit township, was born in Pennsylvania, February 19, 1825, the son of Peter and Frances (Bridenbaugh) Sprankel, natives of Pennsylvania. Mr. Sprankel received his education in the common schools of Pennsylvania, and worked on the farm with his father until twenty-two years of age. He was engaged by Hatfield & Son, in their rolling-mill, which was run by water and situated on the Juniata river. After Mr. Sprankel had worked at the mill for about eighteen months, an overflow of the river bursted the furnaces. This caused the discharge of all single men there employed. It was thus that Mr. Sprankel became persuaded to move west. Failing to find work at Pittsburgh or up the Allegheny river at the Great Western iron works, he took a job of chopping wood until spring, and then came west into DeKalb county, Ind., worked for a short time for a cousin, and then returned east to his father. On May 1, 1849, the father and son traveled west through Ohio, Michigan, Illinois and Indiana, by horse and buggy. They traveled in this way over 700 miles, examining lands at various places. They finally purchased the tract of land on which Mr. Sprankel now lives, buying 400 acres. He then engaged in farming and stock-raising, at which he has continued with good success. The farm now consists of 240 acres. Mr. Sprankel is deservedly popular with the community, and he was thrice elected to fill the office of township trustee, the term then being one year. He was married in September, 1849, at Manchester, Ohio, to Susan, daughter of Jacob Sourse. They have three children: Mary F., Josephine and J. C. F. Politically Mr. Sprankel is a staunch republican.

Alfred H. Bates, of Aboit township, was born in Oswego county, N. Y., October 23, 1836, the second of six sons born to Jeremiah and Lucy (Norton) Bates. The grandfather was Ephriam Bates, a native of Massachusetts, who married Melvina Hopkins, of the same state. Both lived to an advanced age. Jeremiah, who was a farmer by occupation, died in April, 1869. His widow died in July, 1884, at the age of eighty-one years. Mr. Bates received his education in New York, in Mexico academy, and worked on the farm with his father until eighteen years of age. October 23, 1854, he came to South Bend, Ind., where he worked as a farm hand for Judge Green for thirteen months. He subsequently lived at Cherry Valley, Ill., Clinton county, Iowa, and Oneida, N. Y. Then he came to Allen county, and purchased the farm on which he now lives. In stock-raising as well as agriculture he has been quite successful. He pays especial attention to breeding Clydesdale and Norman horses, short-horn cattle, Poland China, Cheshire and Chester white swine, all pure bred. Mr. Bates is a member of the Allen county agricultural society, and has been quite successful as an exhibitor. He was married September 29, 1859, to Ann J., the second daughter of Enoch Turner, late of Allen county. She died June 15, 1865, leaving three daughters: Lucy A., Rose E. and Ann J. October 21, 1865, he was married to Sarah J., the third daughter of William and Jane Stirk, of this township, both natives of Pennsylvania. Mrs. Bates' father died July 19, 1884, and her mother, December 8, 1887. Mr. and Mrs. Bates are the parents of three children: Frank M., Eudora and Arthur M. Mrs. Bates is a member of the First Baptist church of Fort Wayne. He is a member of Harmony lodge, No. 19, I. O. O. F.

William H. Reemer, of Aboit township, was born in Fairfield county, Ohio, October 2, 1849, son of John R. and Hannah (Siple) Reemer. The father, a native of New York, was a farmer by occupation, and died in 1850. In 1852, the mother came to Allen county, and settled on the Vermilyea farm, which she left shortly to spend eighteen months in Wayne township, but returning, made the Vermilyea farm her home for nineteen years. Mr. Reemer was educated in the common schools, and worked on the farm with his step-father until eighteen years of age. He has made farming and stock-raising his life occupation. He was married March 25, 1874, to Emily, daughter of George Wells, a native of Fairfield county, Ohio. She was born in 1854. They are the parents of four children: Ada F., Maggie H., Benjamin A., and William.

John N. Corey, of Aboit township, was born in Seneca county, N. Y., January 27, 1816. His father, Benajah Corey, a native of New Jersey, was a millwright by trade, but followed farming also. He died March 4, 1870. Mr. Corey was educated in the common schools and worked on the farm with his father and at the lumber business until nineteen years of age, when he came to Ohio, and for a while worked on a canal. Then he rented a farm for about eight years. Afterward moving to Whitley county, Ind., he purchased a tract of wood land, built a log hut and began clearing. Here he remained until 1855, when he purchased the farm of 161 acres on which he now resides. Mr. Corey gives some attention to stock-raising also, making a specialty of breeding short-horn cattle and Poland China hogs. He was married to Margaret Fulk, May 31, 1836, by whom he had eight children: Martha J., Hester A., William, Lida and Caroline are living; Theodore died March 27, 1864; Louisa died September 5, 1882, and Emma died January 5, 1858. His wife having died March 13, 1864, he was married in 1865 to Mrs. Mary F. Campbell, who had one daughter, Mary E. Campbell. Mrs. Corey is a member of the Free Methodist church. He is a republican in politics and voted for Gen. W. H. Harrison. He is one of the enterprising men of Aboit township and is highly esteemed.

Austin M. Darroch, of Aboit township, was born at Rockville, Park county, Ind., October 27, 1844. He is the son of John and Caroline (Puett) Darroch, both natives of Indiana. The father was a farmer by occupation, and is still living at Morocco, Newton county, Ind. The mother died in 1852. Mr. Darroch was educated in the common schools; he worked at farming until 1862, when he volunteered as a member of Company E, Ninety-ninth Indiana infantry. He served two years and ten months, and was in the following engagements: Vicksburg, Jackson, Miss., Mission Ridge, Resaca, Kenesaw Mountain and Atlanta. At Peach Tree Creek he had one of his fingers shot off. Being honorably discharged June 28, 1865, he returned to Newton county, and again was employed in agriculture. Two years later he bought a farm and engaged in farming and stock-raising, in which he has been, quite successful. Mr. Darroch, on November 11, 1870, was married to Mary, daughter of William Hamilton, a native of New York, and an early settler of Allen county. They are the parents of six children, five of whom survive: John W., Hugh M., Johanna, Caroline and Fanny. Mr. Darroch is a member of Phœnix lodge, No. 101, K. of P., of Fort Wayne, also Sion S. Bass post, G. A. R., of Fort Wayne. Mr. Darroch's prominence as a citizen and as a democrat, led to his election in 1886 as a representative of Allen county in the general assembly of Indiana, and he filled that position with credit to himself and county.

Thomas Covington, a prominent citizen of Aboit township, was born in Plymouth county, Mass., December 18, 1836. His parents, Thomas and Mahala (Holmes) Covington were both natives of Massachusetts, where the father followed agriculture successfully. His death occurred May 17, 1880, and his wife died February 1, 1887. Thomas Covington received a good education in the public schools of his native state, and was engaged in work upon the farm of his parents until he was twenty-one years of age. He then began farming and stock-raising on his own land, and in these pursuits has been quite successful. He was married April 14, 1859, to Adeline Burt, and they have four children, Elizabeth D., Kate M., Thomas E., and Mary L. Mrs. Covington was called away in death May 7, 1886. Mr. Covington is prominent in the councils of his party, the republican, and being an active and popular citizen, he was elected township trustee in 1886, and in 1888 he was given the compliment of re-election. He is a faithful and discreet public officer.

John R. Schoene, of Aboit township, was born in Germany, May 9, 1828, son of Frederick and Margaret (Schaffer) Schoene. In 1834 the father left his native land and sailed for America. Landing at Baltimore, he came to Dayton, Ohio, and was engaged in a distillery for five years. He then purchased a piece of land in Williams county, Ohio, erected a cabin and moved into the woods. Here he followed farming until his death, which occurred in 1865. In that year John R. Schoene moved to Allen county, Ind., settling in Aboit township where he now resides. In farming he has had remarkable success, and has a place of 160 acres of well improved land. He was married May 6, 1852, to Catharine Strausberger, and they have nine children: Julia, Amanda, Rudolph, Walter, Katie, Dorato, William, Henry and Joseph. The family belong to the Lutheran church.

W. J. Esterline, of Aboit township, was born in Clark county, Ohio, November 7, 1841, son of Adam and Elizabeth (Slaybaugh) Esterline. The father, a native of Maryland, was a shoemaker by occupation, and died in 1855; the mother who was born near Gettysburg, Penn., died July 5, 1876. Mr. Esterline received a limited education in the common schools, and worked as a laborer on the farm until eighteen years of age, when he took up the blacksmith's trade, at which he was engaged until 1870. He then began farming and stock-raising, at which he is still successfully engaged. He purchased in 1870, the farm on which he now resides, consisting of 152 acres. He was married to Nancy Jeffries in

1867, and they had one child, Milly, now deceased. Mrs. Esterline died December, 1868, and in 1871 he was married to Ellen McKinley. They have seven children: Walter, Edward, Albert, Arthur, Otis, Frank and Chester. Mr. Esterline served his country in the late rebellion, being a member of Company I, Seventy-first Ohio infantry, and was in the engagement at Pittsburg Landing. Mr. Esterline is a member of the Lutheran church, also of Columbia City lodge, 189, F. & A. M.

Daniel W. Simmers, of Aboit township, was born in Ohio, December 3, 1845, son of Daniel and Maria (Smith) Simmers. The father, a native of Canada, died February 8, 1875, but the mother, a native Virginian, is living in Wells county, Ind. Mr. Simmers at the age of sixteen years, enlisted in Company C, Fifty-first Ohio infantry, and served one year and ten months. He was in all the engagements from Chattanooga to Atlanta. Returning to Ohio, he engaged in farming for about sixteen years, and then embarked in the milling business, at Auburn, Ind. Two years later he moved to Whitley county and engaged in farming and stock-raising, at which he is still engaged. In 1881 he sold his farm in Whitley county, and purchased the one on which he now lives. Mr. Simmers was married on June 3, 1875, to Amanda, daughter of Jonathan Michael, of Allen county. Of their six children, five are living: John U., Charles W., Jewell C., Roscoe T. and Ermel B. Mrs. Simmers is a member of the Methodist Episcopal church, and he is a member of De Kalb lodge, No. 214, F. & A. M.

Henry Eloph, of Aboit township, was born in Fairfield county, Ohio, May 4, 1835. His parents, Nicholas and Frances Eloph, natives of France, came to America in 1833 and died in 1877 and 1867, respectively. Mr. Eloph received a limited education in the common schools of Allen county, and worked with his father on the farm until seventeen years of age. He remained on his father's farm until 1865, when he enlisted in the One Hundred and Fifty-second Indiana volunteers. After serving about seven months, he received an honorable discharge, and resumed farming and stock-raising, at which he continues, making a specialty of breeding Norman horses. He was married April 20, 1862, to Mary, daughter of Joseph Rhodes, a native of Ohio They are the parents of four children, three of whom survive: Mary, Annie and Alice.

LAKE TOWNSHIP.

Lands in this township were occupied in 1834, by James Hinton, John Ross, William Grayless, George Slagle, Samuel Caffrey, James Pringle, Jacob Pearson, and Clement Ryan, and their families. Nearly all settled in the vicinity of the Goshen road or in the northern sections. The Goshen road, which had been surveyed four years previous, was then the only road in the township, and it was not until 1836 that the second, the Yellow river road, was laid out along the south township line. In the same year the county road from Kraco to

Raccoon village, was surveyed. In 1835 John McClure, a native of South Carolina, settled on section 17, and remained twenty years. His son-in-law, Samson Pierson, arrived about the same time. In the spring of 1836, Francis Sweet entered a tract in section 17, but remained in Fort Wayne until 1844. He became one of the prominent citizens and filled all the local offices, serving fifteen years as justice subsequent to 1846. He was the second postmaster, succeeding John Crawford, who was appointed in 1840, for what was known as the Taw-Taw post-office. Mr. Sweet held the position until 1863, acting also, after the establishment of the Pittsburg railroad, as carrier of the mail from the station. In 1836 the newcomers were John Anderson and James W. Watson, who were natives of Virginia, and Joshua Goheen, from Pennsylvania, a man of great enterprise, and John Savage. Other early settlers before 1840, were Joseph Taylor, William Caster, John F. Gerding and Frederick Reed.

On the last Saturday of May, 1837, the first election occurred at the house of John McClure, who was the inspector. Samuel Caffrey and James Pringle were elected justices, and William Caster, constable. In the following winter the first wedding occurred, Mary Mangan to John Savage. In 1849 the first steam saw-mill was erected by the plank road company, and the next year J. L. Peabody built a saw-mill on the Yellow river road near Arcola, which was in operation many years. The first general stores were opened by the proprietors of these mills, by William Thorpe, who had bought the plank road mill in 1850, and by Mr. Peabody in 1866. In an early day Samson Pierson platted a village on the plank road in sections 16 and 17, named Pierson, but it was abandoned. The only village in the township is Arcola, on the Pittsburg, Fort Wayne & Chicago railroad. It was laid out in 1866.

The firm of Jacob Colter & Co., now the most extensive manufacturers of hardwood lumber in Allen county, was formed in 1873. In 1887 their mill was burned, causing a loss of $3,500, but it was rebuilt at once. At Arcola the firm employs fifteen men, and are equipped to saw 8,000 feet per day. They also have mills at Williams Station, Monmouth, Decatur and Maples. The five mills employ seventy men, and produce annually about 12,000,000 feet of lumber. They furnish lumber to the Pennsylvania company, ship to San Francisco, and export a fine grade to Scotland. In 1885, the tile manufactory of Grosjean Brothers, now Grosjean & Barrand, was established, and John Grosjean in 1888 purchased the general stores of Victor Cavalier and William Rockhill. The latter now conducts a general store. James Baxter is the blacksmith and I. W. Herrold and John Blietschau are shoe dealers.

Edward Rockhill was one of the well-known pioneers of Fort Wayne and its vicinity. He came from his native state of New Jersey in 1826, and settling in the woods near the city, at once began clearing away the timber and opening up a farm. He built a double log cabin, doing the principal part of the work himself, using weight poles instead of nails to hold the roof on. The Indians at this time camped in the woods round about, and made frequent visits to the house of Mr. Rockhill in quest of meal and potatoes. One peculiar habit of this pioneer was to inquire if they had money to pay for food; if they said they had he would direct them to a neighbor telling them he had none to spare, if without money he would furnish them with potatoes and meal. He and the Indians were on very intimate terms. They frequently visited Fort Wayne, and while there would spend what money they had for whisky, and becoming thoroughly intoxicated, often would fall by the wayside in the snow or on the ice. Mr. Rockhill in such cases, would carry them into his cabin, and keep them until sober, often saving lives in this way. He followed farming until his death, which occurred in 1848, at his cabin. Of his eight children, the third, William Rockhill, now a leading citizen, was born July 28, 1829, at the old homestead. His educational advantages were of course limited, and he attended only one school term of three months. After the death of his father he and his brother remained upon the farm until 1851, when they came to Lake township and began clearing up a new farm, doing farm work in summer and hunting deer and turkey, and trapping mink, coon, etc., in winter. He lived here two years and then moved upon his mother's place, where he remained until 1872, when he came to Arcola and engaged in general merchandise, also receiving the appointment of postmaster. In this office he served in a very satisfactory manner for fourteen years. He continued in merchandise until September 8, 1888, when he sold his stock of goods in order that he might tear down the house in which he was doing business, and build one on a much larger scale. He now has a handsome two-story brick, 38x60, with a plate glass front. Mr. Rockhill was married in 1853 to Miss Harriet Bellamy. Of their eight children seven are living: Amanda, Oliver, Louise, Ida, Ellen, John and William.

William Goheen, who has been a resident of this township more than half a century, was born in Cumberland county, Penn., March 30, 1830. His parents were Joshua Goheen, a native of Pennsylvania, and his wife Ann (Pee) Goheen, a native of Maryland. They settled in Lake township, September 13, 1836, on the farm which their son above named now occupies. Here the father died April 9, 1866, and the mother October 5, 1878. William Goheen was educated in the country schools, and at the age of eighteen years engaged in farming for himself. He is a prominent citizen and held the position of township trustee during five years and a half. He is a member of the First Baptist church of Eel River, of Wayne lodge, No. 25, F. & A. M., and of the republican party. In 1851 he was married to Mary Petit, and to their union were born four children: John N., Charles M., Alice and Nathaniel. This wife died August 29, 1860. In 1861 he was married to Catherine Hutsell, and they have two children, Ada A. and Perry A. Mrs. Goheen is a member of the Methodist church.

Cornelius Gearin, of Lake township, was born here, May 1, 1843, son of John and Catherine (Shonchron) Gearin, natives of Ireland, who came to Allen county in 1837. The father is a farmer by occupation, and is still living at the advanced age of seventy-seven in Marion county, Ore., Cornelius was educated in the public schools and worked on his father's farm until the breaking out of the late rebellion, when he volunteered with Company L, First Michigan cavalry, and served three years. He participated in the following engagements: Gettysburg, Wilderness, Spottsylvania, Sheridan's raid to Richmond, Petersburg, Winchester, Fisher Hill, Cedar Creek and the battle of the Five Forks, where he received a grape shot wound in the left shoulder. He was sent to Thunderville Station, then to Petersburg, then to Point of Rock hospital, Hampton general hospital at Fortress Monroe, and finally to Detroit, where he received an honorable discharge. He returned to Allen county, but soon afterward went to Oregon, remaining two years, after which he again came to Allen county and engaged in farming and stock-raising, which he has followed up to the present time, with a marked degree of success. He was married to Lucy A., daughter of William and Mary Manning, of Whitley county, October 2, 1869. Mr. and Mrs. Gearin are members of St. Patrick's Catholic church, of Arcola. Politically he is a republican.

John Grosjean, a well-known manufacturer of Lake township, was born September 14, 1851, son of John B. and Mary (Pirson) Grosjean, both natives of France. His father, John B. Grosjean, at the age of fourteen, left France, his native land, and landing at New York, came direct to Fort Wayne. Here he worked for one year on the canal and then engaged in farming, entering land from the government. He married Mary Pirson, a native of France, and both are now living on this old homestead. Their son John received an ordinary education in the common schools, and worked on his father's farm until twenty-one years of age, when he, with two of his brothers, embarked in the saw-milling business near Wallen. They prospered in this business until the mill burned, seven years later, causing a loss of about $3,000. They rebuilt at Wallen, and continued the business until July, 1888, when John Grosjean sold his interest to his brothers. Owing to the great demand for tile in 1882, they engaged in its manufacture in connection with milling. In 1885, they established a branch tile factory at Arcola. Mr. John Grosjean has done the buying and selling in the lumber business and been general manager of the tile factories. September 8, 1888, Mr. Grosjean, in partnership with Joseph Sallier, became owners of a general store at Arcola, purchasing the stocks formerly owned by Victor Cavalier and by William Rockhill. They are at present doing a large business. He was married October 16, 1873, to Mary, daughter of James Hudson, and they have had two children: Edgar and Abbie, the latter deceased. This lady dying February 14, 1880, he was in 1882, married to Mary, daughter of Jacob Cook, and they have one child: Ernest. Mrs. Grosjean is a member of the Methodist Episcopal church. Politically Mr. Grosjean is a republican.

William Tracy, of Lake township, is a son of the pioneers, Thomas and Mary Dugan Tracy, who came to this township at an early day, and had the experiences of old settlers. The Indians frequently put up with them for the night, wolves would howl at the door, and deer were so plenty that some unusually inquisitive ones would occasionally look in at the cabin window. William Tracy died in 1861, but his widow survives at the age of eighty years. Their son, above named, was born at Bristol, Penn., April 16, 1837. He availed himself of the pioneer schools to the extent of a three months' term each year, and worked with his father until he was twenty-five. Since then he has been engaged in railroading, and also farming and stock-raising, and is doing well. He is a member of St. Patrick's church, and politically is a democrat.

Benjamin Jones, a prominent farmer of Lake township, was born November 12, 1819. His father, John Jones, son of Benjamin and Sarah (Cadwallader) Jones, was a native of Montgomery county, Wales, and a weaver by trade; he married Mary, a daughter of Edward and Ann (Evans) Humphreys, of the same county. Grandmother Jones lived to be of great age yet never wore glasses. She was frozen to death at the age of ninety-five. John Jones came to this country in 1841, and settled at Tarrytown, N. Y., where he resided two years. In 1843 he moved to his present home and there died April 10, 1876. His wife passed away August 18, 1855. Benjamin Jones came to the United States in 1839, and at New York city engaged in various occupations for the period of four years. He then came with his father to Lake township. He is one of six children, four of whom survive: Benjamin, Mary, wife of Albert Garrison, of Fort Wayne; Anna, widow of William Darby; John, a mechanic in the Wabash shops at Fort Wayne. The latter served in Company C, Eighty-eighth regiment, which went into action in August, 1862. He served during the remainder of the war, being promoted to sergeant. Benjamin Jones was married May 18, 1872, to Sarah C., daughter of Joseph and Caroline (Ayers) Carroll. She was born June 18, 1844, near Zanesville, and came to Indiana with her parents in 1846. Mr. and Mrs. Jones have one child, Mary A. They have a well improved farm of forty acres, on which is built a good house and barn. He has served as township clerk, supervisor, school director, etc. Politically he is a republican.

George W. Grayless, a leading citizen of Lake township, was born in Alice county, Iowa, November 14, 1848, the son of Charles and Jane Grayless. The father is a farmer by occupation, and is still living. The mother died in California, May 22, 1854. George W. was educated in the common schools of Allen county, and worked on his father's farm until twenty-two years of age, when he began farming for himself, which occupation he has continued to the present time, together with stock-raising. He was married June 18, 1871, to Barbara A., daughter of Nathan and Barbara Smith, of Churubusco, Ind. Their union has been blessed by two children: Cora L. and Warren. Mr. and Mrs. Grayless are members of the Methodist Episcopal church. He is a member of Churubusco lodge, I. O. O. F. Politically he is a republican.

B. S. Butts, a prominent citizen of Lake township, was born April 25, 1825, in Monroe township, Licking county, Ohio. He is the second of ten children of Samuel and Fanny (Bruff) Butts. The father, a native of Virginia, settled in Ohio in 1799, participated in the battle of Tippecanoe under Gen. Harrison and Capt. Jake Baker, and died in 1845, at the age of seventy-four. The mother is, at the advanced age of eighty-five years, in good health and in full possession of her mental faculties, being able to relate many early incidents. Their son, B. S., was educated in the common schools of Ohio, and at the death of his father, began farming for himself, in which occupation he continued. In 1850 he came to Allen county, purchasing the farm on which he now lives, settling in the woods and opening up what is now a very rich farm. He was married September 14, 1846, to Hannah Larimore, and they have had eight children: Sarah (died in 1869), Alonzo, Allen D., William W., A. J., James D., Annie B. and Mary N. They also raised a grandson, Harry B. Young. Mr. and Mrs. Butts are members of the Methodist Episcopal church and he is a member of Wayne lodge, No. 25, F. & A. M.

William W. Butts, son of the above, was born in Lake township, October 16, 1854. He studied in common schools and worked on his father's farm until eighteen years old, when he began work on the railroad, which he continued for three years. Resuming farming in 1877, he moved to Arkansas where he remained one year. Returning to Indiana, he was employed on the railroad two years, and was then engaged in saw-milling for three years. Then he purchased the farm on which he now lives, and has successfully followed farming and stock-raising to the present time. He was married on October 6, 1877, to Allie, daughter of Simon and Mary I. Harshbarger, old settlers of Whitley county, Ind. Her father, born May 23, 1832, served three years in the late rebellion. The mother was born October 22, 1838. Mr. and Mrs. Butts are the parents of two children, both deceased.

George Kronmüller, a prominent and wealthy farmer of Lake township, was born August 1, 1828. His parents, Leonard and Wilhelmina (Shaffer) Kronmüller, were natives of Germany, where the father was a farmer by trade and owner of a large tract of land. They had eleven children, eight of whom are living: John, residing in Wittenberg, Germany; George, Jacob, Gotlieb, residing at Huntington; William, a well-to-do farmer near Huntington; Wilhelmina, and Mary, wife of Gotlieb Kaine, of Peru, Ind. George Kronmüller came to this country in 1852 and after living a few months in Erie county, Penn., he went to Kentucky, and came to Fort Wayne a short time afterward. After spending about eight years as a laborer in a saw-mill he bought the handsome farm on which he now resides, which is well improved and has a large frame residence and a spacious barn. He was married December 28, 1856, to Mary, a daughter of Jacob and Catharine (Sagar) Weller. Her brother, George Weller, now resides in Nebraska. Mr. and Mrs. Kronmüller have six children: Mary, wife of Charles Byer, of Churubusco; George, of Goshen, Ind.; Wilhelmina, wife of William Sutter; John, Catharine, wife of James Butts, of Churubusco; William C., of Goshen. John is associated with his father in cultivating their farm of 120 acres. Mr. and Mrs. Kronmüller are members of the Lutheran church and are active Christian people. Politically he is a democrat, having voted that ticket all his life.

Wilson R. Stirling was born July 26, 1826, son of Samuel and Delilah (Craig) Stirling, natives of Westmoreland county, Penn., who moved to Ohio in 1830, and remained there until their deaths in 1864 and 1868, respectively. Wilson R. Stirling received a common school education, and worked with his father until twenty-two years of age. In 1852 he came to Allen county, and purchased the farm in Lake township, on which he now lives, and engaged in farming and stock-raising, paying especial attention to Durham cattle, Berkshire hogs, and Southdown sheep. His farm consists of 163 acres. He was married November 30, 1848, to Rachel Harrison, who died September 30, 1849. His second marriage, to Cynthia Grayless, took place January 1, 1852, and they had three children: Josiah, Allen and Alfred, all living. This lady died in April, 1857, and he was married October 5, 1857, to Rebecca Vanmeter, by whom he has four children: Florence, Hattie E., John G. and Clara B. Mr. and Mrs. Stirling are members of the Methodist Episcopal church. He is a member of Wayne lodge, No. 25, F. & A. M.

William W. Madden, a well-known farmer of Lake township, was born December. 3, 1853, the son of William and Rachel (Taylor) Madden, natives of Ohio. He was educated in the common schools and worked on the farm with his father until nineteen years of age, when he began farming for himself. This occupation, together with dealing in stock, he still follows on an extensive scale, cultivating a valuable farm of 160 acres. He was married on August 15, 1878, to Edith A. Hire, daughter of Elisha Hire. They have had four children: Joseph W., Jesse B., William A. and Bessie H., of whom William A. is deceased.

Octave Bœuf was born in the province of Jura, France, May 1, 1818. He is the son of Jacob and Joanna Bœuf, who both lived and died in France. He worked on a farm with his father until 1853, when he left his native land and landing in New York, came directly to Fort Wayne. Here he remained for two months working on the canal and then worked on the railroad for two years. Subsequently he rented a farm and engaged in agriculture, living on rented lands for seven years. At the expiration of that period he bought the farm of eighty acres on which he now lives. He now owns 200 acres in all. Mr. Bœuf follows stock-raising in connection with farming. He was married in France, September, 1847, to Gustine Outier, and have six children: Henry, Mary, August, Eugenie, Josephine and Julian. Mrs. Bœuf died December 29, 1887. The family are members of St. Patrick's church at Arcola. Mr. Bœuf is one of the enterprising citizens of

Lake township, and by industry, integrity and economy he has gained quite an extensive property.

Luderick Welsheimer, of Lake township, was born in Fairfield county, Ohio, February 22, 1829. His parents, Philip and Catharine (Duley) Welsheimer, were natives of Virginia. They died at their farm home in Ross county, Ohio, the mother in 1850, the father in 1868. Mr. Welsheimer was educated in the common schools of Ross county, and worked on his father's farm until twenty-four years of age, when he moved to Allen county. He has engaged in the occupation of farming and stock-raising, making a specialty of short-horn cattle and Poland China hogs. His farm consists of 224 acres, and is one of the best in the township. Mr. Welsheimer has served his township as justice of the peace, and is the present assessor. He was married in 1851, to Elizabeth Lucas, and they have had nine children, seven of whom survive: Laura, Ezra L., Otto, Frank L., Nettie G., Jesse A. and William. Mr. and Mrs. Welsheimer are members of the Methodist Episcopal church.

Thomas Larimore, of Lake township, was born June 12, 1827. His father, Thomas Larimore, a native of Pennsylvania, married Hannah Young, and moved to Licking county, Ohio, where he was killed by a falling tree, in March, 1832. The widow and youngest son moved to Sparta township, Noble co., Ind., in 1849, and eight years later came to Lake township, where Mrs. Larimore died in March, 1866. Thomas was bound out after his father's death, but the master's wife dying a short time afterward the family broke up, and young Larimore was left among strangers. From the age of eight he led a life of hardships and was self-supporting. In 1848 he was married to Mahala Evans, and in the fall of 1850 he moved to Lake township, Allen co., bought eighty acres of land, and with his wife, child and a bound boy, began life in this state without a cent in his pocket nor a cabin on his land, and winter before him. But he was possessed of industrious habits and determination. In November, 1881, he moved to Churubusco, and took charge of the Larimore house, having purchased the property the previous May. Besides this Mr. Larimore owns 400 acres of land in Lake township, and valuable property in Fort Wayne. He is a well-known breeder of short-horn cattle. Mr. and Mrs Larimore are the parents of twelve children, of whom Lydia, Cynthia, Thomas J., Hannah M., Levi B., Eli, Mary, Howard and Charley are living, and Alexander, William F. and Norris are deceased. Mr. Larimore is a member of Churubusco. lodge, 515, F. & A. M., and he and wife are members of the Baptist church. He has held the office of justice of the peace four years, and a number of minor offices. He is devoted to church work and has been active in the Sabbath school since 1851. His home is a very pleasant one, and he has the largest barn in Allen county, in dimensions 88x53, and perfectly equipped.

John Rapp, a prominent citizen of Lake township, was born in Wurtemberg, Germany, July 16, 1849. Five years later his parents,

John and Margaret (Wendlenger) Rapp, with their family, left their native land, and arriving at New York came directly to Fort Wayne, where they lived a short time. They afterward resided in Whitley county ten years, and then moved to Lake township. The father died January 10, 1889, and the mother May 10, 1883. John Rapp was educated in the common schools and worked on his father's farm until twenty-one years of age, when he rented the farm and engaged in agriculture and stock-raising for himself. In 1874 he purchased the farm on which he now lives, of 157 acres. He was married March 14, 1875, to Mahala E., daughter of William and Rachel Barrett, and they have had six children, five of whom are living: John W., Harry H., Agnes, Gertrude and Katie. By industry and economy Mr. Rapp has accumulated considerable property.

Jacob Colter, a prominent manufacturer of Lake township, was born in Bavaria, May 4, 1848. In 1851 he was brought by his parents, Jacob and Caroline (Teppla) Colter, to America, but in forty-two days after landing at Canal Dover, Ohio, the father died. Subsequently his mother married again and he had a home with his step-father until he was twenty-one years old, receiving a common school education. After teaching school one term he removed to Indiana, and settling at Coesse, engaged in the manufacture of hoops and staves in partnership with William Smith. Three years later he removed to Arcola, and with P. W. Smith, established the firm of Colter & Co., which by good business methods, has prospered. Mr. Colter has accumulated a considerable property, and has won the esteem of his associates. He is a member of the Masonic fraternity, and in politics is a republican. In 1878, he was married to Sarah Crawford, and of their six children, five are still living: Olive B., William H., John H., Maud B. and Louise E. The family are members of the Methodist church.

Sebastian Keller, born in Bavaria, Germany, December 10, 1831, son of Sebastian and Magdaline Keller, who both lived and died in their native land; the father was a carpenter by trade. Mr. Keller was educated in Germany, and learned the trade of stone cutter, at which he worked until twenty-one years of age. He then left his native land and arrived at New York, October 12, 1852; after remaining there for two years working at his trade, he moved to Seneca county, Ohio; and two years later came to Fort Wayne, where he followed his trade for twelve years. Subsequently he engaged in business for himself, at which he continued about seventeen years. Selling out, he bought a farm in Lake township on which he has been engaged in agriculture very successfully, having one of the finest farms in the township, consisting of 233 acres. He was married to Miss Mary Shields in 1861, and of their ten children eight survive: Mary, Andrew, Frank, Cecile, Annie, Edward, Harry and Charles. The family are members of St. Patrick's church.

Daniel Keim, a worthy citizen of Lake township, was born in Holmes county, Ohio, July 30, 1839, son of Solomon and Elizabeth (Hostettler) Keim, both natives of Pennsylvania. The father was a farmer by occupation. He died August 16, 1853, and the mother followed July 2, 1868. Daniel was educated in the common schools of Ohio, and sought work at the age of fourteen, being variously engaged until eighteen years of age when he served a two years' apprenticeship at the tanner's trade. At the end of this time he rented a tannery and followed the business for three years. In 1862 he moved to La Grange county, Ind., and started a tannery the following spring, and continued in the business for twelve years. While there he purchased forty acres of land and engaged in farming. In 1881 he moved to Allen county and purchased the farm on which he now lives, which consists of 205 acres. He was married October 6, 1859, to Phœbe Arnold, and they are the parents of nine children, eight of whom are living: George W., Solomon D., Rosette C., Emma G., Clara E., Charles F., William D. and Ada A. Mr. and Mrs. Keim are members of the German Baptist church. Mr. Keim takes a great interest in educational matters, and two of his sons, George W. and Solomon D., are teachers in Lake township.

Jarvis Smith, a prosperous farmer of Lake township, was born June 26, 1844, in Gallia county, Ohio. He is the son of E. J. and Mahala Smith, natives of Ohio. The father, a farmer by occupation, is still living, but the mother died in Lake township in 1867. Mr. Smith was educated in the common schools of Allen and Whitley counties, and worked on his father's farm until twenty-two years of age. He then took up agriculture as his own business, and in this and stock-raising has been notably successful. He was married August 26, 1865, to Katie, the daughter of George Smaltz, of Aboit township, and they have three children: Franklin, Clarence, and Chester. The family are members of the Methodist Episcopal church.

EEL RIVER TOWNSHIP.

This township, so-called from the stream which drains it, received its first settlers in 1828, when William Kellison and his brother, from Darke county, Ohio, settled on section 32. They erected small cabins and made a deadening, and then in 1830, sold out to Adam Hull, sr., and went on westward. Mr. Hull was well-known throughout the county, and in the many rough and tumble encounters which gave zest to days in town, generally held his own. He built the first bridge over Eel river, at his own expense, and established a private toll to which travelers sometimes unreasonably demurred. For several years his was the only cabin in the neighborhood, and was the stopping place of many immigrants going through. In the fall of 1832, one stranger, who was traveling on foot, shared the cabin over night, but being taken sick died the next morning. A few weeks afterward a family stopped, and the children being sick with scarlet fever, two of them died here, and their bodies, with that of the stranger, were the first to be laid in the old graveyard south of Eel river. Such instances as these, though very briefly narrated, reveal much of the hardships of the lives of those who were making new homes in the wilderness. In 1834, Mr. Hull was appointed postmaster, there being a considerable settlement by that time on the Goshen road, to the south. He held the place until his death, September 1, 1838. About 1833, Peter Heller settled, and his name is perpetuated as the title of the neighborhood and postoffice, Heller's Corners. In 1834 Mr. Hull, aided by his neighbors, cut a road from that neighborhood to the east line of the township, which was the first highway. In this year, Joseph and John R. Johnston settled on sections 21 and 28, and on June 11, John Valentine, from Ohio, as were all these early settlers, made his home on section 33. In the spring of 1836 there was a considerable settlement made in the east, in the direction of the Lima road, including John P. Shoaff, from Miami county, Ohio, who settled on section 13, and became justice, trustee, and from 1862 to 1868, representative in the general assembly. Others who came at that date were F. C. Freeman, Samuel Hillegass, Benjamin Mason, Joseph Jones, Henry Bossler who established the pioneer smithy, and Samuel Kniss. In April of this year the first election was held, and the result was as to justice, for which Messrs. Hull and Bond were candidates, a tie. The judge decided the matter by drawing one of the ballots from the hat, and Mr. Hull so won the election. Later, in 1836, Abram Taylor came from Cuyahoga county, Ohio, to the Hull neighborhood, and William Anderson settled in the east. In 1837 William F. Mooney and Uriah Chase settled, and between 1837 and 1840, came R. D. Baird, Solomon Bennett, John Bennett, Caleb Bennett, John McKee, John Hathaway, Mr. Schilling, John R. Mayo, on whose land the first "Hickory school-house" was built and used in 1837, and William Madden. In 1838, Joseph Jones opened a store at his house, on what was afterward known as the Charles Hanna farm. In 1852, Smith & Diffenderfer established a saw-mill on Eel river, and for a number of years supplied lumber for the houses built about that time to replace the log cabins, but it finally went to decay. Near it a steam grist-mill was built by Peter Heller, in 1855, and he operated it successfully until it was destroyed by fire. Mr. Heller had in 1837, succeeded to the postmastership, and the office was afterward called Heller's Corners. In October, 1835, Asa Miller laid out on his land in the southwest corner of section 32, and an adjoining portion of Lake township, the village of "Kraco," the main street of which was 132 feet wide. A circular tract in the center was reserved as "Miller's Park." The town did not materialize.

The first school was taught in a cabin erected for that purpose in 1837, which as it was built almost entirely of hickory logs, was called the "Hickory" school-house. Among its pupils were Thomas and William McKee, John M. Taylor and his sister, Mrs. Altha Hull.

Adam Hull, son of the Adam Hull above mentioned as the first permanent settler of Eel River township, is now the oldest settler of that township living. He was born May 8, 1812, in Pendleton county, Va., and thence emigrated at the age of twelve years to Ohio with his parents,

Adam and Elizabeth Hull. They made their home in Shelby county, Ohio, until 1832, when the family removed to Indiana. After reaching Fort Wayne they remained there nearly one year, and settled on the land which the father had bought in Eel River township. The senior Hull purchased 240 acres and began the work of clearing, in which he was assisted by his son. On this account and the absence of schools he did not receive much education in his youth, but is nevertheless well informed. His recollection of the past is vivid and he recalls many interesting incidents. In his possession are all his tax receipts since he first settled on his farm, and he also takes much pride in a rifle which his father made in Virginia, and which has served to bring much venison to their tables in Ohio and Indiana. Mr. Hull attended the first election held in the township, and was elected constable; his jurisdiction extended over what are now Noble, Whitley and Allen counties. He held this office two years and then resigned. Mr. Hull is now, though in his seventy-seventh year, quite hearty and active, and recalls with pleasure the progress of his life from the time when he began with a capital consisting of a five franc piece, a fiddle and a gun. By nature a pioneer, he has enjoyed the struggle with nature through which he has passed. Mr. Hull was married in 1836 to Elizabeth Crow, by whom he had three children, of whom one, Adam, is living. Immediately after this marriage he entered 125 acres of land from the government, and settled on the same and built a log cabin in 1838. In 1845 he was married a second time to Hester Ann Strean, and they have had seven children, of whom the following survive: Maria, George W., Henry, Jane, Peter and Judson. Mr. Hull is now well-to-do, and is one of the esteemed and respected citizens of the township. He has been a member of the Missionary Baptist church for thirty-six years.

A worthy and popular man in the early days, and one of the first settlers in Eel River township, was John R. Johnston, a native of New Jersey, who died in 1876. When he was seventeen years old, he emigrated to Greene county, Ohio. In 1834, he was married to Belinda Davis, who was born August 13, 1812, and survives her husband. In the same year they removed to Eel River township, and settled on 120 acres of land, which Mr. Johnston had entered. This they never removed from. Here they went through the toilsome, yet ofttimes happy life of the pioneers of civilization. They were deeply religious, and became charter members of the Methodist Episcopal church at Wesley chapel, of which she has been a member for over half a century, and is the only survivor of the first members. These respected people had twelve children, of whom six are now living: David, Mary, Catherine, Susan, Emma and William H. David Johnston, the eldest, grew to manhood on the old homestead, and never lived elsewhere until 1870, when he bought forty acres adjoining, and built himself a neat dwelling and good barn. He received his education in the pioneer schools. Among his first teachers were Elijah Robinson, Mary T. Smith, George W. Done, G. W. Hutchell and Nancy Griswold. He began teaching when about nineteen years of age and taught five terms. In 1857, he was united in marriage with Mary, daughter of Otho and Mary Gaudy, born in 1836, by whom he had eight children, of whom Clara Almeda, Inez I., William M., Serena and John O., are living. He and wife are members of the Methodist Episcopal church, in which he has been class leader and steward, about three years. Mr. Johnston owns a good farm of eighty-seven acres, and is ranked as a prominent citizen. William H. Johnston, the youngest son of John R., was born September 2, 1852. He now lives on and owns the old homestead where he grew to manhood. He received a good common school education and attended one term at the Methodist Episcopal college at Fort Wayne. November 9, 1873, he was united in marriage with Sarah N. Scarlett, by whom he had two children: Florence A., born September 10, 1874, died December 18, 1876; Emma G., born October 1, 1876, died March 16, 1888. Their mother, now deceased, was a member of the Methodist Episcopal church. May 28, 1877, he was married to Lillian J. Scarlett, born January 9, 1861, and they have had two children: Clarence C., born September 10, 1880, and Grace E., born March 21, 1884, died February 15, 1888. Mr. Johnston and wife are both members of the Methodist Episcopal church, and are highly respected.

Another old settler of much prominence, Joseph Johnston, arrived in 1834 with his wife Martha and children, and settled on the farm where his son now resides. He had entered 160 acres here in the previous year, 1833. Mr. Johnston was born in New Jersey, February 15, 1802, and emigrated to Greene county, Ohio, in 1822, where he was married February 14, 1825, to Martha Opdyke, who was born December 18, 1811. He was a distiller by trade. When he came to Allen county his worldly possessions consisted of two yoke of oxen, one bureau, one chest and some old chairs. But in spite of this meagre beginning his industry made him triumphant over disadvantages, and he came to own 400 acres of land, and amassed considerable property. He was a good and valued citizen, a consistent member of the Methodist Episcopal church, and hightly esteemed by all. He served his township as treasurer and clerk of the township board for several years. This worthy pioneer departed this life June 29, 1869, and his wife survived him many years. Perry Johnston, son of the above, was born in Ohio, June 8, 1834. Nearly all his life has been spent in Indiana, and he grew to manhood on the old homestead, which is still his home. In 1855 Mr. Johnston was married to Sarah A. Wells, who was born in 1838, and departed this life in 1880. She was a consistent member of the Methodist Episcopal church, to which he also belongs. He is a member of the Masonic order and is a representative farmer and a worthy citizen.

Jackson Valentine, of Eel River township, is a son of John Valentine, one of the pioneers of the township. John Valentine, a native of Ohio, was married in 1820, to Susannah Peters, who was born in Maryland, January 4, 1799. Her parents were among the pioneers of Fairfield county, Ohio. John Valentine and wife, with little possessions, but with stout hearts, came with their wagon load of household goods into the wilds of Indiana in 1834, and settled in Eel River township, June 11, entering 120 acres of wild land. This pioneer enterprise prospered, and they became the owners of 227 acres of good land. In 1856, John Valentine went west and settled in Iowa, where he bought some land, and property in Knoxville, intending to reside there, but becoming dissatisfied in 1859, he returned to Indiana and made his home with his son Jackson, where he remained until his death, which occurred in 1869. He was a member of the Christian church, and one of the leading citizens and representative farmers. Jackson Valentine was born in Franklin county, Ohio, October 15, 1824. He received a good common school education and remained at home with his parents. January 6, 1850, he was united in marriage with Charlotte Greenewalt, by whom he had three children, one of whom is living, John W. She was born May 29, 1830, was a faithful member of the Christian church, and departed this life May 6, 1876. In 1878 he was married to Mrs. Maria Jones, daughter of Peter and Sarah B. Frysinger. She is a member of the Methodist Episcopal church. He is a member of the Christian church. In 1868 he was a candidate for trustee on the republican ticket against John M. Taylor and reduced the adverse majority about half. Again in 1880, running against C. L. Greenwell, he reduced the majority to six. His desirable farm of 200 acres is admirably maintained and his handsome buildings are a testimonial to his enterprise.

Robert L. Freeman, a prosperous farmer of Eel River township, was born in this township, July 26, 1843. His parents, Frame C. and Betsy (Simon) Freeman, came to Indiana from Ohio early in the thirties, and settled in Eel River township. The elder Freeman, like so many other sturdy pioneers, succeded well, and at the time of his death he owned 240 acres of good land. He was one of the leading citizens during his lifetime, stood well in his community, and his death was mourned by all who knew him. Robert L. was born and lived in childhood in the old log cabin, but about 1849 his father built a two-story brick dwelling which now stands as a relic of bygone days. He enlisted in 1862 in Company E, Eighty-eighth Indiana regiment, under Captain Chauncy Oakley, but was mustered out under Captain C. Brown. He served three years and was in every battle with his regiment except one — Stone River. He received an honorable discharge at Indianapolis, 1865. April 15, 1866, he was united in marriage with Sarah J., daughter of James and Sarah McBride. Of their four children two are living: Winfield S. and Charles Franklin; their mother who was born February 25, 1841, departed this life March 1, 1879. She was a member of the United Brethren church. June 12, 1881, he was married to Katie Ann, daughter of David and Catharine (Hull) Gordon, born January 19, 1862, and they have three children: Goldy Catharine, Sylvia E., and an infant. He has served his township as constable six years. He was a member of the Independent Order of Red Men during the lifetime of that order, and of the Grange.

Ranald T. McDonald

Nelson Hyndman, of Eel River township, is a native of Indiana, born September 24, 1847. His father, John Hyndman, a native of Ireland, was born in 1809 and emigrated to America in 1835 with just enough money to bring him to land. He was four or five months crossing the sea, being ship-wrecked, and landing from life-boats on American soil, without any coat, but fortunately fifty cents in his vest pocket. He settled in Fort Wayne and began work on the canal and afterward at odd jobs until he began blacksmithing, at which he worked several years. In 1844 he entered forty acres of land in Allen county and afterward traded this for eighty acres in Eel River township, where he settled. He lived a bachelor until early in the forties, when he was married to Lucy Jackson, by whom he had four boys and three girls. He and wife were members of the Missionary Baptist church. His life is a remarkable illustration of the success that can be achieved by indomitable will and energy. He was always friendly to schools, churches and all laudable enterprises, and in all ways a leading citizen and representative farmer. He owned at one time 855 acres of valuable land. He was the first man that began the stall-feeding of cattle in Eel River township. He died April 20, 1874. Nelson Hyndman was born in the old log house in Eel River township where he grew to manhood and received a good common school education. In 1875 he was united in marriage with Mary Pumphrey, born March 4, 1852, by whom he had four children, three now living: Ruah Elizabeth, Robert (deceased), Florence A., James A. He administered on his father's estate, which was quite a large one and required four years to make final settlement. His is among the first families of his township. He owns 160 acres of good land, with a good dwelling and barn. Mr. Hyndman still has the clock, now over fifty years old, used by his father in his bachelor days, which cost $40; also a secret drawer in which the old gentleman kept money.

W. W. Shoaff, of Eel River township, of a well-known pioneer family, was born November 15, 1829, in Miami county, Ohio. His father, John P. Shoaff, was a native of Maryland, born October 12, 1804, and at the age of one year was taken to Ohio by his parents, who settled near Dayton. He remained in Ohio until February 5, 1836, when he settled in Allen county, Ind. Here he remained until February 4, 1885, and then removed to Churubusco, where he died February 1, 1887. Mr. Shoaff's pioneer life did not permit any advantages of schooling, but being of a studious turn of mind, he improved what leisure moments he had as a miller, and became quite well informed. February 5, 1828, he was united in marriage with Priscilla Freeman, who was born in Greene county, Ohio, January 4, 1810, and departed this life at the old homestead in Allen county, May 22, 1880. To this union eleven children were born, of whom W. W., John F., Anna E., James B., Jennie, Allen P. and Wade Scott, are now living. Mr. Shoaff was not a member of any church, but was a liberal supporter of that work. He served his township as justice of the peace sixteen years, and three or four terms as trustee. In 1862 he was elected representative to the general assembly, and served three terms. His business shrewdness was early manifested by trading in live stock. By going to Ohio and bringing on milch cows he accommodated his neighbors and also soon began to accumulate considerable property. By good management he increased this so that he came into possession of over 1,400 acres of good farming land which is now in the hands of his children. W. W., his oldest son, was seven years of age when his father settled here, and his first experience in Allen county was in burning brush. He received a common school education, and attended school at Fort Wayne about two years, and the Methodist college two years. On March 10, 1859, he married Eliza J., daughter of Robert and Sarah A. Work, born January 18, 1839. They have two children: John R. and Joseph Y. He and wife are members of the Methodist Episcopal church, and he is a member of the Masonic order. Mr. Shoaff has served as justice eight years, and as ditch commissioner of Allen county seven years. He is one of the representative farmers of his county, and one of the leading citizens, and in politics has been a supporter of the democratic party since its organization. After leaving college he followed civil engineering for the Pittsburg, Fort Wayne & Chicago railroad. He located the line for the road and finished up two sections of forty miles which he had full charge of between Plymouth and Valparaiso.

W. Scott Shoaff, the youngest son of John P. Shoaff, was born December 16, 1847, on the old homestead which his father entered from the government. There he grew to manhood and received a common school education. He remained with his father until he reached his majority, and then adopted farming as his own vocation. In 1885 he was united in marriage with Lena M. Jimmerson, daughter of Thomas and Margaret J. Farmer. She was born August 10, 1868. He is now one of the leading farmers and stock-raisers of Eel River township, and one of the prominent land owners of the county, holding 440 acres of good farming land with substantial buildings. He makes a specialty of draft horses and good grades of cattle. He is a member of the Masonic order.

Stephen Hathaway, of Eel River township, is a native of Michigan, born September 20, 1836. His father, John Hathaway, was born October 12, 1811, in Washington county, N. Y.; emigrated to Michigan early in the thirties, and in 1836, came to Indiana in search of land and entered eighty acres in Eel River township, which he and his wife, whose maiden name was Hannah Chase, and their children, settled upon in 1838. When he settled in Allen county he had one yoke of cattle, one cow, about $300 in wild-cat money, and very little furniture. He succeeded by close application and frugal habits in gaining 340 acres of excellent land, besides some property in Fort Wayne. He was one of the leading farmers of the county and respected by the people of his township. Stephen Hathaway was raised on the old homestead, and received a good common school education, and attended six months at Perry Center seminary. January 22, 1865, he was united in marriage with Mary E., daughter of Henry and Elizabeth (Norman) Fair, born January 11, 1840. They have three children: Orphelia, James Sidney and Emma. He was elected justice of the peace in 1882, on the democratic ticket, and was again elected in 1886. During his terms of office he has had but one case before him in which he had to commit a man to jail, and he has done the bulk of the business of the township. His beautiful farm in Eel River township includes 200 acres, under a good state of cultivation, with substantial buildings. He is a member of the Masonic order.

Levi Chase, a prominent farmer of Allen county, was born in Eel River township December 4, 1845, and is a descendant of a noted pioneer family. His father, Uriah Chase, came with his parents from Michigan in 1837, and settled in Eel River township where the grandfather had entered land in 1836. Here Uriah Chase grew to manhood, bearing his share of the burdens of the pioneer's career. In 1842 he was united in marriage with Mary Jackson, and in her he found a true wife and helper; she survives him and is now in her sixty-sixth year. She is a member of the Close Communion Baptist church. They had five children, two of whom are now living: Louisa and Levi. The latter was raised on the old homestead where he has since resided. In 1869 he was united in marriage with Sarah Bricker, born in 1847; she died in 1873, leaving one child, Chester. April 2, 1874, he was married to Sarah Rhoads, born February 2, 1849, by whom he has three children: Osa, Ida and Ira. He and wife are members of the Baptist church. He is one of the prominent farmers of this township, owning 144 acres of desirable land.

Notable among the old settlers of Eel River township was John McKee. He was born in Virginia in 1804, and subsequently came with his parents to Ohio, and settled near Springfield, Clark county, where he grew to manhood, and married Martha Lansdale, who was born in Maryland in 1799. He was a cabinet-maker and house-joiner by trade. While in Ohio he passed through the cholera plague in New Carlisle, which swept away 130 of the 340 inhabitants, and was kept busy at that time furnishing coffins. In 1836 he came to Eel River township and entered land, and in 1837, he and W. M. Lansdale attempted to drive their wagons through, but on reaching the Black Swamp could only make four miles a day, and at St. Mary's village abandoned their wagons and came through on horseback. They arranged for the building of their cabin, to which they brought the family in the fall of 1837. Mrs. McKee died January 17, 1839, and was the first person buried in the cemetery, conveyed by her husband. Mr. McKee did an important work in the early settlement in the organization of Wesley Chapel church, and was an official member and an ordained minister of the gospel. In his business relations he was both popular and successful and came to hold 220 acres of valuable land. Thomas L. McKee, son of the above, was born in Ohio, June 9, 1827. He received a good common school education in Ohio, and in this county experienced the life of the pioneer. At about the age of nineteen he returned to Ohio, and attended school about six months, then coming here and beginning teaching, at which he was engaged six or seven years, farming in summer. He taught two winter terms in Illinois. He was one of the first teachers in the county to introduce the outline system of teaching geography. In 1852 he was married to Melinda J. Rock, by whom he had two children, one of whom is living, Martha J., wife of Frank Alderman. Mrs. McKee was born in 1834 and died in 1870. In 1874 he was united in marriage with Sarah C. Gilpen, born in 1847, and of their two children, one is living, Zilpha Gertrude. Mrs. McKee is a member of the Methodist Episcopal church. In 1853, Mr. McKee emigrated west and settled in Iowa, where he remained about two years. Returning to Indiana he remained until 1857, after which he resided in Illinois two years, and removed to Kansas. Here he stayed about nine months and lost all he had but $2.00. He subsequently resided in Iowa about one year, in Illinois two or three years and then returned to the old homestead. In 1870 he removed to Fort Wayne and went into the produce and commission business with Solomon Bash and P. D. Smyser, and was so engaged until 1878, when he sold his interest and retired to the farm. He has been a member of the Fort Wayne lodge, I. O. O. F., No. 14, for about twenty-six years. His land possessions include 300 acres in Eel River township.

Julius C. Mooney, one of a pioneer family in Eel River township, is a native of Miami county, Ohio, born September 9, 1825. His father, William F. Mooney, came west in search of land in 1835, and entered 120 acres of land in Allen county, and returned to Ohio, and on February 9, 1837, came with his wife Elizabeth and family and took possession of the cabin he had prepared for them. His life was that of the pioneer in general, little money but abundance of pluck. He succeeded in life, gaining a valuable farm of 160 acres, and made for himself a name for fair and honest dealing. He lived to the age of sixty-five years. Julius C. Mooney was twelve years of age at coming, and aided in the early clearing. He received such an education as could be obtained in the old log school-houses. In 1867 he was united in marriage with Rosa, daughter of Jacob and Mary Morton, and this union is blessed with two children, William F. and Maude. In 1865 he enlisted in Company K, One Hundred and Fifty-third regiment, under Capt. Young, and served about one year. He has made a success of life, and owned at one time 280 acres of good land. He now has a farm of 160 acres, where he lives, on which he has recently built a two-story dwelling.

John S. Benward, of Eel River township, was born in Pennsylvania September 24, 1837, son of Isaac and Elizabeth Benward. The mother was of German, and the father of English, descent. The family emigrated to Allen county in 1838 and settled in Perry township, where the father bought eighty acres, which was improved with a double log house. He began to keep a hotel for the accommodation of emigrants and for teamsters to and from Fort Wayne and remained in this business until he cleared up his farm, when he began farming. After remaining in Perry township eight or ten years he traded for 160 acres of wild lands in Eel River township where his son now lives. He built a log house here, but his land being low and swampy at that time, he rented his old farm in Perry where he lived four years, at the same time clearing his wild lands. In 1852 he went to the gold fields of California and remained about four years, afterward returning to Allen county and settled on his new farm, which in the meantime had been well improved by his family. His death occurred about 1870. He was an industrious man and well-liked. John S. Benward received a good common school education. November 30, 1857, he was united in marriage with Eliza Jane, daughter of Abraham and Rebecca Workman, early settlers of Noble county. This union was blessed with six children, of whom Edmund C., John E., Commodore and Arthur are now living. Mrs. Benward was born November 30, 1839. She is a member of the Missionary Baptist church. In 1865 Mr. Benward enlisted in Company D, One Hundred and Fifty-fifth Indiana regiment, and was discharged at Indianapolis September 5, 1865. He has given much attention to threshing machines during the past thirty-six years and although he never studied engineering, is an expert in the management of an engine. He is popular, prosperous and owns a farm of 160 acres.

John McCarty (deceased), was an early settler in Eel River township, and was a successful farmer. He was a native of Ohio, born June 4, 1817, son of Samuel and Elizabeth (Wood) McCarty. Growing to manhood in Ohio, he attended school during a short period while he was too young to be of service on the farm, and as he grew older he became a necessity to his father, and thus drifted naturally into farming as his occupation in life. He shared the hardships of a pioneer life in Ohio before coming to Indiana. About 1841 he was married to Mary Douglas, born April 7, 1817, by whom he had five children, of whom two are now living: Eunice, wife of James Potter, and John Henry. In 1844 Mr. McCarty settled in Allen county, where he remained until his death, which occurred August 17, 1877. During his first years here he had to suffer not only poverty, but the more dreaded chills and fever, and had to return to his old home in Ohio for a season to regain his former strength. Beginning again with indomitable will, the morning found him with ax and maul, ready for the woods. From then till eve he worked hard felling heavy timber, making rails for fencing, while brush-piles and log-heaps were burned after nightfall. By such hard work and good management, he gathered to himself 328 acres of fertile land. In his wife he found a true helper; in the many vicissitudes of life she proved herself eminently deserving, patient, kind, frugal and industrious. Sharing his toils and hardships, she lived to see them crowned with success. Mr. McCarty was a man of upright character, and was esteemed throughout the community in which he lived. John H., his youngest son, now occupies the old homestead farm, and the old log house in which his father first lived after coming to Allen county, is now standing as a relic of by-gone days. Our subject was born here March 9, 1855. He received a good common school education. January 1, 1880, he was united in marriage with Lucy J. Woods, born January 28, 1855, daughter of Albert and Nancy (Dunton) Woods. This union was blessed with three children, Arthur, Arlington Guy, and Nancy L. She is a member of the Universalist church. He was a member of the Independent Order of Red Men, during the lifetime of that order. He is a leading young farmer, and owns a half interest in 160 acres of land. In his possession is an old English reader, bought by his mother December 10, 1832, which is in a good state of preservation.

C. Luther Greenwell, a popular teacher in the public schools and ex-trustee of Eel River township, is a native of Ohio, born July 17, 1845. His father, George Greenwell, was born of Irish parentage March 14, 1810, at Hagerstown, Md. In 1830 he removed to Miami county, Ohio, and was there married in 1838, to Elizabeth Blickenstaff. They came with their children to Eel River township in 1846, and here he died November 10, 1878, and his widow July 8, 1868. They had five children. Luther Greenwell received a good common school education, beginning in the old log school-houses, and in 1865 he began teaching in Steuben county. He taught one term in a school of sixty pupils, and twenty-two older than he, and then returned to Allen county and began teaching in district No. 7, Eel River township, and taught in the winters of 1866-7-8-9 and 1870, and taught in Perry, district No. 5, in 1871, again in district No. 7, Eel River, in 1872-3, and in 1874 and '75 in district No. 8, Eel River township, '76 in No. 1, '77 and '78 in No. 8. He was then elected trustee of his township on the democratic ticket, and served until 1882, when he again began teaching in 1883, at district No. 8, and '84, '85 and '86, No. 1. He was again elected trustee in 1886, and assumed the office in the spring of '86, and served two years, and in the winter of '88 and '89 taught in district No. 6. In 1866 when he began teaching in the township there were eleven districts, and it so continued until 1878 when Mr. Greenwell as trustee vacated one district. He then renumbered the districts with the intention of making four sections constitute a school district, placing No. 1 in the northeast and ranging west. By the efforts of his successor it was rendered possible, upon Mr. Greenwell's second election, to vacate one more district, leaving nine. He built one brick school-house during his first term of office and three during the last, on the improved plan. November 7, 1872, he was united in marriage with Fannie J., daughter of Samuel and Alvira Mathews, born in March, 1852. Of their four children, Walter S. and Franklin W. are living, and Cora E. and an infant child are deceased.

Samuel Mathews, an early settler and prominent citizen of Eel River township, was born in Richland county, Ohio, June 24, 1826, son of Jacob and Fannie (Smith) Mathews. He was taken by his parents to

Huron county, Ohio, while quite young, and he there grew to manhood, and received his education in the pioneer school-house. When he was ten years old, the death of his father threw upon him the support of the family, in which there were four children besides himself. In 1846 he was united in marriage with Alvira Rice, born March 1, 1828, by whom he had eleven children, nine of whom are now living: Alfred, Fannie J., Mary E., Samuel J., Commodore P., Ellen A., Brittie, John W. and Norah. John W. has attended college at Ann Arbor and graduated in June, 1889. He is a member of the Church of God. Mr. Mathews came to Indiana in 1846 and settled on the farm where he now lives. At that time he was so poor that to pay a man for helping bring his effects here, he had to surrender the top from his wagon. He accumulated subsequently 415 acres of good land, and now lives on a farm of 295 acres. He is one of Allen's prominent citizens and well respected by all. The experience of a pioneer's wife was that of Mrs. Mathews. She took upon herself such tasks as going to the woods after the cows, digging sassafras from which to make tea, helping her husband to pile brush, etc. She would go with him to help neighbors butcher and work all day for some heads and feet, and would sew all day for a chicken, or whatever they would give.

George V. Kell, of Eel River township, was born in Perry township, February 3, 1846, and grew to manhood on the old homestead of his parents, Jacob and Catharine Kell. He received a good common school education and attended Perry Center seminary about five years, studying the higher branches. On October 1, 1867, he was united in marriage with Alice, daughter of N. V. and Abigail Hatch, born December 8, 1846, and they have had seven children: Gertrude, Louie A., Jessie, Beatrice, Robert, Frank and Dollie. In 1867 he and family made a trip by wagons to Iowa, where they remained six years. While there he was engaged in agricultural pursuits, and in 1871 he was elected trustee of his township and served two years. In 1873 he returned to Indiana, and settled on the farm where he now lives, which was then nearly all in timber, but now well improved. Mr. Kell makes a specialty of breeding the trotting stock of horses, and has recently purchased a valuable Hambletonian horse for $1,000. He served four years as justice of the peace of Eel River township, and is now secretary and a director of the Farmers' Mutual Fire association. He has 100 acres of good land of his own, and 177 acres belonging to his father he has full control of and will eventually own. He is one of the leading citizens of his township, and in politics is prominent as a democrat.

Michael Miller, one of the worthy old settlers of Indiana, was born in Pennsylvania, May 1, 1818. He came to Ohio with his parents when only nine years of age, and nine years later removed to DeKalb county, Ind., in the woods, where wolves were so plentiful that they would run the dogs under the cabin. In 1841 he married Elizabeth Trussle, and they had six children, four of whom are now living, Amos, Rebecca J., Martha and Lucy Ann. Mrs. Miller was born in 1823, and died

February 19, 1882. While in DeKalb county he served as constable one year, and after removing to Allen county in 1849, he was elected trustee about 1851; served three years as one of the board, and was assessor in 1856. He has often declined to run for office. He now owns 105 acres of good land, and is one of the leading citizens. His parents, Henry and Elizabeth Ann (Sheets) Miller, natives of Germany, emigrated to America in 1805, without any money, understanding that they would have to work out their passage after their arrival. The captain of the vessel sold their work to the highest bidder; they were both bought by the same man, who was a very hard master, and as Mr. Miller demanded better treatment, they were sold a second time, and this time fell into good hands. They thus worked three years to pay for their passage. With such a beginning, Mr. Miller came to own 310 acres of land in Eel River and two sections of land in Texas, and has given to his children about $5,000, and to churches and benevolent institutions about $6,000. He has been a devoted friend of his church and generous to it.

John W. Holmes, of Eel river township, was born in Wayne township, March 31, 1853, son of Joshua and Mary M. (Fountain) Holmes. In May, 1884, he removed to Washington township, remained until December, and then came to Eel river township and settled on the farm where he now lives. He received a good common school education, and attended the Methodist Episcopal college at Fort Wayne about five terms. In 1873 he was united in marriage with Sarah J., daughter of James and Elizabeth Cartwright, born May 21, 1850, and they have six children: Clara, Florence, Lizzie, Edith, John R., and Eddie. He and wife are both members of the Missionary Baptist church. Mr. Holmes is the present trustee of his township. Though a republican in a township where there was a democratic majority of fifty, he was elected in 1888 by eight majority. He has a beautiful farm of 160 acres, handsomely improved. He is a leading citizen and universally respected.

PERRY TOWNSHIP.

Charles Weeks and William Caswell, who removed to this part of the county of Allen in 1830, were the first settlers and for three years had undisputed sway in its forests. They were famous hunters, and spent much time in the pursuit of deer and smaller game, by which their larders were supplied. Both were also men of industry and cleared farms, but Caswell, a hardy Canadian, of great strength and endurance, was the more energetic and enterprising, and became prominent in the early history. At his house the first election was held in October, 1835, and he was elected one of the justices. At his friend Weeks' house, in 1836, the postoffice was first established, and for two or three years Mr. Weeks was the postmaster. The next comers were Thomas Dunten and his nephew, Horace F. Dunten, who came from Jefferson county, N. Y., and were joined in the fall of the same year, 1833, by Ephraim H., father of Horace. This family was quite prominent; Horace erected the first hewn-log house in 1834, and soon afterward Ephraim H., jr., who settled in 1834, put up a frame store room on what is now a lot of Huntertown. He purchased his goods in Toledo, and had them shipped by way of the canal, and from Fort Wayne by wagons. The store prospered and was continued many years by his sons. In 1835 the Lima road was opened to the rich prairie region of LaGrange county, and it became a great highway for travelers and freight. Upon this highway in the vicinity of Huntertown, Ephraim H. Dunten, jr., opened a tavern, and being a genial host, had as many guests as he could accommodate. Several years later he built a more commodious house. He also, about the same time, opened a brick kiln, which, however, was not profitable. At a later period he was in business at Fort Wayne, but returned to Perry township and died of cholera in 1854. Other settlers in 1833, were Albert Wood, whose daughter Mary was the first white native, and Nathaniel Fitch, who married Miss Sarah De Long in 1836, that being the first wedding of the township. Fitch was the first blacksmith, opening his shop in 1837, in which same year James Vandergrift, in another part of the township, also engaged in the manufacture of plow points and steel traps. Benjamin and Amaziah Parker came from Jefferson county, N. Y., in 1834, and became leading citizens. In the same year came Jason Hatch from Pennsylvania, and settled on Cedar Creek, and erected a saw-mill. He became quite popular and prominent; with him came his wife, Joanna, and their son, Newman V., born in 1815, who married Abigail Parker in 1839, raised a family of seven children, and is still a resident of the township. Philemon Rundels, a settler of the same year, was also a man of ability. In 1836, George Simon came to the farm which was his home thereafter, and James Vandolah and family began their residence; Schuyler Wheeler, a well-educated man, who was elected to the legislature in 1858, also came in 1836. In 1837 there were several notable arrivals. William T. Hunter came and purchased the tract of land including the site of Huntertown; he did much for the advancement of the township. George, Samuel, Henry and John Bowser were others. Some of those who settled after 1837 are Thomas Tucker, James Thompson, Isaac Benward, Rapin Andrews, Jacob Hillegass, Vachel Metcalf, George Gloyd, L. Gloyd, James Tucker, Dr. E. G. Wheelock, August Martin and Samuel Shryock, but the settlers became so numerous that it is impossible to detail their names. The pioneer mill was that of Blair & Hines on Cedar creek, three miles from Huntertown. It was a saw-mill with a corn-cracker attachment, by which corn was hardly ground, but simply cracked, and was of little value. The establishment was sold to Samuel Shryock in 1836, and he put in a run of buhrs, and founded a grist-mill. About 1852 John Stoner became the proprietor, and the mill is now generally known as the Stoner mill. It is still operated, at present by Price West. In 1848 or 1849 the Lima road was made a plank road, and a considerable amount of toll annually came to its projectors. A line of stage coaches was established to Kendallville, and there was a large timber commerce over the road. But after the railroads were built, the business was mostly destroyed, and the planks went to decay and were finally removed.

Huntertown.— After the completion of the Lima road, a number of settlers built their homes upon what promised to be a great highway, and William T. Hunter, one of the most prominent of these, purchased the tract of land embracing the site of the present town which bears his name. No plat was made nor town lots sold until December, 1869. The Grand Rapids & Indiana railroad takes the place of the old wagon thoroughfare as an avenue of commerce with the north. Among the early settlers were the Duntens, Nathaniel Fitch, Jacob Hillegass, John Hippenhamer, N. V. Hatch, A. I. Ketchum, Elbridge Burke, T. M. Andrews, Danford and Omri Parker, Solomon Simons. The first school near the town was taught by Eliza Parker in 1835, in a log cabin on section 6. She was a teacher surpassing the ordinary instructors of her day, and with the financial aid of the settlers did valuable work. Matthew Montgomery established a school in 1837 on section 8; he was an able young man, and in 1846 was nominated for representative by the whigs against Peter Kiser. The village now has a commodious two-story school building, with two teachers. The early business of the town has already been mentioned. There are now general stores kept by J. C. Hunter, who is the postmaster, J. E. Ballou and James Newman; hardware and groceries by Reuben Cone, hotel by William Clutter, notions and groceries by J. C. Gay. E. J. Scott deals in grain and agricultural implements, and N. C. Glazier conducts a wagon shop. A feed grinding establishment and flour exchange is kept by A. Snyder. The population in 1880 was 226.

A prominent fraternal organization at one time was Henry King lodge, F. & A. M., for which a dispensation was granted March 28, 1868. The petition for the establishment of the lodge bore the names of T. M. Andrews, S. A. Thornton, J. O. Beardsley, Ira A. Wert, F. C. Wert, H. F. Boynton, Thomas Vandolah, Henry King, James W. Fleming, Corwin Phelps, David McQuiston, F. C. Bacon, John Anderson, William Ross and William Anderson. The first officers were installed by Sol D. Bayless, June 24, 1869.

William T. Hunter, the prominent citizen whose name is perpetuated in that of the town, is mentioned in connection with his son in another chapter.

Thomas Dunten (deceased), one of the earliest settlers of Allen county, was born in Vermont in 1787. He removed to Jefferson county, N. Y., while quite young, and remained until the early part of 1833, when he came west in search of wild land, which he found in abundance in this region. He purchased about 400 acres in this county and returned for his family, which he brought to the new home in Perry township. He had been married in 1813, to Margaret Mattoon, also a native of Vermont, born July 31, 1789, and this union was blessed with seven children: Francis, Franklin (died 1886,) James A., Clarinda, Lucinda, Sally (died 1871,) and Thomas J. Of this well known pioneer family, Lucinda is the only representative in Perry township. He was a man in good circumstances before he came west, and left a beautiful home in New York state, and 100 acres of land, to seek his fortune in a new country, and as is characteristic of the man, his ambition was to make homes for his children, suffering all the hardships of a pioneer life to gain this end. He was a generous and self-sacrificing man, and he was one of the first in his township to take his cattle and go to the northern part of this state and haul corn for himself and neighbors, to keep them from perishing from hunger in the winter. This was a trip which required some six or seven days to make, and the country through which he traveled was so thinly settled, that he was compelled to sleep in the forest where night would overtake him. Mr. Dunten endeavored to give his children as good an education as could be obtained at that time, and they were naturally above the average in intelligence, and were quick to learn. Miss Lucinda became one of the early and successful instructors in the schools of Allen county, an occupation which she successfully followed for over twenty years. She was a pupil in the first school in Perry township, taught by Eb. Ayres. Mr. Dunten was a leading citizen during his life, and his death, which occurred August 20, 1858, was widely mourned.

Horace F. Dunten, the oldest living settler of Perry township, was born in New York, January 28, 1813, son of Ephraim H. and Abigail (Ball) Dunten, who with their family, came to Indiana in August, 1833. Ephraim was a soldier in the war of 1812. Horace Dunten entered forty acres the first year, and continued to accumulate land as fast as he earned the money, at $16 per month while working on the canal, and $10 per month at other work. Horace F. and Thomas Dunten in 1833, selected the site of the cemetery near Huntertown. In 1837 he was united in marriage with Almena, daughter of Henry and Anna (Broughton) Timmerman, who came to Indiana in 1834. To this union were born ten children: Granville S., Marville N., Orville A., died at the age of twenty-eight; Milton B., Alexander B., Winfield S., Friend B., Henry Clay, Mary Helen and Charles J. Four of the sons served in the war of the rebellion: Orville A., a year and a half; Milton B., three years; Alexander a short time, and Winfield, one year. Eight of the ten were successful school teachers. Mrs. Dunten was born July 22, 1816. She has been a member of the Universalist church since its organization at Huntertown. Mr. Dunten though a leading citizen, never desired office of any kind, and held his only office, that of constable, but about one year, when he resigned, and went with the tide of emigration to the gold fields of California, where he remained about a year and a half. He has succeeded well in life, and owns 200 acres of fine farming land which is under a good state of cultivation, with substantial buildings.

Albert Wood (deceased), an early settler, was a native of Jefferson county, N. Y., born in 1810. He was raised in his native state until 1833, when he emigrated and settled in Allen county. In the same year he was united in marriage with Nancy, daughter of Ephraim and Abigail (Ball) Dunten, and this union was blessed with twelve children, seven of whom are now living: Mary J., who is the first white child born in Perry township; John W., Richard F., Oscar D., Commodore, William and Lucy. Mr. Wood departed this life in February, 1878. Mrs. Wood, who was born in Jefferson county, N. Y., in 1817, is still enjoying the comforts of a peaceful life. She is a member of the Universalist church. Mr. Wood was not a member of any church, but was a friend and supporter of such organizations. Though beginning married life with little, he left his family 110 acres of fine farming land in Perry township, which was well improved. He was a leading citizen of his day and was highly respected.

Nathaniel Fitch (deceased), one of the old settlers of Allen county, was a native of Pennsylvania, born July 9, 1806, son of Nathaniel and Sarah Fitch: In 1832 he became a settler in Allen county. He was a blacksmith, gunsmith and locksmith, having learned the trade without instruction. This he followed in Pennsylvania and continued the work after arriving here. He made all the iron for the canal locks from the Wabash to Fort Wayne. Circumstances denied him educational privileges, but he was intelligent and shrewd. June 4, 1840, he was united in marriage with Sarah, daughter of George and Elizabeth De Long. Her grandfather, George Statler, was a soldier of 1812. This union was blessed with fifteen children, of whom thirteen are now living: Perry, Matthias, Jane, Charles, Amos, Francelia, Fidelia, Harvey, Sarah E., Allen, Ida A., Emeline and David. Mrs. Fitch though born in 1818, is still enjoying life. She is a consistent member of the Methodist Episcopal church. Mr. Fitch, being very poor, had only 15 cents in his pocket when he started from Pennsylvania to Indiana, and consequently made the journey on foot. Beginning under such circumstances, his success was very remarkable. He came to own 2,300 acres of land, and raised a large family in comfortable circumstances. As might be expected, his life was full of adventures. At one time, while at work in his shop, he was compelled to put off an Indian who had a gun to mend, which so enraged the redskin that he sprang at him with drawn knife, and probably would have been hurt with the shovel Mr. Fitch was sharpening had not Chief Chopine interfered. Before he came to Indiana he had been accidentally shot in the leg while on a wolf hunt. Again, while crossing Lake Erie on a side-wheel steamer, they were caught in a gale, and the shaft becoming disabled, they were fast going to ruin, and were only saved by breaking one of the shafts. David N. Fitch, the youngest son of Nathaniel Fitch, now lives on the old homestead farm with his aged mother. He received a good common school education and attended college at Fort Wayne two years. In 1887 he was united in marriage with Emma B., daughter of James C. and Nancy (Kidd) Stirlen. They have one child, James B., born January 26, 1888. Mrs. Fitch was born November 2, 1866. She is a member of the Lutheran church. Mr.

Fitch is a member of the Regulators of Allen county. As a young man he stands high in the estimation of all who know him.

Perry Fitch was born January 6, 1842, in the old log house built by his father in an early day, where he grew to manhood. He received a common school education. In 1864 he was united in marriage with Sarah E., daughter of George B. and Magdalena Gloyd. This union was blessed with twelve children, eight now living: William S., Oliver J., George B., Bert C., Kelsie D., Frank E., Claude P. and Pearl M. Mrs. Fitch was born April 9, 1846. She is a member of the old school Baptist church. Mr. Fitch is a resident of DeKalb county, having removed there in 1864, where he has served his township twelve years as justice of the peace. He has a valuable farm of 140 acres, where he lives, with a two-story brick dwelling and a good barn, and eighty acres in Union township, DeKalb county. He is one of the leading citizens of his county, and respected by all. Mr. Fitch is a member of the Masonic order.

Matthias Fitch, the second son of Nathaniel, was born January 16, 1843. December 1, 1867, he was united in marriage with Frances, daughter of James and Rebecca Vandolah, and this union gave them nine children, six of whom are living: Schuyler, John B., Walter, Bessie, Altha and Beatrice. Mrs. Fitch was born February 19, 1843. He is a member of the Regulators, and was once a member of the F. & A. M. He makes a specialty of raising sheep. He has 240 acres of good land in Perry township, improved, and 200 acres in Iowa. In connection with farming he also runs a water-power saw-mill built by his father.

Amos Fitch, of DeKalb county, was born at the old homestead, June 11, 1849, and there grew to manhood, receiving a good common school education. In 1878 he was united in marriage with Nancy E., daughter of William T. and Jane Hunter, and they have two children; Gladys, born October 15, 1881, and Roland, born September 12, 1884. Mrs. Fitch was born January 22, 1849. She is a member of the Universalist church. He was a member of the Good Templars while that lodge was in existence at Huntertown. He possesses 160 acres of land given to him by his father, and upon which he has erected a two-story brick dwelling. He remained in Perry township on the old home place until 1878, when he returned to DeKalb county and settled on the farm where he now lives. Harvey Fitch, eighth child of Nathaniel and Sarah Fitch, was married in 1880 to Etta P. Parker, daughter of Danford and Parmelia Parker, and they have had four children, three now living: Andra, Nina and Parker. He owns 160 acres of fine farming land.

George B. Gloyd is a name conspicuous in the annals of the early settlement of Allen county. He was born in Virginia in 1812, and when nineteen years old emigrated to Ohio, whence he removed in 1832 to Indiana, entering 240 acres of land. He was a man of considerable executive ability, and devoted much of his time to the construction of public works. His first engagement of that kind in this county was as superintendent of a portion of the construction work on the Wabash & Erie canal. In 1835 he returned to Ohio, and was married September 19, to Madeline Mittler, by whom he had nine children, of whom eight are now living: Jerome D., Lewis, Sarah E., William S., Mary M., Edwin G., Celia A., Verdenia (deceased), and George B. After his return to Indiana he took contracts on various railroads, and at the time of his death was engaged on the Saginaw railroad. He amassed a competency and became one of the leading citizens of his township. His widow, who was born June 3, 1816, yet survives. The children of these worthy parents are now prominent citizens of Perry township, esteemed and honored by a wide circle of friends. Jerome D. Gloyd, the eldest, was born in Perry township, July 12, 1841. In 1875 he was married to Fidelia, daughter of Nathaniel and Sarah Fitch, born in April, 1851. They have four children, Estella, Madella, Otis F., and Norma A. Mr. Gloyd served his township as trustee four years, and evinced such ability in this direction that he was elected county commissioner in 1882, and re-elected in 1884, and served six years. He has a fine farm of 160 acres.

William S. Gloyd was born September 8, 1852, on the homestead, and was there raised to manhood, receiving a common school education. October 11, 1888, he was married to Mary Gunger. He is a highly respected citizen, owns a fine farm of eighty acres, and has just completed a handsome and commodious residence.

Edwin G. Gloyd was born February 19, 1850. He early manifested a natural adaptation to the trade of miller, and though he never served an apprenticeship, he became an expert, and is now proprietor of the Gloyd water-mill. His land possessions are 100 acres, which he cultivates. Mr. Gloyd was married April 4, 1872, to Priscilla Myers, who was born April 20, 1852. Of their seven children but three are living: Charles, Silvia and Gertrude.

George B. Gloyd, the youngest son, was born May 21, 1858, and brought up on the old homestead. He has a fine farm of eighty acres of the original land entered by his father, and is one of the influential young men of the township. In 1885 he was married to Emily, daughter of Edward B. and Lavinia Harwood, and they have one child, Ethel May. Mrs. Gloyd who was born in 1867, is a member of the Reformed Lutheran church, while he belongs to the regular Baptist church.

Solomon Simon, an early settler of Allen county, was born in 1825, in Columbiana county, Ohio. His father, George Simon, was a native of Pennsylvania, and was carried across the mountain in a pack saddle when only six months old, to Washington county, Penn., where he was raised to manhood. About 1809 he removed to Ohio and settled in Columbiana county. He served in the war of 1812 about six months. In the fall of 1836 he removed to Allen county with his wife, Elizabeth Hewitt, and children, and settled in Perry township, where he lived until his death in 1872. In 1852 Solomon Simon was united in marriage with

Mary A., daughter of Daniel and Mary (Carble) Rhoads, who settled in DeKalb county, when there were only six other families in the county. This union was blessed with eight children, seven of whom are now living: Joseph, Etta, James S., George L., Ella, Benjamin A. and Perry B. Mrs. Simon was born about 1830. She and her husband are members of the old Lutheran church, Mr. Simon being now elder. Mr. Simon began life in this country without any money, and made his start by traffic in coon skins and other furs. He is now prosperous, having a handsome property of 225 acres in Perry township, and 120 acres in De Kalb county, also a half interest in four lots in Laotto.

James Vandolah, one of the worthy pioneers of Allen county, came to Indiana in 1832, on a tour of inspection, looking for a situation for a water-mill. This he found in Perry township, and then returned to Ohio. In 1835 he came again, and remained long enough to dig the race for his mill. In the fall of 1836, he emigrated with his family, and settled on the farm where Benjamin Vandolah now lives. He entered about 400 acres of wild land in Eel River township, 520 in Perry township, and 160 acres in DeKalb county. He was a mill-wright, and devoted much time to his trade, having worked in several mills throughout the country. He built the Shryock mill, at Leo; the Dauson mill, at Spencerville; the grist-mill, near Clarksville; his own mill, and a number of others. About 1830 he was united in marriage with Rebecca Tucker. Of their eight children, five are now living: Benjamin, Thomas, Sarah J., Francis and James. Mr. Vandolah served as one of the trustees of his township several terms. He was a leading citizen, and was highly respected by all who knew him. His eldest son, Benjamin Vandolah, was born in Greene county, Ohio, April 14, 1834; he was brought to Indiana when three years of age, and on the farm where he now lives he grew to manhood. On October 4, 1888, he was married to Catharine Aaron, daughter of Michael and Elizabeth (Pierce) Aaron. She is a member of the Lutheran church. He is a prosperous farmer, possessing 180 acres of fine land in Perry township, with substantial buildings. Mr. Vandolah has in his possession a very curious Indian relic, which he unearthed about twelve years ago. Thomas Vandolah, the second son, was born in Greene county, August 31, 1836. His life in Allen county began in the same year. He received such education as could be obtained in the pioneer log school-house. In 1871 he was united in marriage with Elizabeth Vandolah, daughter of Joseph and Drusilla (Nickerson) Vandolah. She was born in 1842. Though never seeking office, he has always taken an interest in politics, being one of the leading democrats of his township. He owns 285 acres of good farming land, and is as prominent socially as he is as a land-owner.

John Surfus, an old and prominent farmer of Perry township, and a pioneer of Allen county, is a native of Ohio, born in 1812, son of Andrew and Betsy (Harless) Surfus. He left his native state in 1833 and settled in Allen county, Ind. Mr. Surfus was denied the privilege of any education, his family being poor and in need of his work. In 1842 he was united in marriage with Ellen Delong, by whom he had twelve children, ten of whom are living: Stephen, George, Samuel, Andrew, John E., Harriet, Mary, Ellen, Celina and Julia. When Mr. Surfus landed in Allen county he possessed a yoke of cattle, table, chest, set of chairs and oven, and their first bed was made by boring holes in the logs of the house and putting in sticks, which he wrapped with bark. In such circumstances Mr. Surfus began life in Indiana, surrounded by bands of Indians and wild beasts. He had no financial advantages and his success in life must be attributed to the energy and perseverance he has displayed in all his undertakings, and the unfailing assistance of his true wife. They accumulated considerable property and at one time owned over 1,000 acres of good land in Perry township. They have lived to see all their children comfortably situated. After giving his children all a good home Mr. Surfus retains a residence elegantly surrounded with all the comforts of life. He and wife are members of the Methodist Episcopal church. Their seventh child, Andrew Surfus, a prosperous farmer and stock-raiser, was born September 8, 1850. He received a common school education and remained with his parents until twenty-five years of age, when his father gave him 140 acres of good farming land, which he now occupies and has well improved. In 1875 he was united in marriage with Mary, daughter of Jacob and Sarah Snyder, born November 18, 1854, and they have three children: Jerry H., born October 16, 1876; Orville, born July 11, 1878; Eva Blanche, born July 25, 1880. He and wife and children are members of the Methodist Episcopal church. He makes a specialty of graded stock.

Schuyler Wheeler (deceased) was one of the pioneers of Allen county. He was born July 22, 1802, in Massachusetts, but was taken to New York by his parents when only six months of age. He remained in Oswego county until fourteen years of age, when he removed to Orangeville, N. Y., where he remained until 1836, when he settled in Allen county, entering 400 acres, in April. Returning to New York he brought his family during the summer of 1836. In 1828 he had been united in marriage with Lydia, daughter of Perry G. and Sophia Smith. This union was blessed with four children, three of whom are living: Julia, Commodore P., now a resident of Missouri; Columbia, the wife of F. C. West, who died April 19, 1888, and Almina, wife of Cyrus Krumlauf. Mrs. Wheeler was born in Berkshire county, Mass., in 1801. She was a member of the Methodist Episcopal church from sixteen years of age. He served an apprenticeship at the tanner's trade, at the age of nine years, and after he became twenty-one he formed a partnership with his father and Luther Briggs, and in connection with the tannery they also ran a boot and shoe store. He had strong elements of character that commanded the respect and confidence of his neighbors and associates. He succeeded financially, leaving 940 acres of good land here, and 1,800 in Missouri, and in public life was honored by the position of representative of Allen county, in the legislature of 1859.

Rapin Andrews, above named as an early settler, came to Perry township with his wife, Mary Brimmer, and their children, from New York in 1839, and began to take a hand in the township's development. He was one of its most valued citizens. He was a Mason, while in New York, during the period of the Morgan excitement, and was a charter member of the first Royal Arch lodge of Allen county. He was one of the eleven voters at the first presidential election in Perry township, in 1840. In 1849 he died at the age of sixty-seven, but his widow survived until 1884, reaching the age of eighty-five years.

Theron M. Andrews, son of the worthy old settlers, Rapin and Mary Andrews, was born March, 1822, in New York state. Theron M. received his early education in the log school-house, and assisted in the poineer work of the family. December 20, 1849, he was united in marriage with Helen L., daughter of Oliver and Clarissa Potter, born October, 1830. To this union were born three children, Mary D., Sidney D., and Ida J. Mr. Andrews is one of the prominent citizens of the county, and during his more active days was among the foremost in its affairs. He served as assessor of his township from 1856 to 1857, and was elected township trustee, an office he resigned in 1857, to accept a higher one to which he was called by the people of the county, that of member of the board of county commissioners, and he held this important position until 1860. He has served since then as one of the drainage commissioners of the county, and has been a member of the board of equalization since that body was created. He is a member of the Masonic order and occupies a high position socially. One of the leading people, he is widely known and he and family are highly respected. Mr. Andrews has a beautiful farm in Perry township of 220 acres, thoroughly cultivated, and provided with substantial buildings.

Dexter B. Andrews, a well-known citizen of Perry township, was born in New York, July, 1825, another son of Rapin and Mary (Brimmer) Andrews. In 1839 Dexter B. emigrated with his parents and settled in Perry township. In 1848 he entered the shops at Fort Wayne to serve an apprenticeship as millwright, but never completed it. Being a natural mechanic, he stood at the head wherever he worked. He followed this trade through life In 1849 he was united to Celeste A. Sauers, born at Watertown, N. Y., October 3, 1832, daughter of Samuel and Mercy Gibson (Parsons) Sauers, early settlers of Allen county. The father cast the first democratic vote in Washington township. He was proprietor of the Washington hotel in Fort Wayne about five years. This union was blessed by four children, three now living: Amelia, wife of J. N. Bassett; Cora M., wife of L. C. Hunter, and Clara G. Mr. Andrews worked a number of years as a daguerreotyper, which art he learned from books alone. He has in his possession pictures he took in 1853, which are as bright apparently as the day they were taken. He continued at this business in connection with his trade until 1865. In 1866, he entered the pension office with S. D. Bayless, where he remained until 1869. In March, 1852, he started on the overland route to the gold fields of California, arriving August 10, 1852. He entered the mining region at the mouth of Nelson Creek, and remained until November, when he removed to Santa Clara, and returned to Indiana in the spring of 1853. He is a member of the Masonic order, of Wayne lodge, No. 25. Mr. Andrews is one of the leading citizens of his township, and a man respected by all. He owns ten and one-half acres of land in Perry, and 140 acres in Eel River township.

David M. Shoaff, one of the pioneer settlers of Allen county, was born in Hamilton county, Ohio, December 16, 1814, son of Peter and Elizabeth (Musselman) Shoaff. He received a good common school education, and served an apprenticeship at the tailor's trade, which he followed about twenty years. In 1836 he was united in marriage with Mary Mendenhall. This union was blessed with five children. Four of his children are now living: Peter, Samuel H., John P. and Emma. Mrs. Shoaff, who was born in 1819, departed this life in 1888. She was a member of the Methodist Episcopal church. Mr. Shoaff and wife came to this country in 1839, with no money, and very little goods. Being poor, he was compelled to work out, and in the winter worked in the snow and storm for 50 cents per day, enough to buy two pounds of coffee of old Squire Jones. His wife's experience in the early days was typical of what the helpmeet of the pioneer had to endure. She would go to the clearing with her two little babes and place them on the ground while she would help pick and burn brush. Mr. Shoaff now has a nice little farm of eighty-four acres, which is under a good state of cultivation. Mr. Shoaff was one of the eleven who voted at the presidential election in Perry township in 1840, and cast his vote for Harrison. In March, 1840, salt sold at $9.00 per barrel in Fort Wayne, and Mr. Shoaff being in need of some, his brother furnished the money, and he and F. C. Freeman made the trip in March, taking twelve days to reach Maumee City. He returned by Fort Defiance on the ice, having very narrow escapes from drowning. When Mr. Shoaff built J. P. Shoaff's and Squire Jones' houses in the fall of 1836, they were the first houses on the road on which he now lives between his home and Heller's Corners, a distance of six miles. Six men helped to build these houses, out of whom two are now living: D. M. Shoaff and Harrison Jones.

Phanuel W. Jackson, a prominent farmer of Perry township, was born in Butterfield township, Oxford county, Me., May 19, 1827. His parents, Lemuel and Mercy (White) Jackson, were also natives of Maine. When he was six years old his parents emigrated to Ohio, and located in a part of Richland county, now a portion of Crawford, where the father died six years later. Here Mr. Jackson passed his boyhood and received his schooling. The advantages for an education were very poor, but he has since, however, acquired a broad knowledge and general information. At the age of fourteen he accompanied his sister and her husband, Eleazer Cummings, to Allen county, and located with them on the farm Mr. Jackson now occupies in Perry township. In December, 1841, he returned to the home of his mother in Richland county. At the age of twenty he accompanied his mother to Whitley county, Ind., and from 1847 until 1850, gave his attention to the well business. May 16, 1850, he was married to Catharine Kell, who was born in France, of German descent, June 29, 1824. She came to America with her parents, George and Magdalena Kell, when she was four years old. Immediately after his marriage Mr. Jackson located on the farm he has occupied nearly forty years. In his chief occupation, farming, he has been successful. He owns a well-improved farm of 120 acres, and has given more or less to his children. Besides being known as a first-class farmer, Mr. Jackson has acquired an extensive reputation as an oculist. It was twenty-five years ago that his attention was especially directed to his ability in this line, when his wife had a very severe disease of the eyes, which had been pronounced incurable by a recognized oculist. He began a systematic study of the subject, determining thoroughly to acquaint himself with it, and the case above mentioned and others with which he was equally successful soon attracted the attention of the public. For the past twenty years he has practiced quite extensively, and has performed a number of difficult cures. He has also devoted much attention to the study of medicine in general, and he is now one of the licensed physicians of Allen county. Mr. Jackson and wife had four children that lived to maturity: Mercy M., Cordelia M., Margaret D. and Melia N., of whom Cordelia M. died in her twenty-fourth year. The wife of Mr. Jackson died January 23, 1887. She was a member of the Baptist church. Mr. Jackson is a member of the same church and in politics is a democrat. He is now serving as justice of the peace, having been elected in the spring of 1886.

Joseph Warner (deceased), one of the pioneer settlers of Perry township, was born in Adams county, Penn., September 1, 1796. He remained in Pennsylvania until 1831, when he emigrated to Ohio and settled in Richland county. In the fall of 1842 he removed to Indiana. He bargained to clear twenty acres for forty acres, and completed the work that winter, and settled the next year on the forty acres. His education was limited, and he had to depend upon his labor for support of his family, and what he made was by honest work and good management. At twenty-five years of age he was united in marriage with Elizabeth Ebley, by whom he had nine children: John (died in the service of the Union at Nashville), Samuel, Joseph, George, Mary, Amos, James, Alexander and Sophia. He and wife were both members of the Catholic church. He served as township treasurer one term, and as supervisor several years during the time of opening new roads. He opened all the roads in his district and proved to be an efficient officer. He resided in Perry township on his original farm until his death, which occurred in 1871. He became a prosperous as well as popular citizen, and at the time of his death owned 303 acres of valuable land. Samuel Warner, his eldest son, is a native of Cumberland county, Penn., born November 21, 1824. He came with his parents to Indiana in 1842, and had the usual pioneer experience. After receiving a common school education he worked at the carpenter's trade about eighteen years, and though he never served an apprenticeship at any trade, he became one of the leading carpenters of his day. On June 4, 1849, he was united in marriage with Julia A., daughter of Benjamin and Sarah (Robinson) Spencer. Of their eight children, seven are living: Benjamin F., Elizabeth A., Addie, Charles H., Lovisa S., William M. and Julia A. Mrs. Warner was born in Alleghany county, N. Y., April 7, 1833. She is a member of the Close Communion Baptist church. Mr. Warner is a member of the Methodist Episcopal church. He was a member of the Regulators. He has a home farm of 131 acres in Perry township, which is well improved, with a two-story dwelling house, and thirty-five and one-half acres in Cedar Creek township.

Among the notable families of Allen county are Jacob Hillegass and wife, pioneers of Perry township, and their descendants. His father, Michael Hillegass, was a farmer and a native of Pennsylvania. He was married to Anna Yeakel, and they had thirteen children. Jacob, the youngest of five brothers, was born February 7, 1818, after the removal of the family to Montgomery county, Ohio. There he was raised, and there he received the education which could be obtained in the early school-houses in the woods. May 26, 1841, in Butler county, Ohio, he was united in marriage with Lucy A. Powell, daughter of John and Barbara Shaffer, both natives of Pennsylvania. This union was blessed with seven children: Josiah D., Jerry, Hezekiah, Isaiah J., Sarah J., Mary M. and Lucy I. Mrs. Hillegass was born July 28, 1822, in Butler county, Ohio. She and husband have for many years been members of the Presbyterian church. Mr. Hillegass is a man in whom the people have always had implicit confidence, and in an early day when the township board consisted of treasurer, clerk and one director, he served as clerk about six years, afterward being elected trustee, a position he held nine years. He has also served as assessor of his township. During his terms in these smaller offices, he became noted among his constituents as a man of energy and much decision of character, and this reputation led to his election as county commissioner in October, 1870. He was re-elected three years later. In this position he acquitted himself with honor. Mr. Hillegass came to Allen county, April 14, 1843, and settled on the farm where he now lives. It comprises 320 acres of very fine farming land, well improved, with a two-story brick dwelling. He has always been a supporter of churches, schools and all laudable enterprises. Though in his seventy-first year he is fully able to enjoy the comforts with which he is so amply surrounded. His manly qualities and honest dealing have gained for him the respect of all who know him. Having been deprived of school advantages in his early years, he bestowed those privileges upon his children liberally. His sons, J. D., Jerry and Isaiah, were graduated at the University of Michigan. The first and third became lawyers, and the second was for several years superintendent of schools of Allen county. Josiah D. died April 2, 1875, and his law partner, John Stahl, husband of Sarah J. Hillegass, died August 16, 1878.

Jacob Kell, an old and successful farmer of Perry township, is a native of France, born July 10, 1818, son of George and Magdalene Kell, both of German descent. At ten years of age he emigrated with his parents to America, and first settled in Wayne county, Ohio. In October, 1843, he removed to Indiana and settled on the farm where he now lives, buying eighty acres of land, and afterward entering forty acres, all timbered land. He began work for Mr. Newhouse, making rails for 75 cents per hundred, and furnished the timber and boarded himself. By this labor he bought his house furniture. He cleared and fenced ten acres, and in the summer following he raised some corn and potatoes. In a few years he had a beautiful farm. In 1841 he was united in marriage with Catharine Weimer, and they had five children, three of whom are living: Solomon, George V. and Amelia E. This wife was born March 27, 1824, and departed this life November 2, 1852. She was a member of the Cedar Creek Presbyterian church. On July 7, 1855, he was married to Catherine M., daughter of John and Mary (Crous) Foner, and they had the following children: Mary Magdalene, John (died at the age of seventeen), Emma, Hiram A. (died aged twenty-one), Edna Viola (died aged five), Bertha May and Frederick Jacob. Mrs. Kell was born in Pennsylvania April 19, 1828. She is a member of the Methodist Episcopal church at Huntertown. Mr. Kell was a member of the Regulators for the protection of property in Allen county. He has served his township as trustee four years. He makes a specialty of the best grades of all kinds of stock. He has prospered in life, and now owns about 1,000 acres of fine farming land in Allen county, and his home place, being the old homestead, consisting of about 800 acres, is handsomely improved, with good buildings. His accumulations have been by industry, not through speculation, and he is esteemed as one of the prominent citizens and representative farmers of his township.

Solomon Kell, of Perry township, was born August 23, 1842, son of the above named Jacob and Catharine Kell. He was raised in Allen county, and received a good education, attending the Perry Center seminary four or five years, and studying all the higher branches, after which he followed the vocation of teacher for five years. Part of this period, subsequent to 1868, he was a resident of Iowa. He was there elected trustee of his township, but after being in office two years, returned to Perry township. In 1865 he was united in marriage with Emeline, a daughter of John and Eliza Krider, born in 1845. Her parents were pioneers of Allen county. This union was blessed with five children: Alice May, Eliza M., Mabel Ellen, Charles E. and Grace Gertrude. Mr. Kell is a constable, or one of the riders of the "Regulators" who have done much in the past to rid Allen county of outlaws. Being a resolute man, he is very earnest in his work, and does his full share in helping to bring to punishment these enemies of law and good society. Like his worthy father, he occupies one of the first places in the estimation of his township. He has a fine farm of eighty acres, with a good two-story frame dwelling house and commodious barn.

Constant Delagrange, one of the prosperous farmers and stock-raisers of Perry township, is a native of France, born May 24, 1831. He is a son of Joseph and Mary (Shottan) Delagrange, natives of France, who emigrated to America, bringing Constant, then only twelve years of age. They settled in Ohio and bought twenty-five acres of land, where they remained eight years and then sold and bought eighty acres, which they improved and lived upon four years. Then they removed to Indiana and settled in Cedar Creek township. They first bought forty acres in the woods, and four years later sold this and bought sixty acres near Leo, where he remained three years, and in 1861 he bought and settled on the farm where he now lives. All of these farms he cleared to a considerable extent and built upon, and his present place is handsomely cared for. In June, 1861, he was united in marriage with Ann Margaret Greavy, by whom he had fourteen children, seven of whom are living: Joseph, Franklin, Constine, Josephine, August, Louis and Julian. Mrs. Delagrange was born in 1837 and died December 27, 1881. She was a member of the Catholic church, to which he also belongs. His vocation has always been that of a farmer and he has succeeded well, now owning a farm of 200 acres which is equal to the best. In stock-raising he makes a specialty of Norman horses.

John B. Masson, a substantial farmer of Perry township, is a native of France, born December 21, 1826. He is the son of Peter and Margaret Masson, the former of whom died when John B. was five years old. He lived in his native country, being employed chiefly in a vineyard until eighteen years old, when he accompanied his mother and step-father to America. Coming directly to Fort Wayne, they settled on a farm in Lake township, two miles from Arcola. There he remained with his mother six years. December 4, 1850, he was married to Amelie Nicolas, also a native of France, born September 18, 1833, daughter of Nicolas and Mary Nicolas, the former of whom died when Mrs. Masson was two years old. She accompanied her mother and step-father to America when she was eleven years old, and they also settled in Lake township. About eighteen months after their marriage, Mr. and Mrs. Masson located on the farm they now occupy. Mr. Masson resides on his well improved farm of eighty acres, and also owns a farm of forty-eight acres in St. Joseph township. He and wife have six children: John N., Jane M., Mary J., Joseph A., Jule J. and Adel J. Mr. and Mrs. Masson and children are members of the Catholic church. In politics Mr. Masson is a democrat.

Florentin Roy, of Perry township, is a native of France. He was born July 26, 1833, to Ferdinand and Josephine (Julliard) Roy, of French nativity, who on March 4, 1846, emigrated to America and reached Fort Wayne June 22. They purchased land in Washington township and remained until 1858, when they removed to St. Joseph township, where the mother died in 1872. The father lived with Florentin until his death in 1878. He reached this country poor in purse, but came to own a farm of eighty acres. He was a worthy man and well-liked by his neighbors. Florentin received his education mainly in this country. His vocation has always been that of farmer, but in connection with farming he was engaged in operating a saw and shingle mill about five years. April 5, 1853, he was united in marriage with Mary Lailliot, born April 24, 1824, and they had four children, three now living: Louis F., Charles J., Philomine. February 15, 1865, Mr. Roy enlisted in Company H, One Hundred and Fifty-second regiment, under Capt. M. W. Wines, and received an honorable discharge at Charleston, August 30, 1865. He served as deputy assessor three years and was elected constable but resigned to enlist in the war. In 1871 he removed to his present home in Perry township, where he owns a valuable farm of 178 acres. Having come here when quite young he and all of his father's family suffered all the privations of pioneer life. He is one of the leading citizens of his township and is well-known as a prominent politician in the democratic party. In 1888 he was elected township trustee. Mr. Roy makes a specialty of his vineyard, and also gives much attention to raising German carp, having a pond of about two acres. He and wife are members of the Catholic church.

George Gump, of Perry township, is a native of Miami county, Ohio, born August 14, 1825, son of Daniel and Margaret (Studebaker) Gump. In 1848 he emigrated west and settled in Perry township, and in 1856 removed to the farm where he now lives. He received the common school education of his day. His occupation has always been that of a farmer. In 1849 he returned to Ohio and was united in marriage with Harriet Agenbroad, born June 1, 1830, and of their thirteen children nine are living: Franklin, Priscilla, Alice, Jane, Madison, Marion, Calvert, Effie and Cora. Mr. Gump served as township trustee four years, his term closing in 1888. He has also done considerable probate business in his township. Mr. Gump had only 60 cents in money when he settled in the woods and began to hew out a farm, but now he looks with satisfaction over a handsome farm of 184 acres. He and wife are members of the German Baptist church.

Martin V. Metcalf, a substantial farmer of Perry township, was born in Ashland county, Ohio, December 3, 1845. His father, Vachel Metcalf, an early settler of Perry, was born September 20, 1816, in Ashland county, Ohio, where his father, Edward Metcalf, was a pioneer. In 1842 Vachel married Amanda Otto, and in 1849 they emigrated to Perry township, settling upon land yet in the forest. When Martin V. was but four years old he accompanied his parents to Allen county, and located on the farm where his boyhood and youth were spent. In winter he went to the district school, receiving a very good education for that day. In early manhood he adopted the vocation of a farmer. January 26, 1870, he was married to Mary E. Duly, a native of Ashland county, Ohio, born September 7, 1845, to John and Elizabeth (Ely)

Duly. From 1870 to 1877, Mr. and Mrs. Metcalf resided on the Metcalf homestead, in Perry township. In the latter year they removed to another farm in the same township. Besides this valuable farm of eighty acres, Mr. Metcalf owns a one-half interest in the old homestead of 140 acres. He and wife have had two children. The first was a son that died in infancy, unnamed. The other is William Edmund, who was born October 29, 1881. Mr. Metcalf is one of his township's most worthy and respected citizens.

Solomon Duly, of Perry township, is a native of Wayne county, Ohio, born November 27, 1838. His father, John Duly, was born in Pennsylvania, and emigrated to Ohio, and in 1849 settled in Perry township on the farm where Solomon now lives. Here he died June 14, 1874. He began life in the Perry township woods with about $900, and succeeded in becoming the owner of 240 acres of good land. He was one of the leading citizens, and he and his wife, whose maiden name was Elizabeth Ely, were highly esteemed. Their son, Solomon, received his education in the log school-houses, now passed away. On December 14, 1871, he was married to Lucinda, daughter of George and Margaret (Kairger) Bowser, early settlers who came from Ohio about 1836, and settled on land which they entered from the government. This union was blessed with two children: Harry E. and Edna I. Mrs. Duly was born July 14, 1842. She is a member of the United Brethren church. Mr. Duly has a fertile and well improved farm of eighty acres.

Eugene Parnin, a successful farmer of Perry township, is a native of France, born January 18, 1844, son of Gabriel and Virginia (Everard) Parnin. He emigrated to America with his parents when only eight years of age, and settled in Lake township, where he grew to manhood and received an education such as could be obtained at that time. His vocation has always been that of a farmer. In the dark days of the rebellion he enlisted in Company I, Forty-sixth Illinois infantry, under Capt. D. S. Pride, and served two years when the war ended; he received his discharge as corporal at Baton Rouge, La., January 20, 1866. On February 28, 1870, he was married to Louisa Delagrange, born September 6, 1849, daughter of Justin and Theresa (Bonot) Delagrange. Of their eight children seven are living: Joseph, Louis, Emma, August, Edward, Mary and George. Mr. Parnin has prospered in his undertakings, and by good management and close economy now owns a valuable farm of 120 acres in Perry township. He gives much attention to breeding Norman horses. He is one of the leading citizens of the township, and is well respected.

Solomon C. Chapman, of Perry township, is a native of Ashland county, Ohio, born May 18, 1838. His father, John Chapman, emigrated from Ohio, October 4, 1852, and settled on the farm where his son now lives, where he remained until his death, July 12, 1861. By honest industry he was enabled to leave a good farm of eighty acres and an honorable name. Solomon Chapman coming to Indiana when about thirteen years of age, grew to manhood on the old homestead and received such schooling as the schools of that day afforded. December 10, 1861, he was married to Hannah Honora, daughter of Patrick and Matilda (Baird) Horn, and they had seven children: Mary J., Sylvester G., Minerva A., Hannah H., Eunice M., Catharine C. and Blanche H. Mrs. Chapman, who was born December 12, 1842, departed this life May 18, 1873. She was a member of the Presbyterian church. Mr. Chapman was deputy assessor of Perry township in 1873. He is a member of the Masonic order. His land-holdings in Perry township amount to 272 acres.

John W. Hursh, one of the prominent teachers of Allen county, is a native of Perry township, born July 15, 1855. He is a son of Jacob and Elizabeth Hursh. Growing to manhood on the old homestead farm, he received a good common school education and afterward attended a term at the Center seminary and at the Fort Wayne college about two years. In 1875 he began teaching in the country schools and has been so engaged since, with the exception of about two years. In 1880 he was united in marriage with Jennie, daughter of George and Harriet Gump, and they have four children: George, John, Donnie and Bertie. He and wife are both members of the Methodist Episcopal church. He occupies the old homestead of 200 acres, of which he owns all but one share. He is recognized as one of the worthy and valuable citizens of his township.

Alexander Stirlen was born in Holmes county, Ohio, December 24, 1832. His parents, Samuel and Delilah (Praig) Stirlen, natives of Westmoreland county, Penn., came to Ohio about 1828, traveling in the once familiar emigrant wagons. In 1853 Alexander settled in Allen county, and was employed about four years as a day laborer. He then farmed on shares two years, after which he purchased land. His schooling was that of pioneer days. In 1858 he was united in marriage with Magdalena, daughter of George and Magdalena Kell, early settlers of Allen county. She was born February 6, 1829. This union gave them five children: Martha, John, William, George and Edgar. Mrs. Stirlen departed this life February 26, 1880. She was a member of the Methodist Episcopal church. Mr. Stirlen has always been an active worker for the democratic party, but has not held office except as a school director four years. When he first came to Allen county he was without resources, and had the usual wearisome experiences of early days. But his success has been remarkable, and he possesses 532 acres of excellent land in Perry and Cedar Creek townships. His home place, in Perry, is handsomely improved.

James McCombs, of Perry township, was born in Ireland, April 4, 1828. His parents, Robert and Margaret McCombs, emigrated to America when James was about two years of age, and settled in Claremont county, Ohio. After landing in Cincinnati, his mother was taken sick and died, and he was bound out to Sampson Newbrough, with whom he remained until twenty-one years of age. In 1850 he was united in marriage with Margaret Simonton, and they have had eleven children: Robert S., Thomas C., John S., Mary C., wife of John Reynolds, Joseph (deceased), James I., Theoppolis M., Emma, wife of Samuel Davis, William S., Hiram E. and David O. Mrs. McComb was born July 21, 1833. She and husband are members of the United Brethren church. Mr. McCombs is a leading citizen and has served as trustee from 1880 to 1884. His landed possessions are 200 acres of fine farming land, which were heavily timbered when he first came here.

Henry A. Treace, an early settler of Perry township, is a native of Pennsylvania, born in 1823, son of Jacob and Elizabeth Treace. He was taken by his parents to Ohio when only two years of age, and there grew to manhood. He received a common school education in the pioneer log school-house. In 1844 he was married to Elizabeth Clayton, born in 1821, and had by this union nine children, eight of whom are living: Margaret, Rosa Ann, Lottie, Jane, William, Frank, George and Robert. He served six years as a school director. He and wife are members of the Methodist Episcopal church. When Mr. Treace settled in Perry township he had but a shilling in money, but by hard, diligent industry he came to own 480 acres of good land out of which he cleared farms, and has given all to his children except 120 acres upon which he now lives. He is one of the leading citizens of his township, and is well respected by all.

Alanson C. Griffin, of Perry township, is a native of New York state. He was born June 29, 1836, the son of Jonathan and Huldah (Dudley) Griffin. The mother, who is in her eighty-first year, is still a resident of New York state. Mr. Griffin remained in his native state until 1864, when he settled in Allen county, and in March, 1866, occupied the farm where he now lives. He received a very limited education, his father having died when he was quite young, leaving much responsibility to him. He began with his brother, when seventeen years of age, the trade of a carpenter and joiner, which he engaged in after coming to Indiana. He and his brother went to Canada in 1857, and built a house for one of his uncles. December 22, 1858, he was married to Mary J., daughter of Charles B. and Rosette (Eddy). They had one child, Viola, born September 28, 1860. The mother of this child was born February 8, 1836, and departed this life August 8, 1863. December 31, 1865, he was married to Henriette, daughter of John and Ellen Surfus. By her he had five children: Effie M., born May 6, 1867; Anna, born September 13, 1869; John E., born November 14, 1870; Aclie S., born January 8, 1872, and Jesse, born May 14, 1876. The mother was born March 25, 1844, and died May 18, 1876. December 5, 1877, he was united in marriage with Sarah J., daughter of James and Rebecca Vandolah. She is a member of the German Baptist church. Mr. Griffin was a member of the Masonic lodge at Huntertown during its existence, and passed through the chairs. He has a fine farm of eighty acres, in Perry township, well improved with perfect arrangements for watering, and supplying water to his house, and 160 acres in Kingman county, Kansas. In connection with farming he also runs a repair shop for farmers.

Fisher C. West was born in 1827, at Syracuse, N. Y., son of Joseph and Joanna (Smith) West. The father was a soldier in the war of 1812, and served about one year. The grandparents on both sides were soldiers in the war for American independence, and the grandfather on the father's side served through the whole struggle and lost an eye in the first battle. Mr. West left his native state when about fifteen years of age, and settled in DeKalb county, where he remained with his parents about one year, and then began to learn the miller's trade, which he has followed more or less ever since. In 1849 he joined the great tide of emigration to the gold fields of California, where he was very successful in mining. He remained about four years, then returned to Indiana and purchased the farm in Perry township on which he now lives. He remained in Allen county about ten months and then began a series of travels, to New York city, then to the Cape Verde, Africa, then to the little island of St. Helena; thence to Rio Janeiro, Brazil; thence to Cape Town, Africa; thence to Fort Phillip, Australia; thence to the gold mines of Australia, where he remained about eight years; then from Melbourne to London, England, where he remained about three months and then returned home. In 1860 he was united in marriage with Columbia Ann Wheeler. Of their eight children, three are living: Price D., Curtis S. and Lena E. The mother of these children was born in 1833, and departed this life in 1888. Mr. West is an extensive land owner, having 937 acres of valuable land in Perry township, with brick dwelling and other substantial buildings. He also owns eighty acres in Noble county, about 300 in Missouri and 1,700 in Tennessee. He is an enterprising man and is now boring for gas on his farm, the well being at this writing about 1,000 feet deep. His home farm is the very best land in Allen county, unsurpassed in its production of grain. Mr. West is a member of the F. & A. M.

CEDAR CREEK TOWNSHIP.

The region about the confluence of Cedar creek and the St. Joseph river appears to have been the seat of villages both of those mysterious people, the mound-builders, and of Indians, at a remote epoch, and here it is probable that missionaries erected the cross at a date never recorded in history. During the present era the first to make a permanent home were Jacob Notestine and family, who in the spring of 1834, went up the St. Joseph in a flat-boat and settled near the mouth of Cedar creek. He found there a man named Wood, who had passed the winter, but eagerly availed himself of the boat to remove his possessions, and start for the east. The early settlers found here traces of former occupation, at least of the visits of the French. William Muller, in 1836, found upon a beech tree a French inscription and the date 1772, and in 1869, John Pring found two feet beneath the surface, in the vicinity of Cedarville, a cross, made of beech wood, fourteen feet in length, with the figures 1772 carved upon it. These facts have led to the belief that this was the site of a French mission, during the Indian occupation. Mr. Pring, some twenty years before, had found on the banks of the creek, buried beneath the surface, fragments of trace-chains, log-chains, etc., and a heap of cinders, which appear to show that a blacksmith's forge had been in operation there at some date previous to the settlement. The same gentleman, on April 28, 1850, found a sword imbedded in the wood of a linn tree, which had been blown down the previous night, and about the same time William Muller discovered a cannon ball on his farm, circumstances which seem to indicate that there had been military operations here which have escaped the cognizance of historians. The memory of these finds aided in causing a great deal of excitement at a subsequent date, when a party of strangers from the west came to Cedar Creek, and letting it be known that they were about to fish and trap, began digging instead, apparently in the search of some hidden treasure. It is said that they finally unearthed and bore away the contents of an old, rotten chest, but further the traditions do not satisfy curiosity, except that it is told by way of explanation that these men came to find treasures buried by Indians, whose descendants, removed to strange lands beyond the great river, had revealed the secret. The only neighbors which the Notestines had during the first year were John Manning and family, who settled on section 15. In 1836, William Muller, coming from Ohio, cut his way through the forest tangles from Beckett's branch to the spot he had selected as his home, and after building his cabin, went to Cincinnati and married the lady who assisted him in his pioneer life. In 1836, also, came Charles C. Nettelhorst and family, Peter Sullivan and John Rogers, two friends of Irish nativity, and John Baker and William Berry, who afterward went west. Moses Sivotts came up from St. Joseph township in 1838, and among the others who came between 1837 and 1840 were William and Joseph Shields, John Hackley, Aaron Poff, William Bowser, John Hagan, Henry Updyke, Abraham Fulkerson, Harmon Lydecker, Joseph Silvers and John B. Blue. The two latter were elected the first justices, and Thomas Wilson, the first constable, at the election in 1837, held at the house of Jacob Notestine. The total poll was twelve votes.

In 1835 the first road was surveyed through the township, which became known as the St. Joseph road. About 1839, James Vandolah built a saw-mill, and afterward arranged for grinding grain. About 1840 Stout Price established a blacksmith forge at the site of Hamilton. In 1847 the Leo postoffice was established near the center of the township, and John Manning was appointed postmaster. John B. Blue was the deputy and kept the office at his store. At this place grew up the village of Hamilton. This was a point on the mail route to northwestern

Ohio and southern Michigan, on which Jeremiah Bowen was contractor and his sons, Mason and Marvin, the carriers.

Settlers becoming numerous about Cedar creek, the village of Cedarville was laid out in the forks of the creek and St. Joseph river, in May, 1838, by William G. Ewing, of Fort Wayne; George M. Ewing, of Cass county, and Messrs. Seymour, Robinson and Peck, of Connecticut; but soon after the platting of Hamilton, in February, 1849, the older town lost precedence. In 1880 the population was 113. One of its earliest traders was Asa Miller, who took a stock of goods there from Fort Wayne about 1839, and built a mill.

In 1852 John Dever established a wagon shop, and afterward a store at Hamilton, and managed the first regular boat line on the St. Joseph. The village, which now is generally known as Leo, had in 1880 a population of 166.

The village of Urbana was laid out May 10, 1867, by J. C. Hursch. Here the Urbana mills have been conducted by M. L. Moudy since 1879.

Jacob Notestine, who has been referred to as a prominent early settler of Allen county, was a native of Lehigh county, Penn., born in 1790, of parents who were natives of Germany. He received a good common school education in his native state, and became a skillful blacksmith, so that after his settlement in Allen county he was called on to weld a collar on the spindle of the buhr of the second flouring mill in Allen county. Like all his work, it was a good job. He was married about 1812, to Barbara Gunder, who was born in York county, Penn., in 1788, and they had thirteen children, of whom six are living: Uriah, Peter, Daniel, Aaron, Isaiah, and Barbara Ann. Jacob Notestine, during the war of 1812, enlisted, but after his company had received their uniforms, they were notified that their services were not needed, so that he did not see actual service. He and his family reached Fort Wayne, July 14, 1830, and first settled near Fort Wayne, near the site of the old Rudisill mill, and there cleared eight or ten acres. In 1834, he entered forty-six acres where his son Daniel now lives, and in March, 1834, the residence of the family in Cedar Creek township began. Here they did a great work in opening and preparing land for cultivation, and no family among the old pioneers more deserves an honorable place in the annals of the county. Possessing the characteristics of true pioneers they succeeded in their herculean tasks, and became well-to-do, and the survivors are now highly esteemed by the people. Jacob Notestine was a prominent citizen in his time, and was one of the board of trustees of his township for two or three terms. He died September 16, 1853, and his widow's decease followed on August 3, 1860. He was a member of the Lutheran and his wife of the Methodist church.

Peter Notestine, the sixth child of the above, was born April 11, 1819, in Fairfield county, Ohio. Being a youth when they settled in Eel River township, he was an important help in the work of clearing and farming, and so busy was he at these duties, that he only obtained three months' schooling in the old log school-house before he was of age.

Afterward he attended but three months more, but his natural shrewdness has compensated him for the advantages he missed. After marriage he began for himself on wild lands that his father gave him to clear, with the right to take what he raised. He now has a good farm of seventy-four acres of the old homestead. June 29, 1843, he was married to Jane, daughter of John Blair, a pioneer of DeKalb county. This union was blessed with six children, of whom five are living: Benjamin F., Emily J., Margaret C., Joseph H. and Cordelia. Mrs. Notestine died February 10, 1860, and on July 27, 1862, he was married to Mary, a daughter of A. D. Rhinehart, an old settler of Knox county, Ohio. To this union have been born three boys: Clermont L., Charles M. and John P., of whom one is living. Mr. Notestine, politically, is a democrat, and was a delegate from his township that helped to organize the convention system in this county. His first presidential vote was for Martin Van Buren, in 1840, and he has never failed to vote at any presidential election since.

Daniel Notestine, the second of the surviving children of Jacob Notestine, was born August 6, 1822, in Fairfield county, Ohio. Since twelve years of age, his life has been spent in Cedar Creek township. February 15, 1843, he was married to Charlotte Lee, who died August 20, 1857, leaving eight children: George W., Andrew, Jackson, John, Elizabeth, Catherine, Sarah and Cordelia. He was married August 29, 1858, to Catherine Wagner, who gave to him six children: Henrietta, Jacob B., William, Nettie O., Annie R., and Daniel, before her death, December 25, 1871. September 8th, following, he was married to Susan McCrory. He and wife are members of the Lutheran church. His political adherence has always been with the democratic party. In early life, Mr. Notestine was a leader in the work of the day as well as in the manly sports, and was distinguished as a hunter of the large game of the olden time. In later life, he has been equally prominent in his influence upon society and the advancement of his township, and he is generally esteemed as a worthy citizen and upright man.

George W. Henderson, one of the early settlers of Cedar Creek township, is a native of Ashland county, Ohio, born September 22, 1827. His father, Samuel Henderson, was born in 1801, in Westmoreland county, Penn., and removed with his parents to Ohio, while a small boy. They first settled in Jefferson county, remained a short time and then removed to Harrison county, where he grew to manhood. Moving to Ashland county he remained there until 1836, when he came to DeKalb county, and settled in Jackson township, where he entered a half section of timbered land, under Jackson's administration. He and one John Watson once had a dangerous experience on the St. Joseph river. Going to Fort Wayne in the winter with corn, and there being no roads convenient, they attempted to drive down on the ice, but after going about five miles the ice began to break. They turned to the shore forty rods distant, the ice breaking at every jump of the horses, and reached land with no injury but wetting. Mr. Henderson's wife's maiden name was

Letty Moody. Their son, George W., came with his parents to Indiana when only nine years of age. His education was of the pioneer sort. At the age of twenty-one he hired to his father and worked for him three years in payment of 153 acres of land on which he now lives. December 28, 1851, he was married to Magdalene Tarney, and they had four children, of whom but one is living: Matilda, born June 22, 1858, wife of Dr. K. K. Wheelock, of Fort Wayne. Mr. Henderson and wife are members of the Methodist Episcopal church at Robinson chapel, of which he has been trustee about twenty-five years. His farm is one of the best improved in the township and he is regarded as a leading man.

Louis Nettelhorst, one of the pioneers of Cedar Creek township, and prominent among the farmers of Allen county, is a native of Hanover, Germany, born October 5, 1826, son of Charles C. and Helena (Schulte) Nettelhorst. The father was born in Prussia, October 16, 1785, the mother, in Hanover, in 1794. The family emigrated to America in 1835, and first settled in Mercer county, Ohio. In the spring of 1836 they settled in Cedar Creek township, he coming down the St. Mary's to Fort Wayne by flat-boat; they found the river so full of driftwood that it took almost a week to make the trip of about sixty miles. As there were few houses along the St. Mary's river at that time, they would put up their tent. This they lighted by burning a piece of pork fastened in a split stick, the other end of which was stuck in the ground. The father entered eighty acres of land which his son now occupies. He erected a log cabin, and began to convert his wooded land into a farm; but not being used to such work, having been in business all his previous life, he soon fell a victim to the malaria of the new country, and died August 11, 1839. His widow survived until August 31, 1860. Thus orphaned, Louis Nettelhorst began a life of hard struggle; being the oldest son of the family the burden of support fell upon him. He had attended school in the old country, but had but three months' schooling in this country. Beginning with little money, with the assistance of his mother as financier, they succeeded well, and raised the family of three boys and three girls. In January, 1837, he was married to Marian, daughter of George and Maria (Bierly) Ziegler, born September 24, 1834, and they had six children, five now living: Laura, wife of W. C. Howey; Charles C., Euphemia, Louis W. and Harriet. He is a member of the Catholic church. In 1873 he was elected trustee of his township, and served two years. As assessor he has served about four years. Mr. Nettelhorst has in his possession his father's memorandum book which bears date October 25, 1810. He has also a violin, which belonged to his father, now over one hundred years of age.

William M. Muller, one of the old settlers of Cedar Creek township, is a native of Germany, born April 29, 1805. He emigrated to America in 1832, and first settled in Mercer county, Ohio, where he remained four years, meanwhile seeking land in Indiana. He bought eighty acres of land where he began clearing and making rails. The first years he kept bachelor's hall, and the wolves at that time were so numerous he was compelled to carry a pitch-fork with him on his visits to neighbors as a weapon of defense. April 19, 1837, he was married to Mary Ann Kansen, born March 18, 1815, of German descent. She was then a resident of Cincinnati; her he brought to his new home in Allen county, a log hut 11x12 feet, so that her first experience in Allen county was attended with much privation. They had thirteen children of whom eight are now living: Herman, Frank, Henry, Victor, Clementine, Mary, Englebert and William. When Mr. Muller came to Allen county it abounded with bears, wolves, deer, turkeys and snakes. On one occasion when he was returning from work, to his astonishment he was met by an angry bear, who stood up to receive him, and was very near him when he began to call for help, which fortunately frightened the animal away. At another time when returning from Fort Wayne, by an Indian trail which lessened the distance home, his horse suddenly refused to proceed, but being urged past a certain large hollow tree, to his surprise on looking up he beheld a large bear on the tree after wild honey. Mr. Muller has been a recognized leader among the Germans, and on July 4, 1844, made a German speech at Fort Wayne, the manuscript of which his youngest son living, William, now has in his possession. He began in this country with little money, and being a baker by trade, and knowing nothing about farming, it is to his credit that he did well and made a success of life. He is now, though in his eighty-fourth year, enjoying good health. Mr. Muller and wife are devout Catholics and he named the postoffice at Hamilton known as Leo, in honor of Pope Leo. He was one of the leaders in building the church at that village, and has been one of the main supporters of the organization.

John Douglass, of Cedar Creek township, is a native of Indiana, born March 8, 1842. His parents, Samuel and Diana (Edgington) Douglass, emigrated from Ohio to Indiana in 1837, and settled on the present homestead, entering 160 acres, which was at that time all heavily timbered. To reach this place they crossed the St. Joe river on a cake of floating ice. John Douglass now lives on this homestead, in the first brick dwelling of the township, and has on his farm the first frame barn built in the township. He was born and raised here and has had his home here all his life, except in the year 1873, when he resided with his family in Missouri. He received a common school education. In 1868 he was united in marriage with Almira, daughter of Davis and Belinda (Fulkerson) Lyons, natives of Ohio, who emigrated to Indiana in 1844, and settled in Cedar Creek township, where they remained until death. Mr. and Mrs. Douglass had four children, only one now living, Hattie, born January 1, 1875. He and wife are members of the Methodist Episcopal church. He is now trustee of the church at Leo, also trustee of the circuit and steward. He is a member of the Sion S. Bass post, G. A. R. In 1862 he volunteered in Company C, Eighty-eighth Indiana regiment, as corporal, and was promoted sergeant in April, 1864. He

Robert B. Shirley

served gallantly three years, was with his company in all its engagements up to his discharge, yet was never wounded, though often grazed by bullets, and in his last battle had one side of his hat shot away. He was with Sherman in his famous march to the sea. He has prospered in agriculture, possessing a good farm of 160 acres in Cedar Creek township.

Albert Douglass (deceased), was one of Cedar Creek township's worthiest farmers. He was a native of Indiana, born June 19, 1848. He was born and raised on the old homestead of his parents, Samuel and Diana Douglass, and received a common school education. On September 10, 1871, he was united in marriage with Jennie Osborn, born November 9, 1850, daughter of William and Emily Osborn, early settlers of Steuben county, Ind., and this union was blessed with three children, Mira A., born February 27, 1874, died February 20, 1877; Elmer A., born December 12, 1877; Harry, born February 8, 1880. He and wife were members of the Methodist Episcopal church. He had but little capital when he began life for himself, but was one of those enterprising and industrious men who worked hard and have done so much for the advancement of this region. He prospered and at his death he owned a valuable farm of 109 acres. Since his death his widow has erected a comfortable two-story frame dwelling. Mr. Douglass was a leading citizen and a man well respected.

Charles M. Gillett, of Cedar Creek township, is a native of Indiana, born September 3, 1841. The father, Wilkes Gillett, a native of New York, born March 21, 1811, came to Ohio with his parents when nine years of age, where he grew to manhood and married Sophia Jones, who was born May 1, 1809. They cleared a farm in Ohio and remained until 1837, when they removed to Milan township, Allen county. At the time of their settlement, their nearest neighbors were two miles distant. In 1863, they removed to St. Joseph township, and in 1881, to Fort Wayne, but soon after died, he on June 15, and she in September, 1881. Wilkes Gillett came here a poor man, and he and family suffered all the hardships known to a pioneer life. The principal food at that time consisted of venison, wild honey and corn bread. He never had the advantages of education, and for the considerable success he had in life, had to depend upon hard work. His wife, however, was well educated, and was one of the early teachers in Ohio. He served as one of the board of trustees of his township, when the board consisted of three members, and was in short, one of the representative farmers of Allen county. Charles M. Gillett was raised on the old homestead, where he received a common school education. On April 26, 1871, he married Harriet, daughter of William and Eliza (Swift) Utter, natives of New York; she was born September 4, 1844. This union was blessed with two children: Wilkes, born June 3, 1877; Ray, born January 26, 1885. He was assessor and appraiser of St. Joseph township two years. On September 13, 1862, he enlisted in the Twenty-third Indiana battery, and served in all the battles in which his battery participated, and received an honorable discharge at Indianapolis, July 2, 1865. After farming with his father about fifteen years, he bought thirty acres in St. Joseph township, sold this and bought another sixty acres, which he sold and removed to Milan township, and a year later came to Cedar Creek township and settled on the farm where he now lives. In 1883, he made a prospecting tour to Washington territory, and in the following June, went with his family, intending to stay, but only remained eighteen months. He has eighty acres in Cedar Creek which are well improved with good buildings erected by himself. He and family are highly esteemed. He now has in his possession a silver watch which was presented to his father on his sixty-ninth birthday, by his friends at Fort Wayne.

Aaron Paff, lately deceased, one of the old settlers of Cedar Creek township, was born January 17, 1816, in Pennsylvania, where he grew to manhood. In his nineteenth year he accompanied his parents, Jacob and Susan (Stinger) Paff, to Ohio, whence after a residence of about seven years, he removed to Indiana and settled on the farm where he now lives, which was then a forest. In 1838, he was united in marriage with Mary A. Reater, and this union was blessed with eleven children, of whom seven are now living: Moses, born November 21, 1839; Susanna, born May 11, 1845; George W., born December 10, 1848; Mary, born November 27, 1851; Harriet, born March 6, 1856; Andrew J., born January 17, 1858, and Daniel E., born January 1, 1861. Mrs. Paff was born August 31, 1817, and died March 28, 1888. She was a member of the Baptist church before coming to Indiana, and he was a member of the Presbyterian church, but afterward they both united with the Methodist Episcopal church, of which he was a class leader about twenty years, and was one of the trustees the same period. His first experiences in Allen county were attended with much struggle and privation, as he began without capital, but by hard work and skillful management he prospered, and owned at his death 120 acres of fertile land, and earned the good will of all who knew him. This worthy citizen passed away in August, 1889.

Simon Bair, a pioneer of Allen county, is a native of Ohio, born February 28, 1815. His father, Christopher Bair, a native of Westmoreland county, Penn., married Barbara Simons, who was born in Washington county, Penn. After her death he came to Indiana and settled in Cedar Creek township, where he remained the rest of his life. Simon Bair at the age of twenty-two years left his native place and removed to Holmes county, where on July 3, 1843, he was united in marriage with Elizabeth Croco, by whom he had nine children, four of whom are now living: Sarah, Adam, Christopher and John. She was born February 22, 1820, and departed this life March 30, 1880; she was a consistent member of the Lutheran church, of which he is also a member. He never had more than the pioneer schooling when there was no work to be done on the farm. When he came to Allen county, September 23, 1845, he had no money, and moving into his little log cabin, his household furniture consisting of one bed, one chest and two chairs, he made some stools and by boring holes in the logs of the walls, he put in some small poles around which he wound cord for his other bed. He remained here on first coming two years, but the country being so sickly at that time he was advised by doctors to return to Ohio. He remained there about nineteen years and then removed to Missouri for two years, returning afterward to his home in Allen county. His possessions are all the fruit of toil, and he has succeeded notably well. He now owns 166 acres of fine farming land in his his township, with good buildings. He has always supported the whig and republican parties, casting his first presidential vote for William H. Harrison.

John W. Hollopeter is one of the pioneers of Cedar Creek township. He is a native of York county, Penn., son of Abraham and Lydia (Myers) Hollopeter. He was taken by his parents to Ohio when two years of age; they settled in Wayne county and remained six years, then resided in Holmes county about four years, and then located in Seneca county where he grew to manhood. In 1845 he first came to Indiana on a prospecting tour. On December 11, 1845, he married Virginia Welch, born September 30, 1825, and they had three children: James A., Oscar E. and Hiram S. This lady became a member of the Methodist Episcopal church while a young girl, and lived a devoted Christian until her death February 6, 1852. On October 6, 1852, he married Mary Zimmerman, who was born December 21, 1833. They have had ten children, of whom are living: Lydia V., Mary V , Brenton S., Clinton L., Samuel E., Luther S., Clarence H. and Levi L. He and wife belong to the Methodist Episcopal church, of which he has been a member since 1840; he is also steward and trustee of church and parsonage. He is a member of the Masonic order, lodge No. 224, was master six years and is treasurer at the present time. He is a carpenter by trade, at which he worked several years. In 1847 or '48 he bought 150 acres, and after selling seventy acres was almost out of debt, but in 1852 the prolonged sickness of his wife and other misfortunes, caused him to lose everything he had and begin life anew, but he now owns eighty acres of excellent farming land and enjoys the hearty esteem of all.

Matthias Hollopeter, of Cedar Creek township, was born in Holmes county, Ohio, November 18, 1833, but was taken by his parents to Seneca county, when two years of age, where he remained until thirteen, then coming with his parents to Indiana. His father, Abraham Hollopeter, was born in Pennsylvania in 1800, and in that state grew to manhood and married Lydia Myers, two years his junior. They moved to Ohio and remained fifteen or sixteen years, then coming to Indiana and buying eighty acres of school land to which was afterward added forty acres. They came here poor but did well. He served as trustee in the days of township boards. He and wife were members of the Methodist Episcopal church. Matthias Hollopeter had his first experience in Allen county in clearing and burning brush, and such pioneer work. He received a good common school education, and at the age of twenty-one began teaching in the country schools and taught five or six terms. He also worked at the carpenter's trade a number of years. In 1856, he married Susan Hannen, by whom he had six children, of whom but one is living: Charles. She was born in 1835, and departed this life in 1873. She was a devoted member of the Methodist Episcopal church. In 1874 he was married to Mary E., daughter of Jacob Stevick, born in 1847, and they have five children: Milton, Bertram, Frank, Lester and Mabel. He and wife are members of the Methodist Episcopal church, of which he is steward and trustee. In 1865 he enlisted in Company G, One Hundred and Fifty-second Indiana Infantry, and served until the close of the war, holding the rank of corporal. He is a member of the Masonic lodge at Leo, No. 224. In connection with farming he has also been running a saw-mill at Leo fifteen or sixteen years. He now owns 108 acres of fine land in good state of cultivation, with substantial buildings. He has served as justice of the peace of his township eight years, being elected through personal regard, as he is an ardent republican, and his township is strongly democratic.

David E. O. Herin is a native of Pennsylvania, born December 10, 1814. His parents, James and Mary (Smith) Herin, removed when he was thirteen years of age to Ohio, where he grew to manhood. He received a common school education, and at the age of nineteen years began the battle of life for himself without resources. He worked as a common laborer until twenty-five years of age, when he built a carding mill in Seneca county, Ohio. He remained in this business about seven years, and then came to Indiana and settled in Cedar Creek township on the farm where he now lives. He first bought eighty acres, and has since added forty acres. In 1839 he was married to Elizabeth Umsted, born in 1812, and they had twelve children, of whom seven are living: Mary E., Melinda J., Francis A., John R., James A., Rolla E. and Jennie E. He and wife are members of the Methodist Episcopal church. He served one term as justice of the peace of his township, and was the first trustee of his township after the institution of the present system, and afterward served two terms in the same capacity. He is one of the leading citizens, and he and family are well respected.

David L. Fulkerson, an early settler, was born in Ohio, September 23, 1820, son of Samuel and Lydia Fulkerson. He lived in his native state until 1842, when he came with his father to Indiana in search of land. In 1846 he bought eighty acres of wood-land, the site of their present comfortable home which his industry has created. He first built a log cabin, and moved in his furniture, one bedstead and two or three chairs. The money with which he bought land he earned by day's labor. In 1854 he was married to Mary Mosier, born in 1831, and they had six children, five now living: Adell, Samuel, Ella, Clara and Matilda. He and wife are members of the Methodist Episcopal church, of which he was class leader about six years. He served two terms as one of the three township trustees in early days, was afterward elected trustee under the present system, and justice of the peace at different times, but declined both offices. He helped to cut the road through his farm known as the Fort Wayne & Leo road. He is a worthy and esteemed citizen.

Capt. William C. Hollopeter, of Cedar Creek township, is a native of Wayne county, Ohio, born August 24, 1833. Thirteen years later his parents, Andrew and Catharine (Edmonds) Hollopeter, both of German descent, came to Indiana and settled in Cedar Creek township. William C. attended the common schools of Ohio and Indiana, farming in the summer season, until he reached his majority, when he attended the Methodist Episcopal college at Fort Wayne. He previously taught one term of school and taught four terms after attending college. In 1858 he was married to Cynthia A. Moore, born April 22, 1839, of Irish descent, by whom he had nine children, of whom eight are living: C. M., Methodist Episcopal minister at Geneva, Adams county; W. M., a teacher and farmer; Ophelia M., Ellen G., a teacher; Rosa B., Herbert S., Lloyd H. and Edith G. In 1862 he enlisted in Company C, Eighty-eighth Indiana Volunteer infantry, as a private; was appointed second corporal same month, and on December 26, 1862, was promoted fourth sergeant; April, 1863, was elected first lieutenant, and November 24, 1863, was promoted captain. He was honorably discharged June 7, 1865, at Indianapolis. He was with Sherman in his celebrated march to the sea; was wounded at Mission Ridge, and at Bentonville, N. C. When Capt. Hollopeter came to Indiana the family settled on the old homestead, where there was about five acres cleared. He is one of the prominent citizens of Allen county, and now owns 200 acres of valuable land.

John W. Moudy (deceased) was born in Pennsylvania, April 18, 1824, son of John and Elizabeth Moudy. At the age ten years, he settled in Ohio, where he grew to manhood. In 1847 he removed from Ohio and settled in Perry township, Allen county, where he remained until 1852. He then removed to Cedar Creek township and settled on the farm, where he remained until his death, May 26, 1888. On January 19, 1843, he was married to Catharine Ann Marshall. Of their seven children, four are now living: Martin L., Elizabeth A., Ralph and William. Their mother died May 17, 1857, aged thirty-six years. On December 27, 1858, he was married to Elizabeth Boger, daughter of Jacob and Catherine Boger, born July 3, 1835, and they had five children, of whom are living: John R., Mary J. and Henry L. He was a member of the United Brethren church; his first wife was a member of the Protestant church and his widow is a member of the Methodist Episcopal church. He served as constable of Perry township one term. His early life in Allen county was one of great exertion and patience, but being a man of great will and courage, success crowned his efforts. He died possessed of a farm property of 160 acres of fertile land in Cedar Creek township and was regarded as one of the county's representative citizens.

Samuel Dailey, of Cedar Creek township, is a native of Seneca county, Ohio, born October 9, 1831, son of William T. and Sarah Dailey. The father emigrated from Ohio in 1848, and settled in this township

August 26, 1848. He then bought the farm where his son now lives and settled on it April 1, 1849. It was then wholly wood-land. Samuel Dailey came to Indiana with his parents and remained with them until their death. His education was received in Ohio in the pioneer log school-houses. In 1858 he was married to Mary McCroy, born July 20, 1835, and they have had eight children, of whom seven are now living: William M., Dora, Frank, Charles, Sarah, Nevada and Absalom. Mr. Dailey has gained his present comfortable surroundings, a valuable farm of 100 acres and handsome buildings, by industrious habits and natural abilities, that cause him to be regarded as one of the township's leading citizens.

Martin L. Moudy, proprietor of the Urbana mills at Hursh postoffice, is one of the early settlers of Allen county. He was born in Ashland county, Ohio, November 2, 1843, son of John W. and Catharine (Marshall) Moudy, with whom he came to Allen county when about five years of age. The family first settled in Perry township where he grew to manhood and received a pioneer education. At his majority he went to Cedarville and engaged in coopering and handling staves, at which he continued about eleven years, when the sickness of his father compelled him to return to the farm and take charge for two years. He then came to Urbana in 1879, and engaged in milling, at which he has continued. In 1865 he was married to Martha E. Opdyke, born October 28, 1843, and they have had seven children, of whom Melvin, Sylvia, Elnora and Isa Belle, are living. Mrs. Moudy is a member of the Lutheran church, and he belongs to the I. O. O. F. lodge, No. 321, at Maysville, of which he served one term as recording secretary. They and their family are highly respected.

Jacob Sauder, a prosperous farmer of Cedar Creek township, is a native of Ohio, born May 7, 1828, to Henry and Elizabeth (Schrock) Sauder, natives of Pennsylvania. He was raised in his native state and received a common school education. He remained until twenty-three years old on the home farm and naturally adopted farming as his vocation, but since coming to Indiana he has taken up cabinet making and masonry, never serving an apprenticeship, but does very good work, and is naturally handy with most tools, making the wood work for his farming implements. In 1848 he settled in Cedar Creek township, where he now lives. He came to Indiana a poor man, but by industry, at one time had 320 acres, and now owns 181 acres of good land, well improved. In 1852 he was married to Elizabeth Troyer, who was born in 1830, and died in 1861. By her he had five children, four of whom are living: Levi, Jonas, Elizabeth and Jacob. In 1861 he was married to Mary Eicher, by whom he had five children, four living: Mary, Lydia, Samuel and Henry. This lady, who was born in 1843, died in 1870, and in 1871 he married Mrs. Sophronia Yerks, who gave to him two children, of whom one is living, Sylvia. This last wife died in 1884.

William W. Trease, of Cedar Creek township, is a native of Ashland county, Ohio, born August 20, 1843. He came with his parents,

Henry and Elizabeth (Clayton) Trease, to Indiana when six or seven years of age, and grew to manhood on the old homestead, receiving a common school education. In 1864 he was married to Samantha, daughter of Henry Spitler, and this union was blessed with one child, Allie, wife of Andrew Metcalf; Mrs. Trease was born January 6, 1847. The family are members of the Methodist Episcopal church, of which he has been steward about fifteen years. He settled on the farm where he now lives, then entirely wooded, in 1866. Early morn then found him with ax and maul in hand, and the "dewy eves" he and wife spent in burning brush. With her assistance and good management, they have done well and now own an excellent farm of eighty acres with good house and barn. He and family have many warm friends.

George W. Trease, of Cedar Creek township, is a native of Pennsylvania, born September 2, 1822. With his parents, Jacob and Elizabeth Trease, he emigrated to Ohio when about seven years of age. There he grew to manhood and received a limited education, the schools being few and poorly taught, and work plenty. At the age of twenty-one years he began work for himself as a day laborer. In 1846 he was married to Rosanna McFee, born in 1826, who gave him eight children, six of whom are living: Jane, Arminda, John, Alice, Eliza and Dayton. This lady, who was born in 1826, joined with him the Methodist Episcopal church, and she was a consistent and devoted member and earnest worker therein until her death in 1875. In 1879, he was married to Margaret Aldign, a member of the Catholic church, born about 1843. In 1853 he emigrated from Ohio to Indiana, and settled on the farm of 128 acres where he now lives, which was partly cleared and had a log cabin and log stable. He wonderfully improved this property, and has continued to add to the same from time to time, until now he owns 352 acres of valuable land. He has lived a life of honorable industry, abstained from all questionable speculation, and is highly respected.

Henry Bacon, an early settler in Cedar Creek township, is now one of the representative farmers of Allen county. He was born in New Jersey, April 8, 1815, son of Jacob and Elizabeth (Shiner) Bacon. The father was of English, the mother of German, descent, and were descendants of revolutionary heroes. When Henry was about nine years old, his father died, and having lost his mother about one year previous, he was alone in the world at a tender age. He never had the advantage of much schooling, but worked on the farm until about nineteen years of age, when he went to sea, coasting at first from Philadelphia to New York and South Carolina. He continued at this about twelve years. About the year 1839 he sent money to his brother who came west to enter land, and in 1850 he removed to Indiana and settled on the farm where he now lives. In 1852 he built a hewn-log house which was at the time one of the best dwellings in the neighborhood. Here he lived alone until October 3, 1853, when he was married to Nancy, daughter of James and Mary (Scott) Scott. Her father was a soldier in the war of 1812 and served through the war. He was followed for three days by an Indian, who sought to kill him, and when he failed declared that his intended victim was not to be killed by a bullet. They had three children: Laura, born 1854, died 1872; an infant deceased, and John S., born March 22, 1860. Mrs. Bacon was born July 18, 1820, received a good education and became a member of the Methodist Episcopal church. Her first experience in Allen county was in helping her husband in clearing, burning brush, and such pioneer work, although she had been raised at Liberty, Union county, and was wholly unused to the toil and hardships she willingly shared with her husband. Starting without money ahead, very little furniture, and living mostly on corn bread and pork, they succeeded well and now own 133 acres of valuable land, with handsome buildings.

Henry W. Beams is a native of Pennsylvania, born September 30, 1846. His father, John Beams, emigrated to Ohio in 1849, after reaching his majority, married his wife, Barbara, and in the spring of 1850 removed to Indiana and settled in Cedar Creek township on the farm where his son now lives. He bought eighty acres of new land in February, and brought his family in May, 1850, to the log cabin he had built. He came to Indiana a poor man, but his industry and honesty won him prosperity and the esteem of his neighbors. At the time of his death, November, 1864, he owned 120 acres of well-improved land. He was a member of the Lutheran church. Two of his sons served in the war of the rebellion. One, George, who enlisted in Company A, One Hundreth regiment, contracted disease in the service and died at Memphis, Tenn. John W. served in Company E, Fifty-sixth regiment. Henry W. Beams came with his parents to Indiana when little over three years of age. He received a common school education. February 3, 1870, he was united in marriage with Anna E. George, born September 25, 1847, who died January 18, 1877, leaving one child, Amedia E. November 4, 1877, Mr. Beams was married to Rebecca A., daughter of Abraham and Jane Johnson, pioneer settlers of DeKalb. This union was blessed with two children: Franklin L. and George H. Mrs. Beams was born December 15, 1847. She is a member of the Lutheran church, of which her husband has been deacon twelve years. In connection with farming, he has for nine years been a partner in a furniture and undertaking business, dry goods, etc. He occupies eighty acres of the old homestead farm in Cedar Creek township, and is one of the leading citizens.

Samuel Zimmerman, of Cedar Creek township, is a native of Pennsylvania, born April 4, 1840. His parents, Andrew and Rachel (Roop) Zimmerman, were both natives of Pennsylvania. The father died when Samuel was about four years of age. In 1846, his mother and family removed to Vanwert county, Ohio, and in 1850, to Perry township, Allen county; in 1854, to Kosciusko county, then to Missouri, where they remained one year, and then to Bremer county, Iowa. He remained there until December, 1859, when he left his family and returned to Allen county, Ind. On August 2, 1862, he enlisted in Company C, Eighty-eighth

Indiana regiment, and served until June 7, 1865, being mustered out at Washington city. He was with Sherman in his march to the sea. He did gallant service and received an honorable discharge at Indianapolis. On December 14, 1865, he was married to Emeline Hollopeter, who was born April 6, 1845, and of their five children three are living: Charles M., Harris H. and Avery R. Mrs. Zimmerman became a member of the Methodist Episcopal church when a small girl, and was a devoted member until her death, March 23, 1880. On April 3, 1883, he married Mrs. Emily Spuller, widow of Joseph Spuller of Adams county. She was born December 17, 1844. He and wife are members of the Methodist Episcopal church. He served as assessor of his township four years, having been elected, though a republican, in the banner democratic township outside of Wayne. He is a member of the F. & A. M. lodge, No. 224, and a comrade of Bass post, G. A. R., of Fort Wayne. He has a good farm of over seventy-five acres, well improved with good buildings. He is one of the leading citizens of his township.

Michael Klopfenstein is a native of Germany, born March 22, 1824, son of John and Catharine (Amstutz) Klopfenstein. He received a good German education, and in 1841 emigrated to America. Settling in Ohio, he remained seven years, and then removed to Indiana and worked as a laborer in Adams county nearly two years. He then settled in Cedar Creek township, first buying 160 acres all in the woods, to which he added from year to year until at one time he owned 485 acres. In 1851 he married Lydia Sauder, by whom he had nine children: Jacob, Eli, Michael, Emanuel, Joseph, Mary, Jeremiah, David and Lydia. This lady, who was born January 14, 1831, died June 11, 1875. She was a member of the Amish church. In 1877 he married Mrs. Rebecca (Conrad) Schlatter. By hard work and good management he has done well in life, and has lived to help all his children to nice farms and to see them comfortably situated. He is one of Cedar Creek's township's best citizens and is well liked and respected. In connection with farming he has been running a saw-mill with his sons since 1876. Mr. Klopfenstein and wife are both members of the Amish church.

James McCrory, an old settler of Cedar Creek township, was born in Ohio, July 13, 1807. When a child he went with his parents, David and Mary (Howey) McCrory, to Pennsylvania, where he grew to manhood and received a common school education. At the age of fifteen he was apprenticed as a blacksmith, which he followed until 1852, when he came to Indiana and settled in Cedar Creek township on the farm where he now lives. In 1828 he was married to Ellen Eichelberger. Of their nine children, six are living: Mary, George, Samuel, William, Frank and Garlerd. The mother, who was born in 1809, died in 1873. February 2, 1877, he was married to Mrs. Caroline Shannon, born in 1840, daughter of Andrew and Rachel (Roop) Zimmerman. To this union was born Leonard M. Mrs. McCrory is a member of the Catholic church. Mr. McCrory holds the title to 320 acres of valuable land in Cedar Creek township, also lots 15, 16, 17, 29 and 2 in Leo. When he settled in Allen county his farm was all in the woods except about twenty-eight acres. He is one of the highly respected farmers of the county, and has served his township as trustee for twelve years in succession.

John Dever, one of the pioneers of Cedar Creek township, is a native of Ohio, born May 31, 1824. His father, David Dever, was a native of Virginia, who served about two years in the late rebellion, in the Missouri state militia, and died at Georgetown, Mo., May 27, 1862. His wife's maiden name was Nancy Shonkweiler. Their son John, grew in his native state to manhood, and received a common school education. He was a wagon-maker, and worked at that trade a number of years in Ohio, in connection with farming. In 1848, he was married to Ellen Dailey, who was born in 1825, lived a consistent member of the Methodist Episcopal church, and died in 1875. They had seven children of whom but two are now living: Martha, wife of O. W. Maxfield, and David D. In 1876 he was married to Clara Dailey, by whom he has one child, Florence. Mrs. Dever is a member of the Methodist Episcopal church. He has served as trustee of Cedar Creek township two years, and built three frame school-houses during his administration. He was elected on the republican ticket, though the township gives a democratic majority of 100. He made a second race in 1886, and reduced the adverse majority considerably. Mr. Dever came from his native state in 1852, and settled at Hamilton, now known as Leo postoffice, and worked at his trade two years. He then opened a general store, which he continued ten years. Then selling his store, in partnership with A. H. Bittinger and E. L. Knight, he had a boat built at Roanoke, which was the first regular boat that ran upon the St. Joseph river; at this he continued about two years, when he resumed his trade and pursued it at Leo about nine years, when he became one of the proprietors of the Leo flouring-mill, which has been his business since that time. He is one of Cedar Creek township's leading citizens.

William C. Howey, the present trustee of Cedar Creek township, was born in Ashland county, Ohio, August 15, 1844. When nine years old, he came with his parents, William and Mary J. (Reed) Howey, and settled in Cedar Creek township, where he has since remained. He grew to manhood on the farm and received a common school education. He is a carpenter and painter by trade, which he worked at until elected trustee. March 28, 1880, he was married to Laura A. Nettelhorst, and they have two children: Ray and Maud. Mrs. Howey was born June 12, 1858, and she was raised in the Catholic church. In 1882 Mr. Howey was elected constable and served two years. In 1886 he was elected trustee of his township by a majority of eighty-nine, and was re-nominated in 1888, and elected by a majority of over 225, an increase which is a rare testimonial to the creditable manner in which he had discharged his duties. He built a two-story brick school-house at Cedarville, at a cost of $2,292.13, a proof to his constituents of his ability as an economist, and many of his friends are urging his name for commissioner of Allen county. Mr. Howey, himself, has never sought office. He is one of the worthy, self-made men, and a natural leader among men. Mr. Howey is preparing to build two more brick school-houses, in districts No. 2 and No. 6.

John Lochner was born in Germany, April 18, 1821, son of Peter and Elizabeth (Pelerof) Lochner. He received a common school education in Germany and remained in his native country until 1853, when he emigrated and settled in Cedar Creek township. Being a poor man, he was compelled to work by the day at first for his living, and wages at that time being very low, he worked many a day in the broiling sun for 50 cents, and thought he was well paid. He accumulated enough to purchase eighty acres of land. His greatest ambition on coming to America was to own twenty acres of land, thinking that he would then be well fixed for life, but he now owns 160 acres of fine land in Cedar Creek township, with excellent buildings. He was a weaver by trade, which he followed in the old country altogether, and on coming here had to learn farming, but under the instruction of Bernard Barwe he soon learned and became a shrewd and competent agriculturist. He has not only succeeded as a farmer, but has made a worthy name for himself with his neighbors. In 1855 he was united in marriage with Margaret Hamm, born in 1838. This union was blessed with four children: Rebecca, Jacob, Mary and Martha. He is a member of the Lutheran church, and his wife of the New Amish church.

Adam Hamm, of Cedar Creek township, is a native of Alsace. He was born near Strasburg, March 3, 1834, the eldest of four children of Adam and Margaret Hamm. He was educated in the French and German schools, and has since acquired a sufficient knowledge of the English language to both read and speak it readily. In 1854, during the excitement incident to the Crimean war, he left his native country, sailed for America and settled in Allen county, where he has since resided. He was followed in 1855 by the family, who also settled here. He first bought sixty acres of unimproved land, forty of which he cleared and upon it erected a log cabin. This property he sold and bought 160 acres covered by woods which by unremitting industry were soon converted into fields of grain. In later years he erected on this farm an elegant frame residence and a commodious barn. In 1882 he purchased a farm near Leo, where he built a two-story brick residence, and this place he exchanged in 1888 for the farm upon which he now lives, which in fertility is unsurpassed. August 28, 1859, he was married to Rebecca Depew, by whom he had seven children: George W., Margaret Delilah, Joseph E., Mary E., Caroline, Martha E., Samantha B., six now living. Mr. Hamm has been a friend to churches and schools and has given his children a good common school education. He and wife hold to the Apostolic Christian belief. The substantial improvements which he has made on the different farms which he has occupied are unmistakable evidence of his industry and public spirit.

John Amstutz, a successful farmer of Cedar Creek township, was born in France, February 16, 1836, and grew to manhood in his native state, where he served an apprenticeship as a machinist. On September 18, 1856, he sailed for America, his business being to bring $900 in gold to some of his relatives, which he did after a voyage of twenty-six days. He first stopped at Fort Wayne for two weeks, and then settled in Cedar Creek township, where he began working at the carpenter's trade. He followed this several years, working as many as twenty-six hands at one time. In 1859 he purchased, where he now lives, eighty acres, and has added to it until he now has 240 acres in Allen county and eighty in DeKalb. October 22, 1859, he was married to Mary Schwartz, who was born in 1837, and died in February, 1879, leaving eight children: Mary, Martha, Lydia, Leah, Eli, Emma, John and Hannah. Mrs. Amstutz was a member of the New Amish church. Mr. Amstutz came to this country a poor man but has done exceedingly well, has one of the best improved farms in the township, and is one of the best citizens. Besides farming successfully, he is a natural-born mechanic, and has been making brick for nineteen years, and during the last two years has conducted a tile factory.

Charles Merkel, a prosperous farmer of Cedar Creek township, was born in Prussia, July 21, 1818, son of Frederick and Lena (Braun) Merkel. He received a good education in his native country, and served an apprenticeship at the shoemaker's trade. At the age of twenty-two years he was drafted for the Crimean war and served six years in the Russian army as a good and loyal soldier, during four years being a sergeant. In 1852 he emigrated to America and first settled at Leistville, Ohio, where he worked at his trade about five years. In 1864 he was married to Mary Fres, who was born in 1824, and they had two children: Ida, wife of Hiram Page, and Huldah, who died in 1886. While in Ohio, during Morgan's raid through that state, he was called out with the militia of Ohio. Later he removed to Indiana and settled on a farm in Springfield township, where he lived until 1875, when he removed to Cedar Creek township and occupied his present property which he has greatly improved, and he has one of the neatest farms in the township, comprising eighty acres of good farming land. He is one of the reliable citizens and is well liked and respected. He and wife are members of the Lutheran church.

Conrad H. Viberg, a prominent farmer of Cedar Creek township, is a native of Germany, born March 6, 1808. He emigrated to America in 1831, and first settled in Fairfield county, Ohio. Six years later he removed to Williams county, Ohio, where he remained about three years; after living in Huntington, Ind., from 1842 until 1857, he removed to Allen county and settled on the farm where he now lives. His first visit to Fort Wayne was in 1840, when all west of the court-house was woods. He came to America without money, and in a strange land his lot was a trying one, but he has succeeded well and at one time owned 372 acres of farming land in Cedar Creek township. In 1833 he was married to Angeline Struckmann. Of their nine children four are living: Sophia, Arseles, George and Sarah. George is the present sheriff of Allen county. Sarah is the wife of Samuel McCrory, and has three children: Calvin, Clyde and Roy. Mrs. Viberg, who was born in 1810, died after a useful life, in 1885. She, with her husband, was a member of the New Lutheran church. Mr. Viberg, while in Huntington county, served as township trustee two years. He has always been one of the prominent citizens of Allen county since his residence here, and is universally respected.

Jacob Stevick, a native of Pennsylvania, was born in Cumberland county, November 7, 1824, son of Jacob and Sarah Stevick. There he grew up and received his education, and in 1859 he came to Indiana and settled where he now lives. In 1846 he was united in marriage to Hannah Snoke, who died April 25, 1853, at the age of twenty-seven, leaving two children: Mary and Jemima. In 1854 he was married to Catharine North, by whom he had two children, one, Lavinia, now living, but this wife died in 1863, aged twenty-eight years. In 1865 he was married to Elizabeth North. Their two children are deceased. He and wife are members of the Methodist Episcopal church. Seven years after settling where he now lives he removed to Newville, Wells county; and engaged in conducting a flouring-mill for five years, and was afterward for seven years in the same business at Wolf Lake, Noble county. Since then he has remained upon his fertile and well improved farm of eighty acres in Cedar Creek township.

William J. McNabb is a native of DeKalb county, Ind., born July 4, 1846. His father, William McNabb, a native of Pennsylvania, removed to Ohio when about sixteen years of age, and began work as a mason and continued until he got money enough to enter 160 acres of land. In 1835 he visited Indiana and entered 160 acres in DeKalb county and in 1836 brought his wife Mary and children and settled. After clearing 100 acres he sold out and in 1859 he came to Allen county and bought 120 acres and cleared the most of this. Here he remained until his death in 1876. He served as county commissioner while in De Kalb county, also as justice of the peace about eight years. He was a member of the Methodist Episcopal church. He came to Indiana with only $5 in money. En route one of his oxen dying he had to yoke up one o his cows to finish the journey. He had the pleasure on one occasio f by ambushing behind a tree, to kill one of the bears which infested the woods, with his ax. William J. McNabb was raised in DeKalb county until thirteen years of age, and has since then resided in Cedar Cree k township. He received his education in the pioneer log school-hou e. In 1866 he was married to Catharine Hursch, born in December, 1846, and they have nine children: John, Christ, Harmon, Maude, Gilbert,

Claude, Lizzie, Maggie and Grover C. He and wife are members of the Lutheran church and are highly respected.

Daniel Van Zile is a native of Ohio, born July 4, 1833, son of Jesse and Mary Van Zile. He was raised in Ashland county, Ohio, and in 1861 came to Indiana and settled in Perry township, where he cleared a farm of forty acres. Seven years later he removed to Cedar Creek township upon the farm where he now lives. In 1854 he was married to Rachel M. Brit, born April 10, 1836, and they have had ten children, of whom eight are living: Thomas, Mary, John, Sidney, George, Aldey, Ida and Samuel. He and wife are members of the Lutheran church. When he settled in Allen county he had nothing, and his early life was attended with much privation and toil, but he has had remarkable success, and now owns 120 acres of good farming land.

August Fox, of Cedar Creek township, is a native of France, born near Strassburg, April 9, 1827, to Anthony and Catharine (Halter) Fox. His parents came to America when he was about two years of age, and first settled in Stark county, Ohio, where he grew to manhood. He received all his schooling in the old pioneer school-house, but is now a well-informed man. He served an apprenticeship at the carpenter's trade, which he has followed through life. In 1851 he was married to Mary Myers, who was born January 15, 1835, by whom he has had eleven children, the following now living: Lena, Anna, Henry, Emma, Clara, Rosa, Agnes, Francis, Charles and Martha. In 1852 he removed with his wife to Noble county, where he bought eighty acres of woodland, paying only $50 down, and then began clearing and working on his farm, and in the summer season he worked at his trade. He paid for his eighty acres, and then added forty acres. He remained on his farm until 1863, when he sold out. After following his trade three years, in 1872 he bought and removed to the farm of 160 acres where he now lives about one-half mile west of Leo. It is one of the best improved farms in the township. His industry and good qualities have made him one of the leading farmers.

SPRINGFIELD TOWNSHIP.

Through this township runs a ridge or water-shed, from Fort Wayne extending toward the lakes, and along this in 1839, the Hicksville or ridge road was surveyed, which has come to be an important highway. Three years previous, in 1836, there had been several settlements in the township. William Sweet and family, from New York, had made a home. Isaac Hall, a native of Pennsylvania, who had lived and married in Portage county, Ohio, came up by way of the Maumee settlement, and became a leading man. At his house the first election was held in October, 1837. He was inspector, and Ezra May, who was another of the 1836 settlers, was elected justice. May was quite enterprising, and in 1837–8 built a grist-mill, and the next year established a blacksmith shop. At his home the first religious meeting was held in 1838 by Rev. True Pattee, and in the same house his daughter, Mary E., passed away—that being the first death among the settlers here. In 1837 there settled Jeremiah Whaley, Henry Gruber, James King, Richard Glaze, Estes Howe and William Ringwalt. In Mr. Gruber's family occurred the first birth, a son named Henry, born in November, 1838. Nathan Lake and family came to the vicinity of Cuba in 1838. Ezra Worden, who came in 1838, settled in 1841. Richard Anderson came in 1839, and in the following year John D. Reichelderfer, now a patriarch among the people of the township, began his labor of clearing away the forest. Thomas Lucas, who came to Fort Wayne in 1831, removed to this township in 1842. In 1840, and afterward, settlers multiplied rapidly, and a list of them is impossible. Several are hereafter mentioned. Soon after the opening of the ridge road, taverns were kept by William Letcher and Ira Johnson, and about the same time John N. Alderman opened a tavern near the site of Maysville. The first postoffice was established at the village of Cuba, in the southwest corner of the township, and here a town was laid out by Andrew Metzgar, in June, 1855, but though it promised to succeed, it has not grown to importance. In 1851 the neighborhood at Hall's Corners was given a postoffice, and it still remains, perpetuating the name of an old settler.

Maysville— The place of Ezra Mays was a center of business at an early date, and in a room of his house, Richard McMullen started a store, in 1847. In May, 1859, Mr. Mays laid out a small plat of the town which bears his name, south of the Hicksville road, adjoining the plat of Harlan, which had been laid out in December, 1853, between the Hicksville and Spencerville roads, by Lewis Reichelderfer. The towns grew into one, and though the name Maysville has now been attached to both, the postoffice is still known as Harlan. Additions were made by Mr. Mays, W. Squires and Lewis and Charles Reichelderfer. The population is now about 700.

In 1859, the Maysville flouring-mill was erected by John Hawkins, which has been an important industry. It has been successively in the hands of Hawkins & Anderson, Timbrook & Ashley, the Eckles Brothers, Eckles, Small & Sturm, and is now owned by the firm of Ober, Mann & Anderson. The next industry was the saw-mill, established by Seymour Coomer and Jacob Bickart, first as a shingle-mill, in 1862. Interests have since been owned by Jacob and Matthias Hollopeter, Joseph D. Stopher, Horace Herrick, William B. Daniels, and John Small. The mill was destroyed by fire in 1867, and rebuilt by Jacob Hollopeter and now owned and run by Cummins & Reichelderfer. The Mayville planing-mill was founded by Isaac Bickart, in 1875, and in 1879, a saw-mill was built by him.

Harlan lodge, F. & A. M., was instituted in May, 1863, and chartered May 25, 1864, with the following members: Peter S. Crisenbury, Ira S. Skinner, Marvin C. Munger, Rev. David Pattee, Rev. J. S. Sellers, William Herrick and George Platter. It now has about thirty members.

Prospect lodge, No. 331, I. O. O. F., was chartered June 22, 1869, with the following members: Arthur M. Taylor, J. S. Crites, John Horn, Jefferson Walter, and Josiah Roller. The first meeting was held November 4, 1869. A building was purchased by the lodge immediately after the organization, which was used for its meetings until the summer of 1889, when the lodge purchased the Maysville graded school building, which it now occupies. The membership is about forty-five.

The first newspaper at Maysville, was the *Harlan Independent*, established by D. M. Allen, who published it until being elected county surveyor, he removed to Fort Wayne, when the paper was discontinued. In March, 1889, a paper was established under the same name by James Forsyth, formerly of New York city, who has proven to be an able manager and editor. This favorite weekly is independent in politics, and aggressive in news gathering. It has steadily grown in popularity and has a circulation of over 1,000 copies, and a steady increase in subscriptions. In 1887, the *Maysville Breeze* was established by J. M. Shutt; this was a creditable paper, but the office was destroyed by fire early in July, 1889. Other prominent business men of Maysville, are: Dry goods — heirs of Samuel Eminger, Grubb & Co., William Reichelderfer; hardware — Oliver Minnie, Hays & James; drugs — J. H. Omo; furniture and undertaking — E. C. Carrington; blacksmiths — James Webber, William Page, George Brown, William Oberholtzer; harness — A. B. Umstead. Charles A. Starr is postmaster and proprietor of the Starr hotel.

Nelson B. Hall, for many years from an early date a resident of Springfield township, is a son of Isaac Hall, the notable pioneer who has been referred to. Isaac Hall was born in Erie county, Penn., in 1804, and while yet a young man, went into the wilds of Ohio. In February, 1833, he was married to Margaret Bardue, and they lived in Ohio upon a small piece of land given him by his father, until 1836, when they came to Allen county, and first went to the settlement in Maumee township, but remaining there only two or three months, then came through the trackless forest to Springfield township, and bought 240 acres of wild land. Here he built his log cabin in the woods, but before he could bring his family to it, he lost his wife by death, a severe blow to him. But aided by his sister-in-law, he went on with his work in the wilderness, and a year later he was married to Jane Bardue, a sister of his deceased wife, and a good mother to his orphan children. Indians were numerous at that time and often came to Mr. Hall's to trade their beads and baskets, and as was peculiar with them always demanded the provisions for which they traded in basketful lots. Game was abundant, and wolves, bear and deer quite numerous. Mr. Hall was widely known and respected as a representative pioneer of the best class. He served as trustee of his township several years, as justice in Scipio eight years, and as county commissioner one term, 1860 to 1863. With the surroundings just described, Nelson B. Hall was raised. He was born in what is now Summit county, Ohio, December 12, 1833. His education was received in the old log school-house, and at the academy at Fort Wayne and at Newville. Being well educated he began teaching at nineteen years of age, and taught during fifteen years. From his salary he saved enough to buy and partially pay for sixty acres of unimproved land. In 1863 he was married to Jennette Moore, who was born November 3, 1838, and by this union had three children, one of whom, Ivan, survives. After marriage he resided in Springfield township until 1887, when he retired from farming and made his home at Hicksville, Ohio, where he has a good two-story dwelling and handsome grounds. He still owns 160 acres of good land in Springfield township, well improved. Mr. Hall is an influential and prominent man, and during eight years served as justice of Springfield township. He and wife are members of the Methodist Episcopal church, in which he is a class leader.

Christian Gruber, an early settler and leading German farmer of Springfield township, was born in Piqua, Ohio, December 29, 1824, son of Christian and Mary (Ruber) Gruber. The father came to Ohio while a young man and was enlisted a short time afterward in the war of 1812, in which he served until the close. Christian came to Indiana in 1837 with his brother and worked as a laborer nine or ten years, and then bought forty acres which he cleared and converted into a beautiful little farm. In 1853 he married Mary, daughter of Simon and Catharine (Harner) House. Of their thirteen children, eight are living: John, Sarah, Joseph, Milton, Ellen, William, Clara and Anna. Mrs. Gruber was born May 9, 1831. She and husband are members of the old Lutheran church, of which he has been an elder about forty years, and is deacon and trustee at present. He served about four years as constable but has declined other offices. When he first came to Allen county there were but three families in his township. With his parents, Mr. Gruber underwent all the trials and discomforts of early days, being deprived of the advantages of schools, but he is nevertheless intelligent and enterprising, and is numbered among the worthy and respected citizens of Allen county.

George P. Lake, of a pioneer family, was born in Vermont, November 24, 1834, son of Nathan and Jerusha (Sheldon) Lake, both natives of Virginia. They moved to Vermont when aged eighteen or twenty years, and there married and remained until 1835, when they left Vermont in search of health, the husband being consumptive. He came with his family of eight children by boat to Maumee City, and then took wagons and struck the Black Swamp where it required three days to travel seven miles. They settled in LaGrange county, but after eighteen months removed to Allen county and settled where Fort Wayne now stands. During the first years there he cultivated forty acres of corn within the present city limits. In the spring of 1838 he removed with his family to where Cuba now stands, built his wigwam covered with bark and moved with his family upon his entry of 120 acres made in 1837. There the father died in 1853. George P. remained on the old homestead until he was twenty-nine years of age, when he bought eighty acres in Springfield township. He remained on this farm fifteen years when he sold, and bought ninety-four acres and settled upon it. When his father first settled in this township there were no roads of any kind, and they had to make their way through an almost trackless forest to get to and from neighbors or to Fort Wayne, where they were compelled to go for the necessaries of life. The forest trees grew fewer before the sturdy blows of their axes, and they were soon repaid for their hard work and energy with fields of growing grain. In 1857 he was married to Rosetta Rupert, born in 1841, and they had three children: Charles C., Rosa and Ora. In 1875 he married Jane Dragoo, born in 1843, by whom he has one child, Nelson, born November 18, 1876. He and wife are members of the United Brethren church. He has a handsome farm of eighty-four acres. In 1865 he enlisted in Company D, One Hundred and Fifty-sixth regiment, under Capt. Sitvers, and served until the close of the war, being discharged at Wilmington, Del.

Cyrus Hollopeter, an old settler of Allen county, was born in Wayne county, Ohio, February 12, 1828, son of Abraham and Lydia (Myers) Hollopeter. At nineteen years of age, he came with his parents to Cedar Creek township, where his father bought eighty acres of land. Here, in the twentieth year of his age, Cyrus cleared seven acres of ground for his father for the balance of his minority. Coming to Springfield township, he bought fifty-three and one-half acres of wood-land nearly three miles from any house. In two or three years he traded this for the forty acres where he now lives. February 25, 1850, he was married to Lydia Conway, in Fort Wayne, by Esquire Du Bois. Of their nine children, six are living: Henry J., Francis E., Avery A., Mary W., Seldon R. and Lydia R. Mrs. Hollopeter was born October 28, 1830. He and wife have been members of the Methodist Episcopal church since they were children, of which he is one of the present trustees. He served as constable ten or twelve years, and has been school director about twenty years. He was a member of the Regulators during their reign in early days. At one time he owned 360 acres of land in this state and Michigan. He is one of the respected farmers of his township.

William H. Ringwalt, a substantial citizen of Springfield township, was born in Indiana October 14, 1844, son of William and Catharine (Staufer) Ringwalt, both of German descent and natives of Pennsylvania. The father in 1835 emigrated to Ohio and settled near Gallion, where he cleared eighty acres of wild land. In 1837 he sold this farm and started to Elkhart county, but when he saw the fine timber of the land in Allen county he changed his mind and entered eighty acres of land in Springfield township. He was well educated in both the English and German languages; served as constable of his township about four years and was present at the time of the organization, when there were only seven voters in the township. He and wife were members of the

United Brethren church, of which he was an official member. He was one of Allen county's best citizens. William H. remained on the homestead farm until seventeen years of age, when he enlisted in the Twenty-third Indiana battery. He participated in the battles with John Morgan, at Brandenburgh, Ky., at Roytown, Tenn., the siege at Knoxville, Buzzard Roost, Ga., Resaca, Ga., Ettawa River, Allatoona Pass, Punkinvine Creek, Kenesaw Mountain, Burnt Hickory, Big Shanty, Marietta, Chattahooche River, Jonesboro, Columbia, Franklin, Nashville. He served two years and nine and one-half months and received an honorable discharge at Indianapolis, July 2, 1865. October 24, 1875, he was married to Anna Maria Boger, born July 12, 1853, by whom he had four children, three of whom are living: May, Orin and Elza. He and wife are members of the Protestant Methodist church. Mrs. Ringwalt is the second of three children of Matthias and Anna (Dressbach) Boger. Her father was born in Ohio, July 14, 1809, son of John G. and Mary (Faust) Boger. He came to Indiana in 1836 and entered 240 acres which he occupied in 1840. In 1870 Mr. Ringwalt embarked in tile and brick manufacturing on the old homestead. He has 120 acres of good land, well improved, with substantial buildings. He is a good citizen as he was a brave soldier. Though beginning poor and deprived of the advantages of schools, except those of pioneer days, he has become a leading citizen and has the esteem and good will of the community.

Estes Howe, one of the pioneer settlers of Springfield township, was born in Saratoga county, N. Y., May 30, 1812, son of Benjamin and Sarah (Stewart) Howe. His father died when he was about one and a half years old. He remained with his mother until eight years of age, when he was taken by an uncle to raise. At fourteen years of age he was apprenticed at the tanner and shoemaker trade, which he followed while in New York; has made his own boots since he was fourteen years of age. He was one of the pioneer shoemakers of Allen county, making all kinds of boots and shoes. On February 25, 1836, he married Susan, daughter of Jeremiah and Susannah (Waite) Whaley. Her maternal grandmother, Mercy Madison, was related to President Madison. By this union were born ten children, seven now living: George B., Charlotte, Ellen, Estes O., Sarah H., Samuel E., Harriet M. and Reeleefee R. Mrs. Howe was born April 16, 1817, in Tompkins county, N. Y. They were married in Oswego county, and in 1837 they settled in Allen county, where Harlan now stands. Here he began working at his trade for Ezra May, and two years later abandoned his trade, except at odd times, and began working out, taking contracts for clearing land for land, and first got eighty acres in DeKalb county, which he soon traded for eighty acres of canal land in Allen county. He continued at clearing several years, and early in the forties settled on forty acres in section 21, in Springfield, which he cleared and afterward bought and added 100 acres. In 1871, he retired from the farm and moved to Harlan, where he now lives. He has cleared in all about

100 acres of land in Springfield township for others besides his own. He never speculated, but has made all he has by hard work, close economy and good management. He served as one of the board of trustees of his township, as treasurer one year and trustee about three years. When he first came to Indiana the first corn be bought he went about fourteen miles for, and bought two bushels at $1.50 per bushel, and then went to what is now called Rudisill's mill, a distance of about ten miles, to have it ground. The next spring after coming to Indiana, he walked eight miles and split 400 rails in one day for one bushel of corn.

Ezra Worden, a substantial farmer of Springfield township, was born in Onondago county, N. Y., July 25, 1827, son of Ira and Charlotte (Wentworth) Worden. His father's father served in the English forces during the revolution, and his mother's father was a soldier on the American side. When eleven years of age, Ezra left home and worked out two years, when he became dissatisfied and hired out to the first man's brother-in-law, and worked three months at $3.00 per month with the privilege of going to school that winter. He hired out the next spring for nine months, for $3.00 per month, and at the end of this time his father had taken up all his wages except $3.00, so that he was disappointed in his expected winter's schooling. His employer gave him cloth enough for a coat, three yards, instead of the $3.00 due him. He then began work for a doctor at $4.00 per month, having previously contracted with his father for his time at $1.00 per month. He continued to work as a farm hand about ten years, and accumulated enough to buy wild lands in Indiana. In 1838, he bought eighty acres of wild land in Allen county, but being too poor to settle, he returned to New York, where he remained three years. In 1841, he married Elizabeth Walsworth, by whom he had nine children, seven of whom are now living: Emma, John W., William Ezra, Ella, Charles, Grant and Freddie. After this marriage he returned to Springfield and made his home in a log cabin on his land. In October, 1861, he enlisted in Company D, Forty-fourth Indiana volunteer regiment, and was with his company in all its engagements. He was wounded at Shiloh by being shot through the right breast and arm, and again at Chickamauga, he was shot in the right side, breaking three or four ribs. In 1862, he was taken prisoner at Stone River and was confined in Libby prison two or three months. Being paroled, he rejoined his company and in the battle of Chickamauga, after he was wounded, was left on the field and was again picked up by the enemy. He is the fortunate possessor of 118 acres of as good land as there is in Allen county, and is one of the county's best citizens. He has served as constable two years. His wife is a member of the Protestant Methodist church.

John D. Reichelderfer, one of the pioneers of Springfield township, was born in Pickaway county, Ohio, October 16, 1812. His parents, John and Christina (Spangler) Reichelderfer, were both born in Berks county, Penn., were married in Pennsylvania and came to Ohio in 1806.

There they raised a family of eleven children, of whom our subject was the fifth, but is the oldest living. He remained with his father until twenty-one years of age. In April, 1832, he married Hester, a daughter of Jacob Markel, born February 19, 1810, and this union was blessed with seven children, of whom two are living: Jacob and Sarah, wife of J. W. Fry. When married, they began on a rented farm, with three cows, horse, and a very little furniture. He remained on this farm six years, and on September 10, 1840, started for Indiana and traveled through to Allen county in wagons. In 1835 he made a prospecting tour on foot, and bought 160 acres, the homestead farm, but only remained a short time. Returned home two years later, he came back and contracted with Henry Gruber to clear two acres, and built a hewn-log house, to which he removed with his family in 1840. He cleared his farm by working almost day and night, his wife helping him in all his work. Often would she work with him in the night time burning logs, and would assist in putting out the crop, and one day she covered ten acres of corn with the old fashioned jumper with a boy to ride the horse, besides doing her own work. They began the struggle of life without anything, but have done well. He has in his possession an old fashioned anvil which was used to hammer out the old Dutch scythe, also the old scythe and whetstone. He also has an old fashioned lamp which has been handed down by five generations. He and wife have been members of the old school Lutheran church, he since childhood, she since sixteen years of age. He, in company with John Zeimmer, cleared several miles of roads in the township of underbrush. He retired from the farm in 1873 to Harlan where he now lives. He has been one of Springfield township's worthiest farmers since his residence here.

Jacob Reichelderfer, son of the above, was born in Ohio, January 3, 1835. He came to Indiana with his parents when only five years of age and helped his father clear the homestead farm. He was one of the first scholars in the first school ever taught in Springfield township. This was taught by Sarah Bracy in a double log dwelling house in Maysville. The teacher would take chalk and mark on the slab benches each scholar's place to sit. On December 30, 1856, he married Sarah, daughter of William and Mary (Rudisill) Harter, who were early settlers of Richland county, Ohio. This union was blessed with eleven children, of whom six are living: Jacob Franklin, Anna S., Joseph E., Lavina H., William H. and Sarah C. Mrs. Reichelderfer was born November 27, 1837. He and wife are members of the old school Lutheran church, of which he has served as deacon several years in succession and is leader of the choir. In 1845 their Sunday-school was organized, he being one of the first pupils. In the early days they would attend in bare feet; the girls were more fortunate than boys, but they would go in their bare feet until within view of the church when they would don their shoes. He now owns eighty acres of the homestead farm.

Lewis Reichelderfer, a native of Pickaway county, Ohio, was born October 9, 1820, son of John and Catherine (Spangler) Reichelderfer. In early boyhood he was remote from schools, but his physical training in the woods developed him well for the hardships of pioneer life in Allen county. In 1840 he came to Indiana on a prospecting tour and purchased a piece of land of 320 acres from his father. Like others of time he came hoping that here he might find a home where patient toil would yield greater results than in the older settlements. When a boy his father bought a clover huller, which furnished work during the winter for him and his brothers, hulling for neighbors when he should have been in school, and one day when the father was away he and brother concluded to break the machine and render it useless, which they did by feeding the same with a large stone, and refusing to work any longer if it was repaired. After coming to Indiana he only made a short stay, but returned to Ohio, and remained two years. He then made another short trip to Indiana, and returned to Ohio, and in 1842 he married Miss Julia Ann Ranck, who was born April 20, 1822. Throughout her husband's pioneer life, she ever comforted and sustained him. To this union eleven children were born, of whom nine survive. Elihu, ex-representative of Allen county; William, ex-trustee of Springfield township; Alden, John, Aaron, Lafayette, Sarah, Hanna and Selena. Mr. and Mrs. Reichelderfer are members of the old Lutheran church. He now owns 195 acres of fine land well cultivated. Mr. Reichelderfer's life has been marked by the strictest integrity, and no one enjoys more fully the esteem and confidence of his fellowmen.

William A. Reichelderfer, a prominent citizen of Harlan, is a native of Pickaway county, Ohio, born July 19, 1848, son of Lewis and Julia A. Reichelderfer. He remained in his native state until sixteen years of age, when he came to Indiana with his parents and settled in Springfield ownship. After being here about one month he enlisted in Company F, One Hundred and Forty-second Indiana volunteers, under Capt. Biglow, and was in the battle of Nashville. He served until the close of the war and received an honorable discharge at Indianapolis. When he returned home he had contracted a cold which disabled him for some time, and his education being limited up to this time, he began going to school at Harlan, and attended about one year. He then began teaching in the country school and taught three winter terms. In 1868 he married Jennie E. Stopher, who was born December 24, 1852, and they have had four children, three living: Charles, Elwood, Frank A., and Lola E. He and wife are members of the Methodist Episcopal church. In 1875 he was elected justice of the peace of his township and served eight years. In April, 1884, he was elected trustee and re-elected in 1886, which is quite complimentary to him, as his township is republican by about forty votes at this time — when he first ran for trustee the republican majority on the state ticket was forty-eight, but he was elected by forty-four majority. He is one of the leading citizens of Harlan, and, highly respected by all. He has always been a democrat and is prominent in his party.

Charles Reichelderfer, an old settler of Springfield township, was born May 11, 1824, in Pickaway county, Ohio, son of John and Christina (Spangler) Reichelderfer. In 1840 he came to Indiana with his family and settled in Maysville. He bought ninety acres in the woods and this he cleared into a farm. He was first married to Louie Allen, by whom he had one child, Maria. The mother was a member of the Methodist Episcopal church. Subsequent to her death he married Louie Kentner, still living, by whom he had four children: Frederick, William, Mary and Jay P. He and wife are both Lutherans. He is one of the leading citizens of Springfield township, and well respected by all who know him.

Ira I. Grubb, an industrious farmer and stock-raiser of Springfield township, was born June 3, 1838, in Wayne county, Ind., son of Nelson and Martha A. (Notestine) Grubb. He came with his parents to Indiana in 1841, who settled in Cedar Creek township, buying sixty acres of uncultivated land. In 1861 he was married to Elizabeth A., daughter of Henry and Anna (Bickhart) Oberholtzer. To this union six children were born, five now living: Charles C., Lochiel L., Herman H., Bern B. and Mary J. The mother was born August 27, 1840. He and wife are members of the Evangelical Lutheran church which was organized in his barn by Rev. Waltinan about 1852. He is a member of the Masonic order. He enlisted in the late war but was not accepted. In 1856 he went west on a prospecting tour, but not being satisfied with the west, he returned and settled at Harlan and embarked in blacksmithing and wagon-making, which business he continued until April, 1866, when he bought and settled on the farm where he now lives. He now has a handsome farm of 149 acres in Springfield township, within one and one-half miles of Harlan, with good buildings. He was the first man in the township to begin the breeding of Jersey cattle; he began in June, 1880. He is an ardent supporter of the democratic party, and on one occasion was nominated by his party for trustee, but was not able to overcome a large adverse majority. He is one of the leading citizens of his township. Mr. Grubb's two oldest sons are graduates of the Valparaiso normal school.

William A. Moore, an old settler of Allen county, was born in New York, November 8, 1824. His parents, Priam and Lois (Calkins) Moore, were born in Genesee county, N. Y., the father in 1796, the mother in 1805. The father remained in New York and followed the shoemaker trade until 1830, when he removed to Erie county, Ohio, where he worked at his trade in connection with farming rented land. Since 1840 he has made his home with his son William A., and is now in his ninety-third year. The mother died at her son's home in 1884. William A. grew to manhood in Ohio, with slight opportunities for education. Being the oldest of a family of eight children it fell to him to help his father to support the others, and he has been the mainstay and support of the family ever since he was large enough to earn wages. He hired out previous to their coming to Indiana to obtain the money that brought them here. On November 15, 1840, they settled in Scipio township. He traded his team for thirty-one acres of wood-land, built his log cabin, and cleared and farmed until 1852 when he sold this place and bought eighty acres in Springfield township. In 1850 he embarked in the saw-mill business and lost all his hard earnings and incurred a judgment debt of $1,600. He had previously run the first thresher in Springfield, and continued in this business about thirty years, by this means arising from his embarrassed condition and paying for his farm of eighty acres. To this he has added eighty acres. June 19, 1842, he married Dorliska Bracy, born April 10, 1822, and they have had ten children, eight of whom are living: Angelia Sarah, Harriet E., Dorliska L., William W., Charles W., Henrietta C., Hiram B. and Cora L. He and wife are members of the Protestant Methodist church. In 1854 he had the misfortune to lose by fire his dwelling house and all contents, and again in 1866 he was burnt out, losing nearly all he had in the house. He served as constable one term in Scipio township and two terms in Springfield township. The first winter he was here he had to go five miles on foot and draw a hand sled with his sack of corn to mill to be ground for bread. In spite of his many misfortunes he is now prosperous.

Frederick Omo, one of the pioneer settlers of Springfield township, was born October 24, 1819. His father, Simon Omo, was a Frenchman and a soldier under Napoleon Bonaparte, being wounded five times. After coming to America he was drafted into the war of 1812, and served till its close. He lived to the good old age of ninety. He was a member of the Methodist Episcopal church. He married Mary Mercer, a native of Pennsylvania, of German descent. Their fourth child, Frederick, in 1836, left his home in Pennsylvania, and settled in Ohio, where he hired out by the month as a farm hand. In 1836 he and his brother-in-law bought 160 acres of wild land in Springfield township, but did not make their home here until 1840. On division of this land he got sixty acres, but was compelled to hire out to get money enough with which to begin farming. In 1843 he was married to Elizabeth Shields, born July 3, 1825. They have had twelve children, seven now living: Mary, William H., John W., Louisa, Adaline, Joseph and Francis. He was a member of the board of trustees of his township in company with Estes Howe and Linas Cutts, and helped to make the first appraisement of school lands in the township. He was a supporter of William H. Harrison for the presidency in 1840, and has adhered to the republican party since its organization. He has prospered in a high degree, and now owns 140 acres in Springfield township, with substantial buildings. He and wife are members of the Methodist Episcopal church, of which he was steward twenty years and class leader four years.

Richard Price, an industrious farmer of Springfield township, was born in 1841, in Allen county. His parents, John and Susan (Oliver)

Price, both died while he was a small child, and he was taken by one Wilson to raise, but after a time he was taken by Abraham Dingman, who married his step-sister. A few years later he found a home with Isaac Claxton, then with James Mills, and then with Henry Miller, with whom he remained seven years. He was living with Alex Baston in 1862, when he enlisted in Company D, Eighty-eighth Indiana regiment, and with the exception of about sixty days while sick and at home on a furlough, he participated in all the engagements of his regiment. He received an honorable discharge at Indianapolis in 1865. On November, of that year, he married Martha E. Hatch, and this union was blessed with one child, Minnie A., born November 5, 1875. He and wife are members of the United Brethren church. After marriage he worked at clearing one winter and then rented farms until 1868, when he bought forty acres of uncultivated lands in Springfield township, which he has converted into a valuable farm. For the last twelve years he has been running a threshing machine in connection with farming. He is a member of the G. A. R. at Mayville, and was a member of the Regulators.

DeGroff N. Herrick, of Springfield township, is a native Hoosier, born in Milan township, October 28, 1849, son of Aruna and Elizabeth (Parent) Herrick. The paternal grandfather was a native of Vermont, born June 26, 1797, who in 1819 married Susan Robbins of upper Canada. They seittled in Jefferson county, N. Y., where they raised a family of seven boys and three daughters. In 1842, they removed to Allen county. The wife died in 1848, and in the fall of the same year he married Mrs. Catharine Lloyd, with whom he lived until death. On coming to Maysville, he became one of the charter members of the Maysville class of the Methodist Episcopal church. He was a devoted member of this church until his death, which occurred March 5, 1877. His wife survived him to the good old age of ninety-three, and died in 1887. She was married at the age of eighty-three years, after her husband died, to Mr. Gothep, who is now living and is ninety-two years of age. Aruna Herrick was a native of Jefferson county, N. Y., where he grew to manhood, and then emigrated west, and settled in Allen county. He received a good common school education, and was a carpenter by trade. In 1847 he was married, and to this union four children were born: John Frank, who died in 1878; DeGroff N., Daniel M., and Clarence M. The mother died in 1854. In 1857, he was married to Mary Boger, by whom he had seven children: Andrew, Adelia A., Susan Ida., Phoebe C., David O., Hattie E., and William. In the dark days of the rebellion, he volunteered in Company D, One Hundred and Fifty-fifth regiment. He resided after the war in Springfield township, until his death January, 1875. DeGroff N. was raised in Milan township, and received a good common school education. November 12, 1871, he married Lydia A., daughter of John and Rachel Zeimmer, and this union was blessed with one child, Ella M., who died in 1876. He and wife are members of the United Brethren church, of which he is one of the trustees of the parsonage. In 1874, he bought and settled upon the farm he now occupies, which he has made one of the best of the township, and has a two-story brick dwelling, with a good barn.

Ephriam Markle, one of the old settlers of Springfield township, was born in Pennsylvania, August 6, 1813, son of Jacob and Catharine Markle. The family moved to Ohio when he was four years of age, and there he grew to manhood and learned the weaver's trade, which he followed about twelve years. In 1834 he married Elizabeth Reichelderfer, and they have had six children, of whom five are living: Margaret, Mary, Henry, Jacob and Jerry. The mother, who was born in 1814, was a member of the Lutheran church, and died in 1846. In 1851 he married Catharine Reezer, by whom he had four children, of whom survive: Daniel, Samuel and Melinda. The mother, who was born April 25, 1817, is a member of the old Presbyterian church. He is a member of the Lutheran church. In 1842 he entered eighty acres of wild land in Springfield township, and built his log cabin, the only house between that vicinity and Maysville at that time, and here began his toilsome career, which has ended so well. He made considerable money in his time, and added to his first entry until he owns 240 acres of well improved land. He has always been one of Allen county's valuable citizens.

Henry Boulton, an early settler of Springfield township, is a native of England, born January 14, 1821. His parents, William and Elizabeth (Hamblett) Boulton, emigrated to America in 1837, and settled in Erie county, Ohio, and in 1849 removed to Scipio township, where the father died in 1863. Henry worked out and helped his father to pay for a piece of land, and in 1843 came to Indiana and bought eighty acres of land in Springfield township where he now lives. Being without money to clear it he returned to Ohio to work for the necessary means, and remained in Ohio until 1847. He then began to improve his land and built his log cabin. After clearing and cultivating about ten acres, he took to himself a wife, Helen Hatch. They have eight children: Louisa, Anna N., Emma, Flora, Mary, Oscar, Ida and Mina. Mrs. Boulton was born May 31, 1831; she and all their children are members of the United Brethren church, while he has been a member of the Methodist Episcopal church since 1850. He has given his children the benefit of all the schooling his township afforded, and then at Fort Wayne college. His son has attended two terms at Ann Arbor. His industry has been rewarded by the possession of 322½ acres of good land in Allen county, and his home place is well improved. He has given each of his five daughters at their marriage $550.

John Zeimmer, one of the pioneer settlers of Allen county, was born in Pickaway county, Ohio, July 27, 1814, son of Abram and Susannah (Chritenbaugh) Zeimmer. His grandfather came from Pennsylvania and settled in Pickaway county, remained five years and removed to Wooster, where he was killed by the Indians. John came to Indiana in 1836, on a prospecting tour, and entered 160 acres, and then returned to Ohio, where he hired out by the month to get money with which to cultivate his new land. In 1843 he returned to Indiana, and after clearing about five acres, erected a cabin, and in 1843 was married to Rachel, daughter of Obediah and Lydia Ann (Markle) Boger. By this union he had eight children, six now living: Martin, Susannah, George, Lydia A., John W. and Mary. The mother, who was born October 31, 1825, was a member of the old Lutheran church. She died November 14, 1878. He and wife settled in their new home in the woods and being a poor man, he and wife had many privations. They were compelled to go to Fort Wayne, at that time but a small village, to mill, and there being no roads it took them about three days to make the trip and return. They would carry axes with them to cut their road. He succeeded in his efforts and came to possess 400 acres of good land in Allen county, from which he has given to his children, but still holds his homestead of 160 acres. On this he has a comfortable two-story brick dwelling and good barn. Mr. Zeimmer served as school director five years, about thirty-five years ago.

Martin Zeimmer, a progressive farmer of Springfield township, son of the above, was born September 4, 1842. He was born and raised on the homestead farm, and being the oldest son, helped his father as soon as he was able. He began to plow when he had to reach up to the plow handles and was too small to release the plow when it became fast, so that he had to invent a mode of using a chain by which the oxen could do that for him. In 1868, he married Mahala A. Burrier, who was born in 1844. To this union two children were born, of whom one survives: Cora A., born May 13, 1871. After his marriage his father gave him forty acres of wood-land, which he has converted into a nice little farm, and has a two-story brick dwelling and good barn.

Isaac Dreisbach, an early settler of Springfield township, was born in Pickaway county, Ohio, April 4, 1820, son of Samuel and Catharine (Bookwalter) Dreisbach. The father was a native of Pennsylvania, the mother of Berks county, Penn., and came to Ohio about 1811, and remained until death. The father was in the war of 1812. Isaac remained with his father until twenty-three years of age, when on April 13, 1843, he married Catharine Metzger, by whom he had six children: John, born September 21, 1847; Samuel, born December 11, 1851; Joseph, December 5, 1857; Frank, March 16, 1861; Mary E., May 17, 1844 (oldest); Levi, March 24, 1854. The mother was born November 7, 1819. He remained in Ohio three years after marriage, and then settled on the farm of 160 acres where he now lives. About thirty acres was cleared at that time, and there was a small cabin, which was the second built in the township. He served as constable one year in an early day. He and wife are charter members of the United Brethren church. He donated the ground on which the church stands, besides $500. He has always been liberal in his donation to churches and gave $50 to the United Brethren church in Fort Wayne, also a smaller donation to a mission church in Nebraska. Through his kindness to relatives in becoming security for them, and his sacrifices in selling lands to liquidate those debts, he was the loser at one time of about $12,000; and about this time had the misfortune to lose his dwelling by fire, without insurance. But he withstood these calamities, and soon erected a beautiful two-story brick dwelling. He has 158 acres of fine land within one mile of Harlan, which is one of the best in Allen county.

Levi Dreisbach, son of the above, and an enterprising business man of Harlan, was born March 24, 1854. He was born and raised on the homestead farm in Springfield township, and remained on the farm until 1882, when he located in Harlan and embarked in the butcher business, which he continued until 1885. On December 27, 1874, he was married to Rachel A. Sapp, who was born April 17, 1852. This union was blessed with three children: Katie, born in 1875; Clyde, born in 1880; Cosie, born May 23, 1883.

Daniel Knisely, of Springfield township, was born May 31, 1826, in Columbiana county, Ohio. He was the fourth child of Solomon and Elizabeth (Rudy) Knisely, both of German descent and natives of Pennsylvania. At fourteen years of age he was bound out to a farmer and remained until twenty years of age. He had only six months' schooling, but through his own industry learned to read, write and figure. On March 2, 1853, he married Mahala Conway. Of their nine children, six are living: David, born December 13, 1856; Delilah, March 12, 1861; Luella, November 29, 1862; Rollin, May 21, 1866; Orlando, April 2, 1868; and Rosa, May 6, 1871. The mother, who was born November 11, 1833, departed this life February 19, 1880. He and wife were members of the Methodist Episcopal church, which he first joined in 1853, and was a steward two years. In 1887 for convenience he took a letter and placed it in the Protestant church. At twenty years of age he hired out on the farm at $10.50 the first summer, and he saved enough to buy him a yoke of cattle and came to Indiana in 1846 to see the fifty acres of wood-land he received as his wages for the six years that he was bound out. The following year he built his log cabin and began to clear. He now owns eighty acres of well improved land and has a two-story brick dwelling. He has served as school director of his district about twelve years.

George R. Snyder, a prominent farmer of Springfield township, was born in Washington county, Penn., August 15, 1836. His parents, Jacob and Margaret (Riggle) Snyder, moved from Pennsylvania to Ohio in 1838, and settled in Ashland county, buying eighty acres of land which they partly cleared. Eight years later, they came to Allen county, Ind., and settled on the farm where George now lives, at that time in the woods. George remained with his parents and took care of them until their deaths. In 1862 he married Sarah Coles, and they have had six children, five living: Rosalie, Jennie, Hattie, William H. H. and Samuel. The mother was born May 12, 1844. She is a member of the Lutheran church. Mr. Snyder has a handsome farm embracing eighty acres of the old homestead. He and family are respected by all who know them.

Horace Herrick, a progressive farmer, is a native of New York, born in Lewis county, July 15, 1824, son of Daniel and Susan (Robbins) Herrick. Mr. Herrick received a good common school education, and remained in his native state until 1847, when he came west and settled on a farm near Fort Wayne, but only remained about one year when he removed to Milan township. Three years later he returned to his birth-place for a short stay, but again located in Milan township, this time near Cuba. He remained here until 1854, when he sold his farm and in the following year removed to Wisconsin. A year later he returned to Hoosierdom and settled on the farm where he now lives. On October 12, 1851, he was united in marriage with Mary, daughter of Jedediah C. and Jane (Forsythe) Mills; she was born June 26, 1826. He and wife are both charter members of the Protestant Methodist church at Maysville, and devoted and consistent members since its organization. He is also a member of the Masonic order at Maysville. Mr. Herrick came to Indiana with only enough money to enter forty acres of wild land, but by close economy, hard work and good management, he has prospered. He has a comfortable two-story brick dwelling with good barn, which is supplied with water from a natural fountain. He takes a great interest in fine stock, and since 1882 has been making a specialty of the Jersey cattle.

Adam Driver, an old settler of Allen county, was born in Maryland, May 2, 1819, son of Wesley and Ruth (Barns) Driver. At sixteen years of age he came to Ohio and settled in Erie county, where his father bought seventy-four acres of timber land. Here he got a foretaste of a pioneer's life. After twenty-one years of age he worked out until 1847, when he had accumulated enough with which he came to Allen county and bought eighty acres of wild lands. In a short time he sold this and returned to Ohio, but two years later, he came in company with his brother, and bought 240 acres of wood-land in partnership. Here he began a real pioneer life. April 9, 1854, he was united in marriage with Almenia S. Bartholomew, who was born in 1834. This union was blessed with three children: Harriet, Adelia and John S. He has been a devoted member of the Methodist Episcopal church for thirty-five years. He now owns 160 acres of well improved land and is one of the substantial citizens of his township.

Alexander Boston, a substantial farmer of Springfield township, was born in Ohio, December 25, 1827, son of George and Mary (Lytle) Boston, both natives of Pennsylvania. He was raised in Wayne county, Ohio, until fifteen years of age, when his father removed to Seneca county. After helping his father clear up a farm in Ohio, he came to Indiana in 1848, on a prospecting tour and in 1849, came again and bought eighty acres in the woods, and by clearing and selling he obtained the 160 where he now lives. This he has improved with a two-story brick dwelling and good barn. After his father's death he bought sixty acres of the homestead farm. In 1851 he married Phoebe J. Price, who was born in 1835. Of their seven children there are living:

Sarah, Alice, Clara, Charles H. and Willis A. He and wife are members Protestant Methodist church. He is the present parsonage trustee, and has served as class leader, steward, etc. He was a member of the Regulators during their operations. He is one of the leading citizens of his township and well respected.

James A. Henderson, of Springfield township, is a native of Ohio. His father, John Henderson, was raised to manhood in Pennsylvania, and his father dying when he was quite young he was bound out, and never had the advantage of much education. He was married in Pennsylvania to his wife Elizabeth, and several years later they emigrated to Ohio and settled in Mahoning county. In 1850 he sold his little farm of twelve acres and came to Indiana and bought eighty acres in Milan township, all wooded except twenty acres. Five years later he sold and bought forty acres in Springfield township, where he remained until his death, which occurred in 1870. He and wife were members of the Lutheran church, and he was one of the leading citizens. James A. Henderson was born while the family resided in Mahoning county, Ohio, July 8, 1840, and came to Indiana with his parents when ten years of age. In 1871 he married Mary Richards, born in 1839, by whom he has two children: Earl and Willard B. He and wife are members of the Lutheran church, of which he has served as deacon, elder and trustee. In 1861 he enlisted in Company E, Thirtieth Indiana regiment, under Capt. Silvers, and served three years and eleven days, being honorably discharged at Indianapolis, October 11, 1864. He began the battle of life as a day laborer, and so accumulated $700, with which he bought a half interest in a saw-mill which he ran about eleven years. He then traded his interest in the mill with other property for eighty acres of land in Springfield township, where he now has a pleasant home.

George W. Nusbaum, a prosperous farmer of Springfield township, was born in Frederick City, Md., September 11, 1822, son of William and Susannah (Devilbiss) Nusbaum. At twelve years of age he went with his parents to Ohio, and settled in Seneca county. Here he rented a farm for three years and accumulated enough to buy a farm in Springfield township, where he now lives, in 1850. He served an apprenticeship at the pump-maker's and carpenter's trades, which he followed in this county in connection with farming. March 25, 1847, he married Mary Fry, born in 1825. Of their five children, four are living: James W., Alice V., Emma C. and Alva A. Mrs. Nusbaum was a member of the United Brethren church, and died in 1864. In 1865 he was married to Sarah C. Sanders, by whom he had three children, of whom one is living, Nettie. He and wife are members of the United Brethren church. When Mr. Nusbaum first came to Allen county, he bought 160 acres of wood-land, which he cleared and converted into a farm, and he has now 280 acres. He is one of the leading citizens of his township, and has served as trustee one year.

Henry Cummins, one of the early settlers of Springfield township, was born in Vermont, February 23, 1816, son of Linden and Maria

C. F. Hettler

(Wilkerson) Cummins. He came with his parents to New York when seven years of age. Thirteen years later they removed to the western reserve of Ohio, and remained about fifteen years, when he came to Indiana and first bought ninety-one and 54-100 acres of wild land and afterward sixty-four more, which was all covered with a dense growth of timber, which he cleared away. In 1838 he was married to Matilda Kilborn, and first settled at Circleville, Ohio, where he worked at the carpenter's trade until he came to Indiana and settled in his little log cabin. Here he spent his golden days, as he was fond of hunting and many a deer fell before his unerring rifle. He has often followed the track of deer nine miles from home when it was almost sundown and no roads led him through a trackless forest. On his last hunt he killed ten or eleven deer in little less than two weeks and sold them at Fort Wayne for about $60. His marriage was blessed with eight children: Mary A., born July 16, 1839; Joseph D., May 12, 1841; Isabel, March 29, 1843; William F., November 29, 1844; Richard A., April 27, 1847, died 1875; Robert M., August 13, 1849; Estella, July 6, 1852; Charles E., December 6, 1854. Mrs. Cummins was born November 17, 1814, and departed this life February 10, 1881. He served as supervisor of the road in an early day when they had to cut the roads through the woods. He now owns 119 acres of good land besides his home property in Harlan, and is one of the respected old citizens of Allen county.

Joseph D. Cummins, son of the above, is a native of Brown county, Ohio, born May 12, 1841. Being the oldest boy of the family, he had experience in pioneer life. In 1862 he enlisted in the late war in Company D, Eighty-eighth Indiana volunteers, under Capt. Scott Swan, and participated in the following battles: Perryville, Stone River, Chickamauga, Lookout Mountain, Mission Ridge (being with the Fourteenth army corps that made the charge that broke the rebel line and gained the victory), Ringgold, Altoona, Peach Tree Creek, Burnt Hickory Atlanta, Jonesboro, and was with Sherman in his march to the sea. At Perryville he received a wound in his right ankle which disabled him about eight weeks, and with the above and the exception of thirty days at home while sick, he was always at his post of duty. In 1865 he received an honorable discharge at Indianapolis. He served in the campaign from Savannah, December 1, 1864, through Georgia and Carolinas, and served in the battles of Averysborough and Bentonville, N. C., then to Galesboro and into camp until April 10. From there they chased Johnston and captured him near Raleigh, N. C., and then marched via Richmond to Washington on foot. When he went to return to his company after his furlough he started via Nashville, but could not get through and went via New York city, taking the steamer Ajax, which was chased by the rebel gunboats and narrowly escaped sinking. When he returned home he was engaged in the blacksmith business at Harlan about three years, and then started for the Black Hills, but was stopped at Fort Kearney, Neb., by the Indian outbreak. On April 20, 1873, he married Orsia Daniels, born June 28, 1852, by whom he has four chilren: Bernice, born January 25, 1874; Otis, March 9, 1875; Ethel, October 18, 1881, and Mildred, August 11, 1888. He and wife are members of the Methodist Episcopal church, of which he is district steward and trustee. She was a teacher in the schools about ten years. He has been engaged in the saw-mill business about twenty years and now owns the saw-mill and planing-mill and band saw and does all kinds of wood work. He has a handsome two-story house in Harlan with all the modern improvements.

W. O. Oberholtzer, the leading blacksmith of Harlan, was born in Ohio, February 15, 1851. His parents, Jacob and Mary (Bickhart) Oberholtzer, are both natives of Pennsylvania. The father was born May 20, 1821, the mother June 14, 1825. The father came to Ohio with his parents when a small boy, and there grew to manhood, and became by occupation a farmer. In 1851 he removed with his wife and two children and settled in Springfield township. He bought eighty acres of uncultivated school lands, and soon added another eighty acres. This he began to clear, but sickened and died, November 2, 1855, leaving his wife and three small children. His wife, a true mother, cared for the family, and improved their new home with a house and barn. Here Mr. Oberholtzer grew to manhood, and being the oldest boy the bulk of the work fell to him. His mother died January 29, 1873, and he began to work at the blacksmith trade, never serving any apprenticeship, but he has mastered the trade. On November 20, 1873, he was married to Sarah M., daughter of Solomon and Harriet (Garman) Myers, both of Pennsylvania, of German descent. This union was blessed with six children: Moses, Birdie, William E., Rolla E., Elnora and Zula Edith. The mother was born September 27, 1853. He and wife are members of the Lutheran church. He is a member of the Masonic order. In connection with his trade he manages his farm of sixty-nine acres, two miles north of Harlan.

Gilbert Starr, an old settler of Springfield township, was born July 20, 1811, son of Comfort and Abigail (Barnum) Starr; the latter was a cousin of the great showman P. T. Barnum. The parents were natives of Connecticut; the father born June 3, 1776, and was married October 27, 1796. They moved to Patterson, Dutchess Co., N. Y., where Gilbert was born. Here the father became a member of the Methodist Episcopal church. Thence they moved to Canfield, Ohio, in June, 1817, and the father was one of five who organized the first Methodist class at that place, July 6, 1848. Gilbert came with his parents to Ohio, when about five years of age. At the age of eighteen years his father gave him his time and he bound himself out to Edmund J. Benton, until twenty-one years of age, and he made this his home about nine years On December 22, 1836, he married Sarah, daughter of George and Susan Flick, by whom he had seven children: Emory L., born December 17, 1838; Susan E., June 23, 1841; Charles A., February 12, 1843; Comfort W., October 13, 1848; Mary M., February 16, 1851; Sarah A., March 31, 1854; Willis C., November 8, 1858. The mother was born

November 21, 1817; she was a devoted member of the Methodist Episcopal church. On October 15, 1865, he was married to Nancy A., daughter of Jedediah and Jane Mills. This union was blessed with three children, twins, who died in infancy, and Gilbert A., born June 2, 1869. He and wife are members of the Methodist Episcopal church. About eight years after his first marriage he left Ohio and went to Michigan, but after about eighteen months he returned to Ohio and remained until September, 1851, when he came to Indiana and settled on the farm where he now lives, which was at that time all in the woods, but three families between him and Spencerville. He never served an apprenticeship at any trade, but was a fair carpenter and got out the timbers and made all the shingles for his house and barn. Mr. Starr was one of the leading farmers of his township until 1876, when he had the misfortune to lose his eyesight. Of the children born to Mr. Starr's first wife all are living but two: Willis C., who died in childhood, and Comfort W., who died March 22, 1889. Comfort removed from Ohio September 19, 1850, and married Martha Cope, February, 1872, who died a year later. November 21, 1873, he married Hannah Reichelderfer, who survives. In 1876 he united with the Methodist Episcopal church at Maysville, and was chorister and a teacher in the Sunday school about ten years. At sixteen years of age he enlisted in Company F, One Hundred and Forty-second Indiana infantry, under Capt. Robert Swann, and became corporal. He served until the close of the war and received an honorable discharge at Indianapolis. He was a member of D. K. Stopher post, G. A. R., at Maysville. He was a lover of music and for many years a singing teacher and a leader of the cornet band at Maysville, and was a teacher of the bands at Payne, Ohio, Leo, Ind., Harlan and Chamberlain. He was a member of the I. O. O. F. C. A. Starr, the genial proprietor of the Starr house in Harlan, is one of the leading citizens. He came to Indiana with his parents when nine years of age. He was married to Eliza J. Lillie, daughter of Thomas and Julia A. (Wakeland) Lillie; she was born February 29, 1844. After marriage he farmed and teamed until April 6, 1874, when he embarked in the hotel business. His wife is a member of the Methodist Episcopal church. He is a member of the K. of P. lodge at Fort Wayne. He is a prominent republican, and has been chairman of its committee since 1880. He was appointed postmaster at Harlan, Ind., in July, 1889.

John Peters, an early settler of Springfield township, is a native of Pennsylvania, born near the famous battlefield of Gettysburg, July 24, 1816. His parents, Abram and Christina (Teters) Peters, emigrated to Ohio when he was seven years of age, and settled in Columbiana county, where he grew to manhood. His father being a poor man and a blacksmith, he was put in the shop when quite young. In 1843 he was married to Sidney A. Mason, who was born July 7, 1843, and they have had four children, three living: Anna, Joseph A. and John A. He remained in Ohio until 1852, when he came to Indiana, and bought and settled on eighty acres of wild land in Springfield township. This he cleared and converted into a farm. He is now a highly esteemed citizen. He and wife are members of the Methodist Episcopal church.

Anthony Snyder, of Springfield township, was born in France, March 15, 1839, son of George and Mary (Stick) Snyder. The parents emigrated with their family to America in 1848, first settling in Pennsylvania, but after a short time, removing to New York state. Four years later, they removed to Fort Wayne where they remained until 1857, when they came to Springfield township and settled on the farm, where they remained the rest of their lives. Anthony remained with his parents until their deaths. In 1868, he married Elizabeth Reichelderfer, daughter of John D. and Hester (Markle) Reichelderfer. This union gave them four children: John, George, Charles and William. The mother, who was born in 1848, died November 16, 1884. She was a member of the Lutheran church. In 1885, he married Margaret Johnson, by whom he has one child: Sophia. He is a member of the Catholic church. He began the struggle of life without money, and when he and his brother bought the eighty acres where he now lives, they went into debt $1,200, and the land at that time was covered with a dense growth of forest. He now owns 125 acres of good farming land in Springfield township and substantial buildings, and is one of the representative farmers.

George Haifley, a prosperous and industrious farmer of Springfield township, was born in Mahoning county, Ohio, December 29, 1837, son of Israel and Sarah (Baker) Haifley, both of German descent. The father was born in Maryland, April 10, 1811, and the mother was born in Kentucky. Israel Haifley, when about twenty-four years of age, emigrated west and settled in Mahoning, Ohio. In 1852 he removed to Indiana and settled in Springfield township, where he remained until his death, July 25, 1871. About a year before coming to Indiana he bought eighty acres of wood-land in Springfield. Having a family of four children, and being a poor man, and settling in the woods, he and family suffered all the hardships known to a pioneer life. He and wife were both members of the English Lutheran church, of which he served as one of the elders about fifteen years. He was a leading citizen. His wife was born May 24, 1808, and died September 24, 1882. Their son, George, was raised in Ohio until about fourteen years of age. He received a common school education, and served an apprenticeship at the carpenter's trade, which he followed in connection with farming several years. June 25, 1863, he married Martha E., daughter of Jonas, sr., and Sarah A. Astry. Of their eight children, six are now living: Joseph B., born May 3, 1864; Clarissa J., born October 13, 1865; Flora B., born July 30, 1869; Nettie May and Perry W. (twins), born February 10, 1877, and George S., born March 25, 1883. The mother was born August 6, 1843. He and wife are both members of the Lutheran church. He was formerly a member of the Masonic order at Maysville. He began for himself by working at his trade, and soon accumulated enough to buy a threshing machine, which in connection with farming and his trade, he ran for twenty-one years. He first bought forty acres, and added to that until he now owns 125 acres, and has become a prominent citizen.

John B. Haifley, of Springfield township, is a native of Ohio, born February 28, 1846, son of Israel and Sarah (Baker) Haifley, above mentioned. He came to Indiana with his parents when about seven years of age, and received a common school education such as could be obtained in the log school-houses of his day. On May 7, 1868, he was married to Martha E. Walter, born May 5, 1846, daughter of Jefferson and Margaret (Whan) Walter, both natives of Columbiana county, Ohio. This union was blessed with two children: Harry J., born October 18, 1868; Myrtle, May 21, 1882. Mr. Haifley and wife are members of the Lutheran church. He has prospered in life, and has a valuable farm of 130 acres, with good and substantial buildings. He is a leading citizen and highly respected.

Absalom Sapp, one of the prosperous farmers of Springfield township, was born in Bedford county, Penn., December 14, 1822, son of Adam and Mary M. (Larbarger) Sapp. When he was seven months old, his parents removed to Ohio, and settled in Knox county, where he grew to manhood. When twenty-three years of age he went to his native state and remained one year, and returning to Ohio, settled in Wayne county. On January 13, 1848, he married Elisabeth, daughter of John and Catharine (Fightner) Flickinger. This union was blessed with nine children, five of whom are living: Rachel A., born April 17, 1852; Daniel M., born January 9, 1856; Samuel W., born November 10, 1857; Elizabeth A., born October 18, 1862; Luther F., born October 18, 1865. The mother was born December 26, 1822. After marriage they began on a rented farm, but one year later he embarked in the hotel business at Smithville, Ohio, at which he continued until he came to Indiana in October 1852, when he settled on the eighty acres where he now lives and which he bought the April previous. He built his log cabin, and began to clear the land. In his young days in Ohio, when his father settled, there were not families enough in one neighborhood to start a subscription school, but in time there were eight or ten families got together, who built a log school-house with stick chimney and puncheon seats, in which he went to school when there was no work for him to do on the farm, as in those days they had to tramp out their wheat and clover seed with horses, an occupation where he was always counted in. He and wife are members of the Lutheran church. He has 113 acres of good farming land in Springfield township, with substantial buildings. He is in politics a democrat. He is one of the leading farmers of this progressive day, but still preserves his old log cabin and stable to commemorate the golden days of the past.

Christopher Zeis, a venerable citizen of Allen county, is a native of Germany, born May 3, 1818. His parents, Martin and Christina (Stross) Zeis, natives of Germany, came to America with their family in 1819, and settled in Maryland, where they remained ten years, then to Seneca county, Ohio, where they remained until death. Christopher remained with his pa━━━━━━━ father's death, in 1852, when he came to I━━━━━━━━━━━━━ghty acres with seventeen acres cleared. ━━━━━━━ ━━45, he married Henrietta E. Nusbaum, and this ━━ion was blessed with eleven children, seven of whom are living: Barbara E., Melissa J., Rufus H., Laura V., George W., Joseph F. and Charles F. The mother was born August 21, 1827. She was a member of the German Reformed church, formerly, but before her death, united with her husband in the Lutheran church, of which he was elder and deacon. November 8, 1887, he married Mrs. Ellinor Miller, widow of George Miller. She is a member of the Protestant Methodist church. He accumulated an estate of 220 acres, which he has divided among his children, except that he has a life lease on the homestead farm.

John W. Fry, a prominent farmer of Springfield township, was born in Seneca county, Ohio, June 30, 1839. His parents, James and Martha (Gilham) Fry, natives of Virginia, came to Ohio about 1837, and located in Seneca county, Ohio, where they remained until the father's death in 1847. He started out just after the treaty with the Indians, with the intention of settling in Indiana, but on arriving in Ohio, was persuaded by his brother to remain. The family remained in Ohio after the death of the father about five years, when John came to Indiana, his brother being his guardian having previously purchased eighty acres of uncultivated land in Springfield township. At the age of fifteen years, he began working at the carpenter trade, which he continued until 1883, and there is many a good and substantial building in Allen county to-day to witness to his industry and workmanship. On January 16, 1862, he was united in marriage with Sarah, daughter of John D. and Esther (Markle) Reichelderfer. This union was blessed with six children, only five now living: Charles E., John W. D., Emma E., Dolpha, and James R. The mother was born June 17, 1838. He is a member of the United Brethren church, his wife of the old Lutheran church. Just after marriage he located on a farm in the northern part of Springfield township. Two years later he removed to the farm where he now lives, and built his house in the dense forest. On April 30, 1883, he had the misfortune to be crippled by the explosion of dynamite, while blowing out stumps, so as to be disabled for work of any kind. In 1875 and 1876 he built a nice frame dwelling. His valuable farm embraces 130 acres, with good and substantial buildings of his own work.

Jacob Friedt, a leading German citizen of Springfield township, was born in Westmoreland county, Penn., April 11, 1824. His parents, John and Lydia (Zimmerman) Friedt, both natives of Pennsylvania, of German descent, emigrated with their family in 1827 or 1828 and settled in Wayne county, Ohio, where they bought eighty acres of uncultivated land, which they converted into a farm with the assistance of their son Jacob. There the latter was raised to manhood. He was never apprenticed, but was what might be called a natural carpenter, learning by himself to make many things which he had never seen made, such as panel doors, etc. In 1844 he married Sarah, daughter of Samuel and Mary Snyder, born April 1, 1823. This union was blessed with eight children, five now living: Samantha, Mira, Lizzie, John and Agnes. He and wife are members of the Lutheran church, of which he has been elder about twelve years. He served as one of the trustees of his township in an early day and was treasurer of the board two years. In 1874 he was elected justice of the peace and served twelve years in succession. After his marriage in Ohio, he worked at his trade until 1852, when he came to Indiana and bought eighty acres of land in Springfield, so overgrown that he had to cut out underbrush to find a site for his log cabin. He began clearing in connection with his trade. But having studied diligently, in 1854 he was able to teach one winter, and about five years later taught another term. There stand now in the township several houses and barns, the mark of his industry in early days. He has a handsome farm of eighty acres.

Samuel Betz, a venerable citizen of Allen county, was born in Columbiana county, Ohio, February 1, 1816, son of George and Susannah (Sommer) Betz. The father and mother were pioneer settlers of Columbiana county, Ohio. There Samuel grew to manhood, and received a common school education. In 1851 he married Rebecca Best, born October 4, 1834, and they had thirteen children, of whom ten are living: Alice, Samantha A., Joel, Jeremiah F., Samuel, George, John, Elizabeth, Sarah and Nettie. After marriage he rented land and worked on the railroad for about two years. In 1852 he came to Indiana, and bought 160 acres of wood-land, built his cabin, and in 1853 moved with his family to his new home. He and wife worked hard and soon the forest yielded to their perseverance. He never learned a trade, but being raised on the farm adopted agriculture as his vocation. His beautiful farm of 163 acres is one of the best in Allen county, and he and family are highly respected by all who know them.

Hiram Houk was born in Starr county, Ohio, November 25, 1841, the second of seven children, born to George and Mary (Shilling) Houk. The father was born in Pennsylvania, the mother in Ohio. George Houk came to Ohio while a youth, and after driving team about a year, learned the miller's trade. He followed milling more or less until 1852, when he settled in DeKalb county, where he now resides. When he began work for himself he had only 50 cents capital, but he saved nearly all he made and when he came to Indiana, was able to pay $3,500 for 160 acres of land where he first settled. To this he added from year to year, until he had over 600 acres. He has been a consistent member of the Lutheran church about fifty years. His wife was formerly a member of the Methodist Episcopal church, but after marriage, she also joined the Lutheran church. He has always donated liberally for the erection of new churches. Hiram Houk received his education mainly in Ohio while a child. In 1863, he was married to Caroline Clemmer, born September 4, 1843, and they have had six children, of whom are living: Clara, Alice, Della and Mary A. Mr. Houk and family are among the leading people of his vicinity, and are highly respected.

Smith Richards, one of the substantial farmers of Springfield township, was born in Wayne county, Ohio, June 13, 1840, sixth of a family of nine children born to Soloman and Matilda (McIntire) Richards. The father was born in Steubenville, Ohio, where he grew to manhood and married. He was a blacksmith by trade. Beginning life a poor man he bought forty acres of new land which he soon sold and bought eighty near Wooster, which he converted into a beautiful farm, and at one time owned 160 acres in Ohio. In 1853 he came to Indiana and settled in Milan township, where he bought eighty acres. After two and one-half years he returned to Ohio and remained until 1857, when he went to California with the view of making money enough to buy homes for his children. He remained two or three months and started home, but was lost at sea in a storm which lasted three days and nights. The captain of the vessel was the father of the wife of President Arthur. At thirteen years of age Smith came with his father to Indiana and after the death of his father he moved to Indiana, in 1862. He traveled a great deal, going to Iowa twice, also to Missouri and other states, until 1864, when he enlisted in Company A, One Hundred and Sixty-sixth Ohio regiment, and served until the close of the war. He received an honorable discharge at Cleveland in 1865. After the war he traveled several years and finally, fourteen or fifteen years ago, he settled on the farm where he now lives. His fine farm of eighty acres is within one mile of Harlan. He is one of the leading citizens of Allen county. His brother John, who was a captain in the war, is now county judge of Atchison county, Mo., and is worth about $100,000.

Samuel Mills, a worthy farmer of Springfield township, was born in New York state, October 21, 1837, son of Jedediah C. and Jane (Forsythe) Mills. The father was a native of New York and the mother a native of Ireland. She came to America when a child, settled in Pennsylvania where she grew to womanhood, and removed to Jefferson county, N. Y., where afterward she was united in marriage with Mr. Mills. In 1853 they came west and settled in Allen county, Ind., where he bought 100 acres of land where Samuel now lives. There were about thirty acres cleared without buildings. He erected buildings and there they remained until death, the father dying in 1857, and the mother in 1881. Both were members of the Methodist Episcopal church. He was a school teacher while quite young and took a great interest in schools all his life. Samuel remained with his parents until their death, and cleared and improved most of the farm. In 1861 he was married to Martha Brown, and this union was blessed with seven children: Charles, Samuel C., Abbie, Carrie, Alice, William and Jesse. The mother was born in August, 1838. He and wife are members of the United Brethren church. He possesses 270 acres of as good farming land as there is in Allen county, with good and substantial buildings. At one time he owned 310 acres of fine land. When his father died he with three others inherited the farm of 100 acres, but he bought out the others, and with this and $100 from his grandfather, he has made all he has. His brother and sisters living are: Mary, Nancy and William.

John Swaidner, an old settler of Allen county, was born in Columbiana county, Ohio, January 13, 1827, the oldest son of Jacob and Barbara (Goodbrake) Swaidner. His father moved to Richland county when John was about twelve years of age. In 1848 he married Elizabeth Raby, by whom he had five children, of whom four are now living: Mary E., Jacob N., John S. and Simon L. The mother was born in 1831, and she died in 1863. She was a member of the Protestant Methodist church. After paying the justice of the peace at his marriage, he only had 75 cents left with which to begin housekeeping. He first farmed rented land with a yoke of oxen, and in five years accumulated about $500 with which he came to Indiana, in 1853, and bought eighty acres of land in the woods. They lived for six months on corn-bread and coffee, then his means ran out and he was indebted to a kind old groceryman for the necessaries of life. In 1864 he was married to Anna Files, born in 1839, by whom he had four children, three now living: Nettie V., Edith A. and Arthur Garfield. He and wife are both members of the Protestant Methodist church. Mr. Swaidner has prospered by honest hard work until he owns 310 acres in Springfield township, one of the best improved farms of Allen county. His second son attended college at Adrian, Michigan, about three years.

Dr. C. F. Swift, a prominent physician of Allen county, was born in Bryan, Ohio, October 11, 1850. His father, Philetus H. Swift, a native of Ohio, born 1820, grew to manhood in his native state, amid all the difficulties of the then pioneer country. In 1848 he was united in marriage to Caroline Cutts, and to this union six children were born. In 1854 he removed to Indiana with his family and bought 115 acres of new land, which he cleared. He remained in Springfield township ten years and then removed to DeKalb county, but two years later settled in Milan township where he remained until his death. He bought ninety-three acres of good land in one body and twenty acres of wood-lands near his home place, and cleared about thirty acres, built a two-story frame dwelling and good barn, and after he had lived in his new house but six weeks he was taken sick and died. He was one of the leading and representative farmers, was trustee of Springfield township two terms, and held the same office in Milan when he died. Dr. Swift attended the country schools of this county, and attended Fort Wayne college three years and Carleton college, Minnesota, one year. Going to Huntington, Ind., he entered the office of Dr. W. C. Chaffee and read medicine one year. He then entered the University of Michigan at Ann Arbor, and graduated three years later. He began the practice of his profession at Harlan amid old friends, and has now a large and lucrative practice. In 1878 he married Nanna A., daughter of William and Mary (Scott) Alderman, and they have had three children: Clarence, who died in 1887;

Lyle and Eugenie. Mrs. Swift was born October 9, 1852. He is a member of I. O. O. F. at Harlan. In 1888 he was elected by the republican party as trustee of Springfield township, succeeding a democrat. He is independent and progressive, and as trustee he does what he thinks best for his township. Although there is considerable opposition to the erection of a new school-house at Harlan, he is about to build a two-story brick building with four rooms. The doctor taught school three years in Springfield.

William H. Harter, of Springfield township, is a native of Ohio, born February 2, 1833, the seventh child born to George and Sarah Harter. He was raised on the farm until five years old, when the family moved to Navarre, Ohio, where his father embarked in the hotel business. William H. received a common school education and attended commercial college at Fort Wayne three months and graduated. At the age of twenty-one he removed to Indiana and settled at Fort Wayne where he accepted a clerkship in the store of J. W. Townley & Co. Six weeks later he was the first person to begin the machinist's trade in the shops of Cooper, Bass & Co. He remained in the shops until 1857, when he went on the road with John H. Bass, and traveled mostly in Iowa, setting up the saw-mills that Mr. Bass sold. He then went to Monroeville, Ohio, and after working at his trade four or five months, returned to Fort Wayne and was sent to Springfield township to repair and take charge of a saw-mill near where he now lives. In 1859 he bought twenty acres of land which he farmed about ten years, and then bought forty acres; to this he has added until now he owns 220 acres of as fine land as there is in the township. He has the largest and best bank barn in the county. August 11, 1859, he married Lorinda Hall, born in 1835. Of their five children, four are now living: Olive Esther, Arthur, Milly and Isaac. He and wife are members of the Presbyterian church at Hicksville. In 1866 he was elected trustee of Springfield and served nine years in succession, and in 1880 was again elected for four years without any solicitation from him. He has been president of the Hicksville fair association for ten years. On two occasions he was nominated as a candidate of the republican party for county commissioner, and in his own township and Scipio, where he is well known, he ran ahead of his ticket, and in his own township ran about three to one ahead of his opponent. Mr. Harter is a leading stock-raiser and makes a specialty of short-horn cattle and thoroughbred Poland China and Chester white hogs.

Jesse Greenawalt, of Springfield township, was born in Montgomery county, Penn., January 16, 1822, son of John and Elizabeth (Connor) Greenawalt. The father was born in Montgomery county, Penn., about 1788, and died about 1872. The mother was born in 1795, and is still living, but has been an invalid several years. The father emigrated with his family in 1835, and settled in Columbiana county, where he remained. He died at a good old age, having gained a comfortable home and 131 acres of good land in Ohio. He and wife were members of the Lutheran church. He served in the war of 1812, and drew $8.00 per month pension a short time before his death. Jesse came with his parents to Ohio, when in his fourteenth year, and learned the trade of a cabinet-maker and joiner, which he followed fourteen or fifteen years, and built all his own buildings. In 1846 he married in Ohio, Susannah Shimp, who was born in Franklin county, Penn., February 6, 1826; of their five children, four are living: John E., George L., Oliver J., and Samuel E. He and wife are members of the Lutheran church, of which he is the present elder. He served as assessor of his township twelve years, and has been solicited to accept other offices, but always declined. In 1854, he bought eighty acres of wood-land in Springfield, and in 1855, moved on the same with his family of three children. Prosperity has come to him through toil and he now has 131 acres of well improved lands, and is esteemed as one of the leading citizens, well respected. His youngest son is a Lutheran preacher, and all his children are well educated.

Lewis Zeis, one of the prominent farmers of Springfield township, was born in Seneca county, Ohio, January 10, 1840, son of Jacob and Elizabeth (Lower) Zeiz. He was raised in Seneca county, on the farm, and received a limited education. At the age of twenty-one years he began working out by the month. In 1855 he came to Indiana with the intention of learning the blacksmith trade, but being sick all the time he returned to Ohio, and remained until 1860, when he came again with his family and settled on the farm of forty acres, where he now lives. To this he has added 120 acres. He started in a poor man but has done well, and has one of the best improved farms in the township. January 1, 1860, he married Barbara Baltz, who was born January 1, 1843, and they have had seven children, of whom four survive: Jacob H., Barbara E., Oliver M. and Perry F. Mrs. Zeis is a member of the Protestant Methodist church. He is a member of the Masonic order at Harlan.

Henry Horn, of Springfield township, is a native of Pennsylvania, born February 22, 1811, son of George and Louisa (Cramer) Horn. He was raised on his father's farm in Pennsylvania, and at seventeen years of age was apprenticed at the wagon-maker's trade which he followed thirty-three years. In 1836, he settled in Ashland county, Ohio, where he followed his trade until 1855, when he removed to Indiana, and on the 16th day of May settled on the farm where he now lives. He continued working at his trade in connection with farming. When he first came to Indiana he bought eighty acres of uncultivated land in Springfield township; he had previously bought eighty acres in La Grange county, which he afterward sold and bought seventy-one and 40-100 acres joining his home farm. May 7, 1840, he married Mary A. Kohler, who was born July 8, 1818, and of their ten children six are living: Uriah K., Walter S., Ezra H., John L., George A. and Frank A. He and wife are members of the English Lutheran church, in which he has been elder over forty years. He has prospered through unremitting

Allen county, and .... on which he has a good .... a prominent and enterprising man .... was born in Mercer county, Penn., October 9, 1838. He remained at his birth-place with his parents, James William and Susan Hood, until 1856, when he came to Fort Wayne and began work as a carpenter, which was his occupation until the outbreak of the rebellion. In August, 1862, he enlisted in the Eighty-eighth Indiana volunteer infantry, and remained in active and faithful service until the close of the war. Then, returning home, he engaged in agriculture on the "old Jackson farm" near the city. In 1871 he removed to Maysville, and there lived until his death November 11, 1882. Though cut off in early manhood, he left a valuable estate, comprising 217 acres of fertile land. He was a member of the Masonic order, having joined Harlan lodge, No. 296, in 1863. He was a brave soldier and a worthy citizen. August 15, 1865, he was married to Julia E. Johnson, who was born in Springfield township, daughter of Ira and Melinda May Johnson, natives of New York. To this union four children were born: Frank, February 20, 1867; Lilly, December 25, 1869, who married Elwood George, November, 1888; Florence, October 3, 1873; James William, April 20, 1876. Mrs. Hood is now a resident of Fort Wayne. She is a member of the Methodist church and is highly esteemed. In the settlement of her husband's estate as administratrix, she displayed business abilities of a high order.

Peter Repp, one of the leading citizens of Springfield township, was born in Pennsylvania, December 28, 1837, son of John and Hannah J. (Omwake) Repp. When sixteen years old he emigrated to Seneca county, Ohio, and in 1860 came to Indiana. He bought forty acres of wild land which he cleared and kept twelve years, and then he bought where he now lives. He served an apprenticeship as a painter, a trade he has since followed in connection with farming. He received a common school education. In 1857 he married Elizabeth Baltz, daughter of Jacob and Barbara Baltz, and they have seven children: Jacob F., Alonzo E., Viola V., Charles E., Lillie, Lulu and Barbara. The mother was born June 27, 1837. She and husband are members of the Lutheran church. His valuable farm includes 163½ acres of good land, well improved.

George Hoffman, sr., a native of Germany, was born November 23, 1815. He is the oldest child of Adam and Elizabeth (Sprau) Hoffman. In 1848 he left his native country and settled in Ohio where he bought sixty acres of land, thirty of which he cleared, and remained there until 1864. He then sold this farm and removed to Indiana and settled on the farm where he now lives. In 1839 he was married to Elizabeth Weber, and this union was blessed with eight children, four of whom are living: George, Elizabeth, Sarah and Henry. Mrs. Hoffman was born in 1820 and died November 3, 1885. She was a member of the

German Reform church, of which Mr. Hoffman has been deacon about twenty years and elder about ten years. He has prospered in his affairs and now owns 156 acres of well-improved land. He is one of the substantial farmers of his township and well respected.

Milton Crall of Springfield township, was born in Seneca county, Ind., March 8, 1840, son of Henry and Melinda (Butler) Crall. In 1844 the family moved to Franklin county, Ohio. There Milton received a good common school education. At the age of twenty years he hired out by the month. In 1864, he married Matilda, daughter of Alexander and Hannah McCauley, born December 25, 1842. To this union were born twelve children, ten living: Samuel, Henry, Geary, Hannah, Arthur, Amos, Clinton, Rosa, Olive and Grover C. He and wife are members of the United Brethren church, of which he was class leader one year. After marriage he first settled on thirty acres of land he had previously bought near the center of Springfield township. Here he remained until 1875, when he sold this and bought fifty acres where he now lives. He is one of the leading citizens and well respected.

Emanuel Hettinger, one of thriving farmers of Springfield township, is a native of Pennsylvania, born January 13, 1832, son of Jacob K. and Elizabeth (Schreffler) Hettinger, both natives of Pennsylvania. The father lived to the good old age of ninety-one, and the mother is now alive in her eighty-eighth year. Emanuel was taken to Ohio by his parents at the age of two years, and his father bought eighty acres of wild land in what is now Ashland county. Here Emanuel grew to manhood and received a common school education. At the age of twenty-three years he removed to Medina county, Ohio, and in 1855 he married Salome Merrifield, by whom he has one child, Carrie, born in 1857. He and wife are members of the Congregational church. In 1861 he enlisted in Company G, Forty-second Ohio infantry, under Capt. Jewett, and was with his company in all its engagements until 1863, at Thompson Hill, where he was wounded in the left ankle. He remained in the hospital four or five months, was home on furlough four or five months and then returned to Camp Dennison, where he was discharged in 1864, and now draws but $6 per month for his injury. His eighty acres in Springfield township is one of the best improved farms in the township. He cleared about thirty acres and has a good and substantial two-story dwelling house. He is a member of 1. O. O. F., at Harlan, and Stopher post, No. 72, G. A. R. His first wife departed this life in 1869, and in 1871 he was united in marriage with Mrs. Emily Monroe, daughter of Samuel and Catharine Walker, born in Summit county, Ohio, in 1827. This union was blessed with one child, Louie E., born October 17, 1872. All the family are members of the Lutheran church.

George W. Hoffman, of Springfield township, was born in Germany, on the Rhine, October 31, 1840, son of George and Elizabeth Hoffman. He came with his parents to America in 1848, and settled in Crawford county, Ohio, where he grew to manhood. In 1861 he removed to Canada and remained four years. On his return to the United States he settled with his parents in Springfield township. In 1869 he married Catherine Eidt, who was born in 1847, and died in 1871, leaving one child, Gideon. In 1876 he married Mrs. Anna Weicker, born in 1855, by whom he had two children: Edward and John. He and wife are members of the United Brethren church, of which he served as steward one year, also trustee three years. When he first married he embarked in the saw-mill business, which he followed about five years, and then he bought eighty acres of uncultivated lands, which he cleared and now lives upon. In connection with farming he still runs his mill in the winter season. He also owns ninety-five acres in Maumee township. He is a leading and esteemed citizen.

William Bauman, of Springfield township, was born in Germany, September 5, 1829, son of Peter and Elizabeth Bauman, both of German descent. In 1839 his parents came to America and settled in Ohio, where he grew to manhood on a farm. In 1854, he married Margaret Lauer. Of their five children, four are living: Melissa, William H., now in Colorado mining, Susanna and George, who is at home with his parents. The mother was born March 14, 1835. She was a member of the Presbyterian church in Ohio, and joined the Albrights in Indiana, while he is a member of the German Reform church. When he was first married, he worked his father's farm for two years, then rented two years, and at the end of this time his father gave him $200, which with his savings, partly paid for the forty acres which he bought in Allen county, and settled upon in 1869. He has increased his land to eighty-eight acres, and has lately built a two-story frame dwelling. His work in early life was so severe that four years ago he had a slight stroke of paralysis which has impaired his health. His wife aided him in every way, and she is also almost broken down by their efforts to make a home for themselves and family.

John S. Lemon, of Springfield township, was born in Dauphin county, Penn., August 19, 1819, son of Simon and Jane (Sweigart) Lemon. He was raised in his native state, and received a common school education. In 1848 he went to Union county, Penn., and worked at the blacksmith's trade about four years. In 1850 he was married to Mary A. Omro, who was born December 31, 1827. This union was blessed with eight children, seven of whom are now living: Anna M. D., Mary A., Margaret E., John W., Joseph L., Simon F. and Ella. He and wife were formerly members of the Methodist Episcopal church. In 1870 he moved with his family to Indiana, and settled on the farm where he now lives, June 22, 1870. His farm includes 120 acres of well improved land.

Latham Moore, a substantial citizen of Springfield, is a native of Ireland, born April 5, 1825, son of William and Margaret (Mahafa) Moore. At the age of twenty-one years, he emigrated to America, and first settled in South Hampton, Long Island. Here he was engaged in oyster fishing, until 1866, when he came to Ohio and bought forty acres for

ANNALS OF THE TOWNSHIPS.

$4,000. He paid down $1,000, and went in debt $3,000, which he paid in six years. In 1881, he sold out and removed to Indiana, buying eighty acres in Springfield township, where he now lives. In 1850 he married Ellen McGee, who was born in 1834. Of their eleven children, nine are living: William, Matthew, James, Moses, David, John, Robert, Nanny J., and Margaret E.

Amariah Johnson, an industrious farmer of Springfield township, is a native of Indiana, born March 19, 1852, son of Amariah and Jane Johnson. The father came from Ohio to DeKalb county in an early day and there the son was born and raised. He received a very limited education, his father being crippled and needing his work. March 18, 1876, he was married to Mary M. Morr, who was born January 8, 1852, and they have five children: Lillie G., Edna M., Charles C., Clyde H. and Maude A. Mr. Johnson began farming by renting land in DeKalb county, and remained there until March 15, 1831, when he settled on the farm where he now lives. He has 100 acres of good land in Springfield township, and is well liked by all who know him.

Isaac Hilbert, of Springfield township, is a native of Harrison county, Ohio, born June 5, 1831, son of Daniel and Catherine (Young) Hilbert. At about fifteen years of age he moved with his parents to Defiance county, Ohio, and remained until twenty-two years of age. He then came to Indiana and settled in Springfield township; two years later he returned to Defiance, but in two years came again to Indiana and bought sixty acres of new land. The father of Mr. Hilbert was born in Maryland, April 27, 1785, and departed this life December 31, 1877, and the mother, who died on the same day of the month fifteen years before, was a native of Pennsylvania. They were both devoted and consistent members of the Lutheran church. On October 23, 1852, Mr. Hilbert was married to Mary J., daughter of Daniel and Sophia C. (Omo) Hassenpflug, born November 26, 1836; the father, a native of Pennsylvania, was born March 21, 1812, and died March 20, 1882; the mother, born in Pennsylvania, May 19, 1815, died January 1, 1883. They were married February 19, 1835, and were members of the Lutheran church. To the union of Mr. and Mrs. Hilbert were born six children: Maria E. A., born March 9, 1859; Rosabelle C., April 29, 1861; Elmer D., August 28, 1864; Edward G., July 2, 1866; Anna J., December 19, 1871; Elsie L., August 7, 1873. Edward G. and Anna J. died in infancy. He and wife are members of the Lutheran church in which he served two years as deacon and two years as elder. He began without a dollar of capital when he first settled in Allen county, but made himself a nice little farm where he remained until 1883, when he removed to Hicksville, Ohio, intending to rest from work, but after five years he' removed to his farm one mile east of Hicksville. He has forty acres of fine land, and house and one-half acre lot in Hicksville. He is the youngest of ten brothers and sisters among whom the first death occurred in September, 1888. His sister Rosabelle is one of the successful teachers in Allen county, and has taught in Indiana and Ohio about nineteen terms.

SCIPIO TOWNSHIP.

This, the smallest township of the county, and most remote from Fort Wayne, received its first settlers in 1836, when Platte Squiers and Jehial Parks purchased their lands and reared their log cabins. The former was a leader in the community, and at the first election after the formation of the township, in 1843, he was chosen justice, a position he held for twenty years. The first birth was in his family, of Lafayette D. Squiers, in 1839, and the first death was the tragic one of Laura Squiers, in April 1840. She was playing about the fire where her parents were boiling sugar, her clothing caught in the blaze and she was burned to death. Parks was a man of great strength of muscle and character, and was highly esteemed. The first religious meeting in the township was held in 1840 at his house by Benjamin Dorsey, and he donated the ground in 1842, for the pioneer burying ground. In 1837 Lucius and Nathan Palmer settled, and they subsequently removed after clearing farms. By Nancy Palmer the first school was taught in 1842. George and Robert Dorsey and Philip Shell came in March, 1838, and became valuable assistants in the campaign of civilization. William Bice and Samuel Wentworth also came in this year, and about 1840 Wentworth's brothers, John and Henry, who had stopped at the Maumee, came on to this settlement. In the latter year Adam Burrier made his settlement. This township, owing to its remoteness from the center of activity, was quite backward in development and the settlers above named had all the hardships and privations of those who settled much earlier in the more central townships. The first road was the Hicksville road, and no postoffice was established within the township until 1862, when John Murphy was appointed postmaster. Two years later the office was removed to Springfield township.

Platte Squiers, above referred to, was a native of Vermont. He was married to Aurilla Goodspeed of the same state, and they removed to Ohio and there remained about one year. Early in the thirties they removed to Allen county and became the first white settlers in Scipio township. He bought a quarter section and cleared over 200 acres of wild land. He settled in the woods with no neighbors nor roads, and when he first went to Fort Wayne to get corn ground, he took his ax and cut his road, taking just one week for the trip. He served as justice of the peace of his township about twenty-four years, and several years as one of the board of trustees. He and wife were devoted and conscientious members of the Christian church; he for over twenty years. Mr. Squiers owned and cleared various tracts of land and must have owned as much as 1,200 or 1,500 acres of land during his lifetime. He was one of the leading citizens and won the respect of all who knew him. He was friendly to churches and schools and a leader in many laudable enterprises. He died at the age of seventy years, deeply mourned by the community. His son, Lafayette D. Squiers, now one of the leading citizens, was born in Scipio township, August 21, 1839. He received a common school education. In 1867 he was married to Rhoda A. Foot, born in 1846, and they have seven children: John, Lincoln, Catherine, Ora, Ada, Archie and Phœbe. He and wife are members of the German Baptist church, and politically he has always been a staunch democrat. He owns 116 acres of good land which he has cleared himself and provided with good buildings.

The Dorsey family, prominent in the history of Scipio township, is one of the most worthy in the county. The ancestry has been traced and brought down to recent date by Mrs. Robert Dorsey, and the genealogy published in 1887. As far back as 1730, in England, whence the family came to this country, William Dorsey married Sarah Wilson, and one of their children, Benjamin Dorsey, was born in England, in June, 1786. He grew up in his native land, and learned the trade of wagon-maker, and also being of a deeply religious nature, became a local preacher in the Methodist church. He was married to Jane, daughter of Robert and Polly Jefferson, born in 1791, and ten children were born to them during their residence at Elloughton, Yorkshire, as follows: William, born July 21, 1814; George, October 11, 1815; Sarah Ann, August 2, 1817; Robert, March 1, 1820; John, March 8, 1822; Thomas, September 5, 1824; Mary Ann, July 3, 1826; Christopher and a twin brother, in 1828; Jonathan, May 13, 1830. Sarah A. and the twins died in England; Mary Ann Boulton died in Scipio township, August 16, 1868; William, who became a resident of LaGrange county, died there August 9, 1872; John died in Scipio, March 9, 1881, and Thomas died in Scipio, April 11, 1885. Benjamin Dorsey and family came to America in 1830, and his wife and the seven surviving children followed him in June, 1831. They first settled in Milan, Erie county, Ohio. Thence the sons, George and Robert, came to Scipio township, March 16, 1838, and the father followed them in 1842. William Andrew Dorsey, a brother of Benjamin, came to this country in 1842 with his family, and settled in Scipio township in 1845. Benjamin Dorsey passed away at his pioneer home, September 7, 1865. Jane Dorsey died before the removal to this state, December 23, 1844. George Dorsey, the oldest surviving member of the family, was married February 24, 1842, to Elizabeth Boulton, who was born February 12, 1819, in Minty, Gloucestershire, England. To them were born the following children: Jane E., August 14, 1843, married R. M. Simmons; Sarah A., July 29, 1847, married McL. McCurdy; Pluma, July 27, 1849, died May 26, 1874; Joseph J., November 30, 1851; Louisa H., October 24, 1851, married H. L. Beach, died December 19, 1882. Robert Dorsey, the second of the surviving children of Benjamin, has always been a farmer by occupation, and shared in the pioneer work of opening the lands of this township. When he came here there were no roads and he helped in the construction of all of them. He first purchased forty acres of wild land, and cleared about eighty acres more, where he built his log cabin. He traded this for eighty acres, and soon sold out and bought the eighty upon which he now lives, then covered densely with forest. His capital at the outset was $45, but now he is one of the wealthy men of the county and owns 329 acres of productive land, thoroughly improved. He has always been friendly to church and school and helped build the first church, a hewn-log cabin, on his farm, and also assisted in building the first school-house, a log building, 14x16, and just high enough for a man to stand inside. To the first forty acres he owned he gave the name of Opossom Knobs, a title that still clings to it. June 3, 1846, he was married to Margaret R. Moore, daughter of Priam and Lois (Calkins) Moore. She was born March 21, 1827, in Ellisburg, Jefferson county, N. Y. Their children are: Rhoda R., born September 3, 1848, married David Nelson; Lois Lovica, October 24, 1850, died June 20, 1862; Martha Ann, September 30, 1853, married to William W. Driver; Elizabeth M., April 8, 1860; Benjamin P., November 19, 1863, married to Hulda J. Williams.

John B. Foote (deceased), one of the early settlers of Springfield township, was the first white child born in Sidney, Ohio. He was born December 5, 1818, to Harvey B. and Eliza A. (Mantona) Foote. He received a good education and became one of the pioneer teachers in the country schools of Indiana. On March 5, 1839, he was married to Catherine Zeimmer, born January 20, 1821, by whom he had eleven children, nine living: Harvey B., Abraham Z., Rhoda A., Maria E., John B., William McL., Joseph G., Mary A., and Oliver M. He and wife were members of the German Baptist church. In 1848, he removed to Indiana, and settled on 160 acres of wild land, where he remained until his death, April 29, 1877. His wife, who survives him, is now in her sixty-eighth year. Her first experiences in Allen county were of the toil of pioneer life. There were no roads and it required three days to make the trip to Fort Wayne and return. Before coming to Allen county, they had lost all their property by fire and were compelled to begin anew. He became a leading citizen and owned 160 acres of land, of which he cleared 100 acres. Harvey B. Foote, son of the above, was born in Darke county, Ohio, May 25, 1840. He received a common school education, such as could be obtained in his day. In 1866 he was united in marriage with Sarah A., daughter of William and Elizabeth (Mulnick) Bailey, who were early settlers of Allen county, Ohio, by whom he had three children: Mathew F., born February 14, 1870; Delma, November 25, 1877, and Harry B., March 27, 1888. The mother was born April 5, 1848. She and her husband are members of the German Baptist church. In 1864 he enlisted in Company F, One Hundred and Fortieth Indiana volunteer regiment, under Capt. Swann, and served until the close of the war, being discharged at Indianapolis in 1865. He has a farm of ninety-five acres in Scipio township which he bought when it was in timber in 1860. He is now one of the leading citizens of the township, and is respected by all.

Thomas Allen, an early settler of Scipio township, was born in Trumbull county, Ohio, December 6, 1830, son of Joseph and Mary (Jackson

Ferd. F. Both

Allen. He remained until ten years of age in his native county, and then came with his parents to Allen county, Ind., and settled in the woods in Scipio township, where he grew to manhood. He received his education in the pioneer log school-house, going two and one-half miles through a trackless forest. In 1858, he married Elmira Babb, born in 1840, and they have two children: Alfred and Arthur. He served as assessor of his township one term. In 1850, he bought and settled on the fifty acres where he now lives, and to this he has added until he now owns 222 acres of valuable land. When he first bought his land it was covered with a dense growth of timber, which his indefatigable efforts have converted into fertile fields.

Martin Waters, a leading farmer of Scipio township, was born in Crawford county, Ohio, January 23, 1837, son of Samuel and Margaret (Burwell) Waters. He came to Indiana with his parents in 1851 and settled in DeKalb county, where his father bought a farm of eighty acres of wild land and here Martin grew to manhood. Being the oldest of the family his experience in this state at that time was clearing, chopping, making rails and other work known to a pioneer's life. He received a common school education such as could be obtained in the old log school-house, walking from a mile to two miles. In 1861 he married Mary Ann Shutt, born October 28, 1841, by whom he had four children: Isaac S., Harriet E., John V. and Mertie R. He began life without a dollar but by hard work and good management he has done well. He now owns sixty-five acres of good land, which he bought in its natural state. He and wife are members of the United Brethren church.

William Beninghoff, an early settler, is a native of Pennsylvania, born in Schuylkill county, April 8, 1825, son of George and Elizabeth (Daubespeck) Beninghoff. When twelve years of age he removed with his parents to Ashland county, Ohio. In 1846 he began an apprenticeship as carriage-maker and followed his trade until by close economy he saved $600, with which he bought eighty acres of land in Noble county. He sold this farm two years later and bought eighty acres of wood-land; clearing this, he amassed more property, and now owns 220 and 115 acres in DeKalb county, and a ten-acre residence place within one mile of Hicksville. In September, 1851, he married Ann, daughter of John and Catharine (Bowmaster) Martin, who was born April 10, 1835. They have had four children, of whom George and John are living. Mr. Beninghoff is a member of the Lutheran church. His companion through life has been a true wife, sharing his hardships and his joys, and often went with him through the work in the fields, doing the work of a pioneer's wife.

Francis A. Johnson, a prominent citizen of Scipio township, was born in St. Lawrence county, N. Y., April 3, 1833, son of Ebenezer and Betsy (Ryan) Johnson. At ten years of age he removed with his parents to Ohio, where he remained from 1844 to 1856, when he came to Indiana and settled in DeKalb county. In 1865 he removed to Allen

25

county, and settled on the farm where he now lives. In 1855 he was married to Margaret J. Hammond, born in 1834, and they have had nine children of whom seven are living: Nancy A., Emma J., John F., Myron A., Charles W., Tryphena M. and Sarah E. He is a member of the Masonic order, and of Stopher post, No. 75, G. A. R. In 1861 he left his wife and two little babes at home, and enlisted in Company F, Forty-fourth volunteer regiment, under Capt. Merrill. At the battle of Stone River he was struck on the hip by a piece of shell, which so disabled him that he had little use of his leg for about six years; for this he now draws the small pension of $10. His grandfather was a soldier in the revolutionary war, and his father a soldier in the war of 1812. Mr. Johnson began the battle of life without a dollar but by hard work has done well. He first bought forty acres of new land in DeKalb county, and then came to Allen county, and bought 120 acres of land, "without a stick amiss," in Scipio township, eighty-eight acres of which he now has under a good state of cultivation.

George W. Warner, one of the thorough-going farmers of Scipio township, is a native of Lincoln county, Ohio, born January 14, 1839, son of Dennis and Rachel (Miller) Warner. The father was of Dutch, and the mother of Pennsylvania Dutch, descent. In 1864 George W. emigrated to the gold fields of Montana and Idaho, but finding gold as hard to accumulate there as here, after one year's stay, returned to his native state, landing February 15, 1865, and then came immediately to Indiana and settled in Scipio township and bought eighty acres for $3,000, on which he lived about two years before marriage. June, 1867, he married Mary Allen, and they have two children: Howard and Florence. The mother was born in 1849. When he first began in Indiana he just had $1,300 to make a partial payment on his land, since then he has paid out for his land $17,400, and now owns 330 acres as handsomely improved as any in Allen county, and a two-story brick dwelling which cost him over $3,000. His farm is ditched and tiled, and altogether, his improvements show that he is one of the leading farmers of the county.

John R. Knapp, a prominent farmer of Scipio township, was born in Luzerne county, Penn., May 9, 1839, son of Walter and Elizabeth (Reed) Knapp. The father was a native of Pennsylvania, the mother of New York. At eighteen years of age he left his home and settled in Ohio, arriving there with $1.50 in money. His parents being poor people he was compelled to make his own way in the world when quite young. March 3, 1861, he was united in marriage with Olive Maxwell, by whom he had one child, Melinda, wife of Coe M. Smith. This wife was born April 21, 1844, and died January 7, 1865. In 1866 he was married to Thalia Boullon, born August 28, 1846, and they had nine children, of whom eight are now living: Joseph W., Walter R., Sarah E., Abbie S., John M., Frederick A., Ida M. and Thomas M. February 9, 1865, he enlisted in Company G, One Hundred and Ninety-first regiment Ohio volunteers, under Capt. Kinney, and served to the close of the war, receiving an honorable discharge at Winchester, Ohio, in 1865. Mr. Knapp began to support himself at an early age, his parents being poor, and his success in life is greatly to his credit. In 1865 he bought and settled on the eighty acres where he now lives, which was at that time densely timbered, which he has cleared and converted into a beautiful farm. He now owns 120 acres of good land in Scipio township, and is comfortably situated, having commodious and substantial buildings.

MAUMEE TOWNSHIP.

A convenient landing place on the river, known as Bull Rapids, because, tradition says, some hunter slew here a buffalo bull, was the site of the first settlement. Gregory Jackson came here in 1833 and built a large log house, which he used as a tavern for the accommodation of those who came up the Maumee, and landed here to look at land in the vicinity. A collection of houses grew up, and as the chief attraction was a groggery, the place became famous for rough life and lawlessness. In 1836, James Shirley, who owned a large tract of land here, laid out town lots and gave the plat the name of Indiana City, but that name did not become acclimated, his town was not settled, and Bull Rapids is still the name by which the locality is known. In 1834 one Barnes settled near the state line, and in the same year William Johnson and Lloyd Lemart settled near the center of the township. Ulrich Saylor, sr., settled on Knagg's reserve in the fall of 1835, and later moved to the state line building, a house which occupied space in both states. Subsequently he made his home upon the canal, near a lock which became known as Saylor's lock. This pioneer planted the first orchard, the first marriage was of his son Matthias to Ann Maneary, the first death was of his son John D., in 1836, and the old gentleman was the first postmaster, keeping it at his store, which he had established in 1853. Ulrich Saylor, jr., came with his parents in 1835, also Solomon Swisher, a son-in-law. In 1836, John Ashley and his son George, were here, and the father contemplated building a dam across the Maumee, and even began the erection of a mill, but abandoned the scheme. In April, of this year, the first election was held at the house of George Platter, and Lloyd Lemart was elected a justice, and Jabez Philips, constable. Among the other early settlers of this township were James Johnson, Charles Harding, Benjamin Johnson, Flint, Crapeau, Washington Corpse, J. N. Sweet and James Shirley.

In September, 1839, Andrew Dykes laid out in section 14, an ample town plat of forty blocks, which he named Geneva, but no trace of it now remains. Another "paper" town which the canal was expected to foster, was "Bengal," laid out by Joseph Sinclair and Thomas Tiger. Mention of these now serves only to illustrate the enterprise of bygone days. Woodburn, a station on the Wabash railway, was platted by J.' K. Edgerton and Joseph Smith, proprietors, September, 1865. To the northwest of Woodburn, on the Maumee, in January, 1871, E. D. Ashley had a tract of land platted as Edwardsburg, and it is the seat of a postoffice.

Ambrose Ashton, who is of German origin, was born December 15, 1822, in Brown county, Ohio. The father, Zachariah, a native of Pennsylvania, was born in 1799, and when a child, moved with his parents to Marietta, Ohio, where he remained about two years, after which they located in Brown county, Ohio, near Fayetteville. In 1840, he married Rebecca Sly and removed to Allen county, settling on a farm at Maysville, where he lived until 1851, when he removed to Paulding county, Ohio, and remained until his death, February, 1863. His wife was born in 1800 in Clermont county, Ohio, and died in Maysville, in 1851. Ambrose, the second of their five children, was educated in the schools of Warren county, Ohio, coming to Maysville with his parents; he remained there until 1848, when he moved to the banks of the Maumee river in Milan township, and one year later moved on a farm in Maumee township, now owned by M. B. Price. Mr. Ashton when he first went to school, was compelled to walk two miles through the woods to a log schoolhouse with puncheon floor, stick chimney and greased paper windows. In those days their clothes were all home-made. He earned his first pair of boots at fourteen years of age, by working out for the money. Before that, he had shoes made by his father. His father would go to the tannery and get a side of leather and make shoes for the family. Near Maysville, there remains on the old farm, an orchard which was set out by Mr. Ashton. In 1846, he removed to Fort Wayne and worked in the mill of Judge Hanna & Bird, nearly one year. Returning to Springfield township, he bought forty acres of wild land of his father, which he traded in 1851, for 107 acres, where he now lives. He now owns in all, 300 acres of choice land in one of the finest locations in the township. He also deals quite extensively in stock. In 1844 he was wedded to Huldah, daughter of William Shields. December 29, 1863, he wedded Mary A., daughter of Henry and Matilda Cummins, and they have five children: George F., Nellie A., Joseph, Lillie D. and Mark. In 1860 he was elected as trustee of his township and served one year. He is at present justice of the peace, and is a member of the Masonic order.

Moses B. Price, one of the prosperous farmers of Maumee township, is a native of Pennsylvania, born April 25, 1838, son of John and Susan (Oliver) Price. They came to Indiana and settled in Allen county, where they soon after died, leaving their son an orphan at the age of ten or twelve years. He worked his way on a canal boat to Cincinnati, Ohio, and from there to Kentucky, and after two years went to Lebanon, Ohio, where he worked as a farm hand about four years. Then returning to Indiana he settled in Allen county, where he has since resided. On January 14, 1859, he was united in marriage with Mary E., daughter of Elisha and Phebe D. (Davis) James. This union was blessed with two children: Charles, born 1861, died 1864; Gabriel, born 1863, died in infancy. The mother was born October 18, 1837. She is a member of the Christian church. He is a member of the

Masonic lodge at Harlan. He began in this country without a dollar but now owns 108 acres well improved with good buildings and well watered with natural fountains. When he first purchased this land it was covered with a dense forest. He is now prepared to enjoy the fruits of a life of labor and spend his declining years amid the comforts of a pleasant home.

Henry Schepelmann, a worthy citizen of Maumee township, is a native of Hanover, Germany, born in 1853. He is one of a family of five children, of Henry and Johanna Schepelmann. The father was born in 1823 in Hanover, and was by occupation a miller and farmer; he is still living in his native country. The mother was born in 1833 in Hanover, Germany, and died in 1871. Henry was educated in the Lutheran schools of Hanover, Germany, and in 1883 emigrated to the United States and located in Maumee township. He is the owner of 244 acres of rich farming and grazing land, with good buildings. In 1880 he was wedded to Miss Augusta, daughter of Henry and Sophia Deister. She is a native of Hanover, Germany, born in 1857. By this union there are five children: Henry, Willie, Otto, Minnie and Christian. Mr. Schepelmann is a member of the Masonic order at Harlan, and his wife is a member of the Lutheran church. Mr. Schepelmann is a farmer, and brick and tile manufacturer, and is prominent in local affairs.

In the spring of 1822 Robert Shirley, sr., and family moved from near Chillicothe, Ohio, to Fort Defiance. The family included the mother, Mrs. Rachel Shirley, and the children, James, Elias, Robert, Ruth, Mary, Nancy and John G. From Fort Jennings to Fort Defiance they saw no white people, and followed the Indian trail along the river Auglaize. The fort at Defiance, built by Gen. Winchester, was then standing, in a good state of preservation, in charge of William Preston, the only other inhabitant of Defiance. Four French families lived in cabins on the Maumee above the point, and three American families on the Auglaize near by. Six miles below lived the families of John Perkins, Montgomery Evans and Mr. Hively. Two trading houses were kept on either side of the Maumee. Here the Ottawa, commonly called Tawah Indians, brought their skins of the otter, beaver, raccoon, bear, muskrat, mink, fox, wild-cat and deer, and beeswax, ginseng, cranberries and gooseberries. No person then lived between Forts Wayne and Defiance, but all the travel from Detroit to Fort Wayne and Chicago passed along the Maumee. Mail was carried by Forts Wayne and Defiance from Piqua to Fort Meigs (Maumee City). When the Shirleys settled at Defiance, Capt. James Riley had not begun the survey of land. Shane, the famous pioneer, was then about fifty years old, and living at Shane's prairie, on the St. Mary's river. Flour and salt were obtained from Swan Creek (Toledo), hauled to the Rapids and brought thence on pirogues. In 1827, through the influence of Nathan Shirley, Elias Pattee, of a family familiar in church history in the Maumee valley, organized the first church at Defiance. James Shirley, who was born in Virginia in 1797, was a man of remarkable shrewdness and natural ability, and at the time of his death at his old home in Ohio, in 1850, he owned over 700 acres of land in Defiance and Allen counties. By his wife, Elizabeth Gilbert, born in 1822, in Kentucky, and still living in Defiance county, he had seven children: a daughter unnamed, William, Robert B., Eliza, Alexander, Levisa and Sylvester. Robert B. is the only one living besides the mother. Robert B. Shirley was born October 24, 1842, and at seventeen years of age became a clerk in a dry goods store at Antwerp, Ohio, but three years later came to Maumee township and began to work on the farm which is now his home. In 1871 he was elected justice of Maumee township, and in 1874 re-elected by a largely increased majority. At the same time he served as deputy land appraiser, and subsequently served as assessor by appointment. In 1880 he was elected trustee, and again in 1888. Though he is a democrat, and a recognized leader in that party, these honors have been bestowed upon him in a township that frequently gives republican majorities. In the 1885 and 1889 sessions of the Indiana legislature, he served as chief engrossing clerk in the house. Mr. Shirley was married May 1, 1880, to Ladora, daughter of William and Catharine (Gray) Faulkner. She was born at Lima, Ohio, in 1856. Mr. Shirley's sister Eliza left at her death one son, Albert H. Little, and his brother William left four children: Della, Alice, Verseneth and Frank.

Horatio A. Little, a young man of good standing in Maumee township, is an offspring of the Shirley family. He inherited 110 acres of land in Maumee township, as fine as there is in Allen county, from his grandfather through his mother, Eliza (Shirley) Little, and he is the only living representative of that noble pioneer lady. He also inherited from the Shirleys that industry and push which characterized the family, and promises to become one of Allen county's worthy and valuable citizens.

MILAN TOWNSHIP.

The early settlement here was mainly on the line of the ridge road which was surveyed in 1839. It passes over the best part of the township, the remainder at that early day being swampy and unattractive. In 1836 Charles Shriner, a native of New Jersey, made his home on a half of section 4, which he purchased. He erected the first frame house two years later. In the same year, Nathan Lake, of Vermont, and his family, having come in 1835, settled on section 3. John Heath settled in this vicinity, in 1836, also, and Wilkes Gillett came from Ohio in 1837. Stephen Heath made an early settlement on the ridge road, and upon the first organization of the township in 1838, he chose for it the name of Milan in remembrance of his native town in Huron county, Ohio. He opened subsequently the pioneer store at his house. In 1833, came John Nuttle, from Huron county, Ohio, whose descendants are still residents here. Alvin Hall, of Connecticut, settled on section 18 in December, 1840, having previously visited the township. He became prominent in local affairs. His house was a favorite stopping place for travelers, and in 1856 he secured a postoffice for his neighborhood, called Chamberlain; Lorenzo D. George became the postmaster. Subsequently the office was removed to St. Joseph township, and has lately been kept at the store of Edson Brooks. In 1837 the settlement at Fairport was begun by George Foxtater. During canal times his house was in use as a tavern by the travelers. Fairport was laid out in section 24, by eastern capitalists during this period, and an attempt made to build up there a town, but with the decay of canal traffic the town reverted to agricultural land. The first election was held here at the house of George Foxtater, in 1842, and Andrew Wakefield was elected justice and John Nuttle, constable. In 1843 a postoffice was established at Fairport, and John Irvin, then appointed postmaster, held until the office was abolished. John Irvin also kept a hotel in canal times. Among the settlers between 1840 and 1850 were William Fitzgerald, sr., Edward Nugent, Daniel B. Strong, Joseph Donner, William Tilbury, the Lynes family, William R. Herrick, Richard Beebe and Samuel Archer. In section 35 the town of Mosier was platted by Joseph Mosier, in 1854, but it did not develop.

Ami D. Nuttle, a prominent citizen of Milan township, was born in that township July 2, 1844. His parents were one of the first three families settling in the township. His father was born in New York, November 8, 1803, and removed first to Ohio, thence to Milan township about 1833, and died November 12, 1852. His mother was a first cousin of Hon. John Jay, one of the distinguished men of the early days of the republic. The mother, a native of Scotland, was born March 16, 1805, and came to America with her parents at the age of twelve and settled in Ohio. She died February 4, 1865. Mr. A. D. Nuttle was married August 27, 1865, to Harriet M. Platter, whose parents were also among the first settlers of the township. Her father, a native of Ohio, was born in 1810, and died August, 1852, in Milan township. The mother, a native of Ohio, was born in 1820. She is living and enjoying fair health. Nine children have been born to Mr. and Mrs. Nuttle: William D., born January 21, 1867; Katie C., born March 4, 1867, died August 17, 1885; John F., born November 30, 1869, died September 7, 1876; Minnie M., born October 22, 1871; Edgar A., March 6, 1875; Walter C., June 9, 1880; Wesley H., September 17, 1882; Toney A., February 21, 1887; Ima J., February 12, 1889. William was married to Miss Adeline Miller, July 16, 1887, and they have one child, Grover. Mr. Nuttle enlisted in the Union army July 16, 1862, in the Fifth Indiana cavalry, and was discharged June 15, 1865. He assisted in the raid that led to the capture of John Morgan, and was in numerous skirmishes. In the east Tennessee campaign he lost almost the entire use of one eye. He served also in the Georgia campaign, and was at the engagements at Resaca, Allatoona Pass, Rome and before Atlanta. He is a member of the G. A. R., Sion S. Bass post,

No. 40, Fort Wayne. He has served his township as assessor for four years and as constable for two years. Mr. Nuttle took possession in 1865, of the farm of sixty-three acres on which he now has a handsome new house and barn and is prepared to enjoy the comforts of life.

Alvin Hall, the early settler referred to above, is a native of New London, Conn., born May 11, 1810, son of George and Betsey Hall, who were natives of Connecticut, and residents of New London. In the defense of that city the father was killed during the war of 1812. Alvin left home at the age of sixteen, and went to Canandaigua county, N. Y., where he remained two years, and then worked at his trade of carpenter in Erie county, Ohio, twelve years. Coming then to Milan township with his wife and family, he bought land of the government and devoted himself to pioneer work. He was married in 1833 to Betsey, daughter of John and Anna Miller. She was born in Connecticut in 1810, and died in 1847. They had seven children. January 7, 1848, Mr. Hall was married to Sylvia, daughter of Stephen and Hannah Heath, who was born in Ohio in 1828, and to them were born six children. Mr. Hall has served his township as a justice, assessor, treasurer, and was elected land appraiser of the county in 1876. Since he built the first frame school-house in 1857, he has been a leader in progress and good works. He made the trip to Allen county in December, 1840, reaching Fort Wayne about Christmas, and built his log cabin upon the land he now occupies.

Curtis C. Lake, of Milan township, was born in 1820, in Chittenden county, Vt., one of a family of eight children, of Nathan and Jerusha Lake, natives of Connecticut. The father, who was a farmer and lumberman by occupation, when a young man moved to Vermont and located at Shelburn, where he remained until 1835, when he and family emigrated west, and took possession of the land which C. C. Lake now occupies. He was one of the earliest settlers, and cut a road through the forest for about six miles to reach the tract of land on which he settled. When he first arrived in Allen county he rented a farm near Fort Wayne, where he could raise something to live on until he got a start in the woods. The family stored their grain at Rudisill's mill on the St. Joseph, and would get a grist as they needed it. Then they went to work to clear away the forest, and the parents lived until they and the children succeeded in creating a comfortable home. On the way here they had lost all the goods and clothing they possessed, which increased their hardships. The parents died on the homestead, the father in 1857, the mother in May, 1866. Mr. Lake helped to build, and was one of the students at the pioneer log school-house, and his children were educated in the same house. The lady who taught the second term of school became his wife. He has a relic of old "Johnny Appleseed" in the shape of an apple tree that measures ninety-three inches in circumference, grown from the seed sown by that famous character, on the banks of the Maumee river. It was set out about 1837, and is still a thrifty tree. His first residence was burned down but he has now a fine home which has since been built upon one of the finest locations in the township. In 1850 he was wedded to Mary E., daughter of John and Asenath Chelles. She was born in 1833, in Rutland county, Vt. Her father was born in 1789, at Kingston, N. H. He moved to Vermont in 1830, and thirty-five years later moved to DeKalb county, near Spencerville. He remained there until 1864, when he made his home with his daughter, until his death in 1865. The mother was born in 1798, in Chester, N. H., and is still living at the age of ninety-one years and is well and active with hearing and sight but little impaired. Mr. and Mrs. Lake have had five children: John N., Alma A., Chauncey H., Hattie A., and Benjamin who died August 6, 1887. In politics Mr. Lake cast his first presidential vote for W. H. Harrison, and the last for Benjamin Harrison. He is one of the venerable and venerated old settlers.

George W. Willbur, a prosperous farmer of Milan township, was born in 1840 in De Kalb county, Ind., one of six children of Charles and Catharine Willber. His father, a native of Vermont, born in 1792, at Windsor, when a small boy moved with his parents to New York, where he remained until he was forty-two years of age, when he came to DeKalb county, where he was one of the earliest settlers. He cleared a farm and erected substantial buildings, and having passed through the hardships of pioneer life, in the spring of 1851 he sold out and came to Milan township, locating on the ridge road, where his son now resides, and where the father died in 1877. The mother was born in 1807, at Watertown, N. Y., and died at the old homestead in the fall of 1856. George W. received the rudiments of his education in the pioneer log school-house. As a farmer, he has flourished, and is the owner of 300 acres of fertile soil, in one of the finest locations in the county, upon which he has handsome buildings. March 25, 1869, he was wedded to Mary, daughter of James and Rebecca Vandolah. She was born in Perry township in 1840 and died in 1880. Her only child, Catharine, died in infancy. In 1882 he was married to Ella, daughter of Solomon and Matilda Richards, by whom he had two children, Mary M. and Goldie M., both deceased. Mrs. Willbur was born in 1852 in Wayne county, Ohio. Mr. Willbur patriotically enlisted in Company D, Thirtieth Indiana volunteer infantry for three years or during the war, and was engaged in the following leading battles of the war: Shiloh, Stone River, Chickamauga, Murfreesboro, Kenesaw Mountain, Lovejoy, Gainesborough, and among many others. He is a member of the G. A. R. and of the Masonic order. He and wife are members of the Lutheran church.

Gottlieb Schafer, trustee of Milan township, was born in Germany, March 21, 1846, and at the age of eight years came with his parents to America in December, 1854. They made their home first in Wayne township one year, and then removed to St. Joseph township, where they resided nine years, finally settling in Milan township in the fall of 1864. Mr. Schafer's father was born in Germany, in June, 1806, and died October 19, 1888; the mother was born October 11, 1815, and is still living, active and bright for her age. Mr. Schafer was educated during one year in Germany, and the remainder of his education he obtained in this country. He has been quite successful in life, and has a good farm of 155 acres which is handsomely improved and well under-drained. He was married August 1, 1872, to Rosina Federspiel, and they have had the following children: Caroline, Frederica, Christina, Louisa, William, Anna, Charles, Wilhelmina, Rosina and Margaret. Mr. Schafer is a popular and influential gentleman, and he and his family are highly esteemed.

Willis B. Brooks, of Milan township, was born in Erie county, Ohio, January 20, 1844. He came with his parents to the farm where he now resides, in 1860. His father was born in New York, January 8, 1817, and came with his parents to Ohio. He cleared the forests from his farm and died November 24, 1882. The mother, who was born in Maryland, October 25, 1819, is living at the home of her son and enjoying excellent health. Mr. Brooks was married to Mary Ann Spindler, November 26, 1865, and eight children have blessed their union: Charles, born October 11, 1868; Mary E., May 20, 1869; John W. (deceased), October 3, 1870; Delbert W., born July 10, 1872; Walter A. (deceased), November 22, 1874; Emma D., born June 1, 1878; Clarence Paul (deceased), May 16, 1881; Grover C., born July 3, 1884. Mr. Brooks lives on an excellent 120-acre farm, where he has followed agriculture as an occupation. He and wife are members of the Lutheran church, and are highly esteemed by a wide circle of acquaintances.

William Ehle, the third child of his parents, was born in Saxony, August 4, 1849. He came with his parents to Fort Wayne in the fall of 1861, and then removed to Adams county, returning to Milan township in 1881. The parents reside in Fort Wayne, the father at the age of seventy-two years, the mother sixty-nine. Mr. Ehle was married June 9, 1872, to Sarah Breiner, who was born in Schuylkill county, Penn., August 18, 1855. Her parents, natives of Pennsylvania, moved to Ohio and then to Adams county, Ind., in 1862. Her ancestors came over from Germany 200 years ago. Her mother's people came from the Palatinate, Germany, and the forefathers on both sides fought in the revolution. Seven children have been born to Mr. and Mrs. Ehle: August (deceased), December 12, 1873; John, January 4, 1874; Alfred September 12, 1876; Maggie, February 6, 1878; Ida, August 4, 1880, died September 13, 1881; Eddie, May 13, 1884; Emma, July 24, 1888. Mr. Ehle worked in a spoke factory in Fort Wayne for some time before he began farming. He is the most successful of the younger farmers of the township, having 280 acres, 200 of which are well under-drained. He has cleared by his own efforts 200 acres of land, and deserves to enjoy his comfortable surroundings.

A worthy and popular farmer of Milan township, William A. Spindler, was born in Delaware county, Ohio, June 25, 1846, and came with his parents to Milan township in April, 1864. He owns a good farm of eighty acres where he resides, and his farm is well improved. Mr. Spindler was married to Harriet Stofer, of German descent, whose parents were natives of Pennsylvania; her father died in 1857; her mother, who is living at the age of seventy-six, is a descendant of one of the Hessian soldiers who surrendered to Washington during the revolution. Nine children have been born to Mr. and Mrs. Spindler: John W., born June 23, 1872; David F., November 24, 1874; Elizabeth A., December 16, 1876; Samuel T., August 24, 1878; Catherine M., April 21, 1880; Jennie M., December 23, 1882; William W., November 4, 1883; Cornelius April 9, 1886; Christopher, November 5, 1888.

Wilson S. Spindler, an enterprising citizen of Milan township, was born in Delaware county, Ohio, October 23, 1843. He came to this township, in which he has been quite successful as a farmer, and ranks among the leading people, in April, 1864, and was accompanied by his parents. Mr. Spindler was married January 1, 1866, to Augusta Hobbs, whose parents were natives of Erie county, Ohio. Her father, who is living, was born January 19, 1821, and her mother was born February 27, 1829. Three children have been born to Mr. and Mrs. Spindler: Minnie R., May 23, 1867; Anna B., September 2, 1869, and George W., July 6, 1871. Minnie was married to R. Richart, July 11, 1886, and they have three children: Walter, born December 15, 1887; Sonora G., December 25, 1888, and an infant, June 20, 1889. Mr. Spindler cast his first presidential vote for Gen. McClellan.

Solomon Doty, a prominent citizen of Milan township, was born in Ohio, February 6, 1840, the oldest of a family of eight children. His father, born August 2, 1812, came to Ohio from the mountains near Wheeling, W. Va., the place of his nativity, in 1816, and is still living in Ashland county, the comforts of his old age shared by the wife of his youth, who was born November 6, 1819. Both parents are enjoying excellent health and their families are noted for longevity. His grandfather Lambricht, was with Gen. Wayne in his memorable campaign. Mr. Doty was married December 31, 1865, to Sarah Gougwer, whose parents emigrated from Pennsylvania about 1820. Mrs. Doty, the eldest of eleven children, was born April 12, 1841. Her father died at the age of sixty-eight, the mother at the age of sixty-six. Four children have been born to Mr. and Mrs. Doty: Emma J., January 27, 1867; Joseph E., April 15, 1869; Philip, June 5, 1874; Estella J., May 6, 1880. Emma was married to E. A. Brooks, August 13, 1885, and they have two children, Guy E. and Orlo P. Mr. Doty has cleared a valuable farm of 133 acres, which was paid for in money earned by teaching. He taught eight terms, mainly in succession, in his home township and two in Indiana. Mr. Doty served one term as constable in Ohio, township clerk for three terms and justice of the peace three years; being re-elected he resigned to remove to Indiana. Settling here November 12, 1875, in ten months he was again elected justice and has served twelve years. These expressions of confidence witness his worth. Such men should be called higher to fill offices of trust in county and state. Mr. Doty and wife are members of the Evangelical Lutheran church, known as Barnett's chapel.

JACKSON TOWNSHIP.

A large portion of this township was entered on the government books as "condemned swamp lands," and an extensive marsh covering its northern portion, dissuaded home-seekers from settling in the region. This region was of the same character as the famous Black Swamp which extended far down toward Lake Erie on the south of the Maumee, and was the terror of pioneers. The soil was a deep muck, overlaying yellow and blue clays. The tract appeared level but gently slopes to the lake. Upon this basin grew a forest of greater density and loftiness than was to be found elsewhere in the interior valley of North America. These gigantic trees standing side by side, enclosed a vast and gloomy solitude, which the sun seldom penetrated to evaporate the water which in places stood to the depth of two or three feet. In this Jackson and Maumee township marsh, known as the "bears' nest," hunting was an exciting pastime, long after large game had vanished elsewhere. Bears were hunted here by persons still living, and deer were found up to a recent period. The first cabin in this township was built by George Hollinger, who improved some land and also spent much time in the chase. David, John and Samuel Neff, from Dayton, Ohio, entered large tracts in the southern part, and deadened the timber, but did not settle. In 1840 Jacob Mooney became a permanent resident on Flat Rock creek, and his brother Robert, who settled at the same time, remained for a few years. In 1848 John Kline, Joshua Dickinson and Douglas Whittaker settled, but the two latter subsequently removed. Other permanent settlers were Meads in 1850, and Peter Boody in 1859. In the fifties a number of French immigrants arrived, among whom may be named such prominent residents as Florant Voirol, Francis Parnin and Constant Pernot. John Cline was another settler before the war of 1861. The population even at this time is small, a considerable part of the lands being owned by capitalists who are non-residents.

The first village platted in this township is Edgerton, on sections 10 and 11, which was laid out in May, 1889.

Thomas Jones was born in Maryland in 1814. He emigrated to Harrison county, Ohio, in early life, and there married Susannah Edwards, April 12, 1836, who was born in that county June 6, 1820. They came to Monroe township in 1841, and located on the farm where the widow still lives. Mr. Jones was a true pioneer, being the twelfth voter in that township. He, with his few neighbors, endured all the hardships incident to back-woods life. After rearing a large family, of which seven survive him, he died May 5, 1874. Jasper W. Jones, the oldest son living, was born on the old homestead, near Monroeville, April 10, 1852. He attended the district school during his youth, and at the age of nineteen entered the Fort Wayne Methodist Episcopal college, where he remained two years. He was industrious and soon acquired a practical education, and also became a good teacher, a profession which he pursued for several years. He was married May 30, 1876, to Catharine A. Malley, who was born in Scotland, July 4, 1851. Five children have blessed this union: Thomas Andrew, born June 24, 1878; Mary Alice, December 22, 1879; Edward Conway, January 6, 1882; Jasper Burt, December 21, 1884, and George Lee, April 10, 1886, who died January 9, 1887. Mr. Jones has been honored by various positions of trust. In 1878 he was elected a justice of the peace of Monroe township; in 1883 he resigned and removed into Jackson township, where, in 1884, he was elected township trustee and re-elected in 1886. In the campaign of 1888 he was elected county commissioner by a majority of nearly 4,000 over a strong competitor, and will assume the duties of the office in December, 1889. Mr. Jones is sociable, confiding and trustworthy, in his nature, never forgetting a friend.

Constant Pernot was born February 6, 1824, in France. He came to Allen county, Ind., December 24, 1852, and lived in Jefferson township until 1859, when he removed to his present location, in Jackson township. His father, Jean Baptiste Pernot, was born in 1790, and died in 1878, and his mother, Frances, was born in 1800, and died March 14, 1835. Mr. Pernot was married February 9, 1847, in France, to Mary Munnier. Her father, Thomas, and mother, Mary Huguenard, were of French descent. Seven children have been born to Mr. and Mrs. Pernot: Mary, November 9, 1847; Francis, July 27, 1848; Robert, in 1850 (deceased); Marcelia, born in November of 1851; Peter, born March 1, 1858; Rosie, born in September of 1860, and Julie, born October 8, 1863. Rosie married Louis A. Ressuche in August, 1884, and has four children: Clara, Marie, Julia and Charles. Mary was married to Emile Jabas in 1873, and has two children: Emma, deceased in 1887, and Emile. Mr. Pernot served in the French army three months, but France being at peace and he being a married man, he was released. He has been assessor of Jackson township for twenty-four years. Mr. and Mrs. Pernot are members of the St. Louis Catholic church in Jefferson township.

Florant Voirol was born in Switzerland, October 16, 1839. He came with his parents to Fort Wayne, thence in June, 1852, to Jackson township, Allen county, where he now resides. His father, Louis Voirol, was born in 1805 and died in 1867. The mother, Celestine, was born in 1813, and died February 10, 1883. Mr. Voirol was married to Miss Euphrasie Socie, February 11, 1873. Her father, Eugene, was born in 1823, and the mother, Frances, was born in 1822. Both are living in Ohio, and came to this country from Switzerland about 1840. To Mr. and Mrs. Voirol have been born ten children: Mary L., December 11, 1873, deceased August 9, 1874; Amelia J., November 15, 1874; Charles A., December 23, 1875; Jule S., October 31, 1877; Eugene L., March 13, 1879; Edward, February 18, 1881; Mary C., December 20, 1882; Joseph F., October 9,

1884; Frances E., November 29, 1885, deceased May 19, 1886; Armin F., January 18, 1887. Mr. Voirol is a prominent citizen and has always been actively engaged in farming. He and wife are members of the St. Louis Catholic church.

Among the energetic sons of la belle France, who have chosen this country for their home, is Francis Parnin. He was born in France, June 9, 1839, and with his parents, Gabriel, born in 1811, and Virginia, in 1809, came to America in 1853, and settled in Jackson township. Mr. Parnin was married to Josephine Eugnard, June 21, 1864. Her father, Peter Cloud, born in Frances in 1811, and her mother, Frances, born in France in 1814, came to America in 1850, and settled in St. Joseph township, where they remained until 1884, when they removed to Fort Wayne. The children born to Mr. and Mrs. Parnin, are: Louis, born August 18, 1865; Victor, born December 4, 1866; August, born June 12, 1868; Francis J., born December 10, 1869; Charles, born May 2, 1871; Joseph, born October 8, 1872; Jule A. (deceased), born January 27, 1874; Armand, born January 31, 1876; Valerie, born December 28, 1877; Aristive, born February 12, 1879; Jule A. (deceased), born October 19, 1881; Jule A. (deceased), born November 12, 1884; Henry L., born August 20, 1885. Mr. Parnin was educated in the schools of France, and as a vocation has always followed farming. He and wife are members of the St. Louis Catholic church.

John Cline was born in Trumbull county, Ohio, November 7, 1827. His father was born in Germany, and his mother in Ohio. She died September 17, 1887. His grandparents emigrated from Germany to Trumbull county, Ohio, and thence came to Jackson township, Allen county, in the fall of 1856. Mr. Cline was married to Adeline Housman, February 5, 1855. Her parents came from Pennsylvania. The father died in Trumbull county, Ohio, in 1854, and the mother in 1883. Her grandparents were from Germany. Four children have been born to Mr. and Mrs. Cline: Mary, July 22, 1856; Sarah J., February 28, 1858, died November, 1862; Amanda, November 6, 1855, and John H., December 11, 1861, died 1862. Their daughter Mary was married to John Holsapple, and they have the following children: Roland, born April 11, 1876; Blanche, January 9, 1878, and Elmer, November 19, 1885. Amanda was married to Washington Blake in 1877. He was born October 16, 1860. There have been born to them: Clarence A., September 5, 1878; Odus L., November 20, 1880; Addie F., October 21, 1882; John V., March 26, 1884, and Norah G., March 9, 1886. Mr. Cline enlisted in the Twenty-third Indiana Battery, James H. Myers captain, and served, lacking a few days, for three years. He has suffered greatly with his eyes from a powder explosion to which he was exposed during the service. He was in eight engagements among the most prominent of which were Kenesaw Mountain and the sieges of Atlanta and Nashville.

Timothy Baldwin, a worthy farmer of Jackson township, was born in Summit county, Ohio, September 13, 1838. His grandparents were natives of Connecticut, and parents of Ohio; the father died in 1855, but the mother survives at the age of eighty-two years. In 1861, Mr. Baldwin came to Jackson township and settled where he now resides. Mr. Baldwin has followed farming and the mercantile business, except during the period of the civil war, when he served gallantly in defense of his country. He enlisted in April, 1861, in the Nineteenth Ohio, and re-enlisted in February, 1865, in the One Hundred and Fifty-second Indiana, serving in the Shenandoah valley, and being discharged September 4, 1865. He is a member of John Stabler post, G. A. R., and is prominent in his township, having been elected justice of the peace for three successive terms. Mr. Baldwin was married March 30, 1862, to Phœbe E. Ball, the first white child born in Jackson township. Her father was a native of Virginia and her mother of New Jersey.

John McConnel, of Jackson township, was born in Hocking county, Ohio, September 8, 1839. His parents, Robert McConnel, born October 20, 1798, and Mary Ann (Stout) McConnel, born January 17, 1807, were natives of New Jersey. Mr. McConnel came to Indiana in 1848, settling in Wells county, and removing to Allen county in 1866, making his home where he now lives in Jackson township. July 18, 1867, he was married to Barbara Ann Townsend, by whom he had the following children: Eva, born May 9, 1868; Eliza A., October 5, 1869; Margaret J., February 16, 1871; William S., July 21, 1872, died September 2, 1873; John A., January 5, 1874; Caleb, August 28, 1875; Adema; Charles F., April 17, 1882. Eva was married December 24, 1888, to Thomas J. Savage. Mr. McConnel went through a long and honorable service in the national army, enlisting September 12, 1861, and serving as corporal of the Thirty-fourth Indiana, until February 4, 1866. He participated in the campaigns along the Mississippi, at Vicksburg, Jackson, and in Louisiana, and near Brazos Island. He is a member of William H. Link post, No. 301, G. A. R., of Monroeville. He is a a popular and influential man in his township, and has twice been elected trustee, the second time without opposition. He and wife are members of Pleasant Grove Methodist Episcopal church.

Mrs. Nancy Wyckoff, the widow of James H. Wyckoff, who died September 27, 1877, has one of the handsomest quarter sections of land in Jackson township. She was born July 31, 1822, at Saybrook, Ashtabula county, Ohio, and was married to James H. Wyckoff, April 20, 1843. With him she removed to Cuyahoga county, Ohio, in May, 1844, and remained there until May 1, 1867, when they located in Jackson township. Her father, Philo Webster, was born in Delaware county, N. Y., June 5, 1795, and died September 19, 1850. Her mother, whose maiden name was Deborah Haywood, was born in Clinton, Duchess county, N. Y., October 19, 1799, and died February 9, 1823. Grandmother Webster traced her ancestors back to the Pilgrim fathers. Both grandparents came from Connecticut, and the grandfather was a soldier of the revolution. To Mr. and Mrs. Wyckoff was born one child, Bethena, September 6, 1849. Mrs. Wyckoff is a member of the Christian church of Monroeville.

Clement Evard, a prosperous farmer of Jackson township, was born in Switzerland, March 2, 1845. He came with his parents to Allen county, Ind., and first settled in Milan township, coming to Jackson township November 8, 1873, where he now resides. His father, David, born October, 1806, died in America, March 29, 1883. The mother, Mary A., was born November 24, 1803. Mr. Evard married Eliza J. Sapping, born November 8, 1868. Her father Jacob, was born in Pennsylvania, March 20, 1817, and the mother Mary, was born in Allen county, Ind., in 1833 and died in Whitley county. To Mr. and Mrs. Evard have been born six children: Margaret, August 5, 1869; Minnie M., September 17, 1870; Celia, July 17, 1873; David M., January 17, 1877; Ida G., July 25, 1880; Hattie E., February 16, 1886. Margaret married Benjamin Mooney November 22, 1888. Mr. Evard enlisted in Company H, One Hundred and Forty-second Indiana volunteers, April 12, 1865, and was discharged July 14, 1865. He and wife are members of the Methodist Episcopal church.

Notable among the settlers of Jackson township who have caused the forests to disappear before their laborious efforts, is John Taylor, who was born December 15, 1839, in Auglaize county, Ohio. His father, William, and mother, Jane, her maiden name being Smith, are natives of Ohio. Mr. Taylor was married to Elizabeth Williams, April 16, 1865. Her parents were from Ohio; the father, John S., was born July 31, 1820, and the mother, May 20, 1825. Mr. Williams was a lawyer and practiced in the Auglaize county courts, and was at one time elected probate judge. To Mr. and Mrs. Taylor have been born six children, all living: Edward, January 19, 1866; Charles, February 28, 1868; John, November 17, 1869; Arthur, December 27, 1871; Ibby, November 2, 1875; David, April 14, 1883. Mr. Taylor's father died when he was young, and being the eldest of the children, the burdens fell upon him. He has followed farming with the exception of three years and three months, when he was in the military service of the United States, in the Seventy-first Ohio. He participated in the battles of Shiloh, Atlanta and Nashville. Mr. and Mrs. Taylor are both consistent members of the Methodist church.

JEFFERSON TOWNSHIP.

It is believed that the first permanent settlement within the limits of this township was made by Jared Whitney and his family. He came in May, 1833, and remained during the summer on the Maumee river, but in the fall took possession of a tract on section 7, which he afterward brought into cultivation. In the summer of the same year, Wilhelm and Henry Tuschknagen and families settled, and became industrious and esteemed citizens. But several years later, one of the sons, while at Fort Wayne, took a piece of cloth from a store and was arrested. One of the neighbors becoming bail, the culprit was released, and returned home, but a few days before the day of trial disappeared forever. The

Jasper N. Jones.

disgrace so affected the family that they were broken in spirit, and the ostracism by the community affected their reason. It is related that the elder men were to be heard night after night breaking stone in the woods, for the purpose, they said, of building a temple. The last survivor was a mental wreck, was known as the "Prophet," and fancied he was divinely directed in every action. During 1833 there also came Christian Wolf, Joseph Grunauer, Mr. Blackmore, a transient resident, William Henderson, Simon Rogers. The latter sold his clearing to Eben Burgess, who took possession in 1834. On this farm the first frame house was erected by one Blakely, and was used as a barn by Mr. Burgess, who erected the first brick house in 1837. William Henderson was married in March, 1835, to Elizabeth Rogers, the first ceremony of the kind in the township. In 1835 the first death occurred, that of a child of Mr. Blackmore. In 1834 a settlement was made by Aretas Powers, who was born in New York in 1800. He brought with him his wife, Sarah Stilson, to whom he was married in 1828, and their children afterward increased in number to eleven. James Post came also in 1834, but was not a permanent settler. A sad event of that period was the loss of a little son of the latter. He strayed into the woods, and his body was found by a party of neighbors many days later in Seven Mile creek. Mr. Powers was the first justice of the peace elected in 1840. In 1835 or 1836, Henry Castleman settled near the center of the township. They were famous hunters, and were known to bring at one load to Fort Wayne, on a home-made sled, forty saddles of venison. Henry Castleman is said to have killed 1,678 deer and twenty-three bears. A celebrated event of the early time was the clearing up the Sugar ridge or Vanwert road. On New Year's eve, 1837, about twenty residents went to a point near New Haven, provided with cooking utensils as well as axes, and began the work. The road had been merely a foot path before, but this winter's campaign made it a well-defined highway.

Alanson Whitney opened the first store in 1850, his stock being a barrel of whiskey and a keg of tobacco, but this was soon enlarged and he did a prosperous business. When the Vanwert road was opened Henry Castleman opened a tavern, and prospered until the day of railroad communication. During this period there was a postoffice on the road, kept by Socrates Bacon subsequent to 1850. The first saw-mill was built by Green & Burgess, near the center of the township, and subsequently a run of buhrs was put in, and these two mills were operated for many years. In May, 1851, the village of Besancon was platted by Peter F. Beugnot.

The quiet little village of Maples had its origin in the lumbering business. Here Lewis S. Maples came in 1852 from western Ohio, to take charge of an engine for a saw-mill. August 12, 1853, the town plat was made by O. Bird and J. Bowser, and Mr. Maples made an addition in 1873. Saw-milling, stave manufacture, and the like have been the leading industries. In 1880 the population was 139. Stores are kept by Adam Crawford and Nicholas Ladig, the former of whom is postmaster.

Lewis S. Maples, for whom the village was named, was born in Greene county, Penn., September 20, 1825. He engaged in the manufacture of staves and heading in 1872, but since 1876 has been farming. He was married to Deborah Ritter in 1853, and they have six children living.

Among the earliest settlers in Jefferson township was Joseph Gronauer, a native of Germany who immigrated in about 1828, and first settled in Virginia. In 1832, putting all his possessions in a one-horse wagon, he set out for Indiana, and established a new home on the Maumee, in the northwest part of Jefferson township. The government had not then surveyed the land, and he was allowed when the lands were opened to settlers, $300 for the improvements he had made. He died November 16, 1872. His wife was a native of Germany, who came to this country in 1834, and she is still living, having made her home on the old homestead for forty-one years. She well remembers the old times, when wolves and Indians were numerous, and the great event when the last Indians were taken west from Logansport. Their son, George F. Gronauer, was born April 28, 1851, in Jefferson township, and is one of the leading citizens. He was married October 5, 1875, to Caroline Muhlfeith, whose parents came from Germany about 1840. The mother died September 19, 1883, but the father is still living. Five children have been born to Mr. and Mrs. Gronauer: Norah, July 12, 1876; Clara, June 22, 1879; Lizzie, March 1, 1882; Julien, September 19, 1884, and an infant March 20, 1889. The remains of the old road and bridges built by Anthony Wayne are to be seen on Mr. Gronauer's farm, also many relics of his expedition have been found.

Edward Harper was born in Jefferson township, March 26, 1856. His grandfather, John Harper, died aged eighty-four. The dates of birth and decease of his grandmother, Elizabeth Harper, are unknown. His grandfather, John Hunter, on his mother's side, died aged eighty-four, and his grandmother, Rebecca McMullin, died at the age of ninety-two years. Edward's father, William Harper, was born in Tyrone county, Ireland, March 10, 1810. He emigrated to this country at the age of twenty-one years, and finally settled in Jefferson township, in 1836. He married Mary Hunter, who was born in Erie county, Penn., December 25, 1812, and they had eight sons and four daughters. Edward's childhood, youth and manhood were passed in Jefferson township. From his early youth he seemed not to care for toys, but greatly enjoyed a hammer and a few nails. The advantages of his district school were for him of short duration. Four of his brothers having entered the army, the responsibilities of home duties rested upon him. He first devoted his attention to farming in which he was successful, but his youthful proclivities now began to manifest themselves so that by his ingenuity and close observation, he soon became an excellent framer. He possesses wisdom and tact in financial matters, and takes good care of his own interests, being a wise manager in business, yet he is a generous and sympathetic man, and has a care for others. He possesses a force of character that has made him successful in life. He was married to Martha A. Shull, January 1, 1883, and has a son, Emmet E. Harper. In 1884 he was nominated by the republican party for trustee, but was defeated. In 1886, he was again nominated, was elected and served a term of two years. In 1888 he was re-elected, in spite of an adverse majority of eighty on the general ticket. As trustee he has shown much executive ability, wisdom and discretion in the selection of teachers, and economy in building. He has raised the average of attendance from thirty-one to thirty-eight per cent., and has proved himself a faithful public servant.

John Tillman, one of the early settlers of Allen county, was born in Philadelphia county, Penn., May 10, 1812. His father, John Tillman, a native of Scotland, in an early day emigrated to Pennsylvania where he wedded Catherine Sook, who was born in Germany, emigrating to Pennsylvania with her parents. To them were born two sons and two daughters. Their son John was reared on a farm, and at the age of twenty-three years, left his native state and settled in Ohio. In 1838, he went to St. Louis, Mo., and remained eight months, and in 1840 came to Allen county, settling on section 26, of Jefferson township, which has been his residence. In 1841 he wedded Sarah, daughter of Henry and Rachel (Saltzman) Castleman. She was born in Starke county, Ohio, September 12, 1819. They have four children: Delilah, David, John L. and Margaret. A fifth child was born, but died at the age of nine years. Mr. Tillman bought of the government a tract of land in Jefferson, and settled in the dense forest. He has done much toward the improvement of the county. He began life a poor man, and now owns a well improved farm of 120 acres. He has now for forty-nine years been identified as a citizen of Allen county and has observed the growth of its civilization from almost its inception. He and wife are members of the German Baptist church and enjoy the esteem of a wide acquaintance. Mrs. Tillman came to this county in 1832 with her parents, who settled in Jefferson township. The father was born in Pennsylvania and the mother in Ohio, and were of German lineage. They died in Allen county after rearing thirteen children, of whom twelve reached maturity. John L. Tillman was born in Jefferson township, April 27, 1852, was reared and educated on a farm and followed farming till 1886, when he removed to Monroeville and went into business. He was married November 25, 1880, to Lucinda Burgart, a native of Allen county, and they have one child: Herman.

Mrs. Elmira Whitney, one of the early settlers, was born in New York, May 11, 1822, and came to Jefferson township in 1843. Her recollection runs back to the time when the Miami Indians were numerous; when the wolf was a frequent visitor, and the bear had not yet disappeared. There were then no paths and but three houses between their home and New Haven. Her parents came to Adams township from New York. The father, Henry Cool, was born March

31, 1794, and died March, 1847. The mother, Catherine, was born September 23, 1791, and died about 1838. The subject of this mention was married to Alanson Whitney, January 16, 1842. He was born in New York, January 13, 1817, and died August 26, 1882. He was a member of the I. O. O. F. lodge of New Haven. Ten children were born to Mr. and Mrs. Whitney: Eliza, July 22, 1844, died November 21, 1864; Jerry M., April 8, 1846, died September 9, 1850; James E., May 22, 1847; Samantha, January 11, 1849, died January 23, 1886; Lenora, June 22, 1851; William J., January 21, 1854; Alanson J., December 30, 1855, died July 24, 1856; Carrie C., December 11, 1857, died October 12, 1870; Sarah, August 1, 1860; Abbie A., March 18, 1863. Eliza was married to David Bowers, May 3, 1864; Semantha was married to Reuben B. Hoops, April 7, 1870; Lenora was married to Adam Crawford, January 4, 1874, and has three children: Carrie, Marion and Gertie; James was married to May C. Wilson in 1874, and has two children, Elmira and Edward. William was married to Amanda M. Snider, October 15, 1878, and has had five children: Alice I., Herschell A. (deceased), Myrtle, Charles Mc. and Lottie Elmira.

Francis Roussey is an early settler of Jefferson township, born July 28, 1828, in France. He came with his parents to America in 1847, and settled where he now resides. His father, Peter Roussey, was born in 1793, and died in 1853; the mother, Frances, and the father were of French nativity. Mr. Roussey was married in August, 1847, to Mary Girardeaux; she died in 1848. He was married in 1850 to Justine Bride, and to them was given one son, Frank, born April 28, 1858. Four years after the decease of his second wife, Mr. Roussey married Rose Bride. To them were born: John, September 4, 1862; Louise, March 25, 1864; Justine, February 25, 1866; Rose, March 29, 1879. Mr. Roussey's school advantages were of the most primitive character. When he came to the county the sight of deer, wolf and bear was a common one. He and wife are members of the St. Louis Catholic church, and are worthy and popular people.

Adolphe Reuille, who was born in France in 1838, came with his parents to Jefferson township in 1852. His father went to France in 1872 and died there, and the mother died in Monroeville in 1884. Mr. Reuille was married May 13, 1863, to Miss Mary Cramer, whose parents came from Germany about 1839, first settled in Ohio, and then removed to Jackson township, Ind. Eight children have been born to Mr. and Mrs. Reuille: Fannie, April 24, 1864; Caroline, May 6, 1866; John, August 18, 1868, deceased October 19, 1870; Mary, December 17, 1872; Ernest, December, 1874; Eli, June 6, 1876; Alice, November 19, 1878; Frank, May 6, 1880. Fannie was married to John Ladig, April 10, 1888. Mr. Reuille and wife experienced much of the hardships of pioneer days, and can well remember when there were no roads and when the wolves howled around their door. They are both members of the St. Louis Catholic church of Jefferson township, and are valued and estimable citizens.

August Pepe, one of the successful and progressive farmers of Jefferson township, was born in France, April 19, 1839. He came with his parents to Fort Wayne in 1853, and removed to Jefferson township, in 1875. His father, Mark Pepe, was born July 5, 1805, and the mother, Threacce, October 5, 1805. Mr. Pepe was married to Miss Sarah Grosjean, December 5, 1861. She was born in Allen county, Ind., June 1, 1844. Her father, Frank Grosjean, was born in February, 1809, and died January 6, 1855; the mother, Johanna B., was born October 2, 1818. They came from France in an early day. To Mr. and Mrs. Pepe have been born nine children: Frank, October 6, 1862; Jule, July 5, 1864; Adolph, April 5, 1866, died November, 1885; Mary, December 28, 1868; Edward, April, 1870, died August, 1877; Clara, August 15, 1872 (deceased); Amiel, October 11, 1875; Hattie, November 6, 1877; Clara, July 10, 1882; Lizzie, November 12, 1888. Frank was married to Martie Girardeaux in May, 1885. Mary was married to George Campbell in 1887. Mr. Pepe has always followed farming. He and his parents came to this country, and settled on 300 acres in Washington township, when bear, wolf and deer were plentiful. Mr. and Mrs. Pepe are members of the St. Louis Catholic church.

John B. Dupeyron, a prominent citizen of Jefferson township, was born in France, November 16, 1822. Emigrating to America in 1841, he reached New Orleans on his nineteenth birthday, and at that city remained until 1851, then he removed to Shelby county, Ohio. The latter was his home until 1857, when he removed to Jefferson township, settling where he now lives, January 2, 1857, upon an eighty-acre tract of land. While at New Orleans he was married, June 8, 1849, to Celestine Sansotte, and their only son, Raymond, was born at that city, January 15, 1850. Mr. and Mrs. Dupeyron are members of St. Louis Catholic church, and as worthy people are esteemed by all.

MONROE TOWNSHIP.

This extreme southeastern township was occupied by the splendid forests which have given it fame, without any encroachment upon their growth, until the fall of 1839, when William and James Black and Joseph Rabbit coming from Carroll county, Ohio, began a permanent settlement on section 32. They succeeded in developing farms and lived there for several years. One Kimsey "squatted" upon a claim in the northwest in the same season, but after his death, which followed soon, his stakes were taken up. Other comers in the same year were Lawrence Umbaugh and his son-in-law, Jacob Drake, on section 32, and Peter Schlemmer, on section 21. During the same season Noah Clem, a Virginian, purchased land on section 33, and by the help of his neighbors built a cabin which received his family in the following spring. He was a settler for life and a prominent man. In 1840 came Moses Ratledge and his sons William and Moses, Elijah Reddinghouse and John Friedline. The latter, by entry and purchase, accumulated 400 acres. Hugh

Anderson and Samuel Clem came in 1841 early, and were enterprising citizens. In the same year John Stephenson settled on section 4, and James Savage and Peter Barnhart near the site of Monroeville. After this date immigration was much more rapid. In April, 1841, at the first township election held at William Ratledge's home, there were thirteen voters, and one of these, Peter Schlemmer, was challenged on the ground of naturalization. His vote was accepted, however, on the proof he made, and it decided a tie between Noah Clem and William Black, opposing candidates for justice, in favor of the former. The next year Squire Clem exercised his function in joining the daughter of Asa Dillon to Eli Bauserman in marriage. In 1843 the first death in the settlement occurred, that of the wife of Peter Schlemmer. She was buried on his farm, and in same spot several others of the old families were laid to rest. The early settlers were compelled to take their grain to Wines' mill, on the Maumee, or Rudisill's, on the St. Joseph, the journey often taking six or seven days, and when Hugh Anderson, in 1844, put in operation a horse-mill, although it was of limited capacity, it was gratefully welcomed and well patronized until Muldoon's mill was established on the St. Mary's. In February, 1848, John Burger laid out the village of East Liberty, on section 29, and it promised to become prosperous. Martin Kemp established a store peculiar to the period, the principal stock being liquor, but leaving soon afterward, Judge Reynolds and James Patterson opened a general store, which was quite successful, and continued so under their successors, David Studebaker and Peter Whipky. Here, in 1851, a postoffice was established, but subsequently removed during the life of John Friedline to his farm. Upon the rise of Monroeville, East Liberty soon declined.

Monroeville.— This enterprising town has justified the expectations of its founders, Jacob and John Barnhart. They established the town in December, 1851, and though for a number of years only a mail station on the Pittsburgh road, it suddenly awakened to life and activity in the "flush" times of the war and the few years subsequent, and gained a start in prosperity which it has not retrograded from, being now an important trade center. Additions were made to the original plat by McGovern in 1865, by Samuel Pool in 1865, and by Alpheus Swift in 1866. Immediately following the war there was a remarkable growth in manufacturing. In 1864 John W. Rout embarked in the manufacture of oil barrel staves and heading, and in 1865 George Webster and James Weiler were associated with him. They erected a building 40 by 60 feet, and added dressed lumber to their products. Mr. Rout retired from the business three years later and was engaged in manufacturing independently until 1872, when he removed to Decatur. Webster & Weiler increased their plant, and established a branch at Benton, Ohio, operating both factories until 1877. The manufacture of staves was also engaged in, in 1865, by Messrs. Hemphill & Ashworth, with a complete plant and a branch factory at Decatur. Mr. Ashworth dying in 1866, the business was continued by the other partner, who resided in

Pennsylvania, and was represented by M. E. Argo. A large business was done, the shipments averaging one car load per day, and twenty-five men being employed. Upon the death of Mr. Hemphill and his widow two years later, the business was suspended in 1879. Rallya & Robertson established a factory in the same line in 1865, and did an extensive business until 1874. In the same year, the Monroeville flouring-mill was established by C. H. Schick. It has subsequently passed through the hands of Alpheus Swift & Co., J. Dague & Bros., with whom Daniel Shank was for several years associated. D. S. Redelsheimer became the owner, and while in his possession, the mill burned in May, 1889. In 1867 the Empire stave company was formed at Monroeville with P. S. O'Rourke president, and Alexander Williamson, secretary and treasurer. Jacob Sweeny was appointed superintendent and supervised the construction of one of the most complete stave factories in Indiana. This was burned down in 1875, while owned by T. S. Heller and E. D. Dague. They had at Decatur a similar factory, and at both towns large general stores, and at Dixon a station for the purchase of timber. In July, 1878, D. S. Redelsheimer & Co. purchased the stave factory of J. B. Worden & Co., which was established by A. F. Beugnot and Daniel Monahan in 1875. This is still operated by Mr. Redelsheimer. A pump factory was established in 1877 by T. A. Long, which did business for several years, and the manufacture of carriages and wagons was begun by Sears & Scherer in 1878. This branch of manufacture has since been discontinued.

The prominent business men of the town are: Dry goods, drugs, etc., D. S. Redelsheimer; general store, Corbaley & Freese; groceries, C. J. Breman, J. W. Edwards, Joseph Lewis; drugs, H. A. Shank; hardware, J. B. Niezer, J. Reuille; furniture, M. Strass, F. Edwards; furnishing goods, E. Finan; jewelry, M. B. Knouse; photographers, Engle & Baster; harness shop, P. Krick; meat markets, Bryant & Meeks, John Casselman; millinery, Angie Somers; hotels, Central house, Charles Eastgate; Railroad house, Mrs. E. Baker; agricultural implements, J. B. Niezer, A. S. Robinson; creamery and fine stock, Martin E. Argo; shoe dealer, C. A. Nill; stock buyers, Krick & Hayes, Tillman & Casselman; saw- and planing-mills, D. C. Purman, Webster & Sons; tile and brick yard, Brandeberry & Myers, William Wright.

The present town officers are: Board of trustees, W. A. Waterman, J. W. Edwards, George Doctor, Henry Ehling, Jacob Colyer; Clerk, C. C. Myers; treasurer, H. A. Shank; marshal, John Rose; justices, John Sheehan, J. D. Alligear, H. E. Drake; notary publics, John Corbaley, C. C. Myers, J. P. Nash. H. Stewart is the present postmaster.

The leading and most prosperous industry, of which the town may well be proud, is the Monroeville elevator, built in 1888, by J. B. Niezer. This is in dimensions, 40x76 feet, and its capacity is 20,000 bushels. The structure cost $5,500. There has lately been added a feed-mill and set of buhrs. The annual business of this important establishment is $65,000.

The medical profession has been represented at Monroeville since an early day, some of the practitioners having arisen to eminence. Since 1880, the doctors have been: C. A. Leiter, W. A. Connelly, A. Engle, Wilder, and S. E. Mentzer. The first, now deceased, was a graduate of the university of Pennsylvania, and was a prominent physician. He was a son of ex-congressman Leiter, of Clinton, Ohio. The latter two named are now the only practitioners and both are able.

The legal fraternity at Monroeville is now represented by E. W. Meeks and Chester Holder. The former acts as assistant prosecuting attorney, and is a native of the vicinity.

In 1862 Monroeville lodge, No. 293, A. F. and A. M., was organized December 30, with the following charter members: Jabez Shaffer, James Weiler, Peter Eckley, J. G. Mariotte, M. E. Argo, J. W. Miller, William B. Rabbit, S. T. Rice, John Shaffer, A. Engle, J. L. Robinson, Jacob Cassiday and J. L. Younker. The lodge is still prosperous.

The I. O. O. F. lodge, known as Monroeville, No. 283, was chartered May 22, 1867, with five members: G. C. Nill, A. F. Brown, E. W. Erick, J. W. Rout and A. A. Baker. The growth was slow until 1872, when the hall was destroyed by fire. After moving to new quarters the lodge increased in numbers and wealth, the membership now being fifty-seven in good standing, and the net assets about $1,800. The following are past grands: M. Strass, J. R. Parker, M. B. Knouse, Henry Smith, J. W. Meeks, Henry Deiwert, V. L. Shaffer, W. A. Waterman, G. C. Hunsicker, C. C. Myers, J. A. Corbaley, J. E. Pillars, J. P. Nash, J. I. Shulte, J. T. Baker and L. E. Wright.

The *Monroeville Breeze*, owned and managed by J. D. Alligear, is one of the most flourishing village newspapers in Northern Indiana. Originally known as the *Democrat*, it was purchased by the present management January 1, 1884, from Frank P. Hardesty, and made independent in politics. It has had a steady growth in subscription from that time from 200 to 700, and has a good job patronage. Thomas J. Foster and Thomas Stephens were former owners.

David S. Redelsheimer, a prominent citizen and merchant of Monroeville, Ind., was born in Germany, May 22, 1836, and is a son of Sigmund and Lena Redelsheimer. He was reared and educated in his native country, receiving a fair German education, and in 1850 came to America and joined his parents at Fort Wayne, they having settled in that city in 1839. After coming to Fort Wayne he attended English schools for two years, and subsequently learned the printer's trade at which he was engaged only a short time. In 1861 he enlisted in the Fifteenth Ohio regiment, and was in the volunteer service for about four months. Then he returned to Fort Wayne and engaged with his father in the wholesale grocery business, in which he remained until 1872. He continued in business at Fort Wayne until 1878, and then came to Monroeville and bought the stave factory that had been established here, and at present owns the only manufactory of the kind at Monroeville. He is also one of the firm of D. S. Redelsheimer & Co., manufacturers of overalls, at Fort Wayne. Soon after locating in Monroeville, Mr. Redelsheimer purchased the drug store of J. B. Worden, and subsequently added other lines of merchandise until he now carries a full stock of general merchandise, perhaps the most nearly complete assortment of any merchant in the county. He is a very successful merchant and does an annual business of about $50,000 at his store. December 22, 1862, Mr. Redelsheimer was married to Charlotte Strass, a native of Bohemia, and they have an interesting family. Mr. Redelsheimer is a staunch republican in politics, and made a very creditable canvass in 1876 as the republican candidate for county treasurer. He is not a member of any church, but was reared in the Jewish faith. He is one of the progressive citizens of the county; is a member of the council, F. & A. M., and the I. O. O. F., at Fort Wayne, and the G. A. R., at Monroeville.

Franklin Freese, a prosperous merchant of Monroeville, was born in Summit county, Ohio, September 8, 1840. His parents, Peter and Anna (Faust) Freese, were born in Lancaster county, Penn., and were there married. Of their eight sons and one daughter, all except one reached maturity. Soon after the parents' marriage, they removed from Pennsylvania, and located in Summit county, Ohio, and in 1846 they removed to Indiana, settling in Marshall county, where the mother died in 1856. The father married a second wife and by her had one son and a daughter. In 1871 he died in Marshall county. Franklin Freese was born and reared on a farm, receiving a common school education. At the outbreak of the civil war, he enlisted April 24, 1861, but his company was not accepted. Subsequently he re-enlisted in Company E, Seventeenth Indiana volunteer infantry, and was mustered into United States service in June, 1861, and in the same company served until June, 1864, when he was mustered out, but immediately went into the quartermaster service at Nashville, Tenn., and here remained until March, 1866. He was one of those gallant soldiers who composed Col. John T. Wilder's lightning brigade. Maj. J. J. Wiler was formerly captain of Mr. Freese's company. Among some of the important engagements in which Mr. Freese took a part were Greenbrier, W. Va., Shiloh, Tenn., Stone River, Chickamauga, and Lookout Mountain. In 1867 he joined the G. A. R. at Plymouth, Ind., and at present is a member of William H. Link post, No. 301, at Monroeville, of which he was the main organizer. In 1866 Mr. Freese returned to Marshall county, and February 8, 1867, was married to Miss Matilda Gilbert, a native of Pennsylvania. She died in 1871, leaving two children: Walter S. and Luella O. In 1874 in Stevenson county, Ill., Mr. Freese was married to Eliza Mishler, by whom he had the following children: Hattie, Freddie, Ida, Frankie, Fannie, and Bessie. In 1879 Mr. Freese formed a partnership with J. A. Corbaley, at Monroeville and Maples, and embarked in general merchandise. The store at Maples has been discontinued, and at present the firm is doing at Monroeville an annual business of about $35,000. Mr. Freese is a republican in politics, and is a member of lodge No. 283, I. O. O. F., of Monroeville.

Jules H. Reuille was born in France, November 14, 1846, and is a son of John Claude and Margaret (Predin) Reuille. The parents were of French birth, were married in France, and their union blessed by eight children, of whom the following reached maturity: Adolphe, Jules H., Fannie and Melanie. John Claude Reuille visited America in 1851, decided upon bringing his family to the United States, and accordingly returned to France, and in 1853, brought his family to Indiana and settled in Jefferson township, Allen county. In 1866, the father returned to France on a business trip, and after returning to this country his health failed him, as did the health of his wife and son, Jules H. These three returned to France in 1873, purposing to plant their home again in their native country. Their hope of health was blasted by the death of the father within sixty days after reaching France. In the fall of 1874 the mother and Jules H. departed for America. On reaching here they located in Monroeville, Ind., and ten years later the mother was called away in death. In 1886, one year after the death of his mother, Jules H. wedded Lena Ehling, and they have two children: John C. H. and Louisa Eve. Mr. Reuille is a member of the Roman Catholic church. He is engaged in the hardware business in Monroeville, where he resides and enjoys the esteem of many friends.

John Hayes, of Monroeville, was born in Limerick county, Ireland, October 23, 1825. His parents, James and Elizabeth (Downey) Hayes, were natives of Limerick county, and their deaths occurred in their native country. Of their ten children, seven reached maturity. John Hayes, the second, was born and reared on the farm, and in the country schools of Ireland received his education. At the age of twenty-one years he secured the position of constable in Ireland, and remained in the service nearly four years. In April, 1851, he set sail at Queenstown, Ireland, and on the 28th of May landed at New York. Previously, August 15, 1850, he was married to Ann Cronen, who was born in the county of Kerry, February 22, 1830, one of six children of Daniel and Catherine (McElstrem) Cronen. Their marriage has been blessed by ten children, of whom James J., Daniel M., Michael L., Henry F., Catherine E., John J. and Anna, reached maturity. Immediately after reaching New York, Mr. Hayes settled at Reading, Hamilton county, Ohio, where he remained till 1854, when he came to Fort Wayne. He secured a position with the Pennsylvania Railway company, in whose employ he remained for the following twenty years and eight months. In April, 1874, the directors of the Indiana State Prison at Michigan City appointed him a prison guard, and he was engaged there two years, the last year serving as hospital steward. Since 1860 his home has been at Monroeville. He began in life a poor man, but by energy and integrity has gained a high station in life. He and family are members of the Roman Catholic church.

Henry F. Hayes, son of the above, was born in Fort Wayne, August 31, 1858. He was reared on a farm and educated in the common schools. At the age of seventeen he went into the telegraph office at

Monroeville, and was appointed operator in 1876, and in 1878 was appointed station agent. He is also the agent for the Adams Express company. In April, 1883, he was united in marriage with Olive, daughter of John D. and Mary (Doren) Stephenson. Mrs. Hayes is a native of this township. They have two children: Edward L. and Henry F. Mr. and Mrs. Hayes are members of the Catholic church of Monroeville.

David Martin was born in Muskingum county, Ohio, July 29, 1826. The father, John, was born in Little York county, Penn., of Irish parents, who immigrated in an early day. He married Margaret Messahcup, a native of Maryland, of German descent, and they had four sons and four daughters, among whom was David. The father had previously been married to Susa Ourie, by whom he had nine children. In an early day the parents removed from Pennsylvania to Muskingum county, Ohio, and subsequently became pioneers of Licking county, Ohio. The father died before David left home, but the mother lived to be nearly one hundred years old, and died in Licking county. David, after reaching his majority, attended school, paying his expenses with his own earnings by farm labor at $8 per month, half of which he had to take in merchandise. In the fall of 1851 he came to Van Wert county, where he resided for the following six years, teaching school each winter and working on a farm in summer. He settled on land in Monroe township, in the fall of 1858. January 29, 1853, he was married to Melinda, daughter of Samuel Clem, an early settler of Allen county. She was born in Champaign county, Ohio. By her marriage she has become the mother of thirteen children. Mr. Martin is now a prosperous and representative farmer. He is a zealous worker in the Methodist church, and for several years has acted as a preacher of the gospel, having been licensed by the Ohio Methodist Episcopal conference in 1883. He is a man of great force of character, and wields a happy influence over all who know him. A. L. Martin, a son of the above, was born in Ohio, August 9, 1858. In 1879 he wedded Louisa Jane, daughter of Nathan and Martha Parker, of Allen county. Immediately after his marriage Mr. Martin settled on a farm in Monroe township. He followed farming till in 1884, when he took charge of the Indiana house, in Monroeville. This he managed for two years, and then, in 1886, went into the livery business. He owns and operates in Monroeville Martin's livery, feed and sale stable, and is an enterprising young business man. His children are: Franklin, David and Melinda Ellen. In politics Mr. Martin is a republican.

David Gibson, trustee of Monroe township, was born in Lycoming county, Penn., in March, 1839. His father, David Gibson, was a native of the Keystone state, and his mother, whose maiden name was Mary Richard, was born in Maryland. Both were born in the year 1811, and they died in Allen county, the mother in 1870 and the father in 1855. To them eleven children were born, of whom five are living. Of the survivors the third born is David Gibson. He was reared on the farm of his parents in his native state, and there gained a good common school education. In 1863 he came to Allen county and during his first year here worked by the month on the farm of Andrew Growmann. In 1864 he began farming for himself, purchasing the land on which he has for twenty years made his home. He has a productive farm of seventy acres, which is well improved. Mr. Gibson is influential in township affairs and prominent as a democrat, and being generally recognized to be an able and upright man, he was in 1888 intrusted by the people with the responsibilities of the office of trustee of Monroe township, a trust which he is ably and conscientiously discharging. Mr. Gibson was married in February, 1865, to Lucy Farrell, who was born in Ohio, in 1833, and they have four children: Agnes and Edward (twins), Henry and Helena. He and wife are members of the Catholic church.

Morris Strass was born in Austria, May 29, 1838. His parents J. L. and Theresa (Pepperkorn) Strass, had eight sons and one daughter. Four sons became emigrants to America, the first being Morris. He came to the United States in 1856, and settled at Albany, N. Y. Here he remained until August 12, 1862, when he enlisted as a private in Company G, One Hundred and Twenty-eighth New York volunteer infantry. He was transferred with his company from Louisiana, after the Red River campaign, to the valley of the Shenandoah, under Gen. Sheridan. Subsequently he joined Gen. Sherman in the march to the sea. July 12, 1865, at Savannah, Ga., he was, as a sergeant, discharged by reason of the close of the war. Mr. Strass returned to Albany, but in 1865 removed to Monroeville, where he has since resided, mainly engaged in general merchandise. He has, however, occasionally changed his lines of merchandise, and at present he is dealing in, and manufacturing, furniture, and acting as undertaker. In business he has accomplished more than ordinary success, being now prosperous and having an annual trade of about $6,000. In 1867 he was married to Anna Strass, a native of Austria, and they have had four children, of whom three are living: Carrie, Lena and Julius. Mr. Strass is one of the prominent citizens of the county. He was appointed postmaster for Monroeville in 1866, and held the office by reappointments until in 1885. In politics he is a staunch republican. He is a member of the William H. Link post, No. 301, G. A. R., at Monroeville; is a Mason of Monroeville lodge, No. 293; and is a past master of Monroeville lodge, No. 283, I. O. O. F.

John A. Corbaley, a merchant at Monroeville, was born at Plymouth, Ind., July 19, 1849, and is a son of Richard and Jane (Croco) Corbaley. The father was born in Marion county, Ind., August 7, 1820, a son of Jeremiah Corbaley, a native of Maryland, of Irish descent, who being a farmer by occupation, became a pioneer settler within the present limits of Indianapolis, cutting his way through forests to the place of settlement. He occupied the grounds on which stands the Indiana state capitol, and there made maple sugar. His son Richard was the first white child born in Marion county. He was reared and educated on a farm, and in an early day settled in Marshall county, where he took up farming. Subsequently, he was elected county clerk of Marshall county, and served two terms. In early life he became a convert to the belief of the Church of God, and in 1879 he and wife emigrated with their family to California, where he engaged in preaching for his church, and at present he and wife reside in Washington territory. Of his six children, John A. is the eldest. He remained under the parental roof till twenty years old. In early life he taught in the public schools, and then went to California, where he worked in divers callings for seven years. In 1872 he returned to Plymouth, Ind., and wedded Lou Miller, daughter of S. W. and Elizabeth Miller. Their children are: Clarence, Earl and Roy. In 1878, Mr. Corbaley returned from California to Indiana, and in 1879 formed a partnership with Franklin Freese, and since has been engaged in general merchandise, living for a time at Maples, Ind. Mr. and Mrs. Corbaley hold a membership in the Church of God, at Plymouth, Ind. He is a member of I. O. O. F. lodge, No. 282. In politics he is a republican. He is a member of the school board in Monroeville. He made a close race for township trustee, cutting the adverse majority of 175 to 22.

William N. Parker, a pioneer of Allen county, was born in Onondaga county, N. Y., son of an American-born citizen, of English lineage. He was reared on a farm, and about 1838 came west, settling in Allen county. In early life he taught school and practiced law, and subsequently settled on a farm in Marion township. He was one of more than ordinary education among the pioneers, and became a well respected man. He was regarded as a man of keen and shrewd judgment, honesty and integrity. He was married in 1838, in Allen county, to Sarah Yager, a native of Pennsylvania, her parents being born in Germany. She died in Fort Wayne, and her husband died in Allen county in 1887. Their only child, John Russell Parker, was reared on a farm. When eighteen years old he secured a position with the P., F. W. & C., Ry. Co., and since 1857 he has been in the employ of this company, excepting, perhaps, two years. In 1861, April 19, he enlisted as a private in Company E, Ninth Indiana volunteer infantry, and July 31, 1861, was discharged by reason of the expiration of time of service. He participated in three engagements: Phillippi, Laurel Hill, W. Va., and near Laurel Hill. After his discharge at Indianapolis he returned to Fort Wayne, and in 1862 he was united in marriage with Sophia, daughter of John and Margaret (Young) Hite. She was born near Youngstown, Ohio, and in 1854 came to Allen county with her parents, who were natives of Germany. To this marriage have been born four children: Lydia E., Alice, Margaret and Sophia. At present Mr. Parker is the pumper for the railway company at Monroeville, where he has resided since 1873. He is a member of the I. O. O. F, Monroeville lodge, No. 283, William H. Link post, No. 321, G. A. R. of Monroeville, and of the Methodist Episcopal church. In early life he was thrown on his own resources, but has been successful and has reared and educated a family of four children, one of whom, Alice, is a teacher in the Monroeville schools.

Edward Finan, a prosperous citizen of Monroeville, was born in Ireland in 1845. His parents, John and Ellen (Mourn) Finan, were born and reared in Ireland, where they were married. Of their seven sons and one daughter, all are living but two. The parents with their family, emigrated to America in 1847, for a while lived in Canada, but subsequently became early settlers in Benton township, Paulding county, Ohio, and at present, live in Painesville, Ohio. Their fourth child, Edward, was reared in Paulding county and received a common school education. At the age of seventeen years, he went to Dayton, Ohio, where he enlisted in 1864, as a private in Company I, One Hundred and Thirty-first Ohio infantry, and was in the service for three months. He then remained at home until 1870, when he located at Monroeville, where he has since resided. He has for the greater part been engaged in the timber trade, but has also done more or less merchandising. He became postmaster at Monroeville and holds the position now. He has held several other positions of trust. He and his family are Catholics. In 1873 he wedded Elizabeth Jane, daughter of John D. and Mary Stephenson, and they have had the following children: John, Roger (deceased), Michael (deceased), and Lewis.

Alexander H. Anderson was born in Wood county, Ohio, May 25, 1844. His father, James McC. Anderson, was born in Butler county, Penn., September 3, 1819, and was married July 22, 1841, in Ohio, to Lucinda Hockemberg, a native of Pennsylvania. To their marriage were born five sons and four daughters. The father's death occurred December 28, 1882, in Paulding county, Ohio, where the mother still resides. Alexander H. was born and reared on a farm, and educated in the country schools. When only eighteen years old he enlisted, in August, 1862, as a private in Company I, One Hundredth Ohio volunteer infantry. He participated in the siege of Knoxville, Tenn., Resaca, Ga., and at Allatoona, Ga., he lost his left arm, in consequence of which disability he was discharged June, 1864. He then returned to his home in Ohio and was there married September 19, 1865, to Hannah Parker, who was born in Fort Wayne, February 11, 1844. In 1870 he located at Monroeville, Ind., where has since resided. Mr. and Mrs. Anderson are members of the Methodist Episcopal church, holding a membership at Monroeville. He belongs to the G. A. R., William H. Link post, No. 301, of Monroeville.

Charles J. Breman, a merchant of Monroeville, was born in Sweden, July 22, 1843. He was reared and educated on a farm in his native country, where he learned the shoemaker's trade. Emigrating to America in 1871, he subsequently took up his trade at Decatur, Ind., and afterward located at Coldwater, Ohio, and there in 1875, he was united in marriage with Bernardina Hantaman, a native of Germany. Of their five children only one, Charles G., survives. In 1883 Mr. Breman located at Monroeville, and embarked in general merchandise in which he has prospered, doing an annual business of about $6,000. He and family are members of the Roman Catholic church at Monroeville. Mr. Breman came to the United States a very poor man, but by means of his industry and sterling character he has become a prosperous and well respected citizen.

John D. Alligear, editor of the Monroeville *Breeze*, was born in Danville, Penn., July 24, 1854. His father was born in Jersey City, N. J., and his mother at Danville, Penn., and are both living. Grandmother Alligear is also living, aged ninety-eight years. Mr. Alligear was married to Melinda Wass, February 7, 1874, and they have two children: Dovie M., born January 26, 1876, and William R., September 3, 1880. Mr. Alligear came with his parents to Allen county in July, 1855. He began to shift for himself at the age of twelve. Starting out as a bootblack, he became carriage-boy for Hugh McCulloch. Subsequently, he was a canal boy, and finally began to learn the trade of a printer in 1869, working during the day at the case, and selling papers in the morning and evening, and sleeping during the night under the depot seats. He passed through all the privations incidental to a youth of poverty. Gaining the esteem and confidence of his employers, he became foreman of the *Gazette* for several years, and then managed the Monroeville *Democrat* for Mr. Foster. He took charge of the Monroeville *Breeze* in January, 1884, and has made it prosperous.

Chichester Holder, attorney at law, was born in Marshall county, Ind., December 21, 1845. His father, Absalom P. Holder, born in Sullivan county, Ind., was married in La Porte county, to Mary Blivin, a native of New York. They had six children, who were reared on the farm, the father being a farmer by occupation. The fifth child, Chichester, attended school in the country until the civil war broke out, when, notwithstanding youthfulness, he volunteered, July 26, 1862, as a private in Company D, Eighty-seventh Indiana infantry. Among some of the engagements in which he participated were: Chickamauga, Mission Ridge, Resaca, Buzzard Roost, siege of Atlanta. He was in the march to the sea, and at the fall of Savannah, marched through the Carolinas to Richmond, Va., and thence to Washington, D. C., where he was discharged as an uncommissioned officer June 10, 1865. Returning to his home in Fulton county, in the fall of 1865 he engaged in carpentering and subsequently entered the employ of the P., Ft. W. & C. railroad as a carpenter and later was given charge of a corps of civil engineers in the employ of that company. Meanwhile he took up the study of law, and became, in 1878, a member of the La Grange county bar, under Judge William A. Woods, now on the federal bench, and of the Noble county bar, and in Rome City opened a law office. He has also been admitted to practice in DeKalb and Allen counties. In the spring of 1888 he located at Monroeville, where he has since enjoyed a lucrative practice. He visited England several years ago on a business trip in the interest of the Sarah Jane West (*nee* Spriggs) estate. He is a self-made man, without early advantages, but from early youth the study and practice of law was uppermost in his mind. In politics, like his father, he is a staunch republican.

Noah Clem, above mentioned as one of the conspicuous early settlers of Monroe township, was born in Shenandoah county, Va., September 27, 1809, son of David and Catharine (Walters) Clem, natives of that county, but of German parentage. The latter had six sons and seven daughters. Noah remained with his parents in Shenandoah county until he was married in 1832, to Mary M. Ridenour. In the fall of 1833 the young couple settled in Champaign county, Ohio, and in March, 1840, they made their home in Monroe township, and began clearing away the forest and here for fifty years he has contributed to the advancement of the county. He is an old line democrat and has taken an active part in politics. By his wife, who died September 27, 1886, he had eleven children.

John D. Stephenson was born in Center county, Penn., November 29, 1816. His parents, Thomas and Eleanora (Dayhause) Stephenson, were American-born, the father being of Irish, and the mother of German, descent. To them were born thirteen children. John D. was reared and educated on a farm in his native county, and at the age of twenty-one years started out for himself, going to Seneca county, Ohio. There he was married in 1841 to Mary Dornan, who was born in Columbiana county, Ohio, November 6, 1822, daughter of James and Sarah (Starkey) Dornan. The father was born in Ohio, of Irish descent; the mother was born in Virginia. They had eight children, of whom Mary is the second. Immediately after their marriage Mr. and Mrs. Stephenson emigrated by wagon to Allen county, Ind., and in 1841 they settled on what is now known as the Ridge road in Monroe township. Mr. Stephenson had just before his marriage (in the fall of 1840) visited the place of settlement, had constructed a log cabin in the woods and sown four acres of wheat. The nearest neighbor on the east was one mile away; at the west, eight miles. The Sandusky Indians were numerous and daily hundreds of them might be seen scouting and hunting through the forest. The Ridge road was the only public highway approaching Fort Wayne from Ohio, and the residence of Mr. Stephenson was a stopping place until the building of the railroad. Mr. and Mrs. Stephenson kept a hotel, accommodating hundreds of travelers. On one occasion over 100 wagons were camped with them. This was a station on the stage line. By energy and perseverance Mr. Stephenson became a very prosperous and highly respected citizen, leaving at death an estate of 840 acres. In politics he was a democrat, and though not a member of any church, was friendly to church and school, and was a liberal and enterprising citizen. To Mr. and Mrs. Stephenson were born the following children: James T., John M., Eliza J., Joseph E. (deceased), Theodore L., Alpheus L. and Mary O. Mr. Stephenson died July 12, 1882. Mrs. Stephenson still survives and resides on the old homestead.

John Sheehan, one of the old settlers of Allen county, was born in Wayne township, Columbiana county, Ohio, June 9, 1824, and is a son of Daniel and Elizabeth (Hutchison) Sheehan. The father was born in Lancaster county, and the mother in Monongahela county, Penn.

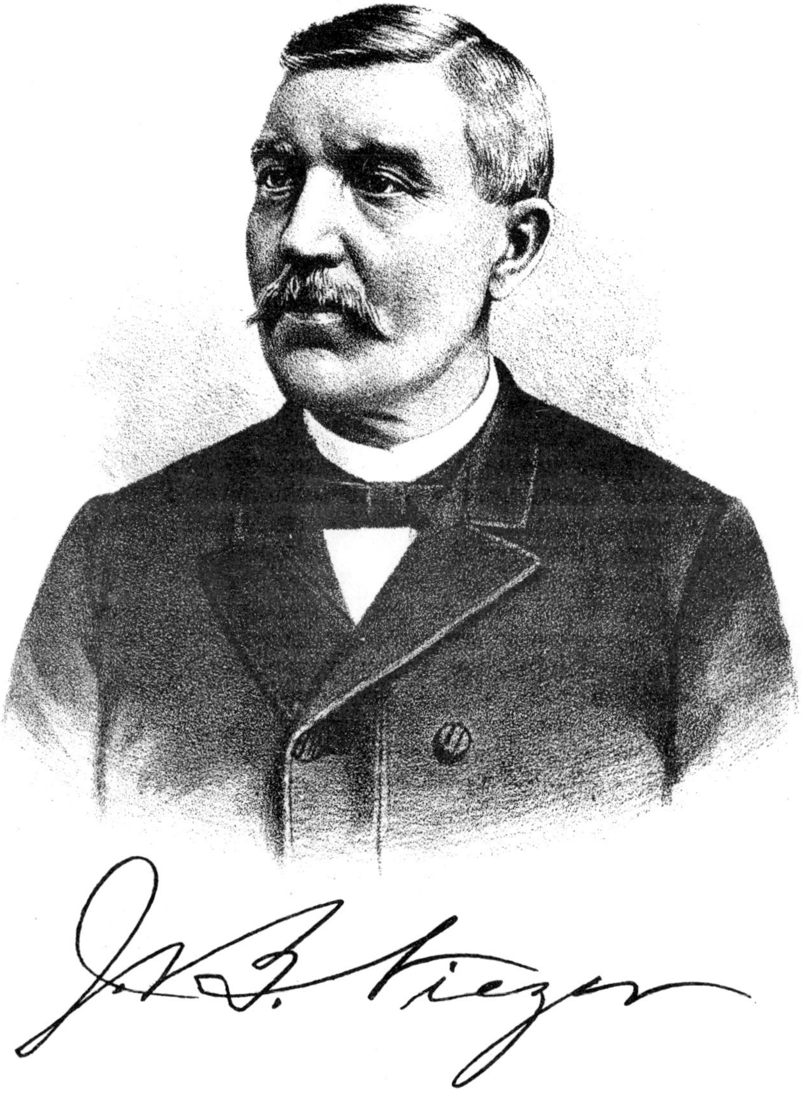

Daniel was a son of William Sheehan, a native of Ireland, who emigrated to the United States. Daniel and Elizabeth Sheehan had five sons and six daughters. With their then living children they removed to Indiana, and in 1845 settled in Allen county, near the site of Monroeville on what is known as the Ridge road, and here the father died in 1876, at the age of seventy-five years; and the mother died in 1878 at the age of seventy-five. With wagons the family drove to their place of settlement, pitched tents, and in the woods built a log hut for a habitation. In this manner was established the home of the family, then consisting of the father and mother and eight children. Of the eleven children, two had died in Ohio, and one, a daughter, now living at New Haven, had married. The father was a hardy pioneer, a sturdy farmer, an esteemed citizen and loved father. He was a zealous member of the Presbyterian church as was also his faithful wife, and they reared their family in the church. John Sheehan was reared on a farm, and received a fair education for his day. He has devoted his life to agriculture in which he has made a practical success. He began a poor man, and under adverse circumstances, but now owns a fertile and well-improved farm of forty acres, in Monroe township. In 1851 he was married to Melissa, daughter of Elias and Anna Shaffer, early settlers of Allen county, and they have had five children: George (deceased), Sarah Jane (deceased), James Monroe (deceased), Louisa, Caroline and Anna. In 1865 the mother of these children was called away in death, and in 1866 Mr. Sheehan married Rebecca, daughter of John and Rebecca Cline, by whom he had seven children, three of whom survive, Eva, Edith Edna and Armina. Their mother died in 1888. Mr. Sheehan is a member of the Methodist Episcopal church, and has lived a good and industrious life. He has held several positions of trust and for a number of years has acted as justice of the peace.

Abraham Brandeberry was born in Columbiana county, Ohio, July 15, 1816. His father Conrad, was born in Germany, a son of Conrad Brandeberry, who in an early day emigrated from Germany and settled in Carroll county, Ohio. Conrad married Susanna Cameron, a native of Scotland, daughter of Alexander Cameron, who in an early day, settled in Carroll county. This marriage resulted in the birth of the following children: Samuel, John, Jesse, Conrad, Mary Ann, Abraham, Elizabeth and Alexander, of whom only Abraham survives. The father was a farmer by occupation, and soon after his marriage he settled in Columbiana county, Ohio. The mother's death occurred in Carroll county, Ohio, and subsequently the father removed to Iowa, where he died. Abraham Brandeberry's life has been devoted to farming. When his mother died, he was not more than ten years old, but he remained with his father till he was twenty, and at his father's second marriage, he started out in life for himself. In 1841, he was married to Elizabeth, daughter of George and Anna Mary (Harse) Eagey, both natives of Pennsylvania and of German parentage. Mrs. Brandeberry was born in Washington county, Penn., May 7, 1820. Her marriage has resulted

27

in the birth of George W. and Amelia A. In 1849 Mr. Brandeberry and family came by wagon to Allen county and settled in Madison township, where they continued till 1861, when they located in Monroeville. He and wife are life-long members of the Methodist church.

Their son George W. Brandeberry was born in Carroll county, Ohio, January 30, 1844; coming to Allen county when a child, he was reared and educated on the farm, receiving a fair common school education. He has followed farming more or less, and at present, is engaged in farming, together with the manufacture of drain tile. In early life he clerked in Monroeville, where his home has continuously been. In the spring of 1884, he became the republican candidate for trustee of Monroe township, and notwithstanding a heavy democratic majority, was elected by a substantial majority, and served one term. March 21, 1872, he wedded Lida A., daughter of John P. and Julia (Wells) Nash. She was born in Starke county, Ohio, April 28, 1847. Their only child is Nora R., born May 29, 1873. Mr. and Mrs. Brandeberry are leading spirits of their community, and enjoy a high social standing. She and daughter are members of the Methodist Episcopal church, of which Mr. Brandeberry, though not a member, is a warm friend.

James Reuille was born in France, March 25, 1845; and is a son of Joseph and Frances Reuille. The parents were born, reared, and married in France, and emigrated to Allen county, where the father has since followed farming for an occupation. James was born and reared on a farm. Though but a youth when the civil war broke out, in June, 1862, he enlisted as a private in Company C, Seventy-fourth Indiana volunteer infantry. His first engagement was at Mumfordsville, Ky. He participated in the battle of Chickamauga and others, was with Sherman on the march to the sea, and remained in the service until the close of the war, being mustered out June 16, 1865. Returning to Allen county, he was married December 3, 1865, to Mary Louya, a native of New York, whose parents were born in France, and settled early in this country. To this union there have been born seven children. Mr. and Mrs. Reuille are members of the Roman Catholic church at Monroeville, where they have resided since 1885, prior to which date Mr. Reuille was engaged in agricultural pursuits. Mr. Reuille is an energetic and progressive citizen.

Ephraim B. Ridenour was born in Monroe township, Allen county, Ind., November 14, 1858, one of twelve children of Lewis and Esther (Brenneman) Ridenour, of German descent. The father was born in Shenandoah county, Va., July 22, 1822, son of Adam and Mary Madeline (Munch) Ridenour. Lewis was reared and educated on a farm in his native county. In 1848 he wedded Esther, daughter of Christian and Anna (Shenk) Brenneman. She was born in Rockingham county, Va., May 11, 1822. Their children are: Anna E. (deceased), Adam P., Lydia M. (deceased), Ephriam B., Catherine and Sarah. In the spring of 1851, the parents removed from Virginia to Indiana, and settled on section 33, Monroe township, Allen county. Here the father's death occurred November 20, 1879. The mother still resides on the old homestead. The father was a hardy pioneer, energetic and persevering, an esteemed citizen and a faithful friend. Ephraim B. Ridenour, the only offspring of this old settler who resides in this county, is a farmer of Monroe township. In 1884 he wedded Catharine, the daughter of John J. and Anna (Cronin) Hayes, early settlers of Allen county. They have had two children, one of whom, Evaline G., survives.

John Griffith was born in Washington county, Penn., April 30, 1835. His parents, Daniel and Jane (Morris) Griffith, were born in Wales, and married in Pennsylvania, and had two children: John and Mary A. In 1839 the mother died in Pennsylvania, and subsequently the father became a soldier in the Mexican war, and later, during the California gold fever, went there where it is supposed he died. At the death of the mother, John and his sister were taken by their maternal grandparents in Portage county, Ohio. John received a fair common school education, and in early life taught school for several years in Ohio, Michigan, Illinois and Indiana. He first came to Indiana in 1859. He taught his last school in 1866–67. In 1862 he was united in marriage with Marvilla, daughter of Thomas and Susannah Jones. She was born in Harrison county, Ohio, March 21, 1838. This marriage resulted in the birth of the following children: Morris, Addie, William and Thomas. In 1864 Mr. Griffith enlisted in Company H, Ninety-first Indiana volunteers, and on December 3, 1864, was transferred to Company F, One Hundred and Twenty-fourth Indiana volunteer infantry, and was discharged August 31, 1865, at Greensboro, N. C., by reason of the close of war. In February, 1865, on account of ill health, he was lodged in the hospital at Washington, D. C., whence he was transferred to Indianapolis in the following June. Since his return to Allen county he has been engaged in farming. He is a member of the Methodist Episcopal church and G. A. R., William H. Link post, No. 301.

Thomas Jones, father of Mrs. Griffith, was an early settler in the Maumee valley. He was born in Maryland, August 1, 1814, son of William and Catharine (Appleton) Jones, natives of Maryland. The father was of Welsh, and the mother of Dutch, descent. They had twelve children, of whom Thomas was the third. April 12, 1836, he wedded Susannah Edwards, who was born in Tuscarawas county, Ohio, June 6, 1820, daughter of John and Charlotte (Trumbo) Edwards. Her father was born in Baltimore of Scotch descent, and her mother was born near Pittsburgh, Penn., daughter of John Trumbo, of German origin, an early settler of western Pennsylvania. Thomas and Susannah Jones had eleven children, of whom the following survive: Marvilla, Rebecca E., Charlotte, Jasper W., Thomas S., Alice and Seymour H. Soon after their marriage they came to Indiana, and in October, 1841, settled on section 9, of Monroe township, in the woods. They came by wagon, requiring fourteen days to make the trip from Harrison county, Ohio. Mr. Jones was a poor man, who by hard toil, soon began to grow prosperous. He was a member of the Evangelical Lutheran church. He was a man of reserved habits, thorough, progressive and enterprising. He was an useful citizen, a faithful friend and kind and loved father. He died May 5, 1874, leaving his faithful wife who still survives and resides on the old homestead.

Charles Whittern, one of the oldest citizens of Monroe township, was born in Awling, Gloucestershire, England, April 4, 1814. His parents, George and Anna (Herbert) Whittern, were born and married in Gloucestershire, and had nine children. The father was a gardener and nurseryman, and Charles was early trained in this vocation. His advantages for gaining an education in youth were poor. He remained under the parental roof until he reached the age of eighteen years, when he started out for himself, and had various employments up to 1839, when he emigrated to America. In January, 1835, he wedded Isabella L. Beauchamp, a native of Gloucestershire. This marriage resulted in the birth of eleven children, of whom two survive. The mother was called away in death in September, 1848. Mr. Whittern and family set sail at Liverpool, purposing to land at New York, but unfortunately the vessel was wrecked off the coast of Long Island. Here they remained until the fall of 1841, when they removed to the vicinity of Cleveland, Ohio. In the spring of 1859, he settled near Monroeville, on a tract of land where he still resides. January 20, 1850, he married Lavinia (Nelson) McBride, who was born near Dublin, Ireland. Her father was of Scotch, and her mother of English, origin. She emigrated to America with her mother and brothers, and by her marriage became the mother of six children, of whom but two survive. Mr. Whittern settled on forest land near Monroeville, and has spent a long life devoted to farming, contributing much toward the improvement of the country. He owns a large tract of land in the county, and it is in good cultivation. He is a self-made man, has become prosperous, and by integrity and fidelity has gained a high position in the esteem of his fellow townsmen. He has been friendly to churches, and is of the Episcopalian faith. In politics, he has since the organization of the party, been a republican.

John M. Tryon was born in Wayne county, Ohio, August 17, 1840, a son of John and Lydia (Sadler) Tryon, he a native of New York, she of Canada. These parents were married in New York, and had eleven sons and two daughters. They were early settlers of Wayne county, Ohio, where they died. John M. was born and reared on a farm, and received a common school education and attended the Ohio Wesleyan university four months. August 11, 1862, he enlisted as a private in Company H, Sixteenth Ohio volunteer infantry, under the command of Captain A. S. McClure. He was with General Sherman in the first attack on Vicksburg, Miss., and at Chickasaw Bayou received a gunshot wound in the left hip. Here he was taken prisoner and placed in the Confederate hospital at Vicksburg. Subsequently, he was lodged at Jackson, then in Libby prison, and later was transferred to Richmond, Va., and here was exchanged May 30, 1863. He was then placed into the Union military hospital at Annapolis, where he remained until September 23, 1863, when he was discharged by reason of disability, as a non-commissioned officer. He returned to Ohio, and in the fall of 1864 settled at Monroeville, soon securing a position with the P., F. W. & C. railway company, in whose employ he has since remained. Since 1865 he has been station agent at Dixon, Ohio, where he now resides. September 22, 1864, he wedded Margaret Lawrence, by whom he had three children, all now deceased. The mother also after twenty-four years as his faithful companion, died September, 1888. Mr. Tryon was once a poor man with many obstacles before him to surmount, and much of his success was due to his worthy wife, who was much loved and respected by all who knew her. Mr. Tryon, throughout life, has been a staunch republican. On one occasion he received the republican nomination as candidate for county treasurer of Van Wert county, Ohio. He had a substantial democratic majority against him which he reduced to nineteen votes, which may well be cited as evidence of his popularity. He is a Knight Templar, and a member of the Grand Army of the Republic.

MADISON TOWNSHIP.

The rich, heavily timbered region now known by this name was not attacked by the pioneers until 1836. In that year one Browning erected a cabin on section 30, and spent his time in hunting, but soon departed. In the fall John Edwards entered a quarter of section 26, and Andrew Meek a quarter of section 36. Both were from Carroll county, Ohio, where they returned and did not live upon their land here until 1837. John Eagy, who had a family at Monmouth, Ind., began the work of clearing for Mr. Meek, and in 1838 brought his family and settled on a forty-acre tract he entered in 1836. Until 1839 the families of these three men were the only inhabitants of the township. In the fall of the latter year they were joined by Charles Peckham and family, also from Carroll county, who contributed many of the first settlers here, John Myers and Jesse Todd, Adam Robinson, and in the northern parts, David Patrick, William Hill, M. Holmes, William Runnolds, and Dawson, Tate and Clear. In this year George Eagy put up the first hewn-log house. In the spring of the following year the settlers held their first election and Andrew Meek, Milton Holmes and Jesse Myers were elected trustees; Martin W. Kemp, clerk; John Myers, treasurer; Adam Robinson, justice; Elias Hobbs, constable. Justice Robinson officiated at the marriage in the same year of Jesse Myers to Polly Meek. In 1840, there came Jacob Marquardt, a worthy man, a native of Prussia, where he married Ann E. Carpenberger. They immigrated about 1826, and lived successively in Virginia, Pennsylvania and Ohio, until 1840, when they came from Springfield, Ohio, to section 11, Madison township. He died in 1852, and his wife, in 1887. They left seven children: Louisa, Lena, Adam, Maria, Philip, Jacob and Margaret. Jabez Shaffer and family settled in 1841. This pioneer was born in Frederick county, Md., May 25, 1793, son of Andrew and Elizabeth Shaffer. Andrew Shaffer's father emigrated from Germany before the revolution, during which struggle the father sympathized with the British so strongly that he disowned his son Andrew, who fought under Gen. Wayne. The latter became a carpenter at Fredericksburg, and married Elizabeth Chambers. They settled near Canton, Ohio, and raised a family of seven children. Jabez was married in 1820, to Susannah McPherson, by whom he had the following children: Amasa, Elizabeth, John, Sarah, William, James, Jabez, Mary Ann, Lydia, Catherine, Albert and Ellen. In 1839 he visited Allen county, entered 160 acres and traded his Ohio farm for 640 acres in Madison township, and settled in 1841. He died November 7, 1849, and his wife died November 10, 1883. Their son John Shaffer, served six years as county commissioner. In 1841 the first road was located, though in a somewhat irregular manner; theretofore the settlers were compelled to take a circuitous route through the woods to Monmouth, to reach mill or market.

Other settlers about this time were: John P. Neff, Charles Jones, Samuel Davis, John Gault and Samuel Stopher. Other well known early settlers were the Hobbs's, father and seven sons, all voters. These eight votes were sufficient at times to carry the township, and as the men invariably went barefooted, it was often discussed when the snow fell early in November, whether the Hobbs family would get to the polls. In 1849 the settlement was given a postoffice at the house of John Shaffer, who was postmaster. This was known as Massillon postoffice, but after 1856 it was removed to East Liberty. The village of Massillon was laid out by Adam Robinson in 1851, and here the first store was established in that year by Wilson & Brown. The village flourished for a time, but is now a quiet hamlet, trade having removed to the neighboring towns of Monroeville and Hoagland. The plat of Centerville, a station on the Pittsburgh road, was made by Urias Mitten, proprietor, in January, 1852. The town has not since attained much importance.

In February, 1872, Stephen Emenhiser platted the village of Hoagland, a station on the G. R. & I. railroad, and an addition was made by Allen Devilbiss, in 1877. The name was given in honor of Pliny Hoagland. The first merchant was Samuel Steadman. The general merchants at present are Merriam & Son, J. L. Robinson and E. E. Jamison. D. L. Small is engaged in the manufacture of brick and tile and Houser Bros. have a saw-mill. James English was the first postmaster and S. Merriam serves at present. J. L. Smith is the physician, H. McWherter, blacksmith. The neat church of the village is owned by the Baptists but is also used by the Methodists, Presbyterians and Church of God. The population in 1880 was ninety-nine.

The Madison Township Agricultural and Horticultural society was organized in the summer of 1878, and held a fair in September. The officers were N. P. Brown, president; John Shaffer, secretary; John H. Brown, treasurer. Christian Yonce was the next president. Forty acres of land was purchased near the village of Massillon, and good fairs were held for a few years, but the association was finally given up.

John Driver, one of the earliest settlers of Allen county, was born in Pennsylvania in 1783, of English descent. He was married in Ohio to Elizabeth Travis, who was born in Kentucky in 1790, and they had the following children: Jane, Samuel, Diana, Eliza, Caroline, David and Charles (twins), Lucinda, George R. and William. John Driver was a gallant soldier in the war of 1812, and for his service in that struggle received a warrant to land in this county. He came to this county soon after the war and settled in Adams township, and lived in the county until 1865, when he was called away in death. He was in politics a staunch republican, as are all his descendants. He was among the early fur traders of Allen county, and was a silversmith by trade and did much work for the Indians. He was a hardy pioneer whose history is of more than usual interest. Besides his own military services, he sent four sons to the war of the rebellion, one of whom was killed at Camp Nevin, Ky. John Driver was a kind father and good citizen, and lived a long and useful life. His son, David D. Driver, was born in Miami county, Ind., February 10, 1830. He has devoted his life to farming, in which he has been successful. He was married in 1852, to Elizabeth Jones, who was born in Hancock county, Ohio. They have the following children: Oscar, Lewis, Florence, John, Ulysses and Orpha. October 14, 1864, Mr. Driver enlisted as a private in Company F, One Hundred and Forty-second Indiana volunteer infantry. He served at Nashville, Tenn., where he was discharged July 14, 1865. He is a representative citizen, enterprising and respected.

Jonathan L. Robinson, a merchant at Hoagland, was born in Madison township, Allen county, August 12, 1855. His father, Joseph Lewis Robinson, was born in Carroll county, Ohio. He came to this county in 1838, and settled in Madison township, where he farmed until 1881, when he went into mercantile pursuits at Hoagland. His death occurred in October, 1884. He was a prominent old settler, enjoyed the esteem of a wide acquaintance; was a zealous member of the Methodist Episcopal Church; and a Master Mason. The mother, whose maiden name was Catherine Roudebush, survives, and is now a resident of Hoagland, and is a member of the Methodist Episcopal church. Of their seven children, five survive. Jonathan L. was reared on a farm and received a common school education. He was married in 1885, to Eddie M., daughter of Joseph and Caroline (Frick) Smith. She was born in Mercer county, Ohio, and is the mother of three children, one deceased. Mr. Robinson went into business in Hoagland in the fall of 1884, and carries on a prosperous trade in general merchandise.

Philip J. Neff was born March 27, 1845, on section 20, Madison township. His father, John P. Neff, a native of Hesse-Darmstadt, Germany, born October 13, 1813, came to America in 1834 and settled on the home farm of 220 acres. He was truly a pioneer. He died February 27, 1887. The mother's maiden name was Elizabeth Keizer.

She was born in Germany, July 29, 1808, came to America, July 1, 1838, and died November 22, 1881, on the home farm. Her parents were natives of Germany; the father born June 15, 1780, the mother August 8, 1778. They died very nearly at the same time, the mother September 6, and the father September 8, 1846. The father was a vineyard man. He started to America July 29, 1840, and landed in New York, September 25, being thirty-five days on the ocean. He came by canal to Toledo, then by wagon to Fort Wayne. He purchased a farm of eighty acres, six miles southeast of Fort Wayne. The names of the mother's five sisters are: Catherine, Barbara, Elizabeth, Christina and Sibylla. Philip J. Neff is a farmer by occupation and a successful one, as his surroundings abundantly testify. He is one of three heirs to the 220-acre farm upon which he resides. A substantial new barn occupies the place of the one destroyed by fire May 21, 1887, at a loss of $4,000. Mr. Neff served the public as constable for nine years, and trustee for two years. He has never married. He is a member of the German Lutheran church.

S. H. Crozier was born in Perry county, Penn., July 27, 1827. His parents, Samuel I. and Mary Ann (Loehr) Crozier, were natives of Pennsylvania. He was of Irish, and she of German, origin. They were married in Pennsylvania and unto them were born the following children: Joseph, Hannah, Mary, Margaret, James, S. Henry, Frederick, Amelia, Robert and Linsey. The parents came to Allen county in 1844, and settled in Marion township in the woods. In 1855 Mrs. Crozier died, and subsequently Mr. Crozier made a few changes of his place of abode, in 1867 making his home with his son S. H., with whom he remained till 1872, when he died. He was a blacksmith by trade. He was first a democrat in politics, later a whig, and died a republican. S. H. Crozier was reared and educated in the country. In 1853 he was married to Mary Jane, daughter of Jedediah and Jane Lewis (Grant) Halladay, natives of New York, he of Scotch-Irish, and she of French-Welsh, descent. Their children are: Hannah B., John Grant, Ellinor B., Mary Jane and Vincent G. Mr. and Mrs. Halladay came to Allen county in 1834, and first settled near Fort Wayne. She died in 1836, and he in 1846, in Wisconsin. He was a trapper and fur dealer. Our subject's wife was born in Dearborn county, Ind., June 3, 1832. Mr. and Mrs. Crozier's marriage has resulted in the birth of the following children: Alice (deceased), Stephen A., Florence A. (deceased), Viola M. (deceased), Martha A., James E., Mary Jane and Henry A., (deceased). Mr. and Mrs. Crozier first made their home in Madison township in 1858. His life has been devoted to farming. He and wife are members of the Protestant Methodist church. In 1864 he enlisted in Company F, One Hundred and Forty-second Indiana volunteer infantry, and was mustered out in July of 1865.

Frederick W. Franke was born in the kingdom of Prussia, December 6, 1841. His parents, Henry and Mary (Berg) Franke, were born in Prussia, the father in 1811, and the mother in 1817. They were married in Germany, and in May, 1845, set sail from Bremen, and in July landed at New York. In August they reached Fort Wayne and within two weeks settled in Madison township, section 20, purchasing forty acres of land and constructing a log cabin. The father died December 24, 1879. He was a member of the German Lutheran church; was industrious, honest and enterprising and by hard toil at the time of death owned 300 acres of land. His wife survives on the old homestead. She is a member of the German Lutheran church and is highly respected. To them were born: Frederick William, Frederick, Wilhelmina (deceased), Mary, Henry, Johanna, Charles, August and Herman. Frederick William was born in Germany but was brought to America when a child. In early life he learned the carpenter's trade, which he followed for ten years. The rest of his life has been spent in farming, in which he has been successful. In 1873 he was married to Karoline, daughter of Christian and Wilhelmina Meyer, natives of Germany, and early settlers of Allen county. Mrs. Franke was born in Madison township, December 10, 1850. The children of this marriage are: Wilhelmina, Mary, Frederick, Eliza, William and Karoline. Mr. and Mrs. Franke are members of the German Lutheran church. He is one of the leading citizens of Madison township and enjoys the high esteem of his fellow townsmen, who elected him trustee in 1888.

Eli Todd, an old and respected citizen of Madison township, was born in Fairfield county, Ohio, October 1, 1827, son of John Todd, a native of Maryland, of English descent, who married Mary Patterson, a lady of Scotch descent. In an early day they settled in Fairfield county, Ohio. Unto their marriage the following children were born: William (deceased), Rachel, Mary (deceased), John, Nancy (deceased), Eli, Elizabeth (deceased), Eliza (deceased), Thomas, Asbury and Sarah. In 1859, at the age of sixty-three years, the father died at his home in Hancock county, Ohio, where his wife died in 1861, at the age of sixty years. Eli Todd spent his early life mainly in Franklin county, Ohio. In the fall of 1848, he came to Allen county, and purchased for $270 a tract of eighty acres in Marion township. He was married May 1, 1851, to Mary Harrod, who was born in Knox county, Ohio, January 28, 1834. She came to this county in the fall of 1849, with her parents, William and Rhoda (Pipes) Harrod, who settled in Marion township. Thirteen children have been born to this marriage, of whom eight are living: William J., Clara L., Mills H., Phillip E., Delilah May, Anna, Lucy and Laura J. Mr. Todd, in 1852, located in Van Wert county, Ohio, but in 1863 returned and settled in Madison township. His life has been devoted to farming and stock-raising, together with trading in live-stock. He has won a comfortable home and a respected station in life. He and wife are members of the Methodist Protestant church. He is a prominent republican, being one of the first in that party. He has held the offices of assessor and justice of the peace, and is a leading citizen. Since 1858 he has been a member of the I. O. O. F., now of Flat Rock lodge, No. 444, of Maples.

William H. Bauserman, of Madison township, was born in Portage county, Ohio, February 15, 1847, son of Henry and Leah (Swarts) Bauserman. The father was born in Shenandoah county, Va., in 1817, son of Jacob Bauserman, a native of Virginia, of German descent. The mother was born in Pennsylvania, daughter of George Swarts, of German descent. To the marriage of Henry and Leah Bauserman were born the following children: Benjamin F. (deceased), Sarah (deceased), William H., Mary L., George, Ida E. (deceased), Nancy J. (deceased), and Flora H. (deceased). In the fall of 1850 the parents removed to Allen county, and settled in Monroe township, where they still reside. They are members of the Methodist Episcopal church and enjoy a high social standing. Their son, William H., remained under the parental roof until twenty-five years old, and March 28, 1872, was married to Hettie, daughter of Charles and Elizabeth (Klopfenstein) Noyer. Mrs. Bauserman was born in Merrill county, Ohio, January 10, 1854. To her marriage have been born the following children: Iola G., Iron R., Irene (deceased), Bertha, William, George, James, Cleveland and Ethel. Soon after marriage Mr. Bauserman settled down in Monroeville, and was for twelve years engaged in the saw-mill business. For the last four years he has devoted his time to farming. In 1880 he settled in Madison township, where he has since resided. He and wife are members of the Evangelical Lutheran church. For five years he has creditably filled the office of justice of the peace. He has a well improved farm of thirty acres.

Frederick Grodrian was born in Brunswick, Germany, December 7, 1807. At the age of three years he became an orphan, and was made the ward of a paternal uncle, who fostered him to manhood. He was taught the shoemaker's trade, and at the age of nineteen years became a journeyman. At twenty-one he became a soldier in the German army, and remained the full term required by law. On returning to his birth-place he was, July 5, 1835, married to Wilhelmina Herrl, a native of Brunswick, born August 8, 1812. They had six children: Frederick (deceased), Charles, August W., Wilhelmina, William and Frederika (deceased). Soon after marriage the parents located in Ottenstein, Germany, and there lived till 1854, when they emigrated, landing at New York, June 22; coming to Fort Wayne, they settled at Maples. Here the father resumed work at his trade, but in 1856 he purchased a tract of land in Madison township on which he thereafter resided. He died February 13, 1863, and his wife survived until July 7, 1869. They were members of the German Lutheran church, and universally respected.

Charles Grodrian, son of the above, was born in Brunswick, Germany, February 1, 1839. He was reared and educated on the farm, and has devoted his life to farming and stock-raising. April 7, 1863, he married Henrietta, daughter of Frederick and Sophia Gable, natives of Prussia, who emigrated with their family to America in 1846. She was born in Prussia, January 28, 1844. Mr. and Mrs. Grodrian have the following children: Wilhelmina, Caroline (deceased), Charles, Nettie, Fred, Frank, Daniel, Herman (deceased), and Clara. Mr. Grodrian is a prosperous farmer and he and wife are members of the German Lutheran church.

August W. Grodrian, a prominent farmer and stock-raiser of Madison township, was born in Brunswick, Germany, December 20, 1841, son of Frederick Grodrian above mentioned. August was reared and educated on the farm. Soon after reaching his majority he was married to Mary Maples, who lived but a short time as his companion. April 18, 1867, he wedded Rachel, daughter of Robert and Mary (Gowen) Mooney, early settlers of Allen county. Mrs. Grodrian was born in Jackson township, September 9, 1849. To them have been born: William, Lewis, Mary, Clara, Charles, Eddie, August, George and John. Mr. Grodrian is a representative citizen, and cultivates a well-improved farm of 160 acres. He and wife are members of the Methodist Protestant church.

William Grodrian was born in Brunswick, Germany, April 2, 1848, son of Frederick Grodrian above mentioned. He remained at the parental home till 1863, at which date he secured a position with the Pennsylvania railway company, in whose employ he remained for eight years thereafter. June 16, 1870, he was united in marriage with Mary, daughter of Henry and Mary (Berg) Franke, early settlers of Allen county. She was born in Madison township, January 10, 1847. To this union have been born the following children: Mary, Emma, Karoline, Henry, William, Martin, Bertha and Amanda. Soon after marriage Mr. Grodrian settled on his present homestead in Madison township, and has since followed farming for an occupation. He is an industrious and progressive man. He and wife are members of the German Lutheran church.

Martin E. Argo, a prominent citizen of Allen county, was born at West Middleburg, Logan Co., Ohio, February 16, 1837. His parents, John and Sarah (McDonald) Argo, were natives of Washington county, Penn. John Argo was the son of Smith Argo, a native of Alsace, then in the French territory, who immigrated to Pennsylvania in an early day, and there married Catherine Pfeiffer, a native of Alsace. They had four sons and five daughters. John Argo and wife removed in 1834 from Washington county, Penn., to Logan county, Ohio, and in February, 1855, they came to Monroeville, which was their residence until their deaths, he passing away in 1862, she in 1863. To them were born four sons and four daughters. Martin E. Argo was reared on a farm, and after coming to this county in October, 1855, he attended the Methodist college and received a liberal education, which enabled him to teach several terms of school in the county. Subsequently, he engaged in the manufacture of oil barrel cooperage at Monroeville, for the Pittsburgh market, at which he was occupied for eleven years. In October, 1878, Mr. Argo was elected auditor of Allen county, a responsible position which he filled with credit until 1883. Previous to his election, in 1865, he had removed to a farm within Madison township, and on his return from Fort Wayne this again became, and is now, his residence. Mr. Argo is a sturdy democrat in politics; in church life he is a member of the Christian body, to which he has belonged for thirty-five years. He was the first master Mason of his township, and is a royal arch Mason and Knight Templar. Previous to his election as auditor he held the office of township trustee for several terms, and in all the positions he has occupied he has won the confidence and admiration of his fellow men. Mr. Argo was married November 28, 1861, to Amanda E., daughter of Hon. Joseph R. Tidball, of Carroll county, Ohio, and they had one daughter, Adella, since deceased. This wife died November 22, 1865, and he was married April 16, 1868, to Marietta, daughter of Hon. Nelson McLain, who is mentioned in the account of the settlement of Marion township. By this marriage Mr. Argo has three children: Zuella, Marietta and Martin Nelson.

George Brouwer, sr., was born in Olsefriesland, Germany, March 2, 1811, and was reared and educated in a German village. His father was a school teacher by profession. In early life George left his native country and landed at New York, and about 1838, came to Allen county, where he has since resided. In 1840 he was married to Phœbe Fry, who was born in Germany in 1823, and came to this country with her parents about 1839. They have had the following children: Mary (deceased), George, Jacob (deceased), Martin, Henry, Mary, Lizzie, and Wilhelmina (deceased). Mr. Brouwer and wife now reside in Madison township, where they have lived since 1856. He has followed farming for an occupation, and his life has been characterized by hard trials and perseverance. For over fifty years he has resided in Allen county, and has been identified with the growth and development of the country. He and wife are members of the German Lutheran church. By industry he came to own 440 acres of land, 200 of which he still holds. George, the oldest living child, was born in Marion township, June 21, 1843, and was raised on the farm. He remained with his parents till December 6, 1867, when he was married to Emma McIntosh, and settled down as a farmer. Mrs. Brouwer was born in Philadelphia, Penn., November 5, 1847, daughter of Benjamin McIntosh, an early settler of Allen county. Mr. and Mrs. Brouwer's children are: Anna Phœbe (a school teacher and graduate of the Fort Wayne high school), Mary Elizabeth, Alexander Henry and Sarah. Mr. Brouwer and wife are members of the Protestant Methodist church; their daughter Annie is a member of the same church, and as a teacher is regarded as very able.

Fred L. Gable (Göbel) was born in Prussia, January 8, 1846. His parents, Frederick and Sophia (Koenbau) Gable, were natives of Prussia, and there they were married. They had the following children: Sophia (deceased), Jacob, Harriet, Frederick L., Caroline and Daniel. In 1846 the family emigrated to America and first settled at Philadelphia, where they remained till 1859, when they settled in Madison township and took up farming for a livelihood. Two years later the parents located in Jefferson township, where they remained till their deaths occurred. The mother died June 28, 1886, aged seventy-two years, and the father June 28, 1887, aged seventy-three years. They are buried in St. John's cemetery, Madison township. Fred L., the fourth of their children, has devoted his life to farming, in which he has been successful. He began with no capital, but has prospered and now owns a well improved farm of eighty acres in Madison township, where he resides. In 1870 he married Annie, daughter of Robert and Mary Mooney, early settlers of Allen county. She was born in Jackson township, March 15, 1848. They have the following children: Jacob H., Frederick D., Bertha M., Alice L. (deceased), Frank A. and Mary S. Mr. and Mrs. Gable are members of the Protestant Methodist church. He is an enterprising citizen, and enjoys the esteem of his fellow townsmen.

Joseph Somers, of Madison, is the son of Andrew Somers, who emigrated to Allen county from Page county, Va., in 1840. He was a native of Virginia, of German descent. Andrew Somers was married in 1845 to Rebecca Lipes, who came from Virginia in 1834, and settled in Marion township. Their union was blessed with six boys and one girl, two of whom are living: Joseph and Julia. Mrs. Rebecca Somers died in 1858. and Mr. Somers married Maria McKissick in 1860, who died in March, 1879. About two years after he married Rhoda Smith. Soon after his marriage, Mr. Somers was taken sick, and after an illness of about a month, died on the 7th of February, 1881. His last wife is still living, and is now a resident of Ohio. Julia, sister of Joseph, married J. W. Surfus, in April, 1871, and resides in Whitley county. Joseph Somers was born December 3, 1848, in Marion township. At the age of eighteen he began teaching school and continued for nine years. He was married to Addie Frances Small, April 15, 1871, and they settled at Middletown. Mr. Somers entered the mercantile business in the spring of 1883, at Hoagland, and conducted a successful business for nearly three years. He then moved on a farm near the village, where he now resides. Mr. and Mrs. Somers have one child: Herbert Lee, born January 25, 1874. In politics, Mr. Somers is a republican, and has been the candidate of his party for the office of trustee. He owns a valuable farm in Madison township of ninety-seven and one-half acres, on what is known as the Wayne trace. Mrs. Somers is a member of the Methodist Episcopal church of Hoagland.

Samuel Hauk, of Madison township, is one of the children of Philip Hauk, who was born in Lancaster county, Penn. After the death of the father of the latter, the widow and children removed to Ohio, where Philip was married to Elizabeth Mock in Stark county, about 1830. While living near Massillon they raised a family of three daughters and two sons; one child was born in Indiana. Philip was a cooper by trade, and was so occupied in Ohio until 1852, when he went to Allen county, settling on a farm in Madison township. He died December 19, 1887, at the age of seventy-five years. Of his children, Rachel died in Ohio; Fanny, who married Peter Gresley; Sarah, who married S. B. Scott, and Elisha, live in Madison township; Mary Elizabeth is deceased. Samuel Hauk was married December 15, 1874, to .Della B., daughter of John M. Smith, of Madison township. They have had six children, of whom the first died. There are living: Amos E., Lewis J., Charles, Rolly, and an infant son. Mr. Hauk lives upon the farm which his father settled upon when coming from Ohio, one mile from the old Wayne trace. This tract the father purchased from the government. Mr. Hauk is a republican in politics, and has been honored by the nomination for township trustee, and made a creditable race against the adverse majority. He, like his father, is a member of the Lutheran church, and is in all respects a worthy citizen, honored and respected by the community.

Charles Houser was born October 24, 1843, the son of Lewis and Theresa (Berich) Houser. They were of German descent, and emigrated to America near the year 1835, first settling in Detroit, Mich., where they resided but for a short time, then removing to Fort Wayne near the year 1840. He was a farmer by occupation, and purchased a farm near Fort Wayne, which he afterward sold and purchased another in Madison township. Subsequently he removed to Wayne township, where he engaged in the dairy business and continued the same until his death, which occurred there August 31, 1863. There are in the family five children: Elizabeth, Henry, Caroline, Joseph and Charles, all of whom are living. Charles, the youngest, spent the earlier part of his life with his father, but at eighteen years of age he began working for N. G. Olds & Sons, of Fort Wayne, in the wheel works, and for twenty-one years, lacking one month, remained with that firm. For twelve years he was foreman of the finishing department. Afterward he engaged in the manufacture of wagon material. He has for the past five years engaged in the business named, in the village of Hoagland, with his brother Joseph as a partner. Charles Houser was married in 1864 to Nancy Augusta, daughter of George Washington and Laura Elizabeth (Strong) Babcock. The father of this family was born in Ohio, May 9, 1823, and both his grandfathers, George Babcock and Luther Reeves, were passengers on the Mayflower. One of them, George Babcock, settled in Connecticut, and during the revolutionary war served until its close, when he took command of a whale ship and was killed off the coast of Newfoundland. The other, Luther Reeves, served on the staff of George Washington during the war, and at its close removed with about fifty others to Ohio, but subsequently removed to DeKalb county, Ind., when the county was new. He was one of the first white people to settle thére. There was in the family of which Mrs. Houser's father was a member, nine children. The oldest of the family and the father of Mrs. Houser, removed to De Kalb county Ind., in 1832. Here he spent the earlier part of his life, his father's death leaving him with the responsibility of providing for the family. They resided in that county until November, 1839, when they removed to Fort Wayne, where the mother died. Mr. Babcock was married in 1846 in Hicksville, Ohio. He first settled in DeKalb county, where one child was born. They subsequently removed to Fort Wayne, where he followed the occupation of a carpenter. There were born to them while in Fort Wayne, one child which died with the cholera. He afterward moved back to DeKalb county, and engaged in the mercantile business. To them were born these children: Nancy Augusta, Harriet, Stephen Sylvester, William Henry, Augustus Sheldon; all but William and Harriet are living. Mrs. Babcock died near the year 1872. The father is at present living in Lima, Ohio, at the age of sixty-six years. After a successful business career he lost nearly all his property through the failure of banks with which he did business. To Mr. and Mrs. Houser were born four children: an infant daughter (deceased), Laura Alice, George Lewis (deceased), and Leola Franceska. Laura Alice was married to James Votrie, by whom she has one child: Jessie Lawrence. Leola Franceska was married to Warren Smitley, and they have one child: Irma Lisle. Mr. and Mrs. Houser are members of the Catholic church St. Rose of Lima. Mr. Houser has been a very successful business man and has made for himself a comfortable and commodious home. He is a democrat in politics and a worthy and respected citizen of the county.

MARION TOWNSHIP.

The rich land within the present limits of Marion township was reached easily in the earliest days, by coming down the St. Mary's river, or by the Wayne trace, and later the Winchester road was the route of those who came "from Willshire down." The first genuine settler was Philo Whitcomb, who occupied forty acres in 1830. Previous to this time a Mr. Douglas rented land owned by Hugh Barnett, of Fort Wayne, and occupied it during 1825. He was succeeded as a tenant by Elisha Harris, who for his shrewdness was known as "Yankee" Harris. He is remembered as the planter of the first orchard in 1830. Mr. Whitcomb proved to be an invaluable citizen, energetic and industrious, and was a leader in his day. He was the first postmaster at Root postoffice, established in 1831, and built the first frame house in 1839. He died in 1842. Heretofore the only road was the trace cut by Gen. Wayne, but in 1830 the Piqua state road was surveyed by Benjamin Lytle, and made in the primitive way, the trees being permitted to lie on either side, to dam up the water which fell, and as the region was marshy, the line of the road was mainly used as a guide through the adjacent dryer ground until it was improved in 1850. On this road, in section 5, Mrs. Mezena Merriman settled with her family in 1830, her husband having died at the Adams county settlement. With the help of her sons she succeeded as well as the sturdier pioneers. In 1833 several new-comers arrived. One, Jesse Heaton, sr., a native of Connecticut, had served in the war of 1812, and had come to Dearborn county in 1818. He lived for many years on section 27. Henry Snider, who settled on the west side of the St. Mary's, was known as "Hunting Henry," but in spite of that cognomen, was an industrious and enterprising man. Michael Spitler, from Preble county, Ohio, settled on section 35, but died in 1834, from exposure while hunting deer. Samuel and Moses Beckner and George Hopple were other 1833 settlers, but were not permanent In 1834 Jared Morton, of Virginia, entered land, and added to his possessions until he had 217 acres of bottom land on the St. Mary's, but he died in 1836, leaving a wife and son George A., whose children own the old farm. Thomas Thompson, an Englishman, came from near Baltimore, about 1834, and entered 100 acres near the Piqua road. The next year he rode horse-back to Piqua, and married Elizabeth Speiser, who returned with him by the same conveyance. His father and four others of the children of the latter were in this settlement, and the descendants of that family are now prominent citizens.

August 4, 1834, John Herber and wife Margaret and family, settled near the Nine Mile house, having just come from Germany. He died in 1867 and his wife in 1876, and only one child survives, John Herber, who was born in Hesse, Germany, in 1820. At the same time came John Hake, hereafter noticed, and the four Sorg brothers, and all made a settlement in the neighborhood now known as Hessen Cassel and its vicinity. A later settler here was John Felger, in 1836. Christopher Lipes and family came in 1834. His son, D. D., after living in the township over half a century, now resides in Fort Wayne. In 1836, Aden Brunson, who was a tenant in Wayne township from 1833 to 1836, came here, and began the clearing of a fine farm of 132 acres. In 1836 there settled Nelson McLain, a native of Muskingum county, Ohio. He assisted in organizing the township, and was a member of the board at the first election, when only nine votes were polled in the township. He followed surveying for several years, and was for seven years postmaster at Middletown. In 1840 he was elected justice of the peace, and in 1845 was appointed county commissioner. On the resignation of George Johnston he was appointed probate judge by the governor, and to this position was elected in 1850. In 1855 he was appointed swamp land commissioner, and in 1859 he served as a member of the state house of representatives. In the fall of 1838, Joseph Small, of Maine, who had been a sailor for fifteen years, then a pioneer near Cincinnati and Cleveland, settled here and became one of the well-to-do people. After 1836 the settlement was more rapid. Jacob Fry and family came in 1839. Notable among those who came prior to 1840 were Henry Drage, Joseph C. Wells, Isaac Harrod, Joseph Hall, William Ward, and Daniel Whitaker. George Doctor, now a leading farmer, settled in 1840. Soon after the arrival of the Thompson family, the father died, the first loss by death in the settlement, and this was soon followed

Yours Truly
B. O'Connor

by the decease of Martha Thompson and Jane Merriman. Old settlers remember, however, that there had been a death within the township previous to this. In the winter of 1827, William McConnaughey, who had been working at Fort Wayne, undertook to go to Ohio on foot. On the next day the Indians brought in word that a man was frozen to death on the road, and the crowd that went out found McConnaughey's body stiff in death. He was buried in the northwest part of section 35. In 1843 the first marriage among the settlers occurred, Elizabeth, the daughter of Philo Whitcomb, to William Cain. On the Piqua road in 1832, there was established a store in a log building south of the site of Hessen Cassel, by Hiram Mooney. In 1839 Miller & King opened a store at the site of the Nine Mile house, and prospered. They also conducted the primitive tavern which had been established by John Karn in 1837. This was subsequently sold to John Trentman, who rented to John Holmes, and the latter built the Nine Mile house in 1850, which is still open to the public. Root postoffice was established in 1831, and Philo Whitcomb distributed the mail for four years, when he was succeeded by Judge McLain. The office appertained to the residence of the postmaster until removed to Middletown by Hiram Barber. The stage coach first made its appearance in 1851. In 1840, a saw-mill, to which was added buhrs for grinding grain, was built by John Depler, at the site of Williamsport. It was subsequently purchased by Charles Muldoon, who built a good grist-mill and conducted it until 1868 or 1869, when it was burned down, and was succeeded by a mill on the other side of the river, built by Morris Cody. For four years the dam has been out and the mill unused. In the year that milling begun here, the citizens cut a road from the mill to the Ohio line, through Massillon. Before the railroad era there was as much expected in the way of development of towns, from the opening of plank roads, as is now anticipated as a result of the laying of the iron railway. In 1850 it was decided to make the Piqua road a plank road and a stage route, and a saw-mill was put up on the land of Louis Lopshire for the manufacture of the needed lumber. He at once prepared for the founding of a town here, and in April, 1851, the town of Middletown was duly platted. William Moody opened a grocery and Benoni McLain a dry goods store, and all the traders and mechanics necessary to a town appeared, but in a few years the railroad came and passed by Middletown, and only a few cabins remain as relics. Its nearest successor is Williamsport, laid out in 1874, on section 29, by William Essig, the proprietor of the site. It is a quiet village, picturesquely situated on the St. Mary's river. Near by a saw-mill is conducted by James Garden, and two general stores are in operation, owned by John Brown and Mrs. McCormick. Many years ago a plat was made of a town that was expected to flourish under the name of Jericho, in this township. The projectors were Benjamin Nickerson and David Hoover. The village never developed.

In 1837, Mrs. Parker taught the first school in the township, in a log cabin, on the land later occupied by John Small's brick yard. She had enjoyed the advantages of a fine education in New York, and opened, in the wilderness, a school of real excellence.

In the winter of 1840, Judge McLain converted the front room of his house into a school-room, and about a dozen scholars came to him for instruction. His school, too, was of a superior order, and like its predecessor, was a subscription school.

The first school-house was erected in the fall of 1841, near the present site of Middletown. Nelson Parker was employed as teacher, and the school was kept up by private subscription during four winter seasons.

In 1845, a hewn-log school-house was erected on the farm of Judge McLain, and was the initiatory step in the system of free schools. For its maintenance, the trustees appropriated the congressional funds belonging to the township, and the residents contributed a sufficient amount to make up all deficiencies. The first teacher was William W. Smith, who received $25 for three months' service. The school had pupils from all over the township, and was held in a log cabin erected by private subscription, on the Piqua road opposite the old Wells house. His father, Thomas Smith, came to Indiana in 1837. The first district school-house was erected in 1853, under the supervision of Judge Vaughn, then trustee of the township.

John Hake (deceased), was one of the pioneers of the upper Maumee valley, and his history is typical of those of the noble forerunners of the present civilization. Born in Prussia in 1807, he emigrated in 1832, and after reaching New York worked in a sugar factory for four years. He then removed to Fort Wayne and began working on the canal. He purchased the land upon which his widow now resides in 1834, and then visited his two brothers at New Orleans, returning soon afterward to clear his farm. He was married in 1837 to Gertrude Neireiter. Her parents, George and Elizabeth Neireiter, had a family of six children. They emigrated to America in April, 1834, and from Detroit came to Fort Wayne with teams, arrriving July 18, 1834, and settled in Marion township. They came in company with the Sorgs and Harbers. They are both now deceased, and the children living are: Gertrude, Caspar, Henry, John, John Allen and Hartman. Mr. and Mrs. Hake began house-keeping in a rude log cabin chinked with clay, at a place so remote from water that the mother frequently had to carry it from the Small farm, three miles away, through the dense woods, finding her path by a blaze. Their toil and hardship was of a degree difficult to comprehend at this day, but they were rewarded by the development of one of the finest farms of the township, and they were blessed with twelve children. Nine of these are living: John, Peter, Catherine, Frank, Jacob, Mary, Henry, George, Gertrude, and are married and live in the township except two, who reside in Illinois. Mr. Hake lived to see his family in comfortable circumstances, and died May 7, 1888, after an illness of four months. He was a member of the Catholic church, and a worthy and respected citizen. His widow survives, strong and healthy at the age of seventy-one years.

Henry Hake, son of the above, resides upon the homestead, his mother making her home with him, in the commodious brick dwelling which was erected in 1874, at a cost of $3,000. He was born in 1854, and was married in June, 1881, to Gertrude Kleber, whose parents were residents of Marion township. They have four children, John Joseph, Mary K., George Otto, and Mary Clara. He owns a valuable farm of 120 acres, and is one of the leading citizens of the township. He and wife are members of St. Joseph Catholic church.

Jacob Hake, son of the pioneers, was born December, 1850. He lived with his parents until about twenty-three years of age, when he began a three years' apprenticeship at the carpenter's trade. Since then he has devoted himself to agriculture. He was married November 9, 1876, to Catherine Kallmeyer, whose parents were of Allen county, formerly of Adams county. They have six children, John Thomas, Catherine Mary, Regina, Clemens Romanius, Henry Barney, George Edward and Clara Gertrude. Mr. Hake owns a valuable farm of 120 acres adjacent to the old Wayne trace. He and wife are members of St. Joseph Catholic church.

George Hake, the youngest son of John and Gertrude, was born April 21, 1859. After working with his parents until his twenty-fifth year he was given by them the farm of 120 acres now owned by him, forty of which is under cultivation. He was married in November, 1884, to Elizabeth Wyss, of this township, and they have a comfortable home place, with commodious frame residence and a large bank barn. They have adopted a daughter. Mr. and Mrs. Hake are members of St. Joseph Catholic church.

Charles W. Berning, a prominent farmer of Marion township, was born in that township, November 30, 1850. He is the son of those worthy pioneers, Henry Christoph and Wilhelmina (Strangeman) Berning. They were married in Germany, their native land, and farmed there until they immigrated. The parents, with the oldest child, Henry, the only one born in Germany, started for America May 3, 1837, and after a perilous voyage of eleven weeks, landed. Proceeding to Toledo he secured a pirogue, and loading into it the goods and the women of the party, the men walked along the shore, while the owners of the craft poled it up the Maumee to Fort Wayne. On September 15, they settled on the feeder dam on the St. Joseph. Renting a farm, he lived there four years, and then left on account of the unhealthiness of the place, and bought 120 acres in Marion township, upon which ten acres were partially cleared and a log cabin erected. He cleared about ninety acres, and on this farm raised a family of nine children, of whom there are now living: Henry, Lisetta, Ferdinand, Charles W. and Wilhelmina. Henry and Ferdinand are residents of Adams county; Lisetta is the wife of Ferdinand Mayland, of Seward, Neb., and Wilhelmina resides with Charles W. The father died in 1882, and the mother in 1870. Upon the death of his father Charles W. came into possession of the farm, and he now lives in the handsome brick residence which was erected in

1877, at a cost of $2,500. He was married in 1880 to Sophia Schoppman, and they have four children: Louise, Ottilia, Charles D. and Frederick. Mr. Berning and family are members of St. John's Lutheran church in Adams county.

The history of the Harrod family in America dates back as far as the middle of the 17th century. Five brothers then emigrated from England, and settled in North and South Carolina. From this original stock has grown a family that is now represented in nearly every state and territory. Little is known of these five brothers, but their descendants became famous as associates of Daniel Boone in the settlement of Kentucky. James and Thomas having come from North Carolina, in 1774, began the first permanent settlement, and the first log house in Kentucky was built by James Harrod. His brother Thomas was killed by the Indians while plowing in his fields. James, as was his usual custom, started on a hunting expedition in the fall of the year, and being never heard of afterward it is supposed suffered the fate of his brother. Samuel, a brother of these, was a soldier in General Wayne's expedition against the Indians at Kekionga. His hatred for the red men knew no limit, as two of his brothers had fallen victims to their merciless cruelty. At one time being sent out as a scout in company with an orderly to find the exact location of the Indians, after traveling some distance in the direction of what is known as the Penn house, he discovered an Indian seated on a log; drawing aim, Samuel told the orderly that he had come 500 miles to shoot one Indian and that his opportunity had come. The orderly remonstrated, but to no purpose; the shot was fired and the Indian rolled off the log a corpse. To their dismay the whole camp began pursuit, and then began a race for life, but the two men succeeded in reaching the fort in safety. Samuel was brought before General Wayne, but his narration of his natural feelings toward the savages mitigated his punishment to the receipt of a canteen of whisky. Levi Harrod, another brother, left North Carolina about the beginning of the revolutionary war and settled in Pennsylvania. He was the grandfather of the family of Harrods of Allen county. There were in his family six sons: Michael, John, Levi, William, Samuel, James, all of whom raised large families and were very successful in life. William, the only one of this family who came to Indiana, was a soldier in the war of 1812, and a farmer by occupation. He was born in Greene county, Penn., but removed with his father's family to Ohio in 1809, and remained there forty years. He was married while in Pennsylvania, to Rhoda Pipes, by whom he had seven sons and seven daughters, ten of whom are living: Delilah, Elinor, Isaac, Eli, Rachel, Elizabeth, Melinda, William, Joseph, Morgan, Mills, John, Mary, Eunice. Delilah, now about eighty-one years old, is the widow of John Le Fevre, of Knox county, Ohio, by whom she had seven children. Elinor is the widow of Isaac Dillon, of Knox county, Ohio. Isaac Harrod, the oldest son of the family, was married in Ohio, to Susan Todd, and came to Indiana in 1838, and settled in section 24, Marion township, in the forest. He was a typical pioneer, hardy, industrious, and a great hunter, having killed more deer than any other man in the township. He had eight daughters, of whom three survive, Rhoda, Emily and Eunice. He died April 29, 1886. Eli Harrod settled on section 27, about 1844. He bought 40 acres of land and laid it out in town lots, founding what was once the flourishing village of Middletown, only a remnant of which remains. He was married to Lucinda Harrod, of Hamilton county, Ohio, and had fourteen children, ten of whom are living. Rachel died in infancy, Elizabeth died at the age of twenty-two years. Melinda was married to Benjamin Sweet, of Licking county, Ohio, removed to Marion township, and has had six children: William, Charles, Martha, Warren, Winfield Scott, Louisa. William and Charles enlisted at the breaking out of the rebellion, in the Eighty-eighth Indiana regiment. Charles served until the close of the war and was wounded. William was discharged on account of disabilities. Warren is a merchant of Fort Wayne; Winfield Scott is a manufacturer of brick and tile at Monroeville; Louisa died in youth; Martha is married to E. C. Smitley. William died at about eighteen years of age. Joseph Harrod came to Allen county in 1850. He was married in Knox county to Anna Ulery. Morgan Harrod came to Indiana when about eighteen years of age, in 1844. Here the people of his township elected him to the office of assessor which he held for six years, after which he was clerk for three years. In 1863 he was elected trustee and served twelve consecutive years. He was married to Belinda, daughter of Cornelius and Elizabeth Beam, and they have eleven children. Theron was married to Nellie Gardner, and resides in Michigan. Marion studied at the Methodist Episcopal college and the conservatory of music, and is engaged in musical merchandise. Charity, a teacher, married Paul Hooper, of Decatur, Ind. Clay was a student of the Methodist Episcopal college, graduated in penmanship from the normal school at Valparaiso, and is engaged in teaching. Mills was married to Mary Lipes, and resides at Williamsport; John studied at the Methodist Episcopal college, is a graduate of the Eclectic Medical college of Cincinnati, and is practicing at Payne, Ohio; Morse was married to Jessie Lipes, and resides in Marion township; Sherman, Clark, Delilah E., and Dessie B., are at home with their parents; all but the last have been students at the Methodist Episcopal college. Mills Harrod graduated at the college at Mt. Vernon, Ohio, and was given a professorship there some time; after about twelve years as a teacher, he entered the ministry of the Christian church and was for a number of years engaged in pastoral work. He is now the business manager of the publishing house of his church, located at Dayton, Ohio. He has had four children, two of whom are dead. He was in the service during the rebellion, with the rank of lieutenant. John Harrod removed in 1849, to Marion township. At the breaking out of the rebellion he enlisted in Company E, Thirtieth Indiana regiment, and served with the army of the Cumberland at the battles of Murfreesboro, Franklin, Nashville, Chattanooga and for 100 days was on the skirmish line between Chattanooga and Atlanta. He served four years and three months without a scar, but during Sheridan's expedition in Texas he was taken with rheumatism and six months after he returned home he died. Mary came to this county in 1849, and subsequently married Eli Todd, of Madison township. Eunice is a resident of Ohio.

No family living at present in Allen county can trace its American ancestry further than the Smalls of Marion township. They are among the descendants of five brothers, Joseph, Joshua, Purington, John, sr., and Taylor, who were passengers on the Mayflower, which landed at Plymouth Rock, November 9, 1620. Joseph Small, jr., the ancestor of the Smalls of Allen county, was the first child born in Old Borden, in 1778. He became a sailor, and followed the seas for thirteen years. He and wife were natives of Maine, and remained there until 1817, when they determined to emigrate to a point four miles above Cincinnati. With seven children — Louis, Maria, Mary, Delilah, Catharine, Emeline and Joseph, they traveled by team until they arrived at the river, and there embarked in a boat of their own construction. After about four years they moved to Cleveland, and Joseph Small purchased a farm in the western reserve. He was for a number of years engaged in surveying the government lands in that part of the state, and was occupied in making brick and such articles as could not be purchased at the supply stores. In 1838, with his family, he cut his way through to Allen county, and settled on section 23. Mr. Small, with the help of his sons, helped to cut the first roads in the township. The wife of this pioneer was Margaret Duncan, whose father was a Scotchman. He was pressed into the British service soon after emigrating to this country, but deserted and went to the mountains of Maine, where he was married and lived and died. Mr. and Mrs. Small raised a family of thirteen children, all but two of whom lived to maturity. Louis, the oldest of the family, died about 1840, leaving a large family, some of whom are living in Michigan and some in Iowa. Maria was married to Lorenzo Holly, and they died in Michigan. Mary Small was married to Riley Hance. She spent her last years at Hoagland, and died in 1886. Fidelia first married Silas Terry, then William Coverdale, and lived and died in Indiana. Catharine Small married Miles Banker, and lived for some time in New Haven. Joseph Small died at the age of twenty-five. Robert Small, one of the oldest settlers of Marion township, was born June 25, 1819, near Cincinnati. He was married October 2, 1841, to Almira Whitcomb, a second cousin of Gov. Whitcomb. Her parents were natives of Greene county, N. Y. They had eleven children, as follows: Elizabeth Whitcomb, born in 1817, was the first bride in the township, in 1843. Her husband, William Cain, died from injuries received from a team he was driving. She is still living in Denver, Col., at seventy-one years of age. Lucinda Whitcomb was married to John Small. Lewis Whitcomb was married in 1844 to Margaret Ann Meach, and had four children. Orin Whitcomb married

Fidelia Hance, both of whom are dead. Jane Whitcomb is living in Michigan, the widow of Joseph Roe. Hiram Whitcomb married Maria Hance, and resides in Wayne county, Mich. Harriet Whitcomb married Jacob Mercer. Martha Whitcomb was married to Benjamin Emerick, and resides in Nebraska. Edward Whitcomb was married to Margaret O'Harra, and is now dead. Almira married Robert Small. Martha Jane married Emory Brown, and had five children: Hiram, Charley, Emma, Warren and Eva, before she died February 13, 1870. Maria, Robert, jr., Albert and Harriet Small died in infancy. Mary A. Small, born March 15, 1850, was married to John M. Brown, March 14, 1865, and has four children. Mr. Brown is the leading merchant of Williamsport. Nellie Small, born April 10, 1852, was married to Calvin Lipes August 9, 1873, and has two children, Robert B. and Elsie Idella, who reside in Fort Wayne; John E. Small, of Fort Wayne, born October 28, 1854, was married to Clara Lipes June 12, 1879, and has three girls: Bessie, Innis, Lida Bell. D. L. Small, born January 7, 1857, was married to Nettie McCague December 3, 1881, and has one child living, Grace. He is at present living at Hoagland, and is engaged in the brick and tile business. Lucinda E. Small was born September 25, 1860, and was married February 15, 1880, to David M. Fonner, who was born on the 26th of February, 1858. His parents, natives of Pennsylvania, were residents of Adams county, but in 1861 settled in Marion township, where the mother still resides, the father having died June 21, 1888. After marriage Mr. Founer removed to Adams county, near Pleasant Mills, where he bought forty acres of land, and cleared a portion. About two years and a half later, he removed to Hoagland, and then to his present place of residence in Marion township. Franklin Small was born July 24, 1865; married March 19, 1888, to Ella Reed. Marion F. Small was born November 11, 1858, the third son of Robert and Almira; at twenty-two years of age, he engaged in the brick business, having learned the trade with his father, near Decatur. He removed to Hoagland, February 14, 1884, and went into business with Thomas Devilbiss, with a general stock of the value of $3,000. Three months later Devilbiss sold to Joseph Somers, who remained a partner about three years, and then sold to Ed. Merriam. March 17, 1888, Mr. Small disposed of his interest, to Mr. Merriam, then opened a store at Allegan, Mich. A year afterward he took charge of his father's farm, where he still resides. Mr. Small was married March 10, 1884, to Emma B., daughter of Lewis Robinson, and they have two children: Blanche M. and Irma M. Mr. Small held the office of postmaster at Hoagland, while in business at that place. George Small, the youngest of Joseph Small's family, was born in 1828. He went to Illinois, afterward to Colorado, then to California, and is now a resident of Nevada. He was married to Julia Beam, and they had five children.

Fred Beckman, of Marion township, was born in the city of Fort Wayne, July 14, 1840. His parents, Henry W. and Caroline Beckman, were natives of Bremen, Germany, and in 1838 became pioneers in Allen county. They first settled in Fort Wayne, and remained four years, during which time the father helped to build the old bank. They then removed to Adams county, but eight years later, returned to Allen county and settled in Marion township, where the father died March 28, 1884, his companion having died eighteen or twenty years before. To them were born six children: Lewis, Fred, Jane, August, Lewis, Francis N. and John, of whom three are living: Fred, Francis N. and Jane. The latter is a resident of Fort Wayne. Fred Beckman began work for himself at twenty years of age, on the farm now owned by him. Soon afterward, he enlisted in the Ninety-first Indiana regiment, and served until the close of the war, in the company of Capt. Joseph Keiffer. At the close of the war, he returned to his farm. He was married October 28, 1868, to Catharine Hake, and they have eight children: Maggie, Louisa, Catharine, Amelia, William, Christian, John, and Benjamin, all of whom are living. Mr. Beckman has succeeded in developing one of the finest farms of Marion township. In the fall of 1868, he erected on his farm a frame dwelling which he now occupies. He and family are members of the St. Joseph Catholic church. He has been successful in business, and is a respected citizen. His wife is a daughter of one of the oldest families in Marion township, John and Gertrude Hake. The father is dead, but the mother is living, at the age of seventy-one years. The eldest child of Mr. Beckman was married to John Wyss in June, 1886, and has one child living: Clara. They are residents of Marion township.

Nicholas F. Beckman, son of John Beckman, was born December 14, 1850, on the farm which his father purchased on coming to the township, and which he, at the latter's death, came into possession of. His handsome improvements reveal his skill as a carpenter as well as his success in agriculture. He was married May 19, 1885, to Maggie, daughter of Rudolph and Mary Hoffman, of Madison township. She was one of a family of ten children, eight of whom are living: Catharine, Mary, Maggie, Caroline, Rosa, George, Simon and Regina. To Mr. and Mrs. Beckman have been born two children: Rudolph F. and William Francis. Mr. Beckman has his farm under a fine state of cultivation, and is, as is evidenced by his crops, a practical farmer. He, like his father, is a staunch democrat; socially he is worthy and respected by all. Successful and enterprising, he has surrounded himself with all the comforts of farm life. He and family are members of the St. Joseph Catholic church at Hesse Cassel. John Beckman was a resident of the township until his marriage with Ellen Herber in 1882, when he removed to Wells county, where he died in the fall of 1885. He left a wife and two children, now residing here.

Philip Snider, of Marion, was born in Botetourt county, Va., August 18, 1818. He is the son of Philip and Nancy (Dolman) Snider, natives of Pennsylvania, who removed to James River, Va., when Philip, jr., was six years old. The father, a farmer by occupation, died in Virginia, during the civil war, at about eighty years of age. In his family were eight children: Barbara, Henry, Tina, Ann, Philip, Sarah, Solomon and Mary, seven of whom removed to Indiana and all but two came to Allen county. Philip Snider came about 1848, alone and without any conveyance, and spent two weeks and a half in making the journey. After about four years he returned on foot, purchased a team and brought back his two sisters. He purchased a farm of 240 acres in section 32, Marion township, at $2.75 per acre, and has added to this until he now owns 390 acres of land valued at $60 per acre. Mr. Snider was married in 1852 to Elizabeth, daughter of John and Delilah Snider, who emigrated in 1853, when Mrs. Snider was three years old, and settled in Marion township. The father was postmaster at Poughkeepsie, afterward Poe postoffice. He raised a family of eleven children: Mary Jane, Rachel, Evan, William Henry, Marinda, Elizabeth, John Wesley, Emily, Philena, Carlisle and David. Of this family John Wesley is a resident of Mexico; Carlisle, of Frontier county, N. C. The latter enlisted in 1861 in the One Hundredth and Thirty-fifth regiment, as a musician, but at Lookout Mountain exchanged his instrument for a musket and was one of the first to reach the summit. Mary Jane became the wife of Judge Nelson McLain. To Mr. and Mrs. Snider have been born six children: Delilah, Mary Kansas, Preston H., Sarah Emily, Minnie and Charley Boyd. Delilah married John Fonner and has one child, Zulu Maud. Mary Kansas was married to Marion Smith and has two children: Stella May and Clements. Preston H. married Tilla Felger and they have one child, Frank Boyd. He is conducting his father's farm. All the children but the youngest have studied at Fort Wayne college, and have received a good business education. Minnie graduated in 1888. Mr. Snider was trustee of the township when there were but three schools, Williamsport, Middletown, and what was called the Center school. He and wife and family, with one exception, are members of the Methodist Episcopal church at Williamsport, which was organized at a very early day, and met for a number of years at the home of Mrs. Snider's father.

Jacob Mercer, of Marion township, was born September 16, 1818, in Cumberland county, Penn. His grandfather was a German who emigrated to America in colonial times. Michael Mercer, the father of Jacob, was a soldier of the revolution. He also served under Gen. Wayne, on his expedition against the Indians of the Maumee Valley. He helped clear the ground on which old Fort Wayne was built and helped in its construction. He was engaged in all the battles with the Indians, on that expedition, and served until the close of that war. When on picket duty one night he saw what appeared to be a large black bear, but its grunt was somewhat peculiar, and he leveled his musket and fired. The thing rolled over dead, and upon examination it was found that the bear skin enveloped an armed Indian. After the war closed, Mr. Mercer returned to Pennsylvania, but soon removed to Columbiana county, Ohio, where he had received 160 acres of land from the government, for services rendered in the revolutionary and Indian wars. He was married while in Pennsylvania, to Susannah Bachte, by whom he had three children in Pennsylvania and eight in Ohio. The only survivor of this family so far as is known, is Jacob Mercer. When the latter was about eleven years old his father died, leaving the family in comfortable circumstances. About 1850 the mother and children removed to the Indian reserve in Pleasant township. She died about 1864, at ninety-four years of age. Jacob Mercer began to support himself at the age of eleven, and when thirteen years old he started for Missouri on foot, to visit a sister in that state, whom he succeeded in finding without much trouble which, considering his age and the condition of the country, was well-nigh miraculous. He learned the trade of "head-sawing" while in Ohio, and followed this occupation in Ohio, Illinois, Missouri, Iowa, and Indiana. Coming to Indiana in 1850 he worked with Edsall, of Fort Wayne, and afterward in the mill of Samuel Hanna, Middletown, where was got out material for the construction of the old plank road, known as the Piqua road. In 1851 he was married to Harriet Whitcomb, whose parents lived in Allen county, and he then removed to Ohio, and purchased eighty acres of land, in Hancock county. Two and a half years later, he returned and purchased eighty acres of land in Marion township, and has since bought eighty acres in Madison township, and twenty acres in Marion township. Mr. Mercer fully realized the amount of toil necessary to make this country a pleasant home, for he had traveled through it long before he came here to live. He has been highly successful as a farmer, as shown by his well tilled fields and his horses and other high grade stock, and is one of the leading citizens. He is a member of the Methodist Episcopal church at Middletown. Mr. and Mrs. Mercer have three children: Robert, Eliza Jane, and Rebecca. Robert residing in Madison township, is married to Nancy McKeeman, and they have three children: John, Frank and May. Eliza Jane is married to William H., son of William Van Horn, of Madison township. They have three children: Carrie May, Cora Rebecca and Jacob William. Rebecca is married to Michael Flaugh, and they have a daughter, Nora Viola.

O. E. Jamison.—The paternal grandfather of the Jamisons of Allen county, was David Jamison, born June 16, 1769, who was married to Ann, daughter of James Springer. James was the son of Carl, the son of Christopher, who came from Sweden in the colonial days and purchased in the region now Delaware, a large tract of land and leased it to others for ninety-nine years. Being a nobleman he returned to Sweden, and left the settlement and the development of the country to those less fortunate than himself. During the lapse of time the land was bought up by innocent purchasers and improved until its value is at present estimated by the millions. It comprises the city of Wilmington and all the region in that vicinity. The task of tracing the title back to Christopher Springer is next to impossible, as the lease or the record of it can not at present be found, though there is little if any doubt that the vast estate legally belongs to the heirs of Christopher Springer, of whom the family of Jamisons are the direct descendants. To David Jamison were born eight children: Mary, Jane, John, Elizabeth, Richard, Ann, Samuel and Rebecca. To Richard, the father of O. E. Jamison, there were born eight children: John R., Anna, Moisella, Rebecca, O. E., Richard, H. G. and Clark. There were in O. E. Jamison's family eleven children, six boys and five girls: Thomas, Samuel, A. B., J. M., L. Bell, Curtis C., Artie M., Everll M., Frank Etta, Elmer E. and Montie W. F. Two of the daughters were for a number of years teachers in the public schools. Thomas Jamison, the eldest of the family, is a farmer of Benton county, Ind., and Samuel is a farmer of Newton county. A. B. Jamison entered the Fort Wayne College of Medicine in 1878, and two years later graduated with honors. He began the practice of medicine in Portland, Jay county, and one year later removed to Decatur where he continued to practice for two years. He then began traveling as a specialist in liver and kindred diseases, and two years afterward went to New York, where he continues his practice as a specialist. J. M. Jamison studied law with L. M. Ninde, of Fort Wayne, and entered the law department at Ann Arbor, where he was graduated. He began the practice of law in Streator, Ill., and one year later was sent as a representative of the Springer heirs, to Europe, where he remained for two years. He afterward located at Grand Rapids, Mich., where he edited the *Progressive Age*, in connection with his law practice. Resigning his position on that journal, he has since devoted his time to the practice of law. Curtis Jamison is a farmer by occupation, upon his father's farm. Elmer E., was a number of years one of Allen county's efficient teachers, but became a merchant at Hoagland, in the spring of 1889, and is conducting a successful business in drugs and groceries. Two of the daughters, Artie M. and Montie W. F., having graduated at the Fort Wayne College of Medicine, began the practice in one of the hospitals of New York, where they still remain. Frank Etta is a graduate of the Mansfield, Ohio, high-school. Mr. Jamison has bestowed upon his children a legacy which will ever remain with them, a liberal education, and all are proving themselves worthy of it. Mr. Jamison came to Allen county, from Fayette county, Penn., and he settled on section 11, Marion township, having purchased 240 acres of land. He has now a farm of 320 acres of very valuable land, and is a successful business man, and a worthy and respected citizen.

John Gresley, of Marion, son of Peter and Barbara Gresley, was born February 18, 1824, in York county, Penn. The grandparents of Mr. Gresley were natives of Germany, who settled in Pennsylvania. Their son Peter settled in Wayne county, Ohio, in 1838, and subsequently removed to Marion township in 1852, bringing his wife and one daughter. He had twelve children: Henry, Peter, Elizabeth, Catharine, Jacob, Sarah, John, Daniel, Susan, Leah, John and Barbara, six of whom are living: Peter in Huntington county; Sarah and Daniel in Michigan; Susan in Marshall county; Elizabeth in VanWert county. John Gresley came in 1852 and purchased 160 acres of land in Marion township for $500. Returning to Ohio he spent two years, and then brought his wife and four children. He was married November 14, 1844, to Sarah Ann Bonewits, one of a family of twelve children, of parents who settled in this township and have succeeded. Mr. and Mrs. Gresley have had eleven children, of whom Margaret, Amelia, Elizabeth, Solomon, and Lewis Wilson are dead. Solomon married Margaret Jane English, and had two children: Sarah Bell and John Leroy. He died December 20, 1878. Peter Miles enlisted when about eighteen years old, 1864, and served until the close of the war. He married Mary C. Mock and has two children: Emma May and John Franklin. He resides in Kansas. Ann Maria married George Adair, of Hoagland, and has three children: Ida Della, Aminda and Cecilia. Mary Ann married Francis Hake, and has two living children: Noah Leander, Financis and John Clifford. John Esli married Mary Elizabeth Neireter, and had two children: Lulu Amelia and Nathan Casper. The mother died in 1889. Lincoln Grant married Sarah C. Hanley and resides in Michigan. Sarah Almira married John Youse, and has three children: Amos, Lewis and Dwight. Noah is conducting the business of the farm. Mr. Gresley occupied the log house he first built, from 1852 to 1865, when he built a more commodious dwelling. He built the first frame barn in Marion township, in 1856. He has a fine farm of 160 acres, and keeps the best breeds of stock. He has by his sociability and honesty, won a large circle of friends.

Early in the century Jacob Smitley, of Loudon county, Va., a worthy young man of Swiss parentage, with the pluck characteristic of that sturdy people, determined to seek a home in the new northwest. He had been married in 1806, to Catharine Youkin, whose ancestors had emigrated to America from Hesse-Cassel, perhaps in the early part of the eighteenth century. In 1817, with his wife and three children, he journeyed a long distance over primitive roads in search of a new home. All of their goods were stored in a four-horse wagon. The husband drove the team and cared for the two older children, while the wife walked the entire distance and carried her babe in her arms. Reaching the site of Adamsville, Ohio, they remained there four years and then settled on an eighty-acre farm two and a half miles south of Chandlersville. There Jacob Smitley died in August, 1868, at the age of eighty-nine years. This venerable age is surpassed by his widow who was born in Bucks county, Penn., December 4, 1787, and is still living, at the homestead. Eleven children were born to the good couple. The eldest, Elizabeth, eighty years of age, is the companion of her mother. Jonathan, Eli, Sarah, Melissa, and another, are dead. Anamiah, now Mrs. Greenfield, resides at Boscobel, Wis., and Elizabeth, Enos, Horace and Selena reside at the old home. Mrs. Aurelia Cassie Jones, the youngest, is fifty-two years old, and resides at Zanesville, Ohio. Jonathan Smitley, the oldest son, was married in 1836 to Ann Smith, daughter of Edward Smith, a native of England, and Jane Shaffer, of French descent. Mr. and Mrs. Smith had eleven children: Jonathan, Thomas, Rebecca, Elizabeth, Martin, Catharine, Ann, Nathan, Eliza and George. The family removed from Virginia to Zanesville, Ohio, in a one-horse cart, accompanied by a number of horses. In the fall of 1852 Jonathan Smitley and family emigrated to Allen county, and settled in Marion township, in the forest. He purchased 110 acres of land, seventy acres of which he converted into fine farming land. In this farm home ten children were born, of whom eight are living: Enos, George E., Horace, Warren, Sarah, Lois, Melissa and Mary. Enos C. Smitley, the oldest son, was born at Muskingum, Ohio, April 19, 1837. At twenty-one years of age he began the carpenter trade, and served an apprenticeship of five years with William Stirk and George Holmes, after which he engaged in contracting and building. He was married July 4, 1860, to Rebecca, daughter of John and Lucinda Small of Marion township. In the winter of 1863, Mrs. Smitley died, leaving two children, who then found a home with their grandmother. One of the children died, but Homer B. survives. On the 3d of September, 1865, Mr. Smitley married Martha J. Sweet, by whom he has had six children, of whom are living: Viola M., Mabel, Cassius, Earl and Paul. Homer B. was educated at the Ft. Wayne college, and the normal school at Valparaiso, and is one of Allen county's most efficient teachers. He was married in June, 1887, to Mary, daughter of Jesse Heaton, of Marion township, and they have two children: Garnet and an infant daughter. Viola M. was married in April, 1889, to William H. Reed, an attorney of Decatur, Ind. Mr. Enos Smitley is a highly respected citizen, and has a profitable business with his brother Warren as a partner. He and wife have been faithful members of the Methodist Episcopal church for twenty years. George E. Smitley, second son of Jonathan, was born August 23, 1838, in Muskingum county, Ohio, and at fourteen years of age removed to Allen county, with his father. He was married in October, 1860, to Sarah Ann Johnson, of Adams county, sister of Mr. George Morton, of Allen county. Three children were born to them; Eliza Jane, Charles A.; Emma Llewellyn, and the mother died February 5, 1886, after long suffering with heart trouble. She was a faithful and devoat member of the Methodist Episcopal church, of which Mr. Smitley is a member at Middletown. Adjacent to that village, Mr. Smitley has a good farm of fifty-three acres, and throughout the township he has many warm friends and is esteemed by all. Warren N. Smitley, son of Jonathan, was born October 5, 1859, on the homestead in Marion township. He worked on his father's farm until twenty-two years of age, and then began the carpenter's trade with his brother Enos, of whom he became a partner five years later. He was married September 16, 1886, to Leolo Houser, and they have a daughter Irma. They reside at Hoagland. Mr. Smitley is a good mechanic and a worthy and respected citizen. Like all those mentioned he is a republican.

Harvey K. Turner, of Marion, was born April 14, 1835, son of William W. Turner. His grandparents were natives of England, who immigrated near the year 1796, and settled in Madison county, N. Y., where they raised a family of four children, and passed the remainder of their lives. William W., their oldest son, was the first white child born in that county. He was married while living in New York, to Welthie Caswell, in the year 1820. After living near Cazenovia some time they removed to Ohio, in 1832, and located in what is now Lake county, where he purchased a farm which was partly improved. There were born to them in New York four children: Clarissa, Mary Ann, John and Harriet, and in Ohio three: William H., Harvey K. and Sarah, all of whom are living. In 1852 Mr. Turner removed to Indiana, and settled in Marion township with all his family, save his wife who died in 1848. He purchased 200 acres of land on the St. Mary's river, of which only about seventy-five acres was cleared. Out of this timber tract, he, with the help of his sons, developed one of the finest farms of the county. Here he died in February, 1879, at the age of seventy-nine years. William H. Turner, son of the above, became a student in the Methodist Episcopal college of Fort Wayne, and graduated with honor in 1883, after which he entered the law school at Ann Arbor and graduated in 1888. After a short practice in Fort Wayne he located at Detroit, Mich., where he is at present. Harriet M. was married to Cyrus E. Miller, a merchant of Fort Wayne, and they have one child, Harvey K. Harvey K. Turner, the youngest son of William W., was married in early manhood to Harriet Essig, by whom he had the following children: Mary, died at the age of four years; Hannah E., who married P. S. Shook, and has one child, Candice; Welthie Jane, who married M. C. Comer, and has two children; Clarence W. and Laura. The mother of these children died in May, 1867, just ten years after her marriage. Mr. Turner was married the second time in September, 1869, to Jane Harris. Mr. Turner's official life began as early as 1865, when he was elected assessor, in which capacity he served four years. He was elected justice of the peace in 1870, but resigned in 1872, the people of the county electing him county commissioner, an office he assumed in 1873. In 1876 he was re-elected, and served with honor until 1879. With enterprising spirit he has been interested in the fair association since its organization, first as director and afterward as president. He is a member the Masonic fraternity, Fort Wayne chapter, No. 19, and Fort Wayne commandery, No. 4, and has attained the highest office of the order in the Olive branch lodge. Mr. Turner came in possession of the farm formerly owned by his father in 1855, and to this he has added until he owns 320 acres, upon which he has erected good buildings. In 1888 he built one of the most handsome farm houses in the township, at a cost of about $2,200.

H. F. Christian Miller, of Marion township, was born in Hanover, February 1, 1841. He was the son of John and Mattie Miller, who emigrated to America in 1854, and settled in Allen county, Marion township, on section 11, having bought 100 acres of Judge Colman. Here he died a short time after his settlement, leaving four children: H. F. Christian, J. H. Harmon, Anna Maria and Anna Gesche, all of whom are living. Christian Miller left the parental abode in 1862 and clerked in a store for some time, then entering the lumber business, at which he was for some time engaged. He afterward began farming, his present occupation. August 16, 1884, he was married to Louisa Wedeking, and they have three children: Christian H. F., Louise C. S. C. and Annie Marie. Mr. Miller was employed during his commercial career in New York, Indianapolis and Fort Wayne, and became known as a very successful business man. He has his home upon a farm of seventy-five acres, handsomely improved. He is a democrat in politics. He and family are members of the Evangelical Lutheran church.

PLEASANT TOWNSHIP.

This region is traversed by both the St. Mary's and Little Wabash, and rivulets rising from springs close at hand, flow according as is the accidental arrangement of knoll and ravine, either to the sunny sands of the Mississippi delta or toward the icy shores of Labrador. Pleasant township was first settled in 1832, or about that year, by a Mr. Cooper and family, who made their home on the Godfrey trace or Bluffton road, at a place called "Green Camp," a favorite spot with Indians and emigrants, on account of a refreshing spring in that vicinity. Some years prior to this settlement the Bluffton road and the older Indianapolis road had been surveyed through the township. In 1832, Horney Robinson, who had settled with his father, Thomas Robinson, in Wayne township in 1826, came to Pleasant township, and afterward became prominent in its history. The first white child born in this vicinity was his son Warren, in November, 1834, and the first death was of his sister, Mrs. Mary Bay, who died in 1841. The first saw-mill was built by him, on the bank of Lost creek, from which it obtained the power, and for many years he operated it successfully, supplying lumber for many buildings in the city. Lumber was hauled from here as far as the Salamonie river in Huntington county. At the home of this same pioneer, the first religious meeting was held by Rev. Ball, in 1834. In 1834 came Edward Kennark, a native of Ireland, who entered land in sections 4 and 10, aided in the building of the Wabash railway, and died in 1872; eight of his sixteen children survive. William Bradbury also came in 1834, and he and Kennark put up the first hewn-log houses. William Watson settled in the spring, but did not remain many years; John Whetton made a permanent settlement in this year. In 1841 Andrew Miller and his sons Christian, Joseph, John and Andrew, of Alsace, were the first settlers on the Indian reserves, and the family is now prominent. Thomas Greer and family settled in 1842. He was one of the fourteen settlers who organized the township and held the first election at the home of Abraham Lutz. These voters were, besides Greer and Lutz, David Hill, Samuel Fogwell, Jacob Kinwell, John Nicodemus, Thomas Bradbury, Edward Kennark, Cooper, Enos Mooney, Benjamin Swett, Hugh

O'Hara, John Whetton and Horney Robinson. Jacob Smith, one of the oldest living settlers, born in Pennsylvania in 1814, came here in 1847 and became the first township trustee under the present system. After 1834 the fertile and inviting land received many occupants, and among the earliest of this period may be named Christian Miller, Nicholas Herber, Jacob Smith, George Woods, Andrew Orrin, John Orrin, Ethelbert Sutton, Alexander Stonebrook, Cornelius Ferrell, Henry Castile, Asa Linscott, Noah Linscott, William Henry, George Mercer, Henry Mercer, Nicholas Rice, Thomas Swank, Zaccheus Clark, Nathan Parker, Washington Parker, Wellington Parker, Thomas Parker, Henry Hall, Carroll Taylor and Jacob Kimmel. In October, 1869, Andrew J. Taylor divided a portion of his lands into town lots, and the name of Sheldon was given to the place, which is a station on the Fort Wayne, Muncie & Cincinnati railroad. In October of the year named, Mr. Taylor established his carriage factory, and adopted the plan of making all sales at auction. His enterprise prospered, and the establishment soon became a prosperous and considerable one. He also, beginning in 1871, conducted a saw-mill, to which he gave his personal attention until he suffered the loss of his left hand in that business. In 1871 an addition to the town was platted by John N. Mowey and Willard S. Hickox. The population at the last census was 166.

Warren Robinson, a native resident of Pleasant township, was born November 30, 1834. His father, Horney Robinson, one of the pioneers of Allen county, was born in Fayette county, Ohio, June 22, 1806, the son of Thomas Robinson, a native of Ohio, whose father was one of the pioneers of that state, and a soldier of the war of 1812. Horney Robinson came to Allen county as early as 1826, when the county was a wilderness and Fort Wayne only a fort and Indian trading post. He first settled in Wayne township, where he entered sixty acres of land, and lived until about 1832, when he entered about 126 acres then in Aboit, but since attached to Pleasant township, where he resided the rest of his life. He was one of the best known early citizens, and was a successful farmer. He was married in about 1829 to Catherine Freshour, a native of Pennsylvania, born about 1816, the daughter of George Freshour, a native of Pennsylvania, and a pioneer of Allen county. The parents were members of the Methodist Episcopal church, Horney Robinson being one of the pioneer Methodists of Allen county. He was instrumental in laying the foundation for the growth of the church in the county. His home was the stopping place for all itinerant preachers and his hospitality was unbounded. The mother died February 27, 1864, and the father on July 22, 1887. To them thirteen children were born, only five of whom survive: Sarah J., wife of Milton F. Ward, of near Topeka, Kan.; Warren; William, a farmer of Lafayette township; Frank, a Methodist minister, now farming in Huntington county; Samantha, wife of Dr. Moffett, of Lafayette, Ind. Warren Robinson attended the country schools and finished his education in the Methodist Episcopal college at Fort Wayne. After teaching school about six years, he

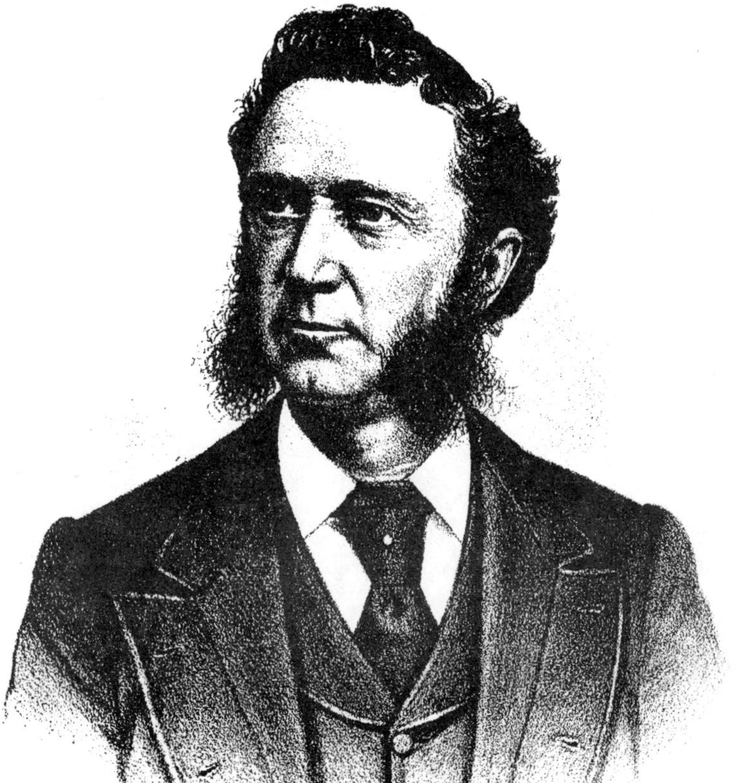

turned his attention about 1861, to stock buying and farming, in which he has met with success. He was married in October, 1865, to Sarah J. Fields, who was born in Wells county, Ind., in 1845, daughter of Morgan Fields, a pioneer of that county. She was a member of the Evangelical Lutheran church; she died in December, 1872, leaving two sons, one deceased. Frank S., born November 27, 1869, lives with his father. Mr. Robinson was married in February, 1877, to Martha J. Wilson, born in Huntington county in 1853. They have one daughter, Ressie. Mr. Robinson has met with success as the result of his industry and enterprise, and has 200 acres of land, 115 of which are of the old homestead. On an eighty-five-acre tract on the line between Pleasant and Wayne townships, he has a good frame residence and one of the largest barns in the township. In politics he is a republican. He is thrifty, energetic and enterprising, and is respected and esteemed by his fellow citizens.

James Cunnison, a well-known farmer of Pleasant township, was born December 17, 1840, in Wayne township, the son of Robert Cunnison, who was born at Dundee, Scotland, in 1799, and coming to America, and to Allen county in 1833, settled in Wayne township. He was one of the pioneers of the township, coming here when Fort Wayne was an Indian village, and the country was little more than a wilderness. His death occurred in 1843. His wife, Margaret Ramsey, was born in Scotland, June 22, 1799. There they were married and their first child, Isabelle, was born on the ocean. She died at the age of four years, and was buried in a graveyard on the site of Brinsley's feed yard in Fort Wayne. The mother is still living, and is the widow of John Whetton, sr., who died in February, 1861. Robert and Margaret Cunnison had three children: Isabelle (deceased), Robert, who was born in 1835, and was killed on July 8, 1880, in a well, leaving a widow and six children, the youngest of whom, now deceased, was born while the father's funeral was in progress; and James. The latter was three years of age when his mother married John Whetton, and removed to Pleasant township, to the farm now owned by himself. He was married in January, 1866, to Mary, daughter of William Dalman. He was born in Derbyshire, England, June 24, 1815, and came to Allen county in 1832. His wife was Rebecca Osborn, who was born in Ohio. Mr. Cunnison has five children: Alex, born June 25, 1867; Margaret Isabelle, wife of Levi E. Koons, of Marion, born March 13, 1870; Will, born August 5, 1871; Frank, born September 18, 1876, and James, born November 30, 1882. Mr. Cunnison has always been an active and prominent citizen of his township. He has met with success in life, and has acquired a competency. His farm is one of the finest in his vicinity, embracing 226½ acres. He also owns two lots and three dwellings on Smith street in Fort Wayne. The old family residence was destroyed by fire in May 27, 1886, and he at once erected a handsome two-story brick on the site of the old home. He also has a good barn and other buildings.

29

He is a member of Summit City lodge, No. 170, F. & A. M.; and Mrs. Cunnison is a member of the Methodist church.

Jacob H. Kimmel, a prominent farmer of Pleasant township, was born on his present farm, nine miles southwest of Fort Wayne, March 25, 1843. His father, Jacob Kimmel, a pioneer of the township, was a native of York county, Penn. He came to Allen county in the fall of 1841, and purchasing 126 acres in Pleasant township, there followed farming the rest of his life. His wife, Jane Newhouse, was born in Virginia in 1807, and died January 27, 1869. The father died September 21, 1873, aged seventy-six years and seven months. They had nine children, eight of whom are living. Five reside in Allen county, one in Wells county, one in Washington Territory and one in Kansas. Jacob Kimmel, the father, was a thrifty and honest man, well-known and well liked, and during his life met with success, accumulating considerable means, he owning 386 acres of land, which he divided among his children as they became of age. He was a member of the Lutheran church, and in politics was a republican. His son, Jacob, is the youngest of the children. He secured a good, practical education and remained on the home farm, taking care of his father in his old age. At his death he became owner of the farm of 126 acres, which he has since increased to 215 acres. In 1876 he erected a large square-roof stable, which is an ornament to the farm, and in July, 1881, built his two-story brick residence, at a cost of $2,300, one of the finest in the township. In 1883 he erected a large barn, which was destroyed by lightning, May 12, 1886, and in 1887 he erected another large barn. His farm, with its improvements, is one of the finest in the township. Mr. Kimmel was married in August, 1869, to Ellen Buskirk, who was born in Allen county, in 1849, daughter of Daniel Buskirk, an early settler. She died in October, 1870, and he was married in May, 1874, to Louisa Fischer, of Fort Wayne, who was born in New York city, in 1849, daughter of Anthony Fischer, a citizen of Fort Wayne. Their children are: Eda, born in 1875, and Thomas H., born in 1883. Mrs. Kimmel is a member of the Lutheran church at Five Points. Mr. Kimmel is a republican in politics and he is a member of Summit City lodge, F. & A. M.

William Dalman, one of Pleasant township's leading men, was born in the township, March 25, 1847. His father Edwin Dalman, was born in England, December 20, 1819, son of John and Hannah Dalman, who in 1833, with part of their family of ten children, emigrated to America, and arrived at Fort Wayne in June. They settled in southern Wayne township, on the Little river, and their home was then the only one between the Indian reservation and the Wabash river. They constructed a rude log cabin and began clearing away the forests, and farming, which was the occupation of John Dalman until his death sixteen years later. He left five children in this country: William, Thomas, Edwin, Frederick and Salina. Edwin a prominent man in his time, was married in 1842 to Mary, daughter of John and Jane McNair, natives of Ireland, who settled in Allen county in 1837. Edwin Dalman died in January, 1864, but his widow is still living at Fort Wayne. To this marriage four sons were born: John, Thomas, William and Charles. John is now a citizen of Pleasant township, of which he has served as trustee nine years, and he has held the position of county treasurer two terms. William Dalman is a farmer by occupation, and was born and reared on the farm and received his education in the pioneer log schoolhouse. In 1870 he was married to Isabel, daughter of William and Susan (Simpson) Beck, early settlers of the county. She was born in this county in November, 1849. To this marriage eight children were born, of whom three are living, Effie, Charles and Naomi. Mr. Dalman started out in life for himself soon after marriage, and settled on the farm in Pleasant township which he has since occupied. He has a fine farm of eighty-six acres and as a farmer is practical and successful. In politics he is a strong democrat. He was elected trustee of his township in 1886, and is now serving his second term to the entire satisfaction of the people. On his second election he for the first time in the history of the township, had no opposition. He and wife are members of the Methodist Episcopal church.

William S. Robison, one of the early residents of Pleasant township, is of a family distinguished among the pioneers. His grandfather, of Scotch descent, was born upon the ocean coming to America. He married Elizabeth Spudy, also of Scotch origin. Their son, James Robison, was born in Mifflin county, Penn., in 1792. In early manhood he learned the carpenter's trade, and while a resident of Mifflin county, married Rebecca Jacobs, who was of English and Irish descent. In 1832 he went to farming in Pennsylvania, and two years later emigrated to Ohio where he remained until 1866, when he became a resident of Allen county. His wife died in 1872, and he passed away in 1875. They were zealous members of the Presbyterian church. Their children are as follows: Mary (deceased), John A. (deceased), Samuel E., William S., Elizabeth (deceased), Sarah, Catherine, James S., David A., George W., Thomas Calvin, Franklin (deceased), Hiram (deceased), Anna E., (deceased). William S. Robison was born in Mifflin county, Penn., December 4, 1821, was reared on the farm, and received a fair common school education. In 1845 he came to Allen county, and settled in Pleasant township, where he has since resided. On first settling, he secured from Hon. F. P. Randall a license to teach and taught thereafter fifteen quarters, teaching and farming alternately. Subsequently, he suspended teaching and since his entire time has been devoted to farming. In the fall of 1846 he wedded Nancy, daughter of Jacob Kimmel, an early settler of this county. The marriage resulted in the birth of the following children: James B., Desdemona J., Harriet E., Theodosia R., Mary E. (deceased), William M. C., Jacob C. and Viola. Their mother, who was born in Starke county, Ohio, in 1828, died in February, 1864. In 1865 Mr. Robison married Mrs. Harriet Robbnei Greenameyer, who was born in Columbiana county, Ohio, in 1828. Mr.

Robison as a farmer has achieved perhaps more than ordinary success. In politics he has ever been an active democrat. He and wife during their lives were members of the Methodist Episcopal church. James B. Robison, eldest son of the above, was born March 3, 1848, in Pleasant townhip. He was reared on a farm and received his education in the country schools. At twenty-two years of age he married and settled down in life as a renter on a farm. May 5, 1870, he wedded Mercy Rice, daughter of Jesse and Mary (Chalker) Rice. Mrs. Robison was born in Trumbull county, Ohio, April 23, 1851. They have one child, Eva. Mr. Robison has devoted his life to farming and stock raising. After his marriage he remained a renter for four years, and then he purchased a tract of land, and by energy and perseverance has come into possession of a well improved farm of ninety-two acres. In politics he is a democrat. He was elected township trustee, in Pleasant township, in 1882, and was re-elected in 1884. He and wife are members of the Methodist Episcopal church. As a citizen Mr. Robison is progressive, and as a farmer he is a representative one. He has been a warm friend to schools, churches and public improvements.

William M. Dafforn, of Pleasant township, was born in Warwickshire, England, May 12, 1840. His parents, William and Mary (Nichols) Dafforn, were born in England and emigrated when he was fifteen years old. They settled in Allen county in 1855. Mr. Dafforn is one of twelve children. In his native country he learned the baker's trade, and at Sutton, gained a good common school education. At the age of twenty-one years, he became a soldier in the United States service, enlisting April 18, 1861, as a private in Company C, Ninth Indiana volunteer infantry. July 1, 1862, he became a private in Company C, of the Fifteenth Indiana. Among some of the engagements in which he took part were: Greenbrier, Va., Marshall's Store, Va., Stone River, Missionary Ridge. At Stone River he was wounded, and because of disability he would have been sent to the hospital, but instead he went into the commissary department. He was discharged at the expiration of term of service, June 25, 1864. He returned to Allen county, where he has since remained, following farming for an occupation. In 1866 he was united in marriage with Eliza, daughter of Elijah and Juliana Ake, early settlers of Pleasant township. Mrs. Dafforn was born in Allen county, December 7, 1848. They have six children: Mary, Samuel, William, James, Delbert and Jennie. When Mr. Dafforn started out in life he had no capital whatever. He is now prosperous and owns a well improved farm of eighty acres.

LAFAYETTE TOWNSHIP.

The remote position of this region with relation to the city and the routes of immigration caused it to be settled much later than other portions of the county of Allen. In the extreme northeast section, Samuel Fogwell, an immigrant from Ohio, settled in 1839, and began a life of industry which he spent on that place. A little later, Frank Morrison and David Overly made their homes in the vicinity, and in 1843, Anthony Krumme moved here from Pleasant township. In 1844 William Jobs came here from Marion township, and in 1845, James Wilson, whose son Isaac A., born May 30, 1846, was the first born in the settlement. Others in 1845 were Isaac Alter, Isaac Hatfield, John Akers, Christian Foley, and John Foley, settled. In 1846 Walter Kress settled, and in 1847 Henry S. Keeley. In 1842 the road known as the lower Huntington road was surveyed through the township, but it was not passable for several years. In 1846 the first township election was held at the house of William Jobs, and Isaac Hatfield was elected justice; William Jobs, constable; Isaac Alter, clerk; James E. Wilson, treasurer, and Samuel Fogwell, James Wilson and John Akers, trustees. The first school-house of the township was the Coverdale, built in 1848, and Eli Ward was the first teacher. The Allen county addition to the village of Zanesville, which lies partly in Wells county, was platted on Henry Sinks' land in February, 1854. In 1849, Henry Sinks erected the first saw-mill, with steam power, and in 1852 he became the first merchant of the settlement. In 1875, a steam grist-mill was built by Conrad Knight. In 1880 Zanesville had a population, in Allen county of ninety-three, in Wells of 135.

George Lopshire, who settled in Lafayette in 1852, is a son of George and Elizabeth (Bender) Lopshire, who came from Pennsylvania to Ohio in 1821, and in 1835 moved to Fort Wayne, where the father built a house on south Broadway, and helped clear the brush from that street. Six of the children of these pioneers are living. John and Elizabeth (Ringer) Denis also settled in 1852 and seventeen children were born to them, of whom thirteen survive. A prominent citizen, not so long a resident of the township, is Adam D. Hill, son of David and Sarah (Fogwell) Hill, who settled in Aboit township in 1837.

Andrew Bowersock, a prominent and well-to-do farmer of Lafayette township, was born April 18th, 1848, in Monroe county, Ohio. Coming to Indiana in 1851, he settled in Lafayette township where he has in since resided. After living with his step-father, William Lahmon, for nine years, he started out for himself, and after buying and selling two farms of forty acres, he purchased the farm on which he now resides. This originally contained sixty acres but now embraces 192 acres of the best land in the township. Mr. Bowersock was educated in the common schools of this township. He was married on September 26th, 1872, to Mary F. Lopshire, who died February 13th, 1874, of consumption. He was again married, December 3, 1874, to Melinda A. Canon. They are the parents of three children: Rilla C., Bertha B., Charles R. Mr. Bowersock was elected trustee of Lafayette township in the spring of 1884 and was re-elected with a large majority in 1886. He is regarded by many as the best trustee the township has ever had. In politics he has been a life-long democrat, faithfully supporting all the nominees of his party, and at the urgent request of members of his party he has now entered the field as a competitor for the office of county recorder, with strong probabilities in his favor of being the successful one. Mr. and Mrs. Bowersock are active members of the Lutheran church.

George W. Mills, a prominent farmer of Lafayette township, was born in Coshocton county, Ohio, March 15, 1828. His father, James Mills, a native of New Jersey, left there at the age of nineteen, and came to Ohio. He was married at Taylorsville, to Eliza Wright, and then moved to Coshocton. They had nine children, eight sons and one daughter, of whom all are living but one son; they are as follows: George W., Robert B., of Oregon; Warren L., of Kansas; Daniel, of Illinois; William B., of Illinois; John C., of Illinois; James G., a farmer of Dakota, and Eliza K., wife of Josiah Bays, of Missouri. James Mills died in Morgan county, Ohio, March, 1845, and the mother died in Ossian, Ind., at the age of sixty-seven, in 1876. George W. Mills came to Indiana in 1848, after his father's death, and brought with him his mother and the children, who depended upon him until arriving of age. He settled in Lafayette township and built a cabin where the Coverdale school-house now stands. He entered forty acres of his present farm in 1849, the deed being signed by Zachary Taylor. He has added to his farm until now it consists of 104 acres of good land. He was married in 1848 to Margaret, daughter of John and Elizabeth (Ryan) Hill. They have had eleven children, eight of whom are living: Robert B., John, Elizabeth, Joseph C., Matilda, Ella, Grant and Jane. Mr. Mills was elected justice of the peace in the spring of 1880 and served four years, filling the office very creditably. In politics he is a republican. He is a member of the Christian church and has been active in church affairs for several years. He was a member of the One Hundred and Thirty-seventh Indiana volunteer infantry, Company D, which went into active service in 1864, and was honorably discharged in the fall of 1864. Mr. Mills is a man of honesty and integrity and is well respected by his neighbors and fellow citizens. He is a member of McGinnis post, No. 167, G. A. R., of Roanoke, Ind.

George B. Lawrence, a substantial farmer of Lafayette township, resides on section 10 in the Zeke reserve, about ten and one-half miles southwest from Fort Wayne. He was born in Wayne county, Ohio, May 1, 1835. His parents, Jacob and Margaret (Johnson) Lawrence, natives of Wayne county, were among the early settlers of Lafayette township. The father purchased and settled upon 160 acres about 1848, and farmed there until his death in 1879, at the age of seventy years. The death of his wife occurred two years previous in her sixty-eighth year. Of their nine children, six of whom survive, George B. was the eldest. In 1863 he came to Allen county and located on a farm of 163 acres in Lafayette township, which he purchased in 1857 from John M. Kinnan and George W. Robison; the land was then entirely unimproved. Mr. Lawrence has since added ninety-one acres to the original farm, and he also owns an interest in a fine farm of 140 acres in Wayne township, in company with his son Oliver. In 1877 Mr. Lawrence erected his large frame residence, and in 1872 built a fine barn, and he has other substantial improvements, making his one of the finest farms in the township. He was married November 23, 1854, to Elizabeth Geitgey, who was born in Wayne county, Ohio, and is the daughter of Adam Geitgey, a pioneer of that county. They have five children: Oliver, a farmer of Wayne township; John, Alice, Ida and Grover C. Mr. Lawrence is one of the leading citizens of Lafayette township, in school, church and public affairs. He has always been a staunch democrat. In the spring of 1889 he was selected by Judge O'Rourke as a member of the county board of equalization, a position he filled quite satisfactorily.

William Branstator, a leading farmer and the largest land-holder in Lafayette township, was born in Clinton county, Ohio, May 10, 1824. His parents, Andrew and Frances (Wilkerson) Branstator, were born, the former in Maryland, June 9, 1782, and the latter in Kentucky, September 13, 1789. Being early settlers of Clinton county, Ohio, they were there married January 19, 1807. To this union thirteen children were born: Sarah, born August 25, 1809, died February 6, 1864; Elizabeth, December 2, 1810, died July 4, 1866; Matthias, August 24, 1812, died January 11, 1842; Catherine, January 28, 1814, died September 1, 1842; Mary, March 17, 1816, died July 13, 1875; James, April 18, 1818, died in summer of 1886; Nancy, January 23, 1820, died July 13, 1875; Andrew, January 12, 1822, died February 1, 1876; William, May 10, 1824; John, September 11, 1826, died April 21, 1871; Marion, November 30, 1828, died June 26, 1847; Frances, November 18, 1830; Thomas, February 22, 1834, died September 29, 1851. Frances is the widow of William O. Jones, of Huntington county. The father died June 20, 1848, and the mother May 15, 1878, in Clinton county, Ohio. In about 1839 the father visited Indiana and purchased a section of land in Allen county and one in Huntington county, and bequeathed to William the west half of the Allen county section, which is his home farm at the present. This he settled upon in 1848. The land at that time was covered with timber. Mr. Branstator erected a log cabin, and, after getting married, began the work of clearing. The farm is known as the west half of the Branstator reserve, part of sections Nos. 1 and 2, in Lafayette township, and sections 35 and 36 in Aboit township. Since then Mr. Branstator has added to his land until he has 597 acres in one body in Lafayette and Aboit townships, and also has a farm of 207 acres in section 36, Aboit township, altogether 804 acres in Allen county. He also owns 243 acres in Warren and Clinton counties, Ohio, the old homestead. In 1871 he erected a large two-story brick residence, one of the finest in the township. Mr. Branstator was married on April 16, 1848, to Catherine A. Hill, who was born in Washington county, Md., May 28, 1829. Her parents, David and Sarah (Fogwell) Hill, the former a native of Pennsylvania and the latter of Maryland, were pioneers of Allen county, where the father died in 1847, the mother dying in Clay county, Ind., about 1873. Of their ten children, seven survive. Mr. and Mrs. Branstator have had twelve children: Elizabeth Frances, born January 11, 1849, wife of Julian J. Cron, of Wayne township; Martin L., March 10, 1851, died March 12, 1857; Sarah E., June 4, 1852, wife of Henry Kress, of Lafayette township; Andrew Dallas, May 14, 1854, farming in Wayne township; Anna C., December 3, 1857, widow ot William McNair; William D., November 15, 1859, farming in Kansas; Jason Douglas, December 15, 1861, living in Aboit township; James, October 22, 1863, died October 22, 1863; McClellan, July 24, 1865, residing at home; Charles W., June 23, 1867, residing at home; Rosa J., December 15, 1869, died December 15, 1869, and Della May, January 23, 1873, died February 2, 1873. Mrs. Branstator is a member of the Five Points Lutheran church. Mr. Branstator has always been a prominent citizen, broad and liberal in his views, progressive and enterprising. He is a democrat in politics, and in 1867 and 1868 was trustee of Lafayette township. He is a member of Summit City lodge, F. & A. M., of Fort Wayne.

CHURCHES IN THE TOWNSHIPS.

Quite important is it, that in an account of the development of that part of the county of Allen which is mainly agricultural in its industries, brief mention, at least, should be made of the rise and growth of the churches. Hand in hand with the school came the church to the early settlers, and both were potent factors in the work of progress. The missionary piercing the trackless wilds, to carry the gospel to the scattered pioneers, could speak with great power to his hearers, for it was apparent that only the love of his cause guided and sustained him. Remuneration he could not hope for, but he never sought in vain for lodging and sustenance for himself and his horse. His reading and preaching and fervent prayer and song brought back the old days at home to the weary toiler in the forest, and cheered him to renewed exertion, that ere long the advantages of church association and the comfort of its sacred rites might be his again. The early church and school often occupied the same rude log cabin, and frequently the shelter was erected primarily for a house of worship of the sustaining Power that the settlers felt was supreme even in the boundless forests, amid wild animals and Indians not long since in savage warfare against his race. These early church classes exerted a great influence for good, and the distinct methods of various denominations in the development of character can be traced to-day in the diverse character of different localities. In the following pages of this chapter a brief account will be given of the establishment and growth of societies of the different denominations, except those elsewhere treated of, throughout Allen county outside of the city of Fort Wayne.

Methodist Episcopal Church.— Without the township of Wayne, in which the earliest settlement was made, the first preaching of the gospel to the American settlers of which record can now be found, was in the Maumee settlement in Adams township. There, at the house of John Rogers, services were conducted by Reuben Nickerson, of the Methodist Episcopal church, in 1828, and he was followed by Rev. James B. Austin, James Holman and Richard Robinson, at the same place previous to 1832. In 1834, Rev. Holman held religious meetings at the home of Richard Andrew in Aboit township, and two years later a class was organized there, which is one of the oldest in the county. There were then twelve members, and they were ministered to by Rev. Stephen R. Ball, once in four weeks. He preached at Fort Wayne, with South Bend and Logansport in his circuit. This pioneer died some ten years ago, in Steuben county. In 1842, a log building was erected to serve alike for church and school. This class is still in existence and now worships at Friendship chapel, built a few years ago, in the Coesse circuit. Another class of similar age is that which was the origin of the Methodist church at Huntertown. Meetings were begun in 1834, at the house of Horace F. Dunten, by Mr. Nickerson, and ministers of various denominations alternated in their visits. In 1836, with six members, the class was organized at the house of James Thompson, by Rev. Ball, and two years later the Caswell school-house became the place of meeting. In 1846, a frame church was erected, 30x40 feet in dimensions, at a cost of $1,500, and this has since been the home of the church. Its present pastor, A. L. Forkner, has a circuit including 180 members in Allen county. Another zealous pioneer of Methodism, the Rev. Mr. Black, preached in Lake township at the home of William Grayless, in 1834, but there was no attempt to organize a class here for many years. Jesse Heaton, sr., a faithful Methodist, had services at his home in Marion township, as early as 1835, conducted by Rev. James Harrison, and their efforts resulted in the formation of a class in 1836, consisting of eight members. At Mr. Heaton's house the little band continued to meet for ten years, and then occupied the school-house at Middletown. In 1852 they erected a comfortable house of worship in the village, at a cost of $800, which has served the society up to the present. To this organization, in its various places of meeting, nearly all the venerable pioneers of Methodism in this region, ministered, and at an early day the membership was quite large. But the organization of more convenient churches for various neighborhoods has decreased the attendants. One of the oldest Sunday-schools in the county was started here in 1837, being first organized by Jared Wharton, as a union school, and it is still conducted on that plan. In 1842, a number of the members organized the Williamsport class, at the house of John Snyder, the meeting being presided over by Rev. Jesse Sparks. A school-house was soon afterward occupied as the house of worship, but that being destroyed by fire, Mr. Snyder's residence was used until the neat church, now in use, was built in 1869, at a cost of $1,200. Both the Middletown and the Williamsport churches are in the Sheldon circuit, in charge of Rev. A. G. McCarter. A flourishing pioneer church class was that organized by Rev. Ball in 1835, in Pleasant township. There were fifteen members, and meetings were held from house to house until 1844, when a log church was erected on land donated by Horney Robinson. This was succeeded in 1866, by Brenton chapel, a commodious frame building, which cost $1,200. It was well attended, but the centers of settlement having changed, and new organizations formed that drew away members, the church finally was disorganized, and now no services are held.

In St. Joseph township, in 1836 or 1837, meetings were held by Rev. True Pattee, one of the first settlers, and Rev. Golthite. About the same time a preacher of much power, Rev. Edward Hickland, of the Methodist Protestant denomination, created a great excitement among his hearers in this vicinity and elsewhere, by preaching the speedy dissolution of the universe. Not content with picturing with startling verbal imagery, the reward of the good, and the future torment of the wicked, he displayed colored cartoons to illustrate his texts. When the day of wrath announced by him, March 2, 1838, arrived, some believers, it is said stood ready in their ascension robes, to ascend to a better world. But the failure of his prophecy ended his influence. The members of the Methodist church in this township kept up their meetings, though irregularly, until the erection of the St. Joseph church, in 1865. It is a frame building, 34x45, and was dedicated by Rev. J. V. R. Miller, Rev. James Greer becoming the first pastor. It is supplied by the New Haven pastor and the membership is consolidated with Wayne Street church, Fort Wayne. In 1836 Rev. Hickland preached in Cedar Creek township and the result was the organization of a class, which met until the members of other denominations, which had united in this, withdrew. In 1845 the withdrawal of the Methodist Episcopalian members occurred, and they organized a class under Rev. Dowd, which met at Silver's school-house until 1851, when a log church was erected. This was the parent church from which Mt. Olivet and Robinson chapel societies sprang, but it soon ceased to exist itself on account of these withdrawals. In 1851 the organization at Leo was effected, and a small frame church was erected, which was used until 1878, when one of larger dimensions was purchased. The Leo circuit includes 203 members, and the pastor is now A. H. Currie. In 1864 the members at Cedarville erected a good frame church, which is included in the Leo circuit.

The beginning of the present flourishing society at Wesley Chapel, Eel River township, was in the winter of 1837-8, when meetings were held at the home of John Valentine. In the spring following the class was organized at the house of John McKee, with about twelve members. John Bennett was class leader, and Rev. James Ross made the class occasional visits. Meetings were held in the old hickory school-house, until 1843, when a hewn-log church was erected. The congregation increased, and in 1865 a handsome frame church was erected at a cost of $2,500, which was dedicated February 18, 1866, by Rev. S. N. Campbell. There are now about seventy-five members and B. Sawyer of the Cherubusco circuit is pastor. In Jefferson township Rev. David Pattee preached in 1838 in the log school-house of the settlement, and several years later a class was formed, which subsequently joined the New Haven church.

In 1838, Rev. True Pattee began preaching in the township of Springfield, and about five years later, in the winter of 1843-4, a class of twelve members: Marcus Brown, Horace Skinner, William Sweet, Richard Anderson, Alphonzo Pattee, and their wives, and Mrs. M. Johnson and Ahira Pattee, was organized at the school-house on section 28. There meetings were held regularly until 1854, when the old Harlan church was built in the town of Maysville. Since 1843 regular pastors have been in charge, the present minister being T. F. Frech, and the church has prospered, having now about 114 members, and a handsome brick church, which was built in 1881 at a cost of about $6,000. Two other churches in the county are included in the Maysville circuit, East Springfield and Scipio, and includes about 180 members in Allen county. The Scipio church is the outgrowth of meetings held at Gehial Park's in 1840, by Benjamin Dorsey.

Brief mention has now been made of the work of the preachers of the Methodist Episcopal church in the township up to 1840, and the organizations which followed their efforts. In the latter named year a church organization was made in Washington township, composed of George Ashley, Daniel Opleger, Uriah J. Rock, James W. Flemming, and their families, and several years later they built a small log church on land donated by Mr. Ashley in the northwest part of the township, and there they first worshipped under the guidance of Rev. J. W. Winans. This primitive building stood many years, and finally became the home of the sexton of the cemetery. In the latter part of 1872 the new church was erected at the village of Wallen, and its first trustees were John Ervin, George Opleger, James P. Ross, George Sunderland and David L. Archer. This prosperous society is part of the Huntertown circuit. The Sunday-school was established in 1844, and has ever since been in existence. In 1841 Rev. Jesse Sparks organized the Massillon class at the house of Charles Peckham, in Madison township. The next year a lot was donated by John Edwards, and a hewn-log church was erected, which was free of debt, as the work was donated by Jabez Shaffer, Charles Peckham, John Edwards, and Adam Robinson. Here the class worshipped until 1856, when the frame church now in use was erected. The membership, at first twenty, increased to seventy-five, but has again decreased. It is included in the Monroeville circuit.

In 1845 the first religious meeting in Milan township was held by Rev. True Pattee, but no organization was formed. The Monroeville Methodist Episcopal church was organized in 1847, with fourteen members. They met at the house of John Barnhart, and were ministered to by Rev. John Palmer. The church lived and prospered, and in 1865 their present handsome church at Monroeville was erected, during the pastorate of A. C. Curry, and dedicated by Rev. John Hill. The present pastor is B. S. Hollopeter, and he ministers to a circuit including about 200 members. In 1849 another class was organized by Rev. Palmer, at the house of William Grayless, in Lake township. In 1850 they erected Lake Chapel, five miles north of Arcola. But the growth of the village of Arcola led to the organization of a class there in 1867, and four years later the latter organization erected a neat frame church, at a cost of 1,600, which was dedicated in September, 1871, by Rev. A. Marine. This drew to some extent from the membership of Lake Chapel. But both are still flourishing and are now in charge of Rev. I. W. Kemberling, of Coesse. In 1850 another society was organized in Perry township, and in the following year a donation of land was made by Andrew Byers, upon which in 1852 a frame church was erected, and dedicated by Prof. Robinson, in honor of whom it was named Robinson Chapel. It is included in Leo circuit.

In 1852, the first class in Lafayette township was organized by Rev. Almon Greenman, at Beach school-house. Meetings were held there, and afterward at Hoosier school-house, but during the time of civil war the membership was much reduced. In 1869 a reorganization was made, and during the next year, a good frame church, 36x50 feet in dimensions, was erected at a cost of $2,200, and was dedicated as Munson chapel. There are now about seventy-five members who are ministered to by J. B. Allemann, of Roanoke circuit.

The class at New Haven was organized July 7, 1861, by Rev. E. W. Erick, of the Massillon circuit, there being but five members, Rev. True Pattee, Lorenzo Pattee and wife, Mrs. Sarah Pattee and Miss Emily Tinkham. The class remained in the Massillon circuit until 1863, when it was assigned to Harlan circuit, and in 1865 it became a separate charge known as New Haven mission, with an appropriation of $125. The building of the Methodist Protestants was used until 1866, when a brick church was erected by Henry Burgess. This was dedicated by Rev. R. D. Robinson, February 24, 1867. The pastor now in charge is J. C. Dorwin, who also has in charge Bower's chapel, in St. Joseph township, which society was organized many years ago, and the circuit includes ninety-five members.

In 1877, as a result of meetings held by Rev. C. H. Brown, at East Liberty, Monroe township, a class of forty members was organized, which held services at first in the United Brethren church. In 1879, a neat brick church, Shiloh, was erected, 32x40 in size, about a half mile north of East Liberty, which is a point in Monroeville circuit. The church at Sheldon is a flourishing one, and A. G. McCarter, now stationed there, has a circuit with 137 members. At Hoagland, in 1888, a society was organized, which now meets in the Baptist church. The various churches of this denomination in Allen county are now under the care of Elder M. Mahin, a veteran pastor.

Among the early pastors who carried the gospel to the pioneers, besides those already mentioned, should be named Elder Hargrave Phelps, Shobe, Joseph Harrison, F. A. Conwell, John P. Jones and D. P. Hartman.

Baptist Church.—In 1835, the courageous and enterprising ministers in the mission work of this church held meetings at various places throughout the county of Allen. At the house of Joshua Goheene, under the ministration of Rev. Gildersleeve, a society was organized which met at the residences of the member named and of John Ross, until 1850, when the Eel River church absorbed the membership.

In Marion township Rev. Robert Tisdel and Rev. William Corbin labored, and so effectually that in 1838, on February 6th, six Baptists, under their leadership, Margaret Rock, Michael Rock, Christopher Lipes, Susanna Lipes, Sarah Morton and Bada Morton, formed an organization and began holding meetings at the house of Christopher Lipes. In 1849, they erected a small church at a cost of $400, which was used twenty-one years. In 1870 the creditable edifice now used, Bethel church, above the village of Williamsport was built, at an expense of $1,200, but the church is not active at present, and there is no regular preaching. The members of this church and the Methodists in union organized a Sunday-school in 1835, on the west bank of the St. Mary's, south of Williamsport.

The Eel River church, above alluded to, was organized December 21, 1844, by Elder Wedge. At the first regular meeting, Appleton Rich was chosen deacon, and John Ross clerk. Rev. A. S. Bingham became pastor May 16, 1846, and was retained in that position more than twenty-five years. In 1850, a frame house was erected near Heller's corners, and dedicated September 28. This was insufficient in later years, and a substantial brick church was built at a cost of $4,400. This was dedicated by Rev. Rider, August 25, 1878.

In Washington township meetings were frequently held by ministers of all denominations, but it was not until 1846 that the First Baptist church was organized by Rev. Alfred Bingham. He remained in charge one year, was succeeded by Elder Adams for a similar period, and then that worthy pioneer of the township, Thomas Hatfield, acted as minister until about the beginning of the civil war. After his resignation, interest in the organization soon flagged, and in a short time it was abandoned.

On the fourth Saturday in October, 1854, ten members of this denomination met at the Beech school-house, in Lafayette township, and organized an "Old School" Baptist church, of which Mark S. Gaskill was chosen deacon and clerk, and Rev. Joseph Williams, pastor. Four years later fourteen members withdrew to join another organization, and the society was therefore much crippled.

A Free Will Baptist church was organized in Lake township in 1852, and a church was erected in the same year, but on account of deaths and removals the society gradually ceased to be, and the church building was transferred to the Methodists.

United Brethren Church.— Some of the most prominent of the pastors of this church who labored in this county during the early years of the organization here were, John Hill and his son, J. W. Hill, M. Johnson, C. B. Whitley, L. S. Parver, F. B. Hendricks, W. S. Bay, W. Miller, W. McKee, J. L. Luttrell, S. T. Mahan and Z. H. Bonnell.

Rev. John Hill, a devoted circuit preacher, who died at Monmouth about 1876, held services at the barn of Samuel Clem, in Monroe township, in 1845, and a church was organized with six members. For several years meetings were held at the houses of members until an arrangement was made by which this society and the Methodists erected a building to be used in common. In 1873 the Bethlehem church was erected at East Liberty, in dimensions 34x46, which cost $1,600. It was dedicated by Bishop J. J. Grosbrenner. The present pastor is W. L. Waldo.

In 1854 a class of sixteen was organized, at the house of John Miller, in Pleasant township, which was the beginning of the congregation which now worships at Liberty chapel. The first church building, a log structure, was erected in 1859, and dedicated by Rev. P. Landen, and served as a place of worship until 1868, when the chapel was erected at Five Corners. T. M. Harvey is now the pastor of the congregation.

The society of this denomination which now meets in a neat church at Cedarville, was organized in February, 1861, at Hamilton, with fifty members, by Rev. Jonathan Thomas, pastor. They erected a church at Hamilton at a cost of $1,200, but sold it in the same year, 1875, to the Methodist Episcopal church, and built a new edifice at Cedarville, which was dedicated by Elder David Holmes in April, 1877. Rev. T. O. Tussing is now in charge of this and the Maysville church. The house of worship of the latter was erected about 1858.

The society which meets at Prairie Grove chapel, in Wayne township, was organized in 1888, but is really a re-organization of an older society, which worshipped there a number of years ago, but had become disorganized. The re-organization was with twenty members, and a local minister, G. W. Carder, is now in charge.

About 1875, the Nine Mile society in Marion township, which met in a log church on the Wayne trace, was disorganized. It was one of the early organizations in the county. The Williamsport church was organized in 1868, with four members. The house of worship was erected and dedicated in 1874, Rev. J. L. Luttrell officiating. At present the membership is thirty, and Rev. J. P. Stewart is in charge.

Presbyterian Church.— In 1836, and subsequently, Rev. Rankin, of Fort Wayne, an able minister of this denomination, held services at a cabin on the site of Huntertown, at the house of Christian Parker, in St. Joseph township, and elsewhere; and several years before, Rev. Chute, of Ft. Wayne, had in 1829, first carried the gospel to the new homes of the settlers of Washington township. But no organizations within this church were made, except near Hoagland, in 1859. This society was organized with fifteen members, and James English and John McConahy as elders. In 1869 a church building was erected at a cost of about $1,000, but the organization is now dissolved.

Christian Church.— In 1865 a society of this organization was formed in west Lafayette township, with eleven members. Rev. E. W. Hammond was the pastor, Stephen Wilson and Thomas Wilkerson, elders, and Isaac B. Dawes and William Jobs, deacons. In 1872 the neat frame church near Beech school-house was erected at a cost of $1,575, and in December of the same year it was dedicated by Elder Smith, of Huntington.

The next church of this denomination to be organized was that in Monroeville, in 1867. For several years meetings had been held at Pool's hall, which was used after the organization for ten years. In 1877 the handsome brick edifice in which the congregation now worships, was built at a cost of $3,500, and dedicated by Rev. L. L. Carpenter.

Universalist Church.— A society of this denomination was organized at the house of Dr. D. Vanderhyden, in 1850, with seventeen members, and William Chaplin of Kosciusko county, visited the church as pastor. In 1851 their house of worship at Huntertown was erected, and dedicated by Mr. Chaplin, who was engaged in 1855 as pastor, the first of a series of able ministers. The society now has no regular minister.

The First Universalist church of New Haven was organized in April, 1865, at the house of H. W. Loveland. The first officers elected were Mrs. Col. Whitaker, president; Mrs. Nancy McDonald, vice president; Mrs. Jane Phelps, treasurer, and Mrs. O. D. Rogers, secretary. In 1878 a lot was purchased for the erection of a church, but it was never built and the society is abandoned.

Evangelical Association.— A society of this denomination was organized in 1850, in the northeast part of Lafayette township, and soon afterward a log church was built, in which meetings were held regularly for many years.

Apostolic Christian Church.— In the fall of 1862, two members of this denomination met at the house of Jacob Schwartz, and organized a society, of which these two were the only members for some time. The first sermon was preached by Rev. John Craybill, of Illinois. The society grew, and in 1878 a house was erected near Hamilton, which was dedicated by Revs. Henry Sanders and Joseph Conrad, who served as pastors afterward.

Church of God.— Ten members of this denomination organized a society at Potter's station, in Eel River township, in 1875, with Rev. John Parker as pastor. In the spring of 1876, a handsome house was built, 40x52 feet, costing $1,360, which was dedicated May 12, 1876, by Rev. Mrs. McCauley, and christened Ari chapel.

Union Chapel, near the center of north Pleasant township, was founded as the result of a meeting held at Prayer Grove chapel in June, 1874, to adopt measures for the building of a place of worship in Pleasant township which should be open to all denominations. The building was begun in August and completed in December, 1874, and was dedicated by Revs. Robinson, of Fort Wayne and T. H. Bernau of Wells county.

Methodist Protestant Church.—An organization under the ministry of Rev. Edward Hickland was effected in about 1838, at New Haven. Among the prominent early members were: Abram Miller and wife, Jeremiah Bateman, Rev. Isaac Bateman, Mrs. Julia Green, E. W. Green, Mrs. Sarah Bateman, Sallie Studebaker, Maria Doyle, Ann Miller, Joseph Young, Abram Hughes, Miss Jane Whitley, Susan McDougal, Mrs. McDougal, Monroe Norton. The congregation used the schoolhouse at first, and in 1857-8 erected a church building, which is still in use.

The Cuba church of this denomination was organized in the winter of 1851, with fourteen members, by Rev. R. S. Widney. In 1854, during the pastorate of Rev. David Pattee, a frame church building, 30x40, costing $500, was built. This building was removed to Maysville in 1866, and was used there until 1878, when a handsome frame structure was erected, which involved an expenditure of nearly $3,000. It was dedicated January 19, 1879, by Rev. McKeever.

Wesleyan Methodist Church.—In 1853 a society of the United Brethren church was organized at Eel River township, with ten members, and it prospered for over twenty years, a neat frame church being erected in the west part of the township in 1860; but about 1874 doctrinal differences between the pastor and congregation resulted in a division, the greater part of the society uniting in the organization of a Wesleyan Methodist church. The meetings of the old church soon afterward ceased, and in 1878 the new organization purchased the old building.

German Baptists.—The members of this church who settled in the northern part of the county at the period of the German immigration, worshipped at a church in DeKalb county for a considerable period. The members in Eel river township withdrew in 1874, chose Jeremiah Gump as pastor, and in 1875 built a frame church 36x50 feet, on section 9, at a cost of $1,500. In Cedar Creek township, a society was organized in June, 1876, which purchased a building formerly used at Hamilton by the Methodists. This was re-dedicated by Rev. Jesse Calberd.

Mennonite Church.—Rev. Kraber held meetings in 1852, at the house of Jacob Saunders, preaching the doctrines of this church, and a society was organized which met at the residences and barns of members until the building of a church east of Hamilton, in 1874. In 1860 there was a withdrawal by a number of members, who met at their private houses.

Allan H. Dougall

HISTORY OF THE GERMAN EVANGELICAL LUTHERAN CHURCH IN ALLEN COUNTY.

By HENRY W. DIEDERICH,
Professor of English Language and Literature in Concordia College.

The Lutheran church is the church of the Reformation. There were reformers in the church before Luther, but there was no successful reformation except which Luther led. It is not necessary to tell the reader who Luther was. As long as history shall be told, and wherever the blessings of religious and civil liberty shall be enjoyed, the name of Luther will be remembered with veneration and gratitude. Of him more than of any other mortal of modern ages, it may be said: THOUGH DEAD, HE STILL LIVETH.

But what is popularly known as the Lutheran church, is not so-called because she is founded on Luther. None can honor and revere the great reformer as a witness for the truth more than does the church that bears his name, but " our faith does not rest upon Luther's authority." Far from it. A pious German prince once said: " We are not baptised in the name of Luther. He is not our Lord and Savior. We do not rest our faith in him. In that sense we are not Lutherans. But if we be asked whether with heart or lips we profess the doctrines which God restored to light through the instrumentality of his blessed servant, Dr. Luther, we neither hesitate nor are we ashamed to call ourselves Lutherans." This is the reason why our church has so cheerfully adopted the name which was first applied to us, by way of derision and contempt, by our opponent, the Roman Catholic church.

Our first name, however, and the name of our own choice, is *Evangelical*. No other word can better characterize our church than this. For the gospel of Jesus Christ, the glad tidings of the Savior of sinners, is the doctrine with which our church must stand or fall. And we hold that the blessings of that gospel are continually presented to us as free as the air we breathe, through the means of grace, God' blessed Word and his holy sacraments. And in accepting them we renounce all dependence upon ourselves, all ideas of human merits, and with a firm and faithful trust cling and cleave inseparably to Christ alone and his merit. Another distinctive trait of the Lutheran church is this At the head of all authority we place the Bible. That book alon determines all questions of doctrine and duty. " It is written," is th only argument to which we submit in matters of religion, our reason feelings, and experience to the contrary notwithstanding.

The Word of God and the Grace of God are therefore the two pillars of the Lutheran church. Hence " all is ours," and we strenuously maintain that liberty of conscience and private judgment are inalienable rights of man. With a conscience free from any state authority, we are equally unfettered by any high church order in our church government. We receive our ministers not as masters of our faith, but merely as our pastors, preachers, brethren, and counsellors. *One is our master, even Christ*, and we are all brethren, and are bound together only by the eternal ties of God's Word. Such are the fundamental principles of the Lutheran church.

Since the days of the apostles, the great object of the Christian church, as an organization, has been " to go into all the world and preach the gospel to every creature." She is appointed to carry the light, liberty and hope of the gospel to the ends of the earth. Her work is not done until the cross is planted in every soil, the banner of redemption unfurled in every breeze, and the wretched and dying of all lands are pointed to the "lamb of God which taketh away the sins of the world." In this great and glorious work the Lutheran church, from the earliest period of the Reformation, took a conspicuous part, as the mother church of Protestant Christianity, she felt that she must lead the van in the work of missions. Accordingly, we find Lutheran princes and church patrons, already centuries ago, directing their attention to the spreading of the gospel among the heathen. Gustavus Vasa, the Lutheran king of Sweden, has the illustrious honor of instituting and establishing the first effective Protestant mission. The great Lutheran hero, Gustavus Adolphus, was of the same mind in these matters, and many other names might be added, that shine forth from the brilliant constellation of Lutheran missionaries and missionary institutions.

It was this missionary spirit first of all, that led to the planting of the Lutheran church in this country. "The English first came hither as adventurers in search of notoriety and gain. The Dutch first came hither impelled by the spirit of mercantile enterprise. The Puritans first came over to escape from religious persecution. But the Lutherans first came hither chiefly moved with the inspiring idea of planting on these newly discovered shores, the pure church of the living God. The plan was conceived by Gustavus Adolphus, and carried into effect by his prime minister, Oxenstiern . . . . . The first permanent settlers on this continent landed in Virginia in 1607. Seven years after the Dutch commenced their settlement along the Hudson. Six years later the Puritans landed at Plymouth Rock. And but thirty years after the first permanent settlement of Europeans upon this continent, the Lutheran colonists, sent forth by royal favor from the kingdom of Sweden, took up their abode in the name of Christ, on the banks of the Delaware. Among the first, if not the very first Christian churches ever built and consecrated in this new world, were those they built. Five years before the arrival of William Penn, a Lutheran minister was preaching the gospel in the neighborhood of where Philadelphia now stands. On Trinity Sunday, 1699, the first Lutheran church in America was consecrated at Christina, Del. . . . . It is also an interesting reminiscence, that the first missionaries who ever taught the gospel of Jesus to the Indians of America, were Lutherans; and that the first book ever translated and printed in the Indian language, was the Lutheran Catechism."

The special mission and work of the Lutheran church in this country has always been chiefly among the Germans and Scandinavians and their descendants. And as the Lutheran church began with the Reformation in Germany, the great majority of Lutherans in this country are Germans and their descendants. It was religious persecution that caused many of them to emigrate from their fatherland and to seek an asylum in America and a home where they might find "freedom to worship God." This was the beginning of a number of Lutheran colonies in Georgia, South Carolina and other states.

But by far the greater number of German emigrants left their homes and all that was dear to them because poverty and starvation stared them in the face in their native country. They entered upon a long and tedious voyage across the Atlantic and endured the perils and hardships which often greeted them upon their arrival in this country, because they knew that with industry and frugality, better prospects and better opportunities for making a living awaited them here than in their own country. There came the titled nobleman who, by misfortune or mismanagement, had lost that affluence which once surrounded his ancestral home. There came the unfortunate merchant who by unwise investments and lack of success in his commercial affairs brought himself and family to the verge of ruin. There came the industrious mechanic who could scarcely maintain a large and increasing family on the small pittance which was his daily support, and who could never hope to get beyond the point of keeping the wolf from the door. There came the sturdy peasant and tenant who was so overburdened with tithes and gatherings that he groaned over the profitless labor he daily performed. There came the strong and promising youth, to escape the demands of his country upon him for military service. There came, in the blush of life, young and unmarried men and women, who could see nothing before them but overcrowded situations; whose circumstances forbade them ever to arrive at the condition of competency in the ordinary pursuits of life, and who therefore felt but too keenly that the Old World had little employment to offer and less bread to spare. Thus *necessity* induced the vast majority of German emigrants to seek their fortune in America. And this class of people has furnished chiefly the field for the mission of the Lutheran church in America. And it was this class of emigrants that laid the foundation to, and built up, the various Lutheran congregations in Fort Wayne and Allen county.

It was on Saturday, October 14, 1837, when a number of German immigrants met in a room of the court-house of Fort Wayne, and by adopting the formula of the discipline of the Evangelical Lutheran hurch organized the first GERMAN EVANGELICAL LUTHERAN CHURCH F FORT WAYNE. This was the first Lutheran church in the state of

Indiana. There were present twenty-three heads of families whose names were entered upon the records of the newly organized congregation. The pastor was the Rev. Jesse Hoover, and the first election resulted in making Adam Wefel and Henry Trier, elders, and Henry Rudisill and Conrad Nill, deacons. Such was the humble origin of St. Paul's church, now on Barr street.

The man who was most active in bringing about this event was Henry Rudisill, who, born and bred in Pennsylvania, had moved to Fort Wayne in the year 1829, when the village had but 150 inhabitants, mostly French and Indians. Mr. Rudisill and his family were the first Germans and the first Lutherans in this part of the country. No happier man than he when, after years of patient waiting, he at last saw the German Lutherans in this frontier village united in a church organization, and supplied with a Lutheran pastor.

Rev. Hoover entered upon his duties with indomitable zeal, serving his people as their pastor and preacher, and sharing with them their hardships and privations. Not content with his work in the settlement, he extended his mission circuit over the greater part of northern Indiana. But unfortunately, after a successful ministry of not quite two years, he died, when but twenty-eight years old. His remains were recently removed from a neglected spot and deposited in the Lutheran cemetery where they have found a prominent and permanent resting place. Blessed be his memory.

The little flock of Lutherans was now without a shepherd. But soon God in His providence led into their midst a man who was not only to supply St. Paul's, but who was to become the patriarch of Lutheranism on this continent west of the Alleghanies. This was the sainted Rev. Wyneken, who only recently had left his native land, and risked the dangers and exposure of a sea voyage, and cast his lot in a new country with its many inconveniences. And why did he do this? For no other reason than to bring the gospel to his German brethren that were scattered over this new country which was then in a most chaotic condition. Nothing but his great love for Christ and His church could furnish the motive. In the autumn of 1838 he came to Fort Wayne and at once entered upon his labors which were many and arduous. The perils and difficulties, trials and exposures which beset him, can scarcely be conceived at this day. And yet his confidence in God remained unshaken. He frequently undertook distant and irksome journeys as far as the states of Ohio and Michigan; sometimes these missionary tours required an absence from home for weeks and months, and subjected him to much persoual inconvenience; yet he cheerfully submitted to all. He was willing to make any sacrifice, endure any suffering, and render any service, however toilsome, that he might advance his mission and bring souls to Christ. He never grew weary in well-doing, but his left hand never found out what his right did in that direction. He had the unbounded confidence of his people, and no man ever deserved it more than he did.

What a hard life many of those early German settlers must have had! After a long and stormy passage, worn out with the toils and sufferings of an overland journey in this wild country before the days of the railroad, they finally reached their destination, only to be disapointed in their expectations. Soon, however, they would gather courage, and many of them began to swing their axes and hewed out the timber for their rude dwellings, and laid the foundation to some of the most valuable farms and estates in Allen county. Bread for themselves, their wives and little ones was all they could expect in the beginning from the fruitful soil of their adopted country. And in many cases the poor immigrant had first to work to pay the expense of his passage to America, as he had to borrow the money to cross the ocean. But we shall not rehearse the touching story of the hardships and strugglings of these heroic men and women, the pioneers in the Allen county wilderness! In spite of it all, wood fires, the only comfort that was plenty, blazed bright, and around the warm hearthstone often was heard the prayers of thanksgiving and the song of praise. Ay, those were men and women of strong faith. They were deeply attached to their church. They read and studied the Bible, and were accustomed to family prayers. They laid the foundation of our Lutheran churches both deep and strong, and deserve to be held in grateful remembrance to all future generations.

After having had their services for years in the court-house, and afterward in a small brick building, on the corner of Harrison and Superior streets, the St. Paul's congregation bought some ground and in 1839 erected a small frame building where the new St. Paul's is rearing its magnificent spires to the skies to-day.

For some years after the first little church had been built, Rev. Wyneken continued to labor among his people with the same untiring zeal, submitting himself to self-denials and deprivations from which most men would recoil. But a call to a Lutheran church in Baltimore, which he accepted, put an end to his work here in Fort Wayne. This occurred in 1845. We can well imagine the scene of leave taking, as the saddened group of people gathered to bid him good-bye and wafted their parting blessings to him. Afterward the reverend gentleman became one of the founders and leaders of the Missouri synod, now one of the largest Lutheran organizations in the country; and for many years he was the president of said synod, where he was frequently and successfully engaged in church difficulties, in restoring peace among the brethren, in encouraging feeble congregations and in performing many other labors in the interest of the Lutheran zion. He died in San Francisco, Cal., in 1877, and was buried in Cleveland, Ohio. The debt of gratitude to him can never be repaid. Wherever his name is spoken his services shall be recounted and his memory hallowed, and his praises dwell living upon the lips of men.

The next pastor of St. Paul's was Rev. W. Sihler, who was installed in 1845. Under his faithful and fostering care the congregation continued to grow and flourish. Soon it became necessary, for want of accommodation, to erect a more commodious house of worship, to which an addition had to be made again in 1862, in the form of a cross.

One of the leading events during the pastorate of Rev. Sihler was the establishment of a theological seminary, of which he was appointed the first professor and director. This institution, years afterward, was tranferred to St. Louis, and the present Concordia college took its place.

In the course of time the congregation became so large that it became necessary to divide it into two parishes. Accordingly, the EMANUEL'S LUTHERAN CHURCH was branched off, and a noble and imposing church edifice erected on the corner of Jackson and Jefferson streets, and Rev. Stubnatzy, who, for years had been Rev. Sihler's most highly accomplished and immensely popular assistant, was made pastor of the new charge. This was done during the years 1868 and 1869.

Rev. Sihler now continued to perform the duties of his sacred office alone until 1875, when the ever increasing work and his decreasing strength induced him to ask for another assistant. Accordingly, Rev. H. G. Sauer, a highly talented Lutheran minister of Mobile, Ala., was called and installed to labor by the side of the venerable senior pastor. The growth of the church was such a rapid one that it soon became apparent that another division would also have to be made. In 1882, therefore, the ZION'S LUTHERAN CHURCH, in the southern portion of the city, was established, with Rev. Dreyer as her first pastor. In June, 1885, Rev. Sihler, who for forty years had so faithfully ministered to the spiritual wants of St. Paul's, was constrained, in view of extreme old age, to resign the pastorate. He lingered on for some months, and died on October 27th of the same year. He went to his grave most highly honored and respected. His stern integrity, his intense earnestness of purpose, his simple and child-like faith, his sense of duty, and his fidelity to the doctrines of his church will always bear honorable mention.

The year 1887 was a year of special interest to the members of St. Paul's, and to the Lutherans of Allen county in general, for it brought the fiftieth anniversary, which was celebrated in a manner becoming the occasion. It was a jubilee of joy and thanksgiving and it was resolved that, though the old church building was still in fairly good condition, to erect a new and more commodious house of worship, and through the extraordinary liberality and devotion of the German Lutheran people, a new church has been built, on the site of the old building that, by universal consent, is one of the handsomest and most imposing structures of the city. At writing of this sketch preparations are being made for consecrating the new building to the service of the Triune God. The present pastor is Rev. Sauer, who assumed the full duties of the pastorate ever since the resignation of Rev. Sihler. That his position offers him no sinecure may be gathered from the fact that no less 3,000 souls belong to his parish. A man more affable in manners, more genial in disposition, and better gifted for pulpit and other ministerial work, than Rev. H. G.

Sauer, it would probably be difficult to find. May this faithful pastor and his good people long continue to enjoy God's choicest blessings in the new temple, and may the means of grace used there redound to the glory of God and the salvation of many souls.

St. John's Evangelical Lutheran congregation was founded in the year 1853. Besides being small and weak, the congregation contained an element that would not tolerate church discipline and order. Consequently, dissensions and conflicts of all kinds that retarded the congregation's growth were not wanting during the first fifteen years. Besides this, frequent change of ministers was a great drawback, for during the time mentioned the congregation was served by four pastors, namely, Hochstetter, Kleineggers, Kuhn and Baumann. This and some other things were the cause why the congregation did not prosper at first as might be expected. In the year 1868 the congregation called the present pastor, Rev. J. Kucher, at that time of Pittsburgh, Penn.

The congregation is now in a flourishing condition. It owns a beautiful church, a school-house, in which 160 children are daily instructed by two teachers, a large parsonage, a dwelling house for the teachers, and a farm near the city. A beautiful cemetery is laid out on the farm. The congregation numbers 1,000 communicants. St. John's church is not in a synodical connection with the other German Lutheran churches of Fort Wayne, but a member of the Evangelical Lutheran synod of Ohio.

The following is a list of the German Lutheran churches (Missouri synod) in Allen county:

St. Paul's, at Fort Wayne.—This is the oldest Lutheran church in the state, and the parent church of the five following. Rev. H. G. Sauer, pastor. The congregation has its own parochial school in which the following teachers are employed: Messrs. J. H. Ungemach, C. Grahl, E. Gerberding, B. M. Hemmann, I. Riedel, C. Strieder and H. K. Mahlich.

The Emanuel's Lutheran Church.—The first pastor of this congregation was Rev. W. Stubnatzy, who, through his polished and pleasant manners, his ardent Lutheran spirit and his eloquent address exerted a most important influence upon the development of the Lutheran church at Fort Wayne. This great and popular preacher died in 1880, and was succeeded by Rev. C. Gross, the present pastor of the congregation. The teachers are: Messrs. G. Kampe, D. Lindemann, D. Roscher, G. Hormel and G. Grimm.

Zion's.—Rev. H. Juengel, pastor. Teachers are: Messrs. F. Klein, J. D. Mangelsdorf and N. S. Zagel.

Martin's.—A model Lutheran country parish near Adam's Station. Rev. S. F. C. F. Stock, pastor. Teacher: R. A. A. Mueller, esq.

Trinity Lutheran Church.—Rev. F. W. Franke, pastor.

St. Peter's Lutheran Church, in St. Joseph township.—This church was organized in 1854, and was served by Rev. R. John, 1854-1859,

and by Rev. C. E. Bode, 1859-1881, and since then by Rev. M. Mic ha
The teacher for more than twenty years has been J. M. L. Hafne

St. John's Lutheran Church, Fort Wayne.

German Evangelical Lutheran Church at New Haven, Allen county, Ind. Rev. F. Kleist, pastor.

German Lutheran Church at Gar Creek, Allen county, Ind. Rev. A. Schupmann, pastor.

The German Evangelical Lutheran Church in Marion township, Allen county, Ind. Rev. C. Zschoche, pastor.

The St. John's German Evangelical Lutheran Church at Hoagland, Allen county, Ind. This congregation was organized October 1, 1849, and has grown from small beginnings under the faithful ministry of Revs. Husmann, Fleischmann, Bauer, Karrer, Rosenwinkel, Zschoche, and of the present pastor, Rev. G. Th. Gotsch, and is to-day in a flourishing condition, having a neat church and a school building and a parsonage, all of brick.

No sketch of Lutheranism of Allen county would be complete without including a description of CONCORDIA COLLEGE. In the "east end" of Fort Wayne, between Maumee avenue and Washington street, there is a tract of land covering twenty-five acres, on which are a number of large buildings and several family residences. The grounds are those of Concordia college, one of the largest German Lutheran educational institutions in this country. This college is mainly a preparatory school for the Concordia Theological seminary at St. Louis, Mo., where from thirty to forty students are graduated each year, to supply pulpits mostly in the Missouri Lutheran synod. Hence almost every clergyman that holds a diploma from the St. Louis seminary has also been graduated at the college at Fort Wayne.

Concordia college was founded in 1839, by a few theologians, in Perry county, Mo. The first college building was a log cabin, and the beginnings were very humble. In 1849, the college was removed to St. Louis, and at the outbreak of the war of rebellion, in 1861, Fort Wayne became its permanent home.

At the time of the change Concordia had but three chairs in its faculty, and these were filled by Professors Schick, Saxer and Lauge. The number of students there was only seventy-eight. In the night of December 28, 1869, the main building of the former seminary was destroyed by fire. Soon, however, not only this part of the institution was rebuilt, but, in time, such other structures were erected as the growing needs of the college required. The main building to-day if 150 feet long by eighty feet wide, and is three stories high. The lower floor is used for class rooms, the second floor for living rooms, and the upper floor for sleeping apartments. Among the latest additions is the gymnasium, built with funds raised by the students, and well equipped with the proper apparatus.

The number of students varies continually. The attendance at present is about 225. These are furnished with every needed accommodation at the college at a surprisingly small cost. No tuition fee is charged to those who propose to enter the service of the church, and as ninety-eight per cent. of the graduates become theological students, very little revenue goes into the college treasury from this source. Concordia college exists and flourishes without one cent for a fund; it depends on the voluntary contributions of the German Lutheran people, upon wise and economical management, and, first and last, upon the Giver of all good things. Thus the German Evangelical Lutheran Synod of Missouri places within the easy reach of its youth all the advantages of a superior education. Thus she supplies her churches with men thoroughly equipped for the arduous duties of the ministry.

On the 25th and 26th days of June, 1889, Concordia was decked and arrayed in her holiday garments. It was her fiftieth anniversary. It was a joyous occasion — one never to be forgotten by those hundreds of students and alumni and guests who were so fortunate as to be present. May Concordia college continue to grow and multiply, and to accomplish great good in the land.

The following is a list of the college faculty: Rev. A. Baepler, director, or president, of Concordia college; Rev. F. Schick, professor of the Latin and Greek languages; Rev. H. W. Diederich, professor of English language and literature. Prof. H. W. Diederich, who for years has been suffering from failing eye-sight and a serious throat affection, was, on July 9, 1889, appointed consul to Leipsic, Germany, by President Harrison, which appointment the professor has accepted, thus creating a vacancy in the chair of English language and literature, which he has filled for sixteen years. In point of service, therefore, the professor was the second oldest member of the faculty, Prof. G. Schick being the senior. Rev. A. Crull, professor of the German and French languages; H. Duemling, Ph. D., professor of mathematics and natural history; Rev. F. Zucker, professor of the Greek and Hebrew languages; O. Siemon, Ph. D., professor of the Latin language; H. Schuelke, Cand. rev. min., assistant professor of the Latin language.

Rev. Henry G. Sauer, pastor of St. Paul's German Evangelical Lutheran church, Fort Wayne, was born in St. Louis, Mo., June 14, 1845, son of Christopher G. and Julia (Waldhauer) Sauer, natives of Germany, who were married in St. Louis in 1844. Both are now deceased. He attended the parochial schools of St. Louis, and at thirteen years of age entered Concordia college, which was then located at that city. While he was a student the college was removed to Fort Wayne, in 1861. He was graduated in 1865, and in the fall entered Concordia seminary, at St. Louis, at which he was graduated in June, 1868. He began his ministerial labors in St. Louis, taking charge of Christ's church for a year and a half, and during the same time teaching the parochial school connected with his church. In February, 1870, he accepted the call of the German Evangelical Lutheran church at Mobile, Ala., and thence in November, 1875, he was called to the position of second pastor of St. Paul's church of Fort Wayne. He acted in that capacity ten years, the late Rev. Dr. William Sihler being the first pastor during the time. Upon the death of Dr. Sihler, in 1885, Rev. Sauer succeeded him, and has filled this position in a very able and scholarly manner. Mr. Sauer was married February 4, 1869, to Maria T., daughter of Rev. Carl and Emma Tuercke. She was born in Füerstenwalde, Germany, September 18, 1845. They have had eight children: Henry T., Herman, Paul E., Charles, Emma, Martha, Maria and Adele, of whom Henry and Charles are deceased. For several years Rev. Sauer has been a member of the board of trustees of Concordia college, and since the death of Rev. Stubnatzy he has been president of the board.

Rev. Charles Gross was called to the pastorate of the Emanuel's Evangelical Lutheran church of Fort Wayne in the fall of 1880, coming with the prestige of thirteen years' successful service as the the pastor of the First Lutheran Trinity church of Buffalo, N. Y. He is of German nativity, born near Frankfort-on-the-Main, September 26, 1834. He came to America with his parents in 1847, and settled with them at St. Louis, where his youth was spent and where the parents remained during the rest of their lives. He began his studies in the parochial schools of St. Louis, and then, at fourteen years, entered Concordia college, then located in Perry county, Mo. He completed his collegiate course in 1853 and graduated from the theological department in 1856. On the 22nd of June, of the year last named, he was ordained a minister and took charge of the German Lutheran congregation at Richmond, Va. He remained there during the trying scenes of civil war, and until 1867, when he removed to Buffalo. This distinguished divine has now for nearly a third of a century labored efficiently in the vineyard of his Master. On May 3, 1857, he was united in marriage with Augusta Westerfeld, a native of Bielefeld, Germany, who died April 7, 1871, at the age of thirty-four, leaving seven children: Charles, Otto W., Martin C., Theodore, Anna, Augusta, and Eddy. The eldest died in his seventeenth year, while a student at Concordia college, and the last child died at the age of three months. Mr. Gross was married June 6, 1872, to Mary, daughter of Rev. John Her, and by this latter marriage has had six sons: Paul (deceased), Gerhard (deceased), Charles Edwin, Walter and Arthur (deceased). The last two were twins. Otto W., the oldest child living, is a member of the firm of Thieme & Gross, Fort Wayne; Martin C. is book-keeper for the firm of Coombs & Co.; Theodore, a graduate of Concordia college, has charge of a Lutheran congregation at New Britain, Conn. Anna is the wife of Louis Hagemann, of Fort Wayne.

Rev. Henry Juengel is a native of Germany, and was born May 13, 1829. At the age of twenty-one he accompanied his parents, Henry and Margaret (Magold) Juengel, to this country, and made his home with them at St. Louis. Two years later, in 1852, he entered the Concordia seminary, then at Fort Wayne, but now located at Springfield, Ill., and after two years' attendance, he began his ministerial labors at Peru, Ind. Six months afterward, he became pastor of a German Evangelical Lutheran church at Liverpool, Ohio, and remained there six years. His next field of labor was at Gootch Mills, Cooper county, Mo., where he was engaged six years and three months. From 1867 he was pastor of St. John's German Evangelical Lutheran church, near Jonesville, Bartholomew county, Ind., until February 1, 1887, when he was called to his present charge, Zion's German Evangelical Lutheran church. For thirty-five years he has been a faithful and efficient worker in the cause. Rev. Juengel was married July 9, 1854, to Sophia M., daughter of Frederick and Sophia (Vajen) Fruechtenicht. She was born in Germany, April 2, 1833, and came to America with her parents when she was nine years of age. This marriage has resulted in the birth of twelve children: Herman, Emma, Elizabeth, Sophia, Johanna, Ernst, Clara, Henry, Paul and Lina, living, and two deceased.

Rev. John J. Kucher was called to the pastorate of St. John's German Evangelical Lutheran church in 1868, and has ever since ministered faithfully and zealously to the spiritual needs of that congregation. This gentleman was born in the kingdom of Wurtemberg, Germany, February 9, 1835, the son of John J. and Elizabeth Kucher. His early education was received in his native country, and when eighteen years of age he entered the missionary institute at Basel, Switzerland, where he pursued theological studies five years, graduating in 1858. He was immediately ordained, and sent by the missionary society, soon afterward, to preach the word among the Germans of the United States. He arrived in this country in October, 1858, and at once began his labors, having served since then congregations at Harrisburg, Penn., Wilmington, Del., Philadelphia and Pittsburgh, before coming to this city. He was married in 1859 to Anna Mueck, who was born at Stuttgart, Wurtemberg, September 21, 1834, and came to America in 1859. They have eight children: Ottilia, Martha, Hermann, Paul, Theophile, Theodore, Otto and Nathanael.

Rev. Simon Frederick Conrad Ferdinand Stock, the able pastor of Martini Evangelical German Lutheran church, of Adams township, Allen county, Ind., was born in the village of Friedrichshoehe, Kur Hessen, Germany, October 3, 1844. He was the son of Frederick William and Florentine (Distelhorst) Stock, the latter of whom died in Germany when he was a little child. In 1851 he came to America with his father and step-mother, and on reaching New York city the family came out westward to Dark county, Ohio, and located near Greenville. In the fall of 1853 they removed to Manitou county, Mo., and located on a farm where both his father and step-mother spent the rest of their lives and where he spent his youth. At the age of seventeen he entered Concordia college of St. Louis, in which, in addition to his other studies, he completed a full course in theology, graduating June 2, 1866. In the meantime, during the last year of his college course, he spent six months at Prairietown, Madison county, Ill., where he performed the duties of pastor of a church and teacher of a parochial school. Shortly after graduating he came to Allen county, Ind., having received a call to the pulpit of Martini Evangelical German Lutheran church of Adams township. He entered upon his charge immediately after his arrival, preaching his first sermon to the congregation on the 8th day of July, 1866. He has filled the pulpit of that church ever since — a period of twenty-three years, and during his pastorate the church has been highly prosperous. During the first twelve years of his pastorate, in addition to his ministerial duties Rev. Stock also taught the parochial school that belongs to his church. Rev. Stock was married November 7, 1867, to Sophia Margarette Wiese, who is a native of Adams township, born January 24, 1849, and was the daughter of Charles and Eleanora (Meyer) Wiese, who were natives of Germany. Rev. Stock and wife are the parents of eight chileren, as follows: Florentine Sophia Wilhelmina, Otto Frederick Ferdinand, John Henry Martin, Ferdinand William Paul, Frederick William Otto, Sophia Mary Wilhelmina, Clara Helene Christena and Christian John Rudolph, all of whom are living. Rev. Stock is an earnest and successful worker in the cause of Christianity, and he is deservedly popular, not only among the members of his own congregation but among all who know him. Rev. Stock's eldest son is now a student in Concordia college of Fort Wayne, preparatory to taking a theological course at Concordia seminary at St. Louis.

Rev. George Theodore Gotsch was born in Leipsig, Germany, December 21, 1825, son of George Mauree Gotsch, D. D., of Leipsig, who emigrated to America in 1852 and afterward served a congregation of the Lutheran church at Memphis, Tenn. He spent the early part of his life as principal of the city schools in Waldenburg, Saxony. He died at St. Louis, Mo., in 1878, after a life of usefulness. Rev. Gotch, the son, emigrated to America in 1851, one year before his father. He came to Fort Wayne and entered Concordia college, and in 1856, began the ministerial work, to which and teaching, he has devoted his entire time. After leaving the college, Rev. Gotsch was called to Jonesville, Bartholomew county, Ind., where he served for some years and then in 1861, removed to Olean, Ripley county. In 1864 he removed to Akron, Ohio and in 1872, to Lombard, Ill., near Chicago, and served as minister and teacher until 1884, when he removed to near Hoagland, where he continues his work as pastor and teacher. He is at present sixty-four years of age, but has the vigor of mind and body of his younger years. His wife is still living and they have eight children: Christian, married in 1875 to the daughter of Rev. H. Juengel, is a teacher in the school at Columbus, Ind. S. M. Gotsch is a teacher in a parochial school in Cleveland, Ohio. He was married in 1883, to Emeline Goltermann. Three of the sons: Emil, Charles and Martin are engaged in business at Altenheim. Oscar is a resident of Altenheim, Ill.; Clara and Bertha live with their parents.

Rev. Andrew Baepler, director of Concordia college, was born in Baltimore, Md., July 28, 1850, the son of Henry and Catherine (Reuwer) Baepler, natives of Germany. He entered Concordia college at the age of thirteen years, and was graduated in 1869. In the fall of the latter year he became a student in the Concordia seminary at St. Louis, where he was graduated in 1874. He was sent to Dallas, Tex., in the following September, and with his home at that place, he performed missionary work in northern Texas and Louisiana, during the following year. In 1875 he took charge of a circuit in Benton county, Mo., and was pastor of the three churches comprised in it until the spring of 1879, when he was called to the pastorate of the German Lutheran church, at Mobile, Ala. He remained there until January, 1882, and during the greater part of the time also had charge of an English congregation at Moss Point, Miss. Following this pastorate, he was engaged as a missionary in southern Missouri, northern Arkansas and eastern Kansas until January, 1884, when he was chosen director of St. Paul's college at Concordia, Mo. This he held until January 9, 1888, when he was called to the directorship of Concordia college. In this position he has proven eminently qualified to advance the interests of this important educational institution. Rev. Bæpler was married July 15, 1875, to Josephine S., daughter of Charles and Charlotte (Miller) Ax. She was born at New Orleans, December 16, 1857, and died May 19, 1881, leaving two sons, Charles H. and Otto J. April 12, 1883, Mr. Bæpler was married to Sophia E., daughter of Joachim and Caroline (Buetner) Birkner. She was born at Long Island, December 10, 1858. They have two children, Louisa M. and Edwin S.

Rev. Henry W. Diederich, for sixteen years professor of English language and literature in Concordia college, Fort Wayne, was born in Pittsburgh, Penn., November 13, 1845. His parents, Nicholas H. and Mary E. (Wesseller) Diederich, were natives of Germany, where they were married. Immigrating in 1845, they settled at Pittsburgh, but now reside at Allegheny City. Henry W. Diederich was graduated at Concordia college, Fort Wayne, in 1866, and at Concordia seminary at St. Louis, in 1869. He entered upon ministerial labors in the Evangelican Lutheran church in central Illinois, and in 1870 was called to the pulpit of St. John's German Lutheran church, of New York city, where he was stationed three years. In 1873 he was appointed to the chair of English language and literature in Concordia college, a position he has since filled in an able and highly satisfactory manner. In 1889 he was appointed by President Harrison counsel to the city of Leipsic, Germany, a pleasing recognition of the professor's high attainments and rare qualifications for service in such capacity. Professor Diederich was married August 23, 1870, to Margaret G., daughter of Frederick and Catherine Stutz, natives of Germany, who now reside in Washington, where Mrs. Diederich was born April 10, 1852. They have two children: Henry Frederick Theodore, born September 2, 1871, and Clara M., born July 25, 1885.

Rev. Otto A. Siemon, Ph. D., professor of Latin and history in Concordia college, is a native of this city, born May 25, 1856. He is the son of A. F. Siemon, of the well-known book firm of Siemon & Bro. Prof. Siemon's education was begun in the parochial schools of his church, in this city, where he remained until he entered Concordia college. This institution he attended from 1867 to 1873, graduating in the latter year. The following autumn he entered the Concordia seminary at St. Louis, and there graduated in theology in 1876. His studies were continued during the following year in the university of Neew York, and in the fall of 1877, he went to Berlin, Prussia, and studied three years in the famous university of that city, perfecting himself in philological acquirements. In March, 1881, the degree of Ph. D. was conferred upon him by the university of Berlin. Upon his return to this city he was selected to fill a vacancy in the chair of Latin and history, at Concordia college, and was made professor in that department in February, 1882, a position he has since filled with much credit to himself as a scholar, and to the good of the institution.

Prof. Gustave Kampe, principal of Emanuel's Evangelical Lutheran school, is a graduate of the Evangelical Lutheran seminary of Addison, Ill., which he attended five years, ending his course in 1873. He has ever since been connected with the parochial schools of Fort Wayne, five years with St. John's Evangelical Lutheran school, and since 1878 with the Emanuel's Evangelical Lutheran school, having been principal during the past four years. He is an accomplished teacher, is a man of sterling character and exemplary habits, and is esteemed as a good citizen. Prof. Kampe was born in Cleveland, Ohio, September 3, 1854, the son of Adolph and Rosina Kampe, who, when their son was eight years of age, removed with their family to Fort Wayne. He was married June 22, 1880, to Clara S. Sulzer, and they have four children: Alma, Clara, Adolph and Frieda. Mrs. Kampe was born in Milwaukee, Wis., October 21, 1857, the daughter of Adolph and Susan Sulzer.

The able and popular principal of Zion's parochial school, Prof. Frederick A. Klein, completed at fifteen years of age a thorough five years' course in the gymnasium at Wiesbaden, Germany, his native land. He did not at that time contemplate teaching, and began the study of pharmacy and chemistry, which he pursued two years at an institution at Brunswick, clerking during the same time in a drug store. In 1878 he he landed at New York, and then held for two years and a half the position of assistant chemist in a large wholesale drug house. While there he was importuned by the pastors of the Lutheran churches of the city to prepare himself for teaching. He accordingly took a course of instruction in Addison college, Ill., graduating in June, 1884, and then took charge of a primary school at Logansport, Ind., remaining there three years. He accepted his present position in June, 1887, and being a thorough and zealous instructor, of wide attainments and fertile in resources, he has achieved notable success. Prof. Klein was married October 27, 1887, to Clara Wefel, who was born in Fort Wayne October 31, 1864, daughter of John W. Wefel, formerly of this city, now of Logansport. Prof. Klein was born July 17, 1861, the son of Leo and Helen Klein.

The efficient first teacher in St. John's parochial school, Prof. Carl C. G. Bez, was born in Wurtemberg, Germany, April 2, 1861, the son of Christian and Mary Bez. He received his education in Germany, graduating from a college at Rottweil, at seventeen years of age, and in his twentieth year, from a seminary at Esslingen. In 1882, he came to America, taught school first at Allegheny, Penn., then at Briar Hill, Ohio, and accepted his present position September 1, 1885. He is a member of St. John's Lutheran church, and officiates as organist and leader of the church choir. He was married October 28, 1886, to Miss Elizabeth Huebner, daughter of Rev. C. Huebner, of Toledo, Ohio. She was before her marriage a teacher. After a married life of but little over a year, she died November 15, 1887. Mr. Bez is a successful teacher and a worthy gentleman.

SCHOOLS OF ALLEN COUNTY.

BY JOHN S. IRWIN.

Of Virginia, in 1671, it was said that "the almost general want of schools for their children was of most sad consideration, most of all bewailed of the parents then." "Every man," said Sir William Berkley in his report to the home government, "instructs his children according to his ability. The ministers should pray more and preach less. But I thank God there are no free schools nor printing, and I hope we shall not have these hundred years; for learning has brought disobedience and heresy and sects into the world, and printing has divulged them and libels against the best government. God keep us from both." Most loyal subject of Jack Cade who tells Lord Say, "Thou hast most traitorously corrupted the youth of the realm in erecting a grammar school; and whereas, before our forefathers had no other books but the score and the tally, thou hast caused printing to be used; and contrary to the king, his crown, and dignity, thou hast built a paper mill." Under this same wise governor, Berkley, on reference of the subject to the king, a printing press was destroyed, and public education, and printing all news or books forbidden. Yet when this same Virginia ceded to the general government her territory northwest of the Ohio river, the congress of the confederation, in accordance with the spirit of the deed of cession, declared in the celebrated ordinance of 1787, for the perpetual government of the ceded lands, article 3, "Religion, morality, and knowledge being necessary to good government, and the happiness of mankind, schools and the means of education shall forever be encouraged." And Washington, in his farewell address, before leaving the presidency, said, "Promote, then, as an object of primary importance, institutions for the general diffusion of knowledge. In proportion as the structure of a government gives force to public opinion, it is essential that public opinion should be enlightened."

Guided by these wise and judicious views, the framers of the first constitution of Indiana, in 1816, adopted as a fundamental principle the following which was verified by the people. "Knowledge and learning generally diffused through a community being essential to the preservation of a free government, and spreading the opportunities and advantages of education through the various parts of the country being highly conducive to this end," "it shall be the duty of the general assembly," "to provide by law for a general system of education ascending in a regular gradation from township schools to a state university, wherein tution shall be gratis, and equally open to all." The language of the revised constitution of 1851 differs slightly from this, but is essentially

J. M. Robinson

of the same import. It makes it the duty of the general assembly " to encourage by all suitable means, moral, intellectual, scientific and agricultural improvement; and to provide by law, for a general and uniform system of common schools, wherein tuition shall be without charge, and equally open to all."

In the enabling act authorizing the state of Indiana, congress, to ensure the carrying out of the directions of the ordinance of 1787, provided that section sixteen in every township should be granted to such township for the use of schools, and also provided that two whole townships should be appropriated to the use of a seminary of learning.

Private and Church Schools.—There is a tradition that the earliest school, in what now constitutes Allen county, was established at a very early day by the Society of the Friends, but no records or reminiscences whatever, concerning such school can be found. In 1821, while Allen county still formed a part of Randolph county, Rev. Isaac McCoy was sent as a missionary and teacher to the Indians by the Baptist missionary society. Opening a school in the old fort for these, he also received the children of such white parents as desired his services. In this school, which was small, he was assisted at various times by Matthew Montgomery, by Mr. and Mrs. Potts, and Mr. Hugh B. McKean.

Leaving Mr. McCoy, Mr. and Mrs. Potts taught school in a house on the banks of the St. Mary's river, near the present gas works office.

In 1825, after the organization of the county, the first school-house built in Fort Wayne, was erected on a lot adjoining the old grave-yard, in the rear of the present jail, and was known as the County seminary. In this building for many years, under the old ideas so admirably and tersely put by "Pete Jones," the young of the place, male and female, were taught by Mr. John P. Hedges and his successors in office. About the same time Henry Cooper, afterward well-known as a lawyer, taught in an upper room in the old log house on the southwest corner of the public square. The barred windows of this primitive school-house must have served to depress the spirits of the scholars in the bright spring weather, while the rough floor and seats could have had little resemblance to the comfortable and even elegant appliances now provided for the scholar.

Mr. Aughinbaugh, after teaching in the old Masonic hall of that day, had charge of the seminary in 1832–3, being followed in 1834 by Smallwood Noel, who died many years later an honored and respected old man. He in turn was followed by Mr. James Requa in the following year. About the same time Mr. Beggs taught in a small building on Columbia street.

In 1835–6 Mr. Myron F. Barbour, a most popular and successful teacher, still living, had charge of the seminary where he laid the foundation of a solid and practical education, to the benefit of many of the best business men and citizens of the town. He was followed by Mr. John C. Sivey, afterward well-known as a civil engineer engaged on the Wabash & Erie canal, who became a resident of Wabash.

An anecdote still lives in the memory of the old men of the city, concerning an applicant for the position of teacher in the seminary, against whose moral character the examineers entertained suspicions, and want of moral character being apparently no ground of action, they endeavored to defeat him by a strict and thorough examination in the essentials, an examination, however, which in less than an hour resulted in the utter defeat of the entire board, and the issuance of the license.

In the spring of 1836, Miss Mann, now the honored wife of ex-Secretary of Treasury McCulloch, and the mother of Charles McCulloch, president of the Hamilton National Bank, and Miss Stabbell, the late Mrs. Royal Taylor, came from the east and opened a school in a room in the old court-house, but after teaching there for a short time joined the Rev. Jesse Hoover, who had, on August 2, 1836, opened a school in the basement of the Presbyterian church, near the corner of Berry and Lafayette streets, then the first and only church in the town. Mr. Hoover was succeeded by the Rev. W. W. Stevens, with Alexander McJunkin, as assistant. Mr. Stevens subsequently built a school-house on West Berry street, where with his wife, he taught for many years.

Probably no teacher of Fort Wayne, certainly none of the earlier ones, has so impressed himself upon the memories and respect of his pupils, as did Alexander McJunkin. After leaving Mr. Stevens, he built a house, now standing on Lafayette street, between Berry and Wayne streets, where he most successfully taught school for many years, until in 1852, when he became the treasurer of the Fort Wayne & Chicago railroad company. A fine scholar, a good instructor, and a stern, strict disciplinarian, he most forcibly impressed his ideas and teachings upon the minds of his scholars, and not infrequently with equal force upon their bodies.

In the fall of 1845 the Presbyterian church opened a ladies' seminary, under the charge of Mrs. Lydia Sykes, which promised great usefulness, but after a year and a half's very successful work, Mrs. Sykes' health failed, and she was succeeded by the Rev. James, who came to the town in 1846. Prion to teaching in the seminary, this gentleman had no permanent school-house, but taught in various buildings successively. Many other small schools were taught in Fort Wayne, with various success, by residents of the town, amongst them the present Mrs. Barbara Ronan.

The Methodist college, now the Fort Wayne college, at the west end of Wayne street, was opened in 1849, for higher education, under the charge of Prof. A. C. Huestis, still living an honored retired life. Mr. Huestis was possessed of marked ability and great originality as a teacher and educator, and it is impossible fully to estimate the good seeds that were sown by his labors, or the fruits that have grown from them. The institution, with a life of varied success and depression, has continued, with some interruptions, till the present time. Under the judicious management of its present president, Dr. Herrick, its promises to regain much of its former strength and importance, and do much valuable work. It is an institution much needed in such a country as ours, and cannot fail, under wise direction, to produce an immense amount of good beyond the reach of the larger and more expensive institutions of the land.

In August, 1853, the Presbyterian academy was re-opened, on the site of the present Central grammar school, in charge of Mr. Henry McCormick, with Jacob Laniers as assistant. This school was continued under various teachers, with varying success until 1867, when it was abandoned as the public schools were more economically carrying out its objects, and the lots sold to the board of school trustees.

In the year 1883, Miss Carrie B. Sharp and Mrs. Delphine B. Wells, two of the strongest and best qualified principals of the public schools, opened the Westminster seminary. This institution has had a career of usefulness and success which the writer earnestly hopes may continue till the present principals and their successors and pupils for many generations, have passed to their higher rewards. Large and well organized parochial schools have, from time to time, been organized under the care and direction of the Roman Catholics, Lutheran and other churches, which are well managed, well appointed, and successful in teaching their pupils the fundamental elements of religion as held by the respective churches, in connection with the more secular subjects of education. So extensively are these parochial schools patronized by the families connected with the respective religious bodies, that in connection with the private and the public schools, no excuse whatever, can exist for an ignorant child or an illiterate adult. Excluding those above the age of fifteen years who are at work, and those out of school on account of ill health or youth, the scholars of the parochial, private and public schools, together, make up nearly ninety-five of the children of school age.

One of the most famous schools outside the city before war times was the Perry Center seminary, incorporated and established in Perry township in 1856, by Nathaniel Fitch, Jacob Kell and George Gloyd. They were moved by a laudable desire to establish a worthy institution of learning, and, with that end in view, erected near the center of the township a large frame building, and in the winter of that year, secured the services of T. W. Tilden as teacher. In 1860 there were formed three departments or grades, and Prof. Tilden was retained as principal with two assistants in the other grades. The pupils of this institution came from Noble, DeKalb, Allen, LaGrange and other counties. The course was academic, including the languages, higher mathematics, philosophy, astronomy, etc. It was a prosperous institution until 1862 or 1863. Then a number of its pupils enlisted in the army, and its principal resigned. Though it never rallied, and the building is now a ruin, its work still lives, and is commemorated in the useful careers of those who studied there.

Public Schools.— The constitution of 1851, which so fully recognized the principles of the ordinance of 1787, in its article 8, section 2, on education, declares that the common school fund shall consist of the congressional school fund and the lands belonging thereto; the surplus revenue fund, the saline fund and the lands belonging thereto; the bank tax fund, and the fund arising from the 114th section of the charter of the State Bank of Indiana; the fund derived from the sale of county seminaries and all properties held for the same; of all fines and forfeitures under state laws; all escheated lands and properties; all lands and the net proceeds of the sales thereof, including swamp lands; and taxes on the property of corporations that may be assessed by the general assembly for common school purposes. Section 3 declares that "The principal of the common school fund shall remain a perpetual fund, which may be increased, but shall never be diminished; and the income thereof shall be inviolably appropriated to the support of the common schools, and to no other purpose whatever."

Under the law of 1852, passed by the general assembly, to give force to these constitutional provisions, Hugh McCulloch, Charles Case and William Stewart were, in 1853, appointed the first board of school trustees to organize and manage the public schools of the city. They found themselves in charge of the school affairs of a city of some 5,000 persons, 1,200 school children, no school building, no school appliances whatever, and not a dollar with which to buy them. They rented the McJunkin school-house, on Lafayette street, in which Isaac Mahurin, and his sister, Miss M. L. Mahurin, began to teach; and a small house, on the site of Henry Paul's present residence, belonging to Mr. A. M. Hurlburd, who with his wife, were engaged to teach in it. Both schools were opened in September, 1853, with a tuition fund for their support of $330.72, and no special fund whatever. To acquire the funds necessary to continue the schools, the trustees, as provided for by law, called a public meeting to vote upon levying a tax for that purpose. The purpose of the meeting ignominiously failed, and the trustees resigned, and were succeeded by James Humphrey, Henry Sharp and Charles G. French. These gentlemen, under a modification of the law, assessed a tax of two mills on the dollar for school purposes.

With the growth of the city the demand for additional school accommodation grew rapidly, but the means under control of the trustees did not grow. In 1855 the board, Mr. Henry Sharp having been succeeded by William S. Smith, determined to do all in their power for the relief of the pressing needs, purchased the site of the Clay school from Judge Samuel Hanna, and that of the Jefferson school from Dr. Charles E. Sturgis, and advertised for proposals to build the Clay school. They adjourned from time to time, but no bids being received, with a magnificent exhibition of moral courage, they assumed a responsibility, the extent and weight of which cannot now be readily appreciated. They proceeded with the work themselves, letting it in portions as they found opportunity and persons willing to assume the risk. After overcoming many and great difficulties, and in the face of innumerable discouragements, they opened the building on February 9, 1857, with appropriate exercises, appointing the Rev. George A. Irvin superintendent. Those, and only those, who have themselves experienced such trials and difficulties can fully appreciate their feelings upon the completion of their labors.

In September of the same year, ten gentlemen of the city mortgaged their personal realty for $500, each lending the full amount to the trustees, who agreed to protect the mortgages and pay the interest as it became due. With this money the trustees built the Jefferson school, which, with the Clay school, furnished accommodations for about 600 pupils. With the heavy debt hanging over them the trustees could do nothing further, although the number of children entitled to school privileges was constantly increasing.

In 1861 the supreme court decided the then school law unconstitutional, and the schools were closed for a short time. A new law was passed, but under circumstances so depressing and disheartening that the constitution of the school board was constantly changing. In June, 1863, the Rev. George A. Irvin resigned the position of superintendent, to become a chaplain in the Federal army, and was succeeded by Mr. E. S. Green, under whose administration a re-organization of the schools and the course of study, was attempted, but owing to the difficulties in the way, without much success.

Early in 1865 the school law was so amended as to empower the city council to elect the school board, to consist of three members, to serve for three years each. In April of that year, the Fort Wayne council elected Oliver P. Morgan, Edward Slocum and John S. Irwin, trustees, who entered at once upon the duties of their office. In the following June they graduated the first class who had passed through the high school, a class of four young ladies of marked ability, two of whom are now teaching in the schools.

At the close of the schools in June, Mr. Green resigned his position as superintendent.

The new school board found the schools with totally inadequate accommodations, themselves the inheritors of a magnificent debt, and not a dollar of money. They had, however, a keen appreciation of the importance of their work, and great faith in the eventual recognition of that importance by the community. They elected Mr. James H. Smart, now Dr. Smart, the president of Purdue university, as superintendent. With a high reputation for teaching ability acquired in the Toledo school, and strong powers of organization, he entered at once upon the accurate and practical grading of the schools, bringing the work within a reasonable number of years, and elevating the standard to the highest practicable level. From this time the growth of the schools, both in numbers and popularity, was rapid and steady.

In 1866 the board purchased part of the present site of the Hoagland school, and, rich in faith but poor in money, built thereon a plain one-story frame building of three rooms, seating when closely filled some 200 pupils. Two rooms were opened in September, but it soon became necessary to open the third. This building has, at various times, been enlarged and modified so that now it contains thirteen classes, all full.

In 1867 they purchased the sites of the present Central grammar, Washington and Hanna schools, and built the high, and Washington, schools, opening them in September, 1868. This was rendered possible only by the liberality of the city council, who, under the provisions of the law, issued bonds, the proceeds of which were applied by the trustees to the erection of the buildings, the sites being paid for in installments out of the special school fund.

In 1869 the Hanna school was built and opened with one teacher to furnish accommodation to the southeast part of the city.

In the same year the German reformed schools were transferred to the board, the east school finding accommodations in the Clay school and the west in its own building on West Washington street which the trustees rented, adding a second story. These schools, much enlarged, still remain under control of the board, greatly to their own advantage as well as to the strengthening of the public school system.

In September, 1870, the one-story frame building, which had been moved from the site of the high school to the northwest corner of Hanna and Jefferson streets, was opened as the Hanna school, with one teacher, but the next year it was necessary to add two more rooms to it.

In 1871 the villages of Boonsville and Bloomingdale, north of the city, were added to the corporation, and the school, a one-story frame, with a single room, opened in September, but it became necessary the next year to add two rooms to this building also.

In 1874 small districts were added to the city on the north, east and south, each having a small school building, which the board immediately occupied. They also rented another small frame building on the north for a grammar school. These districts, with one exception, have been returned to the respective townships to which they formerly belonged.

In 1875 the growth of population on the north side compelled the sale and removal of the frame Bloomingdale school-house, and the erection of a fine substantial brick building of eight rooms in which all the schools on the north side were consolidated. This building has since been enlarged to a twelve-room building and is again full to overflowing.

In 1876 a like condition of things in the east end required the replacing of the frame Hanna building with an eight-room brick building substantially like the Bloomingdale, into which the east German school was moved, and which is now so full as to require one class to recite in the hall.

In 1877 it became necessary to remodel the Washington and Hanna buildings, changing them from four- to eight-room buildings. At the same time a large addition was made to the high school, adding four large recitation rooms, and a drawing room 24x72 feet in size. Since then the Washington and Hanna schools have been enlarged to twelve-room buildings, and the high school building has became overcrowded. Since the last date given, the growth of population in the outer districts of the city has been rapid, and the board, fully realizing the necessity for its relief, and especially for that of the primary scholars residing therein, in 1886, built two-room brick buildings on Boone and Fry streets, northwest, and on Holton and Creighton avenues, southeast, and a four-room brick on Miner and DeWald street, south, for the primary grades, which were all opened in November of that year. These latter buildings are so constructed as to admit of enlargement, and of a second story with comparatively little trouble or expense. In 1888, for the relief of the Hanna school, a four-room brick, similar to the Miner street school, was erected on McCulloch street, east, and two rooms opened in January, 1889.

Fully recognizing the fact that the character of the school largely depends upon the character of its teachers, in 1867, Mr. Smart, under direction of the board, established a training school for the education of teachers. As a rule, graduation from the high school was a necessary precedent to admission to this school. The wisdom of the measure was rapidly manifested in the higher ability of the teacher, the broader, more accurate, and more solid character of their work, and in the rapidly growing reputation of the schools amongst prominent educators. In 1877 the instruction in this school was limited to the primary grades, and another opened for instruction in the higher grades. This latter school was continued for two years only, and the former until June, 1886, when, upon resignation of the principal, the board deemed it wise to discontinue it for the present. The undoubted advantages gained from its work lead to the hope that it may before long, be re-organized. Mr. Smart having been, in October, 1874, elected superintendent of public instruction, resigned his position as superintendent of the city schools in the early part of March, and was succeeded in June following by John S. Irwin, who had for ten years been a member of the board of trustees, and who still fills the position.

The growth, prosperity, and character of the schools have been largely dependent upon the skill and labor of the Hon. James H. Smart. Elected superintendent in 1865, when a young man for the position, he gave to the work abilities of a very high order, energy and perseverance that knew no tiring or defeat, knowledge, theoretical and practical, in his profession, much beyond his years, and brought out of virtual chaos, a system well arranged, with courses of study well adapted to the wants of the community, and productive of practical results, valuable to the pupils, serviceable to the communiny, and honorable to the superintendent and the teachers.

In 1877 the "colored" question, which had given much anxiety and trouble, was satisfactorily settled by placing the colored children in the grades and districts for which their advancement fitted them.

In March, 1878, moved by various considerations, the board changed the name "high school" to its present one, "the Central grammar school." The old name, while giving no additional strength to the schools, at that time excited useless but very unpleasant opposition. The whole term of school life were then divided into primary, intermediate, and grammar grades, of four years each. The standard of the work required has not been in any way lowered, nor its extent lessened. The course of study, while by no means faultless, has proved itself valuable by the success of our graduates, both in higher institutions of learning and in the professional and business walks of life. It is the aim of all in charge not to weaken the schools but rather to strengthen them, and that rather by the thorough and accurate prosecution of a few solid and necessary branches, than by the superficial skimming of the whole field of art, literature, and science.

At present the board have under their charge thirteen buildings with some 4,300 seats, well furnished with desks, apparatus, and reference books, and a general library of over 6,500 volumes. There are 124 teachers regularly employed, of whom six are special teachers, having general charge of drawing, reading, writing, music, stenography, and book-keeping. The school enumeration of the city including transfers from the townships is nearly 12,000, of whom nearly 4,000 are in the public schools, and nearly as many in the private and parochial schools. Of all the children enumerated over the age of fifteen, not more than 300 are in any school whatever, but are almost universally at work. Excluding these and also those whom, by reason of their youth and physical disability, their parents keep at home, it would seem that not more than five per cent. of the school population are out of school.

It has been the fortune of the present superintendent, and except for two years, that of Mr. O. P. Morgan to have been officially connected with the graduation of every class that has left the schools. The first class was graduated in June, 1865, two months after the election of these gentlemen to the board. From 1865 to the present year, both inclusive, there have been graduated from the high school and its successor the Central grammar school: 17 from the post graduate course, 45 from the classical, 163 from the Latin and 141 from the scientific course, of whom 265 have been ladies, and 101 gentlemen. In addition to these, 174 young ladies have been graduated from the training schools.

It is a matter of great gratification that these young ladies and young gentlemen, have proved themselves, with scarcely an exception, honorable and useful members of the communities in which they live, better fitted by the education they have received for the performance of their respective duties, and filled with a higher ambition to perform them in the best and most honorable manner. While, so far as known, none of them have attained to positions of great distinction, they have adorned the more useful walks of middle life. No honorable profession is unrepresented by their number. Many to whom the "res angustae domi" has otherwise denied the opportunity of cultivating the abilities with which they have been endowed have found in these schools ample facilities, most effective and kindly aids toward raising them to spheres of honorable usefulness, and positions that have enabled them to become valuable producers in the community, instead of the wasteful drones and useless consumers of the results of others' labors.

The prudent and business-like management of the school funds by a board of exceptionally strong and successful business men has enabled that board to lessen the number of scholars assigned to a single teacher. This condition of things gives to each scholar a greater personal attention on the part of the teacher, gives to the teacher a better opportunity of studying the individual character of each scholar, and its modifications by heredity and its environments, permits the teacher, therefore, more understandingly, and more successfully to put in practice the best methods under the best conditions; avoids the evil effect to the health, physical, mental and moral of an over-crowded room, and places the pupil in the best conditions to obtain the best results with the least expenditure of life and strength. The course of study has been so carefully arranged, that while due and paramount importance is attached to the so-called common branches, which must form the necessary and only safe foundation for all advanced work, just and weighty consideration is given to those branches which serve not only to supplement the former but also to strengthen them to the better equipment of the scholar for the work of life. The natural relation of the study and the age and capacity of the scholar have been so studied and provided for, that, as a rule, at whatever age a child may leave the school, it leaves it with the best to be attained in the time. The employment of special teachers in drawing, reading, music and writing, and of teachers in the advanced grades of the work specially fitted and educated for their respective fields, enables the board to furnish the highest facilities for a very advanced education with less comparative cost than was formerly necessary to teach the three R's.

As an evidence of the value and accuracy of the work done in the schools, the board can point to the facts that no scholar in the advanced grades has ever gone to a higher institution of learning and failed to take an honorable position for work and conduct, that a larger percentage of our teachers have been educated and fitted for their profession in our schools than in any other city in the country except Boston, so far as they are advised. The facilities for prosecuting scientific study and research are beyond those of many colleges; historical and literary studies are prosecuted with a fuller and closer consideration of original works, and with a breadth and comprehensiveness of scope, which a lustrum ago would have been considered impracticable. The results of the art teaching are seen in many of the houses of this city, and in many of its work shops. A study that raises the capability of a lad to those of a journeyman; which reduces the expenditure of time in a given employment one third; enables a given result to be attained with the use of a third less material, may be ornamental — highly so — but it is also unquestionably eminently practical. A method of study which raises the subject of reading from a mere mechanical repetition of words, or their stilted mouthing, after the manner of a barn-stormer, to an intelligent comprehension and rendering of the ideas of an author, and the ability critically to analyze and discuss the work of that author, may well be regarded as cheaply purchased by the salary of a special teacher. No less can be said for that delightful and humanizing study of music, which enables the child, as well as the youth of more advanced years, accurately and with feeling, to render in sweet and harmonious measures the elevating thoughts that seek their utterance in melody.

All these facilities and more, are freely furnished by a wise and prudently generous board to the scholars of the Fort Wayne schools, almost without money and without price; furnished to a fullness and extent which are equalled in but few cities.

One other point exhibing the wisdom and the foresight of the board. Such strict cleanliness in all the schools, from garret to cellar; in outhouses and yards; such watchful care and attention to light, heat and ventilation in all the rooms and halls; such observance of the laws of hygiene in study, rest, recreation, duration of recitation, and the hundred other points which bear upon the health, strength and comfort of the pupil have been, and are so closely and fully observed, that last year —1886–7—out of an enrollment of 4,097, the whole number of deaths in the schools was eight, a proportion far below the average mortality of even the healthiest country. It is detracting nothing from the homes of the city to say that in many cases the schools largely counteract the evil effects that want of care, want of means, and want of hygienic knowledge, inflict upon the children in their own homes.

Very much the larger part of these valuable results and the marked economy of means by which they have been brought about, is due to the wisdom of the council in keeping in their positions men eminently fitted by their natural abilities and acquired experience, ably and successfully to administer the large, the important, and the delicate interests which must ever attach to the education and building up of the future fathers and mothers of the land. Long may this wisdom in all its conservative power be exercised to the welfare, the prosperity, and the abounding good to the community, of these public schools, so that a grateful posterity may rise up and call all concerned therein blessed.

The present management of the schools is under the following board of school trustees: John M. Moritz, president; A. Ely Hoffman, secretary, and Oliver P. Morgan, treasurer, while Dr. John S. Irwin is just closing the fourteenth year of his superintendency.

The following is a list of the trustees from the organization of the schools in 1853 till the present time, with the dates of their election:

Elected 1853, Hugh McCulloch, served till 1854; Charles Case, till 1854; William Stewart, till 1854. Elected 1854, James Humphrey, till 1857; Henry Sharp, till 1855; Charles G. French, till 1856. Elected 1855, William S. Smith, till 1856. Elected 1856, Franklin P. Randall, till 1856; Pliny Hoagland, till 1856; John M. Miller till 1857; Charles E. Sturgis, till 1858. Elected 1857, William Rockhill, till 1859; William H. Link, till 1857; James Humphrey, till 1859. Elected 1858, Thomas Tigar, till 1861; William Edsall, till 1859; Charles G. French, till 1859. Elected 1859, Samuel Edsall, till 1861; Charles E. Sturgis, till 1861; Oliver P. Morgan, till 1863; Robert E.

SCHOOLS.

Fleming, till 1861. Elected 1861, William Rockhill, till 1863; James H. Robinson, till 1863; John C. Davis, till 1863; Orin D. Hurd, till 1863. Elected 1863, Samuel Edsall, till 1863; A. Martin, till 1863; Christian Orff, till 1865; Charles E. Sturgis, till 1865; Oehmig Bird, till 1865; Emanuel Bostick, till 1865; Virgil M. Kimball, till 1865. Elected 1865, Oliver P. Morgan, till 1873; John S. Irwin, till 1875; Edward Slocum, till 1869. Elected 1869, Pliny Hoagland, till 1880. Elected 1873, Alfred P. Edgerton, till 1888. Elected 1875, Oliver P. Morgan, now serving. Elected 1880, Max Nirdlinger, till 1886. Elected 1886, John M. Moritz, now serving. Elected 1887, A. Ely Hoffman, now serving.

TOWNSHIP SCHOOLS.

Unfortunately the records of these schools, prior to the administration of the present efficient county superintendent, are very meager and unsatisfactory. It is proper to say that under the management of the present superintendent, the schools are making marked progress in all that appertains to them, and the people of Allen county feel and know that their schools are keeping pace with the foremost, and that their children leave the schools well equipped for all the duties and vocations of life. By the reports of Superintendent Felt to May, 1888, to the state superintendent, it appears that the total number of children in attendance upon the county schools, exclusive of the city of Fort Wayne, were, 6,257, out of a total enumeration of 10,623, with an average daily attendance of 4,044. Of the enumeration, 5,557 were white males, and 5,066 white females, no colored children being enumerated in the townships. Of the total attendance, 3,378 were white males, and 2,879 white females, a condition of things not usual in township schools, and one from which it is evident that the farmers' daughters are largely detained at home for household assistance, or have entered upon domestic service in the towns and cities around. In the townships there are 104 brick school-houses, and seventy-one frame, the last log school-house having been abandoned, The value of the buildings, sites, furniture and apparatus is estimated at $175,145, seven of the buildings were newly erected within the year, at a cost of $9,200. These schools were taught by ninety-four male, and ninety-five female teachers, at an expense of $47,730.82, and for incidental expenses of $11,466.69, in addition to which there was expended for permanent improvement a further sum of $10,366.83. The tuition revenues for the year, including balances on hand July 31, 1887, were $85,076.11, and the balances on hand July 31, 1888, $47,730.82. The special school revenues for the year, including balances on hand July 31, 1887, were $40,522.40, and the balances on hand July 31, 1888, $18,662.67, with no indebtedness whatever, except a small one in an incorporated town.

Monroeville Public School.— Monroeville, so far as its educational needs have been concerned, has always endeavored to keep pace with the times. The school was first graded in 1865, but there being but one room in the building, there was great inconvenience until the erection of a commodious building in 1871, by Trustees A. Engle, James Weiler and T. S. Heller. This is 31x71 feet in dimensions, and cost $7,175.50. The first term here began January 2, 1872, under W. A. Dickey, principal. The school has attained a high rank, and the course of instruction includes those branches that are best calculated to prepare its students for practical life. The officers of the board at present (1889) are: President, David Purman; secretary, David Redelsheimer, and treasurer, John Corbaley. Teachers chosen to take charge of schools during 1889-'90, are: J. B. Munger, principal, assisted by the Misses Emma Peckham, Rose Redelsheimer, Minnie McGonagle and Alice Parker. During the past two years Prof. Munger has placed in the schools a library numbering 225 volumes, and the fact that 100 of these volumes are constantly in circulation during the school year, proves that the library is appreciated.

Two classes have completed the course of study, the first in 1887, with W. A. Munger as principal, included Minnie McGonagle, Lena Strass and Mary Debolt. The second class, in 1889, with J. B. Munger as principal, included Rose Redelshennir, Luna Buchanan, May Dewirt, George Glancy, Louis Brown and Ollis Robinson.

The names of the principals since 1871 are: W. A. Dickey, M. E. Crawford, L. M. Dillman, I. O. Jones, O. Z. Hubbell, W. S. Walker, W. A. Munger and J. B. Munger.

The number of pupils enrolled is about 240.

John M. Moritz, one of the prominent men of Fort Wayne, has always taken a deep interest in the welfare of the educational interests of the city, and when President Cleveland appointed the Hon. A. P. Edgerton civil service commissioner, and Mr. Edgerton thereupon vacated the office of president of the school board of the city, Mr. Moritz was elected in his stead, much to the satisfaction of the public. To the same position he has recently been re-elected. Mr. Moritz was born in Adams county, Penn., about nine miles from the since famous battle ground of Gettysburg. His parents were native Pennsylvanians. In 1866 he came to Fort Wayne, and in partnership with his brother-in-law, D. M. Miller, leased the Aveline House, which in 1874 they purchased, and have ever since conducted. The hotel is handsome in all its appointments, and is well-known throughout the country. Mr. Moritz is one of the trustees of the First Presbyterian church, of which he is a member. In politics he is a democrat and prominent in his party. In business and social circles he is highly esteemed.

Dr. John S. Irwin.—In the twelfth century the family of De Irwin, of Norman descent, obtained possession of the lands of Bonshaw in Dumfrieshire, Scotland, and were known as the Irwins of Bonshaw. When Robert Bruce was waging the war for the freedom of Scotland, against Edward I., on one of his fights he stopped at Bonshaw, and finding William De Irwin to be a bright and energetic man he took him with him, making him his armor bearer, a post of distinguished honor.

At the battle of Bannockburn Irwin was instrumental in saving the life of Bruce, for which he was publicly thanked and authorized to take the coat of arms of Bruce, the triple holly leaves with the motto "*Sub sole sub umbra vircus,*" which has ever since been the family motto. He also gave him the barony of Drum in Aberdeenshire, which has remained the seat of that branch of the family, the castle of Drum being the oldest inhabited dwelling in Scotland. In the rebellion of 1680, several members of this family went over to Ireland to help raise the siege of Londonderry. Remaining there after the rebellion was quelled, they received lands in the counties of Tyrone, Londonderry and Antrim, the important branch settling in Tyrone. John Irwin was born there in 1745. He emigrated to the United States early in the revolutionary period and became assistant commissary general at Fort Pitt from 1781 to about 1791, after which he settled in the village of Pittsburgh as a merchant, where he died after an honorable and useful life in 1831. His eldest son, John S. Irwin, born in 1798, was graduated M. D. at the university of Pennsylvania in 1819, but died of consumption in 1832. His eldest son, John S. Irwin, now a citizen of Fort Wayne, was born at Pittsburgh, April 4, 1825, and was there educated, being graduated A. B. at the Western University of Pennsylvania in August, 1842. He entered upon the study of medicine, practical chemistry and pharmacy under Dr. Joseph P. Gazzam of that city, and was graduated M. D. at the university of Pennsylvania, April 3, 1847. He entered immediately upon the practice of his profession, becoming junior member of the medical and surgical board of the Mercy hospital in Pittsburgh. In September he married Miss Mahan, of Carlisle, Penn. He continued the practice of his profession till 1853, when his health completely broke down, and he was compelled to abandon it. Recovering his health partially he became, in December, 1853, book-keeper for the private banking firm of Allen Hamilton, in Fort Wayne, with whom he remained eleven years, becoming then teller in the Fort Wayne branch of the Bank of the State of Indiana. At the end of two years he was elected cashier of the Merchant's National Bank, which position he retained until 1873, when being threatened with serious disease of the brain he was compelled to resign his position, and spent a year traveling as general manager for Indiana, of the United States life insurance company. In April, 1865, he was elected a member of the city school board of trustees, and, upon organization of the board, made secretary and treasurer, retaining the latter position till June, 1875, when the superintendent of schools, Dr. James H. Smart, now president of Purdue university, having been elected state superintendent of public instruction, Dr. Irwin was elected superintendent of the city schools, which position he still occupies. In 1869 Dr. Irwin was elected a trustee of Indiana university, which office he held until elected superintendent, when, becoming *ex officio* a member of the state board of education, he resigned the trusteeship. Upon his resignation he received from the university the honorary degree of LL. D.

Prof. Chester T. Lane, principal of the Fort Wayne high school, was born in Jackson county, Mich., October 31, 1851, the son of David and Minerva J. (Crawford) Lane, both of whom were natives of New York. He remained upon the farm of his parents until he was fifteen years old, and then entered the public schools of Jackson, Mich., whither they had removed. He was graduated from the high school in 1869, and in the fall of 1870 entered the university of Michigan, where he was graduated in June, 1874, after completing a full classical course. He accepted the principalship of the high school at Ypsilanti, Mich., the next fall, and occupied that position five years, coming to Fort Wayne in the fall of 1879, to enter upon the duties of his present position. His educational work during the decade he has passed in Fort Wayne, has been of the highest order in his department of instruction, and he has become widely known as a successful teacher. Socially as well as professionally, he occupies a high rank. In politics he is independent of party and very much interested in the progress of reform of the civil service. Prof. Lane was married August 15, 1876, to Caroline J. Bloomfield, daughter of Giles and Cornelia R. (Williams) Bloomfield. She is also a native of Jackson county, Mich., and was born April 19, 1853. They have four children: Elmer B., Ralph C., Hilda and Winthrop D. Mrs. Lane is a member of the Episcopal church.

Dr. Charles R. Dryer, teacher of sciences in the Fort Wayne high school, is a native of Ontario county, N. Y., born August 31, 1850. He was reared on a farm and at seventeen entered Hamilton college, at Clinton, N. Y., in which he completed a full classical course, graduating in 1871. Meanwhile he had given some attention to the study of medicine, and after graduating he set about a thorough study of that science. For four years he devoted himself to that study and also taught school, being principal during the time, of Phelps Union and classical school at Phelps, N. Y. During the winter of 1871-2 he took a course of medical lectures at the university of Michigan, and he took his second course in the medical department of the university of Buffalo during the winter of 1875-6. He graduated in February, 1876, after which he began practice at Victor, N. Y. In August, 1877, he came to Fort Wayne, since which time he has held the position of teacher of natural sciences in the Fort Wayne high school. Dr. Dryer was married July 28, 1874, to Alice M., daughter of Samuel and Mary Peacock, of Walworth, N. Y. Dr. Dryer and wife have four children: Helen E., Alice J., Reginald P. and Clare M. Between the years 1881 and 1885 he served as a member of the board of pension examiners of Fort Wayne. For ten years he has been professor of chemistry in the Fort Wayne college of medicine. During almost his entire residence here he has devoted much attention to analytical chemistry, particularly toxicology, and he has won in this department a very creditable reputation. Dr. Dryer is a fine scholar and an able educator. Socially his standing is very high. During the summers of 1887-8 he made a geological survey of both Allen and DeKalb counties which is a masterly production and does him much credit. The survey was made for the state geologist and is published in full in the latter's report.

Westminster seminary was first opened in the fall of 1883. The year preceding, one of the principals had been offered the charge of Mr. Moody's seminary at Northfield, Mass.; but was so impressed with the idea of the need of a Christian school in the northern part of Indiana that she refused the offer, and in company with her associate principals they decided to open such a school in Fort Wayne. The right building and location were secured, being the family residence of the Hon. Robert Lowry, who having been elected to congress, desired to lease his home for a term of years. Additions were made to the building; while the home-like character was preserved. A competent corps of teachers was engaged, and the institution opened its first sesson September 13, 1883, with four boarders and thirty-six day pupils, a number far exceeding the expectations of the founders. A course of study was laid out, both classical and English, such as will fit for entrance into any of the higher schools for women, and equal to that of any similar institution in the west or east. A preparatory department was connected with the seminary proper. The numbers increased, and improvements were made from year to year. In 1884 a company of gentleman purchased the property, and continued to hold it for this purpose. Their generous aid and helpful encouragement at all times are striking illustrations of the public spirit and interest in all such enterprises, manifested by many of the foremost citizens of Fort Wayne. In 1886 the seminary graduated its first class, consisting of six young ladies; the exercises were held in the elegant new First Presbyterian church. No essays were required from the graduates, but they listened to an eloquent address from the Rev. Dr. McLeod, of Indianapolis. In 1887 the building was enlarged to meet its growing requirements; it also received a generous gift of money from Mrs. J. L. Williams. Some of the distinctive features of the seminary may be mentioned. The home-life is modelled upon that of a private family, and aims to train the manners and morals of the young ladies as they would be in their own homes. The small number received into the famly makes it possible for the principals to come into direct contact with each pupil. The decipline is based upon the laws of Christian courtesy and mutual helpfulness. Systematic instruction in the Bible is a part of the regular course of study, and of the family life. The methods of instruction are intended to develop the power of thought.

For the inception, as well as the successful management of Westminster seminary, the people of northern Indiana are much indebted to the foresight and executive ability of Miss Carrie B. Sharp. In 1882, having achieved a worthy reputation as a teacher by reason of nearly twenty years' service as principal of the Jefferson school, she was invited by the trustees of the Northfield, Mass., seminary, to take the principalship of that institution. She visited it, and this led to the foundation of Westminster seminary, an account of which has already been given. Miss Sharp has since been identified with it as one of the principals. She began her life work at the age of sixteen, but after teaching one term in Fort Wayne, she entered Holyoke seminary, Mass., from which she graduated in 1862. Returning to Fort Wayne she resumed teaching, taking a position in the Jefferson school. Three years later, at the request of ex-state superintendent, James H. Smart, then superintendent of the city schools, she accepted the principalship of that school.

A devoted teacher, of wide and varied experience, Mrs. Delphine B. Wells brought to Westminster seminary, upon its organization, a well-earned reputation and a thorough professional training. She was born in Bristol, Conn., February 2, 1847, daughter of William G. and Josephine L. Bartholomew. In her infancy the family removed to Weatherfield, Conn., where for six years the father was warden of the Connecticut state prison. Subsequently, they removed to Providence, R. I., where the father held the wardenship four years. Their next home was at Dayton, Ohio, for about six years, and they then removed to Kalamazoo, Mich., where the father and mother passed the remainder of their lives. Their daughter, at an early age entered Kalamazoo college, and after completing the sophomore year, she entered Mrs. Stone's school for young ladies, at Kalamazoo, where she graduated at the age of eighteen years, and during the subsequent year was engaged there as a teacher. She was married at the age of twenty and after a married life of three years, resumed her profession, to which her whole attention has since been given. She was principal of the Irving school at Detroit two years; principal of the high school at Muskegon, two years; teacher of modern languages in the Freeport, Ill., high school, one year; principal of the Plymouth, Ind., high school one year; and principal of the Clay school at Fort Wayne, four years, resigning that position to become one of the founders of the Westminster seminary, of which she is now one of the principals, having charge of the department of language and literature. Mrs. Wells is a member of the First Presbyterian church, and for ten years has taught the adult Bible class in the Sunday school of that church.

James F. Whiteleather, one of the principals of McDermut and Whiteleather's business college, Fort Wayne, is a native of Columbiana county, Ohio, born July 4, 1853. His life was spent in Whitley and Allen counties, Ind., being engaged in boyhood on a farm. At eighteen years of age he took up the vocation of a teacher, and for several years he taught school and attended school alternately, receiving a collegiate education. For the past eighteen years his whole attention has been devoted to school work, either in the capacity of student or teacher. He completed a special course in plain and ornamental penmanship at Huntington, Ind., in 1875, and in 1879 he took a six months' course under P. R. Spencer, of Cleveland, Ohio. In 1882 he became teacher of penmanship in the Fort Wayne business college, and later became one of the proprietors of that institution. For some two or three years he was instructor in penmanship and other branches in the Fort Wayne college. In the fall of 1885 he, in connection with Mr. W. E. McDermut, established the McDermut and Whiteleather business college, to which his main attention has since been given as instructor in penmanship, mathematics and bookkeeping. For two years past he has also taught bookkeeping in the Fort Wayne high school. He is an able instructor and a first class citizen.

Wilson E. McDermut, one of the founders and principals of McDermut & Whiteleather's business college, is a native of Richland county, Ohio, born August 9, 1851. He is the son of Josiah S. and Nancy (Vail) McDermut, natives of the same county. When he was but two years old his parents came to Indiana and located at LaGrange. There his father died in 1858, and in the latter part of 1859 he removed to Ohio, and located at Lima. He remained at Lima four years, attending school in winter and working in a blacksmith shop in the summer. In 1863 he returned to Richland county, and for two years resided there and in Wyandotte county, working upon a farm and attending school. In April, 1865, he began to learn the printer's trade at Upper Sandusky, Ohio, and was thus engaged at Upper Sandusky, until April, 1869, when he came to Fort Wayne, where he has remained since with the exception of three months in 1872, when he worked in Chicago. In July, 1869, he took the position of foreman of the composing room of the Fort Wayne *Daily Sentinel*, and with the exception of an interval of about one year, he continued in the same capacity until January 30, 1880, also acting as telegraph editor during the most of that period. During his connection with the *Sentinel* he had learned stenography, and to this art, in 1880, he turned his attention as a court reporter. In the spring of 1881 he became clerk and chief officer of the Fort Wayne waterworks, a position he held four years, resigning it January 1, 1885, to resume the practice of court reporting, and he has labored in the latter capacity ever since. For the past four years he has also devoted much of his attention to the management of McDermut and Whiteleather's business college, which was established by himself and Mr. James F. Whiteleather, in the fall of 1885. Mr. McDermut was married September 27, 1883, to Miss Lida F., daughter of the late Lewis Embey, of Fort Wayne, and they have one child, Gail, born August 13, 1885. Mrs. McDermut is a member of the Baptist church. He is an Odd Fellow and a member of the A. O. U. W. For the past two years he has been employed as special teacher of short-hand in the Fort Wayne Central grammar school.

During the last twelve years James A. Gavin, a worthy citizen, has served very acceptably as overseer of the Fort Wayne public school buildings. He was born at Glasgow, Scotland, September 10, 1848, son of Robert and Isabelle (Craig) Gaven, with whom he came to America when he was six months old. The family made a brief stop at Cleveland, Ohio, and then came to Fort Wayne, and soon after located on a farm near Leo. Two or three years later they settled on the Comparet farm which is now within the city limits. In 1860 Mr. Gavin accompanied his father to a farm near Bryan, Ohio, where he remained several years. On his return to Fort Wayne he entered upon an apprenticeship as a miller, and served about four years in the old Wines mill and the City mill when ill health compelled him to give up milling. He then obtained employment on the Grand Rapids & Indiana railroad, beginning as a foreman on a construction train, and upon the completion of the road he was promoted to baggage master, and still later to conductor, serving in the latter capacity two years. From the spring of 1872, to September, 1877, he was collector for the Fort Wayne gas light company. In the fall of 1877 he was appointed to his present position. Mr. Gavin was married June 29, 1871, to Sedonia R., daughter of Wesley T. Davis. She was born in Newark, Ohio, April 29, 1850, and died October 23, 1879, leaving one child, Frank W., who was born April 9, 1872. Mr. Gavin is a member of the First Baptist church, in which he has been a deacon for the past seven years, and of the Masonic lodge.

OLD FORT WAYNE.

VALLEY

OF THE

Upper Maumee River

WITH HISTORICAL ACCOUNT OF ALLEN COUNTY AND THE CITY OF
FORT WAYNE, INDIANA. THE STORY OF ITS PROGRESS
FROM SAVAGERY TO CIVILIZATION.

VOLUME II.

ILLUSTRATED.

MADISON, WIS.:
BRANT & FULLER,
1889.

INDEX TO VOLUME II.

GENERAL HISTORY.

	Page.
Amusement, places of	284
Architectural growth	223
Assembly, members of	384
Asylum	225
Attorneys, prosecuting (see Courts).	
Banks	246
Bench and bar (see Courts).	
Berghoff brewery	166
Breweries	165, 166
Buildings, government	224
Business interests	145
Canal Era	17
Centlivre brewery	165
Churches, Catholic	411
Cathedral	415
St. Aloysius	434
St. John the Baptist	432
St. Joseph's	432
St. Joseph's hospital	427
St. Leo's	429
St. Louis	430
St. Mary's	416
St. Patrick's	433
St. Paul's	422
St. Peter's	423
St. Rose of Lima	433
St. Vincent's	431
St. Vincent's orphan asylum	428
Church, Hebrew	314
Churches, Protestant	296
Baptists	301
Christian	315

	Page.
Churches, Protestant.	
Congregational	315
Evangelical Association	315
Lutheran, English	311
Methodists	306
Presbyterian, First	296
Presbyterian, Second	300
Presbyterian, Third	301
Protestant Episcopal	310
Reformed	313
United Brethren	316
College, Fort Wayne	307
County infirmary	381
Courts	439
Common Pleas	460
Circuit, first session	440
Criminal	463
Probate	458
Superior	465
Under first constitution	440
Under second constitution	460
Dentistry	370
Finances in 1825	376
Fire department	257
First election	375
Gas, natural	286
Hospital	284
Improvements, aid to	381
Manufacturing enterprises	86
Medical college	335
Medical profession	330
Medical societies	334
Milling interests	23
Municipal and federal	254

	Page.
Newspapers	317
American Farmer	319
Dispatch	322
Freie Presse	322
Gazette	320
Journal	321
Miscellaneous	319
News	322
Poultry and Pets	322
Sentinel	317
Staats Zeitung	319
Times	319
Officers, city	255
county	383
federal	276
Organization of Allen county	374
Parks	281
Physicians licensed	336
Physicians, Monroeville	369
Police, The	256
Population	390
Postoffice building	224
Public buildings	378
Public enterprises	281
Railroads	54
Statistics, financial	382
political	385
Street railways	288
Transportation, local	288
War record	391
Water-works	259
Wayne Hotel	228
Y. M. C. A. building	224

PERSONAL HISTORY.

	Page.
Adkins, A. W	77
Albrecht, Martin L	133
Alden, S. R	502
Ames, Geo. W	292
Anderson, Calvin	47
Anderson, J. R	84
Andersen, Peter	115
Archer family	35
Auger, Benjamin L	192
Auger, Charles	52
Axt, Moritz	49
Ayres, Henry B	163
Ayres, Henry P	339
Baker, B. H	46
Baker, John	243
Baker, John	46
Baker, Kilian	45
Baltes, M	244
Bandt, Fred	236
Banks, Creed T	362
Banta, H. F	113

	Page.
Bard, Samuel	193
Barnett, W. W	345
Barnum, George P	293
Barr, William J	193
Barrand, John B	39
Barrand Peter F	38
Barrett, James M	502
Barrows, Frank R	174
Bass, John H	93
Bastian, Jacob	194
Baxter, Thomas	271
Beaber, Abraham G	194
Beaver, A. C	139
Beaver, Charles B	85
Becker, Frederich	50
Becks, Rev. Julius	427
Becquett, John B	40
Begue, John C	50
Beighler, John	195
Bell, R. C	498
Bender, Louis	195

	Page.
Benoit, Rev. Julian	423
Bensman, Rudolph	98
Bensman, William J	114
Beverforden, Henry F	195
Bierbaum, F. R	74
Bigger, Samuel	487
Bitler, Samuel D	139
Bitner, John R	111
Blair, Solon K	74
Blair, Thomas W	279
Blakesley, Lyman	77
Bobilya, Louis J	178
Boerger, A. H	178
Boester, F. H	234
Bohne, Carl	117
Boltz, Ferdinand F	100
Boltz, Fred. C	124
Bond, Charles D	252
Bookwalter, E. H	329
Borden, James W	476
Boseker, Christian	228

INDEX TO VOLUME II.

Name	Page	Name	Page	Name	Page
Boswell, Asa C	361	Dudenhoefer, George P	131	Hartmann, Henry	405
Boswell, A. J	360	Dunham, Frank W	104	Hartman, Jacob	205
Bowen, George W	342	Dwenger, Rt. Rev. Joseph	436	Hartman, John H	205
Bowser, Sylvanus F	135	Eckhert, John C	198	Hartman, Joseph H	206
Brackenridge, Joseph	486	Edgerton, A. P	33	Hartman, S. B	372
Brackenridge, G. W	34	Edgerton, Joseph K	63	Hayden, John W	279
Brackenridge, Robert	34, 507	Ehle, August N	199	Hazzard, Louis	275
Brames, Louis	141	Ehrmann, Charles	198	Heaton, Owen H	507
Brammer, Rev. J. H	429	Ellison, T. E	503	Hedekin, Michael	42
Brandt, Diederich	96	Ely, George W	267	Heimroth, Andrew	112
Brannan, John H	405	Eme, Claude F	47	Hench, S. M	497
Braun, John	142	Entemann, Christian	199	Henderson, A. R	182
Breen, W. P	505	Ersig, William A	199	Henderson, S. C	40
Breidenstein, Simpson	192	Essig, Charles O	86	Henderson, Zenas	40
Breimeier, Ernst	233	Ewing, Charles W	472	Henry, James M	232
Brimmer, Joseph	242	Ewing, W. G. and G. W	31	Hensel, Peter	236
Brenton, Samuel	406	Fay, James A	487	Herber, J. F	226
Brink, John J	178	Felts, George F	401	Herbst, Otto P	278
Brinsley, George C	184	Ferguson, John	128	Hetrick, Jacob	356
Brinsley, John C	295	Fink, Frank H	97	Hettler, C. F	265
Brooks, William H	338	Fischer, Henry E	402	Hewes, James C	109
Brossard, John	196	Fisher, Abel	106	Higgins, C. R	277
Brown, Seneca B	370	Fisher, R. J	95	Higgins, Frank P	82
Brown, William H	39	Fitch, Charles B	121	Hilbrecht, Henry	266
Bruebach, George T	343	Fitzpatrick, Bernard	105	Hilbrecht, Henry, jr	269
Bruns, C. W	244	Fleming, Thornton J	169	Hild, Henry	242
Buchman, A. P	351	Fletcher, Charles P	76	Hilgemann, H. F	206
Buck, Charles W	73	Fletcher, Josiah F	292	Hill, Thomas	118
Buckwalter, Louis	111	Foellinger, Jacob	45	Hilton, Charles S	120
Buhr, Henry	197	Foster, David N	149	Hinton, John C	206
Bullerman, Henry F	404	Foster, Samuel M	151	Hoagland, Pliny	62
Bursley, Gilbert E	157	Fox, Louis, and Bro	160	Hoffman, Henry A	237
Busching, Henry	197	France, Joseph S	488	Hull, Lewis O	165
Byrne, Rev. M. J	416	Frank, Mendel	201	Hunt, John T	207
Caldwell, James	355	Franke, A. H	271	Hunter, Lewis C	403
Campbell, Daniel	113	Frankenstein, Max L	200	Hyman, Philip H	139
Carnahan, William L	159	Freeman, Samuel C	44	Iten, Frank	269
Carpenter, Warren	270	Freese, August	200	Jaap, George	235
Carrier, A. H	192	Freiberger, Ignatius	200	Jackson, Thomas	72
Carson, W. W	478	Frestoffer, Henry	201	Jackson, William T	81
Cartwright, Charles	102	Fremion, Joseph	143	Jenson, James O	293
Case, Charles	509	French, Brooks	118	Jocquel, John J	175
Chambers, John D	352	Fulton, Charles W	294	Jones, Fremont L	181
Chapin, A. A	500	Gage, Robert	145	Jones, Joseph H	350
Cody, Maurice	42	Gale, George A	202	Jones, Maurice L	174
Colerick, David H	482	Gallmeier, Ernst	240	Johnson, A	78
Colerick, John	485	Gallmeier, William	240	Johnston, William, jr	114
Colerick, Walpole G	483	Gard, Brookfield	350	Judy, G. H	109
Connolly, William A	366	Geake, J. J	231	Kabisch, Rudolph	207
Coolman, John H	237	Geake, William	230	Kalbacher, Anton	207
Coombs, William H	474	Geller, W. F	203	Kaough, William	277
Cooper, Henry	473	Gessler, Albert F	202	Keefer, Christian	241
Cosgrove, Franklin K	364	Gibson, David N	406	Keel, Aurora C	169
Cosgrove, F. D	400	Gilbert, John	164	Keil, Frederick W	327
Cox, Enoch	70	Gilmartin, Edward	173	Kelker, Anthony	79
Cramer, Matthias	103	Glenn, Thomas M	187	Keller, Henry	140
Cran, Robert	96	Glenn, William M	80	Kendrick, Frank B	229
Cratsley, Frank C	162	Gocke, Anthony	51	Kendrick, William H	231
Craw, Edward L	191	Gocke, Louis H	51	Kern, Jacob J	402
Crawford, John T	238	Golden, Edward J	171	Kerr Murray manufacturing company	115
Cressler, Alfred D	115	Gordon, George P	75	Kintz, A. W	239
Cromwell, Joseph C	137	Gotsch, Theodore O	176	Klett, Jacob	136
Cromwell, Joseph W	246	Graffe, Frederick, jr	161	Kline, C. W	208
Dalman, Frederick	41	Graffe, Henry C	160	Knecht, F. J	209
Dawson, C. M	476	Graham, James A	105	Knight, William	108
Dawson, John W	324	Granneman, H. C	179	Knothe, Charles F	121
Dawson, Reuben J	474	Gray, James P	78	Koehler, John A	144
DeHaven, Perry N	172	Griffith Levi	234	Koehler, Paul	144
Delaney, Rev. J. F	416	Griswold, Crawford	74	Koenig, C. F	209
Derbyshire, Samuel W	360	Green, M. Frances	44	Koenig, Rev. E	422
Detzer, Martin	179	Greenwell, Franklin	367	Koerdt, Rev. Ferdinand	435
Dickinson, Philemon	163	Greenawalt, George L	356	Kollock, Fred. N	84
Diehl, Hugh M	272	Gregg, James S	344	Korn, August	210
Diether, John H	127	Gruber, John Michael	203	Korn, John	210
Diether, Louis	127	Hackius, G. L	116	Kortee, Frederick	241
Dills, Thomas J	351	Haiber, Charles F	204	Kraft, Frederick	239
Dinnen, James M	354	Haiber, George W	204	Kreite, Charles F	314
Dittoe, Albert J	167	Haller, Gottlieb	204	Krock, John	233
Doehrmann, William	268	Hamilton, Allen	250	Krohne, H. H. L	210
Doswell, George W	197	Hanna, Samuel	27	Krusy, H. F. W	211
Doswell, John H	283	Harding, D. L	262	Kryder, John L	363
Dougall, A. H	188	Harrison, Robert H	107	Kuhne, F. W	186
Dreibelbiss, John	191	Harrison, Walter S	245	Kunkle, E. B	136
Dreibelbiss, Robert B	191	Hartman, Rev. B	434		

INDEX TO VOLUME II.

Name	Page.
Laubach, A. J.	354
Landenberger, John M	131
Lauer, Gregory	240
Lauferty, Isaac	253
Lang, Rev. J. F.	415
Law, C. D.	67
Lenz, Frederick	211
Leonard, Nathan R.	326
Leonard, Nelson	143
Lepper, Charles O	180
Leykauf, John N	211
Liebman, E. F	233
Liggett Bros	291
Lillie, John	129
Lindlag, Philip J	142
Lintz, Anthony	43
Loag, George W.	396
Loesch, George H.	180
Long, Mason	167
Longacre, M. P	138
Lowry, Robert	496
Luers, Rt. Rev. J. H	426
McCaskey, George W	357
McCausland, John W.	358
McClellan, Charles A. O	408
McClure, Andrew	83
McCormick, Thomas H.	362
McCulloch, Hugh	248
McDonald, P. J	269
McDonald, R. T.	120
McIntosh, William	53
McKay, James M.	157
McKinnie, W. M., & Co.	228
McLain, Nelson W	403
McMahan, Sylvester	76
McMullen, John	235
McNamara, Washington	103
McNiece, Nicholas R.	212
McNutt, L. D.	288
McQuiston, John W	52
McQuiston, Wilson	124
Madden, James D.	244
Mark, Rev. J. A.	433
Markey, A. C.	212
Martz, Christian	358
Matsch, J. Christopher	96
Mentzer, Simeon E	369
Mergentheim, A	168
Messman, Rev. A.	423
Metcalf, S. C.	348
Meyer, Diedrich	264
Meyer, Frank H.	213
Meyer, Henry William	95
Meyer, John F. W.	152
Meyer, William D.	267
Meyers, Charles F.	289
Meyers Frederick C.	98
Miller, Cassius A.	182
Miller, Frederick	235
Moellering, William	226
Moffat, D. W.	298
Monahan, Dennis	171
Monning, Henry	419
Monning, John B.	127
Moran, Peter A.	212
Morgan, Joseph D.	365
Morgan & Beach	149
Morris, John	480
Morris, Samuel L.	499
Mowrer, Isaac	397
Moynihan, A. J.	328
Muldoon, John W.	242
Munson, Charles A.	399
Murphy, George	364
Neireiter, Conrad	189
Nelson, Isaac DeGroff	409
Nestel, Daniel	53
Newton, Charles H.	71
Niemann, Gottlieb	213
Niezer, John B.	397
Ninde, L. M	508
Niswonger, Henry W	359
Northrop, S. A.	304
Nusbaum, Peter	142
O'Brien, Dennis	265
O'Connor, Bernard	66
O'Connor, B. S.	67
O'Leary, Rev. T. M.	415
O'Rourke, Edward	489
O'Rourke, Patrick S	68
O'Rourke, W. S.	505
O'Ryan, Patrick	273
Oechtering, Rev. J. H	421
Ogden, Robert	243
Olds, N. G., & Sons.	98
Olds' Wagon Works	114
Orr, John W	164
Page, William D	325
Pape, Charles	123
Pape, William C	126
Paulus, Frank D	183
Pearse, James W	289
Perrin, A. C.	294
Peters' Box Co.	123
Peters, John C	122
Pfeiffer, Henry	175
Pierce, Ogden	182
Pixley, George W.	153
Porter, Miles F.	355
Powers, Emmet W.	290
Pressler, John	134
Quinlan, Rev. W. J	433
Racine, Aime	135
Randall, Franklin P.	37
Randall, Perry A.	501
Ranke, Wm	130
Rastetter, Louis	129
Read, H. A.	291
Rehling, Ernst	113
Reidmiller, John M.	52
Reinewald, Rudolph C.	263
Reiter, George	214
Remmert, H. J	117
Renfrew, Robert G	104
Rhinesmith, John	125
Rich, Sanford	227
Rippe, Frederick	237
Robertson, R. S.	493
Robinson, H. H.	499
Robinson, James H.	46
Robinson, James M.	506
Rockhill, William	406
Rockhill, William W.	328
Rodabaugh, Thomas J.	110
Rohan, John H.	119
Romer, Rev. C. M.	421
Romy, Robert L.	190
Rose, Charles	215
Rose, Henry A.	214
Rosenthall, Isaac M.	344
Ross-Lewin, Edward A	132
Ross, James P.	215
Rossington, R. B.	71
Rowe, Nicholas B.	216
Rudisill, Henry	36
Ruhl, Wm. DeLa	367
Rurode, E. C.	158
Ryan, Patrick	265
Sallot, Victor A.	102
Sarnighausen, J. D	324
Sauvain, Samuel H.	216
Schaper, Charles H.	238
Scheid, Peter J.	268
Schiefer, Christian	49
Schlatter, Christian C.	176
Schmueckle, Frederick	267
Schneider, Matthias	216
Schone, H. H.	184
Schroeder, Henry	239
Schroeder, L. S. C.	280
Schultz, Henry	243
Schulz, Adolph F.	118
Schulz, William Fred.	185
Schust, G. Adolph	116
Schust, George A.	271
Schweir, Henry	217
Seaton, John	345
Seavey, Gideon W.	162
Seibold, H. J	180
Shafer, Edward A.	358
Shambaugh, William H.	402
Shea, Michael F.	83
Shordon, Daniel	183
Shrimpton, Alfred	232
Shryock, William W.	373
Shuman, E.	183
Siemon, A. F.	161
Simonson, James H.	126
Singleton, Michael T.	273
Singmaster, Joseph	49
Sites, E. F	372
Sites, Henry C.	372
Siver, Emett L.	359
Slater, John	274
Smaltz, Francis M.	218
Smaltz, John	217
Smead, Frank K.	218
Smith, Cornelius S.	343
Smith, F. M.	177
Smith, J. L.	366
Smith, J. Sion	270
Sommers, H. G.	181
Souder, Daniel W.	396
Sosenheimer, C. J.	264
Spereisen, Jacob A.	218
Spice, John	177
Spiegel, Gottfried E.	219
Spiegel, Gustave	173
Stapleford, L. P.	41
Stellhorn, Charles	172
Stemen, Christian B.	352
Stemen, George B	357
Stephan, William	107
Stier, Jacob J.	97
Storm, J. A. M	177
Strodel, John George	219
Studer, Himerius L.	219
Stultz, Charles E.	362
Sturgis, Charles E.	338
Stutz, John A.	361
Suelzer, John	238
Sullivan, Andrew	220
Summers, James	220
Sweet, Samuel B.	68
Swearingen, H. V.	346
Tagtmeyer, David.	137
Tapp, Herman W	236
Taylor, John M.	398
Taylor, Robert S.	488
Thieme, Frederick	171
Thieme, J. G.	170
Thomas, William A.	125
Thompson, M. M.	401
Thompson, Nelson	137
Thompson, Nelson W.	73
Thompson, Richard G.	70
Tinkham, John P.	220
Torrence, George K.	190
Tower, Alexander M.	112
Trautman, John	274
Tresselt, Christian	48
Trentman, August C.	147
Trentman, Bernard	148
Underhill, Elliot S.	141
Urbine, James	181
Van Buskirk, A. E.	353
Vesey, William J.	504
Veniard, Rev. Felix	431
Viberg, George H.	398
Virgil, Thomas S.	348
Volland, Henry	50
Wagenhals, Samuel	312
Wagner, John C.	175
Wahrenberg, Fred.	274
Weber, Andrew	107
Weil Brothers	185
Weisell, David D.	371
Wenninghoff, Christian	221
Wheelock, E. G.	341
Wheelock, Kent K.	342
White, James B.	154
Wichman, A. C. F.	124

INDEX TO VOLUME II.

Name	Page	Name	Page	Name	Page
Wilder, Joseph H.	99	Winch, Calvin J.	133	Woolsey, Hiram B.	103
Wilkens, Jacob V.	221	Wise, William	222	Worden, James L.	465
Wilkinson, Frank	272	Withers, W. H.	479	Worley, George N.	368
Williams, Jesse L.	61	Wolf, Louis	158	Yergens, William	130
Wilson, John	221	Wood, George W.	322	Zollars, Allen	490
Wilson, Thomas W.	506	Woodworth, Alonzo L.	110	Zurbuch, Joseph F.	222
Winbaugh, George W.	144	Woodworth, B. S.	340		

ILLUSTRATIONS.

Name	Page	Name	Page	Name	Page
Bass, J. H.	96	Griebel, A. L.	288	Old Fort	Frontispiece
Benoit, Rev. Julian	424	Hackett, E. A. K.	320	Page, William D.	320
Boseker, Christian	192	Leonard, N. R.	320	Sarnighausen, J. D.	320
Brackenridge, Joseph	304	Loag, George W.	384	School for Feeble Minded	224
Brooks, W. A.	336	Lowry, Robert	496	Thompson, M. M.	400
Carson, W. W.	480	Moellering, William	256	Tillo, Charles D.	320
Colerick, David H.	448	Monning, Henry	416	White, J. B.	160
Edgerton, J. K.	64	Mowrer, Isaac	468	Zollars, Allen	464
Ferguson, John	128				

THE CITY OF FORT WAYNE,
By W. P. COOPER.

THE MEDICAL PROFESSION,
By B. S. WOODWORTH, M. D.

ORGANIZATION.

CATHOLIC CHURCHES,
By Rev. JOHN F. LANG.

COURTS OF ALLEN COUNTY,
By Judge ALLEN ZOLLARS.

THE CITY OF FORT WAYNE.

THE CANAL ERA.

WHILE journeying from east to west on the New York, Chicago & St. Louis railway, the traveler experiences in western Ohio an uninteresting ride through heavily-wooded districts until, a half hour after crossing the Indiana line, he comes suddenly to a noble river, along whose precipitous banks he is whirled for several miles. Houses multiply, and are seen to be aligned in streets; the smoke of many factories curls about the train, shutting out the glimpses of stately churches, tall business blocks, tasteful residences and the other abundant evidences of a rich and prosperous city.

The journey is now along an abandoned water way. Suddenly, close to the railroad, but high above it, comes in view a modest little park. On a tall staff floats the American flag and from the well kept enclosure a cannon looks out, as if to keep watch and ward against assailants, who may be expected to swarm up from the valley below. In a moment more the train halts and the passengers for Fort Wayne alight.

The river whose meanderings he has followed is the Maumee; the abandoned water way is what remains of the Wabash & Erie canal; the little park with its flag-staff and cannon mark the site of old Fort Wayne, and the traveler stands upon a bustling depot platform which has taken the place of a part of the canal dock along which the business of the town was for many years transacted.

The stores that line the old dock in solid rank have made a right-about face from the line of the canal and front upon a handsome street, but over what are now the back doors of the oldest of them may yet be seen signs of quaint and indistinct lettering advising the world that West India goods, sugar, rope, provisions, rum, and what not, are to be had within.

Not until the days of railroads did the commerce of Fort Wayne begin to forsake the old waterway, and then the city passed forever from an interesting era that people love to chat about. The event of the day, the day of forty years ago, was the arrival of the gorgeous packet. It was drawn by better-whipped mules than those that tugged at the slower freight boats; and was a craft of larger size and fitted with comfortable accommodations for a passage of many days and nights. A packet's approach to a town was always heralded by a great blowing of horns from the deck, followed by a prodigious bustling of the tradesmen on the wharf, and the hurrying to the dock of no small portion of the population. The passengers, having debarked, were refreshed at the public houses, made purchases, were questioned about the places they came from, the object of their journeys, and were thoroughly interrogated for the news that mail and telegraph now supply.

Then the horn summoned on board those who were to continue their voyage, the swaggering driver, in slouch hat and top boots, cracked his whip, away trotted the mules toward the next stopping place and the bustle on the wharf was over until the approach of the next packet boat was sounded.

Though the Wabash & Erie canal has long been a thing of the past, it was the most important factor in the development of Indiana and the northwest, and the accomplishment of its construction will always remain a monument to the memory of a few far-sighted and energetic pioneer citizens. It was a most stupendous work of internal improvement—the largest continuous line of artificial water communication in the world, and did more to give to Fort Wayne its early impetus than all other agencies combined. All of the more important towns of the northern Indiana counties, through which it passed, have similarly prospered, and have grown to be large and wealthy county seats, viz.: Fort Wayne, Huntington, Wabash, Peru, Logansport, Delphi and LaFayette, and by reason of the earlier advantages derived from the canal, have easily outstripped all neighboring places in both population and business. Indeed the first car of progress was not drawn through the Maumee and Wabash valleys by the shrieking locomotive, but by the patient and plodding mule.

The plan for uniting by canal the waters of Lake Erie, with those of the Ohio river is said to have been entertained by Gen. Washington, a practical surveyor, but the glory of the accomplishment of the great undertaking rests principally with Hon. Samuel Hanna and Mr. David Burr of Fort Wayne. It is related that in a familiar conversation had in a summer house, attached to his then residence at the northwest corner of Barr and Berry streets, Judge Hanna first broached the subject to David Burr. The latter was a man of broad character and great ability and much influence. He entered into the spirit of the undertaking with great ardor and in frequent meetings the plans were matured which bore such grand fruitage. For some time before this the project of an artificial waterway from the Ohio river to Lake Erie had been agitated in Ohio, and a survey of the Miami canal was made in 1824, under the direction of Micajah T. Williams, an elder brother of Jesse L. Williams, who was connected with the party of surveyors. This survey was carried to Defiance, on the Maumee and thence to the lake, forming a southern branch of the great system. The canal was anticipated in the treaty of 1826 with the Miami Indians, in which, where the reservations were mentioned, it was stipulated, that the state of Indiana may lay out a canal or road through any of these reservations, and for the use of a canal, six chains along the same are hereby appropriated.

Messrs. Hanna and Burr supplied themselves with facts touching the length and direction of the proposed canal, and became acquainted with the engineering difficulties in the way of the undertaking, and they began a correspondence with the representatives of Indiana in congress, and so impressed upon their minds the importance and feasibility of the project that a survey of the canal by a corps of the United States topographical engineers was ordered. As has been previously mentioned, this corps, under Col. James Shriver, worked heroically on the survey from the mouth of the Tippecanoe to the head of the Maumee rapids, though Shriver and Moore, his successor, fell victims to malaria. The survey was completed to the Maumee bay by Col. Howard Stansbury, who was one of the original party. This work was begun at Fort Wayne in May or June, 1826, and completed in 1828.

Then followed an act of congress, approved March 2, 1827, granting to the state of Indiana "every alternate section of land, equal to five miles in width for six miles on both sides of the proposed line and throughout its whole length for the purpose of constructing a canal from the head of navigation on the Wabash at the mouth of the Tippecanoe river to the foot of the Maumee rapids. This munificent grant of land, amounting to 3,200 acres for every one of the 213 miles of the proposed work, was the first of any magnitude made by congress for the promotion of public works, and initiated the policy of land grants afterward so liberally pursued. A subsequent act approved May 24, 1828, provided for a similar grant to Ohio for the southern branch, and also for the cession to Ohio by Indiana of the territory granted to Indiana within the Ohio boundary. Commissioners were appointed by each state, W. Tillman on the part of Ohio, and Jeremiah Sullivan on the part of Indiana, who arranged a treaty between the two states, by which Ohio agreed to construct the part of the Wabash & Erie canal in her territory in exchange for the land granted to Indiana between the lake and the Ohio boundary.

The prominence into which Messrs. Hanna and Burr grew as the champions of such an important work appears to have excited a strange and powerful opposition, but Judge Hanna, in a hard-fought contest, was elected to the legislature as the special champion of the canal policy. The grant of land was accepted by the Indiana legislature in the session of 1828, and the sum of $1,000 was appropriated to purchase the necessary engineering instruments and make a survey of the summit level. Samuel Hanna, David Burr and Robert John were appointed a board of canal commissioners, and ordered to make the survey mentioned.

Mr. Hanna went to New York, purchased the necessary outfit of instruments and returned by way of Detroit, bringing the instruments from the latter place by horse-back to Fort Wayne. John Smythe, the engineer, accomplished no more, after arriving at Fort Wayne, than to gauge the river and adjust his instruments when he became a victim to the diseases of the region, and Judge Hanna and Mr. Burr were compelled to take it up, with the aid of a surveyor and finish it without the assistance of the engineer. They provided for the construction of a dam on the St. Joseph river six miles north of the town, from which point a feeder canal led an abundant supply of water to a point a mile west of the town, where the main line was intersected. During the year 1830, the middle or summit division was located and prepared for contract by Engineer Joseph Ridgeway. At the legislative session of 1831-2, the canal commissioners were authorized to place the middle division under contract, creating a board of fund commissioners, and authorizing a loan of $200,000 on the credit of the state. At the first meeting of this board at Indianapolis, in the spring of 1832, it was found that the total amount realized from the sale of canal lands was $28,651. During this spring Jesse L. Williams was appointed chief engineer.

Here, to give an intelligent idea of this great work, from an engineering point of view, it will be well to quote the altitudes of various points along its line and at the sources of the streams which were to supply it. The elevation of the Maumee above the level of Lake Erie at the head of the rapids is sixty-two feet, at Defiance eighty feet, at the state line 135 feet, at Fort Wayne 163 feet. The summit level of the water of the canal was 193 feet above the lake, two feet higher than the marsh which is the summit between the Maumee and Wabash rivers. The surface of the head branch of the St. Joseph is at an altitude of 423 feet; Jackson railroad track at north line of Allen county, 270 feet. The reservoir at Rome city, built by the state in 1838, to aid in supplying a proposed canal from Fort Wayne to Lake Michigan, has an altitude of 367 feet. Low water of the Wabash at the forks, 126 feet. The formal breaking of the ground, with such ceremonies as could be performed in a little frontier town, was performed at Fort Wayne just in time to save the land grant under the limitation of the act of congress.

The ceremony attending the commencement of the work of building the canal is interestingly described in the Cass County *Times* of March 2nd, 1832. The preceding birthday of Washington, February 22nd, had been selected as an auspicious time for the beginning, and by order of the board of canal commissioners, J. Vigus, esq., was authorized to procure the necessary tools and assistance and repair to the most convenient point on the St. Joseph feeder-line at 2 o'clock on that day for the purpose named. A public meeting was called at the Masonic hall and was attended by all prominent citizens not only of Fort Wayne, but of the Wabash and Maumee valleys. Henry Rudisill was chairman and David H. Colerick, secretary. A procession was formed and proceeded across the St. Mary's river to the point selected. A circle was formed and the commissioners and orator took their stand. Hon. Charles W. Ewing then delivered an appropriate address and was followed by Commissioner Vigus. The latter after adverting to the difficulties and embarrassments which had beset the undertaking, and referring to the importance of the work and the advantages which would be realized, concluded by saying: "I am now about to commence the Wabash and Erie canal, in the name and by the authority of the state of Indiana." He then struck a spade into the ground and the assembled gentlemen cheered. Judge Hanna and Captain Murray, two of the able advocates of the canal, next approached and commenced an indiscriminate digging, and the procession then marched back to the town.

Laborers were employed in great numbers, among them men who afterward grew to wealth and prominence, and the expenditure of money thus made necessary had a marked and healthful influence on the business affairs of the place. The first letting of contracts was made in June, 1832, under the direction of the then commissioners, David Burr, Samuel Lewis and Jordon Vigus, of fifteen miles, and in the fall, four miles more, including the feeder-dam, were put under contract. Work was done to the amount of $4,180 by the close of that year. In the following May the remaining thirteen miles of the summit division were let, and in 1835 this division of thirty-two miles was completed, at the small cost, including lockage and an important dam, of $7,177. This united the sources of the Wabash with the great lakes, and on the 4th of July, the canal boat "Indiana" passed through the canal to Huntington. At Fort Wayne, on this occasion there was a great celebration of Independence day, with an oration by Hon. Hugh McCulloch.

The work on the line in Ohio was much delayed by financial difficulties, soon also to overwhelm the Indiana division. The dilatory action of the Ohio government led to the sending of Jesse L. Williams as an embassador to Columbus, to hasten the action of that state. The work was hastened but proceeded slowly, nevertheless. In 1843, when the work was completed, Ohio owed $500 for its share of the work and the whole resources and credit of the state was exhausted. The position of Indiana was the same, and the work was carried on under embarrassments now altogether unknown. In this state, the engineer on his own responsibility, procured the printing of notes, bearing interest and receivable for canal lands, which became a part of the currency of that era, and received the picturesque name of "White Dog."

The completion of the canal was celebrated July 4th, 1843, by a grand demonstration held in Thomas Swinney's grove just west of the town. The attendance was beyond any precedent, people coming from Cincinnati, Toledo, Detroit, Cleveland and many other points. There were few delicacies to serve at that feast and it partook rather of the solid and substantial character of the meals of the pioneers and the backwoods men.

Peter Kiser drove a fat ox from the Wea prairie, 145 miles southwest of Fort Wayne, at the rate of ten miles a day for the barbacue. The principal orator was Gen. Lewis Cass, the projector of the great Erie canal in New York state. His speech is still recalled by the older residents as glowingly anticipating the development of the country the canal would make possible, a development he might have added quite beyond the ability of the orator or his hearers to comprehend. The remarks of Gen. Cass were punctuated by frequent firing of a cannon that had been captured from the British by Commodore Perry, and which now does service as a hitching post in front of Hon. F. P. Randall's residence.

Fast fading from the memory of man are the recollections of that historic celebration. The orator has been dead nearly half a century. Judge Hanna and the other projectors of the canal have long since passed away, and there remains of those who gathered in Swinney's grove but a few white haired men and women. Peter Kiser the butcher, survives. He has since served in the legislature, and for thirty years kept a general store, which old settlers made headquarters. He was the last of the earlier merchants, and is nearly the only living connection between the prosperous and wealthy city of Fort Wayne and the straggling village that gathered about the historic fort.

The first canal boat at Fort Wayne, was one built in 1834 by F. P. Tinkham, to add to the pleasures of the 4th of July celebration of that year. In the following year Capt. Asa Fairfield had a boat built, the "Indiana," which under the command of Oliver Fairfield, an old sea captain, started on the 4th of July from Fort Wayne to Huntington, carrying a large party of gentlemen, including Dr. L. G. Thompson, Judge Hanna, Allen Hamilton, Samuel and William S. Edsall, W. G. and G. W. Ewing, Francis Comparet, Capt. J. B. Bourie, William Rockhill, Col. John Spencer, J. L. Williams, D. H. Colerick, L. P. Ferry, James Barnett and others. Thereafter trips were made every day. In 1843, Samuel and Archie Mahon began running packets between Toledo and Fort Wayne, and in the summer of 1844, a regular line was organized by Samuel Doyle and William Dickey, of Dayton, with eleven boats and a steam propellor, for use on both branches of the canal. In 1854, the opening of the Wabash railroad caused the withdrawal of the packet lines forever. Following are the names of the old packet captains: Thomas B. Filton, W. S. B. Hubbell, M. Van Horne, John M. Wigton, Clark Smith, Byron O. Angel, William Sturgiss, Benjamin Ayres, Joseph Hoskinson, William Phillips, George Alvord, James Popple, Nathan Nettleton, Thomas B. McCarty, Elias Webb, William Dale, George D. Davis and J. R. Smith.

In 1847 the Wabash and Erie canal, under the state debt act, passed into the control of the board of three trustees, two of whom were appointed by the holders of Indiana bonds and one by the legislature of Indiana.

That portion of the canal running through Fort Wayne, was, as has been stated, purchased by the New York, Chicago & St. Louis railway company, which has filled it up, turning it into a magnificent right of way through the center of the city. The long acqueduct over the St. Mary's river, was taken down several years since, and near its site has been erected a handsome iron railway bridge. The wide canal just west of the St. Mary's is filled up and converted into a splendid railway yard, capable of the storage of hundreds of cars, and near the point of the junction of the old feeder with the main line of the canal, stands the company's round-house and repair shops.

Early Enterprises.—The earlier enterprises of Fort Wayne, speaking in a mercantile sense, were trading with the Indians for the furs and peltries in which this region abounded, and great packs of the skins of the beaver, the otter, bear, deer and raccoon were regularly shipped in pirogues down the Maumee to Detroit, whence they were taken by lake to Buffalo and other commercial centers.

A peculiar industry was that established on the river bottom near where the jail now stands. It was the trying of fish for their oil. This business was managed by Cincinnati parties, and had a profitable existence of several years. It gave employment to a number of Indians and whites who caught and delivered canoe loads of muskalonge and other large fish, which were then so plentiful that they were often caught on the ripples with the hands of the fishermen or were driven into a cove where they were captured in great quantities.

The forests of northern Indiana have long been celebrated. Nowhere was walnut found of finer grade or in more plentiful quantity. Great oak trees of the white and red variety had lifted their strong arms in the gales of a century and nodded to the straight hickory, the graceful poplar and the stalwart ash. The early settlers who set about hewing farms out of the wilderness gave to the business of saw-milling its early prominence, and at many points where a water power could be had by damming the streams, the sawing of logs into lumber was extensively carried on, the farmer being glad enough to rid his land of an incumbrance so great as a grove of walnut trees. Where the distance to the saw-mills was great these trees were cut up into rails, or oftener still, were burned. The first steam saw-mill of Fort Wayne, and one of the best known in northern Indiana, was that established by George Baker and his two sons, John and Jacob, on lot No. 7, county addition, corner of La-Fayette and Water streets, and lying between the canal and St. Mary's river. The situation was exceedingly advantageous and permitted shipments of logs by canal, river or wagon road. The mill was fitted with two "muley" saws and employed ten men. It is still operated by Killian Baker, but its capacity of 5,000 feet a day is not now often tested.

In 1842-43 William Rockhill and Samuel Edsall built two saw-mills on the north side of the canal and on the east side of St. Mary's river, and having effected a lease with the canal company for water privilege, built two saw-mills and operated them for a number of years.

In 1848 William H. Coombs and Mr. Edsall built a steam saw-mill on the north side of the canal on lot No. 568, Hanna's addition, and in 1862 a large and splendidly equipped saw-mill of two stories in height, was established on the north bank of the canal between Ewing and Cass streets. The original proprietors were John B. Krudup, Louis Schrœder, Fred Brandt and Julius Kenoder, the firm's title being

Krudup & Co. After many changes in partners the mill was sold in December, 1876, to D. Tagtmeyer, who continues to operate it. This mill's average daily work was the sawing of 4,000 feet of lumber. The circular saw was sixty inches in diameter. The capital employed was $6,000.

Other saw-mills were there of H. G. Olds on the north bank of the canal at Coombs street bridge and a saw-mill operated in connection with the Beaver, or Esmond, grist-mill at the crossing of the St. Mary's river by Broadway and the one established on the Maumee river near the foot of Hanover street by Mr. Coles. This mill was afterward sold to Marshall Wines.

But by far the most important of the saw-mills is the one of most recent establishment. Reference is made to the band saw-mill constructed on the south bank of the old canal between Van Buren and Jackson streets in 1868 by Hoffman Brothers. This firm leads all others in America in the extent of its walnut lumber business, and has for a number of years been quoted as the largest owner of this timber in America. The firm is composed of Messrs. A. E. and W. H. Hoffman, and was established nearly twenty years ago. The shops have grown to vast proportions and are occupied in the manufacture of fine hard wood lumber for house furnishing and for furniture. A capital of $300,000 is employed, and the firm has constantly in its employ from 150 to 200 men. Eight timber buyers make purchases in Kansas, Missouri, Illinois, Indiana, Ohio, Michigan, West Virginia, and other states. These mills have cut 125,000 feet of lumber per week. A new 300 horse-power engine has just been added to the works. The yards of the firm have become so extensive that every foot of ground that can be leased within three blocks of their mills is covered by their lumber and logs.

The first grist-mill was built in 1827 by James Barnett and Samuel Hanna on the west bank of the St. Mary's river, near the crossing of the Bluffton road. The mill was sold to Louis H. Davis, who again sold to Asa Fairfield and Samuel C. Freeman, who in turn sold to A. C. Beaver. It was next sold to George Esmund, and was destroyed by fire on February 27th, 1878. Mr. Esmund immediately organized a company of which the late O. A. Simons, banker, was a principal member, and erected on the site of the old structure a splendidly equipped brick mill three stories in height, 44 by 64 feet, fitted with three powerful turbine wheels and five run of stone. The establishment had a storage capacity of 10,000 bushels and could manufacture eighty barrels of flour a day. The failing health of Mr. Esmond induced the sale of this mill to Messrs Tevis & Proctor, and in 1888 it too was burned down and has not been rebuilt.

Along the canal which early became the great highway for grain shipments, a number of good grist-mills and warehouses sprang up. In 1842-43 the City mills were established by Messrs. Allen Hamilton and Jesse L. Williams on the north bank of the canal, between Calhoun and

Clinton streets. The business was very successful. Within a few years Mr. Hamilton retired, and later Pliny Hoagland was admitted as a partner. After some changes Mr. Christian Tresselt was admitted in 1870, and since the death of Mr. Hoagland he has been the principal owner. The power was furnished by an over-shot wheel, supplied with water from the canal, but since the occupancy of the canal held by the New York, Chicago & St. Louis railway, this power has been lost and the mill is devoted to warehousing only.

For many years the Woodlawn mill or Wines mill was one of the best known. It was erected in 1838, by Marshall Wines at a dam thrown across the Maumee river near the foot of Hanover street and a short distance west of the old canal lock. Mr. Wines sold to Samuel Hanna and Ochnig Bird. Subsequent owers were Bostick & Fronefield, Fronefield & Volland, Trentman & Volland, Orff & Volland, Comparet & Haskell, and finally Esthen A. Orff, during whose ownership the mill was burned, ten years ago. The floods have since nearly obliterated the dam. This mill had a capacity of fifty barrels of flour a day, and at the time of its greatest prosperity a capital of $6,000 was invested.

The Empire mills or the "Stone mill," as it used to be called, is one of the few old ones that continue to grind. It is the largest in this part of the state, and is probably the best known. Its building was begun by Samuel Edsall in July, 1843, and it was first put in operation in 1845. Soon afterward Milford Smith was admitted to partnership, and in 1856 the property was sold in its entirety to Messrs. Orff, Armstrong & Lacy. Mr. Lacy died, and Mr. Armstrong retired, and since then the business has been continued by Mr. John Orff. For a long time, however, the active management of affairs has been in the very capable hands of his two sons, Edward A. and Montgomery Orff. The elder son, Mr. John R. Orff, is the miller. A grain warehouse has of late years been added to the mill. The capacity, under the old process, was 200 barrels per day, but under the new process it is twenty-five barrels less. The capital employed is $6,000. The power was originally supplied by a great overshot wheel which was fed from the canal, but a 100 horse-power engine was afterward put in, and since the abandonment of the canal the sole reliance for power is upon steam.

In 1853 George Little and Hugh McCulloch built an elevator on the south bank of the canal near the foot of Maiden Lane. The elevator was afterward converted into a grist-mill, and was the first steam flouring mill to be operated in Fort Wayne. From 1855 to 1859 it was owned and run by William Pratt & Co., who sold to John Brown. In 1867 it was sold to Hill, Orbison & Whiting, and in 1869 was destroyed by fire.

One of the best known among the early business houses was that of Comparet & Hubbell, forwarding and commission merchants. The business was established in 1846 by Joseph J. and David Y. Comparet. In 1850 M. W. Hubbell was admitted to partnership. In 1857 a three-story steam grist-mill was built which, like so many other of the mills, was destroyed by fire. This occurred in 1861. In 1862 Mr. D. F. Comparet having succeeded to the sole ownership of the business erected another grist mill on the same sight. The capital invested was $35,000. The mill was sold to A. Powers in 1871. Next year he died and the business was carried on by L. P. Stapleford & Co. until December, 1876, when fire wrecked the property and the busiuess of milling was not resumed.

The first mill operated by an overshot wheel in this section of the country was that built on the St. Joseph river, a mile north of the city, by Henry Rudisill and Henry Johns, and this is said to be the first of the local mills to manufacture merchantable flour. The building and the dam were commenced in 1830. The mill was first known as Johns' mill and after Mr. Johns' death was known as Rudisill's mill, taking the name of the surviving partner. Mr. Rudisill died February 6, 1858, and was succeeded by his son Henry J. Rudisill. He was succeeded in 1866 by John E. Hill & Co. The mill is not now in operation and is somewhat dismantled. The property has passed into the hands of Messrs. John H. Bass and the estate of O. A. Simons, principal owners of the canal feeder. It has one of the most valuable water powers in the state and its value is being increased by leading water from the level of the canal feeder to the mill, giving a fall of some eighteen feet with an abundant supply of water. This splendid power will be utilized to operate the power station of the Jenney Electric Light company, which has been newly established within a few yards of the mill, and power will be cheaply let to other manufactories by the Fort Wayne Water Power company, which owns the property. The water of the St. Joseph river will be reinforced by Fish lake, in DeKalb county.

Before the heavy tax was laid upon distilled spirits their manufacture in Fort Wayne was profitably carried on. William Rockhill, in 1836, built the first distillery, on the north bank of the canal immediately in the right of way of the Grand Rapids & Indiana railroad. It was constructed of hewn logs and was two stories high. A man named Hays succeeded to the business and the building was abandoned in 1841. By far the best known distillery was that built in 1840, by Francis Comparet on the south side of the canal, just west of where Coombs street now crosses. It was two stories in height. Mr. Comparet conducted the business for ten years, when he leased the premises to Jesse Smith and J. Dudley. They subsequently removed to Peru, and in December, 1848, the common council by ordinance, prohibited any distilling of liquors within the city limits.

The history of a city, however earnest may be the attempt at generalization, can best be told by the narrative of the deeds of the men who worked together for its upbuilding. Of some of those prominent in the history of Fort Wayne, as this account of its progress proceeds, brief mention will be made, and here appropriately may be noticed some of the early residents, sketches of whom have not already appeared in the account of "the village of the fort." Among these now to be mentioned are still honored and leading citizens.

Of Samuel Hanna, whose name frequently occurs in this work, it may be said without exaggeration, that it is impossible to write an adequate account of his life without reciting the history of Fort Wayne, nor is it possible to give a complete history of the city without embodying an account of his career. Loving biographers have detailed the events of his life with much care, and in this work little more than a brief outline can be attempted, in addition to what appears throughout its pages. Samuel Hanna was born October 18, 1797, in Scott county, Ky. His father, James Hanna, removed to Dayton, Ohio, in 1804, and cleared him a farm near the site of that town. Here Samuel's early days were passed, and his educational privileges were no greater than those of most pioneer boys. His first occupation, away from home, was as a post-rider, distributing newspapers to subscribers throughout the country, there then being no mail service for that purpose. In his nineteenth year he was a clerk in a Piqua store, and he and another ambitious young tradesman bought out the store, giving their note for $3,000. Soon afterward these notes were transferred to an innocent purchaser, and a writ of attachment followed, taking the goods away from Hanna and his partner. The notes being pressed for collection the partner pleaded infancy, a valid defense, but Hanna refused to do so, and though he had been swindled, he declared his purpose to pay his obligations in full. When he was able he did so, principal and interest. Such incidents as these explain the remarkable strength he afterward had in the financial world, and the almost unbounded credit which enabled him to assume the main burden of great enterprises. After teaching school some time, he next became prominent as a purveyor at the treaty at St. Mary's in 1818, with his brother Thomas. They hauled provisions from Troy, Ohio, and by their enterprise secured a small sum of money, a little of which was potent in those days on the frontier. At St. Mary's he decided to come to Fort Wayne, and at this little settlement he arrived in 1819. He established a trading-post in a log cabin, the work on which was mostly by his own hands, on the northwest corner of Columbia and Barr streets, thoroughfares at that time, however, unknown. In the Indian trade Mr. Hanna was a notable exception to those harpies who unscrupulously enriched themselves, and his fair and honorable dealing endeared him to the red men, and afterward to the settlers who took the place of his dusky customers. Legitimate profits were the basis of his princely fortune, upon which foundation he built with a rare business sagacity, and an economy which dissuaded him from spending $1 for personal luxuries until he was worth $50,000. During the period of his early trade here, manufactured goods were purchased in Boston or New York, and came by the lakes, and down the Maumee in pirogues, or were brought from Detroit with pack-horses. Provisions of all kinds were brought from southwestern Ohio, by way of the St. Mary's river, in the care of sturdy boatmen who were frequently delayed by fallen trees which barred the stream until they were cut away. These discomforts of commerce early turned the attention of Mr. Hanna to the improvement of routes of transportation. Before the time of canal agitation began he had widely extended his possessions. He had acted several years as agent of the American fur company, and was rapidly acquiring land throughout Indiana. His influence was aided also by his service as the first associate judge of Allen county. The canal project had its inception in a conversation between Judge Hanna and David Burr, at the home of the former, and their efforts secured the land grant by congress. There was opposition to the acceptance of the grant and Judge Hanna was elected to the legislature as a champion of the canal. He had previously served in the house in 1826, and his subsequent membership of that body was in 1831 and 1840. He also served in the senate from 1832 to 1836. He went to New York to purchase the instruments, which he brought on horseback from Detroit to Fort Wayne, when the survey was begun on the St. Joseph river, Mr. Burr acting as rod-man and Mr. Hanna as axe-man, both at $10 per month. The climate vanquished the engineer on the second day, and the two invincible pioneers continued the work alone. They reported to the next legislature, and Judge Hanna being a member, secured the passage of an act authorizing the construction of the canal.

No one contributed more to the success of the work in the early and trying years of its history than Samuel Hanna. From 1828 to 1836 he was successively canal commissioner and fund commissioner, negotiating the money with which the work was carried on, besides acting in the legislature as chairman of the canal committee.

During the same period he took a prominent part in the organization of the financial policy of the state, subsequent to the veto of the United States bank act. The creation of state banks being recommended by the president, Judge Hanna was given an opportunity to consider the proper measures to take in that direction. He strenuously opposed and defeated a measure proposed, and in the next legislature was given, as chairman of the committee having the measure in charge, the duty of drafting a charter. This he did so wisely that the state banking system of Indiana, which stood until the time of civil war, was always substantial, and a credit to Indiana. A branch was at once established at Fort Wayne, of which Judge Hanna was president for a considerable period.

In 1836, Judge Hanna purchased the remaining land interests of Barr & McCorkle, now within the city limits, and until the opening of the canal brought a large increase of population he was much embarrassed by this absorption of his capital. But he never distressed those who had purchased his lands and failed in meeting their obligations, preferring to suffer inconvenience himself, and many landowners owe their prosperity to-day to his kindness. After the building of the canal, an era followed in improvement which may be termed the plank road epoch. Jesse Vermilyea visited some of these highways in the east and Canada, and his report incited Judge Hanna and others, to the construction of such roads for the benefit of Fort Wayne. A route was provided by the canal from east to west, substantially that of the Wabash railway of to-day, and now a route from north to south, a forerunner of the Grand Rapids & Indiana road, was a desideratum. The Fort Wayne & Lima (LaGrange county) plank road company was organized, and stock subscriptions solicited. But cash was very scarce, and subscriptions were mostly made in goods, land and labor. Nearly all the necessary capital was borrowed from the branch bank, and this was expended in erecting saw-mills. Contractors being timid, Judge Hanna himself, took the first ten miles north of Fort Wayne and personally superintended and ax in hand, did much of the work. Like a born general, he led, and as a necessary sequel, others followed. With the efficient co-operation of William Mitchell, Drusus Nichols and others, within two years there was a plank road from Fort Wayne to Ontario, a distance of fifty miles. This, the pioneer plank road of northern Indiana, was followed by the Piqua road, in which Mr. Hanna was also an indispensable factor. Now the era opened in which the prosperity of cities depended upon the building of railroads, and again Judge Hanna led the army of progress. Peculiarly in this direction did he have great influence upon the future of Fort Wayne, in the growth of which the railroad industries have had a predominant part. When that grand national line of railway, which is now the pride and strength of Fort Wayne, and with which his name is forever identified, the Pittsburg, Fort Wayne & Chicago railway, was first projected — beginning with the section from Pittsburgh to Massillon, thence from Massillon to Crestline, thence from Crestline to Fort Wayne, and finally developing in the grand idea of a consolidated continuous line of railway from Pittsburg to Chicago — Judge Hanna was among the first to see, to appreciate, and to take hold of the golden enterprise, that was, in ten years' time, to bring up Fort Wayne from the condition of an insignificant country town, to rank and dignity among the first commercial and manufacturing towns of Indiana. When the construction reached Crestline, Judge Hanna and his friends induced the voting of a subscription of $100,000 by Allen county, which was the turning point toward the completion of the enterprise. He and Pliny Hoagland and William Mitchell took the contract for the construction of the section from Crestline to Fort Wayne, 131 miles, but in a short time funds gave out, the work stopped, and gloom overspread the hopes of the city. Dr. Merriman, the president of the company, resigned. In this emergency, the great strength of character of Samuel Hanna was the unfailing resource. He was elected president, and in three days was in the east, pledging the individual credit of the contractors for the necessary funds. Being successful, he hastened to Montreal and Quebec, and redeemed the iron, which was held for transportation charges. The work was resumed, and in November, 1854, the trains from Philadelphia ran into Fort Wayne.

While yet overwhelmed with the work just mentioned, the Fort

Wayne & Chicago railroad company was organized, and Judge Hanna elected president. Money was to be derived from the sale of stocks and bonds, and stock subscriptions which were paid in cash amounted to less than three per cent. of the cost of construction and equipment. The main part of the subscriptions were paid in land and labor. The sale of bonds was slow and discouraging.

Quoting again the appreciative words of Hon. J. K. Edgertoun: The powerful corporation, now so strong and prosperous, measuring its annual income by well-nigh half a score of millions of dollars, from the fall of 1854, to the close of 1860, passed through a fearful struggle, not only for the completion of its work, but for its own corporate and financial life. The financial disasters of 1857 found the consolidated company with an incomplete road, with meager revenues, and a broken credit. Many of its best friends, even among its own managers, were inclined to grow weary and to faint by the way. Through all this trying period no man worked more faithfully and hopefully, or was consulted more freely, or leaned upon with more confidence, than Judge Hanna. He was a tower of strength to an almost ruined enterprise. He was at brief times gloomy and desponding, but he was a man of large hope, and a robust physical organization, that eminently fitted him to stand up and toil on to a successful end. No man who has ever been connected with the management of the Pittsburg, Fort Wayne & Chicago railroad has had a larger share of confidence of all interested in it than Judge Hanna possessed. In all phases of the company's affairs, in the midst of negotiations involving the most vital interests in Chicago, Cleveland, Pittsburgh, Philadelphia and New York, surrounded by the most sagacious financiers and railway men of the country, such men as J. F. D. Lanier, Richard H. Winslow, John Ferguson, Charles Moran, J. Edgar Thompson, William B. Ogden, George W. Cass and Amasa Stone. There was in Judge Hanna a weight of character, a native sagacity and far-seeing judgment, and a fidelity of purpose to the public trust he represented, that commanded the respect of all, and made him a peer of the ablest of them. Judge Hanna was especially the advocate and guardian of the local interests of the road. He was ever watchful for the home stockholders, the local trade, the rights and interests of the towns and counties on the railway, and of the men who worked on the road. In those dark days, when the company could not, or did not, always pay its men, and suffering and strikes were impending, Judge Hanna sympathized with, and did all he could for, the men on the road who earned their daily bread by the work of their hands. He had always in his mind the welfare of Fort Wayne, and worked unceasingly for the establishment of the immense shops of the company at this city. In this he had the aid of able men, but he had to encounter the opposition of others no less active. By direct demand, by strategy and invincible persistence, in the meetings of the directors, he pursued his object to success. Before the road reached Chicago, the consolidation and formation of the great Pittsburgh, Fort Wayne & Chicago railroad company was accomplished, mainly through the efforts of Judge Hanna, who became vice president. The road being completed to Plymouth, there was sentiment in favor of using another line from that point to Chicago, but Mr. Hanna pressed for an independent through line, and was soon successful.

About three months before the end of his career he was called to a meeting at Grand Rapids of the directors of the proposed Grand Rapids & Indiana railroad company, another project which languished, and was chosen president of the company, though he feared to assume the responsibility. In addition to these greater projects, he was a partner in the establishment of the woolen factory, the great Bass foundry and machine shops, and the Olds manufactories, to the founding of which he contributed capital. His religious training was in the faith of the Presbyterian church, of which his father was an elder for some fifty years. He joined that church in 1843, and was a ruling elder during the greater part of the remainder of his life. His last illness was of short duration. Taken ill June 6, 1866, he died on the 11th. The city mourned as it never had before. The council, passing resolutions of sorrow, adjourned; houses were draped with somber crape; and the railroad shops and buildings were festooned with evergreen, through which ran the inscription, "Samuel Hanna, the Workingman's Friend." The bells of all the churches tolled in unison while a procession two miles in length followed his mortal remains to the grave.

Marked features of Judge Hanna's character were his untiring energy, hopefulness and self-reliance. He was not a polished or highly educated man, but enjoyed the benefits of a higher education than schools can give. He was eminently a leader, a general of civil life, an administrator of affairs. Not a man of minutæ or notably systematic, his office was to call such intellects as lieutenants to his service, while he held in his broad and comprehensive mind the great plan with all its bearings and objects. He was a planter and builder, rather than a legislator. With high elements of statesmanship in his character, the work that lay before him was of the formative kind, and to him was given the opportunity to be higher than a statesman, in that he was one of those great characters of imperishable memory, who are known as the builders of cities and the founders of commonwealths. Like all such men his private character was irreproachable and his family life quaint and lovable. A monument to this noble man stands in Lindenwood, but Fort Wayne itself is his most worthy memorial, and right worthily might be copied for Samuel Hanna that famous epitaph to the architect of the great London cathedral, "Si monumentum requiris, circumspice."

William G. and George W. Ewing, prominent in the early history of Fort Wayne, were sons of Col. Alexander Ewing, who was born in Pennsylvania, in 1753, the third son of Alexander Ewing, a native of Ireland. Alexander enlisted in the revolutionary war at the age of sixteen, and served during the last three years of that struggle. In 1787 he engaged in a trading expedition to the Six Nation Indian tribes, and established a post in the wilderness on Buffalo creek, now the site of the city of

Buffalo. He prospered here, and a few years later settled on a splendid farm, on the Genesee, about sixty miles above Rochester. Here he was married to Charlotte Griffith, a sister of Captain William Griffith, who was one of the garrison at Chicago at the time of the massacre. In 1802 they removed to the river Raisin and settled near where the town of Monroe now is, and in 1807, they moved again and settled in the town of Washington, Ohio, now called Piqua, and lived there and at Troy until 1822, when they came to Fort Wayne. Here Col. Ewing died January 27, 1822. During the war of 1812 he served in a company of scouts under his brother-in-law, Capt. Griffith, and there gained his honorary title. His wife passed away March 13, 1843. Their children were: Sophie C., who married Judge Hood; Charles Wayne, formerly president judge of the eighth judicial circuit of Indiana; William G.; Alexander H., a successful merchant of Cincinnati; George W.; Lavinia, who married George B. Walker, of Logansport; and Louisa, who married Dr. Charles E. Sturgis. William G. and George W. were born during the residence on the river Raisin. In 1827 they formed the firm of W. G. & G. W. Ewing, and by the articles of partnership, all their estate became the property of the firm until one died. During the whole period of their association no settlement was asked for between them, such was their mutual confidence. There were many side branches. William S. Edsall was one of the firm of Ewing, Edsall & Co., and he was succeeded by Richard Chute. At Logansport, G. B. Walker was the partner in the house, and at LaGro was the establishment of Ewing & Barlow. At Westport, Mo., a business was done under the title of W. G. & G. W. Ewing, and many other branches were located in Michigan, Iowa, Kansas, Minnesota, and Wisconsin. Indeed the name of the Ewings was familiar from the Alleghanies to the Rocky mountains. William G. Ewing died July 11, 1854, and his brother then devoted his whole energies to settling up the estate, and this settlement was made to the satisfaction of the administrators, Hugh McCulloch and Dr. Sturgis, in October, 1865. Col. George W. Ewing began his business career at a trading post at Wapakoneta, and he took a prominent part in the subsequent treaties in Ohio, Indiana, Michigan and Illinois. In 1828 he was married to Harriet Bourie and then lived at Fort Wayne until 1839 when he removed to Logansport, which he and a colony from Fort Wayne founded. From 1839, to October, 1846, he lived at Peru, and was then at St. Louis until the death of his brother. He then made his residence at Fort Wayne until his death, December 27, 1865. George W. Ewing, the son of Col. G. W. Ewing, was born at Peru, Ind. He was an esteemed citizen of Fort Wayne, where he died. In 1864 he was married to Mary Charlotte Sweetzer, a native of Fort Wayne. Their son, George W. Ewing, the third of that name, and the only living male representative of the famous family, was born in this city September 26, 1866. He is a well known citizen, and takes an active interest in politics as a republican. In July, 1889, he was appointed a member of the staff of Governor Hovey, with the rank of major.

Hon. Alfred P. Edgerton, a notable citizen of Fort Wayne, who has been prominent in the political history of Indiana and Ohio, was born at Plattsburg, Clinton county, N. Y., January 11, 1813, the eldest son of Bela and Phœbe (Ketchum) Edgerton, who were married at Plattsburg, March 24, 1811. His father, a descendant of Richard Edgerton, one of the original proprietors of Norwich, Conn., was born in New London county, Conn., September 29, 1787. He was a lawyer by profession, a graduate of Middlebury college, a member of the assembly of New York from Clinton county for several years, and died at Fort Wayne, September 10, 1874. His wife, Phœbe Ketchum, was born at Livingston Manor, N. Y., March 27, 1790, and died at Hicksville, Ohio, August 24, 1844. Mr. Edgerton, after graduating from the Plattsburg academy, took the editorship of a newspaper in his native town in 1833, but in the fall of the same year removed to New York city and engaged in commercial pursuits. He removed to Ohio in the spring of 1837, and became the representative of the American land company and Hicks & Co., and established an office at Hicksville, where 107,000 acres of land were sold by him to settlers. He became the owner, himself, of nearly forty thousand acres, which were mostly sold by him to settlers on liberal terms. In 1845 he was elected to the Ohio state senate from a large territory which embraced nearly ten of the present northwestern counties. He immediately took an active part on the side of the democratic minority, and showed himself a master of the important financial questions which were the subject of discussion in the senate by the ablest men of the state. Becoming prominent by a debate with the Whig leader, he was mentioned as a candidate for the governorship of the state, and he was alluded to by a leading democratic journal as "an able and talented statesman; while faithfully adhering to sound democratic principles, his unimpeached private character, high sense of honor and sterling integrity as a gentleman, have commanded the respect of his most bitter opponents." So even and consistent has been the long career of Mr. Edgerton, that this early expression regarding him, may still be truthfully quoted as an estimate of his character. In 1850, after a brilliant career in the state senate, he was elected to the United States house of representatives, and re-elected in 1852. He was second on the important committee of claims during his first term and chairman of that committee on his second term. On the floor his arguments commanded the respectful attention of his associates. From 1853 to 1856 he held the important position of financial agent of the state of Ohio, at New York. In 1856 he was chairman of the committee on organization of the democratic national convention held at Cincinnati, and subsequently he was one of a committee selected by the legislature of the state of Ohio, to investigate the frauds upon the state treasury. In 1857 Mr. Edgerton removed to Fort Wayne, but retained his citizenship in Ohio until 1862. He became lessee of the Indiana canal, associated with Hugh McCulloch and Pliny Hoagland, in 1859, and held the position of general manager of the division from the state line to Terre Haute until 1868. In January, 1868, he was nominated by the Indiana democratic state convention for lieutenant-governor, Thomas A. Hendricks being at the head of the state ticket, which was defeated, it will be remembered, by 861 votes. Other political positions he filled prior to the latter date were those of delegate to the Baltimore convention of 1848 and the Chicago convention of 1864, but since 1868 he has not taken an active part in politics. In 1872 he was tendered the nomination for governor of Indiana by the O'Connor democrats, but declined to endorse that movement. He was for many years a member of the school board of Fort Wayne, and resigned that position to accept the appointment of civil service commissioner tendered him by President Cleveland. This office he held until 1888. The latter position, like all others, was filled by him in a manner satisfactory to his party, and his constituents, with whom he has always been popular. In private life Mr. Edgerton is an accomplished and genial gentleman, and during his residence in Fort Wayne, has been held in high esteem by the whole people.

One of the most distinguished citizens of Fort Wayne in its early days was Capt. Robert Brackenridge, who enjoyed the distinction of being a pioneer in both the cities of Cincinnati and Fort Wayne. He was born at Springfield, Bucks county, Penn., February 8, 1783, and there resided until 1805, when he made a trip as far west as Cincinnati, and then in 1806 became a resident of that place, where he remained ten years. When the war of 1812 broke out, he was one of the first to volunteer as one of a company organized at Brookville, Franklin county, Ind., and when this met with other companies at Lawrenceburgh, for muster, he delivered a patriotic address to his comrades, and was elected first lieutenant. After marching to Urbana, Ohio, they were ordered by Gen. Harrison to remain in Indiana as a reserve force. Subsequently the company was disbanded, and Capt. Brackenridge then held a position in the paymaster's department at Cincinnati until peace was declared. He made his residence at Brookville in 1816, and was appointed cashier of the branch at that place of the territorial bank. In 1829 he was appointed by President Jackson register of the land office at Fort Wayne, and was reappointed, holding the office eight years. He resided at Fort Wayne from the fall of 1830 until his death, May 9, 1859. He was a prominent Mason, and one of the charter members of Fort Wayne chapter. Capt. Brackenridge was a man of conscientious religious convictions, was of incorruptible integrity and filled the responsible positions assigned him with honor and fidelity. He was married July 27, 1820, to Mrs. Hannah Northrup, *nee* Culley, who was born in New York, and died at Fort Wayne in 1870, at seventy-six years of age. They had five children (two now living), of whom the third born is George W. Brackenridge. The latter was born at Brookville, September 28, 1825, but spent his life after his fourth year at Fort Wayne, where he received the education of the pioneer days. One of the teachers to whom he is principally indebted was Alexander M.

McJunkin, a Pennsylvanian, and another is Myron F. Barber, now a resident of this city. For twenty years from 1848 he engaged in farming, and then removed to the city and conducted a spoke factory. He is in politics a democrat of the old school. For two years he was trustee of St. Joseph township, and in 1888 was elected trustee of Wayne township. He was married in 1848 to Mary D. Orwig, who was born in Perry county, Ohio, in 1829, and they have three children: Julia B., Robert O., and Hannah M. He and wife are members of the Methodist Episcopal church.

The Archer family is one conspicuous in the history of the early settlement and mention is made of their achievements under the head of Washington township and elsewhere. Benjamin Archer, the progenitor of the family in Allen county, though an elderly man when he came here, was full of energy, and his usefulness was recognized by the people in his election to the associate judgeship upon the organization of the county. He found time, however, to manage his brick yard in Washington township, and he and his family made the brick for and erected the first brick buildings in Fort Wayne, one upon the first lot west of Morgan & Beach's hardware, the other now owned and occupied by John Schweiters. They also furnished the brick and built the first courthouse, and the first Masonic temple, on the site now occupied by Sol Bash & Co. They also aided in the construction of the feeder division of the canal and the feeder dam. Judge Archer was of Scotch-Irish descent, of the Protestant faith, a whig in politics, of intellectual and moral sturdiness, and many mourned his loss when he died at Fort Wayne in 1833. The Masons, to which order he belonged, buried him in the old grave yard where the county jail now stands. His remains and those of his wife, who was a native of one of the Carolinas, and some grandchildren were afterward removed to the Broadway cemetery, but now nothing remains to mark their resting place. Of the few now living who attended that funeral one is Peter Kiser, and another Judge Archer's son-in-law, Edward Campbell, who lives at Albion, Noble county, and is now about ninety years of age. Judge Archer left three sons, David, John S. and Benjamin, and three daughters, Susan, Elizabeth and Sarah. John S. was a brother-in-law of the Hon. Hugh Hanna, and left one son James S., who married Catherine King, of a family which recently left a valuable estate in the heart of the city. They had three sons and one daughter, now the wife of C. E. Archer. Benjamin Archer, jr., married a Miss Petit. David, the eldest son, married Anna Chrisenbury, a native of Kentucky, and his eldest son, Samuel, married Matilda Whiteside. These were the parents of John H. Archer, now a prominent citizen of Fort Wayne. The Whiteside family were also notable in the early days. The family came from Ireland to Virginia before the war of the revolution, during which the grandfather of Matilda Whiteside made clothing for Washington's men and received a great quantity of continental money in return, which he afterward burned as worthless. His son James and his son Samuel removed to Baltimore, where James married Mrs. Ward, a very handsome and intelligent lady who was related to the Baltimores of Maryland. They came west and settled at Chillicothe, and came thence to Fort Wayne in 1825, accompanied by all the children of Mr. Whiteside. Of the children by his first wife, Madison, John, Harvey, and Jane, and the children by his second wife Mrs. Ward, Jeremiah, Matilda, Malinda and Harriet, all are dead except Jane who is living with a daughter in Kansas. James Whiteside settled near the Archers, and the marriage of the children of the two families above referred to soon occurred. Then Samuel and Matilda Archer moved upon their land, three eighty-acre tracts of canal lands, three miles north of Fort Wayne. They had eight children, six sons and two daughters, five of whom are living: David R. is engaged in real estate business in Omaha; Mary J. is a resident of Fort Wayne, and Anna, of Piqua, Ohio; John H., the eldest son, was born on the farm March 23, 1837, and passed his early life there, receiving such education as was possible to gain by attending a country school three months out of a year. His father died in 1852, en route to California. June 10, 1860, Mr. Archer was married to Anna M. Hopple, born of German parentage in Northampton county, Penn., and they have had five children, all residents of Fort Wayne: Charles E., born March 28, 1861; Joseph F., born January 23, 1864; W. Sherman, born October 19, 1866; Olive Edith, born August 24, 1868, and Mary L., born November 19, 1870. Charles E. and Sherman form the firm of Archer Bros., printers, who have been doing business as the Gazette Job Printing company, and are now located in a handsome office of their own on Clinton street, near the new government building. In 1872 Mr. Archer purchased fifty acres of land in the northern suburbs of the city of Fort Wayne, at a cost of $20,000, and had it platted as Archer's addition. The remarkable advantages of this tract as a residence portion of the city has made it a popular site for many comfortable homes. Mr. Archer has a vivid memory and can recall many historic scenes and characters back to the time almost of his infancy. He is one of the leading citizens of the metropolis he has witnessed the growth of, and his unfailing energy has contributed much to the progress of events. The sixth generation in Allen county of this family are now counted in the census. The family are nearly all republicans in politics, and are independent, manly and honorable in all the relations of life.

Henry Rudisill, a pioneer in manufacturing in northern Indiana, was born at Lancaster, Penn., in 1801. His father subsequently moved to Franklin county, Penn., and at the age of fourteen, Henry was placed in a mercantile establishment at Shippinsburg, Penn. Three years afterward he removed to Chillicothe, Ohio, as an employe of Barr and Campbell, who were then engaged in merchandise at that and other points, east and west. He remained with this firm till 1824, when he moved to Lancaster, Ohio, where he engaged in business on his own account, and was subsequently married to Elizabeth Johns. In 1829 he came to Fort Wayne, and, as the agent of Barr and McCorkle, the original proprietors of Fort Wayne, had charge of their interests here until 1837; and while acting in that capacity, cleared and cultivated a large portion of the "old plat" and "Hanna's addition" to Fort Wayne. Mr. Rudisill was of active and energetic temperament, and a true representative of the men, who, under Providence, have made the western country what it now is. As early as 1830, he, in connection with his father-in-law, Henry Johns, commenced the improvement of the water power of the St. Joseph river, at the point where the St. Joe mills are now located, one mile north of Fort Wayne, and built there a saw-mill and the first flouring-mill capable of manufacturing merchantable flour in northern Indiana. A few years later, he put in operation the first machine for carding wool that was ever used in Allen county; and, several years subsequent, in company with Mr. L. Wolkie, he started the first mill for making oil from flax-seed; and also established the first woolen factory of northeastern Indiana. In church and educational matters also, and in such public improvements as tended to develop the resources of the county, he was always ready and willing to aid. Being of German descent, and for a number of years the only one in the city who could speak both languages, he became the counsellor of many who came from the old world, and there are many in the county who can date their first steps in prosperity to his assistance. He was a prominent supporter of the democratic party, and served as postmaster at Fort Wayne eight years under Jackson's administration, and a term of three years as commissioner of Allen county; and probably did more than any other man, through his personal influence with the Germans, to make the democratic party the ruling power in the county. While superintending some work at one of his mills, he fell in such a way that his spine became affected, causing partial paralysis and subsequent death in February, 1858. His uprightness, kindness, and affability, won for him a host of friends among the early settlers, the survivors among whom cherish his memory.

Hon. Franklin P. Randall, an old citizen, and prominent in the history of Fort Wayne, was born in Madison county, N. Y., June 2, 1812. His ancestors emigrated from England and Mayor Randall is of the seventh generation in descent of the family in America. His grandfather was an officer in the army of the revolution, and commanded a regiment at the battle of Saratoga, and witnessed the surrender of Gen. Burgoyne. His father was an officer in the American army during the war of 1812, and after peace was declared, he resumed his occupation as a farmer in Madison county, where the early youth of the subject of this mention was passed, attending school meanwhile during the leisure of winter. He also was a student in the Cortland and Hamilton academies, and obtained a good education, especially in mathematics and classics. He taught a select school in Oneida county, two years, and then in October, 1835, went to Williamsport, Penn., where he read law in the office of Judge Ellis Lewis, who was for fourteen years chief justice of the supreme court of that state. In February, 1838, he was admitted to practice, and in April of the same year, he removed to Fort

Wayne, and began the practice of law. Soon, however, he entered upon an official career, which has been long and honorable. In 1840 he was elected school commissioner of Allen county, and for four years had the control and management of the school lands and funds of the county. In 1847 he was elected state senator for the district composed of the counties of Allen, Adams, Huntington and Wells. He was commissioned by Gov. Wright as colonel of the state militia for Allen county, and in 1855 was promoted by Gov. Hammond to brigadier-general of the tenth division. In 1856 he was appointed director of the state prison south, by Gov. Willard, and in the same year he was chosen one of the presidential electors who voted for James Buchanan for president. Besides these higher offices, he has from the early years of his residence been closely identified officially with the progress of the city. He prepared the first city charter, which was made a law in 1840, and since then he has thrice been employed to revise the ordinances of the city, and publish them in book form, the edition which he published in 1874, forming an octavo volume of 300 pages. He was city recorder in 1840 and 1841; city attorney for three terms, beginning in 1840, 1853 and 1865, and alderman in 1843 and 1855. He was elected to the office of mayor in 1859, and re-elected at the following dates, 1861, 1863, 1869 and 1871, serving in all ten years. Taking an active interest in the projects for the development of the city, he was for about ten years a director, representing the city, of the Grand Rapids & Indiana railroad company; and for many years, was either president or prominently connected with the county agricultural society during the flourishing days of that organization, to the success of which he contributed in no slight degree. In horticulture and floriculture he is a standard authority, and his handsome residence and grounds on Berry street are filled with rare exotics, a delightful resort for all as enthusiastic as he in the study of the beauties of nature. His interest in the collection and preservation of the remains of the past, have saved to the student many interesting relics of by-gone days, and his memory is stored with a seemingly inexhaustible treasure of anecdotes and reminiscenses of the early history of Indiana and especially of Fort Wayne. His antiquarian collections, Indian antiquities, old and rare books, and cabinet of coins, are among the most valuable in existence. Mayor Randall in social life is genial and hospitable, preserving to this latter day the fine qualities of the gentleman of the old school, and is still remarkably active and vigorous both in mind and body.

One of the pioneer families of the county was that of Peter F. Barrand, who was born in France in 1804. He received a good education and became a teacher in his native land. In 1836 he emigrated and came directly to Allen county. The trip from Toledo to this place he made in a pirogue upon the river as far as the rapids. At the date of his coming the population was small, and there was little but a trading station at the site of the present city. Mr. Barrand's first employment here was with the Indian chief, J. B. Richardville, and he afterward worked on the construction of the canal. November 22, 1838, he was married to Ann J. Poirson, who was born in France, in 1820, and immigrated with her parents in 1834. The family spent a few years at Tandawanda, N. Y., about eighteen miles from Niagara Falls, and then settled on the old plank road four and a half miles from Fort Wayne, where they farmed and kept the "French Mary's Tavern," so-called by the early settlers. Peter and Ann Barrand began farming on the Penn farm, about one and a half miles north of Fort Wayne, and three years later purchased a farm in Washington township, where they have since resided. In 1888, they celebrated their "golden wedding." They have reared nine children out of eleven born to them. Their son, John B. Barrand, born in Washington township, April 23, 1849, is now superintendent of the sash, door and blind factory of Louis Deither & Bro., and an esteemed citizen. Before he left the farm he learned the carpenter's trade, and in 1869, began working at that occupation at Wallen, where he remained ten years. Since 1879 he has been a resident of the city. For the first two years he was engaged in the grocery business, but afterward resumed his trade. In February, 1887, he entered the manufactory referred to, and in the following June was made superintendent. He was married May 24, 1871, to Catharine L. Cremer, of Washington township.

William H. Brown, a popular citizen of Fort Wayne, is one of an honored family of the city's pioneers. He was born here, March 3, 1839. His father, John Brown, was born at Dayton, Ohio, September 10, 1811, by birth, indeed, a western pioneer. He is a blacksmith by occupation, and in 1825 came to Fort Wayne, where he was married in 1833, to Dorcas Rodgers, who was born in Ohio in 1814. They are both living in the city, esteemed and venerated by all. Her father, John Rodgers, born December 9, 1785, died September, 1877. He voted first for Madison, and was afterward on the winning side for Monroe, Harrison, Taylor, Lincoln, Grant and Hayes. William H. is the oldest of their living children, the others being Benjamin H., John C., Alexander M., and Susie. The paternal grandfather was Samuel Brown, a native of Ireland, who was one of the early settlers of Allen county, and died here at an advanced age. The maternal grandfather, Collins by name, was a Frenchman who came to the United States and fought for the independence of his adopted country in the war of the revolution. Early in life Mr. Brown learned the blacksmith's craft, and was so occupied until 1866, since which date he has been engaged in teaming and heavy transfer business. His career has been an honorable and successful one, and he and his family have won the respect and esteem of the community. He is well-known to have a great regard for thorough-bred horses, and among his valued possessions are some of the most handsome of those valued co-workers with man. Mr. Brown was married in 1870 to Cassander Yost, who was born in Preble county, Ohio, in 1833. Mrs. Brown is a daughter of Isaac Yost, who was born in Virginia and died in Cincinnati in 1850, while returning from a trip to California. Her mother was Susanna (Collingsworth) Yost, a native of Ohio, who died there in 1851. Mrs. Brown is one of six children living. Mr. Brown is a staunch republican having cast his first vote for Abraham Lincoln, and his father's first vote was cast for Henry Clay. The residence of the family is at No. 73 Holman street. Mr. Brown has by his first wife, one daughter, Mary, born in 1866.

John B. Becquett, a pioneer citizen of Fort Wayne, was born in Detroit, Mich., January 13, 1824. He is the son of John B. and Theresa (Durett) Becquett, the former a native of the province of Quebec, and the latter of Detroit, Mich. In 1826, their son John B., being two years old, they removed to Fort Wayne and located on the corner of Columbia and Clinton streets. Here the father followed the trade of an Indian jeweler until his death, September 17, 1846. His wife survived him until March, 1884, when she died, aged eighty-four. At eighteen years of age, John B. Becquett began an apprenticeship of three years as brick layer; this trade has been the occupation of his life, and he has pursued it in this city for nearly half a century. Mr. Becquett was married November 16, 1855, to Elizabeth, daughter of George and Catharine Baker, with whom she immigrated from Germany when she was five years old. They located at Fort Wayne where Mr. Baker followed the trade of wagon-maker. He and his wife are now deceased. Mr. and Mrs. Becquett have four sons and four daughters, all of whom are grown to maturity. Their names are: John A., Jacob, Henry, George F., Catharine, Mary, Elizabeth and Theresa. Mr. Becquett and family are members of the Catholich church. In politics he has been a life long democrat. He is one of Fort Wayne's earliest residents now living, having been here for sixty-three years. His memory is good and his recollections of early times are many and varied. He possesses an extensive acquaintance and is highly respected.

Zenas Henderson, who has been referred to in this work as one of the pioneers of the city of Fort Wayne, was born in Cleveland, Ohio, and came to Fort Wayne early in the thirties. He was an interpreter for the Indians and was also in business as an Indian trader. This he subsequently abandoned to engage in hotel keeping, on the corner of Calhoun and Columbia streets. He married Rosina McKee, who was born in Wheeling, W. Va., and died in 1855. His death followed two years later. To these parents seven children were born, five of whom are living. Samuel C. Henderson, one of these, was born December 17, 1841, on the corner of Main and Barr streets, and is now foreman of the tin, copper and flue department of the shops of the Pittsburgh, Fort Wayne & Chicago railroad company. He attended the school at the corner of Clay and Washington streets on the first day that it was opened, and gained a good education in the city schools. At the age of eighteen years he set in to learn the trade of copper-smith, and entered the shops of the Pittsburgh, Fort Wayne & Chicago railroad company for that purpose September 20, 1859, and since that date has been one of the trusted employes of that corporation. Three years after beginning work he was appointed assistant foreman of the copper department, and in 1877 he became foreman. He is a member of the First Presbyterian church, and of Home lodge, No. 342, F. & A. M., and of the National Union. He was married in September, 1876, to Mary Kinnard, who was born at Sidney, Ohio, but reared in Fort Wayne.

Frederick Dalman, a well known and esteemed citizen of Fort Wayne, has had the rare privilege of becoming acquainted when a boy with the tangled forests then covering Allen county, and has enjoyed the pleasure of observing the growth of a beautiful and prosperous city. He was born near Burton-on-Trent, Derbyshire, England, May 30, 1824. His father, John Dalman, who was born in April, 1774, married Anna Burcher, who was born in 1790. They had eight children, of whom Frederick is the youngest, and three of whom survive. The father, a carpenter and joiner, became dissatisfied with life in the old country, and in 1833, to seek a field where his energy and industry would yield better rewards, sailed for America, landing at New York in June, with his family. After stopping two weeks in Madison county, N. Y., they sailed from Buffalo to Maumee City. Being transported by wagon to the head of the rapids, they there embarked in pirogues, and reached Fort Wayne after a week's journey. They located at Barnett's Springs, now within the city limits, but in December removed to land they had purchased in section 33, in Wayne township, a tract of 120 acres on Little river. On this land Mr. Dalman had built a cabin in the dense woods, and there was not to the south of him another habitation of white men for twenty miles. Here the parents lived the life of pioneers, self-sacrificing, patient and persevering. At a ripe old age, they passed away, the father in 1864, the mother in 1868. Frederick remained on the farm, managing it until, July, 1884, when he divided the land amounting to 301 acres among his three children, and removed to town. He still was the owner at the time of dividing the farm of 140 acres, sixty of which is still in his possession. His property in the city includes seven houses and lots, among them his residence at 116 Williamson street, and three vacant lots. The superintendence of his property occupies his time mainly, though he is also superintendent and treasurer of the Bluffton gravel road, in which he was one of the original stockholders, and superintendent of the construction of a portion of it. Mr. Dalman was married in 1846 to Mary M. F., daughter of David Hill, a native of Pennsylvania. She died in 1870, leaving the following children: David, and Jesse, farmers in Wayne township; America E., wife of Thomas King, a prosperous farmer of Pleasant township. In July 1884, Mr. Dalman was married to Louisa Flinn.

Among the early settlers of Fort Wayne, Edward Stapleford will be remembered as one widely known and generally esteemed. He came to this city in 1833, and for many years was a prominent merchant. He was born in Delaware in 1809, and at an early age he accompanied his father and mother and brothers and sisters to Piqua, Ohio, where his father died, and he thence came to this city. He was eminently social in his relations to the public, affectionate to his family, and strictly honorable as a business man. He married Susan E. Powers, and to them was born October 15, 1838, Lucien P., now a resident of this city. The latter gained his education at the Methodist college, in which he completed a full course. He afterward entered the Fort Wayne commercial college, of which C. J. Diedrich was principal, and attended it some two or three years, graduating at the age of nineteen. He acquired meanwhile a high proficiency in penmanship, and has the credit of being one of the best penmen in the city. Up to the time of his father's death, January 1, 1861, he clerked in his store, and after that date became his successor, and successfully managed the business until 1872. Soon after that date he purchased the Comparet mills and warehouse on the corner of Columbia and Lafayette streets, but after remodeling the property and making extensive improvements, Mr. Stapleford suffered the crushing loss of the whole property by fire, a loss of $40,000. For several years past he has given his attention to the livery, coal and wood business and the management of the Herdic coach line, of which he is proprietor. For more than thirty years he has also acted as auctioneer, and in this manner has an extensive acquaintance throughout the whole county. He was married in January, 1871, to Caroline E., daughter of Peter Heller, the founder of Heller's corners, of Eel River township. They have had two children: Leonidas P. and Norris E., the latter of whom died in the ninth year of his age. Mr. Stapleford was reared in the Methodist faith and takes much interest in the Sunday-school work, having been secretary of the Wayne Street Sabbath school five years. He was formerly a Good Templar, and is an ardent temperance man. He is secretary of the Liverymen and Hackmen's protective association, and formerly was secretary of the Audubon club. In politics he is a republican.

Michael Hedekin, frequently referred to as an early settler, was a native of County Westmeath, Ireland. Emigrating to America he was married to Rebecca Pau, a native of Ohio. They came to Fort Wayne in 1834. In 1843 and 1844 he built a three-story brick hotel building on the east side of Barr street south of Columbia, and on May 15, 1846, Calvin Anderson opened it as a tavern. Under various proprietors it was maintained until 1876, since when it has been conducted by Jacob Swaidner. The Hedekin House is a notable monument of early days, and was, when built, excelled in its size and appointments by none in the northwest. Thomas B. Hedekin, son of Michael, who was not a year old when his father came, established a grocery in 1848, which he managed for twenty years.

Maurice Cody, well-known among the early settlers of Fort Wayne, was born in County Cork, Ireland, September 15, 1818, the son of John and Mary (Bolland) Cody. His parents were both born in County Cork, the father in 1790, and the mother in 1804. They emigrated to America in 1825, and settled at Oswego, N. Y., where the mother died in 1829. In the following year the father died at Horseheads, Chemung county,

N. Y. In 1832, Mr. Cody removed to Penn Yan, and from there to Maryland, in the fall of 1833, and in December, 1834, he came to Fort Wayne. His route thither was over the Alleghany mountains to Wheeling, W Va., thence to Columbus, Ohio, and then to Troy and Piqua, and up to St. Mary's, and then overland to Fort Wayne through what was then called the Black swamp country, the difficulties of which may be imagined from the fact that it required three weeks to make the trip, and one six miles of the way required three days to traverse. In company with him were his uncle, Patrick Cody, and Patrick and Garrett, his brothers. On reaching Fort Wayne Mr. Cody engaged in cutting stove wood and other odd jobs, until 1839, when he became a clerk in the pioneer store of Michael Hedekin, with whom he was associated for four years. In 1841 he was interested with Mr. Hedekin in a store one mile east of Antwerp, Ohio, where he lived eleven months, but subsequently he returned to Fort Wayne, was married, and purchased a farm in St. Joseph township. He had occupied this but six months, when he went to Paulding county, Ohio, and was there engaged in merchandise for two years. Returning to Fort Wayne, in October, 1845, he went to Chicago, and became engaged in merchandise at Blue Island. In May, 1847, he resumed business at Fort Wayne, and was in merchandise until 1862, when he went into the milling business on the St. Mary's river, ten miles south of the city, and was so engaged for twenty years. Previously he had been engaged in the ice business for four years, in the city. Since 1882 he has been living in the city, on the same lot, on the corner of Barr and Superior streets, that he rented in 1835, and bought in 1847, and is retired from business, but busies himself in managing his farm. Mr. Cody is a democrat and cast his first vote for Martin VanBuren. For ten years he was councilman for the second ward, and in 1852 was elected marshal of Fort Wayne, and street commissioner at the first election by the people. He is a member of the congregation of the Cathedral. Mr. Cody had the following brothers and sisters: Ellen, John, James, Bridget, Mary, Patrick and Garrett, of whom Mary Bonfield alone survives. February 1, 1843, he was married to Mary Daugherty, a native of Ireland, who died in December, 1859, leaving six children, John H., Margaret, Ellen, Thomas G., Ann E. and Mary R. May 14, 1861, he was married to Mrs. Bridget Muldoon, a native of St. Lawrence county, N. Y.

Among the pioneers who came here at a time when Fort Wayne was a village and Allen county was almost a wilderness, was Anthony Lintz (deceased). Mr. Lintz was born in France, of German parents, in 1806, and emigrated to the United States in about 1832. He spent about two months in New York city, then went to Rochester, N. Y., where he remained almost a year, and then to Detroit. In 1834 he removed to Fort Wayne, and about two months later went to Rochester, N. Y., and was married to Delia Klem, who was born in Baden, Germany, in 1814. When two years old she came to America with her parents, who settled in Rochester, N. Y. In coming to Fort Wayne,

Mr. and Mrs. Lintz went from Rochester to Buffalo by canal, thence to Toledo by lake, and from Toledo came to the head of the rapids by wagon, and then in a pirogue on the Maumee to Fort Wayne. Four weeks were spent in making the trip, which to-day can be made in less than eighteen hours. To Anthony Lintz and wife eleven children were born, eight of whom survive: Delia, the widow of Casper Schœripp, of Marion, Ind.; Mary Wirley, of Rochester, N. Y.; Catherine Bauer, of St. Louis, Mo.; Josephine Martin, of Socorro, New Mexico; Anthony, of Fort Wayne; Carrie Sigl, of Rochester, N. Y., and Theodore L., in business in Fort Wayne. Anthony Lintz was for years in the boot and shoe business in Fort Wayne. In about 1865 he went to Europe on a tour for pleasure and health, and remained nine months. Upon his return, and while in New York city, he met with an accident in which his leg was broken, and his death occurred in that city on February 6, 1866. His remains were interred at Indianapolis. For five weeks before his death his wife was with him in New York city. He was a member of the Cathedral Catholic church of Fort Wayne. In about 1859 the family removed from Fort Wayne to Indianapolis, and continued to live there until 1867, when they returned to Fort Wayne. Mrs. Lintz is among the oldest citizens in point of residence at Fort Wayne, and in December, 1889, she will have been here for fifty-five years. She is a member of the Cathedral congregation. She and husband gave all the black walnut lumber for the pews of the first church, and he was one of ten who bought and donated the land upon which the Cathedral now stands. Before the erection of a Catholic church in Fort Wayne, services were held in Mr. Lintz's residence. In the fall of 1884 Theodore L. Lintz established the China Bazar at No. 12 E. Columbia street.

Samuel C. Freeman (deceased), one of the early settlers of Fort Wayne, was born at Williamstown, N. Y., December 6, 1812, son of Samuel and Sarah (Hoffman) Freeman. At his native place he was married in 1831, to Mary A. Taylor, born in Connecticut in 1810, to William and Electa Hale Taylor. In 1836 Mr. Freeman and wife, and her brother, Royal W. Taylor, came to Fort Wayne, where Messrs. Taylor and Freeman became known as successful and enterprising business men. Mr. Freeman was engaged at different times in milling, merchandise, and the foundry business. His first wife died in 1838, leaving two children. One, M. Frances, who became the wife of Seth R. Green, now deceased, is a practicing physician of the city. The other, Samuel P. Freeman, died in 1873, at the age of thirty. In 1840 Mr. Freeman married Sarah Bigelow, a native of Massachusetts, who formerly had charge of a successful school for young ladies in this city. He died March 7, 1888, his loss being deplored by the many citizens who had for so long had with him pleasant associations. His widow survives in her eighty-first year. Mrs. Green, daughter of Mr. Freeman, graduated from the Women's Homeopathy college of Cleveland, in 1871, and has since then been enjoying a very successful medical practice in Fort Wayne. She is the mother of four children: Freeman R., Malcolm A., M. Gertrude and Seth F. Green.

One prominent among the pioneers of Fort Wayne is Jacob Foellinger, who settled here in the latter part of 1836. He was born in Prussia, December 19, 1817, son of Jacob and Sophia (Goebel) Foellinger, the former of whom died when his son Jacob was fourteen years old. The son found a home in the family of his uncle, George Foellinger, for two years, engaged ⸳ farming and worked at the shoemaker's trade. The latter vocation he followed in France, and at eighteen years of age, April 2, 1836, he sailed for America on the sailing vessel "Majestic," and was seventy-eight days at sea, landing at New York August 19. Arriving at Fort Wayne he worked three years as a journeyman and then set up a shop of his own and conducted it many years, finally becoming a dealer in boots and shoes, to which he gave his attention until 1880. Subsequently, owing to impaired hearing, he has been leading a retired life. In 1872 he removed his family to the beautiful home they now occupy on Fairfield avenue. His residence is a large and handsome brick situated on a tract of ten acres which, owing to its nearness to the city, is very valuable property. He is also the owner of two valuable business blocks on Calhoun street, from the rent of which he realizes a handsome income. He also has a residence property on Harrison street. He possessed nothing whatever when he came to America and his present prosperity speaks creditably of his business ability. Mr. Foellinger was married May 30, 1840, to Margaret Kiefer, a native of Prussia, born March 17, 1818, the daughter of Christian and Barbara Kiefer, with whom she came to America in 1837. Mr. and Mrs. Foellinger have had ten children: Elizabeth, Frederick, Jacob, Christian, Martin, Augusta, Julia, Adolph, Louis and Margarita, of whom Jacob, Martin, Adolph and Louis are living. Mr. and Mrs. Foellinger are members of Emanuel's German Lutheran church. He has been a life-long democrat, and has served as a member of the city council two years.

Kilian Baker, a prominent manufacturer of lumber, is one of a family which were among the pioneers of Fort Wayne. He was born to George and Catherine (Baschinger) Baker, in Hesse-Darmstadt, Germany, December 15, 1830, and five years later the family, including eight children, emigrated, and after landing at New York went to Pittsburgh. In the following year, 1836, the father came to Allen county and entered a piece of land in Cedar Creek township, and removed his family in the spring of 1838 to Fort Wayne, then a town of about 400 inhabitants. He worked at the wagon-maker's trade until 1848, when he erected a saw-mill and began the manufacture of lumber. In this he was associated with his sons, John, Jacob, Henry and Kilian. Two years later the father and John sold the mill to the other brothers. Henry retired in 1867 and Jacob in 1878, leaving Kilian the sole proprietor. This mill, founded by his father, he continues to operate. The mother died in 1850, and the father in 1870. Kilian Baker was educated in the

Catholic schools. He has grown up with the city, and is possessed of many valuable historical reminiscences. His life has been devoted to business, and in it he has achieved a high standing in the community. Mr. Baker was married in 1859, to Annie Daugherty, who was born at Arcola, Allen county, in 1840, of Irish parents, and they have had eleven children, of whom nine survive. He and wife are members of the Catholic church.

John Baker, an old citizen of Fort Wayne, was born in Hesse-Darmstadt, Germany, in 1817, and came to America in 1835 and to Fort Wayne in 1838. He is the son of George and Catherine (Baschinger) Baker, both natives of Germany. The father was one of the early blacksmiths of Fort Wayne, and his son worked with him, the latter doing the wood-work. Later he was engaged in a saw-mill enterprise with his father and brothers, Jacob, Henry and Kilian, but after two years at that business he sold out and began the manufacture of trucks and delivery wagons. He was very successful and built up a large business which he conducted until 1883, when he retired and was succeeded by his son, B. H. Baker. In November, 1841, he was married to Mary Fauth, who was born in Baltimore in 1826, and came to Fort Wayne in November, 1840. To their union, five daughters and three sons have been born. Both Mr. and Mrs. Baker are members of the Catholic church, and are among the most highly respected of Fort Wayne's old citizens.

B. H. Baker, son of the above, is a prominent young manufacturer, being extensively engaged in the production of carriages, trucks and express wagons at Nos. 16 and 18, Lafayette street. He was born in this city in 1856. Mr. Baker was given a liberal education in the Catholic schools, and then entered the factory with his father, and succeeded in 1883, to the business which he is now successfully conducting. He is a member of the Catholic church.

James H. Robinson, born near Morristown, N. J., January 31, 1802, died at Fort Wayne, May 2, 1878, was one of the conspicuous figures in that period of the history of Fort Wayne covered by his residence here. He was a lineal descendant of Rev. John Robinson, the pastor of the pilgrims, and his family had resided in New Jersey for more than a century. At sixteen years of age he went to Newark, and when still a young man became a partner of Caleb B. Shipman in the wholesale boot, shoe and leather trade. The firm of Shipman, Robinson & Co., was one of the most important in the country, and its very large southern trade was attended to in person by Mr. Robinson. He retired from business at the age of thirty-five, with a handsome fortune, and built him a residence at Newark afterward occupied by Gov. Marcus L. Ward. In the panic of 1837, however, he lost most of his possessions, and then he engaged in the wholesale dry goods trade at New York. Removing to Fort Wayne in 1843, he purchased the tan-yards at the head of Columbia street, at the site of the Robinson house. After managing that property for several years he engaged in the boot and shoe trade, erecting the large buildings for that purpose which have subsequently been converted into a hotel. He was the pioneer wholesale merchant of Fort Wayne and carried on a large and profitable trade until 1868, when he retired from business. In 1872 the buildings were refitted for hotel use, becoming the most popular hotel in the city, and of this establishment Mr. Robinson had personal charge two years before his death. Mr. Robinson took an active interest in politics, first as a whig and then as a republican. He represented Newark in the New Jersey legislature in 1840 and 1842, and was the whig leader, enjoying the personal frienship of such men as Governor Pennington and Theodore Frelinghuysen. Further political honors he never sought, though repeatedly asked to become a candidate for mayor of Fort Wayne. He was a leading member of the Presbyterian church, and was a member of the First church, then during the pastorate of Rev. Charles Brechen, of the Second church, subsequently returning to the First church. He was in bearing a dignified gentleman of the old school, in character upright, pure and strong but unobtrusive. He was married in 1822, to Mary Crane, of Newark, who died in 1835, in Georgia. Their four children all died in childhood. In the spring of 1837 he was married to Mary C., daughter of Hon. Obadiah Meeker, of New Jersey, and they had two children: James H., jr., of Chicago, and Henry H., of this city.

Among the old residents should be mentioned Claude F. Eme. He came to Allen county with his parents, who settled in St. Joseph township in June, 1844, and has been a resident ever since. He was born in France, July 8, 1831, son of John H. and Claude Frances (Cotes) Eme, who were born in France, the father in 1808, the mother in 1813, and now live in Fort Wayne. Two of their children are living, Claude F. being the elder. He spent his youth on the farm, receiving a common school education, and in 1851–2 was employed for two seasons on the "state boat," on the canal. He was then employed for a year and a half with A. H. Carier, and afterward for fourteen years with H. R. Schwegman in the dry goods business. In January, 1870, he formed a partnership with Henry Rohs and Frederick Reinking in the dry goods trade, and this firm continued until 1882, when the death of Mr. Reinking occurred, when it was succeeded by the firm of Rohs & Eme, which did business until 1888, when Mr. Eme permanently retired from mercantile pursuits, in which he was successful and prosperous. He was married in 1856 to Adele Duval, a native of France, born in 1836, daughter of Nicholas and Catherine (Bastien) Duval. Her father came to this county in 1844 and died in 1849. They have three children: Julius J., Josephine and Joseph F. Mr. and Mrs. Eme are members of the Catholic church, and he is in politics a democrat.

Calvin Anderson, a venerable and honored citizen of the city, has been a witness of its growth and a participant in its commercial enterprises for the past forty-three years. He was born at Manchester, Bennington county, Vt., July 3, 1803, son of Andrew and Sarah (Sexton) Anderson, natives of the Green Mountain state. The father was born in 1760, and died in 1816; the mother was born in 1769, and died in Ohio in 1837. Of their six children, Mr. Anderson is the only one living now. At the age of twelve he came to Ohio with his parents, and remained on the farm until he was twenty-one, when he embarked in the hotel business, which he followed for thirty years. Nine years of that period was spent in Fort Wayne, whither he came in 1846. In 1855 he opened a grocery and provision store, which he conducted successfully for twelve years, and then retired from business life. He was a pioneer in the settlement of Ohio, and also one of the early settlers of this city. He was married April 13, 1828, to Rebecca Lybarger, born in Pennsylvania, June 26, 1803, still the faithful companion of his life. They are the oldest couple in the city, and are highly honored and esteemed. They have six children: Laura Ann Lydia, Sarah Ann, Mary Eliza, Theresa, Calvin A. and Eli G. Mr. Anderson is a member of the First Presbyterian church. He cast his first presidential vote for John Quincy Adams in 1824, voted for Gen. W. H. Harrison in 1836 and 1840, and has been a republican since the organization of the party.

Christian Tresselt, proprietor of the City Mills, was born in Thuringia, Germany, September 3, 1823. His father, August Ludwig Tresselt, an artist by profession, was born in 1776, and died in Germany in 1838. His wife, Hannah Machold, died in her native land about 1828. Of the eight children of these parents, three survive: Doretha, Benjamin William and Christian. Mr. Tresselt was educated in Germany at the common schools, and in 1838 engaged in mercantile pursuits at Gross Brietenbach, at which he was engaged for seven years. In 1845 he emigrated to the United States, and after his arrival at New York, remaining there fifteen months, clerked in a dry goods store. His residence at Fort Wayne began in 1846, and for four years he was employed as a clerk in the store of Hill, Wilson & Company, afterward, for one season, running a freight boat on the canal. In the fall of 1850 he was a clerk in the City Mill, and from 1851 to 1854 was in the dry goods business with George Wilson as a partner. Then, after one year as a partner of his brother-in-law, H. R. Schwegman, he returned to the City Mills. In 1866 he was engaged with Siemon Brothers, and four years later became a member of the firm of Hoagland, Tresselt & Co., proprietors of the City Mills. Mr. Hoagland died in 1884, and since then Mr. Tresselt has been sole proprietor, the firm now being known as C. Tresselt & Sons. The mill which they operate was established in 1843. Mr. Tresselt was married in 1854 to Elizabeth Siemon, who was born in Prussia in 1829 and came to Fort Wayne in 1853. They have three children: Oscar W., born in 1858; Herman C., born in 1859, and Frederick G., born in 1866. Mr. Tresselt is in politics a democrat, and he is a member of the Lutheran church. His long residence in the city, and worth as a man and honorable in business life, have made him a prominent and respected citizen. He was one of the city commissioners from 1872 to 1885, in which year he was elected to the city council and served for two years.

A well known early business man of Fort Wayne, Christian Schiefer, is now at the head of a successful boot and shoe house of the city, that of Christian Schiefer & Son, of No. 8 East Columbia street. The senior member of this firm, Christian Schiefer, was born at Hamburg, Germany, in 1829. In 1846 he came to America, and going directly to Toledo, came up the old canal to Fort Wayne. He had learned shoemaking in the old country, and as soon as he reached Fort Wayne he began work at his trade. In 1854, he formed a partnership with E. Vordermark, in the boot and shoe business, and they were associated for seven and a half years. After that he was in partnership with one Hood, for about one year, and since then managed the business alone until 1881, when his son-in-law was admitted to the business. Mr. Schiefer was married in 1851, to Elizabeth Harbecker, who was born in Lancaster county, Penn. To them two children have been born, of whom two are living: William D. Schiefer, ex-sheriff of Allen county, now in the boot and shoe business on Calhoun street, and Lizzie, the wife of Herman H. Hartwig. Mr. Schiefer is a member of the Lutheran church, and is a Master Mason. Mr. Hartwig, above named, was born in New York city, December 17, 1855. In that city he was reared and educated in the Lutheran and public schools, and also in commercial college. In 1875 he engaged in the window glass trade in New York city. In 1877, he was married to Lizzie Schiefer, and in 1881 he removed to Fort Wayne, and entered the firm of Schiefer & Co. He is a member of St. Paul's Lutheran church, in which connection he is a trustee of the church and treasurer of the building committee. To his marriage four children have been born.

Moritz Axt, one of the prominent pioneers of Fort Wayne, came to the town when it was in its struggling infancy, and he has witnessed its magnificent growth, and not a little by his industry and good citizenship, aided in the growth of the city. Mr. Axt is a native of Germany, and was born January 29, 1811. In 1847 he immigrated to the new world, and in the same year made his home in this city, from which he has not removed. His life occupation has been the carpenter's trade in which he was a skillful and expert workman. He is an esteemed member of St. Paul's Lutheran clurch. Mr. Axt was married July 12, 1848, to Christena Brackenridge, and their union has given them eight children: William, Henry, Catherine, Charles, Christena, August, Sophia and Moritz, the last two of whom are deceased.

Joseph Singmaster, a venerable citizen of Fort Wayne, was born in Bucks county, Penn., October 2, 1804. His parents, Jacob and Susan Singmaster, were both natives of Pennsylvania. He was reared to manhood in his native county, and in youth learned the tanner's trade. About 1848 he came to Fort Wayne, and worked awhile at his trade, after which for twenty-five years he was employed in the Pittsburgh shops. For the past thirty years he has acted as agent for the Great American Tea Company of New York. Though now eighty-five years of age he still acts in that capacity, and transacts business with as much accuracy as he did twenty-five or thirty-years ago. Mr. Singmaster was married in early manhood to Catharine Stager, who died in September, 1880. He has living three children: Catharine E., Sarah M. and Joseph M. Six others all deceased. Mr. Singmaster is a member of the English Lutheran church, and in politics is a democrat, having cast his first vote for Andrew Jackson. He was very fond of hunting in the early days and frequently indulged in that sport. His memory is still good and his recollections of early times are interesting and varied.

A member of the early German families of Fort Wayne, Frederick Becker, now a well-known citizen, is a native of Fort Wayne, born November 4, 1849, son of Frederick and Margaret Becker, both of whom were natives of Germany. They were married in that country in 1847, and coming to America in 1848, located at Fort Wayne, where the father, who by trade was a blacksmith, died in 1882. The mother is still living. Frederick Becker learned the blacksmith trade with his father very early in life, and the pursuit of it has, thus far, received his entire attention. He makes a specialty of shorseshoeing and for a great many years past has done an exclusive business of that kind. He erected his present shop in 1883. It is a splendid brick building at 13 East Washington street, and is an establishment which does credit to the city. Mr. Becker is a member of the German Lutheran church, and is a democrat in politics. The firm name now is Frederick Becker & Bro.

Henry Volland, one of the prominent millers of northern Indiana, has devoted more than forty years to that business, and has been a resident of Fort Wayne for the period named. In 1847 he came to America and settled in Ohio, coming thence to Fort Wayne on foot in 1849. The two previous years he had been alternating his time between work in a mill and labor upon the farm. Reaching this city he found employment in the city mills for three years, after which he was for nine years engaged in Judge Hanna's flouring mill on the Maumee river. Prior to the war he purchased an interest in this property and held it for three years, subsequently to that period being for fourteen years connected with the mill of John Orff on West Main street. Then the firm of H. Volland & Sons was formed, and for the last four years they have been doing an extensive business at No. 14 West Columbia street. Their mill is equipped in the best manner for the production of an excellent grade of flour, etc., having the full roller process. Mr. Volland was born in Bavaria, January 21, 1827, son of John and Margaret (Shoulty) Volland, who were born and passed their lives in that country. He was married in 1851 to Isabella Billman, born in Ohio, October 4, 1835, of parents who came from Pennsylvania. She died in 1885, leaving six children: Henry J., born 1857; Tillie, 1859; John, 1861; William, 1863; Mary, 1865; Charles, 1871. The family are members of the Lutheran church. Mr. Volland is in politics a democrat.

One of the prominent early manufacturers and worthy citizens of Allen county, John C. Begue, now deceased, was born in Alsace, France, April 11, 1827. When he was but three months old he lost his mother by death. In 1844, he accompanied his father and step-mother to America. They landed at New Orleans, and settled about twenty miles from Dayton, Ohio, on a farm. The son obtained employment with a tanner, and worked at that trade four years, and afterward came to Fort Wayne, in the fall of 1850. On November 23, 1851, he married Marie Beugnot, daughter of Francis and Collet Beugnot, natives of France. She was born at Hautsonne, France, March 24, 1830, and accompanied her parents to this country when she was thirteen years old. They stopped first in Stark county, Ohio, but in May, 1848, settled in Jefferson township, Allen county. For some time after their marriage Mr. Begue and wife resided in Fort Wayne, and then removed to Jefferson township, where he worked as a cooper. In May, 1854, they settled at New Haven, where they resided about twenty-one years, Mr. Begue giving his attention to coopering and the stave manufacture. He aided in the building of the Maumee Valley Mills, and was one of the owners of that property about two years. He helped build a stave factory at Antwerp, Ohio, and was connected with it three years. He was also connected with the Indiana Stave campany, which had three factories at New Haven, and one in Fort Wayne. In the fall of 1875, he removed to Fort Wayne, and was engaged during the remainder of his life as a contractor. He was prominent in politics as a democrat, and served two terms as one of the commissioners of Allen county, from 1869 to 1874. In the fall of 1874 he made a visit to France for the benefit of his health, and remained several months. He died October 2, 1880. Of the eight children of Mr. Begue, only two are living, Mrs. Alice Schoenbein and Mrs. Amelia Baker. The former, who is also a widow, resides with Mrs. Begue at 164 East Wayne street. Mrs. Begue is a member of the Catholic church, as was her husband.

Anthony Gocke, an old citizen of Fort Wayne, was born in Germany, November 3, 1815. In 1851 he emigrated to America, landing at New Orleans, January 25. He came directly to Fort Wayne where he has since resided. Before coming to America his occupation was chiefly that of a coal miner. During thirty years of his residence in Fort Wayne he occupied a position in the wholesale grocery establishment, formerly owned by Barney Trentman and now by his son A. C. Trentman. Mr. Gocke was married in February, 1856, to Elizabeth Rensman, a native of Germany, who came to America at seventeen years of age. They have had eight children: Frank, Anna, Henry, Bernard, Louis H., Theresa, August and Clara, two of whom, Bernard and Theresa, are dead. Mrs. Gocke died January 15, 1875. Mr. Gocke is a member of the Catholic church.

Louis H. Gocke, above named, is occupied as book-keeper for A. C. Trentman. He was born at Fort Wayne, July 20, 1863. November 8, 1887, he was married to Miss Elizabeth Grimme, by whom he is the father of one child, Edward H., born August 10, 1888. Mr. Gocke and wife are members of the Catholic church, and he is a member of the Catholic Knights of America.

Charles Auger, prominent among the citizens of Fort Wayne, of French nativity, has resided in the city since 1853. He has witnessed the great development of his adopted town, and throughout his life has been honored by his fellow citizens. He was one of the first to engage in business as a florist in this city, and has had an extensive business, owning as many as six green houses at one time. Having prosered in his affairs and grown advanced in years, he has retired and turned over his business to his son, Louis B. Auger, who continues it successfully. Charles Auger was born in France, March 4, 1822, the son of John B. and Marie C. Auger. He came to America in 1850, and at first spent two years in New York city. He was married November 25, 1850, to Catherine Thorpe, a native of England, daughter of William and Ann Thorpe, also of that country, but of French descent. Mr. and Mrs. Auger have had two children, Louis B. and Charles W., who died at the age of eleven years and eight months. Mrs. Auger is a member of the Episcopal church. Mr. Auger has made three trips to his native country, and he and wife visited the Paris exposition in the summer of 1889.

John M. Riedmiller, a prominent citizen of Fort Wayne, now deceased, was born in Asbach, O. P., Crailsheim, Koenigreich, Würtemberg, Germany, on March 14, 1836. He emigrated to America in 1853, and came at once to Fort Wayne. He was a shoemaker by trade, and was a prominent and influential citizen until his death, which occurred August 19, 1885. For three terms he was a member of the common council. He was prosperous in business and left his family in good circumstances. Mr. Reidmiller was married May 5, 1857, to Catherine Wolf, who was born in Hesse-Darmstadt, Germany, December 24, 1839, and came with her parents to America in 1852. She is the daughter of William Wolf, an early citizen of Fort Wayne. To the union of Mr. and Mrs. Riedmiller three children were born, as follows: Julia Eliza, born May 15, 1859, now the wife of Fred Rippe, a liveryman of Fort Wayne; Charles John, born October 3, 1863, now in business in Fort Wayne; John M., jr., born August 7, 1866, engaged in the bottling business, and a well-known business man of the city. Mr. Riedmiller was, and all the family are, members of St. John's Lutheran church.

John W. McQuiston is one of the early settlers of Allen county, who has done well financially by bringing shrewd business qualifications to bear upon the early advantages, and by continuous and intelligent application through life has gained a wide fund of information, which well stands instead of the educational advantages now so abundant, but then infrequent. His father, John McQuiston, was born in Westmoreland county, Penn., in 1782, and married Jane McDaniel, who was born in York county, Penn., in 1789. Both were children of revolutionary soldiers, who held rank as officers. They removed to Allen county in 1837, settled in Perry township, and cleared out a farm. The father served as one of Allen county's early commissioners. He died at his home in 1877, having survived his wife two years. John W., the oldest of their eight children, was burn in Westmoreland county, Penn., June 27, 1812. He did his share of the pioneer work, and continued farming until 1887, when he removed to the city. In politics he is a democrat. He was married November 16, 1836, to Eliza Rodgers, born September 16, 1816, in West Virginia, and they have had thirteen children, of whom eight are living: Jane, William Henry, Wilson, Allen Perry, Benjamin, Edward L., Charles and Franklin. Mrs. McQuiston is a member of the Presbyterian church.

William McIntosh was born in Adams township, November 28, 1831. His father, John McIntosh, one of the earliest of the pioneers of Allen county, was born in County Derry, Ireland, and came to America just after the close of the war of 1812. After spending a few years in Pennsylvania and Ohio, he came to Allen county in 1823, and entered land in Adams township. In 1827 he was married to Ruth, daughter of Samuel Brown, and this was the first marriage that occurred in Adams township. Mrs. Ruth McIntosh died when her son William was but three years old, and a few years later Mr. McIntosh married Mrs. Olive Young, who died in September, 1858. John McIntosh spent all the rest of his life in Adams township, his occupation being that of a farmer. He died in December, 1859. William W. lived in childhood on the old homestead where he was born, and followed farming there until December, 1888, when he and wife removed to Fort Wayne. He was married July 4, 1859, to Emily A., daughter of Peter L. and Hannah G. (Kenworthy) Carrier, the former a native of Ohio, and the latter of England. Mrs. McIntosh was born in Trumbull county, Ohio, February 16, 1843. They have had eight children: Grace M., Jessie B., Elmer E., Alice and Helen (twins), and Lila R. and Lulu A. (twins), and Archie W., all living except Grace M., who died aged sixteen months. Mr. McIntosh is a member of the I. O. O. F., New Haven lodge, No. 253, and in politics is a republican. He is an honorable, upright man and he and wife are highly respected.

Daniel Nestel, a worthy and honored pioneer citizen of Fort Wayne, was born in Carlsbronn, Prussia, January 31, 1818, the son of Daniel and Elizabeth (Klein) Nestel. He attended school until he was fourteen, devoting his attention during the last year to the study of veterinary surgery. During six years of his youth he was employed in a grist mill, filling the position of superintendent during the last two. June 1, 1840, he started for America, on the sailing vessel Cotton Planter, commanded by Capt. Harley, and reached New York City August 7, after a voyage of forty-seven days. His entire capital when he landed was but eight cents and the first meal he ate in America was earned before it was eaten. He arrived at Fort Wayne on August 27th, having walked a good portion of the way. He had a companion who had started with him from Germany, Fred. Foellinger. When within thirty miles of Fort Wayne they camped for the night in the woods, after having walked all day long with no food but green walnuts. The wolves in the surrounding forest prowled about them and not knowing what the result might be, Mr. Nestel took occasion to carve upon a tree near by the following inscription: "D. Nestel and Fred. Foellinger, died from hunger and eaten up by wolves." Here he was first employed as a day laborer but soon began to learn the blacksmith trade, and setting up a shop of his own he worked at that trade about twenty-six years. While so engaged he worked sixteen hours a day for more than fifteen years. Mr. Nestel was married June 4, 1844, to Henrietta, daughter of Adam Goebel, who located in Preble township, Adams county, Ind., in 1835. Mrs. Nestel was born in Germany, about 1821. Mr. and Mrs. Nestel have had six children: Henrietta, Charles W., Daniel, Charlotte, Eliza S. and Oscar W., of whom Charles W. and Eliza S. are familiarly known to the world as Commodore Foote and Fairy Queen, and though perfectly developed, weigh respectively but forty and thirty-five pounds. They are highly educated in different languages and have traveled throughout the civilized world, appearing before all the royal personages of Europe. Mr. Nestel traveled with them for eighteen years, visiting all the larger cities in the eastern, western, northern and middle states, and also Canada. For six years after this he was engaged in the dry goods business in Fort Wayne. For the past three years he has owned and conducted the Broadway nursery. In politics he is a staunch republican. He has been a member of the city council two terms. He is one of the city's old citizens, is extensively known and very highly respected. Mr. Nestel, in his extensive travels, had an opportunity to witness the progress of American cities and this excited in him greater interest than anything else. He has for several years past, given some time to the real estate business, besides attending to his nursery. The Commodore and Fairy Queen (Charles and Eliza) have just returned from their second visit to Europe.

RAILROAD DEVELOPMENT.

Few cities are blessed with railroads in number and excellence equal to those which center in Fort Wayne, and have made of this inland city a commercial place of the first class, a distributing point for freight and passengers second only to the very largest of American cities.

It is fortunate that its location is on the forty-first parallel of latitude. On the same parallel New York city is situated and Chicago and Omaha are not far from it, accordingly. Fort Wayne lies directly on the highway which commerce has established between the metropolis by the Atlantic and the great western cities with which it interchanges so much of its vast business. Accordingly it is not strange that three great trunk lines lead from Fort Wayne to New York city with two to Chicago and that another trunk line now in course of construction will connect the lakes with the city by the sea through this bustling place. The fact that six railways enter Fort Wayne and provide easy communication in ten different directions is of the highest importance to the manufacturing and commercial interests of the city. New York, Philadelphia, Buffalo, Cleveland, Toledo, Grand Rapids, Chicago, St. Louis, Indianapolis, Detroit, Louisville, Cincinnati and many other cities are reached without change of cars and generally by two or more through routes.

The fact that the city has the advantage of railway cómpetition has greatly contributed to cheapen freight rates from eastern trade centers and thus enhance the profits and strengthen the business of the wholesale merchant, who can secure his supplies at as low cost as though he resided at Chicago or Cleveland, Indianapolis or Detroit.

The railroads which enter or pass through this city are the Pittsburgh, Fort Wayne & Chicago railway company, operated by the Pennsylvania, the Wabash, the Grand Rapids & Indiana, the Fort Wayne, Cincinnati & Louisville, the Cincinnati, Richmond & Fort Wayne, the New York, Chicago, St. Louis ("Nickle Plate"), and the Fort Wayne & Jackson a branch of the Lake Shore.

Within a few miles of the city these roads intersect other lines which thus become almost as intimate and direct a portion of the general system. For example, the Chicago & Atlantic, the western feeder of the Erie system, is crossed by the Wabash at Huntington and by the Muncie at Kingsland; the Baltimore & Ohio is crossed by the Wabash at Defiance, by the Lake Shore at Auburn, and by the G. R. & I. R. R. at Avilla; the "Clover Leaf" is crossed by the Muncie at Bluffton and by the G. R. & I. R. R. at Decatur; the Lake Shore & Michigan Southern is intersected by the Fort Wayne branch at Auburn, and by the G. R. & I. R. R. at Kendallville. All of these points are within a few miles from the city and the lines there met with regularly contribute to Fort Wayne's commercial prosperity.

The regular time for fast freight shipments between New York, Philadelphia and Baltimore and Fort Wayne has recently been reduced to seventy-two hours, and in some instances of special shipment even below this low figure. Between Boston and Fort Wayne the time is five days; between Fort Wayne and Cincinnati and Chicago fifteen hours, while in the fruit and oyster seasons special trains are run through the city on the schedule of the fastest passenger trains, thus supplying Fort Wayne with the fish of the sea and the fruits of the orchard of delightful flavor and freshness. An immense trade in oysters and fruits has been developed here in consequence of the unusual excellence and cheapness of these staple luxuries.

The Pittsburgh Fort Wayne & Chicago railway is the result of the consolidation, effected in 1857, of the Ohio & Pennsylvania, the Ohio & Indiana, and the Fort Wayne & Chicago railways. The entire road extending from Pittsburgh to Chicago, is 469 miles long and Fort Wayne is the largest city on the line and is the seat of the principal erecting and repair shops.

In January, 1850, the contract for building the entire length of the Ohio & Indiana, from Crestline, Ohio, to Fort Wayne, a distance of 131 miles, was let to Samuel Hanna, Pliny Hoagland and William Mitchell, for $740,000. This sum was to include all necessary buildings and fixtures, but no iron or cars. In January, 1852, the entire contract was sublet. The firm name of the contractors was William Mitchell & Co. In the same year Allen Hamilton donated six acres for depot purposes, the site of the south depot, and Samuel Hanna donated five acres, for grounds for the company's shops. The railroad was completed to Fort Wayne in the fall of 1855, about one year after the contracted time. The track deflected from the present straight east and west line at a point just west of Clay street and swung around to Lafayette street down which it passed northward to the canal basin at the foot of Columbia street, where a frame depot and a frame engine house were erected. These buildings remained until 1857, and marked the western terminus of the road. A principal reason for extending the road to the canal was to secure a profitable interchange of business, and this expectation was substantially realized, the railroad at once receiving great consignments of east-bound wheat from the canal boats. The depot and freight grounds embraced all lands between the canal and the north side of Columbia street, and extending from Barr to Lafayette street. The first locomotive seen in Fort Wayne was brought from Toledo on a flat boat, under the charge of Mr. R. W. Wohlfort. He landed it at the foot of Lafayette street and for several years run it over the road. After its usefulness had ended, by reason of greater perfection in machinery of that character, the old locomotive was stored on the wharf in front of the company's warehouse where it remained for a considerable time an object of much curiosity and interest. It has long since been consigned to the scrap pile and the melting pot. The original depot was a small frame affair, and the original engine-house was a store which was converted to the purpose by tearing out the gable end. This old building may still be seen near the Globe flouring mill of J. B. Monning & Co. The first buildings on the present site of the south depot were of frame and consisted of a passenger depot and a freight house. The depot was removed to a point west of Calhoun street, and was subsequently demolished. The freight house was destroyed by fire. The present elegant buildings were in part erected to take their places but both have been largely added to to meet the wonderful increase of traffic.

Operating this railroad without through business or connecting lines, and extending out into a sparsely settled country, with its agricultural, manufacturing and commercial interests all undeveloped, was by no means as satisfactory as the owners of the stock and bonds find it today.

In 1854 and 1855 the condition of the Ohio & Indiana, and the Fort Wayne & Chicago roads was by no means prosperous. The first had been imperfectly constructed; the ballast was largely of sand or a poor quality of gravel, the bridges and culverts were flimsy wooden affairs, and the imperfect drainage of the country subjected the track to frequent and annoying washouts. The equipment of the road was woefully lacking, and, worse than all, the financial credit had been exhausted by three mortgages, all of which had been inadequate to complete and equip the road. The Fort Wayne & Chicago road was at a stand-still, the track had been laid for a distance of some fifteen miles west of Fort Wayne, when no more money for construction work was available. In this predicament a consolidation of the three lines leading from Pittsburgh to Chicago was proposed at a meeting of the presidents of the Pennsylvania railroad, the Pennsylvania & Ohio, the Ohio & Indiana and the Fort Wayne & Chicago roads. The object of this scheme was to vitalize the stagnant corporations, and its principal champion was Hon. Joseph K. Edgerton of this city, president of the Ohio & Indiana railroad. Mr. Edgerton's plan of consolidation was approved almost unanimously by the stockholders of the various corporations, and the enlarged possibilities that grew out of a great line of travel operated for through business. became at once apparent, and the completion of the road to Chicago was not much longer delayed.

The consolidation, called the Pittsburgh, Fort Wayne & Chicago Railroad company, went into operation August 1, 1856. George W. Cass of the Ohio & Pennsylvania railroad, was chosen president, and Mr. Edgerton, vice president. The first four Indiana directors were Messrs. Samuel Hanna and J. K. Edgerton, of Fort Wayne, William Williams of Warsaw, and A. L. Wheeler of Plymouth.

In 1857 the road became seriously involved financially, and German bondholders applied to the United States court of the Northern District of Ohio for the appointment of a receiver. Mr. Edgerton was appointed, and at once the stockholders and bondholders in the Pennsylvania railroad, who had been gradually acquiring stock in the promising western feeder, opposed the appointment in the courts and Mr. Edgerton resigned, giving way to William B. Ogden, who appeared to be better able to harmonize the conflicting interests. He introduced Samuel J. Tilden, deceased, as a legal adviser, who devised a plan of reorganization. The control of the road was finally acquired by the Pennsylvania railroad company upon foreclosure sale to a purchasing committee of which Mr. Tilden was one and was at once re-sold to a reorganizing committee. The name of the road was changed to Pittsburgh, Fort Wayne & Chicago railway. A lease to the Pennsylvania interests for 999 years followed and the operation of this great line of travel has since been out of the hands of its projectors and builders.

It is probably the best equipped trunk line for freight and passenger business between Chicago and the seaboard, runs solid through trains of royal magnificence and has established in Fort Wayne the finest equipped car shops in the west.

The Pennsylvania company, lessees, now run sixteen passenger trains daily in and out of Fort Wayne. The monthly ticket sales at the Union passenger station are $13,000, about a third of which amount must be accredited to the passenger business of the Grand Rapids & Indiana railroad, which the Pennsylvania company also controls. Mr. C. D.

Law, the enterprising superintendent of the western division resides in this city.

Fort Wayne is the largest city and most important commercial point on the Wabash main line between Toledo, Ohio, and St. Louis, Mo. The company's principal engine shops are located here, and give employment to 550 skilled mechanics who are largely occupied in the building of locomotives, famous for their speed and power. Ten passenger trains arrive and depart from the Wabash depot daily, eight of them being through trains. The affairs of this road have occupied the attention of the courts for many years, and the history of Wabash litigations, arising from the control of Jay Gould, the extension of the system, the creation of the $70,000,000 debt and the various receiverships, would greatly exceed the compass of this chapter. Under the receivership of Gen. John McNulta the road has been magnificently equipped, and its management by General Superintendent K. H. Wade and Assistant General Superintendent G. W. Stevens, has been exceedingly satisfactory to its patrons. The gross receipts at Fort Wayne station are about a million and a quarter of dollars annually and the yearly tonnage is 500,000. The last sale of the road was in June, 1889, under order of Judge Gresham, when the entire property was purchased at foreclosure sale at Chicago by the Wabash Western railway, whose lines are generally west of the Mississippi. It is now operated from St. Louis, and O. D. Ashley is president of the consolidated systems.

The Grand Rapids & Indiana railroad forms a north and south trunk line of vast commercial importance. It extends from the Straits of Mackinaw on the north, through the center of Michigan and on through Fort Wayne in an almost due southerly line 459 miles, to Richmond, Ind., where direct connection is made to Cincinnati. The road is noted for its splendid passenger equipment, and in the summer runs through sleeping cars from Cincinnati to Mackinaw. It is under the control of the Pennsylvania company, and to that company at Fort Wayne it is a principal feeder, delivering thousands of car-loads of pine collected from the Michigan forests, tons of salt, millions of dollars worth of furniture from the factories at Grand Rapids, solid train loads of ice from Cadillac, besides Michigan-grown potatoes, apples and other fruit in great abundance. The road is known among pleasure seekers as the "Fishing Line," and during the summer months a constant stream of tourists seek the cool, refreshing resorts in Northern Indiana and Michigan, by way of this road. Mackinaw, Petoskey, Traverse City, Charlevoux, Michigan and Rome city, Ind., are perhaps the best known of these places of delightful remembrance of the summer tourist. The superintendent of the southern division, extending from Grand Rapids, Mich., to Richmond, Ind., is P. S. O'Rourke. His headquarters are in Fort Wayne. Besides ranking very high as a wide-awake and pushing railway official, he has taken a leading part in politics, and on the subject of a reform of the tariff his views have been widely quoted for many years past.

Like the Pittsburgh, Fort Wayne & Chicago railway the construction of the "Rapids" was attended with great financial difficulties. In 1866, when Joseph K. Edgerton became president of the company, it had for more than ten years held a grant of about two thirds of a million acres of Michigan land, for the construction of a road from Grand Rapids to Traverse Bay, and in 1864, congress had enlarged the grant over 200,000 acres, and extended it to a line from Fort Wayne to Traverse bay. But not a mile was built, nor a bar of iron bought, and the land grant was subject to immediate forfeiture from January 1, 1866. Samuel Hanna, during the three months preceding his death, had initiated movements at Fort Wayne and elsewhere for aid to the road, and his operations were taken up and continued by Mr. Edgerton, with vigor. In December, 1866, iron was obtained to begin track laying on the twenty miles between Grand Rapids and Cedar Springs, the first section required to be built by the land grant, and at the following session of the Michigan legislature, Mr. Edgerton memorialized it for an extension of time. This prayer was granted, though with much opposition. The struggle for the restoration of the company's credit was a long and arduous one, but was finally successful. The company is now in excellent financial condition. Its improvements are of the most substantial character. Its shops at Grand Rapids are of great magnitude and excellently equipped. The city of Fort Wayne is a large owner of its stock, which the mayor votes at the annual meetings held at Grand Rapids. J. H. P. Hughart is the president of the road and C. L. Lockwood the general passenger agent. Eight passenger trains are run through Fort Wayne every day.

The railways heretofore mentioned, run their trains through the south depot on Calhoun street, between Railroad street and Grand street. The Pittsburgh, Fort Wayne & Chicago, and the Grand Rapids & Indiana, occupy a large and finely appointed brick building, which contains a hotel and an eating house, noted all along these lines of travel for the excellence of the cuisine. On the opposite side of the tracks and facing this depot is the passenger depot of the Wabash company, a frame building well adapted to the purposes intended.

There are two other depots and all are connected by street cars, making passenger transfers cheap and expeditious. On the north side of the city, in the Ninth ward, is the union depot used by the Fort Wayne branch of the Lake Shore road and the Fort Wayne, Cincinnati & Louisville railway. These roads form a continuous north and south line from Cincinnati and Louisville on the south to Jackson and Saginaw, in Michigan, and the volume of business transacted is of such rapid growth that the engine service has recently been very largely increased. Both roads are laid with steel rail. The principal shops of the Muncie road are at Fort Wayne and here its general superintendent, W. W. Worthington, who has grown up with the company, has his office.

The latest addition to Fort Wayne's railways is the New York,

Chicago & St. Louis railway, or Nickel Plate, which was built for the sole object of profitable sale to the Vanderbilts, which object was finally accomplished. It parallels the Lake Shore main line from Buffalo to Chicago and so greatly threatened the business of the Lake Shore that after Vanderbilt had denounced it as valueless property, "a string of dirt leading from nowhere to no place," he paid a good round price for it. It has been of the greatest service to Fort Wayne in developing a new country, famous for its hard wood timber and heretofore quite difficult of access.

The Vanderbilt management of the "Nickel Plate" has not directed much attention to its passenger business, though its two daily trains are well patronized, but the road has been devoted almost exclusively to the quick movement of freight, especially live stock, dressed meats and perishable goods generally. Its direct line, from Chicago to Buffalo, with easy grades, permits of such rapid transportation of these food products that the Nickel Plate has long since been dubbed the "Meat Express" line, and the claim is made for it that shipments from the great Chicago packing houses reach New York by this line from ten to twenty hours in advance of all other routes. It is common for the Nickel Plate to haul six long meat trains east through Fort Wayne every night. The road has a very handsome depot located in the heart of the wholesale trade, and in this city are the offices of C. D. Gorham, superintendent of the western division, of trainmaster S. K. Blair, engineer W. McK. Pardee and other officials. The principal shops of the company are at Stony Island, Ill., where they were located to improve the value of real estate owned by the road's speculative projectors. There is reason to expect that these shops may be removed to Fort Wayne, their natural place of location.

An ambitious project in railway building, which, when accomplished will greatly benefit the city, is that of the American Midland company. Its officers assert that its early financial embarrassments have been arranged, and that before many months its trains will be running into and probably through Fort Wayne. An aid of $200,000 has been voted the company, conditioned upon the early construction of the line and the erection and maintenance of its principal shops in this city. The bonds of the company are said to have been placed, and a number of miles of the road are now constructed and in operation. The scheme of the projectors is for a trunk line between Jersey City on the east, to Omaha on the west, crossing the Allegheny mountains at the Red Bank pass, and traversing the country in almost an air-line, paralleling the forty-first degree of latitude. It is planned to lead a branch from Fort Wayne to Chicago, and another from Fort Wayne to St. Louis, making this the junction point of all branches. It is stated that terminal facilities and wharfage of the greatest value have been secured at Jersey City and Philadelphia, and by a traffic arrangement with the Reading and other lines, access to both New York and Philadelphia may be had whenever needed. An item of particular interest here is that an arrangement has been entered into by the Midland company with a large eastern car building concern by which mammoth car shops, which are expected to give employment to at least 1,000 men, are to be located here.

Jesse L. Williams, who was for a period of more than forty years prominent in the history of the public works of Indiana, Ohio, and the whole great west, was born in Stokes county, N. C., May 6, 1807. His parents, Jesse and Sarah T. Williams, members of the society of Friends, removed to Cincinnati, Ohio, and subsequently to Warren county, and in 1819 to Wayne county, Ind. In his early youth he was a student at the Lancaster seminary at Cincinnati for a short time. He early selected the profession of civil engineer as his life work, being inspired by the great schemes of canal improvement then popular. The Erie canal was nearing completion, and the Miami and Erie canal from Cincinnati to Maumee bay was about to be surveyed. At the age of seventeen he accepted a minor position in the engineer corps on this work, and served until the construction of the canal in the Miami valley. In the spring of 1828 he was appointed by David S. Bates, then chief engineer of Ohio, to make the final location of the Ohio canal from Licking summit to Chillicothe, and to construct a division of that work. In his twenty-fifth year he was appointed chief engineer of the Wabash & Erie canal, and two years later, in 1834, the surveys of all other canals in Indiana were placed by the legislature in his hands. In 1836, under an act for internal improvements he was appointed engineer-in-chief of all the canal routes, to which duties were added those of chief engineer of railroads and turnpikes in 1837, giving him supervision of 1,300 miles of public works. In the summer of 1841 he attended thirteen lettings of contracts, and he journeyed during those four months, on horseback, some 3,000 miles, the mental task of mastering the details of construction being at the same time an equally gigantic effort. His work was actively prosecuted until 1841, when the improvements were suspended for want of funds. From March, 1840 until 1842 he was also by appointment of the legislature, ex-officio a member of the board of internal improvements and acting commissioner of the Indiana division of the canal, including the management of the canal lands. In 1847 the Wabash & Erie canal, under the state debt act, passed into the control of a board of three trustees, two of whom were appointed by the bondholders and one by the legislalure. The act required the appointment of a "chief engineer of known and established character for experience and integrity," and Mr. Williams was selected for this position in June, 1847. This was held by him until the canal was sold by decree of the United States district court in 1876. Prior to 1842 there were many criticisms arising from political excitement, but a legislative committee appointed by the legislature in 1842, after making an exhaustive examination of the management of state improvements, completely exonerated Mr. Williams, closing with the words, "every man has his enemies who deserves them." In February, 1854, he was appointed chief engineer of the Fort Wayne & Chicago railroad, which he held until its consolidation in 1856 in the Pittsburgh, Fort Wayne & Chicago railroad. Of the last named company he became a trustee. Mr. Williams was appointed by President Lincoln a government director of the Union Pacific railroad in July, 1864, and held that place until the Union and Central Pacifics met west of Salt Lake, in 1869, being commissioned by three successive presidents. He served on the committee of location and construction, and made frequent tours of inspection through the canyons and over the slopes of the Rocky Mountain ranges, always insisting on the adoption of the lowest possible maximum grade. He made frequent reports to the secretary of the interior, which were communicated to congress and printed as public documents. In his report of November 23, 1866, he described ten distinct routes, describing briefly each proposed line. The lowering of the maximum grade was his object. Congress, for want of preliminary surveys had fallen into the grave error of authorizing by law, a maximum grade of 116 feet per mile. But Mr. Williams, having ascertained that a maximum grade of ninety feet per mile was possible, resisted the establishment of any higher grade, which would limit the load of a train for the whole road. This question was intimately associated with the cost of the road, in which congress had also acted unadvisedly. Mr. Williams submitted a report November 14, 1868, showing that the actual cash outlay for constructing and equipping the entire road of 1,110 miles would be $38,824,821; while the cash means provided by the act of 1862, as a subsidy, together with the company's first mortgage bonds, amounted to $56,647,600, without including the value of the land grant. Mr. Williams' report led to discussion, and the famous "credit mobilier" investigation followed. January 19, 1869, Mr. Williams was appointed receiver of the Grand Rapids & Indiana railroad company, and in October following he resigned his position as director of the Union Pacific, and devoted his energies to the completion of the Grand Rapids road, opening for transportation nearly 200 miles of that road. Mr. Williams was married November 15, 1831, to Susan Creighton, daughter of Judge William Creighton, of Chillicothe, Ohio, who was a representative in congress from the Chillicothe district during the war of 1812, and from 1828 to 1832.

Pliny Hoagland, who was prominently associated with canal, railroad and city improvement of the Maumee valley, began his professional life as an engineer on the Sandy and Beaver canal, in the spring of 1835. In 1838 he was engaged in the same capacity on the Ohio portion of the Wabash & Erie canal, and remained so until the canal was completed in 1843, when he was given charge of the work he had been engaged upon, and of the Western Reserve and Maumee road. In the fall of 1845 he removed to Fort Wayne, and thereafter took an active part in all the schemes for improvement of the city and its commercial avenues. When the Ohio & Pennsylvania road was partly constructed to Mansfield, and the company was hesitating whether to build to Chicago or simply connect with Cincinnati, Mr. Hoagland urged upon the projectors the probable advantages of a Chicago extension, and writing to Hugh McCulloch regarding the situation, he urged that movement of the citizens of Fort Wayne which secured the road. The Indiana legislation in regard to this road was secured chiefly by Mr. Hoagland's efforts, and when the corporation for connecting Crestline and Fort Wayne with the Ohio & Indiana railroad was formed, Mr. Hoagland, Judge Hanna and William Mitchell became contractors for the whole line, except furnishing the iron, and taking the contract January 28, 1852, completed it November 1, 1854. From that time Mr. Hoagland held the position of director of the road, under its various names, and subsequent to 1866 was a director of the Grand Rapids and Indiana road. In 1856 he was elected to the lower house of the assembly, and in 1862 to the senate. His position as senator he resigned to accept the presidency of the Fort Wayne branch of the bank of Indiana, succeeding Hugh McCulloch. When this concern became a national bank he declined the presidency and became vice president. During his service in the city council, beginning in 1865, the system of sewerage, which is hardly excelled in any city of the land, was begun at his instance. Permanent street grades and Nicholson pavements were also begun at that time. In the upbuilding of the schools, models of efficiency, his influence was also strongly felt. His career as a public man was most honorable, and was characterized by a degree of independence and devotion to the public good, that is apparently becoming most rare. This benefactor of the city died January, 1884.

Joseph K. Edgerton, who has been prominent in the railroad and political history of Indiana, is the third son of Bela and Phebe (Ketchum) Edgerton, and was born at Vergennes, Vt., February 16, 1818. His maternal grandfather, Joseph Ketchum, was a merchant and ironmaster at Plattsburg, N. Y., and died in New York, in September, 1794. He is of the fifth generation in direct descent from Richard Edgerton (or Egerton, as the name is spelled in England), one of the band of English Puritans, who, under the leadership of Maj. John Mason, the hero of the Pequod war, removed from Saybrook to Mohican (afterward Norwich, Conn.), and on the 6th of June, 1659, purchased from Uncas and other sachems of the Mohican Indians, a tract of land nine miles square, embracing the site of the city of Norwich, Conn. Another of the English settlers and proprietors was William Hyde, one of whose female descendants, in 1744, married Elisha Edgerton, grandson of Richard. The late Chancellor Walworth, of New York, who was a descendant of this William Hyde, devoted the leisure of the later years of his life to the compilation of a genealogy of the Hyde family. In a letter addressed to the subject of this sketch, he wrote: "I suppose you have seen my Hyde genealogy. I find, by the congressional dictionary you sent me, that fifty-two senators or members of the house of representatives, were either descendants of our ancestor, William Hyde, of Norwich, or married wives who were descendants." Col. Elisha Edgerton represented the town of Franklin in the legislature of Connecticut in 1803, and was a member of the constitutional convention of that state in 1818. His son, Bela Edgerton, born September 28, 1787, was graduated at Middlebury college, Vermont, in 1809; was a lawyer and magistrate in Clinton county, N. Y., and in 1827, '28 and '29, represented that county in the legislature. In 1839, Bela Edgerton removed to Hicksville, Ohio, where for many years he was engaged in farming. In the later years of his life, he resided at Fort Wayne, Ind., in the family of his oldest son, Alfred P. Edgerton, and died September 10, 1874. He was a man of ability and fine social qualities. Joseph K. Edgerton was educated in the common schools of Clinton county, and at the Plattsburg academy, until his sixteenth year, when he became a law student in the office of William Swetland, of Plattsburg — "the great lawyer of northern New York," as he was called by his cotemporaries. In 1835, Mr. Edgerton sought employment in the city of New York, and became a student in the law office of Dudley Selden and James Mowatt. He was admitted to the bar of New York in 1839, and until 1844 practiced law in that city, associated with George B. Kissam, under the firm name of Edgerton & Kissam. He was married in 1839 to Hannah Maria, youngest daughter of William and Elizabeth (Chatterton) Spies, of New York. In 1843 Mr. Edgerton visited the west in the interests of a New York client, and being favorably impressed with the country, he removed to Fort Wayne and established an office here in 1844, occupying the office of ex-Governor Samuel Bigger, with whom he formed a partnership in the following year, which was terminated by the death of his partner in 1846. Mr. Edgerton soon established a profitable business as a land and collection agent, and from July, 1850, to July, 1851, was associated in practice with Charles Case. He was one of the first to interest himself in the progress of the Ohio & Indiana and Fort Wayne & Chicago railroads, and on his own account and on behalf of clients made large land subscriptions, including large tracts in LaGrange county, owned by the New York house of Grinnell, Minturn & Co. Mr. Edgerton was made a director of the Fort Wayne & Chicago road in 1854, and in November, 1855, succeeded Mr. Hanna as president. He was elected director of the Ohio & Indiana road in January, 1856. During the critical period of the existence of these companies, Mr. Edgerton was prominent in their affairs, proposed the consolidation which was effected and the formation of the Pittsburg, Fort Wayne & Chicago railroad company, and negotiated the preliminary contract for that purpose and the final articles. He was the first vice president of the new company, until his appointment as receiver in December, 1859. From 1857 he had also been financial and transfer agent of the company with his office in New York, and from February until December, 1859, was the legal adviser of the company with office at Fort Wayne. Owing to the opposition of the Pennsylvania company, which aimed to acquire the new road, he resigned the receivership, and in March, 1860, he was defeated as a candidate for director, though supported by 37,000 shares. His defeat in this connection was the end of the final struggle of the builders

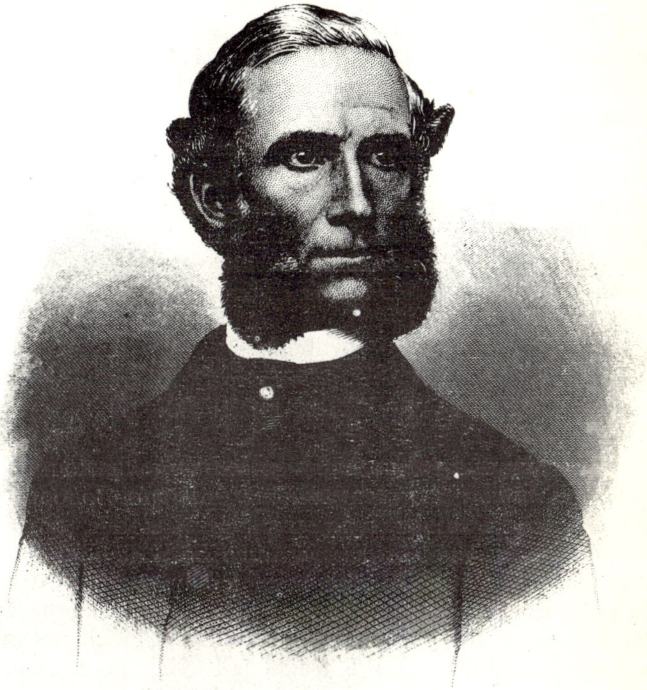

Western Biogl. Pub. Co.

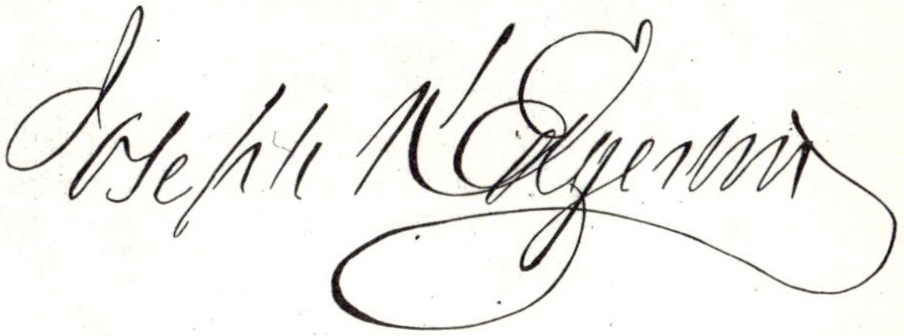

of the road to preserve its independence. The reorganization and sale that followed, at great expense, put the road forever out of the hands of those who had struggled for its success in the early days. In July, 1866, upon the solicitation of the Michigan directors, Mr. Edgerton became president of the Grand Rapids & Indiana railroad company, on the death of Samuel Hanna, and again had an arduous struggle to encounter for the establishment of a great thoroughfare. In August, 1871, after five years' service, Mr. Edgerton left the company on the removal of its offices to Grand Rapids, being succeeded by William A. Howard of Michigan. In the mean time, the land grant had been fully protected by the construction and putting in operation, under a contract with the Continental Improvement company, of 200 miles of the road, from Fort Wayne to Paris, Mich. In the leisure following the cessation of his railroad duties, Mr. Edgerton, in the fall of 1871, crossed the continent to San Francisco.

Mr. Edgerton's political career has also been a notable one. Prior to 1860, though until then never active in politics, he had been a whig, and voted with the party up to 1853. In 1852, after the taking effect of the new constitution making judges elective, he was an independent candidate for judge of the court of common pleas for the district of Allen and Adams counties. Judge James W. Borden was the democratic nominee and was elected, the district being strongly democratic. In October, 1860, Mr. Edgerton made his first political speech in Indiana in favor of Stephen A. Douglas for president. The address was printed, and with other publications from his pen, gave Mr. Edgerton prominence as an advocate of the democratic doctrine of popular sovereignty, represented by Mr. Douglas. In August, 1862, Mr. Edgerton received the democratic nomination for congress in the then tenth district of Indiana, against William Mitchell, of Kendallville, the republican nominee, who had been elected in 1860, by nearly 3,000 majority, and Mr. Edgerton was elected by 436 majority. In the summer of 1863, Mr. Edgerton visited Europe, but just before his departure published a letter in the Indianapolis *Sentinel*, concerning the right to free discussion, which was widely commented upon. It was called out by the military order No. 9, of Gen. Milo S. Hascall, commanding the district of Indiana, following military order No. 38, of Gen. Burnside. In the XXXVIIIth congress, Mr. Edgerton was a member of the committee on naval affairs, but for over two months of the first session was kept from his seat by sickness from small-pox. During his term in congress, he spoke in opposition to the republican measures of confiscation, the constitutional amendment as to slavery, and on reconstruction, taking conservative democratic ground. He was re-nominated for congress in 1864, against Joseph H. Defrees, of Goshen, but was defeated by 580 majority. Pending the canvass of 1864, and the enforcement of the draft of that year, the state was greatly excited, and Mr. Edgerton was invited to attend a meeting at Indianapolis, on the 12th of August, of the democratic state central committee. He was requested to prepare a brief address, in the name of the committee, and his draft, with some modifications, was adopted, and the address published, which was made an occasion by Gov. Morton, for a proclamation "To the people of Indiana." Since engaging in railroad service in 1855, Mr. Edgerton has never fully resumed the practice of his profession, although he has continued to ᴜe an active business man.. He is among the largest owners of land in Allen county, but these for a long period proved more of a burden than a profit. In 1866, he established the Woodburn lumber and stave mills, on his property in the eastern part of Allen county, but the mills were burned in 1867, involving a large loss. In 1871, he aided in establishing the Fort Wayne steel plow works, and in 1875, became sole owner, and so continues. This house manufactures the Fargo harrow, the Pioneer plow and Osborn fanning mill, and is an extensive establishment. In 1878, on its organization, he was made president of the board of trustees of the Fort Wayne medical college, and is the author of the law of Indiana, of 1879, to provide means for obtaining subjects for scientific dissection. For many years, Mr. Edgerton has been a member of the Vestry of Trinity Episcopal church.

Bernard O'Connor, prominent in railroad and telegraph history, was born in Ireland in 1817, and at the age of twelve years journeyed alone to America. Joining an uncle, a Catholic priest at Lancaster, Pa., he resided with him for several years and was educated. About the year 1835, he became a contractor for the construction of a portion of the Susquehanna canal, and from that found his way into the then young science of telegraphy, engaging in line construction. He is now the oldest living telegraph builder in the United States. In 1845 he built the telegraph line from Baltimore to Philadelphia, by Havre de Gras, and Wilmington, which was the first telegraph line built by private enterprise, continuing the first line from Washington to Baltimore, built by the government. Bernard O'Connor became the third operator in the United States, and he was the first to use the ground as one-half of the circuit, in opposition to the opinion of S. F. B. Morse, that such an arrangement would be a failure. Soon afterward, he and Henry O'Riley made important contracts for the construction of telegraph lines, and from Buffalo, N. Y., put up lines to Cleveland, Cincinnati, Louisville, Memphis, Vicksburg and New Orleans. His next important enterprise was the building of the Charleston & New Orleans railroad, and this was followed by the construction of the Keokuk & Des Moines railroad. Obtaining extensive contracts for building levees on the Mississippi, he was there engaged, and next in the construction of the Vandalia & Terre Haute railroad, the St. Louis & Southeastern, and 105 miles of the Houston & Texas Central. In early life he was married at Lancaster, Penn., to Elizabeth McGonigle, and the completion of a half century of happy married life was celebrated by them at their wedding aniversary, October 23, 1888. To them were born five children, of whom four are living. Mr. O'Connor and family made their home at Fort Wayne in the fall of 1858, and they have since resided here. He retired in 1872 from the occupation which had busied him for many years, and in which he had been an important factor in the development of the country north and south. In 1881 he engaged in the establishment of the City National Bank at Dallas, Texas. Bernard S. O'Connor, son of the above, now a prominent capitalist with interests in Fort Wayne and Dallas, Texas, was born in Lancaster county, Penn., in 1842. He removed with his parents to Illinois when eight years old, but returned to Lancaster a year later. From 1852 to 1855 he resided at Dayton, Ohio, and there attended school. He finished his education at St. Mary's Landing, Mo., at a Catholic institution where his brothers also were educated. During this time the family removed to Alton, Ill., where Charles died. In 1859 he came to Fort Wayne, and learned the crafts of machinist and marble cutter. But his father being then engaged in levee work on the Mississippi, Bernard joined him and afterward was engaged with his father in his enterprise. His brothers, John and James, subsequently joined them and the firm of O'Connor & Sons was formed. In the banking business, John F. owns a controlling interest and James C. is president. The latter, in 1873, went to Europe, where he was joined the next year by Bernard S., and they made a trip through England, Ireland and France. Mr. O'Connor, with an energetic spirit, has interested himself in various enterprises. He is a stockholder in the Salamonie gas company, the Natural gas company of 1888, the Summit City soap company, the Gladstone land company, of Kansas City, and has interests at Duluth, Minn. He is a member of the Cathedral congregation. Mr. O'Connor was married November 4, 1878, to Marietta Fox, of Mansfield, Ohio.

C. D. Law, superintendent of the western division of the Pittsburgh, Fort Wayne & Chicago railroad, was born in Philadelphia, November 23, 1844. Three years later his parents removed to Carlisle, Penn., where he was reared, and obtained his early education in the public schools. He then entered the polytechnic institute at Philadelphia, and graduated from the same in 1863. In the same year he enlisted in the army of the Union, in Company G, Thirty-second Pennsylvania regiment, and served from 1864 until 1866 with the United States engineer corps, in the army of the Cumberland. At the close of this service he began his railroad career with the engineer corps of the Philadelphia & Trenton, now part of the united railroad of the New Jersey division of the Pennsylvania road. Subsequently he was engaged with an engineer corps in Connecticut, and in April, 1873, he was appointed civil engineer of the western division on the Pittsburgh, Fort Wayne & Chicago. At this time he became a citizen of Fort Wayne. In February, 1880, he was given the position of roadmaster of the same division, and on November 15, 1881, was appointed superintendent. In 1880 he removed to Chicago, but returned in 1886, and has since made Fort Wayne his home. Mr. Law takes an active interest in political and fraternity affairs. During the campaign of 1888 he served as president of the local Harrison and Morton railroad campaign club. He was made a

Mason at Matteawan, Duchess county, N. Y., in 1868, of Beacon lodge, and has since attained eminence in the order, being past eminent commander of Fort Wayne commandery, No. 4, Knight Templars, and has passed through the chairs of Wayne lodge, No. 25, and Fort Wayne chapter, No. 19. Mr. Law was married in June, 1870, to Josephine Clarkson, of New York city, and they have had three children, of whom two survive.

Patrick S. O'Rourke, superintendent of the Grand Rapids & Indiana railroad company, was born at Newark, N. J., September 25, 1830. His parents, Christopher and Ellen (Flannagan) O'Rourke, natives of county Kildare, Ireland, were married about 1823, and two years later, came to the United States, and made their home in New Jersey. In 1838 they removed to Ohio, and subsequently to Fort Wayne, where they died. Mr. O'Rourke's career, which is a notable illustration of the opportunities for advancement which the development of this country offers to talent and energy, however circumstances may impede at the outset, first found employment on the farm, and gained his early education in the country schools of Carroll county, Ohio. Afterward, he was engaged on a construction train on a railroad, beginning at the humblest point his long and distinguished career as a railroad man. His executive ability and strength of character were soon manifested, and in 1856 he was made conductor of a construction train, the next year freight conductor, three years later a passenger conductor. He became master of transportation in 1866, assistant superintendent in 1871, and superintendent in 1872. He is now recognized as one of the most successful railroad men of the west, thoroughly acquainted with all details, shrewd in conception of enterprises, and of undaunted energy in execution. Mr. O'Rourke has found time also to devote considerable attention to political affairs, and has given the great questions of statesmanship thorough study. He stands high in the councils of the democratic party. He is particularly devoted to the doctrine of tariff reform, which he has ably advocated upon the platform and by the publication of papers upon the subject. His devotion to party is strong but more to what he believes the true principles of the organization than to nominations, so that in 1872, he supported O'Connor in preference to Greeley, because of the latter's protection principles. He and family are members of the Catholic church.

Samuel B. Sweet, a prominent railroad man of Indiana, would be recorded well toward the top of the list, if such a one were made, of those popular men of the state whose place in the general esteem is based upon worthy lives and solid traits of character. Perhaps the key to his popularity and success is to be found in that generous devotion to principle and stalwart resolution which led him, when a boy of sixteen, to enlist in an Allen county company, organized for the defense of the Union, and serve with it, Company C, of the Forty-fourth Indiana regiment, through the active and dangerous duties of that command, until the close of the war. The years of youth usually devoted to higher education or business training he gave with hearty enthusiasm to the nation; and his cherished diploma is an honorable discharge, and his degree that of a private in a gallant regiment, to the hearts of the survivors of which no one of the comrades stands closer. Mr. Sweet's ancestors came to America in 1636, and were leading people in the Massachusetts Bay colony. In 1671, some of the family removed to Guilford county, N. C., and subsequently to Tennessee, where, near Jonesboro, Francis Sweet was born, July 28, 1806. In early youth he settled in western Ohio, and was married December 13, 1827, to Abigail Hammond, who was born in Abbeyville district, S. C., May 27, 1810. She was the daughter of Louis Hammond, born in South Carolina, May 20, 1785, who served in the second South Carolina regiment in the war of 1812, and was killed in a battle near Washington, D. C., in 1813. Her mother was Nancy Buffington, born in South Carolina, September 14, 1791, died about 1856. Francis Sweet came to Allen county in 1835, and in 1836 brought his family by ox-team from Troy, Ohio, and settled in the western part of the county. He was a prominent pioneer, was one of the first Masons in this part of the country, was a leading old line whig, served twenty-five years as justice of the peace, and was postmaster at the old Indian office of Taw-taw, two and a half miles north of the present hamlet, Arcola. His first wife died August 13, 1865, and in 1867, he was married to Hannah, widow of John Peabody of Arcola, Ind. Francis Sweet died at Columbia city, March 25, 1884. In this worthy pioneer family, Samuel B. Sweet was born, near Fort Wayne, March 25, 1845. He is the eighth of ten children born, four others of whom are living: Nancy, born March 8, 1830; Stephen, April 24, 1834; Joshua, February 7, 1836 and Rhoda, May 10, 1841. Mr. Sweet attended the common schools, his first teacher being Edward Litchfield. August 23, 1861, he enlisted in the union army, and was mustered out September 14, 1865. At the battle of Shiloh, he was wounded while serving as a color bearer, the flag of the regiment being repeatedly shot down in the engagement. He also received wounds in the engagements of Stone river and Chickamauga. His brothers, Lewis and Joshua, were members of Company C, Eighty-eighth Indiana, and the former lost a limb at the battle of Bentonville, N. C., and the latter was wounded at Stone river. The former died at Edgerton, Ohio, in 1883; Joshua now resides at Albion, Ind. In 1866, Mr. Sweet entered the employment of the Wabash, St. Louis & Pacific railroad company, and served in various capacities, gradually advancing until in 1874, he was appointed agent at Fort Wayne. In 1884, he was advanced to the position of division freight agent, with headquarters at Peru. Three years later, after a service of twenty-one years with the Wabash company, he resigned the last named position to become assistant general freight agent of the Lake Erie & Western railroad company, with his office at Indianapolis. Mr. Sweet is in politics, a steadfast republican. As a Knight Templar, he is prominent, having been grand commander in 1882. He became a Master Mason in 1868, Knight Templar in 1870,

Scottish Rite, 1882, and thirty-third degree, 1885. He was married September 19, 1867, to Amanda, daughter of Allen Pratt, a pioneer of Allen county, and they have two children, Frank E., born August 30, 1868; and Jessie M., born May 3, 1872.

Enoch Cox, one of the popular men of the city, and a prominent member of the Independent Order of Odd Fellows, was born at Delphi, Ind., December 4, 1842. His boyhood was spent upon a farm, with his parents, and in 1859 he entered Asbury (now Depauw) university, where he took the classical course and graduated in 1864. After his graduation he became connected with the ordnance corps of the United States army, and served eight months, after which he was transferred to the engineer corps, served with Col. W. E. Merrill, chief engineer of the army of the Cumberland, and was engaged with Maj. Burroughs in closing up the engineer depot of that army. Mr. Cox left the service in May, 1867, and engaged in business in Lafayette, Ind., at which he was occupied about two years. A subsequent period he spent at farming and with the Indianapolis, Delphi & Chicago railroad company. In 1876 he went into the newspaper business at Delphi, and conducted the *Journal* at that place until January 29, 1882, when he was appointed by superintendent C. D. Law as store-keeper of the western division of the Pittsburgh, Fort Wayne & Chicago railroad company, at Fort Wayne. This department has been reorganized and very efficiently conducted by him. Mr. Cox is a member of the Delphi lodge, No. 28, I. O. O. F., and in 1879 was elected grand master of the grand lodge of Indiana. In 1881 he received the additional honor of election as representative of Indiana grand lodge at the sovereign grand lodge, at its session at Cincinnati. Mr. Cox was married June, 1870, to Martha M. Jones, of Delphi, and they have three children.

Richard G. Thompson, passenger and ticket agent of the Wabash railroad, at Fort Wayne, is a native of Iowa, born at Lyons, August 3, 1860. His father, Richard G. Thompson, sr., now residing in Michigan, and following the business of contractor and builder, was born near Harrisburg, Pa., May 4, 1825, and married Sarah Harris, who was born in New York, April 29, 1830, the daughter of Judge Davis Harris. Richard G. Thompson was educated at the Reading, Michigan, high school, and began his railroad life in 1880, in the employment of the Fort Wayne & Jackson railroad. He was first stationed at Waterloo six months, and then removed to Fort Wayne. Until 1888 he was in the service of that company, which in 1883, was merged into the great L. S. & M. S. system and the Fort Wayne, Cincinnati & Louisville. During this period he gained an enviable reputation for efficiency and thorough knowledge of the multifarious duties of a railroad agent, and in 1888, he was tendered the passenger and ticket agency of the Wabash road, which he accepted May 1, and now holds. Though a a young man, his thorough grasp of the work in which he is engaged, and his business-like methods and affable manners, have put him rapidly to the front in railroad circles. He is devoted to business, but nevertheless is well known throughout the community and highly esteemed. Mr. Thompson is a member of the Scottish Rite in Masonry, and a member of the Fort Wayne lodge of Perfection. His political alliance is with the republican party.

R. B. Rossington, a native of Allen county, has attained a prominent place in railroad affairs, and is a deservedly popular and highly esteemed gentleman. He was born eight miles north of the city, in 1853. His parents, William and Julia Rossington, the former a native of Cork, Ireland, and the latter of Manchester, England, were married in England, and emigrated in 1844. After spending two years at Tarrytown, N. Y., they came in 1846 to Allen county, where the father died in 1879 and the mother in 1888. Mr. Rossington lived upon a farm until nine years of age, when the family removed to Fort Wayne, and here he attended school until thirteen years of age. Then seeking an occupation he learned the trade of a hatter, but in 1872 took the first step in a career in which he has been notably successful, by entering the railroad office at Auburn, Ind., as a student of telegraphy. Two weeks later he returned to Fort Wayne, and was employed by the American telegraph company until March, 1873, when he became a member of the engineer corps under John Ryall, assistant civil engineer of the Pennsylvania Railroad company. Three weeks later he was taken from outside duty by C. D. Law, and given a position in the Fort Wayne offices. In the fall of 1873 he entered the freight office under J. C. Davis as bill clerk, and in 1875 was promoted assistant cashier, and January 1, 1877, cashier. He was appointed freight agent July 1, 1886, succeeding J. K. McCracken, and in that capacity represents the Pittsburgh, Fort Wayne & Chicago, and Grand Rapids & Indiana railroads. Mr. Rossington is a member of the Masonic order and the I. O. O. F.

Charles H. Newton, freight agent of the Wabash railway at Fort Wayne, is one of the valuable citizens of Fort Wayne, and has while a resident of the city, worked out an honorable career that is deserving of extended mention. His childhood was mostly spent at Clayton, Ill., and he there attended the public schools until sixteen years old, when he began an apprenticeship of three years in a printing office, the last year of which he was employed at Clinton, Mo. In June, 1874, then being in his nineteenth year, he came to Fort Wayne, and took a position as messenger boy for the Wabash company. A few months later he was promoted to a clerkship in the yardmaster's office, where he remained until December 1, 1879, during which he improved leisure moments by completing a course in the commercial college. Leaving the service of the Wabash company, he removed to Clinton, Mo., and engaged in newspaper work, but in September, 1880, he returned to his former place, the freight office at Fort Wayne, and took the position of car clerk, subsequently being promoted chief clerk and cashier. The division terminus of the road being changed from Fort Wayne to Andrews in May, 1882, the yard force at Fort Wayne was placed in the hands of the agent, who appointed Mr. Newton yardmaster, a place he filled until

August 1, 1884, when the freight agent at Fort Wayne was made division freight agent, and Mr. Newton was appointed to his place as local freight agent. Upon the organization of the local freight agents' association Mr. Newton was elected secretary, a position he still holds. He is a thorough railroad man, and his executive ability and rare tact enables him to win the approbation of the company and the esteem of his fellow citizens in the discharge of his duties. He is a member of the Wayne street Methodist church, and has since January 1, 1866, held the position of superintendent of the Sunday-school. He was one of the organizers of the Railroad Young Men's Christian Association, was chosen recording secretary and is now president. He was also one of the organizers and a charter member of the local Young Mens' Christian Association, was recording secretary and is now first vice president. Mr. Newton's parents, John Clark and Mary Jane (Chapman) Newton, were born the father in Connecticut, the mother in New York, and both descended from revolutionary soldiers. In 1851 they went to the Pacific coast, overland, and the father followed his trade of blacksmith in California until his death in 1857. In that state Charles H. was born December 31, 1855. In 1865 the widow and five children removed to Clayton, Ill., where she remained until 1887, when she returned to California where she is now living. Mr. Newton was married June 19, 1878, to Mary J. Wilding, and they have four children, of whom three are living.

Thomas Jackson, engineer maintenance of way, western division, P., Ft. W. & C. railroad, with headquarters at Ft. Wayne, was born at Hockessin, New Castle county, Delaware, March 21, 1845. There he attended the common schools, and later entered the academy of T. Clarkson Taylor, at Wilmington, Del., and finished his education at Westtown Friends' boarding school, in Chester county, Penn. At about the age of nineteen, he became engineer for the Diamond State Oil Company, at Beaver county, Penn., and two years later joined the engineer corps of the Wilmington & Brandywine Railroad, now known as the Wilmington & Northern. Later he was made assistant engineer of the Delaware Western, now a branch of the Baltimore & Ohio railroad, serving until its completion, in 1872. In March, 1873, he was appointed roadman on the eastern division of the P., Ft. W. & C. railroad, and received various promotions on that division. In January, 1880, he was appointed division engineer of the western division, succeeding C. D. Law, now superintendent. In December, 1884, he was appointed roadmaster of the western division, a title which has since been changed to engineer maintenance of way, the duties being those of division engineer and road master combined. During Gen. Trimble's raid on the Philadelphia, Wilmington & Baltimore railroad, in 1864, he enlisted in the Seventh regiment Delaware volunteer infantry, and served sixty days, doing guard duty on the steamer Maryland, at Havre de Grace. Mr. Jackson was married to Anna R., daughter of Spencer Chandler, Esq., of Mill Creek hundred, Delaware, and they have three daughters and one son, the latter is named for Ralph Jackson, an ancestor, who was burned at the stake, June 27, 1556, in Queen Mary's reign.

Nelson W. Thompson, superintendent of bridges and buildings of the western division of the Pittsburgh, Fort Wayne & Chicago railroad, from Crestline to Englewood, was born in Clarendon, Orleans county, New York. His father, Warren Thompson, removed his family to Hillsdale county, Mich., in 1838, and resided there until his death in 1882. When about seveeteen years of age, Nelson W. went to Logansport, Ind., and was there engaged for two years boating on the Wabash & Erie canal. Then going to New York he was for two years employed on the Erie canal. During the next two years he was engaged in erecting railroad fencing on the Lake Shore & Michigan Southern railroad, in Michigan, and in 1854 he and his father graded one mile of the air line branch of that road at Waterloo, Ind., by contract. For some years subsequently he was farming in Michigan, then in Nebraska, working a section on the Lake Shore road, and in 1861, he began work on that road as a carpenter, a trade he subsequently followed on the state line branch of the Panhandle west from Logansport, then on the Peru & Indianapolis road. From 1867 to 1869 he was contracting in Michigan, then worked on the construction of the Muncie railroad, and in 1871-2 had charge of the construction of bridges on the Cincinnati, Richmond & Fort Wayne railroad. He had charge of pile-driving on the Chicago & Kansas Southern road in 1873, and in 1874-5 was foreman of carpenters on the Valparaiso division of the Pittsburgh road, and in the following year was appointed to his present position. Mr. Thompson is a member of Star lodge, No. 93, F. & A. M., at Osseo, Mich., and Hillsdale chapter, No. 18. He was married in 1853, at Osseo, Mich., to Nancy Orcutt, a daughter of Amba Orcutt, a pioneer of that region, one of whose daughters was the first white child born in Florida township, Hillsdale county. Mr. Thompson began his railroad career as a section foreman on the Lake Shore road in Hillsdale county, when he was sixteen years old, and his record since then has been a creditable one.

One of the veteran railroad men of the city, Charles W. Buck, who now holds the position of section foreman, Fort Wayne yards, of the Wabash railroad, began work at Zanesville, Ohio, on what was then known as the Ohio Central road, in 1851. Six months later he entered the employment of the Mad River railroad, so known at that time, where he remained six months, then going to Toledo and taking a position on the Lake Shore road. He then spent four years in Iowa, and on his return to this state was employed seven years with the I., P. & C. railroad. In 1871 he came to Fort Wayne and accepted a position on the Wabash road in 1874, and has since remained in that service. Mr. Buck was born in Saratoga county, N. Y., November 18, 1830. His father, William Buck, was born in England in 1800, came to the United States about 1816, and married Mary Beach, who was born in New York about 1802. Both died in Washington county, N. Y., the mother in 1852, the father in 1853. Of their five children living, Charles W. is the oldest. He was married in 1854 to Louisa J. Durfee, of Sylvania, Ohio, who was born in 1832, and died in this city, in 1880, leaving six children: Lucy, George, Mary, Edward Ada and Charles. In 1883 Mr. Buck married Calista A. Waite, a native of Ohio. Mr. Buck is a member of Bluffton lodge, No. 145, F. & A. M., and I. O. O. F. lodge No. 44, at Indianapolis.

Solon K. Blair, trainmaster on the "Nickel Plate" railroad, is a native of Union county, Ohio, born January 21, 1852. He is the son of Jabez S. and Elizabeth A. Blair, both natives of Logan county, Ohio. While he was a mere child his parents removed to Hardin county, Ohio, and he was reared to manhood at the village of Mount Victory. His father is a physician by profession and is also a minister in the Methodist Episcopal church. In 1868 the family removed to Bellefontaine, and thence to Sidney, Ohio, in 1870. There Mr. Blair began the study of telegraphy, January 2, 1871. He was engaged as an operator until December, 1874, when he was made train dispatcher, and continued in that capacity until June, 1888, a period of fourteen years. He accepted the position of train dispatcher on the New York, Chicago & St. Louis railroad in 1882. In 1883 he was promoted to chief dispatcher, and June 1, 1888, he was promoted trainmaster. Mr. Blair was married December 16, 1879, to Dora F. Mitchell, by whom he is the father of two children: Kenton L. and Mamie E. Mr. Blair is a Royal Arch Mason, and is a member of the Association of Superintendents of Telegraph, and of the National Union. In politics he is an ardent republican.

The position of car inspector on the New York, Chicago & St. Louis railroad has been held during the past seven years by Frederick R. Bierbaum. He is a native of Germany, born April 19, 1847, son of Henry and Elizabeth Bierbaum. He was reared to manhood on a farm and then served in the Franco-Prusian war three years. In 1872 he came to America and located at Fort Wayne. Here he learned the carpenter's trade, and followed it about five years. Since 1877 he has followed the occupation of car repairer and car inspector. He was married in 1873, to Louisa Niemeyer, a native of Germany, who came to America in 1873. They have had seven children: Louisa, Katie, Emma, Clara, Nettie, Albert and Edwig; of whom only Katie, Emma and Edwig are living. Mr. and Mrs. Bierbaum are members of the German Reformed church, and politically he is a republican.

Crawford Griswold, foreman of the bridge gang on the western division of the Pittsburgh, Fort Wayne & Chicago railroad, is a native of New York, born at Chatham, Columbus county, July 27, 1842. His parents took him to Michigan in 1844, but in 1857 they returned to New York, where they remained. The father died in 1872. Mr. Griswold was engaged in mechanical pursuits until the outbreak of the war, and in 1862 he enlisted in the First New York Mounted Rifles, with headquarters at 600 Broadway, New York. He joined the regiment at Suffolk, Va., was promoted to sergeant from time of enlistment and served in that position until the close of the war. He was continually engaged in active service. He was the first to discover the advance of Longstreet upon Suffolk, which place he besieged for two weeks. After the withdrawal of Longstreet's army his regiment joined in the pursuit to the line of the Blackwater river, and Mr. Griswold participated in all the engagements of the army of the James river, and numerous raids as an independent organization. He, with two corporals and ten men, occupied an advanced picket position on the 10th of December, 1864, when Lee made a reconnoissance in force on the right of the army of the James, and held his post until the entire left had fallen back, from early dawn to 3 o'clock P. M., when he was reinforced. At the capture of Richmond his regiment occupied the city as provost guard, for two weeks, and thence went to Petersburg and held that place as provost guard while Sherman's army was marching to the grand review. He was mustered out in front of Libby prison, at Richmond, June 13, 1865. Going to Ohio in the same year, he entered the employment of the Pennsylvania company at Lima, Ohio, March 8, 1868, and came to Fort Wayne in 1880 in the employment of the same company. He was first appointed foreman of the bridge gang in 1875. He is a member of Hope lodge, 114, F. & A. M., at Delphos, Ohio, and of George Humphrey post, 530, G. A. R., at Fort Wayne, of which he was a charter member, and is now junior vice commander. He is a member of Wayne street Methodist Episcopal church. He was married in 1871 to Louisa Kessler, of Middlepoint, Ohio, and they have had five children, three of whom survive: William H., Lena B. and Ethel L.

George P. Gordon, baggage agent of the P., Ft. W. & C., G. R. & I., and C. R. & Ft. W. R. R. companies, and member of the common council of Fort Wayne, was born in Greene county, Penn., June 24, 1833. His father, William D. Gordon, was born in Greene county, Penn., in 1812, and was the son of George Gordon, who was born and reared in Pennsylvania and died in 1832. William D. Gordon removed to Ohio in 1835, where he followed farming until his death, December 28, 1878. His wife was Catherine Keenan, who was born in Ireland in about 1812, and came to America when thirteen years of age. Her death occurred in Ohio in 1879. To them three sons and nine daughters were born, who are living with the exception of four daughters. George P. was reared in Ohio until the spring of 1856, when he went to Madison, Wis., where he remained until 1869, being engaged in traveling for a wholesale establishment. In the latter year he came to Fort Wayne, but remained here only a short time, going next to Lancaster, Ohio. In 1862 he returned to Fort Wayne and engaged in farming in Pleasant township, until the fall of 1865. He next went to Woodburn, Ind., with J. K. Edgerton, and remained one year. Returning to Fort Wayne he took a position on the city police force, and held the same for one year. August 1, 1869, he entered the railroad business as night baggage agent, and six years later was promoted to his present position. Mr. Gordon was married in 1857 at Madison, Wis., to Catherine Ring, who was born in Perry county, Ohio, September 28, 1834. To their union ten children have been born, six sons and two daughters of whom survive. Mr. Gordon was elected to the common council of Fort Wayne in the spring of 1889.

Charles P. Fletcher, a prominent citizen of Fort Wayne, is a native of Nashua, N. H., born June 13, 1827. He is the son of Paschal and Rebecca (Boutwell) Fletcher, the former a native of Lowell, Mass., and the latter of Amherst, N. H. The branch of the Fletcher family to which Charles P. belongs sprang from Robert Fletcher who immigrated in 1630, and settled at Concord, Mass. It is believed he came from Yorkshire, England. The family is of the old English Puritan stock. During his early life Mr. Fletcher was employed in cotton factories at Nashua and Manchester, New Hampshire, and Lowell, Mass. In early manhood he sought the life of a railroad builder, and was occupied for several years, first as common laborer, then roadmaster, and finally as contractor. In 1854 he laid the track of the Pittsburgh railway from Crestline, Ohio, to the Fort Wayne depot, it being the first in the city. In the following year he laid the track of the Wabash railway from beyond Defiance, Ohio, to the Fort Wayne depot. In 1858 he established the first restaurant in the city. In 1859 he erected the Summit City hotel, now the Harmon house. From 1864 to 1878 he was occupied as proprietor of an omnibus line. For several years past he has been the owner of the Academy of Music, having purchased it November 2, 1878. Mr. Fletcher was married to Hannah C. Cline, September 16, 1854. She died November 26, 1856, leaving one child, Luella, who died in 1872, aged sixteen. October 9, 1858, he was married to Jennie Heath. She is a native of Connecticut, but was reared at Rochester, N. Y. Her parents were Schuyler and Sarah (Minton) Heath. By the latter marriage two children were born, Willie Minnie, and a daughter unnamed, both deceased. Mr. Fletcher and wife have also had the misfortune to lose three adopted children. In politics he is a staunch republican. During the war he served between one and two years as deputy provost marshal.

Sylvester McMahan, the oldest passenger conductor running out of Fort Wayne, on the P., Ft. W. & C., was born in Lake township, Allen county, November 24, 1842, son of Jackson McMahon, a native of Maryland, born in 1818, who came to Lake township in 1836, with his parents. In about 1839 he went to Licking county, Ohio, and married Elizabeth Larmore, then nineteen years of age, and returning, made his home on the farm in Lake township, where he resided the balance of his life, following farming. He died in 1868, and his widow in 1878. To their union eleven children were born, eight of whom survive. Sylvester McMahon remained on the farm until his twentieth year, and attended the common schools. In 1862 he went to work on the section force of the P., Ft. W. & C. R. R'y, laying track. He was so engaged seven or eight months, and subsequently came to Fort Wayne and was employed as a brakeman on a freight train of the western division of the Pittsburgh road. He continued at this about three years, and was then promoted freight conductor. In 1872 he was promoted passenger conductor, and was given a run between Fort Wayne and Chicago. He now has the run known as Nos. 1 and 4, which is the through mail train. Mr. McMahan is a member of Fort Wayne lodge, No. 19, F. & A. M., and of Fort Wayne chapter, No. 19, and also of Wayne lodge No. 19, A. O. U. W. He and family are members of the First Baptist church, of which he is one of the trustees. He was married September 26, 1867, to Mary A., daughter of Peter and Catherine Miller, old settlers of Allen county, who were natives of Pennsylvania. To the union of Mr. and Mrs. McMahan two daughters have been born, Ella and Dora.

An old and well-known passenger conductor on the western division of the P. Ft. W. & C., railroad, A. W. Adkins, was born near Toronto, Canada, June 16, 1835. He came to Fort Wayne about 1843, and was reared in and near the city. He began railroading July 20, 1859, as brakeman on the P. Ft. W. & C. road. After about three years of this occupation, he was promoted to a freight conductorship, and in December, 1870, he was promoted passenger conductor, and he now drives the express and mail between Fort Wayne and Crestline. In politics he is a staunch republican.. He was married in 1861, to Mary E. Garrison, who was born in New York, and is the daughter of Albert Garrison, one of the pioneer citizens of Fort Wayne, died about June 1, 1889. To the union of Mr. and Mrs. Adkins five children have been born, one of whom is deceased. Laura, wife of Harry Shafer, Clara, wife of William Holbrock, Albert C., and Jessie E., wife of Fred Gardner.

Lyman Blakesley, a well-known citizen of Fort Wayne, and one of the veteran passenger conductors on the western division of the P., Ft. W. & C. railroad, was born in Putnam county, Ohio, March 14, 1842. He is the son of J. B. Blakesley, who was a native of New York, but resided during the most of his life in Ohio, being employed as a railroad bridge contractor. He died in 1881 or 1882. Lyman was reared in Sandusky City, but when ten years of age left home and for five seasons was a sailor on the lakes, attending school during the winter months. At about the age of seventeen years he began railroading as a brakeman with the old Sandusky, Dayton & Cincinnati railroad. In June, 1861, he enlisted in Company E, Seventh Ohio regiment, and served three years. At Cross Lane, W. V., he was taken prisoner August 26, 1861, and for nine months was in prison at Richmond, New Orleans and Salisbury, N. C. He was honorably discharged at Cleveland in June, 1864, and returned to railroading on the S. D. & C. R. R., where he remained until 1867, and then came to Fort Wayne and entered the service of the P.; Ft. W. & C. R. R., as brakeman. One year later was promoted to freight conductor, and in 1872 he was promoted to passenger conductor, and has since been on the run between Fort Wayne and

Chicago. The time covered by Mr. Blakesley's service in the P., Ft. W. & C. R. R., amounts to twenty-two years, and he is one of the oldest passenger conductors running out of Fort Wayne. He was married September 8, 1864, to Miss Mary J. St. John, who was born near Tiffin, Ohio, July 21, 1844; she died December 4, 1888. To their union three children were born: Harry A., Laura D. and Ralph. The latter died in infancy, and Laura D. died March 15, 1889. For fifteen years Mr. Blakesley has been a member of the Order of Railway Conductors, and he is the oldest ex-chief conductor in Indiana. He is a member of the Third Presbyterian church of which Mrs. Blakesley was also a member, and he is one of the executive committee of the railroad department of the Y. M. C. A.

Among those who have held honorable positions in the railway service should be included James P. Gray, who is also well-known in business circles as a member of the hardware firm of Gruber & Gray. He was born at Wheeler, Steuben county, N. Y., April 22, 1850, son of Daniel Gray and his wife Lydia Myrtle, who were both natives of the Empire state, and born in the same year, 1812. Daniel Gray, now a resident of Goodland, Ind., whither the family removed in 1868, is a prominent republican, and in 1860 and 1862, was elected to represent Steuben county in the general assembly of New York. He took an active part in the Harrison campaign of 1888. He had ten children. James P., our subject, received a common school education in his native state, and after farming with his father two years, came to Indiana, and in 1870, made his home at Fort Wayne, and entered the employment of the Pennsylvania railroad company as brakeman. A year later he was promoted to freight train conductor, and after three years' experience in that capacity, was given the position of passenger conductor in 1875, having charge of fast trains. In this capacity he is a faithful and popular officer. In 1883, he formed a partnership with Joseph L. Gruber, in the hardware business at 364 south Calhoun street, and they are doing a prosperous business. He is a worthy citizen and prominent in business circles. Mr. Gray was married in 1871, to Jane Blackburn, of Goodland, who was born in 1853, at Decatur, Ind. They have one child: Ada L. Mr. Gray was made a Mason in 1879, at Wayne lodge, No. 25, thirty-second degree and commandery in 1888, being member of the Indianapolis consistory and Fort Wayne commandry, No. 4.

A. Johnson, an engineer on the western division of the P., Ft. W. & C., railroad company, holding the position of trial engineer, was born in East Wallingsford, Rutland county, Vt., April 26, 1831. He is the son of James and Nancy (Sweetland) Johnson, the father being a native of New Hampshire, and the mother of Vermont. The parents located in Lexington, Ohio, in 1839, and resided there until 1846, and then removed to Republic, Seneca county, Ohio. They next removed to Leasville, Crawford county, Ohio, and three years later removed to Sandusky City. In about 1850, they removed to Springfield Ohio, and subsequently resided at Dayton, Patterson, Hardin county,

Ohio, and next at Lima, Ohio. In about 1875 they removed to Chicago, where the father died; the mother then came to Fort Wayne, where she died. Mr. Johnson began railroading in 1848, on the Mad River & Erie railway, and in 1851, was promoted engineer on the same road. He next spent a year on the Dayton & Greenville railroad, and in 1856, went into the service of the P., Ft. W. & C. railroad on the eastern division, running between Pittsburgh and Crestline, Ohio. In 1858, he went on the Central Ohio railroad, running between Columbus and Bellaire, where he remained until 1863, and then went on the Pennsylvania Central railroad. Ten years later in 1873, he came to Fort Wayne, and took an engine on the west division. He ran an engine until about 1883, when he was given the position of trial engineer. His duties are to take in charge new engines and get them in running order, when they are turned over. Mr. Johnson has been railroading forty-one years. He is a member of Harmony lodge No. 19, I. O. O. F. Mr. Johnson was married on January 1, 1857, to Margaret Letts, who was born in Mecklinburg, N. Y. To their union six children have been born, three of whom survive, Flora Bell, Carrie A., wife of Seward Morgan, of New York city, and Lizzie E., now the wife of Thomas C. Warner. Mrs. Johnson and two daughters are members of the First Baptist church, and one daughter is a Presbyterian.

Anthony Kelker, a trustworthy and popular engineer of the Pittsburgh, Fort Wayne & Chicago railroad, was born at Lebanon, Penn., March 1, 1835. His father, David Kelker, of an old Pennsylvania German family, moved when "Tony" was a year old, to Waynesboro, Penn., and five years later to Butler, Penn. Three years later the family moved into Ohio and resided successively at Alliance, New Lisbon, Damascus Bank and Lucas. At Damascus Bank the father became a contractor and graded four miles of the road between Pittsburgh and Alliance. At this place Tony Kelker also began railroading as the boss of a gang of graders. Removing from Lucas to Crestline the father graded two miles more of the road, and between the latter place and VanWert, the son helped to lay the track. In 1854 Mr. Kelker began work as a brakeman on the Ohio & Indiana road, and a year later became fireman of a construction train. From this position he became fireman on the locomotive "Pioneer," the first owned by the Fort Wayne & Chicago road, now divisions D and E. In the spring of 1856 he was promoted engineer by D. B. Strope, master mechanic. He had made his home at Fort Wayne on the 18th of the preceding August. In 1858 he took charge of a passenger engine, and has ever since been entrusted with this responsible position. His assignment at this time is the running of trains Nos. 2 and 9, between Fort Wayne and Crestline. His pet locomotive is No. 199, built in Fort Wayne, after the best pattern of the Boone engines. With this powerful machine, Mr. Kelker in 1870, made a trip from Fort Wayne to Chicago which is memorable in the railroad annals of the world. Photographs of the engine and its gallant driver, and a statement of the record were hung in the offices of the railroad magnates of the land, and pointed to with pride as an example of the mechanical perfection and physical nerve of the great west. On September 14, 1870, Mr. Kelker pulled passenger train No. 1, with one baggage car and three coaches, from Fort Wayne to Chicago, 146½ miles, with eleven stops, in two hours and forty-seven and one-half minutes. Making allowance for three minutes at each stop, the speed made by Mr. Kelker was seventy-five and twelve nineteenths miles per hour. Other fast runs he has made are from Plymouth to Chicago, October 2, 1879, with four cars, over eighty-two miles in one hour and thirty-three minutes; seven days later with four cars from Van Wert to Chicago, 179 miles, in three hours and thirty minutes; and several shorter runs at the rate of a mile a minute or faster. In spite of seemingly dangerous speed Mr. Kelker has never had a collision, and the only accident he has encountered was caused by the breaking of a wheel on the forward truck. He escaped unhurt, but his brother-in-law, who was firing, was killed. Mr. Kelker's private life is interesting and happy. Strictly temperate, abstaining entirely from tobacco, he is always clear in mind and ready for prompt action in any emergency. His home is a beautiful one, and he is known as one of the finest amateur florists in the state. He was married March 8, 1857, to Lydia A., daughter of John Arnold, ex-councilman, and a pioneer of the city, having settled here about 1837. They have had three children: Francis A., died June 2, 1869, at the age of twelve; Nannie D., wife of H. S. Rodeheaver, and Harry O., an engineer on the Pittsburgh road. Mr. Kelker is an active republican, and in 1885, running as an independent candidate in the fourth ward, was elected councilman in that democratic stronghold, and re-elected in 1887. He is a Master Mason of Sol D. Bayless lodge, and a worthy member of the Wayne Street Methodist church. His unfailing kindness, uniform courtesy and manly character have made him hosts of friends wherever he is known.

William M. Glenn, a brave soldier of the republic and one of the most prominent locomotive engineers of the west, began his railroad career near Alleghany City, his boyhood home. At nine years he engaged as water carrier on section twelve of the Alleghany valley railroad, one of the oldest in the country. Afterward at Lima, Ohio, he carried water for a construction gang on the Ohio & Indiana, now P., Ft. W. & C. railroad. In 1857 he rose to the rank of brakeman on a gravel train of the latter road, at Lima, and in the following year he went to Upper Sandusky, and held similar positions as well as conductor on extra gravel trains. May 2, 1859, he arrived at Fort Wayne and took the position of fireman on the "Shanghai" engine, "Fort Wayne," a single driver machine of the Richard Norris build. He was thus engaged mostly with passenger trains until August 8, 1862, when he enlisted in the Eleventh Indiana battery, and went to the scene of war. His battery was stationed at Nashville, in the army of the Cumberland, but owing to a blockade, he, with other recruits, was stationed for three months at West Point, Ky., guarding the Ohio river. Joining the battery at Nashville in December, 1862, they remained there until the early part of January, 1863, when they moved to the field of Stone river, but arrived too late to take part in the action. They were then assigned to Lytle's brigade, Sheridan's Third division, Twentieth army corps, and took part in all the engagements of the army of the Cumberland, about Chattanooga, including Chickamauga. He was in the siege of Chattanooga, and during the winter of 1863, was one of a party of twenty-five men, who started from the town with three days rations, consisting of a little hardtack, bacon and coffee, to take 125 horses over the mountains to Bridgeport, a distance of 104 miles by that route. The hardships of the trip may be judged from the fact that all but fifty horses died on the road from starvation. A week later the party returned to Bridgeport on foot. He and his battery shelled the enemy on Moccasin point, in the battle above the clouds, and shelled them also from Fort Wood. He was next at Tunnel Hill, Buzzard Roost, Resaca, Cartersville, the Chattahooche river, and for thirty-two days and nights, threw a shell every two minutes into Atlanta. They accompanied Sherman as far as Jonesboro, and then returned to Gen. Thomas at Nashville. Thence they did scouting duty and subsequently the battery was discharged, but Mr. Glenn and others were assigned to the Eighteenth Indiana battery, being discharged at Indianapolis, July 3, 1865, he again became a fireman on the Pittsburgh road in September. In the following March, he was promoted freight engineer (No. 155), between Fort Wayne and Valparaiso, was transferred to engine 113 in 1869, and April 7, 1871, was given a passenger engine on division C. For twelve years he ran the Lima accommodation train, and in 1883, entered the through passenger service, running between Fort Wayne and Crestline. He began running the limited express in 1885, and now runs the limited west and the fast mail west of Fort Wayne. His best time was made from Crestline to Fort Wayne, 131 miles, in two hours and thirty-two minutes. Mr. Glenn was born in Morgan county, Ohio, May 2, 1842. His parents, Robert and Ann Smyth Glenn, natives of Ireland, of Scotch descent, immigrated in 1835, and settled at Pittsburgh. They resided afterward successively in Morgan county, Ohio, Alleghany city, Lima, Ohio and in 1862, removed to VanWert, where the father died in 1877 and the mother in 1884. Mr. Glenn was married February 22, 1872, to Mary E. Curtis, who was born August 23, 1854, and died October 2, 1883, leaving four children out of six born, Grace C., Robert Burr, Carrie A. and Eliza F. He was married November 28, 1888, to Frances Wright, of Fort Wayne, and they reside at the handsome residence at No. 26, Dewald street. Mr. Glenn is a prominent Mason, being a member of Summit city lodge, 170, F. & A. M., life member of Fort Wayne chapter, No. 19, Wayne council, No. 4, Fort Wayne commandery, No. 4, K. T., Grand lodge of Perfection, Sariah council, Prince of Jerusalem, Indianapolis chapter Rose Croix, and Indiana consistory, 32nd degree.

William T. Jackson, a veteran passenger engineer on the western division of the P., Ft. W. & C. railroad, was born in Detroit, Mich.,

July 30, 1832. His parents removed to Erie, Penn., when their son was quite young, and it was in that city he spent his boyhood and attended the common schools. He began railroading in 1853, as firemen on the Erie & Northeast R. R., a road running nineteen miles from Erie to the New York state line, having only three locomotive engines. He was in the railroad war, in about 1854, between the roads in and about Erie, which was caused by the citizens of that city attempting to prevent the consolidation of the Buffalo & Erie and Cleveland & Erie roads, by tearing up the tracks of the Erie & Northeast road. Mr. Jackson was next engaged on the Chicago & Rock Island road, and in about 1855 was promoted to a switch and construction engine on that road. About one year later he was promoted to a freight train, and continued in that capacity for about two years. He then came to Fort Wayne and run a freight engine on the Wabash railway about twenty-two months. He was next on the Terre Haute & Alton railway about four months, and on the Burlington & Quincy railway, between Chicago & Galesburg, about ten months, and then returned to Fort Wayne, where his family were residing. On March 1, 1862, he entered the service of the P., Ft. W. & C. R'y Co., as freight engineer, and has remained with that company up to the present time. In 1865 he was made passenger engineer and ran passenger trains on both divisions until about 1870. In that year the fast trains were put on between Chicago and New York, and he was given an engine on the fast run between Crestline and Fort Wayne. His was the second engine to be equipped with the Westinghouse air brakes on the western division, in July, 1870. On June 11, 1870, while braking by hand, he made the run between Crestline and Fort Wayne, a distance of 131 miles, in two hours and forty-seven minutes. The run was phenomenal at that time, as the track was not so level as now, the Westinghouse brakes were not in use, and wood instead of coal was used for fuel. The record made then was unbroken for a number of years, but recently, with more favorable conditions, it has been beaten, Mr. Jackson himself making the same run in two hours and thirty-six minutes. Even that has been beaten by William M. Glenn, who has made the run in two hours and thirty-two minutes. In 1871 Mr. Jackson was taken sick and for about eight and one-half months was off duty. Upon his recovery he took charge of the round-house as foreman for about twenty-two months. In 1881 he was given the engine on the limited express, between Chicago and Crestline, and has been on that run ever since. Mr. Jackson is a member of Wayne lodge, No. 25, F. & A. M., which he joined in 1869. He was married December 5, 1852, at Westfield, N. Y., to Mary A. Groat, and they have had six children, four of whom survive: Ada R., wife of George Burger, engineer on the P., Ft. W. & C.; Alice, now Mrs. Albert Cattingham, of Iona, Mich.; Lillie M. and Edwin T., bookkeeper. Mr. Jackson's family are members of the Congregational church.

Frank P. Higgins, one of the oldest passenger engineers in the service of the P., Ft. W. & C. railroad, was born in Ireland, January 14,

1837. He is the eldest son of John Higgins, who removed with his family to America about 1845, and settled in Massachusetts. Frank P. was left with his grand-parents in Ireland, and did not come to America until 1850. His first work was on a farm in Massachusetts, where he put in three years, and then learned the trade of a shoemaker. Upon coming to Fort Wayne, in the winter of 1860, Mr. Higgins entered the service of the P., Ft. W. & C. railroad, as a fireman on freight and passenger engines. Two years later he entered the machine shops and worked about one year, and was then given an engine in the summer of 1864. He ran a freight engine about six years, and in 1870 he was promoted to passenger engineer. The period of Mr. Higgins' service with the Pennsylvania company is twenty-nine years, about nineteen of which has been as a passenger engineer. In 1881 he was assigned the engine drawing the limited express between Fort Wayne and Chicago. Mr. Higgins was married at Webster, Mass., in 1861, to Margaret A. Carney, who was born in Ireland. To their union a son and daughter have been born. The family are members of the Catholic Cathedral. In 1880 Mr. Higgins erected a handsome two-story brick residence at No. 143 East Jefferson street, where he and family reside.

A worthy gentleman now retired from active business, who has faithfully occupied posts of danger, both as soldier and locomotive engineer, is Andrew McClure of Fort Wayne. He was born in Blair county, Penn., November 12, 1841, the son of Joseph and Martha Ann (Ambrose) McClure, natives of Pennsylvania. At the opening of the civil war he entered Company D, Fourteenth Pennsylvania regiment, and served three months, first as private and then as first lieutenant. In February, 1862, he re-enlisted in Company H, One Hundred and Thirteenth Pennsylvania regiment, and served with it two years as private and as second lieutenant. He was appointed captain, but, for some reason, his commission failed to reach him. In the second battle of Bull Run he was taken prisoner, but escaped about eighteen hours later. He was also in the battles of South Mountain and Antietam. He was discharged at Winchester, Va., in June, 1864. Returning to Pennsylvania, he soon became engaged as locomotive engineer, and remained in that capacity with the Pennsylvania company until 1872, when he removed to Fort Wayne. Here he was employed as engineer for the Wabash company. In 1877, on account of exposure during the war, he had the misfortune to lose his eyesight, and he has ever since been totally blind. From 1877 to 1886 his attention was given to hotel keeping. Mr. McClure was married in November, 1861, to Eliza Zeth, a native of Blair county, Penn., the daughter of Jacob and Sophia Zeth. They have one child, Mary E. McClure. Mr. McClure is a member of the Brotherhood of Locomotive Engineers and the G. A. R. In politics he has been a lifelong republican.

Michael F. Shea, railway engineer, is a native of County Cork, Ireland, born September 29, 1851. His parents, Patrick and Mary (Lynch) Shea, came to America when he was but a year old leaving him in Ireland, fearing, on account of poor health, he would not then stand the trip. His parents located in New Haven, where they still reside. After having been here about nine years they sent for their son, who came to this country in company with Daniel Shannahan, whose passage was paid by the parents of Mr. Shea. Michael joined his parents at New Haven and remained with them until he was fifteen, when he was apprenticed to a shoemaker in Fort Wayne, and spent two years learning the trade. Not being satisfied, he returned home and spent one year on a farm to which his parents had removed. In May, 1869, he secured a position as brakeman on the Pittsburgh road, and held it two years and nine months. He then obtained a similar place on the Wabash road and at the expiration of three months was promoted to freight conductor, and held that position one year. Returning to the Pittsburgh road he was employed for a time as switchman, and for five years as fireman. In 1878 he was promoted to engineer, a position he has held ever since. He was married June 22, 1875, to Bridget Broderick, who was born in Jefferson township, August 31, 1851. She is the daughter of John and Ellen (Meehan) Broderick, natives of Ireland, who were married at Fort Wayne. Mr. and Mrs. Shea have had eight children: Joseph P., John S., Dennis (deceased), Helen C., Mamie L., Michael F., Anna A. (deceased), and another that died in infancy. He and wife are members of the Roman Catholic church, and he is a member of the Brotherhood of Locomotive Engineers.

A trustworthy passenger engineer, residing at Fort Wayne, J. R. Anderson, is engaged on the southern division of the Grand Rapids & Indiana railroad, and runs between Fort Wayne and Richmond. Mr. Anderson was born on East Wayne street, November 23, 1852, the son of Alexander M. Aderson, who came to Fort Wayne from Ohio, his native state, about 1830. He made his home about six miles west of the city on the Yellow river road, the Indians still being numerous, and began the work of clearing a farm. Subsequently he was employed in the shops of the Pittsburgh company. The son, J. R. Anderson, was reared to youth on the farm, and at the age of seventeen entered the employment of the Pittsburgh railroad company in the shops, at machine work. This occupation he exchanged four years later for that of fireman, on the Grand Rapids & Indiana road. In 1879 he was promoted to freight engineer, and in 1888, to passenger engineer. He is a member of the Third Presbyterian church; of the Brotherhood of Locomotive Engineers, and of the republican party. He was married September 6, 1881, to Elizabeth Lopshire, who was born in Lafayette township, a daughter of William Lopshire, who was one of the earliest settlers of that township.

Fred N. Kollock, a popular citizen of Fort Wayne, is prominent in railroad circles as agent of the Union line at Fort Wayne, and traveling agent for the Pennsylvania railroad company, and the C., St. L. & P. railroad. Mr. Kollock was born at Burlington, N. J., April 27, 1845, and two years later was taken by his parents to Philadelphia, where he grew to the age of sixteen years. In August,

1862, determined to enlist in the army, he attained his purpose by leaving home secretly, and joining company B, Twenty-ninth regiment, Pennsylvania infantry. He was with the Twelfth army corps in the army of the Potomac, participating in the battles of Antietam, Chancellorsville and Gettysburg, and was then with the Twentieth corps under Gen. Joe Hooker, at the battle of Mission Ridge and Lookout Mountain, and Atlanta, and in Sherman's campaign through Georgia. After nearly three year's service he was mustered out as sergeant in July, 1865. Two older brothers were in the service, one as assistant surgeon in the navy, and the other as surgeon of the One Hundred and Eighteenth Pennsylvania. In 1865, Mr. Kollock went to Milwaukee, and was connected with the Chicago, Milwaukee & St. Paul railroad until 1873, when he engaged in the oil busines in the same city. He returned to the service of the railroad company in 1875, and remained with them until 1880, when in December, he came to Fort Wayne to accept the position of soliciting agent of the Union line. In 1885 he was promoted agent. Mr. Kollock is at present junior vice-commander of Antony Wayne post, No. 271, G. A. R., and chancellor commander of Phœnix lodge, No. 101, K. of P.; of the uniform rank of the later fraternity he is an enthusiastic champion, and on June 4, 1884, he was elected colonel of the Second regiment, Indiana brigade, for a term of four years. Mr. Kollock was married January 13, 1870, to Mary A. Green, of Philadelphia, and they have three children: John K., born November 3, 1871, a graduate of Fort Wayne college, 1886, and now a member of the class of 92, Amherst college; Fred N., Jr., born October 25, 1876, and Lester R., born January 9, 1882.

One of the early manufacturers at the city of Fort Wayne was D. S. Beaver, born in Franklin county, Pa., May 3, 1820, who came to this city in 1839, and took a position in the mill of Samuel Freeman, and made his home with that gentleman. He was foreman for six years, and in 1845 rented the mill, and subsequently purchased the property which he operated until 1876. He then sold out, and had charge of the Fort Wayne poultry yards until his death, December 9, 1888. He was married at Mexico, Oswego county, N. Y., to Sarah J. Lamb, who died April 3, 1849, leaving one child, Charles B. Beaver, born February 17, 1848, now a prominent citizen of Fort Wayne. October 17, 1850, he again married, to Mrs. A. M. Nichols, of Brockport, N. Y., who died October 16, 1851. His third marriage was to Mrs. Agnes E. Hamilton, at West Stockbridge, Mass., April 3, 1854. She died March 20, 1877, leaving two children: Edwin L., born October 6, 1855, and Minnie A., born August 8, 1863. Another child, Frank M., died in 1876. Mr. Beaver united with the Presbyterian church in 1845, was made an elder in 1853, and held that office until death. Charles B. Beaver was engaged with his father until his twenty-first year, when he began an engagement of eighteen months as clerk for a wholesale house in Fort Wayne. After a year spent in railroading, he entered the service of the United States Express company, and has risen through the various positions of driver of a wagon, manager of the business at the depot, messenger between Fort Wayne and Cincinnati, to agent at Fort Wayne, to which responsible position he was appointed July 28, 1880. He has also been agent of the Pacific Express company since it came into the city about 1878. Mr. Beaver is a member of the Presbyterian church. He was married February 17, 1869, to Mary A. Markley, of this city, born in February 27, 1847, and they have had six children, of whom the following are living: Minnie May, Hugh M., Harry C. and Frank M.

The agency of the Adams express company at Fort Wayne is in the hands of Charles O. Essig, a competent and popular young business man. Mr. Essig was born in Williamsport, Allen county, Ind., October 15, 1859, the son of Adam P. Essig, one of the worthy early settlers, who came to this county about 1840, and purchasing land, was occupied in farming until 1871, when he removed to Fort Wayne. He now resides in the city. For ten years after coming here he was in the hotel business. His wife's maiden name was Susannah Mahnensmith. Their son Charles was reared in the city and educated at both the public schools and at the Brothers' schools. In 1878 he became a clerk in the office of the city treasurer, and remained in that position until 1881, after which he was engaged for eight months as general clerk for tracklayers of a railroad. He entered the employment of the Adams express company at Fort Wayne, February 23, 1882, with general duties. In July, 1883, he was promoted to bill clerk, in December, 1887, made acting agent, and in June, 1888, was appointed agent and manager. During this period he also had charge of the business of the American express company which was with the Adams. Mr. Essig is a member of the National Union, and is secretary of the local lodge. He is also a member of the First Baptist church, of which he was treasurer for some time. He was married June 16, 1886, to Ella Brooks, of the city.

MANUFACTURING INDUSTRIES.

From its situation as an inland city, Fort Wayne is dependent to an unusual degree for its prosperity upon the extent of its manufactories. Fortunately its location on the the great avenues of travel between New York and the great cities of the west, has made its shipping facilities of inestimable value, has cheapened its freight rates, and made travel to the great commercial centers easy and pleasurable. More than this its location has been fortunate in being in the center of the great hard wood timber district, which Lieut. Maury once aptly described as the "Steppes of America."

Fort Wayne has never felt the injurious effects of a boom, but has made such regular and substantial additions to its wealth, year by year, which few American cities can boast of. In 1828 the population was but 500; in 1840, 1,200; in 1860, 10,319; in 1880, 25,700; and in 1889, a population of over 75,000 people is shown by the canvass of R. L.

Polk & Co., publishers of the new directory. Eight hundred dwelling houses will be erected this year, and architects estimate that $3,000,000 will not cover the building contracts. So great has been the demand for brick that the yards have been taxed to their utmost capacity, and many thousands have been shipped in from other places.

These observations are preliminary to a sketch of the manufacturing industries of this city. Some of them, it will be noted, are of surprising extent, wide-spread reputation and of financial solidity equal to any in the land.

Let us begin with the great shops of the Pittsburgh, Fort Wayne & Chicago railway company, of which the Pennsylvania company is the lessee. Over 1,100 names are now on the labor rolls, and the company paymaster makes a monthly disbursement in Fort Wayne of over $100,000 per month. Considerably more than half of this great volume of money is charged to the account of the shops proper, and the salaries of the superintendent and other officials is not included. The 1,100 employes referred to, it should be understood, include the men who work in the yards, but not the engineers, firemen, conductors, brakemen, switchmen, sectionmen, freight handlers and clerks in all departments who constitute a distinct regiment of their own.

In order that the magnitude of the company's plant may be better understood the following figures, representing the ground plan areas of buildings, furnished to the writer by superintendent of motive power and machinery, F. D. Cassanave, are here presented: Station and hotel, two stories, 230x35; freight house, 300x35; office building, 55x55; brass foundry, 60x25; machine shops, 320x110; boiler shops, 145x70; engine or round-house with stalls, 39; blacksmith shops, 320x80; planing-mill, 217x75, with two wings, each 187x63; oil house, 35x22.

These great buildings cover a space of four blocks from west to east and two blocks from north to south, nearly every foot of space being made available. They are not, however, the whole of the company's shop plant. Vast as is their extent, splendid as is their equipment, and although the army of men work ten hours a day and often a night force labors until morning, there was a demand for additional manufacturing facilities that must be met with enlarged accommodations. Accordingly, just beyond the eastern limits of the city the company, two years ago, laid out a magnificent yard with ten miles of side track and there erected a vast car shop, built in the segment of a circle, like a big round-house, for the storage of locomotives. This structure has seventeen stalls, reached from a turn table and each capable of holding two freight cars, when in process of construction. When this shop shall have been completed the turn table will be in the center of a mammoth car establishment containing forty stalls and capable of holding eighty cars. The surprising growth of the business of the company promises to make the completion of this great shop necessary within the near future. A large planing-mill is another of the improvements at the east yards. The old and new shops of the Pennsylvania company at Fort Wayne cover a tract of fifty acres. In them will be built this year forty new locomotives of the Class S, or Big Mogul pattern, each capable of drawing forty loaded freight cars at a speed of eighteen miles an hour. Two thousand dairy, refrigerator, box and gondola cars will be turned out, besides an immense amount of repair work to the rolling stock of the entire western division of 279 miles. The performances of the passenger engines manufactured at these shops have so often been referred to in the public press that it were idle to state more here than that they have made the very best of records for speed, power and economy in the use of coal. Not unfrequently the limited express, or vestibule train, as it is variously called, is carried over the western division at an average rate of speed of fifty miles an hour, the train attaining, where there are few railway crossings to stop at, the surprising velocity of seventy miles an hour. Exact records of these performances are kept by the company which claims with its well-constructed track, its perfect system of train dispatching, its unexcelled motive power and equipment to be able to run its trains faster and with less risk to life and property than is done on any road in the country. Mr. G. L. Potter is the general superintendent of the shops, and his corps of assistants are all men of many years' faithful and intelligent service.

The main car shops of the Wabash road are at Toledo, Ohio, and at Springfield, Ills., but the principal erecting shops of the eastern division of the main line, extending from Toledo, Ohio, to Danville, Ills., are located at Fort Wayne and here, until recently, J. B. Barnes, the superintendent of the motive power and machinery, had his headquarters. The building, rebuilding and repair of all the locomotives is done at the Fort Wayne shops. This work is under the supervision of master mechanic, Frank Morse, and Frank Tyrrell, general foreman. The dismemberment of the Wabash property by Judge Gresham's famous decree has had the effect of removing the mechanical work on what were the Peru branch and the Eel River branch and of reducing the number of men on the company's labor rolls at this point. However, 225 men are yet given employment and for their benefit and the benefit of the train men, freight house men and others, the company's paymaster makes a monthly disbursement of $20,000. The Wabash plant at Fort Wayne consists, in buildings, of two round-houses of forty stalls capacity, an erecting shop 100x160 feet, fully equipped with the latest and best machinery, a blacksmith shop 40x160 feet, a wood shop 30x200 feet, a paint shop 30x100 feet, a tin and coppersmith shop 30x40 feet, an oil house 20x30 feet, besides a large freight house, passenger depot, coal sheds, and other smaller structures. The number of locomotives turned out every month, either new or generally overhauled, will average fourteen.

The Fort Wayne, Cincinnati & Louisville railway, the "Muncie" route, has never been as prosperous as some of the east and west trunk lines, and although its management has been generally wise and economical, it has never been able to erect extensive shops anywhere. However, the headquarters for the mechanical department are in Fort Wayne. The principal shop is a large brick structure excellently equipped and carefully managed by master mechanic, Theodore Habenkorn. Fifty skilled men are employed under his direction. The business on the "Muncie" has of late years had a most satisfactory increase, and $4,000 is a fair estimate of the disbursements for all kinds of labor the company makes at Fort Wayne.

The Lake Shore railway, which reaches this city from the north is a branch of the main line leading from Auburn Junction, has no shops at Fort Wayne, although the liberal grant of land made to the company's predecessor, the Fort Wayne, Jackson & Saginaw railway was predicted upon their establishment here.

The Nickel Plate makes Fort Wayne a division point for engine and freight service, and has at Fort Wayne a round-house and repair shop, but the disposition of the management is toward increasing this little beginning, it being well understood that the location of the principal shop plant at Fort Wayne would be most advantageous.

First among the private enterprises that give solidity to the city may be mentioned the Bass foundry and machine works, an establishment so vast as to easily rival the mammoth shops operated by the Pennsylvania company.

It is no easy matter to comprehend, let alone describe, an industry which covers twenty acres, gives employment to 1,100 men and disburses $35,000 per month in wages, besides paying out many times that amount for the pig iron which goes into the blazing cupolas, and for the other material which make up the varied output of this mammoth hive of industry. The manufactured product finds its way either as stationary engines, machinery, saw-mills, etc., to every city in the land, and on nearly all the trunk lines the car wheels used will be found, upon inspection, to be marked with the name of this great corporation. It is a fact, beyond any dispute, that at Fort Wayne, Ind., more car wheels are cast than in any city in the world.

The Bass works were established in 1853, and the company was incorporated twenty years later. The president and principal owner is John H. Bass, the secretary, John I. White, and the treasurer, Robertson J. Fisher. Mr. Bass is president of the First National bank, is an officer in two other national banks, is president of the Star Iron Tower company, of the street railway company, and is identified with many other industries besides. His wealth is estimated at nearly $4,000,000. He is still in the prime of life and the great institution which his energy has built up is ever expanding. Many of the employes have been twenty-five years in his service, and of them, it may generally be said, that there are but few traveling-journeymen and that nearly all are of the better class of thrifty American mechanics, who strive to save from their earnings enough to provide well for their families, to educate their children to traits of industries and frugality, to own a comfortable home and to secure themselves from want in their old age. In the thirty-six years of operation the establishment has never known a strike or even any serious labor trouble. This results from the remarkable degree of confidence existing between the corporation and its employes. Large branches of this establishment are those of the St. Louis Car Wheel company and of J. H. Bass, Chicago.

Everywhere in America where vehicle wheels are bought and sold, the name of H. G. Olds, of Fort Wayne, Ind., is a familiar one, for he is president of a corporation which manufactures more wheels for wagons, carriages and other vehicles than any other. The record shows that in this business as in the business of manufacturing car wheels, a Fort Wayne manufactory excels all others in the extent of its outputs. Think of 90,000 sets of wheels made and shipped in the last twelve months! It would seem that hereafter not only the rich can ride in chaises, but the poor will not always be compelled to walk. Upward of 7,000,000 spokes will be manufactured this year, 1,500,000 strips for felloes will be used, and about 500,000 hub blocks. Vast amounts of timber are annually unloaded from wagon at the works, besides over 2,500 cars, each with an average load of 30,000 pounds. The works are located at the southeast corner of Lafayette street and the Wabash railway, and cover five acres of ground. In the various departments nearly 500 men and boys are employed, and over $16,000 a month is disbursed in wages. The concern retains the name under which business was conducted in the lifetime of Noble G. Olds, and is called N. G. Olds & Sons.

The marvel of the manufacturing establishments in Fort Wayne is that of the Fort Wayne Jenney Electric Light company, its wonderful growth emphasizing the prediction that the electric spark with the vaporized drop of water would revolutionize the world. The company was incorporated in 1881, with a capital stock of $100,000. The five original incorporators were O. A. Simons, now deceased, J. H. Bass, H. G. Olds, P. A. Randall and R. T. McDonald. The business started in a small way in two rooms, in one of the buildings connected with the Fort Wayne Iron Works, on Superior street, and was afterward removed to Mr. Randall's building on East Columbia street. The patents used were at first chiefly those of James A. Jenney, and his son Charles D. Jenney. Mr. McDonald was elected general manager, and he soon began to attract for the new company and its light a reputation that was as surprising as it was gratifying to his friends. In 1887, the capital stock was increased to $500,000, the company by that time had occupied new and enlarged shops at the intersection of Broadway and the P., Ft. W. & C., railway track, gave employment to 500 people, and had won a famous lawsuit in which the Alder Brush company of Cleveland, had sought to cripple the company by suing an Indianapolis firm, which used the Jenney light, for damages for infringement. About this time general manager McDonald secured the services of the distinguished electrician, M. M. M. Slattery, whose ingenius system of producing light by alternating currents of electricity has revolutionized the business of electrical illumination. The works were burned down on the night of November 23, 1888, and have since then been rebuilt on a scale of double the size of the destroyed buildings. The majority of the stock has lately passed into the hands of a Boston syndicate, which controls the Thomas-Houston company. Mr. J. H. Bass predicts that within a few years the shops of the Fort Wayne Jenney Electric Light company, will exceed the Bass foundry and machine works in extent. The Jenney light illuminates a large portion of New York city, and is found in nearly every city in the land and on every navigable lake and river.

The Olds wagon works were established with a capital stock of $200,000, and its plant, including a four-story brick building, 60x412 feet, with a blacksmith shop 75x150 feet, occupies an entire square, in which are extensive drying houses, side-tracks, etc. Its wagons are turned out at the rate of forty and fifty a day and are sold all over America. The company employs 200 men and has a monthly pay roll ot $10,000.

The Kerr Murray Manufacturing company is engaged in building gas apparatus and has put up some of the largest works in the country. The business was established in 1862, the general foundry and machine business being then the principal feature. Mr. Murray had scarce begun the building of gas works when he died and the business has since been prosecuted with wonderful success by a stock company of which his son-in-law, Mr. A. D. Cressler, is president and manager. Large buildings have been erected and are splendidly equipped. The capital stock is $100,000.

Among the gentlemen to newly enter the manufacturing business in Fort Wayne are the Messrs. D. N. and S. M. Foster. The former is at the head of the Fort Wayne Furniture company, whose large works lie at the north end of Lafayette street, to the north of the Nickel Plate track. Two hundred men are employed chiefly in the manufacturing of a patent folding bed, the most valuable and salable in the market. The establishment has been doubled in capacity in the single year of its existence and further large additions must soon be made.

Mr. S. M. Foster is the proprietor of an institution that gives steady employment to over 300 operatives, mostly girls. The business is that of manufacturing shirt waists for children, an industry entirely new hereabouts. An immense building is occupied near the furniture company's establishment.

The Clark & Rhinesmith Lumber company is one of the solid and thrifty industries of Fort Wayne. Their extensive works are situated at the intersection of the Wabash track and Lafayette street, and employ 150 men. Here are manufactured the Anthony Wayne washing machines, which are sold all over the world. The principal products, however, are building materials of all kinds, such as doors, sash, blinds, etc.

The Fort Wayne Organ company is said to pay the handsomest dividends of any manufacturing investment in the city. The company now owns large shops on South Fairfield avenue, and sends around the

Globe organs for the church, the concert hall and the parlor, of surpassing excellence for correctness of pitch, durability of workmanship, and beauty of design. Of late years an immense foreign trade has grown up.

Directly opposite the Fort Wayne Jenney Electric Light works is located the large establishment of Louis Rastetter. The business is the converting of ash timber into buggy bows and other articles of bent wood work, known to the trade. Many thousand dollars are paid to Mr. Rastetter annually by A. G. Spaulding & Bros., of Chicago, for racquet bats, base ball bats and other sporting goods. One hundred men are employed.

A particularly thrify industry is that of the Fleming Manufacturing company in the Ninth ward. The company owns valuable patents for the manufacture of road scrapers and leveling machines which are sold in great numbers from ocean to ocean. The buildings have 40,000 square feet of floorage. Mr. Charles Pfeiffer is the manager.

In the extreme west end of the city are located the works of the Horton Manufacturing company. The large buildings with the lumber yard cover over an acre of ground, and over 100 men are employed. Here are manufactured the Horton washing machine and four styles of corn planters. Mr. John C. Peters is the principal proprietor.

Near to the Horton works the Indiana machine works have built new and large buildings which are devoted to the manufacture of wood working machinery of various kinds, pulleys, etc. An immense business has been built up.

One of the oldest and strongest of the wood manufacturing enterprises in the city is that of the Peters Box and Lumber company, situated in the Ninth ward. The company was founded by Mr. John C. Peters, and its principal industry was long the manufacture of boxes, but the concern is now chiefly occupied with the manufacture of furniture of a high grade, and competes successfully with the big institutions at Grand Rapids, Mich., and other furniture-making centers. Charles Pape, William Fleming and Wilson McQuiston are the proprietors. They have recently added the manufacture of wooden pulleys to their business.

In the extreme east end of the city Winch & Sons have established a hub factory, which gives employment to eighty men.

The White wheel works were organized in 1872. The business is now owned by Capt. James B. White, ex-member of congress, and his son, John W. White. The latter has the management and gives to it his entire time and attention. The works have a paid up capital of $100,000, and the value of the annual output is $150,000. One hundred and thirty hands are employed the year round and the pay roll is $4,000 per month. Fifty thousand dollars is annually expended for material, and nearly all of this large sum is distributed in the near vicinity of Fort Wayne, to find its way again in the local channels of trade.

Made up as Fort Wayne's population is, largely of Germans, and people of German extraction, it is not strange that the business of brewing beer has grown to mammoth proportious. There are two great breweries here. The oldest is that of C. L. Centlivre, an enterprising Alsacian, and it is, perhaps, best known as the French brewery. The situation is a charming one on the bank of the St. Joseph river, a mile north of the city. The brewery bottling works and boat house were entirely destroyed by fire on the night of July 16, 1889, and are to be rebuilt upon a magnificent scale. What, with the brewery, the handsome residences of C. L. Centlivre and his sons, the bottling works, and the fleet of pleasure boats on the river, over $300,000 will be represented.

The Herman Berghoff Brewing company began business in 1888 and erected a magnificent brewery, equipped with the very latest appliances for the manufacture of pure and wholesome beer. The brewery was burned down on August 22, 1888, before it had well begun operation. It was immediately restored and does a business so large that a new malt house is to be erected within a few months. The brewery proper is 120 by 160 feet in dimensions and is six stories high. It has a capacity of 100,000 barrels a year and represents an investment of $175,000. The Berghoffs belong to a noted family of brewers at Dortmunder, Germany, and Dortmunder beer is the name of a principal product of the establishment.

It was not the purpose of this article to describe all of the manufacturing interests of Fort Wayne. Accordingly only a few of the larger ones have been mentioned and these at no great length. There might be added extended notices of an hundred other hives of industry, woolen mills, soap factories, vast pork-packing establishments, tress hoop factories, mattress factories, cigar manufactories, boiler shops, planing-mills, sash, door and blind factories, stave and heading works, harness factories, marble and stone works and so on. But this general description, with such further particulars as are embodied in the following pages devoted to the gentlemen connected with these industries, is all the scope of this work will permit.

John H. Bass, the most distinguished of the men who have built up great manufacturing interests in northern Indiana, is of Kentucky nativity, born at Salem, Livingston county, November 9th, 1835. His father, Sion Bass, was born in North Carolina, November 7th, 1802, and at three years of age removed with his parents to Kentucky. He was a man of great worth, and by occupation a merchant and farmer. After residing in Kentucky until 1866, he came to Fort Wayne, where he died August 7th, 1888. He married Jane Dodd, daughter of John. She was born in Charleston, S. C., June 19th, 1802, and died in Fort Wayne, August 26, 1874. Sion Bass was a son of Jordan Bass, who was born in Virginia in 1764, and died in Christian county, Ky., at eighty-nine years of age. After receiving a thorough academic and business education in Kentucky, John H. Bass removed to Fort Wayne, in 1852, and entered the employment of the firm of Jones, Bass & Co., in 1854, with which he remained until it discontinued business in 1858.

His brother, Sion S. Bass, who came to Fort Wayne in 1848, was a member of this firm and one of the leading business men of this city. At the outbreak of the rebellion, he left his business and assisted in the organization of the famous Thirteenth regiment, which was mustered in September 24th, 1861. Of this regiment, Sion S. Bass was commissioned colonel, and he led the regiment through preliminary movements up to the battle of Shiloh. Arriving on that bloody field the second day of the fight he led his men forward in the face of a terribly destructive fire. In this movement he fell mortally wounded. A more gallant soldier or devoted pariot never lived. John H. Bass, having mastered the manufacturing business at which he had been engaged, became, in 1859, interested in the Fort Wayne machine works, which succeeded the firm with which he had been employed. The stock of this company coming into the hands of Samuel Hanna and Mr. Bass, the partnership of Bass & Hanna became controllers of the business in 1863, the interest of Judge Hanna being transferred to H. H. Hanna. In 1869, through the death of the junior partner, Mr. Bass purchased the entire business, which, under his management has had a wonderful development, and furnishes employment to thousands of men, as well as aiding greatly in the upbuilding of the city. In the same year in which he became sole owner of the plant here, he founded the St. Louis car wheel company, at St. Louis, Mo., of which he has been president and owned a controlling interest since its organization. With confidence that is perhaps unparalleled, he established an extensive foundry in Chicago in addition to his other large investments, in the midst of the panic of 1873, when many were deterred from any new ventures. These latter works are also for the manufacture of car wheels and general railroad work, and have prospered equally with all his other enterprises. The works at Fort Wayne, which are prominent among the manufacturing institutions of this city, are described elsewhere in this work. In 1880 Mr. Bass established a plant for the manufacture of iron in northeastern Alabama, whence iron is shipped to his establishments at Fort Wayne, St. Louis and Chicago. In addition to his manufactories, Mr. Bass has invested heavily in enterprises for the advancement of Fort Wayne. He and Stephen Bond were mainly instrumental in the building of the street railway, and own a controlling interest. He has been for many years a stockholder and director in the First National and Old National banks, and for the past three years has been president of the first named. The famous Brookside farm, adjoining the city limits, is also an outgrowth of his wide-spread enterprise. It is devoted to the importing and breeding of Clydesdale horses and Galloway cattle, and has attained a national reputation. Of the company which manages this farm he is president. The farm embraces more than 300 acres, the property of Mr. Bass, who cultivates about 1,500 acres in Allen county, and owning other large tracts in this county, and many thousand acres in this and other states; notably about 18,000 acres of valuable mineral land in Alabama. Mr. Bass was married in 1865, to Laura, daughter of

Judge Lightfoot, of Falmouth, Ky. They have two children, viz.: Laura Grace and John H., jr. Mr. Bass is, in politics, in favor of tariff reform and has affiliated with the democratic party, to the national convention of which, in 1888, he was a delegate at large. He was nominated as one of the presidential electors in that year. But politics is necessarily subordinated with him, to the tremendous demands of his business. In the splendid development of this he has displayed the rarest executive ability and a brilllant genius for affairs. The fame he has attained however, rests upon him lightly, and he is still a courteous, companionable gentleman to all, and thoroughly occupied with the immediate supervision of his business. The work he has done for his city in promoting its growth will long be remembered. His life work ranks him among those who are the creators of cities.

R. J. Fisher, treasurer of the Bass foundry and machine works, came to Fort Wayne in the spring of 1861, and for about one year was engaged with William H. Brooks, book dealer, and then for two years with Reed & Wall, druggists. He entered the employment of J. H. Bass in 1864, and has ever since remained with him. He was assigned the responsible position of treasurer in 1873, and his fidelity and ability are unquestioned. In politics he is a democrat; is a member of the Masonic order; socially, is highly esteemed, and as a business man occupies a leading position. His father, James R. Fisher, was born in New Jersey in 1802, and was by occupation a furniture dealer. He was married to Henrietta Burnett, and in 1852 removed to Chicago, where his wife died the same year, and he passed away three years later. They had six children, of whom R. J. is the fifth, born at Little Falls, N. Y., September 24, 1845. Mr. Fisher was married October 30, 1866, to Julia M. Holton, a native of Covington, Ky., and they have one child, Laura M. B., now the wife of L. E. Walker, of Los Angeles, Cal.

One of Fort Wayne's enterprising and progressive citizens, Henry William Meyer, has since August, 1886, occupied the responsible position of general foreman of the machine department of the Bass foundry and machine works. He first became engaged in these works in 1866, has become a thoroughly posted, practical and ingenious machinist. After serving as assistant foreman he was promoted to his present place. Mr. Meyer was born in Sylvania, Ohio, October 6, 1850, the son of John M. and Anna M. (Loeffler) Meyer, natives of Bavaria. The father was born July 3, 1823, and died February 11, 1871, in this city, whither he removed with his family in 1858. The mother is living here in her seventieth year. For fourteen years the senior Meyer held the position of section foreman. October 17, 1875, Henry William Meyer married Amelia Buhr. She was born in Fort Wayne, May 5, 1852, and they have three children living: Mamie, Henry and William. A fourth child, Frederick, died November 29, 1886. The family are members of the St. Paul's German Lutheran church, of which Mr. Meyer is one of the trustees. Politically, Mr. Meyer is a pronounced republican.

The foremanship of the core room at the Bass foundry and machine works is intrusted to Diedrich Brandt, a skillful artisan, who though not a native of this country, and having his own way to make in life, has acquired a comfortable home, and become a deservedly popular citizen. He was born in Prussia, September 6, 1850, son of Conrad and Christina (Humke) Brandt. His father, born in the old country, died in 1862, aged sixty-one, and the mother, who was born in 1810, died in her native land in 1855. They had six children, of whom Mr. Brandt was the youngest. He came to Fort Wayne in June, 1867, and having been employed on the farm at home, followed the same occupation in this country for ten months. He then worked two years for Freeman & Rudisill, and entered the employment of J. H. Bass in 1870, where he has since remained, having held the foremanship of the core room for twelve years. He was married in 1879 to Bertha Lohrmann, born in Germany in 1860, and they have four children: Henry, Theodore, Diedrich and Edward. Mr. Brandt and wife are members of the Lutheran church, and he is in politics an active republican.

The foremanship of the cleaning room of the Bass foundry and machine works is held by J. Christopher Matsch, who was born at Kusey, Province Saxony, May 27, 1844. His parents, John Christopher and Dora (Lenz) Matsch, came to the United States in 1854, and settled at Cicero, Ind., afterward coming to Fort Wayne, where the father died in 1874, at the age of sixty-two, and the mother died in 1885. They had three children, now living, of whom the second is Christopher. In the spring of 1858, he entered Concordia college, but after a year and a half study was compelled, by failing sight, to leave school. He then remained upon the farm until 1861, when he entered the employment of A. D. Brandriff, of this city, and afterward that of T. K. Breckenridge in the grocery business, and subsequently was engaged with Conner & Co., merchants. He took a trip during three and a half years, through the west, and upon his return in 1870, served two years as fireman on the Pittsburgh, Fort Wayne & Chicago railroad. Afterward he was with Gillett & Co., and in 1878 became engaged with J. H. Bass, and has since been connected with the works. He was married in 1873, to Sophia Woebbeking, born in Adams county in 1849, and they have three children: Dora, Anna and Emma. They are members of the Zion's Lutheran church.

For ten years the important foremanship of the car wheel department of the Bass foundry and machine works has been in the competent hands of Robert Cran, who is distinguished as an artisan and esteemed as a citizen. He was born in the old city of Quebec, February 14, 1840, the son of Charles and Anna (Madison) Cran. His father was born in England in 1811, the mother in Scotland in 1813. They came to Quebec about 1830. The father now resides at Sandusky, Ohio. Robert Cran was educated in Canada, and at seventeen years of age began at the moulder's trade in Bissel's iron foundry at Quebec. He remained in Canada until 1860, when he came to Fort Wayne. In 1861 he entered the employment of Murry & Benningin, and in 1862, began

Yours Truly
J H Bass

work for J. H. Bass, with whom he has since remained. Mr. Cran was for twenty-two years a member of the Fort Wayne volunteer fire department, and for six years was first assistant chief under Frank Vogel. In May, 1889, the regard and confidence of the community in his worth as a citizen was manifested by his election to the city council from the sixth ward. He is a member of the Presbyterian church. Mrs. Cran, who is a member of the Catholic church, bore the maiden name of Mary Ward. They were married in 1882, and have three children, Anna B., Charles, and Charlotte.

Driving a canal boat on the Wabash & Erie seems to be an occupation belonging to a generation past and gone, but such was the first employment of Jacob J. Stier, who was a boy of twelve years when he began that work, and is now one of the foremen of the Bass foundry and machine works. At fourteen years of age he began learning the moulder's trade with Murray & Bennigan, and in 1866 entered the employment of J. H. Bass, and in the same works has since remained, having been for ten years foreman of the moulding department, and having supervision of eighty men. He was born in this country April 27, 1847, son of Henry and Charlotte (Meyers) Stier, who came to the county at a very early day. He was married in 1876, to Carrie Weaver, who was born in Knox county, Penn., May 16, 1849, and they have six children: Frederick G., Edward, Frank, Joseph, Mary and Anna. Mr. Stier and family are membecs of St. Mary's Catholic church, and he is a Catholic Knight, of branch No. 103. In politics he is a democrat. Mr. Stier is of thorough attainments in his trade, and is esteemed as a citizen.

In 1862 Frank H. Fink entered the employment of J. H. Bass, and has ever since been engaged in the works, ample evidence of his efficiency and value as a skilled mechanic. He has had through life to depend upon his own acquirements, but he has advanced steadily, and is now completing his eighth year as foreman of the moulding department of the Bass foundry and machine works. He was born at Fort Wayne, July 27, 1847, the son of Anthony and Mary (Dahmann) Fink, natives of Germany, who came to this city about 1837. His father died about 1856, and the mother August 4, 1889. This was the second marriage of the mother, and by it she had two children, of whom Frank H. is the youngest. He attended St. Mary's school and commercial college, and obtained a good education. He was married in 1870, to Elizabeth Kartholl, a native of Germany, born in 1848, who was brought to this country in an early day by her father, Joseph Kartholl, who died on the canal boat on the Wabash & Erie canal, this side of Defiance, Ohio, while coming to this city. His body was brought here for burial. Mr. and Mrs. Fink have six children: Caroline, Nora, Mary, Frank, Anthony and Joseph. The family are members of the Catholic church, and Mr. Fink is a Catholic Knight. In politics he is a democrat.

VII

For over thirty years Rudolph Bensman, foreman of the boiler department of the Bass works, has followed the trade of boiler-maker, and in his branch of mechanics and construction, he has few equals in thorough knowledge and practical ability. Mr. Bensman began his trade in 1857, with one McLauchlin, of this city. In 1865 he removed to Norwalk, Ohio, and was there employed ten years in the Lake Shore railroad shops. Upon his return to Fort Wayne in 1875 he entered the employment of the Wabash railroad company, and there remained until 1886, when, in October, he accepted his present position. He was born in Hanover, Germany, November 16, 1843, son of Rudolph Bensman, born in Hanover, in 1804, who married Elizabeth Quint, born in Prussia, in 1807, and removed to Fort Wayne with his family in 1844. He died here in 1867, but his widow survives. They had five children, of whom Rudolph is the youngest but one. He was married in 1865 to Catherine Loran, who was born in France in 1848, and they have five children: William, born in August, 1870; Alice, November, 1880; Mamie May, 1883; Florence, December, 1885, and Gertrude, October, 1888. Mr. Bensman and family are members of the Catholic church, and politically he is a democrat.

In the year 1875 Frederick C. Meyers first became employed at the J. H. Bass works, and has since been one of the trusted men in that great establishment. During the past two years he has been one of the foremen of the moulding department. Mr. Meyers was born in Prussia, May 22, 1857, the son of Frederick and Louis (Dammier) Meyers, both natives of Germany, who now reside in Fort Wayne. They came here with their family in 1872. Frederick was the second born of their five living children, and received his education in the old country. In 1877 he was married to Mary Kirkel, who was born in this city in 1853, and died in 1883, leaving three children: Katie, Charles and Minnie. In 1884 Mr. Meyers was married to Cassie Beierline, who was born in Germany and came to this country when five years old. They have one child, Frederick. Mr. Meyers and wife are members of the Lutheran church, and he is politically, of the democratic faith. He is a worthy and highly esteemed young man, and in his line of activity has a bright future.

N. G. Olds & Sons. — This famous manufacturing establishment was founded in 1861 by Noble G. Olds, who began that year his residence in Fort Wayne, which continued until his death in April, 1876. He was born at Bedford Springs, Penn., in January, 1818, son of Daniel Olds, a native of Pennsylvania, who died in New York at about the eightieth year of his age. The boy, Noble, having removed to the latter state with his parents, began work in a saw-mill, and then turned his attention successively to carpentry and cabinet-making and machine pattern making. In 1848 he removed to Sandusky, Ohio, and the next year became master mechanic of an agricultural establishment. Afterward he established machine works, but sold out, and in 1853 went to Buffalo, N. Y., where he was for one year master mechanic of the Eagle Iron works. His next enterprise was at Sandusky, Ohio, where in 1854 he established the N. G. Olds machine works. In 1859 and 1860 the firm of Olds & Occobach & Co. was formed, to conduct the Sandusky wheel works, but he remained in that city only until 1861. Mr. Olds was in politics a whig and subsequently a republican; was a member of the Baptist church. As an artisan and designer he had remarkable talent, to which were added an executive and business ability of a rare order. In 1838 Mr. Olds was married to Elizabeth Woolsey, who was born in New York in 1815, and died in 1872. They had five children: Henry G., born in 1839; Charles V., 1841, who was drowned accidentally in the winter of 1849-'50; John D., born September 5, 1843; Jay V., 1849, and Charles L., 1855. After the death of Mr. Olds, sr., the business was conducted as a partnership until 1882, when the firm was incorporated as N. G. Olds & Sons, with a capital stock of $400,000, the officers being Henry G. Olds, president; John D. Olds, vice president; Joseph Henry Wilder, secretary; Thomas C. Rogers, treasurer, and so continues. The establishment covers an area of ten acres, is composed of a series of brick and wooden buildings and sheds of large capacity, is supplied with steam power aggregating 600 horse-power, and gives employment to a large force of skillful workmen. It is probably the most complete establishment of the kind in the world, and its output is unrivaled in quantity, and of such excellence that it is in great demand not only throughout this continent, but is also exported to South America, Europe and Australia. John D. Olds, vice president, was born at Syracuse, N. Y., and has been a member of the manufacturing organization since the formation of the old firm in 1873. In 1863 he enlisted in Company C, Seventy-fourth Indiana volunteers, and served three months. He was married in 1866 to Allie C. McLaine, who was born in Knox county, Ohio, in 1843, and they have three children: Egbert C., born 1868; Charles M., August, 1870, and Hugh B., 1878. He and wife are members of the Presbyterian church. In politics he is a republican. In 1868 he became a Mason, of Home lodge, No. 342, and in 1888 became a member of the Scottish Rite, Mystic Shrine and a Knight Templar. He has added to the value of the product of the company by the invention of the Olds compound band hub.

Joseph H. Wilder, above named as secretary of N. G. Olds & Sons, is a native of Holliston, Mass., born in the year 1844, son of Joseph and Sarah (Bruce) Wilder, both natives of that state. Ebenezer Wilder, father of Joseph, lived at Lancaster, Mass., to a great age, and the latter is still living at Holliston, having been a citizen of that place for seventy-five years. His wife died at their home about 1852, when their son Joseph was eight years old. The family is of English descent, the American ancestor having immigrated in the last century. Joseph H. Wilder is the only living descendant of his parents. He received a good common school education and was for three years a student at the Phillips academy at Exeter, N. H. In 1860 he came to Fort Wayne, and in 1863, entered the employment of N. G. Olds & Sons. Upon the incorporation he became a member of the company, and his career in this connection has made him conspicuous as a business man. In politics he is an ardent republican. Mr. Wilder was married in 1867 to Jennie Leland, a native of Massachusetts, born at Holliston, daughter of Alden Leland, and they have one child, Constance.

Ferdinand F. Boltz was born at Saarbruck, Rhenish Prussia, October 26, 1839. His father was a prosperous hotel keeper, of a family which had been in Saarbruck for four generations, though of Bohemian origin. His father's mother was Savnia Lucas, of St. Avold, Lorraine. His mother was Louise Best, daughter of Henry Best, a native of the Palatinate, and a baker, whose failure in business involved the father of Mr. Boltz. Her mother's maiden name was Neizer, and she was a native of Saarbruck. Immediately after this misfortune the father, in the spring of 1848, emigrated, and reaching Fort Wayne in the fall of that year, found employment at his trade of cabinet-maker, and sent for his family. In October, 1849, Ferdinand F. Boltz, and his mother, sisters, Louise, Caroline and Amelia, and brothers, Gus. J., and Fred. C., reached Fort Wayne. Here the family became prosperous and highly esteemed. The father was born November 9, 1809, and is still living, but the mother died in 1874. Ferdinand F. attended school, to learn the language, and then for several years found employment at the home of Thomas Hamilton. At the age of fourteen he became clerk at the store of William Jacobs, and until 1857, was in his employ or in that of John Hamilton, and in the latter year became engaged with James H. Robinson, then manufacturing boots and shoes. At the first call for volunteers for the defense of the Union, Mr. Boltz was ready to serve his country, and his name was the first on the roll of a company raised for three months' service, but which was accepted by Gov. Morton as Company G, Twelfth regiment, and mustered into service, May 11, 1861, with William H. Link as captain. Mr. Boltz was mustered in as first sergeant. The regiment served first in southern Indiana, and after the first battle of Bull Run, in July, 1861, the command joined the division of Banks at Harper's Ferry. Mr. Boltz soon proved himself a soldier of rare merit, and when the time of enlistment of the regiment expired, he was mustered out in May 1862, as sergeant-major of the regiment, a rank to which he had been promoted in the previous August. In August, 1862, under President Lincoln's call for " 300,000 more," the Eighty-eighth regiment Indiana volunteers was organized, and Mr. Boltz, who had been out of the service but a short time, enlisted in this regiment as second lieutenant of Company F, under Capt. Lefevre. As a part of Gen. Lytle's brigade, the regiment had its first battle at Perryville, Ky., October 8, 1862, and lost heavily, though somewhat sheltered by its position. The soldierly conduct of Lieut. Boltz led to his promotion in January, 1862, to first lieutenant, and in December, 1862, he became acting adjutant of the regiment, a position he filled during the battle of Stone River. His regiment was engaged here on December 31, 1862, and January 1, 2 and 3, 1863, and made the last charge, and fired the first volley from the Union lines on that bloody field. Lieut. Boltz commanded his company during the Tullahoma campaign, and in August, 1863, again assumed the adjutantcy of the regiment, serving in that position during the Chickamauga campaign and siege of Chattanooga. Lieut. Boltz was injured at the battle of Stone River by the falling of his horse, and after being promoted captain of his company to succeed Isaac Lefevre, killed at Chickamauga, he was not able to assume command until the Atlanta campaign. In this he served bravely until wounded August 7, 1864, at the battle of Eutaw Springs. Rejoining his command October 1, 1864, he participated in the pursuit of Hood as far as the Tennessee line, and then returned to Atlanta, whence he moved with his regiment with Sherman to the sea, and from Savannah to Goldsboro, N. C. The regiment took a prominent part in the battles of Averysboro and Bentonville. The latter engagement, it was the fortune of Capt. Boltz to open, and being unexpectedly thrown into a situation of great responsibility, he displayed qualities of the best soldiership. On the morning of the battle he had been specially detailed by orders from division headquarters to select a picked detail and take the advance, and go to Goldsboro if he could, Gen. Sherman not believing that Gen. Johnston was near. Capt. Boltz had no hopes of getting through, but declaring that he would try, he moved out on the morning of March 19, with seventy good men. Six miles out they found several hundred foragers gathered, who revealed the presence of the "Johnnies." Deploying as skirmishers, Capt. Boltz's men advanced and were immediately under fire; but drove back the enemy's advance and discovered heavy columns moving up to attack the army of Sherman. Boltz fell back to a narrow belt of timber, and continuing firing, sent a messenger back to warn Gen. Hobart to prepare for battle. In a short time the first division came up, and the battle was begun. Capt. Boltz's courage and promptness in attacking the enemy, gave the Fourteenth corps time to prepare for action, and he received the personal thanks of Gen. Hobart for saving the corps. The military career of Capt. Boltz, so full of honorable deeds, came to a close June 7, 1865, when he was honorably mustered out. He then engaged in the retail grocery business, at Fort Wayne, in which, however, he did not succed, and in April, 1875, he became cashier of the Empire line. Since February, 1880, he has been timber purchasing agent of the firm of N. G. Olds & Sons. Capt. Boltz is a past commander of Sion S. Bass post, G. A. R. He was made a Mason in Perseverance military lodge, No. 1, at Sharpsburg, Va., in 1862, and is now pastmaster of Home lodge, 342, is a member of Fort Wayne chapter, No. 19, is past eminent commander of Fort Wayne commandery No. 4, K. T., is a member of Fort Wayne council, No. 4, lodge of Perfection, No. 2, and Indiana consistory, and of the Murat Temple, No. 1, Indianapolis. He was married September 4, 1864, to Cornelia A. Sowers, daughter of Samuel and Mercy J. Sowers. Mr. Sowers was one of the pioneers of this county in 1834. Capt. Boltz is a republican in politics, and a leading citizen of the city.

For twenty-three years Charles Cartwright has held the position of lumber agent for N. G. Olds & Sons. He was born in Miami county, Ohio, April 24, 1825, the son of Charles and Elizabeth (Paxton) Cartwright, who were born and married in Rockbridge county, Va. About 1819 they emigrated to Greene county, Ohio, and later to Miami county, where the father who was a farmer lived until 1832; his wife survived him until 1846, when she died in Mercer county, Ohio. At sixteen Mr. Cartwright began to learn the tailor's trade, which he followed about twenty-six years, excepting from June 2, to August 7, 1846, during which time he served in the Mexican war, in Company B, First Ohio regiment. His service was cut short by sickness. Prior to this he had worked at Piqua, Dayton, Union, Ohio, Malden, W. Va., and then in Xenia, Ohio. From the war he returned to Ohio, and until 1853 resided at Union and Covington, and in March, 1866, he came to Fort Wayne, and has ever since been employed as lumber agent with the firm of N. G. Olds & Sons. His long engagement is evidence of his steadiness of character and of the value of his services to the prominent firm which he represents. Mr. Cartwright was married November 10, 1848, to Mary, daughter of John Sinks, then of Union, Ohio. Mrs. Cartwright was born in Miami county, Ohio, May 22, 1831. They have had seven children: John C., Jeremiah L., Frank P., Edward A., Burty E., Maud M. and Charles, all of whom are living except John C., who was a conductor on the Pittsburgh railway and was killed on duty, July 12, 1876, at the age of nearly twenty-seven years. Politically Mr. Cartwright has been a life long democrat. He has led a strictly temperate life, having entirely abstained from intoxicants and tobacco.

The superintendency of the N. G. Olds & Sons' wheel works has been entrusted since 1884 with Victor A. Sallot, a careful and accurate business man, who thoroughly fills that position. He was born in France, August 27, 1844. His father, born in France, in 1809, married Josephine Julian, who was born in 1811, and in 1841 they came direct to this city. The father is by occupation a carpenter and cooper, and he purchased the first lots in what is now known as "Frenchtown." Victor A. is the youngest of two children. In 1868 he engaged in the manufacture of sash and doors, and in 1870 the factory was converted to the manufacture of furniture. This business was continued until 1872, when the factory was destroyed by fire. In 1873 Mr. Sallot became associated with Barney O'Connor in cutting out dimensions stuff and shipping the same, which business Mr. Sallot subsequently became sole proprietor of and continued until 1878. He then entered the employment of Boseker & White, in their wheel works, and remained with that firm nearly six years, three years of the time as superintendent, until January, 1884. Mr. Sallot is in politics a democrat, and is a member of the Catholic church. He was married in 1881 to Agnes Baker, who was born in Fort Wayne in 1854, and they have five sons: Remedius, Joachim, Hubert, Stephen and Barnard.

The foreman of the rimming department of the Olds wheel works,

Hiram B. Woolsey, was born in Jordan, N. Y., December 25, 1840. His father, Luther L. Woolsey, born in New York in 1799, the son of Luther L. Woolsey, who lived in New York to the age of ninety-nine years. Luther L. Woolsey died in his native state in 1841, and his wife, whose maiden name was Keturah Bloomer, died in Fort Wayne in 1882, at the age of eighty. Ten of their childeen are living, Hiram being the youngest. When he was twelve years old he went to Sandusky, Ohio, and lived there some time with his brother John, receiving his education at that city. When seventeen years old he returned to New York and enlisted at Syracuse, in Company G, One Hundred and Twenty-second New York regiment. He served for three years, was wounded at Gettysburg and Petersburg, and was honoralby discharged in July, 1864. In the following month he came to Fort Wayne, and began his engagement with N. G. Olds & Sons, which has ever since continued, with the exception of three years he has served during that long period as foreman, a fact which speaks eloquently of his faithfulness and worth as a man and as a mechanic. He was married in 1873, to Ella A. Dresser, who was born at Hillsdale, Mich., in 1849. They have two children, Jay and May. In politics Mr. Woolsey is a republican; he is a Mason, a comrade of the G. A. R., and a member of the Baptist church.

In the month of February, 1865, Washington McNamara, now a popular and worthy citizen of Fort Wayne, entered the employment of N. G. Olds & Sons, and with the exception of two years, he has been connected with the wheel works ever since. For eleven years he has been a foreman, now having in charge the yards and drying department, and he has the good will of all with whom he is associated. Mr. McNamara was born at Mt. Vernon, Ohio, April 12, 1849. His parents, William and Susan (Porter) McNamara, were born in Maryland, the father in 1805, the mother in 1811. The family removed to Indiana in 1855, settled first in Huntington county, and came to Fort Wayne in 1864. The father died in this city in 1868. Seven of their children are living, Washington McNamara being the fifth born of these. He was married October 28, 1885, to Laura Lindsley, who was born September 28, 1864, at Attica, Ind. Mr. McNamara is a member of the I. O. O. F., Fort Wayne lodge, and politically is a democrat.

The foreman of the polishing department at the establishment of N. G. Olds & Sons is Matthias Cramer. He was born in Germany, December 4, 1844, son of Matthias and Barbara (Doppen) Cramer, natives of Germany. The mother died in her native land in 1846, and the father died in Fort Wayne in 1869. Their son Matthias came to Fort Wayne from Germany in 1856. When the war broke out, though only a boy in years, he gallantly enlisted in the cause of his adopted country, August 18, 1861, in Company E., Thirtieth regiment Indiana volunteers, and participated in the battle of Shiloh where he was shot through the head, and on account of his injury was discharged in July, 1862. But he re-enlisted in the following September in Company K, One Hundredth Indiana and served until the close of the war, being commissioned first lieutenant. He was honorably discharged June 29, 1865. During his second enlistment he participated in the battles of Vicksburg, Black River, Jackson, Chattanooga, Resaca, Dallas, Kenesaw Mount, Atlanta, and others, and was with Sherman in his march to the sea. On his return to Fort Wayne he entered the employment of Olds & Sons, and has been with them ever since excepting nine years spent in slate roofing. He is a member of the G. A. R., George Humphrey post, of the Catholic church, and is highly esteemed. Mr. Cramer was married in 1868 to Augusta Miller, a native of France, and they have eight children: Mary, Maggie, Rosa, Elizabeth, Anna, Trácy, Mathia and Cecilia.

One of the boy soldiers of the war of the rebellion, Robert G. Renfrew, enlisted at the age of fifteen, in Company B, Twenty-first Pennsylvania cavalry, and served faithfully during the various severe battles of the army of the Potomac which followed until the close of the war, receiving an honorable discharge, July 17, 1865. In the same month he came to Fort Wayne, and for two years engaged in farming. In 1868 he entered the employment of N. G. Olds & Sons, and has been connected with the works of that firm until the present, with the exception of one year. Twelve years ago he was appointed foreman of the fitting department, the position he now holds. Mr. Renfrew was born at Fayetteville, Penn., March 9, 1848, son of Rea K. and Maria (Bohn) Renfrew, of whose children three others are living. He was married in 1872 to Sarah A. Fox, who was born in Lancaster, Penn., in 1847. She is a member of the Baptist church. Mr. Renfrew is a republican in politics, is a member of Fort Wayne lodge, No. 14, I. O. O. F., a comrade of George Humphrey post, No. 530, and is honored and esteemed as a citizen.

Since 1880 Frank W. Dunham has filled with credit to his skilfulness and business ability, the active and important place of foreman of the spoke turning department of the N. G. Olds & Sons wheel works. He was born at Lucas, Richland county, Ohio, January 28, 1856, the son of James and Frances Dunham. His father, a native of Delaware, was a soldier in the One Hundred and Twentieth Ohio regiment, and died in hospital at St. Louis in 1863. Seven children of these parents are living, of whom Frank W. was the fourth born. A few years after the death of his father his mother died. Mr. Dunham remained on the farm for five years afterward, and then, in 1873, came to Fort Wayne, and found employment in White's wheel works, where he remained four years. He entered the employment of the Olds company in 1879, and his marked ability soon caused his promotion to the foremanship he now holds. Mr. Dunham is well known and popular in the community. He and wife are members of the Berry Street Methodist Episcopal church; he is a member of Phœnix lodge, No. 101, K. of P., and politically he ranks with the republican party. Mr. Dunham was married in 1880, to Jennie Dunfee, who was born at Columbia City, in 1862. They have three children: Charles H., Albert E., and an infant child unnamed.

James A. Graham, general foreman of the car shops of the western division of the P., Ft. W. & C. railroad, at Fort Wayne, was born in Alleghany county, Penn., December 25, 1856. His father, John Graham, was born in the north of Ireland in 1825; emigrated to the United States in 1847, and settled in Alleghany county, where he died February 3, 1889. By occupation he was an engineer in the P., Ft. W. & C. shops, at Alleghany City. The mother of Mr. Graham was Martha (McAleer) Graham, who was born in Ireland in 1827; immigrated in 1847, and now lives in Alleghany city. James A. was reared in Alleghany City, and received his education at the public schools of that place. At thirteen years of age he extered the employ of Elliott & Burges, nurserymen of Alleghany City, where he remained about two years, and then entered the employ of James Calwell; becoming an errand boy, he was promoted to a clerkship. But he became dissatisfied with the life and prospects of dry goods salesman, and determined to learn a trade, and accordingly he entered the car shops of the P., Ft. W. & C. railway at Alleghany City as an apprentice, April 2, 1872. He attended drawing-school during evenings, and faithfully applying himself, advanced until 1884, he was given charge of all passenger car repairs in the Alleghany City shops, and continued in that capacity until September, 1886, when he was transferred to Fort Wayne and given the general foremanship of the car shops in this city. All the different departments, including the east yard shops, are under Mr. Graham's supervision, and the extent of his responsibility and the scope of his duties, will be readily understood when it is known that he has under him no less than half a dozen assistant foremen. In the spring of 1888 Mr. Graham realized the necessity of his company having a different draw gear or draft rigging for freight cars, and at once began experimenting in that direction. In July following he succeeded in inventing a device, of which he made a full-size model, and submitted it to Messrs. J. Wood, then superintendent of motive power, F. D. Cassanave, then master mechanic, and G. L. Potter, then assistant master mechanic, who examined the invention, approved it, and gave Mr. Graham permission to equip ten new freight cars with his draw rigging, and the same proving successful, it was adapted for all cars on the Pennsylvania lines. On September 8, 1888, Mr. Graham filed an application for a patent of his device, and on May 7, 1889, was awarded a patent for the same in the United States. It is no doubt the most valuable draw gear ever invented for durability and cheapness. Mr. Graham is a member of the Fort Wayne lodge, No. 25, F. & A. M., and of the royal arcanum. He was married in November, 1875, at Alleghany City, Penn., to Miss Ella McNurtney, of Little Washington, Penn., and to them two daughters have been born: Martha B. and Minnie A. Mr. and Mrs. Graham are members of the Methodist church.

Bernard Fitzpatrick, general foreman of the machine and erecting shops of the western division of the P., Ft. W. & C. R. R. company, was born at Lancaster City, Penn., August 7, 1850, the son of Bernard and Margaret (Dougherty) Fitzpatrick, the former of whom was born in Ireland and the latter at Philadelphia. The parents removed to Lancaster City in 1845, where they resided the rest of their lives. The father became a prominent citizen and held numerous municipal positions, including that of alderman, for several years. His death occurred in 1872, at the age of fifty-five years, his wife having died in 1857 at the age of thirty-five years. They were both members of the Catholic church. Four sons and one daughter were born, four of whom survive. Bernard Fitzpatrick was reared in Lancaster City and educated in the common schools. In 1867 he began an apprenticeship as machinist in E. S. Norris & Co.'s locomotive works, and after serving four years, in 1871 he entered the Baldwin locomotive works in Philadelphia, where he remained one year, and then went to Altoona. After working at the latter place, he returned to Lancaster on account of the illness of his father, and remained there until after his father's death. In 1872 he worked at Scranton in the D., L. & W. R'y shops. Six months later at Wilksbarre, in the Lehigh & Susquehanna R. R. shops, where he was promoted to gang boss in the above shops under L. C. Braston, master mechanic. He was next with the Lehigh Valley company as machinist, then returned to Altoona, and next went to Zelinople, Penn., on the Pittsburgh & Western, being foreman of the shops at that point for one year. In January, 1882, Mr. Fitzpatrick came to Fort Wayne and entered the P., Ft. W. & C. R. R. shops as a machinist, but a month later was appointed assistant foreman of the round-house, in which capacity he served five months, and on June 1, 1882, he was promoted to his present position. Mr. Fitzpatrick is a member of the Catholic Cathedral and of St. John's Commandery Catholic Legion. Mr. Fitzpatrick was married December 23, 1873, to Louisa Miller, of Baltimore, Md., who was born in that city in 1853. To this union three children have been born: Harry, Willie and May.

Abel Fisher, lumber inspector and foreman of the lumber yards of the P., Ft. W. & C. Ry. at Fort Wayne, was born in Lawrence county, Penn., on March 29, 1844. He is the son of Abel Fisher, born in the same county, whose father was John Fisher, an officer in the war of 1812, and one of the pioneers of Lawrence county, Penn. His wife was a sister to Bishop Roberts, the pioneer Methodist who was bishop of what was then known as the Erie conference, numbering all the Methodist Episcopal churches west of the Alleghany mountains. The mother of the subject of this mention was Polly Gibson, whose father was a native of Pennsylvania and a pioneer of Lawrence county. Abel Fisher, sr., now over seventy years of age, is a resident of Iola, Kan., where he owns and manages a hotel. He also conducts a hotel at Victoria, Kan. His wife died in 1858. Abel Fisher, jr., was reared on a farm in Lawrence county, Penn., and after obtaining a common school education, he learned the miller's trade, and worked at the same until at the age of seventeen years and three months. In July, 1861, he enlisted in Company G, of the Sixty-second Pennsylvania regiment of volunteer infantry, as a private. He served three years, and was discharged at the expiration of his time at Pittsburgh, July 4, 1864. He was wounded in the right wrist at the battle of Gaines' Mill on the Peninsula. Returning to Pennsylvania, he finished his trade and worked at it in Lawrence county until 1869, when he came to Fort Wayne. He was engaged with the railroad company as foreman of the lumber yards, and three months later was made inspector. Mr. Fisher was married in 1869 to Jennie Waddington, of Fort Wayne, who was born in Crestline, Ohio. To them three children have been born: Maude M., wife of E. J. Pirson, of Columbus, Ohio, Walter B. and William.

Andrew Weber, a well-known and valued citizen of Fort Wayne, has been chief pattern maker on the western division of the Pittsburgh, Fort Wayne & Chicago railroad company, since May 2, 1860. He was born in Hesse-Darmstadt, Germany, July 23, 1828, and in his native land learned cabinet and pattern making. In May, 1851, he left his native country and came to New York city, where he worked four years, and then came to Fort Wayne, where he was engaged by Bowser & Story as pattern maker. He began his engagement with the Pittsburgh railroad company as above stated, as foreman of the pattern department, and is the second oldest foreman in the Fort Wayne shops. While at New York Mr. Weber learned mechanical drawing with Commissioner Albert Fink, who is also a native of Hesse-Darmstadt. Mr. Weber was married August 2, 1853, to Anna Guentzer, who was born on the river Rhine, Germany, in 1835. To them one son has been born, Carl Weber, druggist, of Fort Wayne. Mr. Weber is a member of the Catholic church, and for thirty-four years has been the leader of the Cathedral choir. His voice is one of rare compass, two and a fourth octaves, and there are few voices of that range in the country.

William Stephan, chief draftsman of the Pennsylvania company, was born at Saxonia town, Mittweida, Germany, August 4, 1848. He was educated in his native town and attended the Technicum, learning mechanical engineering, in which he graduated in 1868. He followed his profession for one year, and then entered the army and served in the infantry from 1869 to the fall of 1871, participating in the Franco-Prussian campaigns. July 20, 1872, he reached the United States, and coming directly to Fort Wayne, entered Bass foundry as pattern maker, where he remained a year and a half. He then spent about one year at New Haven, and afterward returned to Fort Wayne and entered the employment of the Kerr Murray manufacturing company, in the pattern department, where he remained four years. In 1878 he was engaged by the Pennsylvania company as mechanical draftsman, and worked in that capacity for six years. In 1883 he was appointed chief draftsman for the Pennsylvania company. Mr. Stephan is a member of Home lodge, F. & A. M. He was married in Germany in 1871, to Emeline Baatz, and six children have been born, of whom five are living: Emeline, William, Lina, Charles and Adolph.

Robert H. Harrison, a well known citizen of Fort Wayne, and foreman of the car machine shops of the P., Ft. W. & Chicago railway, was born in Ireland, January 1, 1834. He is the son of Richard Harrison, a native of Ireland, who was the son of John Harrison, who was born in Lancashire, England, but removed to Ireland and spent the remainder of his life. He was an extensive manufacturer of linen and was possessed of large capital. Richard Harrison married Eliza Hamilton, who was the daughter of Glover Hamilton, a titled Scotchman, and her mother was the daughter of George Laird, also a member of the Scotch nobility. These parents immigrated to Toronto, Canada, where they lived until death. Their son, Robert H., was given a good education in the public schools of Toronto, and at the age of seventeen years, he set in to become a machinest in the Toronto locomotive works. In 1854 he removed to Philadelphia, Penn., and about 1858, to Pittsburgh, coming in 1859 to Fort Wayne. He was in the employment of the Pennsylvania railroad company, at Pittsburgh, and he came here in that service. In April, 1861, Mr. Harrison answered the call for ninety days volunteers, and enlisted in Company E, of the Ninth regiment Indiana volunteer infantry, as first sergeant. He also served one year in an Illinois regiment, and was then forced to leave the service by sickness. Returning to Fort Wayne he re-entered the Pennsylvania machine shops, where he has since continued. He was made foreman of the car machine shops in 1872. Mr. Harrison is a member, and has been for twenty years, of Harmony lodge, No. 19, I. O. O. F., and is also a member of Home lodge, F. & A. M. He is a member of the Episcopal church. Mr. Harrison was married in 1865 to Louisa Wittie, of Fort Wayne, who was born in Boston, Mass., in 1839, of German parents. To their union six children have been born: Grace Hamilton, Glover Benjamin, Viola Louisa, George Arthur, Ida May, and Bertha Eliza. In March, 1888, Mr. Harrison received a handsome legacy from the estate of his brother, who died at Toronto.

William Knight, foreman of the east yard car shops of the west division of the P., Ft. W. & C. R. R. company, at Fort Wayne, was born at Croydon, Surry county, England, November 4, 1832, and came to America in April, 1854. Landing at New York city, he remained in that state for a while, and in 1856 came west and located in Fort Wayne. He learned the trade of cabinet making in England, but on coming to Fort Wayne he spent six months in bridge building on P., Ft. W. & C. road. In the winter of 1856 he entered the employ of Jones, Bass & Co. as car builder, and in 1857 he entered the service of the P., Ft. W. & C. R. R. Co., in the same capacity. In 1879 he went to work in the shops of the Fort Wayne, Cincinnati & Louisville R. R. Co., as foreman, and remained there nearly five years. Returning to the P., Ft. W. & C. R. R. Co., on July 1, 1885, he was appointed foreman of the east yard car shops, a position he has since held. He was married in February, 1854, to Eliza Jenner, of Leatherhead, England, and to their union eight children have been born, five of whom survive, and four of whom are married. Mr. Knight is a Mason, member of Summit City lodge, No. 70, chapter No. 19, council No. 4, commandery No. 4, K. T., and consistory S. R. He and family are members of the Episcopal church.

James C. Hewes, foreman of the boiler shops of the Pittsburgh railroad company, was born in Delaware county, Penn., January 26, 1822, the son of Samuel and Margaret (McCullogh) Hewes, both natives of Pennsylvania. The father died about 1860, and the mother four years later. James C. Hewes removed with his parents to Philadelphia when he was about fifteen years old, and after receiving a good education he was taught the trade of boiler-making in that city. Subsequently he removed to Reading, and there remained eleven years. In 1855 he entered the employment of the Pennsylvania company at Altoona, as assistant foreman and was sent to Pittsburgh in 1861 to take charge of the boiler shops of the company there. Coming to Fort Wayne in September, 1864, he took charge of the boiler shops of the company here, a position he has since held, creditably filling a place of much importance. His engagement with the Pennsylvania company has existed now for thirty-five years. Mr. Hewes married at Reading in 1848, to Julia John, a native of that city, born in 1826. To their union three children have been born. A son is deceased and there survive, Ella, wife of William Cherry, of this city; Jennie, wife of John Piper, of Altoona. Mr. Hewes is a member of the Presbyterian church, is a republican, and is a member of Summit City lodge, F. & A. M., and for forty years has been a member of the I. O. O. F., now of Montgomery lodge, No. 59, Reading.

G. H. Judy, foreman of the blacksmith shop of the Pittsburgh, Fort Wayne & Chicago railroad company, was born at Point of Rocks, Frederick county, Md., February 11, 1847. He is the son of Thomas L. and Susan (Garrott) Judy, both natives of Maryland. The father, who was a blacksmith by trade, having been retired from service, came to Fort Wayne in June, 1888, and died here in the following January, at the age of seventy years. His widow survives at the age of sixty years. Their son, G. H., was reared at Cumberland City, Md., and in 1865 entered the employment of the Baltimore & Ohio railroad company at that place. Two years he was engaged with the Cumberland & Pennsylvania company at Mount Savage, Md., and remained there until 1870, when he returned to the B. & O., and was foreman of the blacksmith shops of that company, at the rolling mill department, until 1877, when he again entered the employment of the Pennsylvania company at Altoona, Penn., working until 1880 as forger. In 1880 he removed to Huntingdon, Penn., and took charge of the blacksmith shops of the Huntingdon car and car-wheel works until 1883, when he came to Fort Wayne. He was at first engaged in the Pittsburgh shops here as forger, and received his appointment as foreman in September, 1884. This he has since held to the entire satisfaction of the company and is popular with all. He is a member of the Kekionga council, No. 93, National Union, is a republican in politics, and he and wife are members of the

United Brethren church. He was married in 1868 to Emma Myers, of Cumberland City, Md., who died in 1880, at Altoona, Penn., at the age of twenty-nine years, leaving two sons, David L. and L. W., who are now in the Pittsburgh railroad shops, one in the blacksmith and one in the car department.

Thomas J. Rodabaugh, foreman of the paint shop of the Pittsburgh, Fort Wayne & Chicago railroad company, is one of the veteran railroad men of the city, having been first connected with the work of the railroad with which he is now employed, in 1850, grading the road bed in Ohio. After the track was laid he was engaged in repair work on the section between Louisville and Canton, Ohio, until the spring of 1855. Mr. Rodabaugh was born in Summit county, Ohio, October 9, 1835. He is the son of Adam Rodabaugh, born near Harrisburg, Penn., who was a miller by trade and in early life removed to Lorain county, Ohio, and thence to Summit county, and finally to Stark county, where he died in 1887 at the age of eighty years and over. His wife, Mary Heath, was born in New Hampshire, and died in 1843, at the age of thirty-five years. Their son, Thomas J., was reared on a farm to his twelfth year and was then in a store with his father until he began work at railroading. On June 5, 1855, he came to Fort Wayne in a stock car, and then went to New Haven and engaged in tracklaying on the Wabash railroad between that place and Defiance. In the following August he returned to Fort Wayne and was engaged with J. J. Kammer in learning the painter's trade. Eight months later he found employment at his trade in the Wabash shops, where he remained until June 20, 1860, when he entered the employment in the same capacity of the Pittsburgh, Fort Wayne & Chicago company, with which corporation he has since remained. March 11, 1868, he was made foreman of the paint shops, a position he has held for over twenty years. Mr. Rodabaugh was a volunteer fireman in Fort Wayne for sixteen years and eight months, and was in active duty during all that time. He was foreman of Vigilant company, No. 2, for eight years, first assistant of Mechanic company, the first company, for three years, and was acting chief engineer for a short time. In politics he was a democrat and voted for James Buchanan first, but in 1860 became a republican. He became an Odd Fellow in 1858, and has since been a member of Fort Wayne lodge, No. 14, and has since 1864 been a member of Wayne lodge, No. 25, F. & A. M. Of both of these fraternities he has acted as deputy to the grand lodges of the state. He was married in 1857 to Elizabeth J. Snyder, of Fort Wayne, who was born at Canal Dover, Ohio, in 1841. They are members of the Congregational church.

In 1879 Alonzo L. Woodworth came to Fort Wayne and took a position as tool dresser in the blacksmith department of the Pittsburgh, Fort Wayne & Chicago railroad shops, and in the fall of 1884 he was promoted assistant foreman of the department. Mr. Woodworth was born near Boston, Mass., July 16, 1847, the son of John Woodworth and wife, whose maiden name was Stearns. They came to Indiana in 1852 and settled near Kendallville, where the mother died in 1861. The father came to this city in 1879, and is now living, in his eighty-first year, with his son Alonzo. The latter had hardly reached his fourteenth birthday when he enlisted (1861) in Company C, Forty-fourth regiment Indiana volunteers, as a private. He served bravely throughout the war, being wounded at Chickamauga in the lower jaw, a hurt which disabled him for nine month. He was honorably discharged at Chattanooga in September, 1865, and then came to Fort Wayne and learned the blacksmith's trade at the shops of Murray & Bennigan, remaining there three years. For four years he was employed at Bass's foundry, and then went to Logansport, where he attended Hall's commercial college. After five years at Logansport and one at Terre Haute, he spent a year in travel through the west, before engaging with the railroad company as above stated. Mr. Woodworth is a member of Summit City lodge, No. 170, F. & A. M.; of Kekionga lodge, No. 93, National Union; he is a Baptist, and in politics, republican. Mr. Woodworth was married to Annie Holmes, of Maples, Ind., who died in 1872 at the age of twenty-four, leaving one son. In 1875 he was married to Rosa Bennett of this city. Mr. Woodworth is the father of these children: John, born in 1872; Margery, 1877; Frank, 1886; Newton, 1888.

An esteemed and worthy citizen of Fort Wayne, Louis Buckwalter, is a native of the city of Philadelphia, born October 18, 1831. He is the son of Jacob and Mary (Thomas) Buckwalter, the former of whom was born near Phœnixville, Penn., where his ancestors settled on emigrating to this country from Switzerland, in 1749. At sixteen Louis began the trade of a machinist and served an apprenticeship of five years in the Baldwin locomotive works of Philadelphia, where he remained until 1860. In that year he came to Fort Wayne, and he has ever since been employed as a machinist in the Pittsburgh, Fort Wayne & Chicago railway shops. At no time during this long period has he been off duty more than a month at a time. For several years past he has been an assistant foreman. Mr. Buckwalter was married February 21, 1866, to Mary E. Houenstein, a native of Fort Wayne, and they have had four children: Mary E., Charles H., Clara H. and Mathilde A., of whom the second died in infancy. In politics Mr. Buckwalter has been a republican since 1856. He is a skillful mechanic, and a first class citizen.

One of the skillful machinists who find occupation in the shops of the Pittsburgh, Fort Wayne & Chicago railroad company, is John R. Bitner, who first engaged in that employment in March, 1869. He is the son of Andrew J. Bitner, who was born in Center county, Penn., December 18, 1816, and at the age of ten was taken by his widowed mother to Holmes county, Ohio. June 8, 1846, Andrew Bitner was married to Eliza Nabe, who was born in Franklin county, Penn., July 8, 1827, and had removed to Holmes county with her grandparents in 1836. At Gallion, Ohio, November 23, 1850, John R. Bitner was born to these parents. Three years later the family removed to Roanoke, Ind., where they resided until the fall of 1863, when they returned to Holmes county. Six months later they made their home on the Bluffton road, twelve miles south of Fort Wayne. In 1865 the family came to this city, where the father died November 7, 1887. Mr. Bitner has been one of the trusted men in the Pittsburgh shops ever since engaging there twenty years ago. He was married November 14, 1877, to Emma Helfrich, a native of Crestline, Ohio, and they have five children: Lula M., Andrew C., Charlotte F., Charles L. and Irving E. Mr. Bitner is a member of Wayne lodge, F. & A. M.

Andrew Heimroth, a well-known citizen of Fort Wayne, engaged in the tool room of the Pennsylvania shops, was born in Prussia, January 16, 1819. Coming to America in 1847, he reached New York at four o'clock p. m., August 18. Having learned thoroughly the trade of a machinist in the old country he soon found employment at the West Point foundry, at Cold Springs, N. Y., beginning on the 26th of the same month. In June, 1848, he lost his right eye through an accident in the shops in which he was engaged. In 1852, he went to New York city, and was there engaged until 1855, when he entered the shops of the Camden & Amboy railroad at Bordentown, N. J. After an engagement there of several years he started to Fort Wayne, and on March 9, 1865, took a position in the Pennsylvania shops. For twenty years he was a faithful and valued assistant in the machine shop, and after the close of that period in 1885, he went into the tool shop. Mr. Heimroth is in politics a republican, and he is a member of the Summit City lodge, No. 170, F. & A. M. He was married October 20, 1848, to Catherine Shelton, who was born in Oxfordshire England, November 24, 1830. To them three children were born, of whom two survive; Matilda, now Mrs. Joseph Ellsner, of Chicago; and Sarah, now Mrs. William Hattersley, of Fort Wayne.

A representative of one of the pioneer families of Fort Wayne, Alexander M. Tower, an esteemed citizen, for several years connected with the machine shops of the western division of the P., Ft. W. & C. railroad, was born in Fort Wayne, January 6, 1855. His father, Benjamin H. Tower, a native of Michigan, who came to Fort Wayne during the thirties, resided here until his death in 1872. He was a lumber and furniture manufacturer, and was a prominent citizen. During the days of the old Wabash & Erie canal he was connected with that enterprise, and for some time was paymaster. He was a member of the city council for a considerable period. He married Kate Paul, who died when her son, Alexander, was but three years of age. The latter was reared in Fort Wayne and attended the public schools, receiving a first-class education. He entered the machine shops above named in June, 1872, as an apprentice, and serving out his apprenticeship, he continued as a foreman. In 1884 he went to Scott, Ohio, where for two years he was engaged in the manufacture of patent barrel hoops, but in 1886 he returned to the shops. He is a member of the Third Presbyterian church. Mr. Tower was married September 15, 1880, to Anna A.

Kinnaird, who was born in New York city, June 6, 1855, the daughter of Robert Kinnaird. Mrs. Tower died May 13, 1889, leaving two daughters, Mary W. and A. Louise.

During the past seventeen years, Daniel Campbell, a well-known railroad man of this city, has acted as foreman of the blacksmith department of the Wabash railroad shops. He began working at his trade in Buffalo, and in 1859 came to Fort Wayne, and then entered the employment of the Wabash company, in the department of which he has since served so long and efficient as foreman. He is a skillful workman and a good citizen, and his acquirements in life include those prime factors of happiness, an attractive family and a pleasant and comfortable home. Mr. Campbell was born in Edinburg, Scotland, December 6, 1835, son of Daniel and Ellen (Clapin) Campbell, both natives of Scotland, who spent their lives in that country. He came to the United States in 1853, and at first spent seven years at Buffalo, N. Y. He was married in 1862, to Jeanette Muirhead, and they have three children, Daniel A., Nellie and Jennie. Mr. Campbell is a prominent republican, and is a member of Fort Wayne lodge, No. 14, I. O. O. F.

The foreman of the boiler shops of the Wabash railroad company, Ernst Rehling, has been a resident of Fort Wayne for forty-one years, and has gained during that extended period the good-will and esteem of the community, and a high standing among the leading artisans of the city. Mr. Rehling is a native of Prussia, born March 24, 1841, the son of Frederick and Dora (Tegtmeier) Rehling. The parents emigrated to this country and came to Fort Wayne by the Wabash & Erie canal in 1848. Here the father, who was born in 1792, died in 1861, and the mather passed away in 1872, at the age of seventy years. They had eight children, of whom seven are living, Ernst being the youngest. Mr. Rehling, after receiving his education in the Lutheran schools, began work at the trade of boiler making, in 1857, which has been his life occupation. He served his time with Bass, Jones & Co., and subsequently was engaged by the Pennsylvania railroad company and remained with them until 1871. In 1872, he entered the employment of the Wabash railroad company, and his thorough knowledge of his craft, and trustworthiness as a man, led to his promotion in 1882, to the important position he now holds. He was married in April, 1864, to Sophia Starke, a native of Prussia, born January 3, 1842, who came to this city in 1854. They have four children: Fred. H. E., born December, 1864; Lizzie, born 1867; Ernst C. E., born 1870; and Charles, born 1873. Mr. Rehling and family are members of the German Lutheran church. He is in politics a republican, having cast his first presidential vote for U. S. Grant.

The foremanship of the Wabash railroad paint shop is ably filled by H. F. Banta, who has been a resident of this city since 1853. During his first two years here, he was engaged in the furniture business. In 1858, he entered the employment of the Wabash company, and for twenty-five years has occupied his present position. He is a skillful and com-

VIII

petent man and his services are highly valued by the company. Mr. Banta was born in Hanover, Germany, August 12, 1836, the son of Henry and Anna (Oclgeschleger) Banta, both natives of Hanover, where they passed their lives. Mr. Banta, the youngest of their children, was educated in his native land, and there learned the business of a gardener, a more important occupation there than here. He was married in 1863, to Catherine Schmidt, who was born in Germany in 1838, and came to this country in early childhood. Mr. Banta and wife are members of the Lutheran church, and he is in politics a republican, having first voted, in a presidential contest, for Abraham Lincoln.

One of the responsible men connected with the Wabash railway company is William J. Bensman, a valued citizen of Fort Wayne, who follows the trade of boiler maker. He was born Hanover, Germany, July 24, 1840. His parents, Rudolph and Elizabeth Bensman, were born in Germany, the father in 1807, the mother in 1805, and came to Fort Wayne in 1845, where the father died in 1886, and where the mother is now living. Of their three surviving children the eldest is William J., who being only five years old on his arrival here, received his education in the German Lutheran schools of this city. At eighteen years of age he began the learning of his trade, and since 1873 he has been in the employment of the Wabash railway. He is one of the best qualified in his occupation, and has prospered, having a handsome home, which he built in 1867. On December 5 of the following year he took to his home as wife, Frederica Boseker, who was born in Saxony, June 1, 1844, and they now have two children: Mary, born in 1869, and Della, born in 1883. They are faithful members of the Lutheran church.

Olds Wagon Works.—The famous Olds wagon works were established in 1881 by Henry G. Olds, who was succeeded in 1882 by the present corporation. The works were built by the Hamilton estate, and the buildings are supplied with machinery, operated by a 150 horse power engine. The trade extends to every state and territory in the union. Farm wagons, freight wagons, lumber and cotton wagons are all manufactured, and every piece of material used in their construction is of the best quality. H. G. Olds, the president, is also interested in N. G. Olds & Sons' wheel works. A. H. Hamilton is vice-president, William Johnston, jr., secretary, Charles McCulloch, treasurer.

William Johnston, jr., a popular and capable business man, occupying the position of secretary of the Olds wagon works, was born in New York city, October 10, 1845, to William and Sarah (Pollock) Johnston. The parents were born in Ireland, the father in 1798, and the mother in 1801, and came to this country in 1828. The father died at Foster's Meadow, Long Island, in 1876, and his widow eight years later. William is the youngest of seven children, three of whom are now living. He obtained a common school education in New York, and in 1862 came to Fort Wayne, reaching here March 21. He entered the employment of McDougal & Co., afterward Root & Co., as book-keeper, and held that position for six years, after which he was for ten years in the employment of Coombs & Co. He became connected with the Olds wagon works in 1881, and has acted as secretary since the incorporation in 1882. Mr. Johnston was married January 21, 1878, to Ada B. Fuller, a native of Michigan, daughter of John and Lois Fuller, and they have one child, Grace L. Mr. and Mrs. Johnston are members of the First Presbyterian church; he is a prominent republican; a Mason of the thirty-second degree, and Knight Templar.

Peter Andersen, a skillful mechanic, occupying the responsible position of foreman at the Olds Wagon works, began learning the trade of wagon maker in his native land, Denmark, at the age of fourteen, and in 1870 came to the United States, settling at Racine, Wis., where he lived twelve years, carrying on his business and also doing general carpentry and contracting. He came to Fort Wayne in 1881, and has ever since been connected with the Olds wagon works. He is a practical mechanic and skilled workman. Mr. Andersen was born in Denmark, June 10, 1845, of John and Mary (Henrickson) Andersen, who were born in that country, the father in 1796, the mother in 1811; and died there, the father in 1855, and the mother in 1885. In 1874 Mr. Andersen married Matine Rasmussen, a native of Denmark, born January 17, 1849, who came to the United States in 1874, and both are members of the Lutheran church. They have four children: Matilda C., Thorwald A., Olga R. and Herman A. Mr. Andersen is a republican in politics.

Kerr Murray Manufacturing Co.—Hugh Bennigan, who came to Fort Wayne in 1859, in that year with Jones & McLaughlin, established the Fort Wayne machine works. In 1862, he and Kerr Murray built the foundry near the south depot, which was the beginning of the Kerr Murray works. Kerr Murray became the sole owner in 1868, and in 1881 the concern was incorporated, with a paid up stock of $100,000, and in the same year was built the present brick shops. In 1868 the company commenced to manufacture gas works machinery and holders, to which has been added grain elevator machinery and general foundry and machine work. Their foundry is a one-story building with a cupola, its area is 110x115 feet, and the average melting is thirty tons per day; the machine shop is a three-story building, 60x150 feet, and its machines are run by a 100 horse-power engine; the wrought iron and smith shop is a two-story building, 75x175 feet, having seven forges and one steam hammer, pattern houses, yards, etc., to accommodate their stock, and a railroad track running through their works to facilitate their receiving and shipping departments. Employment is given to about 300 men, and the trade extends to all parts of the United States and Canada. Gas works have been erected by this company all over the continent, a few cities in the list being Pittsburgh, Mobile, El Paso, Dallas, Kansas City, Los Angeles, Davenport, Minneapolis, Detroit, Grand Rapids, Indianapolis, Cleveland, and London, Canada.

Alfred D. Cressler, president and general manager of the Kerr Murray manufacturing company, was born at Lucas, Richland county, Ohio,

July 7, 1852. His parents, George H. and Nancy (Miller) Cressler, were natives of Pennsylvania, the father born in Franklin county in 1811, and the mother in Cumberland county in 1813. The father was a railroad contractor and took part in the construction of the Pittsburgh, Fort Wayne & Chicago railroad. He survived his wife, who died in 1868, until August, 1875. Alfred D. Cressler spent his early life upon a farm, and from 1867 till 1869 worked at carriage making. His uncle, D. M. Miller, of the Aveline House, being a prominent citizen of Fort Wayne, Mr. Cressler came here in April, 1870, and found employment as a cash boy for Foster Brothers. In a few months he had risen from that position to have charge of the dress goods department, and he then entered Eastman's business college at Poughkeepsie, where he spent four months. Returning to the employment of Foster Brothers, he was stationed at Grand Rapids until October, 1874. He was next engaged one year in the dry goods business at Wooster, Ohio, and then returned to Fort Wayne, where he took the position of time clerk for the Kerr Murray manufacturing company. In 1877–8 he traveled for the company and acted as bookkeeper in 1879. On the death of Mr. Murray, May 6, 1880, Mr. Cressler took charge of the business for the heirs, and conducted it during the remainder of the year. In 1881 he organized and incorporated the present company for the manufacture of gas works machinery, and was elected to his present position. He is one of the most prominent and energetic of the young manufacturers of the city. He is a member of the Masonic fraternity, having attained the thirty-second degree and the Mystic Shrine. Mr. Cressler was married October 13, 1874, to Eliza E. Murray, daughter of Kerr Murray.

Since September, 1888, G. Adolph Schust has held the position of secretary of the Kerr Murray manufacturing company. He was born in this city November 1, 1862, the son of J. M. and E. M. (Hoffman) Schust, both natives of Germany, who emigrated to this city in 1849. The family removed to Wheeling, W. Va., in 1864, but returned to this city in 1874, where the parents are still living. The father is now employed in the pattern making department of the Wabash railroad shops. Their son, the subject of this sketch, attended school at Wheeling and Fort Wayne, and in 1877 entered the law office of Jenison & Alden. A year later he became a student at Addison seminary, near Chicago, and remained there until 1882. He then returned to this city and took a commercial course in the business college, afterward taking a position as bill clerk and assistant ticket agent in the Wabash railroad freight office. In 1883 he entered the employment of the Kerr Murray manufacturing company as shipping clerk, and has since been prominently connected with that company. He is a member of the Lutheran church.

Since January 1, 1885, Gustave L. Hackius has occupied a position with the Kerr Murray manufacturing company, and on January 1, 1888, he was promoted treasurer and head bookkeeper of that establishment, a responsible position which he at present fills to the entire satisfaction of the company. He was born in this city February 19, 1867, and was educated in the Lutheran schools, attending also the commercial college, taking a night course during the fall, winter and spring of 1882-3. He was engaged with A. Kalbacher, in the flour and feed trade, as book-keeper and clerk, in 1881-2, and then became a clerk in the shop-clerk's office of the Pennsylvania company from 1883 to 1885. He is the son of Andrew and Mary Hackius, natives of Germany, who came to Fort Wayne in 1854. The father being a copper and tinsmith by trade, was engaged at his trade with the Pennsylvania company at Fort Wayne. He died December 28, 1885, but his widow survives and is living in the city. To them eight children were born, of whom Gustave is the fifth, and all but two are living.

Herman J. Remmert, prominent in the manufacturing interests of the city of Fort Wayne, was born in Prussia, August 5, 1841. When fifteen years of age, in September, 1857, he landed at New Orleans, and after a few months' stay at St. Louis, he reached Fort Wayne in February, 1858. Here he learned the trade of a carpenter and joiner, which he followed for a year and a half. In the fall of 1861 he made a visit to his native country and was absent six months. Upon his return he became engaged with the Bass foundry and machine works, and remained there until the fall of 1863, when he entered the employment of Murray & Bennigan, in their machine shops. In the fall of 1864 he engaged in the retail grocery trade, and though out of the shops not more than three months, continued that business for three years. He has been connected with the same works ever since, through its various changes of proprietorship, a period of twenty-six years. Previous to the organization of the Kerr Murray manufacturing company he acted as general foreman for four or five years, and since the organization of that company in which he is a stockholder, he has been superintendent of the works. Mr. Remmert was married on June 26, 1866, to Mary C., daughter of John J. Koester, of this city, and to their union ten children have been born, six of whom survive. He and wife are members of the St. Paul's Catholic church.

Among the popular foremen of the Kerr Murray establishment should be named Carl Bohne, a skillful pattern-maker. He was born in Hanover, Germany, May 13, 1857, the son of Henry and Engel (Meyer) Bohne. They emigrated to America in 1857, and came directly to Fort Wayne, making their home five miles south of Fort Wayne, where the father followed farming until his death in 1866. The widow then removed to the city, where she still resides. Carl Bohne was educated in the German Lutheran schools, and at the age of thirteen years entered the drug house of his uncle, William Meyer, where he remained two years, and then began an apprenticeship of four years with J. C. Boser & Co., at the trade of pattern-maker. He remained with the above house twelve years altogether, and then entered the employ of the Kerr Murray manufacturing company in 1885. In 1886 was engaged at Kendalville, Ind., with the Flint & Walling manufacturing company, as pattern-maker, for nine months. He then returned to the Kerr Murray manufacturing company as foreman of the pattern department of that establishment, and has continued in that position. Mr. Bohne was married at Kendallville in 1887 to Dora Wehmeyer, who was born at that place in 1865. Mr. and Mrs. Bohne are members of Emanuel Lutheran church.

The foremanship of the boiler and blacksmith department of the Kerr Murray works is in the hands of Adolph F. Schulz, who came to this city in 1883, and having learned the trade of blacksmith and boilermaker in his native land, immediately engaged with this company. He was made foreman in 1884, but in 1885 removed to Decatur, and was for a short time engaged with a machine shop and foundry at that place, going then to Alleghany, Penn., taking charge of a department in a machine factory. In 1886 he returned to this city, and again took the foremanship he now holds. Mr. Schulz was born in Germany, February 28, 1854, and immigrated in 1882, having previously been married, 1877, to Sophia Seidensticker, by whom he has three sons and one daughter. Mr. Schulz is a member of the Reform church, and a worthy citizen.

Fort Wayne Organ Company.— Of this prominent industry, of which mention has already been made, Stephen B. Bond is president, Charles E. Bond, secretary, and A. S. Bond, treasurer and superintendent.

The position of designer and superintendent of case manufacturing in the Fort Wayne organ factory, is held by Thomas Hill, a native of Halifax, Yorkshire, England. He was born January 9, 1839, the son of Richard and Ann (Lockwood) Hill. At thirteen he began to learn the cabinet-maker's trade and after a seven years' apprenticeship, followed his trade at various places in England until 1872. In that year he emigrated to America, locating in Boston; he remained there two years and then had charge of a cabinet shop at Worchester, Mass., three years and a half. After a few months at Boston, he went to Appleton, Wis., and took charge of a factory in which chairs and bed room suits were made. There he was occupied as designer five years and a half. He then went to Chicago, and was with the firm of Story & Clark, organ manufacturers, as designer, five or six years. Prior to this he had spent one year with the firm of A. H. Andrews & Co. In February, 1888, he came to Fort Wayne and accepted his present position. Mr. Hill was married July 9, 1861, to Ellen Stott, a native of Hebden Bridge, England. They have one son, Richard, born July 4, 1871. Mr. Hill is a member of the A. O. U. W., and the White Rose lodge, Sons of St. George.

Brooks French is a native of Wilton, N. H., born November 1, 1845, son of Samuel and Elvira (Grey) French, both natives of the same town. He lived until eighteen on a farm and then removed to Michigan, and became employed in a furniture factory at Battle Creek. Later he held the position of foreman in a table factory, and subsequently worked two years in an organ factory which had developed out of the table factory.

In the fall of 1871, he accepted a position in the Burdett organ factory at Chicago, but the establishment was destroyed by the great fire before he took his situation. He spent the winter of 1871-2 in Gratiot county, Mich., with relatives and afterward came to Fort Wayne, and has ever since been employed in the factory of the Fort Wayne organ company. He has aided in the construction of every organ that has been turned out by the institution, and since June, 1872, has been foreman of the stop action department. During the summer of 1878, he served four months as acting superintendent. He is the inventor of French's stop action, upon which he received a patent March 14, 1882, and of French's grand organ action, patented June 12, 1883. Both patents have been assigned to the Fort Wayne organ company. From 1876 to 1884, in connection with his other duties, he had charge of the fly finishing department, and since 1884 has managed the pedal base double bank department, all the mechanism of which is of his own invention, as well as the labor of draughting and manufacture. Mr. French was married September 14, 1873, to Miss Roberta C. Kent, who was born in DeKalb county, Ind., but was reared at Coldwater, Mich. Mrs. French is a telegraph operator and had worked at her profession two years prior to her marriage. Mr. and Mrs. French have both completed the Chautauqua course, graduating in 1886, and since then Mrs. French has completed a course in the Hailman kindergarten school of La Porte, Ind. She is the founder of the Frœbel kindergarten school of Fort Wayne, established in 1886. She is a member of the Episcopal church. Mr. French is a member of the Apollo club and the Morton club. In politics he is an ardent republican.

The foremanship of the finishing department of the Fort Wayne organ company has been for seventeen years in the hands of Capt. John H. Rohan. He was born in County Clare, Ireland, June 24, 1839, son of John and Bridget Rohan, with whom he came to America in 1845. The family first located at Burlington, Vt., but three years later, removed to Milwaukee, Wis. In early manhood Capt. Rohan learned the trade of a finisher of wood, and followed it in Milwaukee until 1859, and afterward at Buffalo, N. Y. In July, 1862, he enlisted in Company D, One Hundred and Sixteenth New York volunteer infantry and served until the close of the war. He was successively promoted from private to sergeant, first sergeant, second lieutenant, first lieutenant, and in April, 1864, he was promoted captain and served as such with company G, of the same regiment, until the close of the war. He commanded his company in the battles of Port Hudson, Pleasant Hill, Sabine Cross Roads, Cedar Creek, Fisher's Hill and numerous skirmishes of less importance. He received a flesh wound in the left side at the battle of Pleasant Hill, and a scalp wound in the battle of Cedar Creek, but fortunately neither proved serious. He was mustered out at Washington, D. C., June 25, 1865. Returning to Milwaukee he engaged in the grocery business. Two years later he removed to Chicago and until the great fire in 1871 worked at his trade in the factory of the Burdett organ company. After the fire he came to Fort Wayne and has ever since held his present position. Captain Rohan was married May 28, 1868, to Miss Mary Ann Theresa O'Brien, a native of Rochester, N. Y., and daughter of Lawrence and Mary O'Brien. They have had nine children, of whom Lottie J., William H., John F., Edwin G. and Agnes are living, and Mida, Theresa, Maggie and Walter are deceased. Mr. Rohan and wife are members of the Catholic church. He is a member of the uniformed rank of the Catholic Legion, the National Union, and G. A. R. In politics he is a democrat. Captain Rohan was formerly captain of the Veteran organization of the state militia and was promoted to the rank of major and finally lieutenant-colonel, and still serves in the latter rank.

Fort Wayne Jenney Electric Light Company.—Of this very important corporation Henry G. Olds is president, P. A. Randall, vice president, R. T. McDonald, treasurer and general manager, and M. W. Simons, secretary. Ronald T. McDonald, general manager and treasurer of the Fort Wayne Jenney electric light company, is a native of Pennsylvania, born June 24, 1849, at Alleghany City, the eldest of four children now living of James B. and Margaret (Morrison) McDonald. The father was a native of Pennsylvania and died at Fort Wayne in 1886 at the age of seventy-six years. The subject of this mention came to Fort Wayne in 1860, and here has since resided. In 1864 he enlisted in company C, One Hundred and Fifty-second Indiana infantry, and served until the close of the war, when he was honorably discharged as sergeant major. On his return to this city he was engaged first in the dry goods business as a clerk, afterward as a member of the firm of Evans, McDonald & Co., leaving that business in 1881 to engage in the electric light industry. To that he brought all the energy and enterprise which had already distinguished him as a business man, and he has greatly advanced the interests of the company of which he was one of the incorporators in 1882, and which promises to become one of the leading industries of the city. During the few years he has been identified with this industry he has gained a wide repute as one of the prominent men of the country in the electric light manufacture. Mr. McDonald was married in 1876 to Lillie Morse, of Angola, Ind., daughter of Marquis and Elizabeth Morse, and they have one child, Esther. He is a member of Sol D. Bayless lodge, No. 129, 1870, of Fort Wayne commandery, 1872, and of the Indianapolis consistory, 1882. In politics he is an ardent republican.

The master mechanic, with his scientific knowledge of the forces and materials of nature, with careful training and natural ingenuity, is one of the prime movers in the prosperity of Fort Wayne. Such a man is the master mechanic of the Fort Wayne Jenney electric light company, Charles S. Hilton. He began work as a machinist in the employ of the Franklin machine company at Lewiston, Me., in the fall of 1865. He remained there three years, and was then for nine years employed by the manufacturers of the Cottrell & Babcock printing presses in Rhode

Island. During five years of the latter period he held the position of foreman. Removing to Kentucky, he acted two years as master mechanic of the Bowling Green woolen company. In 1882 he came to Fort Wayne, and was in the employment of the Wabash railroad company in their shops, after which he entered the service of the electric light company, first as superintendent of the arc department, and then for two years past as master mechanic. Mr. Hilton was born at South Boston, Mass., July 28, 1846, son of Leonard Hilton and his wife Susan Farnsworth, both natives of Massachusetts, who passed their lives there. Leonard was the son of Daniel Hilton, who was born at Fitchburg, Mass., about 1790, was a soldier in the war of 1812, and died in his native state at about seventy-six years of age. His wife was Julia Sautell, who died in Massachusetts at about eighty-six years of age. Charles S. enlisted in 1863, in Company B, Fifty-sixth Massachusetts infantry, and served in all the engagements of the army of the Potomac after the battle of Gettysburg until the close of the war, being wounded at the battle of Petersburg. He was married in 1882, to Mrs. Mary E. Sands, of Wabash, and have two children, Donna M. and Charles W. He has one child, Hattie, by a former marriage, and his wife one child, May Sands, by her previous marriage. Mr. Hilton is a republican, a comrade of the G. A. R., and a Scottish Rite Mason.

The assistant master mechanic of the Fort Wayne electric light company, Charles F. Knothe, is a native of this city, born February 11, 1851, to J. A. and Louisa (Krochman) Knothe, natives of Germany, who immigrated in 1846, and made their residence in this city in 1848. The mother passed away in 1882, but the father is still living, and engaged in business as a member of the lumber firm of Beaver, Miller & Co. Charles F. Knothe was educated in the public and Lutheran schools of the city, and in 1869 began an apprenticeship as machinist with Louis Rastetter, at which he continued three years. He then worked at various places, and in 1874 became engaged in the railroad shops at East Saginaw, Mich. In 1883 he returned to Fort Wayne, and entered the employment of the Jenney electric light company, as a machinist, and in 1886 was appointed assistant master mechanic. Mr. Knothe was married in 1874 to Elizabeth Billing, who died in 1878, leaving two children, and in 1884 he was united to Polly Frohmuth, by whom he has had two children.

The position of purchasing agent and superintendent of shipping of the Fort Wayne Jenney electric light company is efficiently filled by Charles B. Fitch, one of the most popular young men in the city. He possesses winning social qualities as well as business acumen, and is prominent in Masonry, being a Knight Templar of Fort Wayne commandery, and high in the Scottish Rite. Mr. Fitch was born at Medina, Ohio, May 23, 1859, the youngest of seven children (six now living), of William and Aurelia (Brintnall) Fitch. The father was born in Connecticut in 1817, was a farmer by occupation, and owned one of the best farms in the Western Reserve. He died in 1867, at Medina, and his widow, who was born in 1819, in New York, died at Fort Wayne in 1881. Her family were pioneers in New York and Vermont. The father of William W. Fitch, who had the same name, was born in Connecticut in 1780, settled in Ohio with his family as early as 1825, and died about 1865. His ancestors came from England prior to 1660, and were pioneers in Connecticut and Rhode Island. Mr. Fitch received a good education in the schools at Medina and Fort Wayne high school. He came to this city in 1872, and in 1875 began teaching, at which he was engaged in this county for several terms. From 1879 to 1882 conducted a mercantile and grain business at Avilla, but in the latter year returned to Fort Wayne, and became engaged with the electric light company, with which he has since been prominently connected. He was married in 1881 to Elizabeth Fryer, of Noble county, daughter of Henry Fryer, a prominent farmer.

John C. Peters, as a prominent manufacturer and owner of the famous Wayne hotel, has by his various enterprises contributed in a large measure to the advancement of the city. Mr. Peters was born in this city June 11, 1848, son of Claus and Caroline (Eberlein) Peters, who came to Fort Wayne in 1841, from Germany, their native land. The father, who was born in 1813, followed in this city the occupation of builder and contractor until his death in 1849. His widow still survives. John C. Peters received his early education in this city, and then, in 1862, began learning the trade of piano and cabinet-maker at which he was occupied for four years, from 1865 to 1869, in New York city. In 1873 he was married to Mary Myers, of Fort Wayne, who was born in 1853, the daughter of Frederick Myers. To this union has been born seven children: Frederick, William, Otto, Arthur, Paul, Flora and Bertha. Mr. Peters is a member of the Emanuel Lutheran church; and in politics he takes an active interest in the welfare of the democratic party. He has risen to an honorable place among the foremost citizens of Fort Wayne, by his character as a man, his unfailing reliability as a business man, and his energy and enterprise as a manufacturer. He conducts an extensive business solely his own in hardwood lumber, which he established in 1872. The large building devoted to this manufacture, on Osage and Main streets, is equipped with one band-saw mill, operated by steam, with an average capacity of 7,000 feet per day. Ash, oak and whitewood lumber are principal features of the product, which is to some extent disposed of to local manufactories using a fine grade of lumber, but mainly to eastern factories. Dealing only in perfect stock, the house is popular and the business is constantly increasing. Mr. Peters is also manager of the Horton manufacturing company, incorporated in 1883, with a capital stock of $30,000, whose works give employment to seventy skilled workmen. This establishment manufactures the improved Western washer, hand corn planters, and various wooden novelties; and has a heavy trade throughout Ohio, Indiana and Michigan, throughout the union, and even to Australia. Mr. Peters was also a partner prior to 1873 with Charles Pape and Joseph Schaffer in the Peters' box and lumber company, another extensive enterprise elsewhere mentioned. He is also president of the Indiana machine works, a company organized and incorporated in 1887, with a capital of $75,000. This establishment manufactures patented specialties in woodworking machinery, etc. Mr. Peters built in 1887, the Wayne hotel, described elsewhere, which is already widely known as one of the finest places of accommodation in the country. This brief mention of the enterprises in which Mr. Peters is engaged is sufficient, though but a meagre outline, to give an idea of the activity of his busy life, devoted to the upbuilding of the city of his birth.

The Peters box and lumber company, manufacturers of furniture and hand-sawed lumber, was established and incorporated in 1871, by J. C. Peters, Charles Pape and Joseph Schaffer, with a capital stock of $55,000. The factory is situated at Nos. 79 and 102 High street, and the salesrooms at Nos. 15 and 17 Court streeet. The factory occupies four floors, 50x100, two floors, 40x70, one 50x80, and one 40x60, and the best productions of modern invention are employed in the manufacture. From sixty to seventy-five men here find employment. This product is also shipped extensively over the state and into Ohio, and the hardwood lumber produced is shipped to the cities of the east and to London. A special feature is quartered oak, of which the finest grades are handled. Two band-saws are run with a capacity of 20,000 feet per day, and one venner saw, with a capacity of 10,000 feet per day. Of this institution Charles Pape is president, and Wilson McQuiston secretary.

Charles Pape, prominent among the enterprising men who have established the greatness of the city of Fort Wayne, by establishing manufactories that employ hundreds of men and carry the fame of the city wherever their products are sold, first saw this city in 1850, then being a German lad of thirteen years, fresh from his native land. He worked for several months at such labor as he could find. He then went to Elkhart and remained there two years. Returning to Fort Wayne in 1861, he engaged in contracting, and continued to be thus employed until 1873, when he became connected with the Peters' box factory. In 1878 he purchased a controlling interest in the Peters' box and lumber company, and has since then been president of the company. In 1882 he purchased an interest in the Jonathan Fleming road machine, and established a business which has since become known as the Fleming manufacturing company, of which he is sole owner and one of the most extensive producers of road machines and snow scrapers in the United States. His career has been a remarkable one, and his success is all the more notable as he has been wholly dependent upon his energy and talent for affairs, being entirely without assistance at the outset. Mr. Pape was born at Minden, Germany, December 18, 1837, son of William and Wilhelmina Pape, who emigrated to the United States in 1850, and settled at Fort Wayne, where they both died. He is the eldest of their five children. He was married in 1859, to Wilhelmina

Bierman, a native of Germany. She died in 1871, and in 1872 Mr. Pape was married to Caroline Schroeder. He has eight children. He is a democrat in politics, and was for two terms a member of the city council. He is a member of St. Paul's Lutheran church.

The responsible position of secretary of the Peters box and lumber company is in charge of Wilson McQuiston, who has a thorough knowledge of the business, and performs his portion of it in a way that leaves nothing to be desired. Though a native of this county, his first essay in business was as bookkeeper in the bank of Sigourney, Iowa, in May, 1868. His efficiency won for him in the course of a year, the position of cashier. After six years of experience in that function he turned his attention to newspaper management, and removing to the national capital, became one of the publishers of the *Washington Daily Chronicle*. For four years he held the position of secretary and treasurer of the *Chronicle* publishing company. In 1878 he returned to Fort Wayne, and has since that year, been associated with the lumber manufacturing of the city. He became secretary of the Peters box and lumber company in 1884. Mr. McQuiston was born in Allen county, March 21, 1844, the son of John and Eliza McQuiston, residents of the county, and he received his education in the schools of the city. In the fall of 1870 he was married to Lydia A. Bean, of Delaware, Ohio. He has been a member of Summit City lodge, F. & A. M., since 1865, and is in politics a republican.

The Anthony Wayne manufacturing company, of which John Rhinesmith is president, and Albert C. F. Wichman superintendent, is one of the prosperous concerns of the city. Its product is the improved Anthony Wayne washing machine, the invention of Mr. Wichman, which is one of the most popular contrivances of that kind. Mr. Wichman was born in Prussia in 1835, and came to America in 1849. He first made his home at Cincinnati, but in 1851 came to Fort Wayne, where he resided until 1864. He then removed to Kendallville, and during his residence there served as city clerk from 1869 to 1873. Returning to Fort Wayne in 1880, he for several years held the position of bookkeeper for William Moellering, contractor and builder. In 1886 he entered the Anthony Wayne manufacturing company, and became the superintendent of the works in June, 1887. Mr. Wichman was married in 1857, to Elizabeth Eberlein, who is a native of Bavaria, though reared in Fort Wayne. They have nine children.

The first president of the company named was that well-known and enterprising citizen, Fred. C. Boltz. In the year 1849, being at that time one year old, Mr. Boltz was brought here by his parents from his native town of Saarbruken, Prussia. He was brought up in this city, and enjoyed the advantages of the public schools. He engaged in business in 1864 at the age of sixteen years, and has been identified with different business interests ever since. In 1864 he engaged in the manufacture of cigars, and at present is one of the prosperous men in that branch of business, operating factory No. 201, which produces several brands of fine cigars, the most popular being the "B. & O.," and "Fuss." In 1886 Mr. Boltz became a stockholder in the Anthony Wayne manufacturing company, being one of the organizers, and served as president until 1887, when he resigned, but still holds a directorship. He is also a member of the contracting firm of Boltz & Dehrheimer. From May, 1881, until 1885, he served as a member of the city council. He has been a member of the Masonic fraternity since 1869. Mr. Boltz was married October 8, 1871, to Miss Catherine Best, of New York city. Mr. Boltz's father is yet a resident of this city, but his mother died in 1876.

The Hoosier manufacturing company, A. S. Evans, president, is a well-known establishment. The superintendency of the factory of this company is in the hands of William A. Thomas, a capable business man. He began mercantile life in 1873, in the retail clothing trade at Addison, Ohio. This he sold out in 1880, and in 1881 he came to Fort Wayne, and here was first engaged as assistant bookkeeper for Evans, McDonald & Co., wholesale dry goods merchants. Soon after the incorporation of the Hoosier manufacturing company he was intrusted with the position of bookkeeper, and since January, 1887, has occupied his present position. Mr. Thomas was born in Champaign county, Ohio, September 2, 1851, son of John H. and Elizabeth Thomas. The mother was a native of that county, the father of Rockbridge county, Va. Mr. Thomas attended the district school, and at sixteen entered Denison University at Granville, Ohio, whence he graduated in 1872. He was married June 24, 1874, to Mary F., daughter of Capt. Nathan McConkey, late of Springfield, Ohio. She was born in Clark county of that state. They are the parents of two children, Ross and Stella, both living. Mr. Thomas and wife are devoted members of the First Baptist church. He has been a Mason since the night of his twenty-first birthday, and has attained the rank of thirty-second degree; he is also a member of the Knights of Pythias.

John Rhinesmith, senior member of the well-known lumber firm of Rhinesmith & Simonson, was born in Trumbull county, Ohio, in 1832. His father, George Rhinesmith, was born in Pennsylvania, moved to Ohio when a young man, and after working as a farm laborer about six months, bought land and began its cultivation, continuing as a farmer until his death in 1859. His wife, whose maiden name was Elizabeth Earle, is a native of Ohio. She removed to Fort Wayne in 1862, and now resides at the home of her son John, in her eighty-second year. John Rhinesmith, after leaving school, clerked for a few years, and in 1885 came to Fort Wayne and entered the employment of a produce dealer. Subsequent to 1861 he was a messenger for a few years for the American Express company, and in 1865 he engaged in the lumber business in partnership with John H. Clark. The firm was incorporated as the Clark & Rhinesmith lumber company in 1872, and was succeeded in 1877 by the firm of Rhinesmith & Simonson, J. H. Simonson being the partner. The business of this concern has become very extensive and successful, having increased from a capital of about $33,000 to over $60,000, and the average annual business is now $200,000. The product is sash, doors and blinds, and they do all kinds of factory work, employing between fifty and sixty-five men, and also deal in lumber. Mr. Rhinesmith is also president of the Anthony Wayne manufacturing company, in which he owns a one-fourth interest, and is one of the prominent men of the city.

James H. Simonson, member of the firm of Rhinesmith & Simonson, and secretary and treasurer of the Anthony Wayne manufacturing company, was born at Peeksville, N. Y., in 1838, the son of Isaac and Abby J. (Mosher) Simonson. The father was a contractor of considerable note, and with others built the palace of General Bolivar, at Bogota, S. A. He was one of an old Dutch family whose ancestors came to New York in 1643. He died in 1857, and the mother, who is a descendant of an English family that landed on Block Island in 1736, is now a resident of New York. In that city James H. was raised and educated in the city schools. He was holding a position as bookkeeper in a machine shop at New York, at the outbreak of the civil war, when, being a member of the famous seventh regiment, he went with that regiment to the capital at the call of President Lincoln. As soon as relieved from guard duty Mr. Simonson returned to New York, and in 1862 removed to Pittsburgh and entered the employment of the Pennsylvania company. In 1864 he removed to Fort Wayne, where, until 1867, he was cashier in the freight depot of the Pittsburgh railroad. Resigning his position he entered the employment of Clark & Rhinesmith, and upon the organization of the Clark & Rhinesmith lumber company, in 1872, he became a stockholder and director. Subsequently he and Mr. Rhinesmith succeeded to the business. He is also a fourth owner in the Anthony Wayne manufacturing company. Mr. Simonson was one of the projectors of the Masonic temple, and upon the completion of the opera-house portion in 1885 he was appointed manager of the same, a position he still holds. Mr. Simonson's genial and happy nature has gained him many warm friends, and he is one of the popular men of city. In 1887 he was the republican candidate for mayor, but though making a gallant contest was unable to overcome the adverse majority. He is a member of the Masonic fraternity, of the rank of Knight Templar.

Among the careful and trustworthy foreman of the manufactories of the city, William C. Pape, of the Rhinesmith & Simonson factory, should be creditably named. Though a young man, he was given in 1885, a foremanship at the Peters box and lumber company's works, which he held until 1887, when he accepted his present position with one of the leading firms in wooden manufacture. Mr. Pape was born at this city, May 2, 1863, son of Charles and Minnie (Bearman) Pape. He was educated at the German Lutheran schools, and August 31, 1884, was married to Carrie Paul, a native of Ohio. They have one child, Roy. Mr. Pape is a member of one of the prominent families of the city, and is highly esteemed. He and wife are members of the Lutheran church, and he is politically a democrat.

Louis Diether, senior membr of the firm of Louis Diether & Bro., manufacturers of sash, doors and blinds and mouldings, and dealers in lumber, is one of the notably successful manufacturers of the city of Fort Wayne. His parents, Charles F. and Barbara Diether, natives of Germany, were married in New York city and came to Indiana in 1850 to seek a place to plant their home in the new land. They located in this city in 1850, and here in the same year, their son Louis was born. The mother died at Fort Wayne in 1885. Louis was educated in the city schools, and at the age of twenty years, engaged in the hardware business at Mendon, Mich. He returned to Fort Wayne, however, in July of the same year, and took a position as book-keeper for the firm of Cochrane & Humphrey, one of the oldest lumber firms of the city. He was subsequently with Nuttman & Taylor three years, and was book-keeper for Meyer Bros., wholesale druggists, five years. Afterward he embarked in the lumber business, succeeding the firm of Cochrane & Humphrey. In May, 1887, and on January 1, 1888, the firm of Diether & Bro. was formed by the admission of his brother John to a partnership. The firm ranks with those which do the largest business in the city, and employ an average of thirty-eight men. In addition to their manufactures, which include all kinds of factory work, they deal extensively in rough and dressed lumber and shingles. Their factory, at 100 Pearl street, is one of the prominent concerns of the city, and their lumber yards are located on Superior street.

John H. Diether, junior member of the firm of Louis Diether & Bro., above referred to, was born in this city, January 3, 1852, the son of Charles F. and Barbara Diether. At the age of eighteen years he set out to learn the trade of harness making, and two years later, became a member of the firm of F. Hilt & Co., manufacturers and dealers in saddles and harness, and was so engaged for twelve years, selling out his interest at the end of that period. In January, 1888, he formed the present partnership with his brother Louis. For a time he took charge of the lumber yards of the firm on Superior street, but at present has the management of the manufactory on Pearl street. Mr. Diether was married April 27, 1882, to Malana McIlvaine, of Fort Wayne, who was born in New York city in 1862. They have three children.

John B. Monning, the eldest of five children of the late Hon. Henry Monning, an account of whose life appears in another portion of this work, was born at Cincinnati, Ohio, May 2, 1852. In the fall of the same year his parents began their residence at Fort Wayne, so that the life of the subject of this mention has been almost entirely spent in this city. In the Catholic schools of the city, as he grew in years, he received a good and comprehensive education. When sixteen years old he became deputy county treasurer, serving under his father, then county treasurer, and after his father's retirement from office, for one year with his successor. During this period his father and A.

C. Trentman had established a coffee and spice mill, and John B. Monning engaged in this in 1874, and in 1881, under the firm name of J. B. Monning & Co., began the business of flour milling, at which he is still engaged. His business sagacity and enterprise, joined with that honor and integrity which characterizes his undertakings in all channels of activity, have made him a highly successful man, and one who ranks among the leading citizens of Fort Wayne. He is prominent in the affairs of the city, and being a leader among those who delight in advancing the interests of the whole community, has been secretary of the business men's association since its organization. Mr. Monning was married in 1876, to Mary Luhn, who was born in Cincinnati, March 2, 1852, and their union has been blessed with four children: Mary, Agnes, Anna and John. Mr. Monning and wife are members of the Catholic church, and he is active in the interests of the order known as the Catholic Knights of America. In politics Mr. Monning is a democrat.

John Ferguson, prominent among the leading manufacturers and lumbermen of Fort Wayne, was born near Quebec, June 24, 1834. His father, John Ferguson, a native of Scotland, was born at Westfield, near Alloa, in 1795, and in 1816 went to sea, and for sixteen years continued the life of a sailor. About 1830 emigrated and settled in Canada. Mary Orr, who became his wife, was born in County Armaugh, Ireland, in 1805, and had come to Canada, about 1829. She and her husband settled on a farm and they were occupied in its cultivation until their death. She died March 19, 1879, and his death followed, February 20, 1883. He was a man of great energy and careful habits, and his rugged constitution knew no suffering until just before his life went out at four score and eight years. To these parents were born eleven children, of whom seven survive. Their son, John Ferguson, remained on the farm near Quebec until his twentieth year, when, in 1855, he came to Fort Wayne, which has since been his home. He engaged in the lumber business in 1861, and has ever since been successfully prosecuting that industry, having two large mills on the Fort Wayne & Muncie railroad, the product of which finds market principally in Chicago. His enterprising spirit has led him into other investments for the advancement of the city, and he is a director of the Wayne natural gas company, and for twelve years has been president of the Bluffton gravel road company. Mr. Ferguson's interest in this city, is property valued at $30,000. He owns about 1,000 acres of mostly improved land in Allen, Huntington, Wells and Marshall counties, and also $11,000 worth of property in Lucas county, Ohio. Mr. Ferguson was married November 19, 1861, to Eliza King, a native of Canada, born in 1837, and they have five children as follows: Cora M., Fannie, now Mrs. Palmer, wife of Earl Palmer, who is now engaged in the lumber business with Mr. Ferguson, Eliza K., John K., and Minnie E. He is a prominent republican in politics, a member of Harmony lodge, No. 19, I. O. O. F., and with his family are members of the First Baptist church. Enterprise and energy are the crowning characteristics of his character.

John Ferguson

Louis Rastetter, who has had an honorable career in this city since September 27, 1857, came here at that date, expecting to find employment as a machinist, a trade he had well learned in his native land, and had practiced in America since he landed in 1854, unaccompanied by any relatives, to search his fortune in a new land. He had been employed two years at Rochester, N. Y., and one year at Buffalo, before coming to Fort Wayne. Here he found work in the old Wabash shops. In November, 1859, he went to Germany to visit his parents, and returned in June, 1860, to resume his position in the shops. Marrying soon afterward, he set up a small machine shop of his own, which he conducted with considerable success until 1870, when he sold his business and took the position of master-mechanic of the wheel works of N. G. Olds. Here he remained until the fall of 1876, when, with two associates, he went to Lima, Ohio, and they established a factory for the production of hubs, spokes and buggy bows, under the name of the Lima wheel company. At the end of four years and a half he sold to his partners and established his present factory at Fort Wayne, which was removed to the site now occupied on the corner of Broadway and the Pittsburgh railroad in the fall of 1881. This, the Fort Wayne buggy bow works, is one of the important manufactories of the city, and in its management Mr. Rastetter displays notable ability. Mr. Rastetter was born in Baden, Germany, May 31, 1834, the son of Andrew and Anna Mary (Sutter) Rastetter. He was educated for a teacher by his parents, but his inclinations led him to learn the machinist's trade. He was married August 4, 1860, to Elizabeth Hauenstein, who was born in Fort Wayne, March 27, 1841, daughter of John and Anna Mary Hauenstein, natives of Switzerland. Mr. Rastetter and wife have had seven children, of whom four are living: William C., Helen, Charles and Mary. Mr. Rastetter is a member of the I. O. O. F.

John Lillie, one of the prominent manufacturers and business men of Fort Wayne, was born in Scotland, September 12, 1847, the son of John and Jane (Fowler) Lillie. The parents were natives of Scotland, the father born October 16, 1819, the mother about 1821. The family came to the United States in June, 1850, and settled at Fort Wayne. The mother died at Wells county, this state, in 1852. In 1856 the father engaged in the lime and stone business at Fort Wayne, and in 1875 removed to Columbus, Ohio, where he died May 21, 1885. John Lillie is the second of five children of these parents, of whom three are now living. He received a common school education. In 1872 he became a member of the firm of James Lillie & Co., and in 1883 became sole proprietor. In January, 1884, he admitted Charles A. Munson as a partner in the manufacture of Huntington lime, with their works located at Lillie, Huntington county. The firm also deals in cement, plaster, sewer pipe, etc., and does a large business. Mr. Lillie is a valued citizen, is a representative business man, and is widely known as one of the most prominent Masons of Indiana. He has attained the thirty-second degree, is past eminent commander, Knights Templar, has been grand secretary of the grand lodge of Perfection, A. A. S. R., at Fort Wayne, since its organization March 12, 1887, and is one of the trustees of the Masonic Temple. His prominence in these fraternal connections is a valuable testimonial to his fine social qualities and worth as a man. The esteem in which he is held by those who know him best is shown by his having been elected repeatedly to represent his ward in the city council, though he is a firm republican, and his is the leading democratic ward in the city. Mr. Lillie was married March 9, 1871, to Kate Williams, of this city, who was born in Canada in 1851.

William Ranke, of the firm of Ranke & Yergens, manufacturers, was born in Prussia, September 16, 1838. In 1854, he immigrated and landing at Baltimore, proceeded to Cincinnati, where resided two years. In 1856 he came to Fort Wayne, where he engaged three years later, in the bakery business. After a career of seven years in this line of trade, he formed a partnership with William Yergens in a saw-mill, which they managed until 1871, when they engaged in the manufacture of staves and heading, to which products were added buggy bows, in 1889. Their factory is one of the extensive establishments of the city, employing forty-five to fifty men. The product, which annually amounts to $75,000 to $100,000, is shipped to St. Louis, Cincinnati, Louisville, Boston, Buffalo and other points. The manufactory is situated between Ewing and Griffith streets, fronting on Superior, and extending to the tracks of the "Nickle Plate" railroad. Mr. Ranke was married April 19, 1863, to Sophia Jacobs, a native of Germany, who was born February 18, 1845, and came to America with her parents in the August following. She is the daughter of Frederick Jacobs, a painter by trade, who was one of the pioneers of this city, and died in August, 1879. In the same year his wife died, whose maiden name was Sophia Jacobs. Mr. and Mrs. Ranke have nine children: William, born January 20, 1865; Sophia, July 21, 1867; Henry, March 1, 1870; Louisa, August 3, 1873; Emma, May 29, 1876; Frederick, October 14, 1878; Clara, February 4, 1881; Herman, September 25, 1884; Lydia, April 7, 1887. Mr. and Mrs. Ranke are members of the Emanuel's Lutheran church.

William Yergens, of the above named firm, came to America in 1845, from Prussia, where he was born March 26, 1828, and from New York, came to Fort Wayne by the way of Albany, Buffalo and over the lake to Toledo, thence by the Wabash & Erie canal. His settlement dates June 1, 1845, and though that seems a comparatively recent period, yet he had the experiences of an early settler and pioneer, as there were then not over 500 people in the town, and Indians were almost as numerous as whites. He has seen the town increase a hundred fold. He first engaged in canal boating, but in 1860, started a saw-mill, and embarked in lumbering. The mill was destroyed in 1863, but immediately rebuilt. In 1866, the partnership with Mr. Ranke was formed, which has developed into a prosperous and important business. Mr. Yergens was married in 1850, to Eliza Jacobs, who was born in Germany, November 26, 1834, and came with her parents, Frederick and

Sophia Jacobs, in 1845, to America, and settled at Fort Wayne. They have six children, three of whom are living: William, born in 1854, is married, and is employed in the works; Gustav, born in 1861, is married, and served as deputy revenue collector during Cleveland's administration; and Emma, born in 1864, is the wife of William Moellering, of the city. The family are members of the Lutheran church.

Noteworthy in the roll of young men of the city who are interested in manufacturing, is John M. Landenberger, treasurer and manager of the Indiana machine works. He assumed the duties of his present position April 7, 1888. Mr. Landenberger is a native of Philadelphia, born September 28, 1863, son of Gottleib and Mathilda (Storm) Landenberger, natives of Germany. The father, who was born in 1843, came to the United States in early boyhood, and lived in Philadelphia until his death in 1866. The mother died in the same city in 1871, at about forty years of age. Of their seven children John M. is the fourth. He obtained a common school education, and came to Fort Wayne in 1875, and studied three years at Concordia college, subsequently attending a business college at his native city. He was married October 19, 1887, to Amelia F., daughter of J. F. W. Meyer. She was born in this city in 1863. They are active members of the Lutheran church. Mr. Landenberger is a republican, and cast his first electoral ballot for James G. Blaine.

The City carriage works, established in 1857, is extensively engaged in the manufacture of carriages, buggies, sleighs, etc., and is one of the largest of the kind in the city. The plant includes a brick factory, 60x100 feet, on Clay street, and a large storage warehouse on Clinton street. The firm name of the proprietors is Dudenhoefer, Daniels & Co., the partners being George P. Dudenhoefer, S. S. Daniels, H. E. Bueker and H. P. Sherer, recently of New Mexico. The other gentlemen named are much respected citizens, of long residence in the city, which they have done their part to advance.

George P. Dudenhoefer, the senior partner, learned the trade of carriage-maker with his father, George P. Dudenhoefer, who emigrated from Germany in 1841, and in Pennsylvania married his wife, Mary A., also a native of Germany. They resided four years in Ohio, and came to Allen county in 1845, settling in Marion township, where their son, George P., was born January 27, 1848. The latter, at eighteen years of age, came to Fort Wayne, and worked for eight years in various factories. In 1877 he purchased an interest in the City carriage works, of which he has since been one of the proprietors. Mr. Dudenhoefer was married October 19, 1871, to Minnie Scherer, a native of Marion township, daughter of Louis and Elizabeth Scherer, natives of Germany, who were married in that county, and emigrated and settled at Fort Wayne in 1847. Mr. Dudenhoefer and wife have had three children: Amelia C., Mary S. and Clara C., the last of whom died in infancy. He and wife are members of the St. Paul's Lutheran church. His long experience and talent for business give him a high rank among the manufacturers of the city.

Capt. Edward A. Ross-Lewin, one of the foremost of those skillful men whose work have done so much for the advancement of the city, now foreman of the Fort Wayne furniture company, was born in Ireland, June 12, 1833, son of Francis B. and Susanna (Kenney) Ross-Lewin, both natives of County Clare. The father was born in 1787, came to the United States with his family in 1849, located first at Rochester, N. Y., and in 1857, removed to Elkhart, Ind., where he died in 1858, and was followed in death by his widow in 1864, at the age of fifty-seven. They had eleven children, of whom eight are living, Edward being the second. He was educated in his native country at King's college, at Ennis, and after coming to this country began in 1849, an apprenticeship at the carpenter's and joiner's trade at Rochester, N. Y. In 1854 he went to Elkhart, and was there engaged for five years as a contractor. He removed to Rochester, N. Y., in 1859, and in 1861 enlisted in Company H, Twenty-sixth New York infantry, was elected second lieutenant by his company, in 1862 commissioned first lieutenant, and in the fall of the same year commissioned as captain. His regiment was actively engaged for two years in nearly every engagement in which the army of the Potomac was. His record as a true and faithful soldier was terminated by his honorable muster out in 1863. In 1864 he came to Fort Wayne and for fourteen years he was occupied as foreman of the great wheel works of N. G. Olds & Son. He also acted as foreman in the construction of the Masonic Temple and First Presbyterian church. His connection with the Fort Wayne furniture factory began in 1888. Mr. Ross-Lewin was married in 1858, to Sarah Jane Gardner, of Rochester, N. Y., who was born in 1837, daughter of John and Anna Spencer Gardner, and they have two children: Ida L., now cashier of the Fort Wayne furniture company, and Jennie S. In politics he is a democrat.

Andrew R. Henderson, superintendent of the woolen mill operated under the name of French, Hanna & Co., was born near Auburn, Cayuga county, N. Y., March 31, 1826. His parents, Joel P. and Mary Ann (Rogers) Henderson, the former a native of Connecticut and the latter of Cayuga county, N. Y., removed, when he was a lad of twelve years, to Chautauqua county, N. Y., where at the age of thirteen he became apprenticed in a woolen mill. During almost his entire life he has been employed in woolen manufacture. In 1842 he took a position in a mill at Erie, Penn. In 1848 he went to Waterloo, N. Y. Subsequently he had charge of mills at North East, Penn.; Westfield, N. Y.; Kingsville, Ashtabula county, Ohio. In March, 1856, he came to Fort Wayne to manage the mill now owned by French, Hanna & Co., of which he has now been superintendent for about thirty-three years. Mr. Henderson was married in 1855 to Zervia Berdsley, who died in June, 1858. She was born in Rochester, N. Y. March 22, 1860, he was married to Miss Annetta E., daughter of Harvey M. and Elvira (Lampher) Putnam, natives of Lewis county, N. Y. Mr. Henderson and wife are the parents of an only son, Charles W. Henderson, who was born January

17, 1861, and is now a bookkeeper in the office of the Pittsburg shops. Mr. Henderson is a Knight Templar, and politically he is a republican.

Martin L. Albrecht, carriage manufacturer, is a native of Fairfield county, Ohio. He was born June 6, 1847, the son of Rev. Christopher and Mary Ann (Conrad) Albrecht, who were natives, the former of Baden, Germany, and the latter of Fairfield county, Ohio. Christopher Albrecht was the son of Andrew Albrecht, with whom he came to America in 1832 and located in Tiffin, Seneca Co., Ohio, being one of the earliest settlers. Christopher Albrecht helped to construct the Wabash & Erie canal, and with the money thus earned he took a course in the Lutheran theological seminary at Columbus, Ohio. He then began his ministerial duties in Fairfield county, and labored as a minister for more than forty years, having but four different charges. For more than twenty-five years he was pastor of the Lutheran church at Miamisburg, Ohio. He died near that place in 1887. The mother of Martin Albrecht died when he was but two years old, in Perry county, Ohio, whither his parents had moved. After her death he found a home with his grandfather, Andrew Albrecht, at Tiffin, with whom he remained until he was twenty-one. His education was received in the public schools of Tiffin and at Heidelberg college of that place, which he attended one year. During the greater part of his youth he was employed as a clerk. At eighteen he entered upon an apprenticeship as a carriage painter and served three years. In 1868 he went from Tiffin to Indianapolis where, for a few months, he worked at his trade, after which, in October, he came to Fort Wayne. Here he worked two years for Stanley & Bieber. For six months thereafter he was the owner of a shop in which was done carriage painting. He then formed a partnership in the livery business with James Liggett, and to it his attention was given for a year and a half. For the past seventeen years he has been engaged in the manufacture of carriages, and he has now done a continuous business of that kind longer than any other man in the city. From November, 1876, to January, 1883, he was one of the proprietors of the City carriage works. For the past six years he has been the proprietor of his present establishment on the corner of Barr and Main streets. Mr. Albrecht was married May 10, 1870, to Miss Dora Bloom, a native of Germany, born in 1848, the daughter of Philip Bloom, with whom she came to America when a child. They have seven children: Frank L., Samuel W., Edward, Eva M., Fred, Dora S. and Christopher. Mr. Albrecht and wife are members of the German Lutheran church. He was the first president of the city hospital and is the present incumbent, having held the position for the past six years.

Calvin J. Winch, an old and honored citizen of Fort Wayne, and the founder of Winch & Sons' hub and spoke works, was born near Burlington, Vt., July 14, 1824, the son of Joseph and Almira (Murray) Winch, who were respectively natives of New Hampshire and Vermont. The grandfather, Joseph Winch, was a native of New Hampshire. He was reared to manhood on a farm in his native county, and received a common school education. In the latter part of his youth he learned the blacksmith's trade, and he pursued it for a great many years. In about 1845, he emigrated to Indiana and located in Monmouth, Adams county, where he conducted a blacksmith shop some ten years. He then erected a steam saw-mill at that place and operated it about three years. He then gave his attention to agricultural pursuits until the spring of 1864, at which time he removed to Leo, Allen county, Ind., having purchased a grist-, woolen- and saw-mill. He conducted that property about five years. In the spring of 1869 he came to Fort Wayne, and for about two years he was engaged in the building of gravel roads and streets. He then began the manufacture of hubs in connection with his son, H. D. Winch, the firm name being Winch & Son. The manufacture of spokes has been added, and the firm is now the owner of a large factory in Fort Wayne and another in Jay county, Ind. For two years their business was at Arcola, then at Geneva, Adams county, and still later at Briant, Jay county. The factory in Fort Wayne was started in October, 1886. Another son, W. E. Winch, has been a member of the firm about five years. Mr. C. J. Winch was married when about twenty-years old, to Miss Phebe C., daughter of Calvin T. and Fannie (Bell) Dorwin, who were respectively natives of Vermont and New York. She was born in Richland county, Ohio, in 1834. Mr. C. J. Winch and wife have had eight children: Walter J., born March 9, 1850; Homer Dick, February 24, 1853; Willard E. and Mildred D., April 2, 1858; Sherman P., October 31, 1862; Fannie M., April 1, 1867; Jessie M., July 4, 1869; Howard T., October 29, 1872, all of whom are living except Walter J., who died in the fourth year of his age. Mr. Winch is an ardent temperance man and strongly opposed to monopolies. He is always active in public enterprises, is an honorable, upright man, and very highly respected.

John Pressler, proprietor of the Summit City galvanized iron works, was born at Chambersburg, Franklin county, Penn., October 25, 1845, the second of two children now living of George and Anna Pressler, who were natives of Germany and immigrated to Pennsylvania and there died. In 1863 Mr. Pressler enlisted in Company L, Twenty-first Pennsylvania cavalry, William H. Boyd commanding, but being under age at the time, his father required his release and he was honorably discharged soon afterward. He learned the tinner's trade at Chambersburg, and in 1868 came to Fort Wayne. For three years he was employed in the P., Ft. W. & C. railroad shops, under Joseph Stillwagon, and for a time at the Wabash shops. He was then for some time occupied in the tin and jobbing business, and in 1883 established his present business, which is the largest and most extensive in its line in the city. In 1885 he bought his present business property on the corner of Barr and Columbia streets, which he has greatly improved, to furnish room for his increased business. In addition to his manufacturing he deals in hot air furnaces and metalic shingles, and makes specialties of natural gas and other fittings, and grates and mantels. He was married

July 18, 1868, to Amelia Menze, who was born in Fort Wayne, and they have six children: Rosa, Charles F., John A., Edith A., Carrie and George H. He and wife are members of the English Lutheran church. Mr. Pressler became a member of Sol D. Bayless lodge, F. & A. M., April 28, 1886, and in 1888 became a Scottish Rite Mason. He is an enterprising, active business man, and though beginning in Fort Wayne with small means has prospered, and has a pleasant home on West Main street, which he purchased in 1886.

Sylvanus F. Bowser, a well-known citizen of Fort Wayne, is at the head of the firm of S. F. Bowser & Co., patentees and manufacturers of the Perfect Self-measuring oil tank, and perfecting siphon, also pumps and self-measuring oil wagons. He was born in Allen county, August 8, 1854. His parents, John H. and Eliza (Kieger) Bowser, came from their native state of Penusylvania to Allen county in 1833, and were among the sturdy pioneers, and followed farming in Perry township. The father was born April 15, 1812, and died March 10, 1879; the mother, who was born September 18, 1818, passed away September 9, 1875. To them thirteen children were born, eight of whom survive. S. F. Bowser was reared on the farm of his parents, and received his education in the common schools. In 1882 he took a position as traveling salesman for the Chicago paper house of W. H. Wells & Bro., and was thus engaged until 1885, when he perfected the invention above named, and began its manufacture. Beginning on a small scale, he continued the business until July 1, 1888, when the company was organized, by associating with him August Bowser and William F. Devilbiss. They erected the factory now in use, a three-story frame building, with 20,000 feet of floor space, and are doing a prosperous and rapidly increasing business. Mr. Bowser is a member of the First Baptist church. He was married October 9, 1878, to Sarah F. Russell, of Fort Wayne, and to them four children have been born.

Aime Racine, a prominent citizen of Fort Wayne, has developed here the manufacture of horse collars on a large scale, and the "Racine" horse collar has a national reputation. In 1865 he fromed a partnership in this city for the manufacture of harness, to which was subsequently added the making of collars, and for more than twenty years he has conducted that business. The factory occupies a handsome three story brick building, at the corner of First and North Cass streets, which was erected by Mr. Racine several years ago. In the near vicinity Mr. Racine has two comfortable residence buildings, one of which he occupies. Mr. Racine is not wholly absorbed in his prosperous business, but takes and interest in public affairs, and is prominent as a republican. During two years he served as councilman from the ninth ward. He was born in Switzerland, March 16, 1834, son of John Jacob Racine. In 1849 he accompanied his parents to this country, and they settled first in Washington township, this county. He remained upon the farm until 1865, and then began an apprenticeship in the harness business in Fort Wayne. He worked as a journeyman in Chicago six months; at Lafayette, Ind., six years, and as foreman in a collar factory in Toledo, two years. He was married in 1865, to Louisa Sawdy, of the latter city, and they have living two children: Ollie and Nellie. Mr. Racine is a member of the I. O. O. F.

Erastus B. Kunkle, member of the firm of E. B. Kunkle & Co., proprietors of the Fort Wayne safety valve works, was born at Greensburg, Westmoreland county, Penn., December 14, 1836, the son of Leonard and Harriet C. Kunkle, natives of Pennsylvania and New Jersey, respectively. In his youth he learned the trade of a machinist with his father, and has followed it during life. In 1862, he removed to Alliance, Ohio, where he was employed two years, and then in December, 1864, came to Fort Wayne. During eleven years he was employed in the locomotive department of the Pittsburgh, Ft. Wayne & Chicago railroad shops, and since that period has turned his attention to invention and manufacture. He invented the celebrated Kunkle lock-up pop safety valve, upon which he received a patent May 4, 1875, and another July 24, 1877. In January, 1876, he began the manufacture of the valves, and as it is an article of much importance and solid merit, it finds an extensive sale over the continent. Mr. Kunkle has also manifested his skill and genius in mechanics by the invention of an egg beater, a water gauge, a gauge-cock, and a steam gauge, on all of which he has received patents. He is honored as a citizen, is one of the trustees of the English Lutheran church, of which he and wife are members, and served one year as a trustee of the water-works, to which position he was elected in 1887, but was compelled to resign on account of of his private business. He was married October 22, 1868, to Louisa E., daughter of Emanuel and Harriet Bostick, esteemed pioneer citizens. She was born in Lancaster county, Penn., October 25, 1845. They have these children: Ella A., Eva H., Frances C., Blanche M., Lulu S. and Edith P., all living except Frances, who died at the age of three years.

Jacob Klett, one of the leading citizens of Fort Wayne, of German birth, was born in Wurtemberg, in 1831. In his native land he was educated, and learned the potter's trade. In 1853 he immigrated and in the following year, settled at Fort Wayne. Four years later, he entered the employment of Andrews & Oakley, of Fort Wayne, in their planing-mill, and remained with them until 1860. He became engaged with Clark & Hurd, lumber dealers, in 1861, and continued with the successors, Clark & Rhinesmith, and upon the organization of the lumber company of the same name in 1871, he became a stockholder, and accepted the position of yard foreman and inspector. Having become thoroughly acquainted with the business, he opened an extensive yard on his own account in 1877, and prospering in this business, added in 1889, a large and complete planing-mill plant, and began the manufacture of sash, doors, blinds and general factory work. Mr. Klett's business experience has extended over thirty-one years, and he is one of the leading lumber men of the city. Socially, he has a wide circle of friends and acquaintances. He was married July 6, 1858, to Louisa Sauter, a native of

Germany, who came to this country at about the age of about five years, and they have had eight children, five of whom are living. J. A., the oldest son, is engaged with his father in the lumber business.

The management of the extensive lumber yards of Coombs & Co., of Fort Wayne, is entrusted to Nelson Thompson, who resides at No. 339 East Wayne street. He is a native of Sweden, born November 10, 1844. He remained on the farm with his parents until 1865, and then immigrated. He came west and located at Chicago, where he remained until 1867, and then came to Fort Wayne, where he has since resided. While in Chicago he was employed in laying Nicholson pavement, and he was engaged in that after coming to Fort Wayne until 1877, being occasionally in the employment of the city in repairing bridges, culverts, etc. In 1877 he entered the lumber yard of Coombs & Co., and in 1885 was made manager of the yards. Mr. Thompson is a member of the English Lutheran church. He was married in 1868 to Augustine Pichon, daughter of Alexander A. Pichon, a native of France, who settled in Fort Wayne about 1833, and is now in his seventy-sixth year, making his home with Mr. Thompson. To Mr. and Mrs. Thompson three children have been born: Peter Alexander, John William and Charles Dollies. Mr. Thompson has been very successful in business, and has recently completed a handsome two-story residence on East Wayne street. In politics, he is a republican, and his religious affiliation is with the English Lutheran church.

Joseph C. Cromwell is one of the prominent factors in the great lumber industry of Fort Wayne, and has been connected with the business here since his coming to the city in 1872. His first employment was as bookkeeper and measurer for the lumber firm of Hoffman Brothers, and he remained with them until the summer of 1876, when he became engaged with Coombs & Co., hardware dealers, as entry clerk. In 1880 he assumed the position of chief clerk and head bookkeeper with the Kerr Murray manufacturing company. After four years in this position, in 1884, he engaged in the lumber business on his own account, and now has an extensive trade, manufacturing lumber, and shipping that and logs to home and foreign markets. His mills are in Adams and Jay counties, with headquarters there and in Fort Wayne, and the annual business amounts to $20,000. Mr. Cromwell was born at Frederick City, Md., January 17, 1852, the son of Joseph W. Cromwell, now a worthy citizen of this city, elsewhere mentioned. He received his education in the schools of West Virginia, and in 1868 began his business career as a clerk at Frederick City. He was married in 1880 to Maggie C. Hardt, daughter of John C. Hardt, of the lumber firm of Hardt & Keefer, of Frederick City. She was born November 23, 1850. They have three children. Mr. Cromwell is a member of Sol. D. Bayless lodge, No. 359, F. & A. M., and of the First Presbyterian church.

David Tagtmeyer, a leading lumber manufacturer, embarked in that business in 1861, in company with three partners, and so continued three years, when the mill was destroyed by fire. It was rebuilt, but seemed fated, for two months later the boiler exploded, again destroying the building. A second time it was rebuilt but was subsequently sold. Afterward, Mr. Tagtmeyer and a partner purchased the property and operated it one year, then disposed of it. He was next engaged in the grocery business on Columbia street for one year, and then in 1868, purchased a half interest in the mill he now runs, gaining possession of the entire property five years later. He now manufactures hardwood lumber, the product being about 1,300,000 feet annually, which is mainly disposed of to the railroads. Mr. Tagtmeyer, though now a successful and prosperous manufacturer, started as a poor man. He was born in North Germany, February 5, 1834, and came to America alone in 1853. He came direct to Fort Wayne, disembarking from the canal boat which was his conveyance from Toledo, at the place where Monning's mill now stands. The first four months of his residence he worked upon the construction of the Wabash railroad, and next spent one winter in the woods of Adams county, the epidemic of cholera having brought affairs to a stand-still in Fort Wayne. Mr. Tagtmeyer was married July, 1862, to Caroline Kaysar, who was born in Prussia, in 1834, and died in 1871, leaving two children, of whom one survives. In 1873, he was married a second time, to Sophy Axt, who was born at this city, in 1843. She died in June, 1875, leaving one child, and in November, 1876, he married Christine Tilking, who is a native of Prussia, born in 1854, and they have had five children. Mr. Tagtmeyer is a member of the Lutheran church.

The secretary of the Hoffman lumber company, Milton P. Longacre, is a native of Chester county, Pa., born January 14, 1851. He is the oldest of five living children of David and Hannah B. (Rhinehart) Longacre, natives of Pennsylvania, the father born about 1827 and the mother about 1831. His father is now engaged in farming and stock-raising in Chester county, where the mother died June 14, 1870. Mr. Longacre was educated in the public schools at his home, and remained there until twenty-one years of age, when he went to Pittsburgh and was for six months in the employment of the Wheeler & Wilson sewing machine company. In August, 1872, he came to Fort Wayne, and served four years in the freight department of the Pennsylvania company, under J. C. Davis. He entered the employment of Hoffman Brothers in the fall of 1876, and since the organization of the company has held his present position, becoming favorably known as an alert and capable business man. May 1, 1873, he was married to Rachel Lilly, of Perry county, Penn., born January 3, 1852, who died in March, 1876, leaving one child, Bertha L., born September 20, 1874. September 20, 1880, he was married to Caroline Schlatter, who was born in Allen county, July 12, 1853, and they have four children: Milton G., born November 2, 1882; Hazel I., born October 29, 1884; David S., born March 1, 1886; and Leon R., born February 19, 1889. He and wife are members of the First Presbyterian church.

Philip H. Hyman, a prominent citizen of Fort Wanye, is a native of Germany, born March 19, 1841. In 1852 he accompanied his parents, William and Anna M. Hyman, to America, and the family settled in Huron county, Ohio. In 1866 he engaged in mercantile pursuits in Kirby, Wyandotte county, Ohio, and was so occupied six years. In 1872 he removed to Columbia City, Ind., and was engaged in the lumber and stave business, to which his whole attention has since been given. In 1873 he removed to Portland, Ind.; in 1875 to Versailles, Ohio; to New Washington, Ohio, in 1876; in 1877 to Tiffin, Ohio, changing his residence frequently with the opening of new railroads. In 1882 he came to Fort Wayne. His lumber and stave interests at present are at Payne, Ohio. Mr. Hyman was married August 11, 1868, to Cassie Jetter, who was born in Philadelphia, March 13, 1851, daughter of Jacob and Anna Jetter. They have had nine children: William J., Isabel L., Philip H., Edward A., Minnette E., Arthur F., Estella C., Wanetta J. and Anna M., of whom William J., Isabel L. and Minnette E. are dead. Mr. Hyman and wife are members of the German Reform church. In politics he is a republican.

Samuel D. Bitler, manufacture of cooper's truss hoops, corner of East Wayne and Schick streets, Fort Wayne, was born in Berks county, Penn., November 23, 1845, son of Daniel and Eve (Frees) Bitler. The father was one of seven sons of Daniel Bitler, also a native of Pennsylvania, who was the son of John Bitler, a native of Switzerland, who emigrated to America between 1740 and 1750, and became a soldier of the revolutionary war. He was married to an English lady in Philadelphia. Daniel, father of Samuel D., was a blacksmith and farmer; he died in August, 1867, at the age of seventy years. Eve Frees, the mother, was born in Berks county, of German descent, and died in 1863. Samuel D. Bitler left the farm in 1870, and spent a year with an engineering force surveying the Wilmington railroad. In 1872 he came to Fort Wayne, and for a year and a half was in the employ of N. G. Olds & Son. In June, 1875, he became a member of the firm of H. Stephan & Co., in the manufacture of cooper's truss hoops, and upon the death of Mr. Stephan in January, 1883, became sole proprietor of the business. His trade extends over the entire country, shipments being made to St. Louis, San Francisco, New Orleans, New York, Nashville, and even to Cuba and Germany. Mr. Bitler was married February 9, 1885, to Mary Beidler, of Birdsboro, Penn., and they have one child. He is a member of the I. O. O. F. and K. of P. Was a charter member of Constoga lodge of Morganstown, Penn.

A. C. Beaver, for many years an honored citizen of Fort Wayne, hat witnessed the growth of the city from 1,500 to 40,000 inhabitants, and meanwhile has contributed in a decided manner to this advancement by active and enterprising business operations. He has been uniformly successful in business, and enjoys a well-founded reputation for integrity as well as talent for the successful accomplishment of his undertakings. He was born near Hagerstown, Md., April 19, 1822, the son of John and

Dorothy (Mowen) Beaver, both natives of Franklin county, Penn. The mother died in 1837 and the father subsequently married Elizabeth Best. The family left Maryland in 1842, settled first in Preble county and then in Montgomery county, Ohio, where the father was surveyor for the county for four years, with his residence at Dayton. The father came to Fort Wayne in 1860 and here died about 1881. His widow is now living at Columbus, Ohio. A. C. Beaver started from Preble county for Fort Wayne on foot in February, 1844, and walked the entire distance, arriving here March 1, 1844, with a total capital of 75 cents. He worked at the carpenter's trade, which he had learned in Ohio, until 1852, when he began contracting, at which he was occupied until he went into the lumber business in 1867, with Jeptha Mitchell, of the well-known firm of Mitchell & Rowland, of Cincinnati, as a partner. The business here with a capital of $10,000, was conducted in Mr. Beaver's name for three years, when the latter purchased the interest of Mr. Mitchell, and organized the Beaver-Miller lumber company, still in business, with a capital of $24,000. After the panic of 1873 Mr. Beaver retired from that firm as an active partner, and organized the Fort Wayne lumber company, with a capital of about $10,000 devoted to wholesale trade. The retail business was added in 1888 and the capital increased to $20,000. Mr. Beaver was married in 1848 to Mary Maples, daughter of D. W. Maples, a pioneer of Fort Wayne. She died in 1853, leaving three children: Catherine, Mary E. and Elizabeth, of whom the first only is living. In 1855 he was married to Caroline Spence, a native of Leeds, England, who died in 1858, leaving one child, Clara E., wife of Frank Miller, of Sacramento, Cal. In 1861 Mr. Beaver married Emily Parks, born at North Bend, Ind., and they have two children: Florence E. and Montgomery G., the latter now associated with his father in business. Mr. Beaver united with the Presbyterian church some forty years ago, but recently became a member of the First Baptist church.

The Fort Wayne steam stone works, the leading establishment in its line, is managed by Henry Keller. He is a native of Gemany, born in 1853. He emigrated to America in 1870, and located at Chicago, where he learned the stone cutter's trade, and remained until 1884, being for five years foreman of one of the largest in the state and oldest stone yards in that city. On February 2, 1884, Mr. Keller removed to Fort Wayne and purchased a half interest in the stone works of Frederick Roth. The firm of Roth & Keller has ever since met with success, and at present it is the most extensive in the city, and is the only one in northern Indiana having a steam derrick. Mr. Roth died September 14, 1888, but the firm name is continued. The business was established about twenty-three years ago, and has continued at the same location to the present, passing through various hands. When Mr. Keller entered the firm the business was on a small scale, but each year it has improved. They employ from forty to fifty men and do a general stone cutting business. Contracting is also carried on, and among the buildings for which this firm has furnished the cut stone are the new government building, asylum for feeble-minded children, St. Mary's Catholic church, St. Paul's Lutheran church, Schmitz's, Rich's and Baker's business blocks, at Fort Wayne; First Methodist Episcopal church, Jacob Bros.' residence and I. O. O. F. block at Huntington; the Peru Catholic church; city hall and engine house, Defiance, Ohio; county jail, Decatur, Ind.; court-house in Bluffton, Ind., and Paulding, Ohio, and various others. Mr. Keller was married January 4, 1880, to Ida Scheibe, a native of Chicago, who died in 1882, leaving one son, Frederick. He was married November 11, 1884, to Mary Leitt, born in Germany, by whom he had four children, of whom three are living, Henry, Ida and Mary. Mrs. Keller is a member of the Catholic church.

Elliott S. Underhill, one of the prominent young men of the city, was born at Olmstead Falls, Ohio, December 1, 1858. He is the son of P. S. and Harriet O. Underhill, natives of Vermont and Maine, respectively. When he was quite young, his parents located in Fort Wayne. The father died in 1877, but his widow is still a resident of the city. In 1875, Mr. Underhill engaged in the grocery business and was so occupied for three years. In the spring of 1879, he embarked in the marble business, and in 1881, went to Hicksville, where he was a partner in the same business two years. Returning to Fort Wayne, from 1883 until 1885, he was employed as a letter carrier, and then in the retail oil business. During the session of 1887 of the Indiana legislature, he was employed as a clerk in the house of representatives. He then resumed the marble business, and is now one of the proprietors of Underhill's monumental works, a large establishment at No. 82 Barr street. Mr. Underhill was married April 8, 1880, to Anna E. Scott, by whom he has three children: George E., Jessie and Hattie. In politics he is a republican, and he has for four years been a member of the republican county central committee.

Among the industries of Fort Wayne, a notable one is the manufacture of the various popular beverages of the day. Prominent among those so engaged is the firm of Louis Brames & Co., manufacturers of seltzer and mineral waters, ginger ale, birch beer, etc. Louis Brames, the leading member of this firm, began this business in 1880, the firm being known for the first year as Brames & Ehrman. He does a large manufacture and ships extensively. Mr. Brames was born in Adams county, Ind., near Decatur, January 3, 1847. His father, Christopher Brames, was born in Germany, in 1814, and was married in his native land to Elizabeth Vodde. The family emigrated about 1834, and after spending four years in New York, came to Fort Wayne. He was by occupation a farmer and was an early settler of Allen county. He died at this city, April 25, 1881, and his wife followed him February 12, 1886. Of their seven children three are living, of whom Louis is the second. He attended the common schools and a commercial college at this city, and in 1868 engaged in the grocery business, and three years later became a bookkeeper, successively for Messrs. Oppenheimer & Heilbroner, Abraham Wolf, and Frank Hake & Co. He was married in 1871, to Mary A. Tibett, who was born in Allen county, in 1849, and they have four children: Anna, John B., Antoinette and Louis. In politics he is a pronounced democrat, and in 1878, he was elected to the city council from the first ward, an honor which was again conferred in 1880. He is a member of the Catholic church.

One of the leading and most thoroughly competent brewers of Indiana is Peter Nusbaum, foreman of the celebrated establishment of C. L. Centlivre. He was born in Germany, December 26, 1845, the son of Peter and Margaret (Dietsh) Nusbaum, who were born and passed their lives in that country. The eldest of their seven children was Peter Nusbaum. He received his education in his native land, and in 1859 began to learn the trade he has since followed. In 1871 he came to this country, and settled at Chicago, where he remained seven years, coming then to Fort Wayne. He was engaged by Mr. Centlivre as foreman, and has held the position ten years. His thirty years' experience has made him a valuable man in that business. Mr. Nusbaum was married in 1874 to Susanna Mathy, who was born in Chicago in 1857, and they have seven children: Matilda, Joseph, Mary, Malchen, Victor, Louis and Ida. He is in politics a democrat.

A well-known citizen of Fort Wayne, and a representative of one of the oldest families, is Philip J. Lindlag. His father, C. W. Lindlag, was born in Germany in 1818, and there married Sevilla Kiser, who was born about 1820. They came to Allen county about 1834, and the father was engaged in farming until 1861, when he removed to the city from his Wayne township farm. He worked upon the Wabash & Erie canal during his early residence in the county, and after removing to the city was elected street commissioner in 1862. He also did business as a contractor. He died in 1882, and his widow followed him in 1884. The second of the three living children is Philip J., born at Fort Wayne, December 27, 1854. He received a common school education. For some years he was engaged in the contracting business, and was subsequently for fifteen years, the Fort Wayne agent for Graser & Brand's brewery, of Toledo. In 1889 he became the agent of the Berghoff brewery company, of Fort Wayne. He resides at the old home, 115 Washington street, and owns 213 acres of land in the township, the farm of his parents. He is a democrat in politics, and a member of Phoenix lodge, No. 101, K. of P.

One of the early German settlers in Allen county, was John Braun, who came to America about 1847, stopped awhile in New Jersey, and came to Fort Wayne about 1850. Here he married Barbara Heber, a country woman, who had immigrated about 1852. She is now living in the city. He was a carpenter by trade, and worked at that in Fort Wayne until about 1863, when he removed to St. Joseph, and located on the farm where his son now resides. In 1880, he began the manufacture of brick. His death occurred June 27, 1886. John C. Braun, the son of these worthy parents, was about seven years of age when they removed to the farm. He was educated at the St. Peter's Lutheran school of St. Joseph township, and was confirmed at St. John's school in Fort Wayne. He resided on the farm and worked with his father at brick making, until the latter's death, when he took charge of the yards, and has since conducted the business. The yards are among the most extensive, and have a daily capacity of about 11,000 brick. The average product is about 11,000,000 per year. Mr. Braun and wife are members of St. John's Lutheran church. He was married in the fall of 1887, to Louisa Braun, who was born in Germany, and came to America about 1885. To this union a daughter has been born, Lottie. Mr. Braun has a well improved and valuable farm of fifty-four acres, upon which he has a comfortable two-story brick residence.

The brick industry enlists no more industrious manufacturer than Joseph Fremion, whose extensive yards are located at the north limits of Fort Wayne, between Harrison and Lafayette streets. The daily product of these yards is ten to eleven thousand daily, and the average annual output is 1,100,000. All of this immense product is sold as rapidly as made. Mr. Fremion was born at Lorance, France, April 23, 1829. Coming to America in 1848, he first made his home in Hancock county, Ohio, but in 1853 came to Fort Wayne. In 1869 he engaged in his present business. Mr. Fremion was married in 1854 to Seraphine Perasote, a native of France. They have nine children, of whom seven are living. They are members of St. Peter's Catholic church.

The manufacture of brick, one of the important Fort Wayne industries, is quite extensively engaged in by Leonard & Son. The senior member, Nelson Leonard, was born in Henry county, Ind., in 1825, and came to Allen county in March, 1871, and located on the Leo gravel road, two miles north of Fort Wayne, and established a brick yard. He has followed brick-making all his life, and is one of the pioneer brickmakers of the state. He married Drusilla Llewellyn, who was born near Harrisburg, Va., in 1823, and came with his parents to Indiana when about thirteen years of age. To these parents five children have been born, all of whom are living. The junior member of the firm, Jefferson Leonard, was born in Delaware county, Ind., December 9, 1847. In August, 1863, he ran away from home and enlisted in Company A, Twenty-first Indiana heavy artillery, and was with Sherman in his Atlanta campaign. He was mustered out at Indianapolis, December 20, 1865. After the war he went to southern California, and remained eighteen months, and then came to Fort Wayne and went to work with his father. In 1879 he went to Detroit and took charge of the packing house of Willard Parker & Co., and remained two years. He then returned to Fort Wayne and went into partnership with his father. He was married June 15, 1880, to Aurelia Smith, of Freemont, Ohio, who died February 5, 1884, at the age of thirty-two years and six months. He is a member of Summit City lodge, No. 132, F. & A. M., Royal Arch, and of Harmony lodge, No. 19, I. O. O. F., of which he has filled all the chairs.

Paul Koehler, a well-known manufacturer of brick, was born in Wayne township, February 21, 1856, the son of Michael and Catherine (Kiefer) Koehler. The father was born in Germany and came to this country in about 1841, making his home in the same year at Fort Wayne, and engaging in his business of brick-making. He died March 1, 1881, at the age of fifty-six years. His wife, who was born in Canton, Penn., died in September, 1886. Of their ten children, five sons and five daughters, one daughter is deceased. Paul Koehler was educated in the schools of Wayne township, and worked with his father at brick-making, and after the death of the latter, he took the management of the yard for his mother. In 1883 he engaged in brick making at Decatur, and in the fall of 1884 he went into business for himself, purchasing the yard of Alexander Armison at Decatur. This establishment includes twelve acres, and a two-story brick residence. At the yards are made a daily average of 14,000 bricks, and the annual output is very large. The product finds a ready sale at Fort Wayne, where Mr. Koehler resides. He was married in 1881, to Mary Brown, of St. Joseph township, and they have three children: Andrew, Clara and Charles. Mr. Koehler and wife are members of the St. John's Lutheran church.

John A. Koehler, a prominent manufacturer of brick at Fort Wayne, with residence and yards on Lafayette street, just without the city limits, was born at Fort Wayne, July 6, 1850, the son of Michael Koehler, one of the early manufacturers of brick at this place. The latter was a native of Germany, who came to America in 1847, and made his residence at Fort Wayne in the same year, and died in this city March 31, 1881. John A. received a common school education and remained with his parents until he was twenty-six years of age, when he established himself in business. His yards have a daily capacity of 12,000 brick and the average product each season is very large. Mr. Koehler is also agent for the Grosser & Brand brewing company, of Toledo, Ohio. Since 1886 he has been a member of Phoenix lodge, No. 101, K. of P., and his religious affiliation is with St. John's Lutheran church. He was married in 1871 to Anna Bergeman, of Fort Wayne, and to them seven children have been born, of whom five survive.

The City book bindery of Fort Wayne, though a comparatively new enterprise, is successful, owing to the good business qualifications of its proprietor, George W. Winbaugh. He was born in Indiana, June 11, 1860, and came with his father, John Winbaugh, to Fort Wayne in 1865. The father was a wagon-maker by trade, and followed that calling until his death in 1869. George W. was reared in Fort Wayne and educated at the public schools. About 1872 he entered the employ of Davis & Bros., bookbinders, and served an apprenticeship with that firm, with whom he remained until 1886. He then left their employ and formed a partnership with L. D. Ward, and together they established the City book bindery. In the fall of 1888, Mr. Winbaugh became the sole proprietor, his partner retiring, and he has since conducted the business alone. He does general bookbinding and paper box manufacturing on an extensive scale, supplying a territory within a radius of forty and fifty miles from Fort Wayne. He was married December 25, 1887, to Miss Jenny Titus, of Fort Wayne, and has one son, Charles, born December 21, 1888. Mr. Winbaugh is a member of English Lutheran church, and of Fort Wayne lodge, No. 14, I. O. O. F.

In the spring of 1873, Robert Gage, now a well-known and worthy citizen of Fort Wayne, engaged in the manufacture of brooms in this city, a pursuit which he has continued to the present. His establishment, which is one of the most extensive of the kind in this region, is situated at 318 West Main street, and his trade is a wide one. Mr. Gage was born in Pennsylvania, June 26, 1842, son of Robert and Mary Gage, both of whom were natives of Ireland. They immigrated to this state and three months after the birth of their son Robert, arrived at Fort Wayne, on the night of October 31, 1842. Robert Gage was married November 18, 1867, to Sarah, daughter of John and Sarah Conley. She is a native of Ireland. Mr. Gage has succeeded in his business, is enterprising and popular, and worthy as a citizen. He is a Mason, a member of the Knights of Pythias and a republican in politics.

BUSINESS INTERESTS.

Beginning with a traffic that ramified throughout the west, then wild indeed, Fort Wayne has throughout the major part of its career as a business center been the seat of extensive mercantile transactions. The traditions of its business are of establishments the dealings of which were not confined by state lines, and of pioneers in trade whose names were familiar even to the mountains beyond the Mississippi, and the story of its modern trade is no less flattering to the enterprise of the city. With railroad development came the establishment of wholesale houses at Fort Wayne, which receive goods from manufacturers, or imports from the seaboard, or fruits from the south, as cheaply as they can be delivered anywhere. The same splendid system of railroads enables the retailers in a considerable area of territory in Indiana, Ohio and Michigan, to visit the city more conveniently and receive goods from here more promptly, than is true of any other important point accessible from this region. Consequently, the wholesale business of Fort Wayne is established on a firm foundation, and it is rapidly assuming immense proportions, and will continue to grow, keeping pace with the increasing wealth and population of its tributary territory.

A brief enumeration of the houses engaged in the wholesale trade will convey an idea of the extent of this branch of business which would require much space to give otherwise. The dry goods houses of Root & Co., and George Dewald & Co., are widely known throughout three states. In the grocery trade, and in fruits, there has been the greatest development, and the houses of A. C. Trentman, G. E. Bursley & Co.,

x

Skelton, Watts & Wilt, C. D. C. Huestis, J. B. White, Louis Fox & Bro., William Moellering & Sons, Niswonger & Fox, and Pottlitzer Bros., do in the aggregate an immense trade, their salesmen being sent everywhere throughout the wide region tributary to Fort Wayne. In confectionery the houses of Fox & Brother and H. Barcus are prominent; the millinery trade is represented by Adams & Armstrong, and the wholesale shoe-house of Carnahan & Co., is one of the leading institutions of the kind in the state. The drug house of Meyer Bros. & Co. is one of the famous establishments of the city, and has a large wholesale trade. The field of the wholesale hardware trade is well occupied by the houses of Coombs & Co., established in 1862, Alderman, Yarnelle & Co., established in 1883, Morgan & Beach, who have done business for over thirty years; Pfeifer & Schlatter, established in 1882; G. W. Seavey, a house established in 1875 by Prescott Brothers, and saddlery hardware is sold extensively by J. W. Bell and A. L. Johns & Co. The wholesale paper trade, in its various departments, is represented by Foster Brothers, the Newspaper Union, Siemon & Bro., also prominent in the book trade, and M. R. Yohey.

The Fort Wayne newspaper union, which may be termed a wholesale house, as it is indeed in paper and printers' stationery, is mainly conducted for the furnishing of ready printed sheets to newspaper publishers throughout the large parts of the states of Ohio, Indiana and Michigan, and covers the field quite successfully. It is under the management of Charles D. Tillo, a thorough business man, who is well known among the publishers of the states named.

The local trade of some of the famous retail houses of the city almost reaches the dimensions of the wholesale business, and these establishments are resorted to not only by the people of the city but frequently by the inhabitants of towns at a considerable distance, customers who are drawn to the city by the shrewd advertising of Fort Wayne merchants and by the reputation of the latter for enterprise and attractive business methods.

The importance of organized action by those financially interested in the advancement of the city and the enlargement of its field of trade was recognized in January, 1872, by the incorporation of the Fort Wayne board of trade, the first officers of which were: A. P. Edgerton, president; J. H. Bass and R. G. McNiece, vice presidents; F. S. Shurick, secretary; Charles McCulloch, treasurer. On the 10th of November, 1875, another organization was incorporated, called the chamber of commerce, in which J. D. Bond, Thomas M. Andrews, F. S. Shurick, George T. Fowler and others were members.

The remarkable improvement of the city during the past few years, is no doubt due in large measure to the efforts of the business men of the city to advertise in a systematic way, the advantages of the city, and attract enterprises which would aid in the increase of population. This work has been done mainly through the organization of the Business Men's Exchange. Late in the winter of 1886, A. S. Lauferty, the founder of this institution, caused the publication of several calls for a meeting for organization, primarily to devise ways and means for the establishment of new gravel roads and the freeing of those now entering the city. Several meetings were held during December, and the subject named was exhaustively discussed without result. Finally at a meeting at which were present J. B. White, G. W. Seavey, Fred Eckart, J. B. Monning, D. N. Foster, Frank Alderman, A. J. Moynihan and A. S. Lauferty, the latter introduced a resolution, setting forth the need of united action on the part of business men, and the convenience of having a recognized head center for discussion and action concerning questions relating to the welfare of the city. The proposed association was dubbed the Fort Wayne Business Men's Exchange, and A. S. Lauferty, Fred Eckart and J. B. Monning were selected to canvass for members. At the next meeting the association was formed with sixty members, and it was incorporated January 3, 1887. The first officers were: president, J. B. White; vice president, E. C. Rurode; treasurer, Fred Eckart; corresponding secretary, A. J. Moynihan; financial secretary, J. B. Monning; directors, J. B. White, F. Beach, A. S. Lauferty, E. C. Rurode, Fred Eckart, J. B. Monning, Frank Alderman, D. A. Foster, L. Wolf, G. W. Pixley and O. W. Tresselt; trustees, Charles McCulloch, A. C. Trentman and C. S. Bash.

First amongst the achievements of the Exchange was the securing of the location of the school for feeble minded youth at this city. Representatives of the Exchange interested themselves in the matter, and by their efforts in setting forth the claims of Fort Wayne the legislature was induced to pass by the inducements held out by other localities, including even the capital itself, and direct the establishment of the school at this place.

The locating of the Pennington machine works, the Folding bed company, the Bickford furniture company, at Fort Wayne, are also due to the efforts of this organization, and the piping of natural gas is in a considerable degree the result of its out-reaching for all improvements possible to add to the city's attractions and conveniences. In municipal affairs it is an important factor, and no question of public improvement is left undebated by the Exchange. Its members represent the plucky, brainy and enterprising citizens of Fort Wayne.

The present officers are: Samuel M. Foster, president; G. W. Seavey, vice president; Fred Eckart, treasurer; J. B. Monning, financial and recording secretary.

August C. Trentman.—The leading commercial house of Fort Wayne, and one of the largest concerns in the west, is the extensive wholesale grocery establishment of A. C. Trentman, located on the northeast corner of Calhoun and East Washington streets. The laying of the foundation of this prosperous house dates as far back as 1848, when Bernard Trentman, in partnership with one Mills, established a retail grocery in this city. Two years later Mills retired from the business, and Bernard Trentman continued to conduct a retail establishment until 1864, and then engaged in the wholesale trade. In 1865 his son, August C., was admitted as a partner, the firm then being entitled B. Trentman & Son. The senior partner died in 1874, and his son succeeded to the entire business, but conducted the same under the old firm name until 1878, when the latter was changed to August C. Trentman, as it has since remained, A. C. Trentman being the sole proprietor. The business continued to increase from year to year, until in 1883 Mr. Trentman found it necessary to provide suitable quarters for the same, and in the fall of that year he began the erection of his present business building which is the largest in the city, and one of the largest in the west. The building is of brick, four stories and a basement, built in recent style of architecture, with pressed brick front, and occupies Nos. 111, 113, 115 and 117-19 and 20½ Calhoun street, and Nos. 1, 3 and 5 East Washington street, and has a total floorage of 45,000 square feet. The business is exclusively wholesale, the lines embracing all kinds of groceries, tobaccos and liquors. The territory covered by the six traveling salesmen employed by Mr. Trentman includes Indiana, southern Michigan, eastern Illinois and western Ohio, and the amount of business is enormous, and increases each year. As before stated this is the leading commercial house in Fort Wayne, and the largest wholesale grocery establishment in the state, and as such reflects much credit upon the city as well as upon the gentleman who manages the same as the sole proprietor.

Bernard Trentman, founder of this house, was one of the pioneers of Fort Wayne, and during life one of the most prominent citizens and merchants. Born in Hanover, Germany, in July, 1816, he emigrated to the United States in 1838, and was located first in Cincinnati, where he remained for about two years. In 1840 he came to Fort Wayne, his brother John having settled here two years previous, and he soon afterward engaged in farming in Marion township. Later he worked on the old Wabash & Erie canal, and was employed in the City mills. In 1848 he embarked in the retail grocery trade, and in 1864 converted the same into a wholesale business. He was a self-made man in every respect, coming to Allen county poor, and succeeding by good business qualifications in climbing to a high round in the ladder of prosperity. He was held in high esteem by the community, was a member of the Catholic church and died March 19, 1874. While living in Cincinnati in 1838 he was married to Anna M. Rheinhardt, who was born in Hanover, Germany, in 1817. To their union eleven children were born, seven of whom survive. The mother died in 1859.

August C. Trentman, proprietor of the above establishment, and one of the most prominent citizens of Fort Wayne, was born in Marion township, Allen county, February 20, 1843, and is the son of Barnard and Anna M. (Rheinhardt) Trentman. He was reared in Fort Wayne and given a good education, attending both the Brothers' and the public schools of the city, and finishing at Notre Dame, Ind. In 1864 he entered business with his father, and upon the death of the latter, in 1874, succeeded to the immense business of which he is at present proprietor.

His commercial career has been a successful and brilliant one, and today he is recognized as one of the leading wholesale grocers of the west. Aside from the grocery business Mr. Trentman is connected with other enterprises, being director of the Hamilton National bank, special partner in the business of J. B. Monning & Co., extensive spice and flour millers; stockholder in the Herman Berghoff brewing company, all of Fort Wayne, and he is treasurer of the Kœnig medicine company of Chicago. Success has attended the efforts of Mr. Trentman in all his undertakings, and he is now one of the substantial men of the state. As a citizen he ranks among the most prominent of Fort Wayne; in commercial circles he is recognized as the peer of any man in the state, and his reputation in that regard is spread throughout the west. Enterprising, energetic and liberal-minded, he has always been found ready to assist all movements looking to the advancement of his city, and for that spirit and his many commendable qualities he is esteemed and respected by his fellow citizens. Mr. Trentman was married October 19, 1865, to Jennie A. Niermann, who was born in Fort Wayne, and is the daughter of Herman Niermann, who was one of the old settlers and prominent citizens. Seven children have been born to Mr. and Mrs. Trentman, four of whom survive: May, born in 1871, graduated in 1889 from St. Mary's in the Woods; Carrie, born in 1873; Augustine, born in 1881, and Joseph, born in 1883. Mr. and Mrs. Trentman are members of the Cathedral church, and he is a member of the Catholic Knights of America. Socially Mr. Trentman and family rank among the first in Fort Wayne.

One of the oldest business establishments of Fort Wayne is the house of Morgan & Beach. The hardware business to which it succeeded was begun by Horace Durvy, in 1843, and taken up in 1856 by Oliver P. Morgan, a native of Dearborn county, who has been a resident of the city since 1832. In 1860 the present partnership was formed. Beginning in the retail trade, the house has now an extensive wholesale business. Mr. Morgan is a prominent citizen, is director and vice-president of the Old National bank, and has served as councilman and as school trustee for many years.

David N. Foster was born at Coldenham, Orange county, N. Y., April 24, 1841. His early years were spent on the farm of his parents, John Lyman and Harriet Scott Foster, and when fourteen years old he went to New York city, equipped with such education as he had been able to obtain in the country schools, and found employment as bundle boy in the store of William E. Lawrence, then a prominent merchant of the metropolis. Making rapid progress in his business education, at the age of eighteen, with his brother Scott Foster, he established the firm of Foster Brothers, which soon became one of the leading retail firms of the country, and particularly well known to Indiana people by the large branch establishments maintained at Fort Wayne, Terre Haute and Lafayette. Mr. Foster had an ambition for the profession of law, and having devoted his spare hours to study, in 1860 he sold out his interest to his brother, John Gray

Foster, and entered an academy at Montgomery, N. Y. But his study was soon stopped by the firing upon Fort Sumter. On the morning of the day following the first call for troops by Abraham Lincoln the students at the academy hoisted a flag amid the cheers of nearly all the people of the town, and the excited throng was addressed by Mr. Foster, the orator chosen for the occasion, who concluded by announcing that he should leave at noon to enlist in the Ninth militia regiment, which had tendered its service by telegraph. He was the first volunteer from his native county, and going in as a private, carried a knapsack until December, 1862, when his commission as second lieutenant reached him while lying dangerously wounded in the hospital on the battle ground of Fredericksburg. Soon after the battle of Gettysburg he was promoted captain of his company. But his wounds soon compelled him to leave the service. He was actively engaged in the battles of Harper's Ferry, Cedar Mountain, Rappahannock, Thoroughfare Gap, second Bull Run, Antietam, Fredericksburg, Chancellorsville, and Gettysburg. Returning to New York city, he re-entered the dry goods business, and in 1870 came to Indiana, and established the Terre Haute branch of Foster Brothers. In 1873 he disposed of his interest in the firm to engage in journalism, for which he had a decided taste, and he established the *Saturday Evening Post*, at Grand Rapids, Mich., an enterprise which met with immediate success. In 1878 the health of his brother John having failed, he, at the earnest solicitations of his brothers, disposed of his newspaper and again entered the firm, coming to Fort Wayne, where were its heaviest property interests. Here he has since remained, and the business interests of the city have always found in him an active and valuable friend. (He is the president and manager of the D. N. Foster furniture company, and of the Fort Wayne furniture company, and has recently been chosen president of the Central Mutual fire insurance company of this city. He is the owner of the Aldine hotel, recently completed, is director in the Indiana machine company, and is besides interested in a number of other enterprises.) The people of Indiana are indebted to Mr. Foster for the Public Library bill passed by the legislature of 1881, under which nearly every city in Indiana has since established a public library free to all its citizens. At his own expense he circulated petitions in all the large cities of the state, praying for the passage of the bill he had prepared, and which was introduced in the senate by the late Senator Foster. Mr. Foster has always taken an active interest in the prosperity of the Grand Army of the Republic, and was elected commander of the department of Indiana in 1885. At that time the membership had rapidly grown to nearly 18,000 in the state, but there had been little opportunity for perfecting discipline necessary to the highest good of the order. This work fell to his administration, and so thoroughly was it done that when he turned the office over to his successor there was not a post in the department that was not in absolute good standing. In politics he has always been an active republican, but though frequently named in connection with prominent positions, he ~~invariably~~ *happenually* declined such honors. ~~He is one of the originators of the Morton Club.~~

Samuel M. Foster, son of John L. and Harriet Scott Foster, was born at Coldenham, Orange county, N.Y., December 12, 1851, the youngest of seven children, six of whom were boys. When about fourteen years old he went to the city and entered the New York dry goods store of his brothers. In 1868 he went to Troy, N. Y., and in 1872 formed a partnership with his brother, A. Z. Foster, now of Terre Haute, in retail dry goods. The venture was profitable, so that two years later he found himself able to carry out his cherished plan of securing a collegiate education. Disposing of his business interests, he fitted himself for college, and in 1875 entered Yale, at New Haven, Conn. His career there was a creditable one, and while holding his own in the class-room he found time to serve as one of the editors of the *Yale Courant*, won an appointment on the "junior exhibition," had the honor of being one of the "Townsend men" chosen from 132 competitors, and was named by the faculty as one of ten to represent the class on the platform on commencement day. He received the degree of Bachelor of Arts, June 26, 1879, graduating fourteenth in a class which originally had 200 members. Mr. Foster came west, and in the fall entered the law office of Judge R. S. Taylor, not decided in mind to take up the profession of law, but feeling that the time devoted to the study would be well spent. A few months devoted to alternately reading Blackstone and to regaining the health which had been impaired by his college work, convinced him that his constitution was not strong enough to enable him to win that success in law which he desired, and as a result of this conclusion, in December, 1879, the first issue of the *Saturday Evening Record*, with Samuel M. Foster as editor and proprietor, was issued at Dayton, Ohio. His experience in journalism was short and decisive. The paper was a brilliant success in every respect but a financial one, and though the editor's health gave out before his pocket-book did, serious inroads were made upon both. In 1880 the *Record* (now known as the *Dayton Herald*), was disposed of, and Mr. Foster returned to Fort Wayne and resumed business life in the firm of Foster Brothers. This firm was dissolved in 1882, by the withdrawal of Scott Foster to accept the presidency of a New York bank, and the business of the firm was then divided, Samuel M. Foster succeeding to the dry goods department of the firm's trade. In this he continued until 1886, when he withdrew entirely from the retail trade, to devote himself to manufacturing, a business which he has built up, and which is assuming large proportions, the product going into every state and territory in the Union. Mr. Foster is secretary of the D. N. Foster furniture company, president of the business men's exchange, and devotes much time to many questions of public interest and importance. In politics he was raised a republican but has joined the democratic party on the tariff issue. Mr. Foster was married in June, 1881, to Margaret Harrison, of this city.

John Frederick William Meyer now ranks among the earlier settlers of Fort Wayne, having been a resident for forty years past. His career has been a laudable and excepional one, which justifies in this work a short sketch of his life of activity and usefulness. He traces with much pride his ancesters, in direct lineage, to the year 1417, when John Henry Meyer wedded a modest girl of inferior rank and without domain. Much as this action displeased the parents, they soon became reconciled and they erected for him, conditionally, a small house on one end of the large farm, which remained the home of direct descendants for more than four centuries, until the year 1838. J. F. W. Meyer was born in Holden, province of Westphalia, Germany, December 19, 1824. His parents being in humble circumstance, the average limited education of those days was hardly accorded him, and the greater portion of his earlier days were spent on the greenswarth, herding the sheep. When he was nine years of age his father died, leaving a widow and six children. His mother again married, and in 1838 the old homestead, in which so many generations of one family had passed their days, reverted to the original domain, as conditioned four hundred years previous, and the Meyer family removed to a neighboring village. In 1846 the mother died, and on October 3, the following year, he and his younger brother, Frederick, set foot on American soil at New Orleans. Their goal was Adams county, and after two months of tedious travel by boat and afoot, they reached Monmouth, Adams county, December 3, 1847. The first four months were spent in clearing the woodlands, and in the following March, Mr. Meyer became a driver of a canal boat team. February 7, 1849, he was engaged in the drug house of Hugh B. Reed, as bottle washer, but being of an industrious and ambitious disposition he soon gained a satisfactory knowledge of the business, and in 1853 became a partner in the firm of Wall & Meyer. In 1851 Mr. Meyer, then earning a salary of $15 a month, was married to Caroline Schroeder. One daughter and three sons were the fruits of this union; of the latter one died at the age of two years. Mrs. Meyer died in 1859, and the following year he wedded Julia Gerke. In February, 1862, the firm, then located on what is now East Columbia street, suffered a great loss by fire, but nothing daunted, the ambitious firm had a large consignment of new drugs started from New York in two days. In 1865 the present location on Calhoun and Columbia streets, was taken, and in the same year the branch of Meyer Bros. & Co., was established in St. Louis, which is now numbered among the largest wholesale drug houses in the country. In 1875 the firm established another branch in Kansas City, which has since grown to immense proportions. A fire in 1883 totally destroyed this stock, but the push that has always been characteristic of this house was again called into action, and in a few days sufficed to place then in position to serve the numerous patrons. In 1887 the company also located a house at Dallas, Texas, and the firm of Meyer Bros. & Co., now stands at the head of the wholesale drug business of this country. Being of a religious turn of mind, Mr. Meyer attributes the greater portion of the success that has attended his seeming ventures to an all-guiding Providence, and modestly he asserts, it was so ordained. He has done much for the church and charity, both at home and abroad; always open-hearted and cheerful he counts his friends by legions. A loving wife and seven children, of whom three are married, afford him much comfort, and although already sixty-four years of age, time has dealt leniently with him, and he is as hale and hearty as many young men of half his age. He was honored by a membership in the city council four years, and for many years he has been a water-works trustee. Politically, he is a democrat, and his religious connection is with the Lutheran church.

George W. Pixley, one of the leading business men of Fort Wayne, who has gained a wide fame by his successful operations in the clothing trade, has been engaged in that business since 1872, when he became, at Troy, N. Y., the cashier of the first branch house of Owen Pixley & Co. In 1876 he came to Fort Wayne, and as resident partner established the house of Owen Pixley & Co., at this city. Mr. Pixley was born at Kirkland, N. Y., near Utica, March 1, 1834. His great grandfather Pixley was born in Connecticut, and during the revolution raised, equipped and furnished a regiment at his own expense. His son, David Pixley, was a native of Connecticut, and in 1806 moved to Kirkland, N. Y., nine miles from Utica, with his family, where he lived, kept a tavern and stage stables on the old Seneca turnpike between Utica and Syracuse, where the greater portion of the traffic between the east and west passed over that route before the days of railroads. He died at that place at the age of seventy-seven years, leaving four sons and two daughters. The third son, David, was the father of George W. Pixley, the subject of our sketch. He was born at Bridgeport, Conn., in September, 1798, and died at Kirkland, N. Y., March, 1884. He succeeded his father in the hotel and stage business until what is now the New York Central railroad was built, when he went into the manufacture of brown sheetings and other cotton goods and general merchandise. He was postmaster and justice of the peace for over forty years, and was widely known and very highly respected. He married Charlotte Mygatt, who was born at Berlin, Conn., in March, 1805, and died in July, 1885, at Kirkland, N. Y. The Mygatt family were early settlers in Oneida county, N. Y. The father of Charlotte was Austin Mygatt, who was born in Berlin, Conn., in 1776, and died at Kirkland, N. Y., in 1863. He was the inventor and manufacturer of the first tin lantern, and made a fortune out of it. David and Charlotte Pixley had five children, of whom four survive: Henry D., Eliza J., George W. and Abby M. George W. received his education at the Clinton Liberal Institute, at Clinton, N. Y., and there was occupied in his father's store, then at farming and dairying until he entered his present occupation. In 1885 the old firm name was abandoned and the firm of Pixley & Co. was formed, which is now composed of the following: George W. Pixley, Henry D. Pixley, George W. Pixley, jr., Charles E. Read and

Robert H. Parmalee. In 1888 Mr. Pixley and Mason Long erected the magnificent business building in which the firm is now established at a cost of $75,000. The spacious room is splendidly equipped and there is every facility for the proper display of the immense stock and rapid disposition of their extensive trade, and great credit is due Mr. Pixley for giving to the city such a grand building, which will always remain an ornament and pride to the city. The same firm owns branch stores at Bloomington and Danville, Ill., and George W., jr., and Henry D. own stores at Terra Haute, Ind., Rockford, Ill., Streator, Ill., Sioux City, Iowa, Sioux Falls, Dak., and Oshkosh, Wis. Mr. George W. Pixley was married at Kirkland, N. Y., December 30, 1870, to Sarah A. Lewis, daughter of E. Chauncey Lewis, born at Kirkland, N. Y., December 30, 1851. Mr. Pixley is a prominent member of the F. & A. M., has been a member of Clinton lodge, No. 169, at Clinton, N. Y., since 1855, was made a Knight Templar February 12, 1869, in Utica commandery, No. 3, at Utica, N. Y. Took the Scottish Rite at Indianapolis consistory, in March, 1882, and the thirty-third degree in New York, September 17, 1889. He has held for many years the responsible position of treasurer of the Jenney electric light and power company, and is president of the Tri-State building and loan association, capital, $1,000,000, a newly organized association for the purpose of assisting people in building homes. In politics Mr. Pixley is a republican.

Capt. James B. White, one of the distinguished citizens of Fort Wayne, was born in the town of Denny, Stirlingshire, twenty miles east of Glasgow, Scotland, June 26, 1835. His father was manager of a large calico printing establishment, which gave employment to over 500 hands. His mother, a woman of strong intellect, strict in her religious life, was careful in the bringing up of her four sons and three daughters. At the age of twelve years James B. began a period of two years spent at the trade of tailor, but this he abandoned to take up calico printing, at which he was engaged until nineteen. Emigration being popular at that time, he embarked in a sailing vessel at Glasgow, and thirty-four days later, in the summer of 1854, arrived at New York. Seeking employment at his trade, he was able to obtain work only until November, when, considerably discouraged, he resolved to search for an uncle, John Bains, who had settled near Fort Wayne, then in the far west, some ten years before. He went to Buffalo by rail, thence to Toledo by steamer, and by packet to Fort Wayne on the Wabash & Erie canal. He arrived here in the latter part of November, when his money was exhausted, and he was compelled to deposit his trunk at the packet office at the old Comparet basin in the east end of town, for the sum of $3, still due on his packet fare. He walked six miles out on the Winchester road, and obtained of his uncle the money to redeem his trunk. He obtained temporary work with Wade C. Shoaff, as a tailor, until January, then was employed a few weeks in a machine shop on the corner of Barr and Water streets, and in February began an employment in the stone yard of John Brown, which lasted three months at $3 per week and board.

He was subsequently employed with Mr. Shoaff, and Nirdlinger & Oppenheimer, and in the summer of 1856 opened a tailor shop of his own, upstairs in the building occupied now by Mayer & Graffee. Not being satisfied he went to Cincinnati in the fall, and then to St. Louis, where he was employed first as a shipping clerk, and then in a wholesale dry-goods house, but making only $6 per week, he resumed his trade as a tailor. This was his occupation for a year longer in Fort Wayne, where he returned soon, and opened a shop over the dry goods store of S. C. Evans. During this year, 1857, he was married to the estimable lady who has been his helper through life, Maria Brown, a half-sister of John Brown. They have seven children, four sons and three daughters, viz.: John W., Jessie, Anna B., Edward, Gracie, James B., jr., and Alex B., all of whom are living. Mrs. White was born in Glasgow, Scotland, in 1836, and came to this country in company with her brother in 1853. She is a daughter of John and Jennie (Blair) Brown, natives of Scotland. Her father was a man of more than ordinary ability, and was one of the most extensive contractors and builders of Glasgow, where he died in about 1840, leaving the family in good circumstances. The mother of Mrs. White was known for her well established Christianity and unswerving faith in the doctrine of the Presbyterian church, of which she was a life-long member. She came to Fort Wayne in 1858, and died here in 1874. Mrs. White, like her mother, is a pronounced Presbyterian, and esteemed by all who know her. Mr. White's next enterprise was the acceptance of a position in the establishment of Becker & Frank, Warsaw, and after working there two years, he was able to have a shop of his own, a house and lot and a prosperous trade. The war of the rebellion now broke out, and in August, 1861, he sold his little stock at a considerable loss and assisted in recruiting a company. He was elected captain, and he proceeded with his command to Camp Allen near Fort Wayne, where it was assigned as Company I, of the Thirtieth Indiana regiment. After being equipped at Indianapolis, they were sent to Camp Nevin, Ky., to join the command of Gen. Wood. The regiment was among the first troops to reach Nashville after the battle of Fort Donelson, and they reached Pittsburgh Landing in the command of Gen. Buell in time to participate in the second day's fight. In this battle of Shiloh, during the attack when Col. Bass was killed, Capt. White was wounded in the right side by a spent minie ball, but soon recovered, and took part in the siege of Corinth, and the skirmishes incident to that campaign. The Thirtieth then joined in the movement to Louisville in pursuit of Bragg, and followed the rebel forces back to Nashville. Soon after the return to the latter place, Capt. White resigned his commission in the army. In the spring of 1863, he with Joseph A. Stellwagon, became suttler to the Eighty-eighth regiment, and was so engaged to the end of the war. During this time, he was twice captured by the rebels. Once he lost everything he had, his wagons and merchandise being totally destroyed in the Wheeler raid in the Sequatchie valley, near Chattanooga. The next time he was paroled with little loss. Returning to Fort Wayne at the close of the war he established a grocery and fruit house, and was prospering when his establishment was destroyed by fire in January, 1872. Though his insurance did not cover forty per cent. of the loss, his resolute spirit did not fail him, and on the next day he opened for business in a building opposite his old stand, and had ordered a new stock. Two years later he had repaired his losses, and was again firmly established. Throughout the panic that occurred about this time he abated in no way the daring of his operations, and was uniformly successful. He has invested largely in real estate, and added much to the improvement of Fort Wayne, by laying out new streets, and embellishing the four city additions which bear his name. The foundation of his reputation is his wholesale and retail grocery house, known throughout northern Indiana and northwestern Ohio as the "Fort Wayne Fruit House." This immense establishment, now quartered in a handsome new building on Wayne street, employs seventy-five clerks and employes, and does a business of nearly one-half million a year. He has also, in partnership with his son, John W. White, established a wheel factory, in which are employed about 200 workmen. It has a business which extends to every part of the Union, and is one of the largest establishments of the kind in the United States, producing all kinds of carriage and wagon wheels. John W. White is manager, and has made the business very successful. Capt. White was at one time a partner in the ownership of the Fort Wayne *Gazette*, and has always taken a deep interest in politics, though not often becoming prominent in political campaigns until recently. He was, however, twice elected to the council from the Second ward, a democratic stronghold, and in 1874 he was nearly elected clerk of the circuit court by the republicans, in spite of a democratic majority of 3,000. In 1886 he was prevailed upon to accept the republican nomination for congress as representative of the twelfth district, and though the district had been surely democratic, usually by about 3,000 majority, he was elected by a majority of nearly 2,500, revealing his unbounded popularity. During his term in congress he was noted as a zealous worker, not only for the good of the people of his own district, but for the whole people, and he introduced several measures for the relief of the working people, which though they have not yet been adopted, will be recognized in the future as the proper foundation for legislation for the amelioration of the condition of the wage earners the world over. Such in particular was his Minimum Wages bill. Also, during the fiftieth congress, to which he was elected, he took an active part in debates and particularly on the tariff bills. On the question of protection versus free trade, he was able to speak as a business man, with much weight, and his arguments were widely quoted, The following campaign was fought upon that line, and resulted in the defeat of Grover Cleveland. Since his return from congress Mr. White has settled down to business with undiminished energy, and having so many interests to demand his attention, real estate transactions, the Fruit House, and the factory, he will have little time for politics in the future. Capt. White has long been an attendant upon the First Presbyterian church, though liberal and charitable in his religious views. His kindness and open-handedness to all those who are distressed is as widely known as his name, and his quiet and unostentatious charity has made him beloved in many a humble home. Taken all in all, he is one of those self-made men who have the affection of their neighbors, and never loses an opportunity to serve them to the best of his ability.

Mention of the business interests of Fort Wayne would be incomplete without notice of the famous wholesale house of Gilbert E. Bursley & Co., wholesale grocers. The house was established in 1880, and now enjoys an extensive custom throughout a wide territory. The proprietors have a thorough knowledge of their intricate business, buy in the best markets, and have the brightest and most capable salesmen extending their trade in the prosperous region tributary to Fort Wayne. The house occupies a four-story brick building at Nos. 129, 131 and 133 Calhoun street, having an area of 50x100 feet, and especially fitted for the business. Gilbert E. Bursley, the senior partner, was born at Barnstable, Mass., April 9, 1837. His father, Joseph, son of Lemuel Bursley, a native of Massachusetts, was born in 1791, served in the war of 1812, and died in his native state in 1870. He married Deborah Lothrop, who died in 1840, aged about thirty-seven years. They had twelve children, of whom five are living, Gilbert being the youngest. He lived in Barnstable until sixteen years old, and then went to Boston to seek his fortune. He was first employed in a book store, and then by the Old Colony railroad, and enlisted in 1862, in Company B, One Hundred and Thirtieth New York infantry, and after one year's service, was discharged on account of ill health. He had visited Fort Wayne in 1861, and in 1868 he returned here and made the city his home. He was largely instrumental in organizing the Citizens' street railroad company, and superintended the construction of the road and the operation of it during the first ten years. A few months after the organization of the Fort Wayne organ company, in 1872, he became connected with that enterprise, and was general manager and the largest stockholder for ten years, during which he placed it upon a sound financial basis, and won for it an extensive business and high reputation. He married in 1861 Kate P. Smith, of West Virginia, who died in 1871, and in 1876, married Ellen R. Aldrich, of Providence, R. I.

James M. McKay, junior member of the above named firm, was born in Ontario, Canada, January 21, 1856. His father, Neil McKay, was a native of Scotland, born May 6, 1823, and emigrated with his parents and settled in Ontario, where he was educated and resided, holding the position of "Reave" for several years, until he came to the United States in 1864. He settled at Fort Wayne in 1868, and followed his occupation of railroad contractor until his death, November 26, 1882. He was a man of great energy, and was connected with the construction of many of the railroads of this country. He married Nancy Young, who was born in Canada, December 29, 1833, and died in Fort Wayne, in May, 1872. They had eight children, three of whom are now living: James M., Nannie, wife of Neil McLachlan, and Jennie E. Mr. McKay, in 1880, became a member of the firm of G. E. Bursley & Co., and has attained a high rank among the popular and active business men of Fort Wayne. His career has been entirely the result of personal application, and his success is noteworthy. October 1, 1885, he was married to Elizabeth J. McFee, a native of this county, and they have two children: Neil A. and William. He is a prominent republican and a member of the Morton club.

Louis Wolf was born in Germany, April 23, 1849, the son of Samuel and Fannie Wolf, who lived and died in their native land, the mother passing away at the age of fifty-nine years in 1881, the father in 1889, at the age of about seventy. There are nine children living, of whom Louis Wolf is the second. His childhood was spent in Germany, where he received his earliest education. In 1865 he immigrated and settled first at Warsaw, Ind., where he entered the dry goods business in the employ of Becker Brothers. Two years later he came to Fort Wayne, and for five years was employed by the firm of Frank & Thanhauser. He then went to Plymouth and embarked in dry goods on his own account under the firm name of M. Becker & Co. This business was kept up for four years, at the end of which time he sold out, and returned to Fort Wayne and purchased the interest of Mr. Thanhauser in the firm which had formerly employed him. Two years later he bought out Mr. Frank and ever since he has managed the large and increasing trade. The retailing of dry goods, carpets and millinery is the principal department, though a considerable amount of wholesale business is done. The establishment is located at 54 Calhoun street, and employs fifty to sixty people. Through the indefatigable energy and exceptional business ability of Mr. Wolf the store has come to be widely known as one of the foremost in northern Indiana. He was married in 1880 to Rebecca, daughter of Joseph and Caroline Stiefel, prominent people of Angola, Ind. Mrs. Wolf was born at that town, in 1860. They have three children: Milton, Edgar and Florence. Mr. and Mrs. Wolf are members of the Hebrew church.

Ernest C. Rurode is one of the successful business men of Fort Wayne, a member of the firm of Root & Co., a dry goods house whose extensive wholesale and retail operations make it one of the most prominent institutions of the city, and widely recognized as one of the leading business concerns of the country. The business was established by McDougal Root & Co., in 1860, the present firm succeeding in 1863. They moved into their present building in 1874; it is a three story brick 52x170, fronting on Calhoun street, and 30x50, fronting on Main street, all fitted with the most ingenius of modern contrivances for faciltating business. The wholesale trade is extensive throughout Ohio, Indiana and Michigan, and the firm, being direct importers, compete with all markets. The retail trade is very large, the custom of the house not being confined to the city alone, but extending over a territory of fifty miles in all directions. One hundred and fifteen persons are given employment by the firm. Ernest C. Rurode was first associated with the business in 1860 with the old firm, and in 1862 took an interest in the same. For twenty years he has managed the wholesale and retail departments, and under his careful and shrewd management the business has grown to its present magnitude; thereby Mr. Rurode has gained for himself the widespread reputation as one of the leaders in Fort Wayne's commercial life. Mr. Rurode was born in Hanover, Germany, and is the son of Henry and Catherine (Hier) Rurode, who livied and died in Germany. Mr. Rurode received his early education in his native land, came to America in 1854, and first settled at Terre Haute, Ind., where he was in the dry goods business until 1860. He was married in 1873 to Emma Pedecord, of Decatur, Ill., by whom he has three children. In politics, Mr. Rurode is a republican.

Carnahan & Co., wholesale dealers in boots, shoes and rubbers, is the title of a Fort Wayne house which has an extensive trade throughout four states. The house was established in 1872 by Carnahan, Skinner & Co., and this was succeeded in 1875, by Carnahan, Hanna & Co. In 1886, the present firm Carnahan & Co., composed of William L. Carnahan and Emmet H. McDonald, succeeded to the business. The establishment is located at Nos. 76, 78 and 80 Clinton street, a four-story brick building 60x60, and is stocked with a complete assortment of all grades of foot-wear, including boots, shoes, and India rubber goods. The purchases of the firm are made with such business acumen that the prices it offers are daily recommending it to dealers throughout the vast territory the salesmen of the firm are traversing. With annual sales of from $400,000 to $500,000, and a steady increasing patronage, the future of the firm is a very bright one. William L. Carnahan is the son of James G. and Margaret (Brown) Carnahan, both of whom were natives of Ohio. They removed to Indiana in 1833, becoming pioneers of Tippecanoe county. Settling at Lafayette, the father engaged there in merchandise. At that place William L. Carnahan was born March 5, 1837, and growing to manhood there, attended the city schools and prepared himself for entrance to the state university, at which he was graduated At the close of the year 1856, he went to Nebraska, and remained in that state three years, the greater part of the time in Dakota county, and the city of Omaha, in the latter place being engaged in merchandise, and as clerk in the land office. Mr. Carnahan returned to Indiana in 1860, and established himself in business at Delphi, where he was occupied for two years, after which he removed to Lafayette and embarked in the boot and shoe trade. Two years later he became a traveling salesman for the firm of Carnahan, Earl & Co., of Lafayette, in which capacity he acted for eighteen months, at the end of that period becoming a member of the firm, which did businens under the title of Carnahan Brothers & Co., wholesale dealers and manufacturers of boots and shoes. Attending to the wholesale trade, he spent seven years altogether on the road. In January, 1872, Mr. Carnahan made his home at Fort Wayne and established the business above referred to. Mr. Carnahan's long and successful business career gives him a high rank among the prominent men of the city. He was maried in 1864, to Clara L., daughter of James Bayliss Hanna, of Allen county, and to this union four children have been born.

One of the most destructive fires for many years in the business part of Fort Wayne was the burning of the establishment of Louis Fox & Bro., dealers in foreign fruits, and manufacturers of confectionery and crackers. This fine four-story brick building, 145, 147 and 149 Calhoun, and 1 to 11 East Jefferson streets, was entirely destroyed on the morning of February 16, 1889, entailing a loss of about $55,000. It had been erected but two years before. The Messrs. Fox with characteristic energy set to work to rebuild, and the walls of an equally extensive and elegant building were erected by autumn. The members of this firm, Louis and August Fox, are sons of Joseph R. Fox, of Fort Wayne. The father was born in Germany, March 3, 1820, and came to Fort Wayne in 1848. He followed farming in Adams township four years, then engaged in gardening in the city until 1863, when he began his business of confectioner and restauranteur at 25 East Main street, where he still does business. He was married in 1848 to Mary Schnetz, a native of Switzerland, by whom he had three sons, Joseph in addition to those already named.

Henry C. Graffe has been prominent in the business affairs of the city for many years. He is a native of Germany, where in the early part of this century Ludwick Graffe died at the age of thirty-four, leaving two sons, Frederick and Henry. The latter died in his native land at the age of seventy-four. Frederick, born in Brunswick, January 31, 1809, was married in 1837 to Mary Ann Stark, who was born in 1810, and in 1838, the young couple came to New York. May 28, 1840, they reached Fort Wayne. They brought with them their son, the subject of this mention, who was born at Frankfort, March 1, 1838, the eldest of eight children, of whom six survive. Frederick Graffe was engaged in cabinet-making in the firm of Muhler & Graffe for twelve years, and then with the same partner for twelve years in the grocery business, until Mr. Muhler died. Mr. Graffe, sr., has since been engaged in the galvanized iron cornice, roofing and general tin business with his two sons George W. & C. M. His wife died in this city in 1882. Henry C. Graffe obtained a common school education, and in 1851 entered the jewelry house of Andrew Mayer, in this city, as an apprentice for three years, and after three years' further service went to New York city, and was employed there three years in the same business. He returned to Fort Wayne, and after three years more with Mr. Mayer, went into business on his own account and was quite successful. In 1865 he became a partner with his former employer, the firm being known as Mayer & Graffe, a partnership which continued until the death of Mr. Mayer in December, 1875. The latter was a native of

Respectfully yours
D B White

Germany, and immigrated to Dayton, thence to Fort Wayne in 1844, establishing his business at that date. The business has ever since been continued in the same block on Columbia street. November 17, 1859, Mr. Graffe was married to Eliza A. Myers, who was born at Lancaster, Ohio, March 3, 1838, and they have three children living out of nine born: May E., Cecilia and Harry C. Mr. and Mrs. Graffe are members of the Catholic church, and he is in politics a democrat. From 1874 to 1876 he was a member of the city council, and is now president of the electric light and power company.

Frederick Graffe, jr., a well-known jeweler, is a representative of one of the old and prominent families of Fort Wayne. He was born in the city, September 18, 1853, the youngest of six children of Frederic and Mary Ann Graffe. He gained his education in the Catholic schools and the commercial college of this city, and in 1871 entered the employment of the firm of Mayer & Graffe, and served an apprenticeship of three years. He has since been connected with the same house and that of H. C. Graffe. For five years, from 1879, he had charge of a branch house at Wabash. He was married in 1882 to Jennie Polk, the oldest child of the late Col. Richard Polk, an eminent soldier of the civil war, who died at Wabash in 1877. Mrs. Graffe was born at Wabash in 1858. They have two children: Verva and Thomas. Mr. and Mrs. Graffe are members of the Catholic church, and he is in politics a democrat.

A. F. Siemon, founder of the old and widely known house of Siemon & Brother, dealers in books and stationery, was born in Saxony, Germany, at the city of Ziesar, September 18, 1821. His father, August Ferdinand Siemon, a native of Saxony, was a prominent man, a merchant at Ziesar, and postmaster and mayor of the city for a number of years. He died about 1860. His wife, whose maiden name was Caroline Grams, died in 1821, eight days after the birth of her son. Mr. Siemon received a good education in his native town, completing it at the college of Brandenburg. In 1849 he came to America and traveled directly to Fort Wayne, intending to study at Concordia college. After an attendance there of about one year, he entered the employment of Towley & Freeman, as a clerk, and subsequently held similar positions with W. T. Abbott and Towley & Brother. He founded his present business in 1858, and in 1861 admitted his brother Rudolph as a partner, when the firm became known as Siemon & Bro. In 1885 the interest of Rudolph was transferred to Mr. A. F. Siemon, and the two sons, Henry and Herman, were admitted to the business as partners. At their present place of business, 50 Calhoun street, they have one of the most commodious store rooms in the city, occupying the entire four floors of the building, which is in dimensions 20x170 feet, and they carry a complete stock of books, stationery, wall paper, pictures and frames, doing an average annual business of $50,000 to $60,000. Mr. Siemon is one of the prominent men of Fort Wayne, a veteran in business and highly esteemed in all his relations with society. He is a member of St. Paul's

Lutheran church, of which he was trustee five years. He was married in 1854, to Lisetta Berning, of Hanover, Germany, who died in 1859, leaving two sons. In 1861 he was married to Helena Strunk, who was born in Fort Wayne, and they have three children.

Gideon W. Seavey, proprietor of one of the largest wholesale and retail hardware houses in the country, has in a business career of somewhat varied occupation, shown a notable ability in his different enterprises. In 1864, being seventeen years of age, he left the farm and entered Company D, One Hundred and Fortieth regiment Illinois infantry, and served until the close of the rebellion. The next year he entered Michigan university, and graduated from that institution in 1871, with the degree of B. A., receiving two years later, the degree of Master of Arts. January 1st, 1872, he established the Hoopston (Ill.) *Chronicle*, which he conducted five years, making for it a wide reputation as one of the ablest papers of eastern Illinois. His residence in Fort Wayne began in 1877, when he engaged in the practice of law with P. A. Randall. In 1880, he engaged in the lumber business, which he subsequently disposed of to enter the hardware business in which he is now occupied. He has been decidedly successful in his undertakings and is a valuable and enterprising citizen. Mr. Seavey's father was Winthrop Seavey, born in New Hampshire in 1802, son of Joshua Seavey of that state, who was a soldier in the war of 1812. The latter, who married a cousin of Daniel Webster, died in Illinois in 1862, at the age of ninety years. Winthrop Seavey married Elizabeth Curtis, of New York, who was born in 1809, and in 1834, they made the journey from New Hampshire to Illinois by wagon, in forty-five days, and became one of the pioneer families of Lee county. They died in Illinois, the mother in 1853, the father in 1865. They had six children, of whom Gideon was the youngest. He was born at Palmyra, Ill., February 14, 1848. In 1874 he married Amy C. Randall, born in 1853, at Avilla, Ind., daughter of Judge Edwin and Mary A. Randall. They have two children, Walter R. and Irma M.

Frank C. Cratsley, one of the prominent book firm of Renner, Cratsley & Co., is a native of Fowler, Trumbull Co., Ohio, born December 29, 1856. He is the son of William and Sabrina (Kingsley) Cratsley, the former a native of Onondaga county, N. Y., and the latter of Trumbull county, Ohio. He was reared to the age of sixteen on a farm. His early education was received in the public schools, and later he completed a course in a commercial school at Elyria, Ohio. In early manhood he taught school for six months at Oberlin, Ohio. In 1881 he took a position as bookkeeper with Brown, Eager & Hull, a wholesale and retail book and stationery firm at Toledo. He continued with them in the same capacity until June, 1888, when he came to Fort Wayne, and he has since been a member of the firm of Renner, Cratsley & Co. Mr. Cratsley was married in February, 1881, to Adella, daughter of James and Ann (Bates) Hull. Mr. Cratsley and wife are members of the Baptist church. He is a member of the National Union and Royal Adelphia societies.

Henry B. Ayres, an esteemed and worthy citizen of Fort Wayne, and son of the late Dr. Henry P. Ayres, is one of the native business men of the city, having been born here on the 8th day of March, 1847. He has been associated with the drug business almost all his life, having become initiated in it in the capacity of clerk as early as thirteen years of age. With one exception, he has been identified with this business longer than any druggist in the city, and he has built up an enviable reputation as an honest man and as a competent and reliable pharmacist. He was married in May, 1870, to Miss Margaret A. Kirk, by whom he is the father of two sons: Henry Cooper, born in July, 1872, and Kirk Banard, born in February, 1877. The social qualities of Mr. Ayres are admirably well developed, and though of a retiring nature, he is, to his friends, most genial and companionable. He is a good man and his friends are numerous.

Robert Ogden, in 1858, having just immigrated from England, came to Fort Wayne, and embarked here in the business of plumber, which had been the trade of his father and grandfather in the old country, and which he had thoroughly learned. In October, 1859, he removed to Dayton, Ohio, and in 1870 returned to this city, which has since been his home. He conducts a large plumbing business, with his establishment at 26 East Berry street, and has achieved an honorable reputation. He was the first plumber to establish himself at Fort Wayne. Mr. Ogden was born near Manchester, England, January 9, 1825, son of John and Alice Ogden, and when a small boy began learning his trade with his father. He has been three times married. His present wife, to whom he was married July 3, 1888, is Agnes H., daughter of John Fowles of this city. She is a member of the First Presbyterian church. Mr. Ogden is a member of the Episcopal church, and is a prominent Mason, being a Knight Templar and a member of the lodge of Perfection. He is also connected with the Sons of St. George. He is a republican and a charter member of the Morton club. He stands high in both business and social circles.

One of the leaders in the musical instrument trade in northern Indiana is Philemon Dickinson manager in this city for D. H. Baldwin & Co. He learned the jewelry trade early in life, with his father, and after the war he engaged in the jewelry business at Richmond, Ind., where previous to the war period he had dealt in musical instruments. In 1866 he removed to Des Moines, Iowa, and was engaged in jewelry two years, then going to Troy, Ohio, where he was in business four years, adding musical instruments to his former stock. These two branches of business he continued from 1873 to 1875, at Richmond, Ind., and in the latter year he removed to Indianapolis, and next year became associated with the firm of D. H. Baldwin & Co., of that city, a business alliance that has since continued. In February, 1885, he came to this city and took charge of the large establishment of the firm at 98 Calhoun street, and has since successfully conducted it. Mr. Dickinson was born at Richmond, Ind., September 15, 1839, son of Charles A. and Sarah A. (McCoy) Dickinson, who were pioneers of Wayne county. In June, 1862, he enlisted as a private in Company I, Eighty-fourth regiment, Indiana infantry, and served with the same company in the line for twenty-six months. He was then promoted first lieutenant, and transferred to Company H, One Hundred and Fortieth Indiana, and served as acting quartermaster until the close of the war. He participated in the battles of Chickamauga, Dalton and those incident to the Atlanta campaign, and was mustered out at Greensborough, N. C. Mr. Dickinson was married April 29, 1862, to Olivia Lefevre, who died in June, 1872, leaving two children, Clarence and Laura May. He was married December 15, 1873, to Emma Thompson, by whom he has one child, Mary Olivia. Mr. and Mrs. Dickinson are members of the Third Presbyterian church, and he is a comrade of the G. A. R.

John Gilbert, a business man of the city, was born in Bohemia, March 9, 1833. In 1846, he came to the United States, and made his home at New York city, where he remained until 1854. He then removed to Canada West, where he served an apprenticeship as a pharmacist. A year later, his brother having gone to Rockford, Ill., he followed him there, and was engaged eight years at that city at the drug business. He came to Fort Wayne in 1866, and for fourteen years held the responsible position of manager of the wholesale and retail departments of the famous drug house of Meyer Bros. & Co. In 1880 he was appointed manager for the Standard Oil company, at Fort Wayne, and now has charge of their immense business at this point. Mr. Gilbert was married at Rockford, Ill., in 1861, to Harriet P. Mandeville, a native of New York state, and daughter of Michael Mandeville, a pioneer of Winnebago county, Ill., who died in 1885, at the age of ninety-four years. Mr. Gilbert is a member of Sol. D. Bayless lodge, F. & A. M., and is a charter member of Plymouth Congregational church.

John W. Orr, a prominent gentleman, who is now engaged in the oil business with Joseph Hughes & Co., was born in Brooke county, W. Va., May 2, 1829. When ten years of age he removed with his parents to Belmont county, Ohio, and there most of his boyhood was spent. He was educated at Barnesville academy, in that county, under Professor Thomas Merrill, now president of the Newton (Iowa) college, and Professor N. R. Smith, formerly of Boston. After leaving school he went to Wheeling, W. Va., and served an apprenticeship as machinist. After four or five years he returned to Ohio, following his trade and clerked in a store. About 1860 he went to Illinois and followed farming and school teaching for two years. October 1, 1862, he came to Fort Wayne and engaged as a machinist with the P., Ft. W. & C. railroad company, and later was in charge of an engine on the same road. In 1868 he took an engine on the Wabash railroad under W. F. Ray, master mechanic, and was so engaged until 1872, when he entered the Wabash round-house as assistant foreman, and was promoted foreman of the same. He held this position until June, 1887, when he quit railroading and took the position of bookkeeper with the house of Joseph Hughes & Co. During the absence of Mr. Hughes in Europe, from July, 1888, to July, 1889, he had the management of the business. Mr. Orr has always been a democrat, and has taken an active interest in the party affairs. He has been a Mason since 1854, and is a member of Summit City lodge. He is a member of the First Presbyterian church. Mr. Orr was married December 27, 1853, at Fairview, Ohio, to Ellen, daughter of Joseph Carlisle. To their union five children have been born: Joseph H., who holds a position in the First National bank of Fort Wayne; Charles W., assistant cashier in the Hamilton National Bank; Flora E., wife of Charles S. Bash, grain and commission man; Kate C., a teacher in the city schools, and James A., a stenographer for Bash & Co.

Lewis O. Hull, one of the leading business men of Fort Wayne, came to this city in 1865 at the close of the war, and in 1870 he engaged in house and sign painting. Nine years later he undertook his present enterprise, dealing in wall paper, paints and decorative materials, artists' materials, etc. He also carries on the business of painting and decorating, and does a large business in all departments, standing in the front rank in Indiana. He was born in Lucas, Richland county, Ohio, August 7, 1849, son of Wesley and Elizabeth (Deems) Hull, the first of whom was born in Ohio in 1817, the latter in the same state in 1826. In 1863 the parents came to Fort Wayne, and here the father died in 1888, but the mother survives. Mr. Hull enjoys the distinction of having been one of the youngest soldiers in the war of the rebellion, having enlisted as a drummer boy August 10, 1862, at the age of thirteen years and three days. He was a member of Company B, One Hundred and Twentieth Ohio regiment, and saw hard service, participating in the battles at Vicksburg, Arkansas Post, Jackson, Miss., Mobile, run the blockade on the Mississippi at Vicksburg, was with the army of the Gulf, was on the Red river campaign, and was honorably discharged November 5, 1865. Mr. Hull is prominent as a republican, and he is a member of the Masonic order. He was married October 25, 1875, to Viola C. Markley, of this city, and they have three children: Grace, Clara and Mabel.

On the west bank of the St. Joseph river, a mile and a half northeast of the court-house and a short distance beyond the limits of the city, Charles L. Centlivre, a native of one of the Rhine provinces, established a brewery nearly twenty-five years ago. There were at that time seven other concerns of the kind in Fort Wayne, one of considerable extent being owned by Franz J. Beck. The new enterprise thrived remarkably, and now many thousands of dollars that went to other cities for this beverage, is spent at home, to the great profit of the city. The brewery was established on a strip of ground between the feeder canal and the river, the difference in the levels of which is twenty feet, and thus a constant supply of water was obtained. The cellars were supplied with a patent cooling apparatus which constantly maintained a very low temperature throughout the extensive area in which the beer is stored. At first a white frame building was the principal structure and this gave way to a handsome brick building, which was destroyed by fire, July 16 1889.

Among the improvements of recent years, are the artesian well, which furnishes a constant supply of the purest water. Two new cellars of immense size were added in 1887, greatly increasing the storage capacity, and now the original plat of ground is nearly all excavated, and devoted to cellar room. The new building which takes the place of the one destroyed by fire, exceeds the old one in extent and is perfectly adapted to the requirements of the business.

The immense proportions to which this business has grown may be inferred from the fact that the real estate, buildings, machinery, cellars, etc., are valued at over $300,000. The output in 1887 was 20,000 barrels. Associated with C. L. Centlivre in the management of this great establishment are his sons, Louis A., general manager, Charles F., superintendent of the works, and John B. Reuss, general agent. Mr. Centlivre has been very enterprising in improving the approaches to his establishment, and invested $9,000 in a street car line, which connects with the Citizens' railway, and he was a prominent promoter of the macadamizing of Spy Run avenue. The boat house, and the improvement of the delightful sylvan surroundings of that vicinity, are due to the enterprise of this house.

The Berghoff brewery, which was founded in 1887 by the Herman Berghoff brewing company, is one of the prominent establishments of the kind in the west, and has a wide-spread reputation for the purity and wholesomeness of its product. The company makes a specialty of purely malt and hop products, being the only house in the west of that kind, and it has an extensive trade throughout the northwest and western states. The special export brands, "Salvator" and "Dortmunder," the latter named after the birthplace of the Berghoffs, are well known. The capacity of the establishment is about 100,000 barrels a year. The building of this company is conspicuous in the eastern part of the city, near the eastern end of Washington street, and is six stories in height, with a ground plan of 100x160 feet. It is equipped throughout with all the new and improved machinery for this industry. This building was erected in 1888 to replace the first one destroyed by fire. The company, of which Herman Berghoff is president and Henry C. Berghoff secretary and treasurer, was incorporated in 1887, with a paid up capital stock of $100,000. The estimated value of the plant is $250,000. Herman Berghoff, president of the company, a man of remarkable business and executive ability, is a native of Germany. He came to Fort Wayne in June, 1870, and has been engaged in mercantile business ever since. Henry C. Berghoff came to this city in 1872, and has since been engaged in business, and was for eight years treasurer of the city of Fort Wayne, an office he filled to the general satisfaction.

Albert J. Dittoe, the well-known proprietor of the Boston tea store at Fort Wayne, was born in Perry county, Ohio, August 23, 1845. His parents were Jacob A. and Catherine (Cluny) Dittoe, the former of whom was born in Perry county, the latter near Wheeling, W. Va. Mr. Dittoe had his home upon the farm of his parents until he was twenty-three years of age, receiving his education in the common schools, and in St. Joseph's college in his native county, which he attended two years, after having passed the common branches at the early age of fourteen. At eighteen years of age he accepted a position as teacher in St. Thomas's Catholic school at Zanesville, Ohio, for one term, and during the winter which followed he taught in Perry county. In the spring of 1869 he came to Fort Wayne, where he has since been an active and prominent citizen. For two years he held deputyships in the offices of the county recorder and the clerk of the circuit court, and was for four years employed as bookkeeper and cashier of the wholesale hardware firm of A. D. Brandriff & Co. In the season of 1873-4 he was engaged in the ice business with his father-in-law, the late Peter Moran. Afterward becoming a clerk in a grocery store, he held that position until July, 1882, when he purchased the store, which he has since conducted with marked success. It is recognized as one of the leading establishments of the kind in the city and is popularly known as the Boston tea store. Mr. Dittoe was married January 25, 1870, to Margaret G. Moran, and they have had nine children: Mamie C., Charles W., Loretta A., Vincent A., Anna G., Peter A., Margaret May, Alice G. and Burnadette, all of whom are living save Anna G., who died in childhood. Mr. and Mrs. Dittoe are members of the Catholic church.

Mason Long, a citizen of Fort Wayne whose career is widely known, has thus epitomized his life in his famous volume entitled "The Converted Gambler, and Save the Girls": "My story is that of a bleak and cheerless childhood, a youth of ignorance and hardship, a manhood of intemperance and vice." This, however, he wrote from a standpoint he had attained of prominence among those who labor for the good of their fellow men. He was born in Luray, Licking county, Ohio, September 10, 1842, and six years afterward his father died. He went with his mother, Margaret Long, a noble woman, to the home of her father, in Ashland county. There, when Mason was ten years old, his mother died, leaving him to the mercy of the world. He was bound out to a wealthy farmer of Medina county, and his life for seven years afterward was one of slavery, doomed to cruelty, incessant toil, and deprived of education. This service finished he went to Illinois, where he worked and went to school a short time. In the spring of 1862, he enlisted in the One Hundred and Twelfth Illinois regiment as a private. Throughout the war he served, performing brave and patriotic duty with his regiment, which participated in the memorable defense of Knoxville, the bloody battle of Franklin, and the defense Nashville, under Gen. Thomas. During the service, having had no early training as a guide to conduct he entered recklessly into the gaming which was resorted to in order to pass away tedious days in camp, and here the bent of his life, for many years to come, was formed. In August, 1865, he came to Fort Wayne and opened a grocery store, and abandoned cards, devoted himself to business, and for a while did well. But about a year later he accepted the invitation of a saloon-keeper to drink, and the invitation of a prominent citizen to play, and from that time his business was sacrificed. Fort Wayne was at that time a paradise for gamblers and confidence-men, and some of the largest games in the United States were maintained. In 1866 and 1867, the city was also the headquarters of as desperate a gang of pick-pockets as could be found in the country, thoroughly organized under the leadership of one Edward Ryan. They exercised a potent influence in politics and carried things with a high hand. Finally, Ryan robbed an old man named Tucker at the saloon which was the headquarters, and the latter attempted to shoot him. The result was the burning of the saloon by a mob, and the end of the gang. Mason Long, thrown into such surroundings, became known as a gentlemanly gambler, elevated above his associates by business-like honesty, manliness, high-mindedness and remarkable generosity to the poor. He had been an occasional attendant at the church of Rev. J. R. Stone, but the influence of that good man did not seem to be felt. In 1877, during the great temperance revival, when the the rink was crowded nightly, and the good women of the city labored heroically for the reformation of the community, a struggle was made for the enlistment of Mr. Long in this movement, he having attended the meetings out of curiosity, and finally he yielded and signed the pledge. The struggle that followed against his habits was a fearful one, but he conquered and soon became a famous speaker in the temperance cause. A great revival followed, the results of which for good are of incalculable extent. He was admitted to the Baptist church in 1878. Since then he has carried on the work of temperance agitation far and near, and has made many warm friends, and has done great good in many localities.

A. Mergentheim, proprietor of the most extensive retail millinery house in northern Indiana, was born in the province of Westphalia, Germany, June 18, 1847, and in 1862 began the millinery business in Bremen, Germany. In 1865 he emigrated to the United States, and settling in Philadelphia, was there for three years a clerk in the wholesale notion house of Metz Brothers. In 1870 he came to Fort Wayne and embarked in the notion business in a small way. His custom rapidly increasing he located at his present place of business in 1883, and the establishment now employs twenty-seven people. Mr. Mergentheim is the fourth of seven living children of Joseph and Bertha (Gans) Mergentheim, natives of Germany, who both died in their native land, the father in 1864, at the age of sixty-two, and the mother in 1854, at forty-five years of age. He was married in 1875, to Josephine Hirsch, born in Newark, N. J., in 1856, and they have one son, Morton A. Mr.

Mergentheim has been very successful in business, which testifies to his sagacity and enterprise, and is a popular and worthy citizen.

Thornton J. Fleming, a prominent merchant of Fort Wayne, has been engaged in merchandise since his majority, when he entered the dry goods business in Jay county. In 1883, he went to Dakota and returned to Fort Wayne the next year, and purchased what was known as the "old Kiser stand," where he has since done a flourishing business in dry goods, notions, and all kinds of gentlemen's furnishing goods. His father, J. W. Fleming, who now resides in this city, is a native of Virginia, and married Nancy Sunderland, who was born in Montgomery county, Ohio, in 1819, and was killed by a railroad accident at Detroit, Mich., August 17, 1888. Thornton J. Fleming, the sixth of ten children, seven of whom are living, was born near Huntertown, December 30, 1849, and spent his youth upon the farm, receiving a common school education. He is a member of Sol D. Bayliss lodge, having become a Mason in 1885; in politics he is a democrat. The building occupied by Mr. Fleming is an historic one, the date of its erection being 1838 or 1839.

Aurora C. Keel, dealer in books, stationery, etc., at 139 Broadway, was born in Stark county, Ohio, July 19, 1835, son of Joseph and Elizabeth (Chestnutwood) Keel. The parents, who were natives of Pennsylvania, removed to Ohio when young, and were married in Stark county, where they resided the rest of their lives. The father died August 8, 1877, at the age of seventy-two, and the mother died October 18, 1882, aged seventy-eight years. Aurora C. Keel was reared on the farm and educated in the common schools. At the age of seventeen years he entered the hardware store of James A. Saxton, at Canton, Ohio, and three years later took a position as traveling salesman for the wholesale grocery and drug house of Weimert & Steinbacher, of Akron, Ohio, with whom he remained until the breaking out of the rebellion, April 18, 1861; enlisted in Company G, Sixteenth regiment, Ohio volunteer infantry, for three months' service, and went into quarters at Camp Jackson, Columbus, whence the regiment was sent to West Virginia. It took part in the first battle of the war, at Phillipi, and was at Laurel Hill, when General Garnet tried to make his escape down Cheat river, and was engaged at Garrett Ford, where Garnet lost his life. The regiment then returned to Ohio and was mustered out after four months' service, receiving as payment $11 in gold per month. September 7, 1861, he re-enlisted in the Nineteenth Ohio regiment and was elected second lieutenant of Company F. The regiment was assigned to duty in the army of the Cumberland. During the winter of 1861-2 they were in camp at Columbia, Ky., and after the battle of Mill Springs joined the army at Bowling Green. At the latter place Mr. Keel was taken with typhoid fever and was sent to Louisville. Recovering from his illness he joined his command at Corinth, having been promoted first lieutenant April 30, 1862, and participated in the siege of that place. They were next at Battle Creek, Tenn., and with the army during Buell's movement from Chattanooga to Louisville. He was at the battle of Perryville, and afterward participated in the battle of Stone River. Just before the close of the last day of that battle he received a gunshot wound in the right arm which caused excission of the elbow joint, rendering that arm useless during life. He was placed in a field hospital, and later returned home on furlough. In the following September he rejoined his command at Chattanooga, having been promoted captain on July 22, 1863. His disability unfitted him for field duty and he was recommended for the veteran reserve corps, and received his commission as second lieutenant of such from President Lincoln, March 8, 1864. He was on duty at Camp Rendezvous Distribution, at Washington city, performing exacting and arduous work, until June, 1865, and received promotion from President Johnson to first lieutenant, and was sent to Concord, N. H., to assist in mustering out state troops. He resigned his position November 30, 1865, and returned to Ohio. In 1866 he removed to Ligonier, Ind., and engaged in the grocery and provision business. March 17, 1868, he came to Fort Wayne, and in company with H. V. Sweringen, M. D., established the Broadway drug store. The establishment was destroyed by fire in 1873, after which he was engaged in the preparation of an atlas of the state of Indiana. In 1876 he established the Broadway news depot and added thereto the present extensive stock. Mr. Keel is a member of the G. A. R. and the I. O. O. F. He was married in 1866 to Miss Mary G., daughter of Sarah J. McKenzie, of Ligonier, Ind., and they have had five children, one now deceased.

J. G. Thieme, the senior merchant tailor of the city, in years of business career, was the senior member of the firm of Thieme & Bro., which was organized in 1850, and did business for many years at the corner of Columbia and Clinton streets, Since February, 1889, the firm has been known as J. G. Thieme & Son. They do an extensive merchant tailoring business and manufacture clothing on a large scale, employing forty to fifty hands. Mr. Thieme is a prominent citizen, and a member of the board of Concordia college, an institution which he helped to build and organize. He is a native of Saxony, born March 20, 1821, son of Andrew Thieme, who was born in Germany in 1791, and died in his native land. J. G. began to learn the tailor's trade at eight years of age, and in 1846 came to the United States and settled at Fort Wayne in 1847, having spent the intervening time at New York. By his first wife, Mr. Thieme had one daughter, Engel, born in 1850. In 1851 he married Sophia Blecke, his present wife, who was born in Prussia in 1833, daughter of Christian Blecke, who was born in Germany in 1800, and settled at Fort Wayne in 1839. Mr. and Mrs. Thieme have the following children: Pauline, born 1853; Mary, born 1855; Traugott, now a minister at South Bend; Gottlieb, born 1860; Clara, born July 25, 1864, and Emma, born 1868. Mr. Thieme and wife are prominent members of the Lutheran church. Gottlieb C. Thieme, the junior member of the firm, was born at this city, February 20, 1860, graduated at Concordia college in 1880, and in the fall of that year went into business with his father, being admitted to the firm in 1889. He is one of the popular young men of the city, and is an earnest democrat.

The late Frederick J. Thieme was, during his active life, a leading spirit in some of the beneficial enterprises of the city of Fort Wayne. He was a good business man and prospered in his private affairs, but besides this, his public spirit led him to engage in projects for the general good. He was a prominent Lutheran, was one of the charter members of Immanuel's church, and for many years a trustee. He was also the first president of the Lutheran Mutual Insurance company. He was one of the founders of the City hospital, and its first president, a position which he held for three years. Mr. Thieme was born at Leipsic, Germany, February 7, 1823, and immigrated in 1854, settling at Fort Wayne the next year, when he engaged in the clothing trade and merchant tailoring with his brother, J. G. Thieme, as a partner. The firm was first located on Calhoun street, subsequently removed to the corner of Calhoun and Clinton streets, and there lost everything by fire in 1862, but rebuilt in 1863. The firm continued in business until the death of Frederick J. Thieme, December 16, 1887. His wife died on October 14th of the previous year. Her maiden name was Clara Weitzmann; she was born in Saxony, in May, 1832, and was married to Mr. Thieme, July 12, 1852. They left the following children: Lonnie, born 1855; Theodore, born 1857; John A., born 1859; J. G., born 1863; Frederick J., born 1865; Pauline, born 1867; Hugh P., born 1870, and Matilda, born 1873. John A. and J. G. are leading merchant tailors of this city, at 12 West Berry street, under the firm name of Thieme Brothers. They are among the most promising and enterprising young men of the city, and are active republicans.

Edward J. Golden, of the firm of Golden & Monahan, whose business career has been a brilliant and successful one, is a native of the city, having been born here January 17, 1854, son of Patrick and Mary (Barrett) Golden, natives of Ireland. The father was born in 1810, and emigrated to this country when a young man. He was a contractor by occupation, and was engaged in the construction of the Wabash & Erie canal. The mother was born in 1815 and died at this city in 1880. In the same year the father passed away suddenly, dropping dead in the court-house. Of their six living children, Edward is the fifth. He was educated at the Brothers' school, and in 1877 began business in partnership with Dennis Monahan, dealing in hats, caps and men's furnishing goods, and manufacturing shirts. In 1886 they established a branch store at Defiance, Ohio, under the name of Golden, Monahan & Co., and in 1889 another branch at VanWert, Ohio, all doing a good business. The firm is the leading one in its line in this part of the west. Mr. Golden was married in November, 1881, to Louisa Hutzell, a native of Fort Wayne, born 1861, and they have two children: Charles E. and Edward G. He is a member of the Catholic church, and is a democrat in politics.

Dennis Monahan, of the well-known firm of Golden & Monahan

was born in Jefferson township, February 27, 1846. His father, John Monahan, a native of Ireland, born in 1811, married Catherine Driscoll, a daughter of the Emerald Isle, and they came to Allen county in 1834, after which he was engaged upon the Wabash & Erie canal. The father died in 1866 and the mother in 1885. They had six children, four now living, of these latter Dennis being the youngest but two. He worked upon the farm and attended the common schools until December, 1863, when he enlisted in Company B, One Hundred and Twenty-ninth Indiana regiment and served until the close of the war, participating in the battles of Resaca, Kenesaw Mount, and the engagements about Atlanta and Kingston, N. C. Upon again taking up peaceful pursuits after this worthy military career, he engaged in the merchandise of men's furnishing goods in 1868, having an interest in the firm of Harper & Co., and in 1877, he formed his present partnership with Edward J. Golden. He is one of the prominent men of the city, is in politics a democrat, has served on the city council in 1886-7, and is a member of the Catholic church. He was married in September, 1872, to Elizabeth Golden, who was born in Fort Wayne in 1849, and they have eight children: John J., Franklin G., Grace B., Thaddeus B., Alfred E., Benadette C., Dennis L., and Edith J.

One of the oldest tailoring establishments of Fort Wayne is that of Joseph M. Clark & Co., of which firm a valued member is Perry N. DeHaven, one of the enterprising young business men of the city. Mr. DeHaven is a native of Wayne county, Ohio, born May 20, 1853. His father, Harrison DeHaven, married Nancy Stonehill, and they came many years ago to this city, where the mother died in 1872. Both parents were natives of Ohio. Of the three surviving children, Perry N. is the oldest. He received his education in the city schools, and in 1867 entered the employment of Joseph M. Clark, who had been doing business here since as early as 1857. February 7, 1889, Mr. DeHaven became a member of the firm. Their establishment at 32 East Berry street, is one of the finest of the kind in the city and eight to ten skilful workmen are constantly employed. Mr. DeHaven is a popular citizen, is a past chancellor of Fort Wayne lodge, No. 116, K. of P., and in politics is a democrat.

A worthy ex-official of Allen county, Charles Stellhorn, is a native of northern Prussia, and was born May 27, 1838. He remained upon the farm of his parents and attended the common schools until fifteen years old, when he learned the trade of boot and shoemaker. In 1856 he emigrated to America, landing in New York city on Novem- November 2nd. He came directly to Fort Wayne, where three of his uncles were living, and began work at his trade. In 1870 he engaged in business for himself at his present stand, at 146 Calhoun street, at first doing only custom work, but in 1886 he added a stock of books, stationery, cigars, tobacco and notions. In 1886 he was elected coroner of Allen county on the democratic ticket, and served two years. Previous to that he served as clerk for the coroner two years. Mr. Stellhorn was married in 1860 to Frederica Ohm, of Fort Wayne, and they have had six children, four of whom survive: Louisa, Frederica, Charles William, Frederica, Henry. Mr. and Mrs. Stellhorn are members of the Emanuel Lutheran church.

For a considerable number of years Gustave Spiegel, a worthy German citizen of Fort Wayne, has been engaged in the retail boot and shoe business, at No. 132 Broadway. He is a native of Prussia, born March 8, 1823. In July, 1846, he immigrated, and landing at New York, city, remained there until October, 1850, when he came to Fort Wayne. Having learned the trade of boot and shoemaker in Germany, he followed that as an occupation until about 1860, when he opened a shop of his own, carrying a small stock of ready-made goods. About 1870, he opened a regular boot and shoe store at his present place, and has since carried a full line of all kinds of boots and shoes, and also does general repairing. Mr. Spiegel was married in 1847, to Mary E. Baals, of New York city, who was born in Bavaria, and emigrated to America in 1846. To their union nine children have been born, six of whom survive. He is a member of the Lutheran church, is an elder and a member of the school board, of Emanuel's church.

Edward Gilmartin of Fort Wayne, an extensive dealer in telegraph poles and lumber, is a native of Queens county, Ireland, where he was born January 13, 1840. He came to America in 1860, landing in New York city on July 4 of that year. He came directly to Columbus, Ohio, and engaged with the Western Union telegraph company at that place. In the winter of 1861 and 1862 he was sent south to build military telegraph lines after the army of the Potomac, and was engaged in that work for about two years. Returning to Columbus, Ohio, the Western Union telegraph company assigned him to work for the Pennsylvania railway company on the east end. In 1864 the company sent him to Fort Wayne, and he was given charge of the western division of the Pennsylvania line until 1870, and then transferred to the G. R. & I. He built all that railroad line, in all six or seven hundred miles. He was engaged with G. R. & I. until November, 1887, when he resigned to attend to his private business. During his service in the Western Union and Pennsylvania companies he never lost a day in twenty-seven years. He had previous to that time been dealing in telegraph poles and lumber, and his business having greatly increased, his resignation was necessary. He now supplies the Western Union electric light and telephone companies, and Pennsylvania and G. R. & I. companies, shipping as far as Texas. In 1862 while laying a cable from Cape Charles to Fortress Monroe he was ship wrecked losing all personal effects. He was married in May, 1867, to Katherine Lynch, who was born in Dublin, Ireland, and came to America with her parents when a child. To their union eleven children have been born, nine of whom are living: Kate, now the wife of W. D. McDonald, superintendent of electric light works, Fort Wayne; Michael J., William P.,

Mary A., Edward, Nellie, John F., Loretta and Alice. He is a member of the Cathedral congregation, and Catholic Knights.

Frank R. Barrows, one of the leading photographers of Indiana, was born at Sturgis, Mich., August 5, 1854, son of Julius M. and Eliza (Hammond) Barrows. His father, a native of Hartford, Conn., born in 1829, resides at Sturgis, and is well-known in that region as a skillful architect and builder. His mother was born near London, England, in 1830. There are three living children of these parents, of which Frank R. is the second in age. He was educated in the schools of Sturgis and Lansing, Mich., and spent about three years in the profession of architect. In 1876, however, he engaged in photography, an art for which he has shown the highest adaptability, and in which he has risen to the front rank, mastering all the remarkable advances which have been made by science, and combining with artistic skill such business methods as commend him to the public and at the same time assure his own prosperity. Three years after turning his attention to the art he came to Fort Wayne, and was until 1882, in partnership with Francis H. Clayton, under the firm name of Clayton & Barrows. At the latter date Mr. Barrows purchased the entire business and four years later, Mr. Clayton died at Chattanooga, Tenn. In October, 1888, he occupied his establishment at the corner of Berry and Calhoun streets. The patronage of his gallery is not confined to the city, but embraces many of the neighboring towns of Indiana. It is noted that the largest direct photograph to be obtained in the city, bears the name of Barrows. Socially he is one of the most popular men of the city. He was married March 22, 1877, to Abbie Hanson, born in Massachusetts, and they have two children, Lulu G. and Ray H.

Maurice L. Jones, a leading photographer, and dealer in photographic supplies, was born at North Manchester, Wabash county, Ind., August 11, 1848. His father, Rufus T. Jones, is a native of New York, and now resides at Bunker Hill, Ind., engaged in farming. During the war he enlisted, in 1862, in Company A, Thirty-ninth regiment, and was placed on detail service. Maurice is the oldest child by the second marriage of his father, which was to Mary A. Burr, who was born in Jamestown, N. Y. In 1863 he enlisted in Company H, One Hundred and Eighteenth Indiana infantry, and subsequently served in the Thirty-ninth regiment, and the Eighth cavalry, until the close of the war, marching with Sherman to the sea. Being honorably discharged in 1865, he came home and entered Bryant & Stratton's commercial college of Indianapolis, from which he graduated in 1867. Until 1870 he was in the lumber business with his father at Bunker Hill, and then for four years in the employment of the Howe sewing machine company at Peru, Ind. There he engaged in photography, being a partner in the firm of Moore & Jones, and in 1876 came to Fort Wayne, where he is the second oldest photographer, and ranks among the best in this part of the state. In politics he is a republican; he was a charter member of Mythra lodge, K. of P., at Peru, and is a member of Loyal lodge, of Fort Wayne, and is a comrade of the G. A. R.; was married in 1870, has a son and daughter. His son, Harry A., is now engaged in business with his father at 44 Calhoun street, Fort Wayne.

More than a half century ago John J. Jocquel became a resident of Indiana. Born in France in 1812, he immigrated in 1832, and settling first at Cincinnati, then at Milton, Ohio, in 1836, he came into Indiana, and made his home first at Logansport, then at Peru, and in 1854 came to Fort Wayne. For a year he was foreman for Derry & Maple, stove and tinware dealers, and then engaged in business for himself. In 1871 he began dealing in oil and lamps, but in 1876 changed his business to books and stationery, at which he continued until December 1, 1887, when he retired from active life. While at Peru he was married to a daughter of Capt. Louis Drouillard, an Indian trader. She died in August, 1876. Mr. Jocquel, now in his seventy-seventh year, is one of the oldest members of the congregation of the Cathedral, for which building he furnished all the tin and galvanized iron work. He retains his mental faculties in a surprising degree, with an excellent memory of the early days. He was succeeded in business by his son, Louis Jocquel, who was born at Peru, in 1849. He was educated in the Catholic schools, and in 1871, engaged in the book and stationery business. From this he retired in 1876, to accept the appointment of deputy assessor of Fort Wayne. After holding this position for three years he was in 1880, elected by the council to fill an unexpired term as assessor, and in 1882 and 1884 was elected by the people. He conducts a first-class bookstore on Calhoun street, making a specialty of Catholic books. He was married November 5, 1872, to Philomena, daugther of Jacob Glutting, of Fort Wayne.

John C. Wagner, one of the foremost in the piano trade in this city, came to Fort Wayne in 1875, and soon became generally known as a skillful piano tuner. He has been busily engaged in this, and during the past five years has also dealt extensively in pianos, his present establishment being at 27 West Main street, where he has built up a successful business. He is unusually skillful in his profession and as a business man, and socially possesses the esteem and confidence of the community. He was born in Germany, October 4, 1851, son of Sebastian and Elizabeth Wagner, and received his early education in his native country. At the age of seventeen he came to America, leaving his relatives in the old country, and from 1868 to 1875 made his home in New York city. Mr. Wagner was married June 3, 1873, to Maggie Schield, daughter of John and Margaret Schield. She died September 4, 1886, leaving three children: Bertha, Louise and Sophia.

Henry Pfeiffer, senior member of the hardware firm of Pfeiffer & Schlatter, had his introduction to the business in 1866 at Dillenburg, Germany, where he continued until the fall of 1868, when he immigrated and settled at Fort Wayne. After attending the common schools some time he entered the employ of Morgan & Beach, and continued with them for more than thirteen years. In May, 1882, he formed his present partnership, and is now doing a handsome business, and is recognized as one of the leading young business men of the city. He was born in Prussia, April 17, 1851, son of Peter and Mary (Gick) Pfeiffer. The father was born in 1793, and died in his native land in 1858. He had nine children, of whom Henry is the youngest. Five are deceased. In 1873 he was married to Mary Meyer, who was born in New York city in 1850, and they have had four children: Henry, born 1874; Flora, born 1880; Albert, born 1882, and Bertha, born 1887. Mr. Pfeiffer and wife are members of the St. Paul's Lutheran church, and he is in politics a democrat.

Christian C. Schlatter, of the hardware firm of Pfeiffer & Schlatter, was born in Cedar Creek township, Allen county, September 13, 1851. His father, Sebastian Schlatter, is a native of France, who came to the United States in 1838, and lived first six years in Wayne county, Ohio, settling then in Allen county, where he died in 1871, having devoted his life to the occupation of farming. He married Rebecca Conrad, who was born in Wayne county, Ohio, in 1821, and now resides in Cedar Creek township. They had eleven children, of whom eight are living, C. C. Schlatter being the fourth born. He was raised on a farm, and at eighteen years of age went to Wooster, Ohio, and for two years attended high school, at the expiration of that period entering the employment of D. D. Miller, hardware dealer. A year later he came to Fort Wayne, and was for ten years in the employment of Morgan & Beach, acquiring a thorough knowledge of the business, which enabled him, when he embarked in trade for himself in partnership with Henry Pfeiffer, at the expiration of the service referred to, to speedily gain a high rank among the enterprising and trustworthy business men of the city. He was married in 1876 to Addie Zimmerman, who was born in Cedar Creek township, May 6, 1856, and they have one child, Harry C., born October 26, 1885. Mrs. Schlatter is a member of the Methodist Episcopal church.

Theodore O. Gotsch, a prominent hardware dealer, of the firm of Smith & Gotsch, was born at Kendallville, Ind., June 25, 1860. His father, Julius H. Gotsch, was born at Leipsic, Saxony, in 1830, came with his parents to America when a young man, first settled in Fort Wayne, and in 1860 removed to Kendallville, where he died in 1872. He was a jeweler by trade. He married Lena Muessing, who was born in Frille in Kresse-Menden, Prussia, in 1835, by whom he had five children, three of whom are living, Theodore being the second. The latter received a common school education at his birth place, and in 1877 came to Fort Wayne, and the next year took a position with Prescott Bros. & Co., hardware merchants. In 1881 he began a six years' employment with Morgan & Beach. He embarked in business independently in 1888 in partneaship with Fred M. Smith. They purchased the store of T. J. Nolton, and are now doing a prosperous business. Mr. Gotsch made his own way in life since he was nine years of age, and is highly esteemed as a citizen. He was married

November, 1884, to Carrie Johnson, who was born at Waterloo, N. Y., in 1860. She died April 18, 1886. Mr. Gotsch is a member of St. Paul's Lutheran church.

Fred M. Smith, of the hardware firm of Smith & Gotsch, was born at Watertown, Jefferson county, N. Y., son of Willett and Zilpha (Baker) Smith, both natives of that state. His father, born in 1834, died in 1887, at Watertown, and his mother, born in 1834, died at the same place in 1880. Mr. Smith, the second of three living children, attended the schools of his town, and then, in 1880 entered the Potsdam Normal school, whence he graduated in 1886. He was for two years principal of the Parishville graded school, and then in 1888, came to Fort Wayne, and engaged in the hardware business, purchasing the stock of T. J. Nolton. He carries a general line of light hardware, and is doing a good business. Politically he is a democrat, and socially he is highly esteemed, being generally classed among the prominent young business men of the city.

Joseph A. M. Storm, who is a native of Germany, arrived in America with his parents in 1863, settling first at Philadelphia, where he resided until October, 1864, when he removed to Fort Wayne. In January, 1865, he entered the hardware store of Morgan & Beach, where he remained five years, then spending seven years in the same business with McCulloch & Richey. Subsequently, after three years' experience with Coombs & Co., as traveling salesman, he bought out the firm of McCulloch & Richey, and since has had that success in business that his twenty-three years' experience in his chosen line, and his natural ability in commerce have led his friends to expect. Mr. Storm was born in Germany on the river Weser, January 18, 1847, son of Conrad and Sophia (Reiking) Storm. His father was born in 1802, in the town of Oberkirchen in Hesse and when he emigrated to the United States, settled at Philadelphia, where he lived until his death in 1884. He was by occupation a glass engraver. The mother of Mr. Storm was born in 1808, at the village of Haevern on the river Weser, and now resides at Philadelphia. Mr. Storm is the sixth in a family of eight children, of whom six survive, and received his education in Germany. He was married in 1873, to Caroline Paul, born in 1853, and they have one child, Matilda. They are members of the German Lutheran church. In politics Mr. Storm is a democrat, and as such from 1885 to 1887, represented the Fifth ward in the city council, serving as a member of the finance committee during his membership, one year as chairman.

In about the year 1855, John Spice, a native of County Kent, England, came to the United States, and settled at Buffalo. In 1861 he came to Allen county, and settled on a farm in Lake township. He was appointed superintendent of the county poor farm in 1869, and held that position until 1880, when he made his home at Fort Wayne, and engaged in business, dealing in pumps, pipe, and fittings, lightning rods, drive wells, water elevators, etc., and as agent for the Star wind mills. Established first on Broadway, the business was removed in 1885 to

XII

No. 48 West Main street. The business was founded in 1865 by A. P. Kyle, who was succeeded by J. Y. Keyser, and he in October, 1880, by John Spice & Son. In July, 1887, John Spice retired from business, and removed to Hudson, Steuben county, where he and wife, whose maiden name was Frances Craft, are living a retired life. They had five children: John W., born in England, in 1841, died in 1877: Charlotte, died in chilhood; Fanny, born in England in 1853; Herbert, born in New York in 1857, died in 1880, and Robert, born in New York, June 6, 1859. The latter succeeded to the business in which he had been a partner, in 1887, and has a large trade throughout a territory included in a radius of twenty miles. He was married in July, 1878, to Alice E. Richey, daughter of James Richey, of this city, and they have had five children, two of whom are deceased. Mr. Spice is a member of the Knights of Pythias.

Louis J. Bobilya, one of the brightest and most active young business men of Fort Wayne, occupies the responsible position of general agent for J. F. Sieberling & Co., of Akron, Ohio, manufacturers of the Empire mowers, reapers and binders. He is a native of the county, born August 9, 1857. His father, August Bobilya, married Susan Buva, in their native country, France, and they then immigrated, settling first in Ohio, and removing to Allen county in 1851. The father died in the thirty-fourth year of his age, and the mother survived him until 1886, when she died in her fiftieth year. Louis was the third of five children, of whom four are living. After the death of his father he made his home with an uncle at Defiance until he was twelve years of age, when he entered the employment of Frank Alderman, in the agricultural implement business. Five years later he engaged with J. F. Sieberling & Co., as general agent for the state of Indiana. He is a Mason, and in politics a democrat. He has made his own way in life, and his success in business and good standing in all the relations of life, are highly gratifying to his many friends.

One deserving mention among the young business men of the city is Alexander H. Boerger, a prominent young druggist, a native of this city, born July 15, 1867. He is the son of William and Elizabeth (Spring) Boerger, old and esteemed citizens of Fort Wayne. He received his early education in the public schools of the city, both English and German branches. At sixteen he took a position as clerk in a drug store, and a year later entered the Cincinnati college of pharmacy and attended two terms. Returning home, he spent a few months in the capacity of clerk, after which on August 1, 1887, he opened a drug store at No. 316 Hanna street, where he has since done a successful business. He is a member of the Salem Reformed church. Mr. Boerger is an upright young man, and a competent and reliable pharmacist.

In the year 1884 John J. Brink established himself in the drug business at 43 Wells street, and has since enjoyed a profitable custom. He is prominent in his business, an enterprising and popular young citizen. Mr. Brink was born in this city March 30, 1857, the son of Jacob and

Catherine (Wismer) Brink. When he was eight years old he lost his father by death. In 1871, being then fourteen years old, he began his experience in business with his employment as a drug clerk, and he continued to be engaged in that capacity until opening a store of his own.

Martin Detzer, one of the most trustworthy druggists of the city, began his study of pharmacy in 1867, when he accepted a clerkship in a drug store at Defiance, Ohio. A year later he was employed in the same capacity at Napoleon, and four months afterward came to Fort Wayne. He was subsequently compelled by sickness to give up his position, and he was then employed for a few months at Bryan, returning then to this city and taking a position with August L. Selle, druggist. In 1878 he and his brother, August J. Detzer, became the successors of Mr. Selle, purchasing the stock after his death, and the firm of Detzer & Brothers prospered for nearly eight years. December 14, 1885, Martin Detzer became the sole proprietor, by purchase of his brother's interest. His establishment at 260 Calhoun street, is one of the prominent drug stores of the city, and is enjoying a lucrative business. Mr. Detzer enjoys the confidence of the community as an honorable and upright man. He was born in Williams county, Ohio, May 23, 1851, the son of Rev. Adam J. and Charlotte (Neidhardt) Detzer, natives respectively of Bavaria and Alsace. When Martin was a small child the family removed to Defiance, Ohio. The mother died at Desplaines, Ill., September 26, 1873; the father, a minister of the Lutheran church, resides at Holgate, Ohio. Mr. Detzer first came to Fort Wayne at the age of eleven as a student in Concordia college, where he remained five years. He was married in December, 1874, to Lizzie, daughter of Rev. W. S. Stubnatzy, formerly a Lutheran minister at Fort Wayne. She was born in Illinois, in April, 1852. They have had four children: Phebe W., Charlotte E., Paul F. W. and Edith, the first and last being deceased. Mr. Detzer and wife are members of the Lutheran church.

One of the popular young men of the city, and well equipped by taste and education for his business as a druggist, Henry C. Granneman, was born in Osage county, Mo., August 18, 1867. His parents are Charles H. and Minnie (Fisher) Granneman, natives of Germany, the father born in 1822 and the mother in 1826. They came to the United States about 1856, and subsequently removed to Missouri, but are now residents of the city. To them six children were born, of whom three are living, the youngest being Henry C. He came to Fort Wayne with his parents in 1873, and received his education at the Lutheran schools. He entered the drug business in 1883, in the employ of the well known firm of C. B. Woodworth & Co., with whom he still remains. He studied his profession in the Chicago college of pharmacy, of which he is a graduate, and he is a member of the Indiana state phamaceutical association. He is a member of the Lutheran church, and is one of the Fort Wayne light artillery, Company G, of the first regiment. He is a republican in politics, and cast his first presidential vote for Benjamin Harrison.

After a seven years' experience with the late Henry G. Wayne as a drug clerk, Charles O. Lepper, at present proprietor of the popular drug store at 66 West Jefferson street, embarked in business on his own account, September 27, 1886. Mr. Lepper possesses a thorough knowledge of pharmacy, is a conscientious and trustworthy young man, and possesses in a marked degree those desirable business qualifications which insure success. He was born in Washington township, Allen county, January 27, 1864, the son of Lewis and Margaret (Good) Lepper. The father was killed in 1870 by the explosion of a boiler in his grist-mill, at New Haven, and soon afterward the mother and children removed to this city. Mr. Lepper began his engagement with Mr. Wayne in the drug trade in 1879. He is a member of the Salem Reformed church, and also of the Salem literary society, being treasurer of that organization.

George H. Loesch, the well known druggist at No. 96 Barr street, is a native Indianian, born in Marshall county, October 31, 1856. He is the son of Christian and Augusta L. (Hamm) Loesch, both natives of Germany. The father was born at Heidelberg, and is a graduate of the university at that place, and the mother was born forty of fifty miles from there, in the state of Baden. They were married at Pittsburgh, Penn., about 1851, and now reside at Plymouth, Ind. About ten years before their removal to the latter place, their son George H., was born, and his early education was received in the schools there. In November, 1870, he took a clerkship in a drug store there, and after two or three years' experience, went to Chicago, where he spent over three years, having employment as a drug clerk, and also taking one course in the Chicago medical college, and two in the college of pharmacy, graduating from the latter March 11, 1876. In the latter part of the following month he came to Fort Wayne, and obtained a clerkship with the late George B. Thorp. A year and a half later he purchased the establishment, and has since conducted the business very successfully. He is quite prominent among the business men of Fort Wayne, is accomplished in his profession, and socially occupies a high standing. He was married October 29, 1878, to Mary M., daughter of John and Mary M. (Mahler) Hohan, who was born at Lake Maxinkuckee, April 17, 1857. Her father, an old settler of Marshall county, is living at Plymouth, but the mother died in November, 1875. Mr. Loesch is a Knight Templar and a member of the lodge of Perfection.

H. J. Seibold, superintendent of the Keller medicine company, of Fort Wayne, and a member of the Fort Wayne bill poster company, was born in Allen county, nine miles west from Fort Wayne, in 1856, the son of George and Dorothea (Seigel) Seibold, both of whom were natives of Germany. They emigrated to America in 1845 and coming directly to Allen county, located in Lafayette township, upon a farm. The mother died in 1875, at the age of fifty-seven, and the father has now passed his seventy-ninth year. Mr. Seibold was reared on the farm until fourteen years old and was educated in the country schools.

Subsequently he came to the city and engaged, in April, 1873, in the drug business with T. M. Biddley. He remained in this position until the fall of 1879. He then engaged with C. B. Woodworth for two years and became a half partner in 1881. On July 1, 1886, he engaged in the hotel business as one of the proprietors of the Robinson hotel. He was thus engaged until 1888, when he took his present position in the Keller company. Mr. Seibold was married June 23, 1887, to Chloe, daughter of Captain H. C. Eastwood, one of the proprietors of the Brunswick hotel. Mr. Seibold is a popular citizen; is a member of the Elks, of the Evangelical association and the Apollo musical club.

One of the handsomest drug stores of the city, that at 35 Calhoun street, is under the able management of Henry G. Sommers, one of the enterprising young business men of the city, who became proprietor in the fall of 1887, purchasing the stock and the valuable business property which the store occupies. Mr. Sommers is a thorough druggist, and is in all respects adapted to carry on the business successfully. He is energetic, courteous and deservedly popular. Mr. Sommers was born at Fort Wayne, September 16, 1863, and is the son of Frederick and Jennie (Mergel) Sommers, former residents of the city, now deceased. At fifteen years of age he became employed in the drug store which he now owns, as clerk for his uncle, Henry G. Wagner, then proprietor. Under the tutelage of that prominent druggist he acquired a complete knowledge of the business.

James Urbine, a well-known business man of Fort Wayne, is a native of Allen county, born February 18, 1849, son of John B. Urbine, a native of France, who was born in 1821, son of Nicholas Urbine, who died in this county about 1860. John B. Urbine came to Fort Wayne in 1833, and helped in the excavation of the Wabash & Erie canal. He married Adeline C. Litot, who was born in France in 1822. Five of their children are living, James being the oldest. He received a common school education, attended the commercial college, and in 1875 entered the employment of Dreier Brothers, and began his life occupation as a druggist. After seven years' experience he became engaged with J. F. W. Meyer & Bro., where he is at present. In 1881 he was married to Mary T. Golden, who was born in Ireland in 1859, and they have two children: Catherine C., born April 22, 1882, and James Ralph, April 22, 1886. Mr. Urbine and wife are members of the Catholic church. They reside at 52 East Williams street.

Fremont L. Jones was born in Grant county, Ind., August 10, 1855, son of David W. and Jane (Atkinson) Jones. His father was born in Montgomery county, Ohio, in 1821, son of Obadiah Jones, a native of North Carolina, who died in Jonesboro, Ind. His mother was born near Dayton, Ohio, in 1821, and died at Fort Wayne in 1882. There are six children of these parents living, of whom Fremont L. is next to the youngest. He came to Fort Wayne with his parents in 1863, and received his education in the common schools and Fort Wayne college. In 1876, he removed to Grand Rapids and served an apprenticeship in the laundry business, returning the next year and establishing the now widely known Troy steam laundry, which is conducted under the firm name of F. L. Jones & Co. The establishment employs fifty people the year round, and does a great business, its custom extending widely throughout the adjacent counties. In politics, Mr. Jones is a republican, and is a member of the Morton club. He and wife are members of the Methodist Episcopal church. He was married in 1879, to Gertrude M. Hatch, who was born in this county in 1859, daughter of N. V. and Abigail (Parker) Hatch, who were among the first settlers of the county. Mr. and Mrs. Jones have four children: Bessie L., David V., Ralph L. and Walter B.

Ogden Pierce, one of the proprietors of the Troy steam laundry, above mentioned, was born in Green county, N. Y., March 19, 1830. His father, Eli Pierce, was born in the same state about 1775, and married Sarah Burgess, who was born in Philadelphia about 1797. They removed to Allen county in 1844, and here the mother died ten years later, and the father in his eightieth year. They left seven children, of whom Ogden is the fourth. He was raised on a farm, obtained his education in the public schools, and in 1856 went to Milwaukee, Wis., where for some time he was engaged in the produce business, returning to Fort Wayne in 1870, where he has since resided. In 1871 he was appointed to the position of railway postal clerk on the Eel river line from Detroit to Logansport, which route he held until two years later, when he was transferred to the Michigan Southern line from Toledo to Chicago, and after two years to the fast mail between Cleveland and Chicago. In 1876 he was transferred to the Pittsburgh line railway postoffice, and given charge of a car from Crestline to Chicago, which position he retained until January, 1884, gaining a reputation as one of the most valuable and efficient men in the service. He became a partner in the Troy steam laundry with his brother-in-law, F. L. Jones, in 1877, and since 1884 has given the business his personal attention. He was married in 1870 to Martha A. Jones, born in Grant county in 1848, and they have five children: Ogden, Ethel, Robert B., Howard and Martha.

Cassius A. Miller is an enterprising young business man of Fort Wayne, having been engaged with his father in the furniture business since completing his education. During an interval of two years, however, 1875-7, he was in California, and while there he cast his first presidential vote for President Hayes. He has remained an earnest republican, and is now one of the vice presidents of the Morton club. He is a representative of one of the oldest families of the city. He was born at this city, January 10, 1853, to John M. and Sarah (Noble) Miller, and is the second of three living children of those parents. He received his education in the public schools and the commercial department of Fort Wayne Methodist Episcopal college. January 10, 1883, he was married to Minna A. Wright, a native of Allentown, Penn., daughter of Judge Robert E. and Maria Wright. Judge Wright died January 10, 1887.

Mr. Miller is a member of the Methodist Episcopal church, and his wife of the Episcopal charch. Their residence is at 103 East Washington street.

E. Shuman, dealer in furniture, was born in Mainville, Penn., May 15, 1841, son of Isaiah and Mary Ann (Miller) Shuman, natives of Pennsylvania, in which state his father died and his mother now resides. He is the second of four children living. After receiving a common school education he came to Fort Wayne in 1863, and was for eight years in the employment of John M. Miller, furniture dealer, and then spent four years in Grand Rapids in the same business, returning to Fort Wayne to embark in the business on his own responsibility. For nine years he has been doing a successful business, also giving considerable attention to pawnbroking. He is a republican in politics, and is a member of the Masonic order. In 1869 he was married to Amanda M. Grover, who was born in Pennsylvania in 1844, and they have seven children: George, Frank, Gilbert, Katie, Arthur, Annie and Robert. Mr. Shuman is an admirer of fine horses, and has owned some noted animals, and in March, 1889, he purchased at Cambridge City, Ind., the famous mare, Lady Wonder, record 2:25, for $925. She has a colt, Anna Wonder, foaled June 1, 1889. Mr. Shuman's life has been active one, and he is noted for industry and application to business.

Daniel Shordon the senior dealer in agricultural implements of Fort Wayne, embarked in that business here in 1870, and has been notably successful in his enterprises. He is also prominent as a citizen, and generally esteemed. In 1887, Mr. Shordon was elected a member of the city council for the second ward by a majority of twenty, he being a candidate on the straight republican ticket. He was born at Syracuse, New York, March 15, 1837, son of Stephen and Catherine (Keifer) Shordon, both natives of France. His father was born in 1808, the mother in 1807, and they came to America in 1835, and after stopping four years in New York, settled in Springfield township, Allen county, Ind., in 1839, being one of the first families in the township. The father died here in 1882, and the mother lives in the city. Daniel is the oldest of their twelve children, of whom six are living. He attended the public schools and one year at the Notre Dame university, and also taught school for some time. In 1862, he enlisted in Company D, Eighty-eighth Indiana regiment, and served gallantly at the battle of Chickamauga, at which he was wounded, Stone River, Resaca, Peach Tree Creek, during the siege of Atlanta and at Jonesboro, the last battle of the war, and was mustered out in 1865, as sergeant. On coming home, he went to farming, and while so engaged, served one term as trustee of St. Joseph township. He was married in 1871 to Susan Lau who died in 1874. In 1881 he married Augustine Joly, born in Allen county in 1845. They are members of the Catholic church.

Frank D. Paulus, who deals in engines and threshers and other agricultural implements at 53 East Main street, has had a long experience in the trade, and few men are better qualified for success in that business. Two years after the close of the war, he entered the employ of the firm of J. F. Sieberling & Co., of Akron, Ohio, and was with them ten years, after which he was employed by Aultman, Miller & Co., for thirteen years. He came to Fort Wayne in 1875, and is now principally handling Walter A. Woods' binders and mowers, and the Huber threshers and engines. Mr. Paulus was born at Akron, Ohio, November 23, 1842, son of Isaac and Elizabeth (Girrl) Paulus. Both parents were born in 1812; the father died in 1845, and his widow now resides in Michigan. Frank, the youngest of three children, worked out for his board and clothes from nine to fourteen years of age, and then was employed by the month on a farm until October, 1861, when he enlisted in Company G, Sixty-fourth Ohio infantry, with which he served until December, 1864, participating in the battles of Shiloh, Stone River, Chickamauga, siege of Atlanta and battle of Franklin. He was married December 31, 1868, to Mary C. Bolender, born in Stark county, Ohio, in 1846, and they are members of the Reformed church. He is a comrade of the G. A. R., a Mason and Odd Fellow, and in politics an earnest republican.

Henry H. Schone, a prominent young business man, of the undertaking firm of Schone & Wellman, was born in this city December, 1859. His father, Henry J. Schone, a well known citizen, was born in Germany, September 15, 1815, came to the United States in 1840, and in the fall of that year settled in Fort Wayne. He is a tanner by trade, but for nineteen years was engaged in the grocery business. He is a faithful member of the Catholic church, and is highly esteemed by the community. He was married in 1843, and by this union had one child Elizabeth. This wife died in 1857, and in 1858 he was married to Margaret Damon, who was born in Germany in 1821. She gave him one child, Henry H. The latter was educated at the Catholic schools of this city and afterward attended the commercial college. In 1874 he took a position as clerk in a dry goods store, and was so engaged for twelve years. In October, 1887, he embarked in his present occupation with Henry Wellman as a partner, and their business has prospered, even beyond their expectation. They are fully equipped for the proper and comely performance of their offices, do embalming according to the best methods, and in every way justify the noteworthy popularity which they enjoy. Mr. Schone was married October 18, 1880, to Jennie E. Henry, who was born at St. Joseph, in 1858, and they have two children, Alnoria G. and Julian J., and Mary and Aloysius, deceased. He and wife are members of the Catholic church.

George C. Brinsley, dealer in illuminating oils and gasoline, at No. 85 West Main street, was born in Cheshire, England, April 25, 1826. He was reared in Staffordshire, and in 1850 came to America, and settled in New York. Two years later he removed to New Jersey, where he remained two years. He afterward resided successively in New York city, New Jersey, Pennsylvania (Schuylkill county), New Jersey, New York city and Crestline, Ohio. On November 12, 1864, he enlisted in Company

B, One Hundred and Seventy-ninth regiment, Ohio infantry, and served until his muster out near Nashville, Tenn., in June, 1865. He then returned to Crestline, Ohio, and was engaged in railroading with his residence there until 1883, when he came to Fort Wayne and engaged in the oil business. He does a successful retail and wholesale business. Mr. Brinsley is a member of the Methodist Episcopal church, and of Sion S. Bass post, G. A. R. He was married in England, in 1849, to Sarah A. Hibbs, who died in 1876, leaving five children. In 1877 he was married at Mansfield, Ohio, to Sarah R. Nunamaker, by whom he had two children, one of whom is living. The children by his first marriage are: Louis S., born in 1851, now farming in Kansas; George C., born in 1853, in business with his father; Mary Ann, born in 1855; William, born in 1857; Charles E., born July 1, 1861, and the surviving child by his second marriage is Harry A. Charles E. was born in Cresline, Ohio, and remained ther until 1880, receiving a public school education. He resided four years in Springfield, Ohio, and then came to Fort Wayne, and went into the oil business July 1, 1887. He was married November 7, 1887, to Hattie E. Phillabaum, of Fort Wayne, and they had one child, Mabel S., born November 19, 1888, and died March 24, 1889.

Weil Brothers & Co., a prosperous firm, doing a large business in pelts, furs, wool, etc., at 92, 94, 96 and 98 East Columbia street, is composed of Isaac and Abram Weil, both worthy and enterprising men. They began doing business as a firm in 1877 on Calhoun street, and four years later removed to 87 and 89 East Columbia street, where they remained until July, 1887, when the stock was destroyed by fire. The same year they built the present business house, sixty feet front, and 130 feet deep. They employ more than fifty people, have an annual trade of $600,000, and do a business which is among the most extensive in this part of the country. The Weil brothers are children of Jacob and Rosa Livingston Weil, natives of Germany, who came to the United States about 1850, settled first in Cincinnati, and in 1858 came to Fort Wayne. They now reside here. Isaac Weil, the oldest of their four children, was born at Cincinnati, December 13, 1855. He was educated in the Fort Wayne schools, and in 1870 began to learn the trunk business, at which he was engaged two years, abandoning it to deal in hides, pelts, etc., on Bass street, where he remained five years. He is a member of Wayne lodge, No. 25, F. & A. M. He was married in 1888 to Rena Rothschild of Terre Haute. Abram Weil, the other member of the firm, was born at Cincinnati, December 16, 1857, and is an enterprising business man.

William Fred Schulz, a well-known German citizen of Fort Wayne, and a leading sewer contractor, was born in Prussia on August 21, 1839. Emigrated to America in 1865. Learned his trade in Germany; came direct to Fort Wayne, and went to work for an employer, with whom he remained for fifteen years. Began contracting in about 1885, as one member of a partnership in the sewer business, and the next two years with Joseph Derheimer, still with him in sewer work. They do most of the city work, and recently took three large contracts. Married in 1866 to Wilhelmenia Kreger, who was born in Germany. Three children have been born to them, five altogether, two dead. Member of the St. Paul's Lutheran church.

The Abstract Office.— Among the oldest and most reliable abstract companies of Indiana is that of F. W. Kuhne & Company, which began business as early as 1870. F. W. Kuhne, the senior member of the firm, is a native of Prussia, born in 1831, and he was raised and educated in that country. In 1856 he came to America, on a visit merely, but liking the country, its people and institutions he concluded to remain, settled at Iowa City and became naturalized. February, 1866, he accepted the position of deputy auditor of Allen county, Ind., and moved to Fort Wayne. He served the county as deputy auditor from March, 1866, to October, 1875, and as deputy treasurer from 1875 to 1879, gaining in those positions a broad familiarity with the the lands of the county. In 1870 he became associated with John M. Koch and C. M. Barton in the abstracting of titles of real estate. Later Mr. Kuhne purchased the interest of Mr. Barton, and about the same time David P. White became a partner in the firm. About 1875 Mr. Kuhne bought the interest of John M. Koch, and upon the death of Mr. White, he admitted his sons to the firm. Paul F., the eldest son, was born in Iowa City, Iowa, November 16, 1860, received a good business education, and in 1877 entered the employment of the First National bank, where he remained six years. Richard H. was born January 14, 1862, and Charles W. Kuhne, the youngest son, February 5, 1864, both in Iowa City. The latter was educated in Fort Wayne and in the university of Michigan, graduating from the law department in 1887. He was admitted the same year to the Allen county bar, and is making a specialty of realty law and probate matters. The firm, thus composed, and headed by F. W. Kuhne, is a strong one, and does an extensive business in preparing abstracts, and placing mortgage loans, making collections, and selling exchange on Europe.

John W. Hayden, a prominent citizen of Fort Wayne, was born in Brown township, Franklin county, Ohio, May 18, 1837. His father, Isaac Hayden, was born in Fayette county, Penn., March 21, 1809, and was married in 1833, to Elizabeth Crabb, who was born in Franklin county, Ohio, August 15, 1815. He was of English descent, she of Scotch, and their parents both served in the war of 1812, his father being at the battle of the River Raisin. Their only other child was Emeline, born in 1835. In 1848 the family removed to Kosciusko county, Ind., where they settled in a cabin on 160 acres of land, and here, without the advantage of good schools or church privileges, except such as the itinerant preacher furnished, John W. grew up to the age of nineteen, when he was sent to Fort Wayne college. He completed the course here in 1860, but on account of a slight misunderstanding with the president, refused to accept his diploma. He began the study of law with Hon. Isaac Jenkinson, and was admitted to the bar. On April 22, 1861, when President Lincoln called for three months' enlistments, he became a member of Company G, of the Twelfth Indiana volunteers. Being appointed second sergeant, he held that position until the expiration of his enlistment, when he re-enlisted for one year, but on account of disability contracted while in line of duty he was discharged at Poolsville, Md., August 31, 1861. Returning home he was engaged for several years in the pension office at Fort Wayne, and subsequently began the practice of law. August 12, 1875, he was appointed register in bankruptcy by Judge W. Q. Gresham, which office he held until the repeal of the law in 1878. On the organization of the United States district court at Fort Wayne, he was appointed deputy by United States Marshal W. W. Dudley, and he held this place until the change of administration in 1884. In the meantime he had built up a large and lucrative real estate and loan business, at which he is now occupied. Mr. Hayden is a Methodist, as were his parents. Born a whig, he became an enthusiastic republican, and early in life adopted for his political motto, "Colonization and qualified suffrage," a doctrine which he still believes could have saved the union its tremendous sacrifice in settling the question of slavery. He was united in marriage May 18, 1866, with Sarah M., daughter of Dr. Samuel J. Green, of Wayneton, Ind., and they have had five children, two of whom are living: Grace G. and John R. Mr. Hayden is a Mason of the thirty-second degree, a Knight Templar and a member of the G. A. R.

One of the most prominent and trustworthy passenger conductors in the service of the Pennsylvania company is Thomas M. Glenn. Has also of late years, when off duty, devoted much time to real estate, more particularly to the development of the south side, where his was one of the first offices of the kind established. His energy, candor and manly principles, have earned him an enviable standing among all classes. He entered the service of the Pennsylvania company in the year 1858, at Lima, Ohio, as water boy on a gravel train, under the direction of the late O. A. Simons, and rose through nearly all the subordinate positions in the service, to the position of passenger conductor in 1879, on western division between Fort Wayne & Chicago, since which time he has resided in Fort Wayne with the exception of about a year's leave of absence traveling with his family in California and Mexico. He occupies a high position in his calling. His gentlemanly and courteous manners and watchful care of his passengers, has made him popular with the traveling public, and given him the perfect confidence and esteem of his officers and associates. Mr. Glenn was born in Allegheny county, Penn., March 1, 1848, son of Robert and Ann (Smith) Glenn, who were both natives of County Antrim, north of Ireland, of Scotch descent. His father was born in 1813, and mother in 1817. They came to America in 1839, and settled in Pennsylvania, subsequently removing to Van Wert, Ohio, where his father died in 1876, and his mother in 1883. Thomas M. was the fifth born of their seven children, five of whom are now living. He was married at VanWert, Ohio, March 22, 1871, to Miss Viola C. De Puy, the accomplished daughter of Dr. W. W. De Puy, an old and prominent physician of northwestern Ohio. She was born at Laketon, Wabash county, Ind., January 24, 1853, and they have three children living: Walter D., Robert W. and Viola B. Her mother's maiden name was Elizabeth Bonner. Mrs. Glenn has been a member of the Second Presbyterian church of Fort Wayne, for many years. In 1874 Mr. Glenn took his first degrees in the order of Freemasonry, at Longmont, Col., St. Vrain lodge, No. 23, A. F. & A. M., and is now a member of Fort Wayne commandery, No. 4, Knight Templar, Valparaiso chapter, No. 137, Royal Arch Masons, and Porter lodge, A. F. & A. M.

Capt. Allan H. Dougall was born in Glasgow, Scotland, July 17, 1836. Twenty-two years later he emigrated with his father, John Dougall, and the younger portion of his father's family, arriving in Fort Wayne, June 2, 1858. The family settled in St. Joseph township in July, 1858, where they engaged in farming. During the agitation in Great Britain for the abolition of human slavery in the British colonies, his father took a prominent part, and at the outbreak of the rebellion, foreseeing that American slavery had to succumb ere peace would be restored, he willingly permitted the subject of this sketch and his brother William, to enlist in the army. Although comparatively unknown, Allan H. Dougall enlisted as a private in Company D, Eighty-eighth Indiana volunteer infantry, in July, 1862. He served with distinction at the battles of Stone River and La Vergne, Tenn., also in the Tullahoma and Chattanooga campaigns. He was severely wounded in his right arm and shoulder while leading his company against a rebel battery at the battle of Resaca, May 15, 1864. This wound crippled his entire right side and rendered him ever after unfit for manual labor. July 1, 1864, he was promoted adjutant of his regiment, and while serving as such he was shot through the left leg at the battle of Peach Tree Creek, July 20, 1864. From the commencement of "Sherman's march to the sea," to the close of the war, he was topographical engineer of the first brigade, first division, fourteenth army corps, under Gen. H. C. Hobart, and aid to Col. C. E. Briant, commanding the right wing of the brigade, composed of the Thirty-third Ohio, Eighty-eighth Indiana and Ninety-fourth Ohio volunteers infantry. At the battle of Bentonville, N. C., he was wounded and left on the field, but succeeded in regaining our lines by Acorn run, and assisted in re-forming the brigade in support of the massed artillery which so materially assisted in deciding that battle. He was mustered into the G. A. R. in August, 1866, and is one among the oldest members in the department of Indiana, of which he has been chief mustering officer. He is past commander of Anthony Wayne post, and is at present a member of the national council of administration. For some time after his return from the army he was engaged in the milling business at New Haven, and was for several years clerk of that town and one of the school board, and commenced the first set of books for both these corporations. He is now engaged in the pension, government claim and insurance business. His peculiar adaptation to details, acquired in the adjutant's department, makes him especially fitted for executive work, and in whatever position of life he is planted, he is sought out for this work. The captain has always been a republican. He took an active part in the election of Abraham Lincoln, and in every campaign since. In 1872 he was a candidate for the legislature, running ahead of his ticket, he receiving more votes than the governor and congressman in the county. He has been, at different times, and is at the present time, secretary of the republican central committee. Although of a retiring disposition he is sought out and urged to fill these positions. He was one of the prime movers in the organization of the Morton club, and has held official position in that flourishing political organization. In Masonic circles he stands high, and is past master of Newman lodge of New Haven, Ind., past high priest of Fort Wayne chapter, and past illustrious master of Fort Wayne council, vice-president of the Fort Wayne Caledonian club. In August, 1862, he married Josephine Griffin who, with their two sons, John I. Dougall and Arthur H. Dougall, and their daughters, M. Inez Dougall and Winnie J. Dougall, are well known in Fort Wayne social circles. On coming to this country he brought with him his transfer from the old kirk of Scotland and affiliated with the First Presbyterian church of this city in 1858, and is still a worthy and honored member. Like his nationality he is a man of strong convictions, and when once convinced of the right, no power will induce him to turn. He is always known to fight for his principles to the last, and if need be, go down with them. His counsel is therefor eagerly sought after in whatever position in life he may be placed either in society, politics or elsewhere.

Conrad Neireiter, general insurance agent and notary public, has been for years one of the prominent men in business life in Fort Wayne. He came to the city in July, 1848, having then been but little over a year a resident of the United States. After landing at Baltimore, May 18, 1847, he had settled in Pennsylvania, and there passed the intervening time. He was first occupied here as a clerk in the general store of I. Lauferty, which position he held for four years, resigning it to go into business for himself. For some time he conducted a grocery, then for seventeen years was in the harness and saddlery business, was four years a wholesale leather merchant, and then for several years engaged in the manufacture of trunks. In all these pursuits his correct business principles and upright dealing gained him the confidence of the public and the general esteem. For the past six years he has devoted his talents to insurance agency, managing the interests here of the German insurance company, of Freeport, Ill., the Williamsburg City fire insurance company of New York, the Rochester German, of Rochester, N. Y., and the Concordia, of Milwaukee, all reputable and responsible organizations. Socially Mr. Neireiter enjoys in a marked degree the good-will of the community, and has many warm friends among his wide acquaintance. In politics, he is a democrat, and was at one time honored by that party with a membership in the city council. He was married October 27, 1852, to Harriet Lepper, who was born in Germany, March 5, 1834, and came to Allen county in 1845. They have three children: Kittie M., born October 1, 1858; Nettie F., July 11, 1862; Emma E., April 7, 1871. Mr. Neireiter and wife are members of the German Reformed church. Mr. Neireiter was born in Germany, June 11, 1829, and is the eldest of five children living of Conrad and Mary Ann Neireiter. His father was born in 1804, and died at Fort Wayne in 1872; his mother born in 1808, died January 2, 1889. They came to Fort Wayne in 1860.

George K. Torrence, of the firm of George K. Torrence & Co., real estate and loans, was born in Fayette county, Penn., August 11, 1835. His father, Robert Torrence, was a native of the county, born in 1800, by profession a civil engineer. He married Sophia Kemp, who was born in Hagerstown, Md., in 1804. They resided in Dayton, Ohio, from 1850 until their deaths, which occurred, the father's in 1878, the mother's in 1879. They had four children, Emma R., George K., Mary A., who in 1867 married Edward Edmondson, who died in San Jose, Cal., in 1884, and Isaac M., now ticket agent at Denver, Col., of the Santa Fe railroad. In 1857 George K. went to New Orleans, and was engaged until 1867 in the sugar business, handling also sugar making machinery. In the latter year he returned to Dayton, Ohio, and there resided until 1870, when he came to Fort Wayne and entered the employment of Hoffman Bros., with whom he remained four years. In 1874 he went to South America and for one year was occupied in shipping fine cabinet woods to New York. Upon his return to Fort Wayne he was in the lumber business for several years, and then engaged in his present occupation. In politics he is a democrat; is a Mason, having been Master of Sol D. Bayless lodge, No. 359; and he and wife are members of the Presbyterian church. He was married July 10, 1867, to Alice Belknap, who was born at Frederick City, Md., in 1849.

Robert L. Romy, upon coming to Fort Wayne in 1866, found employment for the first few months as a day laborer, and for twelve years following was engaged in farm life. In 1882 he embarked in the real estate and loan agency in the city, and is now one of the most successful in that calling, and in good circumstances. He is a native of Switzerland, born near Bern, March 2, 1851, son of Fredrick and Barbara (Lutth) Romy, who were both born in Switzerland, of French-German descent. The family immigrated in 1854 and settled in Wayne county, Ohio, where the mother died in 1861. Robert is the third of eight children. He was married March 18, 1871, to Catherine Yerks, born in Canada in 1841, who came to Fort Wayne with her parents in 1851. They have five children: James L., Nora M., Viola, Catherine A., and Ida C. Mr. Romy's residence is three miles northwest of the court-house. He owns 920 acres of land, 390 of which lie in Allen county. He and wife are members of the Grace Reformed church, and he is an Odd Fellow, and in politics a democrat. At present, he is justice of the peace of Washington township.

The Dreibelbiss Abstract of Title Company, one of the successful business associations of Fort Wayne, is composed of, and under the exclusive management of, John and Robert B. Dreibelbiss, who are prominent as business men, and in addition to their abstract business, which has assumed large proportions, do an extensive real estate and loan business, and are associated in various manufacturing enterprises, being stockholders in the Indiana machine works, and the Old Fort manufacturing company. They have offices in the Pixley-Long building, East Berry street. John and Robert Dreibelbiss are sons of John P. Dreibelbiss, born in Bavaria, November 28, 1829, who was three years later brought by his parents to America. The family came to Fort Wayne by ox-team from Buffalo, N. Y. In 1852, John P. Dreibelbiss was married to Anna Saurer, who was born in Switzerland, April 24, 1829, and seven children were born to them: John, Christian G., Christiana R., Conrad W., Mary L., Robert B., and Edward D. The father died December 31, 1886, aged fifty-seven years, and his widow is still living. John was born March 24, 1853, and was married to Kate M. Darrow, October 11, 1877. He is in politics a republican. Robert, next to the youngest of the family, was born October 19, 1861, at Huntington, Ind., is unmarried, and is politically a democrat. The brothers began in December, 1883, the laborious task of copying from the deed, mortgage and court records, all matters pertaining to the title of real estate in Allen county, and after completing this, incorporated, January 1, 1887, the company above named.

Edward L. Craw, engaged in the real estate and loan business, was born in Cleveland, Ohio, February 7, 1846. His father, James A. Craw, was a native of New York, born in 1812, and was a stone mason and contractor. For sixteen years he was city sexton at Cleveland, for two years deputy provost marshal, and two years marshal of the city. He married Rhoda L. Lynde, born at Newark, Ohio, in 1819, who died June 26, 1846. He died November 11, 1864. Of these parents the youngest of three living children, raised at Cleveland, is Edward L. After receiving a good business education at the Cleveland institute he came to Fort Wayne in 1862, and until 1869 was in the postal service of the city, under Postmaster Drake. During the next two years he served in the Cleveland postoffice under Postmaster Benedict. Returning to this city, he was for twelve years a traveling salesman with A. S. Evans & Co., then for two years in the real estate and loan office of D. C. Fisher. Shortly afterward he engaged in the business on his own account, and has been eminently successful. He was married in 1874 to Maria Rockhill, born in 1852, daughter of the late Hon. William and Elizabeth (Hill) Rockhill, and they have one child, George R., born in March, 1875. Mr. Craw and wife are members of the Episcopal church; he is a leading Mason, being a member of Sol D. Bayless lodge, No. 359, Fort Wayne chapter, No. 14, council No. 4, and grand lodge of perfection. In politics he is a republican.

August H. Carier, a resident of Fort Wayne during the past thirty-eight years, is a native of France, born December 30, 1827, the fourth of five children of Claude and Rosa (Melnotte) Carier. The father and mother were both born in 1796, and both died in France, their native land, he in 1876, she in 1856. Mr. Carier was educated in France, and was a student at the seminary of Pont a Mouson, department of the Meurthe. In 1851 he immigrated and settled at Fort Wayne, where for about three years he engaged in teaching the French language. He then embarked in the wholesale liquor trade, and was so occupied until 1859, when he entered the insurance, loan and real estate business, in which he has been successful in a notable degree. His religious affiliations are with the Catholic church; in politics he is a democrat, and for two terms, 1869 to 1873, he was a member of the city council. He was married in France, in 1847, to Clemence M. Bourdon, who was born in 1828. They have three children, Juliette, now the wife of Henry Lingenfelser, of Milwaukee, Helene, and Clemence.

Simpson Breidenstein, a well-known real estate and loan agent, made his debut in that occupation in June, 1872, when he entered the office of John Hough. He remained there until the death of his employer in 1875, when he accepted a similar position with Fisher & Tons, who took charge of Mr. Hough's business. He was with this firm until 1882, when he embarked in the real estate and loan business on his own account, and has built up a prosperous agency. In politics he is a republican. Mr. Breidenstein was born in Fort Wayne October 16, 1854. His father, Mathias Breidenstein, was born in Columbia county, Ohio, in 1815, came to Allen county in 1840, and is by occupation a carpenter. He married Margaret Doctor, who was born in Hesse-Darmstadt in 1825, and died at this city in 1883. Of their two living children, Simpson is the younger. He was educated in the public schools and attended Fort Wayne college about two years. October 4, 1880, he married Margaret Rothefluoh, born in New York state in 1859, and they have one child, Jerome H., born in 1881.

Benjamin L. Auger, one of the leading florists of Fort Wayne, was born in this city February 22, 1853, the son of Charles and Catherine (Trapp) Auger. The father was born near Versailles, France, in 1824. He was the son of a French florist and worked in the leading gardens of Europe, principally of France. He immigrated to America, and after spending some time in New York city, came to Indiana and located at Marion. In 1852, he came to Fort Wayne and engaged in market and flower gardening. Later, in 1869 when the city had sufficiently developed, he confined his business to that of a florist, exclusively, and is the pioneer florist of Allen county, and one of the oldest in the state. He is still a resident of Fort Wayne, being in his sixty-fifth year. His wife, who is now in her fifty-fifth year, was born near London, Eng.,

Christian Boseker

and came to America at about the same time as her husband, to whom she was married in New York city. Benjamin L. Auger was educated in the Fort Wayne public schools, and spent three years at Notre Dame. After leaving school, he came into the business with his father. About 1873, he went to Cincinnati and had charge of the establishment of Cooke & Co., the leading florists of that city. Returning home in 1876, he engaged in business with his father and succeeded the latter upon his retirement, in 1883. He conducts an extensive establishment and has probably the largest cut flower trade in the city. His place at No. 16 East Washington street, occupies 62x150 feet space, and in 1887, he started a growing house, 150x150 feet, at Creighton avenue. In 1879, Mr. Auger was married to Lilian, daughter of James Bird, of Fort Wayne, and they have three children. Mr. Auger is a member of the National and State Florists' associations, Sol D. Bayless lodge, F. & A. M., the I. O. O. F., K. of P,. and Trinity church.

Samuel Bard, a well-known and respected citizen of Fort Wayne, was born in Montgomery county, Penn., June 10, 1825, the son of Samuel and Mary (Yates) Bard. The former was a native of Montgomery county, Penn., and the latter of Philadelphia. The boyhood of Mr. Bard was spent in his native county, but in 1840 his parents removed to Stark county, Ohio, where he spent his youth and early manhood. He learned the carpenter's trade with his father, beginning at the age of sixteen. At twenty he became a teacher in the district school and altogether taught four winter terms. When not thus engaged he worked at the trade he had learned, and between his first and last terms of school he attended college at Meadville, Penn., two years. He was married in Stark county, Ohio, in 1850, to Mary, daughter of John and Mary Niesz, who was a native of Stark county. For a number of years after his marriage Mr. Bard gave his whole attention to the carpenter's trade. In 1864 he removed to Fort Wayne, and in 1865, in connection with N. B. Freeman, began the erection of a paper mill at Fort Wayne, which was completed and Mr. Bard continued to be one of its proprietors until 1869. In 1871 he removed to Logansport, where he was the proprietor of a paper mill for ten years. For two years thereafter he conducted a paper mill at Mansfield, Ohio. Mr. Bard returned to Fort Wayne in 1883, and here has since led the life of a retired citizen. He has had a career of activity and industry, and is now permitted to spend his declining years in comfortable circumstances. He is the owner of a valuable business block recently erected on Berry street, besides other property in the city. In politics Mr. Bard is a democrat. He and his wife have two children living, Frank I. and William A.

Though a young man, William J. Barr has spent all his business life in Fort Wayne, and has become well and favorably known in business circles and generally. He was born at Springfield, Clark county, Ohio, February 3, 1860, the son of Thomas and Mary Barr, who were born and married in Ireland, and emigrated to America in 1854. When William J. was but eight years old his father died and soon afterward

XIII

he accompanied his widowed mother to Fort Wayne, their subsequent residence. As early as thirteen years of age he became engaged as clerk in a grocery store, and he has since been connected with a grocery store, either as clerk or proprietor, almost continuously. For a period of nearly fourteen years he was employed as clerk in the Yankee grocery, formerly one of the largest establishments of the kind in the city. In October, 1887, he engaged in the grocery business for himself, and he is now the proprietor of a large store at No. 25 West Main street, and enjoys a good trade. Mr. Barr was married April 5, 1883, to Cordelia, daughter of William and Susan Winget. They have two children: Walter A. and Jessie. Mr. Barr is a member of the K. of P., the F. & A. M., the Patriotic Circle and the A. O. U. W. In politics he is an ardent republican.

Jacob Bastian, mail carrier under Postmaster Kaough, is one of the younger citizens of Fort Wayne, who has made his own way in life and achieved a noteworthy degree of success. He was born in Germany, August 23, 1853, to George and Catherine (Hans) Bastian, natives of that country. He came to Allen county with his parents in 1868, and here his father died in 1870, at the age of seventy-eight years. His mother, who was born in 1807, still lives in this county. Mr. Bastian received his education in the common schools and the Fort Wayne commercial college, and first worked for some time at common labor. From 1884 to 1886 he was in the bakery business for himself, and since 1887 has been connected with the postoffice. He is a democrat and influential in politics. In 1878 he was married to Maggie Scherer, a native of Allen county, born December 14, 1879, and they have one child, Ida E. C. Mr. and Mrs. Bastian are members of the Lutheran church; they reside at 205 Madison street.

A venerable citizen of Fort Wayne, Abraham G. Beaber, was one of the pioneers of Ohio, having removed to Tuscarawas county with his parents, Christian and Margaret (Gimmins) Beaber, in 1821. He was then thirteen years old, having been born in Westmoreland county, Penn., October 6, 1808. On October 20, 1831, he was married to Anna Mary, daughter of Isaac and Anna Mary (Flack) Thomas, of Tuscarawas county. In 1848 he removed to Wells county, Ind., and farmed there for fourteen years, after which he came to Fort Wayne, where he has since resided, his home now being at No. 150 Broadway. During the greater part of his residence here he has been engaged as a carpenter. He is a member of the English Lutheran church, and in politics a republican. During five years of his stay in Wells county, he has held the office of justice of the peace. During early life he taught eight terms of school. Mr. Beaber and wife lived happily together within four days of fifty-six years, when she passed away, October 16, 1887. They have had these children: Jemima, Elizabeth, Harriet (deceased), John T. (deceased), Isaac (deceased), Daniel D., Lafayette and Columbus C. Elizabeth, the second daughter, was born in Tuscarawas county, Ohio, October 23, 1833, and was married September 10,

1854, to Elijah W. Sink, a farmer and school teacher by occupation, who was born in Tuscarawas county, March 30, 1834. He died December 8, 1860, leaving three children: Genoa Sebastian, Mary Alice, and Florence Elizabeth, all of whom are living.

John Beighler, a prominent citizen of Allen county, was born in Fairfield county, Ohio, February 16, 1833. His parents, Enoch and Mary C. (Buskirk) Beighler, were both natives of Ohio, the former the son of a worthy German father, who settled in Fairfield county in an early day, and died there in 1812. Both Enoch and Mary Beighler were born in Fairfield county, in 1810 and 1812, respectively, and they both died there, the mother at the age of about forty-four years, the father in 1888. John Beighler is the oldest son among their eight living children. He was reared on a farm, and received a common school education, fitting himself for teaching, which he was engaged in for five years in Ohio. He then engaged in farming, an occupation in which he has been notably successful, and was so occupied for four years before he came to Indiana. Removing to Allen county in 1857, he settled on the farm in Lafayette township where he now resides. The land was then unimproved, and he took it covered with forests, and was compelled to cut a road to his land from five points in order to have an outlet to the world. This is all changed, however, through his intelligent industry, and he has a beautiful farm of 160 acres, well improved. He was married in 1853 to Nancy Nonamaker, a native of Fairfield county, Ohio, a daughter of Jacob Nonamaker, who with his wife, was drowned in Walnut creek, Ohio, in 1849. Two children of this union are living: Dorothy Alice and Frances May. Mr. Beighler and wife are members of the Grace Reformed church of Fort Wayne, and he is a member of Harmony lodge, No. 19, I. O. O. F. In politics Mr. Beighler has always been a steadfast friend of the democratic party, and ever active for the success of its tickets.

Worthy of mention among the enterprising cigar manufacturers of Fort Wayne is Louis Bender, a native of Germany, born June 24, 1845. He learned the cigar maker's trade in his native land, and came to America in 1869, proceeding directly to Allen county. He settled first at Maples, ten miles east of Fort Wayne, but in 1871 returned to the city, and in 1872 began the manufacture of cigars, at No. 30 W. Main street. In 1878 he built his present property, at No. 168 E. Washington street, where he has since resided and carried on his business. He manufactures the following leading brands: "Polly," "Morning Star," "L. Bender's No. 4," "Boquet," and "Casino." He manufactures extensively for the local trade and also does a retail business. Mr. Bender was married in 1869, to Christina Braun, of Maples, and to them have been born ten children, six of whom are dead. Mr. Bender and wife are members of St. Paul's Lutheran church.

Henry F. Beverforden, the well-known druggist, was born in Hanover, Germany, December 30, 1852, the son of August M. and Johanna E. (Reffelt) Beverforden, the former of whom now resides in Fort

Wayne. The mother died March 22, 1889. At the age of fifteen Mr. Beverforden accompanied his father to America. They reached New York city July 25, 1868, and came directly to Fort Wayne. The mother and other children came in the following year. On September 1, 1871, Mr. Beverforden took a position as apprentice in the drug store of the late H. G. Wagner, and remained with him until September 1, 1876. A recommendation which Mr. Wagner gave him at the end of that time states that during three of the five years he had exclusive control of the prescription department, for which he is peculiarly adapted. He further recommends him as being thoroughly posted in all branches of pharmacy and as a sober and industrious young man. A few days after giving up his position with Mr. Wagner, he went to Kansas City, Mo., where he clerked in a drug store about fourteen months. Late in the fall of 1877 he returned to Fort Wayne and soon after engaged in the drug business in partnership with the late George B. Thorp. Six months later Mr. Thorp sold his interest to D. B. Strope, to whom Mr. Beverforden sold his interest March 28, 1882. He then erected a building at 294 Calhoun street, and started a new drug store May 1, 1882. On November 25, 1885, he removed his stock to No. 286 Calhoun street, where he is doing a prosperous business. This, known as the Depot drug store, is well situated, and is in every respect a first-class store. He was married December 10, 1878, to Emma S., daughter of Frederick Kroemer, a pioneer of Washington township. She was born in Washington township, March 10, 1858. Their marriage has resulted in the birth of four children: Bertha, Laura, Ella and Otto, of whom Bertha and Laura are deceased. Mr. and Mrs. Beverforden are members of the Emanuel's Lutheran church. He is one of the most competent druggists of the city, and is an honorable, upright man, one in whom the public has full confidence. His residence which he erected in 1882, is at No. 284 Harrison street. He also conducts a branch drug store, having erected and stocked a new building on the corner of Calhoun and DeWald streets, in 1889.

The residence in Fort Wayne of John Brossard, who has since May, 1885, been doing a prosperous grocery business at 84 Wells street, began on December 28, 1854, when he arrived in this city from New York, having landed a few days previously from his native land. He was born in Bavaria, May 12, 1834, the son of Andrew and Apollonia Brossard. There he worked at farming and at his father's trade, blacksmithing, until his emigration. Soon after reaching here he was employed for five seasons on the Wabash & Erie canal between Toledo and Lafayette, and then resumed the blacksmith's trade and worked at it for twenty-eight years, all but the first three of which were spent in the Pittsburgh shops. Mr. Brossard was married November 13, 1861, to Carrie, daughter of Caspar and Elizabeth Heingardner, early settlers of Fort Wayne. They have had three children, John P., Clara T. and Frank E., the first of whom died at the age of thirteen years. Mr. Brossard and wife are members of the Catholic church. He is a democrat in politics.

Henry Buhr, for many years a farmer of St. Joseph township, and lately an extensive dealer in feed, at No. 20 Harrison street, Fort Wayne, was born in France in 1844. He was brought to America in 1845 by his father Henry Buhr, who was also born in France. The father came directly to Fort Wayne, then a small village, and two years later removed to a farm in St. Joseph township, going first upon the Rudisill farm, where he remained five or six years. He subsequently occupied Judge Hanna's farm seven years, and then bought a farm of eighty acres in St. Joseph township, four and a half miles north from the city, on the St. Joseph river, where he now resides, in his seventy-eighth year. His wife died in 1871. To these parents nine children were born, two of them in France, and but two survive. Henry Buhr, one of these, was reared on the farm in St. Joseph township, and was educated at the public schools and the Brothers' school in Fort Wayne. In 1864, he enlisted in Company B, Fifty-third Indiana regiment, and served in the Seventeenth army corps with General Sherman, and was discharged at Indianapolis in 1865. In 1869 he began life for himself and has ever since been engaged in farming on his father's farm. He was married in 1865, to Lorinda Combs, by whom he had five children, of whom four are living, Charles Francis, George Edward, Catherine, and Henry Jacob. Their mother died in March, 1880, and subsequently Mr. Buhr was married to Mary Miller, by whom he has four children.

For more than ten years Henry Busching has been one of the well known grocers of Fort Wayne. He is a native of Germany, born December 9, 1854, the son of Christian and Wilhelmina Busching. Until the age of seventeen he remained in his native country, attending school until he was fourteen, and then assisting his father in the latter's nursery until he was seventeen. At that age he emigrated to America, reaching New York about April 1, 1872. He at once came to Fort Wayne where he has since lived. During the first year here he was in the employ of the Hon. Holman Hamilton. For two years thereafter he was employed as laborer on the Pittsburgh railway, and then one year in a restaurant. For four years following this he was engaged as a clerk. In 1878 he embarked in the grocery business at No. 272 Hanna street, where he has ever since had a successful trade. Mr. Busching was married January 11, 1880, to Katie Garmann, a native of Allentown, Penn., daughter of Adam and Katie Garmann, the former a native of England, the latter of America. They have three children: Rosa, Emma and Elnora. Mr. Busching and wife are members of Zion's German Lutheran church.

George W. Doswell, prominent as a wholesale and retail florist of Fort Wayne, is a native of Wisconsin, born September 20, 1854, the son of J. H. Doswell, elsewhere mentioned. Mr. Doswell began business in Fort Wayne in 1877, establishing a green house at his present place of business, on West Main street, near Lindenwood cemetery. He began on a small scale, with one house, 10x40 feet, with 400 feet of glass, but under his skillful management the business has prospered, and now about 8,000 feet of glass are required to cover his stock. He deals in cut flowers and plants exclusively, and has a trade which extends over a considerable territory outside of the city. His business amounts to about $2,500 annually, and he ranks among the leading florists. Mr. Doswell is a member of the Episcopal church, and of the Canton lodge, No. 14, I. O. O. F and Sons of St. George, and several beneficiary societies. He was married in 1876 to Lucy Jocker of this city, who died in October, 1881, leaving one child. In 1885 he was married to Mary Webb of this city, and to their union three children have been born, one of whom is deceased.

John C. Eckert, an enterprising citizen of Fort Wayne, and manufacturer of cigars, was born in Dauphin county, Penn., April 22, 1836, the son of John C. and Sarah (Turner) Eckert, both of whom were natives of Pennsylvania. The father died about 1844, and the mother in April, 1871. John C. was reared in Harrisburg, Penn., and in 1851 he began the cigar maker's trade there and was engaged in it at that city until 1857. He then went to Ohio, but in 1859 returned to Harrisburg. In August, 1862, he enlisted in the state troops of Pennsylvania, joining the One Hundred and Twenty-seventh regiment, being one of the nineteen regiments called out by Governor Curtin for nine months' service. In May, 1863, he was mustered out, and in September following he came to Fort Wayne, where he has since resided. Upon locating in Fort Wayne he went to work at his trade, and in 1870, he opened an establishment of his own and began the manufacture of cigars, making a specialty of the brand "39", which has been widely popular for over nineteen years. His factory is at No. 39, and his place of business at No. 85 Calhoun street. Mr. Eckert is a member of Harmony lodge, No. 19, I. O. O. F. He was married February 8, 1857, to Rachel A. Walters, who was born in Dauphin county, Penn. To this union six children have been born: Charles H., born April 30, 1859; William, March 26, 1861; David, February 4, 1865; Jesse, June 13, 1868; Catherine G., July 19, 1870, and John C., May 8, 1874.

Subsequent to the war of the rebellion, in which he did patriotic service, Charles Ehrmann resumed the trade of blacksmithing. His apprenticeship was interrupted by enlistment, and he is now proprietor of an extensive establishment on West Main street, and ranks among the successful men of the city. He is a native of Bavaria, born July 21, 1842, son of John M. and Mary Ehrmann. The family came to America in 1852, and settled in this city, where his parents passed their lives. He enlisted in Company K, Eighty-ninth Indiana regiment, on August 16, 1862, and was mustered out at Mobile, July 22, 1865. Mr. Ehrmann was married January 21, 1867, to Mary Lahmeyer, and they have had thirteen children, of whom Louisa, Mary C., Charles, Wilhelmina, Herman, Ferdinand, Clara and Otto Herbert are living; and John, Matilda, Emma, and two others are deceased. Mr. Ehrmann is an Odd Fellow, a member of the G. A. R., and affiliates with the German Reformed church. In politics he is a republican. He is a valued citizen and a first-class mechanic.

One of the best known cigar manufacturers and dealers of Fort Wayne is August N. Ehle, who was born in Germany in 1825. He came to America in 1851, and first settled at Rochester, N. Y., where he remained four years. Coming to Allen county in 1855, he made his home upon a farm in Lake township, and was there engaged in 1865, when he was accidentally shot and in consequence of the wound lost his left leg. He subsequently removed to the city and learned the trade of cigar maker. He embarked in the manufacture for himself in 1867, and this has since been his occupation. Since 1870 his place of business has been at No. 178 Broadway, factory No. 128. His leading brands are the "No. 36," which has been a popular cigar for sixteen years, "No. 5," and the "Nightingale." He employs four men and does a flourishing wholesale and retail trade. Mr. Ehle is a member of the Emanuel church. He was married in 1853 to Christina Gahn, of Germany, and of their seven children born three are living: Frank, in business with his father; Henry and Ernst also with their father.

An enterprising citizen of Fort Wayne, Christian Entemann, was born in Wurtemburg, Germany, May 17, 1840. His father, John George Entemann, was born in 1804, and took to wife Barbara Schneider. He was by occupation a glazier and painter. In 1852 they emigrated and settled at Toledo, where the mother died in the same year, and the father died in 1886. Christian was the second youngest of their five children. He received a common school education, and in 1861 engaged in business at Toledo, entering the wholesale and retail grocery business in 1865. This he continued for six years, and until 1877, was connected with the business interests of Toledo. He then removed to Fort Wayne, and in 1889, bought out the Globe chop-house, which he rechristened Entemann's restaurant, wholly remodeling and refurnishing it, and is now doing a prosperous business. Mr. Entemann was married in 1862, to Caroline Zimmer, born in Bavaria, May 9, 1840, and they have three children: Lena, born in Toledo in 1866; Ernst, born in Toledo, in 1875; and Charles, born in Fort Wayne in 1882. Mr. Entemann is a member of the I. O. O. F., Concordia lodge, No. 228, the Patriarchal circle, Fort Wayne temple, No. 1, and Phoenix lodge, No. 101, K. of P.

One of the valued mechanics of Fort Wayne, William A. Ersig, was born at St. Mary's, Ohio, September 13, 1856. He is the son of Christian and Mary Ersig, both natives of Germany. They yet reside at St. Mary's, Ohio. The boyhood of Mr. Ersig was spent on a farm, and at sixteen he entered an apprenticeship in the carriage maker's trade at Fostoria, Ohio. He served four years, and then worked four years as a journeyman in Fostoria, Ohio, after which, in September, 1879, he went to Dunkirk, Ohio, but in November following he came to Fort Wayne. Here his whole attention has been devoted to his trade, and since June, 1887, he has conducted a shop of his own on Harrison street. He makes a specialty of horseshoeing, and gives to it his exclusive attention. He was married in June, 1880, to Miss Caroline, daughter of Frederick and Mary Smith, born in Fort Wayne, January 9, 1857. Mr. and Mrs. Ersig have three children: Edward, Mamie and William H. Mr. Ersig is a member of the K. of P., and the Patriotic circle.

Max L. Frankenstein, a prominent druggist at the corner of Washington and Burr streets, Fort Wayne, was born in Olbernhau, Saxony, May 22, 1849, the son of Conrad C. and Julia S. (Fleischer) Frankenstein. He attended school in his native land until he reached the age of eighteen, when he began an apprenticeship at the drug trade, serving three years. He was then employed for three years as clerk in a drug store, after which he served one year in the German army. In April, 1875, he came to America, and proceeded to Chicago, where for four years, he was head clerk in the drug store of C. C. Clacius & Co. In 1879 he returned to Germany, and entered the university of Leipsic, and graduated there in the spring of 1881. He then took a seven months' course in analytical chemistry, at Wiesbaden, Germany. In October, 1881, he took a position as manager of a large prescription store in Hamburg, and held that position until August 15, 1885. On the 22d of the same month he started to America again, and in January, 1886, engaged in the drug business at Fort Wayne. He first located at 66 West Jefferson street. In October, 1887, he became the proprietor of the handsome drug store where he is now doing a very successful business. He was married October 4, 1887, to Mrs. Bessie Fairman, *nee* Wilcox, who is a native of Toronto, Canada. They have two children: Edith R. and Beatrice, the former of whom was born to Mrs. Frankenstein by a former husband. In politics Mr. Frankenstein is an ardent republican. He has been thoroughly schooled in every branch of pharmacy and the drug trade, and is recognized as one of the most competent prescriptionists in the city.

August Freese, an enterprising grocer of Fort Wayne, whose business place is No. 184 Fairfield avenue, was born in Germany, September 14, 1859. He is the son of Frederick and Dorothea Freese. He attended school until he was fourteen, after which he learned the miller's trade and worked at it in Germany until he was twenty-two. In 1882 he came to America, landing at New York, August 11, and came directly to Fort Wayne, which has since been his home. In January, 1883, he became a clerk in a grocery store and held the position until November, 1884, when he set out for Germany to visit his parents. After an absence of four months, he arrived home, and on February 15, 1885, he became a partner in the grocery business. He was married May 31, 1885, to Miss Christena, daughter of Henry Kiel. She came to America from Germany at the age of sixteen, in 1873. They have three children: Frederick, August and Hermann. Mr. Freese and wife are members of Emanuel's German Lutheran church. In politics he is a democrat.

Ignatius Freiberger, foreman of J. B. White's fruit house, spent his childhood on the farm of his parents in Pleasant township, and at the age of thirteen, began his commercial life as a clerk for Gerardin Bros., with whom he remained five years, during that time also attending commercial school. For the past sixteen years he has been engaged with J. B. White, eleven years of the period as foreman of the famous establishment to which his abilities have been devoted. Politically, Mr. Freiberger is a democrat, and his religious affiliation is with the Catholic church, he and wife being valued members of St. Paul's, he also having a membership in the Catholic Knights of America. He was married in 1882, to Mary Schweiters, who was born in Allen country in 1859, and they have three children: Frank, born in 1883; Marcullus, born in 1885, and Amelia May, born in 1888. Mr. Freiberger is a native of France and was born September 16, 1854, came to this country with his parents in 1857, and since childhood, has made his own way in life. He is the son of Ignatius and Tracy (Gerardin) Freiberger, who were born in France, the father in 1816, the mother in 1819, and since 1885, have resided in this city.

Mendel Frank, proprietor of a grocery and provision store and meat market, is a native of Russian Poland, born October 15, 1852. He is the son of Abraham and Bessie (Joseph) Frank. The father of his mother lived to be one hundred and nine years of age. His grandfather, David Frank, was a man of great wealth and lived to the still more remarkable age of one hundred and nineteen. Abraham Frank, who was a contractor by occupation, lived to see the age of eighty-eight. Mendel Frank received a good Hebrew education, and at eleven years of age began to learn the trade of a stone and brick mason with his father. To this occupation his attention was devoted throughout his youth and early manhood. He was married in the early part of July, 1869, to Mollie Nauvelatsky, daughter of Levy and Jennie (Isreal) Nauvelatsky. In the spring of 1870 he emigrated to America, his wife joining him in this country about thirteen months later. Mr. Frank remained six months in New York city, and then came to Fort Wayne, and for several years worked at his trade in summer and did a huckster business in winter. In 1877 he engaged in a grocery and retail meat business which he has conducted ever since. Mr. and Mrs. Frank have seven children: Jennie, Bessie, Joseph, Rachel, Jacob, Lillie and Anna. All belong to the Hebrew church. Mr. Frank is a member of several secret orders and a democrat in politics. To the union of Mr. Frank's parents these children were born. Barney, Sarah, Levy, Asha, Mendel and Libbey. Sarah is the wife of Jacob Koffman, Asha of Harvey Provewinskey, and Libbey of Samuel Neiman. His father and mother departed this life at Lasday, Russian Poland.

It has been said that there is no better appointed horseshoeing establishment in the state than that of Henry Freistroffer, No. 41 West Main street, Fort Wayne. Mr. Freistroffer is a native of Columbus, Ohio, born September 17, 1854, son of Simon and Elizabeth Freistroffer, the former of whom was born in Lorraine, France, the latter at Milheusen, in the same region. When Henry was four years old his parents came to Allen county, and located in Adams township, where his boyhood was spent on a farm. When he was fifteen they removed to Hesse Cassel, where they still reside. At nineteen he came to Fort Wayne and entered upon an apprenticeship at the blacksmith trade and served over two years. His entire attention has ever since been given to this occupation, and since April 29, 1879, he has conducted a shop of his own, doing an exclusive horseshoeing business. He erected his present establishment, a substantial brick building, in 1884. Mr. Freistroffer was married October 23, 1879, to Mary E. Crouser, a native of Ohio, born January 18, 1860. She is the daughter of Victor Crouser, a native of Lorraine, France. They have one child, Charles S., born August 13, 1880. Mr. Freistroffer and wife are members of the Catholic church, and he is a member of the Catholic Knights of America.

Capt. George A. Gale, a prominent citizen of Fort Wayne, who has since January, 1889, been retired from active business, was born at London, Canada, November 1, 1839. His parents, Anthony and Rachel (Sawyer) Gale, were born and married in Ireland. They emigrated first to Hartford, Conn., and in 1831 removed to Livingston county, Michigan, thence to Canada, in 1839. In 1845 they moved to Buffalo, N. Y., and became residents of Fort Wayne in 1861. Here the mother died in 1870, and the father died at Buffalo in 1873. Capt. Gale received a good early education, and during his youth worked for several years as a printer, beginning at sixteen. In April, 1861, he enlisted in the Union army, and on May 22, 1861, was mustered in Company G, Thirty-third New York regiment. Enlisting as a private, he was appointed first sergeant upon muster, and May 20, 1862, was promoted second lieutenant. He was promoted first lieutenant October 17, 1862, and captain December 20, 1862, which rank he held until muster-out, in June, 1863. He participated in fifteen engagements, among them the seven days' fight before Richmond, the second Bull Run, South Mountain, Antietam, Fredericksburg and Chancellorsville. At the siege of Yorktown he was wounded by a ball in the left thigh, April 6, 1862. On leaving the army he was engaged as messenger by the United States express company five and a half years, and then acted two and a half years as assistant division superintendent. He then became connected with the Chicago house of correction, acting six years as chief clerk, and nine years as deputy superintendent. In 1888 he returned to Fort Wayne, and for a few months was engaged in the grocery business, but was compelled by failing health to retire from business. He is a man of excellent business qualifications, and fine executive ability. He is a Mason, of the rank of Knight Templar. In 1873, Capt. Gale was married to Caroline M. Gable, a native of Adams county, and daughter of Christian and Mary Gable. He and wife are members of the Protestant Episcopal church.

Albert F. Gessler, an enterprising and successful young business man, is proprietor of one of the leading meat markets of the city, at No. 60 East Main street. He was born at Dayton, Ohio, September

29, 1855, son of Frederick and Victoria (Schmidt) Gessler, both natives of Germany. In 1857 the family came to Fort Wayne, and the father was engaged here as a butcher until his death. The mother is still living in the city. Albert F. Gessler learned his father's trade early in life, and in June, 1877, purchased a meat market at his present stand, and has done business there for twelve years. His establishment is one of the largest and most attractive in the city, and his custom is quite large. Mr. Gessler was married May 29, 1882, to Rosa, daughter of James and Mary King, formerly of Jefferson township, where she was born. Mr. and Mrs. Gessler have four children: Clarence F., Laura, Florence M. and Albert J. Mr. Gessler is a member of the Catholic Knights, and he and wife are members of St. Mary's church.

W. F. Geller, confectioner and baker, was born in Fort Wayne, March 27, 1859, the son of Peter and Catherine (Martin) Geller, natives of Germany. His father was born in 1839 and came to this country at fifteen years of age, settling in New York city. Three or four years later he visited Fort Wayne, remaining a few weeks, but returned to New York and did not settle in this city until ten years later. He served eighteen months in Company H, Seventh New York infantry. His wife was born in 1839 and died in Fort Wayne in 1872. Five of their children are living, of whom W. F. is the oldest. He received a common school education, and in 1874 began learning the baker's trade. He embarked in business on his own account in 1881 at 104 and 106 Broadway, and in 1886 bought his present business house at the corner of Broadway and Washington, a three-story brick building, 30x100, a well situated and valuable property. Here he has an extensive and lucrative business, and employs fifteen to twenty people. Mr. Geller is ranked as one of the leading bakers and confectioners of the city. He was married in 1881 to Cecilia Neal, a native of Darke county, Ohio, and they have one child, Mabel V., born July 15, 1888. They are members of the Lutheran church.

Fourteen years' experience as a retail grocer, has given John Michael Gruber a well earned prominence in the business circles of Fort Wayne. Mr. Gruber is a native of Germany, born September 5, 1828, son of Frank and Rachel (Henry) Gruber. He was reared in his native country, and attended school until he was fourteen, after which he learned the tailor's trade and followed it until 1852, when he immigrated, landing at New York June 5. He remained in that city, working as a tailor until the next fall when he came to Fort Wayne, arriving November 8. Here he continued the tailor's trade with the exception of one year, during which he was employed in the Pittsburgh shops, until September 13, 1875. Since that date he has been engaged in the grocery business at No. 16 Wilt street, and has enjoyed a good trade. Mr. Gruber was married July 31, 1855, to Veronika, daughter of Vitus and Elizabeth Huhn. Mrs. Gruber came from Germany in 1852, landing early in July. They have had eleven children: Mary M., John W.,

Mary E., Charles, Frank J., John Jacob, Veronika, Edward J., Michael, Caroline and a son that died unnamed. Mary M., John W. and Charles are also dead. Mr. Gruber and wife are members of the Catholic church. He is a member of the Catholic Relief society.

Though one of the young business men of Fort Wayne, George Wallace Haiber, has devoted many years to the retail grocery trade and none in that line are better informed. He is a native of Massillon, Ohio, born April 7, 1860. He is the son of Frederick and Margaret (Good) Haiber, the former a native of Germany, who came to America about 1852, and the latter a native of Ohio. In 1863 the family came to Fort Wayne. Mr. Haiber received his early education in the German Lutheran school and the city schools. During his boyhood he worked two summers at gardening, after which at the early age of eleven, he was employed one year as clerk in the grocery store of George Heger. Afterward he took a position in the Fruit house, and for ten years was in the employ of Hon. J. B. White. He began as a cash boy but was regularly promoted order boy, clerk, produce buyer, and finally he was given charge of the stock. In 1881, he engaged in the grocery business for himself, and is now the proprietor of a well-stocked grocery and provision store, and in connection with it conducts a meat market and deals in flour and feed. He was married May 17, 1881, to Miss Mary Kaiser, who came with her parents from Germany, when seven years old. They have four children: Edward Frederick, Bertha Mary, Eleanora Theresa, and Lorenz Francisco. Mr. and Mrs. Haiber are members of the Catholic church, he having joined it at the age of nineteen. He is a member of the Butchers' national protective association of the United States, and of the Catholic Benevolent Legion.

Charles F. Haiber, grocer and proprietor of a meat market at No. 122 Wells, and another at No. 15 High street, was born in Stark county, Ohio, August 21, 1858, the son of Frederick and Margaret Haiber, the former a native of Germany and the latter of Pennsylvania. When he was six years old his parents came to Fort Wayne, where they still reside. October 2, 1877, he opened a meat market at No. 110 Wells street, and he has since remained in that business. January 1, 1889, he added a stock of groceries. He was married April 25, 1881, to Mary Ellen Clark, who died April 21, 1882, and was buried just one year from her wedding day. He was married March 8, 1885, to Alice A. Kelsey, his present wife. By the latter marriage he has two children, Edna B. and Byron C. Mr. Haiber is a member of the A. O. U. W., and he is a republican in politics. In May, 1886, he was elected a member of the city council by a majority of 225, a great testimonial to his worth, as the democratic majority in the ward ranges from 225 to 250. In May, 1888, he was re-elected, and is now serving his second term.

Gottlieb Haller is a native of Switzerland, born November 6, 1849. He was the son of Gottlieb and Anna Haller, the latter of whom died when their son was but two years old and the former when he was eleven. He worked on a farm and attended school until he was fourteen, when he learned the butcher's trade, to which his attention has been given ever since. He pursued that business in his native country, later in Germany about six months, and in France about two years. In 1872 he emigrated to America and at once located at Fort Wayne. Here, after two years' employment, in 1874 he opened a market of his own and is now doing a prosperous business at 366 Calhoun street. Mr. Haller was married November 7, 1878, to Mollie, daughter of Anthony and Margarita Fischer, born in Fort Wayne, September 23, 1859. Mr. Haller and wife have one child, Anna, born November 8, 1885. They are members of the German Reformed church. Mr. Haller is a member of the Odd Fellows lodge, the K. of P., and the Patriotic circle. He is a staunch republican in politics, and is a member of the Morton club. He is president of the local Butchers' union, and is a member of the Business men's exchange.

Jacob Hartman was born in Marion township, this county, September 11, 1862. His father, Joseph, was born in Germany, on February 2, 1834, and in 1851 came to Allen county and settled in Marion township. The mother, whose maiden name was Caroline Hoffman, was born in 1839. Mr. Hartman remained on the farm, receiving a common school education, until sixteen years of age, and was then until 1883, a clerk in a grocery store. In July of the latter year he embarked in the grocery and provision business, and in 1886 engaged in his present business at No. 267 East Wayne street. Mr. Hartman is a prominent member of the Catholic Benevolent legion. He has held different positions of honor, and has also taken active part in the Emmett commandery, No. 123, a branch of the order of the Knights of St. John, and is a member of St. Julian council, No. 89, and a faithful worker in the Catholic church. He was married October 18, 1883, to Anna Aukenbruck, who was born in this city, September 17, 1862, daughter of Bernhard Aukenbruck. They have two children, Augusta and Andrew. Mr. Hartman is a democrat in politics.

John H. Hartman, a prominent grocer of Fort Wayne, whose place of business is at No. 126 East Washington street, was born in this city, April 15, 1855. He was the son of Herman and Anna Hartman, both natives of Germany. They sailed to America on the same ship, and were married in 1854, at Peru, Ind. In the following year they removed to Fort Wayne, a short time before John was born, and they have ever since resided in this city, being old and respected citizens. Their son, John H., learned the tinner's trade in his youth, devoting about two years to it. After this he was variously employed until 1875, when he engaged in the grocery trade, in which business he has remained and been quite successful. He began with very moderate means, and at the time was carrying an $800 debt. He has not only been able to free himself from indebtedness, but has accumulated much property. He erected his two story brick business block at No. 126 East Washington street in 1885, and is also the owner of several residence properties from which he realizes a considerable income. Mr. Hartman was married October 24, 1876, to Louisa, daughter of Joseph and Amelia Aubrey. They have two children: Eve and Clements. Mr. Hartman and wife are members of St. Mary's Catholic church. He is a member of the Catholic Knights and the Catholic benevolent societies.

Joseph H. Hartman, of the grocery firm of Hartman Bros., is a native of Peru, Ind., born August 23, 1860. He is the son of Adolph and Theresa (Weachman) Hartman, both natives of Germany. When he was two years old his parents came to Fort Wayne, but a year later emigrated to Shakopee, Scott county, Minn., where they resided nearly seven years. In 1872 they returned to Fort Wayne where the father died in 1883, and where the mother still resides. In his youth Joseph H. Hartman learned the butcher's trade. At eighteen he became a clerk in a grocery store and continued in that capacity about six years. On February 14, 1885, he engaged in the grocery business for himself, and he is now one of the leading grocers of Fort Wayne. In the spring of 1887 his brother Henry became a partner, the firm being known as Hartman Bros. He was married August 26, 1886, to Miss Josephine, daughter of Daniel Jennings. She is a native of Boston, Ind., born April 26, 1861. Mr. Hartman is the father of two children: Clementina and Charles H. Mr. Hartman and wife are members of the Catholic church, and he is a member of the Knights of St. Charles.

Henry F. Hilgemann, who is a native of Fort Wayne, and has resided in the city continuously with the exception of three years and a half, was born January 31, 1851, the son of Henry and Frederika Hilgemann, natives of Germany. For five years and a half after he was sixteen, he was employed in the Summit City woolen mills. He then held the position of shipping clerk three years in the wholesale house of A. S. Evans & Co. From 1875 to 1878 he resided at Huntington, Ind., and owned a half interest in a woolen mill. Returning to Fort Wayne, he was engaged until the spring of 1881 as shipping clerk for the notion firm of Hanna, Wiler & Co. For two or three years he was employed as general agent for the Chicago installment book company, and in the fall of 1884 he embarked in the grocery business at 121 West Jefferson street, where he has done a successful business. He has erected a business block at 123 West Jefferson, and now occupies both rooms. This additional room was necessary to accommodate his trade, which, though on the first day of business it amounted to only $4, increased to $13,000 in 1888. Mr. Hilgemann was married September 4, 1873, to Lisette F., daughter of Frederick and Sophia Bueker. She came from Germany with a brother in 1870. They have six children: Franklin H., Charles H., Oliver H., Walter H., Harry H. and Victor H., the first and last two of whom survive. Mr. Hilgemann and wife are members of the German Reformed church. In 1889 Mr. Hilgemann, who is a staunch democrat, was elected to the city council, and is now an honored member of that body.

John C. Hinton, a popular and successful restaurateur, proprietor of the Boston restaurant at 270½ Calhoun street, a native citizen of Fort Wayne, was for fifteen years connected with the railroad interests so important in the history of the city. In 1871 he entered the employment of the Pennsylvania railroad company, and for thirteen years was a freight conductor, earning a well-deserved reputation for efficiency and trustworthiness. In 1886 he left the road and engaged in his present business, in which he is quite successful, having made his restaurant very popular. He is in politics a republican, is a member of the Patriarchal circle and of the Conductors' Brotherhood. He was married January 10, 1889, to Anna J. Welton, daughter of J. W. Welton, of this city. She is a member of the German Reformed church. Mr. Hinton was born October 18, 1852, son of Samuel and Johanna (Smith) Hinton. His father is a native of New York, his mother of Germany. They came to Fort Wayne at an early day, and yet reside here.

An enterprising business man of Fort Wayne, John T. Hunt, was born in this city, February 16, 1856. His parents, Henry and Ellen (Griffin) Hunt, were natives of Ireland, and emigrating, settled in Massachusetts. About 1854 they came to Fort Wayne, where the father, who was a shoemaker by trade, died in 1856. His widow, who was born about 1838, is still living in this city. Mr. Hunt attended the Catholic Brothers' school while receiving his education. In 1878 he was married to Sarah Trout, who was born in Delaware county, Ohio, and they have an adopted son, Albert F. Mr. Hunt has been engaged for ten years in the refreshment business, and he also conducted a livery and sale stable. He bought his present place of business in 1886. He and wife are members of the Catholic church, and he is in politics a democrat. In 1886 he was elected a justice of the peace, receiving every vote in the township but five.

In 1852 Frederick and Louisa Kabisch, who became worthy and esteemed citizens of Fort Wayne, came to this city from Saxony, their native land, with their family. The father died, about the year 1868, and the mother in 1882. Their son, Rudolph Kabisch, now the proprietor of a popular meat market at No. 156 Fairfield avenue, was born in Saxony, August 29, 1836. He was in the butcher business three years before he learned the plasterer's trade which he learned soon after coming to Fort Wayne and worked at it about three years. He then turned his attention to the butcher's business and it has been his vocation ever since. In 1884 he engaged in the business for himself. Mr. Kabisch was married in July, 1860, to Miss Katharina Elett, who was born in Hesse, Germany, and came with her parents to America in about 1854. Mr. and Mrs. Kabisch have six children: Frederick C., John P., Louisa, Jeanetta, Rudolph and Katharina.

Anton Kalbacher is the fifth of ten children of Marx and Ursula (Dieringer) Kalbacher, who at the time of his birth, August 24, 1841, were living at their native place, Hohenzollern Hechingen, in Germany. All the family are now deceased, save Anton and his sisters, Caroline and Matilda. The family emigrated from Germany in 1852, and settled at Delphos, Ohio, whence in 1855, they came to Fort Wayne, where the father died in 1886 in his seventy-eighth year. The mother died at Delphos in 1854, at the age forty-three. Anton was employed in a grocery store at Delphos, and after coming to Fort Wayne was so engaged for about seven years, when he entered the employment of Beaver & Dunham, flour and feed merchants, with whom he remained four years He then spent two years in the wine and liquor business, and then embarked in the trade in flour, feed, grain and produce, in which he has since continued, with a marked degree of success, gaining a reputation as one of the enterprising men of the city. In 1878 he erected his grocery building on Grand street, and formed a partnership with John Sheffer. In 1882 he purchased the Sedgwick mills and removed the business to Columbia street, and sold out to H. W. Bond, in 1887. In 1882 he became associated with William Potthoff in his present business, under the firm name of A. Kalbacher & Co. He is a democrat and takes an active part in politics. In 1865 he was married to Jane Schobe, born in Fort Wayne in 1845, daughter of Eberhart and Maria Angela (Daman) Schobe. Mr. and Mrs. Kalbach have five children: Sister Aquineta, of the order of Sisters of Notre Dame, Kate, Theresa, Edward and Lenore. Both parents are members of the Catholic church.

Jacob Klett, one of the leading citizens of Fort Wayne, of German birth, was born in Wurtemburg in 1831. In his native land he was educated, and learned the potter's trade. In 1853 he immigrated, and in the following year settled at Fort Wayne. Four years later he entered the employment of Andrews & Oakley, of Fort Wayne, in their planing-mill, and remained with them until 1860. He became engaged with Clark & Hurd, lumber dealers, in 1861, and continued with the successors, Clark & Rhinesmith, and upon the organization of the lumber company of the same name in 1871, he became a stockholder, and accepted the position of yard foreman and inspector. Having become thoroughly acquainted with the business, he opened a yard on his own account in 1877, and beginning without capital, has to a remarkable degree prospered in this business. He added in 1889 a large and complete planing-mill plant, and the establishment is equipped for general factory work. Mr. Klett's business experience has extended over thirty-one years, and he is one of the leading lumber men of the city. His business career has been successful through his adherence to honest and straightforward methods and now his word is as good as gold and his standing in the business world is unimpeachable. Socially, he has a wide circle of friends and acquaintances. Mr. Klett was married July 6, 1858, to Louisa Sauter, also a native of Wurtemberg, who came to this country at about the age of five years, and they have had eight children, five of whom are living. His sons, John A. and William B., are engaged with their father in the lumber business.

C. W. Kline, a native of Perry county, Penn., was born October 7, 1844, son of Benjamin and Catherine (Hicks) Kline, both natives of that state. The father died on the old Pennsylvania homestead in 1880, at the age of eighty years, and the mother, who was born in 1803, died in about 1870. His paternal grandfather, C. W. Kline, was born in Berks county, Penn., and died in the same county. The subject of this mention, who was next to the youngest of ten children, enlisted in 1864 in the Two Hundred and Eighth Pennsylvania regiment, in Company F, and served until mustered out in June, 1865. He was afterward engaged in business at various places, five years in Philadelphia, and afterward at Youngstown, Ohio, and Virginia City, Nev., returning to Philadelphia in 1876. In that year he settled at Lancaster, Ohio, and remained until 1884, when he came to Fort Wayne and engaged in the wine and liquor trade, at 242 Calhoun street. He is a member of the German lodge, K. of P., of Fort Wayne.

An enterprising young citizen and a leading florist, F. J. Knecht, is a son of one of the early settlers of this city from beyond the sea. His father, Dominick Knecht, a native of Switzerland, came to Fort Wayne about 1848, and was for a considerable period engaged in the manufacture of shingles, and later embarked in business as an undertaker, which he followed until his death in 1863, at the age of fifty-five years. His wife was Katherine Miller, a native of Germany, who died in 1875, at the age of forty-four years. Both were members of the St. Mary's Catholic church, and highly esteemed. Of their six children five are living. F. J. Knecht was born in this city, September 28, 1860. After receiving an early education in the St. Mary's Catholic schools, he began work in 1875 as a florist, and becoming proficient, in 1885 opened an establishment of his own, and removed to his present place on the corner of East Wayne and Harmer streets, in 1887. His greenhouse is covered by about 3,500 feet of glass, and he uses over half an acre for bedding purposes. Making a specialty of cut flowers and bedding plants, he finds a ready market in the city. Mr. Knecht was married in 1882 to Anna Zahn of this city, and they have two children. He and wife are members of St. Mary's Catholic church, and he is a member of the Catholic Knights.

Among the worthy German families of the city of Fort Wayne, is that of William and Charlotte Koenig, who arrived in this city from Germany, September 4, 1869. William Koenig was born June 11, 1830, son of Ernst and Margaret Koenig. He learned the blacksmith trade in his native land, and was married November 30, 1853, to Charlotte, daughter of Frederick and Wilhelmina Kammier. She was born May 3, 1831. Mr. Koenig's occupation in this city has been that of a boiler-maker. He and wife have had five children: William, who married Wilhelmina Rodenbeck; Henry, married to Sophia Rodenbeck; Frederick, married to Emma Haase; Christian, married to Mary Schweir; and Charles, married to Charlotte Haegermann. All of the family are members of the Lutheran church. Christian F. Koenig is a well-known grocer, having his store at the corner of East Washington and Harmer streets. He was born in Germany, December 3, 1859. He received his education at St. Paul's parochial schools and in his youth, worked somewhat

XIV

at the boiler-maker's trade and as a newsboy. He clerked in a grocery store two years, and then worked at the shoemaker's trade six years. He engaged in the grocery business January 8, 1883, and has since prospered, having a well stocked grocery and an excellent custom. Mr. Koenig was married March 7, 1886, to Mary, daughter of William Schweir, a native of Fort Wayne, and they have one child, Otto. They are members of the German Lutheran church. Mr. Koenig is an enterprising young business man, and deserving of confidence.

In 1875, August Korn engaged in the grocery business at 194 Broadway, where he has ever since done a successful business. He was born in Germany, May 15, 1849, the son of Jacob Korn. In his native land he attended school until he was fourteen, and during his youth assisted his father at farm work a part of the time. In November, 1869, he landed at New York, where, and at Union Hill, N. J., he remained three years. At Union Hill he learned the baker's trade. From New York he came to Fort Wayne in the spring of 1872. Here he was employed three years and a half as a baker. Mr. Korn was married in 1874 to Dora, daughter of George and Johanna Jacobs. She came with her father from Germany in 1868. Mr. and Mrs. Korn have had six children: Mary, George, Mamie, Henry, August and Edward, of whom the first four are deceased. They are members of St. John's German Lutheran church.

For several years, John Korn, of Fort Wayne, has been doing a prosperous business as proprietor of a meat market at No. 134 Fairfield avenue. He was born in Germany, October 21, 1853, the son of Jacob Korn. He was but two years old when his mother died. He attended school until he was fourteen, after which he learned the carpenter's trade. In 1871 he emigrated to America, and after spending six months in New York city he came to Fort Wayne. Six months later he returned to New York, but after a few months again came to Fort Wayne, where he has since lived. During the first years of his residence here he worked in a stone yard. In 1880 he engaged in the retail meat business, and he has been the proprietor of his present market ever since. He was married June 20, 1878, to Lizzie Bender, a native of Fort Wayne, born June 20, 1856. Mr. and Mrs. Korn have had five children: Clara A., Carrie, Lillie, John W. and Henry A., of whom Clara A. died in infancy. Mr. Korn and wife are members of the German Lutheran church.

A well-known citizen of Fort Wayne, Herman Henry Ludwig Krohne, was born in Germany, October 27, 1847, the son of Ludwig and Mary Krohne. In his youth he clerked in a store in his native land three years, and in early manhood served four years in the Franco-Prussian war, participating in sixteen battles. In 1874 he came to America and located in Fort Wayne. Here he worked a short time at the carpenter's trade, and subsequently for four years he was employed as driver on the street car line. In April, 1883, he became one of the proprietors of a gun and ammunition store, at No. 79 Calhoun street.

His partner having since died, he has conducted the store alone. Mr. Krohne was married April 14, 1887, to Lena Mary Rice, also a native of Germany, the daughter of William Rice. She came to America about 1882. Mr. Krohne and wife have one child, Arthur Henry, who was born August 16, 1888. They are members of Emanuel's German Lutheran church.

Henry Frederick William Krusy, a well-known dairyman of Fort Wayne, was born on the Atlantic ocean while his parents were on their way from Germany to America, September 14, 1845. On reaching this country his father, William Krusy, came to Indiana, and he is now a venerable resident of Fort Wayne. His mother died before her son was a year old. When a small child he was bound out, and during his entire early life his home was among strangers, living at different times with five families. In early manhood he learned the carpenter's trade, and followed it several years, during the last few of which he was a contractor in Fort Wayne. For the past twelve years he has been engaged in the dairy business and is now the proprietor of the City dairy. Mr. Krusy was married September 8, 1870, to Sophia Wilhelmina, daughter of Christian and Sophia Kramer. She is a native of Fort Wayne, but her parents were born and married in Germany, and emigrated to America on the same vessel that brought the parents of her husband. They have five children: William P. C., Frederick G., Frieda, Alma and Edmund. Mr. Krusy and wife are members of St. Paul's German Lutheran church.

Frederick Lenz, though not long, comparatively, in business, has prospered in his enterprise. He is a native of Germany, born November 27, 1855, son of Joseph Lenz. His mother died when he was but three years old. In 1866 he accompanied his father and step-mother to America. On reaching this country the family came directly to Fort Wayne, where they have since resided. He quit school at thirteen and learned the shoemaker's trade, working at it four years. Between the ages of seventeen and twenty-eight he was in the employ of the Pennsylvania railroad company, being employed two years in the yard and for nine years in the shop oiling line shafts. In June, 1884, he engaged in the retail meat business and has ever since been the proprietor of a market at No. 170 Hanna street. Mr. Lenz was married November 28, 1879, to Miss Louisa Mannawich, who is a native of Fort Wayne, born May 20, 1861, daughter of Frederick Mannawich. They have four children: Frederick, Louisa, George and Oscar. Mr. Lenz and wife are members of the German Lutheran church.

Since the year 1858, John Nicholas Leykauf, a reliable business man, has been a citizen of Fort Wayne. He is a native of Bavaria, Germany, born May 20, 1830, the son of Nicholas and Catherine Leykauf. The latter died when their son was five years old, and the former died when he was twelve. He attended school until his fourteenth year, after which he learned the baker's trade and followed it in Germany until 1858, when he emigrated to America. The first work he did here was butchering, which he followed about a year. He then resumed the baker's trade. In 1862 he became employed in the Pittsburgh shops. He resumed his trade in 1864, and from April of that year until November, 1865, he conducted a bakery business for himself. In 1866, he made a visit in Germany, and on his return, resumed work in the Pittsburg shops and continued there until March, 1872. Since then he has conducted a bakery at No. 209 Broadway. Since 1875, he has also carried a stock of groceries, and has done a poultry business. Mr. Leykauf was married August 24, 1863, to Mrs. Charlotte (Blume) Bolman, by whom he is the father of three children: Henry, Elizabeth, and John N. By her first husband, Christian Bolman, Mrs. Leykauf had these children: Theodore, Christian F., Frederick W., Bertha, Charlotte, Albert, and Otto, all living. Mr. and Mrs. Leykauf are members of St. John's German Lutheran church.

On August 14, 1888, Nicholas R. McNiece, an energetic young business man, became one of the grocery firm of Markey & McNiece, at Fort Wayne. He is a native of Porter county, Ind., born January 18, 1861. His parents, William H. and Elizabeth McNiece, were both natives of Pennsylvania. When he was a small child his parents removed to Valparaiso, where his boyhood was spent. At fifteen he accompanied his parents to Hobart, Ind., but soon afterward he returned to Valparaiso and there learned telegraphy. He took a position as operator at Wanatah, Ind., and continued in that capacity in several of the states during ten years. He then, in June, 1886, engaged in the grocery business at Lake Elmo, Minn. His store was destroyed by fire in February, 1888, and in June, of that year, he came to Fort Wayne, and subsequently he engaged in the grocery business with Albert C. Markey. Mr. McNeice was married June 16, 1883, to Miss Delilah A. Hively, a native of Whitley county, Ind. They have one child, Ora L., born October 17, 1884. While a resident of Lake Elmo, Minn., Mr. McNiece served as postmaster eight months, resigning the position when he was burned out.

Albert C. Markey, an enterprising young business man of Fort Wayne, of the grocery firm of Markey & McNiece, is a native of New York city, born October 18, 1864. His parents, Lawrence and Eliza Markey, came to Fort Wayne in 1869, and still reside in this city. Mr. Markey's early education was obtained in the Fort Wayne schools, and later he pursued the studies of German, French and Latin in Calvary college of Wisconsin. During five years of his early manhood he was in the employ of different railroad companies, his work being of a clerical character. For more than three years past his attention has been given to the grocery business and he is now one of the members of the firm of Markey & McNiece, at No. 356 South Calhoun street. Mr. Markey is a member of the Catholic church.

Peter A. Moran, the well-known ice dealer and prominent young citizen of Fort Wayne, is a native of this city, born April 13, 1855. His father, Peter Moran, came to America from Ireland, his native land, in early manhood, and was married to Miss Rachel A. Neusbaum, in

Maryland, April 23, 1846. In 1849 they located at Fort Wayne. The father was a tanner by trade, but from 1859 was engaged in the ice business until his death, November 17, 1880. The mother is still living, and now makes her home with her son Peter A. The latter was occupied with his father, and when he died succeeded him in the ice business. It is the oldest enterprise of the kind in the city. Mr. Moran was married May 24, 1881, to Miss Mary E., daughter of John and Mary (Faut) Baker, the former a native of Germany, and the latter of Baltimore, Md. Mrs. Moran was born at Fort Wayne. They have had five children: Peter J., Bernard E., Mary M., Gertrude E. and Alphonsus H., of whom Gertrude E. died in childhood. Mr. Moran and wife are members of the Catholic church.

A life of persevering industry has given to Frank H. Meyer, a respected citizen of Fort Wayne, a well-earned leisure in his later years, and a comfortable competency. Mr. Meyer is a native of northern Prussia, born January 11, 1836. When he was three years old his mother died, and two years later he was bereft of his father, August Meyer. Finding a home in the family of a relative, he attended school, and then at the age of fifteen began work at the trade of blacksmith. After six and a half years at this employment, he left his native land and reached New York about October 1, 1857, with $2.50 in his pocket. He found a friend to advance the fare to Fort Wayne, but the short stop at New York so exhausted his capital that he could afford to take but one meal while coming overland, a trip which occupied four days. He worked five months in the shop of Daniel Nestel, was occupied a short time on the farm of Frederick Meyer, and then began an engagement with John Brown which lasted until 1863. In that year he rented a shop and began business on his own account. Three years later he built his blacksmith, carriage and wagon shop on the corner of Calhoun and Superior streets, in which he did business for twenty-two years. In the spring of 1888 he retired from business, having prospered remarkably, and gained a reputation as a reliable and honest man. Probably no man who started here as he did, pays a larger tax than he. He expects soon to make an extended visit to his native land. He was married September 16, 1860, to Louise Stegman, with whom he first became acquainted on shipboard, though they had lived within a mile of each other in the old country. She was born October 18, 1834. They have six children: Fred H., William H., Charles, Henry, Lizzie and John.

Gottlieb Niemann, grocer at No. 148 Calhoun street, Fort Wayne, is a native of Germany, born in the kingdom of Hanover, March 24, 1843, the son of Gottlieb and Sophia Niemann. His youth was spent in his native country, and he was chiefly employed as steward in hotels. At seventeen he emigrated to America, reaching New York, June 8, 1862. He came directly to Fort Wayne and went to Wabash, and there was employed in a stone quarry three months. In the spring of 1863 he took a position as clerk in the bakery and store of John B.

Krudop, of Fort Wayne, but after a few months he became a clerk in the grocery store of Heitkamp and Hambrock. Ever since that time he has been in the grocery business. For the past thirteen years he has been engaged in the business at No. 148 Calhoun street, and he possesses a good trade. He is the owner of the building occupied by his store, which from its location, is very valuable property. Mr. Niemann was married October 18, 1866, to Louisa Rodenbeck, also a native of Germany. She is the daughter of Frederick and Maria Rodenbeck, with whom she came to America when she was eight years old. Mr. and Mrs. Niemann have had five children: Henry Gottlieb Frederick, Louisa Sophia, Henry Diederich Richard, Frederick William, and John Henry, the last of whom died aged two years. All are members of Emanuel's German Lutheran church. In politics Mr. Niemann is a democrat.

One of the best known cigar manufacturers of Fort Wayne, George Reiter, was born in Reading, Berks county, Penn., August 21, 1827, son of John and Catherine (Kuntzmann) Reiter, both natives of Berks county. The mother died in 1835 and the father in 1836. In 1840 George Reiter went to Hamburg, Penn., and learned the cigar maker's trade. After 1844 he was for several years in various cities, but in 1848 located at Albany, N. Y. He subsequently resided at New York city, Suffield, Conn., Peekskill, Baltimore and Philadelphia, where he was married. In 1854 he left Baltimore for Cincinnati, Ohio, and six months later went to St. Louis, Mo. After a sojourn at Baltimore and Suffield, Conn., he went to Westfield, Mass., in 1857, where he remained until 1864, and while there his wife died. He then went to Cleveland, Ohio, and on May 7, 1866, arrived at Fort Wayne, where he opened a cigar manufactory and began making the celebrated "Pony" cigar, which is the oldest brand made in the city. He has continued the manufacture of the "Pony" cigar for twenty-three years. His establishment is at No. 30 Calhoun street, where he carries on his manufacturing business, and also deals at wholesale and retail in a general line of cigars of his own manufacture. Mr. Reiter became a member of the Masonic fraternity in 1852 in Baltimore. He is a member of the Fort Wayne chapter, No. 19, Fort Wayne council, No. 4, and Fort Wayne commandery, No. 4, K. T. He is also a member of Fort Wayne lodge, No. 1,547, K. of H., and of Howard council, No. 246, Royal Arcanum. Mr. Reiter was married in 1850 to Mary C. Von Camp, who was born in New Jersey in 1828, and died in Westfield, Mass., in 1863, leaving four children, of whom George W., Henry H., and Winfield S., survive. Mr. Reiter was married in 1874, to Mary A. Payne, of Chicago, Ill.

Henry A. Rose, an esteemed and worthy citizen, well known as a leading blacksmith of Fort Wayne, is a native of this county, born in Adams township, January 27, 1858. His parents, Anthony and Louisa Rose, were natives of Germany, and came to America. His mother's parents, Christian and Louisa Meising, located in Adams county, Ind., at a very early day. At sixteen years of age, Henry A. took up the blacksmith's trade, which he has worked at ever since. He has followed his trade in Fort Wayne since July, 1878. He was married April 16, 1882, to Miss Minnie Hartmann, a native of Adams township, and daughter of Henry and Kate Hartmann. Mr. Rose and wife have had four children: Henry W., Adolph, Minnie and Herman, of whom Adolph died, aged about sixteen months. Mr. and Mrs. Rose are members of St. Paul's German Lutheran church.

Charles Rose a prominent young grocer of Fort Wayne, was born in Adams township, Allen county, November 18, 1863. He is the son of Anthony and Louise (Miesing) Rose, both natives of Germany. The father came to America and settled in Allen county in a very early day, and the mother immigrated with her parents and located in Adams county, Ind., about 1837. They were married in Fort Wayne, in about 1849. The father who was a farmer, by occupation, was accidentally killed by a hay fork while unloading hay, July 15, 1876. The mother now lives at No. 28 Lavina street, Fort Wayne. Charles Rose left the farm at fifteen, and clerked in a grocery store one year, after which he worked four years at the blacksmith's trade. He then engaged in the grocery trade at Nos. 75 and 77 East Wayne street, where he has ever since done a large business. He also deals in flour and feed. Mr. Rose was married February 25, 1886, to Dora, daughter of county commissioner, Henry Hartmann. They have two children: Martha and Ervin. They are members of Emanuel's German Lutheran church.

A prosperous business man and hotel proprietor at Fort Wayne, James P. Ross, was born in St. Joseph county, Ind., March 5, 1836, the son of Benjamin and Rachel (Helmick) Ross. In youth he worked upon a farm in his native county and attended the common schools, and in early manhood attended the old Methodist college of Valparaiso, Ind., six months. He continued upon the farm until his marriage, April 1, 1862, to Marietta Kingdon. She was born in Allen county, March 22, 1842, daughter of William and Mary Kingdon. Immediately after his marriage Mr. Ross located in Eel River township. He removed to Washington township in 1870, where his attention was divided between farming, saw-milling and merchandise, until 1880. He also served as postmaster about seven years in the village of Wallen. In 1880 he removed to Kansas City, Mo., where, on the 15th day of April, 1881, his wife died. In 1882 he returned to Indiana and located at Fort Wayne. Here he has conducted a meat market ever since, and for the past three years he has also been the proprietor of the Columbia House. He is now also conducting a grocery and bakery. He was married April 9, 1885, to Mrs. Mary E. Ayres, who was born near Syracuse, N. Y., March 17, 1836. Mr. Ross by his first wife became the father of ten children: Wilbert A., Judson K., Millie Ann, Charles L., Eva Estella, James P., Frank S., Jessie R., Benjamin M. and Marietta E., of whom Charles, James, Frank and Benjamin are deceased. Mr. and Mrs. Ross are members of the Methodist Episcopal church.

Among the leading market proprietors of Fort Wayne should be named Nicholas B. Rowe, whose establishment is at No. 189 Broadway. He was born in Utica, N. Y., February 12, 1838, the son of Nicholas S. and Nancy E. (Smith) Rowe, the former a native of Utica, N. Y., and the latter of Johnstown, N. Y. His father died when he was but seven years old. He received a common school education, and during his youth when not in school he clerked in a grocery store. In 1856 he went to Lawton, Van Buren county, Mich., where he clerked for three years, after which he engaged in the grocery business for himself. In 1868, he became superintendent of the Michigan Central iron company, and continued in that capacity five years. In 1875 he removed to Garrett, Ind., where he did a grocery business and conducted a meat market until 1880. In July, 1880, he came to Fort Wayne, where he has ever since been the proprietor of a meat market. He was married in Lawton, Mich., December 24, 1860, to Miss Mary M. Waldo, who was born in Erie county, Penn., March 2, 1842, daughter of George W. and Susan M. (Prescott) Waldo. They have two children: Mary J. and Herbert G. Mr. Rowe and wife are members of the Methodist Episcopal church; he is a member of the Masonic order, and in politics is a republican.

A worthy citizen of Fort Wayne, Samuel H. Sauvain, came to this city when eight years old, from his native county of Wayne, Ohio. He was born April 4, 1846, son of Abraham and Mary Ann Sauvain, who were natives of Ashart, Switzerland. At the age of fifteen he entered upon an apprenticeship at the confectioner's trade, and served three years and a half. He then in March, 1864, entered the Union army in Company K, Twenty-fifth New York cavalry, under Gen. Custer, and served till the close of the war. He was discharged at Hart's Island, N. Y., in July, 1865. Returning home he learned the blacksmith's trade, and has pursued it with but little interruption ever since. He is the inventor of a fire pot upon which he received a patent in 1882, and since that time he has spent two years traveling throughout the country introducing it. Mr. Sauvain was married in September, 1870, to Amanda L., daughter of John Line. Mr. Sauvain and wife have had five children: Mertie, Clarence, Minnie, Charles R., and HuburtS., the three oldest of whom are deceased. He and wife are members of the Methodist Episcopal church, and he is a comrade of the G. A. R. In politics he is a republican.

A worthy and industrious citizen of Fort Wayne, Matthias Schneider, was born at Wolfurt, Austria, May 26, 1849. He is the son of Jacob and Juditha Schneider, by whom he was brought to America when two years old. They made their home at Findlay, Ohio, but in 1853, returned to Wolfurt, Austria, where the mother died in 1860. Matthias remained at Wolfurt and between the ages of eight and twenty worked in a brick yard, and afterward for two years at the tinner's trade. In the meantime the father had returned to America in 1862, and settled in Minnesota, but in 1873 he once more returned to his native place in Austria, where he now lives in his seventy-seventh year. At the age of twenty-two Matthias started out for America again. He reached New York, February 2, 1872, and went directly to Minnesota where he worked at farming in Brown county two years. In 1874 he removed to Findlay Ohio, where he clerked in a grocery for an uncle twenty months. After four months in Minnesota he worked fifteen months at the butcher's trade at Fremont. In September, 1877, he went to Sacramento, Cal., being engaged there and at Woodland, Cal., ten months. He came to Fort Wayne in August, 1878, and since then he has pursued the occupation of a truckman. For five years he did all the truck work for Morgan & Beach. Mr. Schneider was married November, 1882, to Mary, daughter of John McCarty. She came from Ireland in 1873. Mr. and Mrs. Schneider are members of the Catholic church. In politics he is a democrat.

Henry Charles Schweir, an estimable citizen of German birth, was born in Lade Kreismenden, Westphalia, December 20, 1833, son of William and Christina Schweir. In his native country he attended the regular school until he was fourteen and spent his youth on a farm. In 1855 he entered the German army, and in 1856, appointed corporal until 1858, served four years. Upon receiving his discharge, he at once started to America and arrived at Fort Wayne, August 26, 1859. Here he learned the trade of a boiler-maker, and from 1859 to 1883, was in the employ of J. H. Bass, working all the time at his trade. For the past six years he has been engaged in the grocery business at No. 176 Montgomery street, having opened his store at that place May 28, 1883. Mr. Schweir was married October 6, 1866, to Catharine E. Barnhardt, who was born in Hesse-Darmstadt, January 25, 1846, the daughter of Thomas Barnhardt. She came to America with her father and mother when she was seven years old. Mr. and Mrs. Schweir have three children: William Gottfried Charles, Catharine Sophia Christina Mary and Sarah Charlotte. Mrs. Schweir is a member of St. Paul's German Lutheran church.

In 1853, John Smaltz, having reached his twenty-first year on February 20th, left his native county of Hancock, Ohio, and settled in Aboit township, Allen county, and engaged in farming and carpentry. He is the son of Henry and Christina Smaltz, both natives of Fairfield county, Ohio. His paternal grandfather was John Smaltz, and his maternal grandfather, Philip Kramer, a native of Fairfield county. In February, 1865, Mr. Smaltz entered the Union army in Company G, One Hundred and Fifty-second Indiana regiment, and served until the close of the war, being mustered out at Charleston, W. Va., August, 1865. In 1872, Mr. Smaltz removed to Fort Wayne, and was occupied at his trade several years. He was married May 24, 1854, to Martha, daughter of Hamilton Scott, of Hardin county, Ohio. She was born May 9, 1830. Their only child is Francis M. Smaltz, proprietor of a well-known grocery and dry goods store at 307 West Main street, where the father has been engaged since 1877.

Francis M. Smaltz was born in Aboit township, April 13, 1855. At seventeen years of age he came to Fort Wayne and for five years worked at the tinner's trade. In 1877 he engaged in the grocery business, and his whole attention has since been given to the retail trade. Since the spring of 1879 he has done a successful business at his present location, and for the past five years he has also carried a line of dry goods. Mr. Smaltz was married April 22, 1877, to Miss Libbie Manchester, of Elkhart, Ind. She is a native of Mahoning county, Ohio. They have had two children, Florence M. and Hugh M., the former of whom died in childhood. Mr. Smaltz is a successful business man and socially stands very high.

Frank K. Smead, manager of the Union Pacific Tea company, at Fort Wayne, was born in Florence, Switzerland county, Ind., February 14, 1861. He is the son of Charles and Charlotte (Krutz) Smead, both natives of Vevay, Ind. At the early age of fourteen, Mr. Smead made his way to Denver, Col. He spent eighteen months there, six months in Wyoming Territory, and a year in Kansas. During this time he was engaged at mining, herding cattle and hunting. Returning home he spent one year on the farm, but set out again in 1879, going to Kansas City, and there completed a course in the commercial college, graduating in 1880. For six months after this he was in the employ of W. D. Faunce & Co., of Boston, jobbers in teas and coffees as salesman at Kansas City. Early in 1882 he went to Cincinnati, and entered the employ of the Union Pacific Tea company, with which he has since been engaged in the capacity of manager. He has been the manager of tea stores in Cincinnati, Richmond, Cleveland and Peoria. In the spring of 1889, he came to Fort Wayne, and has ably and successfully managed the business here. Mr. Smead was married at Cincinnati, October 8, 1885, to Mamie A., daughter of Michael Sheridan, a boot and shoe dealer of that city. Mrs. Smead was born in Cincinnati, May 1, 1865. They have had one child, Stella F., born July 5, 1887, who died September 26, 1888. Mr. Smead is a member of the I. O. O. F.

Since 1856 Jacob Alexander Spereisen has been one of the worthy citizens and mechanics of Fort Wayne. He was born in Switzerland, November 2, 1833, son of Ursus Joseph and Mary Anna Ida (von Arx) Spereisen. In his native country he attended school and served a three years' apprenticeship as a blacksmith with his brother. He worked at his trade as a journeyman in different places in Switzerland until he was twenty-two, at which age he accompanied his father and mother to America. The family landed at New York on May 1, 1856, and at once proceded to Fort Wayne, where the father and mother spent the rest of their lives, the latter dying January 2, 1860, and the former July 22, 1869. For many years after coming to Fort Wayne our subject worked at his trade as a journeyman. In May, 1870, he set up a blacksmith shop of his own, which he has conducted ever since. His present establishment is at No. 156 Fairfield avenue. Mr. Spereisen was married May 24, 1864, to Elizabeth Baker, who is a native of Fort

Wayne, born July 15, 1843, daughter of John and Mary (Faut) Baker, both natives of Germany. Mr. and Mrs. Spereisen are members of the Catholic church. He is a member of the Catholic Knights of America, and also of the St. Paul school and Pius benevolent societies.

For nearly a quarter of a century Gottfried Ernst Spiegel, one of Fort Wayne's popular grocers, has been doing business at the rooms he now occupies. He first engaged in the grocery business as a clerk at the age of fourteen, and on August 1, 1866, became a proprietor at his present stand. Mr. Spiegel was born January 4, 1845, in the village of Juedendorf, province of Saxony, Germany. He is the son of August and Sophia (Wehr) Spiegel, with whom he came to America in 1857. The family landed at New York August 17, after having spent seventy days on the ocean. They at once proceeded to Detroit, but about four months later came to Fort Wayne, arriving on December 15. The entire family still resides in this city. Mr. Spiegel was married May 23, 1867, to Miss Christina Wolf, who was born February 22, 1846, in the village of Leutenbach, Wurtemburg, Germany, the daughter of Christian and Dora Wolf. She accompanied her mother to America in 1852, her father having died in Germany. Mr. and Mrs. Spiegel have five living children: Anna, Minna, August, Tenea and Christian. They are members of the St. John's German Lutheran church.

John George Strodel, a popular Fort Wayne business man, was born in Bavaria, September 4, 1845. His father, John George Strodel, born in Bavaria in 1802, was a butcher by trade, who immigrated and settled at Huntington, Ind., in 1855, and there resided until his death, May 6, 1877. He was the father of thirty-two children, of whom seventeen are living, an interesting fact, for which few if any parallels can be found in modern life. The mother of the subject of this mention bore seventeen of these children, he being the second. Eight of these are living. She was born in Bavaria in 1825, and now resides at Huntington. Mr. Strodel was given a common school education, but throughout his subsequent career has been wholly dependent upon his own exertions. At the age of twelve years he came to Fort Wayne, and found work with his brother in the butchering business for ten years. In 1866 he engaged in the saloon and restaurant business, and has been so occupied ever since, being notably successful, and being generally known as an enterprising and popular citizen. In politics he is a democrat. For twenty-one years he was connected with the fire department of the city, a long and honorable service, from which he withdrew as assistant chief. He was married April 8, 1866, to Christina Wuersten, who was born in this city July 3, 1847, to Jacob and Catherine Miller Wuersten, who immigrated from Germany and settled here at an early day. He was the founder of Bloomingdale, and died in 1855. Mr. and Mrs. Strodel have six children living of eight born: Martha, Pauline, Herman, Otto, Frank and Emma. The family are members of the Lutheran church.

Himerius Leopold Studer, a manufacturer and dealer in mineral waters and other popular and refreshing beverages, engaged in the business here in 1871, having emigrated from Switzerland the previous year. He has been quite successful, and in 1888 erected the business building in which he is now located at a cost, including the lots, of more than $7,000. This is on West Main street, Nos. 228, 230 and 232. He was born in Switzerland, November 14, 1842, son of Anton and Anna Mary (Meyer) Studer. The parents were born in that land, his father in 1804 and the mother in 1813. The father died in 1864 and the mother in 1884, both in their native country. The subject of this mention was the youngest of three sons, and received his education in Switzerland. He was married February 7, 1875, to Anna Mary Steinhauser, who was born in Germany October 13, 1851, and came to Fort Wayne in 1872, and they have four children: Anna J., born in 1876; Rosamond, 1880; Alma, 1884; and Bertha, 1886. Mrs. Studer is a member of the Lutheran church.

One of the leading dealers of coal and wood at Fort Wayne, Andrew Sullivan, was born in New York state, May 7, 1852. Coming to Fort Wayne in 1869, he soon afterward was occupied in railroading on the Pittsburgh, Fort Wayne & Chicago. In 1877 he went to Lawrence county, Penn., and was there engaged in the saw-mill business for several years. He returned to Fort Wayne in April, 1884, and then engaged in the wood and coal business at the corner of Grant and Oliver streets, an occupation in which he has been successful. He was married October 26, 1875, to Mary D. Cole, a native of the state of New York. To this union five children have been born, of whom one is deceased. Mr. Sullivan is a member of the Cathedral congregation, of the Catholic Knights, St. Julian council, No. 9, and Catholic benevolent legion. In politics he is a democrat.

One of the successful business men of Fort Wayne, James Summers, was born in county Kilkenny, Ireland, August 8, 1835, the second and only survivor of six children of Michael Summers. The latter was born in Ireland, and there married Ann Delaney, who died in her native land. The father came to America and died at Fort Wayne at eighty years of age. James Summers came to the United States in 1853, and settled first in Vermont, where he resided one year. In 1854 he came to Fort Wayne, and for five years acted as clerk at the Rockhill house. In 1861, he engaged in business in this city, and at this has since been occupied. Mr. Summers was married in 1863, to Catherine Nelligan, who was born in Ireland, and they have five children living out of twelve born: Mary, Ella, Anna, Lizzie and Frank. In politics Mr. Summers is a democrat. He is a prominent member of the Catholic church, and is active in the Catholic Legion and the Catholic Knights of America.

John P. Tinkham, a prominent dealer in wood and coal at Fort Wayne, was born in Delaware county, Ohio, January 13, 1832. His father, Isaac Tinkham, a native of Vermont, married Sarah Mapes, a native of New York, and about 1820 they became pioneer settlers in Delaware county, Ohio. In 1837, they joined the advance guard of civilization in Indiana, settling in Adams county, where the father died in 1844. The mother then removed to Whitley county, thence to Lafayette, and then to Allen county, where she died about 1877. They had four children, of whom two survive, the subject of this mention and Benjamin F. Tinkham. The latter enlisted in the Twentieth Indiana, in 1861, and served three years. He was taken prisoner and confined in Libby prison, and was on ship board during the disastrous storm off Hatteras Inlet, and suffered all the hardships of war. He is now a resident of Fort Wayne. John P. Tinkham spent his early years upon the farm of his parents, their last location being near New Haven, and after leaving the farm, was employed on packet boats on the Wabash & Erie canal during the summers, spending the winters at Fort Wayne for five or six years. Afterward he engaged quite extensively in shiping wood and lumber to Cincinnati, from Fort Wayne by way of the canal. This occupied him for several years. About 1874, he opened a wood yard at Fort Wayne, which he has since conducted. He was married in 1861, to Mary Parant, who was born in Ohio in 1838, and died about 1872, leaving three children of whom two survive, Cora and Frank. In 1876, he was married to Matilda M. Eldridge, born in Steuben county, in 1851, and they have five daughters: Mabel, Gracie, Blanchie, Nellie and Eva. Mr. Tinkham has been successful in business, and is highly esteemed as a citizen.

Since April, 1868, when he made his home at Fort Wayne, Christian Wenninghoff has been extensively engaged in the manufacture of cigars, and the wholesale and retail trade. His establishment was for many years on Calhoun street, but has been lately removed to his present commodious quarters at 110 West Jefferson. In his factory (No. 142), are employed ten men on the average, and his products, "Copyright Red Bird," "Xenophon," "Nelson" and "Triple Extra," are well known. Mr, Wenninghoff was born at Bramsche, Hanover, October 12, 1842. In 1866, having learned the trade of cigar maker, he came to the new world, and made his home first at Steubenville, Ohio. April 1, 1869, he was married to Amelia Wieman, of Williams county, Ohio, and they have seven children: Sarah, Amelia, Lilly, Christian, Flora, Arthur and Edgar. Mr. Wenninghoff is a member of Emanuel Lutheran church, and a worthy citizen.

During the past decade Jacob V. Wilkens has been a successful business man at Fort Wayne, and one of the proprietors of a meat market which does a flourishing business. He was born in Ohio, April 8, 1857, the son of Chris Wilkens, a native of Germany, and Katherine, his wife. He came to Fort Wayne with his parents in 1863. He learned the butcher's trade with his father, and this has been his vocation. He was married September 3, 1883, to Miss Sarah Sutter, a native of Wells county, Ind. He has three children: Grace, Emma Leoni and Maud May. Mr. and Mrs. Wilkens are members of the English Lutheran church. He is a good business man and a first-class citizen.

John Wilson, a leading dealer in coal and wood at Fort Wayne, is a native of England. He was born at Suffolk, August 25, 1823, and was reared in London, whither his parents moved when he was young. The father was a school teacher, surveyor and map-maker, and assisted materially in his son's education. At the age of fourteen John was apprenticed, an engagement which he abruptly terminated. Then he secured a position in a grocery store in London, and afterward was in the employ of a wholesale cheese dealer, for whom he traveled. In the fall of 1844 he married and engaged in general merchandise at Black Friar's, London, until 1848, when he emigrated with his family to Albany, N. Y. In July, 1851, he made his home in Allen county, on the "Ryder section," in Lake township. He taught school, graded in 1853 one mile of the Pittsburgh railroad, and next invested in timber land and managed a saw-mill, selling the product to the railroad, until 1878, when he had cleared 560 acres of land. Leaving his sons on the farm, he took a position in the lumber yards of J. N. Coombs, at Fort Wayne, and remained exactly four years. Mr. Wilson embarked in the coal and wood business in April, 1882, in partnership with Edward Gilmartin and B. B. Rossington. A year later he purchased the interests of those gentlemen, and in 1884 his son Walter was admitted to the business, and in 1885 his son J. C. became a partner, the firm style now being John Wilson & Sons. Mr. Wilson was married first to Harriet Pryor, who was a native of Hertfordshire. She died in 1876, leaving three children: John C., Walter B. and Mary A., now Mrs. Whitney, and in 1878 he was married to Mary Rossington, also a native of England. Mr. Wilson is a member of the Episcopal church, and is a highly esteemed citizen.

Since August 10, 1880, William Wise has been enrolled among the busy and successful mechanics of Fort Wayne. He was born near Mansfield, Ohio, September 3, 1854, son of Henry and Mary (Bosler) Wise, the former of whom was a native of Pennsylvania. He was reared on a farm and received a common school education. At nineteen he entered upon an apprenticeship at the blacksmith's trade in Mansfield, Ohio, and served three years and a half. He then conducted a shop at the old Wise homestead, in Richland county, two years. On coming to Fort Wayne he first worked a while as a journeyman. But in the spring of 1882 he and Mr. Farnin became the owners of a blacksmith shop on Lafayette street. The partnership was dissolved in the following autumn, and on September 22, 1882, Mr. Wise opened up his present shop at No. 363 South Calhoun street. Mr. Wise is a member of the English Lutheran church.

A skillful mechanic and worthy citizen of Fort Wayne during the past eight years, Joseph F. Zurbuch, conducts a prosperous business at No. 387 West Main street. Mr. Zurbuch was born in Mercer county, Ohio, April 12, 1861. His father, Xavier F. Zurbuch, came to this country with his parents, from Alsace, in 1833, and was married in Ohio in 1856, to Elizabeth Rentz, a native of that state. When their son Joseph was ten years old they removed to Lawrence county, Tenn, but in 1877 returned to Ohio, settling near Carthagena. In 1880 they came to this city, their present home. On the return from Tennessee, Joseph F. Zurbuch found employment at farm work in Mercer county, Ohio. In the fall of 1877 he came to Allen county, and for three years he served an apprenticeship at the blacksmith's trade at New Haven. In the spring of 1881 he came to Fort Wayne where his attention has ever since been given to his trade. He has made a specialty of horseshoeing, and for the past four years he has conducted an establishment of that kind for himself. He was married November 18, 1884, to Christena M. Reinhardt, who is a native of Fort Wayne, born February 20, 1865, the daughter of John and Louisa M. Reinhardt, both natives of Germany. Mr. Zurbuch and wife are members of the Catholic church. He is a member of the Knights of St. Charles society.

ARCHITECTURAL GROWTH.

The architectural improvement of Fort Wayne during the last few years has been remarkable, both for the number of new buildings erected, and for the elegance and substantial qualities of these additions to the attractions of the city. Before this era of improvement began, and within the memory even of the young men of the city, Calhoun street, the principal thoroughfare, now having the additional distinction of being the wholesale street, was a muddy road, bounded by poor sidewalks, making pretensions to business at the north end, and with a few eating houses and drinking houses at the south depot. Between Washington and Baker streets was a motley array of buildings too variegated in character to give the street a substantial appearance. Here, handsome buildings now stand, which are a credit to the city and its people. At the "old Townley corner" the buildings occupied in part by George Dewald & Co. have been wonderfully improved, and this old seat of trade is not behind more recent business blocks in striking appearance. The handsome five-story building of A. C. Trentman, 60x65 feet frontage, the five-story building of E. A. K. Hackett, adjoining the Rich building, distinguished by its handsome cut stone front, the attractive four-story building, 50x100, occupied by the wholesale house of Bursley & Co., the Fleming building, which so closely escaped destruction in the fire of February, 1889, the metropolitan Pixley-Long block, erected by George W. Pixley and Mason Long, with front of Michigan sandstone, the Fox wholesale block, risen from the ashes of a disastrous conflagration, the Schmitz building, the stone exterior of which is the most elaborate and ornate of any business building in the city, the Rich, Wayne and Aldine hotel buildings, which have supplemented so efficiently the entertaining capacity of the older Aveline and Robinson hotels—these are some of the more prominent improvements in the city's business accommodations. Of the many handsome and luxurious residences which have grown up recently, and of those elegantly appointed ones that have stood for many years, attesting the good taste and faith of their builders in the future of the city, it would be impracticable to make detail in this work. The splendid temples of worship and other church institutions now adorning the city, are described in a more appropriate connection. There remain to mention, the buildings of a public character, and of these, and the circumstances attending their erection, a brief account will here be given.

The Government Building.— The Fort Wayne building has been pronounced by competent judges, the handsomest and best building, size and cost considered, that the government has yet erected, yet the work was done so honestly and economically that $6,000 of the appropriation remained unexpended at the completion of the work. The movement for this public work was begun by the citizens during the congressional term of Hon. Walpole G. Colerick, and through his exertions, the first appropriation of $50,000 was made by congress. The subsequent appropriations were obtained through the efforts of Hon. Robert Lowry, who earnestly devoted himself to this enterprise. The total estimate was $221,000, of which $34,000 was for the site. The first superintendent of the work was the late Col. George Humphrey, who was appointed in April, 1884. He was relieved by the appointment of Christian Boseker about the time that the work had progressed as far as the laying of the second floor supports. William Moellering was the contractor, and faithfully performed the work he undertook. It was occupied by Postmaster Kaough on the night of February 14, 1889. The building is fire-proof throughout, and the walls are built of Michigan bluff sandstone, from the quarries of S. B. Bond, at Stony Point, Mich., a very handsome material. The ground plan is eighty-five feet square, and the top of the roof is sixty-six feet above the ground. At the northwest corner a beautiful bastion tower rises to the height of 115 feet. The building affords a working room for the postoffice, 26x80 feet, as well as offices, on the first floor, and the second floor contains, besides offices of various departments of government service, a court room, 26x53, elegantly appointed, and furnished with benches and tables of solid cherry. This superb building is the pride of the city and a great gratification to all who labored for the securing of it.

Y. M. C. Association Building.— For a number of years a Young Men's Christian Association, railroad branch, had flourished in the city and furnished a commodious reading room near the depots on Calhoun street. But the necessity of an extension of this noble enterprise and the organization of a regular association in Fort Wayne of a general character, was recognized early in 1886, and the matter was debated in the meetings of the executive committee of the railroad department. At the suggestion of E. D. Ingersoll, railroad secretary for the international committee, a committee consisting of E. A. K. Hackett, E. S. Philley and C. H. Newton was appointed to formulate a constitution, and Messrs. Ingersoll and D. F. More were added as advisory members. This committee reported a plan of organization to the meeting called at the parlors of the railroad association March 18, 1886, at which

INDIANA SCHOOL FOR FEEBLE-MINDED YOUTH.
FORT WAYNE, IND.

time the organization of the city association was made with 100 charter members. The first officers were E. A. K. Hackett, president: E. S. Philley, S. R. Smith, W. T. Ferguson, August Detzer, vice presidents; C. H. Newton, secretary, and J. A. Tyler, treasurer. Trustees: J. K. Edgerton, John Ferguson, O. P. Morgan, John H. Jacobs, George W. Breckenridge and John M. Miller. The association at once began considering the erection of a building as a permanent home for the association, and though the project was a vast one for the young organization, the brave hearts of its founders were not discouraged. In January, 1887, it was officially resolved to purchase the lot of J. B. White adjoining the *Sentinel* building, and erect a building 40x100 feet, and the plans prepared by Wing & Mahurin were adopted. The work of digging for the foundation was begun before the frost was out of the ground, and the contract was let to William Moellering. A building committee was appointed, who vigorously and efficiently prosecuted the work, Hon. A. A. Chapin, chairman; J. W. Cromwell, W. S. Harrison, H. C. Schroeder, and George O. Bradley. The corner stone was laid with appropriate services, and an address by Dr. Munhall, on June 6, 1887, and in about a year the building was occupied. It is a handsome structure with an attractive stone front, and cost, the lot included, about $40,000. It is elegantly furnished throughout, and contains a lecture hall, a spacious reading room and ample space for athletic exercises, fully equipped with apparatus. On September 16, 1889, a new constitution was adopted, whereby the two branches of the association in the city are brought under the control of a board of directors, of which W. D. Page is president; C. H. Newton, vice president and H. C. Schroeder, secretary. Of the association just described, E. A. K. Hackett, whose untiring energy and popularity have contributed so much to the success of the institution, remains as chairman, with George B. Shivers, secretary, and James McKay, treasurer. The general secretary is D. F. Bower, lately of Reading, Penn., and E. F. Gage is physical director.

The State Institution. — By the state legislature of 1887, there was enacted a law for the establishment of a state institution, to be called the Indiana School for Feeble-minded Youth, taking the place of a similar institution formerly connected with the home for soldiers' orphans. There was a lively struggle in the legislature for the location of this new institution, and the pluck and perseverance of Fort Wayne citizens was well illustrated in the campaign which ended in their victory and the establishing of the location at Fort Wayne. A board of trustees was appointed of which E. A. K. Hackett, of this city is president. On the 19th of May, 1887, they purchased of William L., and Clara L. Carnahan, a tract of fifty-four and one-half acres, one and a half miles from the city, and on this the erection of a building was begun in the spring of 1888. For this and site there was at first appropriated $50,000. The trustees decided to erect a building which should be able to adequately meet the wants of the unfortunate children, long neglected, and the plans were

xv

prepared by Wing & Mahurin of this city. The contract for the main building, which was all that could be attempted under the first appropriation, was let to William Moellering, of Fort Wayne, who finished it in the fall of 1888, waiting for the state's financial condition to improve before receiving his pay. The contract for building the wings, hospital, cold storage building, boiler house and laundry, was let subsequently to Brooks Brothers, and the entire structure, it is expected, will be ready for receiving its inmates in the spring of 1890. The building has a 400 foot frontage, and has a capacity of accomodating 1,000 children. The central portion, or administration building, contains, in addition to the various offices, dining rooms, chapel, culinary department, etc. The additions to the east and west are dormitories. The building is constructed with particular care to provide those conveniences necessary to the character of its occupants, being heated by steam, with a complete system of water-works, and fire protection, an electric-light plant of its own, complete sanitary arrangements and fire escapes, and is most thorough in its adaptation to the uses for which it is designed. The halls and all dining rooms are tiled, and the building is as near fire proof as possible. By the last legislature aditional appropriations of $187,000 were made, and the building when completed will have cost including land about $230,000.

William Moellering, one of the leading contractors and builders of northern Indiana, was born in Prussia, April 7, 1832, the youngest son of August and Dorothea (Rackeweg) Moellering. The father, a native of Prussia, died there when William was about three years old, and the mother, a native of Hanover, died in Prussia about 1844. William Moellering obtained a good common school education, and in 1849 emigrated to the United States, making the voyage in sixty-three days. He reached Fort Wayne, which has since been his home, in August, 1849. In 1850 he began the trade of stone mason and brick layer, and three years later, had so thoroughly perfected himself that he began the business of a contractor, in which he has since been so successfully engaged. He is also one of the most extensive brick manufacturers of the city and has extensive stone quarries at Wabash. Mr. Moellering has erected many well-known public buildings in this part of Indiana, among them, six of the public school buildings in Fort Wayne, St. Paul's cathedral, 1886, St. Paul's Lutheran church in 1888, the United States court-house and postoffice at Fort Wayne, and he is now building the State School for Feeble-minded Youth, near the city. He has been very successful in business, and occupies a high rank among the enterprising men of the city. He is a member of the Evangelical Lutheran church, and in politics is democratic. Mr. Moellering was married in 1854, to Anna Hambrock, who was born in Germany in 1834, and came to Fort Wayne in 1851. They have ten children: William F., Eliza, Minnie, Henry F., Anna, Sophia, Charles E., Mathilda, Edward and Clara.

In the year 1884 J. F. Herber embarked in business as a carpenter at Fort Wayne, and in 1888 began contracting, in which he has been quite successful, having a good custom and employing a number of men. He was born in Marion township, October 3, 1862, the son of Nicholas and Mary (Hoffman) Herber, both of whom were born in Germany. The father immigrated in about 1850, came directly to Allen county, and buying a farm in Marion township began farming. He is now one of the prosperous farmers of that township. His wife came to America in 1832, and her father was Gunderum Hoffman, was one of the pioneers and a well-to-do farmer of Marion township. She died in 1875, at the age of forty-six years. Both parents were members of the Catholic church. To them nine children were born, eight of whom are living. Their son, J. F., was reared on the farm until his seventeenth year, when he began working at the carpenter's trade. He owns a handsome two-story frame residence on South Wayne street, on a forty-foot lot. Mr. Herber is a member of St. Mary's Catholic church.

Sanford Rich, owner of Rich's Hotel, is a native Indianian, born in Washington township, Rush county, September 30, 1840. His father, Joseph Rich, was born in Adams county, Ohio, August 1, 1818, the son of John Rich, a native of North Carolina, who was one of the pioneers of Adams county, Ohio, settling there in 1804. He died in that county at middle age, and his widow removed to Fayette couuty, Ind., about 1824. When Joseph was about seventeen years of age he removed to Rush county, and was there married in 1839 to Melinda Lightfoot, who was born in Kentucky in 1822. In 1847 he moved to Wells county, and settled in what was known as the Indian reserve, when there were only about a dozen families living in the township. His occupation was farming and stock dealing. He died in Wells county, December 12, 1877, his wife having passed away in 1854. They had five children, of whom Sanford Rich is the oldest. The others are: Edwin, born in 1842; Permelia, born in 1844; Angeline, born 1848; and William, born 1851. Sanford was raised on the farm, and obtained his early education in the pioneer schools of Wells county. The first school-house at which he attended was known as the Uniontown school-house, and was the first erected in Union township, Wells county. His father donated the ground and was one of four men who put up the building in 1848. The first teacher was John Mulrine. In 1864 he came to Fort Wayne, and for about two years was engaged in the meat business, afterward, in the fall of 1865, returning to Wells county, where he was occupied in farming and stock dealing until his return to the city in 1873. Until 1880 he was again engaged in conducting a meat market, at Fort Wayne, but in the year named he removed to Chicago, and there followed the same business for seven years, doing a business of nearly $100,000 a year. Throughout his career he has maintained a reputation as a shrewd and careful business man, and an upright and worthy citizen. He is now a resident of Fort Wayne, where in 1885 he built Rich's Hotel, which is one of the leading and most popular hotels of northern Indiana. In politics he is a democrat; and he is a member of the Masonic and I. O. O. F. orders. He was married in 1863 to Elizabeth E. Walker, born in Rush county, in 1839, daughter of William Walker, a pioneer of that county. Mr. and Mrs. Rich are prominent members of the Christian church.

The Wayne Hotel, built by J. C. Peters, in 1887, is famous over the land as a strictly first-class hotel, with perfect appointments and thoroughly equipped with all those many provisions of comfort which the civilization of to-day has devised for the convenience and pleasure of the wayfaring public. The building is of brick and stone, four-stories high, with an area of 110x150 feet, and contains 128 furnished rooms for guests. On the ground floor are the office, lounging room, washroom, bar and barber shop, five sample rooms, ample dining rooms, and a large lobby, all richly frescoed and decorated, and furnished with an exquisitely tiled floor. There are three capacious entrances, two elevators and wide stairways, and four fire escapes, to make entrance and exit comfortable and safe under all possible circumstances. To provide for comfort, there are two parlors with fireplaces, though the building is heated by steam; and the Hess electric system of call and return call extends throughout the house. Ample sample rooms on the second floor are ready for the many commercial travelers who make their headquarters here. The best ventilating and sanitary engineering have found scope in the Wayne, and the furniture is of a high order of elegance. In the respects named the house is first class, but an essential feature of a successful hotel has not yet been mentioned — its management. This, in the hands of W. M. McKinnie & Co., the active partner being Captain Henry McKinnie, leaves nothing to be desired in the *tout ensemble* of the Wayne Hotel. Capt. McKinnie has the sole control, and to him the unparalleled success of the establishment is due. Under his careful supervision the service is uniformly satisfactory, the *cuisine* is all that the most fastidious could wish for, and all guests receive the most courteous attention. Capt. McKinnie is also interested in the management of the Hotel Anderson, at Pittsburgh, the Manhattan Beach and Oriental hotel at Coney Island, and the Niel Hotel at Columbus, Ohio.

Christian Boseker, a prominent citizen of Fort Wayne, and well-known throughout northern Indiana, was born in Saxony, Germany, May 8, 1841. His parents, Peter Boseker and wife, were natives of Saxony, and five years after the birth of Christian came to the United States, settling at Fort Wayne in June of 1846. Here the father followed his occupation, that of miller. The parents passed away after gaining the esteem of their acquaintances in their new home, the father in 1857, and the mother in 1865. Christian Boseker is the youngest son among eight children, four of whom survive. He received his education in the common schools, and in 1859 began work at the trade of carpenter in the employment of A. C. Beaver, with whom he remained until the outbreak of the war of the rebellion. In the summer of 1861 he enlisted in Company E, Thirtieth Indiana volunteer infantry, and served until March 28, 1863, when he was discharged on account of physical disability. Returning to his home, he resumed the carpenter's trade in the fall of 1863, and in 1864 he entered the employment of J. D. Silver and was his foreman in the construction of the DeKalb county court-house. He embarked in the business of contracting in 1865, forming a partnership with Jacob Forbing, which continued until 1868. The executive ability and genius for construction manifested by Mr. Boseker in these early years of his career made him prominent as a builder, and he soon began to engage in the construction of public buildings involving the expenditure of large sums of money. In 1868-9 he engaged in the remodeling of the Allen county circuit court room. He subsequently built the court-houses of Defiance county, Ohio, and Adams county, Ind., and the Allen county jail. Leaving this business for a season he embarked with J. B. White, in the fall of 1875, in the manufacture of wheels, in which he continued for eight years. His next work was the completion of the Masonic temple, which had been commenced in 1881, but for lack of funds was not completed. This work was finished by Mr. Boseker in the fall of 1884. During this year he also took the contract for the erection of the First Presbyterian church, which he completed in 1885. In September of the latter year he was appointed by President Cleveland superintendent of the erection of the government building at Fort Wayne, which was completed in April, 1889. In 1889 Mr. Boseker took the contract for building the Wells county court-house, which is to be completed in the fall of 1890. In politics, Mr. Boseker has always been a democrat, casting his first vote for Gen. McClellan. In 1881 he was elected water-works trustee for one year, and in 1882 was elected for three years. In 1888 he was elected to fill the unexpired term of J. F. W. Meyer, and in 1889 he was again elected for three years. He has taken an active part in political affairs and in the improvement of the city. In 1888 he purchased the Fort Wayne *Journal*, the proprietorship of which he held for eighteen months, then disposing of it on account of his other business. Mr. Boseker was married September 28, 1863, to Cornelia Hinton, who was born in Fort Wayne in 1843. To them two children have been born, Lida E. and Harry C.

Frank B. Kendrick, a well-known and popular architect, took up the study of architecture in Philadelphia, in 1869, under the direction of B. D. Price. In the fall of 1871 he began the practice of his profession at Lancaster, Penn., and continued there until May, 1874. He then spent three years at Salem, Ohio, and one year at Springfield, and in February, 1879, came to Fort Wayne, where he has since resided and successfully pursued his profession, being also engaged for eight years in contracting, in partnership with Alfred Shrimpton. During that period they built the residence of H. J. Trentman, in 1880, the Catholic library in 1881, the addition to St. Augustine Academy, the "Nickel Plate" depots, the Wayne Hotel, St. Vincent's asylum, and many other conspicuous residences and public structures. In 1888, Mr. Kendrick withdrew from the business of contractor. He is a valued citizen, and is in politics a republican. He was born at Lancaster, Penn., August

13, 1850, son of W. G. and Louisa Kendrick, natives of Maryland and Pennsylvania, respectively. The father, who was born in 1815, for ten years subsequent to 1837, followed the life of a sailor. For three years he served as a captain in the Union army, under Gen. George H. Thomas, and was honorably discharged after the battle of Chickamauga. The mother, whose maiden name was Stoddard, was born in Philadelphia about 1830. Frank B. is the oldest of seven children, and received his early education in the schools of Lancaster. He was married in 1874, to Miss L. Souders, who was born in Pennsylvania, and they have one child, Sallie.

William Geake, senior member of the firm of William & J. J. Geake, the well known cut stone contractors of Fort Wayne, was born at Bristol, England, June 26, 1849, the son of Martin T. and Sarah (Hill) Geake, both natives of England. The family emigrated to Canada, in August, 1854, and returned to England in 1858, where they remained. William returned to America on May 2, 1868, and after making a stay at Oswego, N. Y., in the following November came west to Toledo, Ohio, where he learned the stone cutting trade. He then spent the time between 1868 to 1873 following his trade in Boston, Chicago, and various other cities, and in the latter year settled at Toledo and began contracting in cut stone work in partnership with J. J. Geake, his present partner. From Toledo he went to Petoskey, Mich., where he took up a homestead of 160 acres of land, and was one of the first white settlers of that region. After spending six years there, he located permanently at Fort Wayne. Before bringing his family here, however, he had come to Fort Wayne and was foreman of the work of erecting the Masonic temple. The firm of William & J. J. Geake was re-established here in 1882, and the business has grown remarkably, now giving employment to thirty to forty skilled workmen. Evidences of their skill are to be seen in the Hall block, Toledo, the finished stone work of the Masonic temple, the First Presbyterian church, the Y. M. C. A. building, and the lodge entrance at Lindenwood cemetery, the St. Paul's Cathedral church, Pixley and Long block and the Nathan and Rothschild residence, Fort Wayne, the court-house and the Michigan Central railway depot at Kalamazoo, Mich., the large stone residence of C. C. Bloomfield, Jackson, Mich., stone residences of A. B. Robinson, Jackson, Mich., and C. H. Brownell, Peru, Ind., National bank, Peru, Ind., and the court-house at Columbia City, Ind., now building. Mr. Geake is a member of the Summit City lodge, F. & A. M., No. 170. He was made a Mason in 1871, passed through the chapter in 1872, Knight Templar commandery in 1882, Scottish Rite in 1882, the chair of Worshipful Master of Summit City lodge, and has filled all the chairs of subordinate lodge. He was for three years H. P. of Fort Wayne chapter, No. 19, and Eminent Commander of Fort Wayne commandery for nearly three years, and T. P. G. M. of Fort Wayne lodge of Perfection, and A. & A. S. R., northern Masonic jurisdiction of Fort Wayne. He received the thirty-third degree on the 17th of September,

1889, at New York city. He is also a member of the Royal Arcanum, and Sons of St. George, of which he was first president. Mr. Geake was married November 5, 1874, to Alice E. Clayton, of Toledo, Ohio. To them seven children have been born — three boys, four girls, all of whom are living.

J. J. Geake, member of the firm of Wm. & J. J. Geake, proprietors of extensive stone works at Fort Wayne, learned the craft of stone cutter with his father, while his family were residents of Canada. After being engaged in the business about six months they removed to Toledo, in 1865, and he then began taking contracts for stone work of all kinds, which business he has subsequently pursued. The first firm of which he was a member was that of Kilt & Geake, the next Simmons & Geake, and in 1873 he formed a partnership with a cousin, William Geake. This was afterward dissolved by the removal of William to Michigan, but in July, 1879, J. J. removed to Fort Wayne, and his cousin having also made his home here, the old firm was re-established in 1882. Their firm is very prominent in the trade, the field of operations extending throughout Indiana, Ohio and Michigan. The works employ twenty to thirty skilled masons, are supplied with all the best appliances, and much of the work is done by steam power. All forms of ornamental as well as plain stone work is produced, and such buildings as the Y. M. C. A., Masonic temple, First Presbyterian church, and many others, show the quality of the work of the firm. Mr. Geake was born in Onondaga county, N. Y., February 6, 1836, the son of Edward and Susanna (Jenkins) Geake, who were natives of Devonshire, England, and emigrated to this country in 1832. In 1842 they removed to Canada, and in 1865 to Toledo, where the father died in 1871 and the mother in 1870. Mr. Geake was married March 8, 1861, to Rebecca H. McClear, of Ireland, who was born in 1841, came to Canada with her parents when a child, and died January 4, 1888, leaving seven children living, out of nine born.

William H. Kendrick, a prominent stone, brick and pressed brick contractor at Fort Wayne, began learning the trade of brick and stone mason in Lancaster, Penn., and finished it at Springfield, Ohio. In the latter city he began the business of a contractor in 1881, taking all kinds of brick construction. He came to Fort Wayne in 1886, and here engaged in the same business making a specialty of construction in pressed brick. He also began contracting in stone work in 1888. His business is extensive and he does all the pressed brick work in the city. Among the handsome buildings he has constructed are Trentman's on Calhoun street, and Fox's building, which he is also rebuilding. Mr. Kendrick is a member of the International bricklayers' association, and and at its meetings in 1888 and 1889 at Boston and Cleveland, he was the representative of northern Indiana. Mr. Kendrick was born in Lancaster, Penn., July 14, 1857, and his childhood and youth were spent there until 1875, when he removed to Springfield, Ohio. He was married in

1881, to Susie Kulp, daughter of Levi Kulp, a contractor of Springfield, Ohio, and they have had one daughter, who is deceased.

One of the successful and practical contractors of Fort Wayne is Alfred Shrimpton. He is a native of London, England, born October 2, 1836, son of Joseph and Elizabeth (Smith) Shrimpton, natives of that city. The parents, who were both born in 1811, immigrated in 1837, and first settled in New York city, afterward removing to Hamilton county, Ohio, where they now reside. The father is a cabinet-maker by trade, but has been carrying on farming for twenty years. The mother is a daughter of Capt. Smith, of the East India company's service. Mr. Shrimpton attended school in New York, and at the age of fourteen, began an apprenticeship of seven years in carpentry and stair building. In 1857, he went to Cincinnati, Ohio, and worked at his trade until 1861, when he enlisted in the Second Kentucky regiment, and was honorably discharged, and on account of physical disability, was unable to re-enlist. On his return from the service, he was engaged in building and re-fitting opera-houses. In the spring of 1880, he came to Fort Wayne, and shortly afterward engaged in contracting and building, in partnership with F. B. Kendrick, which association continued until February, 1888. Since then he has been doing business alone. He is a worthy citizen, and is one of the leading contractors of the city. In politics he is a republican.

James M. Henry, prominent among the contractors and builders of Fort Wayne, was born in Parkersburg, W. Va., March 5, 1856. His father, Gabriel Henry, was born at Steubenville, Ohio, in 1837, and when quite young was taken by his parents to West Virginia, where they farmed near Parkersburg. He followed steamboating on the Ohio river about fourteen years, as an assistant pilot. Afterward he learned the carpenter's trade and was for a number of years engaged for a Pittsburgh company in erecting derricks, putting up machinery and opening oil wells in the oil region. In 1865 he removed to Noble county, Ind., and purchased a farm, to which he has since given his attention. His wife, whose maiden name was Sophia McKinzie, was born in Williamstown, W. Va., in 1837, her parents being natives of Glasgow, Scotland. James M. Henry passed his early years on the farm, and attended the country schools, then the schools at Marietta, Ohio. He began the trade of a carpenter at Kendallville, and was there engaged until July 3, 1882, when he came to Fort Wayne and entered the employment of Kendrick & Shrimpton. He was foreman of the establishment of that firm until 1887, when he formed a partnership with E. T. Liburn, in general contracting and building. They have a large and increasing business. Mr. Henry is a member of Summit City lodge, F. & A. M., Fort Wayne chapter, being at present high priest: Fort Wayne council, No. 4, the grand lodge of Perfection, and the Royal Arcanum. He was married April 7, 1886, to Laura Hoover, of Wabash, Ind., and they have two children.

A prominent contractor and builder, Ernest F. Liebman, senior member of the firm of Liebman & Henry, became a resident of this city in 1865. He then learned the trade of a carpenter, and subsequently for several years had charge of the erection of public buildings for various contractors, being so engaged at Decatur, Defiance, Wabash, LaGrange, and elsewhere, gaining during that time much valuable information and experience, so that he is to-day one of the most competent men in his profession. In 1881 he formed a partnership with Charles Boseker, but a year later engaged in business on his own account and so continued four years. The present partnership, with James M. Henry, was formed April 1, 1887. Among the principal buildings he has erected are R. T. McDonald's residence, several houses for Mrs. M. Hamilton, Mrs. W. Williams, the Rothschild and Nathan residences. Mr. Liebman is a native of Saxony, born in 1845, the son of William and Emma Liebman, who immigrated to New York in 1850, and are still residents of that city. He received his education in the German and English schools of New York. He is a member of the Masonic order, Knight Templar and Scottish Rite, of the I. O. O. F., Royal Arcanum, and politically is a democrat. Mr. Liebman was married in 1874 to Catherine Try, of Circleville, Ohio, and they have two daughters.

The family of Caspar and Barbara (Hoffman) Krock is associated with the earliest German settlement in the Maumee valley. The parents came to America in 1837, and settled in Marion township the same year, upon a farm. The father enlisted in 1863 in the National army and being discharged in the fall of 1864, on account of illness returned home to die shortly afterward. The mother had died in 1849. The children were five in all; three sons and two daughters. One of the sons, John Krock, now a prominent contractor and builder at Fort Wayne, was born in Marion township, June 4, 1845. He remained on the farm until his nineteenth year, and attended the free schools and the Catholic school at Hessen Cassel. In 1863, he went to Springfield, Ohio, and remained about eighteen months, returning to Fort Wayne to begin the carpenter's trade. Eighteen months later he went again to Springfield, and resided there four years, and then returned to Fort Wayne, and engaged in carpentry. Nine years he spent in the employ of the Fort Wayne steel plow works. In 1882 he began contracting, at which he has continued. He was married at Springfield, Ohio, July 29, 1869, to Mary Dahman, of Fort Wayne. To their union twelve children have been born, four of whom: Annie J., Mary, Emma and Matilda, are living. Mr. and Mrs. Krock are members of St. Mary's Catholic church.

Ernst Breimeier, one of the leading contractors and builders whose work has adorned Fort Wayne, is a native of Westphalia, Germany, born April 24, 1837. In 1855 he came to America alone and located at Chicago, and having completed his school studies, and learned his trade, in his native land, he immediately obtained work, and was engaged in that city four years. In 1860 he removed to Fort Wayne, and three years later began contracting, which has been his occupation to the present time. Among the buildings he has taken important building contracts upon, are: Emanuel Lutheran church, German Reformed church, Concordia college, new addition to St. Joseph's hospital, Orphan's home, Trentman's, De Wald's and Bursley's business buildings. Mr. Breimeier was married in 1861 to Sophia Eliza Fos, who died in 1863, leaving one son, Ernst, jr. In 1865 he again married to Julia Gerke, who was born in this city and died in 1881, leaving five sons: Louis, Gustave, Herman, Frederick and Theodore. In 1884 Mr. Breimeier was married to Eliza, daughter of Capt. Koch, and they have had two daughters, Bertie and Julia. Mr. Breimeier and wife are members of the Emanuel Lutheran church, and he is a director of the Concordia cemetery.

One of the early carpenters of Williamsport, Allen county, was James M. Griffith, a respected citizen, who came there from Adams county in 1857, and during his residence was the postmaster. He came to Fort Wayne in 1863, and resided here until about 1874, when he moved to near Decatur, Ind., but returned here in 1888 to reside with his son. His wife, Margaret Comfort, was born in 1814 and died in 1874. He was born in 1813, was a native, as was his wife, of York county, Penn., and after their marriage they moved to Ohio, and in 1854 to Adams county, Ind. In Washington county, Penn., November 13, 1842, their son, Levi Griffith, now a prominent contractor and builder at Fort Wayne, was born. His childhood was spent in Ohio, where he received his education in the public schools. At sixteen years of age he began learning the carpenter's trade at Williamsport, and when about nineteen years old began work at Fort Wayne, which has ever since been his home. He began contracting with W. S. Patten in 1869, and was engaged with him about four years, and since then has been alone in the business of general contracting and building. Mr. Griffith is a prominent citizen, is a republican in politics, and in 1887-8 served on the city council for the sixth ward. He is a member of Summit City lodge, No. 170, F. & A. M., chapter No. 19, council No. 4, commandery No. 4, K. T., lodge of Perfection, Princes of Jerusalem, the consistory at Indianapolis, and Howard council, R. A. Mr. Griffith was married in the fall of 1865, to Sarah A. Morton, who was born in Adams county, and they have had five children, four of whom survive.

Fred H. Boester, carpenter, contractor and builder, with office at 164 Griffith street, Fort Wayne, is well known as an enterprising citizen. He was born in Hanover, Germany, September 9, 1841, son of August and Mary (Huge) Boester. June 1, 1860, he started from his native land for America, and came directly to Fort Wayne after landing. Here he set in to learn the carpenter's trade, and becoming a master of his craft, began contracting in 1873, and at this he has been quite successful. Mr. Boester is a member of the German Lutheran church, and in politics is a democrat. He was married in 1866, to Frederika Neuer, who was born in this city in 1847. Seven children have been born to them, of whom five are living.

Frederick Miller, of the firm of Miller & Schele, contractors and builders, began to acquire a trade at the age of fifteen, when in his native land, Germany, commenced to learn the bricklayer's craft. This was his occupation for a considerable period, part of the time in this city, whither he came when he immigrated in 1866. For fifteen years his business has been that of a contractor, and he has been a member of the firm with which he is now connected for ten years. He has built some of the best residences in the city, and one of his most important undertakings is the erection of the new works of the Fort Wayne Jenney electric light company. He is an honorable and capable man, highly esteemed by the community, and is a practical builder, with a thorough knowledge of his work in all of its details. He is ranked as one of the leading contractors. Mr. Miller was born in Germany, October 3, 1841, son of Frederick Miller and Mollie Plenge, both natives of Germany. His father was born in 1806, and is living in his native land, where the mother, who was born in 1816, died about 1869. Six of their children are living, of whom Frederick is the oldest. He was married in 1869 to Louisa Menze, who was born in Germany in 1848, and they have nine children: Frederick, Lizzie, Mary, Herman, Sophia, Charles, Clara, William and Arthur. Mr. Miller is in politics a democrat, and he and family are members of St. Paul's German Lutheran church.

While in his native country, George Jaap, now one of the leading contractors in cut stone, learned his trade, and upon arriving at New York in 1873, he engaged in contracting in masonry. Two years later he removed to Allegheny, Penn., afterward spent fourteen months at Canton, Ohio, and then went further west, and was engaged for two years in the cattle business, making his home with an uncle, Andrew Ritchie, a wealthy cattle raiser at Fayette county, Iowa. In 1881 he became engaged with Pierce, Morgan & Co., contractors at Lafayette, Ind., in the erection of the county court-house. He was afterward foreman in the construction of the court-house at Terre Haute, and then came to Fort Wayne in 1885. Going first upon a farm in this county for two years, he returned to the city, and in May, 1888, began contracting, purchasing the business of Henry Paul & Co., on Columbia street. He does a good business, contracting and dealing in lime and cement, with office and yards at Nos. 79 and 81 East Columbia street, and gives employment to an average force of four stone cutters and four laborers. Mr. Jaap was born at Kilmarnock, Ayrshire, Scotland, in 1855. He was married in July, 1884, to Mary Dignan, of this city, and they have had four children, three now living. He is a member of Fort Wayne Temple, No. 1, Patriotic Circle; Liberty Assembly, No. 2,315, Knights of Labor; No. 101, Pheonix lodge, K. P., and Caledonian Society, Fort Wayne branch.

In 1868 John McMullen came to Fort Wayne, having emigrated from his native land in the previous year. He began an apprenticeship as a carpenter at once, and advancing rapidly in his trade, began contracting in 1876. He also furnished designs and drawings for buildings, and in all branches of his business has been quite successful. He was born in county Antrim, Ireland, April 10, 1844, the son of Michael and Mary (Duncan) McMullen. The father died in 1859, and in 1875 Mr. McMullen brought from Ireland his mother, two sisters and two brothers, who, with the exception of one brother who went to Australia, all reside in the city. Mr. McMullen was married in 1876, to Elizabeth Franks, of Fort Wayne, who died in 1878, leaving one child, who died a month later. He is a member of the congregation of the Catholic cathedral.

Particularly in his specialty of bridge abutment building, Herman W. Tapp ranks with the leading contractors and builders of Fort Wayne. He was born in Berlin, Germany, December 14, 1856, the son of Ferdinand and Wilhelmina (Siedschlag) Tapp. The family emigrated to the United States in 1860, and resided at Chicago until 1865, when they removed to Fort Wayne, their present home. The father is a bridge contractor, and is engaged with his son Robert W., under the firm name of F. Tapp & Son. Herman W. Tapp studied in childhood at the Lutheran schools, the Clay street public school and the Fort Wayne commercial college. At the age of fifteen years he began work as a stone cutter, and pursued that trade about six years, then engaging in contracting. Mr. Tapp is a member of Wayne lodge, No. 25, F. & A. M., Fort Wayne chapter, No. 19, R. A. M., and Fort Wayne commandery K. T. He is also a member of Harmony lodge I. O. O. F. Mr. Tapp was married in 1879 to Lizzie M. Winter, who was born in Allen county in 1857. To them three daughters and one son have been born: Ruth, Fred, Bessie and Elsie. Mrs. Tapp is a member of the Third Presbyterian church.

A well known contractor of Fort Wayne, Peter Hensel, is a native of the south of Germany, born January 15, 1845. In his native land he learned the trade of brick and stone mason, and in 1867 emigrated to America, and came to Fort Wayne in July of the same year, where his hopes of prosperity have been amply realized. He worked at his trade in this city until 1877, and then embarked in contracting for brick and stone construction, at which he has since been engaged, and a large number of first class buildings display his handiwork. Mr. Hensel was married in 1869, to Caroline Dissellhot, a native of Prussia, and to them six children have been born. Mr. Hensel is a member of the German Reformed church.

Among the prosperous contractors and builders should be named Fred. Bandt, who is a native of Prussia, born December 11, 1850. He came to the new world in 1872, and reached Fort Wayne September 10, 1872. He had learned his trade in his native land, and this occupied him after reaching Fort Wayne until 1879, when he began the business of contracting. Among the buildings which show evidence of his skill are Sidel's block, Fleming's block, part of the Kerr Murray shops, Olds' wheel works, etc., and a number of business houses, and numerous residences, such as the Dewald and William Dryer residences. Mr. Bandt was married in 1876 to Wilhelmina Bock, who was born in

Prussia, and came to America in 1870. To them have been born seven children, of whom five are living: William, Fred, Charles, Louisa and Gustave. He and wife are members of the Emanuel Lutheran church.

A well known contractor in masonry at Fort Wayne, Frederick Rippe, was born in Bremen, Germany, on May 5, 1845. He was educated in the public schools of his native country and began the trade of brick and stone mason when fifteen years of age. This he followed in the old country until 1871, and then emigrated and came directly to Fort Wayne, where he has since resided. He began contracting about 1879 and was so occupied about three years. He was foreman for Henry Paul for five years and then resumed contracting. He was married in 1872, in Fort Wayne, to Adelheit Beyer, and to them seven children have been born, four of whom are living: Mr. and Mrs. Rippe are members of St. Paul's Lutheran church. Their children that are living are: Henry, Lizzie, Louis and Charles.

Among the enterprising men of Fort Wayne engaged in contracting and building, a creditable place is occupied by Henry A. Hoffman, who embarked in the business in 1879. Mr. Hoffman's father, Peter Hoffman, was a native of Germany, who was brought to Ohio in childhood by his parents, who afterward removed to Adams county, Ind., where Peter Hoffman married Mary Fuhrman, of the same nativity. There their son Henry A., was born, November 15, 1847. In 1853, the family came to Allen county and settled at Mechanicsburg, a suburb of Fort Wayne, the father having rented the farm he had entered in Adams county. Peter Hoffman was employed at Fort Wayne as a carpenter until his death about 1855, and his widow then returned to the Adams county farm, where she now resides. These parents left seven children, one besides Henry A., residing in this city. The latter received his education in the Lutheran schools here and in Adams county, and at nineteen years of age began work as a carpenter's apprentice, and speedily became one of the leading men in his calling. He has been a resident of Fort Wayne since his fifteenth year, with the exception of a period during 1869-70, spent in the western states. He was married in 1874, to Emily Bly, of Adams county, and they have four children: Susan, Ellen, Louis and Anna. Mr. Hoffman and family are members of the Lutheran church.

John H. Coolman, contractor, a valued citizen of Fort Wayne, was born at Medina, Ohio, in 1850, and came to Fort Wayne when quite young, his parents making their home in Allen county in the same year. His father, William Coolman, a native of Ohio, being a farmer by occupation, purchased a farm four miles north of the city, where he lived until his death in 1863. After the death of his father, John H. Coolman returned to Ohio, and there learned his trade. He engaged in contracting in 1871, and has done an extensive business. From 1877 to 1879, he was in California, and was there engaged in the same business, and in 1881 made his home at Fort Wayne. Mr. Coolman was married in

1874, to Mary J. Corderay. He is a member of the Cathedral Catholic church.

John Suelzer, one of the prominent contractors of Fort Wayne, embarked in that business in the spring of 1882, and since then has built the Berghoff brewery, since the fire, St. Paul's Catholic church, the asylum for feeble-minded children, the Catholic church at Peru, schoolhouses in Columbia City, and Wabash, and Louis Fox's building. He was born near Cologne, on the German bank of the Rhine, November 26, 1853, the son of Peter and Elizabeth (Neuhauser) Suelzer. He lost his mother when he was twenty-three weeks old, and his father when he was six years of age, so that he was at an early age dependent upon his own resources. When he was fifteen he learned the carpenter's trade, and at nineteen emigrated to the United States. Landing at New York, he immediately purchased a ticket for Dallas, Texas, at which place he spent twenty-two months. He was afterward engaged at Conway, Ark., Morrillton, Memphis, Cario, Cape Girardeau, Mo., and Kankakee, Ill., before coming to Fort Wayne. In September, 1881, he went to Germany and was married January 31, 1882, to Catherine Suelzer, who was born April 8, 1856, and then returned to Fort Wayne, which has since been his home. Mr. and Mrs. Suelzer, and their children, Agnes, Mary, John, Bertie and Annie, are members of St. Peter's Catholic church.

John T. Crawford, contractor and builder at Fort Wayne, residing on the corner of Butler and Clinton streets, was born five miles west from Fort Wayne, on June 14, 1854, and is the son of James and Rachel (Mood) Crawford, both of whom were natives of Ohio. The parents came to Allen county in 1843 and located on a farm in Aboit township, and were among the pioneers of that region. The father died in 1883 at the age of fifty-seven years, and the mother died in 1885 at the age of fifty-three years. John T. Crawford was reared on the farm and attended the country schools. He came to Fort Wayne in 1878 and finished the carpenter's trade, and worked at the same until 1884, when he began the business of contractor and builder, at which he has since continued, meeting with success. Mr. Crawford was married in 1878 to Clara E. Crawford, who was born in Lowell, Ind., and to their union three daughters have been born: Ettie May, Nellie Blanch, and Alma Ethel. Both Mr. and Mrs. Crawford are members of the First United Brethren church.

A leading contractor and builder of Fort Wayne, Charles H. Schaper, was born in Adams township, Allen county, July 8, 1860, the son of Goodlet and Louisa (Weese) Schaper. His parents, who are natives of Germany, on coming to this country, settled first at Fort Wayne and then removed to Adams township, where they have since resided. Mr. Shaper was reared on the farm, and received his early education in the country schools. He began the learning of the trade of carpenter in about 1878, and in 1881 he removed to Fort Wayne, and finished the acquirement of the trade. He worked as a carpenter until

1884, and then began taking contracts, and being successful has since been engaged as a contractor. He did the carpenter work on the Fort Wayne Jenney electric light works, and was engaged in the rebuilding in 1889 and has been engaged on many other buildings, notably St. Paul's Lutheran church, the new Lutheran school building, and the large barn for Ryan Bros., and makes a specialty of heavy buildings, framing barns, etc. He employs on the average, fifteen men.

Well known as a contractor in the construction of brick and stone work, is Ambrose W. Kintz, member of the firm of Pratt & Kintz, of Fort Wayne. He was born in Ohio, February 22, 1842, the son of Alexander and Phœbe (Echenrode) Kintz. His parents were both of German descent, but natives of this country, and became residents of Allen county in 1844, first settling on a farm near the city. The father is a practical brick-mason, having followed that trade most of his life, and in 1846 he came to this city. He is now a resident of the ninth ward, in his seventy-first year, and his wife is aged sixty-nine. Mr. Kintz was reared in the city, attending the public schools, and when about seventeen years of age, learned the trade with his father. In 1885 he began contracting, and in 1886 formed the partnership with Benjamin Pratt. They are actively engaged in general contracting in brick and stone construction. In 1862 Mr. Kintz enlisted in Company E, Fifty-fifth regiment Indiana volunteers, and served both in that regiment and in the Ninety-first Indiana. He was married in 1874 to Lucia Miller, of Fort Wayne, and to them three children have been born: Daniel, Frank and Lulu. Mr. Kintz is a member of Fort Wayne lodge, K. of P., and of Sion S. Bass post, G. A. R.

One of the old settlers of Fort Wayne was Henry Schroeder, who was one of the pioneer marble cutters of the city, and a worthy and highly esteemed man. He was the proprietor of a marble yard for a number of years. He died in 1870 and his wife, Barbara Weipert, passed away nine years afterward. They were both natives of Germany. Herman C. Schroeder, son of the above, born at Fort Wayne, February 3, 1857, is the eldest of five children born, all of whom are living with one exception. He was educated in the Lutheran schools, and learned the carpenter's trade with Frederick Hostmeyer. He worked at his trade until 1888, then embarking in the general contracting business, at which he is successful to a notable degree. Mr. Schroeder was married in 1885 to Anna Osterman, of Allen county, and they have one daughter, Lizzie. He and wife are members of the Lutheran church.

Frederick Kraft is a member of one of the early German families, that of Ernst and Louisa (Eichkoff) Kraft. Ernst Kraft came to Allen county about 1842 or '43, and worked on the old Wabash & Erie canal. He next purchased a piece of land of forty acres in Marion township, and in 1845 he returned to Germany and moved his family to his new farm home. He followed farming the balance of his life, and added to his original tract about fifty acres. His death occurred in 1849, in his fifty-fourth year, and the mother died in 1879 in her seventy-third year. To them five children were born, four of whom survive. One of these, Frederick Kraft, who was born in the south of Germany, January 28, 1841, is now a prominent contractor and builder. He received his education in the Lutheran schools, and remained on the farm until his twenty-fourth year, during the winters learning the carpenter's trade. In 1865 he removed to Fort Wayne and went to work at his trade. In 1870 he began contracting, at which he has been notably successful. Among the buildings which Mr. Kraft has erected are the Trentman block, Sidel's block and Bursley's block, on Calhoun street, Pixley & Long block on Berry street, L. M. Ninde's building on Berry and Harrison streets, two foundry buildings for Mr. Bass, and the Olds' wheel works and many others. He was married March 5, 1865, to Lizzetta Mauzan, who was born in Allen county in 1848, and died in 1868, leaving one son, Henry, who has since died. He was married a second time, March 8, 1872, to Sophia Henning, who was born in Germany in 1850. To this union eight children have been born: Louisa, Charles, Minnie, William, Louis, Emma and Sophia. Fred, the fifth child, died in 1883. Mr. and Mrs. Kraft are members of the Lutheran church.

Among the worthy German families that have become valued residents of Allen county during the past forty years, is that of Christian and Mary (Huxoll) Gallmeier, who came to this country in the spring of 1850, and settled on a farm in Adams county. They passed their lives happily, the mother dying August 14, 1874, and the father December 3, 1887. Their son, Ernst Gallmeier, was born November 10, 1849, was about six months old when the parents settled in this county, and he grew up upon the farm, gaining his education in the public and Lutheran schools. In 1866 he came to Fort Wayne, and began learning the carpenter's trade, which has since been his occupation in this city. Mr. Gallmeier was married May 1, 1879, to Minerva Waldo, of Fort Wayne. He and wife are members of St. Paul's Lutheran church. Mr. Gallmeier is one of the capable and enterprising men in his business, and is a good citizen.

A well known contractor and builder of Fort Wayne, William Gallmeier, was born in North Germany, May 6, 1845, and emigrated to the United States in 1865. He was educated in the public schools of Germany, and then learned the carpenter's trade. Upon arriving in America, he located in Fort Wayne and obtained work at his trade. In 1872, he began contracting, forming a partnership with Frederick Korte, with whom he has continued in business. Mr. Gallmeier was married in 1870, to Eliza Meier, who was born in Hanover, Germany. To them nine children have been born, four of whom are dead. The living children are: Louisa, Frederick, Mary, Clara and Annie. Mr. Gallmeier and family are members of St. Paul's Lutheran church, of which he has been one of the trustees since about 1884.

One of the successful contractors of Fort Wayne, Gregory Lauer, first engaged in contracting in the spring of 1884, and is doing a good business, employing four men. Mr. Lauer is a native of Germany, born October 21, 1850, to John G. and Maggie (Hargerreiter) Lauer. The next year the father emigrated to New York to find a new home for his family. He settled in New York and sent for his wife, who started with her three children to join her husband, but she was taken sick at Havre, France, and died, leaving the children, the eldest of whom was sixteen, to make the voyage alone. After five years' residence at New York the father and children came to Allen county, where he purchased a farm about ten miles south of Fort Wayne. After twenty years of farming he sold his place and removed to the city, where he now lives. Gregory Lauer left the farm in his eighteenth year, and began learning the carpenter's trade at Fort Wayne. September 8, 1874, he was married to Catherine Trampe, a native of this county, and they have had seven children: George, Catherine, Gustave, Christina, Jesse (deceased), Jacob and Gregory. Mr. Lauer and family are members of the St. Mary's Catholic church.

One of the successful contractors and builders of Fort Wayne, Frederick Korte, was born in Westphalia, Germany, October 25, 1847. He emigrated to America in 1865, and came at once to Fort Wayne, where he learned the carpenter's trade, and worked at the same until 1872, and then began contracting in partnership with William Gallmeier, with whom he has since continued in business. They have erected numerous buildings in the city, including both business and dwelling houses, and have met with much success. He was married May 6, 1870, to Sophia Berghorn, a native of Germany, and to them ten children have been born, six of whom survive: William, Elizabeth, Minnie, Sophia, Henry, and Ernst. Mr. Korte and family are members of St. Paul's Lutheran church, and in politics he is a republican.

Formerly a partner of Frederick Roth and S. Keller in the stone cutting business, and now engaged with the firm of Roth & Keller, Christian Keefer, of Fort Wayne, is well-known as one of the masters of his craft. He was born in Preble township, Adams county, Ind., March 4, 1845, the son of John N. and Sophia (Gabel) Keefer. His parents were natives of Prussia and came to Indiana in 1838 among the early settlers, settling first in Adams county. In 1861 they removed to Fort Wayne, where they died, the father in 1864 and the mother in 1874. To these parents three children were born, of whom one son is deceased. Christian Keefer was reared in Adams county, and came with his parents to this city in 1861. The next year he went west, and for nine months drove the stage and carried the United States mail between St. Joseph, Mo., and Council Bluffs, Iowa. Then returning to Fort Wayne he began learning the stone cutter's trade, which has since been his occupation. In 1870 he formed the partnership above referred to, under the title of S. Keller & Co., which was subsequently changed to Keefer & Roth. He retired from the firm in 1882. Mr. Keefer was married in 1873 to Louisa King, of Fort Wayne, and to them a son and daughter have been born, Edward and Emma. Mr. Keefer in

XVI

politics is a liberal democrat, and he is a member of Concordia lodge, No. 228, I. O. O. F.

John W. Muldoon, practical painter, located at No. 12 East Berry street, Fort Wayne, is a native of this county, born in Marion township, August 11, 1858. His father, Patrick Muldoon, a prominent man among the early settlers, was born in Ireland in 1827, and immigrated to this country, and was for a while engaged in contracting, then for some time in the milling and grocery business at Williamsport, subsequently being occupied in agriculture, until his death, which occurred February 19, 1864, in Allen county. He was married on Jannary 30, 1851, to Margaret Killen, who was born in Pennsylvania in 1833, and now resides at 280 East Lewis street, this city. They have seven children, of whom four are now living, John Muldoon being the youngest. At twelve years he came to Fort Wayne, and when eighteen began to learn the painter's trade. When twenty-one years old he went to Chicago, and a year later returned to this city, and was for a year and a half in the employment of the Pittsburgh, Fort Wayne and Chicago railroad, as fireman. In 1884 he resumed the painting business, and is now doing a good business, employing eight men, and has an extensive reputation as a skillful and accurate painter. Besides the general business he gives considerable attention to the finer branches of his art. He removed to his present location in March, 1889. He is a democrat, politically; is a member of the Catholic church, and of the Catholic Knights of America; and socially is one of the popular young men of the city.

Joseph H. Brimmer has been engaged in sign painting, giving attention also to the finer departments of his art, such as the painting of pictures, banners for societies and the like, in Fort Wayne, since 1872, when he came to this city from Chicago, where for one year he had been occupied in his profession. He is now regarded as one of the leading artists in his line in this part of the state. Mr. Brimmer was born in Lancaster, Penn., February 13, 1850, son of Joseph and Mary (Hutchinson) Brimmer, natives of that state. His father, born in 1808, died in 1885; his mother now resides in Pennsylvania at the age of seventy-three. They had ten children, of whom three are living, Joseph being the second of these. In 1865 he began learning sign painting, and in 1868 embarked in the business, removing in 1871 to Chicago. He is a worthy citizen; politically is a republican; fraternally is a Mason of the degree of Knights Templar; and he and wife are members of the English Lutheran church. He was married in 1875 to Rhoda E. Buckles, a native of Ohio, and they have had these children: John E., Mary E. and Clara L., living, and one Joseph H., jr., deceased.

Henry Hild, a well known carriage and sign painter, has been a resident of Fort Wayne since 1872, and has during that period achieved substantial success in his business and is held in esteem as a worthy and valuable citizen. He was born March 8, 1846, at Pittsburgh, Penn. His father was a native of Germany, born in 1813, who came to America in 1837, followed teaching as a profession, and died at Pittsburgh in 1869. He married Elizabeth Marquardt, born in 1809, and died in Iowa, November, 1888, and they had five children, of whom three survive, Henry being the second of these in age. In 1862 Henry Hild began learning the painter's trade in Pittsburgh, and followed it there until 1872. In 1870 he was married to Caroline Schust, who was born in Germany in 1848, and came to this country when an infant with her parents, who settled at Fort Wayne. They have three children, Albert D., Otto G., and Emma W. Mr. Hild is a republican, and he and wife are members of the German Lutheran church.

Among the worthy citizens of German birth should be mentioned Henry Schultz, a well known contractor and plasterer. He was born in Prussia, November 18, 1840, and immigrated to the United States in 1864, coming directly to Fort Wayne from New York. While in the old country he learned the trade of mason, but after arriving in this country he engaged in plastering, to which he has since given his attention. He began contracting in about 1879. Mr. Schultz was married in 1869 to Henrietta Brink Kroager, who was born in Prussia. To their union ten children have been born, eight of whom survive: Louisa, William, Caroline, Sophia, Henrietta, Katie, Henry, Frederick and Albert. Mr. Schultz and family are members of St. Paul's Lutheran church.

In the business of slate and tin roofing and manufacture of tin and galvanized iron work, John Baker, of Fort Wayne, is conspicuous. He was born in this city April 24, 1849, son of Conrad and Bridget (O'Donnell) Baker. The father was a native of Germany, and was born in 1821. He emigrated to America and afterward came to Fort Wayne. He was a shoemaker by trade, and followed that occupation for a number of years. He served as street commissioner of Fort Wayne two years, and was afterward in the saw-mill business at Decatur, Ind. His death occurred in this city, April 11, 1884. His widow, who was born in Ireland in 1821, and was married to him at Pittsburgh, Penn., now makes her home on West Berry street, this city. John Baker was reared in Fort Wayne, and was educated in the Catholic schools. In 1865 he set in to learn the slate roofing and tin and galvanized iron work, and has followed that trade ever since. He began contracting in 1871, forming a partnership with John H. Welch, with whom he continued in business until December, 1886, when the firm was dissolved, Mr. Baker buying the business. In February, 1887, he sold out to T. O. Gerow, and subsequently re-engaged in business, and continues at contracting. Mr. Baker was married September 14, 1875, to Fanny Welch, who was born in Ohio. Both are members of the Catholic cathedral.

In 1858 Robert Ogden, who had just immigrated from England, came to Fort Wayne, and embarked here in the business of plumber, which had been the trade of his father and grandfather in the old country and which he had thoroughly learned. In October, 1859, he removed to Dayton, Ohio, and in 1870 returned to this city, which has since been his home. He conducts a large plumbing buiness, with his establishment at No. 26 East Berry street, and has achieved an honorable reputation. He was the first plumber to establish himself in Fort Wayne. Mr. Ogden was born near Manchester, England, January 9, 1825, to John and Alice Ogden, and when a small boy began learning his trade with his father. He has been three times married. His present wife, to whom he was married July 3, 1888, is Agnes H., daughter of John Fowles, of this city. She is a member of the First Presbyterian church. Mr. Ogden is a member of the Episcopal church, and is a prominent Mason, being a Knight Templar and a member of the lodge of Perfection. He is also connected with the Sons of St. George. He is a republican, and a charter member of the Morton club. He stands high in both business and social circles.

James D. Madden, a prominent plumber of Fort Wayne, was born in county Derry, Ireland, March 25, 1856, the son of Patrick and Rose (McGuigan) Madden. He was reared in his native land until he reached the age of seventeen, when he came to America, and shortly after reaching this country entered upon an apprenticeship with Hoolihan & Barry, of Philadelphia, with whom he spent five years learning the plumbing business. In the spring of 1878 he opened a plumbing establishment on the corner of Second and Vine streets, Philadelphia, and two years later came to Fort Wayne. He is now the proprietor of a handsome plumbing establishment at 101 Calhoun street, and enjoys a large custom. He is industrious in business, is full of energy and enterprise and possesses more than ordinary tact and ability. He married in Philadelphia, February 12, 1877, to Ellen Crilly, who died August 22, 1877. He was married to Hannah Lyons, his present wife, September 9, 1882, by whom he has three children: Lawrence, Rose and Patrick Henry. Mr. Madden and wife are members of the Catholic church. In politics he is a republican.

Among the leading plumbers of the city is enrolled C. W. Bruns, one of the enterprising young business men of Fort Wayne. He was born in this city, November 24, 1865, the son of William and Rosa Bruns, who reside at 130 Gay street. He received his early education at the German Lutheran schools, and between the ages of fourteen and seventeen, learned the trade of painter. At the age of eighteen he graduated from the Fort Wayne business college, and then turned his attention to plumbing. He spent a year and a half with the firm of McLachlin & Bowen, and was then employed four years as bookkeeper for Robert Ogden. In the fall of 1888 he opened a plumbing and gas fitting establishment at 166 Calhoun street, and is laying substantial foundations for business success.

M. Baltes, a well-known German citizen of Fort Wayne, and a manufacturer of white lime and dealer in lime, stone, cement, sewer pipes, fire brick, clay, etc., at No. 3 Harrison street, residence at No. 63 Harrison, was born in Prussia in 1836. In 1854 he emigrated, landed at New York city, and came at once to Indiana and for several years worked in the neighborhood of Huntington. He next engaged in wheat dealing, and subsequently in the marble business at Huntington. In 1861 he settled at Fort Wayne, and engaged in contracting, and dealing in lime, brick, stone, etc., and continued at contracting until about 1879, when he abandoned that branch of the business, since when he has carried on his manufacturing and mercantile business. The lime kilns situated at Huntington were built in 1868, and have a capacity of 2,500 bushels per day. The stone quarries of Mr. Baltes are also located at Huntington, and produce large quantities of all kinds of building stone. Mr. Baltes has figured conspicuously in the politics of Allen county. He has taken a prominent part in city public affairs, has served in the common council, and is at present a trustee of Saint Mary's church. Mr. Baltes was married in 1862 to Miss Margaret Gabele, of Fort Wayne, and to this union one child was born. Mrs. Baltes died in 1863, and her child died a month later. In 1865 Mr. Baltes was married to Caroline Gabele, and they have had four children, two of whom survive, Clara and Edward.

Walter S. Harrison, sign and ornamental painter, was born at St. Louis, Mo., July 5, 1853, son of Dr. Abram W. Harrison, who was born in Greenville, Tenn., in 1800, graduated at the Indiana medical college at Indianapolis, in 1842. He was the first freight agent at that city for the Bellefontaine railroad, and was appointed postmaster at Laporte, Ind., during the administration of President Jackson. In 1859, he removed to St. Louis, amd there practiced medicine until 1862, when he became a surgeon in the U. S. army, being first stationed at Jefferson City, and afterward at the Washington hospital at Memphis, Tenn., where he remained until the close of the war. He was a prominent Mason. He died at Chillicothe, Mo., April 13, 1867. In 1851 he married Priscilla C. Bush, born in Rockingham county, Va., in 1832, who came to Indiana with her parents in 1834, and settled in Boone county. She died December 5, 1888, at Indianapolis. Of this marriage Walter S. is the only child living. He learned his trade with George Peisch & Bro., at St. Louis, and in 1877, engaged in the business at Indianapolis. In 1885 he came to Fort Wayne, where he has been successful, and also gained a reputation as an active and public spirited citizen. His business location is at No. 32 East Columbia street, and 134 Broadway, and he is a member of the firm of Hull & Harrison. He is a member of the Y. M. C. A., one of the building committee, and one of the members of the first and second board of directors. Of Summit City lodge, No. 36, A. O. U. W., he was the organizer, and is a past masterworkman of that order. He is of that lodge, past chancellor, and a member of Fort Wayne lodge, No. 116, K. of P., and past chief of Knights of the Golden Eagle and member of Wayne Castle, No. 2. He and wife are members of the Baptist church, of which he is the clerk, and he is secretary of the Fort Wayne Baptist association, composed of eighteen churches of that denomination. He was married September 11, 1879, to Mary L. Moore, who was born at St. Louis in 1859, and they have two children: Edgar J. and Edna L.

Joseph W. Cromwell, a lumber dealer and prominent citizen of Fort Wayne, Ind., was born at Newburg, Orange county, N. Y., in 1825. When twenty-one years of age he went to Maryland and lived for ten years in Frederick City, being engaged in the lumber business. Going next to West Virginia, he was a citizen of Fairmount, that state, during the war. While at Fairmount he had a government contract for furnishing walnut gunstocks for Springfield rifles, and in the year 1863 that section being invaded by Confederate forces, his mills were burned by the rebels, destroying in the neighborhood of 25,000 or 50,000 gun stocks, which with the mill were a total loss to him. He was provost marshal of the district, including Fairmount, and had several narrow escapes, and was captured at one time but paroled. In 1870 he made his home at Fort Wayne, where he has since resided. After coming here he was interested for five years in the lumber business with Hoffman Bros., and then began for himself. In connection with his son he owns a mill in the Indian territory, handling black walnut timber exclusively. Mr. Cromwell has been treasurer of the Y. M. C. A. since its organization, and was one of the building committee. He has given a large share of his time and money to that work during the past fifteen years. He is a prominent advocate of temperance, and in all respects a worthy citizen. His church connection is with the First Presbyterian church, of which he is an elder, and for several years he was president of the Allen county Sunday School Union, and also for the district composed of Allen, Huntington and Wells counties. Mr. Cromwell was married in Maryland, and losing his wife married again in West Virginia. He has three sons: William O. is a student; Clarence W., is in Indian territory, and Joseph C. is in the lumber business in Fort Wayne.

BANKING HOUSES.

The sound financial basis on which business is conducted in Fort Wayne, is due no doubt in a considerable degree, to the general confidence in the safe management of the banks. There has never been a bank failure in this city, and there has never been a time of financial depression when there was any alarm for their perfect solvency or any demand for deposits that was not fully and promptly met.

The first bank and for a long time the only one in the city, was the Fort Wayne branch of the State Bank of Indiana, which was established here in August, 1835. Its president was Allen Hamilton, known and respected everywhere for his integrity, who was succeeded in 1841 by Samuel Hanna; the cashier was Hugh McCulloch, late secretary of the treasury. These men were the founders of the banking system of Fort Wayne, which was built upon the strong foundation stones of integrity, fair dealing and thorough and exact knowledge of finance. The charter of this bank expired January 1, 1856, when it was re-organized as the branch of the Bank of the State of Indiana, with Hugh McCulloch, president, and Charles D. Bond, cashier. In 1865 it was merged in the Fort Wayne National bank, with Jesse L. Williams president, and Jared D. Bond, cashier. The Old National bank is the successor of the Fort Wayne National bank, and although the name is changed the business has continued from as far back as 1835. The First National bank was organized in 1863, by J. D. Nuttman. In 1883, at a meeting of the directors, Mr. O. A. Simons was elected president. Mr. Simon's sudden death in 1887, demanded another election of officers, and J. H. Bass was chosen president; Hon. William Fleming, vice president; Lem R. Hartman, cashier; W. L. Pettit, assistant cashier.

Upon the retirement of Mr. Nuttman from the presidency of the First National bank, he immediately opened a private bank under the name of Nuttman & Co. Mr. Oliver S. Hanna is cashier. The bank enjoys a splendid reputation.

Stephen B. Bond was admitted to partnership in the banking house of Allen, Hamilton & Co. in 1855, and in 1860 Charles McCulloch was also admitted as a partner.

The firm was dissolved on July 1, 1874, and the Hamilton National bank was immediately organized to succeed to its business. Charles McCulloch was elected president; John Mohr, jr., cashier, and Joseph D. Mohr, assistant cashier. The first board of directors which has remained almost unchanged, was Charles McCulloch, Jesse L. Williams, Montgomery Hamilton, William Fleming, Frederick Eckert, August Trentman and Edward P. Williams.

The officers of the Old National bank are S. B. Bond, president; O. P. Morgan, vice president; J. D. Bond, cashier, and James C. Woodworth, assistant cashier.

The combined capital of the three National banks is about one million two hundred thousand dollars, and the deposits in round numbers two million of dollars. The paid in capital stock of the Hamilton National bank is $200,000, of the First National bank, $300,000, and of the Old National bank, $350,000. The stockholders of these banks are the active business men of the city, and they will see that there is no suffering from lack of bank accommodation.

The Merchants' National bank was organized on March 15, 1865, and was chartered on May 1, 1865. The first location was on the northwest corner of Berry and Calhoun streets. It was afterward removed to the northwest corner of Main and Calhoun streets, where it remained until discontinued. Peter P. Bailey was the first president, and Dwight Klinck, cashier. In July, 1868, S. C. Evans was elected president, and Dr. John S. Irwin was elected to succeed Dwight Klinck, who had resigned. In February, 1873, Dr. Irwin resigned and C. M. Dawson was elected to succeed. The bank had an authorized capital of $300,000, and a paid up capital of $100,000.

For many years Isaac Lauferty has been engaged as a private banker in the Aveline House block, but discontinued business in the spring of 1889 because of ill-health.

Hon. Hugh McCulloch.— In the latter part of May, 1833, Hugh McCulloch was examined by the judges of the supreme court of Indiana and licensed to practice law in all the courts of the state. He had chosen his profession but had not decided where he would locate. Alhough northern Indiana was mostly a wilderness, he was advised to go north, a..d in a few weeks afterward he began the practice of law at Fort Wayne. For a short time he filled the position of judge of the common pleas court, but fate had decreed that he was not to continue a lawyer. In the winter of 1833 and 1834 the State Bank of Indiana was chartered, and when the branch of that institution was established at Fort Wayne, he was appointed cashier and manager. Although he had no practical experience in banking, and had not yet decided to abandon the profession which he had chosen, he went to work with a determination to establish the bank upon a good financial basis and then resign. This resolution, however, was overcome by circumstances. He became interested in the business in which he had made a temporary venture, and was soon made one of the active directors of the bank, and meeting four times a year with the managers of the other branches, at Indianapolis, he formed acquaintances that materially assisted him toward future promotions in life. The State Bank of Indiana, although established in a new state, and committed to the charge of inexperienced men, was a very successful institution, and in addition to helping materially in the improvement of the state, it secured to the commonwealth a net profit of nearly three millions of dollars, which became the basis of her large and well-managed school fund. The Bank of the State of Indiana commenced business January 1, 1857, as a successor to the State bank, and Hugh McCulloch was chosen president of all the branches, with headquarters at Indianapolis. The business of this institution was equally successful until the national banking system was established, when, congress having passed a law taxing the circulation of all state banks, it went into liquidation. In 1863, Salmon P. Chase, then secretary of the treasury, offered to Mr. McCulloch the position of comptroller of the currency, and being appointed by President Lincoln, he assumed the organization of the national bank bureau of the treasury department, and the management of the national banking system. Within less than two years the state banks throughout the country were superceded by the national, and all was accomplished without any disturbance to the current business of the people. The labors of the first comptroller of the currency were severe and incessant, but in later days he could well feel rewarded in the knowledge that he was instrumental in establishing the best system of banking that this country or any other has ever seen. When Mr. Lincoln's second cabinet was formed Mr. McCulloch was the leading name mentioned in business and financial circles for the position of secretary of the treasury, on account of his recognized ability and success as a financier, and in March, 1865, he became the chief of the treasury department. He immediately announced his policy to be: First, to raise money by loans to pay the soldiers of the great Union army, and all other demands upon the treasury; second, to fund and put in proper shape all obligations of the government; third, to take the first steps toward an improvement of the value of the paper currency, with the ultimate view of a return to specie payment. The war had just ended, vast sums were due from the government and the responsibiity of the management of the treasury department was enormous, and the work to to be done greater than that of any secretary from that time to the present day. The work was well done, and the policy adopted by Mr. McCulloch was steadily pursued by succeeding secretaries until gold, silver and paper currency became of equal value, in conducting the business of the country. For twenty-five years Mr. McCulloch did not lose a day from rigorous attention to business. His health being good, his body robust, his active mind was always at work upon the problems and financial questions of the day, even when he was not at his desk. During his administration over one thousand millions of short-time debts of the United States were funded into long-time bonds and therefore required no attention for twenty years, except in payment of the annual interest. In 1870 Mr. McCulloch went to London as the resident and managing partner of the banking house of Jay Cooke, McCulloch & Co. Immediately (it could almost be said) did the business of this firm grow into large proportions, so that in a year's time no foreign firm was doing a larger or more profitable business with this country. Mr. McCullough was a partner in the London house only, and therefore could give no advice concerning the management of business in America. Had he been consulted he certainly would have advised the firm of Jay Cooke & Co. against attempting to furnish means for building so great a railroad system as the Northern Pacific. This was a project that would have tested the resources of a government, and the natural result was the failure of Jay Cooke & Co., and the financial panic of 1873. Having established good credit abroad, Mr. McCulloch kept the London firm from going down in the general wreck. As the interests of the American partners had to be withdrawn, the banking firm of McCulloch & Co. was established, which continued for a number of years, until on account of advancing age, Mr. McCulloch determined to retire from active business, and return to his home in the United States. He owned a farm about eight miles from the city of Washington, and as no part of his varied life had been so thoroughly enjoyed as the small part of it which had been spent on the farm; he hoped to spend his remaining years in the cultivation and improvement of his land. The resignation of Walter Q. Gresham, then secretary of the treasury, in 1884, to become circuit judge of the United States, induced President Arthur to request Mr. McCulloch to accept the management of the treasury department a second time, and help him close up his administration. When Mr. Cleveland became presidient, March 4, 1885, Mr. McCulloch again retired to private life, but he takes a deep interest in public affairs and political and economic questions of the day.

In politics Mr. McCulloch has always been conservative. He never sought office, nor was elected to one. His experence in public life has led him to conclude that a protective tariff is detrimental rather than beneficial to the best interests of the country. To quote his own words, he believes that what is needed by our manufacturers (to say nothing about our farmers, whose wants are becoming powerfully pressing) and will become more and more needed as their productive power increases, was wider markets for their manufactured goods, the very markets of which they have to a large extent been deprived by the measures that have been thought necessary to secure for them the control of the markets at home. Combinations to limit supplies and maintain high prices are the necessary outgrowth of our protective tariff. In his opinion a tariff for revenue only, and as largely as may be practicable upon luxuries, is the only protection this country needs. Mr. McCulloch, in the winter of 1887 and 1888, wrote a book entitled, "Men and Measures of Half a Century," which contains brief sketches of the prominent men that he became acquainted with, the political events and measures of the country, with his views upon them from a non-partisan standpoint. He is at the time that this article is written eighty years old, but in good health and enjoying the reward of a well spent life. He was married March 15, 1838, to Susan Man, of Plattsburgh, N. Y., and on March 15, 1888, they celebrated their golden wedding, surrounded by their four children, their grandchildren, and a large number of relatives and friends. Charles McCulloch, their oldest son, was born September 3, 1840, at Fort Wayne. He went into the bank of the State of Indiana, at an early age, afterward became a member of the banking house of Allen Hamilton & Co., and later was elected president of the Hamilton National bank.

In the group of strong and enterprising men who are prominent in the history of Fort Wayne, a notable one was Allen Hamilton. He was a native of Ireland, born in the county of Tyrone, in the year 1798, the son of Andrew Hamilton, an attorney, and his wife, Elizabeth Allen, a woman of noble qualities of mind and heart. Young Hamilton, at the age of eighteen, while listening to the recountal of the experiences during a visit to America, by a gentleman of some talent, determined to seek a new home in the western world. Accordingly, in July, 1817, having acquired sufficient means, he set sail for Quebec. A few days after arrival he was taken with ship fever, and for six weeks was confined to bed with this malady. When convalescent he sought a milder climate, but before he could go further than Montreal he was taken with a relapse, and upon his recovery found himself with very little money left. He was compelled to sell part of his wardrobe to obtain funds to make the journey to Philadelphia, which, however, he found it necessary to make in large measure on foot. Arriving there without means and friends, pale and weak from illness, he wandered about the streets in search of employment. He was finally attracted by a notice of laborers wanted, posted on the door of a store, and though he had already been refused a position as porter, he applied at this place, and by good fortune found a good Quaker, who promised his assistance. A few days later young Hamiltnn found himself in possession of a clerkship, with a salary of $100 a year and board. With an increased salary he remained there until the spring of 1820. He had a cousin, James Dill, previously a general in the army, and learning that Dill resided at Lawrenceburgh, Ind., Hamilton journeyed to that place, and found his cousin holding the office of clerk of the circuit court. An arrangement was soon made whereby the young man entered that office, writing six hours a day for his board and the use of the library as a student of law. There he formed the acquaintance of many men of note, among them Jesse L. Holman, one of the first judges of the supreme court of Indiana, and later associate justice of the United States district court, to the oldest daughter of whom Mr. Hamilton was subsequently married. In 1823 Mr. Hamilton was induced by Capt. Samuel C. Vance to visit Fort Wayne, at which the latter was appointed register of the land office, and the young law student concluded to remain here and perform the duties of deputy register while he pursued his reading. But perceiving that the country was thinly populated and that the law therefore was not a profitable occupation, he turned his attention to commerce, and purchased a small stock of goods on credit. His trade, which was principally with the Indians, was prosperous, and he soon enlarged his stock, and becoming associated with Cyrus Taber, he advanced rapidly in wealth and influence. Mr. Hamilton was largely indebted to the Indians for his start in business as he often averred, but his dealing with them was such that he always had their confidence and esteem, and he was especially liked by the Miamis, who confided their business to him. Chief Richardville, during his later years, entrusted his affairs to Mr. Hamilton, and never ventured upon any matter for himself or his tribe, without first consulting with his friend. Immense sums of money were frequently placed in his charge by the Indians, and large amounts were often disbursed by him to them. During the administration of Gen. Harrison, he was appointed agent for the Miamis, a position he held from 1841 to 1844, and during this period he disbursed $300,000 to $400,000 to the red men, to the satisfaction of both them and the government. His association with Richardville was marked by many a jocular contest. On one occasion Mr. Hamilton, riding a fine horse, passed the chief in front of the store of Hamilton & Taber, when the Indian exclaimed, "I strike on that horse, Mr. Hamilton," using a phrase common with the Indians when they wished to intimate their desire for anything as a gift of friendship. Mr. Hamilton at once turned the horse over to the chief, and waited for his revenge, which came while riding with Richardville along the Wabash, in sight of Indian reservations. Then he "struck" for a section of beautiful land, the deed for which the chief made without a murmur. In 1824 Mr. Hamilton received the appointment as sheriff, for the purpose of organizing Allen county, an office he subsequently held two years by election. In 1830 he was chosen county clerk, and held the office seven years. He was appointed as secretary of the commissioners to negotiate a treaty with the Miamis, and was tendered the same place in 1838, but declined the office. In 1840, though politically opposed to the administration of Van Buren, he was appointed one of the commissioners to treat with the Miamis for the extinguishment of their land titles in Indiana, and their removal to Kansas, and in that position he rendered the government valuable service. Of the important constitutional convention of 1850, Mr. Hamilton was a member, being elected by a large majority over a very popular democratic competitor, and as chairman of the committee on currency and banking, he was an important and valued member of that famous body. In the summer of 1857 he visited his old home and other places in Europe, and soon after his return in 1858 he was elected to the state senate, and was a member for four years, worthily representing the people of northeastern Indiana. He had been for several years president of the branch bank of Indiana at Fort Wayne, and the name of Allen Hamilton is still perpetuated by the Hamilton National bank, of which he was president until his death. He continued to devote himself to his large business interests until 1864, when he died at Saratoga, N. Y., August 23rd. His widow, a sister of Congressman W. S. Holman, was spared for many years, to witness the wonderful development of the city she was so long associated with, and died August 16, 1889, at the age of seventy-nine years. Mrs. Hamilton was born in 1810, and she was married to Mr. Hamilton at Aurora, in 1827. In the same year her residence at Fort Wayne began, first at the old fort, and subsequently in the Hamilton mansion, which was erected in 1838, and with its beautiful grounds, occupied an entire square. In religious and social affairs Mrs. Hamilton took a leading part, and the narration of the virtues and many acts of kindness and benevolence of this noble woman would tax the narrow limits of this sketch. Her elder son, Andrew Holman Hamilton, was a member of the Forty-fourth and Forty-fifth congresses, and now manages the estate. The other surviving children are Montgomery Hamilton, Mrs. Samuel Wagenhals, Mrs. H. M. Williams, and Miss Margaret V. Hamilton.

Charles D. Bond, formerly one of the foremost bankers of Indiana, was also prominent as a citizen of Fort Wayne. He was born at Lockport, N. Y., October 13, 1831, the eldest son of Stephen B. and Adelia L. (Darrow) Bond. The father, at one time prosperous, incurred financial disaster through indorsements made for others, and brought his family to the west in 1842. They settled first at Fort Wayne, but after remaining here two years went to Wisconsin. In 1846 the family again made their home at Fort Wayne, and in the following year the father died, leaving Charles D. Bond at the age of sixteen the main support of his mother and three younger brothers, without friends or means. On the return to the city Mr. Bond obtained employment with Hon. Peter F. Bailey, then engaged in merchandise in Fort Wayne, but a short time afterward he accepted a position in the postoffice under Postmaster

Samuel Stophlet. Several years later he became a bookkeeper in the branch of the State bank at Evansville, of which Mr. Rathbone was president, a position he held for about a year, when anxious to return home he secured a position in the Fort Wayne branch of the State bank, of which Hon. Hugh McCulloch was then cashier. He entered upon his duties as bookkeeper and assistant teller, succeeding his brother, Stephen B. Bond, who took the position of cashier with Allen Hamilton & Co. September 25, 1855, Mr. Bond was elected teller to succeed M. W. Hubble, and on October 26, 1856, he became cashier of the Bank of Indiana, which succeeded to the business of the branch of the State bank, and opened for business January 2, 1857. Of this, Mr. Bond became a director. In 1865 when the business was adapted to the national banking act, under the title of the Fort Wayne National bank, Mr. Bond was elected president, a place he held until his death. Thus, at the age of thirty-four he stood at the head of the financial interests of Fort Wayne. Many public and private enterprises also had his assistance, among which may be mentioned the Fort Wayne gas-light company, the Fort Wayne, Jackson & Saginaw and Grand Rapids & Indiana railroads, Fort Wayne organ company, Citizens' street railroad company, and others. He was one of the four partners of the banking house of Bonds, Hoagland & Co., of Peru, and of the Citizens' National bank of that place. Of the Lindenwood cemetery company he was one of the incorporators and foremost promoters. Mr. Bond was married March 27, 1854, to Lavinia Anna, daughter of the late Charles W. Ewing, and seven children were born to them. He was a man of deep religious convictions, and at an early age became a member of the Trinity Episcopal church. Of this he was for many years a member of the vestry, and also superintendent of the Sabbath-school. Mr. Bond died December 7, 1873, from the effects of an exposure to a rain storm in November preceding.

Isaac Lauferty, who has recently retired from an active business career of forty-five years' duration in the city of Fort Wayne, has been throughout that time intimately connected with its business history, and especially with the important financial operations during a large part of that extended period. He was born on the boundary line between France and Germany, August 2, 1820, of French parentage. His father, Lazarus Lauferty, was born in 1769, son of Frankel Lauferty, a native of France, born about 1730, who was a quarter-master in Napoleon's army, and a very wealthy man. He died on the Franco-German line, at one hundred and four years of age. Lazarus Lauferty was one of Napoleon's life guards, and was a man of imposing stature, six feet in height. He was a merchant, and in later life was a citizen of Philadelphia, whither he emigrated in 1846, until his death, which occurred while he was on a visit to this city. His wife, whose maiden name was Sarah Rothschild, was lost at sea while coming to this country, May 6, 1846, at the age of seventy-two. Of the seven children of these parents, Isaac Lauferty was the youngest, and is the only one now living. He came to the United States in 1839.

He engaged in merchandise at Wilmington, N. C., in 1842, but in 1844, came to Fort Wayne, and here continued in mercantile pursuits at the corner of Columbia and Clinton streets, until 1871, when he established Lauferty's bank, with which he was actively connected, making it one of the prominent institutions of the city, until 1889. Mr. Lauferty was married in 1848, to Betty Munchweiler, who was born at Frankfort-on-the-Main, December 11, 1824, and they have four children: Alexander S., Sarah, Blanche and Agatha. The family are members of the Hebrew church. Mr. Lauferty has been a Mason since 1852, and in politics is a democrat, but before 1856 was an old line whig.

MUNICIPAL AND FEDERAL.

A land office was located in Fort Wayne in the summer of 1822, and the land immediately about the fort enclosure was sold by the agent to John T. Barr and John McConkle, the latter a wealthy citizen of Piqua, Ohio. The original plat of the town was surveyed by Robert Young of Piqua, in August, 1822. It is designated in the latter day maps as the "original plat," and was recorded in the office of the recorder of Randolph county, at Winchester, and subsequently at Fort Wayne, in recorder's record A, page 316, of the records of Allen county. It contains 118 lots with three streets, running north and south on a variation of 3° 30' west of magnetic north, namely: Calhoun, Clinton and Barr, and five streets running at right angles to the same variation, namely: Wayne, Berry, Main, Columbia and Water streets. The public square was laid off on this plat with Court street on the east side of the same. The name of Water street has since been changed to Superior street.

The county addition was laid out by the commissioners and recorded in recorder's record A, page 315. It contained seventy lots and fractional lots. Its position is immediately east of and adjoining the original plat; the lots were laid off on either side of Lafayette street between Berry street and the St. Mary's river, continuing Water, Columbia, Main and Berry streets from the original plat.

Next, Cyrus Taber laid off an addition of forty lots including all of the military tract lying between the south boundary of said tract and the canal. Main and Berry streets were continued through the county addition. The remains of the fort reservation, by an act of congress, had been set apart for the benefit of the canal and with other lands at Logansport and subsequently sold at public auction.

Ewing's addition was laid off by G. W. and W. G. Ewing. It contains thirty-four blocks or fractional blocks of 278 lots, including all fractional lots. Cass, Ewing and Fulton streets were laid out to run north on a magnetic bearing of 15° 30' west. Jefferson, Washington, Wayne, Berry, Main and Pearl streets, continued west from the original plat. Lewis street was laid out south of Jefferson street and was the first street to be established running due east and west

Judge Samuel Hanna, platted and recorded Hanna's first addition, containing 299 lots and fractional lots. Clinton, Barr, Clay, Monroe and Hanna streets were laid out on a magnetic bearing of north 15° 30' west. Wayne, Washington and Jefferson streets were continued west from the original plat. Madison street was laid out north of, and parallel with, Jefferson street, and running from Barr street east.

Rockhill's addition, which includes a principal portion of the city lying west of Broadway, was the next large addition. It contained 182 lots and fractional lots. This addition extended north to the canal and on either side of Market street, now Broadway; between Main and Berry streets, a space was left for market purposes. The original plat and the additions named comprise the first five wards of the city. The number of wards is now ten.

The incorporation of Fort Wayne as a town, dates from September 7, 1829, when an election was held and it was certified to the board of county commissioners, by William N. Hood, president of the meeting, and John P Hedges, clerk, that a majority of two-thirds of the persons present favored the plan.

Accordingly, on the 14th of the same month, at the house of Abner Gerard, esq., the first town election was held, which Benjamin Archer, president of said election, and John P. Hedges, clerk, certified as resulting in the choice of Hugh Hanna, John S. Archer, William G. Ewing, Lewis G. Thompson and John P. Hedges, as trustees for one year.

The town government differed little from that of other young places. The town funds were meager; of public buildings none warranting the name. The streets were not improved and were of the muddy and impassable character of the ordinary country road. The needs of the thrifty town soon outgrew the usefulness of this primitive manner of government and the subject of a city charter and the corporate powers it should contain were matters of frequent and earnest discussion.

The original city charter was written by Hon. Franklin P. Randall and was carefully compiled to meet the requirements of a better government. It was submitted to the legislature of Indiana at its session of 1839–40, and was passed on February 22, 1840. It provided for the incorporation of the city of Fort Wayne, and for the election by the people of a president, or mayor, and six members of the board of trustees (or common council), and the election of general officers by said board or council.

City Officers.— The first officers were: mayor, George W. Wood; recorder, F. P. Randall; attorney, F. P. Randall; treasurer, George F. Wright; high constable, Samuel S. Morss; collector, Samuel S. Morss; assessor, Robert E. Fleming; market master, James Post; street commissioner, Joseph H. McMaken; chief engineer, Samuel Edsall, and lumber measurer, John B. Coconour.

The first common council consisted of William Rockhill, Samuel Edsall, Thomas Hanneton, William S. Edsall, Madison Smiltser and William M. Moon. Of all these gentlemen there now survives but one,

Hon. F. P. Randall. He is actively engaged in the insurance business, and his enjoyment of his green old age is shared by his fellow citizens, who have learned to respect and love him.

Hon. George W. Wood was twice elected mayor, and resigned on July 5, 1871. Subsequent mayors were: Joseph Morgan, Henry Lotz (two terms), John M. Wallace, M. W. Hurford (three terms), William Stewart (five terms), P. G. Jones, Charles Whitmore (two terms), Samuel S. Morss (two terms), Franklin P. Randall (five terms), James L. Worden, Henry Sharp, C. A. Zollinger (five terms), Charles F. Muhler (two terms) and Daniel L. Harding, the present incumbent.

The first board of health was in 1842, and consisted of Dr. John Evans, Dr. William H. Brooks and Dr. Bernard Sevenick.

The seal of the city of Fort Wayne was designed by Hon. F. P. Randall about 1858. Upon its face are a pair of scales; under the scales are a sword and Mercury's wand inverted, crossed at their points. Above the scales is the word in a semi-circle, Ke-ki-on-ga, the Indian name of Fort Wayne, and around the outside edge are the words "City of Fort Wayne."

The present city officers are: Mayor, Daniel L. Harding; treasurer, Charles J. Sosenheimer; marshal, Henry C. Franke; assessor, Charles Reese; city attorney, Henry Colerick; civil engineer, Charles S. Brackenridge; chief of police, Frank Wilkinson; chief of fire department, Henry Hilbrecht; street commissioner, Dennis O'Brien; weigh master, Patrick Ryan; market master, William Ropa; pound master, Fred Woehnker. Secretary board of health, Dr. S. C. Metcalf. Trustees of water works, Christian Boseker, J. Sion Smith, Charles McCulloch. Trustees of public schools, John M. Moritz, O. P. Morgan, E. A. Hoffman. City commissioners, J. Dickerson, A. F. Glutting, U. Stotz, George Fox, P. H. Kane. Councilmen—First ward, William D. Meyer, John C. Kensill; second, Fred Schmueckle, Maurice Cody; third, H. A. Read, Joseph L. Gruber; fourth, George W. Ely, H. F. Hilgemann; fifth, Henry Hilbrecht, Louis P. Huser; sixth, F. W. Bandt, Robert Cran; seventh, Peter J. Scheid, George P. Morgan; eighth, John Smith, H. P. Vordermark; ninth, Louis Hazzard, Charles F. Haiber; tenth, V. Ofenloch, William Bruns.

The Police.—The city was without a police force until 1863, the people having no other protection than the sheriff and his deputies, the city marshal and his assistants and a few constables. In May of that year a police force was established, and consisted of a captain, a lieutenant and two patrolmen from each ward. Their hours of service were fixed at twilight to daylight.

The first chief was Conrad Pens, a German sailor. The others in their order of service were: William Ward, Fred Limecooley, Patrick McGee, Detrick Meyer, Michael Singleton, Hugh M. Deihl, Eugene B. Smith and Hugh M. Diehl, again. The latter resigned in June, 1889, and Lieutenant Frank Wilkinson was appointed by the police commissioners to fill the vacancy. Patrolman Leonard Fuchshuber was appointed

William McElroy

lieutenant. Within the last year the offices of deputy marshals have been abolished and the five officers who are subject to the directions of the marshal are known as day policemen. The present marshal is Henry Franke.

The first police station was established in a small brick building on the east side of Court street, opposite the court-house. An office occupied the front room communicating with a cell room in the rear fitted with three iron cages. Upon the upper floor were two rooms in which female prisoners, but oftener tramps, were confined. The station was removed two years since to better quarters in the Barr street market house.

The night force consists of the chief, lieutenant, eighteen patrolmen, two drivers of the patrol wagon with a day and a night clerk at headquarters. The marshal and five patrolmen are on duty in the daytime. Important aids to the efficiency of the department is supplied by the new police patrol and telegraph system, which cost the city nearly $3,000. It consists of twelve sentry boxes, located in different portions of the city, each electrically connected with headquarters and each supplied with a telephone. The direction of the whole force from the central office is thus made easy, and the patrol wagon which supplements the system, is at the ready call of an officer who may need assistance or who may by this means, send his prisoners to the lockup without leaving his beat.

Fire Department.—The fire department of Fort Wayne, like that of all cities, had its origin in the volunteer companies. The department was organized in 1856. Prior to that time there were two independent companies, one called the Anthony Wayne, organized in 1841, and the other called the Hermans, organized in 1848. The Anthony Wayne company owned a Jeffries " gallery engine " and a two-wheel hose cart. The engine house was on the north side of Clinton street, north of Main street.

The Hermans' engine house was on the west side of Clinton street, north of Berry. It contained a side brake Button engine and a two-wheel hose cart. Each company had a fair supply of leather riveted hose.

The Hermans' was succceded by the Alert engine and hose company, which used all of the Hermans' apparatus until January 13, 1868, when it was given back to the city and the company reorganized as an independent hook and ladder company known as the Alerts.

The Mechanics' engine and hose company was organized August 7th, 1856.

On December 3, 1848, the common council defined the fire limits as bounded on the east by Barr street, on the west by Harrison street, on the south by Main street and on the north by the canal.

The first steam fire engine was purchased from Pittsburgh, Penn. With a hose reel the expenditure was $3,000. The engine was of the Amoskeag manufacture, and was second-hand, but was in a very serviceable condition. This was in the summer of 1867, and in September of the same year, a company called the Vigilants was organized to operate the new purchase. This engine is still in service. Various purchases of hand-engines, pumps, etc., more experimental than satisfactory, were made from time to time. In the spring of 1872, the city purchased of George Hannis, Chicago, at a cost of $2,300, the hook and ladder truck which has been in active service ever since.

In the fall of 1872 a notable addition was made to the apparatus by the purchase of a fine rotary steamer from the Silsby manufacturing company. It was called the Anthony Wayne, and cost $4,800. It was originally designed as a reserve engine to be used only in case of large conflagrations.

In 1861 there was purchased from the Silsby company, a rotary steam fire engine which was named the Frank Randall, and later from the Clapp & Jones factory, was purchased another steamer, called the Charley Zollinger, both in honor of the mayors of the city at the times of purchase.

The second ward engine house, at the northeast corner of Court and Berry streets, was built in the summer of 1860, and shortly afterward the old engine house which stood in the rear was demolished and the ground was partially occupied by an extension of the new structure to provide accommodations for the increasing amount of apparatus.

On August 15th, 1875, the national fire alarm telegraph service was introduced with fifteen boxes, eight miles of wire and other apparatus at a cost of $5,000, and nine years afterward, the Gamewell system was substituted, giving vastly greater satisfaction. The number of boxes were increased and keys were placed in the possession of responsible persons in various parts of the city. It is a peculiarity of the boxes that a key when once used cannot be released except by the use of the private key of the chief engineer. This effectually prevents the turning in of false alarms at least more than once by the same person.

In 1875, the present system of unhitching horses by electricity and the suspension of swinging harness in front of the apparatus was inaugurated. The men and horses were perfectly drilled and severe discipline was introduced in all branches of the service. Sleeping rooms were fiitted up in the second story of the engine house and the firemen, instead of tumbling down flights of stairs to answer a night ring, slid down brass rods to the lower floor and the well trained horses having been electrically released from their stalls, were found in their places. A few snaps of the swinging harness were made, and the department was off to the scene of the fire in an incredibly short time, the boiler containing water heated by a stationary lamp which warmed it while the engine stood in its accustomed place.

Two years ago a handsome hose wagon was added to the apparatus. It is a vast improvement over the old reel and can be worked with much less effort. From time to time liberal purchases of hose have been made until now there seems only to be lacking an extension ladder which will be of the greatest service should fires break out in the tall buildings.

At first water was supplied to the department by laying long lines of hose to the canal, and later, the system of fire cisterns was inaugurated. These reached, in 1876, the number of thirty-four. All were abandoned and filled up upon the completion of the water-works system.

The names of the principal volunteer organizations which have done excellent service for the city are, the Alert engine company, the Torrent engine and hose company, the Eagle engine and hose company, whose hand engine was stored in the Broadway market house, the Vigilant engine and hose company, the Mechanics' engine and hose company, the Protection engine and hose company, which succeeded the old Wide-Awake engine and hose company, and the Hope hose company.

The various chief engineers of the fire department were: L. T. Bourie from 1856 to 1858; George Humphrey, 1858 to 1860; O. D. Hurd, 1860 to 1861; Joseph Stellwagon, 1861 to 1862; L. T. Bourie, 1862 to 1863; Munson Vangeison, 1863 to 1866; Henry Fry, 1866 to 1867; Hiram Poyser, 1867 to 1868; Thomas Mannix, 1868 to 1873; Frank B. Vogel, 1873 to 1874; Thomas Mannix, 1874 to 1875, and Frank Vogel, 1875 to 1879.

Mr. Vogel was the last of the chiefs under the volunteer system. It was succeeded in 1881 by the paid fire department, of which Henry Hilbrecht was appointed chief engineer. He has held the position ever since, and with such satisfaction to the people that his successive candidacy before the common council has met with no opposition. John McGowan is first assistant, and John Becker, second assistant.

Besides these officers two full paid men are attached to each piece of apparatus, as follows: two steamers, three hose carriage and one ladder truck. Then there six "minute men" on half-pay attached to each of the three hose carriages. They are expected to respond to every alarm and to carry the hose under the direction of the chief engineer and his assistants. These men are really subjected to the greatest danger of any of the firemen.

The growth of the city has for many years made it apparent that the fire department could not be handled with advantage from a single station, and after repeated recommendations by the chief engineer the city in 1885 built at a cost of $3,000, a handsome engine house in the seventh ward, from which the great manufactories of that district may be easily reached. With a perfect system of water-works and a well-trained department, the city now has good fire protection.

Water-works.—As early as 1875 the necessity of a system of water supply was thoroughly canvassed, and in the spring of 1876 the common council decided to establish water works in Fort Wayne. Moses Lane, an hydraulic engineer, was engaged to prepare and submit plans and specifications. These were submitted by him, and referred to the proper committee. Before this committee reported the canal owners presented a proposition, in the form of a carefully written contract, to construct water-works under the Lane plan, using the canal feeder as a source. This proposition required the expenditure of $380,000 for the construction of 21.18 miles of pipe and the erection of a stand-pipe five feet in diameter and 200 feet in height. The majority of the common council as then constituted, was in favor of this proposition, but certain citizens obtained a temporary restraining order, and before the final adjudication an election was held, and the issue presented in the several wards of the city being as to the adoption or rejection of the Lane plan, not one candidate who favored that plan was elected.

On the 15th day of May, 1879, the common council authorized the trustees of the water-works to employ any competent hydraulic engineer whom they might select. They employed J. D. Cook, of Toledo, who, on the 5th day of July, 1879, submitted plans and specifications. The water-works committee and a majority of the council opposed the Cook plan because it contemplated the construction of a reservoir, and the question as to the adoption of the plan was, on the 5th day of August, submitted to a popular vote. In order that the people might vote intelligently, the plan was printed and published in pamphlet form in the German and English languages, and a copy given to every voter in the city. The Cook plan was adopted, by a majority of 2,533, the total vote being 3,094 for, and 561 against, it.

The common council ratified the decision of the people and ordered the construction of the water-works as they are now, except as to reservoir and supply. There were in 1888, 29.9 miles of pipe, two engines and 239 fire hydrants, of which twenty-four are Lowry hydrants, at a total cost of $262,930.

Mr. Cook's salary was fixed at $2,500 a year, and the trustees were to receive $150 a year.

On October 21, 1879, the following contracts were let: Two engines and four boilers from Holly & Co., Lockport, N. Y., $30,500. Pipe and pipe laying, R. D. Wood & Co., Philadelphia, $126,380.17. Valves, Ludlow Valve Co., Troy, N. Y., $3,377.30. Hydrants, Matthews Hydrant Co., of Philadelphia, $8,490. Reservoir construction of building, etc., on the Olds' property, John Langohr and M. Baltes, $59,627.36. Engine house, Moellering & Paul, $8,490.

The whole footed up $236,865.36. Mr. Cook's estimate was $270,000, and after deducting the aggregate contracts from the estimate of Mr. Cook, there was $33,134.36 left for contingencies. Ground was broken in the fall of 1880, and the construction of the works, as originally planned, was carried forward and completed with the exception that the elevated reservoir, in the seventh ward, has not yet been finished, although such a course is strongly recommended by the commissioners, the work to be resumed in the spring, the same to cost not to exceed $20,000.

A source of supply that should be adequate in quantity and of wholesome quality was a subject of contention that was warmly fought over in the city council, in the room of the water-works commissioners and in the columns of the public press. Many favored pumping water from the St. Joseph river. The owners of the feeder canal sought to sell that property to the city, and it was urged that the canal being some twenty-five feet higher than the St. Joseph river, would not only furnish the needed water, but would supply the power to force it through the mains. A third source of supply and the one which was finally adopted, was Spy Run, a brook which enters the city from the north and falls into the St. Mary's river a short distance east of the Clinton street bridge. The water of the run was said to be superior in quality to that of the other sources under consideration, but of the sufficiency of the supply there were grave doubts. Nevertheless by the side of this brook, at a point just east of North Clinton street, the city erected its pumping house, equipped it with a costly low pressure engine, capable of pumping three millions of gallons in twenty-four hours, a fine high-pressure engine, a battery of boilers, etc.

Between the pumping house and Spy Run, a great basin was scooped out of the gravel, and several strong springs were struck at the bottom. From the run to this basin, influent pipes, fitted with rock filters were laid; some twenty miles of pipe were put down and the contractors for the reservoir worked with amazing zeal in raising the great clay embankment into which it was designed to force the water, and from which it would gravitate back and down as needed by the consumers. The elevation of the reservoir was so great that it was estimated that water from this source could easily be thrown upon the highest buildings in the principal part of the city by making a mere hose connection. The very first summer's drought that followed the completion of the works and the general use of the water demonstrated fully the inadequacy of the supply, and water had to be obtained from the canal owners by tapping the aqueduct over Spy Run. This additional supply was never positively refused, and in cases of extreme drought when a conflagration would have found the fire department helpless, it was always to be had, but the relation between the canal owners and the city government became strained and other means of re-inforcing the inconsiderable volume of water of Spy Run were sought. A long pipe was finally laid from the pumping basin to the St. Joseph river, and a large rotary pump was set at work forcing water into the pumping basin from the Rudisill pool, being that level of the river above the Rudisill dam. This plan proved to be only a temporary relief. The same interests that had sought to sell the canal feeder to the city, owned the Rudisill dam, and it was cut, and in the early summer, with a water famine staring the citizens in the face, the board of commissioners were brought to face their most serious perplexity.

As a last resort, in 1888, a series of wells were bored. They were put down along the channel of Spy Run, below the pumping basin, and pump connection was made with them as fast as they were completed. The water in the pumping basin was falling rapidly under the steady consumption from the parched city, and it had actually fallen to but a few inches above the top of the big suction pipe when a few of the wells were made to yield and a strong stream of pure wholesome water began to add its steady volume to the basin. It was welcomed by the citizens as the traveler across the desert welcomes a well or river.

These wells are eight inches in diameter and are driven to an average depth of fifty-two feet. They are thirty in number, and are all connected with a great suction pipe which leads directly to the big engines in the pumping house. Eight millions of gallons in twenty-four hours is a fair estimate of the amount supplied by the six wells first connected with a temporary suction pipe and when all have been so connected at least forty millions of gallons can be regularly relied upon. So fully satisfied are the water-works commissioners of the adequacy of this supply of pure spring water that they are now seriously considering the advisability of drawing the water from the pumping basin and cementing its bottom and sides so that none of the Spy Run water, once so much longed for, may enter. Thus has the problem of water supply for this growing city been settled at a great cost, but it is believed to the entire satisfaction of the consumers forever.

During the summer of 1889 a large addition was made to the pumping house at an expense of $16,000, and a triple expansion, low pressure Gaskill pumping engine, costing $30,500, has been put in service. This giant piece of machinery is warranted to pump 6,000,000 of gallons in twenty-four hours.

It was unfortunate that the original plan of pipe distribution was not on a scale sufficiently large for all demands, and many of the mains have been taken up and replaced by larger ones. Then, too, the growth of the city and the establishment of manufactories in the outlying wards, has demanded a general increase of the pipe service until now there are thirty-one miles of mains in the streets and alleys. When the reservoir shall have been completed and the direct pressure system will be abandoned, the expense of operation will be greatly curtailed, and as perfect and economically managed water-works will be found in Fort Wayne as in any city in America.

After many changes in the board of trustees, the "old board," Messrs. McCulloch, Monning and Boseker was re-elected in 1889, because of the great popular confidence in their management of affairs, and Mr. Frank Iten remains as inspector. This gentleman supervises all the extensions and repairs of water mains, which the city never lets to contractors, and it is said that no work he has approved has ever needed subsequent renewal. The water-works with all improvements up to the summer of 1889, have cost the city $269,000.

Daniel L. Harding, mayor of Fort Wayne, was born January 8, 1843, in Kings county, Ireland, son of Robert and Dorethea (Minchin) Harding, natives of Ireland. The father was born about 1793, and died in 1867, and the mother, who was born about 1801, died in 1847. Both passed their lives in their native land. Prior to coming to America Mr. Harding was engaged for five years in civil engineering, and this he continued after emigrating in 1866, for eight months, in the employ of the Fort Wayne, Cincinnati & Louisville railroad. He then went to

Omaha, and was engaged two years on the Union Pacific railroad, until the road was completed. He remained in the active practice of this profession in various parts of the country until 1877. He then embarked in the real estate and insurance business in Fort Wayne, and has been so engaged ever since, except one year spent in England. In this business he has been quite successful and has won the confidence and esteem of the community. In politics he is a republican. In 1880 he was elected justice of the peace and re-elected in 1886. In the spring of 1889, Mr. Harding was prevailed upon to accept the republican nomination for mayor, although there had been but one republican mayor elected since the organization of the city, and that was twenty-two years previous, and the regular democratic majority was about 2,000. The democrats nominated C. F. Muhler for re-election, and the canvass which followed was very spirited, resulting in the election of Mr. Harding by a majority of 909. Mayor Harding signalizing his election by a proclamation demanding the rigorous enforcement of the laws regarding the closing of the traffic in intoxicating liquors on the Sabbath day, and this and the good results which followed, elicited laudatory comment in all parts of the country. Mayor Harding is prominent in Masonic circles, having been made a Mason at Tullamore lodge, Ireland, in 1865. He is also a member of the I. O. O. F. and K. of P. He was married in 1869 to Mary A. Fleming, who was born in Ireland in 1850, and came to the United States in 1869. They have four children: Robert F., Emily, Grace and Edith.

Rudolph C. Reinewald, city clerk of Fort Wayne, is a native of this city, born March 22, 1857. He is the oldest son of William F. and Lousie (Reffelt) Reinewald, who were born in Germany, the father in Blahsheim, Russia, and the mother in Bramshe, Hanover. They came to this country in 1855, and settled in Fort Wayne, and have resided here ever since. The father found employment in the Wabash shops, where he has been engaged during the past thirty-two years. Both parents are living, and in 1882 they celebrated their silver wedding. To them twelve children have been born, of whom nine are still living, five sons and four daughters: Rudolph C., John M., Henry W., William H., and George A. Reinewald, Mrs. William Bevesforden, Mrs. Charles Ostman, and Lotta and Mamie Reinewald. Rudolph C. Reinewald was educated in the Emanuel German Lutheran schools, and later took a business course in the Fort Wayne commercial college. At the age of fourteen he entered the employment of C. Wenninghoff, as an apprentice in the cigar trade. Subsequently, he began the manufacture of cigars for himself. Through his business career he became widely known and respected, and his friends urged him to make the race for the office of city clerk, which he did, but was unsuccessful in obtaining the nomination. In 1887 he again became a candidate for the same office, and was defeated by a small majority. In May, 1889, he was urged to make the race again, and this time was successful in securing the nomination over a number of candidates for the same office, and at the election on

May 7th, he was elected by an overwhelming majority of 1,853 votes, the largest majority of any candidate on the democratic ticket, receiving a total vote of 4,078, the largest vote polled by any candidate at the election. Mr. Reinewald was married October 21, 1886, in this city, to Mary A. Meeks, of Greenville, Ohio, who was born in Huntington, Ind. Her father, Jeremiah Meeks, is still living at Greenville, Ohio. Mr. and Mrs. Reinewald are members of the Emanuel Lutheran church.

Charles J. Sosenheimer, city treasurer of Fort Wayne, was born in Philadelphia, Penn., February 21, 1854, the son of John and Mary A. (Miller) Sosenheimer. The father was born in Germany, May 20, 1815, and coming to America in 1848 and settled at St. Mary's, Penn., finally making his residence at Fort Wayne in 1880. Charles J., when twelve years of age, served an apprenticeship at the tinner's trade with his father, and five years later he went to Crestline, Ohio, and was engaged with his brother one year. He then returned to Pennsylvania and worked with his father one year. At the end of that time he went to Crestline again and purchased a third interest in a hardware store, in which business he was successfully engaged for four years. But becoming dissatisfied, he sold out his interest and removed to Fort Wayne with the intention of going into the hardware business. But sickness in his family prevented, and he obtained employment at the Wabash railway yards at $1.50 a day, and after four days went to the Pittsburgh shops at $1.60 per day, in the tin and copper department. He was promoted from time to time until he gained the position of assistant foreman under S. C. Henderson, which place he has held since. In 1887 Mr. Sosenheimer was nominated for city treasurer on the Union Labor ticket and was defeated, but in 1889 he entered the campaign as the democratic candidate for the same office, and having been nominated by a majority of ninety-four was elected by a majority of 1,026. He took possession of this office in September, 1889. He speaks both the English and German languages fluently, is well educated, and bids fair to be a popular officer. Mr. Sosenheimer was married May 4, 1875, to Emma A. Myers, of Crestline, Ohio, and they have four children: Alice, Charles, Frederick and Lillian. He and wife are members of the Cathedral Catholic church.

Diedrich Meyer was first elected to a position on the police force of the city of Fort Wayne in 1866, and he served twelve years, five of which were spent in the capacity of jailor. The faithfulness and ability he had displayed in important positions led to his appointment May 12, 1881, as deputy marshal. He held this position three years, nearly, and then, upon the resignation of Marshal Frank Falkner, Mr. Meyer was appointed to fill the vacancy, and in 1884 was elected marshal, and re-elected in 1887. He has been a trustworthy and popular official. Mr. Meyer has long been a democrat, and cast his first presidential vote for Stephen A. Douglas. He is a native of Germany, born July 15, 1829, son of John and Margaret Meyer, who spent their lives in that, their native land. Diedrich was the youngest of seven children, of whom three are living. He was educated in Germany, and there learned the miller's trade. In 1856 he immigrated and settled in Fort Wayne, and was for a time engaged on the Pittsburg, Fort Wayne & Chicago railroad, and then for two years at boating on the Wabash & Erie canal. He was married in 1882 to Lucretia M. Munson, who was born in 1845 in this city. He and wife are members of the Lutheran church.

Dennis O'Brien, street commissioner of the city of Fort Wayne, was born in county Wexford, Ireland, March 25, 1834. His father, William O'Brien, was born in 1782, and married Mary Brady. In 1852 the family came to America, and settled at Huntington, Ind., where the father died in 1865, and the mother in 1873, at the age of ninety-three years. The youngest of their four children now living is the subject of this mention. On coming to America he was first employed in railroad work, and for twelve years was in the employment of the Wabash & Erie canal, being for eight years foreman of the state boat. Since 1865 his residence has been at Fort Wayne. In politics he is a democrat, and in 1877 his integrity and industry were recognized by election to the position which he has held continuously ever since. He was married in 1872 to Nancy Sheridan, who was born in this county in 1846. They have seven children: John D., William P., Robert E., Frank B., Albert, Helen M., and Annie. Mr. O'Brien and family are members of the Catholic church, and he is a member of the Catholic Knights.

The functions of weigh-master and wood-measurer of Fort Wayne have been efficiently discharged since 1875 by one person, Patrick Ryan He is a native of Ireland, born March 15, 1832, the fifth of nine children of James and Johanna (Bohan) Ryan. His parents were natives of the Emerald Isle, the father born 1774, died 1845; his mother born 1782, died in quarantine below Quebec, 1847. In the latter year Mr. Ryan settled in Massachusetts, and remained there fifteen years, coming to Fort Wayne in January, 1862. While in the east he had learned the trade of shoemaker, and this he followed here until 1875, with the exception of one year in military service. He enlisted in 1864 in the Ninety-first Indiana infantry, and was honorably discharged in 1865. Mr. Ryan is a worthy and popular citizen; is a democrat in politcs, and he and family are members of the Catholic church. He is a Catholic Knight and member of St. Joseph and St. Patrick benevolent societies. He is a strict temperance man and has been a member of Father Matthew's society since 1873. Mr. Ryan was married in 1853 to Margaret Sheedy, who was born in Ireland in 1832, and they have had fourteen children, of whom eight are living: Mary E., James, Hannah, Patrick H., Margaret A., Agnes, John and Joseph.

Christopher F. Hettler, now assistant purchasing agent for the Pennsylvania company, was born in Hohenhaslach, county Vaihingen, Wurtemberg, Germany, April 1, 1834. He received a liberal education in that country, and in 1857 he emigrated to the United States, landing at New York city August 8 of that year, and then proceeded to Preble county, Ohio, where he remained until the fall of 1861, when he came to Allen county and for one year lived at New Haven, and then in 1862 located in Fort Wayne and accepted a position at the Pennsylvania shops. Considered by Gov. O. P. Morton as being a true, loyal American citizen, he was appointed recruiting officer at Fort Wayne in 1864, in which position he enlisted a large number of recruits. In September, 1864, he selected a company from these recruits, of which he was commissioned captain, and his command was assigned to duty as Company C, One Hundred and Forty-second regiment, and was given place in the army of the Cumberland. The regiment was mustered out July 14, 1865, after which Captain Hettler resumed his position with the Pennsylvania company, and since 1871 he has been assistant purchasing agent for that company. Since 1862 he has been prominent among the citizens of Fort Wayne, and has taken a leading part in public affairs, whenever he could work for the general good. From 1873 to 1882 he represented the second ward in the city council, and during his service he was ever on the alert to obtain the greatest possible advancement for the city with the lowest possible per cent. of taxation. He was instrumental in the introduction of the fire alarm telegraph system and other improvements for the fire department. In 1876 he delivered the first speech in the interest of city water-works and in which he advocated the idea that the city should build, own and control her system of water-works instead of their being in the hands of private companies. The question came before the people in 1879, and received a majority vote of 2,533 as against a minority vote of 561. Mr. Hettler has held the position of treasurer of the Fort Wayne building and loan fund and saving association, the largest organization of the kind in Indiana. He is a prominent member of Harmony lodge, No. 19, I. O. O. F., Sion S. Bass post, No. 40, G. A. R., and Fort Wayne saengerbund. Captain Hettler was married March 26, 1861, to Catherine Furthmiller, then of New Haven, but was born in Stark county, Ohio, August 26, 1840, and they have one son, Herman Henry, born June 17, 1862, now extensively engaged in the lumber trade in Chicago. Mrs. Hettler is a member of the W. R. C., the Evangelical association and is an active, energetic member of various charitable and benevolent interests. Mr. Hettler possesses an untiring energy and in all his business transactions he has been very successful. Though of foreign birth he is thoroughly American in all his views and emphatically advocates allegiance only to that grand old flag, the stars and stripes.

Henry Hilbrecht is a native of Germany, born January 4, 1828, the son of Diedrich and Louisa Hilbrecht. In his native country he attended school until he was fourteen, after which he learned the trade of a blacksmith. In 1848 he emigrated and after spending three days in New York and a week in Buffalo, came to Fort Wayne where he has now been known as an upright and useful citizen for more than forty years. Here he found employment as a blacksmith, an occupation, which owing to his knowledge of the locksmith's trade, he soon was proficient in. He followed blacksmithing for a period of thirty years. Since 1878 he has served two years as deputy trustee, three years as deputy assessor and two years as trustee of Wayne township, and with these exceptions, has led a quiet retired life. Mr. Hilbrecht was married August 16, 1848, to Miss Sophia Mesing, a native of Germany who came with her parents to America when a child. They have had five children: Henry, Lisette, Louisa, Sophia and William, of whom only Henry and Louisa are living. Mr. Hilbrecht is a member of Emanuel's German Lutheran church. Mrs. Hilbrecht, who was also a member of that church, died December 24, 1879. In politics Mr. Hilbrecht is a democrat. He was elected a member of the city council in the fifth ward in the spring of 1888, and at present holds that position. In public life as in private, he is the same reliable, trustworthy man in whom the people place full confidence. In 1873 Mr. Hilbrecht visited his native land, where he spent about three months with his father and other relatives and friends.

William D. Meyer was born in Germany in 1848, the son of Conrad and Louisa Meyer. His childhood and youth were spent in Germany, where he was raised on a farm and taught the shoemaking trade. In 1867 he immigrated to America, and made his home at Fort Wayne. Here for one year he was engaged in teaming, and during eleven years following worked at his trade, conducting a shop of his own during the latter eight years of that period. In 1881 he engaged in the grocery business to which his attention has since been given. In politics Mr. Meyer is an ardent and influential member of the democratic party, and in 1887 he was elected to the city council from the first ward, an office which he holds at present. Mr. Meyer was married in 1869, to Mary Dicke, a native of Germany, who came to this country in 1867. They have three children: Louise, Henry F., and Mary. Mr. and Mrs. Meyer are members of St. Paul's German Lutheran church.

The present representative of the second ward in the city council is Frederick Schmueckle, a worthy citizen. He was born in Wurtemburg, Germany, January 3, 1839, of parents who lived and died in their native land. The father, Gottlieb, was born in 1800, and died in 1877, and the mother, whose maiden name was Fredericka Ferber, was born in 1805, and died in 1880. The eldest son of their three living children is Frederick, who received his education in Germany, and at the age of fourteen years began work at the tanner's trade, which was his occupation until 1859, when he emigrated to the United States. He resided for one year at Milwaukee, Wis., and then came to Fort Wayne, which has since been his home most of the time. He is now engaged in the hotel and restaurant business, and doing well. In politics he is a democrat, and in 1888 he was elected to his present position on the ticket of that party. He is a member of Goethe lodge, K. of P. Mr. Schmueckle was married in 1867 to Mary Edringer, of Chicago, who died in 1870, leaving one child, Albert. In 1873 he married Louise Clemens, a native of Germany, by whom he has one child, Frederick.

Among the leading men of the city council of Fort Wayne should be named George W. Ely. He became a citizen of Fort Wayne in 1863, engaging at that time in the grocery business, which he conducted until

1875. In 1884 he was elected to the council as an independent, from the fourth ward, and in 1886 was re-elected, but on account of a contest occupied a seat in that body only five months. In 1888 he was again elected. Mr. Ely was born at Owego, N. Y., June 22, 1836, son of Daniel and Lois (Kelsey) Ely, natives of New York. The father was born in 1802, served as postmaster at Owego, by appointment of President W. H. Harrison, was colonel at one time in the militia of the state, and died at Owego in 1845. The mother was born in 1811 and died at Wooster, Ohio, in 1887. George W. was the third of five children, of whom three are living. He received a common school education, and at fourteen years of age removed to Wooster, Ohio, and entered a clothing store as clerk. In 1863 he was married to Theresa R. Anderson, who was born in Ohio, August 11, 1842, daughter of Calvin and Rebecca Anderson, old settlers of this city. Mrs. Ely is a member of the First Presbyterian church.

William Doehrmann, a successful business man of Fort Wayne, is also worthy of note as a prominent member of the city council, to which he was first elected for the eighth ward in 1881, and has since been three times re-elected. He is the oldest member in years of service, is chairman of the committee on finance, and is also a member of the board of police commissioners. He is a deservedly popular citizen. Mr. Doehrmann is a son of Conrad and Minnie (Zwick) Doehrmann, who immigrated from Germany and settled in Adams county fifty years ago. He, the fifth of their children, was born in Preble township, Adams county, December 27, 1850. After receiving a common school education he came to Fort Wayne and began clerking in a grocery store. Five years later he became a grocer on his own account, at Decatur, and after two and a half years, in 1875 returned to this city and has continued in the business. In 1880 he was married to Sophia Schroeder, born in Marion township, February 8, 1862, to William and Caroline (Kroemer) Schroeder, natives of Germany. They have four children: William C., born 1881; Frederick H., born 1884; Martin H., born 1886, and Alma C. M., born 1889. Mr. Doehrmann and wife are members of the St. Paul's German Lutheran church.

Peter J. Scheid, assistant foreman of the machine shops of the Pittsburgh, Fort Wayne & Chicago railroad company, was born in Lancaster, Penn., October 18, 1847. He attended the public schools there, and began learning the trade of machinist when fifteen years old with Norris Bros. In 1863 he enlisted in Company B, One Hundred and Ninety-fifth Pennsylvania infantry, for three months, and afterward enlisted in the Seventy-ninth regiment, and served to the end of the war. He then returned to the establishment where he had begun his trade, and finished it. In 1867 he secured a position in the shops of the Pennsylvania company, at Pittsburgh, and in 1869 came to Fort Wayne. After many years' faithful service he was made assistant foreman in 1881. Mr. Scheid is prominent as a citizen and as a member of the democratic party, and was elected to the city council for the seventh ward in 1881, again in 1884, and again in 1888. He is a member of the church of the Holy Trinity, of Wayne lodge, F. & A. M., and of Sion S. Bass post, G. A. R. Mr. Scheid was married in 1867, to Mary Ruck, of Lancaster, Penn., and they have had seven children: Frank, William, George, Clark, and Lotta (deceased), Crover C. and Cecilia.

Henry Hilbrecht, chief of the the Fort Wayne fire department, was born in this city, August 26, 1849. His father is Henry Hilbrecht, now a resident of this city, who was born in Germany in 1828, and married Sophia Mesing, a native of the same country who died in 1878. The senior Hilbrecht came to this city in 1848, and was by occupation a blacksmith, but is now retired. The subject of this mention is the elder of two children now living. He was educated in the Lutheran schools, and then for sometime worked at the blacksmith's trade, after which he was engaged as a machinist about nine years. In 1873 he became a member of the fire department, and since 1875 has been in continuous service. He soon became distinguished for bravery and efficiency, and was elected chief of the department. He was married in 1876 to Christina Dreibelbiss, of this city, born in 1854, and they have two children, Clara and Flora. The family are members of the St. Paul's Lutheran church, and he is in politics a democrat.

The position of inspector of the Fort Wayne water-works has been held since their establishment by Frank Iten, who has in that capacity rendered the city valuable service. He had previous experience, having been appointed to a similar position for the city of Dayton, Ohio, at the age of twenty-eight, holding the same for five years. Subsequently, he was engaged in business at Ada, Ohio, for over two years, and then for three years at Tiffin, returning to Fort Wayne, which is his birth-place, in 1879. Mr. Iten was born December 14, 1841, son of Scott and Catherine (Wagner) Iten. The father, who was a native of Switzerland, emigrated to the United States in 1827, and soon afterward became one of the pioneers of Fort Wayne. He was engaged in the flouring business some time, and died in 1848. His widow now resides in the city, in her eighty-sixth year. They had seven children, of whom four survive. Frank Iten was educated in the Catholic schools, and at twenty-one years of age learned the steam and gas fitting trade with A. Hattersley & Co., with whom he remained until he removed to Dayton, excepting his service in the war of the rebellion. He enlisted in 1861 in the Thirtieth regiment, and went through three years' faithful and patriotic service. In 1865 he was married to Sophia Young, of this county, who was born in 1845, and died at Tiffin, November 25, 1879, leaving three children who are yet living. He was married November 24, 1881, to Mary A. Daly, of Sanpierre, and they have had three children, one of whom survives. Mr. Iten and wife are members of the Catholic church, and he of the Catholic Legion.

As deputy in the city clerk's office for eight years, from 1875 to 1883, and as secretary of the city water-works, which position he has held since Jaduary 1, 1888, P. J. McDonald has rendered the city careful and efficient service. He is a native of the city, born December 22, 1858, son of Philip and Catherine (Summers) McDonald, who were natives of Ireland and immigrated and settled at Fort Wayne at an early date. They were married in this city, and had two children, both of whom are living. Philip McDonald conducted a grocery store in the city a number of years, and served one term as deputy for Sheriff McDonald. He died in 1862 at the age of thirty-six, and his wife died in 1873 at the age of forty-one. P. J. McDonald was married in August, 1885, to Gertrude E. Donally, of Wooster, Ohio, and they have two children. Mr. McDonald is a member of the Catholic church, and of the Catholic Knights of America. He received his education in the Brothers' schools and at Notre Dame university, attending that institution in 1873-4. After serving eight years as deputy city clerk he spent a short time in the west, and on his return was for a short time again employed in that office.

J. Sion Smith, one of the trustees of the water-works of Fort Wayne, is a native of Salem, Livingston county, Ky. He was born August 3, 1849, the son of W. B. and Emily J. (Bass) Smith, the former of whom was born in Virginia in 1815, and the latter, a sister of J. H. Bass, of Fort Wayne, was born in Kentucky in 1832. The family came to Fort Wayne in August, 1865, and two years later, Mr. Smith, who had by this time obtained a good common school education, engaged in the coal and iron business under the firm name of Bass & Smith. He was thus occupied until 1876, after which, for two years, he conducted a flouring-mill at VanWert, Ohio. Returning to Fort Wayne, he took his present position at the Bass foundry and machine works, which he has since held. Mr. Smith is influential as a citizen and is interested in the advancement of the city. In politics he is a pronounced democrat, and he was elected by his party as councilman for the sixth ward, a position he held from 1883 to 1885. Upon the death of the late Henry Monning Mr. Smith was elected to fill out the unexpired term of the former in the important office of trustee of the water-works of Fort Wayne. Mr. Smith is a member of the Masonic order. He was married in 1870 to Alice Shoaff, who was born in this city in 1853, and they have two children: Claude S. and Maude M.

The post of engineer at the water-works is occupied by Warren Carpenter, who is a thorough master of his calling. He was born at Lafayette, Ind., October 20, 1852, and after receiving his education in the city schools, entered a carriage shop in 1871 to learn the trade of a painter, but in the early winter of the next year he took a position as fireman on the Wabash railroad. This he held for five years, then being promoted engineer, and assigned a locomotive. He remained with the Wabash until the great strike of 1876, in which he was prominently engaged. He afterward accepted a position as locomotive engineer with the Chicago & Atlantic railroad, and was next employed as engineer of a planing-mill in this city. In 1883 he was appointed assistant engineer of the water-works, and in June, 1886, appointed first engineer for the period of three years. He was married in 1877 to Catherine Hinton, who was born in Fort Wayne in 1855. They have one son, Wilbur Garfield, born in 1879. Mr. Carpenter is the son of Augustus and Caroline (Williams) Carpenter, natives of New York, who came to Indiana in the thirties and settled in Lafayette, removing thence to Delphi, Logansport, and Chicago, successively, returning afterward to Lafayette, and thence coming to Fort Wayne in 1872, where the mother died in 1875. The father removed and now resides at Butler, Ind., an invalid, having been paralyzed by a sunstroke in 1884.

An assistant engineer of the city water works, A. H. Franke has done efficient service for several years. He is a native of this county, born in Madison township, April 6, 1853, son of Henry and Mary Berg Franke, natives of the same village of Prussia, where they were married. They came to America in 1840, and settled on a farm in Madison township. The mother still lives there, but the father died December 24, 1879. They are reckoned among the worthy early settlers, to whom the present advancement is so much indebted. Their son, A. H., received his education in the German free schools, and at the age of fifteen came to Fort Wayne and worked at the shoe business for thirteen years. He then became engaged in the water-works, first as fireman for five years and then was promoted to his present position in 1885. Mr. Franke was married June 9, 1881, to Miss Scherer, who was born in this city April 12, 1857, and died September 30, 1882, leaving one child. January 6, 1884, he married Louisa Schafe Schaper, of this county, born September 30, 1856, and they have two children, one of whom is living. Mr. and Mrs. Franke are members of the Lutheran church.

Since July, 1883, Thomas Baxter has faithfully served the city as one of the skilled employes at the water-works. He was born in England, January 16, 1859, son of Joseph and Phœbe (Foster) Baxter, both natives of England, who brought their families to America in 1861, and came directly to Fort Wayne. Joseph Baxter was an engineer, and followed that calling until his death, which occurred in 1887, he being then sixty-two years old. The mother is still living at the age of fifty-nine years, and resides in Fort Wayne, on Spy Run avenue. To these parents thirteen children were born, of whom three sons and three daughters survive, and reside in Fort Wayne. Thomas Baxter was married in Fort Wayne, and was educated in the public schools. At the age of seventeen years he entered the plow factory of J. K. Edgerton, where he remained five years. He was next in the employ of T. R. Pickard & Sons, three years. In July, 1883, he entered the city water-works as night fireman, and after three years was promoted to day fireman, and holds that position at present. He was married February 5, 1885, to Emma, daughter of John Smith, born in Fort Wayne in 1860, and they have one daughter: Edith M., who was born March 19, 1886. Mrs. Baxter is a member of Emanuel Lutheran church.

George A. Schust, night foreman at the Fort Wayne water-works, was born in Fort Wayne, December 19, 1854, the son of George A. and Mary (Betzler) Schust. His parents were both born in Germany, the father in 1827 and the mother in 1830. The father emigrated to America in 1849, and coming directly to Fort Wayne, has since made this city his home. He has been engaged as a carpenter, and for thirteen years was steward of Concordia college. His wife came to America about 1852. To them eleven children were born, of whom eight are living. George A. Schust was reared in this city, and received his education in the Lutheran and public schools. In 1872 he entered the carpenter shops of the Wabash railroad, and was engaged there until 1886, when he took his present position. Mr. Schust was married November 30, 1885, to Minnie Krannichfeld, a native of Buffalo, N. Y. They have had two children, of whom a daughter, Hedwig, is living. Mr. Schust and wife are members of the St. Paul's Lutheran church.

Hugh M. Diehl, ex-chief of police of Fort Wayne, was born at Philadelphia, October 21, 1844. His father, Charles H. Diehl, was born in Northampton county, Penn., in 1819, and now resides in Philadelphia, where he was in business many years as a contractor and builder. He married Mary C. Martin, who was born in Ireland in 1819, came to America at the age of nineteen years, and died in 1865. Hugh M. was the second of their eight children, all of whom are living. He received his education in the schools of his native city, and in 1860 went to Scranton to learn the trade of a machinist. His work was, however, interrupted in 1861 by the war of the rebellion. His father enlisted in Company C, Seventy-sixth Pennsylvania, and served three and a half years. The son also enlisted in the same month of the outbreak of war, in Company C, Eighth regiment, and served three months, the time of enlistment. He then came home and worked at his trade until July, 1863, when he again enlisted, as a ninety-day man, in Company H, Thirtieth Pennsylvania, being honorably discharged at the close of his term of enlistment. After a short time spent at Scranton he went to Philadelphia, and in 1865 removed to Chicago, and in January, 1866, to Fort Wayne, where he has since resided. Until 1876 he was employed in the shops of the Pittsburgh, Fort Wayne & Chicago railroad company. In the latter year he was appointed chief of police of Fort Wayne, and in 1878 elected marshal on the independent ticket. In 1881 he was again chosen chief of police and held the position until 1889. His service in this important capacity was marked by fidelity and efficiency, and he has become one of the most popular men in the city. He is prominent as a Mason, which order he joined in 1874, entering the Scottish Rite in 1886, and becoming a Knight Templar in 1887. Mr. Diehl was married in 1867 to Ada Jones, a native of New York, and they have three children, Lillie, Alice and Fred.

Frank Wilkinson, chief of police of Fort Wayne, was born in Troy, N. Y., May 1, 1836. His father, William, was born in Ireland, of English parents, and married Joanna Quinlin, a native of the same county (Cork). They immigrated in 1830, and settled at Troy, N. Y., where they remained until 1838, coming then to the village of Fort Wayne. Here the father died in 1848 and the mother in 1878. Five of their children are living, the oldest being Frank. At this city, which has been his residence more than half a century, his first occupation was as fireman for the Pennsylvania railroad company. He then engaged in business for nine years, and on June 8, 1876, was appointed lieutenant of the police force, a position which he held until appointed chief upon the resignation of Hugh M. Diehl, in June, 1889. He has been a popular man in his social, business, and official relations, and will doubtless fill his present position with credit. He was married in July, 1878, to Margaret H. Gordon, a native of Scotland, and they have four children: Josie, Ella, Edith and Frank. He is a prominent democrat, a member of the Catholic church and of the Catholic Knights of America.

From 1871 to 1875, the position of chief of the Fort Wayne police force was held by Michael T. Singleton. He was born in county Cork, Ireland, November 1, 1841, the son of John and Ellen (Dannahy) Singleton. In 1854 he came with his mother to America, and his father and the younger children followed two years later and joined them at Fort Wayne whither they had come from New York city in 1855. The father and mother spent the remainder of their lives in this city, the latter dying in February, 1881, and the former January 29, 1883. Their son Michael, during his youth attended school, worked as a driver of a canal boat, and also as the driver of a cart on the Pittsburgh railway. During three years he was employed as an assistant at gas fitting. For three years and a half following this he served in the capacity of jailor. In 1865 he became a member of the city police force. He was elected chief of the force in 1871, and served as such four years. From 1876 to 1882, he operated a truck line. On the 10th of May, 1883, he resumed his position on the police force, which he has since held. Mr. Singleton was married October 26, 1862, to Catharine, daughter of Michael and Catharine Myers. She is a native of Kentucky. They have three children: Michael, John P. and Michael T., the first of whom died in infancy. The others are both grown and are promising young men. Mr. Singleton and family are members of the Catholic church.

One of the oldest and most trusty members of the Fort Wayne police force, Patrick O'Ryan, is a native of Ireland, born January 17, 1837. He is the son of Patrick and Anna (Eagan) O'Ryan, both natives of Ireland, the father born in 1814, the mother in 1819. The family immigrated in 1840, and lived for eleven years at Philadelphia, removing then to Covington, Ky. The father died in Fort Wayne in 1882, and the mother now resides in Cincinnati. Of their thirteen children Patrick O'Ryan is the eldest, and only two others are living. In 1859 he came to Fort Wayne, and here followed the carpenter's trade which he learned with his father, until 1876, when he accepted a position on the police force. For eleven years he has served on the night division and three years on the day division, and he is regarded as one of the best men who are serving the city in that capacity. He was married in 1861 to Mary Maddigan, who was born in Ireland in 1844, and they have eight children living: John, James, Anna, Mary, Katie, Frank, Flora and Genevieve. Mr. O'Ryan and wife are members of the Catholic church. He is a charter member of the Catholic Knights, and was the first vice president of the order in this city.

John Trautman, an old and valued member of the Fort Wayne police force, was born in Stark county, Ohio, October 23, 1835. He is the son of George and Mary M. (Lehrman) Trautman, who were natives of Germany, but came to America in 1833 and were married soon afterward. In 1836 they came to Allen county and settled in Marion township, the father also conducting a blacksmith shop, and in this John Trautman received a partial knowledge of that trade as well as farming. He worked at the trade in 1858 in Menominee, Wis., and afterward at St. Louis, Mo. In the spring of 1859 he returned home, and after two years on the farm, came to Fort Wayne, where he has resided since 1862. He worked in the Pittsburgh shops six years, followed teaming seven years, and on June 11, 1876, took a position on the Fort Wayne police force, a place he has honorably filled ever since. He was married October 8, 1864, to Mary Guttermuth, a native of Adams county, Ind. They have had eleven children: George, Emma, Henry, Louisa, Rebecca, Jacob, Gertie, John, Sarah, Mary, and Samuel, all living except Rebecca, who died, aged three days. Mr. and Mrs. Trautman are members of St. John's German Lutheran church.

Since March, 1881, Frederick Wahrenburg has been one of the efficient, brave and honorable members of the Fort Wayne police force. He is a native of Prussia, born January 21, 1852. His parents, Henry and Sophia (Martin) Wahrenburg, were born in the same country, and there the father died when his son Frederick was about five years old. The mother is now a resident of this city. Mr. Wahrenburg has been a citizen of Fort Wayne since 1866. He took up the trade of carpenter, and was for nine and a half years in the employment of Koch & Humphreys, subsequently carrying on his trade by himself. He was married in 1875, to Mary Summers, a native of Fort Wayne, and they have six children living: Sophie, Fredrick, Maria, Henry, Ernst and Christina. He is a member of the Lutheran church, and in politics he is a democrat. Subsequent to the death of his father, his mother was married to Diedrich Martin, who for many years has been janitor of Emanuel's Lutheran church. Previous to this engagement he was employed by the Wabash railway company for over thirteen years. His married life has now been thirty years, and he has had four children, the three survivors of whom are residents of the city.

John Slater, of Fort Wayne, assessor of Wayne township, was born in Litchfield, Staffordshire, England, June 28, 1837, the son of Joseph and Elizabeth (Wood) Slater, both natives of England. The father died in 1866, in his fifty-sixth year, but the mother is still living, residing in England, and is now in her seventy-sixth year. John Slater was reared in England, and after attending the common schools, began an apprenticeship at the blacksmith trade. In 1857 he emigrated to the United States, and came direct to Fort Wayne, reaching this city on June 15. James Baxter, with whom he began an apprenticeship in England, had preceded him to Fort Wayne, and had located at Heller's Corners, and Mr. Slater at once joined him and after working for him the two formed a partnership at blacksmithing, and continued in business together for two years, when Mr. Baxter retired, and Mr. Slater continued for two years for hinself. In 1862 he removed to the city and entered the service of the P., Ft. W. & C. railroad company, in the blacksmith department. In 1868 he went into the employ of J. H. Bass, where he remained until 1872, and then entered the Wabash shops. In 1873, while in the employ of the Wabash shops, he returned to his old home in Litchfield, England, on a visit, taking with him his son Willie, then only twelve years of age. After a visit of four months in England, Mr. Slater returned to Fort Wayne, and was in the Wabash shops, until 1886, and then returned to the Pittsburgh shops, where he is employed at present. In 1886, Mr. Slater was nominated by the republicans for the assessorship of Wayne township, and was elected by a majority of between 600 and 700, notwithstanding the democrats had a majority of 2,000 in the township. He was the first republican elected in the township in a straight out fight, which speaks volumes for his popularity. During the strike on the Wabash railroad in 1885, Mr. Slater was quite conspicuous and was chairman of the local grievance committee. While the strike was in progress, he was sent west to Moberly, St. Louis, Springfield, and other points as a delegate of the Knights of Labor, to to confer with Master Workman Powderly, and others. Mr. Slater emerged from the fight with credit, having always worked for law and order as well as justice. He is a member of Summit city lodge, No. 170, F. & A. M., of Robin Hood lodge of Sons of St. George, No. 216, Kekionga Council of the National Union. He is a member of the First Baptist church, and was instrumental in erecting the present church building of that congregation, he collecting over $800 in contributions for the same. Mr. Slater was married at Heller's Corners, April 20, 1859, to Jane E. Dafforn, who was born in Staffordshire, England, March 20, 1837, and came with her parents to America in 1855. To this union thirteen children have been born, four of whom survive: William M., born September 20, 1861, now married and residing in Kansas City, Mo., Rosetta M., born October 15, 1864; Ada, born October 20, 1873, and Herbert G., born April 6, 1876. Mrs. Slater is a member of the First Baptist church.

Louis Hazzard, inspector of oils for the Twelfth Indiana congressional district, and a member of the common council of Fort Wayne, was born in Newburg, on the river Rhine, Germany, August 12, 1844. He is the son of Bernhard Hazzard, who emigrated to America with his family in 1849. His wife, daughter, and infant child, died at Indianapolis in three days' time while en route from New York to Fort

Wayne. Bernhard Hazzard while living in Germany was a wholesale and retail wine and provision merchant, but on reaching Allen county settled on a farm in Washington township, and followed farming until his death, which occurred February 26, 1874, at the age of sixty-two years and six months. Louis Hazzard was reared on the farm, and secured such education as was possible in the country schools. February 29, 1862, he enlisted in Company E, Nineteenth United States infantry, and served until February 29, 1865. He was with the Army of the Cumberland, and among the important engagements he participated in were Fort Donelson, Shiloh, Corinth, Nashville, Franklin, Stone River, Buzzard's Roost, Chattanooga, Mission Ridge, siege of Atlanta and Marrietta, Ga., from which latter point he was sent back to Lookout Mountain, where he remained until discharged. Returning to Fort Wayne, in 1865, he went to work for the firm of Clark & Rhinesmith, lumber dealers, and a few months later entered the employment of N. G. Olds & Son. While with that firm, in June, 1865, he met with an accident which caused the loss of his right arm. In the spring of 1870, he removed to Sheldon, Allen county, where for six years he dealt in groceries and provisions, then in boots and shoes and groceries, during which time he also acted as ticket agent for the Muncie railway, was postmaster of the town, and supervisor of the district in which Sheldon is located. In 1876 he returned to Fort Wayne, and soon afterward was appointed bailiff for the superior court of Allen county, a position he held about four years. In 1882 he was appointed oil inspector for the Twelfth congressional district, by Governor Gray, and is holding that position at present, having been re-appointed and commissioned March 1, 1889. In 1887 he was elected a member of the city council from the Ninth ward for a term of two years: re-elected to serve two years more, time expires 1891. Mr. Hazzard is a member of Phœnix lodge, No. 101, K. of P., of Summit City division, No. 12, U. R. K. of P., of Sion S. Bass post, No. 40, G. A. R., and of the Patriotic Circle. He was married December 20, 1865, to Anna Sargent, of Allen county, and they have one son, William Ellsworth, born October 22, 1866.

Federal Offices.— The "federal relations" of Fort Wayne have been a prominent part of its history from the very inception of the settlement. Before the earliest settlers under the present regime had thought of migrating hither, the United States flag floated from the old fort, and the soldiers of the garrison were for some time the main part of the population. Here treaties were made with the Indians and land offices established by the United States. In later days, here was the site of a federal camp for the enlistment and drilling of troops from the "Old Tenth" district, and following the war of the rebellion a pension agency was established here, at which a large volume of business was transacted until the consolidation of Indiana agencies at Indianapolis, which agency was during the Cleveland administration, in charge of Col. C. A. Zollinger, of Fort Wayne. Now, Fort Wayne is a seat of the United States circuit court for Indiana, presided over by Hon. W. A. Woods, and possesses one of the handsomest government buildings in the country, in which the postoffice also finds quarters.

The first postmaster at Fort Wayne, Samuel Hanna, opened his office in 1822 one door east of Colerick's hall. He was succeeded by Henry J. Rudisill, who kept the office in a frame building on the north side of Columbia street, between Calhoun and Clinton. In the same place the office remained during the terms of Oliver Fairfield and Smallwood Noel, but William Stewart, who was appointed in 1845, removed the office to the west side of Calhoun street, between Berry and Main. Samuel Stophlet was appointed in 1849, and John G. Maier in 1853, and during the latter's term the first mail arrived by railroad, and he was the first postmaster appointed by the president. Moses Drake succeeded in 1861, and he established the office, which had been kept in various places by his predecessors, on Court street, where it remained until the government building was erected. Peter P. Bailey filled out the unexpired second term of Mr. Drake, and was succeeded by Jacob J. Kamm, who was chosen by a popular election in 1869, there being a considerable number of candidates. He served eight years, and was followed by Frederick W. Keil, who held until the appointment of William Kaough, in August, 1885. Four years later the present incumbent, C. R. Higgins, took charge of the office.

William Kaough, an energetic and prosperous citizen of Fort Wayne, who has filled a conspicuous position in the political history of the city as a democratic leader, was in August, 1885, appointed postmaster by President Cleveland, and the functions of this important office have been by him ably and faithfully performed. He has been a resident of the county during his entire life, was raised on the farm of his parents in Washington township, and educated in the public schools. In 1872 he removed to Fort Wayne, became engaged in the agricultural implement trade, in which he was quite successful, taking a prominent place among the active business men of the city. His interest in political affairs has always been an absorbing one, and he has done the party of his choice valuable service. In 1885 he acted as chairman of the democratic central committee. He is a worthy member of the Catholic church. Mr. Kaough was born in Washington township, June 11, 1844. His father, Nicholas Kaough, was born in Ireland in 1800, came to Allen county more than half a century ago, and was one of those who cleared away the timber from the present site of the Cathedral. He married Margaret Brown, who was born in 1823, and they have had five children, of whom William was the second born. The father died in 1876, but the mother is still living, making her home in this city.

Cecilius R. Higgins, postmaster at Fort Wayne, late chief clerk of the western division of the Pittsburgh, Fort Wayne & Chicago railway company, is a native of Ohio, born at Kalida, Putnam county, January 21, 1847. Afterward his parents removed to Delphos, Ohio, where he was raised to manhood, and educated in the public schools, and where he began his career as a railroad man. His first employment was as a messenger boy, and while serving in this capacity he learned telegraphy, and was given a position as an operator. About the year 1867 he was appointed ticket and freight agent of the Pittsburgh & Fort Wayne road at Delphos and Ada. January 1, 1868, he was called to Fort Wayne to accept the important position of train dispatcher of the western division, which he filled during nine years. He then acted two years in the capacity of wood and tie agent for the company, and in 1879 was appointed chief clerk, and this responsible position he held until the summer of 1889. Those admirable qualities of character which have made him so successful in railroad life have also made him popular with his fellow-citizens in all social relations. Having always taken an active interest in politics, he was, in 1886, tendered the republican nomination for auditor, a trust which he accepted. He made a gallant contest for the success of the ticket, but was unable entirely to overcome the tremendous adverse majority in the county, although he ran 2,700 votes ahead of his ticket. During the exciting campaign of 1888, Mr. Higgins served as treasurer of the Allen county republican central committee, and as a director of the Morton club, and rendered efficient service to the republican national ticket. In recognition of his services, and that executive ability he has manifested in other positions, he was appointed by President Harrison, June 18, 1889, postmaster at Fort Wayne, which position he assumed July 9, 1889. Mr. Higgins was married May 6, 1874, to Ella S. Hale, of West Virginia, a niece of O. W. Jefferds, with whom she was raised, and they have two children: Celia and Adah. Mrs. Higgins is a member of the First Presbyterian church.

The important position of deputy postmaster, an office in its duties closely related to the public, is satisfactorily filled by Otto P. Herbst, who has been a resident of Fort Wayne since 1865. He received his education in the public schools and at Concordia college. For several years he was engaged in the meat market business in this city, but on September 1, 1885, was tendered the position of stamp clerk in the postoffice. He served in that capacity until January 1, 1887, when he was appointed deputy postmaster. He is an enterprising citizen, and is prominently connected with building and loan associations, being president of the German association No. 1, and secretary of German No. 5, Summit City, Wayne, German Allen and Jefferson associations. Politically he is prominent among the young democrats. He was married December 5, 1877, to Mary Bullerman, a native of this city, born May 7, 1858, and they have three children: Frederick H., Clara D. and Henry W. They are members of the Lutheran church. Mr. Herbst was born at Indianapolis, November 8, 1857, son of Frederick and Dora (Turkopp) Herbst, natives of Germany. The father, who was born April 10, 1825, came to the United States in 1854, and after living two years at Columbus, Ohio, removed to Indianapolis. There he enlisted in 1861, in Company K, Forty-seventh Indiana infantry, and served faithfully three years, receiving an honorable discharge in 1864. He came to Fort Wayne with his family in 1865, and was accidentally drowned March 12, 1886, in the old canal. His widow resides in this city; she was born February 5, 1824. Two of their children are living, Otto P. being the elder.

John W. Hayden, a prominent citizen of Fort Wayne, was born in Brown township, Franklin county, Ohio, May 18, 1837. His father, Isaac Hayden, was born in Fayette county, Penn., March 21, 1809, and was married in 1833, to Elizabeth Crabb, who was born in Franklin county, Ohio, August 15, 1815. He died in 1862. He was of English descent, she of Scotch, and their parents both served in the war of 1812, his father being at the battle of the river Raisin. Their only other child was Emeline, born in 1835, who died in 1857. In 1848 the family removed to Kosciusko county, Ind., where they settled in a cabin on 160 acres of land, and here, without the advantages of good schools or church privileges, except such as the itinerant preacher furnished, John W. grew up to the age of nineteen, when he was sent to Fort Wayne college. He completed the course here in 1860, and began the study of law with Hon. Isaac Jenkinson, and was admitted to the bar on April 22, 1861. President Lincoln having issued his proclamation for 75,000 three months' volunteer troops, he enlisted in Company G, of the Twelfth Indiana volunteers. Being appointed second sergeant, he held that position until the expiration of his enlistment when he re-enlisted for one year, but on account of disability contracted while in the line of duty he was discharged at Poolsville, Md., August 31, 1861. Returning home he was engaged for several years in the pension office at Fort Wayne, and subsequently began the practice of law. August 12, 1875, he was appointed register in bankruptcy by Judge W. Q. Gresham, which office he held until the repeal of the law in 1878. On the organization of the United States district court at Fort Wayne, he was appointed deputy United States marshal by W. W. Dudley, and held this position until the change of administration in 1884. In the meantime he had built up a large and lucrative real estate and loan business, at which he is now occupied. Mr. Hayden is a Methodist, as were his parents. Reared a whig, he became an enthusiastic republican, and early in life adopted for his political motto, "Colonization and qualified suffrage," a doctrine which he still believes could have saved the Union its tremendous sacrifice in settling the question of slavery. He was united in marriage May 18, 1866, with Sarah M., daughter of Dr. Samuel J. Green, of Wayneton, Ind., and they have had five children born to them, two of whom are living, Grace G. and John R. Mr. Hayden is a Mason of the Thirty-second degree, a Knight Templar and a member of the G. A. R.

Thomas W. Blair, deputy United States marshal for the northern district of Indiana, was born in Defiance county, Ohio, September 15, 1850. His father, Joseph Blair, was born in Ohio, September 10, 1824, and was a farmer by occupation, and a worthy and highly esteemed man. He married Jane Ritchhart, also a native of Ohio, born August 8, 1829, who died in Defiance county, December 28, 1865. The father died in Paulding county, April 7, 1882. Thomas W. Blair is the eldest of their three children, and his childhood and youth were spent upon the farm of his parents. After receiving a common school education he began work in 1872, at the trade of cooper, at Antwerp, Ohio, and he followed that occupation until 1881, when he came to Fort Wayne and established himself in business as a cooper. He was so engaged until January, 1886, when he sold his business and embarked in the grocery business, in which he continued until January, 1888. Mr. Blair was married February 10, 1876, to Amanda J. Smith, who was born in Paulding county, Ohio, in 1853, the daughter of Judge Ezra Smith. He is a member of Harmony lodge, No. 19, I. O. O. F., and of Phœnix lodge, K. of P., No. 101, and is a member of the supreme body of the order of the National Union. In politics Mr. Blair is an active republican, and in 1886 he was the nominee of his party for the office of senator for the district composed of the counties of Allen and Whitley, the opposing candidate being Col. I. B. McDonald, of Columbia City. Mr. Blair made a splendid contest against overwhelming odds, and going into the canvass with an adverse majority of 3,500, reduced it to 671. In May, 1889, he was appointed deputy by United States Marshal Dunlap, of Indianapolis, and he has already made an honorable record. In an early day, counterfeiters were not rare in northern Indiana, but for many years a counterfeiters' den had not been found, until Marshal Blair, early in September, 1889, discovered a complete outfit for the production of spurious coin in the garret of D. D. Rhynard, near Monroeville. On this case Mr. Blair worked three days and nights, and the culprit was safely lodged in jail. He resigned the deputy marshalship, September 23, 1889, to accept the position of assistant mailing clerk in the post-office.

Louis S. C. Schroeder, a deputy collector of United States internal revenue, stamp department, is a native of Fort Wayne, born September 10, 1857. His father, C. Louis Schroeder, was born in Germany, January 1, 1827, arrived in America June 24, 1852, and on March 13, 1856, was married to Eliza Rippe, who was born in Germany, April 10, 1838, and came to America June 18, 1854. They had two children, of whom the younger, Charles J. H. Schroeder, was born in Fort Wayne, February 4, 1860, married Louisa Lahmeyer, October 4, 1883 (she was born February 27, 1861), and has one child, Carl Louis, born January 14, 1889. Louis S. C., the elder, received his education in the English and German schools of Fort Wayne, and at fourteen years of age entered the drug store of Dreier Brothers, where he remained five years. Then, in May, 1877, at the age of twenty, he formed a partnership with his brother, who was seventeen, and embarked in business as druggists. It is probably the youngest firm of the kind on record, but they succeeded in their enterprise, and now at the corner of Broadway and Washington streets, are doing a prosperous business. Louis S. C. Schroeder is also president of the Schroeder medicine company, of Fort Wayne, of which his brother Charles J. H. is treasurer and Carl Weber is secretary. The Schroeder medicine company is a thriving young industry, organized March 1, 1889, for the purpose of manufacturing four specialties: "Weber's Catarrh Cure," "Weber's Toilet Lotion," "Weber's Corn Cure" and "Weber's Tooth Ache Drops." Though yet in its infancy, the prospects for this enterprising concern are of the most flattering nature. Mr. Schroeder is an active adherent of the democratic party, and he was in August, 1886, appointed to the deputy collectorship. He was married in November, 1879, to Lauretta, born in Fort Wayne, March 5, 1860, daughter of Orlando E. Bradway, who was born in Massachusetts, March 10, 1834, and married in 1857 Ellen Grusch, who was born in Pennsylvania, April 3, 1836. Mr. Schroeder and wife are members of St. John's Lutheran church.

PUBLIC ENTERPRISES.

Parks.— The city has no centrally located public park, and many visitors to Fort Wayne go away in the belief that in these needful places of recreation there is a woeful deficiency. On the contrary, there are parks in abundance, situated at no great distance from the business center, but in the need of money for water-works, streets, sewerage and other public works that made more imperative demands upon the municipal purse, they have until late years been somewhat neglected. The present purpose of the common council is to speedily remedy this defect, and appropriations for shade trees, flower beds, graveling of walks, drainage and fencing, seats and so on are cheerfully voted. Within the past twelve months much money has been intelligently expended in this direction, and before long Fort Wayne will have delightful breathing places for its populace, which, while they may not be made strikingly attractive by reason of the level character of the ground, may nevertheless become models of landscape, gardening and exquisite floriculture.

The city owns a large tract of land in the ninth ward, between North Cass street and Spy Run, which was years ago set apart for park purposes. A line of street cars makes it accessible from all parts of the city, and pedestrians will be occupied but fifteen minutes in a walk from the court-house, crossing the St. Mary's river by either the Clinton street or the Wells street bridges. On the east side courses Spy Run which the city proposes to deepen and widen into a lake of sufficient size for pleasure boats. The ground is elevated, the soil of gravel, overlaid with sand, and so is easily drained. During the present year a large appropriation was made for shade trees which have been planted. It is planned to erect on this property permanent buildings of graceful and attractive design, reserving always enough of the grassy lawns for games of base ball, quoits, cricket, Scottish games and other athletic sports, with possibly a track for bicycle riders. The water-works pumping house with its two monster low pressure engines, its great supply pool, fed from a series of deep flowing wells is a short distance to the north and afford objects of interest and attraction to the pleasure seeker. A little further off are the St. Vincent's orphanage, the power house of the electric light company with its great engine and powerful dynamos, and but a little farther the Centlivre boat-house where a fleet of pretty pleasure boats invite to breezy rides over the waters of the majestic St. Joseph river.

By the will of the late Thomas Seomney it was provided that the beautiful Seomney park of sixty-one acres, which lies in the bend of the St. Mary's river in the west end of the city, shall revert within a few years to the public use. The cleared portion of the property is on a gentle slope, the rest is covered with a heavy growth of forest trees. It is on these grounds that the Northern Indiana fair has been held for many years past. They contain a half-mile race track, several hundred horse and cattle stalls, and a few large buildings which have been used for exhibition purposes. Street cars run to the principal gate.

A delightful place for recreation is Williams park in the sixth ward. It is reached by the Belt line cars which pass the principal entrances. The park is amply shaded by a thick growth of young forest trees, has been thoroughly drained and been made beautiful in various ways. The boundaries of Williams park are Creighton and Hoagland avenues, Pontiac and Webster streets. The grounds are the property of the heirs of the late Hon. Jesse L. Williams, and the improvements are made by them.

The same gentlemen have beautified the site of old Fort Wayne, and have placed there the flag staff and the cannon, with mention of which this chapter begins.

Hayden Park takes its name from Hon. T. J. Hayden. It is a nearly triangular piece of ground in the eighth ward. It is not quite a block in extent, and though small is situated in a thickly settled portion of the city, admirably adapted to the greatest usefulness to the public. Numerous shade trees have been set out, flower gardens planted and it is planned to make this little park a gem of landscape gardening.

A large park, designed especially for the benefit of the citizens of of the west end, was thrown open to the public last year. It is called McCulloch park after Hon. Hugh McCulloch, ex-secretary of the treasury, who gave the land. This park will be made especially attractive. It is reached by the Belt line of street cars.

In this connection may appropriately be mentioned Lindenwood cemetery, the beautiful city of the dead, to which tender and solemn associations draw many visitors. Here, covered by the gentle hand of nature are the graves of many whose names are recorded in this history, and many a magnificent monument commemorates the prominence of worthy men and women who have passed away. This property was purchased on July 5, 1859, by Jesse L. Williams, Hugh McCulloch, Charles D. Bond, David F. Comparet, Royal W. Taylor, Allen Hamilton, Alexander M. Orb, John E. Hill, Pliny Hoagland, Alfred D. Brandriff, Oehmig Bird and I. D. G. Nelson, for the sum of $7,627.50. The title was first in the name of Mr. Williams, for the use of the company, and was deeded to the association on May 14, 1860. On the latter day the organization was completed by the election of I. D. G. Nelson as president, and Charles D. Bond as secretary and treasurer. The grounds were set apart with solemn ceremony on May 30, 1860, by a remarkable coincidence anticipating the observance of a day now dedicated to the deceased soldiers of the republic. The grounds were then in a wild, unattractive state, and much money has been expended for their improvement.

Lindenwood cemetery now comprises 124 acres, of which seventy acres are used for burial. The grounds are surrounded by an iron fence, 1,700 feet in length, is five feet high, set upon stone posts, three feet in the ground. It cost $2,652.25 and will last for generations.

The "Gate Lodge," built in a picturesque style of Gothic architecture, is located just inside the entrance gates covering a space 35x31 feet. The floors are laid with black and white marble tile, and the various rooms wainscoted with marbelized slate, and the walls and grained ceilings neatly frescoed. A circular bell-tower breaks out in one of the angles, and at the base is an open *loggia* leading to both the private office and reception room.

On the 17th day of March, 1884, the trustees sold about three acres lying on the west border of the cemetery grounds, to the Achduth Veshalom congregation, for their exclusive use for burial purposes.

A large sum of money has been expended in winding walks, and several miles of cobble stone gutters have been put down. The company secured by a substantial culvert over the old canal feeder, and by a finely graded pike such an approach from the city as few cemeteries possess. The place is visited annually by thousands of strangers, who praise its unrivaled beauty.

Two of the corporators of the association now sleep within the confines of the cemetery, Hon. Jesse L. Williams and O. A. Simons. Their demise has made changes necessary in the corporators and trustees. The former board is now composed of Hugh McCulloch, S. B. Bond, I. D. G. Nelson, O. P. Morgan, A. P. Edgerton, George H. Wilson, J. H. Bass, W. O. H. Hoffman, J. D. Bond, A. E. Hoffman, E. H. McDonald and John Orff. The board of trustees consists of Messrs. I. D. G. Nelson, O. P. Morgan, S. B. Bond, George H. Wilson and John H. Bass. The superintendent and landscape architect, is John W. Doswell.

Since the opening of the cemetery, John H. Doswell has held the position of superintendent and landscape architect. This esteemed citizen was born in the city of London, November 3, 1827. His childhood was spent in that metropolis until he was about nine years of age, when his parents removed to the vicinity of Southampton, where he was reared to manhood. He served an apprenticeship with a florist, and followed that calling in England until 1852, during a portion of which time he was in the employ of W. D. Page at Southampton, and for four years was in the gardens of the Earl of Radnor, near Salisbury, Wiltshire, from where he went to the Royal Botanical Gardens at Kew. Afterward he was head gardener for Sir William Medlican, at Venhall, Somerset. In September, 1852, he emigrated to the United States and spent the following winter at Cincinnati, where he was in the employ of the late William Resor, having charge of his green houses. He next went to Wisconsin, purchased some land and engaged in farming, but in the fall of 1859 returned to Cincinnati. In December, 1859, he came to Fort Wayne and took charge of Lindenwood cemetery. In the summer of 1888 he was engaged in laying out and improving all the city park plats. Mr. Doswell was married in England in July, 1852, to Catherine J. Humphries, who was born in Gloucester, England, April, 1825. Of their ten children, the following are living: Haidee, wife of W. H. Brady; George, florist; Alfred, florist; H. J., assistant superintendent of Lindenwood; Emma, wife of I. B. Adams; Nellie L.; A. C., florist. Mr. Doswell is a member of the Episcopalian church.

City Hospital.— No worthier institution of more humane ends is to be found than that conducted at the southwest corner of Washington and Barr streets by the City Hospital association, incorporated November 2, 1878, which may embrace any philanthropical person who will sign the constitution and by-laws. The property is that formerly known as the Hanna house, a massive brick building excellently adapted to the purposes. Mrs. C. L. Smith is the matron, and her Christian and motherly interest in the welfare of the patients, commends her to their affectionate regard. The lady is assisted by a corps of professional nurses. The hospital has accommodation for thirty patients and derives nearly its entire income from free gifts. A well equipped ambulance will shortly be put in service. The affairs of the hospital are managed by a board of nine directors, of whom M. L. Albrecht is president; W. D. Page, secretary, and E. F. Yarnelle, treasurer.

Places of Amusements.— With places of amusements Fort Wayne has been fairly well supplied. In 1853 Mr. E. F. Colerick erected Colerick's hall on the north side of Columbia street, in the middle of the block, between Clinton and Barr. This was the first public hall of any consequence, and it was opened on December 26, 1853, and for many years was a popular resort. The stage was small. In the rear of the auditorium was a gallery running across the room. In 1864 the place was refitted, the gallery was extended around the room, and private boxes were added, and the whole theater was handsomely decorated. A few years afterward it passed into the hands of Capt. J. B. White, who rechristened it White's opera house, and was twice gutted by fire. It has since been rebuilt for business purposes.

In 1868 Hervey Brothers, of Montreal, contracted with an association, called the Rink association, to erect a skating rink covering lot 95, original plat, on the north side of Berry street, between Clinton and Barr. The building was afterward turned into a tobacco factory, and in 1878 was sold and refitted as a place of amusement. A stage was put in and the floor was raised. The name of the Academy of Music was bestowed upon the property. For a time it was used as a roller skating rink, but is now devoted to general theatrical purposes. The present owner is Mrs. Charles Fletcher, and the lessee is Fred C. Baltz.

The Olympic Theater was built by the executors of the Washington Erving estate, at the southeast corner of Clinton and Columbia streets, in 1868. It had a seating capacity of 1,300. One year later it was leased by Robert L. Smith, who changed the name to the Bijou. On February 1st, it was partially destroyed by fire, and was rebuilt. On May 17, 1881, it was again gutted, and after a number of months was rebuilt for business purposes. The Bijou was a first class variety theater.

The Princess rink is a creature of the roller skating craze of three years ago. It was opened in April, 1876. It is the largest place for holding popular meetings in northern Indiana, has a seating capacity of 2,800, and covers a plat of ground 100x150 feet, at the southeast corner of Main and Fulton streets. It was erected by B. S. O'Connor, John C. Eckart, and W. A. Foote, the former gentleman owns a half-interest. The Princess is lighted with electricity and heated with natural gas.

By far the handsomest theater ever built in Fort Wayne is that erected by the Masonic temple association at the northeast corner of East Wayne and Clinton streets. The building cost $75,000, and besides its splendid opera-house provides on its three upper floors accommodations for Fort Wayne commandery, No. 4, K. T., the most elaborate in the state, with rooms for the occupancy of the four blue lodges.

The Masonic temple association was formed in the winter of 1877-78 and included in its membership many prominent citizens who were not Masons. A subscription amounting in round numbers to $30,000 was raised, and in June, 1879, the contract for enclosing the building, according to the plans of Architect Thomas J. Tolan, was let to Hueston & Co., of Dunkirk, Ohio. This firm put in the foundation and had made some progress in erecting the walls when they failed, and on February 25, 1880, abandoned the contract. The unfinished walls were boxed up and not until 1882 was work resumed by the association, issuing bonds to the amount of $30,000 and running twenty years. A majority of these bonds were taken by Hon. James Cheney of this city, who became trustee of the bond holders. The contract for the completion of the building was let to Christian Boseker. Material changes were made in the plans in the way of cheapening the construction of the upper stories.

On November 6, 1884, the Masonic temple, as the theater is called, was opened to the public with a series of brilliant concerts by the Emma Abbott grand opera company. The actual number of seats is 846, but with the four beautiful boxes and with other accommodations that can be made available, seats may be provided for 1,000 people. On June 18th last, at a meeting of the Masonic temple association, the sum of $1,000 was appropriated for new scenery, new carpets and the introduction of natural gas. Masonic temple has a Clinton street frontage of seventy feet and a depth of 120 feet on Wayne street.

The Catholic library hall is a handsome contribution to the city from the efforts of Very Rev. J. H. Brammer, vicar general of the diocese of Fort Wayne. It stands on Calhoun street at the southwest corner of Cathedral square, and is of noble and commanding appearance. The corner-stone was laid June 3, 1881, by Rt. Rev. Bishop Spaulding, of Peoria, Ill., who delivered an eloquent address. The hall is of magnificent proportions and has a well appointed stage, two galleries, etc. The building cost $65,000.

Natural Gas.— The important matter of how best to secure a supply of natural gas for Fort Wayne first took definite shape at a meeting held in the circuit court room in 1886. Robertson J. Fisher was chosen president and C. B. Woodworth secretary. Earnest speeches were made and under the belief that boring at Fort Wayne would be attended with the same success as at Findlay, Ohio, and places in Indiana to the south, a company was organized and called the Fort Wayne natural gas and fuel mining company. Four wells were sunk to the average depth of 1,400 feet, one near the Berghoff brewery, one near the Gay street over-head bridge, one near White's wheel works and one near the Centlivre brewery. In all of these wells gas was "struck," but in an insufficient quantity to reward the projectors of the scheme. The first well, however, that near Berghoff's brewery, has not been unprofitable. It was sold to the brewery company and continued for two years to supply a constant and considerable supply of gas to the boilers. After expending $12,000 this company abandoned further effort, and a new company, organized by J. C. Peltier, E. L. Craw and others, to make further search for gas. A well was bored in the east end of the city and another on the Peltier farm, three miles west of the city. These efforts were no more successful than those of the first company. Gas in small volume was invariably found but with it came a strong flow of water that choked the wells.

Matters were in this shape when, in the spring of 1887, the Salamonie mining and gas company was organized for the purpose of piping gas to this and other towns and cities from lands leased in Blackford county, Ind., forty to forty-five miles south of Fort Wayne, and near the line of the Fort Wayne, Cincinnati & Louisville railway. Hon. R. C. Bell was elected president of the company and Superintendent W. W. Worthington of the Fort Wayne, Cincinnati & Louisville railway, was elected secretary and treasurer. The company first bored four wells near Montpelier and piped and supplied that town. The success of this undertaking straightway attracted attention from Fort Wayne capitalists, and the project of piping gas to this city was then given its first serious consideration. The capital stock of the company was $50,000, and of this amount, there was but $10,000 paid in. It was agreed that if a favorable ordinance could be secured from the common council of Fort Wayne, that more capital could be enlisted and the work could be prosecuted to success.

In the fall of 1888, after long and weighty deliberation and many annoying delays, the council passed such an ordinance as warranted the great undertaking. The company was at once re-organized and its capital stock was increased to $600,000. About $350,000 of this amount was subscribed in Fort Wayne, and $250,000 was taken in New York city. At an election of officers, Hon. William Fleming was made president, and Henry C. Paul, vice president, treasurer and general manager.

Contracts for pipe and pipe laying, aggregating $400,000, were let, and within ten days thereafter the pipe was being delivered at Millgrove, Blackford county, Fort Wayne and many points along the line of the Fort Wayne, Cincinnati & Louisville railway.

The services of Max Hofman, an expert engineer, were secured, and an office was opened on Clinton street, in part of the same building long occupied by the postoffice. The work was carried to a successful completion last fall, and at once prepared Fort Wayne for the greatest stride in her history. The company has long leases on 10,000 acres of gas-bearing land, and with its twenty wells, can furnish forty million cubic feet of gas in twenty-four hours, enough to supply many cities of the population of Fort Wayne.

The main pipe enters the city from the south, near the old Wabash gravel pit, and the gas is conducted at a high pressure through two principal east and west mains, laid along Creighton avenue and Washington street. From these mains it is supplied through specially constructed automatic valves to the other mains, the valves admitting only so much gas as will give to the consumers the small pressure at which it can be used to the most advantage. The entire plant from the wells to and through the city represents ninety-eight miles of pipe. The connection having been completed there was a display of natural gas at the reducing station southwest of the city, witnessed by many people, on the evening of September 19, 1889. At that date the company had fourteen wells, with a capacity of fifty to sixty million feet per day, and intended to add sixteen wells during the season. A well known expert at that time declared that the Fort Wayne plant is the best in the United States.

The advantages of natural gas are so obvious that they need not here be recited. Among the chief points of excellence claimed for it over other fuels are cleanliness, no dust, no soiling of furniture, saving in the wear and tear of removals, uniform temperature, and freedom of the consumer from colds, is noiseless, regular and convenient; there is no dusty cellar, no carrying up of wood and coal and down of ashes, no search for kindling, no change of price and as to cost, it is at least 30 per cent. cheaper than any other fuel. It is worthy of note that the best stores and private houses in Fort Wayne will be warmed this winter with natural gas and the fuel used in the increasing number of factories comes from the same inexhaustible source.

Local Transportation.— During the era of stage lines, those conveyances were numerous, for the city was the center of a large system of diverging routes, for the transportation of mail and passengers to all parts of northeastern Indiana. Many of these ran daily, and at the smaller towns they visited, at least, were the objects of much interest. The first omnibus line in Fort Wayne, was established by James Walker in February, 1857, and for a considerable period the local passenger traffic was performed by the omnibus and hack lines exclusively. Finally in 1871, the desire for a cheaper and more convenient mode of transportation was so strongly felt that an association was formed, which filed its articles September 8, 1871, under the style of the Citizens' street railway company. Of this corporation John H. Bass was made president, Gilbert E. Bursley, secretary, and H. M. Williams, treasurer; directors, S. B. Bond, Samuel T. Hanna, John H. Bass, R. S. Taylor and H. M. Williams. On October 10, 1871, the city council passed an ordinance authorizing the company to lay lines of railway on Calhoun, Creighton, Wallace and Lafayette streets. The first superintendent of the system was Gilbert E. Bursley. This older corporation was succeeded in 1887, by the Fort Wayne street railroad company, of which John H. Bass is president; S. B. Bond, vice president; James M. Barrett, secretary; A. S. Bond, treasurer, and L. B. McNutt, superintendent. Another street car line, running from the intersection of Calhoun and Superior streets, along Spy Run to the French brewery, was built by C. L. Centlivre, and was completed in 1888.

Lorenzo D. McNutt, superintendent of the Fort Wayne street railroad, has devoted his life to the thorough study of the methods of successful and proper management of city transit facilities, and his efficiency in his present position is evidence that his career has been and will be one valuable to the public. He was born in Sandusky county, Ohio, June 30, 1849. His father, Calvin P. McNutt, was born in New York in 1805, was a farmer by occupation, and married Jane Slults, who was born in New Jersey in 1806. Both died in Lucas county, Ohio, he in 1870, and she in 1880. They had eleven children, eight now living, of whom Lorenzo D. was the youngest. He was raised on the farm, receiving a common school education, and remained there until 1872, when he removed to Toledo, and entered the employment of the street railroad company. He remained with that company until 1878, making such rapid advancement that at the end of that time he was given the foremanship of the Minneapolis street railway company. He was afterward for several years engaged in laying street railway track in various cities. In the spring of 1887 he went to Cleveland, and entered the employment of F. D. H. Robinson, as assistant superintendent of Superior street railway, and in the fall of that year came to Fort Wayne and accepted the superintendency above mentioned. Mr. McNutt was married in 1868 to Emeline M. Barnes, who was born in Illinois in 1849, and

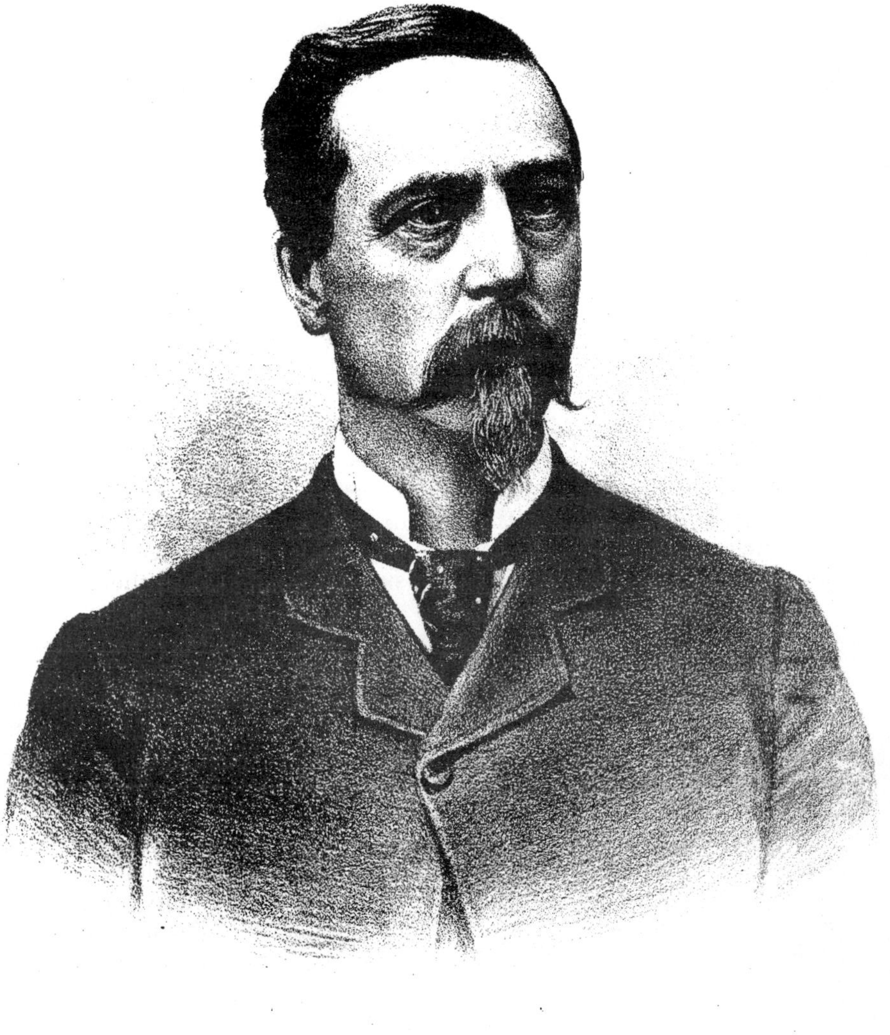
A. L. Griebel

they have four children: Willard C., Elizabeth J., Henry T. and Norian V. He is in politics a republican, and he is a member of the Masonic order.

Charles F. Myers, a worthy pioneer citizen of Fort Wayne, was born at Vintheim, Prussia, May 14, 1828. His parents, Frederick and Mary (Hansarms) Myers, coming to America in 1836, he was early introduced to the new world. Their voyage occupied nine weeks, and landing at New York, they came directly to Fort Wayne, arriving here November 11. Two or three years later the family settled on land in Preble township, Adams county, Ind., where the father was occupied at agriculture until his death in 1860, his wife surviving him until October, 1865. Charles shared their pioneer toil until he was fifteen years old, when he started out for himself, and first found employment for three years at Fort Wayne, as chore boy at the home of Hon. F. P. Randall. Then he was engaged for a year on a farm near town. After that he was for six years chiefly employed driving team for William Ewing and Hugh McCulloch. Saving his earnings he bought a team, and about this time, November 21, 1851, was married to Sophia Caroline Hitzemann, who was born at Hobbenzen, Germany, September 28, 1831. She came to this country with her mother at the age of thirteen, her father, Christian Hitzemann, having emigrated six years previously. During 1853, Mr. Myers engaged in canal boating, and in 1854 he removed to Adams county, where he farmed until 1862, when he made his home permanently at Fort Wayne. In 1863 he became engaged in the business of street sprinkling, and for several years he, or the firm of which he was a member, did the entire sprinkling for the city, and during the twenty-six years he has been so engaged, he has done an extensive business. Much of his attention since 1862 has also been given to the purchase and sale of horses, and for several years he has conducted a livery stable at Nos. 112 and 114 Webster street. His long residence here has made him a host of friends, and his acquaintance is very extensive. By all he is highly esteemed. He has six children: Mary Sophia Susanna, Sophia Christina Mary, William Christian, Henry Frederick William, Carl Henry Ferdinand and William Frederick, of whom the second and third are dead. William Frederick is a veterinary surgeon and a graduate of the Chicao veterinary college. The family are members of the Emanuel Lutheran church.

James W. Pearse, formerly superintendent of the Citizens' street railroad, has had a varied and successful business career. On first leaving his Fairfield county, Ohio, home, he served one year in the quartermaster's department during the civil war; then became engaged in the dry goods business at Newark, Ohio, where he remained unt. 1869. After that date he traveled for the Ohio Valley glass works, of Wheeling, W. Va., until 1872, then beginning an engagement of one year as traveling salesman for E. R. Taggart & Co., of Philadelphia. For five years up to 1878 he engaged in agriculture in Adams township, Allen county, removing in February of that year to Lancaster,

XIX

Ohio, where he was proprietor of the Mithoff house, the leading hotel of that city, for two years. In 1881, having returned to this city in the previous year, he was appointed superintendent of the street railway, which responsible position he held for about six years. At the time of his resignation, January 1, 1887, to take effect in March, he had already engaged in the dairy business, and to this he gave his attention until the next fall, when he was for a short time engaged in buying and selling horses. In February, 1888, he became the proprietor of a livery barn at No. 263 Calhoun street, which he has since conducted. Mr. Pearse was born near Lancaster, Ohio, March 24, 1844, son of James W. and Hannah D. (Ward) Pearse, natives respectively of Fairfield county, Ohio, and Syracuse, N. Y. He was married February 16, 1871, to Frances M. Bowser, daughter of Jacob C. and Delilah (Click) Bowser, both of Fairfield county, Ohio. Mr. and Mrs. Pearse have had four children: Fannie, Charles J., Harry W. and Bessie C., the first two of whom are deceased. Mr. Pearse is a member of the Knights of Pythias. In politics he is a prominent worker on the side of the republican party. During the campaign of 1888 he served as chairman of the political committee of the Morton club, doing effective service. He is an honorable and upright citizen.

Emmet W. Powers, a prominent business man of Fort Wayne, was born in Wayne township, Allen county, April 7, 1848, the son of John A. and Margaret (Parrent) Powers, the former of whom, a native of New York, became a pioneer of this county. The parents removed to this city when Emmet was a small child, and this has ever since been his residence. He received his education in the city schools, and in 1858 became engaged in the manufacture of handles with his father. In 1870 he became a partner of C. P. Fletcher, in the baggage and transfer business. In 1878 Mr. Fletcher sold his interest to Messrs. Angell & Barnett, and the firm was then known as Powers & Barnett until October 1, 1879, when Mr. Powers retired and removed to a large farm which he had purchased in Huntington county. This property, which contained 615 acres of good land, he cultivated until the spring of 1881, when he sold it, and in September following, returned to Fort Wayne. From the fall of 1880, he was engaged in the purchase and sale of horses and cattle until the spring of 1882, when he re-purchased an interest in the transfer, and the firm of Powers & Barnett has since done an extensive business. They are the proprietors of the immense establishment on East Wayne street, and conduct the only exclusive baggage and transfer business in the city. Mr. Powers for several years past has also given much attention to the breeding and training of fast horses, and owns a stock farm four miles south of the city. In 1887 he became a member of the Fort Wayne importing and breeding company, of which he is now a prominent member. Mr. Powers is active and successful in businiss life, and in all relations has a high standing. He is an Odd Fellow, and a republican.

Asahel Jackson Read, an old and respected citizen, is one of the worthy pioneers. He was born in New Hampshire, March 27, 1815, the son of Asahel and Esther Read, natives of that state. When he was four years old his parents removed to Syracuse, N. Y., where he grew to manhood, receiving a common school education. In 1844 he accompanied his parents to Allen county, and they settled in Cedar Creek township, removing two years later to Wayne township, where Mr. Read was engaged at farming until 1852, when he came to the city and entered the livery business, in which he has now had thirty-seven years' experience in this city. In 1868 he built his large barn on West Wayne street. He was married in April, 1837, to Fannie Aiken, who died in 1847, leaving one son, Henry A. In April, 1849, he was married again to Maria Patterson, his present wife, by whom he has a son, Charles Read, one of the proprietors of the Pixley clothing house, of Fort Wayne, and a daughter, Esther, the wife of George Brown, of Lafayette, Ind. Mr. Read is one of the city's worthiest citizens, and his life of industry permits him to spend his declining years in comfortable circumstances. Dr. Henry A. Read, eldest son of the above named, was born near Salina, Onondaga county, N. Y., December 21, 1838. After his father entered the livery business he assisted him until 1855, when he was employed as an express deliverer. He determined to devote himself to veterinary surgery, and in 1859 entered the school of veterinary surgery and medicine of Boston, where he was graduated in 1860. He has ever since practiced his profession in this city, with the exception of a period in 1865-6 spent as agent for the Merchants' union express company. From that time up to 1870 he also was engaged in the livery with his father in addition to his practice. During a subsequent period, 1879 to 1885, he again resumed that business. He has attained a high rank in his profession, and is highly esteemed by the community. In his practice he has made a specialty of the application to the treatment of animals of the principles of neurotomy, and his success in this specialty has made him a reputation throughout the United States. Dr. Read was elected to the city council in 1885, from the third ward, and re-elected in 1886 and 1888. He was married February 25, 1863, to Mary E., daughter of Owen Owens, formerly of Marion township.

The popular livery establishment of Ligget Brothers, was founded in 1873, the partnership then being formed between Robert A. and James Ligget. Their parents were John and Nancy (Young) Ligget, the father a native of Maryland, the mother of Jefferson county, Ohio. About a decade subsequent to their birth in 1852, the parents removed this county and settled in Lafayette township, where the youth of the brothers was spent on a farm. Robert A. Ligget, the elder, was born in Jefferson county, Ohio, May 10, 1842. At nineteen years of age he began to learn the trade of plow-maker, and spent an apprenticeship of three years in the works of A. D. Reid, of Fort Wayne. He then enlisted in Company A, Twelfth regiment Indiana infantry, November 17, 1864; was with Sherman from Savannah to Washington, and participated in Bentonville, and several skirmishes. He was honorably discharged at Louisville, July 17, 1865, and then resumed work at his trade here, Ft. Wayne. In 1867, he and Charles Messing bought the factory in which he worked, but sold it at the end of a year and a half. He continued to work at his trade until 1873, the last two years of that period being occupied at Rock Island, Ill. He was married September 9, 1879, to Mrs. Rebecca Sorg, and they have one child: Roy, born May 9, 1881. Mr. Ligget is a Mason, and in politics a republican. James Ligget was born in Carroll county, Ohio, August 26, 1843. He first worked at a trade as carriage maker at Zanesville, Ind., but this was interrupted by his enlistment August 8, 1862, in Company H, Seventy-fifth Indiana volunteers. He served until the close of the war, participating in the battles of Chickamauga, Mission Ridge, the battles between Chattanooga and Atlanta, and the capture of that city, and the march to the sea. Upon his muster out, June 6, 1865, at Washington, he came to Fort Wayne, and for about seven years was engaged at his trade, leaving that in 1872, to embark in the livery business. Mr. Ligget was married June 18, 1873, to Fannie E., daughter of Amos and Eliza Davis. She is a native of Sulphur Springs, Ohio. They have six children, each alternate one being a son: Phraortes C., Grace B., James A., Blanche, John W., and Nellie. Mr. Ligget is a member of the G. A. R., and past grand of Harmony lodge, No. 19, I. O. O. F., and a member of the encampment.

Among the leading liverymen of the city is Josiah F. Fletcher, who was born in Nashua, Hillsboro county, N. H., September 27, 1833, the son of Loami and Mary Ann (Boutelle) Fletcher. His father is a native of Massachusetts. Mr. Fletcher was reared in his native town, and was chiefly employed in a cotton mill in his youth, though he also learned the carpenter's trade and the making of whips. At about eighteen years of age he went to Boston, Mass., and worked at the whip trade three or four years. He then made his way to Chicago, and for several years engaged there in the manufacture of coffee and spices. Mr. Fletcher came to Fort Wayne in 1861, and has since lived here. For two years he conducted a hotel, and then turned his attention to the livery business, at which he has since been successfully occupied. He was married April 19, 1862, to Margaret Fay, who was born in January, 1834. Mr. Fletcher's present place of business is at No. 32 Barr street.

In 1867, for the purpose of giving his children superior educational advantages, George W. Ames, who had since 1838 been engaged in agriculture in Adams county, removed to Fort Wayne, where he still resides. During fifteen years of his residence he was proprietor of a truck line, and prospered in business. He is now retired, esteemed as an honorable and upright man and worthy citizen. Mr. Ames was born in Bradford county, Penn., December 12, 1822, the son of Rufus and Amy (Head) Ames, natives respectively of Massachusetts and New York. When he was three years old the family removed to Tioga county, Penn., and nine years later to Delaware county, Ohio, leaving there in 1838, to settle in Adams county, Ind., where the father passed the remainder of his life, nearly thirty years. Mr. Ames was married in Adams county, September 6, 1843, to Mary A., daughter of Ezekiel and Cornelia (Swazey) Hooper, who was born in Fairchild county, Ohio, April 13, 1824. They have had nine children: Ezekiel H., Rufus, Aaron S., Francis M., Samuel B., Benson C., George F., Ida H. and Lemuel M., of whom Aaron, Francis and Lemuel are deceased. The two eldest sons served in the war of the rebellion. Mr. and Mrs. Ames are members of the Methodist Episcopal church; in politics he is a republican.

Dr. George P. Barnum, the well known veterinary surgeon and liveryman, was born in Keeseville, N. Y., July 18, 1831, the son of Platt and Hannah (Hull) Barnum, both natives of Vermont. When he was but six months old, his parents removed to West Chateaugay, Franklin county, N. Y., where his boyhood was spent on a farm. At the early age of thirteen he started out for himself and made his way to Burlington, Vt. where he secured a position in the veterinary hospital of William I. Richardson, a prominent surgeon of that vicinity, and a graduate of a college in London. He remained there until he was nearly twenty-one years of age, having had full charge of the establishment after he reached the age of sixteen. He removed to Milwaukee, Wis., arriving there November 1, 1852, and soon afterward to Madison, where he was for one year employed by the month in his profession. Going to St. Paul, he practiced his profession one year, and then moving to Grant county, Wis., farmed and practiced until 1861. In April of that year, he engaged in the livery business at Marion, Iowa, and remained there until October, 1865. He continued to practice his profession, and in 1868, went to Omaha, Neb., and conducted a stable and practiced until April, 1870, when he came to Fort Wayne. Until 1871 he gave his time here to the profession, but in that year began the management of a large livery barn, to which he has given much attention in connection with the breeding and training and campaigning of fast horses. Mr. Barnum was married March 15, 1852, to Eliza Curtis, of Burlington, Vt.; she died in October, 1856, and March 1, 1857, he married Mary White, of Jones county, Iowa. She died in October, 1866, and on Christmas eve, 1871, he was married to his present wife, Salina Mercer, of Owasso, Mich. He had one child by his first wife and two by his second, but all are dead. He has adopted three children, since deceased. He is in politics a republican. While in Wisconsin he served five years as deputy sheriff. Mr. Barnum is a second cousin of the veteran showman, P. T. Barnum.

At the early age of twelve years, James O. Jenson, now a prosperous citizen of this city, started from his native town of Lockport, N. Y., and turned westward to seek his fortune. He found a position at Nashville, Barry county, Mich., where he spent his youth clerking in a general store, being ten years in the employment of William A. Aylesworth. Removing to Big Rapids, Mich., he spent three years in lumbering, and prospered, but at the end of the period named his large saw, planing, shingle and lath mill was destroyed by fire, at a loss of $26,000. Since then Mr. Jenson has devoted his attention to horses, dealing in them extensively. In the fall of 1885 he came to Fort Wayne, and in December, 1888, became a partner in a livery barn, which he aids in managing in connection with his business. He is prospering, has accumulated considerable property, and the energy which inspired him to start out in life single handed in a strange land, has enabled him to overcome the effects of his severe losses. Mr. Jenson is a member of the Odd Fellows, and is in politics a democrat. He was born May 22, 1859, the son of John and Abby Jane (Dunning) Jenson, who were natives of New York.

Ashley C. Perrin, prominent among those engaged in the livery business in Fort Wayne, traces his ancestry to John Perryn, who was born in England in 1614, and sailed to America in the ship "Safety," landing at Braintree, Mass., in 1635. He died September 13, 1674. His son John had a son John, born October 12, 1668, who also had a son John, born March 8, 1692, and the latter a son, Jesse, born January 24, 1726. Jesse married Rachel Ide, and their son Asa was born July 18, 1775. The latter married Rebecca Thatcher, and their son Austin, born July 18, 1801, and his wife Mary, daughter of Nathan Johnson, were the parents of Ashley C. Perrin. He was born in New York, March 21, 1828, in the eighth generation of the Perrin family in this country. In 1829 his parents became pioneers in Wayne county, Mich., where he grew to manhood. In 1852 he started for California, and en route was shipwrecked and delayed on the southern coast of Mexico about two months. In California he mined one year, and was then engaged seven years in transporting freight. Soon after his return home he engaged in hotel-keeping at Plymouth, Mich. In 1864 he was for a year and a half occupied in the livery business at Ypsilanti, and then conducted a furniture store at Plymouth, finally returning to the livery business. In May, 1873, he came to Fort Wayne, and has ever since conducted a large livery barn at No. 62 East Wayne street. Mr. Perrin was married January 1, 1861, to Mary Ann Dodge, who died in January, 1865, leaving two children, May and Eloise. February 27, 1867, he married Ellen Dodge, sister of his first wife, and they have one son, Robert Ashley, born December 3, 1881. Mr. Perrin is a Royal Arch Mason, and a member of the council in that order. In politics he is a democrat.

Among the prosperous liverymen of Fort Wayne should be named Charles W. Fulton, who embarked in his business at Burgettstown, Penn., September 12, 1877. He came to Fort Wayne in the fall of 1888, and is now the proprietor of a barn at No. 13 Pearl street. Mr. Fulton was born in Washington county, Penn., September 20, 1852, son of John J. and Margaret (Canon) Fulton, both natives of that county. He spent his boyhood on a farm, and then learned telegraphy, and for about one year had charge of an office at Oakdale, Penn., on the Pan Handle railroad. Then for three years he was engaged in hotel keeping at

Burgettstown. Mr. Fulton was married March 28, 1878, to Laura Bell McFarland, a native of his home county. She was born March 2, 1856, the daughter of Andrew McFarland. In politics, Mr. Fulton is a democrat.

John C. Brinsley was born at Stoke-on-Trent, Staffordshire, England, October 7, 1828. He is the son of Charles and Mary Jackson Brinsley, the latter being the sister of the Rev. Thomas Jackson. She died when her son was but four years old. In his early youth he served an apprenticeship of three years at the moulder's trade, and at sixteen was employed in a pottery, where he worked about four years. In 1849, the father, son and one sister, immigrated and settled at Washington, Middlesex county, N. Y. Subsequently, John C. was employed at boating between New Brunswick, N. J., and New York city, and afterward found employment as a potter, at South Amboy, N. J., one year; at Pottsville, Penn., nearly two years; at Patterson, Penn., 1852 to 1854; at Covington, Ky., until the fall of 1855. He then removed to Crestline, Ohio, where he was engaged first as a clerk in the office of the Adams express company. In 1856 he entered the employment of the Ohio & Indiana railroad company, as brakesman, and at the end of one year he was promoted conductor, which position he held seven years, five of which he was conductor of passenger trains, his run extending from Kent, Ohio, to Dayton, Ohio. For seven months he served as passenger conductor on the Indianapolis Junction railroad, from Hamilton to Indianapolis, and then accepted the same position on the Fort Wayne, Muncie & Cincinnati, and in two months was promoted master of transportation, which important position he held for eight years. Meanwhile, in 1871, he had removed his family to Fort Wayne, and this city has since been his home. Since 1881 he has conducted a feed and sale stable, having an extensive and lucrative custom. He erected his large building on Pearl street, known as the Red Lion stable, in 1887. He is prominent as a citizen, in Masonry has attained the degree of Knight Templar, and membership in the lodge of Perfection, is a past president of the St. George society, and in politics is a republican. He was married at Middleport, Penn., October 27, 1852, to Harriet Gibson, who was born at Old Mines, near Wilkesbarre, Penn., March 11, 1831, daughter of Thomas and Maria Gibson. They have had five children: Alfred (deceased), Alvina L., Charles M., John C., and Herbert. Mr. and Mrs. Brinsley are members of the Episcopal church.

CHURCHES OF FORT WAYNE.

Beginning with the earliest settlement, as will be seen in the succeeding pages, and elsewhere in this work, where the Catholic and Evangelical Lutheran churches are treated of, missionary labor and the preaching of the gospel had their inception at Fort Wayne. These early labors in the cause of religion bore good fruit, and to-day the vigorous and earnest church organizations, and the stately temples and educational institutions they have built up, form no small part of those evidences of intelligence and progress which the citizen of Fort Wayne is disposed, with just pride, to present to the world. As has been intimated the history of two powerful denominations are elsewhere presented, and the following pages will be devoted to an account of other organizations of importance.

First Presbyterian Church.*—The history of the First Presbyterian church of Fort Wayne embraces the whole period of the growth of the city from a small collection of frontier settlers to the present time. The roots of the church are intertwined with those of the city, and many leading citizens have been embraced in its communion. This brief sketch is chiefly compiled from a history of the church up to October, 1882, prepared the late Jesse L. Williams, who was one of its ruling elders from January, 1834, until his death, October, 1886. The first Protestant minister known to have visited Fort Wayne was the Rev. Matthew G. Wallace, a Presbyterian, who accompanied the army as chaplain when Gen. Harrison marched to the relief of the garrison in 1812. But the first Presbyterian minister to preach to the settlers by ecclesiastical appointment was the Rev. John Ross, one of the heroic pioneer missionaries of Indiana, familiarly known as "Father Ross," who had been appointed by the Presbyterian general assembly missionary for this frontier region. His earliest visit was made in December, 1822. Coming with a companion from Warren county, Ohio, through the wilderness, the wolves howled around their camp at night, and meeting a snow storm and intense cold they were obliged to leave their conveyance frozen fast in the mud, and leading their horses, it being too cold to ride, walked the last part of the way to Fort Wayne, where arriving late at night the missionary found a warm and hospitable welcome from Samuel Hanna, who afterward became a ruling elder in the church. The settlement then comprised about 150 souls, including French and half-breed families, mainly engaged in the Indian trade. The field of "Father Ross's" missionary labors was too widely extended for him to remain long at one place, but he visited the settlement here five times from 1822 till 1826.

In 1829 the Home missionary society, in response to an appeal made by Allen Hamilton the previous year, appointed the Rev. Charles E.

---
* By Rev. David W. Moffat.

Furman as missionary to Fort Wayne. Mr. Furman arrived November 13, and remained till the following summer. Writing to the mission rooms in New York, February 20, 1830, he said: "From this place, one hundred miles in every direction, it is a wilderness. * * This county contains only seven or eight hundred inhabitants." Of Fort Wayne, he said: "The people are hospitable and have more intelligence and liberality of feeling than any similar town I have found in the country." He also suggested the organization of a Presbyterian church. In June, 1831, the Rev. James Chute visited Fort Wayne, and at the request of the Presbyterians residing here, on July 1, 1831, organized the First Presbyterian church with eleven members, and continued ministering to the young church till his death, December 28, 1835. There was no house of worship. The services connected with the organization of the church were held in the open air under a rude shelter of boards near what is now the junction of Columbia with Harrison streets; and for six years following, the congregation met for public worship wherever it could find a place, successively occupying a carpenter shop, a school-house, the Masonic hall and the court-house, till in 1837 they found rest in a frame church forty feet square which they erected on the south side of Berry street, between Barr and Lafayette streets. After the death of Mr. Chute, the Rev. Daniel Jones, and following him for a few months in 1837 the Rev. Jesse Hoover, a Lutheran, ministered to the congregation.

In October, 1837, the congregation having occupied their church building, the Rev. Alexander T. Rankin began his ministry which continued till September, 1843. All these ministers, already mentioned, had been either missionaries or stated supplies, but now, well established, vigorous and growing, the church desired to have a pastor, and in May, 1844, called the Rev. W. C. Anderson, D. D., to that office. The same month six members were dismissed, who, with others, were organized into the Second Presbyterian church of Fort Wayne. Dr. Anderson declined the call tendered him, but occupied the pulpit for six months, when by reason of failing health, he was obliged to retire. By his advice a call was extended to the Rev. H. S. Dixon, who accepted, and in September entered upon his work as the first pastor of the church. The building erected in 1837 was becoming too small to accommodate the increasing congregation, and in 1845 a larger edifice of brick was begun, the site being at the southeast corner of Clinton and Berry streets. The basement was occupied for public worship in 1847. In the fall of that year, Mr. Dixon resigning, the pulpit was supplied for six months by the Rev. Hawes, and in August, 1848, the Rev. J. G. Riheldaffer accepted a call to the pastorate, in which he continued till 1851, when he resigned.

In November, 1851, the Rev. Jonathan Edwards, D. D., having been called, became pastor, and in the next November the church at the corner of Clinton and Berry streets was completed, dedicated and wholly occupied for worship. The pastorate of Dr. Edwards continued till

July, 1855, when he resigned to accept the presidency of Hanover college. He was succeeded by the Rev. John M. Lowrie, D. D., who was installed in November, 1855, and remained pastor of the church till his death, September 26, 1867. During Dr. Lowrie's pastorate, the church edifice was enlarged, a mission in the south part of the city was established, and all the arrangements were made in pursuance of which, December 2, 1867, thirty-four members were dismissed to be organized into the Third Presbyterian church of Fort Wayne. The site chosen was at the northeast corner of Calhoun and Holman streets. It was contributed by a lady of the church, and upon it, the members of the congregation placed a commodious brick church, fully equipped at a cost of $15,000. Dr. Lowrie was succeeded in the pastorate March, 1868, by the Rev. Thomas H. Skinner, D. D., who resigned September 18, 1871, to accept a call from the Second Presbyterian church of Cincinnati. February 5, 1872, a call was given to the Rev. David W. Moffat, D. D., then pastor of the Georgetown Presbyterian church, Washington, D. C., and, having accepted it, May 1, he entered upon his pastorate which still continues.

Saturday evening, December 16, 1882, the church edifice was destroyed by fire. One year's delay in rebuilding was occasioned by the determination of the congregation to select another location. During the next summer the old site was sold to the United States government, and is now occupied by the postoffice building. A new site was purchased two squares south, at the northeast corner of Clinton and Washington streets, and in the spring of 1884, the new edifice was begun. The congregation continued to meet for Sabbath worship, in the circuit court-room until May 1, 1883, and after that in the Jewish synagogue for two years and five months. The first Sabbath of October, 1885, they began to meet in the lecture room of the new church, and May 1, 1886, the auditorium was open for public worship. The church is a majestic and beautiful stone structure, the style of architecture being a modification of the gothic, and the total width east and west 100 feet; and the total length north and south 134 feet. The interior, which is complete in all its appointments, is handsomely finished in California redwood. The pews, pulpit, pulpit furniture and wood-work of the organ are of cherry. The north end, divided from the auditorium by a partition, has two floors. On a level with the auditorium are the lecture room and Sabbath school rooms, and on the floor above are the church parlors. The cost of the site was $12,000, and of the building proper, with the spire yet unfinished $65,879. The total cost of the building including organ, pews, furniture, etc., and excluding the site has been $81,855. The number of members in the full communion of the church is 450, the congregation aggregating about double that number.

The Rev. David W. Moffat, D. D., pastor of the First Presbyterian church, Fort Wayne, was born of Scottish parents, January 9, 1835, in Morris county, N. J. His father, David Douglas Moffat, was a farmer. The next year the family emigrated to Madison, Ind., and, on a farm on one of those beautiful hills which overlook the city and the Ohio river, the boyhood of David was spent. He attended school in Madison, and afterward entered Hanover college, six miles distant, from which he was graduated in 1858, his parents meanwhile having removed to the vicinity of Vernon. With a little aid from his father he paid his own way at college, earning the money principally by teaching part of each year. It was a time of intense political agitation and he took a deep interest and active part in the great anti-slavery debate and movement to prevent the extension of slavery into the new territories. Having chosen the profession of law while in college, he began, after his graduation, to prepare himself by private study at Vernon, for entering a law school, and it was while thus engaged that the course of his life was changed. Though religiously trained by Christian parents, he had become indifferent to the personal claims of religion upon him, and in his opinions vibrated between extreme liberal views of Christianity and skepticism. Judging that every professional man ought to have a settled and intelligent knowledge of the teachings of the Bible, he entered upon a systematic study of it. Becoming, as he progressed, more and more interested in his biblical studies, they encroached on, and at length wholly absorbed the time he had allotted to Blackstone and Kent. He reviewed the Christian evidences, and though they seemed satisfactory, he found the most powerful evidence of Christianity to be Christianity itself as unfolded in the biblical revelation. The result was a firm persuasion of the divine origin of that revelation, faith in Jesus Christ as the Son of God and Saviour of men, and a decision to live a Christian life. He united with the Presbyterian church in July, 1859, his own convictions of the teachings of the Bible leading him into the church of his fathers. The desire to preach sprang up at once and soon overcame his love for law and for political life. In January, 1860, he entered the theological seminary at Princeton, N. J., in which the Rev. James C. Moffat, D. D., his oldest and only living brother, has been professor of church history since 1861. He graduated from the seminary in May, 1862, was licensed to preach in June of that year by the Presbytery of Madsion, in session at Hanover, and in April, 1863, was ordained to the ministry. After preaching a year in Clinton county, and two years at Vernon, in Jennings county, in 1866, he accepted a call to the First Presbyterian church of Madison. In 1870 he was unexpectedly called to the Presbyterian church in Georgetown, D. C., and although bound to Madison by the strongest ties he decided it was his duty to go. He began his work at Georgetown in February, and two years afterward returned to Indiana in response to a call from the First Presbyterian church of Fort Wayne. May 1, 1872, he entered upon this pastorate in which he has remained until the present time. January 20, 1870, he was married to May J., eldest daughter of Samuel Cochran, of Madison. She died at Fort Wayne, October 29, 1882, leaving one son and two daughters, since which he has remained a widower.

Second Presbyterian Church.—This, one of the strong and flourishing religious organizations of the city, was organized May 5, 1844, with twelve members. Henry Ward Beecher, then a young preacher of the new school faith at Indianapolis, was called here by those who inclined to that doctrine, and he made the trip to Fort Wayne, arriving here on horse-back for the purpose, as he jocularly remarked to Mrs. J. L. Williams upon his arrival, of "splitting the church." The new church was founded successfully but now is at one with the older organization, and under the same general church government. On June 4, 1844, Rev. Charles Beecher was invited to become the stated supply for one year, and he remained in that capacity until April 28, 1850, when he was installed as pastor. In the same summer he removed to the east, and while there resigned his charge. This first pastor was a zealous worker and thorough student, and preached with such effect that his congregation was increased to over 100. By his exertions was erected during the early years of his ministry the church building which was in use for many years. After Mr. Beecher's resignation, the church did not remarkably flourish for some time, and during this period the supplies were Revs. Isaac W. Taylor, David C. Bloose, Mr. Ray, and Amzi W. Freeman. In November, 1854, Rev. E. Curtis was called by the church, and the membership was considerably increased during his pastorate. He was succeeded by W. R. Palmer in 1861, and Rev. George O. Little in May, 1866. The latter served until August 18, 1870. W. J. Erdman, who did important and valuable work for the church, was stated supply until June, 1874, and during his service Glenwood chapel was erected and dedicated for use as a Sunday-school mission. Rev. Joseph Hughes succeeded in July, 1874, and was followed by Rev. W. H. McFarland, who served from June, 1876, to June, 1886, when he resigned and went abroad for his health. From April, 1887, to October, 1888, Rev. J. M. Fulton acted as pastor, but ill health compelled him to resign. During his service, the movement was inaugurated for the abandonment of the venerable temple and the erection of a new one on the same site. This edifice was soon begun, and has progressed rapidly, through the great energy of those in charge, systematic organization, and the liberal contributions of the congregation and many friends throughout the city. This new building, one of the finest in the state, it is expected will be occupied by the close of 1889. It has a beautiful stone front, the side and rear walls being of brick with stone finish. The spacious plans afford an auditorium capable of seating 600 persons, ample Sunday-school rooms and social parlors. The ceiling and sides of the interior are ornamented with quartered oak and fresco, and the seats are of quartered oak antique, and cherry finish. The total cost is about $30,000. Memorial windows have been placed in the new building as follows: by Hon. Hugh McCulloch, Mrs. Susan McCulloch, the heirs of D. S. Beaver, Fred W. Antrup, Col. C. B. Oakley and Mrs. O. J. Wilson, the latter two to the memory of Benjamin W. Oakley and Harriet Oakley. The church has included in its membership a considerable number of those prominent in the history of Fort Wayne and the country. The only survivor of the first members is Mrs. Susan McCulloch, wife of Hon. Hugh McCulloch. Hon. W. H. H. Miller, now attorney general of the United States, was a trustee of the church in 1869. At present the membership of the church is about 300. The pastor is Rev. James L. Leeper, of Reading, Penn., who accepted an unanimous call in November, 1888, and has been an earnest worker for the good of the organization and its building enterprise. The trustees at the present time are Solomon Bash, F. W. Antrup, Joseph Hughes, H. V. Root and C. B. Beaver.

The Third Presbyterian church, a daughter of the First church, was organized as has been mentioned, in 1867, and the church building was completed in 1869. This edifice has lately been repaired to a considerable extent and re-frescoed. For a short time after the organization, the congregation worshiped in a frame building on Holman street, afterward temporarily occupied by the Episcopal church. The church has flourished, is one of the prominent religious organizations of the city, and now has a membership of 250. A Sunday-school is maintained, with an average attendance of 220. The first record of official action by the organization bears date December 8, 1867. Rev. N. S. Smith, under whom the church was organized, was the pastor until the winter of 1873, after which the office was supplied by Rev. John Woods until the spring of 1874. The succeeding pastors have been: Harlan G. Mendenhall, installed May 6, 1875; W. B. Minton, installed June 20, 1878; J. Vance Stockton, installed June 4, 1880; S. Ferre Marks, installed May 29, 1882; David Scott Kennedy, installed May 3, 1886; J. M. Boggs, installed January 6, 1889. The first elders were: W. N. Andrews, J. B. McDonald and Andrew Wallace, and since then have served M. P. Longacre, John M. Wilt, N. D. Lindley, B. M. Herr, and the present elders, C. E. Shultze, who was installed May 5, 1872, O. B. Fitch, A. E. Van Buskirk, J. D. Chambers, J. C. Mudge, W. D. Page, W. Meyers. The deacons in service are: Thomas Sinclair and J. W. Donavin; trustees, G. W. Morgan, W. Diffenberger, A. M. Tower, W. Harrison, F. M. Wilt, and the congregational officers are William Creighton, president, E. G. Schulze, secretary.

The First Baptist Church.—The history of the Baptists of Fort Wayne, writes E. G. Anderson, esq., dates back to the year 1820, when Rev. Isaac McCoy, under the appointment of the Baptist Triennial convention, came as missionary to the Miamis and Pottawattomies, tribes of Indians whose reservations were located in this vicinity. Elder McCoy found it a difficult task to reach a people who were very suspicious of any advance of the white man, and it was a long time before he could gain their confidence and tell them of a Saviour's love. He succeeded, however, in gathering some fifty children together and instructing them in the truths of the gospel. But few white people had ventured into this country at that time, partly on account of the terrible malaria that was then so prevalent. But the success that attended Elder McCoy's work induced the society to still further occupy this important field. In 1821 Rev. John Sears received the appointment as missionary among the Ottawas, and arrived at Fort Wayne August 1, 1822. He was accompanied by his wife and brothers. Reinforced by these new recruits Elder McCoy organized a church and adopted articles of faith. The names of eight whites, two Indian women and one black man appear on the roll.

This church was short-lived, Elder McCoy going west with the Miamis, and Elder Sears and his wife prostrated with malarial fevers, were compelled to return to New York, leaving his brother alone in the field, but after twenty-three days of labor he also succumbed, dying with typhus fever, November 3. Thus the little church became extinct.

For the next fifteen years we hear no more of the Baptists in this locality. In 1835-6 we learn that Revs. Tisdale, French and Moore preached here occasionally to the Baptists, who had moved to the village and vicinity, and in January, 1837, the brethren who had been worshiping with other denominations began the organization of a church of their own faith, and after the earnest efforts of Rev. Robert Tisdale it was consummated. On Saturday, April 15th, 1837, by previous invitation, Revs. Tisdale, Moore and Fry, met with the church to complete its organization. The Presbyterian congregation kindly gave them the use of their church for the occasion. After appropriate exercises the following persons appeared and signed the roll of membership: Richard Worth, Elizabeth Worth, John Fairfield, William Worth, Sarah Swop, Hannah Worth, Meriam Sawtelle, Ann Archer and Elizabeth Morgan.

It was a joyous yet solemn beginning, ten souls agreeing in solemn covenant to maintain the faith once delivered to the saints in all its purity and simplicity. On the following Sabbath the First Baptist church of Fort Wayne was duly re-organized, Elder Moore preaching the sermon, Elder Fry extending the right hand of fellowship assisted by Elder Tisdale. Services were continued for several days and some new converts were baptised, among them Ann Girard, known to the older members.

The progress of the new church was at first very slow. A good deal of difficulty was experienced in securing and maintaining a pastor. Elder Tisdale remained with the little flock for a few months. He was followed by Revs. William Corbin and William Cox, in short pastorates. The need of a church building was sadly felt and meetings were held at the homes of the different members, and when the preacher came, the little brick school-house was secured. After the resignation of Brother Cox, the church was without pastoral care until October, 1841, when Rev. William Gildersleeve became the pastor, at a salary of $300 a year. During his ministry, some progress was made and new hopes inspired the membership. Many additions were made to the church, among them, Messrs. Lewis Embry and Jeremiah Mason, both of whom have gone to their heavenly reward. The Eel River church was organized during the pastorate of Mr. Gildersleeve, and the frame church was built on "Clay Hill," on a lot donated by Hon. Samuel Hanna. March 11th, 1843, Rev. J. H. Dunlap was invited to the pulpit. He remained for two years. During this period, severe trials came upon the church and serious troubles arose among the membership which were never fully healed until death removed all parties concerned. About this time Mr. E. M. Ferris and family were admitted by letter. Rev. George Sleeper supplied the pulpit for a few months after the resignation of Mr. Dunlap, but declined continued service. April 4, 1846, Rev. H. D. Mason became pastor. By his earnestness, new life was infused into the work of the church and a new inspiration was given all along the line. The lot on the corner of Berry and Clinton streets was secured, and in the summer of 1848, the frame church was moved upon it. No obstacle was allowed to hinder the best interests of the church.

After two years of faithful service Mr. Mason resigned and for nearly two years thereafter the Baptists were without any regular pastor. Preaching, however, was maintained by the Rev. Mr. Searls as a supply, until he was stricken down by malaria. Elder D. W. Burrows then supplied the pulpit for more than a year.

In May, 1850, Rev. J. D. Meeson began his pastoral labors. He was sustained in part by the Home Missionary society. His ministry was one of great power and Zion put on a new life, for God was with her and the Spirit seemed to find ready access to many hearts. A revival of great power followed, Brother Mason preaching. Among those who came into the church were Mrs. R. Cothrell, Emily Philley, Eliza Coombs and Charlotte Rupert, N. Sibray and wife and sister, Sarah Holmes. All of these are still active members. The retirement of Rev. Mr. Mason was a great loss to the church. May 1, 1853, Rev. U. B. Miller was called. He was a man of more than ordinary force in the pulpit, and was an earnest worker for the Master. For three years the church enjoyed his ministry, and the cause of Christ was greatly advanced. But the Home Missionary society declined to extend further aid and Pastor Miller resigned for lack of sufficient support.

Rev. C. W. Rees, a young man who had just graduated from the Kalamazoo college, became pastor on September 4, 1856. He was a mighty power in God's hands, and in a little over a year sixty were added to the church membership, mostly by baptism. Mr. Rees resigned October 31, 1857. He is now pastor of a church at Glensburgh, Ore. The next pastor was Rev. Stephen Wilkins. He was a man of considerable power in the pulpit and strongly impressed his hearers with his quaint way of putting the gospel truths. He served the church for two and a half years with great satisfaction. No pastor succeeded him for several months and there was only occasional preaching by such supplies as could be obtained. February 6, 1861, Rev. William Frary accepted an invitation to preach. He was invited to resign, and ended his connection with the church on June 2, 1861.

Dr. G. L. Stevens became pastor September 25, 1861. He was a valuable servant, an excellent man, and a good preacher. During his ministry there was a large increase of membership. At this time the necesssity of a new house of worship became very apparent and plans for building were set on foot. The pastor, together with Messrs. Sanford Lumbard, Isaac Dripps and Thomas Stevens, aided by a self-sacrificing people and sympathizing friends, reared and dedicated to God, our present beautiful church home. Dr. Steven's pastorate was continued over a period of over seven years.

March 1, 1869, Rev. J. R. Stone, D. D., was called. This man of blessed memory needs no words to speak his praise. He was an exemplary Christian gentleman as well as an ideal pastor. He was an honor to his calling. A man of genial though dignified habits, by his life and daily walk the Baptist cause received an impetus and recognition never before accorded it. After years of faithful service he resigned, to accept a call to the church at Lansing, Mich., where after a brief pastorate, he fell asleep mourned by all who knew him. Truly blessed is the memory of such a man. Many were begotten of the Lord through his labors, and were he to speak to-day, he would say: Be thou faithful, that ye may also enter into the rest prepared for those that love our Lord Jesus Christ.

After Dr. Stone's resignation, correspondence was immediately opened with several clergymen with a view to settlement as to pastor, and by special request, Rev. S. A. Northrop met the committee of the church as Rome City where it was agreed that he should preach from the vacated pulpit two Sabbaths. He came, we saw, he conquered and on September 1st, he entered upon his duties. Of the first four and a half years of Dr. Northrop's pastorate it may be said: "O Zion, how stately have been thy steppings, how grand thy conquests! The glory of the Lord has risen upon thee, and thy power has gone out through all the land."

From 190 the membership has increased to nearly 700. The latent power of the church has been brought into action, and to-day the Baptist people are a faithful band of earnest workers, fully awake to the necessity of the hour, and ready for any work in the Master's vineyard. The handsome house of worship was this year greatly improved in appearance and considerably enlarged by the building of a new front. The attendance is generally limited only by the seating capacity of the large auditorium.

Rev. Stephen A. Northrop, the distinguished pastor of the First Baptist church of Fort Wayne, was born at Granville, Licking county, Ohio, April 7, 1850. His father, William R. Northrop, a native of Gallipolis, Ohio, is also a clergyman of the Baptist church, and is at present engaged at Monroe, Mich. The son, Stephen, spent the first ten years of his life in his native state, and then accompanied his parents to Michigan. At twenty years of age he entered Denison university at Granville, Ohio, and pursued the classical course three years, then entering Madison university, Hamilton, N. Y., where he was graduated with the degree of A. B., in June, 1876. He stood first in his class in Greek literary work and oratory, and was noted as a debater. While

Brackenridge

in college he was a member of the Delta Kappa Epsilon fraternity. Subsequently his Alma Mater conferred upon him the degree of A. M. In the fall of 1876 Mr. Northrop entered upon a course of theological study in the Rochester seminary, Rochester, N. Y., a Baptist institution, meanwhile filling the pulpit of the First Baptist church at Ashville, Chautauqua county, N. Y. On July 1, 1877, he received a call from the First Baptist church of Fenton, Mich., where is located the Baptist ministers' home for the states of Indiana, Ohio, Illinois, Michigan and Wisconsin. Here he remained over five years, during which period more than 200 were added to the church. In July, 1882, he received the unanimous call of the First Baptist church of Fort Wayne, to succeed the late Rev. J. R. Stone, D. D., and this call he accepted and assumed the pastorate September 1, 1882. Immediately afterward improvements were made in the house of worship to the value of $6,000. Rev. Northrop is now serving his eighth year, and during this time between 700 and 800 have been added to the church. In 1887 he was elected president of the board of managers of the Baptist ministers' home, for a term of two years, and he is also one of the trustees of the Baptist assembly at Laporte, Ind. In politics Mr. Northrop is a republican, and he had the honor of offering prayer at the Wednesday session of the national republican convention at Chicago, in June, 1888. He was married August 16, 1877, at Hamilton, N. Y., to Leitie A. Joslin, who was born at that place September 8, 1856, and is a graduate of Hamilton female seminary. Her father, William C. Joslin, a businessman of Hamilton, led the choir in the Baptist church there for forty-three years. This musical talent is shared by his daughter, a charming vocalist, who has filled the position of soprano singer in the choir of her husband's church since his residence in Fort Wayne. They have one child, Laura May. Pastor Northrop has been able to solve the vexing problem, "How to reach the masses." He has succeeded in this respect beyond his highest expectation. Throngs of our people have sought the door of the Baptist church for years, till the congregation was obliged to enlarge their house of worship, at an expense of $8,000, increasing the seating capacity to 1,600. The value of the property is $45,000.

The only other Baptist church in the county of Allen, that of Eel River township, may here be appropriately mentioned. It was organized December 21, 1844, mainly through the efforts of Elder Wedge, and the first members were John Ross, Appleton Rich, John J. Savage, Mary Ross, Sarah Rich, Mary Crow, Mary Savage and Sally Lowen. The organization was effected in the log school-house near the present site of the church, and that primitive building, 16x24 feet in dimensions, was used as a church until a short time after April 15, 1848. At that time trustees were elected, and a building committee appointed for a new church, which was not, however, completed until the summer of 1850. This building was 24x30, and cost $250 besides labor. Many years later the congregation had outgrown its quarters and a meeting was held August 19, 1871, which resolved to build a new church. There wrs a delay until January, 1877, when Thomas Larimore, William J. Mayo and John M. Taylor were appointed a building committee, and they prosecuted the work so vigorously that the congregation has worshiped for several years in a handsome church built of brick, in dimensions 40x60 feet, with a spire 120 feet high. The first pastor of the church was A. S. Bingham, who was chosen in the May following the organization. He served most of the time for thirty years. The first deacons were Appleton Rich and John Ross. Elder Bingham was a faithful worker, and though the church was not much developed in that time in benevolence and Sunday school work, it was nevertheless abreast of the church development of that day. Nearly 200 members were added during Elder Bingham's pastorate, which ended October 1, 1875. During the latter part of this period he was assisted by Elder A. Latham. Elder Jones served one year from November, 1878, and was succeeded by D. D. Spencer for one year. J. H. Winans served the church two and a half years in connection with Churubusco, until January, 1885, and left the church prospering. In the following August, B. F. Harman was called, who served a short time, after which the church was supplied by Rev. C. V. Northrop, then a student for the ministry. Rev. W. S. Kent, the present pastor, took charge in November, 1886, and has since the first year, given the church half of his time, doing valuable service, through which there have been thirty-three additions. The church has been much adorned and beautified. It is an imposing church building, having cost $5,000, and the cemetery adjoining is one of the largest in the county.

Methodist Episcopal Churches.—In the year 1824, James Holman, one of the famous Holman family, of Wayne county, Ind., a local preacher of the Methodist church, removed with his family to Fort Wayne, then a small village, and purchasing a farm in what is now a part of the city north of the St. Mary's river, made his residence in a log cabin near where now the New York, Chicago & St. Louis railroad crosses the river. True to his vows, Mr. Holman preached the gospel to as many as would come to his house to hear him, or would gather where he went, throughout the county. These meetings continued until in the latter part of 1830. Alexander Wiley, then a presiding elder of the Ohio conference, came to Fort Wayne to establish a mission, to be embraced in his district. About the same time Nehemiah B. Griffith was appointed by the Ohio conference to take charge of this mission. He was succeeded by Richard S. Robinson, and the latter by Boyd Phelps, under whose ministration it was named Maumee mission. The last missionary sent by the Ohio conference was Freeman Farnsworth. During this period the meetings of the class were held at various convenient places. In 1832 the class consisted of six members, Judge Robert Brackenridge and wife, James Holman, wife and daughter, and Miss Alderman, afterward Mrs. Simon Edsall. After Rev. Farnsworth had served one year, the conference of Indiana having just been formed, sent to this place Rev. James S. Harrison, and Maumee mission became Fort

Wayne circuit. During the pastorate of Rev. Harrison, 1835-36, an attempt was made to build a church, and have a regular place of worship. A lot on Main street, between Cass and Ewing, was secured, and a large frame was erected, with an imposing steeple, gothic windows, etc. But the congregation finding itself unable to complete, abandoned the structure and the frame was afterward taken down and the lot reverted to the Ewings. The congregation continued to hold services where places could be found, in the Masonic hall, a two-story brick building where Bash's elevator now stands, or in a carpenter shop on the lot where Root & Co.'s store now is, and sometimes in the school-house, then located on the site of the county prison.

Fort Wayne circuit was served successively by Revs. Stephen R. Ball, James T. Robe and Jacob Colclazer. During the pastorate of the latter, Alexander M. McJunkin, whose name is worthy of prominence in the history of the Maumee valley, generously gave the use of his school-house to the Methodists, where they worshiped and held Sunday school until the second and this time successful attempt was made to build a house of worship. A frame building was erected, finished and occupied in 1840, on the corner of Harrison and Berry streets. In this year the circuit became Fort Wayne station, to which F. A. Conwell was appointed. He was succeeded by George M. Boyd, Hawley B. Beers, J. S. Bayless, Samuel Brenton, Amasa Johnson, William Wilson, Homer C. Benson and Milton Mahin. In 1849 the membership was 217, and at this time, under the eldership of Samuel C. Cooper, William Wilson being pastor in charge, the congregation was divided, and the withdrawing members founded Wayne Street church, building a house of worship on the corner of Wayne and Broadway streets. The first frame church built on Berry street in 1840 gave way twenty years later to the brick edifice, known as the Berry Street church. Since the division in 1849, resulting in two Methodist Episcopal churches, three additional churches have been founded and buildings erected, Simpson church in the south part of the city, Trinity in the north, and St. Paul's on the east side.

Berry Street church has 416 members, and its house of worship is valued at $22,000, parsonage $8,000. The present pastor is W. M. VanSlyke. At Wayne street there are 478 members; church, $22,000, parsonage, $4,000; pastor, R. M. Barnes. Simpson street, G. B. M. Rogers, pastor, has sixty-five members and a church valued at $6,000. St. Paul church, M. E. Cooper, pastor, has 219 members, and the property is estimated at $4,000. Trinity has a church worth $2,000, and 123 members under charge of D. M. Shackleford. The total number of members of the Methodist Episcopal churches of the city at the last report was 1,301.

Fort Wayne College.—At the third session of the North Indiana conference of the Methodist Episcopal church, held at La Porte, Ind., in September, 1846, the Fort Wayne female college was organized. The first session, which was informal, of the board of trustees was held on the 28th of the same month and year, and the board regularly organized under a charter, June 19, 1847. The corner-stone of the college building was laid on the 24th of June, 1847, Rev. Samuel Brenton delivering an address on the occasion. Hon. A. C. Huestis was the first president, serving from September 1847, to May, 1848, when he was succeeded by G. H. Rounds, who held the position until July 30, 1849. Upon his resignation the vacancy was filled by the appointment of Rev. Cyrus Nutt, who served until September 3, 1850, and then resigned. A. C. Huestis was acting president until April 19, 1852, when Rev. S. T. Gillett became president, serving until September 24 of the same year. He was succeeded by Rev. Samuel Brenton until August 4, 1855, when Rev. Reuben D. Robinson became president, serving until December 18, 1866. Several changes occurred in the management of the institution until March 20, 1872, when Rev. R. D. Robinson again became president, serving this time for five years. He was succeeded by Rev. W. F. Yocum, who continued in the management of the institution for the eleven succeeding years, tendering his resignation as president June 14, 1888. At the same time Rev. H. N. Herrick was elected to the presidency and sustains that relation at the present time, September, 1889.

During these years the progress of the institution was not the most satisfactory, and steps were taken, as occasion seemed to demand, to remedy existing deficiencies. At a meeting of the trustees, March 1st, 1849, the president laid before them a communication from Rev. Samuel Brenton, on the subject of having a male department in connection with the college, which was referred to a committee consisting of Messrs. Edsall and Williams. At a subsequent meeting of the board, a resolution looking to the consummation of this end was laid on the table. In March, 1850, the faculty united in a written request to the board asking the privilege of admitting male students at the commencement of the next term This request was granted, and at a meeting of the board on the 17th of August, 1852, it was resolved " that in the opinion of the board, it is expedient to establish a college for the education of males at this place, to sustain the same relation to the North Indiana conference that the Fort Wayne college does, and that we will co-operate with the North Indiana conference and the friends of education, in carrying into effect such a project." On the 10th of October, 1855, the "Fort Wayne female college" and the "Fort Wayne collegiate institute for young men" were consolidated into an institution known as the "Fort Wayne college." The history of the college has been that of one continuous struggle from its beginning. Sometimes the indications seemed favorable for its establishment upon a good financial basis, and yet none of its plans have been fully accomplished. Rev. R. D. Robinson, D. D., who presided over it for seventeen years, and Rev. W. F. Yocum, D. D., for eleven years, deserve great credit for what has already been accomplished, having been ably assisted by such men as William Rockhill, Allen Hamilton, Joseph K. Edgerton, John M. Miller, George Breckenridge and many others.

At a meeting of the National association of local preachers held in the college chapel, Fort Wayne, September 11th to 14th, 1886, the committee on education recommended: that the efforts of the association shall be confined and directed to only one institution of learning at a time, and that such benefactions shall be continued until such institution be placed on a firm financial basis, and be thereby made permanently an honor to the association thus fostering it; the committee proceeded to state certain favorable facts and concluded: Your committee, in view of these facts, also in view of the action your body heretofore had, and that said college is the first applicant, therefore, and in consideration of its central location, its healthy Christian work and influences, and the promising field of its operations, we recommend that the Fort Wayne college be selected by the association to be the recipient of its benefactions, and be declared to be under its patronage.

There was cited in this report the following communication from the trustees, signed by H. C. Hartman, vice president:

DEAR BRETHREN:— In view of the favorable action taken by your association, in behalf of the Fort Wayne college, at its session in Brooklyn in 1885, we feel emboldened to present our institution again to your consideration.

We have adopted resolutions providing for special rates and facilities for students who are local preachers of the Methodist Episcopal church, and also for the children of local preachers, and for students who are preparing themselves for missionary work.

We desire your endorsement as an association. In the event of your aid to the extent of the endowment of a chair in our college, we suggest that it be named in a manner to become a permanent record of your munificence and practical aid to the cause of education. Should your association be enabled, in the providence of God, to do more than this, we would meet it in a corresponding spirit and give you an equitable representation upon the board of trustees. You would then be joint owners with us of our college, for the legal title is the trustees of the Fort Wayne college.

This association had at each of its annual sessions since the above was passed taken favorable action in behalf of the college, and at the joint meeting of trustees and visitors held June 20, 1889, Hon. Chauncey Shaffer, of New York, in behalf of the friends of Bishop William Taylor, and Dr. C. B. Stemen and William B. Chadwick, the educational committee of the National association of local preachers, made a proposition that they would secure for the institution certain liberal financial aid on condition that the name of the college be changed to William Taylor college, or university, as might be mutually agreed upon. The joint board accepted the proposition, appointed the proper committees, and at the present time the indications are very encouraging for the change in name as soon as it can be legally accomplished and for the institution's beginning an era of real satisfactory prosperity.

The Protestant Episcopal Church at Fort Wayne. — Over half a century ago, in the spring of 1839, Rev. Benjamin Hutchins, a missionary of the Protestant Episcopal church, came to Fort Wayne, and through his efforts Christ church was organized, May 27th, of which the first vestrymen were Thomas Broon, William L. Moon, James Hutchinson, Samuel Stophlet, and Merchant W. Huxford. The meeting for organization held at the Academy, was presided over by Allen Hamilton, and Robert E. Fleming was secretary. Other members than these named were: W. W. Stevens, Samuel Hanna, Thomas Pritchard, M. W. Hubbell, James Parry, Dr. Beecher, P. G. Jones, and Joseph Pickens. This organization continued and the name being changed, was the foundation of Trinity church. On May 25, 1844, Trinity church was organized, with Rev. Benjamin Halsted as rector, and the following officers: Jacob Hull, senior warden; Peter P. Bailey, junior warden; Lucien P. Ferry and R. M. Lyon, vestrymen; Ellis Worthington, clerk, and I. D. G. Nelson, treasurer. Mr. Halsted administered the first communion on July 7, 1844, to seventeen persons. Services were held for several years at the old court-house. There was an effort made in 1846 to supply the needed edifice, and Willian Rockhill offered to donate a lot if $1,000 were raised for the building, but the amount not being secured, that lot was abandoned, and a lot purchased for $85 on the southeast corner of Berry and Harrison streets, where the first church was erected, a small building, in which was placed "an organ with four stops," as appears from an official paper at that time, and all was paid for. On April 6, 1848, Mr. Halstead was succeeded by Rev. H. P. Powers, and he was followed by Rev. Joseph S. Large, who arriving in November, 1848, served the church a considerable period, both at this and at a later time, and by his spiritual power and self-devotion accomplished much for the church. During his first pastorate an addition was made to the church building, largely increasing its capacity, and it was consecrated, May 23, 1850, by Rt. Rev. Bishop Upfold. In the fall of 1857 Mr. Large was succeeded by Rev. E. C. Pattison, who was in a short time followed by Rev. Caleb A. Bruce, and he by Stephen H. Battin, of Cooperstown, N. Y., in May, 1859. Rev. Large was called again by the church in September, 1863, and in November, C. D. Bond was authorized to purchase the site for a new church on the corner of Berry and Fulton streets, which was secured at a cost of $3,000. The corner stone was laid in 1865, and a handsome church was completed August 1, 1866, the total cost of the building being $21,050. The building is a fine specimen of ecclesiastical architecture, built of stone, in pure gothic style, with apsidal chancel the full width of the nave. The seating capacity is 450. At the time the church was built, Peter P. Bailey was senior warden, I. D. G. Nelson, junior warden, and the vestrymen were C. B. Bond, F. P. Randall, Warren Withers, John S. Irwin, Philo Rumsey. Messrs. Bond and Irwin held the keys of the edifice after completion, and no services were held until it was entirely paid for. The church is now building a rectory and a parish building, which are to be of stone, to harmonize in plan with the church, which they adjoin, so as to form a quadrangle. The total cost will be $10,500. Colin C. Tate became rector of the church in 1872, and remained until the fall of 1879, when he was succeeded by Rev. William N. Webbe. In December, 1888, the latter was succeeded by Rev. A. W. Seabreese. Hon. I. D. G. Nelson, who has been a warden for forty years, is now senior warden, a position he has held for about thirty years. Hon. F. P. Randall, now and for twenty-five years junior warden, has been a member of the vestry thirty-eight years, and Dr. John S. Irwin, one of the present vestrymen, has performed that function since 1855. The other vestrymen are W. L. Carnahan, Stephen B. Bond, H. W. Mordhurst, B. D. Angell and Charles E. Bond.

On May 24, 1869, a petition was presented for the organization of another parish east of Calhoun street, and the church of the Good Shepherd was established. A building was purchased of the Third Presbyterian church and moved upon a lot on Holman street, which had been purchased, and here services were held for a few years, first by Rev. John Gay, afterward by Rev. Walter Scott, but many of the members removing, the building was sold and vacated. Of the organization, still in existence, Dr. John A. Irwin is senior warden, Hon. A. P. Edgerton, junior warden, and W. L. Carnahan, S. B. Bond and William Playfair, vestrymen.

Trinity English Evangelical Lutheran Church.—The origin of this congregation dates as far back as 1836, when Rev. Jesse Hoover, a Lutheran minister, came from Woodstock, Va., as a missionary to gather and organize the scattered Lutheran families in Allen and neighboring counties. The formal work of organizing was effected October 14, 1837, by the adoption of the "Formula for the Government and Discipline of the Evangelical Lutheran Church," approved by the Evangelical Lutheran General Synod of the United States. Provision was made for services in both English and German. After Rev. Hoover's death in 1838, Rev. F. Wyneken assumed charge and continued the mission work in the self-sacrificing spirit of his predecessor until his resignation in 1845. During his ministry the accessions to the congregation consisted mainly of German immigrants who settled in and around the city. His successor, Rev. W. Siehler, being able to minister only in German, it became necessary for those desiring English services to effect a reorganization. Accordingly, with the approval of their German brethren, the preliminary steps for the establishment of an exclusively English congregation were taken March 22, 1846, and on the 19th of April following a constitution was adopted in which the Unaltered Augsburg Confession and the Small Catechism were designated as the doctrinal basis. Among the seventeen charter members were many who had been instrumental in effecting the original organization in 1837.

The first board of officers consisted of Elders S. Cutshall and E. Rudisill; deacons, H. Rudisill and C. Ruch. A small frame church at the corner of Berry and Lafayette streets, in which the Presbyterians had formerly worshiped, was at once purchased and the services of Rev. W. Albaugh secured. He was succeeded in 1850 by Rev. A. S. Bartholomew, who severed his connection by resignation, April 28, 1856. The resulting vacancy continued until 1859, when Rev. W. P. Ruthrauff became pastor. During his ministry the present site was purchased, having a frontage of 185 feet on Wayne, and 150 feet on Clinton, street. In 1863 a fine church and commodious parsonage were erected. Rev. Ruthrauff resigned in 1867 and was succeeded by Rev. A. J. Kunkleman, who nine months afterward removed to Philadelphia, Penn.

The present pastor, Rev. S. Wagenhals, was elected while yet a student of theology, and assumed charge June 14, 1868. The property has been improved from time to time, and extensive additions to both church and parsonage were made in 1885. The membership at present numbers 437, with a flourishing Sunday-school.

The church has a national reputation among Lutherans as the place where the general Synod was divided in 1866 and the general council organized in 1867.

Rev. Samuel Wagenhals, D. D., pastor of the Trinity English Evangelical Lutheran church, Fort Wayne, was born at Lancaster, Ohio, January 17, 1843, son of Rev. John and Catharine (Ludwig) Wagenhals. His education was begun in the schools of Lancaster, which he attended until fourteen years of age, when he entered Capital university, at Columbus, Ohio. Being limited in means he was compelled to withdraw from college during his junior year in order to secure the necessary funds, which he did by teaching school. He then resumed his studies and graduated at the age of nineteen. During his senior year he also acted as a tutor in the preparatory department. In July, 1862, two weeks after his graduation, he enlisted as a private in Company A, One Hundred and Fourteenth Ohio volunteer infantry, commanded by Col. Cradlebaugh. He took part in the battles of Chickasaw Bluff, Arkansas Post, and many of the skirmishes of Grant's initial movement on Vicksburg. After the battle of Port Gibson, he was promoted sergeant-major of the regiment, and served in that rank in the battles of Champion Hills, Black River Bridge, and the siege of Vicksburg. Subsequently, he went with his regiment to the department of the Gulf, where it was engaged in campaign and garrison duty, until the spring of 1864, when it joined the Red River expedition under Gen. N. P. Banks. In the summer of 1864 he was commissioned first lieutenant of Company B, and held that rank until the close of the war. He also participated in the investment and siege of Mobile, and during this last campaign served as assistant engineer of the second division, thirteenth army corps. Two weeks after being mustered out at Columbus, Ohio, Mr. Wagenhals entered the Evangelical Lutheran Theological seminary, at Philadelphia, Penn., where he studied three years, and was ordained a minister of this demonination June 10, 1868. Two days later he arrived in Fort Wayne, and has ever since been a resident of the city and in charge of his present congregation. In years of continuous service he is the oldest minister in the city, and his long acquaintance with the people has only the more endeared him to them. He is a man of scholarly attainments, and is one of the ablest divines of the city.

The Reformed Churches of the city are of great importance, containing large congregations, having spacious houses of worship, and pastors of notable intelligence and piety, who work unceasingly for the welfare of their charges. The original church, the German St. John's Reformed, was organized in 1844, with fourteen members. Three of these are, now living, Henry Hilgemann, Philip Ruehling and Daniel Bashelier. At first the little congregation worshiped in the Sunday school room of the Presbyterian church, but in the same year of organizing the lot was purchased which is still held by the society, and a frame church was under roof in 1845, and was slowly finished. This was about a quarter of a century later sold to the African church, and the present commodious church building was begun in 1869. It was completed in 1871 at a cost of $20,000, and dedicated September 3. It has a seating capacity of about 800. The church also has a school building, which cost about $3,000, built in 1883, in which a school is maintained, and the total value of the church property is about $30,000. There is a flourishing Sunday school of 360 attendance, a ladies' society of 100 members, and a young men and young ladies' Christian association of about sixty-five members. The first pastor was Rev. Mr. Karroll, who served but a short time, being succeeded by J. A. Beyer, who was soon followed by F. B. Altamatt. K. Bossard served about eight years from 1848, and H. Benz during the year following. J. H. Klein was called in 1855, remained thirteen years, and following him F. B. Schwedes served five years and A. Krahn two years. In 1876 began the pastorate of Rev. Carl Schaaf, one of the prominent ministers of the denomination in the west, who is still in charge of this church. The membership is about 700.

An offshoot of the above is the Second German Reformed Salem church which was formed by about forty members of the older church, who purchased for their first place of meeting the old Baptist church which stood on Clinton street, between Berry and Wayne. Subsequently the society purchased the lot on the opposite side of the street of which they now occupy part, the south half having been sold as the site of the Masonic temple. Here a church was erected in 1870–71 at a cost of $10,000. In 1879 the parsonage was built, and an addition was made to the church in 1886. Rev. C. Cast was the first pastor and served until 1871, when he was succeeded by Rev. Muhler. He remained about two years, C. Baum two and a half years, and Rev. Kriete, the present able and esteemed pastor, began his work here in November, 1875. There are now 350 members.

Grace Reformed church, the Fort Wayne organization of the English branch of the denomination, was organized May 13, 1883, by Rev. T. J. Bacher, with fifty charter members. The church first worshiped in the old Jewish synagogue on Harrison street, but immediately began a movement toward the building of a church of its own. On June 13,

1883, a lot on East Washington street was purchased for $4,000, and on October 29, of the same year, it was resolved to build, provided there could be $500 raised in the church and $500 outside. The congregation at once subscribed $819.50, and sufficient other funds being raised, the contract was let December 10. There was then erected a building which is intended as a part of a larger structure to be built in the future, and this was dedicated July 27, 1884, at which time the whole amount of the debt, $500, was raised. The ladies provided carpets, seats, etc., and all worked together with such zeal, that in May, 1889, the church had raised and expended $11,664.57. A parsonage has also been provided at a cost of $2,000. Rev. Bacher continued as pastor until April, 1888, when he was succeeded by Allen K. Zartman, now officiating.

Rev. Charles F. Kriete became a supply pastor of the Salem Reformed church, in the latter part of 1875, and on January 1 of the following year accepted the call to the pastorate. He was licensed to preach February 16, 1876, and ordained March 2. Since that date he has ably ministered to this congregation, being a worthy and devoted pastor. Mr. Kriete was born in the province of Westphalia, Prussia, August 18, 1851, son of John H. and Catherine S. (Stuckman) Kriete. The family came to America in 1856, and settled on a farm in Sheboygan county, Wis. At sixteen years of age he entered the Reformed college and seminary of Sheboygan, called the Mission House, and remained three years, during which period he also taught school three months. In August, 1870, he entered the Heidelberg college at Tiffin, Ohio, and graduated in the classical course in 1874. He then entered the theological seminary of the same institution, and studied until coming to Fort Wayne. He was married May 7, 1878, to Caroline C., daughter of Rev. John H. Klein, D. D., of Louisville. She was born in Fort Wayne, March 11, 1857. Mr. and Mrs. Kriete have had five children: Emilia C., Theodore H. C., Charles D., Laura A., and Edwin H., the last of whom died in infancy.

Achd'uth Veshalom synagogue, of B'nai Israel, of Fort Wayne, was organized in 1848, the moving spirits being A. Oppenheim, Sigismund Redelsheimer, J. Lauferty, F. Nirdlinger and others. For several years after the organization the congregation met at the home of Mr. Nirdlinger, but the membership increased to such proportions that in 1857 a building was purchased on Harrison street, and subsequently dedicated as a synagogue. The first rabbi was Rev. Solomon, who officiated until 1859, when he was succeeded by Rev. Rosenthal, and the latter in 1861, by Rev. E. Rubin. In 1874 the congregation erected a magnificent temple, one of the finest in the west, at a cost of $25,000. This is built in the gothic style, presents an imposing appearance, and the interior is exquisite in finish and design. It affords a seating capacity for 800, besides gallery for the choir, Sabbath school rooms, lecture rooms and vestry rooms. This splendid structure was dedicated with appropriate ceremonies, the address on the occasion being delivered by Rabbi Wise, of Cincinnati. Rev. Rubin, in whose term this structure was begun and completed, died in 1880, after nineteen years' service, and the congregation then elected Dr. Israel Aaron, a student from the Hebrew Union college of Cincinnati. He came after a lapse of one year and remained three years, then taking a position with a congregation in Buffalo. He was succeeded by Rabbi T. Shanfarber, also a graduate of the Hebrew Union college, who after two years was called to Baltimore. Rabbi A. Gutmacher, from the same college mentioned, is the present incumbent, and is highly esteemed for his many scholarly accomplishments. In 1887 the congregation purchased a beautiful tract of land, adjoining Lindenwood cemetery, which has been handsomely improved as a cemetery. The present membership is about fifty, and the present officers are: Simon Frieberger, president; M. Frank, vice president; L. Lumley, secretary; L. Falk, treasurer; trustees, A. Oppenheimer, Solomon Rothschild, Julius Nathan and Mac Fisher.

The Evangelical association, a denomination of that family of churches, of which the Methodist Episcopal is the greatest member, has one society at Fort Wayne which was organized May 18, 1867, with sixteen members, as the result of services held at the Third Presbyterian church by Revs. D. S. Oakes and M. W. Steffey. The latter was the first pastor of the new organization, which proceeded at once to build a frame church at the corner of Clinton and Holman streets, at a cost of $2,000. The membership is now eighty-five, and the trustees are John Rabus, F. Schoch and David Rentschler. The succession of pastors has been: J. N. Gomer, W. Kreuger, J. Schmidli, E. Evans, P. Roth, Joseph Fisher, M. Hoehn, Joseph Fisher (second term), Jacob Miller and D. D. Speicher.

Plymouth Congregational church of Fort Wayne, was organized September 20, 1870, by Dr. N.A. Hyde, of Indianapolis, with twenty-five members, who met at first for worship in a building opposite the present church. In the following year the congregation undertook the erection of a house of worship, which was completed in 1872, a frame building on the corner of Washington and Fulton streets. The cost of this structure was $5,500. The first pastor was John B. Fairbank, who served five years. He was succeeded by Anselm B. Brown, who served one year, and was followed by Joel M. Seymour, who labored for the church energetically and successfully for nearly eight years. Edwin A. Hazeltine was then pastor for eighteen months, and was followed by Jeremiah C. Cromer, who was called in May, 1889, to a church in Chicago. The church has at present about 130 members. The officers are as follows: deacons, John Gilbert, B. H. Kimball, James Cairns and N. H. Fitch; trustees, W. V. Douglas, James Cairns, G. W. Pixley, W. E. Mossman and E. O. Poole; treasurer, T. J. Rodabaugh; clerk, P. L. Potter.

Christian Church.—This was organized in 1870, by Rev. John N. Aylesworth, who was the first pastor. There were but seven charter members of this society which has been successful in its growth, and these and those admitted from time to time, met for a few years in Anderson's hall. The seven charter members were Mrs. Eliza Rhinesmith, Susan Rhinesmith, Mrs. Elizabeth Bartlett, Mr. Ketchum, Matilda Stirk, Mrs. Hathaway and Mr. Rhodes. The building of the church edifice on the corner of West Jefferson and Griffith streets, was begun about the time of the panic of 1873, and consequently it was not ready for the church to occupy until 1875. Mr. Aylesworth, the first pastor, was succeeded by L. L. Carpenter, and the succession since then has been Thomas Mason, William Aylesworth, George P. Ireland, George P. Slade, M. L. Blaney, George H. Sims. The officers of the organization are: Trustees, John Rhinesmith, John Dalman, B. W. Rambo, Israel B. Adams; elders, John Dalman, C. W. Halberstott, Allen P. Jackson; deacons, David Braden, John N. Broom, Gilbert E. Hutchins, B. W. Rambo; clerk, Miss Lizzie F. Erwin; treasurer, Dr. T. H. McCormick. The present membership is about 350.

The United Brethren church at Fort Wayne was organized in 1875, by Rev. R. L. Wilgus, and among the original members were Charles McNair and wife, William Fox and wife, John Stites and wife, J. Q. Kline and wife, and Catherine Wingate. They met during the first three years of the church's history, in a building on the corner of Fulton and Washington streets, which they rented, and they subsequently occupied a frame chapel on East Lewis street, opposite the site of the present brick church, which was erected in 1883, at a cost of $4,000, including the site. This building was dedicated by Bishop Weaver. The pastors from the beginning have been R. W. Wilgus, J. L. Luttrell, D. A. Johnson, J. P. Stewart. The latter, who was a student at, and is now a trustee of, Otterbein university, entered the ministry in 1873. He came to Fort Wayne in 1882, and during his pastorate of seven years, the building of this congregation was erected, and also that of the Second church, which he organized. During his ministry here he received about 300 persons into the church fold. He was succeeded by John W. Lower, the present pastor. The membership of this organization is now 148. The trustees are G. H. Judy, James Trythall, J. T. Crawford, O. J. Bowser, A. D. Craig; stewards, A. A. Bowser, P. Titus. The Second church, organized in 1886, has a church edifice at the corner of Boone and Fry streets, and the present pastor is Rev. Mr. Spray.

The German Lutheran and Catholic churches will be found in separate chapters in another part of this work.

NEWSPAPERS OF FORT WAYNE.

The situation of Fort Wayne, with reference to other cities of metropolitan pretensions, is exceedingly favorable to the growth of her newspapers. Toledo is ninety-six miles away; Chicago, 148 miles; Indianapolis, 120 miles, and Cincinnati, 160 miles. Accordingly a large and fertile field for the distribution of live newspapers from this central point has attracted the attention of many publishers, probably too many, for the opinion is generally shared that if there were fewer dailies in Fort Wayne their quality and usefulness might be expected to improve. At the present time no less than six daily papers are published here. Of these the *Gazette* and *Journal* appear in the morning, and the *Sentinel, News, Staats Zeitung* and *Freie Presse* in the afternoon.

The oldest of the city newspapers is the *Sentinel*. It is also, with one or two exceptions, the oldest newspaper in the state. Its first issue bears the date of July 6, 1833. The publishers were Thomas Tigar and S. V. B. Noel, two citizens who were among the most prominent in all public affairs for many years. Strangely enough these gentlemen differed radically in politics. Mr. Tigar was an uncompromising democrat and Mr. Noel was a stalwart whig. Accordingly, the paper was not at first noted for strong allegiance to either party, but generally observed a neutral course. The population of Fort Wayne was then about 300 people, and the publication of the little weekly was an ambitious undertaking of very doubtful financial success. It was a hard struggle. There were few merchants to advertise, and there were slight resources for news. Moreover the purses of the proprietors were slender enough. But it managed to survive and has long since rounded its half century of usefulness, and is one of the most valuable newspaper properties in the state. It was first issued from the old Masonic hall building, on lot 154, original plat, being on the north side of Columbia street, opposite where the Wayne hotel now stands. Mr. Noel retired within a few months with more experience than wealth, and the publication of the paper was continued by Mr. Tigar, who at once announced its policy as democratic, and held it firmly to that creed, until in 1837, it was sold to Hon. George W. Wood. The new proprietor was a whig, and the politics of the paper were at once changed, and it continued to be anti-democratic during his ownership, but has since his retirement been a firm and steadfast supporter of the democratic party. Mr. Wood conducted the *Sentinel* for three years, and in 1840, sold to Hon. I. D. G. Nelson, still a resident of the city. Mr. Nelson restored the paper to the democratic party, and continued the publication until January, 1841, when he sold to Thomas Tigar, one of the founders, who continued to be its active head for nearly twenty-five years.

The next owners were Hon. W. H. Dills, now a resident of Auburn, and I. W. Campbell, who, after a checkered life, is again working at the case in a St. Louis job printing office. These gentlemen had shortly before purchased from Hon. John W. Dawson the Fort Wayne *Times*, democratic, and the two papers were merged under the name of the *Times-Sentinel*.

In January of the next year, 1866, there was another change, Messrs. E. Zimmerman, best known as the proprietor of the Valparaiso, Ind., *Messenger*, and Hon. Eli Brown, afterward prominent in Whitley county politics and as member of the state senate, becoming owners. The name of the paper was now changed to that of *Democrat*. Steam power was introduced and the paper was generally improved. Within the next few years there were many other owners and partners, Judge Robert Lowry, who purchased Mr. Brown's interest in 1868, Robert D. Dumm and L. A. Bruner, a firm known as Burt & Tucker, John W. Henderson and Frank Furste. In the fall of 1870 Mr. Bruner sold his interest to Hon. William Fleming, who also purchased Mr. Lowry's interest. R. D. Dumm & Co. issued the *Democrat* as a morning paper for a short time, but the change was not satisfactory and the evening publication was resumed.

On January 30, 1873, the ownership passed to R. D. Dumm and Hon. William Fleming, who restored the name of *Sentinel*, and in April, 1874, the paper was purchased by the *Sentinel* Printing company, composed of Hons. A. H. Hamilton, R. C. Bell, William Fleming, S. B. Bond, M. Hamilton, F. H. Wolke and other prominent democrats. The price paid for the paper was $50,000. The *Sentinel* Printing company had an active existence until the spring of 1877, when the paper passed into the hands of Hon. William Fleming. Until the 16th of April, 1879, he was its sole proprietor, and he then transferred the paper to William R. Nelson, a son of Hon. I. D. G. Nelson, and Samuel E. Morss, the latter of whom had had principal editorial charge while Mr. Fleming was proprietor. The new firm enlarged the paper's facilities and improved it in many ways, Mr. Morss's keen "nose for news" and his facile pen quickly bringing the *Sentinel* to the front rank of state papers. The city was raked for local news as with a fine tooth comb, and in every department there was a force and sprightliness that won much favor for the new firm.

On August 1st, 1880, Mr. E. A. K. Hackett purchased the *Sentinel* and has been since in possession. Under E. A. K. Hackett's management the paper has been more prosperous than at any time in its previous history. It is now considered not only the best paper in the city of Fort Wayne, but one of the leading papers in the state. It has the exclusive control of the Associated and United press associations, has its own special telegraph wire running into its office and has all the facilities for publishing a metropolitan newspaper. The *Weekly Sentinel* is read by almost every farmer in Allen county, and has the largest circulation of any weekly newspaper outside the city of Indianapolis in the state of Indiana. It is printed in its own building at No. 107 Calhoun street, one of the neatest, handsomest and best arranged newspaper buildings in the state. It is of brick, 25x70 feet in size, three stories high, with a basement. In the basement is the engine and press room. The first floor contains the counting room, job printing department and stock room. The second floor contains the editorial, reporters' and telegraph operators' rooms. The third floor contains the composing room and book bindery.

The American Farmer was established six years ago by E. A. K. Hackett. It has a circulation that reaches all over the United States and Canada. It is published as a premium paper, and is the original publication in that field. It is edited by S. D. Melsheimer and printed in the *Sentinel* building.

Thomas Tigar commenced in May, 1843, the publication of a German paper called *Der Deutsche Beobachter von Indiana*. The late Dr. C. Schmitz was editor. The publication was not long continued.

In 1856 a German paper called the *Democrat* was published in Fort Wayne, E. Engler was the editor. The *Democrat* was short-lived.

The Indiana *Staats Zeitung* first saw the light in 1858. Mr. G. B. Newbert was its first editor, and its politics were from then until now democratic. The *Staats Zeitung* seems not to have attracted great attention until 1862, when Hon. John D. Sarnighausen, a scholarly gentleman, came to Fort Wayne and assumed editorial control. He infused into the sheet new life. Within a year or two he became sole owner and the paper has since grown to be a power among the German thinking people of northern Indiana. Mr. Sarnighausen has been in editorial charge all these years except when called to serve his country in the state senate. The *Daily Staats Zeitung* was established in 1877, and has proved a success from the beginning.

Public prints of more or less longevity, and which require no extended notice, are the *Evening Transcript*, published by William Latham and Henry Cosgrove; the *Indiana Freemason*, a monthly, Sol D. Bayless, editor; the *Casket*, by the students at the Methodist college; the *Alert*, whose publisher is forgotten; the *Plow Boy*, an agricultural pamphlet; *The True Democrat* (pamphlet), by R. D. Turner; *The Standard and Weekly*, by D. W. Burroughs; the *Jeffersonian*, the *Laurel Wreath*, the *Call*, by W. R. Ream; the *Republican*, by P. P. Baily; the *Boys' World*, by W. J. Bond; the *Item*, by George R. Benson; the *Volksfreund*, by Rudolph Worch, and the *Mail*, by W. J. Fowler. The *Volksfreund* deserves some special mention. The editor was a positive man who wrote strong and fierce leaders and attracted to his paper for a time some of the patronage that the Germans had regularly bestowed upon the older *Staats Zeitung*.

But all these papers have passed away. In their day they served useful purposes no doubt, but most of them lacked the essential element of presenting the news of the day, and to this fact their early decay can probably be principally attributed.

The Fort Wayne *Times*, when it had a separate existence, by which is meant before it was merged with the *Sentinel*, had for editors strong writers, and it was a power in local and state politics. It was established in 1841 by George W. Wood. He sold to Henry W. Jones, who continued it until the end of the year 1844. In March, 1844, Mr. Wood commenced a campaign paper called the *People's Press*, and after the close of the campaign of that year, the two publications were united under the name of the *Times and People's Press*. A sale of this property was made in March, 1848, to T. N. Hood and Warren H. Withers. On August 31, 1849, Mr. Withers retired and George W. Wood was admitted. Messrs. Hood & Wood continued as partners until September 7, 1853, when Mr. Wood leased his interest for one year, to Mr. John W. Dawson. The firm of Dawson & Wood changed the title of the paper to the *Times*. Within a few months Mr. Hood sold his interest to Messrs. Dawson & Wood. On July 16, 1854, Mr. Wood having retired, Mr. Dawson began issuing the *Daily Times*. The daily edition was discontinued two years later, but on February 1, 1859, was revived and continued until October, 1864. The publication office was situated at the northeast corner of Columbia and Clinton streets, in the second and third stories. This building, which was known as the *Times* building, was destroyed by fire March 28, 1860, and was at once rebuilt. The paper and job office were sold in 1865, to Messrs. Dills & Campbell, and was subsequently merged in the *Sentinel*. Mr. Dawson served for a time as territorial governor to Utah. His widow, Mrs. Amanda Dawson, still resides in this city.

The Fort Wayne *Gazette*, the leading republican organ of northern Indiana, like the *Sentinel and Times*, has had numerous changes of ownership, but never since its initial number has it failed to be the consistent and stalwart champion of the principles of freedom and equal rights to all men of whatever race or color, under the constitution. It was established as an afternoon paper in 1863, by D. W. Jones, who came from Grant county, Ind., for that express purpose. The first place of publication was the old *Times* office corner, which has sheltered so many young newspaper enterprises. Mr. Jones was not only the publisher but the editor. A few months later Hon. Isaac Jenkinson purchased an interest and became editor. In October of the same year a new cylinder press was put in and a portable engine was added to the office. The *Gazette* thus became the first successful steam printing house in Fort Wayne.

In March, 1864, Mr. Jones sold his interest to H. C. Hartman, esq., and the new firm enlarged the paper to a seven-column folio. Mr. Hartman retired in 1867, and in October, 1868, Mr. Jenkinson sold a third interest to James R. Willard, and a third interest to Amos W. Wright, and in the spring of 1869, the entire business was transferred to these parties. For the next few years changes of ownership were frequent. Gentlemen owning interest in the paper at various times were Robert G. McNiece, who had been principal of the high school, and is now a clergyman of much distinction at Salt Lake City, D. S. Alexander, M. Cullarton, John N. Irwin and J. J. Grafton. The organization

JOHN D. SARNIGHAUSEN

E. A. K. HACKETT

W. D. PAGE

C. D. TILLO

N. R. LEONARD

had by this time assumed the form of a joint stock company, and all of the stock was sold to Capt. J. B. White, who sold a half interest to Gen. Reub. Williams and Quincy A. Hossler, now successful publishers at Warsaw.

Williams & Hossler lost money on the purchase, and in July, 1876, the *Gazette* was sold to Keil Brothers. D. S. Keil, now deceased, became business manager, and Fred W. Keil, editor. Silas McManus, better known as a dialect poet, and W. J. Fowler, were among the best known city editors. Under the Keil management the paper prospered. It was enlarged and its circulation greatly expanded. The owners also began the publication of "patent insides" for country weeklies, and had over 100 on their list when this part of the business was sold to Chicago parties and became the nucleus of the Newspaper Union, an establishment which has since grown to vast proportions. The Keils sold the *Gazette* to Messrs. B. M. Holman and Theron P. Keator, who conducted a remarkably vigorous campaign against the democratic party. In February, 1887, the new proprietors having failed to make good all their financial obligations, on motion of the Keils a receiver was appointed and Judge O'Rourke of the circuit court named John W. Hayden, esq. At the end of a few months the paper was sold by the receiver to Messrs. N. R. and Frank M. Leonard, and has since been conducted by them under the style of N. R. Leonard & Son. The senior partner had been professor of mathematics and astronomy in the Iowa state university, and the junior partner had been a practical newspaper man for many years. On January 1, 1889, F. M. Leonard retired, and the paper is now conducted solely by N. R. Leonard. The *Gazette* is a clean, honorable, fair dealing journal, and while vigorously republican is always deferential to opposite political views.

The Fort Wayne *Morning Journal* is the offspring of the Fort Wayne *Weekly Journal*, which was founded December 14, 1868, by T. S. Taylor and Samuel Hanna. It was originally a republican paper, the object of the gentlemen named being to make it the republican organ of the county, displacing the *Gazette*. In this attempt they failed and the *Journal*, after passing through various hands, notably those of Mr. Clark Fairbank and the late Judge Samuel Ludlum, became in 1880, the property of Thomas J. Foster, then state senator, and the price was reduced to a cent. Senator Foster turned the paper into a dyed-in-the-wool democratic organ and it has remained so ever since. After the deplorable death of Senator Foster the paper was purchased by Ironsides & Co., of Louisville, Ky., who soon sold to M. V. B. Spencer. The latter found the business unsuitable to his tastes and organized a stock company which took the paper. Among the stockholders, besides Mr. Spencer, were Col. C. A. Zollinger, Hon. C. F. Muhler, Hon. Allen Zollars, Dr. L. S. Null, Samuel Miller, M. A. Null, F. C. Boltz, and others. G. W. Lunt was the first business manager under the new *regime*, and George F. Shutt was the first editor. Mr. Shutt retired and was succeeded by W. P. Cooper and Mr. Lunt was succeeded by Mr. Miller. The latter conducted the business very successfully, and purchased from the other stockholders nearly all of their holdings. Mr. Miller died in January, 1887, and on the first day of March of the same year the Miller shares were purchased by Col. C. A. Zollinger, who shortly sold to Christian Boseker. The latter conducted the paper with success, increasing its reputation and its circulation, and on June 10, 1889, sold his stock to W. W. Rockhill and A. J. Moynihan, who are now in charge. Mr. Rockhill is president and business manager of the company, and Mr. Moynihan is secretary and treasurer, besides performing the duties of editor. The *Journal* prints the united press report, and its publishers promise that it will increase its usefulness to the public.

The Daily News.— Perhaps the most successful daily newspaper in Fort Wayne is the youngest, and to careful and prudent management, and a consistent following out of a policy thought to be for the people's best interests, is its success to be ascribed. The *Daily News* originated with W. D. Page, its present proprietor and editor, who in its establishment associated with himself, Charles F. Taylor. The early issues were printed on a platen press and the paper was so small that an opposition afternoon paper sneeringly referred to it as a "hand bill," and prophesied its collapse within ninety days. But what it lacked in size it made up in sprightliness. Its popular city editor, the late A. V. D. Conover, was a brilliant and pungent paragrapher. Within a month the *News* had a *bona fide* circulation of 1,600 copies, and to-day it claims to print more papers than any other city daily. In November, 1887, Mr. Taylor sold his interest to Mr. Page, and with it, his half-interest in *Poultry and Pets*, a monthly publication which leads its class in America, and which is devoted to interests its title sufficiently explains. The *Daily News* is conspicuous among other successful dailies from the fact that it has never had a dollar of the patronage from the city, county or state government, that has been extended more or less generously to all of its rivals. It has carved out an honorable place for itself in the newspaper world, and fills it admirably as "the people's paper."

The *Dispatch* occupies a position among Fort Wayne newspapers that is peculiarly its own. It was started a little over ten years ago, and it has been independent in politics, but with a strong leaning at times toward the theories of the greenback party. After the defeat of Gen. Weaver, its candidate for the presidency, the interests of the labor party were taken up. The paper is the uncompromising foe of anything that looks like a clique, a monopoly or a trust, and more than any other city paper its columns bear the personality of its editor, Mr. James Mitchell.

The *Freie Presse*, at the head of which is Mr. Otto Cummerow, is a daily paper which challenges the older *Staats Zeitung* for the support of our German citizens. It is of neat appearance, its local and editorial matter are well prepared. From the large amount of patronage secured it is evident that the *Freie Presse* has come to stay.

George W. Wood, one of the pioneer printers and editors of Indiana, was born in Goshen, Orange county, N. Y., on the 4th day of September, 1808, and resided in that state, where he learned the art of practical printing, and also devoted much time to the study of the law, until about 1834, when he removed to Ann Arbor, Mich., and thence, in 1836, to Fort Wayne. Here he entered the *Sentinel* office, then owned by Thomas Tigar, esq., and is entitled to the distinction of being the second newspaper man at Fort Wayne. In 1837 he purchased the *Sentinel* from Mr. Tigar, and published it until 1840, when he disposed of it to I. D. G. Nelson. A month afterward, he purchased a newspaper establishment from H. B. Seaman, of Defiance, Ohio, and moving it to Fort Wayne, founded the Fort Wayne *Times*. In March, 1840, he was elected mayor of Fort Wayne, being the first person elected to that position after the city was incorporated under a charter. He resigned the office, however, on the 5th of July, 1841, and Joseph Morgan was elected to fill the vacancy. February 18, 1843, he leased the *Times* to Henry W. Jones, who conducted it about two years, when Mr. Wood resumed control of it, combining with it the *People's Press* and calling it the Fort Wayne *Times and People's Press*. He continued its publication until March 23, 1848, when he sold it to Messrs. Withers & Hood. In August, 1849, he re-purchased the interest of Mr. Withers, and the paper was conducted by G. W. Wood & Co. until September 9, 1855, when it was leased to Hood & Dawson until the next June, when he sold his entire interest to John W. Dawson. On the 25th of June, 1849, a telegraph line was established from Toledo to La Fayette, and Mr. Wood became the first operator at Fort Wayne, and continued for some time in that capacity. He is also entitled to the honor of establishing the first daily newspaper in Fort Wayne, which he placed under the management of Messrs. Latham & Rayhouser. Immediately after this, he entered the office of Hon. Samuel Hanna, where he remained until the death of the latter, managing the vast public and private interests of that gentleman for many years, and after his death, acted with Samuel T. Hanna, as administrator of the estate. Besides these positions of personal trust, he was appointed register of the land office by President Fillmore, in 1849, and held the office until it was removed to Indianapolis. After the organization of the Ohio & Indiana railroad, he became the agent of the company for the sale of the lands received for stock subscriptions, and from 1854, when the first cars commenced running to Fort Wayne, until 1860, he was actively associated with Samuel Hanna in the management of that corporation. In all these positions he discharged his duties creditably and with honor, and proved himself to be man of large capacity, good judgment and incorruptible honesty. He was an uncomproming whig, and an ardent admirer of Webster and Clay. He was remarkably simple and unostentatious in appearance and demeanor, a man of few words, except with his family, and with those whose good fortune it was to be admitted to his intimate friendship. With these he was uniformly genial and companionable. His editorials embodied in plain language, the most forcible logic, and were admirably fitted to the manners and customs of his day. An address upon "Intellectual and Moral Education," published in the *Times*, November 4, 1843, another delivered before the students of the Fort Wayne female college, published in the *Times and Press*, January 27, 1848, and his "Life and Character of Hon. Samuel Hanna," published in 1869, as well as his editorials and eulogies of Henry Clay, are evidences of his abilities and the wide range of his studies. He departed this life Saturday, November 11, 1871, leaving no family except a devoted wife.

John W. Dawson, a well known member of the early Allen county bar, and also distinguished as an editor, was born October 21, 1820, a son of John Dawson, an early settler of Cambridge, Ind. John W. came to Fort Wayne in 1838, and became a clerk in the office of his brother-in-law, Col. Spencer, receiver of public moneys. Beginning with 1840, he studied two years in Wabash college, and then entered the law office of his brother-in-law, Thomas Johnson. In 1843 he was admitted to the bar, and then practiced at Augusta, the old county seat of Noble county. He practiced afterward at Fort Wayne, and attended law school in Kentucky, but his health failing, he did not return to Fort Wayne until 1843, when in company with T. H. Hood, he leased the Fort Wayne *Times*, a whig paper, then owned by G. W. Wood & Co. Mr. Dawson became its sole proprietor in 1854, and through this organ became a leader in the new anti-Nebraska party. This party nominated him for secretary of state, and he made a vigorous canvass. Shortly after the inauguration of President Lincoln, he was appointed governor of Utah. His administration was vigorous, and he so incurred the hatred of the saints, that on his return from Salt Lake he was way-laid, robbed and maltreated so that he never fully recovered from the effects of the outrage. Mr. Dawson was an honest politician, of strong convictions and courage to stoutly maintain the right as he saw it. His death occurred September 10, 1877.

John D. Sarnighausen, veteran editor of the *Staats Zeitung*, is the son of a prominent civil officer in the former kingdom of Hanover, and was born October 31, 1818. He attended the colleges at Stade and Luneburg, and the university at Gottingen, and became teacher and minister. In 1860 he came to this country, and to Fort Wayne in 1862. He was at first engaged as editor of the *Indiana Staats Zeitung*, then a small weekly paper owned by Messrs. A. F. Simon and Fred. Meyer, which he bought in 1863, and changed it to a tri-weekly paper in 1867, and to a daily in 1877. The weekly was of course continued. Connected with him as partners were Mr. A. C. Kampe from 1866 to 1868, when the partnership was dissolved by mutual consent, and later, Mr. L. A. Griebel was associated with him from 1876 to 1882, when the latter retired, having been elected auditor of Allen county. Mr. Sarnighausen was elected as a democrat on the independent ticket, state senator from Allen county in 1870, by a majority of about 400, but lost his seat through trickery. In 1872 he was re-elected on the democratic ticket as senator from the counties of Allen and Adams by a majority of 6,184, and in 1876, as senator from Allen, Adams and Wells (under the new apportionment law of 1873), by a majority of 6,630. In 1877 and 1879 he was chairman on the committee on education in the Indiana senate. When Mr. Sarnighausen assumed the editorship of the *Staats Zeitung* he found not a single copy of the paper, nor a file, nor a copy-book, nor any other papers in reference to the former years of its existence. The paper had been established in October, 1858, but had until January, 1862, when he took charge of it changed proprietors and editors time and again and none of them had taken the slightest interest in it, as it was considered an enterprise with which not only no money but much loss was connected. Since 1863 it has been under the same control and will continue so long as life or health of the present owner will permit. It is in politics a strong and effective supporter of the democratic party.

William David Page, editor and proprietor of the *Daily News*, is a lineal descendant of Luther Page, an officer in the English army, who came to America a few years after the landing of the pilgrims at Plymouth Rock, and settled in Massachusetts. From the latter came all branches of the New England Page family. David Page, paternal grandfather of William D., was prominent as a manufacturer in Vermont a century ago. His wife was Elizabeth Minot, of Massachusetts, a member of the well-known Minot family, after whom was named the famous light-house, "Minot's Ledge." Rev. William Page, father of William D., was a prominent Presbyterian clergyman of a half century ago; was a graduate of Middlebury college; preached for some years in New York city, and was afterward for many years prominent in home missionary work in the early days of Michigan's history. He numbered among his close personal friends such well-known characters as William Lloyd Garrison, Garrett Smith, Harriet Beecher Stowe, Henry Ward Beecher, John G. Saxe, and nearly all the leading Presbyterian clergymen of his time. William D. descended, on the maternal line, from a French Huguenot family, named Durand, the maiden name of his mother being Frances Sheldon Durand. She was born at Bethlehem, Conn., in 1807, and is still living, having been an intelligent and deeply interested witness of the progress of this country during the most remarkable century in the world's history. Mr. Page, the editor and proprietor of the *News*, was born at Monroe, Mich., August 16, 1844. He began his career as a printer at eight years of age, at Adrian, Mich., being locked in a room without any companion, and compelled to learn the rudiments of the "art" of type-setting by simple practice with the letters before him. He attended grammar school at Ann Arbor at twelve. Subsequently finishing his trade at Adrian, he was working as a journeyman printer at Milwaukee when the war broke out in '61. He enlisted in Company B, Fifth Wisconsin, and participated in the quelling of the memorable bank riots at Milwaukee, which grew out of the collapsing of the old wild-cat banks of the state, and was mustered out of the service early in June, by order of Brigadier-General Rufus King, on account of youth. Then having his attention turned to education he graduated at the West Rockford high school in 1862, prepared for college at Clinton, N. Y., and entered Hamilton college in 1863. In the fall of 1864 he went into the Shenandoah valley; was chief abstract clerk at twenty years of age at General Sheridan's headquarters at the post at Winchester, and remained in the South until the close of the war, being present at the grand review of all the armies at Washington. He became editor and joint owner of the Adrian *Expositor* in 1865, the office where he had learned his trade. Subsequently he entered the employ of Clark Waggoner & Son, of the Toledo *Commercial*, where he remained until he came to Fort Wayne in 1871, as superintendent of the job department of the Fort Wayne *Gazette*, under McNiece & Alexander. He was connected with the *Gazette* until June, 1874, when, with C. F. Taylor, he established the *News*, which he still publishes.

Nathan R. Leonard, editor and proprietor of the *Gazette*, was born November 29, 1832. He is a native of Franklin county, Ohio, whence his parents moved to Burlington, Iowa, in 1844, settling on a large farm a few miles north of that city. Here Mr. Leonard grew to manhood, devoting the summers to labor on the farm and the winters to study in the school, academy and college in the adjacent village of Kossuth. From this college he graduated in 1857, and having been from childhood fascinated with scientific and mathematical research, he attended lectures upon those subjects at Harvard university. Returning to Iowa in 1860, he became professor of mathematics and astronomy in the state university at Iowa City. This chair he filled for twenty-seven years, contributing in great measure to the development of that institution. He was dean of the college faculty, and at various periods, ranging from six months to three years, acted as president. He also filled the office of state superintendent of weights and measures, and in that capacity ably advocated the introduction of the metric system. Aside from his routine duties he did much in the way of independent research, and contributed a number of valuable articles to the scientific journals, mainly on astronomical subjects. In 1875 he was elected a fellow of the American association for the advancement of science. In 1887 Mr. Leonard came to Fort Wayne, and purchasing the *Gazette*, has since devoted himself to the upbuilding of that influential newspaper, and it has prospered under his management. Having been a republican since the organization of the party, the *Gazette*, in his hands has become an influential champion of that party. He is an ardent temperance man, but strongly opposed to the organization of parties for reform in this direction. He is a prominent member of the Presbyterian church, and represented the Iowa City presbytery in the general assembly of the United States in 1881. Mr. Leonard was married in 1853, to Elizabeth Heizen, who still lives to bless his home with her cheerful presence. They have four children living: Levi O., editor and proprietor of the *Anaconda* (Montana) *Review*, and superintendent of the Rocky Mountain telegraph company; Charles R., a member of the law firm of Maxwell &

Leonard, Creston, Iowa; Frank M., who was for a time associated with his father in editing the *Gazette*, now of the *Inter-Mountain*, at Butte City, Montana; and Minnie E., who makes her home with her parents at their pleasant home on Washington street.

Frederick W. Keil was born near Hamilton, Butler county, Ohio, and lived on the farm until seventeen years of age, when he was apprenticed to learn the carpenter's trade. When that was completed, he entered Wittenberg college at Springfield, Ohio, and graduated in June 1856. In 1857 he entered the law office of Isaac Robertson, at Hamilton, and completed the prescribed course of two years' reading, as required in Ohio, and was admitted to the Butler county bar. He at once entered upon the practice of law, forming a partnership with Abram C. Martz, and continued in the practice until the breaking out of the rebellion in April, 1861, when he enlisted as a private in Company F, Third Ohio, April 17th and served until mustered out, August 18th. He re-enlisted as private in Company C, Thirty-fifth Ohio, August 20th, and was soon thereafter appointed first lieutenant in the same company. The regiment entered Kentucky via Covington, September 26, 1861, and took possession of the Kentucky Central railway between Cynthiana and Paris, guarding bridges until November, when it was ordered to join the brigade under Col. Bob McCook, which, however, it did not unite with until the battle at Mill Spring, January 6th. He followed the fortunes of his regiment from Mill Spring to Nashville, and marched with Buell from Nashville to Shiloh, reaching the field at the close of that contest; took part in the siege of Corinth, and moved with Buell up the Tennessee valley and thence after Bragg, into Kentucky; took part in the battle of Perryville and the pursuit of the rebel forces, which took the army back as far as Nashville. The regiment served in the Fourteenth corps, and was with the same in all its campaigns up to the capture of Atlanta. Mr. Keil had command of his company nearly two years, and was commissioned captain in the Atlanta campaign. In 1865 he came to Fort Wayne to enter upon the practice of the law, but was induced to purchase a book establishment, and form the partnership known as Keil & Bro. In this enterprise he engaged until 1875, when on account of failing health he spent a year in Europe, under the direction of his physician. On his return the Keil Bros. purchased the Fort Wayne *Gazette*, July, 1876, and he became managing editor. April, 1877, he was appointed postmaster at Fort Wayne, to succeed J. J. Kamm. He held this position during two terms, and was removed by Cleveland on the charge of being an "offensive partisan," being connected with the Fort Wayne *Gazette*, a paper advocating views opposite to those held by the administration. He has been connected for ten years with the management of Island Park association, being strongly impressed with the importance of the summer assembly movement, as a means of substantial popular education. The beneficial effect which those assemblies have over a community is seen in a marked manner within the communities where held, and upon the people that attend the sessions. No attempt at the popular culture of the masses has surpassed in effect what these assemblies have already accomplished.

William W. Rockhill, president and manager of the Fort Wayne *Journal* company, owning a controlling share of the stock, is a native of the city and son of one of its most distinguished pioneers. His father, Hon. William Rockhill, was born in Burlington, N. J., in 1792, and was married to Eliza Hill, who was born at Baltimore, Md. William Rockhill came to Fort Wayne as early as 1823, and at once took a leading position in the affairs of the rising settlement. He was one of the first county commissioners in 1824, and when the city was organized he was a member of the first council, in 1840, and in 1843 was elected city assessor. For several years he was a member of the school board. He was elected to the Indiana senate in 1844, served for one term, and four years later was elected as the representative in congress of the large district of which Fort Wayne was the principal town. Politically, he was always a democrat. This notable pioneer died at Fort Wayne in 1865. His wife died at this city at about the age of forty-five years. To them seven children were born, of whom five are living. Their son, William W., was born August 23, 1849. He was reared and educated in the city, and becoming a prominent and popular citizen, was elected in 1881, city clerk, a position which he held by successive re-elections, until June 10, 1889, when he assumed control of the *Journal*. In this property his associates in ownership are Andrew J. Moynihan, the estate of Samuel Miller, deceased, the former proprietor, Judge Allan Zollars, and M. V. B. Spencer. Mr. Rockhill acquired a reputation during his clerkship as one of the most efficient officers the city has had, and he possesses business qualifications of a high order. He is prominent in fraternal circles, being a Knight Templar, an Odd Fellow and a Knight of Pythias. He was married in 1875, to Sarah Holt, of Huntington, who died in 1877, leaving one child, Sadie M.

Andrew J. Moynihan, editor and one of the owners of the *Journal* since the change in its management in June, 1889, has been for almost a score of years connected with newspaper work in Fort Wayne. He was born in Dromulton Paddocks, county Kerry, Ireland, March 15, 1858, and when five years of age accompanied his parents, Martin and Joanna Moynihan, to America. They settled first at Elizabeth, N. J., where they remained four or five years, then coming to Fort Wayne at the solicitation of Robert Townley, who formerly lived at Elizabeth, and became the founder of the dry goods house of Townley, DeWald, Bond & Co. Mr. Moynihan was reared in Fort Wayne and was educated in the Catholic and public schools. His editorial career was begun about the year 1882, having previously passed through a career in the mechanical department, first with Dumm & Fleming, then proprietors of the *Sentinel*, and subsequently with the succeeding proprietors of that office. During this period he began the study of medicine, and attended a medical college at Chicago, but his love for journalism drew him back to his original profession. He served as telegraph editor of the *Sentinel* two years, and then was given local and editorial charge of that paper, in which position he continued until June, 1889. His energy and notable tact and success as a newsgatherer have made him conspicuous among the newspaper men of Fort Wayne.

Elias H. Bookwalter, a popular and well known citizen of Fort Wanye, is a native of Wabash county, Ind., born May 9, 1854. His parents, Josiah and Elizabeth (Riley) Bookwalter, were respectively natives of Ohio and Pennsylvania. They located in Wabash county in 1850, and there resided on a farm until 1868, when they removed to Fort Wayne, and are now worthy citizens of this city. Elias H Bookwalter has lived in Fort Wayne ever since he was a lad of fourteen, and and he was formerly no less favorably known as an honest, industrious, straightforward youth, than he is now as an honorable, upright man and a worthy and useful citizen. Shortly after coming to Fort Wayne, he became employed in the mechanical department of one of the city papers, and it was not long until the mysteries of the printing office were fully solved and understood. He has continued to be thus employed, and for the past fifteen years has held the responsible position of pressman on the Fort Wayne *Daily Gazette*. In addition to this, for the past twelve years Mr. Bookwalter has been a manufacturer of printers' roller composition, and for seven years, he has been a wholesale and retail dealer in printers' supplies. His honesty and courtesy, united with a disposition to please, have enabled him to build up a large trade, and his acquaintance with the newspaper fraternity has consequently become very extensive. Mr. Bookwalter was married September 3, 1874, to Katie L., daughter of James and Kezia (McWorter) Perrin. Her parents were natives of Franklin county, Ind., but, in an early day, located in Marshall county, where she was born. Mr. Bookwalter and wife are the parents of an only son, Clyde, who was born July 16, 1875. Mr. Bookwalter is a member of Harmony lodge, No. 19, and Summit encampment, No. 16, I. O. O. F., and in the latter is a past chief patriarch. He is also a member of E. S. Walker camp, No. 159, Sons of Veterans, in which he has held the position of quartermaster since the organization. Politically, he is an ardent republican. Mr. Bookwalter's friends are numerous, and socially both he and wife stand very high.

THE MEDICAL PROFESSION.

BY BENJAMIN S. WOODWORTH, M. D.

Looking back half a century in the practice of medicine in the valley of the Upper Maumee, it is apparent that great changes have occurred, not only in the treatment of diseases, but in the quantity of drugs used. It has been a question among physicians whether diseases have changed their type, or physicians themselves have changed. The writer is inclined to the latter theory. Physicians have discarded the vast quantities formerly used, and have become much more conservative, both in quantity and quality. Less than forty years ago it was considered necessary to administer immense doses of calomel, drastic cathartics, tartar emetic, to say nothing of bleeding. Now, what is called the expectant plan, in other words, ignoring drugs in great measure, is most in favor. On the other hand, in the early days, physicians heard nothing of those diseases called septicæmia and pyæmia, that are now said to cause the death of so many women, and in twenty-five years, the writer does not remember meeting a case of puerperal fever, and no doctor thought of using such precautions as carbolic acid, bichloride of mercury, and other antiseptics. We are still without remedies that will cure many if any of the diseases called malignant, such as phthisis and cancer, to say nothing of the real croup, diphtheria and scarlatina.

The ague, or "chills and fever," as the early settlers called it, or the malaria, as later sufferers describe it, was in the early days as now the great endemic of the Maumee valley, as it is of more than half the habitable world. These manifestations, so familiar in the early days, have passed away. Then it was a terror to new comers. It appeared to be aggravated by the opening up of the new land. Its hours of attack recurred with frightful precision. Chills, with spasmodic attacks that shook the movables in the cabin, alternated with fevers that seemed to consume all the vitality that had not been shaken out of the afflicted body. Quinine, the only effective medicine, seemed to add to the general discomfort of the victim, and he was in fact, woe-begone, disconsolate, sad, poor and good-for-nothing. With all our progress in the past half century, we still rely on bark and its preparations for a remedy, and hope that the drainage of swamps, marshes and all filthy places will act as a preventive, though the exact poison that causes malaria yet remains to be discovered. But the days of ague for everybody at least once a year, with the enlarged spleens called "ague cakes," have passed away forever. Before quinine came into general use, while the Wabash & Erie canal was building, nearly all the inhabitants confidently expected to have the ague, and not being able to obtain quinine, or not knowing its efficacy, dragged out a miserable existence. It was said of the Panama railroad that every tie cost a life, and the fatality attending the construction of the canal in that region is familiar to more recent readers. Similar dangers attended the construction of the Wabash & Erie canal. The work was done in proximity to a large, sluggish river, and the deep rich soil was stirred up from the depths necessary for the canal, and it seemed as if more than a Pandora's box of evils were let loose upon the devoted pioneers.

An interesting view of Fort Wayne in 1848, from a medical standpoint, was given by Dr. Daniel Drake, in his Principal Diseases of the Valley of North America, and is quoted below:

"Where the town of Fort Wayne now stands, * * is a post-tertiary plain, at the junction and on the right or eastern side of the two rivers which form the Maumee. This plain rises above high water mark; but is overspread with basin-like depressions in which foul waters and rain water accumulate, to be acted upon by the sun. At a depth of twenty or thirty feet, hard well water of an excellent quality is obtained. Between the town and the river there is a slip of low ground, which, although subject to inundation in the spring, formerly became dry in summer, but is now kept wet by the leakage of the canal. On the opposite side of the St. Mary and of the Maumee rivers, there are rich, alluvial grounds under cultivation. About two miles west of the town a grassy marsh or wet prairie begins, and stretches off indefinitely, to the southwest. Its width is from a few hundred yards to a mile and a half. The St. Mary as it comes from the southwest, flows through the eastern edge of this swamp. Beyond the low lands, which have been mentioned, there is on every side a post-tertiary plain; which, at the distance of a few miles to the east of Fort Wayne, becomes a wooded swamp—the western edge of the "Black swamp," known here as the "Maumee swamp." Doctor Charles E. Sturgis, in a communication from which this description has been made out, says, 'I could name several instances where families settled in the unbroken woods, and clearing a very small space only, enjoyed uninterrupted health for three or four years; when other immigrants arrived, and extensive clearings were made, with the consequent breaking up of a great deal of new soil, and intermittents appeared among the whole.' As to Fort Wayne, from the time it was settled as a military post, down to the present day, it has been infested with intermittents and remittents; which, according to Doctor Sturgis, still occasionally present a malignant character. Of the prevalence of these fevers a judgment can be formed from the fact, stated by Doctor Sturgis, that about 400 ounces of sulphate of quinine are annually consumed by the people of Fort Wayne and its vicinity."

Subsequent to the great drought of 1838, as Dr. Drake records, there was an outbreak of the "autumnal" or malarial fever, of such severity as had not been known before. From that time until the cholera scourge of 1849, there was nothing unusual in the category of afflictions of the settlers of the valley.

In May, 1845, there was a terrible outbreak of cholera at Lahore, in far distant India, and there started what may be termed a wave of infection that was felt with disastrous and terrifying effects in the valley of the Upper Maumee. Twenty-two thousand died at Lahore; the disease was carried down the Indus river and into the Persian gulf; thence it spead into Russia; it attacked the armies of the Kossuth war with greater fatality than the shock of battle; it spread over Europe in three months, and there were 33,000 cases in Paris. The disease reached New York and New Orleans late in 1848, in the south attacking the soldiers of the Mexican war, and causing the death of Gen. Worth. Spreading rapidly over the interior, as fast as the infected victims could travel, it reached the Maumee valley. It was a cold, wet season, which appeared to favor the disease, and whenever the northeast wind blew, which was frequent, there was a severe outbreak of the disease. The origin is supposed to have been with a laborer on the canal, who died in the eastern part of the town, and strangely the disease was most severe on East Washington steet, and was almost entirely confined to East Washington, Wayne and Jefferson streets. There were very few cases until August and September, and during that season there was no ague, or very little. There were about 200 deaths in the little town, which considering the population, was a severe mortality. A great panic resulted, and many fled from the region. Medical treatment was ineffectual here as elsewhere, and only one case is remembered where a patient recovered who was taken with purging and cramping. Doctors Sturgis and Wehmer worked together during this epidemic, in every family. The favorite remedy was tremendous doses of calomel, the panacea of that age, and cayenne pepper. Dr. Cartright was another who practiced during the panic. The village of New Providence, down the Maumee, was depopulated by the cholera, and at Perrysburg the greater number of the prominent citizens were carried away. The disease lingered with less fatal results in various parts of the country, until 1852, when there was another violent outbreak, and in July the disease was very fatal at Sandusky and Dayton, coming thence to this locality, where there was another season of great mortality. In the same way the disease lingered in Europe, and broke out with tremendous violence in Russia, in 1853, and spreading over the continent again the infection was so general that there were that year twenty-eight vessels carrying cholera cases that arrived at American ports. This produced the epidemic of 1854, which was also severely felt at Fort Wayne and vicinity. During each of these years, 1849, 1852 and 1854, there were about 200 deaths here. At times the smallpox caused a considerable number of deaths, but it never was prevalent enough to cause a panic. These diseases no longer threaten the country, thanks to quarantines and the preventive measures which compel cleanliness and drainage, and stop these terrible scourges of the past at their fountain head.

"The short and simple annals of the poor" doctors who were the pioneers of the practice in the Upper Maumee valley were soon told if we were to rely upon any written statements in their history, and even the traditions are very meagre. Their contemporaries are nearly all long ago dead. The oldest person now living, who may be said to have been connected with them, is the widow of Dr. Lewis G. Thompson, now residing on South Broadway. The oldest physician whom this chronicler remembers was Doctor Henry Cushman, who lived near New Haven. He died previous to 1845. A nephew of his, a rather wild young man, practiced in Fort Wayne in 1845-6. He had formerly practiced dentistry, but studied and graduated at the university of New York in medicine. Going to the west, he died some thirty-five years ago. Next after Cushman was Dr. Lewis G. Thompson, of whom appreciative mention is made in Hon. Hugh McCulloch's "Men and Measures of Half a Century," as follows:

"Lewis G. Thompson was for many years the leading physician of Fort Wayne. He had that instinctive knowledge of diseases which distinguishes the born physician, and without which medical knowledge derived from books is a snare. Belonging to the old allopathic school, he believed in medicine, and gave evidence of his faith by prescriptions which were the reverse of homeopathic, but so accurate was his intuition in locating diseases that he was rarely at fault in treating them. I admired Dr. Thompson for his medical skill and for his many noble and manly qualities, but more than all for the conscientiousness and humanity which compelled him to treat with equal carefulness and attention those were able to pay for his services and those who were not."

"Dr. Thompson died suddenly while away from home engaged in a canvass for election to congress, against Andrew Kennedy. He had a younger brother who had been, but for one fault, fitted to wear the mantle of the elder. A contemporary and partner of Dr. Thompson, Dr. Charles E. Sturgis, was for many years the leading practitioner here. Dr. James Ormiston, among the earliest physicians, was a graduate of the college of physicians and surgeons of Fairfield, N. Y. He returned to Otsego county, N. Y., where he died a few years ago. His daughter is the widow of Thomas Hamilton. One of the earliest prominent physicians in the Maumee valley was Dr. John Evans. He was born in Bourbon county, Ky., January 16, 1794, studied medicine in Philadelphia under the talented Dr. Rush, after whom the younger brother of S. C. Evans was named. Dr. Evans in February, 1823, took possession of a log cabin left by Gen. Armstrong's wagoner at Camp No. 3, four miles down the river from Fort Defiance, and here his son S. C. was born. He was a very energetic man, filled many offices, and died in 1842 at Defiance, while on a business trip. The writer well remembers being told by Dr. Evan's daughter, the late Mrs. Pliny Hoagland, of her going in the night, with Dr. Thompson, to visit her father in his last illness.

The most prominent physician in Fort Wayne forty-three years ago, was Dr. Lewis Beecher, who came here from New York, a graduate of the Fairfield college of physicians and surgeons. He retired from the general practice of medicine and kept a drug store on East Columbia street. He was a man of great natural force of character, with one exception, and that lack was a most unfortunate one. He was a cousin of the great Beecher family, and possessed some of their peculiar, eccentric traits of character. The family is now scattered and none remain here. Dr. Carl Schmitz, who died about a year ago, had resided here half a century or more, and having an extensive and lucrative practice, accumulated a large estate. His name will be fitly perpetuated by the magnificent block which his widow is erecting at the corner of Calhoun and Washington streets. He and Dr. Bernard Sevenick were the easliest German physicians. The latter besides attending to his surgical practice, conducted a brewery where he dispensed beer in profusion. Dr. H. P. Ayres, who practiced here about fifty years, had a large clientele. After practicing a few years, he graduated at the university of New York in 1845–46. Dr. James W. Daily practiced here for twenty-five to thirty years, and had an extensive reputation as a surgeon. He graduated at the Jefferson medical college of Philadelphia. His widow, the daughter of the venerable Calvin Anderson, resides here.

John M. Josse, a German physician, who left his native land after the troubles of 1848, practiced here from 1860 to 1880. He was born in 1818, and died in April, 1880.

The names of the doctors who have practiced here are legion, and some of them were quite clever, but most have not left an enduring name. Of the living, among whom are some of the veterans in the profession, it is not within the province of this sketch to speak. One other may be mentioned as a type of a class. From about 1844 to 1855, Alexander Tollerton, who died here a few years ago, did a large business and accumulated much money. He called himself an uroscopic doctor. The wealth that he amassed was spent in various ways before his death.

The practice of medicine in the pioneer times, and indeed for many years subsequent to that period, was beset with many difficulties. Physicians in the town were called out to a great distance in the country, and these trips which they were compelled to make to minister to the necessities of the sick had generally to be made on horseback, as the roads would not permit of the safe use of carriages. Not infrequently physicians yet living in the city lost their way in the pathless forests. The remuneration was of course often insufficient, and the practice was in a large degree a generous sacrifice to suffering humanity.

Medical Societies. — The Allen county medical society was organized in 1860. The early records are not available, but it is believed that the charter members of this society were Henry P. Ayres, William H. Brooks, Thomas P. McCullough, Charles F. Mayer, W. H. Myers, Isaac M. Rosenthal, B. S. Woodworth, C. A. Smith, Charles Schmitz, John M. Josse, and George T. Bruebach. The first president was Dr. Schmitz. The society was conducted in a somewhat irregular manner, though profitable meetings were held, attended by physicians from neighboring counties, until June 6, 1866, when it was reorganized, with a large membership, including several physicians of prominence in neighboring counties. The officers then elected were R. V. Murray, president; G. T. Bruebach, vice president; A. J. Erwin, secretary; William H. Brooks, treasurer. The society held regular meetings, and yearly sessions which were largely attended, until May 5, 1874, when the society was reorganized under the auspices and control of the state medical society, and only practitioners in the county were eligible to membership. The society has always held a high rank, and some of its members have occupied positions of honor in the state organization. H. P. Ayres was president of the state society in 1871, James S. Gregg, president of the society in 1885, Isaac M. Rosenthal, vice president of the state society in 1870, B. S. Woodsworth, president of the state society in 1860. The society is still in existence, although its meetings are somewhat irregular. The present officers are A. P. Buchman, president; Howard McCullough, secretary; T. J. Dills, treasurer; board of censors, M. F. Porter, G. L. Greenawalt, W. H. Myers.

The Fort Wayne Academy of Medicine, a society independent of all other organizations, was organized June 7, 1886. Its objects as set forth in the articles of association, are more efficient means for the cultivation and advancing of medical knowledge, and other desirable professional ends. All regular physicians in good standing are admitted, and no code is imposed. Meetings are held semi-monthly, at which papers are presented and clinical cases reported. The officers are elected yearly. The first were: President, B. S. Woodworth; vice president, M. F. Porter; secretary and treasurer, H. McCullough; librarian, J. D. Chambers. The other charter members were Drs. McCaskey, Dills and Stemen. There are now fifteen members.

Medical Education.—On the 10th day of March, 1876, the medical college of Fort Wayne was organized by the election of a board of trustees and a faculty, and the regular incorporation of the institution under the laws of this state and obtaining what is known as a charter. Prof. B. S. Woodworth, M. D., was elected dean, and Prof. H. A. Clark, M. D., secretary of the faculty, and Rev. R. D. Robinson, D. D., president of the board of trustees. The first regular session opened on the 1st of October of the same year, and continued until the 1st of March, 1877. During the summer at the meeting of the American medical college association at Chicago, the college was elected to membership in this association. In October of that year the second session began with a good class of students, much larger than the previous session. But during this term there was a good deal of internal dissension.

After the commencement exercises of this session, a meeting was called of those interested in the enterprise. After some deliberations the college was disbanded. Fort Wayne medical college was then organized, many of the leading citizens signing the articles of association. A board of trustees was elected, composed of the best and most influential men in this city, who at once proceeded to organize a faculty. Prof. W. H. Gobrecht, M. D., was elected to the chair of anatomy, and came from

Philadelphia early in the session and gave an interesting course of lec tures on anatomy.

In August, 1878, the trustees, failing to raise the amount of money which was thought necessary to successfully carry forward the enterprise, abandoned this, the second medical college organization in this city. Almost immediately there was organized under a new charter, a new medical college of Fort Wayne, which at once elected a faculty and issued their first annual announcement, and in October opened the first session. For four years the announcement was made and the lectures were given regularly, until the session of 1882-3. During the summer following the illustrations and fixtures were sold to satisfy a judgment against the college, the entire institution selling for $50. It should be remarked, however, that there was but one college here to bid on the property, and many things did not sell for the same as they cost, as the ordinary citizen has but little use for skeletons, bones, monstrosities, dissecting tables, etc. About the same time that the above-named college was organized, a number of citizens with Prof. W. H. Gobrecht and other physicians organized the Fort Wayne college of medicine. Hon. A. H. Hamilton, then member of congress from this district, gave to the enterprise some money and the building which was occupied, free of rent for one year, other citizens also contributing money and aiding the enterprise. A board of trustees was elected by the corporation, consisting of the Hon. Charles McCulloch, Hon. R. C. Bell, Hon. Henry Monning, Hon. Montgomery Hamilton and A. C. Trentman. This board organized by the election of Hon. Charles McCulloch as president, and A. C. Trentman, secretary. The Fort Wayne college of medicine is still in existence and is prospering.

The following is the present faculty: C. B. Stemen, A. M., M. D., LL. D., dean, professor of surgery and clinical surgery; William P. Whery, M. D., secretary, professor of diseases of women and obstetrics; George W. McCaskey, A. M., M. D., professor of theory and practice of medicine; Joseph L. Gilbert, M. D., professor of theory and practice of medicine; Charles R. Dryer, A. B., M. D., professor of chemistry and toxicology; I. Ellis Lyons, A. M., M. D., professor of obstetrics; Kent K. Wheelock, M. D., professor of diseases of the eye and ear; George B. Stemen, M. D., professor of materia medica and therapeutics; Walter W. Barnett, M. D., professor of anatomy; Alpheus P. Buchman, M. D., professor of diseases of children; Neal Hardy, M. D., professor of physiology; H. D. Wood, A. M., M. D., professor of abdominal surgery; Vesta M. W. Swarts, M. D., lecturer on dermatology; R. W. Thrift, M. D., emeritus professor of gynecology; James S. Gregg, M. D., emeritus professor of surgery.

County Licenses.— In 1885 the law requiring the licensing of physicians went into force, and in that year the following persons received this local authority to practice the healing art in Allen county: James M. Dinnen, John W. Younge, Isaac M. Myers, Franklin Greenwell, George W. Bowen, Joseph D. Searles, William Whery, Charles C. F.

Wm. H. Brooks M.D.

Nierchang, George L. Greenawalt, J. W. Causland, George A. Ross, William T. Ferguson, Hiram C. McDowell, Marion F. Williamson, Samuel C. Metcalf, Amandus J. Laubach, Thomas H. McCormick, Thomas S. Virgil, Thomas J. Dills, Joseph H. Jones, Joseph L. Smith, J. D. McHenry, Horace E. Adams, G. T. Bruebach, Hiram Van Sweringen, Joseph H. Omo, Charles W. Gordon, George E. Chandler, Lewis Payton, Christian Martz, M. Frances Green, William de la Ruhl, Thomas P. McCullagh, Hershel S. Myers, William H. Myers, Kent Kave Wheelock, Clarence F. Swift, Robert F. Lipes, Robert S. Knode, Joseph D. Morgan, Lycurgus S. Null, John W. Bilderbach, John L. Kryder, Christian B. Stemen, Lyman P. Harris, John M. Shutt, Howard McCullough, Charles M. Fiser, Carl Pragler, Brookfteld Gard, Fred Glock, Charles A. Leiter, Cornelius S. Smith, James S. Gregg, Charles E. Heaton, Benjamin S. Woodworth, Jonas Emanuel, Henry G. Wagner, Mrs. Amelie Wagner, John Seaton, Harry G. Gould, Lewis C. Shutt, George N. Worley, Ammill Engel, John D. Chambers, Franklin H. Cosgrove, Isaac M. Rosenthal, George W. McCaskey, Emmet L. Siver, Samuel D. Sledd, William A. Connolly, Siemon E. Mentzer, John W. Gunther, Jacob Hull, George Murphy, E. L. Reed, A. E. Vanbuskirk, Philip Blade, Louis T. Sturgis, Abraham J. Rauch.

Since 1885 the following have registered: A. P. Buchman, Jacob Hetrick, Abraham J. Kesler, George C. Stemen, Joseph E. Stultz, Gustavus G. Brudi, Miles F. Porter, Charles Stultz, George F. Hesler, Daniel M. Allen, Elmer E. Polk, John A. Stutz, Benjamin F. Lamb, Thomas R. Morrison, Isaac W. Martin, George Wirt Hathaway, Mary Tufts Hathaway, Walter Wynn Burnett, Edward J. McOscar, Lloyd Houghton, James Ellsworth Miller, Ella F. Harris, Creed T. Banks, George W. Cutshaw, Andrew J. Boswell, John M. Coombs, William Bevier, Lafayette Balcom, Ulysses G. Lipes, James H. Manville, Augustus Soper, Louis A. Prezinger, Jacob W. Coblentz, Herman A. Borger, David B. Cary, Mary A. Whery, Oliver Theodore May, Carl J. Gilbert, S. Justin Derbyshire, Emma S. Atwood, Henry W. Niswonger, Noah R. Wenger, Walter L. McKinley, A. G. Holloway, Maria L. Holloway, Luella Derbyshire, Marshall Beaty, Rudolph Deppeloa, Columbus M. Pickett, John K. Geary, Carl Shilling, James W. Worden, Charles M. Goheen, P. W. Jackson, John L. Shirey, Asa C. Boswell, George B. McBower, Joshua Simon, J. Ellis Lyons.

One of the early physicians at Fort Wayne was the late Dr. Charles A. Schmitz. He was born in Borgloh, Hanover, Germany, November 24, 1809. In his native land he prepared himself for the practice, graduating from a medical college at Bonn. He came to America in 1837, and after spending a year and a half in Philadelphia he came to Fort Wayne. He continued in the active practice of his profession many years, but for some time prior to his death had retired. He was married August 27, 1840, to Henrika C. Lans, who was born at Deventer, Holland, January 13, 1810. She came to America in 1838, and until her marriage lived with relatives at Elkhart, Ind. Doctor and

XXII

Mrs. Schmitz had six children. Of these Lisette H., wife of Rev. Adolph Biewend, of Boston, Mass., and Carrie S., wife of William V. Douglass, of Fort Wayne, are living. The four deceased were Amanda P., Florenz C. A., who graduated at the United States naval academy, spent twenty-one years as a lieutenant commander in the naval service, and died at Mare's Island, off the coast of California, May 20, 1883; Godfrey and Alloysius. Florenz left one child, Charles Albert Schmitz, who is now a student in the Fort Wayne schools. Dr. Schmitz died March 10, 1887. He was well-known in Fort Wayne and vicinity, and highly respected.

Dr. Charles E. Sturgis, formerly a prominent citizen of Fort Wayne, and a pioneer in the medical profession, was born in Queen Anne county, Md., January 1, 1815. He came to Indiana before reaching his majority, and settled at Richmond. Afterward removing to Logansport, he married Louisa Ewing, daughter of Col. Alexander Ewing. Not long afterward he came to Fort Wayne and was engaged in the practice of medicine for thirty years. He was a graduate of the Ohio medical college, and was peculiarly adapted by nature for a successful physician. His warm-hearted, gentle and attentive presence alone was beneficial in the sick room. He was kind to the poor and by all loved and respected. He was at one time a partner of Dr. S. B. Woodworth. He was identified with the development of the city and contributed toward its advancement. In both houses of the state assembly he represented the county, was for a long time a member of the school board, and in 1868 represented this congressional district in the national democratic convention at New York. He died November 24, 1869. His son, Louis T. Sturgis, was born in this city, July 23, 1848, and was educated in the city schools, also attending the state university one year and studying in Philadelphia one year. He clerked in a drug store in early life, and in 1872 engaged in the drug business at Huntertown, remaining there until 1879, also studying medicine. He attended the medical department of Michigan university during 1879-80, then practiced medicine at Huntertown and subsequently graduated from Rush medical college, Chicago, in 1882. In December, 1885, he came to Fort Wayne, and has since practiced here. He is also the proprietor of a drug store at No. 275 Hanna street. He was married October 26, 1879, to Miss Caroline M. Work, born in DeKalb county, November 21, 1848, to Robert and Sarah (Emery) Work, and they have two children: Sarah L. and Alida K. The doctor and family are members of the First Presbyterian church, and he is a member of the K. of P., and the Allen county and Indiana medical societies.

That veteran physician of Fort Wayne, William H. Brooks, M. D., whose forty-six years of practice here is, without doubt, a longer period than that of the professional career in this city of any other of the medical fraternity, was born in Worcester county, Mass., February 18, 1813, son of Reuben and Anna Brooks. The family removed to Windsor county, Vt., seven or eight years after his birth, and he worked there upon the farm, studying in the common schools, and at an academy at Randolph, Orange county. He taught school two terms in Vermont and two in Ohio. At the age of twenty he began the study of medicine, and in 1834 attended a medical college at Worthington, Ohio. After four courses of lectures there he began practice at Norwalk, Ohio, and in the spring of 1841 established himself at Fort Wayne. During the last two years he has virtually retired from practice, closing a long and honorable professional career, though he still attends occasionally to the calls of friends. He has been married four times, and has four children living, two having deceased. One of the latter, a son, died in the service of his country, from the effect of a wound received in battle. Mrs. Henry G. Olds and Mrs. James M. Kane are daughters of Dr. Brooks. The elder son, William H. Brooks, jr., is now in California, and his other son, Oscar H., is in the employ of Henry G. Olds. Dr. Brooks is a member of the Allen county and state medical societies; is a Mason and Odd Fellow, and in politics is a republican.

Henry P. Ayres, M. D., late a prominent physician of Fort Wayne, was born in Morristown, N. J., September 1, 1813. When he was four years old his parents emigrated to Ohio, and made their home at Dayton, where three years later the father died, leaving seven children to the care of his widow. She, a woman of strong character and religious devotion, proved worthy of the trust, and though the surroundings were not favorable to such a result, brought her children up to habits of industry and reverence of the nobler ideals of life. The son, Henry, was ambitious in the way of study, and while engaged in daily work prepared himself to enter Hanover college at the age of nineteen years. After three years of study his means were exhausted and he taught school at Dayton, Ohio, and for several years at Piqua. During a portion of this period he taught night school also, and among his pupils in this school at one time was he who afterward was Bishop Luers, of this diocese of the Episcopal church. In obedience to a request in his father's will, he also spent some months in learning a trade, taking up cabinet making. But his ambition was to enter the profession of medicine, and to this he devoted much time. Within this period he was married, September 2, 1839, to Kate E. Rowen, of Piqua. During the wirter of 1841–2, he attended a medical college at Louisville, and in June, 1842, came to Fort Wayne, and began the practice, in which he had immediate success. In 1846 he entered the medical department of the university of New York, and graduated. He prospered in his practice, but eighteen years before his death, symptoms of paralysis began to appear, which gradually compelled him to relinquish his work. During his busiest years he was a frequent contributor to the leading medical journals, and to secular and religious papers, and was an active member of the American medical association, and the professional societies of the state and county. In no wise did he neglect the duties of religious devotion, but having united with the Presbyterian church at at Dayton, at the age of fourteen, a membership which he transferred to

Fort Wayne on coming here, he continued through life to be a zealous and useful worker in that denomination. In 1857 he was elected a ruling elder of the church, and held that position until death. The Sunday school also attracted his energies, and he was superintendent nine pears between 1847 and 1866. In all relations to society he was kind, generous and helpful, manifesting to the poor and needy the widest Christian sympathy. He died December 25, 1887, leaving besides his wife three children: Dr. S. C. Ayres, the noted oculist of Cincinnati, Mrs. A. M. Babcock, and H. B. Ayres, the well known druggist of Fort Wayne.

Benjamin Studley Woodworth, M. D., the Nestor of the medical profession in the Maumee valley, has encountered in his career all those experiences that make up the history of the medical profession in that region. Born at Liecester, Mass., in 1816, he went when a boy to Rome, N. Y., to reside with his sister. He was fitted for college in a private school, at which among his fellow students were boys afterward known as Daniel Huntington, a famous artist; Judges Caton and Miller, of Illinois; Dr. D. D. Whedon, of Michigan university; Hon. N. B. Judd, of Chicago; John B. Jervis, engineer of Croton aqueduct. He entered Hamilton college at the age of fifteen, but before graduating, was compelled to begin to prepare himself for a profession. He began reading medicine at the age of eighteen, with Dr. A. Blair, of Rome, N. Y. He attended lectures at the college of physicians and surgeons at Fairfield, N. Y., whose only rival in that state was the college of the same name in New York. Its faculty was then as eminent as any this side of the Atlantic. He afterward attended Berkshire medical college, and received his degree at the age of twenty-one. He remained in Massachusetts until the spring of 1838, when he removed to Ashtabula county, Ohio. One beautiful morning, in the last of December, he rode into Perrysburg at the foot of the Maumee rapids, and his admiration was divided between the landscape and an immense hotel building five or six stories high, erected by Chicago people, which a few years later was torn to fragments by a tornado. This place was then the county seat and was larger than Toledo, which the Doctor visited after enjoying the hospitality of a Doctor Dwight. Returning to Ashtabula county, he resolved to soon emigrate to where "Potatoes did grow small, and they ate them tops and all, on Maumee." In March he rode on horseback to Cleveland, and went by a small steamboat to Perrysburg at the foot of the rapids. He carried a letter of introduction to Dr. H. Burnett, of Gilead, at the head of the rapids, with whom he became a partner. He made his home at Providence, opposite the village of Grand Rapids. Here he had the honor of delivering the fourth of July address in 1839, under the shadow of a big elm. The proceedings were under the auspices of the late Gen. James B. Steadman, then building a dam across the Maumee, for a feeder to the canal. After he had been at Providence a few months he began to shake with the ague, and not knowing of the value of quinine in sufficient doses, he suffered unutterably until the following May, with jaundice, dropsy and enlargement of the spleen. His practice was full of hardships, for a delicate and feeble man, trying indeed for the most robust. He rode over Lucas, Henry, Fulton and Defiance counties, as they are now called, to the Indiana line, on horseback. Tired of a practice so wearisome and without much financial profit, he went to Fort Wayne in the spring of 1846, and here has ever since resided. There were then about 4,000 inhabitants, such roads as there opened were almost impassable and the canal was the commercial outlet. Malarial fever predominated, and it was treated with infinitesimal does of quinine and immense portions of calomel, with antimony, drastics, cathartics, and frequently bleeding. This terrible practice was reformed, and old settlers give the credit for the great advance in treatment to Dr. Woodworth. The venerable doctor has devoted his life to the practice of his profession. The honors conferred upon him in this department have been frequent. He has been president of various local organizations, of the state medical society, and of the American medical association. The only civil offices he has held have been the postmastership under Polk's administration, and a clerkship in the New Orleans custom house under Senator W. P. Kellogg. Still active and energetic he continues to devote the results of a half century of successful practice to beneficent work among the sick and suffering.

Dr. Elbridge Gerry Wheelock, one of the pioneers of Allen county, both in its settlement and in the upbuilding of the medical profession, was born in Burlington, Vt., November 25, 1814. Of notable ancestry, his own career reflected great credit upon those from whom he inherited many good qualities of mind and heart. The Wheelocks are of Welsh descent, and came to Massachusetts during the wars of Cromwell or about the time of the rebellion of the Duke of Monmouth. The American ancestors were three brothers of considerable estates. Dr. Wheelock's grandfather, Thomas, was first cousin of Eleazer Wheelock, first president of Dartmouth college, and his wife, whose maiden name was Dodge, was first cousin of the mother of Daniel Webster. Phineas, son of Thomas, was born at Winchester, or Surry, N. H., February 21, 1781. He became a silversmith at Boston, and was there twice married, first to Margaret Hennessy, by whom he had three children: John, Margaret and William. His second marriage was to Elizabeth Hennessy, by whom he had the following children: Louisa (Mrs. Murphy), Elbridge Gerry, Sarah (Mrs. Bacon), Catherine (Mrs. Dr. Long), and Elizabeth, who died at five years of age. Mrs. Elizabeth Wheelock died at Plattsburgh, N. Y., October, 1823, at the age of thirty-eight years. She was born at Boston; her father was a native of Londonderry, Ireland, and her mother was of Puritan extraction. Phineas Wheelock died in Perry township, August 1, 1848. Dr. E G. Wheelock obtained his early education at the Plattsburgh academy, being a schoolfellow with A. P. and J. K. Edgerton. Coming to Cleveland he taught school and read medicine, but never graduated, the urgent demand for doctors in the new settlements not permitting the time. He began practice on the Wabash & Erie canal while it was in construction, and settled at Woodburn, in Maumee township. Afterward he removed to Huntertown, and in 1849 he bought a farm in that vicinity of 160 acres. In 1861 he removed to Leo, now his residence. At Huntertown he married Esther Hatch, by whom he had several children, the only one of whom that grew to manhood was Elbridge Gerry. Gerry, as he was called, was a man of brilliant talent and unusual culture. He studied medicine at the university of Michigan and graduated at Cleveland medical college. As an extemporaneous orator on any subject called for, he was without a peer in the county, and his retentive memory was stored with the classics of literature. He practiced at Huntertown until April, 1877, and then took his father's practice at Leo, at which place he practiced, except a brief period at Fort Wayne, until his death, November, 1883. Dr. E. G. Wheelock was married, subsequent to the death of his first wife, to Hannah, daughter of Daniel Moody, of DeKalb county, and they have had these children: Thomas Phineas (deceased), John Davis, Elisha Kent Kane.

Kent K. Wheelock, M. D., the youngest son of the above, was born in Perry township, June 9, 1857. At the age of fourteen he entered the dental office of Loag & Brown, of Fort Wayne, where he remained two years. In the fall of 1874, he entered the preparatory department of the university of Michigan, and completed the course, then entering the medical department of the institution, and pursued his studies there two years. In 1879 he matriculated at the Bellevue hospital medical college, of New York, and graduated in 1880. He began the practice of medicine at Huntertown that spring, but in November came to Fort Wayne, and here has successfully practiced to the present. In 1883-4, he was a student and assistant surgeon in the New York eye and ear infirmary. He is a member of the county and state medical societies, and the academy of medicine of Fort Wayne, and is professor of ophthalmology and otology in the Fort Wayne college of medicine. January 19, 1881, he was married to Matilda Henderson, and they have three children, George H., Gerra C. and Margaret. Dr. Wheelock is a Mason and past chancellor of the K. of P. Politically he is an active democrat, and held the office of coroner of Allen county from April, 1882, to November, 1884.

George W. Bowen, M. D., who has been engaged in the practice of medicine at Fort Wayne since March, 1852, is a native of Delaware county, N. Y., the son of Calvin and Charlotte (Watson) Bowen. In 1836 he came west with his parents, who settled first in Monroe county, Mich., and in 1843 in Will county, Ill. Four years later he went to Chicago and was a clerk in the postoffice two years. He then began the study of medicine and graduated from the Hahnemann medical college of that city, also attending the Cleveland medical college. After some practice in Chicago he came to this city, which has since been his home. With a single exception, he is the oldest practicing physician in the city.

During the earlier years of his career he was an earnest student, by the light of the candle perfecting his knowledge of his science, and extending his acquaintance with general literature. His literary attainments are notable, and many of his published poetical efforts have attracted attention. His life has been one of strict temperance, honesty and integrity, and his character is honored wherever he is known. He occupies an enviable rank, professionally, and is now president of the Indiana institute of homeopathy, and member of the American institute and western academy of homeopathy. Dr. Bowen was married May 3, 1860, to America J. Welsheimer, a native of Ohio, daughter of Daniel and Catherine (Taylor) Welsheimer. The doctor comes of a family of great longevity. His parents were married February 14, 1803, and lived together seventy-two years. His father at death was nearly ninety five years old, his mother ninety. They had twelve children who reached maturity. The paternal great-grandfather attained the age of one hundred and five years.

Cornelius S. Smith, M. D., was born in York county, Penn., May 31, 1820. His father, Abraham Smith, was born in the same county in 1796, and died in Adams county, Penn., in 1874, and his wife, mother of Cornelius, a native of the same county, died in 1830. In 1847 he began the study of medicine, and graduated from the Philadelphia medical college in 1850. The same year he settled near Springfield, Ohio, then removed to South Bend, and in May, 1854, to Fort Wayne, where he has since resided successfully practicing his profession. For the past seven years he has devoted particular attention to rectal diseases, and has gained a wide reputation for skill in that branch of medicine, patients seeking him from all parts of the country. Dr. Smith is a member of the Masonic order and of the Methodist Episcopal church. He was married in 1856 to Charity R. Ramsey, who was born June 14, 1825, in Wabash county, Ill., to Dorsey and Hannah Ramsey. They have two children: Spencer R. and Carrie A.

George Theodore Bruebach, M. D., a learned and skillful physician of Fort Wayne, was born at Grossalmerode, Germany, March 3, 1830. In the gymnasium of the city of Cassel he received a thorough collegiate education, between 1840 and 1849, and after passing the examination of "maturity," that required for admission to special study in theology, medicine or jurisprudence, he entered the university of Marburg, and began the study of medicine and natural science, passing the examination in the latter in 1851. He then entered the university of Wurzburg, Bavaria, where he had to direct him in the study of his profession such famous lights as Virchow, Scauzoni, Kolliker, Marcus and Texter. In 1853 he returned to Marburg for further study and final examination, and graduated December 23, 1854, as Doctor Medicinæ, Chirurgiæ, et Artis Obstetriciæ. For several years following he was an assistant physician at the "Landkrankenhaus zu Cassel," but in 1858 he came to America. Locating at Fort Wayne soon after his arrival, he began here the practice of medicine, in which he has occupied a place in the front rank, and has enjoyed nearly thirty years of lucrative work in his profession. He is a member of the American medical association, has served as president of the Allen county society one year, and is examining surgeon of the Hartford and Germania life insurance companies. He has been a devoted student, a faithful physician, and is deservedly popular.

Since May, 1860, Isaac M. Rosenthal, M. D., has been numbered among the leading physicians of Fort Wayne. He was born in Wurtemberg, Germany, October 31, 1831. At seventeen years of age he came to America, and after residing at Philadelphia about three years he removed to Cleveland, Ohio, where he attended the medical college. In 1853 he began practice in Bedford, Ohio, and in 1855 he removed to Indianapolis and thence to Fort Wayne. Dr. Rosenthal was married in Cincinnati, November 30, 1857, to Ada Rauh, and they have seven children: Charles H., Rebecca, Edwin A., Mina, Maurice, Hattie and Milton. The doctor has been a member of the Allen county medical society since 1860, of the state medical society since 1859 and of the American medical association since 1867. He served as president of Fort Wayne board of health about eight years, and he has occupied the position of surgeon and physician to St. Joseph's hospital during nearly the whole time since it was established.

James Sansom Gregg, M. D., is the son of William and Susannah Gregg, both natives of Washington county, Penn. There he was born December 16, 1830, and named for James Sansom, then a prominent Methodist preacher of that state. Seven years later his parents removed to Delaware county, Ohio, where he spent his youth on a farm, receiving a good education, however, including two years' instruction in the Ohio Wesleyan university. In 1852 he settled in Whitley county, Ind., and soon afterward began the study of medicine. After taking a course of lectures in the Cleveland medical college he began the practice in Columbia city. Removing to Missouri, he was engaged in his profession there until the war broke out. During the war period he was first surgeon of the Southwest battalion of Missouri, and then of the Eighty-eighth Indiana regiment three years until the close of the war. He then returned to Columbia City, and during the winter of 1865-6 attended Jefferson medical college of Philadelphia, there graduating. He then located in Fort Wayne, and became one of the prominent physicians of the city, being particularly successful in surgery. He is a member of the Allen county and state medical societies and the American association. Of the state society he served as vice president in 1885 and president in 1886, and was for ten years professor of medicine in the college of medicine of Fort Wayne. He is a member of the Masonic order, of the thirty-second degree, a Knight Templar, a comrade of the G. A. R., and in politics an earnest republican. For seven years he was surgeon of the Wabash railway at Fort Wayne. Since 1880 Dr. Gregg has been an invalid, suffering with locomotor ataxia, a disease resulting from his severe army service. He was married at

Columbia City, May 29, 1866, to Lizzie Morrison, daughter of Andrew M. and Sarah A. (Edwards) Morrison. The former was born at Mercersburg, Penn., October 22, 1808, the latter at St. Thomas, Penn., January 18, 1819. At the latter town Mrs. Gregg was born October 11, 1837. She is a member of the First Presbyterian church. Dr. Gregg and wife have had three children: Fannie Eudora, born November 29, 1867, died April 11, 1870; Stella Mayse, born December 14, 1873; and Fred Morrison, born September 26, 1878.

John Seaton, a skillful oculist of Fort Wayne, is a native of Ohio, born in Carroll county, April 15, 1836. His father, Robert Seaton, was born in county Donegal, Ireland, October 11, 1799, son of Jeremiah and Mary (Patterson) Seaton, who passed their lives in Ireland, the latter reaching the age of one hundred and four years. Robert Seaton came to America in 1819, and was married at Philadelphia, November 15, 1827, to Rachel Liggett, a native of Cecil county, Md., born April 3, 1803, to Alexander and Nancy (Neal) Liggett, natives of Scotland, who emigrated to Ireland and thence to America in 1799. John Seaton received an academic education, and on August 20, 1862, enlisted in Company I, Fortieth Ohio regiment, and served until the close of the war. He participated in the battles of Chickamauga, Lookout Mountain, Mission Ridge, Ringgold, Resaca, and at Kenesaw Mountain, was wounded June 27, 1864, by a ball in the left leg, on account of which he was in a hospital two months at Nashville. Then after a furlough he regained his regiment and participated in the battles of Franklin and Nashville. December 20, 1864, he was transferred to the Fifty-first Ohio, and about the same time was, owing to an attack of conjuntivitis he was sent to the eye and ear hospital at Chicago, where he remained until ordered to Cairo for muster out. For four years thereafter he was almost entirely blind, and a part of the time quite so. In May, 1866, he came Fort Wayne, and three years later began the study of medicine. He has taken two courses of lectures in the Fort Wayne college of medicine. He has made a specialty of the treatment of diseases of the eye and ear, and has performed some remarkable cures. Dr. Seaton was married October 20, 1870, to Mary E. Dudgeon, who died September 14, 1877, leaving two children, Sophia C. and Mary R., the latter of whom has since died. October 15, 1878, he was married to Maggie H. Harter, daughter of Michael and Mary Harter. He and family are members of the Second Presbyterian church, and the doctor is a member of the F. & A. M., K. of P., and G. A. R. In politics he is a democrat. During the administration of President Cleveland he served eighteen months as deputy collector internal revenue.

W. Wynn Barnett, M. D., a young physician of notable ability, is a native of Ohio, born in Louisburg, Preble county, July 18, 1857. His father, Rev. William C. Barnett, was a native of Franklin county, Penn., and his mother, Frances M. Sullivan, was born in Dayton, Ohio. When he was three years old his parents removed to Wapakoneta, Ohio, and in 1868 they settled at Butler, Ind., going thence to Florence, Ky., two years later. There the mother died November 25, 1880. The father now resides at Dickson, Tenn. In 1875, Dr. Barnett entered Wittenberg college, Ohio, and there attended until he had completed the junior year. He began the study of medicine in 1881, at Cincinnati, and in 1882 returned to Butler, Ind., where he continued his reading with his uncle, Dr. J. S. Barnett. During the collegiate years of 1883-4 and 1885-6 he attended Fort Wayne medical college, and was graduated, and then began the practice of medicine in this city. Since graduation he has occupied the position of demonstrator of anatomy in the college, and in 1887 his brilliant attainments were recognized by appointment to the chair of professor of anatomy, both of which positions he ably fills. He is a member of the Allen county medical society and the Indiana state medical society. His religious affiliations are with the Lutheran church.

Hiram Van Sweringen, A. M., M. D., one of the distinguished members of the medical profession in Indiana, is a descendant of the doughty Garrett van Sweringen, of whom it is related in history as well as by tradition, that upon the surrender of the Dutch colony in America to the English, he broke his sword across his knee and throwing the fragments right and left, renounced all allegiance to the Dutch government. He was a notable man, the younger son of a noble family, born at Roensterdwan, Holland, in 1636, served the West India company, and was supercargo of the "Prince Maurice," which sailed to the Dutch colony on the Delaware. He married in April, 1669, Barbara de Barrette, of Valenciennes, France, and had two children, Bacharias and Elizabeth. The family was naturalized by act of the general assembly at St. Mary's, and records of this and many other interesting facts concerning the family are to be found in colonial histories and documents. The family, in its migrations, spread principally southward, though it is now represented in every state, the late W. C. Ralston, president of the bank of California, being a descendant. While the family is well represented in each of the principal professions, that of medicine seems to have been the choice in the great majority of instances. Dr. R. W. Sweringen, of Austin, Tex., has long been the health officer of that state, and is at the present time president of the Texas state medical society. Dr. H. V. Sweringen was born on the 5th of October, 1844, at Navarre, Stark county, Ohio, the ninth of eleven children, of whom two boys and four girls reached maturity. The eldest son, Dr. Budd Van Sweringen, was thoroughly educated in the classics and modern languages, was graduated as a physician and surgeon, and appointed surgeon to Gen. McCook's brigade, but died after a short service at the age of twenty-eight. He was also at one time principal of the high school at Fort Wayne, Ind. The resources of the parents having become exhausted, the son Hiram was obliged, at the age of sixteen, to seek his own maintenance. Coming to Fort Wayne in May, 1861, he enlisted in the Forty-fourth Indiana regiment, but his parents and friends obtained his release on account of his youth, and he was given a position as clerk in the drug store of

Hugh B. Reed, colonel of the regiment named, and this gave him an opportunity to prepare himself in a very important branch of the profession of medicine. While thus engaged, and notwithstanding he had received but a common school education, " Harry," as he was familiarly known, became very popular as a public reader and speaker. In 1864 he was invited to, and did, deliver the 4th of July oration at Huntington, Ind., where twenty-three years subsequently he delivered an address at the annual meeting of the Huntington county medical society. Upon decoration days, at celebrations, as well as at private gatherings, he has been a welcome participant in the proceedings. In 1865, during a protracted meeting at the Berry Street Methodist Episcopal church in Fort Wayne, when an unusual interest in religion was awakened in the young people of the city, he united with the church, and was earnestly entreated for years after to enter the ministry, but declined. In November of the same year, he was married ty Miss Elna M. Hanna, a poor orphan girl, who has been a faithful helper through his early struggles. Becoming a member of the American pharmaceutical association, he read a paper at its Chicago meeting in 1868, which was well received and admitted to publication in its transactions. About this time he removed to the west end of the city, and at the southwest corner of Jefferson and Broadway a building was erected, which he and a partner who furnished the capital, a few hundred dollars, occupied with a drug store. He also began the preparation of a work on pharmacy, which, after several years spent upon it under the most trying difficulties, was published by Lindsay & Blakiston, Philadelphia, upon the very favorable opinion and recommendation of Professor John M. Maisch, of that city. The book, "A Pharmaceutical Lexicon," was very well received, and had it not been for the panic of 1873, the edition would have been exhausted much sooner than it was. Dr. H. Van Sweringen had meanwhile been practicing medicine though surrounded by embarrassing environments. Failing to accumulate a sufficient amount to justify him in leaving his family to attend a medical college, he ventured to hang out his sign as a physician and surgeon and happily succeeded in obtaining a good, living practice from the start. A few years later he was able, with the voluntary aid of generous friends, to enter Jefferson medical college, Philadelphia, where he was agreeably surprised to find his way smoothed by the high esteem in which his work on pharmacy was held by the faculty of that renowned college. After one term of lectures, and passing, with great credit and honor to himself and alma mater, the examinations, he received the degree of M. D. in March, 1876. In 1878 he was elected professor of materia medica and therapeutics in the medical college of Fort Wayne, which chair he held until the college ceased to exist, the reason for which, and a very good one too, was the fact that the city was not large enough to furnish the necessary amount of clinical material, which is the life and blood of a first-class medical college. In 1883 Dr. H. V. Sweringen was honored by the Monmouth college, Illinois, with the degree of A. M., or master of arts, and in

1884 he was invited to accept the chair of materia medica and therapeutics in the college of physicians and surgeons, at Chicago, an honor he regarded very highly, but which circumstances not under his control, forced him to decline. In June, 1885, he was appointed the republican member of the board of examining surgeons for the pension department. Dr. Van Sweringen's career is a notable example of the success that can be attained by patience and perseverance even in the face of the most discouraging circumstances. These qualities have won for his rare talent and exceptional professional ability, a field of exercise for the good of his fellow men, and he has attained great prominence both professionally and socially. While not devoting himself to any specialty in his profession, he has won particular distinction and renown in the field of obstetrics, or midwifery, and in that of diseases of women and children. The doctor and his estimable wife have been blessed with nine children, two girls and seven boys, two of whom died in infancy. His oldest son Budd, also a physician and a graduate of the university of Pennsylvania, is practicing his profession in Kansas City, Mo.

Thomas S. Virgil, M. D., born May 23, 1836, died January 1, 1889, was a prominent and successful physician at Fort Wayne, during twenty years of his life, and was held in high esteem for his many good qualities, manifest in all the relations of life. He was a native of Cochanut, Penn., son of Rev. Almon Virgil, a minister of the Baptist church, who now in his ninetieth year, survives his son. When Dr. Virgil was quite young, his parents removed to New York, and lived at Penfield, Schenectady and Albany, successively. He completed a commercial course at Schenectady, and after teaching school somewhat, graduated from the Albany medical college, at the age of twenty-one. After remaining at Albany two years as a physician in charge of the hospital, he began practice at Rome, and three years later went to Cape Vincent, N. Y. Being afflicted with poor health, he spent about three years traveling, and made several trips to Europe as ship surgeon. In 1869 he made his home at Fort Wayne, and soon had gained a large practice. June 3, 1871, he was married to Anna E. Stratton, who was born near Finley, Ohia, November 11, 1841, daughter of Thomas and Celia (Jones) Stratton. Her parents, natives respectively of New Jersey and Virginia, were married about 1835. The father died May 27, 1864, and the mother, who was but fifteen at her marriage, is living with children in Kansas. Mrs. Virgil is a member of the Baptist church, to which her husband also belonged. For two years prior to his death he was unable to practice his profession, having been attacked with paralysis February 9, 1887, a malady from which he did not recover.

Dr. Samuel C. Metcalf, an able and successful physician of Fort Wayne, was born in Ashland county, Ohio, February 14, 1844, and is the son of Vachel and Amanda (Otto) Metcalf, who were respectively natives of Ashland county, Ohio, and Bedford county, Penn. His father was born November 20, 1816, the son of Edward Metcalf, who was a native of Virginia. Edward Metcalf was the son of Daniel Metcalf, a native of England, who came to America and served as a colonial officer in the revolutionary war. At the close of that war he settled in Virginia. In about the year 1804 he removed, with his family, to Washington county, Penn., where he spent the rest of his life. His son, Edward, after his marriage, removed with his wife and two children, Thomas and John, from Washington county to Ashland county, Ohio, which county continued to be his home during the rest of his life. He died, however, in about the year 1854, at the age of seventy-four years, in Allen county, Ind., while visiting at the residence of his daughter, Mrs. Rachel Crawford, of Perry township. His first presidential vote was cast for Thomas Jefferson. The mother of Dr. Metcalf was born September 27, 1821, and was the daughter of Mathias and Elizabeth Otto, who were of German descent, and removed to Bedford county, Penn., from Maryland. The parents of Dr. Metcalf were married in Ashland county, Ohio, about 1842. In 1849 they came to Allen county, and settled in Perry township, where the father had purchased a tract of unimproved land two years previously. A good farm Mr. Metcalf developed out of the wilderness, and upon this, which is known as the old Metcalf homestead, the father and mother resided for a period of nearly thirty-five years. The latter died on the old home place May 19, 1884. The former survived her until January 8, 1886, when he died at the residence of his son, Martin V. Metcalf, of Perry township. Dr. Metcalf was reared to early manhood on the home farm. At seventeen he became a teacher in the district schools and taught school during the winters of 1862-3 and 1863-4. His early education had been obtained in the district school and in Perry Centre seminary. He began the study of medicine in the spring of 1866, with Dr. E. G. Wheelock, sr., of Leo, Allen county, and in September, 1868, he entered the Charity hospital medical college, or the medical department of the university of Wooster, at Cleveland, Ohio, where he was graduated in February, 1870. He then made his home at Fort Wayne, where he soon became the possessor of a lucrative practice and is now a well known physician. He received the Ad Eundem degree from the medical department of the Western Reserve university of Cleveland, March 15, 1882. Altogether Dr. Metcalf has served about seven years as a member of the Fort Wayne board of health, and since 1884 he has served as secretary of the board or as the health officer of the city. The Doctor was married November 18, 1875, to Miss Amelia T., daughter of John H. and Elizabeth (Lark) Hill, the former a native of Plymouth, England, and the latter of Canada. Her father was the son of William R. and Elizabeth (Tolly) Hill. Her mother was the daughter of Thomas and Elizabeth (Webster) Lark, the former of whom was a ship builder of Chattam, Canada West. The father of Mrs. Metcalf settled at Fort Wayne in 1836, and followed the pursuit of an Indian trader. Mrs. Metcalf was born in Fort Wayne, October 15, 1854. Dr. Metcalf and wife have had three children: Edward, born November 1, 1877, died November 14, 1877; Holman Sinclair, born

December 18, 1880, died July 16, 1881, and Tulip Lillian, born January 31, 1886. They also have an adopted daughter, Miss Maggie Metcalf, who was born December 12, 1871. In politics Dr. Metcalf is a democrat, and takes an active part in political affairs for the promotion of the welfare of his party.

Brookfield Gard, M. D., was born in Preble county, Ohio, January 14, 1833, son of Joseph N. and Sada (Bishop) Gard, both natives of the same county. Joseph Gard was born August 11, 1811, son of Levi Gard, of Pennsylvania, who was a soldier with Gen. Wayne's expedition through Ohio as far as Fort Recovery. Sada Gard was born February 19, 1810, daughter of Rev. Nathan Bishop, a pioneer Baptist preacher in Preble county, a native of Guilford Court House, N. C. In his youth Dr. Gard attended Miami university, at Oxford, Ohio, two years, teaching between the terms of his attendance. In 1858 he began the study of medicine, and entered the Eclectic medical college at Cincinnati in 1860, graduating in 1865. His first practice was at Eldorado, Ohio, in 1861. He abandoned this in 1864, and mustered Company B, One Hundred and Fifty-sixth Ohio regiment. He assisted in equipping the regiment, and was commissioned hospital steward. Three brothers also enlisted: James F., now a prosperous physician at Cherryvale Kas., served five years as hospital steward of Battery M, First Indiana heavy artillery; Samuel G., bugler of the Ninth Indiana cavalry, died at Pulaski, Tenn.; and Martin A., of the Seventy-fifth Ohio, died at Franklin, W. Va. After a service of four months, Dr. Gard resumed his medical studies, and in February, 1865, made his home at Huntington, Ind. April 1, 1870, he removed to Fort Wayne, where he has since successfully practiced his profession. He has been married twice, his present wife being Henrietta A. Francisco, to whom he was united October 17, 1887. Two daughters are living: Anna E. and Lizzie E., of his first wife. Dr. Gard is a member of the I. O. O. F.; he is a republican and cast his first vote for Gen. Fremont.

Dr. Joseph H. Jones began practicing medicine in this city in 1871, and though at that time totally blind, a condition that still exists, he has had a large and lucrative practice, not only in this city, but in various towns throughout Indiana and Ohio. His parents are John and Margaret (Hurren) Jones, natives of Fayette county, Penn., the mother being a sister of Capt. Joseph Hurren, who served under Gen. Hull at Detroit. The parents removed to Ohio, and Dr. Jones was born in Harrison county, December 17, 1832. Seven years later the family removed to Morgan county, Ohio. When he was fourteen years old they moved to Athens county, Ohio, and he then found work for himself, being engaged at driving for a canal boat. He attended Athens college one term, was employed for one year with a drover, making three trips over the Alleghany mountains, and was afterward variously employed until 1857, when he began the study of medicine at Terre Haute, his first preceptor being Dr. Clepinger. Afterward studying with Dr. James B. Armstrong, he began practice with him. April 1, 1861, he fell from a scaffolding and sustained serious injuries, the most deplorable of which was the loss of sight in his left eye. In 1869, the other eye also became totally blind. For a year or so after this injury Dr. Jones was engaged with James Spear & Co., Chicago, but in June, 1863, he settled in Columbus, Ohio, and resumed the practice of medicine. He afterward practiced at Urixville and Cadiz, Ohio, Winchester, Dunkirk, Red Key and Hartford City, until 1868, when he established a drug store at Mt. Pleasant, Ind., in connection with his practice. Removing to Bluffton two years later, he was there married to Lydia D. Lewis, born in Warren county, Ohio, January 28, 1843, daughter of George W. and Eliza A. (Mills) Lewis. In April, 1871, Dr. Jones and wife removed to Fort Wayne, and they now have a handsome residence at 320 West Jefferson street, erected in 1873.

Thomas Johnson Dills, a widely-known physician, noted as a specialist in the diseases of the eye and ear, is a native of Indiana, born at Spencerville, DeKalb county, August 10, 1847, son of Jacob Dills, who was born in 1800, and died in DeKalb county in 1868, and his wife, Christina Dawson, born in Dearborn county, in 1812, died in DeKalb county in 1870. The ancestors of Mr. Dills immigrated from Holland and settled in New Jersey and Long Island as early as 1840. His paternal grandfather, John Diltz (as it was then spelled), entertained General Washington and staff at his home in New Jersey, during the war of the revolution. The family removed to Indiana as early as 1820, settling in Dearborn county, and in DeKalb county in 1844. Thomas J. Dills was the youngest of ten children, of whom three are living. At fifteen years of age he entered Otterbein university, remained two years and a half, and then engaged in teaching school. In 1867 he began the study of medicine in the office of Dr. William D. Meyers, and the next year entered the university of Michigan, where he was graduated in 1871. His first practice was at Avilla, and after a year there he came to Fort Wayne. In 1873 he attended Bellevue hospital college, and in 1875 again went to New York, and for two years studied the diseases of the eye and ear under Dr. Knapp. He spent some time in Europe in 1883 to perfect his studies. In the practice of his profession he has been eminently successful. He is a member of the Masonic fraternity, of the Episcopal church, and of the democratic party. He was married in 1878 to Lizzie Appleton, who died in 1880, and he was married in 1883 to Mabel Horton, of this city. He has two children, Clara B. and Margaret C.

A. P. Buchman, M. D., began the practice of medicine in Tuscarawas county, Ohio, after a thorough course of study, which embraced two years at Union college, work in the hospitals of the Cincinnati college of medicine, and a two years' course in that institution, from which he graduated in 1870. Since 1875 he has resided at Fort Wayne, where he has had a successful career. He is a member of the Allen county and Indiana medical societies, and the American association, and is a lecturer in the Fort Wayne medical college. He was born in Westmoreland county, Penn., November 17, 1844, son of Henry and Mary Buchman, natives of that county, where his paternal ancestors had lived since 1734. Several years previous to that date his great-great-grandfather had immigrated from Switzerland and settled on the east shore of Maryland, where he married a French Huguenot lady, named Marchant. The Doctor's mother is of Saxon descent. When he was four years old his parents removed to Stark county, Ohio. During the summer of 1862, he attended college at Mt. Vernon, Ohio, but in August he enlisted in Company D, One Hundred and Seventh Ohio regiment, with which he served until honorably discharged August, 1865, at Cleveland. The next month, at Union college, he resumed his studies. He was married December 29, 1870, to Dora Painter, daughter of Joseph and Sally Ann Painter, and they have had two children: Emma J. and a son who died in infancy. Dr. Buchman is a Mason, a comrade of the G. A. R., and a republican.

John D. Chambers, M. D., who has enjoyed a lucrative practice in this city since his establishment here in the spring of 1875, is a native of Alabama, Genesee county, N. Y., born July 19, 1844, son of James B. and Mahala (Mandeville) Chambers. His father was born at Salem, Washington county, N. Y., and his mother at Ovid, Seneca county. In 1848 the family removed to Lenawee county, Mich., where his childhood was spent on a farm. He prepared for college at the Tecumseh high school, and the fall after his graduation, in 1867, he entered the university of Michigan, and four years later was graduated as a batchelor of science, June, 1871, and as a doctor of medicine in 1874. While preparing for college he taught school, in all ten terms, and before his graduation had charge of the Marine City, Mich., high school one year, in this manner paying for his education. He still retains his early interest in educational matters. After the establishment of the Chautauqua literary and scientific circle he and his wife completed its four years' course, graduating in 1888, and he has served as president of the local circle, and is its vice president now. Leaving the university he began the practice of medicine at Fredonia, Washtenaw county, Mich., but in the spring of 1875, settled at Fort Wayne. He filled the chair of chemistry in the Fort Wayne medical college one year, and was then elected a professor, but preferring to give his whole attention to his practice, declined the position. He is a member of the academy of medicine, the Allen county and state medical societies and the American medical association. He is a prominent member and elder in the Presbyterian church, is vice president of the city department Y. M. C. A., and one of the board of directors, and served as chairman of the Christian Work committee three years. Dr. Chambers was married November 15, 1877, to Jennie C. Sinks, who was born at Union, Ohio, daughter of John and Julia (Baer) Sinks.

Christian B. Stemen, A. M., M. D., first became associated with the medical profession of Fort Wayne, when, in 1876, yet being a resident of VanWert, he was elected professor of the theory and practice of medicine in the Medical college of Fort Wayne. He filled that chair three years, meanwhile in 1878, removing to this city and engaging in practice, in which he has been notably successful. He is a member of the Allen county and state medical societies, the American and British medical associations; is chief surgeon of the western division of the Pittsburgh, Fort Wayne & Chicago railroad, and local surgeon of the Wabash, St. Louis & Pacific. He has given particular attention to railway surgery while in Europe studying the methods prevailing in that country, has written extensively on the subject and is editor of the *Journal of the National Association of Railway Surgeons*, published at Fort Wayne, and secretary of that association. In 1884 he was elected professor of surgery in the Fort Wayne college of medicine, and is now dean of the faculty. Dr. Stemen was born in Fairfield county, Ohio, December 3, 1836, to Henry and Rachel Stemen, of Swiss descent. The grandfather, Henry Stemen, was one of the first voters of Ohio, and for forty years was a bishop of the German Mennonite church. Three years after the birth of Dr. Stemen his parents removed to Hocking county, and when he was sixteen, to Franklin county, and later to Allen county, Ohio. After he was nineteen he taught school eight terms, and also studied medicine, so that in 1860 he entered the Eclectic Medical Institute of Cincinnati, and graduated in 1864. Later in life he received the degree of A. M. from Baldwin universiity of Berea, Ohio. He began practice in 1859 at Elida, Ohio, and subsequently practiced at Fort Jennings, Kalida, Piqua and VanWert. In the fall of 1874 he entered the Medical college of Ohio, and graduated in March, 1875, in May being appointed demonstrator of anatomy in that institution, which position he filled one year. He was married November 7, 1858, to Miss Lydia Enslen, by whom he has eight children: Kate S., John H., George C., Charles M., Margaret E., William E., Harriet F., Mary L., all living except John H. Dr. Stemen is a member of the Methodist Episcopal church, in which he is a local preacher. In 1886 he represented the local preachers of that church as a delegate to the National Association of Wesleyan Methodists, which was held at Liverpool. At that time he spent four months in Europe. In Masonry he has attained the thirty-second degree and is a Knight Templar.

Aaron E. Van Buskirk, M. D., now a well known and successful physician of Fort Wayne, began the study of his profession in the spring of 1872, while teaching school for his support, at Millersburg, Holmes county, Ohio. In 1873 he attended the medical department of Wooster university at Cleveland, and after attending one term of lectures, began the practice in March, 1874, at Monroeville. Next year he entered the medical college of Ohio, and graduated in 1876. His practice at Monroeville was continued until March 20, 1877, when he removed to Fort Wayne, and now has an extensive practice. Dr. Van Buskirk was born at Harrisburg, Carroll county, Ohio, September 27, 1847, to Jacob and Mary Ann (Elliott) Van Buskirk, and his early life was full of adversity. His parents soon after his birth removed to Adams county, Ind., and afterward to Mercer county, Ill., where the father died in 1857. Aaron accompanied his mother to Carroll county, Ohio, where he was bound out to an uncle, and he there worked upon the farm until about eighteen years old. He then removed to Madison township, Allen county, and engaged in farming, in winter teaching school. During the winter of 1869–70 he taught in Richland county, Wis., and the next summer, farmed in Tama county, Iowa, returning the next spring to Ohio. He was married June 1, 1876, to Mary J. Gray, daughter of Robert F. and Mary Ann (McKee) Gray, who was born in Holmes county, Ohio, September 1, 1848. They have had five children: Minnie B., Myrtle E., Robert J., Bertha M., and Harry F., of whom only the first survives. Dr. Van Buskirk is a Mason, and he and wife are members of the Presbyterian church.

A. J. Laubach, M. D., a physician of prominence and of scholarly attainments, is a native of Pennsylvania, born in Northampton county, December 9, 1844, of Peter and Amelia (Becker) Laubach. His father was the son of Peter and Catherine (Neligh) Laubach, and for several generations the family has resided in Northampton county, the original immigration having been about 1684, two years after the arrival of William Penn. The mother of Dr. Laubach was the daughter of Rev. Cyrus J. Becker, D. D. Dr. Laubach received his early education in the district schools, Weaversville academy and Freeland seminary (now Ursinus college). In August, 1862, he enlisted in Company D, One Hundred and Fifty-third Pennsylvania regiment, as a private, but was at once promoted second sergeant, and at the battle of Chancellorsville was promoted first sergeant. At Gettysburg he was wounded, captured and paroled, and exchanged in September following. He took up the study of medicine on his return home, but in August, 1864, was appointed by Gov. Curtin captain of Company F, Two Hundred and Second Pennsylvania regiment. He commanded his company at the battle of Salem, Va., and after Lee's surrender he was sent to Heckscherville, Penn., to quell the riots in that vicinity. He was mustered out September, 1865, and the next month entered the medical department of the university of Pennsylvana, and in March, 1866, entered the Long Island medical hospital college, where he was graduated the following June. For four months following he took private instruction from Prof. Austin Flint, at Bellevue medical college, and in March, 1867, was graduated by the medical department of the university of Pennsylvania. He began practice at Kreidersville, Penn., removed to Allentown in 1869, and in 1872–3 practiced in Philadelphia and studied further in the university. After returning to Allentown, he was in January, 1875, appointed acting assistant surgeon, U. S. A., and served in the department of Dakota until July 10, 1878, when he resigned and established himself at Fort Wayne. He is a prominent citizen, a comrade of the G. A. R., and president of the Morton club.

James M. Dinnen, M. D., a prominent citizen of Fort Wayne, and one of the leading physicians of the state, is a native of Vermont, born at Burlington, August 29, 1856. His father, Michael Dinnen, was born in Ireland, December 25, 1810, came to the United States in 1841, settled in Vermont, and in June, 1857, removed to Chicago, where for fourteen years he was engaged in business at Nos. 54 and 97 North Clark street. His mother, whose maiden name was Anna Riley, was born in 1823, in Ireland, and died in Chicago, August 14, 1887. Dr. Dinnen was the next to the youngest of six children who lived to maturity. He attended school first in Chicago, then at Notre Dame, Ind., two years at St. Rose's near Springfield, Ky., and one year at Cincinnati. In 1873 he returned to Chicago, and began the study of medicine in the office of Dr. Marguerett. In 1876 he entered the Rush medical college, and graduated in 1879. March 10, the same year, he established himself at Fort Wayne. His knowledge of his profession, various scholarly acquirements, and pleasing social qualities have combined to win for him notable success in life, and general esteem. In 1884 he was elected coroner of Allen county, and is now city physician, to which position he was first appointed in 1881. In the same year he was appointed physician of St. Joseph's hospital. He is also physician of St. Vincent's orphan asylum, and is surgeon for the New York, Chicago & St. Louis, Lake Shore & Michigan Southern, and Fort Wayne, Cincinnati & Louisville railroads. He was married November 27, 1879, to Kate S. Fleming, daughter of Hon. William and Helen (Myers) Fleming, and their children are four in number: William F., Helen F., James F., and Mary C. He is a member of the Catholic church. In August, 1889, Dr. Dinnen was appointed a member of the board of special pension examiners at Fort Wayne.

Miles F. Porter, M. D., a leading physician, is a native of Indiana, born at Decatur, Adams county, September 27, 1856, son of Dr. John P. and Elizabeth (Drowin) Porter. His father was born in Stark county, Ohio, April 21, 1822, and the grandfather, Dr. Alexander Porter, was born in 1794, and died at Decatur, September 20, 1861. Dr. John P. Porter was surgeon of the Eighty-ninth Indiana infantry, and was killed by guerillas near Lexington, Mo., November 1, 1864. His wife, a native of Ohio, died at Fort Wayne in 1886, aged about sixty years. Dr. Miles F. Porter, after receiving a common school education, began the study of medicine in 1875, and graduated from the medical college of Ohio in 1878. After practicing one year in Adams county, this state, he came to Fort Wayne in February, 1879, and his practice here, then begun, has largely developed, and his reputation as a skillful and successful physician has been firmly established. In 1888 he went to Europe, and there added to his medical acquirements. He was married in June, 1878, to Lillie Wilding, who was born at Syracuse, N. Y., in 1854, and they have four children, Lucile A., Charles D., Clara P. and Miles F. The doctor and his family are socially highly esteemed, and he is a member of the Masonic order and of the Knights of Pythias.

James Caldwell, M. D., is a native of Harrison county, Ohio, born

September 19, 1836. His father was born in Fayette, and his mother, whose maiden name was Sarah Reed, in Westmoreland county, Ohio. He spent his childhood and youth upon his father's farm, and devoted a great deal of his time to study. He prepared himself to enter the university of Michigan, where he took a literary course and graduated from both the literary and medical departments. At Antrim, Guernsey county, Ohio, he began the practice of medicine in 1875, going thence two years later to Kansas City, where he pursued his profession eighteen months. Since 1879 he has resided at Fort Wayne, and achieved success and substantial rewards in his profession. He joined the United Presbyterian church when but fifteen years of age, and has been an active member ever since. To this church his wife also belongs. In politics he is a democrat. He was married in Westmoreland county, Penn., April 21, 1864, to Mary A. Caldwell, who though she bore the same family name as her husband, is of distinct lineage. She is a native of the latter county, and daughter of William and Elizabeth (McKinlay) Caldwell. The Doctor and wife have three children: David H., Sadie E. and Laura B.

George L. Greenawalt M. D., second son of Jesse and Susanna Greenawalt, was born in Mahoning county, Ohio, September 6, 1851. His parents came to Indiana and settled in Springfield township, this county, when he was three years old. At the age of eighteen he began teaching, and taught eight terms, was principal of the school at Leo one year, and superintendent of the school at Bourbon, Marshall county, one year. In 1874 he took up the study of medicine in an interrupted manner, in 1877 entered the office of Dr. Henry M. Beer, of Valparaiso, and the next fall matriculated at Bellevue hospital medical college, New York City, where he was graduated in a class of 142, March 1, 1880, coming to Fort Wayne and beginning practice the following month. In 1884 returned to Bellevue hospital and took special courses. He is a member of the Allen county society, Indiana state medical society, and the American medical association, was a member of the ninth international medical congress, held at Washington D. C., in 1887. Dr. Greenawalt was married September 5, 1883, to Mary E. Jeffords of this city, daughter of Oliver and Mary Jeffords.

Jacob Hetrick, M. D., a successful physician and worthy citizen of Fort Wayne, is a native of Clarion county, Penn., born November 1, 1846, the son of Michael and Mary Hetrick, both of whom were natives of Juniata county, Penn. When he was eight years old his parents emigrated to the state of Ohio, and made their home in Crawford county for five years. They then removed to VanWert county, Ohio, where the youth of Dr. Hetrick was spent upon the farm. He became the proprietor of a drug store at Celina, Ohio, in 1873, and in 1878 removed to Middlepoint, the same state, and there continued in the drug business two years. He devoted his leisure time to the study of medicine, and in 1879 entered the Fort Wayne college of medicine, where he was graduated in 1881. In the meantime he had begun in 1880 the practice of his profession at Fort Wayne, where he has ever since enjoyed a lucrative practice. Dr. Hetrick is also the proprietor of a drug store, at No. 303 East Washington street, which has a first-class patronage. The doctor was married November 3, 1867, to Mary E. Plikerd, daughter of John and Julia A. Plikerd. She is a native of Allen county, Ohio. To this union two children have been born: Minnie M. and Julia E. In 1864 Dr. Hetrick served from four to five months in the Union army as a member of Company A, One Hundred and Fifty-first Ohio national guards, and he is now a member of the Grand Army. He is also a member of the Masonic fraternity, and he and wife are members of the Methodist Episcopal church. In politics he is a republican, and while a resident of Celina, Ohio, he held the position of revenue assessor one year, and was deputy postmaster three years. Dr. Hetrick is a man of great worth, as a citizen stands very high, and is honored in his profession.

Dr. George W. McCaskey, a prominent physician of Fort Wayne, is a native of Fulton, Ohio, born November 9, 1853. He is the son of John S. and Catharine (Davis) McCaskey, both of whom were born in northeastern Ohio. He was reared to manhood on a farm, and in 1873 entered upon the study of medicine. He was graduated at the Jefferson medical college at Philadelphia, in 1877, and immediately afterward began the practice of his profession in Paulding county, Ohio. In 1880 he took a special course in the university college of London, England, and on his return to America located at Fort Wayne, where he soon became the possessor of a lucrative practice, and of which city he is now a leading physician. He has finished all the studies embraced in a full collegiate course, and he passed the examination and received the degree of Ph. B. from DePauw university with the class of 1881. In 1884 the same institution conferred upon him the degree of master of arts. Dr. McCaskey was married May 4, 1884, to Louise Sturgis, daughter of the late Dr. Charles E. Sturgis, who was one of the pioneer physicians of Fort Wayne, and who occupied a high place in his profession, and ranked among the best physicians of the city. Dr. McCaskey and wife are members of the First Presbyterian church. The former is a member of the Fort Wayne academy of medicine, the Allen county medical society, the Indiana state medical society, and the American medical association. During nearly the whole time since its organization he has occupied the position of professor of theory and practice in the Fort Wayne college of medicine. He is a very successful practitioner, and socially his standing is very high.

George B. Stemen, M. D., a young physician of promise, was born in Allen county, Ohio, April 27, 1858, son of Rev. Anthony M. and Mary Ann (Baker) Stemen, both natives of Pennsylvania. He graduated from the VanWert high school in 1878, having previously taught school for several terms, and after graduation he clerked in a store in VanWest and at Ada, Ohio, then coming to Fort Wayne where he clerked for Foster Brothers two years, at the same time studying medicine. In 1880 he entered the Fort Wayne college of medicine, and graduated in the spring of 1882. He began practice at Antwerp, Ohio, where he was in partnership with Dr. Adam McDaniels, but eight months later he returned to Fort Wayne, where he has been prosperous. For the past four years he has occupied the chair of materia medica and therapeutics in the medical college. He was married May 25, 1882, to Mary Ann Andrew, daughter of David and Nancy Andrew, and they have two children: James Brainard and Agnes Elizabeth. Dr. Stemen and wife are members of the Methodist Episcopal church, and he belongs to the order of K. of P.

Christian Martz, M. D., was born at Fairfield Center, DeKalb county, Ind., September 23, 1852, son of John G. and Mary A. (Saurer) Martz, natives respectively of Germany and Switzerland. At the age of fifteen he entered Concordia college at Fort Wayne, and attended three years, afterward for several years studying elsewhere and being otherwise employed. About 1877 he began the study of medicine, and in the fall of 1879 entered Hahnemann college at Chicago, and there graduated in 1882. He established himself at Fort Wayne at once, and has gained an extensive practice. He is a member of the Indiana institute of homeopathy. March 9, 1882, he was married to Susie Lehmann, daughter of Dr. Henry Lehmann, late of Waterloo, Ind. She was born in New York city, November 7, 1864. They have three children: Lottie, Robert and Agnes.

John W. McCausland, M. D., was born in Williams county, Ohio, February 7, 1856, son of George and Sarah (Wagstaff) McCausland. His father, who was in early life a school teacher, and afterward a merchant, was born in Scotland, immigrated at the age of seven years, and died in Williams county in 1881. His widow, who was born in Morrow county, now lives in Williams county, Ohio. They had three children, two of whom are living, Dr. McCausland the elder. He attended the Bryan and Toledo high schools, and at the age of nineteen began the study of medicine in the office of Drs. Long & Riggs at Bryan, Ohio. He matriculated at Rush medical college, Chicago, and was graduated in 1880. He embarked in the practice of his profession at Bryan, but in 1883 came to Fort Wayne and in this city has been enjoying a good practice and has achieved a creditable standing in his profession. He was married February 22, 1881, to Eva C. Snedeker, of Westfield, N. Y.

Edward A. Shafer, M. D., is a native of Germany, born September 28, 1840, to Charles T. and Philipina (Koehler) Shafer. He came to America with the late Henry G. Wagner, when a lad of thirteen years, and reached Fort Wayne on his fourteenth birthday. He attended school and clerked four years, and then went to Cincinnati, where he was variously employed for three years until the outbreak of the rebellion. In 1861 he enlisted in Company A, Fifth Kentucky regiment, and served six months, then returning to Fort Wayne, where he clerked for two years in the drug store of Henry G. Wagner. In 1864 he and his brother, Reinhard, engaged in the drug business at Huntington, Ind., and after the dissolution of the partnership in 1867, Dr. Shafer became the partner of S. M. Blount at the same place. In 1870 he entered the medical department of the Northwestern university, and graduated in 1872, beginning then the practice of medicine at Huntington, giving that his entire attention until 1883. He then came to Fort Wayne, where he has since been engaged in the practice and as a druggist. November 10, 1874, he was married to Louise Voght, and they have three children: Anna L., Harry V., and Laura B. Dr. Shafer is a Royal Arch Mason.

Emett Lucine Siver, M. D., prominent among the young physicians of Fort Wayne, was born in New York, June 17, 1858. His parents, Harvey and Elizabeth (Keith) Siver, were born in that state also. The father served three years in the war of the rebellion, enlisting in Company D, One hundred and Forty-ninth New York, and was mustered out as second lieutenant. He died in his native state at the age of thirty-one years, but his widow, who was born in 1839, survives him, and lives in New York. Their only child, Dr. Siver, was educated at Phœnix academy, N. Y., and began the study of medicine at Big Rapids, Mich., in 1878, in the office of Dr. W. A. Hendryx. In the fall of 1880 he entered Michigan university and studied in the medical department one term, and in 1882 studied in the college of physicians and surgeons at Baltimore. He graduated from the Fort Wayne medical college in 1884, and took a post graduate course at Bellevue college, N. Y., in 1886, thoroughly equipping himself for the practice of medicine, which he began at Fort Wayne in 1884, and which he has since successfully prosecuted, confining his attention to the diseases of the nose and throat. He is a member of the Allen county medical society, the State medical society, and the American rhinological association; also major and surgeon of the Second regiment Indiana legion. He is a member of the Masonic order, Wayne lodge, No. 25, and of Loyal lodge, Knights of Pythias, he is a leading member, having been the first chancellor commander of the latter, and is now deputy grand chancellor for the third district, and captain of Summit City division No. 12, uniform rank, K. of P. Dr. Siver was married April 27, 1887, to Adelle McClellan, born at Waterloo in 1864, daughter of Judge C. A. O. McClellan, congressman from this district. Mrs. Siver studied four years at Michigan university. They have one child, Charles McC. L.

Henry W. Niswonger, M. D., passed his early life in Stark county, Ohio, where he was born October 27, 1849, to Abraham and Rachel (Sechrist) Niswonger. He attended school at Marlboro, and clerked in a store, and at the age of fourteen joined the Union army as a bugler. Four months later he enlisted as a private in Company E, Sixth Ohio cavalry. He was in the battles of the Wilderness, Chancellorsville, Gettysburg and many other engagements. In the Wilderness he was wounded, and captured, but after a short experience at Libby prison was exchanged. He was discharged at Washington, February

17, 1865, but was for more than two years thereafter unable to do work. Part of the years 1867 and 1868 he spent in Montana and other portions of the west, and in the fall of the latter year he entered the Physio-medical college at Cincinnati, and took one full course. Then for two years, at Marlboro in his native county, he studied and practiced medicine with Dr. C. C. Lewis. He afterward resided at Rochester, Ind., Piqua, Ohio, Millville and Jonesburg, Mo., returning finally to Marlboro. In 1879 he engaged in business at Rochester, and was afterward for two years a dealer in boots and shoes at that place and the same period at Macy, Ind. He re-entered the practice of medicine at Argos, and in September, 1884, came to Fort Wayne, practicing here ever since, and receiving from Fort Wayne college of medicine in March, 1889, the degree of M. D. He is a member of the Methodist Episcopal church, to which Mrs. Niswonger also belongs, and is a Mason and comrade of the G. A. R. He was married February 12, 1871, to Maria D., daughter of Henry and Mary (Quigg) Barcus, born at Plymouth, Ind., August 5, 1851. They have two children, Emma B. and Roland C.

Samuel J. Derbyshire was born in Putnam county, Ohio, September 28, 1860, son of Jesse C. and Lydia (Pierce) Derbyshire, the former a native of Fayette county, Penn., and the latter of Champaign county, Ohio. He was reared in a farm home, and at the age of twenty began teaching, being a teacher in all, during nine terms. In 1885-6 he was principal of the high school at Warren, Ind. He attended the national normal, at Lebanon, Ohio, three terms, and graduated from the Northwestern Ohio university, at Ada, in 1884, with the degree of B. S., recieving afterward the degree of M. S. In 1885, he came to Fort Wayne and began the study of medicine, mostly with Dr. K. K. Wheelock. He took a course of lectures in the Fort Wayne medical college, and during the following winter (1887-8), attended the medical college of Ohio, graduating March 7, 1888, immediately thereafter beginning his practice in this city. He is a member of the Fort Wayne academy, and the Allen county and Indiana medical societies. He was married July 21, 1885, to Luella M. McKinley, born in Allen county, May 25, 1864, daughter of Perry and Sarah A. McKinley, natives of this county. She is a graduate of the Fort Wayne medical college, class of 1888, and both she and her husband have a good practice.

Andrew J. Boswell, M. D., a prominent young physician, was born in Grant county, Ind., January 3, 1855. His parents are natives of Champaign county, Ohio, where his father was born December 28, 1820, and his mother, whose maiden name was Mary Smith, December 20, 1820. They have resided in Grant county for the past forty-five years. Andrew was the sixth of a family of eleven children. After attending the Marion high school, he began teaching school at the age of eighteen and taught for three years. Afterward he began the study of medicine with Drs. Smith & Blount, at Wabash, and completed his studies at the medical college of Ohio. He has practiced his profession for ten years, first in Huntington county, and since 1886 at this city. He is a member of the I. O. O. F. Dr. Boswell was married October 20, 1885, to Miss Ella Peterson, daughter of Matthias Peterson, late of Lafayette. The latter was one of the pioneers of Lafayette, coming there in 1828, from Knoxville, Tenn., where he was born in 1803. He superintended the construction of the Wabash & Erie canal from Lafayette to Attica. Subsequently, he was editor of the *Advertiser*, which afterward became the Lafayette *Courier*. He sold the paper to the late W. S. Lingle in 1841. He early in life freed eight slaves which were bequeathed to him, and during his life was a member of the republican party. Among the policies which he earnestly advocated in early life, which are now essential parts of state policy, was the system of general taxation for the support of schools. Mr. Peterson's profession was the law, but this he was forced to abandon on account of failure of sight. He was married in 1848 to Susan Rebecca Stoops, of southern Indiana, who was born in 1827, and died in March, 1879, and was followed on May 6, next, by her husband.

Dr. Asa C. Boswell was born February 2, 1861, and spent his boyhood on the farm with his parents, attending the common schools. He entered the normal college at Marion, Ind., preparatory to the profession of teaching, which he entered in the fall of 1879, in Huntington county. After teaching one year, he attended college at Terre Haute, Ind., and at the completion of the course at the state normal, continued teaching until 1885. He then commenced the study of medicine with his brother, Dr. A. J. Boswell. In the year 1886, he entered the medical college of Ohio, at Cincinnati. During his attendance he completed the special courses in histology, pathology and bacteriology, and received personal instruction in causes, diagnosis and treatment of diseases of nose, throat and chest. He graduated from the medical college of Ohio, March 7, 1889, and then entered a partnership with his brother in medicine and surgery.

John A. Stutz, M. D., a prominent young physician, was born in Washington City, October 31, 1860, son of George Frederic and Catherine (Knorr) Stutz, both of whom were born near Stuttgart, Germany. He attended at childhood a parochial school at Washington, and when thirteen years old came to Fort Wayne, and for three years was a student in Concordia college. He completed at Washington the studies of the high school, and in 1880 entered the Capital university of Columbus, and graduated in 1882. Returning to Washington he began the study of medicine under the preceptorship of Dr. T. S. Verdi, and in 1883 attended the medical pepartment of the university of Georgetown during one course. In 1884 he entered the New York homeopathic medical college, and graduated in 1886. In June of the same year he came to Fort Wayne, and has since established a lucrative practice. He is now physician to the reform orphan's home, and to Concordia college. He was married September 15, 1887, to Emma K. Deitz, of Washington City, who was born October 18, 1863, and they have one child, Jerome

H. He and wife are members of the English Lutheran church, and both occupy a high rank socially.

Charles E. Stultz, M. D., was born in Whitley county, Ind., April 19, 1862, son of Joseph and Harriet Stultz. When he was a small child his parents removed to Huntington county, where his early life was spent. At seventeen years of age he entered the Central normal school at Danville, Ind., and there completed a commercial course. In the spring of 1884 he began the study of medicine, and in the following fall entered the Fort Wayne college of medicine, whence he graduated in 1886. He at once began practice in the city, and has since enjoyed a lucrative patronage. He is a member of the Allen county medical society, stands well in his profession and is highly esteemed.

Creed T. Banks, who was a successful practitioneer of medicine for twenty years, came to Darke county, Ohio, when ten years old, from Virginia, where he was born October 13, 1820. His parents, James and Lydia C. Banks, were natives of that state. When Dr. Banks was twenty-two he began teaching and followed that a short time, teaching one of the terms in this county. In 1845 he took up the study of medicine, and graduated from the Starling medical college, of Columbus, Ohio, in 1849. In June, of that year, he began practice at Lynn, Randolph county, Ind., and was the second settler in that town. In 1855 he removed to Deerfield, and in 1859 to Wayne township, this county. Subsequent locations were at South Whitley in 1860, in Forest, Whitley county, in 1865. He continued in the practice until the fall of 1869, when he removed to Liberty Mills, Wabash county, and was engaged until 1886 in milling, merchandise and sale of live stock. Since March, 1886, he has been conducting his farm one mile southwest of Fort Wayne, and residing at his pleasant home at 219 West Washington street. Dr. Banks is a member of the Masonic order, and is a republican. He was married in Darke county, August 23, 1846, to Elizabeth A., daughter of John and Barbara (Kaufman) Coombs, born in Perry county, Ohio, August 26, 1823. Dr. Banks and wife have had the following children: an infant daughter, died unnamed; William T., Reuben F., Eugene T., Samuel C., Charles R., Virginia V. J. and Elmer E., of whom Samuel and Reuben are deceased.

Thomas H. McCormick, M. D., was born in Tuscarawas county, Ohio, May 16, 1840. His parents, Henry and Mary (Armstrong) McCormick, were natives of Pennsylvania, and died in Ohio, whither they emigrated. Three of their children are living, Dr. McCormick being the only son. He was raised on the farm, attending the public schools of his native county, and at the eighteen of age years began the study of medicine. He began the practice at Liberty Center, Ohio, and remained there until 1867, when he removed to Indiana, and established himself at New Haven, Allen county. In 1881 he graduated from the Fort Wayne medical college, and in 1888 came to the city, and is now engaged in active practice, with substantial success. In 1862, he enlisted in Company D, One Hundred and Twenty-fourth Ohio regiment, and served some time, until discharged on account of physical disability. He is a republican in politics; a Mason; comrade of the G. A. R.; member of Allen county and Indiana medical associations and the American medical association. He was married in 1861, to Rosina Yagerlehner, and they have these children: Minnie M., Della C., Pearl R., Firman C., Thomas H., jr., Ada M. and Harry B. He and wife are members of the Christian church.

Dr. John L. Kryder, the leading physician of Cedarville, is a native of Stark county, Ohio, born December 22, 1833. His father, John Kryder, a native of Pennsylvania, emigrated to Ohio while a youth with his parents, and afterward taught in the country schools. He was engaged in merchandise in Stark county, Ohio, and subsequently at different places until nearly 1840, when he sold out his business and embarked in the hotel business at New Berlin, Ohio. In 1843 he removed to Indiana and settled in Fort Wayne, where he remained about two months, then settling on Cedar Creek, where he purchased eighty acres of land. In 1863 he sold this land and removed to Cedarville and purchased 140 acres in the forks of the St. Joseph and Cedar Creek, and built his dwelling in Cedarville, where he has since lived. He served many years as one of the board of trustees in an early day, as assessor several terms and as justice of the peace about twenty-five years. His last election was at the age of seventy, and he served out that term and would not receive any other. He was called on by the people to serve in some township office as long as he would accept. In this politics had no part, as he is a republican and the township democratic. Though born October 11, 1800, he enjoys remarkably good health. His wife was Eliza Pepple, a native of Maryland, born October 21, 1805, who died August, 1879. She was a member of the Lutheran church, of which Mr. Kryder is a member. Their son, John L., came with his parents to Indiana when about nine years of age, and received the education that the country schools then afforded. At the age of nineteen he began teaching in the country schools, receiving for his labor $10 per month and boarding himself. He taught about four winter terms, and studied medicine in the summer. He began the practice of his profession in 1858, and continued until 1873, when he attended lectures at Keokuk, Iowa and graduated in 1876. In 1861 he was married to Martha J. Earl, born June 1, 1840, daughter of Avery F. and Carlista (Greene) Earl, who emigrated from New York state and settled in Noble county in 1847. This union was blessed with three children: Clarence M., John E. and Harry P. In 1858, the doctor removed to DeKalb county and practiced there about eleven years. While there he was elected trustee of Richland township and served two years. In 1869 he removed to Clinton county, Mo., and after practicing six years, returned to Cedarville, where he has since remained. A brother, Alonzo T. Kryder, was also one of the early practitioners of Allen county. In 1852 he began practice at Leo, where he remained two years, and removed to DeKalb county, and located at Fairfield Center, but the country being so sickly, he soon fell a victim to the typhoid fever. In 1867, Dr. J. L. Kryder, then living in DeKalb county, became a candidate for clerk of the circuit court on the republican ticket, and although he had an up-hill race from the start, succeeded in reducing the adverse majority. The doctor has a talent for poetry, and among his best productions are "Now and Then," "Retrospection," "A Sunset Scene," "Sometimes Somewhere," "Going Away," "Indian Summer," "Fate," "By-past Times," "A June Day Dream," "The Exile's Lament" and "Memorial Day."

Franklin K. Cosgrove, M. D., one of the leading physicians of the northeastern part of Allen county, was born at New Carlisle, Clark county, Ohio, March 18, 1827. When quite young his parents moved to Cincinnati, where his father died. He was then taken to Essex county, N. J., and cared for by relatives. Attending school here until 1842, he returned to the west to visit relatives at Warsaw, Ind., and and on his route he tarried in Fort Wayne a few days, at the tavern then kept by John Lillie. At the breaking out of the Mexican war, Dr. Cosgrove enlisted in Company I, Fourth regiment Ohio volunteer infantry. He served as one of the color guards of his regiment during his entire period of enlistment and never missed a day's duty. After the close of that war, he read medicine in the office of John Tutman, M. D., of DeKalb county. He graduated at the Ohio medical college and commenced the practice of his profession in Antioch, Ohio, in 1850; soon after removing to Maysville, where he has since resided. In 1850 he was united in marriage with Melinda Phelps, a step-sister of Mrs. Laura Suttonfield, Mrs. Eliza Hanna, Mrs. Elvira Dubois and E. P., L. M. and Horace Taylor, and their union was blessed with seven children. At the breaking out of the war of the rebellion, the doctor devoted his entire time and a large amount of money to raising troops, enlisting men particularly for the Thirtieth and Forty-fourth regiments, as well as for a number of other regiments and batteries, for which he never received any remuneration. When the Forty-fourth regiment was organized, he was mustered with it as captain of Company D, and he went with it to the front. The regiment distinguished itself at Shiloh, and on the second day of that battle Captain Cosgrove received a severe wound in the left arm from a minie-ball, but he refused to leave the field until the battle was over. His wound was not dressed until the last shot was fired and the victory won. His wound proved so severe that he was detailed for duty at Camp Chase, Ohio, where he remained until September 3, 1862, then receiving an honorable discharge. Later he traveled through the territories and the Pacific slope and Central America, after which he returned to his old home and resumed the practice of his profession.

Dr. George Murphy, the leading physician of Leo, was born in Ohio, June 24, 1838. In his fourth year he lost his father, and was taken by his mother to New Hampshire two years later. They lived there three years and then came to Indiana, and settled at Huntertown, where the mother died, leaving Mr. Murphy an orphan at the age of ten. During the next four years he was cared for by relatives in Michigan. At sixteen years of age he entered the office of Dr. E. G. Wheelock, and began the study of medicine, at the same time studying in the high school and graduating in the commercial college at Fort Wayne. Having no resources but his own efforts, he was also compelled to teach school seven terms while studying. In 1866 he entered the Charitable hospital medical college of Cleveland, and took one course of lectures, then practiced until 1870, when he graduated. In 1872 he took another course of lectures in Cleveland, and in 1874-5, attended Jefferson medical college at Philadelphia, and took a course of surgery at the school of anatomy in the same city. He practiced first at Leo, in 1860, and in 1861 enlisted as a private in Company E, Thirtieth Indiana infantry, under Capt. J. M. Silvers. He served three years and was wounded, first at Murfreesboro, then at Chickamauga, and a third time at Dallas, Ga. He was mustered out as first lieutenant, and was commissioned captain, but his wounds prevented acceptance of the latter. Returning home he practiced his profession at Leo until 1869, and then removed to Spencerville, DeKalb county, remaining there until 1880, and afterward one year in Waterloo. Since then he has been a resident of Leo, and now enjoys a large and lucrative practice. During two sessions of of the Fort Wayne medical college he lectured on chemistry and toxicology. His career is a very creditable one, particularly in view of its unauspicious beginning, and it has won for him the esteem of all. He was married in 1866 to Nancy L. Dever, by whom he had these children, all of whom are living, Mary J., Rosamond and George. In 1882 he was married to Florence Knight, who gave to him three children, Mary E., Irma, and John R. Mrs. Murphy is a member of the Methodist Episcopal church, and the Doctor is a member of the Masonic order, and of the G. A. R.

Joseph D. Morgan, M. D., was born in Cummingsville, VanBuren county, Tenn, October 21, 1857, son of Dr. Isaac Clinton and Lou Emma (Cummings) Morgan. The father was born in Georgia of Welsh lineage, and located early in VanBuren county, subsequently becoming a physician of more than ordinary fame. The mother was born in VanBuren county, Tenn., of a prominent family, of Irish descent, the father being an early settler, in honor of whom Cummingsville was named. Dr. Morgan received his education in the Burritt college of VanBuren county, and subsequently entered the Eclectic medical college of Atlanta, Ga., by which he was graduated in 1881. In 1882 he located at Dixon, Ohio, where he now resides, and has a large and lucrative practice. He is of more than ordinary ability as a physician; is a self-made and energetic man with a bright future before him. March 1, 1885, he was united in marriage with Ella Bowers, daughter of Jacob Bowers, an early settler of Allen county, Ind. The Doctor is a Master Mason of the VanWert lodge, Ohio. In politics he is a democrat, and as a citizen he is enterprising and universally respected.

William A. Connolly, M. D., a physician of Monroeville, Ind., was born in Newark, N. J., November 25, 1847, one of nine children of William and Margaret (McGuire) Connolly. The parents were born in Ireland, but their marriage occurred in New Jersey. About 1850 the parents removed from New Jersey and settled at Johnsville, Morrow county, Ohio. Here the father followed his trade of tanner, and though poor, gave his children the advantage of attending the public schools. Of their nine children, six became teachers, and with teaching as a stepping stone they educated themselves in the main. Three of the sons, James, John and Frank, became lawyers. Ella is deceased, Maggie, a literary graduate of Erie, Penn., has her home with the doctor, with whom the mother also lives. The father died at Monroeville in 1884. William was but a child at the outbreak of the civil war, but in 1863 he enlisted in Company F, Twenty-fifth Ohio veteran volunteer infantry as a private; he was discharged in 1865 by reason of the close of war. He returned to his parental home in Ohio, and subsequently began the study of medicine. In the fall of 1867 he entered the medical department of Michigan university. After remaining here for six months he located at Denmark, Ohio, and began practice. November 19, 1868, he located at Monroeville, where he has since established a large and lucrative practice. On coming here he formed a partnership with Dr. D. W. Champer, but for several years he has been alone in the practice. In 1876 he wedded Miss Nancy Graham, who died in the following year. The Doctor is recognized as able and skillful in his profession. For over twenty years he has been in active practice. He is a member of the Roman Catholic church.

J. L. Smith, M. D., engaged in the practice of medicine at Hoagland, Allen county, was born in Dayton, Ohio, February 7, 1852. His father, Joseph H., was born in Trenton, N. J., November 26, 1809, son of Cideon Smith, who was born in New Jersey, and was a carpenter by trade. The latter's father was foreign-born, and emigrated to New Jersey. He was a soldier in the war of the revolution, and was at the battle of Trenton. The gun he used in that struggle is in the possession of a descendant. The father of Dr. Smith was a shoemaker and farmer, and emigrated when a young man to Green county, Ohio, where he was married to Caroline Frick, who was born at Lancaster, Penn., in April, 1827, daughter of Jacob Frick, a native of Pennsylvania, of German lineage. To them were born one son, J. L., and four daughters. The parents are now residents of Cold Water, Ohio. The father, prior to his marriage with Caroline Frick, had been united in marriage with Lavina Kirkwood, who lived to become the mother of three sons and two daughters. J. L. Smith received his education in the schools of Mercer county, Ohio, and in March, 1872, took up the study of medicine under Dr. A. M. Kyser, of Cold Water, Ohio, and in the winter of 1874 and 1875, entered the Eclectic medical college of Cincinnati, where he graduated in 1878. In the meantime he practiced at Hoagland, where he first located in 1875, and there has since been in active practice. December 9, 1875, he wedded Allie Emenhiser, a native of Muskingum county, Ohio, born September 24, 1852. She is a daughter of Joseph Emenhiser, of Madison township. They have had six children, of whom one is deceased. The Doctor is an able physician of the eclectic school. When but a very young man he located at Hoagland, but with perseverance and enterprise and a determined purpose to succeed in life he has gained the confidence and practice of many people who regard him as an able and skillful physician. He is a member of the I. O. O. F., St. Mary's lodge, 167, at Decatur.

Dr. Franklin Greenwell, the leading physician of Huntertown, was born in Allen county, April 8, 1851. He is a son of George and Elizabeth Greenwell, of Eel River township, already mentioned. His father, of Irish descent and a native of Maryland, settled in Allen county in 1846, and both parents passed the remainder of their lives in this county. Dr. Greenwell received a good common school education, and attended one term at the Methodist college at Fort Wayne, after which he taught two terms of district school in the country. In 1872 he entered the Cleveland medical college, where he remained during the terms of 1872, '73 and '74, and after a year's practice at Huntertown, he was graduated with honors in 1876. He established himself at Huntertown, and by close attention to his business and skillful attendance upon the wants of the sick, he has made for himself an enviable professional reputation and gained a lucrative practice. In 1876 he was united in marriage with Jennie M., daughter of William T. and Jane Hunter, and they have had two children, one of whom is now living, Louise. Mrs. Greenwell was born in 1845. When Dr. Greenwell began the practice it was among his friends and acquaintances, and he made it a rule when called upon at first, to attend a patient whose case he did not thoroughly understand, to candidly offer and do all he could, but also advise the employment of a doctor of more experience. This candor and caution in the beginning of his practice won him the confidence of the people, and now with his many years of study and practice, he enjoys a large and lucrative practice. The Doctor also takes a lively interest in politics, always supporting the principles of the democratic party, and has been prominently spoken of at different times as a candidate for the office of representative, but he has always declined such proposals.

William De La Ruhl, M. D., a member of the American medical association, was born in Galion, Crawford county, Ohio, March 21, 1856. His parents, James Henry and Lucinda (Traul) Ruhl, were natives, the father of Shrewsbury, Penn., the mother of Stark county, Ohio. James H. Ruhl was the son of Jacob and Sarah Ruhl, whose parents were natives of Germany and settled in Pennsylvania, where they raised a family of six children. In 1831 Jacob and father moved to Crawford county, Ohio, and purchased a tract of land which embraced the site of the present town of Galion, which Jacob Ruhl and his brother laid out. James was married to Lucinda Traul in the year 1854, and two years afterward came to Root, in Adams county, and resided there about three years. He then came to Marion township and was engaged in the lumber business until 1860, when he settled on the farm he now owns on the Piqua road. He has five sons and two daughters, William being the oldest. He was born and reared on a farm. By attending the public schools, Dr. Ruhl gained a thorough common school education, to which he added a four-term course in a high school taught in Marion township, by John W. English, A. M. At the age of eighteen years he took up the study of medicine under Dr. Allen De Vilbiss, now of Toledo, Ohio. Afterward one year, he was under the instruction of Dr. Benjamin S. Woodworth, of Fort Wayne, then for two years he was with Dr. William H. Myers, of Fort Wayne, for one year he was home physician in the St. Joseph hospital of Fort Wayne. February 28, 1878, he graduated from the medical college of Fort Wayne, and in 1879, received an honorary degree, M. D., from the same medical college. He located at Middletown in 1878, and began active practice in the profession, removing in 1879 to Sheldon, where he has since continued and extended his practice. He was married November 10, 1878, to Mary L. Shookman, born in this county August 1, 1855. Of their five children, three are living. He and wife are members of the English Lutheran church.

George Nelson Worley, M. D., was born at Upper Sandusky, Ohio, the son of Nathan and Elizabeth (Moore) Worley, who were natives of Ohio. Mrs. Worley's father was a pioneer teacher near Canton, Ohio, having taught for eighteen years in one district, and she received all her instruction from him. Nathan Worley was a tailor, and worked at his trade in Upper Sandusky the greater part of his life. He died in 1879 from injuries received by a fall. There were born to them eight children: William H., Mary Ellen, Lena, Harry, George N., Jeremiah, Franklin, Julius V. William H. is at present marshal of Cameron City, Mo. Mary Ellen, Lena, Harry and Jeremiah are deceased. Franklin was in the employ of a railroad in Virginia for some years, but is now engaged with the Union Pacific. Julius V. is a railroad conductor, now on the Clover Leaf line. Dr. Worley was a teacher in Nelson's commercial college in Cincinnati for about a year, and then removed to Ossian, Ind., and engaged in the drug business, at the same time studying medicine under John I. Metts, one of the oldest practitioners of Wells county. This he continued three years and then took private instruction under Prof. Van Vleck, of Cincinnati, in surgery. Dr. Worley began the practice of medicine at Williamsport. In 1879-1880 he took a course in the Fort Wayne college of medicine. He has been engaged in the practice of medicine in Williamsport without interruption since 1873, and has been very successful. He has made interesting contributions to medical literature. Dr. Worley was married to Serepta Lucretia Metts, on December 19, 1873, and they have three children: Alfred Minor, born December 19, 1874; William H., July 2, 1877, and Maud Myrtle, July 26, 1885.

Simeon E. Mentzer, M. D., of Monroeville, Ind., was born in Mahoning county, Ohio, February 21, 1862. His parents, Jacob and Mary (Swartz) Mentzer, were born, reared and married in Ohio, and had four children, all of whom are now living. Of these Simeon E. is the third. In 1865 with his parents he went to Adams county, Ind., here was reared on a farm up to the age of sixteen years, when he came to Monroeville. He had gained a fair common school education and he was then engaged in teaching, three years in the public schools, meanwhile attending for six terms the Northern Indiana normal school at Valparaiso. Subsequently, he began the study of medicine at Monroeville, under Dr. C. A. Leiter, as preceptor. He studied for one year and then entered the Ohio medical college at Cincinnati, and completed the course, graduating in March, 1885. He then located at Monroe, Adams county, and there practiced for one year. Dr. C. A. Leiter, then practicing at Monroeville, died in March, 1887, and immediately Dr. Mentzer moved here and assumed the greater part of the practice of his former preceptor. He has now established an extensive practice. He is cultured and capable, energetic, and recognized as an able man in his profession. His home is with his mother at Monroeville, where he enjoys the esteem of a wide acquaintance.

Medical Profession of Monroeville. — The medical profession of Monroeville has been well represented since an early day. In it there have been physicians who have reached the top-most round in the ladder of success, some of whom are now sleeping in the silent tomb. Since 1880 the following named gentlemen have represented the medical profession of Monroeville, viz.: Dr. C. A. Leiter, Dr. W. A. Connolly, Dr. A. Engle, Dr. Wilder and Dr. S. E. Mentzer. The first of whom was Dr. C. A. Leiter, who stood at the head of the profession of Allen county. He was not only a successful physician, but a man of very high intellectual attainments, and has since succumbed to the effects of an attack of chronic gastritis. He was a graduate of the university of Pennsylvania and of the Starling medical college, Columbus, having previously taken two courses of lectures in the Ann Arbor medical college at Ann Arbor, Mich. He was a son of Ex-Congressman B. F. Leiter, of Canton, Ohio. Dr. Wilder has since moved to Michigan, where he went to continue the practice of his profession. Dr. A. Engle, the pioneer physician who, after having practiced his profession for forty years, has retired, going to his country home about five miles distant. The present representatives of the medical profession of Monroeville are Dr. W. A. Connolly and Dr. S. E. Mentzer. Dr. Connolly being a graduate of the Columbus medical college, has practiced in this his first location for twenty-five years. As a physician he has been very successful and ranks high in the profession of the county. Dr. S. E. Mentzer, a student of the eminent Dr. Leiter, completed his studies in the Ohio medical college, Cincinnati, Ohio, graduating from that institution, March 5, 1885. After having graduated, he entered into a partnership with his preceptor, and at the expiration of the year he located at Monroe, Adams county, Ind., where he continued to practice his profession until the death of his preceptor (Dr. Leiter) when he again located in Monroeville, since which time he has succeeded in going to the front of his profession in Monroeville. As a physician and surgeon he has been successful and bids fair to stand as one of the leaders of his profession.

Dentistry.— The physician of the early days gratified, as best he could, the desires of those who had aching teeth to be freed from, and the more delicate work of dentistry of to-day was entirely unknown. When the profession began its remarkable modern development, Fort Wayne was fortunate in becoming the home of practitioners of more than ordinary merit. About 1850 Dr. Von Bonhurst became the first dentist in Fort Wayne. He subsequently removed to Lancaster, Ohio. He was followed here by Drs. Talbert, Wells, Knapp, Snyder, George W. Loag, Seneca B. Brown, in the order named, who are the oldest practitioners in the city.

Seneca Buel Brown, M. D., D. D. S., was born August 11, 1834, at Marlboro, Windham county, Vt. His father, John Brown, was born at the city of Rochester, county Kent, England, August 28, 1787, and came to America and located at Rutland, Vt., in 1820. He married a daughter of Archelaus Dean, a native of Massachusetts, of Puritan ancestry, who served through the revolutionary war and died in Vermont in 1846. She was born at Brattleboro, March 19, 1799, and died at Marlboro, Vt., September 30, 1877. She was a member of the Baptist church. John Brown, who was a member of the church of England, and in politics a free soil democrat, died at Westminster, Vt., March 3, 1851. To the latter town, the family removed when Dr. Brown was four years of age. Here farm life occupied him until 1852. In the meantime, the district schools and three terms at Westminster seminary, completed his education. November 1, 1852, he entered the office of Oramel R. Post, D. D. S., at Brattleboro, Vt., as a student at dentistry, and on January 1, 1854, he began the practice at Ticonderoga, N. Y., on a circuit including Ticonderoga, Westport, Essex, Elizabethtown, and Schroon Lake, in Essex, and Chestertown, in Warren, county, He came west and located at Piqua, Ohio, October 23, 1855, and there, on June 9, 1864, he was married to Nannie Louise, eldest daughter of Hon. Stephen Johnson, of that city. July 6, 1874, nine years after their removal to this city, she died, leaving an only child: Katie, then seven years of age. February 14, 1888, he was married to Minne Russell Graves, oldest daughter of Charles E. Graves, of this city. Dr. Brown came to Fort Wayne May 3, 1865, when the population of the city was 15,000, and is now the only resident dentist who was practicing in his own name in this city in 1865. He soon acquired a marked degree of respect and confidence. Eminent skill and personal character were the commanding influences which won an extensive clientelage, and a satisfactory meed of success. For twenty years he has been a member of both the American and Indiana state dental associations. He received the degree of doctor of dental surgery from the Pennsylvania dental college, March, 1870; was elected secretary of the Indiana dental association June 29, 1869; received the degree of doctor of dental surgery from the Ohio college of dental surgery March 1, 1871; was elected president of the Mississippi valley dental association, the oldest in the world now in existence, March 6, 1874; was elected a member of the board of Indiana dental examiners, June 29, 1880, holding the office seven years; was elected president of the Indiana state dental association, July 1, 1885; and member of the board of trustees of Indiana dental college, March 3, 1886; received the honorary degree of doctor of medicine from Fort Wayne college of medicine, March 6, 1888, and March 6, 1889, was elected president of the Indiana dental college. Dr. Brown is in politics a republican; in religion a protestant.

Dr. David Daniel Weisell, a prominent dentist of Fort Wayne, was born near Ithaca, Tompkins county, N. Y., August 23, 1832. He attended the district school until sixteen years of age, and subsequently studied two terms at Hiram college, and one term at Mt. Union college. While at the former college he made his home with the parents of Mrs. James A. Garfield. When he was seventeen he began teaching in the district schools, and taught five terms. His study of dentistry began when he was twenty-four, in the office of Dr. H. M. Beadle, of Chautauqua, N. Y. He began practicing, at the same time studying medicine, at the village of Lordstown Center, Trumbull county, Ohio. He entered the medical department of the university of Michigan, in 1859, and after completing his course of lectures, began the practice of that profession at Northville, Mich. A year and a half later he became the successor of his preceptor at Lordstown Center, and there practiced medicine until the fall of 1863, when he settled at Avilla, Ind., and practiced both his professions over three years. This he continued at Zanesville until the fall of 1873, when he abandoned the practice of medicine, to which he had been giving his main attention, and removing to Fort Wayne, devoted himself to dentistry, in which he has since gained distinction. He is a member of the Masonic order, the Royal Arcanum, and the Chosen Friends. He possesses a genius for invention and has received patents on various contrivances, among them a farm gate, a seat lock for vehicles, carriage springs, road cart, railroad rail, railroad nut lock, pneumatic mallet, artificial teeth, dental vulcanizer (spiral spring), pitman for dental burring engines, and other dental appliances, and a washing machine. He was married at Albion, April, 1864, to Anna E., daughter of Jefferson and Harriet (Harner) Smith, and they have six children: William Ellis, Jefferson Garis, Carrie Delia, Alfred Tennyson, Irma Jane, and Edward McIntyre. Dr. Weisell is a son of Michael G. and Catherine (McIntyre) Weisell, the former a native of Pennsylvania, and the latter of Huntington, N. Y. His father was born September 27, 1787, son of Michael and Catherine (Garis) Weisell, his mother January 14, 1793, daughter of Robert and Rebecca (Quackenbush) McIntyre. They were married in 1817, and in 1834 removed to Trumbull county, Ohio, where the father died September 18, 1870, and the mother January 19, 1875.

Dr. Henry Clay Sites, one of the successful dentists of Fort Wayne, was born at Lancaster, Fairfield county, Ohio, July 12, 1841, son of Emanuel and Frances (Beery) Sites. The father was born in York county, Penn., the mother in Fairfield county, Ohio. Dr. Sites was reared on a farm, and received a common school education. Taking full advantage of his educational opportunities, he was able at the age of eighteen to teach a term of school. At the beginning of the war he enlisted in Company B, Seventeenth Ohio regiment, and served nearly four months. Returning home he attended school about three months, and then enlisted again in Company F, Eighty-eighth Ohio, as a second lieutenant, and served four months, receiving his discharge at Columbus, Ohio. Dr. Sites began the study of the profession in which he has became prominent in about 1870, and since then has devoted all his time to its study and practice. He established himself at Fort Wayne in May, 1874, and has practiced here successfully ever since. Dr. Sites is a member of the G. A. R., the I. O. O. F., and the Knights of Pythias. At the June session of the grand lodge of the Knights of Pythias, for Indiana, Dr. Sites was elected grand master at arms. In political faith he is a republican. He was married June 28, 1870, to Jennie, daughter of John C. Perry, born at Savannah, Ga.

Dr. S. Brenton Hartman, a prominent dentist, born in Fort Wayne, October 5, 1849, is a son of Rev. D. P. Hartman, formerly a prominent Methodist pastor of Fort Wayne, and one of the founders of the Wayne Street Methodist Episcopal church. Dr. Hartman obtained his education in the public schools and in the Fort Wayne Methodist college. In 1871 he began the study of dentistry, and in September, 1876, he entered the dental department of Michigan university, where he was graduated March 28, 1877, and had the honor of being president of his class. Soon after graduating he opened an office at Fort Wayne. He is a member of the Indiana state dental association. He is also a member, and at present is recording steward, of the Wayne Street Methodist Episcopal church.

Dr. Edward F. Sites, a prominent dentist of Fort Wayne, was born near Lancaster, Fairfield county, Ohio, April 21, 1855, being the son of Emanuel and Frances Sites. He was reared on a farm, and in addition to a district school education he pursued his studies two years in the Southern Ohio normal school of Pleasantville, Ohio. In the fall of 1876 he entered upon the study of dentistry, and in order the better to fit himself for its practice he spent between one and two years in the Fort Wayne college of medicine. In the fall of 1878 he entered the dental department of the university of Michigan, from which he graduated in the spring of 1879. He immediately began the practice of his profession in Fort Wayne, and he is now recognized as one of the leading dentists of the city. Dr. Sites was married May 27, 1885, to Miss Carrie L. Pfeiffer, by whom he is the father of two children: Mabel M. and

———. He is a Royal Arch Mason and a member of Fort Wayne lodge of Perfection. He not only possesses an excellent knowledge of dentistry, but also those other qualities which are necessary to put it into successful practice. He is deservedly popular in his profession, and socially his standing is very high.

Dr. William Wilson Shryock, one of the leading dentists of Fort Wayne, began the study of his profession in September, 1876, in the office of Dr. S. B. Brown, with whom he remained three years. He then spent one year in the dental school of the university of Michigan, and subsequently, in 1881, spent eight months as assistant to Dr. George W. Loag, of Fort Wayne, and four months in Auburn, in charge of the office of Dr. Ellison, of that place. In the fall of 1881 he entered the Indiana dental college at Indianapolis, and graduated in February, 1882. He established an office at Fort Wayne, and soon won a large and lucrative practice. His dental parlors are at 27 West Berry street. Dr. Shryock is a member of the Indiana and American dental associations. He is a native of DeKalb county, Ind., born May 25, 1857, son of Joseph and Ann E. (Shoaff) Shryock, both natives of this state. At the age of ten years he entered the Fort Wayne schools, first in the Methodist college, and then in the public schools. At fourteen he began the study of music under Prof. S. B. Morse, and pursued that study six years, graduating from the Indiana conservatory at nineteen years of age. He was married December 3, 1885, to Emily L., daughter of Horatio N. and Christina Ward, of Fort Wayne. She was born at Louisville, Ky., November 16, 1858. The Doctor and wife are esteemed members of the Episcopal church.

ORGANIZATION OF ALLEN COUNTY.

Gen. John Tipton, who came to Fort Wayne in 1823 as Indian agent, was a leading spirit in the movement for the formation of a new county, of which Fort Wayne should be the seat of justice, and in the following session of the legislature a bill was passed and approved December 17, 1823, entitled, "An Act for the formation of a new county out of the counties of Randolph and Delaware," concerning which, and the territory then attached to Allen county, full mention is made in the chapter upon the "Courts, Bench and Bar."

At the suggestion of Gen. Tipton it was provided that after the 1st of April, 1824, the new county should be known by the name of Allen, in memory of Col. John Allen, of Kentucky. This act also provided that Lot Bloomfield and Caleb Lewis, of Wayne county, Abiathar Hathaway, of Fayette, William Connor, of Hamilton, and James M. Ray, of Marion, should act as commissioners for the locating of a seat of justice for the county, and meet for that purpose at the house of Alexander Ewing, on the fourth Monday of May following. The commission met on the 24th of May, as ordered, and had little difficulty in determining the location of the county seat. There appears to have been some competition, however, and an offer was made by Messrs. John McCorkle and John T. Barr, proprietors of the plat of Fort Wayne, in which they agreed, if the county seat were located there, to pay Allen county $500 cash, and donate the following tracts for public use:

"All of that oblong square or piece of ground situate and being in the town of Fort Wayne, aforesaid, and stained red on the plat of said town, as recorded in the recorder's office in Randolph county, in said state, which is granted as a public square, whereon public buildings for said county are to be erected, and bounded by Main, Court, Berry and Calhoun streets; also a lot, or piece of ground four rods square, laid out at right angles, at the northwest corner of the plat of Fort Wayne, west of and adjoining said plat, which is donated and granted for a church and public burying-ground, to be occupied by no particular denomination, but free to all — except so much of said lot as may be necessary for said church, which may be occupied by the first church of professing Christians in said county, who may erect thereon a house of worship of convenient size, of suitable materials; also, a lot of land, of the same size as the regular lots in said town, to be laid off east and adjoining the lots of land last above mentioned, as a place whereon to erect a seminary of learning; also, lots numbered 8, 9, 101, 102, 103, and the lots regularly numbered from 104 to 118, inclusive; also, a tier of lots along the south side of said plat, to be laid off immediately opposite the tier of lots on the first recorded plat of said town (opposite 104 to 118), which are to be divided from said last tier by an alley, and, in size and otherwise, to conform to the plat of the town lots numbered regularly from 92 to 100, inclusive of each."

This proposition was accepted, and subsequently a deed was made of the land described, to John Tipton as county agent. Meanwhile, Gov. William Hendrick, had issued a commission to Allen Hamilton as sheriff of Allen county, dated April 2, 1824, to be in force until an election should be had, and Sheriff Hamilton at once issued a notice to the people of the county to hold an election on May 22, 1824, for the purpose of electing two associate judges of the circuit court, one clerk of the circuit court, one recorder and three commissioners. This first election, of which all records have vanished, was duly held by the handful of settlers, and resulted in the choice of Samuel Hanna and Benjamin Cushman as associate judges; Anthony L. Davis, clerk and recorder; William Rockhill, commissioner for three years, James Wyman for two years, and Francis Comparet for one year. Subsequently, the election of Mr. Cushman was contested by Alexander Ewing, and that of James Wyman and Francis Comparet, by Marshall K. Taylor, unsuccessfully, however, in each case. The commissioners-elect met at the house of Alexander Ewing at noon on May 26, 1824, and producing their certificates issued by Sheriff Hamilton, proceeded to business, their work that day consisting of the appointment of Joseph Holman as county treasurer, who was required to give bond, with two sufficient sureties, in the considerable sum of $1,000. On the next day, Col. Tipton was appointed county agent, and he filed his bond in the sum of $5,000 with Alexander Ewing and Samuel Hanna as sureties. He was then ordered to pay to each of the commissioners who had just concluded their duties in the selection of a county seat, the sum of $3 a day each, for their services. This ended the preliminary session of the commissioners, who next met, in their first regular session, Monday, May 31, at the same house, afterward known as Washington hall. The following appointments were made: Hugh B. McKeen, lister of taxable property; Lambert Cushovis, constable; Robert Hars, inspector of elections; William N. Hood, inspector of flour, beef and pork, for the township of Wayne; Samuel Hanna, road supervisor for the township of Wayne; John Davis and Alexander Coquillard, overseers of the poor, in Wayne township.

At this term it was ordered that the county of Allen be constituted as one township, and called the township of Wayne. John Tipton, county agent, was ordered to construct a pound, of suitable size, which appears to have been the first public building ordered on the public square, but the order was rescinded February 14, 1825. The board also ordered that the sheriff " advertise an election, to be held at the house of Alexander Ewing, if permitted; if not, at some other suitable place in the township of Wayne, for the election of three justices of the peace, on the first Monday in August next." They also selected thirty-six names from which to choose a grand jury, and forty-eight names from which to choose a petit jury for the circuit court. The board had powers now rarely assumed and fixed the first tavern rates as follows:

For dinner, breakfast and supper, each, 25 cents; keeping horse, night and day, 50 cents; lodging, per night, 12½ cents; whisky, per half-pint, 12½ cents; brandy, per half-pint, 50 cents; gin, per half-pint, 37½ cents; porter, per bottle, 37½ cents; cider, per quart, 18¾ cents. At the same session, the board fixed the following rates of assessment on personal property, for county purposes, for the year 1824: On every male person over the age of twenty-one years, 50 cents; horse, gelding, mare or mule, three years old and upward, each, 37½ cents; work oxen, three years old and upward, 18¾ cents; stud horse, the rate at which he stands per season; gold watch, $1.00; silver watch, 25 cents; pinchbeck watch, 25 cents; pleasure carriage, four wheels, $1.50; pleasure carriage, two wheels, $1.00.

Gen. Tipton, who had been appointed agent for the county, an office long since abolished, had for part of his duties, the disposition of the land deeded to the county, in consideration for fixing the county seat. He was ordered to sell lots 8, 9, and 101 to 133, and 92 to 100 at public sale, and the report that he made shows that these valuable lots in the heart of the city sold for from $10.25 to $51 each. By subsequent orders he sold the remaining lots. Of the cash donation ten per cent. was appropriated for a county library, and $174 went to pay the county seat commissioners, and when Mr. Tipton retired from his office, he paid over to G. W. Ewing, his successor, $215.75, as the net amount collected up to that time. Some of this went to partly pay for the first jail.

On the first Monday of September, 1824, the county commissioners passed out of office under a law passed by the previous legislature which gave their powers to the justices of the peace of the townships, who were to sit in a body as the board of justices of the county. This cumbrous machinery transacted the county business until the fall of 1829, when the system of commissioners was again established. There being but one township at this time in Allen county, and only three justices elected for it, the law at first really made very little change in the transaction of business. The justices who first came into power were Alexander Ewing, William N. Hood and William Rockhill, who met at Washington hall, on October 22, 1824, and adopted as their official seal a scrawl inclosing the initials, "B. C. J." One of the first acts of the board of county justices was to receive the report of Benjamin B. Kercheval and Samuel Hanna, who had, as representatives of Allen county, acted with representatives from counties south in surveying and locating the Winchester road, the first highway of the county, extending to Vernon, Jennings county.

At the January, 1825, session of the board, the county treasurer, Joseph Holman, presented the first exhibit of the condition of the county's finances as follows:

Total receipts from organization................ $437 98¾
Total disbursements for same period............ 406 40

Balance on hand........................ $31 58¾

Mr. Holman's report was submitted on the 5th day of January, 1825. The day following, William G. Ewing was appointed his successor for a term of one year. At the July session of that year, the following allowances were made:

To Allen Hamilton, sheriff, for six months' services, ending April 9, 1825, the sum of............... $20 00
To Anthony L. Davis, for services as clerk of the board of justices and of the circuit court, for one year, ending June 30, 1825.................... 45 00
To grand and petit jurors, each, per day.......... 50

Among the other interesting items to be gleaned from the records of this body is the licensing the American fur company's Fort Wayne department, for the sum of $25, to vend foreign merchandise in the town for one year; an order in May, 1828, authorizing the clerk to procure a seal for county business, and the fixing of rates for ferriage across the St. Mary's river, the license fee charged being $1 per year. On January 3, 1825, Adams township was set apart, to be bounded on the west by the line which divides ranges 12 and 13, and on the north by the "contemplated boundary line of Allen county." The financial showing made by Treasurer Ewing for the second year of the county's organic existence, was: total receipts, $283.31; paid out, $22.41; balance, $260.90. Thomas Forsythe was then appointed as the successor of Mr. Ewing.

In October, 1829, a new board of county commissioners came into power, composed of Nathan Coleman, William Caswell and James Holman, who had been elected at a special election on the 12th of that month. One of the first acts of this body was to fix the rate of taxation for 1830, at 40 cents on every hundred acres of first rate land, 30 cents on the same amount of second rate, and 20 cents on third rate.

By act of congress of May 31, 1830, the county acquired a right of pre-emption of twenty acres of the military reservation of forty acres and the county agent, then Francis Comparet, was authorized, at the October session of the board, to procure money by loan or otherwise sufficient to make the purchase, and he was empowered to "pledge the faith of the county therefor, if necessary." The purchase being made, the agent was ordered to lay off the land in lots, and he having made a plat of seventy lots, he sold them by authority of the board at prices that were reasonable for those times. The county agent had multifarious duties to perform, being called on by an order of the commissioners in August, 1831, to cause the cutting off of the brush and stumps from the public square, the work to be let to the lowest bidder at public sale. In the following March the agent was authorized to lease to James Wilcox thirty feet front by fifty back at some remote corner of the public square; the rate being fixed, at the corner of Main and Calhoun, at $10 per year, at the corner of Main and Court, $8, and at the corner of Court and Perry or Barr $6. At a subsequent session, in 1834, the agent was authorized to lease to David Colerick, 25x40 feet at the northwest corner of the square, at $10 per year. These were necessary arrangements for the revenues of the county were extremely small, and not easily collected. The first legal notice ordered printed was directed to be published in the Fort Wayne *Sentinel*, January 6, 1834. In May, 1835, the rate of taxation for county purposes was fixed at 33⅓ cents of every $100 of property, for road purposes 1 cent per $100, and the poll tax was fixed at 75 cents. A bounty was fixed for the killing of wolves, in September, 1840, the financial condition of the county having by that time become such as to warrant such a procedure, in conjunction with the bounty offered by the state. The state having offered to pay the county 50 cents for each wolf scalp of an animal under six months old, and $1 for those over that age, the board thereupon offered $3 apiece for scalps of wolves over six months old and $1.50 for those of wolves under six months. The expenses of the county were very light at that time, as appears from the record of an offier by G. W. Wood to do all the county advertising for one year from March, 1841, for $9.50. The offer was accepted.

On September 9, 1841, the board authorized the county agent to procure a seal for the board of commissioners, bearing the following device and letters: "A sheaf of wheat in an upright position with a sickle sticking therein; and, in the background, a field of corn with a reaper at work. And in a circle surrounding said device, the following words: 'Commissioners of Allen county, Ia. Seal.' The word seal to be in M. and the sheaf of wheat." At the session of December 8, 1841, an additional bounty for wolf scalps was offered, making $5 for a full-grown wolf, and $2.50 for every scalp of a half-grown wolf, killed in the county. Because of the progress made in building a new court-house, there was a necessity for removing the obstructions on the public square, to put the area in a more presentable shape. The board, at the March term, 1843, directed the county agent to cause the buildings east of, and adjoining the, auditor's office, to be removed from the public square; also, the *stable* on the square; to grade the square, and grade and curb the sidewalks on Calhoun street.

For the use of the First Presbyterian church in Fort Wayne, the board at the June term, 1843, authorized the county agent to deed the trustees of the church, lot No. 63, in the county addition. In the following September, the board adopted a county seal, substantially that proposed by the county agent on September 9, 1841.

Public Buildings.—During the first few years following the organization of the county, the courts were held in the primitive taverns, either that of William Suttenfield or at the famous Washington hall. The first step toward the erection of a building for the county offices and courts was taken by the county commissioners at the May session of 1831, when the clerk was ordered to advertise for bids on such a building. Notice having been given, the board let the contracts for the building of a court-house to John S. Archer to furnish the brick, James

Hudson to lay up the brick and furnish the lime and stone, and Hanna & Edsall to do the carpenter work and furnish all lumber, timber, nails, glass, etc., for the total amount of $3,321.75. The citizens of Fort Wayne subscribed $499 in material and labor, and $149 in cash. The rest was paid out of the county treasury. This building, which was ill adapted to the purposes contemplated, was never much more than a shell, with some of the rooms partially finished, while others were scarcely tenantable. The first meeting of court in this new edifice was on the 7th of May, 1832, just one year from the date of its original projection, though the building was not completed, as the record shows. After that date, however, it was nominally completed, but was never a substantial building, though used, in the absence of a better, until the fall of 1841, when, it having become apparent that the old building was totally unfit for the purpose and insufficient in capacity, action was taken by the board preparatory to the building of a new one. On the 9th of September, 1841, it was ordered that an allowance be made to A. Miller for the best draft or plan for a court-house, the cost not to exceed $15,000. This draft had been drawn by Porter & Rice, of Hudson, Ohio, as architects for Miller, and in answer to an advertisement by the commissioners for drafts and plans.

The county agent was then authorized to sell the first court-house to the highest bidder, the building to be removed from the public square in thirty days after the sale. It appears that no purchaser was found, for on December 8, 1841, the board ordered that John Spencer be allowed the sum of $300 and the old court-house, for his building on the public square, the court-house to be removed one year from this date. During the existence of the old building, and after it became unfit for occupancy, a one-story edifice, designed as a temporary court-house, was built on the southeast corner of the square, fronting on Berry street, in the summer of 1843, the contract for which was let by the county board on the 11th of March of that year, to Benjamin Mason, Charles French and John Ocanour. The price was not named, the order stating that it should be suitable for one court room and two offices. At the same time a further order was made for a building to be put on the northeast corner of the public square, to be used as offices for the treasurer and auditor. The old clerk's office was on the northwest, and the recorder's office on the southwest, corner of the square.

The new court-house in contemplation at that time, the second one built in the county, was a two-story brick building, and was completed by Samuel Edsall, the contractor, in 1847. It served for a decade before there was a demand for more room. This demand was so strong by the time of meeting of the commissioners in June, 1858, that they made a levy of 15 cents on every $100 for the purpose of providing for a new court-house. By this levy $7,183.56 was collected, and then an additional levy of 20 cents was ordered, which brought in the sum of $12,271.03. Plans were advertised for in 1859, and finally at a special session in July, 1859, the board purchased the plans of Edwin May and

Samuel McElfatrick, and paid each of those architects $100, discovering in each plan desirable features. At another special session in August, the board adopted the plan of Edwin May, by a majority vote, T. M. Andrews dissenting, and Mr. May was subsequently appointed superintending architect. The bids on the construction of the proposed edifice were opened January 12, 1860, and it was found that there were thirteen of them, the estimates varying from $62,700 to $94,000. The contract was awarded to Samuel Edsall, Virgil M. Kimball, Oehmig Bird and Lewis Walkie, at their bid of $63,613 under the name of Samuel Edsall & Co. Two months later Mr. May was discharged from the supervision of the work, and that position was given to Samuel McElfatrick. This gentleman officially announced to the commissioners on July 23, 1862, that the building was completed, and it was then officially accepted. The final settlement of the account of the contractors was made by J. K. Edgerton, E. R. Wilson, J. L. Williams, I. D. G. Nelson and Pliny Hoagland, showing that the contractors had been paid $74,271. Added to this were other expenses, which made the house cost the county in the aggregate about $78,000. This imposing building is still used by Allen county, and though less expensive than some built by counties of much less population and wealth, it is still a substantial building.

The first public building for which the commissioners provided was one for which no private building could be made available, a jail for the confinement of the unruly members of society. Not only these, but unfortunate debtors in those days found lodgment in the jail occasionally. In he first jail, built in the public square in 1825, by the contractors, David Irwin, Robert Douglass and William N. Hood, there were two rooms, the lower one for criminals and the upper for debtors. Three years later glass was put in the debtor's room for lights, and the room was plastered for the first time. This pioneer jail stood on the southwest corner of the public square until it was destroyed by fire in 1847. A high board fence surrounded it to add to the difficulties of escape, and attached to the building was the residence of the sheriff. In 1847 a lot, No. 518, had been purchased as a site for a new jail, but this was sold and another, the one upon which the present jail stands, was bought in June, 1847. An election was held in that year by which the people decided in favor of a new jail by a vote of 1,192 to 332. A levy of 20 cents on the $100 was made on the assessments of 1848 and 1849, and the building was erected at a cost of $4,955.34, in the spring of 1850. Steps were taken toward the erection of a new jail, the one now in use, in 1872. On October 4th, the auditor was ordered by the commissioners to advertise for bids for the erection of a sheriff's residence and county jail, the work to be commenced March 1, 1873, and completed October 1, 1874. On December 5th, the contract was awarded to Christian Boseker, on his bid of $81,498, and the building was constructed accordingly. It is a fire-proof structure, substantial and commodious.

The County Infirmary.— It appears from the record of the commissioners made in 1834 that a building had been furnished for the poor, and a farm for them to reside upon. In that year William Rockhill was appointed as superintendent of the poor-house and poor-farm, and authorized to select a suitable person to take charge of the place. On the 6th of January following the poor-farm was let for six years to Jeremiah Bowers, he to take care of the poor, and clear twenty-five acres of land, eighteen inches and under, and make a fence six rails high and "double rider" the same, for $2 per week. In June, 1853, the county purchased the northeast quarter, and the west half of the southeast quarter and the east half of the east half of the northwest quarter of section 29, in Wayne township, for a poor farm, and a contract was made with John A. Robinson for the building of a suitable house for $750. To this an addition worth $300 was built in the following year. At this new farm George L. Parker was the first to whom the place was let, and he was paid $600. In July, 1860, a new and better plan was adopted, and James M. Reed was appointed superintendent of the asylum for a period of two years, on a plan similar to that now followed. It was soon discovered, however, that the buildings were insufficient and the farm too remote from the city, and in September, 1863, plans for a new building were purchased. And in December, a tract of land on the west side of the St. Mary's, near Beaver's mill, was purchased of Robert E. Fleming for $50 per acre. On this land the new building was erected by David J. Silvers, the contractor, who had been the builder of the court-house. He completed the structure in the spring of 1865, and was paid for the same $15,676.12. Other buildings have been added for the greater convenience of caring for the county's wards, and the management of the institution has been creditable to the benevolence of Allen county.

Aid to Improvements.— The county has as an organization, as well as through the munificence of individuals, contributed to the improvement of the country by furnishing gradually better routes of transportation as commerce and its necessities grew toward their present ample proportions. The first action taken by the board, as has been seen, was toward the improvement of the Winchester road, leading toward Randolph county, which just previous to the organization of Allen county, embraced the latter. The county board also had jurisdiction of the ferries, then important on account of the greater volume of the rivers, and various persons were licensed to keep ferries at the points of crossing, under the regulations of the state laws on the subject. At the April session of the board, 1851, it considered the propriety of subscribing for stock in the proposed Ohio & Indiana railroad, now a part of the Pittsburgh, Fort Wayne & Chicago system. The people had voted on the subject, and the result had been 1,647 in favor of a county subscription and 334 opposed. The commissioners consequently made a subscription for $100,000, and Samuel Hanna was appointed as agent of Allen county, to execute the coupons or interest warrants. Subsequently,

Auditor Robert Starkweather was given this latter duty to perform. To pay the interest on the railroad bonds to be issued by the county, a levy of 20 cents on $100 valuation was made, which was followed in 1852, by another levy of 22 cents. The special agent of the county, for the transaction of business connected with the railroad, with power to vote at meetings of stock-holders, was, first, Robert S. Fleming, then Pliny Hoagland, and then Oehmig Bird. In 1855, Franklin P. Randall was appointed, who held the position until 1861, when Byron D. Minor was appointed, and soon afterward W. W. Carson was associated with him for the final disposition of the stock. Mr. Randall reported in June, 1856, that he had received 351 shares of stock, which was the interest on the stock owned by the county, up to January 1, 1855, and that there was still due the county, interest from that time to the date of the report, about $9,000, making of interest paid and due, $26,550. Mr. Randall, by order of the board, voted for the consolidation of the roads, and subsequently reported that he had received of the Pittsburgh, Fort Wayne & Chicago railroad company, 2,000 shares for the original subscription and 796 shares for the interest due. After the re-organization, by which process the stock was greatly depreciated in value, agents Carson and Minor were ordered to sell the stock at as advantageous terms as possible, and they reported in March, 1863, that they had sold $39,800 worth for $24,830.75, but did not feel justified in selling the remaining $100,000 worth at prices ranging from 55 to 67 cents, without instructions from the board. Finally the county transferred to Samuel Hanna the $100,000 worth of stock in exchange for $87,000 worth of bonds of the county.

Financial Statistics.—The auditor's annual report, showing the financial condition of Allen county, for the year ending May 31, 1889, shows that the cash in the treasury June 1, 1888, amounted to $243,969.57; to which was added the treasurer's receipts for the fiscal year, $499,078.66. The total outgo, reckoning in this item a small amount of orders afloat, was $514,524.69. In the expenditures a considerable amount represents payment in part for improvements, such as gravel roads, bridges, and other debts incurred, for part of which bonds are extant. The debt statement is: Bonded debt, June 1, 1888, $185,000; bonds redeemed since June 1, 1888, $15,000; bonded debt June 1, 1889, $170,000. The total valuation of the property of the county for purposes of taxation is $26,414,330. It will be interesting to quote here the expenditures for county purposes for each fiscal year ending May 31st, since 1840. During the war period there were also heavy expenditures for bounty and relief, and the figures cited for recent years are those which occur in the auditor's report under the title, "county orders issued." In 1840 the total expenditure for county purposes was $4,606.82; 1841, $3,413.00; 1842, $5,963.60; 1843, $6,255.18; 1844, $9,170.29; 1845, $8,154.48; 1846, $6,825,57; 1847, $7,050.12; 1848, $6,857.07; 1849, $7,496.77; 1850, $10,988.08; 1851, $7,441.74; 1852, $10,904.76; 1853, $10,310.93; 1854, $22,059.78; 1855, $17,568.87; 1856, $19,484.46;

ORGANIZATION OF ALLEN COUNTY. 383

1857, $16,025.53; 1858, $20,329.86; 1859, $23,587.29; 1860, $25,447.68; 1861, $38,390.69; 1862, $72,972.25; 1863, $53,237.74; 1864, $48,707.54; 1865, $57,118.00; 1867, $59,335.03; 1868, $157,050.52; 1869, $109,731.63; 1870, $102,601.25; 1871, $115,552.17; 1872, $125,079.91; 1873, $117,108.32; 1874, $222,855.51; 1875, $137,770.47; 1876, $118,428.25; 1877, $138,689.94; 1878, $147,644.69; 1879, $141,930.58; 1880, $172,985.17; 1881, $172,449.26; 1882, 188,350.32; 1883, $231,115.39; 1884, $187,811.98; 1885, $182,115.32; 1886, $161,981.47; 1887, $137,548.91; 1888, $141,233.68.

County Officers from the Organization of Allen County.— Clerks of the circuit court: 1824, Anthony L. Davis; 1830, Robert N. Hood; 1831, Allen Hamilton; 1839, Philip G. Jones; 1845, Robert E. Fleming; 1853, Joseph Sinclair; 1854, I. D. G. Nelson; 1863, William Fleming; 1871, William S. Edsall; 1875, Frank H. Wolke; 1879, M. V. B. Spencer; 1882, Willis D. Maier; 1886, George W. Loag.

Auditors: 1824, Anthony L. Davis; 1830, Robert N. Hood; 1831, Allen Hamilton; 1839, Philip G. Jones; 1841, Samuel S. Morss; 1845, Henry W. Jones; 1850, Robert Starkweather; 1857, John B. Blue; 1857, Francis L. Furst; 1861, G. F. Stinchcomb; 1865, Henry J. Rudisill; 1873, William S. Abbott; 1877, Martin E. Argo; 1882, A. L. Griebel; 1886, John B. Niezer.

Treasurers: 1824, Joseph Holman; 1825, William G. Ewing; 1826, Thomas Forsythe; 1827, Thomas Thorpe; 1829, John Forsythe; 1829, L. G. Thompson; 1832, Benjamin Cushman; 1833, Joseph Holman; 1834, Thomas W. Swinney; 1839, Samuel Hanna; 1840, George F. Wright; 1841, Theodore K. Breckenridge; 1847, S. M. Black; 1850, Thomas T. DeKay; 1852, Oehmig Bird; 1836, Alexander Wiley; 1860, Oliver R. Jefferds; 1862, Alexander Wiley; 1866, Henry Monning; 1870, John Ring; 1874, Michael Schmetzer; 1879, John M. Taylor; 1883, John Dalman; 1887, Isaac Mowrer.

Sheriffs: 1824, Allen Hamilton; 1826, Cyrus Taber; 1827, Abner Gerard; 1831, David Pickering; 1834, Joseph L. Swinney; 1837, John P. Hedges; 1838, Joseph Berkey; 1842, Brad. B. Stevens; 1846, Samuel S. Morss; 1850, William H. McDonald; 1854, William McMullin; 1855, William Fleming; 1860, Joseph A. Strout; 1862, William T. Pratt; 1866, John McCartney; 1870, Charles A. Zollinger; 1873, Joseph D. Hance; 1876, Platt J. Wise; 1876, Charles A. Munson; 1880, Franklin D. Cosgrove; 1882, William D. Schiefer; 1884, Nelson DeGroff, died May 27, 1887; 1887, George H. Viberg.

Recorders: 1824, Anthony L. Davis; 1830, Robert N. Hood; 1831, Allen Hamilton; 1837, Robert Fleming; 1844, Edward Colerick; 1855, Platt J. Wise; 1863, Clement A. Reckers; 1871, John M. Koch; 1874, Joseph Mommer, jr.; 1884, Thomas S. Haller; 1888, Milton W. Thompson.

Surveyors: 1835, Reuben J. Dawson: 1837, S. M. Black; 1846, Henry J. Rudisill; 1849, J. M. Wilt; 1855, William A. Jackson; 1857, William McLaughlin; 1861, J. W. McArthur; 1865, Nathan Butler;

1867, J. S. Goshorn; 1870. William H. Goshorn; 1882, D. M. Allen; 1884, C. B. Wiley; 1888, Henry E. Fisher.

Coroners: 1852, C. E. Goodrich; 1854, John Johnson; 1856, W. H. McDonald; 1858, John P. Waters; 1874, Augustus M. Webb; 1876, William Gaffney; 1882, K. K. Wheelock; 1887, H. F. C. Stellhorn; 1889, A. J. Kesler.

Superintendents of Schools: 1861, R. D. Robinson; 1867, James H. Smart; 1873, Jerry Hillegass; 1885, George F. Feltz.

Board of Commissioners—First district: 1824, William Rockhill; 1829, Nathan Coleman; 1831, Francis Alexander; 1834, David Archer; 1839, Christian Parker; 1841, David McQuiston; 1842, Robert Briggs; 1843, Nelson McLain; 1846, Rufus McDonald; 1847, William M. Parker; 1840, Noah Clem; 1850, Simeon Biggs; 1853, Henry Dickerson; 1859, John Shaffer; 1865, William Long; 1868, John Begue; 1874, Frank Gladio; 1883, Henry Hartman; 1889, Jasper W. Jones.

Second district: 1824, James Wyman; 1829, William Caswell; 1833, Abner Gerard; 1834, Joseph Burkey; 1835, L. S. Bayless; 1840, R. Starkweather; 1843, F. D. Lasselle; 1846, James S. Hamilton; 1849, William Robinson; 1854, F. D. Lasselle; 1858, Michael Crow; 1861, Byron D. Miner; 1864, John A. Robinson; 1870, Jacob Hillegass; 1876, Jacob Goeglein; 1882, Jerome D. Gloyd; 1888, H. F. Bullerman.

Third district: 1824, Francis Comparet; 1829, James Holman; 1834, Nathan Coleman; 1835, Nathan Colman; 1835, Joseph Townsend; 1838, Horace B. Taylor; 1842, Joseph Hall; 1845, True Pattee; 1848, Henry Rudisill; 1851, Peter Parker; 1854, William T. Daly; 1857, T. M. Andrews; 1860, Isaac Hall; 1863, David H. Lipes; 1870, John C. Davis; 1873, Harvey K. Turner; 1879, Timothy Hogan; 1882, William Briant; 1885, John H. Brannan.

Members of the General Assembly.—The first senatorial district of which Allen county was a part was composed of the counties of Allen, Wayne and Randolph, which was represented in 1824-5 by James Raridan, of Wayne. In 1825-9 Amaziah Morgan represented the district composed of Allen, Rush, Henry, Randolph, to which Delaware was added in the latter part of his term. Daniel Worth, of Randolph, was elected in 1829 for the district of Allen, Randolph, Delaware and Cass, and served until 1832, during that time the district being changed, first by the addition of St. Joseph and Elkhart, and then by the substitution of these new counties for Cass. For the last described district, Samuel Hanna was elected in 1832, and he represented during one term the counties of Allen, Wabash, Huntington, Elkhart, LaGrange, St. Joseph and Laporte. The last district was represented by David H. Colerick in 1835-6, and in his second term his district was reduced to Allen, Wells and Adams. He was succeeded by William G. Ewing, 1838-41, and he by Joseph Sinclair, 1841-4, Huntington county being added to the district. William Rockhill served 1844-7. For the district of Allen, Adams and Wells, then renewed, Franklin P. Randall was elected in 1846; Franklin S. Mickle, 1850; Samuel Edsall, 1852; Samuel L.

Geo. W. Loage

Rugg, of Adams, 1854. At the next election the district was composed of Allen alone, and Allen Hamilton was elected in 1858; Pliny Hoagland, 1862; W. W. Carson, 1864. He was succeeded by Oehmig Bird, who represented the counties of Allen, Adams and Wells, again joined in a district, who was succeeded by John Sarnighausen, 1871-2, James K. Babo, 1871-2; John Sarnighausen, 1872-9. Allen county being again made an independent district, was represented in 1873-5, by Oehmig Bird; 1875-8, by Robert C. Bell; 1878-82, by Thomas J. Foster. In 1880 Robert C. Bell was elected for the joint district of Allen and Whitley counties, and he was succeeded in 1882 by Eli W. Brown, Lycurgus S. Null being elected senator for Allen county the same year. Mr. Brown served until 1886, when he was succeeded by Isaiah B. McDonald, and he in 1888 by Frederick J. Hayden. James M. Barrett was elected senator for Allen county in 1886.

From 1824 to 1828, Allen was joined with Randolph, the two embracing then a very large part of Indiana, in a representative district, and was represented first by Daniel Worth, of Randolph, to 1826. Samuel Hanna served from 1825 to 1826, and was succeeded by Mr. Worth, who was succeeded in 1828 by Anthony L. Davis, representing the district of Allen and Cass. Joseph Holman was elected for this district next. Samuel Hanna represented Allen, Elkhart and St. Joseph in 1831, George Crawford the same counties with Laporte and LaGrange added in 1832, David H. Colerick the same district, 1832-3, William Rockhill, Allen and Huntington, 1833-4, Lewis G. Thompson the same, 1834-5, since which time Allen county has had one or more representatives independently, as follows: 1835, William Rockhill; 1836-39, Lewis G. Thompson; 1839-40, Samuel Hanna; 1840-41, Marshall S. Wines; 1841-42, Lewis G. Thompson; 1842-43, Lucien P. Ferry; 1843-44, Samuel Stophlet; 1844-48, Christian Parker; 1846-47, Peter Kiser; 1849, Oehmig Bird; 1850-53, I. D. G. Nelson; 1853-55, Francis D. Lasselle; 1855-57, Charles E. Sturgis; 1857-58, Pliny Hoagland; 1858-61, Nelson McLain and Schuyler Wheeler; 1861-63, Moses Jenkinson and Conrad Trior; 1863-67, Oehmig Bird and John P. Shoaff; 1867-68, John P. Shoaff and Peter Kiser; 1868-71, Allen Zollers and B. B. Miner; 1871-72, Robert Taylor and Jacob S. Shute; 1872-75, Jefferson C. Bowser and Mahlon Heller; 1875-77, Mahlon Heller and Patrick Horn; 1877-79, Thomas J. Foster and Charles B. Austin; 1879, Elihu Reichelderfer and Oliver E. Fleming; 1881, Lycurgus S. Null, Hiram C. McDowell, Samuel E. Sinclair; 1883, Albert W. Brooks, Joseph D. McHenry, Erastus L. Chittenden; 1885, Albert W. Brooks, Joseph D. McHenry, Fred. J. Hayden; 1887, William H. Shambaugh, Austin M. Darroch, joint, Benjamin F. Ibach; 1889, William H. Shambaugh, Francis Gladio, joint, William A. Oppenheim.

Political Statistics.—The records of the earliest elections in Allen county are not available. The total vote in 1831 was 208; in 1832, 224; and at the presidential election of 1836, 358. In 1840 the county gave a large whig majority, casting for W. H. Harrison 640 votes; for Van

Buren, 399; but four years later the democratic vote had begun to show a rapid increase toward that great preponderance which subsequently characterized the political history of the county. The total vote in 1844 was for Henry Clay, 861; for James K. Polk, 849. The vote at subsequent presidential elections is given below, by townships:

PRESIDENTIAL, 1848.

Townships.	Cass and Butler.	Taylor and Filmore.
Wayne	347	351
Washington	69	103
Scipio	6	14
Springfield	43	31
St. Joseph	45	35
Perry	61	55
Pleasant	28	23
Maumee	8	1
Monroe	27	17
Madison	36	21
Marion	82	53
Milan	21	10
Lake	45	26
Lafayette	20	21
Jefferson	38	17
Eel River	35	54
Cedar Creek	70	53
Adams	50	65
Aboit	28	41
	1,059	991

VanBuren and Adams received 13 votes.

PRESIDENTIAL, 1852.

Townships.	Pierce and King.	Scott and Graham.
Aboit	42	54
Adams	122	72
Cedar Creek	88	59
Eel River	50	74
Jackson	8	1
Jefferson	31	28
Lafayette	56	33
Lake	66	43
Madison	70	49
Marion	122	57
Maumee	12	5
Milan	52	13
Monroe	47	40
Perry	65	65
Pleasant	91	50
Scipio	2	12
St. Joseph	66	64
Springfield	72	50
Washington	142	95
Wayne	710	361
	1,964	1,225

PRESIDENTIAL, 1856.

Townships.	Buchanan and Breckenridge.	Fremont and Dayton.
Aboit	63	70
Adams	193	80
Cedar Creek	142	69
Eel River	44	58
Jackson	14	3
Jefferson	159	46
Lafayette	121	63
Lake	93	67
Madison	72	35
Marion	165	55
Maumee	10	10
Milan	67	25
Monroe	53	22
Perry	112	71
Pleasant	111	78
Scipio	7	49
Springfield	93	135
St. Joseph	107	59
Washington	159	114
Wayne	1,425	484
	3,211	1,593

PRESIDENTIAL, 1860.

Townships.	Douglas and Johnson.	Lincoln and Hamlin.
Wayne	1,327	976
Washington	108	137
Adams	191	141
St. Joseph	91	92
Jefferson	182	58
Madison	93	58
Monroe	67	61
Marion	139	81
Milan	96	49
Maumee	9	21
Springfield	96	163
Scipio	22	54
Cedar Creek	124	82
Eel River	63	111
Lake	97	66
Aboit	75	91
Lafayette	112	92
Pleasant	138	102
Perry	102	90
Jackson, rejected	11	9
Bright P.	81	18
	3,224	2,552

Bell 32, Breckenridge 42.

ORGANIZATION OF ALLEN COUNTY.

PRESIDENTIAL, 1864.

Townships.	McClellan and Pendleton.	Lincoln and Johnson.
Wayne	2,334	833
Washington	143	123
Adams	278	107
St. Joseph	129	82
Jefferson	193	68
Madison	166	41
Monroe	133	47
Marion	175	60
Milan	149	44
Maumee	23	34
Springfield	127	170
Scipio	30	45
Cedar Creek	148	48
Eel River	92	106
Lake	171	75
Aboit	88	89
Lafayette	155	97
Pleasant	148	84
Perry	138	62
Jackson	25	12
Bright P.	87	17
	4,932	2,244

PRESIDENTIAL, 1868.

Townships.	Seymour and Blair.	Grant and Colfax.
Wayne	421	191
Washington	161	129
Adams	196	62
St. Joseph	147	86
Jefferson	204	86
Madison	167	72
Monroe	197	105
Marion	174	78
Milan	164	61
Maumee	33	40
Springfield	163	194
Scipio	39	54
Cedar Creek	174	117
Eel River	114	117
Lake	163	66
Aboit	49	106
Lafayette	171	113
Pleasant	170	97
Perry	158	75
Jackson	54	23
Bright P.	85	22
Fort Wayne	2,190	1,065
New Haven	180	91
	5,604	3,047

PRESIDENTIAL, 1872.

Townships.	Greeley and Brown.	Grant and Wilson.
Wayne	136	147
Washington	125	130
Adams	122	28
St. Joseph	127	79
Jefferson	159	95
Madison	164	92
Monroe	187	135
Marion	161	73
Milan	93	58
Maumee	33	63
Springfield	127	191
Scipio	35	57
Cedar Creek	112	124
Eel River	101	106
Lake	110	59
Aboit	46	101
Lafayette	177	106
Pleasant	155	100
Perry	115	75
Jackson	20	16
Bright P.	68	20
Fort Wayne	2,404	1,675
New Haven	189	111
	5,176	3,541

O'Connor, independent democrat, received 119 votes.

PRESIDENTIAL, 1876.

Townships.	Tilden and Hendricks.	Hayes and Wheeler.
Wayne	293	142
Washington	184	141
Adams	192	41
St. Joseph	234	96
Jefferson	221	133
Madison	224	83
Monroe	307	133
Marion	217	86
Milan	230	70
Maumee	84	71
Springfield	170	239
Scipio	48	66
Cedar Creek	204	113
Eel River	165	105
Lake	221	85
Aboit	107	126
Lafayette	210	134
Pleasant	270	108
Perry	221	92
Jackson	45	31
Fort Wayne	4,476	1,825
New Haven	250	93
	7,732	4,013

Scattering, 17.

PRESIDENTIAL, 1880.

Townships.	Hancock and English.	Garfield and Arthur.
Wayne	319	191
Washington	209	213
Adams	211	42
St. Joseph	247	107
Jefferson	219	135
Madison	220	104
Monroe	278	101
Marion	211	102
Milan	233	76
Maumee	54	55
Springfield	111	230
Scipio	52	57
Cedar Creek	13	127
Eel River	63	128
Lake	19	98
Aboit	107	114
Lafayette	249	129
Pleasant	277	116
Perry	220	105
Jackson	47	31
Fort Wayne	3,605	2,466
New Haven	230	88
	7,791	4,815

Weaver and Chambers received in all 84 votes.

PRESIDENTIAL, 1884.

Townships.	Cleveland and Hendricks.	Blaine and Logan.
Wayne	376	210
Washington	138	92
Adams	223	53
St. Joseph	291	117
Jefferson	225	143
Madison	258	109
Monroe	290	120
Marion	221	86
Milan	245	99
Maumee	58	71
Springfield	198	244
Scipio	45	53
Cedar Creek	220	118
Eel River	168	120
Lake	205	106
Aboit	137	114
Lafayette	248	117
Pleasant	251	129
Perry	233	87
Jackson	59	35
Fort Wayne*	4,534	2,599
New Haven	281	110
	8,904	4,932

*Includes city in Washington.
Butler and West received in all 104 votes, and St. John and Daniel, 85.

PRESIDENTIAL, 1888.

Townships.	Cleveland and Thurman.	Harrison and Morton.
Wayne	411	265
Washington	137	120
Adams	279	90
St. Joseph	254	120
Jefferson	242	159
Madison	246	110
Monroe	299	136
Marion	211	80
Milan	243	109
Maumee	82	57
Springfield	196	229
Scipio	55	63
Cedar Creek	250	100
Eel River	157	130

Townships.	Cleveland and Thurman.	Harrison and Morton.
Lake	204	109
Aboit	119	119
Layfayette	232	120
Pleasant	258	129
Perry	229	100
Jackson	79	55
Fort Wayne*	5,280	2,856
New Haven	229	91
	9,692	5,456

The total prohibition vote was 162, united labor, 95.
*Includes city in Washington.

Congressional Elections.— Indiana's representation in the congress of 1823, consisted of three members, the districts which they represented being of course very extensive, though of small population. The district which included Fort Wayne, the third, extended from the Ohio river to the Michigan boundary, and was first represented by John Test, of Lawrenceburg, who held the office from 1823 to 1827. He was succeeded by Oliver H. Smith, who was elected in 1826. In a work concerning early days in Indiana that gentleman has described his experience in a trip for electioneering purposes from Randolph county to Fort Wayne, riding his horse through rivers, stopping over night with Indians, and other hardships much exceeding those of candidates of these days. He made a speech from the porch of the hotel at which he stopped, which was perhaps the first of the kind in Allen county. He was elected, defeating John Test, who was rather too progressive a man, and had the temerity to talk of railroads to some of his constituents in the south of the state, improvements in which they had no faith. But Smith was disgusted to find, that while he received a majority of 1,500 in his district, Allen county gave him but ten votes in all as a reward for his tiresome pilgrimage. John Test was elected again in 1829, and was succeeded in 1831 by Jonathan McCarty, who served in twenty-second, twenty third and twenty-fourth congresses. Andrew Kennedy, of Muncie, was first elected in 1841, and served three terms. In 1843 he was elected to represent the tenth district, composed of the counties of Adams, Allen, Blackford, DeKalb, Delaware, Grant, Huntington, Jay, La Grange, Noble, Randolph, Steuben, Tipton, Wells and Whitley. His opponent was Dr. Lewis G. Thompson, who received 739 votes in this county to 646 for Kennedy. The latter, however, had a majority in the district of 260. In 1853, the tenth district included the counties of Allen, DeKalb, Elkhart, Kosciusko, La Grange, Noble, Whitley and Steuben, forming the "Old Tenth" district, which during war times, contributed valiantly to the support of the government. Allen was afterward in the ninth district for a few years, but has for fifteen years been a part of the twelfth district, the counties joined with it being varied from time to time.

Below is gived the vote of the county in congressional elections for the leading candidates from 1845 to the present time. The first name given in each instance is the democratic candidate; the successful candidate is marked with a star, and the majority named is the majority of that candidate in the district, over the other candidate named:

1845, Lewis G. Thompson, 843; Andrew Kennedy,* 755; majority, 355. 1847, William Rockhill,* 866; Ewing, 878; majority, 176. 1849, Andrew I. Harlan, 964; David Kilgore,* 709; majority, 411. 1852, James W. Borden, 1,100; Samuel Brenton,* 1,112; majority, 377. 1854, E. N. Chamberlain, 1,907; Samuel Brenton,* 1,538; majority, 1,604. 1856, Robert Lowry, 3,006; Samuel Brenton,* 1,725; majority, 710. 1857, James L. Worden, 2,169; Charles Case,* 1,401. 1858, Reuben J. Dawson, 2,707; Charles Case,* 1,949; majority, 1363. 1860, P. N. Kenkle, 2,493; William Mitchell,* 2,445; majority, 2,889. 1862, J. K. Edgerton,* 3,825; William Mitchell, 1,813, majority, 436. 1864, J. K. Edgerton, 4,622; J. H. Defrees,* 2,223; majority, 580. 1866, Robert Lowry, 4,944; William Williams,* 2,823; majority, 1,272. 1868, Robert Lowry, 5,488; J. P. C. Shanks,* 2,834; majority, 941. 1870, John Colerick, 5,055; J. P. C. Shanks,* 2,835; majority, 394. 1872, John E. Neff,* 6,434; J. P. C. Shanks, 3,343; majority, 24. 1874, Allen

H. Hamilton,* 6,034; Robert S. Taylor, 3,735; majority, 1,695. 1876, Allen H. Hamilton,* 7,681; W. A. Bonham, 3,973; L. M. Minde, 675; plurality, 6,365. 1878, Walpole G. Colerick,* 6,676; John Studebaker, 2,838; majority, 6,355. 1880, Walpole G. Colerick,* 7,350; Robert S. Taylor, 5,104; majority, 770. 1882, Robert Lowry,* 6,274; W. C. Glasgow, 3,327; majority, 3,363. 1884, Robert Lowry,* 8,859; T. P. Keator, 4,960; majority, 2,550. 1886, Robert Lowry, 6,428; James B. White,* 6,126; majority, 2,484. 1888, C. A. O. McClellan,* 9,209; James B. White, 5,910; majority, 1,311.

Statistics of Population.—Trustworthy figures regarding the population at a very early date are very meagre. In 1830 there were 252 males of voting age in the county, and in 1830, the officers of the United States census enrolled 992 persons, all told. The totals of the subsequent enumerations are given below by townships:

TOWNSHIPS AND CORPORATIONS.	1840.	1850.	1860.	1870.	1880.
Wayne	*2,080	†998	*10,366	†1,742	†2,100
Fort Wayne		4,282		17,718	26,880
Washington	595	1,305	1,496	1,628	1,615
Aboit	235	539	876	906	918
Maumee	272	93	164	394	437
Madison	185	561	919	1,278	1,477
Milan	221	361	786	1,183	1,451
Jefferson	108	563	1,061	1,445	1,582
Eel River	317	655	1,002	1,217	1,287
Marion	465	1,095	1,358	1,319	1,375
Perry	283	842	1,180	1,280	1,254
Adams	260	1,012	1,773	*2,388	*2,558
New Haven, town				912	858
St. Joseph	227	748	1,065	1,373	1,521
Lake	254	578	951	1,309	1,338
Cedar Creek	189	814	1,228	1,713	1,584
Springfield	110	702	1,505	1,749	1,899
Monroe			414	610	*1,479	*1,612
Monroeville, town				630	578
Scipio		173	346	420	514
Pleasant		658	1,207	1,280	1,641
Lafayette		524	1,320	1,471	1,425
Jackson			93	202	295
Total	5,944	16,817	‡29,243	43,428	54,557

* Including town. † Excluding town. ‡ Including 22 Indians.

ORGANIZATION OF ALLEN COUNTY.

Allen County in War Times.—Though all scenes of warfare at or near the site of Fort Wanye ceased with the war of 1812, the people who settled this region and their descendants were to become familarized again with military affairs, witness the pomp of martial array and feel the bereavements with which war is inevitably associated. Less than thirty years after the soldiers had been withdrawn from the old fort, the declaration of war with Mexico occurred, and at the first call for troops, two full companies were organized at Fort Wayne, composed of citizens of Allen county. The companies started on the canal to the east, June 1, 1846, followed to the lower lock, five miles from town, by a long procession of parents and friends, and went by way of the Miami canal to Cincinnati, thence to New Albany. There they were mustered in June 20, 1846, as companies of the First Indiana Mexican volunteers, under Col. James P. Drake, and served on guard duty near the mouth of the Rio Grande, but though doing much tiresome marching in a mountainous country, saw no fighting. The commissioned officers of these companies were: Company F—Captain David W. Lewis; first lieutenant, Brad. B. Stevens, second lieutenants, Samuel H. Chapman and William Hunter. Company E, or "Mad Anthony Guards"—Captain John McLain; first lieutenant, Thomas Lewis; second lieutenants, Charles Colerick, George Humphrey. These companies returned home in 1847, and on second call, another company was recruited by Capt. Lewis, whose lieutenants were Thomas K. Lewis, John B. Sawtell and Ira G. Williamson. This became Company K, Fifth regiment, under Col. Lane, and was mustered out July 28, 1848, after doing guard duty on the frontier.

To fitly record the part which Allen county soldiery took in that great conflict which began in April, 1861, would require a volume of itself. A summary of the record has already been published, from the pen of the distinguished colonel of the Thirtieth regiment, J. B. Dodge. It must suffice in this connection to make such brief mention of the regiments and companies which were in large part enlisted in this county, as will serve to indicate how generous was Allen county in her response to the Nation's appeals for help in the hour of extremity. During the period when it was thought that three months' service would suffice to crush the rebellion, the Ninth Indiana regiment was organized, and it was one of the first in the field in West Virginia. To this regiment, which was commanded by Col., afterward Gen., Milroy, Allen county contributed Company K, under Capt. William P. Segur; lieutenants, Henry A. Whitman and William S. Story. The next call was for three years' service, and fifty men from this county at that time joined the Eleventh regiment, under Col. Lew Wallace, in Companies B, C, and E. The Twelfth regiment, which was organized for one year's service from May 11, 1861, was the second regiment to march through Baltimore, and served in Virginia until its time expired. Soon after reaching Virginia, William H. Link, of Fort Wayne, who had been lieutenant colonel, became colonel. The major was George Humphrey; adjutant, Oscar M. Hinkle;

sergeant-major, Ferd F. Boltz. Two companies were organized in this county, of which the commissioned officers were: Company F, Captain George Nelson; lieutenants, Oscar M. Hinkle, John M. Godown; Company G, Captain Arthur F. Reed; second lieutenant, Elbert D. Baldwin, The Twelfth was re-organized for three years' service, and musterec in August 17, 1862, with Col. Link commanding, and Jared B. Bond, adjutant. Of Company B, the captain was E. D. Baldwin, afterward major and lieutenant colonel, and his lieutenants, Frank H. Aveline and William H. Harrison, were subsequently promoted to the captaincy. George Nelson's company became Company K, with John M. Godown, first, and James O'Shaughnessy, second, lieutenant. The regiment was captured almost entirely at Richmond, Ky., and Col. Link killed, but being exchanged, it served during the remainder of the war in Gen. Logan's corps, taking part in twenty-eight severe battles. The Thirteenth regiment, which participated in much severe fighting in Verginia, throughout the war, first under Gen. Milroy, and then under Gen. Butler, was mustered in June 19, 1861, with eighty-two of its men from Allen county. The Fifteenth regiment mustered in June 14, 1861, served three years, and some of its men re-enlisted at the end of that time in the Seventeenth. It had severe service in the Tennessee campaigns, and lost 197 out of 440 men, at the battle of Stone River. Company C was enlisted in Allen county, under Captain John M. Comparet, promoted major and lieutenant-colonel; lieutenants, Oliver H. Ray, John F. McCarthy. Sergeant J. F. Monroe, subsequently became captain. In the Twenty-second regiment were thirty-nine men from this county, who served about one year, through the Atlanta campaign, and in the siege of Nashville, and in the Twenty-ninth there were thirty-three men, mostly recruits.

During this time Hugh B. Reed, under a commission from Gov. Oliver P. Morton, had been serving as post commandant at Fort Wayne, and aiding in raising and organizing the Twelfth regiment. He also aided in organizing the Thirtieth and Forty-fourth regiments, which with the Eighty-eighth, containing a large number of, and being officered principally by, Allen county men, are conspicuous in the military history of the county.

The Thirtieth contained three companies from the county and afterward received about 150 recruits. It was organized at Fort Wayne and went into camp at Camp Allen, on the "old fair-ground," on the St. Mary's, a short distance above where the canal aqueduct crossed that stream, August 20, 1861. It was mustered in September 24th, with Sion S. Bass, as colonel; Joseph B. Dodge, as lieutenant colonel, and Orrin D. Hurd, as major. Other regimental officers were: Adjutant, Edward P. Edsall; quartermaster, Peter P. Bailey; assistant surgeon, Samuel A. Freeman; sergeant major, Nellis Borden. At the organiza tion, Company A had for captain, George W. Fitzsimmons; lieutenants, Henry W. Lawton and Edwin R. Stribley. Lawton became captain, and John Stirling and Thomas J. Kennedy, lieutenants. Company D was organized with J. W. Whitaker, captain; Charles A. Zollinger and Douglas L. Phelps, lieutenants. Of Company E, Joseph M. Silver was the first captain, then Isaiah McElfatrick, promoted from lieutenant. The lieutenants doing service were: Joseph Price, Thomas Hogarth, Charles M. Jones. The regiment did heroic duty at Shiloh, where Col. Bass was killed, at Stone River, with Thomas at Chickamauga, and was actively engaged in the Atlanta campaign. The last of the Thirtieth in service was a residuary battalion, with the Thirty-sixth, which was mustered out in Texas. On the re-organization of the Thirtieth, Henry W. Lawton was colonel; Thomas H. Notestine, quartermaster. Company A was commanded by Dennis J. Kennedy and Company F by Thomas Hogart.

The Thirty-second regiment, or First German, contained a small number of Allen county men, among them John M. Josse, surgeon; John Orff, musician; members of the band, and members of Companies A and C. Allen county contributed some men also to the Thirty-third, Thirty-fourth, Thirty-fifth, Thirty-eighth, Fortieth and Forty-second regiments.

The Forty-fourth was the second regiment organized at Fort Wayne, and was mustered in November 22, 1861. It had on its rolls 260 men from this county. It did conspicuous service at Forts Henry and Donelson, Perryville, Stone River and Chickamauga, and remained at Chattanooga until September, 1865. It lost 350, killed and wounded. Its colonel was Hugh B. Reed at the organization; adjutant, Charles Case. At Fort Wayne were raised Companies C and D, of the First, of which Philip Grund was second lieutenant and afterward lieutenant-colonel of the regiment. Franklin D. Cosgrove was the first captain of the latter company, and lieutenant, Charles H. Wayne. David K. Stopher became a lieutenant and George Shell and George W. Squeirs became captains. The Seventy-fourth regiment was the next organized at Camp Allen, was mustered in August 21, 1862, and "marched to the sea." Company C was raised in the county, and of it, Carl C. Kingsbury, Joel F. Kinney and F. T. Beck, were successively captain, William H. Anderson, Ananias Davis, George A. Craw and Calvin Anderson, lieutenants. The Eighty-eighth regiment was organized at Fort Wayne, and mustered in August 29, 1862, with 344 men and officers from Allen county. It fought gallantly through the campaign of the army of the Cumberland and with Sherman through Georgia. At the organization, George Humphrey was colonel; Cyrus F. Briant, lieutenant-colonel, afterward colonel; adjutants, H. B. Dubarry and Allen H. Dougall. Charles S. True was captain of Company B. Company C, organized in the county, was first commanded by Nelson P. Guffy, afterward by Philip W. Silver. Company D, organized in the county, had for its first captain, Cyrus F. Briant, afterward Scott Swann; lieutenants, J. D. Stopher, Isaac Bateman, I. A. Slater and Milton Thompson. Company E, also organized in the county, was first officered by C. B. Oakley, captain; Richard Williams and John G. Goheen, lieutenants. Augustus Brown was afterward captain and Jerry Heffelfinger, lieutenant. Company F, also organized here, had for its first captain Isaac H. Lefevre, who was succeeded by Lieut. Ferd F. Boltz. The last regiment organized at Fort Wayne in 1862, was the One Hundredth, mustered in September 10th, under Col. Sanford J. Stoughton, containing a comparatively small number of Allen county men.

Other regiments organized early in the war, in which Allen county citizens were enrolled, were: Forty-seventh, under Col. J. R. Slack; the Fifty-fifth, three months' service, to which Allen county contributed Company E, under Capt. Charles Emery; the Fifty-ninth, which received recruits from the county; the Seventy-fifth, which contained forty-five men from Allen county, in Company H, commanded by William McGinnis; the Eighty-ninth, in which several citizens of this county enlisted; the Ninetieth or Fifth cavalry, which was engaged in the pursuit of Morgan, and contained one company from Allen county, under Capt. Harry A. Whitmam; the Ninety-first, which contained two companies of one-year men enlisted in Allen county in 1864, Company H, under Capt. Charles Emery, and Company K, under Capt. Joseph H. Keever. To each of various other early regiments, the county contributed one or more men. To the One Hundred and Twenty-fourth and One Hundred and Fifty-second regiments, organized in 1864, the companies that were raised for the Ninety-first were partly transferred, and there were also a considerable number of men raised in the county for the One Hundred and Twenty-sixth, One Hundred and Twenty-seventh and One Hundred and Twenty-eighth. The One Hundred and Twenty-ninth regiment, partially organized at Kendallville, contained 109 men from Allen county. The organization was completed at Michigan City, with Charles Case as colonel, and Charles A. Zollinger as lieutenant colonel. This regiment, and the One Hundred and Twenty-fourth fought together through the Atlanta campaign, at Franklin and Nashville, and in North Carolina. Company B contained most of the men from this county, and was first commanded by C. A. Zollinger, then by James Harper. The Thirteenth cavalry contained nine men from the county, and the One Hundred and Thirty-seventh and Thirty-ninth regiments, a larger number. The two last named were organized for one hundred days' service, and of the first of the two, Company E, under Captain James Sewell, had forty-five men from the county. The latter named one-hundred-day regiment was commanded by Col. John Humphrey, Adj. Chauncey B. Oakley, and Company H had eithty-five men from the county, G. W: Bell being first lieutenant. The One Hundred and Forty-second regiment was mustered in at Camp Allen, November 3, 1864, under Col. John M. Comparet, Lieut. Col. C. B. Oakley, and had about 350 men from the county. The regiment experienced war at the famous siege of Nashville. The Allen county men were mainly in Company C, under Capt. Christopher Hettler, Company E, under Capt. David Howell, and Company F, under Capt. Alonzo Bigelow, succeeded by Robert W. Swann. The One Hundred and Fifty-second regiment contained 200 men from Allen county, and was one of those organized in 1865, for garrison duty, Joseph W. Whitaker was lieutenant colonel, and Companies C, G and H contained the most of the county's citizens, the two latter being commanded respectively by William A. Kelsey and Marshall W. Wines. The One Hundred and Fifty-fifth, organized about the same time for the same duty, contained eighty men from the county, in Company D, under Capt. Joseph M. Silver.

The artillery branch of the service was contributed to by Allen county, and the batteries in which the patriotic sons of the county did service saw bloody work in all the great battles of the west. The Fifth, mustered in November 22, 1861, had on its muster rolls twenty-six men from Allen county, and served four years, at the end of that time fifteen men becoming veterans in the Seventh battery. The Eleventh was recruited almost entirely at Fort Wayne, and contained 222 men from the county. It was mustered in December 17, 1861, with Arnold Sutermeister as captain, and served three years, some of the men at the end of that time veteranizing in the Seventh and Eighteenth batteries. At Chickamauga the battery lost one-fourth its number. The Twenty-third battery, mustered in November 8, 1862, contained sixty-one men from this county, under Capt. James H. Myers. It served in the Atlanta campaign, at Nashville, and in North Carolina, principally.

The following sums were raised for bounty and relief in Allen county:

	Bounty.	Relief.
Wayne	$75,000	$17,550
Washington	6,750	1,875
Springfield	7,960	1,192
Perry	7,300	1,500
Madison	5,950	1,500
Monroe	5,000	1,250
Marion	7,500	1,500
Maumee	220	50
Milan	5,980	1,300
Lake	6,980	1,400
Jefferson	7,500	1,500
Eel River	8,000	1,800
Cedar Creek	10,000	1,500
Adams	10,500	2,000
Aboit	6,882	1,500
Pleasant	8,660	1,500
Scipio	1,400	160
Lafayette	5,000	1,450
Jackson	250	100
Fort Wayne	13,750	....
	$550,145	$73,853
Miscellaneous	2,000	
Total	....	$625,998.72

George W. Loag, D. D. S., clerk of the circuit court of Allen county and a representative and public-spirited citizen of Indiana, is a native of Philadelphia, Penn. His childhood from five to sixteen years of age, was spent upon a farm with his parents, and his education was received at Philadelphia and at Allen seminary, in Chester county. In October, he began the study of the profession to which he has largely devoted his life, dental surgery, at Philadelphia, in the office of McKowen and Haines, with whom he remained four years. Going then to eastern Maryland, he followed his profession there until the fall of 1862, when he located in Chicago. In the spring of 1863 he came to Fort Wayne, and here has since resided, practicing with marked success his profession. He is one of the oldest dentists in the city, and is widely known. He has always taken an active interest in politics, and devoted much of his time and means to the welfare of the democratic party, to which he belongs. In 1886 he was nominated by that party for clerk of the circuit court, and was elected by a majority of 1,611, to a term which expires November 16, 1890. He has proven to be an efficient officer, and his career in office has added to his notable popularity. In 1888 he was elected a member of the democratic state central committee for the twelfth district, and was a delegate to the state convention. Dr. Loag is a Mason of the thirty-second degree, a Knight Templar, and a member of the I. O. O. F. Since February, 1887, he has been one of the stockholders and directors of the Indianapolis *Sentinel*. He is a lover of thoroughbred animals, and has some fine horses and dogs. He was born October 6, 1839, the seventh of ten children, of William Ross and Eliza (Strong) Loag, natives of Pennsylvania. The father was born in 1802, and died in Philadelphia, March 16, 1883. The mother was born in 1804, and died April 23, 1884. Dr. Loag was married in 1868 to Anna R. Henderson, who was born in this city in 1843.

Daniel W. Souder, acting clerk of the superior court, is a native of Pennsylvania. His parents were natives of Perry county Penn., the father, George Souder, having been born in 1817, and the mother, Mary (Wentz) Souder, in 1818. The father was a farmer, and first followed that occupation in Perry county, where Daniel W., the oldest of his five children, was born June 14, 1848. In 1849 the family removed to Richland county, Ohio, where the father is still living, the mother having died at the Ohio home in 1886. Daniel W. Souder was raised on the farm, and after receiving a common school education applied himself to the carpenter's trade, which was his occupation in Ohio until 1872, when he came to Fort Wayne, and found employment in the car shops of the Pittsburgh, Fort Wayne & Chicago company. He remained there until 1874, and was then for a year in the employment of the Fort Wayne organ factory. Resuming his place in the car shops he worked there until 1876, then going upon the road as brakeman, which occupation was terminated October 10th, by an accident which caused the loss of both his feet. Two years later he entered the auditor's office, served there until April, 1879, was then clerk of the criminal court until its abolition in 1884, and since then he has held the office of acting clerk of the superior court. Mr. Souder is a democrat in politics, and in 1886 was a candidate for clerk of the circuit court. He is a deserving and popular citizen, and is highly respected. He was married in October, 1870, to Hannah C. Fireoved, who was born in Richland county, Ohio, March 6, 1849, and they have four children: Willis H., Mary E., Estella C., and Anna A. He and wife are prominent members of the Reform church. He was made a Mason in 1873, and for ten years has been secretary of Summit City lodge, No. 170.

John B. Niezer, county auditor, and one of the leading citizens of Allen county, is a native of Milan township. His parents, Bernard H. and Christina Niezer, are natives of Germany, the father born in 1809, and the mother in 1816. In 1843 they emigrated and settled in Allen county, where the father was engaged in farming until his death in 1854. John B., the fourth of seven children, was born July 21, 1846. All of the children are living except Henry, who died at Louisville, Ky., while in the service of the Union, in 1863. At seven years of age John B. Niezer came to Fort Wayne with his parents, and here received his education. At fourteen years of age he began an apprenticeship as a tinner, and worked at that trade seven years, leaving it in 1865, to go to Monroeville, to establish a hardware store, a business in which he has ever since been engaged, with considerable success. His political and official career has been a prominent and honorable one. He was first called upon to serve the community as trustee of Monroeville, a position he held for three years. In 1880 he was elected trustee of Monroe township, and re-elected in 1882, and for seven years he served as treasurer of the Monroeville school board. All these official positions were in some degree a preparation for the important office he now fills so satisfactorily. For this he was nominated by the democratic party in September, 1886, from six candidates, and was elected by a majority of 1,620. Mr. Niezer was married in 1869, to Sarah T. Eyanson, who was born in Philadelphia in 1846, and they have six children: John T., Maurice L., Charles L., Louisa H., George B. and Marguerite C.

Isaac Mowrer, treasurer of Allen county, was born in Wayne county, Ohio, May 16, 1840. His father, John Mowrer, was born in Chester county, Penn., in 1810, and now resides in Wayne county, whither he emigrated with his father in 1830, and became one of the early settlers. The grandfather died in 1864 at the age of seventy-one years. John Mowrer married Sevilla Steel, who was born in Berks county, Penn., in 1812, and came to Wayne county in 1816, and they had eleven children, nine of whom are living, Isaac being the third born. His early life was passed on the Wayne county farm, in Ohio, where he received a common school education. Starting out for himself in 1863, he engaged in farming in his native county until 1869, when he came to Allen county, and settled on the southeast quarter of section fourteen in St. Joseph township. Of this 160 acres only twenty were then cleared, and his first years in this county were spent in making a farm out of this wood-land. He now has a valuable farm of 180 acres, well improved. Taking a leading part in politics, he received in 1886, the democratic nomination for treasurer, and was elected by a majority of 1,191, and in 1888 was re-elected by a majority of 3,990 votes. He is one of the popular men of the county, and has made one of Allen county's best treasurers. Mr. Mowrer was married September 30, 1862, to Elizabeth Lightfoot, who was born in Wayne county, Ohio, in 1842, and they have had three children, two of whom are living: John W., who now resides in Burt county, Neb., and Mary V. He and wife are members of the Methodist church, and he is affiliated with the Masons, the I. O. O. F. and K. of P.

George H. Viberg, sheriff of Allen county, was born in Huntington county, Ind., July 8, 1848. He is the son of Conrad H. Viberg, a pioneer of Ohio and Indiana. The latter was born near Hanover, Germany, March 6, 1809, son of Conrad and Caroline Viberg, and came to this country in 1834. He settled in Fairfield county, Ohio, and there was married to Angeline Abright, March 6, 1835. She was also a German by birth who had emigrated in 1834. Five years later they removed to Williams county, Ohio, and began to clear a farm of eighty acres, but sought employment on the Wabash & Erie canal, and became a foreman under Col. Lemuel Jones. After the completion of the canal, he removed to Huntington county, Ind., and purchased the "Roanoke farm" of Col. Jones. Subsequently, he removed to Cedar Creek township, Allen county, where she died. He and wife had nine children: Lucinda, Harmon B., Sophia, Mary, Russellas L., Eliza, Lemuel A., George H. and Sarah J. Mr. and Mrs. Viberg were both prominent members of the Lutheran church, and he is a democrat in politics. Their son, George H., was raised on the farm and received a common school education. His residence in Allen county began with the removal of his parents here in April, 1855. He then was engaged in farming in Cedar Creek township until he was appointed sheriff of Allen county in 1887, to fill a vacancy. In November, 1888, he was elected to the same office by the decisive majority of 4,286. He has demonstrated his capability for the office and fidelity to the public trust. Sheriff Viberg was married in 1871, to Mary Shambaugh, a native of Ohio, and they have two children, Russellas and Daisy C. Mr. Viberg is a prominent worker in the democratic party, and is a member of the Masonic order and Knights of Pythias.

John M. Taylor, ex-treasurer of Allen county, was born near Cleveland, in the Western Reserve, in 1831. His father, Abraham Taylor, of English descent, married Roxy Ann Lane, of Scotch-Irish descent, and they moved with their families to Indiana in 1836, and settled in Eel River township, where Mr. Taylor now lives. Here he grew to manhood and received a good common school education for those days, and being of studious and reflective habits of mind, became in later life well informed, and the general adviser of the township in legal and other subjects. After he had become sufficiently educated, he began teaching in 1849, and until 1868 taught almost every winter. In 1854 he was married to Mary J. Bennett, and they had three children: Judson M., George A. and Carrie A. Mrs. Taylor was a consistent and devoted member of the Missionary Baptist church. Mr. Taylor served as clerk of the board of trustees of his township a number of years, and then as sole trustee about twelve years continuously. In 1878 his eminent qualifications were recognized by election as treasurer of Allen county. He was re-elected in 1880, serving with credit in this capacity four years. He is a member of the Masonic order. Mr. Taylor is one of the notable self-made men of our times, a worthy product of the era of industry and privation in which his family was prominent. The lessons then learned have made him a very successful man. He is now engaged in agriculture, being an extensive land owner in Eel River township, holding 560 fertile and valuable acres, and his farm is thoroughly improved.

Charles A. Munson, former sheriff of Allen county, was born in Fort Wayne, March 27, 1843. His father, James P. Munson, was born in Wolcottville, Conn., March 11, 1816, and in 1840 came to Fort Wayne and engaged in tne mercantile business, in which he continued until 1848, when, his health failing him, he went east, and soon afterward died, in Bristol, Conn. His wife was born in the county of Tyrone, Ireland, July 1, 1813. When six years of age she came to America with her parents, and for many years resided in western New York, afterward removing to Hamilton, Ohio. At this place, in 1830, she was married to J. P. Munson. After the death of Mr. Munson, in 1849, she was married to Henry Cooper, of Fort Wayne by whom she had one child, William P. Cooper. Henry Cooper died March 26, 1853. Mr. Munson's mother was again left with her little family to be supported by her needle. Young Munson's opportunities for obtaining an education were limited, as necessity made busy his youthful years. For a short time he was employed as a messenger in the telegraph office, afterward as a clerk in Hamilton's boot and shoe store, and at Kurtz's and Heller's grocery and provision stores. During two or three winters, failing to find other employment, he sawed and split wood for the merchants and other citizens of Fort Wayne. His industry attracted the attention of George L. Little, of the commission firm of Little & McCulloch, and by them he was engaged to purchase grain, pork, etc. Desirous of taking part in the war, he relinquished his position, and August 13, 1862, enlisted in the United States navy, under Capt. Robert Getty, at Cincinnati, Ohio. He was soon passed from the grade of a "landsman" to that of an "able-bodied" seaman. In December, 1862, he was ordered to the iron clad "Chillicothe," then defending Louisville, Ky., from an expected attack of the rebel Gen. Bragg. Shortly afterward, his vessel was ordered to Vicksburg, and here for a time he served on the United States steamer "Red Rover." He passed rapidly through the petty grades, and after a thorough examination by Capt. K. Randolph Breeze, upon the recommendation of Capt. St. Clair, of the "Chillicothe," and Capt. Wells, of the "Red Rover," he was on his twentieth birthday commissioned master mate, and made third officer in command of his vessel. After the fall of Vicksburg, and the opening of the Mississippi river, Munson gave up his commission and returned home. In the latter part of 1863, he went to Stevenson, Ala., and was employed by Capt. P. P. Baily and Nellis Borden, sutlers in the army of the Cumberland. Returning to Fort Wayne, after the close of the war, he engaged in the retail grocery business until 1868, at which time he was employed by Huestis & Hamilton, wholesale grocers, as a "commercial tourist." He was engaged in this capacity for eight years. At the expiration of four years, he was admitted as a partner into the firm. His yearly sales exceeded $200,000, which were confined to a portion of the states of Ohio, Indiana and Illinois. In 1875 he was elected alderman on the democratic ticket; was chairman of the committee on finance and public printing. At the democratic convention in June, 1876, he obtained the nomination for sheriff, on the ninth ballot, over eight opponents. He was elected and in 1878 he was again elected by a majority of 4,370 over his highest competitor; this was 593 votes over the state ticket, and the largest majority ever given a sheriff in Indiana. In 1886 Mr. Munson was honored by the democratic nomination for auditor of the state of Indiana, but with the rest of the ticket suffered defeat by a small majority. In 1888 he was renominated, but his zealous work for the success of his party again proved unavailing. These nominations, however, attested his remarkable popularity throughout the state. Mr. Munson is of a genial nature, frank and outspoken. As sheriff he was indefatigable, courageous and discreet. He is a member of the Masonic fraternity, Odd Fellows and encampment. Mr. Munson is now a member of the firm of Lillie & Munson, manufacturers of Huntington white lime.

Franklin D. Cosgrove, jr., is a native of the Upper Maumee valley, born at Maysville, Allen county, Ind., November 23, 1851. In early manhood he took a position in the drug store of his father, Dr. Franklin K. Cosgrove, a veteran physician at Maysville. He also assisted his father in the duties of postmaster. September 16, 1873, he was married at Niles, Mich., to Ella V. A., daughter of Delos and Eliza W. Cox. She was born in Berrien county, Mich., April 19, 1852. Mr. Cosgrove was appointed deputy sheriff of Allen county, by Sheriff J. D. Hance, in November, 1874, and in the following February he removed from Maysville to Fort Wayne. He served under Sheriff Hance until the death of the latter in May, 1875, then under his successor, P. J. Wise, nine months, and under Sheriff Charles A. Munson, four years. At the expiration of the term of the latter, Mr. Cosgrove succeeded to the office, having been elected in 1880, at the age of twenty-eight years, by a majority of nearly 2,000. He served one term very acceptably, and then, in August, 1882, engaged in the livery business, in which he remained until October, 1888, when he became one of the proprietors of the pump and wind-mill establishment on Harrison street. Mr. Cosgrove has had four children: Edna, Franklin D., DeWitt W. and Anna,

Milton M. Thompson

the first of whom died in infancy. He is a Mason of the thirty-second degree, a member of the I. O. O. F. lodge and encampment, and of the K. of P.

Milton M. Thompson, recorder of Allen county, comes of a family that were pioneers of Portage county, Ohio. There his father, Milo Thompson, was born February 4, 1818, and died January 9, 1872, and his mother, whose maiden name was Esther F. McKelvey, was born in the same county in 1820, and died in 1854. Milton M., the second of their six children, was born December 28, 1840. He was raised on the farm, and attended the country schools there until 1852, when he came to Allen county. Before he reached his majority the rebellion caused the call to arms by President Lincoln, and one of the first to respond was Mr. Thompson, who enlisted April 12, 1861, in Company F, Twelfth Indiana volunteers. He served in this regiment one year, and August 6, 1862, re-enlisted in Company D, of the Eighty-eighth regiment, in which he served until the close of the war, being mustered out October 17, 1865, as first sergeant. He fought gallantly with his regiment, and at the battle of Bentonville, N. C., after the rebellion was nearly crushed out, lost a leg, seriously crippling him for life. On his return to Allen county, he engaged in the tin and hardware business at New Haven, and on February 1, 1867, was appointed postmaster at that place, a position he held for nine years. In 1877 he resumed his early occupation of farming and continued at that until 1888. In politics he is a democrat, and in 1886 he was elected county recorder on the ticket of that party. This office he has filled with ability, and his unfailing courtesy has made him many friends. In the spring of 1888 he removed to Fort Wayne. He is a member of the I. O. O. F. and of the G. A. R. He was married June 7, 1874, to Lucy M. Bacon, who was born in this county in 1850.

George F. Felts, the efficient superintendent of schools of Allen county, has devoted his life to the work of edudation, and has attained a familiarity with the best methods, which united with his natural energy, integrity and faithfulness to public trust, render him without a superior in the office he now fills. He was born at College Corner, Wells county, Ind., March 20, 1857. His father, Edmund W. Felts, was born in Rush county, Ind., in 1829, was by occupation a farmer, and married Lydia Harman, who was born in Tuscarawas county, Ohio, in 1834. They settled in this county in 1860, where the father died in 1861, and the mother survives. George F. is the second of four children. He was raised on the farm, and studied in the country schools until the college session of 1879–80, which he spent in Purdue university. Designing to prepare himself for teaching, he attended during the next three years, the Michigan state normal school at Ypsilanti, at which he was graduated in 1883. He taught school in Allen county for five years, and became so well known as a teacher of more than usual ability that he was in June, 1885, elected superintendent. He rendered faithful service and was re-elected in 1887, without opposition and again elected in 1889. Superintendent Felts was married July 7, 1886, to Aristine Noyes, born in Plymouth, Mich., in 1854, who graduated from the Michigan state normal school in 1883, and for two years taught Latin and history in Fort Wayne college. In politics Mr. Felts is a democrat, and he is a member of the Summit City lodge, F. & A. M.

Hon. William H. Shambaugh was born in this county, December 24, 1858, son of Daniel and Sarah E. (Yeiser) Shambaugh, natives of Pennsylvania. His father was born in 1816, and his mother in 1830, and they are now residents of this county, whither they came about 1854, from Ohio, to which state they had emigrated from Pennsylvania. Of their five children Mr. Shambaugh is the youngest. He spent his boyhood on the farm, and gained his early education in the conntry schools. In 1877 he entered the Lebanon (Ohio) normal school, in which he was graduated in 1879. In the fall of the same year he took charge of the Fremont, Ind., School, and taught three years at that place. Coming to Fort Wayne in the fall of 1882, he read law in the office of S. R. Alden, and was admitted to the bar of Allen county in the following year. Since 1885 he has been carrying on the practice of law successfully and has achieved a creditable rank in a bar that is distinguished for able and experienced attorneys. Mr. Shambaugh is an earnest democrat, and he was the nominee of his party in 1886 for representative in the general assembly. He was elected by a majority of 1,900, and in 1888 was re-elected by a majority of 4,233, and during the latter session was prominent among the leaders of his party in the house. He is a member of the I. O. O. F., a Mason, of the rank of Knight Templar and Scottish Rite of the class of 1889.

Henry E. Fischer, surveyor of Allen county, in his youth received a common school education, and at thirteen years of age he entered the office of the Indiana *Staats Zeitung* to learn the printer's trade. In 1869 he took up civil engineering, and in the year 1880 he returned from Colorado to Fort Wayne, and for four years was engaged as city editor of the Indiana *Staats Zeitung*, and then became manager of that journal, holding the position when elected to his present office in 1888. He is a democrat. Mr. Fischer was born at Ofenstadt, Prussia, March 5, 1848. His parents emigrated in 1853, and settled at Fort Wayne, where they died soon after.

The work in the office of the clerk of the circuit court in a county like Allen, is of great importance, and the successful performance of even a single department of its multifarious duties, requires a high degree of ability and special training. Under these circumstances no higher compliment can be paid Jacob J. Kern, who has for over ten years officiated as deputy clerk, than to record that he has efficiently met all the demands of his position. Mr. Kern was born in Union county, Ohio, May 15, 1851. His father, Casper Kern, was a native of Bavaria, born in Neubreitenstein, September 24, 1821, and came to this country in boyhood with his parents, and settled in Union county, Ohio. He was married to Elizabeth Spindler, who was born at Bethlehem, Penn., May

20, 1826, and in the fall of 1857, they removed to Allen county. He died here April 15, 1885, but his widow survives, living on the old homestead. Seven of their children are living, of whom Mr. Kern is the oldest. He was reared on the farm, studied in the common schools and two years in Concordia college, and in 1869, made his home in the city, engaging in the drug business with Meyer Bros., with whom he remained six years. In the fall of 1878 he was appointed deputy clerk. He is an earnest democrat. Mr. Kern was married May 20, 1874 to Charlotte Paul, a native of Fort Wayne, and they have three children: William C., John H., and Ida. He and wife are members of the Lutheran church.

Hon. Nelson W. McLain, one of the prominent men in the history of Allen county, was born in Muskingum county, Ohio, March 10, 1810, and removed to this county in 1836. He assisted in organizing Marion township, and was one of the election board at the first election held in that township. His occupation for several years was surveying. During seven years he was postmaster at Middletown. In 1840 he was elected justice of the peace, and in 1845 was appointed county commissioner. His ability and integrity was further recognized, subsequently, when upon the death of Hon. George Johnson, he was appointed by Governor Whitcomb, probate judge, to which office he was elected in 1850. In 1855 he was appointed swamp land commissioner, and in 1858 was elected a representative of Allen county, in the state house of representatives. His son, Charles J. W. McLain, deputy county auditor, was born October 17, 1855, in Marion township, of this county, where he resided until 1873. He then removed to Wabash, and learned photography, in which business he continued until March, 1879, when he came to Fort Wayne, and accepted his present position. He also has served as clerk of the board of turnpike directors since February, 1884. Mr. McLain is a prominent promoter of out-door sports, and was projector and assisted in organizing the Fort Wayne bicycle club, a flourishing organization of about seventy-five members, of which he has served as secretary and captain and is now president. He is also captain of the Fort Wayne canoe club. In his acquirements as bookkeeper, accountant and designer, he has few equals; socially he occupies a high rank, and as an officer is one of the best the county has had. Mr. McLain was married December 24, 1879, to Dora E. Bruner, daughter of Jacob R. Bruner, of Wabash, and they have two children: Marie L. and Nelson B.

That part of the duties of the county administration assigned to the offices of the auditor and treasurer, require in a considerable degree the services of a skillful accountant, and by reason of his acquirements in this direction Lewis C. Hunter has given valuable service both as deputy auditor, which position he held two years, beginning in 1883, and as deputy treasurer, at which he has acted since 1885. Mr. Hunter received a common school education in his native township of Perry, and for eleven years succeeding his twenty-first year he served the Grand

Rapids & Indiana railroad company as telegraph operator and station agent. He is the inventor of Hunter's improved farm gate, a valuable contrivance, which was patented May 18, 1886, and a second patent granted him on an improvement October 23, 1888. October 11, 1883, he was married to Cora M. Andrews, who was born in this county in 1863, and they have two children: Stella May and William T. Mr. Hunter is an influential democrat. He is the son of William T. Hunter, a prominent early settler, who was born in Cumberland, England, April 9, 1802. Immigrating, he landed at Boston, August 12, 1828. Four years later he returned to England from New York, but returned in 1833, with a party of countrymen. The next year he removed to Ann Arbor, Mich., and two years later married Mrs. Jane Buckingham, and moved to St. Joseph county, Mich. In 1837 he came to Perry township, then mainly in woods, and began clearing a farm. Shortly afterward he established a hotel, and was successful. At the time of the bands of horse thieves and counterfeiters, he did valuable service as a member of the regulators. Three years, beginning in 1852, he spent in California, engaged in mining and other pursuits. He was an enterprising and honorable citizen, and will always be remembered in the history of the county. He died in January, 1887. His wife was the daughter of Robert and Margaret Ranney, of Sheffield, Mass., and was born November 24, 1815. She was married in Monroe county, N. Y., in 1833, to John Buckingham, who died in 1835. She passed away November, 1886. There were seven children born to William T. Hunter and wife, of whom six are living, Lewis C. being the youngest.

Henry F. Bullerman who was elected county commissioner for the second district, in 1888, is a prominent member of the democratic party, and also well-known throughout the county as a leading and intelligent citizen. He was born March 26, 1850, at Fort Wayne, son of Frederick and Maria Bullerman, who came to this county from Germany. He received a good education in the Lutheran schools and attended Concordia college one year. In 1877, in company with his brother, he made a trip to the gold fields of California, and beginning there as a laborer in the mines his diligence and intelligent industry in two years won for him the position of superintendent of the Quaker Hill mines. After holding this position about a year and a half, he had the misfortune of losing his right arm in the machinery. He then resigned his position, and returning to Indiana, settled in St. Joseph township, which has since been his home. Soon attaining prominence, he was elected road superintendent of the township in 1882. In 1884 he was elected trustee of St. Joseph, and during his efficient service for two terms, he gained a familiarity with the details of the business which is of great value to him in his present position. In the democratic county convention of 1888 he was nominated for commissioner on the first ballot over three worthy competitors, and his election followed by 3,611 majority. His service in this position has been faithful and commendable.

One of the leading men of the county, and one who has received a substantial expression of the public esteem by election to the office of county commissioner, is John H. Brannan. He was elected on the ticket of the democratic party to which he has long adhered, in 1884, and chosen again in 1888. He has honorably filled an office which peculiarly demands painstaking, prudence and integrity in its occupants. Mr. Brannan was born in Lake township, Allen county, November 19, 1840, son of Thomas and Julia (Brown) Brannan, who were born in Ireland, the father in 1803, and the mother in 1814. The latter came to this country with her parents in 1835, and in 1837 settled in this county. She is still living in the city, but the father died in 1855, October 5. Of their eight children, seven are living, John H. being the second born. He received a common school education, and in 1860 came to the city, and for five years was employed in the Pittsburgh, Fort Wayne & Chicago railroad shops. In 1865 and 1866 he was upon the police force of the city, and then removed to Columbia City, and for eight years was engaged in the grocery business at that city. He returned to this city in 1875 and carried on the same business until July, 1887. While a resident of Columbia City he was a member of the council of that city. He was married in 1864 to Bridget Stanton, who was born in 1840, in Illinois. They are members of the Catholic church.

Henry Hartmann, a leading citizen of Adams township, and a member of the board of county commissioners, was born in Hanover, Germany, June 13, 1829, son of John F. W. and Wilhelmina (Harmening) Hartmann. He was reared to youth in his native country, and attended school between the ages of six and fourteen, and afterward worked on a farm. At seventeen years of age he accompanied his father and mother to America. They started on the 12th of May and landed at Quebec. They settled in Fairfield county, Ohio, where the mother died in 1855. He remained there until 1857, when he came to Adams township, and he has occupied the same farm ever since. His father came to Allen county in 1861, and settled in Wayne township. Some three or four years later he returned to Fairfield county on a visit, and while there he died. The sole occupation of Mr. Hartmann has been farming, and in this he has been successful. He was was married October 24, 1854, to Anna Catharine Hermann, a native of Germany, the daughter of George Adolph Hermann. She came to America with her parents about 1851. Mr. and Mrs. Hartmann have had five sons and four daughters: William, John, Catharine, Wilhelmina, Dorothea, Pauline, Henry, August and Adolph, all of whom are living except Catharine who died in her twentieth year. Parents and children are members of the German Lutheran church. In politics Mr. Hartmann is a democrat of much prominence. He has served six years as assessor of Adams township, and he is now serving his second term as county commissioner, having been elected in the fall of 1882, and re-elected in the fall of 1886. He is one of the substantial farmers of the county and a worthy man in whom the public have full confidence, and has proved to be an excellent commissioner. He owns 160 acres of land in

Adams township, besides 120 acres which he has given to his two sons, William and John.

David N. Gibson, a well known citizen of the county, now serving as trustee of Marion township, an office to which he was elected in the spring of 1888, was born March 12, 1839, in Lycoming county, Penn. His father, David Gibson, was a native of Pennsylvania, born January 4, 1811, and was married in that state to Mary Reichard, who was born in Maryland, February 21, 1811, but was raised in the Keystone state. These parents had eleven children. In 1864, they removed to Marion township and here they died, the father, March 21, 1885, and the mother May 26, 1880. David Gibson is one of the five children surviving. He was raised and educated in Pennsylvania, and in 1863, removed to Marion township, where he worked upon a farm five years, and then bought a tract of seventy acres, which he has since cultivated, and upon which he has a comfortable home. He was married February 14, 1865, to Lucy Farrell, daughter of Edward and Margaret (Denny) Farrell, natives of Pennsylvania, who settled in this county in 1849. Mrs. Gibson was born in Ohio. To this union four children have been born, Agnes, Edward and Henry and Helena, twins. Mr. Gibson is in politics, democratic, and he is a member of the St. Joseph's Catholic church at Hesse Cassel. He is, as his official position indicates, prominent as a citizen, and he and his family are highly esteemed by all.

Hon. Samuel Brenton, notable both in the ministry of the Methodist church and in the political agitation against slavery, was born November 22, 1810, in Gallatin county, Ky., son of Robert and Sarah Brenton. He entered the ministry of the Methodist church in 1830, and was connected with it throughout his life, though at various intervals he was otherwise engaged. In 1834, while at Danville, for the sake of his health he took up the study of law, and was engaged in a successful practice for six years. In 1841, returning to the ministry, he was stationed at Crawfordsville, Perryville, Lafayette, and finally at Fort Wayne, where he labored until he lost the use of the right half of his body from paralysis. His political career was brilliant and useful. He served in the Indiana legislature in 1839 and 1841 as representative from Hendricks county. In 1850 he was nominated for congress by the whigs, and though the race was considered hopeless, went into the canvass with such vigor that he was triumphantly elected to represent the district including Fort Wayne, and was re-elected in 1854 and 1856. The convention at which he was nominated for congress in 1854 was held at Albion, Ind., and was attended by four delegates from Allen county, Mr. Brenton, John W. Dawson, O. V. Lemon and John H. Rerick. He assisted in the organization of the republican party, but the arduous labors of his campaigns and his public duties deprived him of the enjoyment of that party's triumphs. He died before the expiration of his last term in congress, at his home in Fory Wayne, March 29, 1857.

Hon. William Rockhill, one of the early representatives of the tenth district of Indiana, in the congress of the United States, was prominent among the people of Fort Wayne, from the time of the opening of land to settlement until the era of civil war. He was born at Burlington, N. J., February 10, 1793, the son of Joseph R. and Mary (Richardson) Rockhill. Those parents were residents of Fort Wayne in their later years, and died here, the father in August, 1830, at the age of sixty-five years, the mother in June, 1838, at the age of seventy. Coming to Fort Wayne in 1823, William Rockhill purchased by entry from the government a large tract of land, the eastern limit of which is now known as Broadway. This land, which he partly cleared and cultivated in his day, has been added to the city at successive periods, and now the Rockhill additions are a considerable part of Fort Wayne, and present a scene wonderfully different from that which met the eye of their first owner. Mr. Rockhill was a leading citizen from the beginning of his residence, took an active part in politics, and was honored by the people with various important trusts. He was a member of the first board of county commissioners, with James Wyman and Francis Comparet, in 1824, and when the functions of that body were transferred to the board of justices of the county, he was one of three who composed that tribunal. In 1832 he was elected as representative of Allen and Huntington counties in the state legislature, and re-elected in 1834. He took an interest in educational matters, and was among the foremost in establishing the foundation for the school system of Fort Wayne, as a private citizen and member of the school board. He also rendered efficient aid in the organization and building of the Fort Wayne college, an institution by which his memory is cherished. When the city organization was made, Mr. Rockhill was elected as one of the first aldermen, serving with Thomas Hamilton, Madison Sweetzer, Samuel Edsall, W. S. Edsall and W. M. Moon. In 1843 he was elected assessor of the city, and he was appointed to take the census of the city at a time when the total population was about 1,000. In 1844 Mr. Rockhill was elected to the state senate, and in 1846 was elected as representative to congress, in which he served one term with ability and honor to himself and his district. Mr. Rockhill was a man of integrity and notable strength of character. In his relations to the community he was enterprising and active for the public good, and aided greatly in the founding of the now prosperous city. In 1838 he began the erection of the Rockhill House, a considerable enterprise for that day, the interior of which was not finished until 1853. The hotel was opened to guests in 1854, and was a popular resort until 1867. At this hotel on July 4, 1860, a meeting of old settlers was held, which was generally attended by those notable in the settlement and founding of the city, and over which Mr. Rockhill presided as chairman. The hotel was closed in 1867, and the building is now known as St. Joseph's hospital. Mr. Rockhill passed away full of years and honors, January 15, 1865. Several of his children are now numbered among the most highly respected people of the city, in the early days of which this worthy pioneer had so conspicuous a part.

Three daughters of his first wife, Theodosia, who died August 16, 1833, aged thirty-six years, are living: Mrs. I. D. G. Nelson, Mrs. Rebecca Rumsey, now residing at Santa Fe, New Mexico, and Mary, wife of Nelson Wheeler, of this city. Five children by a subsequent marriage to Elizabeth Hill, who died May 9, 1859, in her thirty-ninth year, are living: William W., proprietor of the *Journal;* Ann Maria, wife of E. L. Craw; Hugh McC., Jesse D. B., and Howell C.

Hon. Charles A. O. McClellan, representative in congress of the twelfth district of Indiana, composed of Allen, DeKalb, Noble, LaGrange, Steuben and Whitley counties, has been for many years a prominent citizen of Auburn, DeKalb county. He was born May 25, 1835, at Ashland, Ohio. His parents, William and Eliza (Wiggins) McClellan, were natives of New Jersey. His mother was of German descent, and his father of Scotch-Irish extraction. The father was a mechanic, and followed his trade during life, excepting the last ten years, during which time he was engaged in publishing county maps in Ohio and Indiana. In youth Judge McClellan enjoyed only such advantages of education as were furnished by the common schools of that day, and at the age of sixteen, entered the shop to learn the trade of his father. During the time of his apprenticeship, he became an expert penman by attending evening schools, and for two years, gave instruction in penmanship during the winter, and during the summer worked upon a farm. In 1856 he came to Indiana, arriving at Auburn the first day of April, where he had an uncle, who was then auditor of DeKalb county. He was at once appointed deputy auditor by his uncle, which position he held for four years; during this time he acquired a taste and felt an inclination for the profession of law, and during leisure hours and evenings, devoted his time to its study. He was married in the fall of 1859, to Elizabeth A., daughter of Samuel D. Long, one of the pioneers of DeKalb county. To this union three children have been born: Jennie L., now wife of Don A. Garwood, of Danville, Ill.; Della, now wife of Dr. E. L. Siver, of Fort Wayne, and Charles. In 1860 he was appointed United States deputy marshal to take the census of DeKalb county, which duty was performed to the satisfaction of the government. In the spring of 1861 he moved to Waterloo, and engaged in the real estate business, at the same time pursuing his law studies. He also published a map of DeKalb county, and made an abstract of the records of said county during that time. In 1862 he was admitted to the bar, and in 1863, entered into co-partnership with Judge James I. Best for the practice of law, and formed the firm of Best & McClellan, which became one of the most noted law firms of the state. For ability and conscientious fidelity as well as for successful effort and magnitude of business, they were excelled by few. In 1872 he was appointed judge of the fortieth judicial circuit of Indiana, and until the end of his term discharged the varied and important duties of that office, in such a manner as to win the respect and esteem of the bar, as well as the confidence and commendation of the public. Judge McClellan as a lawyer occupies a distinguished position, and in the trial of causes has been unusually successful. He has always been a leader in public improvements; was a stockholder and director of the Fort Wayne & Jackson railroad company, and in 1868, in company with James I. Best, built the star flouring mills of Waterloo, which were in operation but a short time when they were destroyed by fire, without insurance. In 1873 he established the DeKalb bank of Waterloo, which has always commanded the confidence of the people. In 1880, he moved his family to Ann Arbor, Mich., for the purpose of educating his children, and in 1885, moved from there to Auburn, and in the same year became a stockholder and president of the first national bank of Auburn, which position he holds at the present time. He has, however, never given his personal attention to the banking business, but has applied himself almost exclusively to his profession. He has been the builder of his own fortune, and his position is assured. Judge McClellan is orthodox in sentiment, but is a member of no church. He is in no way a professional politician, although a pronounced democrat and always ready and earnest in his support of his political convictions. On the 9th day of August, 1888, at Kandallville, Ind., he was nominated on the fourteenth ballot, by the democratic party, as its candidate for congress in the twelfth congressional district. Hon. R. C. Bell, P. S. O'Rourke, M. V. B. Spencer, of Allen county, C. K. Green, of Noble, and William F. McNagny, of Whitley, were candidates in the convention. Judge McClellan was sucessful at the election, by a plurality of 1,311 votes over Hon. J. B. White, the republican candidate. Judge McClellan is now in the prime of manhood, and well qualified to perform the duties of the office to which he has been elected.

Isaac DeGroff Nelson, a citizen of Fort Wayne, who has for many years rendered honorable and valuable service to the community, county and state, was born in Poughkeepsie, N. Y., July 2, 1810. His father, Leonard Nelson, was a farmer, the son of John Nelson, a revolutionary soldier who received 500 acres of land in Tompkins county, for his heroic services. Leonard Nelson was married to Mary, daughter of Moses DeGroff, one of a family conspicuous for hazardous duty along the Hudson during the revolution. The DeGroffs were on duty between Pougkeepsie and Tarrytown at the time of the capture of Major Andre. When the subject of this mention was sixteen years of age his father died, leaving him, the only son, to care for a feeble mother and three young sisters, one of whom was an invalid, by labor upon a farm that was considerably encumbered. At twenty years of age he started a country store with the aid of an uncle, and by this enterprise, in connection with farming, he supported the family until 1836, when he and his sisters moved to Fort Wayne. Two years later, August 23, 1838, he was married to Elizabeth, daughter of William Rockhill, a distinguished early settler of Fort Wayne. Mr. Nelson's father was a leader in political life and prominent in the democratic party, and the son, with similar inclinations, has in great part devoted his career to public affairs. He was elected a school commissioner at twenty-one years of age, and during his residence in the state of New York, held various other offices. At twenty-five years of age he represented his county as a delegate to a democratic state convention of 128 members, whose action led to the election of Martin VanBuren as president. At Fort Wayne, Mr. Nelson continued his public activity, and was elected as one of the committee on invitation and reception for the celebration of the opening of the Wabash & Erie canal, at which Gen. Cass declared that "our descendants will come to keep the day that we have come to mark." In June, 1840, he purchased the *Sentinel*, then a whig paper, and made it an influential democratic organ. In 1851 he was without opposition elected a member of the first general assembly under the new constitution, as representative of Allen county. This session lasted six months, and during it Mr. Nelson did valuable service, particularly in passing the measure known as the "Nelson railroad bill," a law under which with some slight changes, all the railroad companies of the state have been organized. Subsequently, he assisted, at Logansport, in June, 1852, in the organization of the Wabash railroad company, under the general law referred to. Mr. Nelson has held office under the national government as receiver of public moneys at Fort Wayne, beginning in 1843, and as paymaster of annuities to the Miamis, in which latter function he introduced the system of paying silver directly to the Indians. He was twice elected clerk of the Allen circuit court. In 1873 he was unanimously nominated by a convention of both parties for state senator, an honor which he, however, declined. Of Purdue university he was one of the first trustees by appointment of Gov. Baker. In 1877 he was appointed by Gov. Williams one of the new state house commissioners, a trust which he worthily discharged. Mr. Nelson's home life also has been active in various channels. He has given much time to agriculture, stock-raising, horticulture and landscape gardening, having a very attractive rural home, Elm Park, four miles east of the city. In the scientific advancement of these departments of industry he was a pioneer and has continued to be an investigator and writer. He was one of the first twelve incorporators of Lindenwood cemetery, one of the finest and most noted in the country, and was the first and is the present president of the association. Mr. Nelson has been a member of Trinity Episcopal church for many years.

THE CATHOLIC CHURCH IN ALLEN COUNTY.

By Rev. JOHN F. LANG,
Chancellor of the Diocese of Fort Wayne.

The history of the Catholic church in Allen county is probably best recorded by tracing it from its earliest known sources here, as a unit, so to speak, until about the year 1848, when language and numbers became factors in the formation of additional congregations. Until the year just named, the sketch herewith presented runs along in one general statement, but after the year 1848, the subject assumes greater proportions and is consequently best treated by tracing the organization and continuance of each church or congregatian in the county, from the date of its origin to the present time.

The first evidences of Catholicity in Allen county seem to be the visit of the Jesuit missionary, Father Allouez, between the years 1665 and 1675. Statistics show that this pioneer priest labored among the Pottawotomies and Miami Indians, among whom we find him as early as October, 1665. Reliable tradition also tells of a white man coming at a very early day to this vicinity as "a missionary of the gospel of peace and offering the sacrifice of mass somewhere near the site of the present St. Joseph hospital."

The early French explorers who came over the Maumee and down the Wabash to the Ohio and Mississippi, learned of this route from the French priests, who, no doubt had come hither from their mission on the St. Joseph river of Lake Michigan, and after visiting the Indians here returned to Montreal, going down the Maumee to the head of Lake Erie. Circumstances show pretty conclusively that there is a reasonable certainty of the visits of the early missionaries to this historic spot. As we come to years within our own cycle we find the venerable Very Rev. Stephen Theodore Badin, the first priest ordained in the United States, visiting the early settlers of Allen county. Father Badin was vicar general of the diocese of Bardstown (now Louisville), Ky., and of the diocese of Cincinnati, to which latter this part of the country at that time was accredited. His first visit to Fort Wayne was in 1831, on which occasion he offered mass in the residence of Francis Comparet.

The first baptism of which there is any record was administered by this zealous missionary. Translated from the French, the record reads as follows:

At Fort Wayne, Diocese of Bardstown, I the undersigned, Priest and Missionary Apostolic, baptized Peter David, born the 5th of October, 1830, of the civil marriage of Peter Gibaud and Mary Gibaud. The sponsors were John Baptist Becket and Theresa Duret his wife.

STEPH. THEOD. BADIN,
V. G. of Bardst. and Cinc.

The first marriage of record in our church annals is the following:

In the year 1831, the 13th February (the contracting parties hereinafter named, for several years residents of Fort Wayne, in Indiana, of the diocese of Bardstown, residing far distant from a priest, the nearest being 130 miles, were for this reason obliged to contract civil marriage before William Ewing, Judge-probate of the county of Allen), I the undersigned, priest, having come to preach a mission at Fort Wayne, above named, have given the nuptial benediction to James Aveline, the eldest son of Francis Aveline and Genevieve Cardinal, and to Catharine Comparet, eldest daughter of Michael Comparet and Agnes Jeanne, who have signed the present Register, together with John Baptist Godfroy, Francis Renaud, John B. Becquette and Peter Courveille, who have signed with us or affixed their mark.

JAMES AVELINE.
Her
CATHARINE × COMPARET.
mark.
STEPH. THEOD. BADIN,
Vic. Gen. of Bardst. and Cincinn.

JEAN B. GODFROY,
His
FRANCIS × RENO,
mark.
His
JNO. B. × BECQUETTE,
mark.
His
PIERRE × COURVEILLE,
mark.

} Witnesses.

In 1832 Rev. L. Picoh, of Knox county, came on a brief visit, and ministered to the Catholics here. After him again came Rev. S. T. Badin in December, 1832, January, 1833, in October, 1833, and in January, April, June and September, 1834. A study of the church records shows that on the 8th of June, 1834, and subsequently, Father Badin departed from his usual signature of S. T. Badin, Vicar General of Bardstown and Cincinnati, and wrote instead, S. T. Badin, Protopriest of Baltimore.

In May, 1835, S. P. Lalumiere served in Fort Wayne. In August of the same year the old church books show that Rev. Felix Matthew Ruff ministered for a short month, and after him came Rev. J. F. Tervooren. From January to August, 1836, we find the signature of Rev. Mr. Jeancoir, who was succeeded by the first resident pastor, Rev. Louis Mueller, who was here four years.

During the year 1835, a portion of the present cathedral square had been purchased. The partial payments made upon it had been gathered mostly from the canal diggers. Father Badin was instrumental in establishing the location. The property, it appears, was purchased in the name of Francis Comparet, and afterward by a universal demand of the members of the church, was deeded to a committee as follows: From Samuel Hanna and Eliza Hanna, to Francis Comparet, Francis D. Lasselle, John

B. Bruno, Charles Hillsworth and Michael Hedekin. This, as the records show, was June 7th, 1837, and was signed in presence of Thomas Johnson and J. B. Dubois. The property was afterward transferred to the ecclesiastical authorities in trust for the congregation.

The first house of worship, a frame building, known as St. Augustine's church, was constructed in 1837 upon the present cathedral block, and remained a long time without being plastered. It was poverty's offering of a weather-board shanty in keeping with the struggles of the early settlers. When preparations were made for the building of the present cathedral, the old frame church was moved to the east side of the square, facing Clinton street; but before many summers passed, the building was destroyed, as is supposed, by incendiarism.

The great bell, which hung in the building at the time of the fire, was ruined. It had been cast in 1814, and was presented to Father Benoit by friends in his native France, and shipped from that country. After the fire, portions of the metal were recast into two small bells, one of which is in daily service at the brothers' school and the other in St. Augustine's academy. Their silvery sounds ring out upon the air and call the urchins to books and desk these many, many years.

Almost the entire south half of the present cathedral square was used as a grave-yard. When the march of the future city began to encroach upon the cemetery, a great many of the remains were removed to sites more distant. When the new cathedral was begun, and later when excavations were made for library hall, wagon loads of bones were carted to grave-yards less disturbed by the stride of advancing life. It may interest some people to know that the remains of John B. Richardville, the whilom Canadian who became the famed Indian chief, were, however, not disinterred. They remained where they had been originally placed. The spot is just at the south edge of the cathedral, between the forward side door and the first buttress of the wall.

In 1840 Rev. Father Shaw visited Fort Wayne and delivered lectures, principally on the doctrine of the church. He was an eloquent preacher and quite a few conversions to the faith were the reward of his zeal.

Some among the first Catholic settlers were J. Peltier, J. B. Bourie, L. P. Ferry, J. Godfroi, J. B. Becquette, Minnius, J. Trentman, P. Wagner, M. Forbing, F. D. Lasselle, F. Comparet, M. Hedekin, J. Urbine, Cath. Duval, W. Reed, J. Donahue, M. Cody, T. Lyons, Fuchstetter, J. B. Richardville, J. and H. Stier, B. Philips, George Baker, Jorgs, P. Fox, Lannon, and Bonfield.

Ground was broken on the canal toward the east in March, 1832, and to the west in 1837. Among the men who labored on these public works, was a large proportion of Catholics, and the Rev. Fathers Lalumiere, Ruff, Mueller, and Benoit, spared no efforts in giving them religious services, even though obliged to follow them for miles as they extended their line of work. When sickness broke out in its dangerous phases among these people, especially in Father Benoit's time, there were many sacrifices and hardships endured by the faithful minister of the gospel.

Father Benoit's missionary field extended over several counties, east, west, south and north. His labors multiplied upon him and the bishop sent him as an assistant the Rev. J. B. Hamion, who died here in 1842. He was succeeded by F. J. Rudolph, who remained three years. Next came in succession Revs. Alph. Munschina, A. Carins, L. Baroux, E. Faller, and Rev. Doctor Madden.

In 1844 the sisters' school was built by Contractor John Burt, who in exchange received three acres of land north of Fort Wayne from Rev. S. T. Badin, and in 1845 Father Benoit brought three sisters of Providence to Fort Wayne from St. Mary's, Vigo county, who opened the first Catholic school. The sisters of this religious order still continue here in the same avocation, though where there were only three in 1845, there are now twenty-two engaged in the same work. Later on Father Benoit opened a separate school for boys, in a whilom carpenter shop, which was ere long supplanted by the present brick structure on Jefferson and Clinton streets. After several "lay teachers" had taught some years, the Brothers of the Holy Cross were placed over these boys' schools, and they still continue in this successful work.

In 1852 Father Benoit transferred in trust for the Catholics of Fort Wayne, the remaining half of the cathedral square to Rt. Rev. Bishop de St. Palais, of Vincennes, to which diocese Fort Wayne then belonged. It may be stated here that as a rule all church property belonging to Catholics, in most of the states, is held in the name of the bishop of the diocese for all the congregations. Every bishop is obliged, within three months after taking his oath of office, to make his will, and bequeath the church properties to his successor in office, in trust for the Catholic congregations, to whom the properties belong, and to name two executors of his will.

When Rev. J. Benoit went to New Orleans, Rev. A. Bessonies was appointed his successor in Fort Wayne. From January, 1853, till February, 1854, Father Bessonies labored perseveringly, both here and among the settlements surrounding Fort Wayne. At New Besancon he built a church, and started them at building one at Leo. In Fort Wayne he built a good brick pastoral residence, which stood on the corner of Lewis and Calhoun streets, until it gave way to library hall in 1880. Father Bessonies contributed $200 toward the cost of this residence. The building committee was M. Cody, John Burt and Henry Baker. John Brown, brother-in-law of Hon. J. B. White, was the contractor.

In 1857 the diocese of Vincennes, which comprised the entire state of Indiana, was divided, and the north half was organized into the diocese of Fort Wayne, which city became the Episcopal See. Of Rt. Rev. J. H. Luers, the first bishop of Fort Wayne, we speak in a special sketch.

After the organization of St. Mary's congregation in 1848, St. Augustine's church continues in its history until merged into that of the

Immaculate Conception, which is the name given to the new metropolitan church. In 1859 Bishop Luers and Father Benoit began the erection of the new

CATHEDRAL.

The building committee was Henry Baker, Michael Hedekin, Maurice Cody and Jacob Kintz. The cost of the building, without its furniture, exclusive of $9,000 expended for the organ, pews, and other furniture, was $54,000. Fourteen thousand dollars were realized from subscriptions, and $2,600 were gathered by a bazaar. In 1860 Father Benoit visited New Orleans and solicited funds for this cathedral. It remains true that only $16,600 were gathered in Fort Wayne to build this church, yet it is nevertheless clear of debt, which is due to the generosity of the venerable pastor that built it. The architect was Thomas Lau, who also had the contract for the carpenter work. The brick work was done by contractor James Silver. The present Episcopal residence was built by Rev. J. Benoit, at a cost of $16,000, of which amount the diocese paid $2,000, the remainder being expended by Father Benoit from his own resources.

Rt. Rev. Bishop Luers died in June, 1871. He was succeeded by Rt. Rev. Bishop Dwenger in April, 1872. Father Benoit remained pastor of the cathedral under the new bishop for some years, when, on account of his advanced age, he relinquished the charge, but he continued to reside with the bishop to the end of his days. In 1867, Rev. E. P, Walters, who for several years had been with Father Benoit, was appointed pastor of St. Bernard's church, at Crawfordsville, and was succeeded at the cathedral by Rev. J. H. Brammer, who came in 1868. Among the other clergy who have been stationed at the cathedral were Rev. A. M. Meili, Rev. W. F. M. O'Rourke, Rev. J. M. Graham, Rev. M. E. Campion, Rev. J. Grogan, Rev. P. M. Frawley, Rev. J. R. Dinnen, Rev. J. M. Hartnett, Rev. L. A. Moench, Rev. H. A. Bœckelman and Rev. P. F. Roach. At present the clergy of the cathedral are: Rt. Rev. Bishop Dwenger, D. D., Very Rev J. H. Brammer, Vicar General, Rev. J. F. Lang, Chancellor, Rev. T. M. O'Leary, Rev. J. F. Delaney and Rev. M. J. Byrne. A biographical sketch of Rt. Rev. Bishop Dwenger and of Very Rev. J. H. Brammer are elsewhere given.

Rev. J. F. Lang is secretary to the bishop, and chancellor of the diocese. He is a native of Delphos, Ohio, born February 15th, 1848. After his collegiate course at Mt. St. Mary's, Cincinnati, he studied logic at Montreal, and a three years' course of theology at Cleveland. He was ordained to the priesthood in the cathedral at Fort Wayne, February 22nd, 1875. After seven and a half years on the missions, he was appointed to his present position, in May, 1882.

Rev. T. M. O'Leary was born at Lafayette, Ind., June 8th, 1854. He graduated in his collegiate course at Notre Dame university, and completed his theological studies at St. Meinrad's, Ind. He was ordained to the priesthood for the diocese of Fort Wayne by the Rt. Rev. Bishop Rademacher, D. D., in St. Mary's church, Fort Wayne, January 26th, 1885.

Rev. J. F. Delaney was born in Thompsonville, Conn., January 15, 1860. He made his collegiate course in the seminary of Our Lady of Angels at Niagara, N. Y. He completed his theological studies at St. Vincent's, Pennsylvania, and was ordained a priest by Rt. Rev. Bishop Dwenger, in the cathedral of Fort Wayne, June 29, 1887.

Rev. M. J. Byrne is a native of Butler county, Ohio, and was born October 18, 1859. He studied at Mt. St. Mary's seminary, Cincinnati, and at Niagara, and completed his theology at St. Vincent's, Pennsylvania. He was ordained to the priesthood in the cathedral of Fort Wayne, June 29, 1888.

In 1888 Bishop Dwenger purchased four lots fronting on Fairfield avenue to the west and to the south on Durier street, in the southwest portion of the city, at an outlay of $4,000. His intention is to begin, without unnecessary delay, the formation of a new congregation. A school has already been organized and numbers nearly 150 children. The new edifice will be called St. Patrick's church.

ST. MARY'S CHURCH.

In 1848 the thirty German families of Fort Wayne, who hitherto had attended St. Augustine's church, manifested a strong desire to build a house of worship wherein they could have the gospel preached in their own language. They accordingly purchased a few lots at the present intersection of Lafayette and Jefferson streets, for $1,700. To secure the payment of this money Bernard Meyer, Nicholas Jostvert, Henry and Lucas Hoevel, and Bernard Voors gave a mortgage on their farms. The first church council was Rev. E. Faller, Joseph Sommers, B. Rekers, Martin Noll, G. Fox and H. Engel. The building committee was Father Faller, B. Rekers, Lorentz Meyer, Ulrich Rehne, Herman Engel and Joseph Sommers. Lorentz Meyer dug the first earth for the foundation of the new brick church, which at present serves as a girls' school. The dimensions of the building were 32x64 feet. In August of the same year, the cholera interrupted the progress of the work, but the church was finally brought to completion in November, and on the 29th of the month these thirty families moved in procession from St. Augustine's church to take possession of the new building. Rev. F. X. Weninger, the zealous missionary, who has since gone to his reward, who had been preaching a mission for the German Catholics for a week previous, conducted the solemn entry into the church and dedicated it to the services of God under the tutelage of Mary, and named the edifice "The Mother of God Church." Revs. J. Benoit and E. Faller, who became the pastor of the new church, took part in the dedicatory services. A small one-story frame house was erected to serve as a pastoral residence. The school-house that had served the Germans was moved

Respectfully Yours
Harvey Morning

from Calhoun street one year after opening the new church, and placed in the rear of the pastoral residence.

In 1850 Bishop de Saint Palais, of Vincennes, visited St. Mary's, administered confirmation, and gave the church $500. The little edifice served its purpose from 1849 for ten years. In 1858 a subscription was started for the erection of a more commodious church. The plans were made by Thomas Lau. The contracts were let, for the brick work, to Thomas Lau; for the plastering, to N. Meyer and N. Alter; for the wood work, to Thomas Lau, except the inside wood finish which was done by Herman Wilkens, George Link and Henry Pranger. The brick were purchased from Samuel Lillie at $4 a 1,000. The sand was donated by Edward Smith. B. H. Schnieders who owned one horse, succeeded in borrowing another and placed the service of the team at the disposal of the building committee during the summer. Another team belonging to B. Trentman, another to Lorentz Meyer and another to Joseph Zimmerman were kept busy during the season. Struggle and sacrifice, good cheer and hard work, figured largely among the early church builders of Fort Wryne. The building committee of the new church was B. Trentman, H. Nierman, John Trentman, M. Noll and B. H. Schnieders. The foundation was begun under the administration of Rev. E. Faller, but he was shortly afterward transferred to New Albany. He was succeeded by Rev. Joseph Wentz, in 1857.

In 1857 the diocese of Fort Wayne was established as is elsewhere stated. Rt. Rev. J. H. Luers, the first bishop of Fort Wayne, arrived here in January, 1858. He laid the corner stone of this new church in the summer of the same year, and preached to the assembled multitude. Another sermon, in German, was preached by a Rev. Mr. Snyder, of Hesse Cassel. In 1859, on the second Sunday of November, Rt. Rev. Bishop Luers dedicated the new St. Mary's, under the same title given its predecessor in 1848. Mr. Henry Monning traveled over the country with Rev. J. Wentz, soliciting contributions to pay for the structure, which had been erected at a cost of $30,000, and upon which a heavy debt remained for many years. In 1871, during the absence of Rev. Mr. Wentz, who had gone to Europe on a visit, Rev. F. Van Schwedler had charge, and in the meantime completed the spire. The assistant priests to Father Wentz were in turn Revs. A. Heitman, A. Young and B. T. Borg.

In 1872 Rev. J. Wentz resigned the pastorate of this church, and Rt. Rev. Bishop Dwenger, who had succeeded to the See of Fort Wayne upon the death of Bishop Luers, appointed Rev. Joseph Rademacher to take charge. Rev. Charles Steurer became his assistant. After some seven years in his pastorate of this church, Rev. J. Rademacher was transferred to LaFayette, and a few years afterward became bishop of Nashville, Tenn. Rev. J. H. Oechtering was appointed to take charge of the Mother of God church, July 14, 1880. His assistants were successively Revs. C. Steurer, C. Ganser, L. A. Moench and C. M. Romer. The last baptism administered in this church was to an infant that was christened John B. Ahrens. The last marriage that was contracted in it was between Bernard Weber and Catharine Wuest. The last funeral was of the child, Joseph G. Rissing. The last Sunday services were by the pastor, Rev. J. H. Oechtering, and the last sermon was by Rev. C. M. Romer. His subject was "Christian Education."

January 13, 1886, will be memorable in the history of this church for many years to come. At half past one o'clock in the afternoon the boiler beneath the church, from which the steam heating was generated, exploded, and the great edifice was a disastrous scene of wreck and ruin, a scene of total destruction. The shock was felt in every part of the city. The fireman was killed and he carried with him the secret of the cause of this disaster. A little girl passing the church at the time of the accident, was struck by a door which was blown from its holdings, and instantly killed. The pastoral residence was also greatly damaged. An elegant new structure graces the scene of disaster, erected at a cost of about $75,000. S. M. Lane, of Cleveland, was the architect. The corner stone was laid by Rt. Rev. Bishop Dwenger, on the 11th of July, 1886, amid an immense throng of people. The great structure finally became a finished monument to genius, an elaborate out-fit of church architecture, and a tribute to the liberality and almost unequalled generosity of the members of the congregation and of citizens generally, even non-Catholics of the city responding cheerfully.

The church was dedicated by Rt. Rev. Joseph Dwenger, D. D., on the third Sunday of Advent, 1887, who also preached the sermon. Rt. Rev. Bishop Rademacher, of Nashville, sang Pontifical mass on the occasion, and was attended by a goodly number of priests from far and near, who had come to rejoice with their reverend friend, upon the completion of his new church. This was a day of great joy to the pastors and congregation of St Mary's church, and their sacrifices in the erection of this beautiful house of worship are worthy of the good and noble people.

St. Mary's church, St. Paul's church and St. Vincent's orphanage were built in the same year, and the Catholics of Fort Wayne, together with many of their non-Catholic friends, came to the aid of all these three great and costly institutions.

There remains the comparatively small debt of about $29,000 on the new structure, the dimensions of which are 190x72 feet. Additional ground was purchased from Michael Kelly, for a pastoral residence, the old house having been taken away to make room for the new church in its greatly increased dimensions over the old church. The boys' school building and the (male) teachers' residence were erected in 1860 and 1877, respectively, at a total cost of $12,000. The girl's school is taught by six sisters, known as the school sisters of Notre Dame, whose mother house is in Milwaukee. There are nearly 500 pupils attending the two schools attached to this church. There are 450 families in this congregation, and about 2,400 souls.

Hon. Henry Monning.—In the narrative devoted to old St. Mary's occurs the name of one who gave much of his time in aiding the pastor to gather funds toward paying the debt of the church. He gave the same earnest and disinterested services to the present rector of the church, both as to time and means, in rearing the stately edifice that to-day is the pride of St. Mary's congregation. Indeed, it can be truthfully said of Henry Monning, that he was ever interested in building up the church and parish, and to every pastor of St. Mary's he was loyal and ready to aid him. The above sketch of St. Mary's had just been completed when the news became current through the city that Mr. Monning, who had gone to Europe three short months before, was expected to land in New York. Preparations were being made to give him a reception of welcome and a joyous entry to his home and friends. But the result was far different. The telegram announcing his arrival also announced his death, which occurred twenty-four hours after landing. To people who knew Mr. Monning it is unnecessary to say what widespread sorrow this information cast upon the community. We do well to chronicle the life and death of such men as Henry Monning. His example should be borne to posterity, for his life was noble; his aim and objects were pure; his faith strong; his trust in God was firm and never wavered; his abiding profession of his religious tenets made him esteemed of men. It is but fitting that his sketch enter into the history of the congregation with which he was so long identified and whose growth and prosperity were his solicitude, his joy and his comfort. The following is from the Fort Wayne *Journal:*

"Mr. Monning was born at Osnabrueck, Westphalia, sixty-two years ago last April. He came to this country and located at Cincinnati, where in 1851 he was married to the lady who survives him. In 1852 he came to Fort Wayne, and has since been identified with its best interests, aiding not a little in its growth and contributing largely to its prosperity. His first business venture was in a soap manufactory with the late John Trentman. He next engaged in the grocery business on the site of Mr. Fred Eckert's meat market, and later conducted a book store. He held various offices of trust, and some time in 1858 was chosen market master. He served in the council from 1863 until 1866, when he resigned to accept a nomination for county treasurer on the democratic ticket. His election followed, and he left the place of trust as becomes a good and faithful servant. He was one of the original members of the board of water-works trustees, and, after serving his term, was appointed oil inspector for this district. He was a member of the board of water-works trustees at the time of his death. He next was chosen one of the directors of the prison north by the legislature, and occupied the place for four years, serving the last two as president of the board. He was widely known throughout the state, and exerted considerable influence in the councils of his party at home and abroad, for he was one of the democratic leaders and he always had a seat of honor at the banquets of the Iroquois club at Chicago. In the meantime he had, with A. C. Trentman and his son, J. B. Monning, established the coffee and spice mill on Main street, and four years ago Mr. Trentman and he disposed of their interest to Henry Monning, jr., the youngest son of the deceased. Mr. Monning was an ardent Catholic, and was one of the founders of the St. Joseph hospital. He was always amiable, and no man stood higher in the community than Hon. Henry Monning. As husband, father and friend he was true to a fault, and about him were the traits of nobility. He has gone to his reward leaving a memory that will live after him for the good he has done, and such a monument is not made of marble or gold."

The press of the city, without exception, was quite pronounced in its eulogy of the subject of this sketch. An extract is herewith given from the *Daily News*, touching upon the funeral rites of August 2, 1889:

"Immediately following were ex-Mayor Randall, Mayor Harding and all the city officers, the council included. Then came the floral conveyance, which was literally filled with a downy bed of roses; a reminder of the gentle manner and amiable disposition of the deceased. The last of the procession had not started when the head stopped in front of the church. The police force marched up the steps of the church and were arranged in a line on each side of the door, facing each other, and extending from the entrance of the church to the sidewalk. The city council and officers were arranged in the same manner next to the policemen. The casket containing the remains was lowered from the hearse. It was almost encased in a bed of rare, richly perfumed and vari-colored roses. The pall-bearers, with their precious burden, entered the sacred precincts of the church that was the pride of the later years of Henry Monning and whose tenets he had so faithfully kept for so many years. To the sad-hearted living it was the most important period of their remembrance of a faithful disciple of the teachings of the Catholic church, and as the last remains of what was once Henry Monning were borne silently between the long ranks of respectful friends, every head was uncovered and every brow was bent in kindly reverence and respect. Spacious as is this noble edifice of public worship, it was filled to overflowing in an incredibly short space of time, and many turned away on account of the lack of room."

Another Fort Wayne daily which had devoted two columns to eulogizing the subject of this sketch ends as follows in its " closing tributes, to the honored life of the late Henry Monning " : " The funeral of the late Henry Monning occurred yesterday morning from his home on East Wayne street and the cortege was one of the longest seen in years. The city officers were all in line doing honor to their colleague, and besides this there were ninety-nine carriages. At St. Mary's church the services were solemn and impressive, for the Catholic church has great regard for the dead. The rector, Rev. J. H. Oechtering, preached the funeral sermon in the German tongue. His words paid golden tribute to the life and citizenship of Mr. Monning, and tender, indeed, was the testimony he bore of his worth in Christian paths."

The following resolutions adopted by the Fort Wayne board of underwriters, of which Mr. Monning was a member, are deemed a fitting close to this sketch.

"*Resolved*, That in his death this board has lost one of its most honored and distinguished members, our city one of its most worthy and cherished citizens, and his family a kind, amiable and indulgent father and companion. In his several relations in life he enjoyed that respect of this community to which the excellence of his character so eminently entitled him. His simplicity of manners, his honesty of purpose, his kindness of disposition never failed to surround him, with a host of true and ardent friends in life, and left him without a single enemy in death. Inflexible integrity was one of his most prominent traits of character. In his intercourse with the world the justice, propriety and benevolence of his conduct rendered him a model worthy of imitation. Kind and forbearing himself he had a sedulous regard to the feelings of others. His practical good sense enabled him to meet any emergency with calmness and self control. The loss of such a man is not alone to relations and friends, but equally so to the city and community in which most of his active life has been spent. Thousands of our citizens feel their loss and their hearts are full of sorrow that the hand of death has laid low one of the purest and best of men.

" F. P. RANDALL,
" A. H. CARRIER,
" S. C. LUMBARD,
" C. NEIREITER,
     " *Committee.*
" C. E. GRAVES,
     "*Secretary.*"

Rev. C. M. Romer, assistant priest at St. Mary's church, was born June 9, 1856, in Würtemburg. He studied classics at Einsiedeln, and philosophy at Lucerne, Switzerland. He came to America at the age of seventeen and entered St. Francis seminary, Milwaukee, for philosophy. He studied theology at Mt. St. Mary's seminary, Cincinnati, and was ordained for the diocese of Fort Wayne, June 21, 1879, by Rt. Rev. Joseph Dwenger, D. D. For three years he was at St. Mary's church, Michigan City, after which time he was appointed to his present position.

Rev. J. H. Oechtering, the rector of St. Mary's church, was born December 23, 1845, in Lingen, Hanover. He visited the schools of his native city until twelve years of age, after which he spent one year at the gymnasium, a school for the higher branches of literature and science, in the same city of Lingen. In 1858 he was sent to college in Münster and remained seven years, after which he spent two years at the university in the same city. In 1867 he entered the American college of Louvain, Belgium, as a candidate for the priesthood. He was ordained for the diocese of Fort Wayne, by the coadjutor archbishop of Malines, May 21, 1869. Father Oechtering came to America the same year, and was assigned to Elkhart, residing, however, at Mishawaka. He had charge of Elkhart one year, when he was transferred to St. Joseph's church at La Porte, where he remained ten years. July 14, 1880, he was appointed pastor of St. Mary's church, Fort Wayne. In 1888 he was named "Immovable Rector," of the same church. During his pastorate in Fort Wayne, Father Oechtering published a pamphlet on capital and labor which attracted favorable attention throughout the United States and in Europe.

ST. PAUL'S CHURCH.

During the winter of 1864 some thirty-five German-speaking Catholics gathered at the residence of the Rekers Brothers, and after some deliberation set to work in erecting a church in the west end of the city. These same Rekers Brothers had been managing a general home for orphans and aged people which was supported by private charity, county funds, and church aid, from 1847 till about 1864, when the orphanage was opened at Rensselaer, and the St. Joseph hospital was established in the hotel property known as the Rockhill House. The institution above referred to was known as the St. Vincent's orphan asylum and the St. Joseph hospital, the same names given to the new homes in a later day. The Rekers asylum has long since made way for the elegant residence now occupied by A. C. Trentman.

Property for the new church was purchased adjoining the corner lot on the southeast crossing of Griffith and Jefferson streets, and a frame church erected upon it; the lot cost $1,100, and the building cost $3,700. The corner lot upon which the present brick school-house stands was secured several years later. This edifice was erected about 1870. Two lots had been bought on the northwest corner and a frame school-house erected. (These lots were sold a few years since.) Later on, the northeast corner was purchased and a commodious pastoral residence erected on the lot adjoining the corner, costing about $7,000. In 1886 the new church, which graces the northeast corner at the intersection of Griffith and Jefferson streets, was begun and the corner stone was laid the same year by Rt. Rev. Bishop Rademacher, of Nashville, and dedicated. The church was dedicated on the first Sunday of November, 1887, by Rt. Rev. Bishop Dwenger. The cost of the church is about $30,000. There is some debt upon the building, which in the course of a few years will be completely liquidated. St. Paul's numbers 152 families. The schools are taught by one man, and two sisters of the community of Poor Handmaids. There are about 200 children attending the schools. The congregation is composed of a thrifty and prosperous class of people.

Rev. E. Koenig, the pastor of St. Paul's church, was born in Westphalia, September 1, 1827. He graduated in theology in the seminary at Münster and was ordained to the priesthood in 1852, by Rt. Rev. Francis Drepper, D. D., Bishop of Paderborn. After serving in a parish a short while he was appointed chaplain of an asylum for insane people, where he labored for ten years. He came to Fort Wayne in December, 1865, was appointed pastor of St. Paul's congregation, where he still labors with energy and zeal. Mention of Father Koenig's name occurs in the sketch devoted to the St. Joseph hospital of this city.

ST. PETER'S CHURCH.

In 1872 a few dozen families living in the southeast part of Fort Wayne, most of whom had worshiped in St. Mary's church, formed themselves into a congregation. They began the erection of a large brick structure, divided into two stories. On the lower floors are four commodious school-rooms, whilst the second floor serves as a house of worship. The corner stone was laid in the spring and the church was dedicated December 29, 1872, by Rt. Rev. Bishop Dwenger. The approximate cost of the building was $8,000. Rev. J. Wemhoff was appointed pastor of the new church, which he faithfully served for eight years, until the time of his death, which occurred in December, 1880. The schools were opened in 1873. Eight years afterward sisters from Milwaukee were secured to teach. They belong to a community known as "School Sisters of Notre Dame." They have at present writing 275 pupils in the schools attached to St. Peter's church. In 1882 the congregation purchased a house and three additional lots for a pastoral residence. The property belonging to this church is known as "St. Peter's Square." It runs from Warsaw street west to Hanna, containing the entire strip between DeWald and Martin streets. I 1887 a two-story brick building was erected for a sister's residence. The entire property is without any incumbrance, and there is a good amount of cash on hand as the beginning of a building fund toward the erection of a new church which will probably be commenced in the near future.

The present pastor, Rev. A. Messman, is the successor of the lamented Father Wemhoff. Father Messman came to America from northern Germany, when a boy, and located at Cincinnati. After some years he began his studies for the priesthood. He graduated at Mt. St. Mary's seminary, Cincinnati, and was ordained priest for the diocese of Fort Wayne by Rt. Rev. Bishop Luers. Immediately after his ordination, which took place Jannary 6th, 1870, he was appointed first resident pastor of Kentland, Newton county, Ind. He remained there until called to his present pastorate, in December, 1880.

Rt. Rev. Julian Benoit, Vicar General, was born in France, in the year 1808. Having completed his studies he received deacon's orders. Being too young to receive the order of priesthood, he accepted a position as private tutor, and wrote for a journal in the city of Lyons. He came to America for the diocese of Vincennes in June, 1836, remained a short while at St. Mary's seminary, Baltimore, and was ordained in 1837. After laboring three years in southern Indiana, excepting a short period of which he spent in Chicago, Ill., he came to Fort Wayne in

1840. Father Benoit secured valuable church property while here; he also brought the sisters of Providence to open schools as early as 1845. He made some purchases of real estate which in the course of time, showed that his prudence was well directed. He acquired quite a little wealth in this manner during his lifetime, but he carefully distributed every dollar among charitable and educational institutions, so that shortly before his death he had not enough left to buy a cheap coffin. Father Benoit visited Europe in 1841. In 1848 he accompanied the Indians from Allen county to their new government reservation in Missouri.

RT. REV. JULIAN BENOIT,
First Vicar General of the Diocese of Fort Wayne.

When the diocese of Fort Wayne was established in 1857, Rev. Julian Benoit was appointed his vicar general by the new bishop, Rt. Rev. J. H. Luers, D. D. In 1865 he again visited Europe, and was absent thirteen months, four and a half of which he spent in Rome; and in 1874 he visited Europe as a member of the First American pilgrimage. He attended the four provincial councils of Cincinnati. In 1866 he accompanied Bishop Luers to the Second National council of Baltimore. After the death of Bishop Luers, until the appointment of Bishop Dwenger, he was administrator of the diocese, and upon the arrival of the new bishop, he was again appointed vicar general. In June, 1883, Father Benoit was named by Pope Leo XIII. to the office of

Papal Prelate, giving him the purple and the title of Monseigneur. His labors among the early settlers, the Indians and the white people, his persevering attention to the scattered missions for miles and miles, riding horseback as far as Columbia City and Warsaw, to South Bend, to LaGro and Wabash, to Decatur, to the French settlements, in Noble county, to the south again as far as Muncie, and his constant care for those near at home, are placed to his credit as to a faithful and heroic servant of God and of the people. He was esteemed and beloved by citizens of all denominations. He took great interest also in building up the young and growing village in which he had made his home. He was a man of wonderful benevolence, and his charity to the needy was one of his characteristic and predominant features. He was greatly esteemed by his fellow citizens as appears from the following extract from a tribute that appeared in the Fort Wayne *Sentinel*, following his death, which occurred December 26, 1886:

"Monseigneur Benoit died last night at 8:15 at the Episcopal residence. This simple announcement will moisten the eyes of thousands and grieve a legion of hearts attached to the venerable prelate by all the ties that are good, noble, holy and true. Coming here when Fort Wayne was in its infancy, the people grew up with and about this priest to love and revere him. To the poor Indians he was priest, counsellor and friend. He taught them the way of the righteous, guarded them against the wily "traders," and watched over them with a fatherly care. It is not to be wondered at that he softened their savage hearts and enjoyed their devotion, for he knew not deceit. The Protestants esteemed Father Julian for his rare virtues, Christian fortitude and princely characteristics. So ardent was their admiration that his every effort met with their warmest approval and received their most substantial assistance for they knew his energies and that every moment of his life would be devoted to the glory of God and the best interests of mankind. In his own church he was honored and renowned. No pen can describe the degree of affection between him and his flock, neither can time efface it, for it will go down from generation to generation as a rare jewel that brightens and beatifies with age. Among the clergy and ecclesiastics of the church of Rome, Father Benoit was venerated for his virtues, extolled for his grand work and elevated for his learning. In the pulpit he was earnest, sensible and brilliant. At the vatican he was listened to with respect and honored for his manly conduct. In his death Fort Wayne loses one of its founders, as well as one of its greatest and grandest citizens. When this city had no inviting prospects Father Benoit was the nucleus about which the pioneers and substantial people gathered. He encouraged every one to build up the city and led the work himself by erecting the most magnificent church edifice in the west. All through his life Monseigneur Benoit enjoyed the best of health and Almighty God seemed to especially bless him for the holy work of his long clerical career. A few months ago symptoms of cancer manifested themselves and the disease increased in severity until pyæmia added its deadly fangs to its fatal predecessor. Up to within the past few days his mind was clear and his faculties retained their vigor, but as the blood poison permeated the system his reason flitted on its throne. Only one endowed with indomitable will power and almost superhuman nerve could have battled so long against disease in so malignant a form."

Rt. Rev. J. H. Luers, first bishop of Fort Wayne, was born near Munster, Germany, September 29th, 1819. He came to the United States with his parents in 1833, and settled near Minster, Ohio, and shortly afterward engaged as clerk in a store in Piqua. Incidentally meeting with Bishop Purcell, the young clerk made known to him his desire of entering the priesthood and was accepted as a student for the diocese of Cincinnati. He completed his studies at the seminary of St. Francis Xavier, in Brown county, Ohio, and was ordained a priest in 1846. The young clergyman was stationed at St. Joseph's church, Cincinnati, where he completed the half-finished church edifice and erected a substantial school-house. When, in 1857, the See of Fort Wayne was established, Rev. J. H. Luers was chosen the first bishop, and was consecrated January 10th, 1858. In a day or two afterward Bishop Luers departed for his new home; he lost no time in taking possession of his See, and in commencing the arduous work before him. He gave his early attention to the erection of a cathedral, for which Rev. Julian Benoit had already matured the plans, and in the spring of 1859, the present metropolitan church was begun. Bishop Luers attended the provincial councils of Cincinnati and the second plenary council of Baltimore. He was excused by the pope from attending the Œcumenical council held in the Eternal city. In the year 1866 the bishop intended to erect an orphan asylum on a piece of land in the suburbs of Fort Wayne, but delays occurred. In the meantime he learned of a large tract of land, 933 acres, in Jasper county, known as the Spitler farm, which he bought for $18,000. There was a frame house upon it which served as an orphan asylum for a number of years. In the visitations of his diocese, and in the labors among his flock, Bishop Luers was untiring. He visited town and village to instruct the people, administer confirmation, dedicate new churches and establish new parishes and schools. The bishop was noted for his charity to the poor, and to the orphans he was a kind and provident father. In June, 1871, Rt. Rev. Bishop Luers, went to Cleveland to administer holy orders. When his task had been completed he started for the railway station, but had scarcely turned away when he fell upon the sidewalk, a victim to apoplexy. He was carried back to the house and expired twenty minutes afterward. The Bishop's remains were carried to Fort Wayne in a funeral train draped in mourning, escorted by clergymen and laymen from both dioceses; other delegations joined the sad cortege at various points along the way, and on arriving at Fort Wayne, every honor which veneration, love, and religion could suggest, was paid to his memory. His funeral took place in the cathedral of Fort Wayne, July 4, 1871, and was attended by Archbishop Purcell, Bishops De St.

Palais, O'Hara, McCloskey, Toebbe, and Borgess, and a large delegation of clergy and laity. His remains were deposited in a vault under the cathedral sanctuary. The age of Bishop Luers was fifty-one years and nine months.

St. Joseph's Hospital.— In 1866, in behalf of Rt. Rev. Bishop Luers, Rev. E. Koenig wrote to his friend, the Vicar General Spaller, of the diocese of Paderborn, to interest himself toward obtaining a colony of sisters from Dernbach to establish a hospital in the prosperous little city of Fort Wayne. The effort was successful. Dernbach is a village romantically situated in the former district of Nassau, southern Germany, almost a day's journey from Coblentz, through the valley of the Lahn. Eight sisters were sent to the new mission in America, in the year 1868. Citizens of Fort Wayne took a lively interest in this matter of establishing a hospital in the future railway center, and were very generous in their contributions toward the enterprise. The Hotel Rockhill was purchased for $20,000, of which the mother convent at Dernbach temporarily supplied one-half the purchase price. Sister Rosa was the superior of the little band. She returned to Europe in 1872. The other sisters were Mary Eudoxia, who is now superior of St. Vincent's orphan asylum; Mary Hyacinthe, assistant superior of the hospital; Sisters Facunda, Henrica, Bella, Matrona and Remigia. They first settled, for a short time, in Hesse Cassel, eight miles from Fort Wayne, from which place three went to Chicago, to take charge of the orphan asylum at Rose Hill, of which they still retain the management. In May, 1869, the hospital was opened and the number of sisters was increased from Europe by seven. In 1884 the new convent with an elegant chapel, for the use of sisters and patients, was built at a cost of $33,000. The community is known as the Handmaids of Christ. The mother home of America is the convent in the city of Fort Wayne.

In 1887, at the invitation of Most Rev. Archbishop Feehan, of Chicago, these sisters began the erection of a large hospital in the city of Chicago, which is patronized to its fullest capacity. The total number of sisters belonging to the community in America is 154, and eighteen novices. Forty-six of these came from Europe, of whom seven died and four returned. The others are native Americans. The total number of patients in the hospital from May, 1869, to December 31, 1888, was 4,145, of which 436 died. The number of patients nursed in private houses (in their homes) was 364. From the 29th of March to the 25th of April, 1881, and from the 1st of December, 1881, to the 6th of May, 1882, the sisters nursed seventy-nine patients in the pest house, during the small-pox epidemic in Fort Wayne. The present superior is Mother Lecunda.

Rev. Julius Becks, the chaplain of St. Joseph's hospital, was born in Laer, Westphalia, October 8, 1836. He made his collegiate course in Munster, Germany. In 1858 he came to America, landing in New York, June 26. He entered upon his theological course in Mt. St. Mary's seminary, Cincinnati, and after about three years he was ordained to the priesthood, in the cathedral of Fort Wayne, by Rt. Rev. Bishop Luers, December 25, 1862. He was at once appointed pastor of Decatur, Adams county, and two years afterward he became pastor of Michigan City, where he remained for twenty-one years. During his administration in Michigan City, he erected a large and beautiful church at a cost of $25,000. He built a pastoral residence and also purchased a grave yard, all of which are paid for. In February, 1885, Father Becks was appointed chaplain of St. Joseph's hospital, Fort Wayne, where he still labors in persevering energy and devotedness to duty.

ST. VINCENT'S ORPHAN ASYLUM.

The magnificent structure that crowns the elevation at the northern edge of the city limits is the diocesan orphan asylum for girls. The building has a frontage of 126 feet by 100 feet deep. It is four stories in height and is supplied with water, gas, steam heating and fire protection, and will accommodate 300 children. There are three flights of stairs in the house. The school-rooms are commodious and well ventilated. The recreation halls are large and airy. The chapel is a gem of its kind. Twenty-five acres of ground, containing a large grove, belong to the building. The corner stone of the asylum was laid by Rt. Rev. Bishop Dwenger, July 4, 1886, and the building was by him dedicated September 27, 1887. The structure cost $49,289.37, of which amount $13,265.17 were derived from individual donations, $13,300 from other sources, $11,800 from sale of land at Rensselaer, and $2,130.81 from a special diocesan collection, making a total receipt of $40,495.98. The debt of $8,793.37 that remains upon the building is, however, no cause for uneasiness, nor will it hover over it for any great length of time. Children are admitted from any part of the diocese upon application to the bishop, who issues a permit to the pastor applying for the admission. The orphans are entrusted to the care of sisters of charity, known as Poor Handmaids of Christ. Sister Eudoxia, the superior, has eight sisters with her, some of whom look after the domestic affairs whilst others are engaged in teaching. There are about 100 children in the institution this year. Rev. B. T. Borg is the chaplain. The asylum is supported by collections taken in every church of the diocese on Christmas day and forwarded to the bishop who disburses the moneys; occasionally, too, private contributions are offered. Two sewing societies are great auxiliaries of the asylum and are much appreciated by the sisters. One is known as the "Kraenschen" (a garland), and the other as L'orphelin (the orphan). They provide from their own treasury, the goods they make up, which together with their services are donated to the asylum. Aside from these, there are no organizations as yet, whose object is the support of the orphanage. Possibly, it is rather early to look to individuals in this comparatively new section of country, for any great endowments, but in the course of time, as wealth is accumulated, charity will probably find its way to the support of benevolent institutions, such as orphan asylums and homes for the aged poor.

Very Rev. J. H. Brammer, V. G., was born in Hanover, Germany, October, 1839, of Lutheran parents, in whose faith he was reared. During his early years he was apprenticed to learn the carpenter's trade, which he followed for some time subsequent to 1854, when he came to America and settled in St. Louis. While attending a series of lectures given by Jesuit fathers, the young man became interested in Catholicity and made it his study for a year or more, and was finally received into the churth, the 18th of September, 1859. About a year afterward he entered college to prepare for the priesthood. He attended the well known institution of St. Vincent's, and St. Michael's of Pittsburgh, Penn., finishing his theological course at Mount St. Mary's seminary, Cincinnati, as a student of the diocese of Fort Wayne. He was ordained a priest in the cathedral in this city, by Right Rev. Bishop Luers, May 11, 1868. His first appointment was assistant to Father Benoit, in the cathedral congregation. During the declining years of this venerable pastor, Father Brammer was appointed his successor, and has ever since worked in that capacity. In 1878 he visited Europe. Among other places of note he spent some time at Lourdes and Rome, where he met Leo XIII. In 1880 he began the erection of one of Fort Wanye's monuments, the beautiful edifice known as library hall. The corner stone was laid by Right Rev. Bishop Dwenger, and the sermon on the occasion was preached by Bishop Spalding, of Peoria, on the 3d of July, 1881. The building cost about $65,000. During Bishop Dwenger's absence in Rome, from March 4, 1885, to October of the same year, Father Brammer was administrator of the diocese. In 1886 Bishop Dwenger appointed him vicar general, to succeed the lamented Father Benoit. In 1888, during the absence of the bishop in Europe, Father Brammer was again administrator of the diocese. He still gives his services to the people of the cathedral, and from present indications, will continue to do so for many years to come.

CHURCHES IN THE TOWNSHIPS.

St. Leo's Church.—While Fort Wayne was still a village, though not without honest pretensions toward metropolitan prominence, a few sturdy families had formed a settlement in the wilderness on the romantic banks of the St. Joseph river, about fourteen miles to the north of Fort Wayne, and called the place Leo. The plat is designated on the record as "Hamilton," and if the writer is correctly informed, the record was never changed to Leo, though this is the only name by which the place is known in every-day life. Among the first Catholics were P. Sullivan, John Rogers, William Mueller, and one Lawler. In 1838 Rev. Mr. Mueller, of Fort Wayne, visited these people, said mass and preached, in the residence of Charles Nettelhorst. Rev. J. Benoit came a few times during the following decade of years. Rev. A. Bessonies in

1853 took an interest in these people. He went to them once a month, and after several visits succeeded in encouraging them to build a church. Two lots were purchased by the congregation, and two were bought by William Mueller, and donated to the church. After Father Bessonies' departure from Fort Wayne, Rev. E. Faller regularly attended Leo, and amid much difficulty succeeded in erecting the present church. It was dedicated by Rt. Rev. J. H. Luers, D. D. The name of the church is claimed by some to be St. Leo, whilst a few maintain that it is St. Mary. In the course of time Rev. Mr. Dechamps attended Leo from St. Vincent's church, at New France. It was next attended by Rev. Mr. Schaefer from Avilla. Rev. Mr. Holz was the first resident priest, and remained two years. Again the place was attended from Avilla, now by Rev. D. Duehmig. Rev. M. Zumbuelte then became resident pastor, and during his administration pews, a bell, and a grave-yard were secured for the church, and new life seemed to enter the congregation and the village as well. Rev. A. Young succeeded to the place, and after him came Rev. P. Franzen. After a little time the church was given in charge by Bishop Dwenger, to a Father of the Holy Cross, Rev. Thomas Vagnier being appointed resident pastor. After eight years Father Vagnier was transferred to Benton county. Rev. M. J. Byrne, of the cathedral, attended Leo for several months, when it was again given in charge of Fathers of the Holy Cross, residing in the settlement of New France, the Rev. M. Robinson devoting himself to the mission of Leo and the neighboring Pierr's settlement known as St. Michael's church.

Church of St. Louis.—The Catholics of Besancom, Jefferson township, were visited by Rev. A. Bessonies, who was the first priest to hold services in the settlement. The first mass was offered in the house of Joseph Dodane, in 1853. Father Bessonies had charge of this place, which he visited from time to time from Fort Wayne, for one year during, which time he erected a frame church. He was succeeded in his visits by Rev. J. Benoit. In 1865 came Rev. Mr. Grevin, who erected a pastoral residence. He, after one year, was succeeded by Rev. J. C. Carrier, who is still living, in St. Lawrence college, near Montreal. Next came Rev. F. M. Ruiz, then Rev. A. de Montaubricq, and after him, for a few months, the Rev. A. J. M. Vandervennet. In 1869 Rev. A. Mignault had charge for three months. In 1870 Rev. A. Adam became the pastor and remained five years. During his administration the present elegant church was constructed at a cost of about $10,000. Father Adam went to France in 1875. Rev. G. Demers, of Notre Dame, took charge, and, after one year, was succeeded by Rev. C. Manjay, who remained two years. In 1880 Rev. Felix Veniard, of the Order of the Holy Cross, took charge. This good father succeeded in paying a debt of $3,000 that hung over the church. Father Veniard is still pastor of Besancom. He told the writer that the lamented Father Benoit contributed $500 to this church. There are about 100 families in the congregation. They are all, with very few exceptions, French people. From appearances one would judge them to be a thrifty and prosperous class of farmers.

The tasty little "God's Acre," in close proximity to the church, is a model of devotion to the " departed " of the parish.

Rev. Felix Veniard, C. S. C., is a native of Normandie, France, born May 13, 1824. His preparatory studies and the greater portion of his theological course, were successfully passed in his native land. He was ordained to the priesthood by Bishop Bourget, of Montreal, in the church of St. Laurent, in the village of St. Laurent, near Montreal, on the 4th of December, 1853, for the Order of the Holy Cross. Father Veniard was the parish priest of this place until 1877, when he became pastor of St. Joseph's church, South Bend. The Catholic churches of South Bend are all in charge of the Fathers of Holy Cross. At the earnest appeal of Bishop Dwenger and Father Benoit after a few years at South Bend, the good Father took charge of the French congregation, where to-day he is the idol of the people. Though nearly sixty-six years old he is still vigorous in the performance of his duties; his health is very good, as is proverbially the case with most men of his nationality at his advanced age.

St. Vincent's Church.— About 1840 a few French families, chiefly from Franche Compte, formed a settlement about six miles north of Fort Wayne, and called it New France. In 1843, Rev. J. Benoit visited these families, and offered mass in the house of Isadore Pichon. Father Benoit continued to attend these families until 1853, when he was succeeded, until 1854, by Rev. A. Bessonies. The first house of worship was erected in 1846. The first frame cottage for pastoral residence was built about 1855, when Rev. Mr. Dechamps became the first resident pastor. Father Dechamps died in 1858. He was succeeded by Rev. Mr. Grevin. During this period the congregation had grown to about eighty families. In 1861 Rev. A. Adam became pastor. During his administration a new church was built, which still serves its purpose. A new residence for the priest was constructed, and an academy of large proportions was erected for the education of young ladies. This educational institution was placed in charge of Sisters of the Holy Cross from Notre Dame, Ind. The school is prosperous. Mother Arsene is still the able superior of this school, which is known as the Academy of the Sacred Heart. In 1870, St. Vincent's church was placed in charge of a priest of the Holy Cross. The fathers of this community still continue to minister to the spiritual wants of the congregation. Rev. B. Roche, who for ten years gave his services to St. Vincent's, is at present laboring in the interests of religion in far off India, among the people of Bengal, whither he was sent by his superior. He was succeeded at St. Vincent's by Rev. P. J. Franciscus, who has since been appointed president of a college in the Eternal city — Rome. He in turn was followed by Rev. J. Lauth, the present incumbent, and Rev. Mr. Robinson who attends the neighboring churches of Leo and Pierr's settlement.

Church of St. John the Baptist.—Rev. Mr. Botty visited the Catholic families of New Haven, and said mass in the house of N. Schuckman, in the latter part of 1857. During this same year he organized the congregation. Among the original settlers and principal constituents were George Schlink, Herman Schnelker, N. Jostvert, N. Schuckman and B. Schnelker. The first *"* church council" was composed of H. Schnelker, B. Schlink and N. Jostvert. These men gave their individual notes to Henry Burgess for the purchase price of the land bought for church purposes. Rev. Mr. Grevin came once a month to give services, and he also aided in pushing to completion the new church edifice, which was erected at a cost of $4,000. Rev. G. W. Giedel became the first resident pastor, taking charge of the church in 1861. About 1871 Father Giedel secured the services of Sisters of St. Agnes from Fond du Lac, Wis., for the parochial schools attached to his church. Sisters of this community still have charge of these schools, which are in excellent condition. The school buildings were erected in 1872 at a cost of $8,000. Rev. G. W. Giedel died in 1873, and was succeeded by the present incumbent, Rev. B. Wiedau. During the administration of Father Wiedau, a new and handsome house of worship has been erected at a cost of about $17,000. There is a small debt of $1,500 upon this entire church property. There are about ninety families, and about 540 souls in the congregation. Most of them are farmers, and all of them are enterprising and thrifty. One hundred and forty-seven children attended the parish schools in 1888 and 1889.

St. Joseph's Church.—As early as 1834, Peter and John Schmidt, Joseph Auth, John Sorg, John and Henry Herber, J. Ziegler and Martin Klug, came with their families from Chur Hessen, Germany, and located upon their present possessions in Marion township. These were the first Catholics in the settlement. Rev. L. Mueller was the first to offer the sacrifice of mass for the settlers in this locality. His temporary chapel was in the house of John Sorg, and he usually visited these people when on his way to preach to the Catholics of Decatur. Rev. J. Benoit succeeded him, and persuaded the few Catholics to erect a little church; they built a neat and roomy log cabin which served as a church for fifteen years or more. When Rev. Mr. Schulze became pastor of Decatur he took charge also of Hesse Cassel and visited the place once a month. Rev. Messrs. Rudolf and Force were also among the attending clergy. Rev. Jacob Mayer became the first resident pastor. He began the present brick church in 1862. At this time there were probably fifty-two families. The church cost a little more than $5,000. The log chapel then became the pastoral residence. Rev. Joseph Nussbaum was the next pastor. He built a brick residence. His successor was Rev. W. Woeste, who was succeeded by Rev. W. Geers. Rev. J. H. Hueser, D. D., was the next pastor. He built a brick school-house and sisters' residence, costing $3,000. In 1880 Rev. Dr. Hueser was succeeded by Rev. J. A. Mark, the present incumbent. Thus the settlement steadily grew from its quiet beginning to a congregation of sixty-three families and 471 souls, possessing beautiful church property without any incumbrance upon it. The congregation is composed of industrious and thrifty farmers and they are a united people.

Rev. J. A. Mark is a native of Wuerzburg, Bavaria. He was born April 1st, 1826. He made his college studies with the Benedictine Fathers in Vienna, his theological course at All Hollows college, in Ireland, and was ordained to the priesthood, August 16th, in Nova Scotia by Most Rev. Archbishop Walsh. Father Mark served therefor six years and then joined the diocese of Alton, Ill., where he remained sixteen years. He came to the diocese of Fort Wayne in 1876 and labored in the missions of Attica and Covington. The Rev. Father was appointed pastor of St. Joseph's church, Hesse Cassel, in 1880.

St. Patrick's Church.— The early Catholic settlers of Arcola had their first visit of a priest about the year 1845. This priest was the same pioneer missionary that we meet with so frequently in the history of this county, Rev. Julian Benoit. He held services the first time in the house of Victor Muneir. Rev. Dr. Madden afterward visited these people at intervals for about one year. He was succeeded by Rev. Mr. Schaefer, of Columbia City, who built the little church that will probably be replaced ere long by a handsome edifice in keeping with the prosperity and growth of the congregation. The early settlers of the place were John Dougherty, John Owens, Thomas Brannan, Nicholas Eloph, Michael Donahoe, B. McLaughlin, W. Brown and William Rawley. The first resident priest was Rev. Theodore Van der Pohl. He remained five years and was succeeded by Rev. H. T. Wilkens whose successor, after eight years, was Rev. B. Hartman. After several years at Arcola, Father Hartman was succeeded by Rev. James Twigg, who after a few months' residence there, died. His successor was Rev. J. A. Werdein, who after two years was transferred to LaPorte county, and the present incumbent, Rev. W. J. Quinlan, became the pastor. There are about seventy-five families belonging to this church, and there is no indebtedness on their property. The ground upon which the school-house is built was donated by a Mr. Welsheimer, and the ground for the church was given by Patrick Ney.

Rev. W. J. Quinlan was born in Syracuse, N. Y., April 16, 1864. When William was four years old his parents moved to Valparaiso, Ind., where the boy received his school education. He made his collegiate studies and his course of philosophy and theology in St. Francis seminary, Milwaukee. Rev. Father Quinlan was ordained to the priesthood in the cathedral of Fort Wayne, by Rt. Rev. Bishop Dwenger, June 29, 1888. Almost immediately afterward the bishop appointed the Reverend Father pastor of St. Patrick's church, Arcola, where he still labors in the interest of the flock confided to his care.

Church of St. Rose of Lima.— Rev. J. Benoit visited Monroeville and ministered to the few Catholics as early as 1850. He said mass in the homes alternately, of one Jeffroy and of a family named Griffith. In the course of time, these visits were made at regular intervals, by both Rev. J. Benoit and Rev. Mr. Madden. After a few visits, a room in the house of John Hayes was made a temporary chapel. In 1868, Rev. E. P. Walters came from Fort Wayne once a month to hold services. He erected a frame church 50x28, which served its purpose for nineteen years. A debt of $300 remained upon the building, which was paid during the administration of Rev. E. P. Walter's successor. The clergymen who next attended Monroeville were successively Revs. J. H. Brammer, J. M. Graham, A. M. Meili, A. Heitman, T. Hibbelen, J. Grogan, H. T. Wilken and B. Hartman. During Rev. H. T. Wilken's ministration, the congregation secured a cemetery. A pastoral residence was built in 1882, during Rev. B. Hartman's attendance. The two gentlemen last mentioned, attended Monroeville from Arcola, whilst formerly it had been attended from Fort Wayne. Rev. J. Grogan was appointed the first resident pastor, in 1884. He was succeeded in the same year by Rev. J. Hoss, who in 1887, was succeeded by Rev. B. Hartman, the present incumbent.

In October of the year just named, the church was destroyed by fire. A subscription of $4,500 was immediately raised, a handsome amount being contributed by the non-Catholic residents. The foundations were begun in the spring of 1888, and on the 1st of July, of the same year the corner stone was laid by Bishop Dwenger. The new church is of brick, built in Gothic style. Its dimensions are 92x35 feet, with a spire of 102 feet. Its total cost is $9,500, and there is a comparatively small debt of $650 remaining. The edifice was dedicated May 12, 1889, by Rt. Rev. Joseph Dwenger, attended by Rev. B. Hartman, Very Rev. J. H. Brammer, Revs. H. T. Wilken, L. A. Moench and M. J. Byrne. A special train of fifteen coaches, packed with people, came from Fort Wayne. All the priests that attended Monroeville are still living except Fathers Benoit, Madden, Graham and Hoss.

Rev. B. Hartman, the present pastor at Monroeville, came to America from Germany when a boy, and located at Alton, Ills. He graduated in theology at St. Francis seminary, Milwaukee, and was ordained to the priesthood by Rt. Rev. Bishop Dwenger, February 22, 1875, in the cathedral at Fort Wayne. His first appointment was to the chaplaincy and management of the orphan asylum at Rensselaer and afterward in the same position in St. Joseph's boys' orphan asylum at LaFayette. After some years he was appointed pastor of Arcola, and in 1887, became pastor of Monroeville.

St. Aloysius Church.—In the autumn of 1858, Rev. Jacob Mayer, of Decatur, visited the scattered Catholics living in Pleasant township. He held religious services at the residence of Frederick Weaver. This was the first time so far as is known that mass was offered in this neighborhood. The year following, the erection of a small church was agreed upon. The Miller and Harber families were the pioneers of the settlement, and principally constituted this new congregation. They took charge of building the new edifice, which was 29x36 feet. Christian Miller donated three acres of land east of the so-called Bluffton plank road. An additional acre was purchased in 1878 for a cemetery. Mrs. Christian Miller, whose energetic services in the interest of the church were cheerfully recognized, was asked to select the name of a saint under whose tutelage the church should be dedicated to the worship of God. She selected the name "St. Aloysius." Rev. J. Mayer was succeeded in his pastorate of this mission by Rev. M. Kink, and he by Rev. A. L. Meile, who attended the place from Hesse Cassel. They were succeeded by Revs. T. Hibbelen, W. Woeste and J. Nussbaum. During the administration of the latter, the church was enlarged and a spire built at an expense of $1,500, leaving a debt of $400. The first resident pastor was Rev. F. Koerdt, the present incumbent. He took charge July 30, 1876. There were then sixty-five families in the parish. Father Koerdt began at once to decorate the interior of the church, and to pay off the debt resting upon the building. October 17, 1876, he opened his new school, a little frame building, the first parochial school of this church, with thirty-eight pupils. In the year 1877 he had completed a pastoral residence at a cost of $4,000. In the interim of a year and a half the young pastor had been a guest of John Harber. In 1882 a commodious two-story brick school-house was erected at an expense of $4,000. The teachers who successively taught in this congregation were G. Smoll, Mr. Kenning, R. Gruber, and Miss Philomina Wolford. The pastor continually shared the labors, with few exceptions, of the two first named teachers. In 1883 two sisters of St. Agnes from Fond du Lac, Wis., took charge of the schools. They continue to give great satisfaction to pastor and people. No debt worth speaking of rests upon all this church property. The premises have been singularly beautified. The congregation is made up of sturdy people who have grown in wealth and education, and are strong in a commendable spirit of unity and peace among themselves, and with their pastor. There are now but forty-seven families in the congregation, numbering about 260 souls. There are fifty-four children attending the school.

Rev. Ferdinand Koerdt was born in Oestinghausen, Westphalia, August 23, 1853. During his boyhood days, he visited the schools of his native village, and at the age of twelve years he began his collegiate course at Paderborn. After six years in college he entered the Royal academy of Munster, and three years later the young man began his course of philosophy and theology. The "May Laws," probably better known as the "Kultur Kampf," became very obnoxious, and made life exceedingly unpleasant for a many a student preparing for the ministry. In consequence, young Mr. Koerdt departed for America in 1875. He entered Mount St. Mary's seminary, Cincinnati, as a student for the diocese of Fort Wayne, in October of the same year. Ten months afterward the young gentleman was ordained to the priesthood by Rt. Rev. Bishop Dwenger, July 8, 1876, in the cathedral, Fort Wayne. Father Koerdt was appointed pastor of the St. Aloysius church, Sheldon, to whose people he still devotes his services.

RT. REV. JOSEPH DWENGER, D. D.

Joseph Dwenger was born in Auglaize county, Ohio, in 1837. When about three years of age his father died; the mother then moved to Cincinnati. The boy received his early education in the schools of Holy Trinity. At the age of twelve the boy's mother passed from earth and he was cared for by Rev. Andrew Kunkler, the provincial superior of the religious community known as the Precious Blood. With these fathers the boy completed his collegiate course, but in the higher branches, theology and the accompanying studies, he graduated at Mount St. Mary's, Cincinnati. He was ordained to the priesthood, for the community above named, by Most Rev. Archbishop Purcell, at the early age of twenty-two years, by papal dispensation of course, on the 4th of September, 1859. The young priest was immediately appointed professor and director in the seminary of his order, a position which he held for three years, and he also founded the new seminary at Carthagena, in Mercer county, Ohio, which to this day is a flourishing institution. The young clergyman was next engaged in parochial work, from which, after five years, he was called to a more difficult duty.

In 1866 Father Joseph, as he was then familiarly known, accompanied Archbishop Purcell to the second plenary council of Baltimore as the representative of the order to which he belonged, and also in the capacity of theologian to the archbishop. From 1867 to 1872 Father Dwenger was exclusively occupied in preaching missions throughout Ohio, Indiana and Kentucky. He also held the office of secretary and consultor, in the meantime, in the community of the Precious Blood. Upon the death of Bishop Luers, Rev. Joseph Dwenger, at the age of thirty-four and a half years, was appointed second bishop of Fort Wayne. He was consecrated for the exalted position, in the cathedral of Cincinnati, by Archbishop Purcell, April 14th, 1872, and without any delay took charge of the diocese entrusted to him.

In 1874 Bishop Dwenger went to Europe with the first American pilgrimage, of which he was the acknowledged head. The objective points of visit were Rome and Lourdes. In 1875 he undertook the erection of an asylum in which he intended placing the orphan boys, who up to this time had been cared for together with the orphan girls, at the orphanage at Rensselaer. He procured fifty acres of land adjoining the city of LaFayette, upon which he erected a commodious four-story brick building, at a cost of $30,000. The new asylum is called St. Joseph's orphan asylum and manual labor school, and has an average of 110 boys; ten sisters of Charity and two brothers have charge under the direction of a reverend chaplain. In 1879 the bishop appointed a diocesan school board, selecting ten clergymen, to whom he gave the supervision of matters pertaining to the parochial schools of the diocese. There is a president and secretary of the board though the bishop is ex officio the superior officer. The diocese is divided into seven school districts, and all the schools in every district is visited once a year and examined by one or more members of the board. A printed pamphlet of about 100 pages, containing a report from all the schools, is annually submitted to the bishop. This is known as the *Diocesan School Report*. This same system was afterward adopted by the provincial council of Cincinnati and by the national council of Baltimore, and in its main features is established in many dioceses of the United States.

In 1883 the Rt. Rev. Prelate paid his official visit to Rome. During his absence Very Rev. J. Benoit was administrator of the diocese. In 1884 Bishop Dwenger celebrated his silver jubilee, the twenty-fifth anniversary of his ordination to the priesthood. All the priests of his diocese, and a number from other parts, gathered in the cathedral to attend the ceremony. Rt. Rev. Bishop Rademacher, of Nashville, preached on the occasion.

In November and December, 1884, the bishop attended the Third National council of Baltimore. Among the thirteen archbishops and seventy prelates, he was the nineteenth bishop in point of rank and seniority. The council lasted about six weeks. In March, of the following year, he left for Rome in the interest of the late Baltimore council, as the representative of the American Hierarchy. The bishop spent seven months in the Eternal city. To his indefatigable labors, and to his knowledge of affairs pertaining to the church in America, are due to a great extent the sanction of the college of cardinals and the approbation of the Pope, of the deliberations of the last council of Baltimore.

During his stay in Rome, the Bishop was the guest of the North American college. The 4th of July was at hand. The authorities of the college were somewhat timid about hoisting the American colors in such close proximity to the Quirinal palace, almost in sight of King Humbert's dwelling. But the bishop came to the fore, and as an American citizen commanded the flag to be sent to the top of the staff, amid the joy and patriotic exuberance of all the students, who though beneath Italian skies, never forget their native America, nor allow an occasion to pass without singing the praises of fair Columbia's shores.

In 1886, Bishop Dwenger carried out a long cherished plan of erecting a suitable home for orphan girls. The asylum was built on a twenty-five acre plat of ground within the limits of the city of Fort Wayne. A special notice is given this asylum elsewhere in this sketch, devoted to the Catholic church in Fort Wayne.

Bishop Dwenger again went to Europe, in September, 1888, on an official visit, and was in consultation with the cardinals, and also had private audience with Leo the Thirteenth. The immense debt that rested upon the diocese when Bishop Dwenger took charge, has been cancelled long since. Thousands upon thousands of dollars have passed through his hands in meeting demands that came upon him in the earlier history of his regime, also thousands upon thousands again, have been carefully expended in the erection of two commodious orphan homes. Large amounts of money are contributed to him during the years, but all find their way into channels that provide bread for the needy, and charity for the homeless child.

The diocese over which Bishop Dwenger presides comprises about one-half of the state of Indiana, being the northern portion, and contains forty-four counties. There are at present in this diocese 120 priests, 130 churches and twenty chapels. There are, one university, sixty-five schools and about 9,000 pupils; orphan asylums two, and hospitals five. During his administration as Bishop, Mgr. Dwenger has conferred the order of priesthood upon many young men. He has traveled over his entire diocese as a rule once in every two years, sometimes oftener, either to administer confirmation and preach, to dedicate a church or perform some other Episcopal function. Bishop Dwenger is still in good health, though his silvery hair, whitened beyond his age, makes him appear older than he is.

Summary.—In the city of Fort Wayne there are, one bishop, eleven priests, four churches and three chapels. There is one hospital, one orphan asylum, one academy, six schools, with about 1,800 pupils. There are about 1,600 families in these four churches, numbering about 7,800 souls.

In Allen county there are twelve congregations, with a total of 2,177 families, the total souls ranging at 10,840. Catholicity has probably gained more in Allen county from the ranks of non-Catholics than she has lost from her own fold. Catholic Christianity is advancing as a rule, within this county, and is at peace with the entire community.

BENCH AND BAR OF ALLEN COUNTY.

BY JUDGE ALLEN ZOLLARS.

The territory now comprised within the limits of Allen county was carved, almost wholly, out of the county of Randolph, although the act creating the county was entitled, "An act for the formation of a new county out of the counties of Randolph and Delaware." That act was approved on the 17th day of December, 1823. At the suggestion of Gen. John Tipton, the new county, whose legal existence was to begin in April following the passage of the act, was named Allen, in memory of Col. John Allen, of Kentucky, who was killed at the battle of the River Raisin, on the 22d day of January, 1813.

By the third section of the act, Lot Bloomfield and Caleb Lewis, of Wayne county, Abiathar Hathaway, of Fayette county, William Conner, of Hamilton county, and James M. Ray, of Marion county, were appointed commissioners to determine and locate the seat of justice for the new county. It further provided, that said commissioners should convene at the house of Alexander Ewing, at Fort Wayne, on the fourth Monday of May thereafter, and proceed immediately to discharge the duties assigned. Fort Wayne was determined upon, and fixed as "the seat of justice."

It was provided in the eighth section of the act, that certain territory, which now constitutes the county of Huntington, the whole of Adams and Wells counties, as now bounded, except one row of townships on the south; the whole of DeKalb and Steuben counties as now constituted, and one row of townships off the east side of Noble and LaGrange counties, as now constituted, "shall be attached to the said county of Allen; and the inhabitants residing within the said bounds shall enjoy all the rights and privileges that to the citizens of the said county of Allen shall or may properly belong; and that said county of Allen shall have jurisdiction, both civil and criminal, over the territory so attached, in all cases as though the same were a constituent part of the said county of Allen."

Pursuant to the first section of the act, "for carrying the laws into effect in the new counties," William Hendricks, governor of the state, by commission dated April 2, 1824, appointed Allen Hamilton sheriff of Allen county, until the next general election, and until his successor should be elected and qualified—should he so long behave well. Under that appointment, and in compliance with a further provision of the said section, Mr. Hamilton, as such sheriff, gave notice to the qualified voters of Allen county, authorizing and directing them to hold an election on the 22d day of May, 1824, for the purpose of electing two associate judges of the circuit court, one clerk of the circuit court, one recorder, and the commissioners of the county. Samuel Hanna and Benjamin Cushman were elected associate judges; Anthony L. Davis, clerk and recorder; William Rockhill, commissioner for a term of three years from the 22d day of May, 1824; James Wyman for two years, and Francis Comparet for one year from said date.

Under the judicial system in force during the existence of the constitution of 1816, the circuit courts consisted of a president, and two associate judges. It was not essential that the associate judges should be lawyers. The president alone, in the absence of the associate judges, or the president and one of the associate judges in the absence of the other, might hold a court. The associate judges, in the absence of the president, might also hold a court, and hear and decide causes, except capital cases and cases in chancery. The circuit courts in each county in the state had common law and chancery jurisdiction, as also complete criminal jurisdiction, subject to restrictions, imposed by law, and probate jurisdiction.

The state was, from time to time, divided into judicial circuits, as the business required. The president judge was appointed by joint ballot of the two houses of the general assembly. He was required to live in the circuit, and had jurisdiction co-extensive with the limits thereof. The associate judges were for the county in which they lived, and were elected by the people of such county. From 1816, when the territory was admitted as a state into the Federal Union, until 1818, all judicial matters relating to the vicinity of Fort Wayne were settled in Vincennes. In 1818 Randolph county was constituted, with Winchester as the seat of justice, and embraced within its boundaries, until the formation of Allen county, all this portion of the state extending to Lake Michigan.

By an act of the legislature approved January 14, 1824, Allen county was made a part of the third judicial circuit, which embraced the counties of Randolph, Wayne, Union, Fayette, Franklin, Dearborn, Switzerland, Ripley and Allen. The extent of territory over which the jurisdiction of the judge of that circuit extended cannot be known, except approximately, without an examination of the several statutes fixing at that time, the boundaries of the several counties. It will suffice here to say, that the circuit extended from the Ohio river on the south, to the Michigan line on the north. The first term of the circuit court in Allen county, was held at the house of Alexander Ewing, commencing on the 9th day of August, 1824, and lasting three days. The court was held by the associate judges, Samuel Hanna and Benjamin Cushman, the president judge of the circuit not being present. The grand jury returned seventeen indictments: two for adultery, one for assault and battery, four for playing at a game (of cards), and ten for retailing spirituous liquors. The ten indicted for selling liquor pleaded guilty and were fined by the court $3.00 and costs respectively, except one, whos fine was $4.00 and costs. Two of those charged with "playing game," submitted their case to a jury and were fined $10.00

and costs. One charged with adultery was tried by a jury and acquitted, while the female charged with the same offense was convicted and sentenced to fifteen days' imprisonment in the county jail. The followances were made: To each of the grand jurors for his services, $1.50; to Robert Hood, as constable for the court, 75 cents per day; to Allen Hamilton, sheriff, for four months' services, $16.62; to the prosecuting attorney, for his services for the term $5.00. At that term, William G. Ewing was admitted and sworn as an attorney of the Allen circuit court, and CHARLES W. EWING was appointed by the court prosecuting attorney. The law at that time made it the duty of the circuit court in each county to appoint some person, legally authorized to practice as an attorney and counsellor at law, as prosecuting attorney in such county, who should hold his office during good behavior, to be adjudged by the court, and who should receive for his services, in addition to the fees allowed by law, such compensation as the judges of the court, in their discretion, might allow, to be certified by the court, and paid out of the county treasury. The same act, however (January 20, 1824), provided that after the second Monday of the following August, the governor should appoint a prosecuting attorney for each judicial circuit, who should hold his office for one year, and receive as compensation an annual salary of $250, payable out of the state treasury, and $5.00 in each conviction, to be taxed against the party convicted.

Of the associate judges, who held that first term of the court, it is not necessary to speak at length here, as they were not lawyers. Samuel Hanna acted as such associate for four years. He was a business man of great sagacity, and uprightness of character. He died in Fort Wayne in 1866, a man of great wealth, and universally esteemed and honored.

By an act of the legislature, approved on the 12th day of February, 1825, Allen county was attached to the Fifth judicial circuit. It is sufficient to state here, that the circuit was large enough to include Marion county, in which Indianapolis was, and is, situated, and a large portion of the eastern part of the state.

HON. BETHUEL MORRIS,

of Indianapolis, was the judge of that circuit, having been appointed on the 9th day of January, 1825, and hence, became the judge of the Allen circuit court. He was a native of Virginia, but became a resident of Centerville, Ind., in 1818. Four years later he removed to Indianapolis, and until 1834, except the time that he was on the bench, was engaged in the practice of the law. In that year, he abandoned the profession, and became president of the old State Bank of Indiana, which position he held for many years. He continued to be a resident of Indianapolis until his death.

The second term of the Allen circuit court was held at the residence of Alexander Ewing, commencing on the 6th day of June, 1825, and lasting five days. Judge Morris was present as president judge, Samuel Hanna sitting with him as associate judge. At that term, James Rariden, of Richmond, Calvin Fletcher, of Indianapolis, and Henry Cooper, of Fort Wayne, were admitted to the bar. In after years Rariden won an honorable distinction as a lawyer and a legislator.

At that term CALVIN FLETCHER was sworn in as prosecuting attorney for the term, the prosecuting attorney being absent. He was born in Ludlow, Vt., in 1798. In early life he was inured to physical labor, and had but meager advantages of education, but so improved his opportunities as to acquire more than an ordinary education for that day. In 1817 he worked his way, mostly on foot, to Urbana, Ohio, where he obtained labor as a hired man for a time, and then taught a school. There he studied law and was admitted to the bar in 1821. In the fall of that year, with his young wife, he started for Indianapolis in a wagon, and after a journey of fourteen days, camping out the same number of nights reached the town, where there were a few newly erected cabins. He commenced the practice of the law there, and continued the practice for about twenty-two years. In 1825 he was appointed prosecuting attorney for the fifth judicial circuit. In the following year he was elected to the state senate, and continued a senator for seven years. In 1834 he was appointed by the legislature one of four to organize a state bank, and to act as sinking fund commissioner. He held that position for seven years. From 1843 to 1859, he was president of the branch of the State Bank at Indianapolis. He was a good and successful lawyer. He died at Indianapolis in 1866, very wealthy, and very highly respected by all. Of Mr. Cooper, mention is made hereafter.

The third term of the court was held at the house of William Suttenfield, commencing on the 21st day of November, 1825. The president judge not being present, the court was held by the associate judges, Samuel Hanna and Benjamin Cushman. Calvin Fletcher was present as prosecuting attorney. He was fined $5.00 for contempt of court, but the fine was remitted. Oliver H. Smith, then a resident of Connorsville, in Fayette county, attended that term of court. In his "Early Indiana Trials," he gives the following description of a trip to Fort Wayne, and the incidents of a trial before the associate judges, which will be of interest to the lawyers of this day, as well as to others:

"The fall term of the circuit courts found Judge Eggleston and myself, well mounted, once more on the circuit, the Judge upon his pacing Indian pony, the same that I afterward rode through an electioneering congressional campaign, I then rode my gray 'fox.' We were joined at Centerville by James Rariden, mounted on 'Old Gray,' one of the finest animals I have ever seen. Our court was to be held on the next Monday at Fort Wayne. We reached Winchester late in the evening and took lodgings at the hotel of Paul W. Way, but no newspaper heralded the arrival. How different was the circumstance that occurred when I was in the senate of the United States. Silas Wright, Thomas H. Benton and James Buchanan, for recreation, ran up to Philadelphia; the next day the *Pennsylvanian* announced that Senators Benton and Buchanan had arrived in that city, and taken lodgings at the United States Hotel. A few days after the three distinguished senators were in their seats. I sat at the time in the next seat to Gov. Silas Wright; turning to the Governor, 'I see by the papers that Mr. Benton and Mr. Buchanan have been in Philadelphia and taken lodgings at the United States Hotel; how did it happen that your name was not announced, as you were with them?' 'I did not send *my* name to the printer.' So it was with us.

"After early breakfast we were once more upon our horses, with one hundred miles through the wilderness before us. There were two Indian paths that led to Fort Wayne, the one by Chief Francis Godfroy's on the Salamonie river, the other in a more easterly direction, crossing the Mississinewa higher up and striking the "Quaker Trace," from Richmond to Fort Wayne, south of the head waters of the Wabash river. After a moment's consultation, Mr. Rariden, who was our guide, turned the head of 'Old Gray' to the eastern path, and off we started, at a brisk traveling gate, in high spirits. The day passed away; it was very hot, and there was no water to be had for ourselves or horses. About one o'clock we came to the Wabash river, nearly dried up, but there was grass upon the bank for our horses, and we dismounted, took off the saddles, blankets and saddle-bags, when the question arose, should we hold the horses while they grazed, tie them to bushes, spancel them, or turn them loose? We agreed that the latter was the best for the horses and easiest for us, but I raised the question of safety, and brought up the adage, 'Safe bind safe find.' Mr. Rariden.— 'You could not drive Old Gray away from me.' Judge Eggleston. — 'My Indian pony will never leave me.' I made no promise for my 'Gray Fox.' The bridles were taken off, and the horses turned loose to graze. A moment after, Old Gray stuck up his head, turned to the path we had just come, and bounded off at a full gallop swarming with flies, followed by the pacing Indian pony of the Judge, at his highest speed. Fox lingered behind, but soon became infected with the bad example of his associates, and away they all went, leaving us sitting under the shade of a tree that stood for years afterward on the bank of the Wabash. Our horses were, a week afterward, taken up at Fort Defiance, in Ohio, and brought to us at Winchester on our return. It took us but a moment to decide what to do. Ten miles would take us up to Thompson's on Townsend's Prairie. Our saddles and blankets were hung up above the reach of the wolves. Each took his saddle-bag upon his back, and and we started at a quick step — Rariden in the lead, Judge Eggleston in the center, and I brought up the rear.

"The heat was intense. None of us had been much used to walking. I am satisfied we must all have broken down, but most fortunately there had fallen the night before a light rain, and the water lay in the shade in the horse tracks. We were soon on our knees, with our mouths to the water. — Tell me not of your Croton, ye New Yorkers, nor of your Fairmount, ye Philadelphians, here was water, 'what *was* water.' Near night we reached the prairie worn down with heat and fatigue. The thunders were roaring and the lightnings flashing from the black clouds in the west. A storm was coming up on the wings of a hurricane, and ten minutes after we arrived at Mr. Thompson's it broke upon us in all its fury, and continued raining in torrents during the night. We were in a low, one-story log cabin, about twenty feet square, no floor above, with a clapboard roof. Supper, to us dinner, was soon ready. Three articles of diet only on the plain walnut table, corn-dodgers, boiled squirrels and sassafras tea. Epicures at the 5 o'clock table of the Astor, St. Nicholas, Metropolitan and Revere, how do you like the bill of fare? To us it was sumptuous and thankfully received. Supper over, we soon turned in, and such a night of sweet sleep I never had before or since. The next morning our saddles and blankets were brought to us from the Wabash. The landlord provided us with ponies and we set forward at full speed, arrived at Fort Wayne that night, and took lodgings at the hotel of William N. Hood. In the morning court met, Judge Eggleston, president, and side judges, Thompson and Cushman, on the bench. Fort Wayne contained about 200 inhabitants, and the county of Allen some fifty voters. There were no cases on docket to try of a criminal character. Court adjourned early, and we all went up the St. Mary's river, to Chief Richardville's, to see an Indian horse race.

"The nags were brought to the ground, a gray pony about twelve hands high, and a roan, rather larger, like Eclipse and Henry, to contest the superiority of stock between the bands of Miamis and Pottawattomies. Six Indians were selected as judges — two placed at the starting point, two at the quarter stake, and two at the coming-out places. 'Riders up — clear the track,' and away they went under whip and spur. The race over, the judges met, the spokesman, a large Miami, says, 'Race even, Miami grey take first quarter, Pottawattomie roan take last quarter,' and all are satisfied. In the evening the grand-jury brought in a bill against Elisha B. Harris for stealing an Indian pony. Judge Eggleston.— 'Any more business before you, Mr. Foreman?' Gen. Tipton.— 'None sir.' 'You are discharged.'

"Judge Eggleston.— 'There is but one case on the docket for trial, an appeal case, damages claimed $5. I feel quite tired, and will be obliged to my associates to try the case.' Judge Cushman.— 'Certainly.' The case was called. Henry Cooper for the plaintiff, and Hiram Brown for the defendant. Case submitted to the court. The action was for damages, $5 claimed, for killing the plaintiff's dog. The witness swore that he saw the defendant running with his rifle, across his yard; saw him lay it on the fence; saw the smoke; heard the crack; saw the dog fall; went to where the dog lay, and saw the bullet-hole just behind the foreleg. Here Cooper rested with a triumphant air, and indeed, to a common eye, the case seemed beyond hope, but to the mind of the skillful advocate, capable of drawing the distinction between positive and circumstancial evidence, a different conclusion was come to. "Breckenridge's Miscellanies, and Phillip's Evidence, stating the danger of listening to circumstantial evidence, and enumerating many lamentable cases of convictions and executions for murder upon circumstantial evidence, when the convicts were afterward proved to be entirely innocent, had been widely circulated and extensively read by courts and lawyers until the tendency of the courts was to reject circumstantial evidence. My friend, Mr. Brown, an ingenious attorney, of fine talents, and, by the way, rather waggish, said: 'A single question, Mr. Witness — can you swear you saw the bullet hit the dog!' 'I can swear no such thing.' 'That's all, Mr. Cooper; a case of mere circumstantial evidence, your honors.' Cooper's countenance fell; defeat stared him in the face; the case was submitted to the court without further evidence. Judge Cushman — 'This is a plain case of *circumstantial* evidence. Judgment for the defendant.' Cooper, with great indignation, with his eyes on Brown:—'When I die I wish it engraved upon my tombstone, here lies Henry Cooper — an honest man.' Brown, rising as quick as thought:— 'Pope says an honest man is the noblest work of God. There have been atheists in this world — Bolingbroke of England, Voltaire of France, and Tom Paine of America, with a host of infidel writers who may be named: they have all done nothing against the Almighty. But let Henry Cooper be held up in the mid heavens, by an angel, for the whole race of man to look upon; and let Gabriel, with his trumpet announce to the gazing worlds, *this is God's noblest work*, and all the human race would become atheists in a day.' We returned to Winchester on our borrowed ponies, took our horses that had been brought from Defiance, and reached the Wayne circuit court in good time."

By an act of the legislature approved on the 21st day of January, 1826, Allen county was attached to the Third judicial circuit, of which Hon. Miles C. Eggleston was president judge. Of that circuit it is sufficient to say that it extended far enough south to include Jefferson county, on the Ohio river, at the county seat of which, Madison, Judge Eggleston lived.

The fourth term of the Allen circuit court was held at the house of Alexander Ewing, on the 13th day of February, 1826. It was held by the associate judges, Hanna and Cushman, the president judge being absent. Two indictments were returned by the grand jury: one against an Indian known as Sa-ga-naugh, for murder, and one against Elisha B. Harris, known as "Yankee Harris," for larceny. Harris is said to have lived on the St. Mary's about seven miles from Fort Wayne, and to have adopted as his life-motto, "to be as honest as the nature of the circumstances would admit." Calvin Fletcher was present as prosecuting attorney. Hiram Brown, of Indianapolis, and Moses Cox were admitted and sworn as attorneys, at that term of the court.

JUDGE EGGLESTON.

The fifth term of the court met on the 13th day of August, 1826, and was held by the president judge, Hon. Miles C. Eggleston, with associate Judge Cushman. Judge Eggleston was one of the leading lawyers of the state, and was regarded at that time as one of the best *nisi prius* judges of the state. Hon. AMOS LANE, of Lawrenceburg, was prosecuting attorney at that term, and continued as such until the next year. Mr. Lane had been a member of the legislature of 1816, the first under the state constitution, and was already a lawyer and a man of note. He was the father of Hon. James H. Lane, who in after years was a resident of Kansas and achieved distinction. At that term Benjamin Cushman, one of the associate judges, was indicted for selling liquors. He was tried by a jury and acquitted.

The next and sixth term of the court was held at the house of William Suttenfield, commencing on the 13th day of August, 1827. The president judge, Eggleston, and associate judges, William H. Hood and Benjamin Cushman, presided. At that term, William Quarles, afterward a prominent lawyer of Indianapolis, was admitted to the bar.

At that term, also, OLIVER H. SMITH was sworn in as prosecuting attorney. He was born on Smith's Island, near Trenton, N. J., in 1794. Until 1813 he attended a school "off and on," in a building near his home. On account of the death of his father, he left home that year to make his own living, and found work in a woolen mill at Philadelphia. In 1817 he came to Indiana, and settled at Rising Sun, but in a short time removed to Lawrenceburgh, and commenced the study of the law. In 1820 he was examined by Judge Eggleston and licensed to practice. Soon afterward he removed to Versailles, in Ripley county, and opened an office, but in a few months removed to Connorsville in Fayette county, where he continued to reside until 1839, when he became a citizen of Indianapolis. In 1822 he was elected a member of the legislature, and made chairman of the judiciary committee. While prosecuting attorney, under an appointment in 1824, Mr. Smith prosecuted some persons in Madison county upon a charge of having killed some friendly Indians. In a public address in after years, he thus referred to that prosecution: "I was circuit prosecuting attorney at the time of the trials at the falls of Fall Creek, where Pendleton now stands. Four of the prisoners were convicted of murder, and three of them hung, for killing Indians. The court was held in a double log cabin. The grand jury sat upon a long in the woods, and the foreman signed the bills of indictment, which I prepared, upon his knee; there was not a petit juror that had shoes on — all wore moccasins, and were belted around the waist, and carried side-knives used by the hunters." In 1826, Mr. Smith was elected to congress from the Third congressional district, which comprised one-third of the state, and extended from the Ohio river to the Michigan line. He served with distinction in the house, and in 1836 was elected a senator of the United States. He served his term in the senate with ability and distinction, and at intervals, when at home, and after the close of his term, conducted a large practice at Indianapolis. As a lawyer, he was in the front rank with the greatest lawyers of the state. He died in 1859. At the term last above mentioned, associate judge, Cushman, was indicted for carrying concealed weapons; notwithstanding these indictments, Judge Cushman was regarded as a good citizen.

The seventh term of the court was held at the residence of Benjamin Archer, commencing on the 12th day of May, 1828, associate judges, Hood and Cushman, presiding, the president judge being absent. At that term Charles H. Test was sworn as prosecuting attorney for the term, the prosecutor for the circuit being absent. It was at this session that the first will was recorded in Allen county, the will of Abram Burnett.

The eighth term of court was commenced on the 10th day of November, 1828, associate judges, Hood and Cushman, presiding, the president judge again being absent. At this term the first conviction on a charge of felony occurred.

At this term also, DAVID WALLACE was appointed and sworn in as special prosecutor for the term. He was born in Pennsylvania in 1799. When he was a small boy his father emigrated to Ohio, and settled near Cincinnati, in the vicinity of Gen. Harrison's residence. Harrison, who was then in congress, had young Wallace appointed a cadet at West Point. He graduated there in 1821, and for a short time was a tutor in that institution. He then entered the army as a lieutenant of artillery, and in about one year resigned his commission. His father in the meantime, having settled at Brookville, Ind., he returned to his paternal home and commenced the study of the law in the office of Judge Eggleston. He was admitted to the bar in 1823, and soon had a good practice. In 1828, 1829 and 1830 he was elected to the legislature. In 1831 he was elected lieutenant-governor of the state, and was re-elected in 1834. In 1837 he was elected governor of Indiana. While holding that office he issued a proclamation appointing a day of thanksgiving and prayer. It was the first paper of the kind issued by a governor of Indiana, and it established a precedent which has been followed to the present day. After the expiration of his term as governor, he resumed the practice of the law. In 1841 he was elected to congress from the Indianapolis district. After the expiration of one term he again resumed the practice. During two years subsequent to the expiration of his term in congress, and prior to 1850, he resided at Fort Wayne, engaged in his profession. By 1850 he had become a resident of Indianapolis, and in that year was elected a member of the convention to frame a new state constitution. In 1856 he was elected a judge of the court of common pleas, and held the position until his death in 1859. As a judge, he was impartial and able, and it has been said that in that position he made the best record of his life. Governor Wallace was not a money-getting nor money-saving man. He took more pleasure in acquiring knowledge and an honorable position than in gaining property. At one time he entered into a business venture at Fort Wayne which cost him his entire estate. It has been said of him that "as an orator he had few equals in the state. With a voice modulated to the finest precision, an eye sparkling and expressive, a countenance and person remarkable for beauty and symmetry, he stepped upon the speaker's stand, in these respects, far in advance of his compeers."

The ninth term of the court commenced on the 11th day of May, 1829. Judge Eggleston, the president judge, and associate judges, Hood and Cushman, presiding. At that term, Martin M. Ray, who afterward became a distinguished lawyer, was sworn in as prosecuting attorney for the circuit.

By an act of the legislature, approved January 20, 1830, Allen county became a part of the sixth judicial circuit, composed of the counties of Randolph, Henry, Wayne, Union, Delaware, Fayette, Rush, Elkhart and Allen. Here, again, the exact size of the circuit cannot be determined without an examination of the several acts bounding the counties, and fixing their territorial jurisdiction. Of that circuit

HON. CHARLES H. TEST

was the president judge. At that day he was already a lawyer of note. He acted as president judge of the Allen circuit court until 1833. During the legislature of 1845, Governor Whitcomb, being opposed to the continuance upon the bench of the supreme court of the state, of Judges Dewey and Sullivan, sent the names of Judge Test and Andrew Davidson to the senate as their successors. The senate not being on friendly terms with the governor, rejected the nominations. From 1849 to 1853 Judge Test was secretary of state. In subsequent years, he was for a long time judge of a circuit court in the northwestern part of the state. He also lived for some years at Indianapolis, and died at Lafayette, subsequent to 1883.

The tenth term of the Allen circuit court, and the first after the county became part of the sixth circuit, commenced on the 10th day of May, 1830, Judge Test, the president judge, and associate judge, Hood, presiding. At that term, and until the latter part of the year 1831 JAMES PERRY was prosecuting attorney. He lived at Centerville, Wayne county, and continued to reside there in the practice of the law until he was nearly ninety years of age. At that term also, David H. Colerick, then a young lawyer from Ohio, was sworn in as an attorney, *ex gratia*, for the term. For a proper notice of the subsequent brilliant and useful life of Mr. Colerick, we refer to subsequent pages. William J. Brown was prosecuting attorney at the April term of the court, in 1832, and Samuel C. Sample at the October term of the same year. During the year 1830 and until the April term, 1831, Messrs. Hood and Cushman remained the associate judges. At the April term, 1831, and during the remainder of Judge Test's service, Messrs. Hood and L. G. Thompson were associate judges.

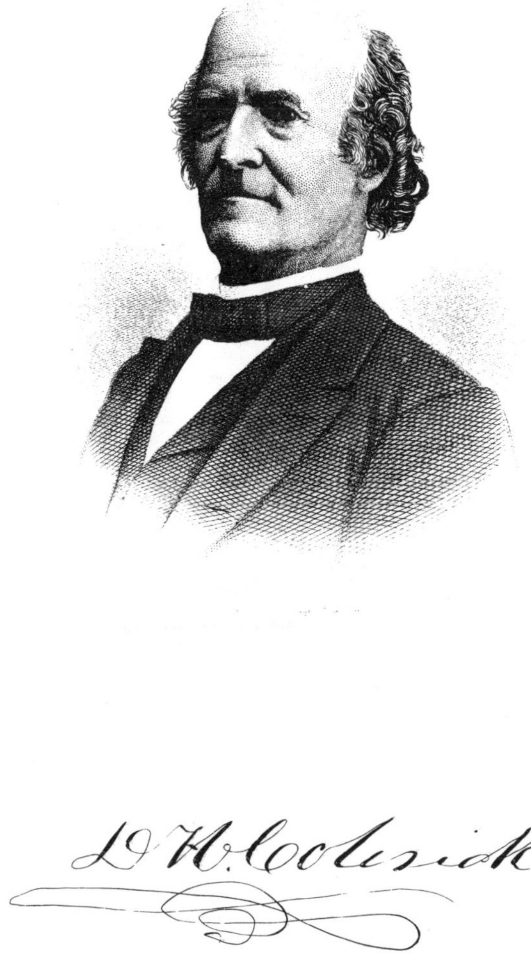

By an act of the legislature, approved on the 2nd day of February, 1832, LaGrange county was organized and made a part of the sixth circuit, along with Allen. The boundaries of the county were fixed as they now are, but by another section of the act, all the territory lying east of the county, to the Ohio state line, and south so as to include all of what now is DeKalb and Noble counties, except one row of townships on the south, was attached to the county for civil and judicial purposes. The county was named, as stated by one of the state historians, "in respect to the residence of General Lafayette in France."

By an act of the legislature approved on the 7th day of January, 1833, the eighth judicial circuit was created, embracing the counties of Carroll, Cass, Allen, LaGrange, Elkhart, St. Joseph, LaPorte, Huntington, Wabash and Miami. The boundaries of the three last named were fixed by an act of February, 1832. A section of the act provided that the several parts of the new counties should remain as they then were, for judicial purposes. The boundaries of Wabash and Miami counties were further defined by an act approved on the 30th day of January, 1833. Huntington county, as stated in the act first above mentioned, was named in honor of Samuel Huntington, one of the signers of the declaration of independence. Wabash county is supposed to have taken its name from the Wabash river, and Miami from the confederacy of Indians which inhabited this portion of the state. Miami county was fully organized under an act approved February 1, 1834, Huntington county, under an act approved February 1, 1834, and Wabash county under an act approved January 22, 1835. Of that circuit

GUSTAVUS A. EVERTS

was judge, and continued to act as judge of the Allen circuit court from the April term, 1833, until after the March term, 1836. He was about forty years of age, and resided at South Bend, the county seat of St. Joseph county. He was a lawyer of moderate ability, and not especially popular with a portion of the bar at Fort Wayne. The associate judges who presided during that period were Messrs. Hood and Thompson, above mentioned, William G. Ewing, David Rankin and Peter Huling. During that period also, John B. Chapman and Samuel C. Sample were prosecuting attorneys, the former for two years, and the latter for one year.

In 1834 Carroll county was taken from the eighth circuit, and made a part of the first. The boundaries of the counties of Noble, DeKalb, Steuben, Adams and Whitley were fixed by an act of the legislature approved February 7, 1835. By an act approved February 6, 1836, the county of Whitley was attached to Huntington county in the eighth circuit, for judicial purposes. The county is said to have been named in honor of Col. William Whitley, of Lincoln county, Ky., and of the bravest and most hospitable pioneers of that state, who fell at the battle of the Thames. Noble county, as stated in the act, was named " in honor of the late Hon. James Noble." The county was organized as a county under an act of the legislature, approved February 4, 1836, and attached to the eighth judicial circuit. Adams county was named in honor of President Adams. It was fully organized under an act of the legislature approved January 22, 1836. By an act approved February 4, 1836, it was attached to the eighth judicial circuit, as were also the counties of Fulton, Kosciusko, Marshall and Porter. The eighth circuit, thus, in 1836, embraced the counties of Cass, Miami, Wabash, Huntington, Allen, LaGrange, Elkhart, St. Joseph, LaPorte, Porter, Marshall, Fulton, Kosciusko, Noble and Adams, including the territory attached to the several counties for judicial purposes. Of that large circuit,

SAMUEL C. SAMPLE

became the president judge in 1836. His first service as judge in Allen county was at the September term, 1836. As already stated, he had been prosecuting attorney during the time Judge Everts was on the bench. He lived at South Bend, and was about forty years of age when he went upon the bench. He was the president judge of the Allen circuit court for less than one year. He represented this district in congress, and subsequently went into the State Bank at South Bend, where he died. During the time he was upon the bench, the associate judges were Peter Huling and David Rankin.

During that time JOSEPH L. JERNEGAN, of South Bend, was prosecuting attorney. He was a very brilliant man, and one of the best lawyers in northern Indiana. He subsequently removed to New York city, and accumulated a fortune by the practice of the law.

The county of Steuben was fully organized as a county under an act approved January 18, 1837, and named in honor of Baron Steuben, a Prussian officer of distinction, who joined the American army during the revolutionary war, and rendered valuable service to the struggling colonies. DeKalb was fully organized as a county under an act approved January 14, 1837, and was given its name in memory of Gen. DeKalb, a revolutionary officer of German descent, who was killed in the battle of Camden. By that act also, the county was attached to the eighth judicial circuit. The boundaries of Wells county having been fixed by the act above mentioned, approved February 7, 1835, the county was fully organized under an act approved February 2, 1837.

By an act approved on the 9th day of December, 1837, the eighth judicial circuit was reduced in size and made to embrace the counties of Cass, Miami, Wabash, Huntington, Allen, Adams, Wells, Jay, DeKalb, Steuben, Noble, LaGrange and Whitley. Jay county had been organized under an act approved January 30, 1836.

CHARLES W. EWING

was president judge of the eighth circuit in 1837, and remained the judge of the Allen circuit court until after the March term, 1839. As we have seen, Mr. Ewing was appointed prosecuting attorney at the first term of the Allen circuit court, in 1824. The father of Mr. Ewing was born in Pennsylvania, and was of Irish parentage. Charles W. was born in the state of New York, his father having become a resident of that state. In subsequent years the father moved with his family, first to what is now Monroe, in the state of Michigan, and then to Washington, now known as Piqua, Ohio, and resided at the latter place and at Troy, seven miles away, until 1822. In that year he moved to Fort Wayne, and died in 1827, leaving a valuable property. It is said by those who knew him, that Judge Ewing was a good lawyer for his day, and quite an orator, but eccentric. He came to an unfortunate death, when he ought to have been in the vigor and prime of his life. During the time he was president judge, the associate judges were Peter Huling, Nathaniel Coleman, Michael Shiras and Marshall S. Wines. During the most of that time, Thomas Johnson was prosecuting attorney.

By an act of the legislature approved January 22, 1839, the eighth judicial circuit was made to embrace the counties of Cass, Miami, Wabash, Huntington, Allen, Whitley, Noble, LaGrange, Steuben and DeKalb. Of that circuit

HENRY CHASE

became president judge by appointment in August, 1839, and remained the judge of the Allen circuit court for a little over one year. Judge Chase lived in Logansport, the county seat of Cass county. He was about thirty-nine years old when he went upon the bench, and as we have been informed by a lawyer still living, who was acquainted with the early judges of the different circuits to which Allen county was attached, he was one of the best judges of his day. During the time he was judge of the Allen circuit court, the associate judges were Nathaniel Coleman and Marshall S. Wines. During that time John W. Wright was prosecuting attorney. The circuit was the same when

JOHN W. WRIGHT,

of Logansport, who had the year before been prosecuting attorney, became the president judge in 1840. He remained the judge of the Allen circuit court for about two years.

Judge Wright was born at Lancaster, Ohio, in 1811. He graduated at the Ohio university in 1832, and went to Logansport, Ind., a year later, and began in a short time the practice of the law. He was judge for five years, including two years that Allen county was in his circuit. After retiring from the bench he was elected mayor of Logansport. He also had somewhat to do with banking and railroad affairs. In 1858 he was elected to the legislature on the democratic ticket, but declined the office, and went to Kansas to take part in preventing the state from becoming a slave state. The same year he was elected to the Kansas constitutional convention, and afterward to the legislature of the state, and was made speaker of the house. A few years subsequent he returned to Logansport. A short time after the inauguration of President Lincoln he removed to Washington, D. C., and made that his permanent residence until the time of his death, on the 9th of October, 1889. It is said that he prospered in his profession there, and left a competency to his children.

During the time that he was judge of the Allen circuit court, the associate judges were Nathaniel Coleman, Marshall S. Wines and J. H. McMahon. During the most of that time LUCIEN P. FERRY was prosecuting attorney. During the balance of the time the office was held by WILLIAM H. COOMBS, a proper notice of whom is given hereafter.

By an act of the legislature, approved December 14, 1841, the judicial circuits were changed and a new, and twelfth judicial circuit was created, embracing the counties of Allen, Adams, Wells, Huntington, Whitley, Noble, Steuben, LaGrange and DeKalb. Of that circuit,

JAMES W. BORDEN

became president judge in 1842, and remained judge of the Allen circuit court until 1851. During that period the associate judges were Nathaniel Coleman, R. Starkweather, J. H. McMahon and Andrew Metzgar. During that time, William H. Coombs was prosecuting attorney for more than one year. For one year of the time, L. C. JACOBY was prosecuting attorney. He resided at Fort Wayne for many years thereafter, but finally located in the practice of the law in the west, where he still is. He was a lawyer of fair ability, but had some peculiar eccentricities. For two years during the period named, ROBERT L. DOUGLAS was prosecuting attorney. He lived at Angola, the county seat of Steuben county. He was a good lawyer, a man of culture, and an accomplished orator. In 1851 he removed to Council Bluffs, Iowa, engaged in the practice of the law, and accumulated a forture. He died a number of years ago while on a visit in Florida.

Following Mr. Douglas, ELZA A. MCMAHON was prosecuting attorney for one year, commencing with the year 1846. Following him, and beginning with the year 1847, JOSEPH BRACKENRIDGE was prosecuting attorney for three years. For an adequate notice of him, reference is made to following pages. Of his successor, also, JAMES L. WORDEN, who served as prosecuting attorney for three years, beginning with the year 1850, mention is hereafter made at length.

When Judge Borden retired from the circuit bench, the twelfth circuit was still the same as when he became judge.

ELZA A. MC MAHON

became the president judge of the circuit in 1851, and remained the judge of the Allen circuit court until 1855. As already stated, he had been prosecuting attorney during the year 1846. He lived at Fort

Wayne, having come from Ohio about 1845. He was about forty-two years of age when he went upon the bench and was unmarried. The writer is informed by a lawyer at Fort Wayne who knew him, that he was a fair lawyer, high-minded, and pleasant as a judge. Although delicate in health, and occasionally melancholy, he was at times witty and fond of humor. He was judge until 1855. A year after that, he removed to Minnesota, and died there about fifteen years ago, almost a mental wreck. During the first year that he was judge, and until the statutes of 1852 went into effect, abolishing the office of associate judge, Nathaniel Coleman and Andrew Metzgar were associate judges. During about three years of Judge McMahon's term, James L. Worden was prosecuting attorney. During the last year of that term Edwin R. Wilson filled that office.

During the term of Judge McMahon, by an act of the legislature, approved June 17, 1852, the state was re-districted for judicial purposes, and the tenth judicial circuit was formed, embracing the counties of Adams, Wells, Huntington, Wabash, Whitley, Allen, Noble, DeKalb, LaGrange, Steuben, Elkhart and Kosciusko. By the subsequent act of January 21, 1853, also during the term of Judge McMahon, the counties of Huntington and Wabash were taken from the tenth circuit and added to the eleventh circuit. Thus stood the tenth circuit in 1855, when JAMES L. WORDEN became the judge. As already stated, he had been prosecuting attorney during a part of the terms of Judges Borden and McMahon. He remained judge until 1858. During one year of his service EDWIN R. WILSON was prosecuting attorney. During two years of his term S. J. STOUGHTON held that office. Mr. Stoughton lived at Auburn, DeKalb county. He subsequently removed to Ligonier, Noble county and later, removed to the state of Kansas, where he died. REUBEN J. DAWSON was appointed by the governor in January, 1858, to fill out the unexpired term of Judge Worden, who had resigned. Of the former, a sketch is hereafter given. During the time he served upon the bench S. J. Stoughton was prosecuting attorney. In the fall of 1858,

EDWIN R. WILSON

was elected judge of the circuit, and remained the judge of the Allen circuit court until 1864. Judge Wilson was born on the 27th day of January, 1827, in Fairfield county, Ohio. His father was born in the north of Ireland, of Scotch parentage. His mother was born in Lancaster, Penn. The parents, with the son, came to Indiana in 1840. Mr. Wilson studied law with Gov. Joseph A. Wright, and was licensed to practice at Indianapolis by Judge Wick and Delano R. Eckels in 1850. He located in Bluffton in Wells county in 1853. In the spring of 1854 he was appointed prosecuting attorney of the tenth circuit, to fill out the unexpired term of Hon. Jas. L. Worden, who had resigned. At the next general election, he was elected to the same office on the democratic ticket over Hon. John W. Dawson, the whig candidate.

He was elected judge of the tenth circuit in the fall of 1858 on the republican ticket. After serving his term of six years upon the bench, he was appointed bank examiner for Indiana by President Johnson. After serving in that capacity for one year, he resigned because not in accord with the administration. In 1867 he removed to Madison, in Jefferson county, Ind., and engaged in the practice of the law as a partner of his brother, Maj. J. L. Wilson. He was elected to the state senate in the fall of 1878, and served for four years. In the fall of 1883 he moved back to Bluffton, where he has since been engaged in the practice of the law as a member of the firm of Wilson & Todd. Judge Wilson was a young man when he entered official life, and when he went upon the bench, but he was studious and energetic, a successful and reputable lawyer, and a careful and acceptable judge.

JAMES L. DEFREESE, of Goshen, was elected prosecuting attorney of the circuit in 1858, and served for a short time while Judge Wilson was upon the bench. He died in the early part of 1859, and Mr. JOHN COLERICK, of Fort Wayne, of whom further mention will be made in subsequent pages, was appointed to fill out his term. Assuming that Mr. Colerick's appointment expired with the fall election in 1859, Mr. Moses Jenkinson, of Fort Wayne, and G. D. Copeland, were candidates at that election for the office, and Mr. Jenkinson, having received a majority of the votes, claimed to have been elected to the office. The governor, however, decided that Mr. Colerick should fill out the unexpired term for which Mr. Defreese had been elected, viz., until the general election in 1860.

Mr. JENKINSON, on his father's side, was of English, and on his mother's side of French, origin. His father was an officer in the war of 1812. In 1825 he was engaged in a commercial enterprise which took him to New Orleans, where he died with the yellow fever. The subject of this sketch was but fifteen years old at the time of his father's death, having been born in Cincinnati on the 5th day of November, 1810. Upon the death of his father, it became necessary for the son to help support the family by his labor. His mother was a lady of cultured intellect, and resolute of spirit, and inspired the son with a laudable ambition. He devoted his early years to the aid of his mother and the acquiring of an education. He commenced the practice of the law in Fort Wayne about the year 1840. He was a man of quick perceptions, and rapid in his actions both physically and mentally, and hence capable of much work. He was a successful lawyer, and universally liked by his brethren of the bar, and the people. In addition to being a successful lawyer, he was an enterprising business man, and was largely identified with the growth of the city. In 1861 he was elected a member of the legislature and continued such for two years, and made an efficient member. He died on the 1st day of November, 1865, after a brief illness. Upon the announcement of his death to the courts, by the late Hon. David H. Colerick, they adjourned in respect to his memory, and the bar, at a subsequent meeting, resolved to attend his funeral in a body, and wear a badge of mourning for thirty days.

From October, 1860, to October, 1862, during the term of Judge Wilson, AUGUSTUS A. CHAPIN, then a resident of Kendallville, in Noble county, of whom montion is made hereafter, was prosecuting attorney. During the last two years of his term, JAMES H. SCHELL, then a resident of Goshen, the county seat of Elkhart county, was prosecuting attorney. When elected, Mr. Schell was a young man, and full of promise. He was a man of good ability, well equiped for the duties of the profession, and was a successful prosecuting attorney. He was twice elected to the office and served for two terms of two years each. During his incumbency in office, he became a resident of Fort Wayne, and engaged in the general practice of the law. His health soon gave way, and he died several years ago, at a time when he ought to have been in the strength and vigor of mature manhood. In 1864

HON. ROBERT LOWRY,

then a resident of Goshen, of whom mention is made hereafter, was elected judge of the tenth circuit, composed of the same counties that constituted the circuit during the incumbency of Judges Worden, Dawson and Wilson.

The circuit remained the same until the 11th day of March, 1867, when the counties of Elkhart, LaGrange, Steuben, DeKalb, Noble and Kosciusko were, by an act of the legislature, taken from the tenth circuit and made to constitute a new circuit, thus leaving the tenth circuit embracing the counties of Allen, Whitley, Wells and Adams. Prior to the passage of that act, Judge Lowry had become a resident of Fort Wayne, and thus remained a resident within the tenth circuit. By an act of the legislature approved May 5, 1869, the tenth circuit was made to embrace, besides the counties above named, the county of Huntington. By an act approved December 14, 1872, Huntington county was taken from the tenth circuit and made a part of a new circuit. By an act approved March 6, 1873, the state was re-districted, and the counties of Allen and Whitley were constituted the thirty-eighth judicial circuit. By an act approved March 9, 1875, Allen county was constituted the thirty-eighth judicial circuit, and so remains (1889). Judge Lowry remained the judge of the several circuits of which Allen county was a part, until 1875, when he resigned to resume the practice of the law at Fort Wayne. For two years of the time that he was judge, James H. Schell, above mentioned, was prosecuting attorney.

In 1866, T. M. WILSON, then an attorney at Bluffton, was elected prosecuting attorney for the circuit. He was then a young man, having been admitted to the bar in 1863, but filled the office with ability and credit. He continued to reside and practice law at Bluffton until a few years ago, when he located at Fort Wayne, and is now (1889), engaged in the practice of the law in that city.

In 1868, when Wells county was in the tenth circuit with Allen county, JOSEPH S. DAILY, of Bluffton, was elected prosecuting attorney. He was re-elected in 1870, and in 1872. Under his last election he was the prosecuting attorney for the Allen circuit court, until, by an act of the legislature, approved March 6, 1873, Allen and Wells counties became parts of different circuits. When he was elected he was a young man, but able and energetic. Since then he has resided at Bluffton, and has been one of the leading lawyers. At different times he has been a member of the legislature. Some years ago he was nominated for congress, but was defeated along with his party. In 1886, he was elected judge of the circuit court for the circuit embracing the counties of Wells and Huntington, and is now (1889), serving as such to the entire satisfaction of the bar and people. As has been seen by the act of March 6, 1873, re-districting the state for judicial purposes, Allen and Whitley counties became the thirty-eighth judicial circuit. By reason of Wells county being thus disconnected from Allen, and Mr. Daily being a resident of the former county, the thirty-eighth circuit was left without a prosecuting attorney.

To fill that vacancy Governor Hendricks, on the 29th day of March, 1873, appointed JACOB R. BITTINGER, of Fort Wayne, to serve until the succeeding election. The act provided that an election should be held in the proper counties on the second Tuesday of October, 1873, to elect judges and prosecuting attorneys in place of such judges and prosecuting attorneys as might, at that time, be holding by appointment of the governor. An election was accordingly held, and Mr. Bittinger was elected prosecuting attorney of the thirty-eighth judicial circuit, and commissioned to serve for two years from the 27th day of October, 1873. That was a special election, as by an act approved April 26, 1869, the general elections, commencing with 1870, were to be held each two years thereafter. It was provided in that act that at such general elections all offices, the terms of which "will expire before the next general election thereafter, shall be filled," etc. In 1874, Mr. Bittinger was renominated, and, at the general election that year, re-elected and commissioned to serve for two years from the 27th day of October, 1875, the end of the term for which he had been commissioned in 1873. It will thus be seen that during about two years of the latter part of Judge Lowry's service upon the circuit bench, Mr. Bittinger was prosecuting attorney. He served under his last commission until the 27th day of October, 1877, with credit to himself and acceptably to the public. At the present time he is the attorney appointed by the circuit court to defend, in that court, all accused persons who have no means of employing counsel.

Upon the resignation of Judge Lowry, Hon. WILLIAM W. CARSON, of whom further notice will be given in this work, was appointed by Governor Hendricks to serve as judge of the circuit until the succeeding general election in 1876.

At the general election referred to, Hon. EDWARD O'ROURKE was elected judge of the Allen circuit court. He is still on the bench, having been elected for the third term of six years each, in 1888. Of him a proper notice appears later.

In 1876, JAMES F. MORRISON was elected prosecuting attorney for the circuit court for a term of two years, commencing on the 27th day of October, 1877. He served that term and was re-elected for a term of two years, to commence in October, 1879. On November 6, 1880, he resigned the office and removed to Kokomo, the county seat of Howard county, where he has since been engaged in the practice of the law.

Upon the resignation of Mr. Morrison, C. M. DAWSON, of Fort Wayne, was appointed by Governor Williams to serve for the balance of his term. At the October election of that year, Mr. Dawson had been elected prosecuting attorney for a term of two years to commence in October, 1881. In 1881, a constitutional amendment was adopted and a law enacted, fixing the annual general elections on the first Tuesday after the first Monday in November, 1882, and biennially thereafter. That change in the time of general elections necessarily extended Mr. Dawson's term under his election, until the general election in November, 1883. The act of 1881, like the act of 1869, above mentioned, provided that at such general elections, " all offices, the terms of which will expire before the next general election, shall be filled," etc. At the general election in 1882, Mr. Dawson was elected for a term to commence in November, 1883; and again at the general election in 1884, he was electecd for a term to end in November, 1887. Under the appointment, and his several elections, Mr. Dawson served as prosecuting attorney for about seven years. When he was elected, and during a part of his first term, there was a criminal court in Allen county, having exclusive criminal jurisdiction, and a separate judge and prosecuting attorney; but by an act of the legislature, approved on the 12th day of April, 1882, the duties of the prosecuting attorney of that court were devolved upon the prosecuting attorney of the circuit court, after the expiration of the term for which the prosecuting attorney of the former court had been elected. In Allen county, the term of the prosecuting attorney of the criminal court expired with the general election in November, 1882. After that election, therefore, it became the duty of Mr. Dawson to prosecute the pleas of the state in the criminal court. As prosecuting attorney, he did himself credit, and was entirely satisfactory to the people. He is a son of Judge Dawson, already mentioned. He has spent most of his life, and all of his business life, in Fort Wayne, where he is now engaged in the general practice of the law. He graduated from the Albany, N. Y., law school in May, 1877. He is a vigorous man, physically and mentally, and is now in the prime of life.

At the November election in 1886, JAMES M. ROBINSON was elected prosecuting attorney for the circuit court for a term of two years, to commence in November, 1887. At the general election in November, 1888, he was elected for a second term, to commence in November, 1889.

He is now in the discharge of the duties of the office. He has made an efficient prosecuting attorney, and met fully the expectations of his most ardent friends. Mr. Robinson is a young man yet, and is entitled to much credit for what he has made of himself, being a self-made man. He is a careful and painstaking lawyer, and a forcible advocate.

PROBATE COURTS.

An act of the legislature, approved on the 29th day of January, 1829, provided for the establishment of a probate court in each county of the state, the judge of which was to be elected by the people of the county. It was not required that the judge should be a " professional character," but in order to receive a commission from the governor he was required to produce a certificate by a' judge of a circuit court, or of the supreme court, that he was qualified to discharge the duties of the office. A more elaborate act upon the same subject was approved on the 10th day of February, 1831, and carried into the revised statutes of that year.

WILLIAM G. EWING became probate judge in Allen county in 1830, and served for three years, when he resigned the office. As stated early in this article, he had been admitted to the bar at the first term of the Allen circuit court, in 1824. He was a brother of Judge Charles W. Ewing.' He did not devote much time to the law, but early went into business with his brother, George W. Ewing, and accumulated a fortune.

In 1834 HUGH MCCULLOCH became judge of the probate court and served as such for about one year, when he resigned the office. He graduated from Bowdoin college in 1826. After having taught school for some time he commenced the study of law, and completed his course in Boston in 1832. In April, 1833, he came west, and after spending a few weeks in the office of Judge Sullivan, at Madison, Ind., he went to Indianapolis, and was admitted to the bar of the supreme court. He came from Indianapolis to Fort Wayne on horseback and liking the place, and believing that it had a promising future, determined to remain there. The State Bank of Indiana, chartered in 1833, was organized for business in 1834. In 1835 a branch was established at Fort Wayne, and Mr. McCulloch was soon appointed its cashier and manager. We cannot here trace the subsequent career of Mr. McCulloch until he became secretary of the United States treasury, and one of the most capable and widely known financiers of the country. His appointment as cashier and manager of the Fort Wayne branch of the State Bank, took him from the law, and the office of probate judge, to which he had been elected.

In the latter part of 1835 Gov. Noble appointed THOMAS JOHNSON probate judge to fill the vacancy caused by the resignation of Mr. McCulloch. He presided as probate judge until August, 1836, when his successor was elected. Mr. Johnson at that time was a young man and lawyer of much promise. The year after he ceased to be probate judge he became prosecuting attorney of the circuit court, and served as such for two years. He was born on a farm near Chester, in Delaware county, Penn., on the 26th day of July, 1807. At an early age he moved with his parents to Belmont county, Ohio, where he commenced the study of the law. In 1832, at Richmond, Ind., he was admitted to the bar, soon after which he became a resident of Fort Wayne, and engaged in the practice of the law. He started in life without money or other help except his own resources. By his ability, unbending integrity and industry he soon acquired a large practice, an honorable position and a competency. Courteous and gentlemanly in his deportment, generous and charitable toward the failings of others, he had no enemies, and was esteemed by all who knew him. He was an estimable man and a good citizen. He died on the 18th day of September, 1843, from the effects of a cold which he had contracted but a few days before his death, in returning with Lucien P. Ferry from Bluffton, where they had been in attendance at court. On the day following his death, the late Hon. D. H. Colerick announced the fact to the Huntington circuit court, when it adjourned in respect to his memory. A bar meeting was at once called, at which Mr. Henry Cooper of Fort Wayne presided, and Lucien P. Ferry of the same place acted as secretary. Messrs. Colerick, William H. Coombs, of Fort Wayne, and the late Gen. James R. Slack, of Huntington, were appointed a committee to prepare suitable resolutions, expressive of the esteem in which Judge Johnson was held by the court and bar, and of their sorrow and condolence with the bereaved family. Of the lawyers who acted as officers of that meeting, and prepared the resolutions, all have followed Judge Johnson to the great court of final reward, except Judge Coombs, who is still living in Fort Wayne, in retirement and in ripe old age.

Mr. Johnson's widow remained a respected resident of Fort Wayne, until her death a short time ago. His daughter, Miss Lizzie Johnson, still resides at Fort Wayne.

In August, 1836, LUCIEN P. FERRY was elected probate judge for a term of seven years. He discharged the duties of the office until February, 1840, when he resigned. The same year in which he resigned the office of probate judge he became prosecuting attorney of the circuit court and served as such for about one year. He, too, was a young man and a lawyer of promise. In 1844 he died at the early age of thirty-three years. His family for years after his death resided in Fort Wayne. His widow is still a resident here. One of his sons lives at Seattle, and has just been elected (1889) governor of the new state of Washington. Upon the resignation of Mr. Ferry as judge of the probate court, REUBEN J. DAWSON, already mentioned as judge of the circuit court at a subsequent date, succeeded him, and held the position until the 9th day of November, 1840.

He was succeeded at that time by SAMUEL STOPHLET, who held the position until 1844, when he resigned. Mr. Stophlet was not a lawyer. In the language of the act creating the court, he was not " a professional character." He died many years ago, a reputable citizen of Fort Wayne.

Upon the resignation of Mr. Stophlet, Gov. Whitcomb appointed GEORGE JOHNSON probate judge. He held under that appointment until August, 1844, when he was elected to the office by the people. He held the position under that election until 1847, when he resigned. He was esteemed as a most worthy and intelligent young man. After his resignation he seems to have turned his attention to theology. While attending a course of theological studies at Gambier, Ohio, in December, 1850, he lost his life by the accidental discharge of a gun.

In 1847, NELSON McLAIN became judge of the probate court, and served as such until the establishment of the common pleas court under an act of 1852, and the transfer to that court of all probate business. Mr. McLain was not a lawyer.

COURTS OF COMMON PLEAS.

Prior to the general act of the legislature creating courts of common pleas in all the counties of the state, there were a number of special acts creating, regulating, and abolishing such courts in different counties. For example, by an act approved on the 18th day of January, 1848, such a court was established in Tippecanoe county. By an act approved January 5, 1852, that court was abolished. By an act approved on the 4th day of January, 1849, such a court was created in Marion county, and by an act approved January 12, 1852, it was abolished. By a general act approved on the 14th day of May, 1852, courts of common pleas were created in all the counties of the state, and the counties of Allen, Adams, Huntington and Wells were constituted a district. The act provided for the election of a judge at the October election in 1852, and fixed the tenure of the office at four years. The act also gave to the court exclusive probate jurisdiction.

At the October election in 1852 Hon. JAMES W. BORDEN, already mentioned, was elected common pleas judge of the district of which Allen county was a part, as above stated, and he opened the court in Allen county on the 3rd day of January, 1853. He was re-elected in 1856, and held the office until 1857, when he resigned. As we have seen, the act creating the court gave it exclusive jurisdiction of probate business. But as prior acts had clothed the circuit court with probate jurisdiction in certain cases, an act was passed on the 14th day of January, 1853, transferring to the common pleas court all probate business pending in the probate and circuit courts.

Upon the resignation of Judge Borden, in 1857, Hon. JOSEPH BRACKENRIDGE, already mentioned, was appointed judge to serve until the succeeding election. At the general election in October, 1858, he was elected to fill out the unexpired term for which Judge Borden had been elected in 1856. Under that election he held the office until the general election in October, 1860, when he was elected for a full term of four years, and held the office until the general election in 1864. A more extended notice of Judge Brackenridge is given elsewhere. At the October election in 1864, Judge Borden was again elected judge of the common pleas court, and held the office until the 29th day of October, 1867, when he resigned.

Upon his resignation, Governor Baker appointed ROBERT S. TAYLOR, of Fort Wayne, of whom a further notice will be given, to serve as judge of the court until a successor should be elected and qualified.

At the October election in 1868, Hon. DAVID STUDEBAKER, of Decatur, the county seat of Adams county, was elected judge of the common pleas court. He held the position until 1870, when he resigned. Mr. Studebaker, had for years been a resident of Decatur, engaged in the general practice of the law. Since his retirement from the bench he has been a resident of that place, and engaged in the practice of the law, banking and other business enterprises. He is a good lawyer, and while upon the bench, gave general satisfaction to the bar and the people. Added to this, he is a man of good character, and a valuable citizen.

Upon his resignation Hon. WILLIAM W. CARSON, already mentioned, was elected to fill out the term which expired with the October election in 1872.

At that election, SAMUEL E. SINCLAIR was elected for a term of four years. He held the position until March, 1873, when the court was abolished by an act of the legislature. Judge Sinclair was born in Fort Wayne in 1840. His father was one of the pioneer settlers and a worthy and respected citizen. He was elected clerk of the circuit court in 1853, and died in office, after having served less than one year. The subject of this brief sketch was thus left at the age of thirteen to make his way without the aid and influence of a father. He early determined to prepare himself for the law, and after availing himself of such advantages as the public schools afforded, he entered the law school at Albany, N. Y., and having pursued the prescribed course, graduated from that institution. Before returning, however, he was admitted to the bar of the court of appeals, the highest court in New York. He commenced the practice of the law at Fort Wayne about 1868, and was soon afterward appointed deputy prosecuting attorney. In 1880 he was elected a member of the legislature, and served for one term. Soon after his return from that service, he was appointed by the circuit court to defend, in that court, such accused persons as were not able to employ counsel. Except during the time that he was on the bench, he was engaged in the general practice of the law at Fort Wayne. Judge Sinclair filled the public positions to which he was elected with credit and fidelity. He was a man firm and outspoken in his convictions, brave and just with his fellows, and gentle, sympathizing and generous to the poor and afflicted. To his friends he was loyal and faithful. He died on the 25th day of March, 1887, greatly lamented by his relatives, friends and all who knew him.

An act approved June 11, 1852, provided for the election of district prosecuting attorneys, at the October election in that year, who should hold their offices for two years, and prosecute the pleas of the state in the common pleas courts of such districts. At that election David Studebaker, already mentioned, was elected prosecuting attorney for the district of which Allen county was a part, as above stated, and served during the term of two years.

At the October election in 1854, JOSEPH BRACKENRIDGE, already mentioned, was elected prosecuting attorney for the district, and served as such until 1856. At the October election in that year, W. B. SPENCER was elected prosecuting attorney for the district, and served for one year.

At the October election in 1857, WILLIAM S. SMITH was elected to that office, and served for one year, the unexpired term for which Spencer had been elected. Mr. Smith was born at Harper's Ferry, Va., in 1816. His father died when he was a young boy. The necessities of his mother required that he should go to work at once, and help provide for the family. He procured work with a gunsmith, and never had an opportunity to go to school. During his early manhood he worked at at his trade of gunsmithing at Cincinnati, Ohio. In 1845, 1846 and 1847, he was a member of the Ohio legislature from the Cincinnati district. Subsequent to that, he moved to St. Mary's, Ohio, and became mayor of that town. He came to Fort Wayne on the 3d day of August, 1853, where he continued to reside until his death on the 21st day of May, 1868. Having been deprived of the advantages of an education in youth, Mr. Smith resolved to educate himself, which he did, while working at his trade. Prior to coming to Fort Wayne, and after that time, he studied law while working at his trade. After the expiration of his term as prosecuting attorney, he devoted himself to the general practice of the law, and in 1861 was elected city attorney for the city of Fort Wayne, and served as such for two years. Soon after the beginning of the late war, he was appointed enrolling and draft commissioner, and served as such until the close of the war. After that, he again engaged in the general practice of the law, and was so engaged until his health gave way, a short time before his death. Mr. Smith was a forcible public speaker, and took an active part in many political campaigns.

At the October election in 1858, JOHN COLERICK, already mentioned, was elected prosecuting attorney for the common pleas court, for a term of two years, ending with the general election in October, 1860. He held the office until May, 1859, when he resigned to accept the position of prosecuting attorney for the circuit court, tendered him by Gov. Willard.

Upon his resignation, JOSEPH S. FRANCE, of whom a further notice will be found in a subsequent part of this work, was appointed to act as such prosecuting attorney until the following election. At the October election in 1859, he was elected to serve out the remainder of the time for which Mr. Colerick had been elected.

At the October election in 1860, Mr. D. T. SMITH was elected prosecuting attorney for the common pleas district, of which Allen county was a part. Mr. Smith was then a young man and lawyer, residing at Bluffton. He filled the position with credit until the end of his two years' term. He is still residing at Bluffton, engaged in the general practice of the law.

At the October election in 1862, Mr. DAVID COLERICK, of Fort Wayne, was elected prosecuting attorney, the district being the same as formerly. He was re-elected in 1864, and served until the October election, 1866. Mr. Colerick was a son of the late Hon. David H. Colerick, a brother of Hon. John Colerick, who died in 1872, and of Hon. Walpole G. Colerick, and Messrs. Henry and Philemon B. Colerick. He studied law with his father, and in subsequent years, and until the death of his brother, the Hon. John Colerick, was a partner with him in the practice of the law. Mr. Colerick was a young man of fine talents, generous impulses, and pleasing and affable manners. As prosecuting attorney he was, though young, able and efficient. He died on the 10th day of June, 1872, at the early age of about thirty-two years.

At the October election in 1866, Mr. JOSEPH S. DAILY, of Bluffton, of whom mention has already been made, was elected prosecuting attorney for the common pleas court. He held that position until the end of his term in 1868.

At the October election in 1868, Mr. BENJAMIN F. IBACH, of Huntington, the county seat of Huntington county, was elected to the office. He was re-elected in 1870, and held the office until the October election in 1872. Mr. Ibach was then a young man, but discharged the duties of the office with ability, fidelity and efficiency. He still resides at Huntington, engaged in the practice of the law. For many years he has been the city attorney for Huntington. In 1886 he was elected a member of the legislature from the counties of Allen and Huntington, and made a careful and valuable member.

At the October election of 1872, JACOB R. BITTENGER, of whom mention has already been made, was elected to the office for a term of two years, and held the position until the office, and the common pleas court, were abolished by the act of March 6, 1873.

CRIMINAL COURT OF ALLEN COUNTY.

By an act approved on the 11th day of May, 1867, a criminal court was established in Allen county, with exclusive criminal jurisdiction. The act provided for a judge and prosecuting attorney for that court, and also provided for the appointment of those officers by the governor until the next ensuing general election. In pursuance of the act the governor, soon after its passage, appointed JAMES A. FAY, of whom further notice is given hereafter, judge, to hold the office until the election and qualification of a successor. At the October election in 1867, Judge James W. Borden, already mentioned, was elected judge of the court for a term of four years. It was by reason of that election that he resigned his place on the bench of the common pleas court. His term extended until 1871, but by reason of the annual election having been dispensed with by the act of 1869, already mentioned, it became necessary to elect a judge of the criminal court at the general election in 1870, whose term should commence in October, 1871. At that election Hon. Joseph Brackenridge, already mentioned, was elected judge, and held the office until October, 1875. At the general election in 1874, Judge Borden was again elected judge, and was re-elected in 1878, for a term of four years. He died in office on the 26th day of April, 1882.

The Hon. WARREN H. WITHERS, of whom more adequate mention will be given hereafter, was appointed judge of the criminal court, by Governor Porter, a few days after the death of Judge Borden, to serve until the election and qualification of a successor.

At the November election in 1882, SAMUEL M. HENCH, of whom more will be said hereafter, was elected judge of the criminal court, and held the office until the 31st day of October, 1884, at which time the court ceased to exist, by virtue of an act of the legislature, approved February 27, 1883.

At the time the governor appointed Mr. Fay judge of the criminal court, he also appointed Robert S. Taylor, before mentioned, prosecuting attorney of that court, with a like term. At the October election in 1867, Edward O'Rourke, of whom mention has already been made, was elected prosecuting attorney of that court, for a term to end in October, 1869. But as there was no election in that year, by reason of the change in the election laws in 1869, he held over until the election in 1870. At the October election in the latter year, he was re-elected and served the full term. At the October election of 1872, JOSEPH S. FRANCE, of whom mention has already been made, was elected prosecuting attorney of the criminal court. He died in July, 1874, before the expiration of the term, and Samuel M. Hench, of whom mention has been made, was appointed by Gov. Hendricks on the 16th day of July, 1874, to serve until the election of a successor. Having been nominated for the office by the democratic county convention in June of that year, he was elected to the office at the succeeding October elections. In 1876 and in 1878 he was re-elected, and, a controversy having arisen as to the length of the term as fixed by the statute, he held the office under his last election until the 10th day of January, 1881.

At the October election, in 1880, WILLIAM S. O'ROURKE was elected prosecuting attorney of the criminal court, and served as such until November, 1882, the end of the term for which he had been elected, and until the office of prosecuting attorney for the criminal court ceased to exist by virtue of the act approved April 12, 1881, already mentioned. Mr. O'Rourke was quite a young man when he was elected

Allen Zollars

to the responsible position, and had but recently been admitted to the bar. He was, however, a young man of ability, energy and integrity, and made a good prosecuting attorney. Shortly after quitting the office he was appointed to the responsible position of attorney for the Grand Rapids & Indiana railroad company in Indiana, and filled the place with ability and success until about August, 1889, when he removed to Chattanooga, Tenn., where he is now engaged in the general practice of the law. Mr. O'Rourke is a son of Mr. Patrick S. O'Rourke, of Fort Wayne, superintendent of that portion of the Grand Rapids & Indiana railroad which is in Indiana, extending from the state line on the north to Richmond, south. He was born in Fort Wayne, and was educated there and in Pennsylvania. He also graduated from the law department of the university of Michigan.

SUPERIOR COURT OF ALLEN COUNTY.

The superior court of Allen county was established by an act of the legislature approved on the 5th day of March, 1877. Soon after the passage of the act, Gov. Williams appointed Allen Zollars judge of the court, but as the act was not to take effect until the following August, the commission was not issued until the 7th day of that month. Under that commission Mr. Zollars would have been entitled to hold the office until the October election in 1878. After hearing some habeas corpus cases in vacation, he formally opened the court on the 10th day of September, 1877, and presided until about the 20th day of the month, when he resigned and resumed the practice.

Upon his resignation, Hon. ROBERT LOWRY, already mentioned, was appointed judge of the court, and held the office until the general election in October, 1878. At that time he was elected by the people for a term of four years, and held the office until after the general election in November, 1882.

At that election, Hon. JAMES L. WORDEN, already mentioned, was elected judge for a term of four years. He died on the 2d day of June, 1884. On the 15th day of the same month, Hon. LINDLEY M. NINDE, of whom further notice will be taken hereafter, was appointed judge by Governor Porter, to serve until the general election in November of the same year. His successors, S. M. HENCH and AUGUSTUS A. CHAPIN, are both mentioned further on in this work.

The biographical sketches of lawers following were not written by Judge Zollars, except that of Judge Worden. They were prepared at the instance of the publishers.

James Lorenzo Worden was born on the 10th day of May, 1819, in Sandisfield, Berkshire county, Mass., the son of John and Jane Worden. His father died when he was about eight years old, and a year or two later he moved with his mother to Portage county, Ohio. His youth was spent upon a farm, where he had the benefit of a common school education, and devoted himself, to some extent, to literary pursuits. He began the study of law at the age of nineteen, and in 1839 entered the office of Thomas T. Straight, at Cincinnati, Ohio. In 1841 he was ad-

XXX

mitted to the bar of the supreme court of Ohio, at Lancaster, and for two or three years thereafter, was in the practice at Tiffin, Ohio. In the spring of 1844 he removed to Columbia City, in Whitley county, Ind., and opened a law office. In the presidential campaign of that year he took quite an active part, being then as he continued to be through life, a democrat.

In the spring of 1845 he was married to Miss Anna Grable, the daughter of Benjamin Grable, then county treasurer of Whitley county, and an honorable and estimable citizen. Through the remainder of his life, the wife shared with him his successes and disappointments, whatever they may have been, and is still a resident of Fort Wayne. She is now, and always has been, very highly respected by all who have known her, for her ability, culture, and refinement, and for her estimable qualities as a wife, mother, citizen, neighbor, and friend. In the fall of 1845 Mr. Worden removed to Albion, in Noble county. He soon became known there, and acquired as good a practice as the county afforded. In 1848, while a resident of Albion, he won quite a reputation, and made friends in Fort Wayne by the brilliant manner in which he conducted the prosecution of a man who had been indicted for murder in Noble county, and had taken a change of venue to Allen county. In conseqence of the solicitations of these new friends, he removed to Fort Wayne in 1849, where he resided until his death. In 1850 he was elected prosecuting attorney for the twelfth judicial circuit, embracing the counties of Allen, Adams, Wells, Huntington, Whitley, Noble, Steuben, LaGrange and DeKalb, and held the office for three years.

Two years after his election, the state was redistricted for judicial purposes, and Allen county became a part of the tenth circuit, which embraced the counties of Adams, Wells, Huntington, Wabash, Whitley, Allen, Noble, DeKalb, LaGrange, Steuben, Elkhart and Kosciusko. A year later, the counties of Huntington and Wabash were taken from the circuit. Of that circuit, Mr. Worden was appointed judge, by Gov. Joseph A. Wright, in 1855, to fill a vacancy. At the general election that year he was elected judge of the circuit for a full term of six years, without opposition. Judge Worden was a lawyer and not a politician, and hence did not desire an office which would take him from the profession. In 1857, however, while he was on the bench, his popularity was such, that contrary to his known inclination, his party associates made him their candidate for congress. The district being largely republican, he was defeated with his party. In 1858 he resigned the position of circuit judge to accept the appointment by Gov. Williard, as judge of the supreme court of the state, to fill a vacancy caused by the resignation of Judge Stuart, of Logansport, and delivered his first opinion, in the case of Mills et al. vs. The State ex rel. Barbour, et al. (10 Ind., 114), in open court, on the first day of the May term of that year. In 1859 he was elected a judge of the supreme court for a full term of six years, ending in January, 1865. In 1864 he was renominated for an election to another term but was defeated with his party at the general election.

In January, 1865, after the close of the term for which he had been elected in 1859, he returned to Fort Wayne and engaged in the general practice. In May following, he was elected mayor of the city, and after having held the office for about one year resigned in order to give his full time to his practice which had become large and important. From that time until January, 1871, he was a partner with Hon. John Morris, who was his life-long, and most intimate and confidential friend. In 1870, he was again elected by the people of the state as judge of the supreme court. In 1876 he was again nominated for re-election to the same position. After the state convention, an individual whose name need not be mentioned here, being disappointed, and dissatisfied with some appointments which had been made by the supreme court, raised an unreasonable and unfounded clamor about the expenses of that court. Some of the judges who had also been renominated by the same convention, unwisely and unnecessarily, concluded to decline the nomination, and so informed the state committee. That committee, just as unwisely and unnecessarily, accepted the declination, and concluded to leave the matter to be settled by the democrats of each of the supreme court judicial districts. Judge Worden was thus called upon, as all men long in public life are, to meet the complaints and charges of the jealous, envious and disappointed.

The state was then, as it is now, divided into five supreme court judicial districts, corresponding with the number of the supreme court judges. The constitution of the state required, and still requires, that a judge of the supreme court shall reside in each of those districts, although they are elected by the people of the whole state. Judge Worden's district comprised the counties of Allen, Whitley, Huntington, Wells, Adams, Grant, Blackford, Jay, Delaware, Randolph, Howard, Madison, Hancock, Henry, Wayne, Fayette, Union and Franklin. In compliance with the order of the state committee, a convention was called and assembled in that district, and was largely attended by the leading, influential, and substantial men of the party. Judge Worden's private and official life was not only approved and commended, but it was unanimously resolved that he should stand as the candidate for the position of supreme judge. That decision was approved by the people, and he was re-elected by a handsome majority, running abreast with the most popular men on the ticket. By virtue of that election, Judge Worden entered upon his third term as judge of the supreme court in January, 1877. That term would have ended in January, 1883. In 1882, his friends at home, and over the state, insisted that he should again be a candidate for election to another term upon the supreme bench. He, however, felt, that having served in that capacity, and performed the arduous and exacting labors of the position for almost nineteen years, he should not further prolong the service, and declined. Upon that declination becoming known, his friends at home determined to place him upon the bench of the superior court of Allen county, and he was nominated and elected without opposition to that position at the general election in November, 1882.

That election, and the acceptance of the office, rendered it necessary for him to resign his position upon the supreme bench, which he did soon after the election. He at once entered upon the discharge of the duties of judge of the superior court and was holding that office at the time of his death, at 9:30 p. m., on the 2d day of June, 1884. His death created the greatest sorrow, not only upon the part of the people at his home, but over the entire state. A meeting of the bar was held on the 4th day of June, at which addresses of the highest commendation of the deceased were delivered by Judge Morris, Hon. J. K. Edgerton, and other members of the Allen county bar; by judges of the supreme court, the governor of the state, Senator McDonald, Hon. David Turpie, and other state officers, and distinguished men of the state. At the funeral, the judges of the supreme court of the state who had been Judge Worden's associates upon the bench, and his successor, and Judge Morris, who had long been his partner when in the practice, and also associated with him as a commissioner of the supreme court, acted as pall bearers. At the opening of the term November, 1884, of the supreme court, a meeting of the bar of the state was held, when Judge Morris, in behalf of that bar, presented an address, upon the life, character, and work of Judge Worden, which the court ordered to be spread upon its records, and published in one of the reports of the decisions of the court.

Judge Worden made no pretence to florid oratory, but in his addresses to the court, and jury, he was logical, practicable and convincing. In the trial of causes, his thorough knowledge of the law and the rules of practice; his fine analytical powers, and logical and methodical manner of thought, enabled him to readily discern and grasp the salient points in a case, and handle them with consummate skill. As a *nisi prius* judge, he had but few, if any, equals in the state. His quick perceptions, and knowledge of the law, and practice, very much lightened the labors of the practitioner, by rendering unnecessary to a large extent, the hunting up and presentation of authorities. Of him it may be truthfully said, that in no office which he was called upon to fill did he fail to come up to the full measure of the requirements of the position. Judge Worden's work upon the bench of the supreme court is what has more certainly secured for him an honorable and enduring place in the history of the state. He went upon that bench when a young man, thirty-nine years of age. His work there was such as would adorn any bench in the land. As has been said upon another occasion, he was a man of unusually strong common sense. His mind was clear, logical and discriminating. He had also a broad sense of right and justice, and could readily discern upon which side they were in a legal controversy.

He was not a man of circumlocution, either in thought or word. There is a clearness, conciseness and directness of expression in his opinions that may well serve as a model for judges and lawyers. He was by nature a lawyer and judge, having the faculty, in an unusual degree, of brushing aside all that might tend to becloud and confuse, and seeing readily the real question for decision, and determining what the decision

Isaac Mowrer

should be to conform to the rules of the law, and work out substantial justice to the parties interested. His opinions not only show his ability, and his learning in the law, but they show also, that they were prepared with labor and care. He had no toleration for the weak and abused idea that the reputation of a judge, upon the bench of a court of final decision, is to be established, or the value of his labors measured, by the amount that he may write, and was governed by the sensible, and the only sensible idea, that the reputation of the judge upon such a bench, will rest, finally, upon the character, and not upon the number of his written opinions, and that the value of his labor will be, and can only be, properly measured by the character, and not by the number of his written opinions. He acted upon the idea, that care in the decision of causes, and in the writing of opinions, lessen the business in the supreme court by lessening litigation below, while haste, and the consequent looseness in expression, in an attempt to multiply opinions, necessarily result in misunderstandings on the part of the profession, the multiplication of suits below, and an increase in the number of appeals. He knew, as any lawyer of experience and observation knows, and especially, as every judge of observation knows, that suits are very frequently commenced which have no other foundation than a dictum found in some case, which ought not to be there, and which would not be there but for the haste of the judge who wrote the opinion. Such cases invariably go to the supreme court, and thus, haste in such a court, instead of lessening, in fact increases its business.

Judge Worden perhaps, wrote as few cases in the same length of time as any judge who has ever been upon the bench of the supreme court, but in the way of reputation, he was in the front rank, if not indeed, the first man in the rank. By the lawyers of the state and by the courts, including the supreme court, his opinions are read and cited with a feeling of security. There is a feeling that he was not only capable of deciding and stating the law correctly, but that he had bestowed the labor, and taken the time, necessary to enable him to state it correctly. It is for this reason that his opinions are the more frequently cited and relied upon, not only in Indiana, but elsewhere. Again, as has been said elsewhere, by his work upon the bench of the supreme court, as embodied in his written opinions extending over so many years, Judge Worden erected his own monument and wrote his own inscription. He needs none other.

While Judge Worden was a democrat, and a firm and conscientious believer in the principles and doctrines of that party, he was, in no sense, an aggressive or active partisan. The result was that he was singularly free from the assaults of party opponents, which almost invariably, every public man has to meet. Indeed, Judge Worden always received quite a large vote from persons in the opposite party, who knew him well. On one occasion only, was he assailed with anything like violence, and that assault was absolutely unfounded, and more unjust than it was violent. He never took the trouble to meet and overthrow the assault—

indeed, could not well afford to do so, while he was upon the bench of the supreme court. The time has now come when, in justice to his memory, the facts ought to be made known.

In 1869 a law was passed which dispensed with the annual general elections, and provided that, commencing with the year 1870, a general election should be held biennially on the second Tuesday in October, and that at such elections all offices, the terms of which would expire before the next general election thereafter, should be filled. So long as the elections were held in October, the terms of county officers commenced, and ended in that month, subsequent to the general election, and they were so commissioned. In April, 1880, some constitutional amendments were submitted to the people of the state for adoption or rejection by popular vote. One of those amendments provided for a change of the date of the general elections from October, to the first Tuesday after the first Monday in November. Almost immediately after the vote had been taken, the question was made and insisted upon, that the amendments had not been adopted by the requisite vote. The controversy soon assumed the form of a legal contest in court, and went upon appeal to the supreme court. It will be readily seen that if that court should hold that the amendments had been adopted, the next election, in the fall of 1880, would be in November instead of October, and the four-year terms of many county officers would expire in October before the November election in 1882. In that event, in order to comply with the law of 1869 above mentioned, it would be necessary to elect successors to such officers in 1880.

Acting upon the assumption that the amendments had been adopted, there were in Allen county, where Judge Worden lived, quite a number of candidates for the nomination for the four-year county offices by the democratic convention, soon to assemble. If the amendments were not adopted there would be no expiration of terms in such offices before the election in 1882, and hence no vacancies to be filled by election in 1880. By reason of the candidates above mentioned, Judge Worden's friends, at home, thought it would be best to know, if possible, before the assembling of the county convention, whether or not the amendments had been adopted. The convention was called to meet on Saturday of the week in which the case was argued in the supreme court. If the amendments should be held to have been adopted, it would be necessary to nominate candidates for the four-year offices; otherwise not. While the argument was in progress, a prominent citizen of Fort Wayne was at Indianapolis, and in a conversation with Judge Worden, in the presence of a close friend of each, spoke of the condition of things in Allen county, and, without an intimation as to whether he wished a decision one way or the other, that, in fact, being a matter of no consequence at all, requested that if a decision should be reached before the coming Saturday, the judge should telegraph him at home what it was. The case was decided before the coming Saturday, and it was held, Judge Biddle writing the opinion, that the amendments had not been adopted by the requisite vote. After the opinion had been read, and approved by the court, and had thus become open for the inspection of all, Judge Worden met the friend who had been present at the conversation with the Fort Wayne gentleman, and said to him that the decision was, that the amendments had not been adopted, and requested him to telegraph the fact to the boys at Fort Wayne. That conversation was overheard by a newspaper reporter, and he has contended that the judge requested the friend to "telegraph it to the boys," not mentioning Fort Wayne. Whether he might have been wrong or not, in that contention, is a matter of no consequence, and cannot affect the real truth in the matter, because Judge Worden had, and could have no thought except to have the fact communicated to his friends at home in compliance with the request before mentioned, which friends he called the boys. He was a man of too much dignity, and too high a sense of propriety, to speak of any except his intimate friends at home as "the boys."

But for the peculiar political condition in Indiana at that time, doubtless no notice at all would be taken of Judge Worden's innocent remark. Indiania was then just entering upon one of its most exciting political campaigns. Up to that time the general elections had been held in October. The state was one of the few states known in the political world as an October state, and having been regarded as a close and pivotal state, the presidental campaigns had always been exciting, and closely contested, a large portion of the great speakers of both parties from other states usually being present, taking part in them. A president of the United States was to be elected in 1880. The friends of Gov. Hendricks in Indiana were making a vigorous effort for his nomination by the democratic national convention. The convention was about to assemble at Cincinnati, and many of the delegates were already there, when the decision of the supreme court was rendered. Although the opinion in the case was written by Judge Biddle, who had not been elected as a democrat, and never had been a democrat, yet, as a majority of the court had been elected as democrats, for the purpose of turning every possible thing to political advantage in the close and fierce contest that was just opening, Judge Worden's innocent statement was tortured and twisted from its true, and only reasonable meaning, and it was contended that his purpose was to have the fact telegraphed to the delegates at Cincinnati, and that therefore, the decision had been rendered for the purpose of assisting in the nomination of Gov. Hendricks.

The real facts in the case, as above stated; Judge Worden's high character, dignity, and sense of propriety; his well known and uniform personal, official and judicial integrity, and the judgment of all who knew him well, fully meet and overthrow such an unreasonable contention, and such an unjust and unreasonable torture of his statement made as above recited. There is no method of judging of a man's character and integrity so reliable as the judgment of the people amongst whom he has lived for a life-time, and who thus have had the opportunity of knowing him as none others can. Judge Worden was a resident of Indiana a few months over forty years. As prosecuting attorney, judge of the circuit court, mayor, judge of the supreme court, and judge of the superior court of Allen county, he was in the public service for more than twenty-seven years of that time. His life was thus, in a large measure, an open book, to be read by all. When not in the public service, he was in the practice of the law at home, and in a large number of surrounding counties, and was thus, in a sense, in public life. At no time, did the people, who knew him best, have more confidence in his integrity than in the later years of his life. As already stated, less than two years before his death, and after his long service upon the supreme bench, he was elected judge of the superior court of Allen county, without opposition. Such a manifestation of enlightened confidence is, of itself, more than sufficient to meet and overthrow the unreasonable and unjust imputation above mentioned.

It is a matter in which his widow, children and friends, may have a just pride, that after having spent the greater part of his business life in the public service, he went to his grave respected and honored by the people who knew him, and by the bar and courts of the state, as an honest and honorable man, and as an honest and faithful public servant. So long as Indiana shall be a commonwealth, so long as its people shall have laws and courts, his name will be known and honored. How much good he may have accomplished for the people of the state may never be fully appreciated by the people generally, but it will be, in a measure at least, by the profession and the more observing.

Judge Worden was not only a great lawyer and judge, but by extended reading and study, he was a man of refined taste and culture. He left surviving him three sons, one of whom, Charles H., is a lawyer. He was born in Fort Wayne on the 14th day of September, 1859. He was educated in the schools of the city, and in 1878 entered the university of Michigan, where he remained two years, pursuing the course of study prescribed by that institution. He was admitted to the bar of the courts in Allen county in 1882, and has since been admitted to the bar of the federal courts in Indiana. He is a member of the law firm of Worden & Morris, and is prominent among the young attorneys of the city and state. He was married on the 10th day of June, 1884, to Miss Elizabeth M. Hoffman, of Fort Wayne, and they have one child, Alice.

Charles Wayne Ewing, at one time president judge of the eighth judicial circuit, was the oldest son of Col. Alexander Ewing. He was born October 13, 1798, near Geneseo, N. Y., and received his collegiate education in Ohio. His first study of law was with Judge Eeste, of Cincinnati. On being admitted to practice he began his career as a lawyer at Fort Wayne. At the first session of court in Allen county he was on August 9, 1824, appointed prosecuting attorney. In 1826 he presented a design for a court seal, which was adopted. Previous to this time he had become a member and the first secretary of Wayne lodge, No. 25, F. & A. M., organized in 1823 by Gen. Tipton. In 1827 Mr. Ewing went to Detroit, where he practiced law about two years, and was married June 5, 1829 to Abigail B. Woodworth. In 1832 he removed to the settlement at Logansport, Ind., where he became eminent as a lawyer, and was judge of the circuit court for several years. Resuming the practice at Peru, he removed to Fort Wayne in 1835, where he became the leading lawyer, and again was called to the bench. He died on January 9, 1843. Judge Ewing was an accomplished gentlemen, and brilliant in social life as in his profession. Impulsive, warm hearted and generous, he won the friendship of all his associates. In the earlier pages of this work is quoted an appreciative tribute from one who knew him during his brief but brilliant career.

Henry Cooper, a noted lawyer and prominent citizen of Fort Wayne in an early day, was a descendant through his mother, of Irish Protestants, who were among the first followers of Lord Baltimore, to Maryland, where they settled near Cambry. His paternal progenitors, who were English Protestants, arrived in Maryland at a later period. He had a maternal uncle who served under the unfortunate Admiral Byng, at Minorca, and in the English West India fleet during the French war. His maternal grandfather was an ensign in the Maryland volunteers during the revolutionary war. One of his paternal uncles was taken prisoner by the Hessians in New Jersey, and was detained a long time on board one of the prison ships at New York. Henry Cooper, son of James and Leah Cooper, was born at Havre de Grace, Md., June 8, 1793, and was left fatherless in his tenth year. Influenced by the slender state of his resources, he commenced a sea-faring life in 1810, but finding there was no chance of preferment without a knowledge of navigation he entered himself as a student of that science under the tuition of Mr. Ackworth, in Baltimore. Determining to follow the sea, he did so until 1818, and by perseverance and good conduct, rose to the command of a vessel. About the year 1818, he abandoned the sea and came west. After coming to the west, the small amount he had saved from his hard earnings was sunk in the Mississippi river during a storm. He made a fresh effort in a new profession, and, in 1822, commenced the study of law under the direction of the late Mr. Wing, of Cincinnati, Ohio. About the year 1825, he removed to Fort Wayne, and after three years of unremitting study, was admitted to the bar of the circuit courts of this state, and in May, 1829, to practice in the supreme court of the state. Mr. Cooper had a very extensive practice in the circuit and supreme courts in Indiana, and in the United States courts in the state. A few of the many interesting cases in which he was engaged have been reported, either by Judges McLean, Blackford or Smith. At the January term, 1833, he was licensed in the supreme court of the United States. In February, 1833, Mr. Cooper married Mary C. Silvers, of Hamilton county, Ohio, who, before her decease, bore him seven children, five of whom have long since died. The two survivors are now engaged in mercantile business on the Pacific slope. In July, 1850, he married Mrs. Ellinor Munson, widow of James P. Munson, and mother of Charles A. Munson. The only child by the last marriage is William P. Cooper. Mr. Cooper was never a candidate for any political office, but was a leading whig, and during the presidential candidacy of his old personal friend Gen. Harrison, he was chairman of the committee which organized such a successful campaign in Allen county. Mr. Cooper had an extensive practice in the courts of Indiana, and frequently of Ohio, and, during the period from 1845, to the time of his death, few lawyers had presented the result of more labor and research to the supreme court than he. As a speaker he made no effort at flowery declamation, but in a methodic and logical argument, presented his case, analyzed the testimony and concentrated it on the point at issue. His memory was wonderful, a decision once read became indelibly impressed on his mind, and he could repeat not only the substance, but give the page and volume with astonishing accuracy. Lawyers yet practicing, remember the kind assistance he always tendered, and the great pains he ever took to thoroughly explain or apply a point of law. Mr. Cooper died suddenly, on Friday, March 25, 1853, from a congestive chill.

Judge William H. Coombs, of Fort Wayne, was born in Brunswick, Maine, July 17, 1808, the son of Andrew and Susannah (Jackson) Coombs, also natives of that state. In December, 1811, his parents removed to Cincinnati and in the following spring they located on a farm twenty miles east of that city, in Clermont county, where Judge Coombs spent his boyhood and early youth. He went to Cincinnati, in 1826, and until 1831 he worked as a carpenter in that city and its vicinity. In 1831 he settled at Connorsville, Ind., where he entered upon the study of law with Caleb B. Smith. He was admitted to the bar at Connorsville in the spring of 1834 and for a short time practiced his profession with Mr. Smith. In 1835 he removed to Wabash, and there practiced until the fall of 1837, when he came to Fort Wayne. Here he practiced law until 1849. In that year he went by way of Cape Horn to California. Arriving there in the fall of 1850, he remained, engaged at the practice of law and farming until the fall of 1855, when he returned by way of the Isthmus to Fort Wayne. In the following spring he removed to Middleport, Ohio, but returned to Fort Wayne in 1859 and here continued in the active practice of his profession until about 1886, since when he has led a retired life. Upon the resignation of Judge Worden of the supreme court, in the fall of 1882, Judge Coombs was appointed by ex-Governor Porter, to fill the vacancy, and he served until his successor was qualified in January, 1883. Judge Coombs has served one term as prosecuting attorney in the judicial district composed of the counties of Allen, Adams, Wells, Whitley, Noble, LaGrange, Steuben and DeKalb, and he also served one term as prosecuting attorney for Alameda county, Cal. He was married at Fort Wayne, May 25, 1837, to Jane Edsall, a native of Ohio, with whom he has passed more than fifty-two years of happy married life. To them eleven children have been born, only four of whom are living: John M., a prominent hardware merchant of Fort Wayne; Joseph, of

William, removed in 1732 to a new home near Beaufort, S. C., where James W. Borden was born February 5, 1813. He was early left fatherless, and his education was due to his mother, Esther Wallace, a lady of rare talents, who sent her son to Fairchild academy, N. Y., and subsequently to Windsor, Conn. James W. Borden read law first in the office of Abijah Mann, jr., then a member of congress, and he was admitted to the bar of the supreme court of New York, in 1834. About this time he was married to Emeline Griswold, and in 1835 he removed to Richmond. Ind. There he was elected mayor, a position he resigned in 1839 to remove to Fort Wayne, and take charge of the United States land office. In 1841 he was elected president judge of the twelfth judicial district, then composed of nine counties. When the people of the state, in 1850, decided to hold a convention to revise and amend the state constitution, Judge Borden prepared the bill to provide for the same. He was elected a delegate from the counties of Allen, Adams and Wells, and resigned his judgeship. In the proceedings of this important convention he took an active part, and the plan of referring the different parts of the old constitution to various committees in such a way that every member should be placed upon one or the other of them, originated with him, and though meeting the opposition of such men as Owen, Bright, Kilgore, Rariden and Petit, contributed materially to give the constitution its present form. Judge Borden was placed at the head of the committee to whom was referred law reform, and was the author of that section of the constitution which has given rise to the present practice. On the subject of currency and banking, there were repeated and animated debates, extending through the entire session of five months. The convention at an early day divided into two parties, one favoring a State bank and branches only, the other a free banking system. Judge Borden vigorously opposed both systems, contending that the state had no authority to issue a paper currency, either in shape of treasury notes, as it had recently done in the case of the bills of credit or currency called " white dog," or indirectly through a State bank or local banks. He held that currency and banking were entirely distinct and separate matters, having no legitimate connection, and their union in the legislation of the United States and the states had been productive of untold evil; that it was the intention of the framers of our government to vest the issue of a circulating medium, whether of silver or gold or circulating notes to operate as money, exclusively in the general government; that banking properly speaking, was a subject upon which the general government could not act; that the regulation of banking was left entirely with state governments; that the time had or soon would come when the best interests of the people required their complete and final separation. Judge Borden, in 1852, was elected judge of the common pleas district of Allen, Adams, Huntington and Wells. These duties he performed until 1857, when he was appointed resident minister at the Hawaiian Islands. He returned home in 1863, and, in the year following, was again elected to the office of judge of the court of common pleas. In

1867 he was placed on the bench of the Allen criminal court, which office he held until his death, April 25, 1882. While he was a law student he compiled a history of the two great political parties, which he claimed to be merely a compilation from original papers and speeches. This was published in pamphlet form by Messrs. Chapmans, of Terre Haute, Ind., and sown broadcast over the state. Gov. Whitcomb frequently declared that this pamphlet had greatly tended to indoctrinate the people of Indiana in Jeffersonian democracy. As late as 1842, the democrats of Allen county had never effected an organization. A few of the more active members of the party in the city, usually, but quietly, named the candidates. This, however, did not suit the farmers, and the result was a meeting of several prominent men from the townships, at Peter Kiser's place of business, who sent for Judge Borden, and requested him to draw up a plan of organization, which he did. A delegate convention was called, and the plan, through Col. Woodard, a farmer from Aboit township, was adopted, and has ever since, with the exception of one or two unimportant amendments, controlled the action of the party. Judge Borden was full six feet in height, well proportioned, of commanding presence, positive but affable in manner, of fine conversational powers, and possessing great energy of character. Judge Borden had five children by his first wife: Esther Anna (deceased), Rebecca Kenyon (deceased), William James, Lieut. George Penington (of the United States army), and Emeline (wife of Capt. Hargou, also of the army). On the 15th of August, 1848, Mr. Borden was married to Miss Jane Conkling, a native of Buel, N. Y., a daughter of Brewster Conkling. They had one child, Henry D. Borden, born April 29, 1863.

Judge William Wellington Carson, a prominent jurist and pioneer citizen of Fort Wayne, was born in county Mayo, Ireland. In childhood he emigrated with his parents and settled at Cobourg, Canada, where his father died in 1835. The mother, born in 1794, died at Fort Wayne in March, 1889. In 1837, during the rebellion in Canada, Mr. Carson, being too young for service, traveled into this country, and reached Fort Wayne in November, 1837. Here he found employment with Marshall S. Wines, then a large contrator, and becoming attached to his employer, remained with him until the death of the colonel, about 1842. During that time he had access to the library of Col. Wines, and improved his opportunities, and also gained from the colonel, who was an old-school Presbyterian deacon, a liking for that church which led to his becoming a member. He took a two years' classical course with Mr. McJunkin, of Fort Wayne, and then for two years read law and taught school in the city. In 1846 he was admitted to the Allen county bar on the same day on which were admitted Judge Brackenridge and Thomas Coombs. He was licensed to practice by Judges James W. Borden and Chamberlain of Goshen. In the fall of 1846 he was appointed deputy clerk and recorder of Adams county, under Samuel L. Rugg. He remained in Adams county two years, and while there was the whig candidate for representative of Adams and Wells counties, but was defeated.

He had not yet had the opportunity to attend lectures in law, and in 1848 he attended the law department of the state university at Bloomington, and graduated in 1849. In April, of that year, he returned to Fort Wayne, and in the same year was elected prosecuting attorney for Adams county on the ticket of the democratic party, which he had by this time joined, and to which he has since adhered. In 1850 he was chosen city attorney of Fort Wayne, a position he held for six years. In 1858 he was nominated for judge of the circuit court, then composed of twelve counties, but on account of his refusal to make pledges to be guided by anything but the law in administering justice, he was defeated by the Regulator vote. In 1860 he was appointed attorney for Allen county, which he held until 1863, before the expiration of his service, however, making a trip to Europe in 1862. Upon his return he was elected to the state senate, of which he was a member until 1870. Though he resigned three times, he was three times re-elected. His service was valuable and conspicuous. He was the author of the law regarding city charters, which governs all the cities of Indiana at the present time. Making a second trip to Europe in 1869, he was upon his return elected judge of the court of common pleas, a position he held with distinguished ability until nearly the time of the abolition of the court. He then made another visit to Europe. In 1874 Judge Carson was appointed by Gov. Hendricks judge of the thirty-eighth judicial circuit, succeeding Judge Lowry, and this place he held until 1876. In 1864 Judge Carson was married to Emily, daughter of George Fleming, of county Westmeath, Ireland. She died in 1871, and in 1874 he was married to Mrs. Jane Allen, also a native of Ireland, by whom he had one son, William Washington. Judge Carson and wife are members of the First Presbyterian church.

Warren Hastings Withers was born at Vincennes, Ind., July 16, 1824. His parents were William L. Withers, of the Virginian family of that name, which is prominent in the history of that state, and Christiana Snapp, daughter of Abraham Snapp, one of the pioneers of the northwest territory. His parents dying while he was a mere boy, he was thrown upon his own resources, and without wealth or influential friends, alone and unaided, commenced the battle of life. Unable to enter college, he spent three years in the printing office of the Vincennes *Gazette,* under the instruction and fatherly guidance of his life-time friend, R. Z. Carrington. Subsequently, he spent some time in St. Louis, New Orleans, and other parts of the south, and, finally, in October, 1842, settled at Anderson, Ind., where he purchased a small printing office, but about the time he was to issue his paper, the printing office at Muncie was burned, and its editor was thrown out of employment, with a family to support. To him young Withers relinquished his paper, and applied himself diligently to the study of the law, and was admitted to the bar at Anderson in the spring of 1843. He entered into partnership with the venerable John Marshall at Muncie, and was afterward associated with John M. Wallace, late judge of the Logansport circuit. Not satisfied, however, with the remuneration afforded by the law practice of that day, and having in early boyhood inbibed a taste for politics, he purchased a printing office, and, in 1846, commenced the publication of the Muncie *Journal*, in which he continued till the spring of 1848, when he came to Fort Wayne and succeeded the late George W. Wood as editor of the Fort Wayne *Times*. He edited this paper during the Taylor campaign, and afterward sold the establishment to Mr. Wood. In September, 1859, he married Martha, eldest daughter of Capt. Henry Rudisill, one of the pioneers of Allen county. Mr. Withers was an Episcopalian, and was one of the active officers of Trinity Episcopal church. He was an ardent whig until the dissolution of that party; and on the birth of the republican party, gave it a devotion born of principle, and increased by years of reflection. But he was not an office-seeker, and in all his active life, held but two offices. The first was that of collector of internal revenue, by appointment of President Lincoln in 1861, at the time the office was created; he was thus obliged to organize and arrange a department of public business of whose workings no one knew anything until then. He held the office until July, 1869, discharging the duties in an able an conscientious manner. In 1874, he was the republican candidate for judge of the criminal court, and was only defeated by a majority of 100, in a county where the usual democratic majority is about 3,000. The other office held by him was that of councilman for the Fifth ward of the city of Fort Wayne, to which he was elected in the spring of 1876, though the ward was democratic by a majority of over 200. In every political campaign for thirty years, he was an earnest worker on the stump. On retiring from the editorial chair, he re-entered the active practice of the law at Fort Wayne; first, as a partner of Mr. Colerick, afterward with Col. Charles Case, until the latter was elected to congress. He then formed a partnership with Judge John Morris, which firm continued for some sixteen years, when Hon. J. L. Worden became a partner and remained in it until he was elected to the supreme court, after which the firm of Morris & Withers continued until 1874. On the death of Judge Borden in April, 1882, Mr. Withers was appointed by Governor Porter judge of the criminal court, but he had enjoyed this honor only a few months when his death occurred, November 15, 1882.

Hon. John Morris.—Jonathan Morris, the father of the subject of this sketch, was born in Loudon county, Va., on the ninth day of June, 1788. Actuated by the motives and ambitions which peopled the then new west with the best blood from the old states, he emigrated to, and settled in, Columbiana county, Ohio, near New Lisbon, as a farmer, and followed that occupation through life. There he married Sarah Snyder, who was born in that county in 1790. Starting thus together in life in the early years of Ohio, as a state, those people by their energy, industry and sterling integrity, made for themselves a home and competency, and won the esteem and highest regards of those among whom they lived. Full of years, and honored by their children and all who knew

W. W. Pearson

them, the husband and father died in 1865, and the wife and mother in 1875. As is most always the case, the son doubtless owes much of his success in his profession, and in life, to the native ability of his parents, and their example and training in early youth. John Morris, the son of those worthy parents, was born on the home farm near New Lisbon, on the 6th day of December, 1816. After receiving his early education he began the study of law in the office of William D. Ewing, at New Lisbon, and was admitted to the bar there in 1841. In the same year he was married to Miss Theresa J. Farr, an estimable young lady of that county, who, as a model wife and mother, has been the helpmeet in fact, sharing with him the anxiety of the young beginner, and the successes of the accomplished lawyer. Three years subsequent to his marriage he removed to Indiana and opened a law office in Auburn, the county seat of DeKalb county. He was not long in achieving a position in the front ranks of the profession in his adopted county and northern Indiana. But a few years after settling at Auburn he was elected judge of the common pleas court, the district embracing a number of counties, and discharged the duties of the office with such faithfulness and ability as to merit the good will and highest commendation of the bar and the people. In 1857 he sought a wider field, and began at Fort Wayne an extensive and successful practice, which has made his name well known throughout the state. In the active practice, Judge Morris is eminently a lawyer of resources. Always a student, careful in the preparation of his cases, and quick to see and anticipate difficulties which are, or may be, encountered, he is never discomfited by them, but is able to so shape his cause as to avoid them, when that is possible. Truthful in his own life, he has the faculty in a large degree, of knowing when a witness is telling the truth, and the whole truth, or when he is concealing the truth or falsifying. While he is always kind, courteous and gentlemanly in dealing with witnesses, the false witness generally has abundant cause to regret his wrong after passing through the searching cross-examination by him. In his long and active practice, Judge Morris has not only retained his reputation among the people for integrity and high character, but has been fortunate in retaining the uniform good will and kind regard of the lawyers with whom he has practiced. Vigorous and aggressive in the trial of a cause he never allows himself to descend from the high standard of a gentleman. His successes in the practice have been numerous, but his laurels have been won with such grace and modesty, that envy and emnity have not assailed him. In politics Judge Morris was an ardent whig during the life of that party, as was his father, and since the organization of the republican party he has been an earnest advocate of its principles. He has never sought official preferment, but on the contrary, having often been solicited and urged by his party to accept nominations for some of the most important political offices when an election was certain, but has uniformly declined. In 1881, an act of the legislature provided for the appointment of five supreme court commissioners by the judges of the supreme court to assist that court in its important work. Judge Morris was selected and appointed as one of the commissioners in April, 1881, accepted the position and served until November, 1883, when he resigned to resume the practice at Fort Wayne. It was a compliment to him to have been appointed largely upon the recommendation of Judge Worden, who had been a judge of that court for years, who was a lawyer and judge of great ability, and who as a partner of Judge Morris for years, knew better than any one else, his ability and fitness for the position. His patient and systematic study of the law, his long and varied experience at the bar, and his power of analysis, greatly aided him in his work as a supreme court commissioner. From the first, and continuously, he was regarded by the supreme court, and the bar of the state, as one of the ablest and safest of the commissioners. His written opinions while commissioner, published in the Indiana reports, would be a credit to any judge. Some of them will be regarded as leading cases. To perpetuate his memory with the bench and bar of the state at least, his work upon the supreme bench will be a sufficient monument. Since his retirement from that bench, Judge Morris has been engaged in the active practice of the law at Fort Wayne. Although beyond the age at which men generally engage in active business, he is still (1889) in his usual robust health, both physically and mentally.

David H. Colerick was a leading member of the bar of Indiana, and with hardly an exception was the most graceful and accomplished speaker in the state. He possessed in an eminent degree all the elements of an orator; a vigorous imagination, a pleasing presence, a rich clear voice, and a great command of language. He was invariably gracious and affable in manner. David Hoge Colerick was born in May, 1805, at Washington, Washington county, Penn. His father, John Colerick, was a distinguished Irish patriot, who worked with Robert Emmet in the great struggle for the liberation of Ireland and the cause of human freedom, and in the interests of the cause to which he was devoted, published and edited a paper in Ireland. Upon the arrest of Emmet, many of his followers made their way to the United States, but just as Mr. Colerick was about to leave Ireland, he was arrested and on political charges was incarcerated for sixteen months. Finally escaping he came to America and joined the settlement of Irish patriots at Pittsburgh, then a small trading post. At that place he published and edited for many years the *Western Telegram*, which was the first newspaper printed west of the Allegheny mountains. Subsequently, he removed the paper to Washington, Penn., where he conducted it until his death in 1807. David, then two years old, was subsequently taken by his mother to Zanesville, Ohio, where, when a youth, he entered the store and afterward the law office of Gen. Philemon Beecher, a successful merchant and eminent lawyer, who had represented the Lancaster district in congress. After the death of Gen. Beecher, David H. Colerick finished his studies of the law in the office of the famous Thomas Ewing, who was afterward United States senator. He was admitted to the bar at Lancaster and soon afterward, in 1829, moved to Fort Wayne, where he practiced law until 1872, when he retired from the cares and duties of his profession. In his early years he was active in politics as a whig, and was an enthusiastic follower of Henry Clay. He served in both houses of the Indiana legislature, being elected to the house in 1832 and to the senate in 1835, on both occasions having as his opposing candidate, W. G. Ewing, one of the wealthiest and most influential men of northern Indiana. The district which he represented, extended from the Wabash river to the Michigan state line, and from Ohio to Illinois, and the legislature during his service was composed of the ablest men of the state, many of whom rose to great prominence. He decided to never again accept office, at the close of his senatorial term, and was steadfast in this resolution, though twice offered subsequently the nomination to congress. After 1854, he allied himself with the democratic party, and in 1864 was unanimously selected as a delegate to the Chicago national convention which nominated George B. McClellan for the presidency. Mr. Colerick was married while a member of the senate to Elizabeth Gillespie Walpole, a woman of fine culture, by whom he had nine children, of whom four are living, Walpole G., attorney, who was elected to represent the twelfth district in congress in 1878 and again in 1880, Henry and Philemon B., both attorneys, and Mrs. John Larwill. David H. Colerick died November 6, 1887. On the following day a meeting of the Allen county bar was held, at which, eloquent addresses concerning him were made, and the following resolution presented by the committee consisting of Robert S. Taylor, Joseph Brackenridge, L. M. Ninde, John Morris, Edward O'Rourke, and F. P. Randall, is here quoted as a just estimate of his character. "As a husband, father and friend he was kind, affectionate, steadfast and devoted. As a lawyer, he knew no end but his client's interest, no means but honorable advocacy, and spared himself no pains or labor to attain success. A kind providence has spared his life so far beyond the common span, that his fame as an orator has become a legend of the bar. It is only the older ones of us who can remember his unrivalled skill and eloquence as an advocate, and who can testify, as we do, with grateful recollection, to his fatherly kindness to every young attorney, the gentle courtesy of his manners, and the unbounded goodness of his heart, in the days when he stood among the leaders of the Indiana bar. After a long day of active life, and a long evening of peaceful retirement in the bosom of his family, he has gone to the night of his eternal rest, to be broken only by the morning of a glorious resurrection. We shall hold him always in affectionate remembrance."

Hon. Walpole G. Colerick was born in Fort Wayne about forty-four and one-half years ago. He belongs to an honorable and distinguished family on both his father's and mother's side. He is a son of the late Hon. David H. Colerick, and his mother's name before marriage was Elizabeth Gillespie Walpole. He also belongs to families of lawyers. Three of his mother's brothers were lawyers. John G. Walpole was a practitioner at Fort Wayne, where he died many years ago, and Robert L. and Thomas D. Walpole were distinguished lawyers at Indianaplis. He is one of six sons of the late Hon. and Mrs. David H. Colerick, all of whom were, and are, successful lawyers. His older brother, the Hon. John Colerick, one of the most promising and brilliant of the younger men of the state, died in March, 1872. David Colerick, another older brother, and a lawyer of ability and promise, also died in 1872. Each of these brothers had, in early life, been trusted and honored by the people, not only by a large practice in their profession, but by the bestowal of public office. Still later, Thomas Colerick, a younger brother died when a young man, and when he was just entering upon what promised to be a successful and brilliant career as a lawyer. He was not only a young man of fine ability and character, but he had the industry and methods of study which always bring their reward by way of success in the learned professions. Messrs. Henry and Philemon B. Colerick, younger brothers, are both practicing and successful lawyers in Fort Wayne; the former has been attorney for the city of Fort Wayne for twelve years, The subject of this sketch was educated in the city schools of Fort Wayne, the course of study in which is equal to that of many colleges. He, however, did not, and has not, depended upon what may be learned in pursuing the ordinary course of study provided by institutions of learning, but has pursued such reading and study as was best calculated to fit him for the learned profession of his choice. He has had advantages which not many enjoy, in preparing for, and entering upon, the duties of a profession. He not only had the benefit of his father's learning, experience, example, advice and encouragement, but also the help, advice and encouragement of a mother of fine ability and culture. He had gone through a course of study in the law, been admitted to the bar, and became a partner with his father, before he was twenty-one years of age. From that time until now he has been one of the leading and most successful practioners at the Allen county bar. He is able and patient in the preperation of his causes for trial, and in the trial of them he is skillful and successful. In the preparation of a cause and in presenting it to the court and jury, he has few equals in discovering in advance the controlling points, and in so marshaling the testimony and handling it in the argument, as to produce the conviction that the cause of his client is just and ought to prevail. He is a good judge of human nature, and is remarkably conversant with the modes of thought on the part of jurors. With these qualifications, and his natural facilities in the way of a public speaker, he is forcible and successful as an advocate in jury cases. Added to his other elements of success is that of sincerity, which has no little weight with both the court and jury.

Mr. Colerick has always been popular with the people, and has been peculiarly fortunate in having many friends among them who, on all occasions, are ready to make his cause their own. In 1878, when but thirty-three years of age, he was nominated over a strong competitor, and elected to congress from the Fort Wayne district. He was re-elected in 1880. In those campaigns, whether alone, or in joint debate with his competitor, Mr. Colerick more than met the expectations of his friends, in the eloquent, learned and logical manner in which he discussed the questions at issue. As a member of congress, he was able, faithful and diligent, always in his seat, or at work with committees. And although he was of the party in the minority, and voted with it upon all questions dividing the two parties, and made earnest and strong speeches in advocacy of its principles, he was popular with the opposition, and was thus enabled to get favors from them in the way of help in the passage of measures in which his people were interested. It was thus that he was enabled to procure the passage of the laws providing for the holding of terms of the federal courts at Fort Wayne, and for the construction of the government building, for the accommodation of those courts, the postoffice, and other government offices. After retiring from congress he was engaged in the practice of the law at Fort Wayne until November, 1883. In that month the supreme court of the state, without solicitation on his part, and without his knowledge in advance, tendered him the position of supreme court commissioner. While the position was subordinate to that of a judge of the supreme court, it required no less ability and learning to fill it properly. Causes were distributed to the commissioners for examination, decision, and the writing of opinions, as to the court. And while the court ultimately decided the causes, by adopting or rejecting the opinions prepared by the commissioners, very much depended upon their work. After some hesitation, Mr. Colerick accepted the proffered position, and entered upon the discharge of its duties on the 9th day of November, 1883, and served until the expiration of the commission, by operation of law in 1885. In that position, Judge Colerick again more than met the expectations of his friends, and of the supreme court. His opinions from the first, showed that he had the ability, learning and habits of industry and care, to render him a reliable, and valuable judge upon the bench of the supreme court. Those qualities at once commanded confidence upon the part of the supreme court, and the bar of the state. His statements of causes are concise and clear, and his opinions upon the law applicable and controlling, are able, accurate and forcible. His written opinions are singularly free from circumlocution, unnecessary matter, or dictum which might tend to mystify or mislead. When they are read by a lawyer, there is left no doubt as to what the case was, nor as to the law therein declared. Since retiring from the bench, Judge Colerick, in the vigor of mature manhood, both physical and mental, has been engaged in a large and important practice at Fort Wayne.

John Colerick, who became one of the most distinguished citizens of Fort Wayne, was born at Indianapolis, September 20, 1837. He was a son of David H. and Elizabeth Colerick, above mentioned. His mother carefully guided his early life, and supplemented the instructions of the celebrated Alexander McJunkin, under whom several well-known citizens of Fort Wayne pursued their studies. In 1854 Mr. Colerick entered Wabash college, at Crawfordsville, where he remained during one college year, then entering Hanover college, near Madison, where he finished his education. He began reading law with his father at nineteen years of age, and found no better school than the attentive study of his father's methods. Soon after his admission to the bar he was elected district attorney for the twentieth judicial district, a position he held until 1859, when he resigned it to accept the appointment of prosecuting attorney for the tenth circuit then composed of ten counties. In 1861 he removed to Indianapolis and practiced there until 1864 when he returned to Fort Wayne. He became widely known as successful in criminal practice, first as a prosecuting attorney, and then in the defense on such cases. There was hardly a criminal case in Allen or adjoining counties in which he was not engaged for the defense. But his civil practice was equally extensive, and his practice grew to immense proportions. Mr. Colerick's unusual power as a speaker, and his intense feelings, led him into the field of politics, where he was a force no less potent than at the bar. In 1869 he was a candidate on the democratic electoral ticket, and assisted in the canvass. In 1870 he was unanimously nominated as the democratic candidate for congress as representative of the ninth district, and he made a gallant canvass, and considerably reduced the large adverse majority. Mr. Colerick's excessive exertions began to tell upon his strength about this time, and those remarkable efforts of imagination and eloquence and reason which so charmed his hearers, gradually made inroads upon his endurance. On the 7th of March, 1872, he passed away, and sorrow overspread the city at the news of the early death of one so brilliant and full of promise of still greater achievements.

Joseph Brackenridge, one of the veteran lawyers of northern Indiana, is also an old resident of Fort Wayne, having lived here since the fall of 1830, when he accompanied his parents to this city. He was born at Brookville, Franklin county, Ind., August 7, 1823. Receiving his early education at Fort Wayne, he soon began the study of the law with his uncle, Robert Brackenridge, a distinguished citizen elsewhere mentioned in this work. He was licensed to practice and admitted to the bar of Allen county, October 22, 1846. He served as prosecuting attorney for several terms, and in 1856 was appointed judge of the court of common pleas by Governor Ashbel P. Willard, to fill the unexpired term of Judge Borden. Subsequently he was elected to the same office and served a term of four years, and at a later date, he was elected judge of the criminal court, a position he also held for four years. These responsible offices he held with honor, and discharged the duties pertaining to them with impartiality and a high sense of responsibility to the public. Judge Brackenridge was introduced at an early period in his career as an attorney to the railroad practice, in which he is still engaged, and he has won a high reputation in this branch of the law. He served as solicitor for the Pittsburgh, Fort Wayne & Chicago railroad company in the state of Indiana in connection with Robert Brackenridge, for some years prior to the execution of the lease of that railroad property to the Pennsylvania railroad company, and continued in the same capacity with the latter company, until the assignment of that lease to the Pennsylvania company in 1873. He has continued to act as solicitor of the latter company, in charge of the legal business connected with the Pittsburgh, Fort Wayne & Chicago railroad company, in the state of Indiana, until the present time. As a citizen, Judge Brackenridge is very highly esteemed by the community of which he has been a prominent member for so many years. He is a member of the Berry Street Methodist Episcopal church, in politics is a democrat, and is a member of the Masonic order. Judge Brackenridge was married in 1861 at Ypsilanti, Mich., to Eliza J. Walpole, and they have three children: Will P., Robert E., and Edith.

James A. Fay, first judge of the criminal court of Allen county, was born May 10, 1813, at Northampton, N. Y. After attending school there, he came west with an engineering party, for his health, and finally taught school at Centerville, then the county seat of Wayne county. Becoming acquainted with Hon. John Newman there, he studied law with him, and was admitted to the bar on motion of the distinguished Caleb B. Smith. Of the latter Mr. Fay became a partner at Connorsville, and was soon well known as a promising lawyer. In 1858 he came to Fort Wayne, which was his home until his death, April 9, 1876. Here he took high rank at once as an attorney, and when the criminal court was established he was appointed judge by Governor Baker, at the unanimous request of the bar. Judge Fay was in many respects a remarkable man, notably so in his high conception of manhood and profound convictions. Arriving at his conclusions by thorough consideration he maintained them without hesitation, and with remarkable moral courage. His mind was active, and at times almost painfully intense in action. His home life, at a beautiful suburban home, was delightful, and he was tenderly devoted to his wife, Julia P. Paine, to whom he was married June 20, 1849, and their three children, but one of whom, Mrs. P. A. Randall, survived him.

Samuel Bigger, governor of Indiana, was born in Warren county, Ohio, March 20, 1802. He received his education at Athens university, in that state, and prosecuted legal duties at Lebanon. His professional life was commenced in Indiana. He first practiced in Union county, and afterward in Rush, in both of which he attained eminence as a sound and successful lawyer. He was elected to the legislature from Rush county, in the year 1834, and was a distinguished member of that body during that and the succeeding year. He was then elected president judge of the circuit court, and served until 1840, when he was elected governor of the state. With the aid of another gentleman, he revised the statutes of the state, and produced the large volume known as the "revised statutes of 1843." In his last message to the legislature, Governor Bigger recommended the establishment of a state hospital for the insane; acting on which recommend action the legislature levied a tax, and took other suitable measures for the establishment of the "Indiana hospital for the insane," now in extensive and successful operation. Under his administration the affairs of the state were managed with prudence, economy and ability. He retired from office with less pecuniary means than he possessed when he entered upon the discharge of its duties, but with the consciousness that he was regarded by his whole constituency as an honest man, and a faithful public officer. On his withdrawal from public life, he resumed the practice of the law in Fort Wayne, and at the time of his decease had an extensive practice. He died in 1845.

One of the prominent attorneys of Fort Wayne during the war period and subsequent decade was Joseph S. France, who was born in Indiana county, Penn., September 9, 1824. At the age of seventeen years he commenced teaching school in his native county, and continued to do so for three years. He then went to Pittsburgh and studied medicine, and after receiving his diploma, he practiced for a short time, but abandoned it for the purpose of taking up the study of law. He was subsequently admittted to the bar. In 1852 he moved to Illinois and established a newspaper at Piqua. In 1858 he came to Fort Wayne and resumed the practice of law, which he pursued until his death. He held several official positions, among them that of city attorney in 1859 and '60; prosecuting attorney of the common pleas court in 1861–62–63; and prosecuting attorney of the criminal court from 1872 until his death in 1874. He was a democrat of prominence, a well educated and brilliant speaker, both in English and German. He married Rachel Cook, daughter of George and Rachel Cook, a native of Pennsylvania, born in 1829. She and four of their five children still survive, residents of the city.

Robert S. Taylor, one of the foremost attorneys of Indiana, has been an honored citizen of Fort Wayne for thirty years. Through his efforts during this period in the practice of law, and devotion to politics, few men are as well known throughout northern Indiana, and esteemed alike by those whose cause he has advocated and those he has opposed. Judge Taylor was born May 22, 1838, near Chillicothe, Ohio, son of Rev. Isaac N. Taylor and his wife, Margaretta Stewart. The father was a Presbyterian minister who devoted his life to the arduous duties of a pioneer preacher, first at Celina, and St. Mary's, in Ohio, and subsequently in Jay county, Ind., whither he removed in 1844. A few years later, inspired by devotion to the cause of education, he founded Liber college, near Portland, where many of the boys and girls of that region laid the foundation of future usefulness. At this school Robert S. Taylor graduated June 30, 1858, and within a few minutes after receiving his diploma, he was married to his class mate, Fanny W. Wright. His attention was soon turned in the direction of law, and he began his studies with Judge Jacob M. Haynes, at Portland. These he further pursued and completed at Fort Wayne, where he arrived in October, 1859. Here his home has ever since been. At first, upon beginning his residence at Fort Wayne, he taught school part of a year, and in November, 1860, he entered the office of L. M. Ninde, as a clerk and office assistant. Two years later he was advanced to a partnership, and the firm of Ninde & Taylor was formed. In 1866, Col. R. S. Robertson was added to the firm, which was one of the prominent ones of northern Indiana. Upon the organization of the criminal court in 1868, R. S. Taylor was appointed its prosecuting attorney. In the same year, the firm of Ninde, Taylor & Robertson was dissolved, and Mr. Taylor was appointed judge of the court of common pleas. This position he held until the next election, when he was elected as a representative of Allen county to the Indiana house of representatives, being the only republican ever sent to that body from Allen county. The prominence thus obtained in the political field led to his nomination in 1874 as the republican candidate for congress, against Holman H. Hamilton, and again in 1880, as the candidate against Walpole G. Colerick. He was defeated on each occasion, but in the last instance especially, the great reduction of the adverse majority, clearly demonstrated the hearty esteem in which Judge Taylor is held by the people of the district. He still takes an active part in political discussions, and is a popular speaker in all important campaigns. In March, 1881, he was appointed by President Garfield, a member of the Mississippi river commission, to succeed Gen. Benjamin Harrison, who had been elected United States senator. This position occupies a great part of his time now and has since his appointment, though he is still a valued citizen of the city, active in all movements for the public good, and ever earning the continued esteem and confidence of his fellow citizens.

Edward O'Rourke, judge of the thirty-eighth judicial circuit, was born October 13, 1841, at Newark, N. J., the seventh of eight children. His parents Christopher O'Rourke and Ellen Flannagan, were natives of county Kildare, Ireland. Patrick O'Rourke, his grandfather, had a lease of a farm for a term of three lives, or ninety-nine years. The oldest son, John, succeeded him, as is the custom and law of Great Britain, and his son, James, now occupies the same farm. The ancestors of both Christopher and Ellen, had lived in the same county for many generations, and were noted as honest, good farmers, as far as their history can be traced. Christopher O'Rourke and Ellen Flannagan, were married about the year 1823, and left Ireland for America, in 1825. They first went to Dublin, thence to Liverpool, and thence, in sailing vessel, to New York, and settled in New Jersey, where Edward was born. They remained there several years, but his father on account of ill health, removed, with his family, to Carroll county, Ohio, some months after the birth of Edward, and purchased a farm there, so that the subject of this sketch has no recollection of the place of his nativity. After several years' life upon the farm, the father became a contractor for building the Pittsburgh, Wellsville & Cleveland railroad, and afterward built several miles of what is now the Pittsburgh, Fort Wayne & Chicago road. He then returned to Ohio, and resumed farming operations near Mansfield, Ohio, but finally removed to Fort Wayne, where he died in 1875, his widow surviving him about six months. Both were respected by a large circle of acquaintances, and their loss was sincerely mourned by friends and descendants. Edward O'Rourke obtained a primary education in the public schools of Ohio, and being fond of books, soon acquired a good knowledge of grammar, arithmetic and algebra; and while attending literary and debating societies in the common schoolhouses, acquired a taste for declamation and debate, which first gave him the idea of entering the legal profession, and from that time the energies of his mind were bent in that direction. He first came to Fort Wayne in the fall of 1859, and entered the Fort Wayne Methodist college, remaining there about a year. In the spring of 1863, he entered Notre Dame academy and remained there one term, going, in the summer of that year, to the French college in Montreal, remaining there as a student, until 1865, engaged in a classical and mathematical course, and acquiring the French language so as to read and converse in it with fluency. His literary taste led him into mental philosophy, poetry and history, and his scientific taste, to excel in mathematics, having a retentive memory for dates and numbers. In the fall of 1865 he entered the law office of Worden & Morris, as a student, and remained with them until he was elected prosecuting attorney of the criminal court, in 1867. He was a successful prosecutor for five years, after which he was in the general practice of the law until 1876, having in 1875, entered into partnership with Hon. Robert Lowry, and Col. R. S. Robertson, the partnership continuing until he was elected judge of the circuit court in 1876, re-elected in 1882 and 1888, which position he now holds, having earned the reputation of an upright, conscientious and painstaking judge. He was married in November, 1871, to Miss Ada L. Abrams, of Wells, Ohio. His mental and moral characteristics he inherits to a considerable extent from his father, who was a man of extraordinary memory, and had a great taste for history and poetry. Becoming a citizen of the United States as soon as he could after his arrival here, he became much attached to the principles which underlie our system of government and taught his son to revere them. With few advantages for education, he was a great reader, and seemed never to forget an important fact he had read. His mother also was of energetic, active mind, and was very vivacious and fluent in speech, and to such parents Judge O'Rourke, no doubt, owes much of his own success in life.

Allen Zollars, the subject of this sketch, was born in Licking county, Ohio. The ancestors of Mr. Zollars were of German extraction, and migrated from Prussia to this country at an early period. They belong to that robust and intelligent class of early emigrants who, to secure their political and religious freedom, were ready to encounter the privations and hardships of an unknown and unbroken wilderness, and the dangers arising from the frequent hostilities of native savages who claimed the whole county as their rightful and undoubted heritage. It was fortunate for the succeeding generations of America, that the circumstances attending the first settlement of the country were somewhat forbidding and such as to invite to its shores only the liberty-loving people of Europe. The sturdy ancestors of Mr. Zollars contributed their share in the struggle for independence, and helped to secure for themselves and those to come after them, that complete national freedom and personal liberty which all enjoy to day. His paternal great-grandfather was an officer in the war of the revolution, and served his country with distinction, for more than five years. Mr. Zollars's father was born in Washington county, Penn., and at twelve years of age removed with his parents to Jefferson county, Ohio. At that time Ohio had been a state in the Federal union but thirteen years, and was, in a large measure, an unbroken forest. Until his manhood and marriage the father of Mr. Zollars lived in that county, when he moved to Licking county, of the same state. There, in the course of time, he became the owner of flouring, lumber and woolen mills, which he operated with success. Subsequently he disposed of those properties and engaged in farming and raising of fine stock. In 1868, in good health, mentally and physically, he retired from business, and until his death in March, 1889, at the age of eighty-seven years and three months, he lived in happy retirement, managing his property, and enjoying the most devoted love and affection of an unusually large number of direct descendants. But a short time before his death he had assembled under his own roof five generations of his family, himself and wife, with whom he had lived for more than sixty-five years, and who survives him, some of his children, some of his grand-children, some of his great-grand-children, and one great-great-grand-child. He was a man not only of remarkable health and strength physically, but also, as self-educated, a man of strong mental power, and extended reading. Upon many subjects his thoughs were in advance of those among whom he lived. It was a source of very great comfort to his family, that during his long and active life they never knew him to give the least sanction, by word or act, to anything that was immoral, dishonest or dishonorable, but on the contrary, uniformly condemned all such things in the strongest terms. In early boyhood young Zollars attended the common schools of the neighborhood, evincing much interest in his books and studies. His parents, observing with pleasure and with pride the fondness of their son for books and his desire for knowledge, determined to aid him in acquiring such training and education as should prepare and equip him for such pursuits in life as he might choose to adopt. After going through the common schools of the neighborhood, he was placed in a private academy, and there thoroughly prepared to enter college. He entered Dennison university, at Granville, Ohio, pursued a classical course, and graduated in 1864, receiving the degree of A. B. Three years later the university conferred upon him the honorary degree of A. M., and, in 1888, the degree of LL. D. It would be alike interesting and profitable to trace the persistent efforts and struggles by which young Zollars secured a thorough and complete education, and that full and elaborate preparation which, in after life, has rendered the acquisition of knowledge easy and pleasurable. The proposed brevity of this sketch will not, however, allow this. Having finished his college course and attained his manhood, the time had come for Mr. Zollars to decide for himself what should be his life pursuit. He chose the law. He entered the law office of Judge Buckingham, of Newark, Ohio, where he studied law for a while. He then entered the law department of the university of Michigan, and graduated in 1866, receiving the degree of LL. B. Being thus prepared for the practice of his chosen profession, Mr. Zollars located at Fort Wayne, Ind. He at once made a favorable impression upon the bench, the bar and the people. All regarded him as a young man of fine attainments, high moral character and great professional promise. It was not long until he had his share of business, and felt assured of success in his profession. Having thus overcome the difficulties and doubts that lurk in and beset the beginning of the way of professional life, Mr. Zollars found himself in a position to support a family. In November, 1867, he was married to Miss Minnie Ewing, of Lancaster, Ohio, a lady of culture who has contributed much to the subsequent success of her husband. Mr. Zollars is a democrat. In 1868 he was elected to the legislature. He took a prominent part in the debates of the house, and was much esteemed as a member of that body. He did not seek a re-election, though the place was easily within his reach. In May, 1869, he was chosen city attorney of Fort Wayne, and continued to serve in that capacity for six years. Upon the establishment of the superior court of Allen county, he was appointed by Governor Williams judge of that court. He held the office for a short time and then resigned in order to resume the practice of his profession, which he found to be much more profitable than the judgeship of the superior court. In 1882, Judge Zollars was nominated by the democratic party of the state as a candidate for supreme judge. He was elected, receiving in the northern part of the state, where he was best known, much more than the party vote. He was nominated by his party for the same office in 1888, but was, with the rest of the democratic ticket, defeated. As judge of the supreme court, Judge Zollars more than met the high expectations of his friends, and so discharged the duties of his high office as to receive the hearty approval and warm commendation of the bar of the state, without regard to party. As a judge he was industrious, careful and singularly painstaking. In his high office he was independent, fearless and honest. It is but just to say, and it is infinitely creditable to Judge Zollars that it may be truthfully said, that no political bias, prejudice or zeal could deflect or move his mind from its honest and intelligent convictions. There is not a judge nor a lawyer in the state of Indiana that does not know and who would not assert this. It is by no means unfortunate for Judge Zollars that, though for a day, through political excitement, a few impulsive friends may have been estranged, the occasion was presented which enabled him to demonstrate the fact that, though a staunch democrat, on the bench he was not and could not be a partisan. The written opinions of

Judge Zollars found in more than the last thirty volumes of our reports, attest his fitness for judicial position. His style is lucid, unstrained and vigorous; his statements full and comprehensive; his analysis perspicuous and complete. His opinions show great research, industry and care. They challenge approval, and must commend themselves to bench and bar. The writer is somewhat acquainted with the bar of the state, and he has yet to hear an unfavorable criticism of any opinion prepared by Judge Zollars. As a lawyer, Judge Zollars has always stood high. He has had a large practice, civil and criminal, and has been unusually successful. He has argued many cases in the supreme court, and has lost but few. No one knows better than Judge Zollars the necessity for thorough preparation in the trial of cases, and no one more industriously prepares his cases than he. He could hardly be induced to enter upon the trial of a cause without complete preparation. He knows and realizes the fact that it is the prepared man who, as a rule, is successful. Though of a warm and ardent temperament, Judge Zollars is, in the trial of a cause, always master of himself. He is rarely not at his best. He is always courteous and deferential toward the court; kind and forbearing toward his adversaries. He examines a witness carefully and thoroughly, but treats the witness with respect, and, as a general rule, so as to secure his good opinion and make him feel that he has been treated kindly and forbearingly. While subjecting the witness to the most severe tests, he so questions him that the witness never seems to realize the fact. As a speaker, Judge Zollars is always direct, logical and forcible. His treatment of his case is always full, comprehensive and accurate; his analysis of the facts is clear and exhaustive. He sees, without effort, the relation and dependence of the facts, and so groups them as to enable him to throw their combined force upon the point they tend to prove. He has now just attained mature manhood, and returns to the profession with the assurance of success. Judge Zollars is rather below the medium size; his head and chest are large, his frame is compact and vigorous. He is graceful in action, in manner courteous, forbearing and genial. He is popular with the people, and his future is full of promise, and no one is better prepared to meet and profit by its hidden mysteries than he. In his domestic life and surroundings Judge Zollars is most fortunate. Surrounded by a most estimable family, every member of which is thoroughly devoted to him and striving to add something to his comfort and happiness — a family that has deserved all the affections of his heart, stimulated his pride, increased his hope and contributed to his success in life and augmented his happiness.

Col. Robert S. Robertson.—Robert Robertson, a native of Scotland, born in October, 1756, emigrated from Kinross-shire in the latter part of the eighteenth century, and settled in Washington county, N. Y., where he died November 6, 1840. His son, Nicholas Robertson, was born at North Argyle, Washington county, May 12, 1803, and was for many years a justice of the peace and postmaster of his town. He married Martha Hume-Stoddart, of New York city, who was born March 20, 1812, and died January 20, 1867. She was a descendant of two Scotch families, the Humes and Stoddarts, the latter name being derived from Standard, the first of the name having come to England with William the Conqueror, as standard bearer for the Vicompte de Pulesden. Their son, Robert S. Robertson, now a distinguished citizen of Fort Wayne, was born at North Argyle, April 16, 1839. His early life was spent under the influences of a strict Scotch Presbyterian element planted in that region of New York about 1764, by Capt. Duncan Campbell, under the patronage of the Duke of Argyle. He studied in the common schools and at Argyle academy, and when not so engaged worked with his father in the saw-mill and grist-mill of the latter. Early in 1859 he entered the office of Hon. James Gibson, at Salem, N. Y., and commenced the study of the law, and at New York city continued his studies until December, 1860, under Hon. Charles Crary. He was admitted to the bar in November, 1860, his examination being conducted by Hons. J. W. Edmunds, E. S. Benedict and M. S. Bidwell; Judges Josiah Sutherland, Henry Hageboom and B. W. Bonney presiding in general term. He then settled at Whitehall, N. Y., but in the summer of 1861 commenced raising a company for the war. The recruits, as fast as enlisted, were placed in barracks at Albany, where in the winter of 1861-62 an order was received to consolidate all parts of companies and regiments and forward them at once to Washington. Under this order, his men were assigned to Company I, Ninety-third regiment New York volunteer infantry, but refused to go unless Robertson would go with them. Rather than desert the men he had enlisted, he at once mustered into the service as a private, but was soon made orderly sergeant of his company, and donning knapsack and shouldering his musket went to the front with his regiment. In April, 1862, he was commissioned second lieutenant, and in February, 1863, was promoted to first lieutenant, Company K. He was in all the campaigns of the army of the Potomac until discharged from the service. For a time, and during the Gettysburg campaign, he was acting adjutant of his regiment. Soon afterward, in 1863, while his regiment was guard at army headquarters, he was tendered, and accepted the position of aide-de-camp on the staff of Gen. Nelson A. Miles, then commanding the fighting first brigade, first division, second army corps. While on this duty he was twice wounded, once in the charge at Spottsylvania, May 12, 1864, when a musket ball was flattened on his knee, and again on 30th of May at Tolopotomoy Creek, when he was shot from his horse in a charge, a minie ball passing through his abdomen from the front of the right hip to the back of the left, at which time he was reported among the mortally wounded. With a strong constitution he recovered sufficiently to go to the front before Petersburg, but his wound broke out afresh and he was discharged September 3, 1864, "for disability from wounds received in action." For his services he was the recipient of two brevet commissions, one from the president conferring the rank of captain by brevet, and another from the governor of New York, conferring the rank of colonel, both of which read, "for gallant and meritorious services in the battles of Spottsylvania and Tolopotomoy Creek." He was in eleven general engagements and numerous skirmishes, and was never off duty until he received his second wound.

During two years following the war he was engaged in the practice of law at Washington, D. C., and while living there was married, July 19, 1865, at Whitehall, N. Y., to Elizabeth H. Miller, whose grandfather, Alexander Robertson, immigrated from Blair Athol, in 1804. They have five children: Nicholas, Louise, Robert, Mabel and Annie. The residence of Col. Robertson and family at Fort Wayne began in 1866. His ability and devotion to the cause of the republican party at once made him prominent, and in 1867 he was elected city attorney for two years. In 1868 he was nominated by his party for state senator from the counties of Allen and Adams, and made a thorough canvass in the face of overwhelming odds. In 1871 he was appointed register in bankruptcy and United States commissioner; the former office he resigned in 1875, and the other in 1876. When the republican state convention met in the latter year, he was nominated, entirely without his seeking, for the office of lieutenant-governor. He entered the canvass with great vigor, but after he had spoken in thirty-one counties he was taken with malarial fever, by which he was prostrated for more than a month. In 1886, there having been a vacancy created in the office of lieutenant-governor by the resignation of Gen. M. D. Manson, both the republican and democratic parties nominated condidates for the office, and after a memorable campaign, Col. Robertson was elected. At the time appointed by law he was declared elected and took the oath of office as lieutenant-governor in the presence of the general assembly. By this time, however, the opposition had decided to regard the election for that office as unauthorized by law, and as it had the majority of the senate, over which, by virtue of law, the lieutenant-governor was the presiding officer, Col. Robertson was forbidden to assume the function of his office. Attempts were made to obtain a judicial decision, by the opposition, by means of two injunction suits, but these ended in the ruling of the supreme court that the legislature had exclusive jurisdiction. Upon a second demand for the rights of the lieutenant-governor, Col. Robertson was forcibly excluded from the senate chamber. Great excitement resulted, in which the calm, dignified and courageous bearing of Col. Robertson had great effect in preventing a calamitous outcome of the deplorable affair. He counselled that no attempts at force be made in his behalf, but that the question should be submitted to the peaceful arbitration of the people, and doubtless prevented a serious outbreak which might have proven disastrous to the welfare and dignity of the state. In all other functions of the office to which he was elected Lieutenant-governor Robertson performed his duties without hinderance. While holding this office, he was for two successive years elected president of the state board of equalization, by that body, an office theretofore always held by the governor. Since 1883 he has served as a trustee of the Indiana university, and as chairman of the library committee has done much creditable work in replacing the library destroyed by fire in 1883, by a new one consisting of some 10,000 well selected volumes, and in planning the beautiful library building now in process of erection. Col. Robertson has devoted much time to historical and scientific studies, and has a collection of minerals, fossils and pre-historic curios of great value. He is a member of the American Association for the advancement of science, of the State Historical Society and of the Congres International des Americanistes, of Europe, and his papers have appeared in the Smithsonian reports, *Magazine of American History*, *North American Review*, and other publications. He has also made valuable contributions to the war history publications of the Loyal Legion. Soon after the inauguration of President Harrison, Governor Robertson was tendered the position of judge of the Indian territory. This he declined, and in May accepted the unsolicited appointment as member of the board of registration and elections of the territory of Utah.

Hon. Robert Lowry, of Fort Wayne, Ind., was born in Ireland; removed in early youth to Rochester, N. Y.; was instructed in the elementary branches at private schools, and had partial academic course, but education was mainly self-acquired; was librarian of Rochester Athenæum and Young Men's association; studied law; removed to Fort Wayne in 1843; was elected by the common council, while yet under age, city recorder; was re-elected but declined; was admitted to the bar; commenced practice in Goshen, Ind., in 1846; was appointed by the governor, circuit judge in 1852, to fill vacancy for an unexpired term; was unexpectedly nominated by the democrats in 1856, in a district having a large adverse majority, as a candidate for congress, and defeated only by a close vote; in 1860 was president of the democratic state convention, and one of the four delegates at large to the democratic national convention; in 1861 and 1862, while still retaining residence and practice in Indiana, he had a law office in Chicago; in 1864, was nominated by the democrats and elected circuit judge for a term of six years; while yet occupying the bench, was again nominated by the democrats in 1866, and re-nominated in 1868, as a candidate for congress in heavily republican districts, and defeated, but by reduced majorities; in 1867 he resumed his residence in Fort Wayne; was re-elected circuit judge on the expiration of his term in 1870, without opposition; was delegate at large to the democratic national convention in 1872; resigned the circuit judgeship in January, 1875, and resumed practice in Fort Wayne as a member of the firm of Lowry, Robertson & O'Rourke; in September, 1877, he was appointed by the governor on the unanimous recommendation of the bar, as judge of the newly-created superior court, and afterward elected as such in 1878 by a unanimous popular vote; was elected the first president of the Indiana State Bar association, in July, 1879; on the expira-

Yours very truly,
R. Lowry

tion of his term as judge, in 1882, he was elected to the Forty-eighth congress, and was re-elected to the Forty-ninth congress, as a democrat, receiving 19,502 votes, against 16,957 votes for his republican competitor. Upon the close of his second term in congress he resumed the active practice of the law in Fort Wayne, extending it throughout the district, an exemplar of the activity and industry which ought to characterize the lawyer, and which have been such marked features in the professional career of this distinguished veteran of the Indiana bar. Judge Lowry's career in congress was characterized by unwearied diligence in the interest of the people of his district, close application, especially to all calls made on him in the interest of the veteran soldiers of his own and other districts, and was always found on the side of the people in all questions before congress. During his services he took an active interest in procuring appropriations for the splendid government building lately erected in Fort Wayne, and to him more than any one else is justly due the several and liberal appropriations voted for it from time to time. Blessed with vigorous health, of stalwart frame, fully alive to the multiform phases of the great social, political and economic activities of this marvelous age, Judge Lowry gives to the questions of the day that calm, judicial examination which only a trained intellect can bestow, and which enters so largely into shaping public opinion on great public questions.

Hon. Samuel M. Hench was elected judge of the superior court to serve out the time for which Judge Worden had been elected, and served until the general election in 1886, and the qualification of a successor. Judge Hench was born on the 22nd day of June, 1846, near Port Royal, Juniata county, Penn. His father was a civil engineer and architect. In his early years he worked with his father and attended the public schools. He was afterward a student at Airy View academy and far along in his course when, in the early part of 1862, he enlisted in Company F, of the One Hundred and Twenty-sixth regiment, Pennsylvania volunteers, and entered the service in the late war. On the 13th day of December, 1862, he was severly wounded at the battle of Fredericksburg. He was mustered out with his regiment at Harrisburg in 1863. He came west to Fort Wayne in September, 1863. There he engaged in work upon a farm in the vicinity of the city, and in the city, until 1864, when he enlisted in Company F, of the Eighty-third regiment of Indiana volunteers, entered the service again, and was mustered out in 1865, after the close of the war. During the remainder of 1865, and the years 1866 and 1867, he attended a commercial college at Fort Wayne, took private instructions with Prof. Robinson, of the Methodist college, and with Prof. Smart, and taught school in the country. In the fall of 1867, he went to Council Bluffs, Iowa, and taught a term of school near the city, and at the same time commenced reading law with Messrs. Clinton & Sapp, a firm of distinguished lawyers of that city. He was admitted to the bar in 1869. While reading law he was a deputy sheriff from January, 1868, until October, 1869. He was also chairman of the democratic county central committee of Pottawatomie county, in which Council Bluffs is situated, from 1869 to 1871, both inclusive. After his admission to the bar he practiced law at Council Bluffs until 1872, when he returned to Fort Wayne and again engaged in the general practice of the law. Subsequent to that he was appointed and elected prosecuting attorney of the criminal court, and elected judge of the criminal court, and of the superior court, as already stated. After his retirement from the bench of the superior court in November, 1886, Judge Hench again engaged in the general practice at Fort Wayne, until the fourth day of August, 1888, when he was appointed by President Cleveland to the important position of chief of the law and miscellaneous division in the second comptroller's office in the treasury department at Washington. Judge Hench is a man of ability and energy, and made a most efficient prosecutor, and a painstaking and acceptable judge. While judge of the criminal and superior courts, he decided important cases, from the decisions of which appeals were taken to the supreme court.

Hon. Robert C. Bell, a prominent attorney of Indiana, was born at Clarksburg, Decatur county, Ind., July 13, 1844. His grandparents were of Virginian descent, and his grandfather, John Bell, was a soldier in the war of 1812. His father, Hiram Bell, a native of Maysville, Ky., married Mary J. Clark, a native of Lexington, of the same state, whose father, Woodson Clark, was the founder of Clarksburg, Ind., whither he emigrated about 1820. Hiram Bell lost his life by an accident, in 1879, but his widow survives. Of their eleven children, all of whom are living, Robert C. is the oldest. He was brought up on a farm, receiving a common school education, and academic training preparatory to the university of Michigan, at which he was graduated in 1868. Previous to this, he enlisted in the union army and after a short period of service in the field, was assigned to detached duty at Nashville, Tenn., where he remained until the close of the war. He provided the means for his education by teaching, and before graduation he was admitted to the bar in 1867. His first law partnership was with Hon. Alfred Kilgore, at Muncie, Ind., and during the time that that gentleman was United States attorney for Indiana, he held the position of assistant. In 1871, he made his home at Fort Wayne, and formed a partnership with Hon. John Colerick, which continued until the death of the latter. He then entered the firm of Coombs, Miller & Bell. Upon the removal of Miller to Indianapolis, his place in the firm was taken by Judge John Morris. This firm was changed upon the appointment of Judge Morris as supreme court commissioner, to Coombs, Bell & Morris, and upon the retirement of Mr. Coombs, the firm became as at present, Bell & Morris. Mr. Bell's record as an attorney is one of distinction, of continued and honorable successes, and he has a high reputation throughout the state. He has been attorney for the county commissioners of Allen county for the past ten years, is attorney for Indiana for the New York, Chicago & St. Louis railroad, and general attorney for the Ft. W., C., & L., and Whitewater railroads. He has always taken an active part in politics as did his father beforehand, on the side of the democratic party. He held the position of United States court commissioner, but resigned it upon election to the state senate, to which he was elected in 1874 and again in 1880. During his last term in that body, he occupied the important position of chairman of the Judiciary committee. In 1884 he was delegate at large for the state in the democratic convention at Chicago. Mr. Bell is prominent also in Masonic circles and in Oddfellowship, being a Master Mason, Knight Templar, and thirty-second degree Scottish Rite. During the year 1876 and 1877 he made an extended visit to Europe. Mr. Bell was married April 5, 1868, to Clara E. Wolfe, daughter of Adam and Elizabeth Wolfe, of Muncie, Ind.

Henry Harrison Robinson, son of James H. Robinson, mentioned in another portion of this work, was born February 2, 1841, at Newark, N. J. He studied three years at Princeton college, leaving before graduation to enlist in the Fifty-fifth regiment Indiana volunteers. Afterward turning his attention to law, he was graduated with the degree of LL.B., at the university of Chicago, in 1865, and was admitted to the bar of the supreme court of Illinois in the same year. He practiced his profession in Wisconsin two years, and upon his return to Fort Wayne, in 1867, he engaged in business with his father. On the 4th of July, 1868, he delivered an oration of striking merit, which was published at the request of comrades of the G. A. R., and in the following autumn he accepted the nomination as republican candidate for state representative and made an active canvass. Though not elected to the legislature, he filled the position of reading clerk of the house at that session with great ability and wrote popular letters to the Fort Wayne *Gazette* over the nom de plume of "Harrison." He was recommended by the state officers and republican legislators for the secretaryship of one of the territories, but did not press his application therefor. From 1870 to 1872 he published the Wabash *Republican*, then one of the leading weeklies of the state. While in Wabash he was appointed United States commissioner, and served in that capacity until his return to Fort Wayne. He also made a campaign in Wabash county for the legislature, but was again confronted by an impregnable adverse majority. Mr. Robinson returned to Fort Wayne in 1873, and engaged in the practice of law and journalism, being at one time editor of the *Gazette*. In the summer of 1874 he was urged to become a candidate for congress on the independent ticket, but declined the honor. On February 1, 1876, he closed his law office to take charge of the Robinson house, and he managed that popular establishment until 1882, since when he has occupied himself in professional and literary pursuits. Mr. Robinson was an early admirer of Gen. Benjam Harrison and advocated his nomination for governor of Indiana in the Wabash *Republican*, now the *Plaindealer*, in 1872.

Samuel L. Morris, one of the prominent attorneys of the city of Fort Wayne, is a native of Indiana, born at Auburn, September 15,

1849. He is the son of Judge John Morris, of this city, and his residence here began when the latter removed from Auburn to Fort Wayne, in 1857. He received his preparatory education in the Fort Wayne public schools, graduating from the high school in 1868. He then entered Princeton college, New Jersey, and was graduated by that institution in 1873. He then began reading law in the office of Withers & Morris, and in 1875 was admitted to practice. For six years he was a partner of Judge R. S. Taylor, and since then has been associated, first with W. H. Coombs, now with Robert C. Bell. Mr. Morris is an earnest republican. He was married at Columbus, Ohio, October 10, 1877, to Carrie E. Ambos, and they have three children: Gertrude E., Samuel L. and Jeannette.

Augustus A. Chapin, present judge of the superior court of Allen county, is a lineal descendant in the eighth generation of Deacon Samuel Chapin, who migrated from England to America about 1635, took the freeman's oath at Boston in 1641, and settled at Springfield, Massachusetts Colony, in 1642, where he died in 1675. Deacon Chapin was prominent in civil and church affairs, and is believed to be the progenitor of all persons bearing that name in the United States and Canada. Through the liberality of the late Chester W. Chapin, president of the Boston & Albany railroad, a statue to the memory of the Deacon was erected and unveiled with appropriate ceremonies at Stearns Park in Springfield, on Thanksgiving day, November 24, 1887. The figure is of bronze, of heroic size, resting upon a granite pedestal, and represents the sturdy old Puritan on his way to meeting on the Lord's day, with staff and Bible and a determined face set strongly toward his destination. The great grandfather of Judge Chapin was an officer in the revolutionary war, and at the battle of Bunker Hill, and the records show that eight bearing the family name in one regiment were in the battle of Lexington. At the close of the war his great-grandfather moved from Uxbridge, Mass., and settled in Windham county, Vt. The Chapin family is believed to have been originally of French descent, but on his mother's and grandmother's side it is of Scotch and Scotch-Irish descent. In 1833, his father, Col. Alexander Chapin, of Wardsboro, Vt., with three of his neighbors, came west and selected a location in the northwestern corner of the then unorganized county of Steuben, Ind. They came to the U. S. land office, at Fort Wayne, and having made their land entries purchased a dugout canoe and in it paddled down the Maumee to Toledo, Ohio, whence, via the Lake and Erie canal, they returned to their New England homes. In 1836, Col. Chapin removed with his family to his new location and with his associates laid out and platted the present village of Orland. The first settlers were almost exclusively from Vermont and for many years the village was known throughout the country as "Vermont Settlement." Col. Chapin was the first postmaster at the place, the first school fund commissioner of Steuben county, held several other positions of trust and died at Orland in 1849 at the comparatively early age of forty-four years, leaving a wife and five young children. Judge Chapin was born in Wardsboro, Windham county, Vt., and grew up from childhood in his father's home at Orland. His early education was obtained at a district common school and at a single term at what was then known as the Ontario collegiate institute near Lima, in LaGrange county, Ind., but subsequently he prepared for college, and in 1855 entered the classical department of the university of Michigan, at Ann Arbor, and graduated in the fall of 1859. He then read law and located at Angola, Steuben county, and followed his profession in that town until the spring of 1865, when he removed to Kendallville. He practiced law in Noble and adjoining counties until the fall of 1883, when he removed to the city of Fort Wayne. He has devoted his time chiefly to his profession and has had but very little to do with politics or political life. In 1860 he was nominated on the republican ticket and elected and served one term as prosecuting attorney of the tenth judicial circuit, which then embraced ten counties in the northeastern corner of the state of Indiana, Allen county being one of them. There were two terms of the circuit court each year, and the judge and prosecutor were obliged to go from most of the counties to others to hold court, either on horseback or in lumber wagons or the primative hacks of that day. At different times he has held some minor offices such as township trustee, city clerk and school examiner. In the fall of 1886, he was nominated and elected judge of the superior court of Allen county, which position he still holds. November 1, 1863, he was married at Angola, to Almira Emerson. They have a family of five children, four daughters and one son. Judge Chapin is a member of the First Presbyterian church, of Fort Wayne, and is a ruling elder in that body.

Perry A. Randall, a well-known attorney of Fort Wayne, was born at Avilla, Noble county, Ind., July 24, 1847. His father, Edwin Randall, born at Lenox, N. Y., May 18, 1807, was a son of Rodley and Amy (Rhodes) Randall. Rodley, born at Winfield, N. Y., May 24, 1783, died at the same place August 1, 1847, was a son of Nicholas R. and Content (Phillips) Randall. Nicholas, born at Uniontown, Conn., May 21, 1753, died September 23, 1814, at same place, was a son of Nathan and Eleanor (Cottrell) Randall. Edwin Randall, as early as 1836, came west and selected lands in Noble county, on which he settled in 1841. He married Mary A. King, who was born in New York, December 18, 1824, and who survives her husband, who died at Avilla, September 14, 1873. Of the three children of these parents, the second is Perry A. Randall. In 1867 he graduated from the Fort Wayne high school, and graduated in 1871 from the university of Michigan, then entering the law department of that university where he graduated in the spring of 1873. Coming to Fort Wayne in 1873, he was admitted to the bar and begun a practice which has been successful and lucrative. In 1881 he formed a partnership in the practice with Will J. Vesey, which still exists. Mr. Randall is one of the best business men of the city. He was married September 7, 1876, to Julia P. Fay, daughter and only child of Judge James A. Fay. They have three children: Fay P., Anna B., and Carrie L.

Hon. James M. Barrett, a prominent member of the bar of Allen county, and well known throughout the state as a leading member of the upper house of the legislature, was born February 7, 1852. His parents were born in Ireland. The father, Benjamin Barrett, born in 1809, son of William, who died at Peru, Ill., married Elizabeth Barrett, who was born in 1814, and in 1834, the family removed to the United States, and settled first in Belmont county, Ohio, afterward, about 1848, changing their home to LaSalle county, Ill. There James M., the eighth of eleven children, was born. The father, who was a farmer, died in Illinois in 1876, but his widow is still living. Mr. Barrett remained on the farm until 1869, also attending the common schools, and then entered Mendota college, in Illinois, where he remained one year, going then to Ann Arbor, Mich. After one year in the high school, he entered the university of Michigan and was graduated in 1875. He immediately began the study of law, and in the fall of 1875, entered the office of McCagg, Culver & Butler, of Chicago, and afterward studied at Princeton, Ill. In March, 1876, he came to Fort Wayne, and was admitted to the bar in the same year. He is now a member of the firm of Morris & Barrett, and has gained an honorable distinction as a lawyer. He is in politics an active democrat, and by that party was elected to the state senate in 1886. During his first session, he took a prominent part in securing the establishment of the asylum for feeble minded youth at Fort Wayne, and during the more important session of 1889, was the acknowledged leader of his party in the senate, as chairman of the judiciary committee, member of many other important committees, and author of a number of most important bills. He has achieved distinction, not only by his merits as a ready and eloquent speaker, and force in debate, but by a reserve strength of character that assures him a brilliant and useful career. Mr. Barrett was married in 1877, to Marian A. Bond, of Fort Wayne, and they have three children: Florence E., Charles D. and Walter A.

Samuel Rockwell Alden, a prominent attorney of Fort Wayne, is the only child of Harlow Alden and his wife, Mary Ann, *nee* Imson. His father, a carpenter and cabinet-maker, was the youngest of ten children of Spencer Alden, a Baptist clergyman, and his wife, Miriam Rockwell. Published genealogies of the descendants of the Puritan John Alden, one of the passengers of the Mayflower, give the history of the Alden family since 1620. His mother, a teacher, was the second daughter of Elias Imson, a thrifty farmer of English and Irish descent, and his wife, whose maiden name was Hunsicker, and was born February 14, 1820, at Oswego, N. Y. Their only son, Samuel Rockwell, was born at South Wilbraham, Mass., August 30, 1847. When he was nine years old his parents removed to Whitewater, Wis., and here he completed the high school course at thirteen years of age, and subsequently studied winters, while engaged on a farm, until he was eighteen, when he went to Beloit to complete his preparation for college. Soon afterward, he was dangerously hurt while attempting to stop a runaway team. The Whitewater normal school having been completed he entered it in 1868 as pupil and teacher, and during the third year held the position of professor of English and elocution, having prepared himself in the latter during vacations. From 1871 to 1874 he was associated with Prof. Horace Briggs, at Buffalo, N. Y., in conducting the Buffalo classical school, preparatory for colleges and universities, Mr. Alden having charge of mathematics and scientific studies. In July, 1874, he went to Germany, prepared for lectures and took the university courses under Windschied at Leipsig in Roman law, and under Bluntschli at Heidelberg in international law, traveling during his vacations through Germany, Switzerland and Italy. He spent part of 1875-6 in Paris, learning lectures on art, science and languages at the Sorbonne. While abroad he gave much attention to the study of people and their customs and languages, and his only use of English at that time was the reading of standard law texts. The following year was spent in Columbia law school, and in the office of Weeks & Forster, New York, and in the fall of 1877 he was admitted to practice at Milwaukee. In 1878 at the solicitation of an old friend, W. T. Jenison, he removed to Fort Wayne, and was a partner with the latter until he removed to Denver, Col., in the winter of 1879. One of his first cases was carried to a successful issue in the United States supreme court, contrary to the opinion of leading lawyers. His practice is exclusively civil, and he has been, in this field, quite successful. In studying legal questions he has adopted the plan of giving the matter full deliberation before consulting authorities to verify his conclusions or discover in what respect they are faulty. Mr. Alden was married December 17, 1884, by Rev. Charles Williams, at All Souls' church, New York, to Carrie, only daughter of Auguste Francois Savin, and his wife, Sarah Jane Staniford. Her father was a shipping merchant, commanding and sailing one of his own vessels the greater part of his life. He was the son of Augustin Pierre Savin, a lawyer of Bordeaux, France, and his wife, Sophie Marie Francoise, *nee* de Maigron, daughter of a French nobleman and army officer, born July 5, 1816, on the island of Guadeloupe. Mr. Alden's wife's mother was the daughter of Samuel Thorndike Staniford, of Beverly, Mass., and his wife, Catherine Chappel, of Hackensack, N. J., born February 7, 1828, at Lansingburgh, N. Y.

Thomas E. Ellison, an attorney at law, was born at LaGrange, Ind., August 12, 1852. He is the son of Andrew and Susan (Tuttle) Ellison, now residents of this city. Andrew Ellison was born in county Tyrone, Ireland, January 12, 1817, and when three years of age emigrated with his parents to the United States. His childhood was spent in New York, where his parents first settled. In 1836 he came to Indiana and became a resident of LaGrange county. He was admitted to the bar of the court of Indiana in 1843, and continued the practice of law until

1879, becoming widely known in the state as one of its ablest attorneys. Mrs. Susan (Tuttle) Ellison is a native of Lockport, N. Y., born September 13, 1829. Of their seven children the oldest is Thomas E. The latter attended the LaGrange schools, was a student at Notre Dame university for some time, and in 1874 graduated from the law department of the university of Michigan. He was admitted to the LaGrange county bar, in 1873, to practice in the supreme court of Indiana, in May, 1874, and in the United States court in 1875. He remained in the practice of his profession at LaGrange until 1878, when he came to Fort Wayne, and entered into a law partnership with Judge L. M. Ninde, with whom he remained five years. Since 1883 he has been practicing his profession independently, meeting with such success that he has attained a high rank as a civil lawyer, not seeking criminal practice. In 1882–3, Mr. Ellison was retained as the attorney of the county, and all the free gravel roads in the county, except one, were built during that time. Their establishment was largely due to him. During his term of office as county attorney, the board of commissioners acting on his advive, and at his suggestion, made great reductions in the fees that had been paid by the county to its various officers, by reason of which the county has saved several thousands of dollars every year while and since he was in office. While he was county attorney, the question as to whether or not the various railroads that passed through the county were properly assessed, came up for discussion, and Mr. Ellison representing the county, appeared before the state board of equalization at Indianapolis, which board raised the valuation of the various railroads in the county several hundred thousand dollars, thus giving the county a large increase of taxes. The great improvement in Allen and Huntington counties known as the Little River drainage, which was effected by constructing forty miles of large ditches, at a cost of about $200,000, was established and constructed very largely according to his advice and skill, he having been attorney and adviser of the petitioners for, and the superintendent and engineer who constructed, the same. Forty thousand acres of waste land were reclaimed, and 80,000 acres beneficially affected. He was married in January, 1879, to Emma S. Stockbridge, who died in March, 1884. They had three chlldren: Pheobe, Andrew S. and Robert W.; the latter has since died. December 14, 1887, he was married to Hannah Hall, a resident of Logansport, Ind., at Topeka, Kan.

William J. Vesey, attorney at law, is one of the younger members of the bar, but has won a rank highly creditable to himself. He became a resident of Fort Wayne in 1878, and entered the office of Ninde & Ellison. The same year he was admitted to the bar, and he has since been actively engaged in the practice. In politics he is an earnest worker in the republican ranks, and socially is highly esteemed. He is a member of the Masonic order, Knights of Pythias, and A. O. U. W. Mr. Vesey was born in LaGrange county, at Lima, April 19, 1857, son of Benjamin W. and Sarah W. (Waterhouse) Vesey, both natives of

New England. His father was born in Vermont, February 28, 1829, and his mother in Maine, February 8, 1836, and now resides at Goshen, Ind. His grandfather, William Vesey, who was born in Vermont in 1801, removed with his family to Ohio in 1837, and in 1839 to Goshen, where he died in 1870. William J. Vesey was raised on the farm in LaGrange county, and received a common school education. He was married July 25, 1882, to Margaret E. Studebaker, daughter of Judge David and Harriet (Evans) Studebaker, pioneers and prominent citizens of Adams county. Mr. and Mrs. Vesey have four children: Margaret S., Sallie W., Dick M. and William J.

William Straughan O'Rourke, former prosecuting attorney of the criminal court, was born at this city, January 6, 1858, son of P. S. and Eliza (Boulger) O'Rourke, being the fourth of eight children born to them. He attended the Fort Wayne public schools, and in 1875 entered St. Vincent's college, in Westmoreland county, Penn., at which institution he was graduated in 1877. In the fall of that year, he began the study of law in the office of Judge Allen Zollars, and in the fall of 1879 entered the law department of the university of Michigan. March 24, 1880, he graduated there. He was admitted to the Allen county bar in 1879. In politics he is a democrat and a tariff reformer. In June, 1880, he was nominated for prosecuting attorney of the criminal court of Allen county, by the democratic party, and was elected in the October following, holding the office until the abolishment of the criminal court, at the close of the term for which he was elected. At the time he was elected, S. M. Hench was prosecuting attorney, and refused to surrender the office, in consequence of which Mr. O'Rourke brought suit to obtain possession. Mr. Hench took a change of venue to Kosciusko county, where the case was tried before Judge VanLong, now chief justice of the United States court of the territory of New Mexico, resulting in favor of Mr. O'Rourke. His contestant appealed to the supreme court, where Mr. O'Rourke's title to the office was affirmed by Hon. George V. Howk, chief justice. In 1882 he was appointed attorney for the Grand Rapids & Indiana railroad company, a position he has since held. He was married in 1883, to Margaret G. Garvey, a graduate of the university of Michigan, who is a native of Springfield, Mass. They have two children, Genevieve and Allen G. Mr. and Mrs. O'Rourke are members of the Catholic church.

William P. Breen, a young attorney who has won marked prominence in the bar of Allen county, was born at Terre Haute, Ind., February 13, 1859. His father, James Breen, was born in Ireland, in 1820, emigrated about 1840, and in 1845 settled at Terre Haute, removing thence to Fort Wayne in 1863. He was a merchant by occupation, and was for several years a member of the Fort Wayne city council. His wife, whose maiden name was Margaret Dunn, was born in Ireland in 1818, and died at Fort Wayne in 1888, having survived her husband five years. Their only child, William, was educated at the Brothers' Catholic school, and entered Notre Dame university, near South Bend, and graduated there in 1877. In the fall of the same year he entered the office of Coombs, Morris & Bell, as a student of law, and in May, 1879, was admitted to the bar. In September, 1879, he formed a partnership with Warren H. Withers, which continued until the death of Judge Withers, November 15, 1882, since when Mr. Breen has had no associate in his practice. Mr. Breen is in politics a democrat, and he and wife are members of the Catholic church. He was married May 27, 1884, to Odelia Phillips, of this city, who was born March 13, 1859.

During ten years, Thomas W. Wilson has been a successful practitioner of law at Fort Wayne, and now has a good business, and is highly esteemed. He was born in Trumbull county, Ohio, September 26, 1837. His father, John J. Wilson, was born in Pennsylvania, in 1804, became one of the early settlers of Wells county, Ind., in 1849, and died there in 1873. He married Margaret Harris, who was born in Vermont in 1817, and died in Wells county in 1873, and they had five children, one of whom served in the Thirty-fourth Indiana infantry, as orderly sergeant. The eldest is Thomas W. The latter attended the common schools, entered a select school at Warren, Ind., in 1857, and after a period of study there taught school three months. He then attended Fort Wayne college three terms, and in 1858 taught school in Iowa. He began the study of law at Bluffton, in 1861, was admitted to the Wells county bar in 1863, and practiced there ten years. In 1873 he removed to his farm in Wells county, and was engaged in agriculture until 1880, when he came to Fort Wayne. He is a pronounced republican, and cast his first vote for Abraham Lincoln. In 1868 he was elected prosecuting attorney of the tenth judicial circuit, then composed of ten counties. He owns a farm in Whitley county, and has a comfortable residence in this city. Mr. Wilson was married in 1860 to Elizabeth E. Davis, a native of this state, and they have four children: George C., born in 1861; Columbus T., 1863; Frank D., 1865; and Talbott M., 1867. They are all mechanics, and one lives in Louisville, Ky.; one in Chicago, Ill.; the other two in Fort Wayne. Mr. Wilson and wife are members of the Methodist Episcopal church.

James M. Robinson was born in a log cabin in Allen county, Ind., in 1861. He remained upon the farm, attending the public schools till he was ten years of age; removing then to the city, he attended school till he was thirteen, the last two years of which time he carried newspapers and cleaned street lamps to secure books and clothes for himself. In 1875, he was collector for the *Daily News*, and in 1876, began work at N. G. Olds' wheel works as a machine hand. While at work from 1877, he studied law, being kindly aided by the well known firm of " Colerick Bros.," one of whom, Mr. Thomas W. Colerick, giving him, as Mr. Robinson frequently remarks, his start in life. In 1881, the subject of this sketch left the shop and began study with the above firm, and in 1882 was admitted to practice at the bar of the United States and state courts. Mr. Robinson rose rapidly in his profession, and by industry and close application to business, secured a lucrative practice early in his career. He began practice before he was of age and is much attached to the profession for which he has a special adaptation. His political career began with his candidacy for prosecuting attorney before the democratic convention in 1884. His shop mates carried one-half of the city for him, but he failed. He was nominated without opposition in 1886, and again in 1888, for prosecutor of the 38th judicial circuit, the former year running 700 ahead of the state ticket and the latter year elected by 4,218 majority. As prosecuting attorney, he has made a brilliant record and is esteemed as one of the best prosecutors the county has ever had. In his first term there was over 100 convictions for felony and but two acquitals. Mr. Robinson is forcible and brilliant as a speaker, is a trustworthy officer and is essentially a self made man. His father, David A. Robinson, and mother, Isabella (Bowen) Robinson, were born in Ohio, the father in 1834, and the mother in 1833, and came to Allen county in 1855. James M. is their youngest of three children. Mr. Robinson is a member of the Masonic and Knights of Pythias fraternities.

In the list of young attorneys of Fort Wayne, the name of Owen N. Heaton deserves honorable mention. He is a native of Allen county, and was born September 2, 1860. His father, Jesse Heaton, was born in Dearborn county, Ind., September 6, 1829, and about four years later, in 1833, was brought by his parents to Marion township, this county, where he resided, following the occupation of farming and stock-raising until his death, May 5, 1889. He married Samantha C. Larcom, who was born in May, 1834, in Tompkins county, N. Y., and they have had eleven children, of whom eight are living, the fourth being Owen N. The latter began his education in the common schools, and in 1882 entered Fort Wayne college, where he spent three years. In 1885 he began reading law in the office of William P. Breen, and was admitted on September 5 of the same year to the bar. He is a prominent member of the K. of P., being chancellor commander of Fort Wayne lodge, No. 116. In politics he is a republican. Mr. Heaton was married December 12, 1885, to Rhoda A. Webb, who was born in this county July 29, 1862. He and wife are members of the Baptist church.

Robert Brackenridge (now deceased), for many years a prominent lawyer and resident of Fort Wayne, was born at Rockville, Ind., in September, 1818. He moved to Fort Wayne with his uncle, Capt. Robert Brackenridge, in 1830, and became a clerk in his uncle's office, who was register of the United States land office. At an early age he commenced the study of law, and was admitted to the bar at the age of twenty-one. He was a partner with Charles W. Ewing until his death in 1843. He early distinguished himself at the bar, and from the first had a large and lucrative practice. From the time the Pittsburgh, Fort Wayne & Chicago railroad company, and the Grand Rapids & Indiana railroad company were organized, until his death, he was their attorney in Indiana. He died in Fort Wayne in 1873, leaving a widow, two daughters and four sons, one of whom, Charles S., is now city civil engineer, and has been for many years. The day following his death the following appeared in the Fort Wayne *Sentinel:*

"Few men in Fort Wayne, or in the state, were better known than Robert Brackenridge, and he was a man sure to be known wherever he went, for he carried with him a marked individuality. For more than forty-two years he has gone in and out before the people of Fort Wayne until we may say, almost without exaggeration, everybody knew him, and few there are who will not miss, with a sense of sadness, his familiar form and voice. Never an office holder, we believe, nor, so far as we know, an aspirant for office, he was essentially a public man. A man of strong faculties and bold self-assertion, could not be hidden. He was a natural leader, and therefore, in his chosen profession of a lawyer, inevitably became a leader among his brethren at the bar. It is no disparagement of any of the able men of the Fort Wayne bar, or of the bar of the state, to say that Robert Brackenridge was among the ablest of them, and in some elements of the highest order of forensic ability he was their superior."

In a public address a short time ago (October, 1889), Judge John Morris, of Fort Wayne, who knew Mr. Brackenridge long and well, and who is entirely competent to speak of his abilities as a lawyer, said: "Robert Brackenridge was a young man when the courts opened in this county. He was from the beginning a good lawyer, quick, apt, and always at himself and at his best. His power of perception was remarkable. He seemed to see at a glance the bearing of every question raised or involved in a case. He appeared to be a sort of legal gladiator, clad in full armor, self assured, confident, and ready for the contest, and he who opposed him, if not thoroughly prepared at every point, was lost. He was not, hardly needed to be, studious, and yet it was surprising how much more he seemed to know than those who were. He was hardly a good speaker, and yet he was very successful. In argument he was pointed, incisive and forcible. He stood the equal of the best lawyers at the bar. He was kind and generous, and never failed to assist the young members of the bar with advice. Many now at the bar owe him much. He died comparatively young, respected and esteemed by all who knew him."

The publishers of this work have used every effort to make this mention of the leading attorneys of the Fort Wayne bar as near complete as possible. Some of the leading men of the profession in the earlier days of the county's history that are still living, have long since ceased the active practice. Most of these are mentioned in other portions of this work in connection with those subjects that they have made more important by their efforts. Notable among these may be named Hon. Joseph K. Edgerton, and Hon. Franklin P. Randall. Some not here mentioned that are now in the practice are omitted for want of the requisite information. Of these Hon. Lindley M. Ninde deserves a more prominent mention. In the foremost rank of the bar of northern Indiana he enjoys a reputation that is at once enviable and meritorious.

A forcible and skillful advocate, he is also distinguished for his almost unerring judgment of the law which is based upon a deep knowledge of the common law. Though lacking many of the qualities of a polished orator, he is nevertheless one of the most convincing speakers before a jury that has ever practiced at the Fort Wayne bar.

Another lawyer of earlier times that stood high in the profession was Charles Case. He practiced at the Fort Wayne bar for many years and rose to distinction as an attorney of unusual high order. He represented the Fort Wayne district in congress for two terms. His popularity was sufficient to defeat Hon. James L. Worden in 1857 for that place, and the following year was elected over Hon. Reuben J. Dawson by a majority of 1,363 in the district. He is remembered by those of the bar who knew him with much kindness, and his abilities were undoubtedly strong.